About This Book

Worlds of History offers a flexible comparative and thematic organization that accommodates a variety of teaching approaches and helps students make cross-cultural comparisons. Thoughtfully compiled by a distinguished world historian and community college instructor, each chapter presents a wide array of primary and secondary sources arranged around a major theme.

New to This Edition

Over 25% new documents offer new perspectives, topics, and broader geographical coverage. New primary source documents range from depictions of gender in classical societies to Facebook posts from the Arab Spring. New secondary source selections include Shlomo Sand's thought-provoking argument about the origins of the Jewish people and Heonik Kwon's theory regarding the origins of the Cold War.

New chapters feature topics sure to engage students. This edition includes new chapters on empire and government in China and Rome; trade, travel, and migrations in Eurasia, Africa, and the Pacific; and a new chapter on new democracy movements from 1977 to the present.

New "Thinking Historically" exercises help students build skills. New skills include "Making Comparisons," "Sifting Factors," "Appreciating Context," and "Detecting Ideological Language." These and the other "Thinking Historically" exercises focus on developing a specific analytical skill appropriate for the documents and themes in each chapter.

New step-by-step instructions for document analysis and "Historical Thinking, Reading, and Writing Skills for AP World History." An expanded introduction for students explains how to approach primary and secondary sources. The new edition also features an in-depth skills primer by Dave Neumann of The History Project at California State University, Long Beach, that prepares students for the historical thinking, reading, and writing skills that they need to master for the AP World History exam.

Maps and images are now available for presentation. Instructors have access to downloadable files of images from the book, including maps and illustrations, many in full color. Along with the revised Instructor's Resource Manual compiled by Kevin Reilly, these can be ordered at **bedfordstmartins.com /highschool/reilly/catalog**.

Worlds of History

A Comparative Reader

Worlds of History

A Comparative Reader

Fifth Edition

Kevin Reilly
Raritan Valley College

Bedford/St. Martin's
Boston • New York

For Bedford/St. Martin's

Publisher for History: Mary Dougherty
Executive Editor for History: Traci M. Crowell
Director of Development for History: Jane Knetzger
Senior Developmental Editor: Laura Arcari
Production Editor: Katherine Caruana
Production Supervisor: Samuel Jones
Senior Marketing Manager: Paul Stillitano
Editorial Assistant: Victoria Royal
Copyeditor: Susan Moore
Cartography: Mapping Specialists, Ltd.
Photo Researcher: Naomi Kornhauser
Permissions Manager: Kalina K. Ingham
Senior Art Director: Anna Palchik
Text Designer: Janis Owens
Cover Designer: Marine Miller
Cover Art: Top left: *Spring Scything*, 1974 (color litho). Chinese School (20th
    Century). © Private Collection/DaTo Images/The Bridgeman Art Library.
    Top right: Wall painting from the tomb of the scribe Ounsu. © Réunion des
    Musées Nationaux/Art Resource, NY. Bottom left: Ms Fr 2810 f.86v. *Trade
    in the Gulf of Cambay*, India, from the *Livre des Merveilles du Monde*,
    c. 1410–1412 (vellum). Boucicaut Master (fl. 1390–1430) (and workshop).
    © Bibliotheque Nationale, Paris, France/Giraudon/The Bridgeman Art Library.
    Bottom right: Candido Portinari, *Coffee*, 1935. © Art Resource, NY.
Composition: Cenveo Publisher Services
Printing and Binding: RR Donnelley and Sons

President, Bedford/St. Martin's: Denise B. Wydra
Presidents, Macmillan Higher Education: Joan E. Feinberg and Tom Scotty
Director of Marketing: Karen R. Soeltz
Director of Production: Susan W. Brown
Associate Director, Editorial Production: Elise S. Kaiser
Managing Editor: Elizabeth M. Schaaf

Manufactured in the United States of America.

1   2   3   4   5   16   15   14   13   12

For information, write: Bedford/St. Martin's, 75 Arlington Street, Boston, MA 02116
(617-399-4000)

ISBN 978-1-4576-1782-9 (Volume 1)
ISBN 978-1-4576-1783-6 (Volume 2)
ISBN 978-1-4576-1785-0 (High School Edition)

Preface

Teaching introductory world history to college students for forty years has helped me appreciate the enduring truths that have governed the framework of this book since its inception. When asked what has made *Worlds of History* such a successful supplemental or stand-alone text for their world history courses, adopters point to the accessible and engaging selections; the choice of interesting themes and topics presented comparatively that address the interests of students while respecting the integrity of the field; and the inclusion of "Thinking Historically" sections that show teachers and students how the study of history can not only teach broad trends and comparative experiences but also develop critical thought. I have continued all of these features in this fifth edition.

To engage students who are not only new to the college experience but new to reading source material as well, I have continued my efforts to provide accessible readings that pique student interest. This new edition aims to maintain that high level of reader interest with new selections that are real page-turners, like the diary of a young man on a doomed slave ship and Pu Songling's story of a mysterious "Lady Knight," along with some new, more accessible translations of established classical sources like *The Tale of Genji*. As in previous editions, I have also included secondary as well as primary texts. In some chapters the secondary text introduces an issue that the primary sources address, while at other times the secondary source offers a summary or suggestions for new directions. My strategy is that students will learn how texts, whether primary or secondary, talk to each other—and without having to buy separate books of each.

As a framework, the reader continues to have a **thematic and topical organization** that also proceeds chronologically, with each chapter focusing on a captivating topic within a particular time period. I have long found a **comparative approach** to be a useful tool for approaching world history, and for the fifth edition, I have continued to use this tool, examining two or more cultures at a time. In some chapters students can trace parallel developments in separate regions, such as the development of society in ancient Greece and India in Chapter 3, or the advent of nationalism in Japan and India in Chapter 23. In other cases students examine the enduring effects of contact and exchange between cultures, as in the chapter on Mongol and Viking raiding and settlements from the tenth to the fourteenth centuries, or Volume Two's chapter on the scientific revolution in Europe, the Ottoman Empire, China, Japan, and the Americas. Even the normally bipolar study of the Cold War in Chapter 26 can be opened up to more comparisons with new documents relating to the fight to control the emerging "Third World."

I have long felt that we should teach "habits of mind" as much as subject matter. This view is becoming more pervasive in recent years, emphasized by the College Board in its AP World History course, and as evidenced by the spreading appeal of assessing common goals for the study of history that is currently winning the endorsement of the American Historical Association. To encourage these "habits of mind," I continue to include a wealth of **pedagogical tools** to help students unlock the readings and hone their criticalthinking skills. Each chapter begins with **"Historical Context,"** an introduction to the chapter's topic that sets the stage for directed comparisons among the readings. A separate **"Thinking Historically"** section follows, which introduces a particular critical thinking skill—such as asking about author, audience, and agenda or distinguishing causes of change—that is designed to mine the chapter's selections. Headnotes preceding each selection provide additional context, while document-specific "Thinking Historically" paragraphs pose questions to encourage close analysis of the selections using the critical thinking skill introduced at the beginning of the chapter. **Explanatory gloss notes** and **pronunciation guides** throughout ensure comprehension of the readings. A set of **"Reflections"** that both summarizes and extends the chapter's lessons concludes each chapter.

To enrich the instructor's experience teaching with this reader, I have written an **instructor's resource manual**. Available online at **bedfordstmartins.com/reilly/catalog,** this manual provides the rationale for the selection and organization of the readings, suggestions for teaching with the documents, an alternate table of contents organized by topics, and information about additional resources, including films and Internet sites. At the same site, instructors can also access and download all of the maps and images from this book, many in color, for presentation. All of the maps from the book are also available for download in Make History at **bedfordstmartins.com/makehistory.**

■ NEW TO THIS EDITION

While I am continually testing selections in my own classroom, I appreciate input from readers and adopters, and I want to thank them for their many suggestions for exciting new chapters and selections. Having incorporated some of this feedback, I think those who have used the reader previously will find the fifth edition even more geographically and topically comprehensive, interesting, and accessible to students. More than a quarter of the selections are new, which has allowed me to introduce fresh material into almost every chapter. In addition, I have included three new chapters, which explore empire and government in China and Rome (Chapter 4); trade, travel, and migrations in Eurasia,

Africa, and the Pacific (Chapter 8); and New Democracy movements from 1977 to the present (Chapter 27).

One more change to this edition of *Worlds of History* has, I hope, made the book more accessible. I significantly expanded the Introduction for Students to give students an idea of how I conceive the purpose of this reader, how it might work with a textbook, if they use one, and how they might read primary sources without abject fear. For instance, I encourage them to ask the basic who, what, where, when, why questions of each source—keeping in mind that it is their understanding of the source that matters most, not what the author of the source may have wanted them to learn.

I am not a believer in change for its own sake; when I have a successful way of teaching a subject, I am not disposed to jettison it for something new. Consequently, many of my most satisfying changes are incremental: a better translation of a document, the addition of a newly discovered source, or additional questions to further inspire critical thinking. In some cases I have been able to further edit a useful source, retaining its muscle, but providing room for a precious new find. I begin each round of revision with the conviction that the book is already as good as it can get. And I end each round with the surprising discovery that it is much better than it was.

■ ACKNOWLEDGMENTS

A book like this cannot be written without the help and advice of a vast army of colleagues and friends. I consider myself enormously fortunate to have met and known such a large group of gifted and generous scholars. Some were especially helpful in the preparation of this new edition. They include: William Baller, Worcester Polytechnic Institute; Peter Burkholder, Fairleigh Dickinson University; Jessica A. Coope, University of Nebraska–Lincoln; Matthew Crawford, Kent State University; Eric Cunningham, Gonzaga University; Vefa Erginbas, The Ohio State University; Ken Faunce, Washington State University; Alan W. Fisher, Michigan State University; Judy Ann Ford, Texas A&M University; Dana Goodrich, Northwest Vista College; Andrew Goss, University of New Orleans; Candace Gregory-Abbott, California State University–Sacramento; Kyle Griffith, California State University–San Marcos; Andrew Hamilton, Viterbo University; Jesse Hingson, Jacksonville University; David M. Kalivas, Middlesex Community College; Sandra LeBeau, Colby-Sawyer College; Jonathan Lee, San Antonio College; George E. Longenecker, Vermont Technical College; Erik C. Maiershofer, Hope International University; Michael S. Mangus, The Ohio State University; Deena C. McKinney, East Georgia College; Heather McNamee,

Arkansas State University; Craig Miller, Pennsylvania College; Dayo Nicole Mitchell, University of Oregon; Jason Neidleman, University of La Verne; Kenneth W. Noe, Auburn University; Patrick M. Patterson, Honolulu Community College; Mark Peach, Southern Adventist University; Laura Ryan, Southwestern College; Steven Seegel, University of Northern Colorado; Jonathan Seitz, Drexel University; Matthew G. Stanard, Berry College; Lisa Tran, California State Fullerton; Teresa Fava Thomas, Fitchburg State University; Doug Tompson, Columbus State University; Karen M. Teoh, Stonehill College; Sally West, Truman State University.

I'd also like to thank the following high school instructors who provided guidance and expertise: Jeffrey Filson, Glen Burnie High School; Deborah Johnston, Lakeside School; Dana Ann Landesman, Bronxville High School; Drew H. Maddock, Harvard-Westlake School; and Kaylene Schliesser, Clements High School.

Over the years I have benefited from the suggestions of innumerable friends and fellow world historians. Among them: Michael Adas, Rutgers University; the late Jerry Bentley, University of Hawai'i; David Berry, Essex County Community College; Edmund (Terry) Burke III, University of California–Santa Cruz; Catherine Clay, Shippensburg University; the late Philip Curtin, Johns Hopkins University; S. Ross Doughty, Ursinus College; Ross Dunn, San Diego State University; Marc Gilbert, Hawai'i Pacific University; Steve Gosch, University of Wisconsin–Eau Claire; Sue Gronewold, Kean University; Gregory Guzman, Bradley University; Brock Haussamen, Raritan Valley College; Allen Howard, Rutgers University; Sarah Hughes, Shippensburg University; Karen Jolly, University of Hawai'i; Stephen Kaufman, Raritan Valley College; Maghan Keita, Villanova University; Craig Lockard, University of Wisconsin–Green Bay; Pat Manning, University of Pittsburgh; Adam McKeown, Columbia University; John McNeill, Georgetown University; William H. McNeill, University of Chicago; Gyan Prakash, Princeton University; Lauren Ristvet, University of Pennsylvania; Robert Rosen, University of California–Los Angeles; Heidi Roupp, Aspen High School; John Russell-Wood, Johns Hopkins University; Lynda Shaffer, Tufts University; Ira Spar, Ramapo College; Robert Strayer, California State University–Monterey Bay; George Sussman, LaGuardia Community College; Robert Tignor, Princeton University; John Voll, Georgetown University; and Peter Winn, Tufts University.

I also want to thank the people at Bedford/St. Martin's. Joan Feinberg and Denise Wydra remained involved and helpful throughout, as did Mary Dougherty, Traci Crowell, and Jane Knetzger. Victoria Royal provided invaluable help in reviewing the previous edition, and she coordinated the development of the instructor's manual, ensured the book's images and maps all appeared online for download, and provided invaluable behind-the-scenes support for the reader. I want to thank my production editor, Katherine Caruana, for overseeing the entire production process of design, copyediting, and page composition. I would also like to thank Susan Moore for copyediting, Marine Miller for the cover design, Sara Hillman for designing promotional materials, and Paul Stillitano, Katherine Bates, and Dan McDonough for expertly marketing the book. Thanks also to photo researcher Naomi Kornhauser and to Heather Salus for clearing the text permissions. Finally, my deepest appreciation goes to Senior Editor Laura Arcari for her editorial guidance, forcing me to make it a better book than I had any right to expect. None of this would have been possible if I had not been blessed in my own introduction to history and critical thinking at Rutgers in the 1960s with teachers I still aspire to emulate. Eugene Meehan taught me how to think and showed me that I could. Traian Stoianovich introduced me to the world and an endless range of historical inquiry. Warren Susman lit up a room with more life than I ever knew existed. Donald Weinstein guided me as a young teaching assistant to listen to students and talk with them rather than at them. And Peter Stearns showed me how important and exciting it could be to understand history by making comparisons. I dedicate this book to them.

Finally, I want to thank my own institution, Raritan Valley College, for nurturing my career, allowing me to teach whatever I wanted, and entrusting me with some of the best students one could encounter anywhere. I could not ask for anything more. Except, of course, a loving wife like Pearl.

Kevin Reilly

Introduction for Students

When most people think of history books, they think of books that tell a story about the past. It may be a small part of the past, like a presidential election or the making of the atomic bomb, or a large chunk of the past like the history of China or the history of warfare. In either case, these are books that tell a continuous story from beginning to end. The story might evolve gradually or reveal a conclusion at the start. It might be dramatic or plodding. There may be quotations from various people scattered throughout or indented in long paragraphs, but the book is written by a single author (or sometimes a few who agree on what to say) and presented with a single voice. The voice of a single storyteller gives this kind of history book a strong sense of authority. The reader is not invited to question anything, much less disagree. Any doubts are met by an implicit: "Wait, let me finish," and the author's conclusions follow inevitably from the facts that he or she has determined best fit the story.

The book you are holding in your hands is a different kind of history book. It does not tell a single story, but many. And while these selections are gathered by a single editor (a not unimportant matter), they were originally crafted by hundreds of different people. These people came from various places throughout the world, lived at different times, and were addressing different subjects, often with no awareness of what any of the other authors in this book said — or even of their existence.

This book contains many different stories. But it contains much more. Most of the selections are not stories in the way that history books are. First of all, most were not written by historians. Some of the stories in this book are literary or imaginary, while others come from personal letters or diaries. And many are not even stories. There are selections from treaties, philosophy books, scientific treatises, holy books, telegrams, and posts from Facebook. Further, some of the selections are not even writings. There are paintings, art works, photographs, pictures of things, and cartoons. There would be music too, if it could fit into a book.

The point is that this book contains what are called **historical sources** rather than histories. Historical sources are the raw materials that historians use to construct histories. Of course, when you think of all the possible sources available to historians, you realize that even a book of this size can contain only a miniscule number of sources. There are in fact whole libraries devoted to archiving historical sources — from presidential libraries that contain the papers of a president to the archives of government offices. In addition, museums, university libraries, film archives, and ever-expanding online collections include sources ranging from newspapers, magazines, and books to images, letters, e-mails, and more.

Historians use these collections in order to find the sources they need to tell a particular story. The sources are as varied as the questions historians ask. Say, for instance, you are studying the history of individuality and you want to see if the use of the pronoun *I* increased in the late Middle Ages. There happens to be an archive that includes every scrap of writing from a medieval Jewish community in Cairo that saved everything on the chance that a piece of paper might contain the word for God, and therefore, under Jewish tradition, could not be destroyed. With this archive, tedious work, and a good computer, you could chart the use of a single word like *I* over the hundreds of years in which these papers were gathered. It would be within one community, to be sure; but there are few, if any, comparable source collections for this period. Someday a historian may even try to figure out what college students were thinking in the last years of the Age of Reading by a study of your e-mail, essays, or other personal possessions.

This book, then, is one of the two types of books most often used in a history course. The first type is the survey textbook. This book is the second type. It is variously called a "reader," "source book," or an anthology, and it collects a variety of sources in one book. It is designed to introduce you to working with historical sources. The reason for using a reader in addition to, or instead of, a survey text is that it allows us to do those things that the text makes so difficult. It allows us to interpret sources on our own, ask questions, solve problems, and actively build our understanding. Sources can engage our minds in ways that narrative textbooks, with their sense of authority and finality, do not.

Many source books contain only what are called **primary sources,** pieces from the past that were created in the period we are studying. This book contains some **secondary sources** as well. Secondary sources are pieces *about* the period we are studying. They are usually written by scholars. Most of the secondary sources in this book were written fairly recently by modern historians. My reason for including secondary sources is to provide some context or perspective to consider the primary sources (which make up most of the selections in each chapter). Historians read and write secondary sources, continually checking and revising them to conform to primary sources—the actual evidence from the past.

Primary sources can be difficult to interpret because they were often written in a time that is not familiar to us, and the context specific to their creation may be unknown. They use funny words, address weird issues, say strange things, and are sometimes written in a language that we have to struggle to make sense of. I have tried to minimize some of these problems with footnotes, pronunciation help, and some modernization of the language.

I've also included headnotes before each source that give you some historical background about the author and the source. But I can't do too much of that because it is important for you to appreciate the unfamiliarity of these sources in order to do your own analysis. A wise novelist once said: "The past is a foreign country: They do things differently there."[1] These sources were created in a different time, which often makes them seem foreign and remote. So it is precisely this context of a different time that we have to immerse ourselves in to understand the source and the world from which it came. Primary sources require and enable a kind of time travel to knowledge in which we have to leave many of our assumptions behind as excess baggage.

Because the authors of primary sources were not writing for us, and indeed had no idea we'd ever exist, they can't lie to us (at least as they might have, had they been given the opportunity). They tell us so much more than they intended. Primary sources can also be full of deceit, based on illusion, and riddled with error. They can even seem bonkers—and by those very characteristics, tell us much. Working with primary sources is like being a fly on the wall or being able to see things while remaining invisible. It is like having a superpower—gained from the study of history.

Throughout both volumes of this reader you have chapters in world history, which deal with particular historical periods and topics. Some topics cover long periods, like the rise of civilization and patriarchy (Chapter 1) or migrations, travel, and trade from 3000 B.C.E to 1350 C.E. (Chapter 8). Some topics cover brief periods, like the First Crusade from 1095–1099 (Chapter 10) and the Black Death from 1346–1350 (Chapter 12). Most fall in between these extremes. There are, for example, chapters on the topics of women, marriage, and family in most of the large periods that divide the book, i.e., ancient, classical, medieval, and early modern. There are also chapters that compare different societies: classical India and Greece, the Roman and Chinese empires, and Mongols and Vikings. There are chapters on such conventionally defined topics as the Atlantic Slave Trade, the Scientific Revolution, the Enlightenment, the First and Second World Wars, and the Cold War. There are also chapters that pose new historical frameworks like secularization, democratization, and globalization.

As you learn about historical periods and topics, you will also be learning to explore history by analyzing primary and secondary sources systematically. The "Thinking Historically" exercises in each chapter encourage habits of mind that I associate with my own study of history. They are not necessarily intended to turn you into historians, but rather, to give you skills that will help you in all of your college courses. Indeed, these are skills for life: for jury duty and the voting booth; for writing letters or drafting memos on the job; for weighing options and making smart decisions. Hopefully these new habits of mind will also expand your interests and nourish your self-confidence.

[1] L. P. Hartley, *The Go-Between* (New York: NYRB Classics, 2002), 17. First published in London in 1953.

These skills are organized from the simple to the more complex. Since skill building is cumulative, your ability to understand, analyze, and use sources will become increasingly sophisticated as you read through this text. But you need not wait for the end of the course to begin your analysis of these sources. Rather, it would be useful to develop the habit of asking the basic questions that journalists are trained to ask whenever they are assigned a story: who, what, where, when, and why?

Whether the source is primary or secondary, a piece of writing or a work of art, a run-through of these basic "w" questions is a good place to start when analyzing sources:

- **Who** wrote or created the source? If the author is unknown or anonymous, what sort of person does the author appear to be? An observer, participant, or eyewitness? A later historian? This will establish whether it is a primary or secondary source. Are there any clues to the identity of the author in the source itself? Are there signs of the author's social class, political position, and attitudes toward the subject of the source?

- **What** is the source? Is it a history by a modern historian and, therefore, a secondary source? Or is it a primary source from the past? If so, what kind of primary source? Is it an engraved stone, a poem, a love letter, a diary entry, a chapter from an ancient book of philosophy, a prayer?

- **Where** does it come from? China? Ancient Mesopotamia? France? Paris? Has it traveled from one place to another, or has it always been in the same place?

- **When** was it created? If it is writing, was it revised? Was there an earlier written or oral version? Is it an example of an older style? How new is it?

- **Why** was it created? To entertain, exorcise, instruct, persuade? **What** was the purpose? **Who** was the audience?

Ultimately, our answers to these questions might help us answer the most important question of all: **What** does this source tell us about the world from which it came?

World history is nothing less than everything ever done or imagined, so we cannot possibly cover it all; we are forced to choose among different places and times in our study of the global past. Our choices do include some particular moments in time, like the one in 111 c.e. in the first half of this reader, when the Roman governor of Bithynia consulted Emperor Trajan about proper treatment of Christians. But our attention will be directed toward much longer periods as well. While we will visit particular places in time like Imperial Rome in the second century or Africa in the nineteenth century, typically we will study more than one place at a time by using a comparative approach.

Comparisons can be enormously useful in studying world history. When we compare the raiding and trading of Vikings and Mongols, the scientific revolution in Europe and Japan, and the Cold War in Cuba and Afghanistan, we learn about the general and the specific at the same time. My hope is that by comparing some of the various worlds of history, a deeper and more nuanced understanding of our global past will emerge. With that understanding, we are better equipped to make sense of the world today and to confront whatever the future holds.

Contents

1. Prehistory and the Origins of Patriarchy: Gathering, Agricultural, and Urban Societies, 40,000–1000 B.C.E. 1

The agricultural revolution ten thousand years ago and the urban
revolution five thousand years ago were probably the two most important
events in human history. Did they "revolutionize" the status of women
or begin the age of male domination? Thinking in "stages" can be more
useful than thinking in years.

4. Empire and Government: China and Rome, 300 B.C.E.–300 C.E. 119

Roughly two thousand years ago the Chinese Empire and the Roman Empire spanned Eurasia. In comparing these ancient empires, we seek to understand how they were governed. Both required officials, armies, and governing ideologies, but these and other tools of rule were not the same. How was the government of the Chinese Empire different from the Roman? What were the consequences of those differences?

HISTORICAL CONTEXT *119*

THINKING HISTORICALLY: **Making Comparisons** *122*

7. The Spread of Universal Religions: Afro-Eurasia, 100–1000 C.E. 235

Christianity, Buddhism, and later Islam spread far across Eurasia often along the same routes in the first thousand years of the Common Era. Perhaps Judaism did as well. What made these religions so expansive? How were they alike and different? Who converted whom? What did they change, and what did they leave the same?

8. Migrations, Trade, and Travel: The Movement of People, Goods, and Ideas in Eurasia, Africa, and the Pacific, 3000 B.C.E.–1350 C.E. 278

World history is not just the story of different civilizations. It is also the story of the movement and blending of peoples, things, and ideas across oceans and continents. Migrants, travelers, and traders have remixed almost every aspect of life: political, social, economic, and cultural.

9. Love, Sex, and Marriage: Medieval Europe and Asia, 400–1350 319

Love and marriage make the world go 'round today, but not a thousand years ago. Love, sex, and marriage were also not always experienced in the same relationship, even ideally. These words meant different things to different people throughout Europe and Asia. We use cultural comparisons to find out more.

10. The First Crusade: Muslims, Christians, and Jews during the First Crusade, 1095–1099 360

The First Crusade initiated a centuries-long struggle and dialogue between Christians and Muslims that would have a lasting impact on both. To understand how it happened, we must be prepared to hear and weigh differing narratives from different communities. At times like this, there are more than two sides to a story.

11. Raiders of Steppe and Sea: Vikings and Mongols, Eurasia and the Atlantic, 900–1350 398

From the late ninth through the tenth century, waves of Viking ships attacked across Europe; a few centuries later, beginning in 1200, the Mongols swept across Eurasia, conquering all in their path and creating the largest empire the world had ever seen. What was the impact of these raiding peoples on settled societies and vice versa? In considering this question and the violent and destructive nature of these "barbarian" raids, we will consider the relationship of morality to history.

12. The Black Death: Afro-Eurasia, 1346–1350 447

The pandemic plague ravaged the population of Afro-Eurasia, killing about one-third of the population of Europe and Egypt. In this chapter, we examine the impact of the plague in various locales while also contemplating its causes and the relation between cause and effect.

13. On Cities: European, Chinese, Islamic, and Mexican Cities, 1000–1550 482

What did increasing urbanization from the medieval period on mean for those who lived in cities and those who did not? Wandering through some of the great cities of medieval Europe, China, and the Islamic world, we attempt to answer this question while also considering the validity and merits of one historian's famous comparative thesis about urbanization.

14. Environment, Culture, and Technology: Europe, Asia, Oceania, and South America, 500–1500 519

Since the Middle Ages, the most significant changes have occurred in the fields of ecology, technology, and science. In this chapter we read and assess three grand theories about the origins of our technological transformation and our environmental problems, drawing on written and visual primary source evidence to develop our conclusions.

15. Overseas Expansion in the Early Modern Period: Asia, Africa, Europe, and the Americas, 1400–1600 560

Both China and Europe set sail for global expansion in the fifteenth century, but China's explorations ended just as Europe's began. What were the factors that led to their similar efforts yet different outcomes? We examine primary and secondary sources in search of clues.

16. Atlantic World Encounters: Europeans, Americans, and Africans, 1500–1850 609

European encounters with Africans and Americans were similar in some ways, yet markedly different in others. The cultural clash created a new Atlantic world that integrated and divided these indigenous peoples. We compare primary sources, including visual evidence, to understand these first contacts and conflicts.

17. State and Religion: Asian, Islamic, and Christian States, 1500–1800 657

In this chapter, we view the relationship between religion and political authority through the prism of Chinese, Japanese, South Asian, and Western experience in the early modern period. By examining the competing and sometimes cooperating dynamics between church and state in the past, we explore the history of an issue much debated in our own time and gain new insights on church-state relations today.

18. Women, Marriage, and Family: China and Europe, 1550–1700 684

With the blinds drawn on the domestic lives of our ancestors, one might assume their private worlds were uneventful and everywhere the same. By comparing different cultures, we see historical variety in family and economic life and the roles of both men and women.

19. The Scientific Revolution: Europe, the Ottoman Empire, China, Japan, and the Americas, 1600–1800 726

The scientific revolution of the seventeenth and eighteenth centuries occurred in Europe, but it had important roots in Asia and its consequences reverberated throughout the world. In this chapter we seek to understand what changed and how. How "revolutionary" was the scientific revolution, and how do we distinguish between mere change and "revolutionary" change?

20. Enlightenment and Revolution: Europe, the Americas, and India, 1650–1850 768

The eighteenth-century Enlightenment applied scientific reason to politics, but reason meant different things to different people and societies. What were the goals of the political revolutions produced by the Enlightenment? A close reading of the period texts reveals disagreement and shared dreams.

21. Capitalism and the Industrial Revolution: Europe and the World, 1750–1900 799

Modern society has been shaped dramatically by capitalism and the industrial revolution, but these two forces are not the same. Which one is principally responsible for the creation of our modern world:

the economic system of the market or the technology of the industrial revolution? Distinguishing different "causes" allows us to gauge their relative effects and legacies.

22. Colonized and Colonizers: Europeans in Africa and Asia, 1850–1930 846

Colonialism resulted in a world divided between the colonized and the colonizers, a world in which people's identities were defined by their power relationships with others who looked and often spoke differently. The meeting of strangers and their forced adjustment to predefined roles inspired a number of great literary works that we look to in this chapter for historical guidance.

25. World War II and Mass Killing: Germany, the Soviet Union, Japan, and the United States, 1926–1945 *957*

The rise of fascism in Europe and Asia led to total war, genocide, war crimes, and civilian massacres on an almost unimaginable scale. How could governments, armies, and ordinary people commit such unspeakable acts? How can we recognize the unbelievable and understand the inexcusable?

26. The Cold War and the Third World: Vietnam, Cuba, Argentina, and Afghanistan, 1945–1989 999

The Cold War was not only a conflict between the United States and the Soviet Union in which both superpowers avoided direct military confrontation; it was also a series of hot wars and propaganda battles, often played out with surrogates, for the creation of a new "post-colonial" world order and the control of an emerging "Third World." A war of words is a good place to look for hidden political meanings.

27. New Democracy Movements: The World, 1977 to the Present 1038

Demands for democracy are on the rise, challenging and sometimes sweeping away old empires, petty tyrants, military dictatorships, and one-party states. Even "old" democracies are pushed to raise the bar to include social justice, economic opportunity, and a right to education. Where are these movements coming from? Are they connected or coincidental? Are they for real?

28. Globalization: The World, 1990 to the Present 1089

Globalization is a word with many meanings and a process with many causes. What are the forces most responsible for the shrinking of the world into one global community? Do the forces of globalization unite or divide us? Do they impoverish or enrich us? We undertake the study of process to answer these questions.

List of Maps

Geographic Contents

Middle East (West Asia)

Central Asia

South Asia

East Asia

Southeast Asia

Australasia and the Pacific

Europe and Russia

The Americas

Interregional Contacts

Historical Thinking, Reading, and Writing Skills for AP* World History

Dave Neumann, Director, The History Project
at CSU Long Beach

Students and adults alike often grumble that history is just a bunch of facts to memorize. While it's true that studying history requires data, information, and yes, facts, that's not the essence of what history is. History is a way of thinking about the world by looking at the past. It is a reconstruction of the past, drawing on both imagination and interpretation. In this effort historians use a number of skills to interpret facts about the past. This skills primer will help you develop those historical thinking skills you need to succeed in Advanced Placement World History and on the exam. It will also enable you to improve critical thinking, reading, and writing skills that will be useful in college, or in whatever endeavor you pursue after high school.

■ HISTORICAL THINKING SKILLS FOR WORLD HISTORY

AP World History addresses four major skills, each with at least two components, that represent the ways historians think about the past. These skills have been described as "habits of mind." This useful phrase should remind you that a skill needs to be practiced repeatedly until it becomes second nature. Because practice is an integral part of learning to think historically, the sections below include exercises to help you develop these "habits of mind." Like shooting free throws, rehearsing dance moves, or playing scales, historical thinking skills need to be exercised regularly until you can use them easily and almost effortlessly.

While the skills described here are shared by all historians, world historians use them in distinctive ways. That's because world history deals with a much larger region (often the entire globe) and a much longer period of time (thousands of years) than, for example, United States history. Thus, world historians practice historical thinking from a very broad point of view. Even though we discuss each skill separately below, these skills overlap in many ways. For example, you can't make a

* AP and the Advanced Placement Program are registered trademarks of the College Board, which was not involved in the production of and does not endorse this product.

historical argument without also evaluating evidence. So as you develop one historical thinking skill, you will also be learning other skills.

Skill 1:
Crafting Historical Arguments from Historical Evidence

The first historical thinking skill focuses our attention on using evidence to make historical arguments. The word *argument* reminds us that any attempt to explain the past requires interpretation, since our understanding of the past is limited. Arguing means making a logical—rather than an emotional—case for your interpretation of a particular historical question or controversy. To be convincing, your interpretation has to present supporting evidence. This evidence consists of both historical facts and information from primary sources.

Historical Argumentation

Historians make arguments about what life was like in the past, how or why things changed, and why those changes matter. Their arguments are informed by their deep knowledge about the subject and careful reading of primary sources. But because evidence from the past is often incomplete or difficult to understand, historians make inferences to fill the gaps in their knowledge. Not all historians make the same inferences, so there are often a variety of interpretations about most historical events.

For example, most scholars agree that the decision of some people to adopt agriculture about 11,000 years ago marked the beginning of a major world-historical development. But because this development preceded writing, the only evidence scholars have comes from archaeology and anthropology. Consequently, historians disagree about whether agriculture led to permanent settlement in a particular location—or vice versa. Many scholars also believe that the development of agricultural surpluses introduced disparities in status. Critics disagree, however, pointing to tomb evidence from foraging (that is, non-farming) people that suggests that significant differences in status existed already among some pre-agricultural peoples.

To develop this historical thinking skill, ask yourself how historians think they know what they know about a particular event. What evidence do they provide? Does their language suggest hesitancy or uncertainty about their interpretation? Do they offer alternative explanations?

➡ **Exercise:** On pages 19–25 of this text, how does Margaret Ehrenberg explain the contributions of women to the agricultural revolution? What inferences does she make?

Appropriate Use of Relevant Historical Evidence

Historians make arguments about the past based on primary-source evidence. A primary source is something produced in the era under investigation. In contrast, a secondary source is something about the era under investigation, produced long after the fact. It is usually the result of scholarly research of primary sources, or a distillation of such research. The introductions and headnotes of this textbook, for example, are secondary sources. Traditionally, primary sources have consisted overwhelmingly of written sources. In fact, some historians referred to any time before writing as "pre-historic."

In the last few decades, historians have increasingly moved beyond relying exclusively on written primary sources by turning to visual sources — paintings, photographs, architecture, artifacts, and so on — and evidence from other fields of knowledge. For example, using scientific and medical information, historians have come to see the role that disease has played in history — destroying Native populations in the Americas after Europeans arrived, for example. Since no historian can be an expert in every field, historians also make use of the secondary-source scholarship of others who have studied primary sources such as ancient DNA or pottery shards in their own specialized studies.

In assessing primary sources, you need to begin with a careful examination of the source itself. But understanding evidence requires more. You also have to pay attention to the information that you know or can find out about the source so you can make good inferences. This is known as the *context* of the source. Primary sources are creations from a particular time and place, often created for someone else, so determining the author, purpose, and audience of a source is essential to your understanding of it. Ask Reilly's list of basic "w" questions from page xiii when analyzing a source to help you gain a more sophisticated understanding of the document.

➡ **Exercise:** What information in Chapter 2 provides a context for the documents in that chapter?

Skill 2: Chronological Reasoning

Chronological reasoning means thinking logically about how and why the world changes — or, sometimes, stays the same — over time. While all fields of knowledge offer arguments based on evidence or make comparisons, historians are uniquely concerned about the past and its relationship to the present. How is the world different now than it was 50 years ago, 500 years ago, or 5,000 years ago? Why did the world change? How have some aspects of the world remained relatively the same over long periods of time? On what basis do historians simplify the long and complicated past by breaking it into smaller eras?

Historical Causation

Causation has to do with explanations about how or why changes take place in world history. Sometimes there is an obvious connection between an event and its consequence, like a cue ball striking the eight ball and making it move. And some events *are* fairly straightforward: The attack on Pearl Harbor prompted President Roosevelt to ask Congress for a declaration of war against Japan. But even this seemingly simple example is more complex. Why did Japan attack the United States? What role did the American embargo on the sale of oil have on Japan's decision? Why did the United States enact this embargo? All of these other events took place just a few years before the Pearl Harbor attack. If we go even further back, we'll gain additional insight about the larger context of the Japanese government's decision.

Just as there were many factors behind the Japanese decision to bomb Pearl Harbor, most examples of historical causation involve multiple causes. Historical causation also involves large processes, unintended consequences, and contingencies, as this chart describes.

Historical Causation involves:	
Multiple causes	Most events or developments such as the Japanese attack on Pearl Harbor occur from a combination of factors, not just one.
Large processes	Many changes take place through major processes that are larger than any one person. Urbanization is a complex set of changes resulting from the actions of countless different individuals.
Unintended causes	Many changes take place accidentally, like the large-scale deaths of Native Americans during the Columbian Exchange due to diseases Europeans weren't aware they were carrying.
Contingency	Events are not preordained, and history could have turned out differently. This is known as *contingency*. Because we read major events in history already knowing their outcome, we have a tendency to think they were bound to happen, but that is not the case. The initial Spanish conquest of the Incas was very precarious, for example, and early on they might have been defeated.

You can begin to develop the skill of determining causation by asking yourself, whenever some significant change in world history is described, what reasons explain the development? If the answer seems simple, keep digging, because there's bound to be a more complicated (and longer-term) explanation.

➡ **Exercise:** The essays by Jared Diamond, Terry Hunt, and J. R. McNeill in Chapter 14 explore the collapse of Easter Island. How do these historians explain the causes for this collapse? Which of the types of explanations from the box on page xlix do they use in their explanations?

Patterns of Continuity and Change Over Time

Historians are interested in both historical changes and persisting patterns, or "continuities." Change is easier to see: When one empire overthrows another one, that event often becomes part of the historical record. But some things stay relatively the same for long periods of time. Because continuity (such as a network of trade that remains in existence for hundreds of years) is less dramatic than change, it can be harder to spot.

What counts as continuity depends on the scale of time you're working with. The Soviet Union was continuous throughout most of the twentieth century. However, in the time frame of Russia's history since the formation of Kievan Rus in the ninth century, the Soviet era looks more like a short-lived exception to tsarist rule.

When historians talk about continuity, they're not implying that a particular pattern applied to everyone in the world or even in a particular region. Nor are they claiming that absolutely nothing changed in the pattern they're describing. For example, agricultural production has been continuous for thousands of years. But there are exceptions to this broad statement: On the one hand, some people have continued to be foragers; on the other hand, methods of farming have changed substantially with technology. So the continuity of agriculture is a generalization but not a completely unchanging pattern nor a pattern that applies to everyone on the planet.

To work on developing this skill, look for places in your text where an author directly indicates that a historical pattern persisted over time and explains *why* that pattern persisted. But even when an author focuses on change in world history, you can still find continuity by inference, since few things ever change completely. When the text describes a new development, ask yourself what *didn't* change. For example, while Buddhism became popular after its introduction into China, Confucianism remained an important force in Chinese culture.

➡ **Exercise:** Look at Reilly's Reflections section at the end of Chapter 7: The Spread of Universal Religions on pages 275–77. What language does he use to convey that he is talking about patterns of continuity?

Periodization

Periodization refers to the ways that historians break the past into separate periods of time. Historians look for major turning points in history—places where the world looked very different *before* some event than it did *after*—to decide how to break the past into chunks. They then give a label to each period to convey the key characteristics and developments of that era.

Because the past is complex, particularly when talking about a subject as vast as world history, any attempt to create eras and give those eras labels can provoke disagreement. Periods are, after all, constructed by historians and reflect the particular context in which they are writing. Some world historians, for example, argue for a major division at 1000 C.E., which would highlight the beginning point of roles of nomadic peoples in the period between 1000 and 1450. Others prefer to maintain a single period from about 600 to 1450, since they don't think nomadic empires significantly interrupted a larger period of Afro-Eurasian contact. These disagreements often carry over into the classroom. The AP World History course used to make a break at 1914, instead of 1900. The older periodization made World War I a major turning point. Pushing the period back to the beginning of the twentieth century in 1900, as the AP World History course now does, places the war in the context of other important modern developments—including developments less focused on Europe, such as the rise of nationalist movements among colonial peoples.

As you develop this skill, pay regular attention to the chapter you're in, noting what major era it is described as being a part of, and thinking about what the different labels for that era say about the main "story" of that era, at least according to your teacher, your textbook, or the College Board.

➡ **Exercise:** Compare Reilly's periodization in Chapters 1 and 2 to the College Board's historical periodization. How do Reilly's dates and titles compare to the College Board's? What explains these differences?

Reilly	College Board
Chapter 1: Prehistory and the Origins of Patriarchy: Gathering, Agricultural, and Urban Societies, 40,000–1000 B.C.E.	**Period 1:** Technological and Environmental Transformations, to c. 600 B.C.E.
Chapter 2: The Urban Revolution and "Civilization": Ancient City Societies in Mesopotamia, Egypt, and Peru, 3500–1000 B.C.E.	**Period 2:** Organization and Reorganization of Human Societies, c. 600 B.C.E. to 600 C.E.

Skill 3:
Comparison and Contextualization

People don't learn things in isolation, but in relationship. Historians are no different. The third category of historical thinking skills reflects the ways historians make sense of the past by placing particulars in some larger framework. For example, they understand historical events and processes by comparing them to related events and processes to see how they're similar and different. Second, historians recognize that historical evidence, including artifacts, photographs, speeches, and historical narratives (secondary sources) can only be adequately understood by knowing something about their context, that is, the time and place when they came into existence.

Comparison

Comparisons help world historians understand how empire development in the past was similar to or different from another development, and in this way determine what was distinctive. For example, through comparative study, scholars have concluded that empires that developed over the last two thousand years share key features. First, rulers have to legitimize their rule through religious or ideological traditions. Second, they have to maintain political unity by dealing with people on the peripheries of the empire. Finally, since empires develop by conquering other groups of people, empires have to deal with ethnic diversity.

But while these patterns hold true for all empires, each one addresses these challenges in its own way. The Ottoman Empire justified its rule through Turkish tradition as well as Islamic belief. They rewarded loyal elites on the margins of their empire through tax breaks. And they dealt with minorities by creating the *millet* system (whereby Ottoman subjects were divided into religious communities, each ruled by its religious leaders). Through the tool of comparison we understand how Ottoman rulers handled common problems in unique ways.

As you develop this skill, practice comparing two nations that existed at the same time—like the Ottoman and Mughal empires—and also compare the same government at two different points in time. For example, how was government in Song China similar to—and different from—government in Tang China? Be sure that the two things you're comparing are relatively similar, or else the comparison doesn't make much sense.

➡ **Exercise:** Look at Reilly's comparison of empire and government in China and Rome in Chapter 4. Is it fair and appropriate to compare these empires? How are these empires similar to one another? Why are they alike? What key features are different? Why are they different?

Contextualization

Just as historical events make more sense when they're studied alongside similar events, historians know that any event can only be understood in "context." Context refers to the historical circumstances surrounding a particular event. World historians look for major global developments in any era to help determine context. They typically think in terms of two levels of context: an *immediate* (or short-term) context and a *broad* (or long-term) context.

The easiest way to begin thinking about context is to figure out when a particular event (or document) took place. Then brainstorm the major developments of the era. Ask yourself, "How might these larger events have shaped this event (or document)?"

For example, when reading the Vietnamese leader Ho Chi Minh's "Declaration of Independence" on page 1006 note that it was written in 1945. What were the major *immediate* geopolitical developments of the mid-point of the twentieth century? World War II had just ended when he made this speech, so you can count on that being important to understanding the speech. After the war, the two major trends were the Cold War and decolonization movements based on nationalist ideologies. Both of those trends are crucial for understanding what Ho was calling for—and why countries (including the United States) reacted to him the way they did. The *broad* context of European imperialism thus forms the background that helps explain Ho's anger.

➡ **Exercise:** Look at the images of the Black Death on pages 468–70. What *immediate* developments in the fourteenth century influenced the scenes depicted in these illustrations? How does the *broad* context of the Medieval period help you understand these images?

Skill 4:
Historical Interpretation and Synthesis

You first learned about how historians make arguments; now you'll practice evaluating those arguments and making your own. Since history requires making inferences about the past, it's inevitable that scholars will come to different conclusions. It can be very helpful then to study different historical interpretations about a particular event or movement over time, as interpretations often change. The final skill component, synthesis, is also related to argumentation. It is the culminating skill because it requires you to integrate all the other skills in creating your own argument.

Interpretation

Historians interpret both primary and secondary sources, evaluating points of view and considering context to create their own interpretations. Through analyzing different historical interpretations, you will see how historical interpretations change over time. We have already established that formulating a historical argument requires making inferences from evidence. The background of a particular historian (age, gender, nationality, political philosophy, time of writing, etc.) often shapes the way he or she understands or interprets the past. In many cases, knowing something about the context of a historian can help you understand his or her argument better—in the same way that understanding the context of the author of a primary source helps you understand the primary source. Sometimes, this information can help you identify the prejudices or limitations of a particular interpretation.

For example, in the early 1960s a British historian claimed that Africa had no history until Europeans took over the continent. Subsequent scholarship has shown this conclusion to be quite false, and we can assume that this historian's context as a citizen of an imperial nation writing during decolonization influenced his outlook. About the same time, an American scholar developed an influential model of modernization for "Third World" countries. Later scholars have argued that this model oversimplified the world by assuming all countries would grow economically the same way the United States had.

Be careful when analyzing historical interpretations. You can't simply assume that because a scholar has x background he or she will make y argument. There are far too many exceptions for such a rule. Instead, begin by finding out what you can about a scholar's background and then make a hunch about how this background might shape his or her views. Then, as you read the scholar's argument carefully look for evidence that the author actually makes the kinds of arguments you anticipated. If you don't find such evidence, discard your hunch.

➡ **Exercise:** On pages 402–08 of this text, Gregory Guzman describes how historians have often ascribed negative attributes to the pastoral nomads known as "barbarians." Why have interpretations of these nomadic people varied over time?

Synthesis

Synthesis is a culminating skill that reflects your ability to make persuasive arguments of your own from evidence. It draws on all of the other historical thinking skills—historical argumentation, appropriate use of relevant historical evidence, causation, continuity and change, periodization, comparison, contextualization, and interpretation—along with two other elements. First, you may need to draw on evidence outside the field of history. This will most likely come from the social sciences: archaeology, anthropology, economics, sociology, and so on. The other element is the ability to apply insights from historical evidence to a new setting. This is a creative form of comparison. Most likely, you will link some moment in the past to a contemporary problem, such as ongoing struggles in the developing world based on the process of decolonization. In so doing, you will be using the past to shed light on the present. You will have taken a major step in historical thinking, as making connections is a key part of what historians do.

■ GETTING THE MOST OUT OF READING WORLD HISTORY

Active reading means reading for meaning. The big challenges of reading are length and detail. If you understand the "big picture," you can read much more quickly and effectively, because you can "see the forest for the trees." That is, you can see the main ideas and recognize how specific information is provided to illustrate those big ideas. The three stages of reading described below will help you understand the "big picture" when reading this text and others.

Pre-reading

When approaching a text such as this one, it is helpful to spend a few minutes pre-reading the material. During the pre-reading stage, you are simply getting prepared for what you will be reading. This involves two steps. First, try to determine chronology, theme(s), and region(s). Do this by looking at chapter dates, the part or unit that includes this chapter (keeping in mind that not all books are divided into parts), the chapter that came before and the one that comes next, and the chapter title. Note that the next main section of a chapter may not describe something that happened later in time; it may simply reflect a different theme about the same time and place. Second, try to determine the major changes, comparisons, and connections discussed in the chapter by scanning the section titles, images and captions (maps, charts, photos, etc.), and any pedagogical tools included (chronologies, key terms, document headnotes, review questions, etc.). Also, skim the introduction to the chapter — usually reading the topic sentences of this section is sufficient.

➡ **Exercise:** Let's practice by pre-reading Chapter 2: The Urban Revolution and "Civilization": Ancient City Societies in Mesopotamia, Egypt, and Peru, 3500–1000 B.C.E. Scan the chapter opener and without writing anything down, answer the following questions.

- **Chronology:** Looking at the dates for Chapter 2 on page 32, what is the chronology of this chapter? How much time does this chapter cover? What does the topic sentence in the first paragraph of the Historical Context section say about this chapter's chronology?

- **Theme:** Read the topic sentences in the Historical Context section. What is this chapter going to be about? Why is the topic important? Using the contents list on page xv, what chapters come before and after this one? How do they fit together?
- **Region:** Read the chapter title and scan the document titles in this chapter. Does Chapter 2 focus on particular regions or larger global processes? How do you know?

You haven't read the chapter yet—and you haven't taken a single note. But by spending 5 minutes pre-reading the chapter you already have a good idea what the chapter's all about. By taking this time, you'll be able to read with a clear focus, saving yourself a lot of time later on. Now that you have a good idea of the "big picture," you're ready to begin actually reading the text.

During Reading

As you read chapters of this text, remember that reading is an active process—so stay focused. The meaning will only become clear as you work at it. The author has intentionally written an organized textbook and wants you to be able to follow along, so take advantage of the clues he's provided, especially titles and headings.

Active readers use four skills to understand texts: *questioning, clarifying, summarizing,* and *predicting.* These steps don't have to happen in a particular order. In fact, once you become comfortable with them, they'll pop up on their own without you trying in whatever order they choose, perhaps several at the same time—that's when you know that they've truly become habits of mind. Use these skills along with note taking to get the most out of your reading.

Questioning

Historians look at the world in a particular way, and they usually organize their writing around the historical thinking skills discussed above: cause and effect, comparison, interpretation, and so forth. By questioning you can identify these patterns.

For every chapter of this book you want to find out the major subject. The easiest way to do this is to ask the "reporter questions": Who? What? Where? When? Why?

1. *Who* is the chapter about? History texts are almost always about people. Is the focus an individual? A social group? A political entity?
2. *What* does the section say about this person or group? Texts usually describe some major event or pattern. Did they do something important? Did something happen to them?

3. *Where* did the subject being described take place? Physical location is often crucial in history. Does this location help make sense of the subject in some way?

4. *When* did the events take place? Like physical location, chronology forms part of the historical context that makes events understandable. Does the text describe something unfolding over a very short period—or a longer one? Are there crucial events that came before that make the description understandable?

5. *Why* did the event or pattern being described take place—and why does it matter? Whether talking about a dramatic development or a continuity that endured for a long period of time, historians always attempt to understand what led to it. What reasons does the text provide for the event or pattern? How is the significance of the development explained?

Clarifying

Are there any words you don't understand? If they're crucial for making sense of the passage, can you define them using a dictionary or other outside source? If there are any sentences you didn't understand, did they become clearer as you reread them or as you read on in the text?

When it comes to vocabulary, use good judgment. Is the word crucial for understanding the passage? If not, read right past it. If it *is* a crucial word, you may need to look it up in a dictionary. Before you take the time to look it up, however, check that it hasn't been defined already for you in the text.

When a longer passage throws you off, usually clearing up difficult vocabulary will help make the passage clearer. If it doesn't, simply reread the sentence a few times (slowly!). If you're still unclear, back up—usually to the beginning of the paragraph—and try again. The most common way skilled readers get clarification is simply by rereading.

Summarizing

A summary is a brief review of the "big picture" of a particular section or chapter. After reading, briefly explain what each chapter is about in one sentence—being sure your summary answers all five questions from the *Questioning* section.

Predicting

Based on your reading of an entire section or chapter, what do you think will come next in the text? How do you know? You may think predicting what's coming next is a waste of time, but it's a really good test of how well you understand the flow of the text. If you're in a car with your family going to visit your grandmother, you probably know the route to get there. If your mother takes an unanticipated turn, it alerts you that something is different from what you were expecting—and prompts you to ask why. So if your prediction based on reading is wildly off, it may alert you to the fact that your previous idea of the "big picture" of the section was off for some reason. You may need to back up and reread a section, or at least move forward more alert to where the author is going.

Note Taking

Of course, simply reading the text is not sufficient. You'll never remember everything that's important unless you take notes. Students experience many pitfalls when taking notes. You should only write notes *after* you understand what you have read. Actively *question, clarify, summarize,* and *predict* in your head (or out loud) as you read each chapter; then go back through the subsections and take brief notes representing the key ideas of that section.

Brief is generally better—don't wear yourself out in the notes themselves. Find some consistent abbreviations for frequent words and use symbols. For example, an up arrow to indicate growth, a flat arrow to indicate cause/effect, and an "=" to indicate a definition, and so on. Don't write everything; ask yourself if a particular point is a main idea or just an example. If you own your textbook, make annotations in the margins. If not, get a stack of sticky notes and place them in the margins for your comments.

➡ **Exercise:** Let's practice these four skills with a secondary source from Chapter 2: "Cities and Civilization" by Kevin Reilly on pages 35–44.

- **Questioning:** What was the urban revolution? Who was involved in the urban revolution? Where did it occur? When did the urban revolution take place? Why did agriculture emerge? Why did cities develop?

- **Clarifying:** What does the author mean by "civilization"? If there were any sentences you didn't understand, did they become clearer as you reread them or as you read on in the text?

- **Summarizing:** Briefly explain what this source is about in one sentence.

- **Predicting:** Based on the source you've just read, what do you think will come next in the text? How do you know?

Now that you know what this selection is about, what brief comments are worth writing down in your notes?

Post-reading

Reflecting on what you've read places information you've just learned into long-term memory. Post-reading involves doing the same kind of summarizing you've done section by section, but now for the entire chapter. In essence, it is a summary of your summaries. While it might seem enough to summarize the chapter verbally, writing down key ideas helps place them into long-term memory. Read through the notes that you've taken for the chapter, particularly the summary of each section. Then try to write a master summary of the entire chapter using no more than 50 words that captures the key point of each section of the chapter, as well as the chapter as a whole.

➡ **Exercise:** Write a master summary of Chapter 2 now.

■ WRITING ABOUT WORLD HISTORY

This skills primer began by introducing you to the patterns of thinking you need to really understand history. The next section pointed out ways to be smart about reading your textbook. This third and final section turns to the writing skills you need to develop for the AP World History course and exam. Our focus shifts away from your *receiving* input toward your *providing* output: sharing your understanding of historical thinking skills through writing.

Most of this section will address the specific challenge of each of the three types of essays in AP World History. But first, it's important to understand two essential skills that apply to all of the essays you'll encounter. First, to successfully demonstrate what you know, you have to answer the question that has been asked. Sounds simple, but many students get in trouble on the exam by failing to address the prompt in front of them.

Every prompt contains three elements, and you need to pay attention to all of them as you plan your response to the prompt. First, there is a periodization or date range expressed in years. Obviously, you need to be sure your response addresses this era. One of the most common problems in student essays on the exam comes from providing historical information from the wrong era. Second, there is a task expressed as the main verb of the prompt: *compare, describe, explain, analyze,* and so forth. Pay attention to this task verb, as these tasks are not the same.

Finally, each prompt deals with a subject, expressed in two important types of nouns. A *proper noun* refers to a specific historical entity—Confucianism, the Mali empire, the Silk Road. A *common noun* typically refers to a historical concept: a key historical idea (monotheism, nationalism) or process (diffusion of culture, expansion of empire). Sometimes this process is limited in time, but often it is a pattern that occurs repeatedly in world history.

It doesn't matter how strong your content knowledge and historical skills are if you can't communicate clearly what you know. Every essay needs to have a specific, focused *thesis* that makes an argument addressing the prompt. Your thesis should be as brief as possible, while still addressing the complexity of the topic. If you explicitly respond to each of the three prompt elements clearly and accurately, you will have a strong thesis—and you'll be on your way to a persuasive essay.

Every essay needs to be organized into distinct *paragraphs*. The number of paragraphs depends on the complexity of the prompt. Typically, however, two body paragraphs won't be sufficient to address the topic thoroughly. What's most important is that you clearly announce the point you're going to make in each paragraph through a *topic sentence* that effectively covers the subject of the paragraph. Any content in the paragraph that doesn't support the topic sentence doesn't belong there.

Finally, every essay requires you to make use of *evidence* to support your claims. The type of evidence also differs depending on the type of essay. The Document-Based Question (DBQ) requires you to reference each of the documents included with the question, while continuity-change and comparative essays require you to draw on factual information.

While many of these writing suggestions would apply equally to essays in other academic subjects, the essay types on the AP World History exam are all geared to the concerns of historians. Each type of essay requires the use of the historical thinking skills discussed above, often in combination with one another. For example, every essay type requires you to discuss the *historical context* of the subject you're writing about and to *appropriately use relevant evidence*.

Essay type	
Continuity & Change Over Time	Examine one historical subject across two (or more) eras of world history.
Comparative	Examine two (or more) historical subjects during the same era of world history.
Document-Based Question (DBQ)	Examine multiple primary source documents as evidence for an argument.

Continuity-and-Change-Over-Time Essay

This type of essay question tests your ability to explain change and continuity. As we discussed above, historical study typically focuses on changes. In this essay type, you have to identify major changes and explain the significance of those changes—that is, why the changes matter—for the topic described in the prompt. You will also have to analyze *why* something changed. But because some things continue largely the same for hundreds of years or more, you also have to identify continuities, explain their significance, and explain why these patterns persisted for so long.

Your essay response must clearly address both elements—continuity and change. A strong argument must do more than simply *identify* some continuities and changes. It has to *analyze* why both the continuities and changes existed and why they mattered. It's a good idea to weigh the relative value of continuities and changes. In other words, do you perceive continuities to have been more powerful than changes on the topic addressed in the prompt, or vice versa? Why do you think so? In terms of structure, avoid the temptation to organize your essay into two large paragraphs, one for continuities and one for changes. Instead, identify important topics or categories of comparison—governmental structure, trade patterns, or gender relations—and use those topics as the body paragraphs. Then, in each body paragraph, address *both* continuities *and* changes, being clear to signal your transition from one to the other.

In the same way that identifying change is an easier historical thinking skill than identifying continuity, change is also easier to write about than continuity. Historical narratives devote a lot of time to, say, reasons for the fall of the Han empire—a significant change in East Asia. So if you're writing an essay about states in that era, that information will come to mind more quickly.

After brief reflection, however, you'll realize that the Han empire endured for more than 400 years—a significant continuity. Hopefully you'll also remember what you learned about how Han rulers governed their empire. Their techniques of government help explain why the empire lasted as long as it did. Therefore, in an essay about change and continuity in the Han empire you would want to identify a major political continuity in the era (the continued existence of the Han empire), discuss why this was significant (this large dynasty influenced a large region of East Asia), and explain why it endured (its governing techniques).

Comparative Essay

As discussed above, comparison is one of the most basic ways historians make sense of any subject and the AP World History exam asks you in this type of essay to write about two similar historical phenomena. You should begin your analysis by identifying broad similarities and differences. When you place two religions, two empires, or two trade patterns side-by-side, what do you notice? How are they similar? How are they different?

Once you move beyond the most basic level of identifying broad similarities and differences, you need to be more precise. You should begin by teasing out both categories in more detail, providing specific evidence to support your broad generalizations. For example, in broad terms neither the American nor the French Revolution significantly expanded the citizenship rights of students. But a more precise statement might explain that in neither case did women get the right to vote or hold public positions. Just as with change and continuity, it's often worthwhile to indicate whether you think similarities are more significant than differences, or vice versa, and why.

You need to be careful about the structure of this essay. Many students fall into the trap of simply describing topic one in a body paragraph and topic two in a separate body paragraph. They assume that readers will be able to recognize the differences between the two topics this way on their own. But you'll never earn a high score that way. Your comparisons need to be explicit and concrete.

Always begin each paragraph with a topic sentence that introduces the category or topic you want to compare. Be sure to use clear signal words that identify that you are shifting from similarity to difference ("Despite these similarities _____, the two trade routes differed dramatically.") In the contrast portion of your essay be clear about the particular difference, making use of contrast words such as *conversely, unlike,* and *however* to signal your point to the reader.

In brainstorming similarities, try to step back a bit and think in more abstract conceptual terms so you don't miss deep similarities that seem different on the surface. For example, students sometimes say that a king is different from an emperor, because they focus on the different titles. But both are hereditary monarchs typically viewed as having divine authority to rule. That makes them very similar in deep ways, despite the different labels. They are much more like each other than they are to, say, a stateless society or to a democracy.

Students sometimes wonder whether they should start the paragraph with similarities or differences first. One way to approach this is to deal with the less significant topic first, get it out of the way, and move on to the more significant topic. But that is really a matter of taste. What *is* important is that you provide a clear transition when you move from the compare to the contrast portion of your essay (or vice versa): "These similarities [that you've just discussed], however, were much less crucial than differences in *x*, *y*, and *z*." If this sounds like a repeat of your thesis statement, that's because it is. In the body of your essay, you want to echo the road map—your thesis—to help your reader know that you are making the transition that you indicated in the introductory paragraph that you would be making.

Document-Based Question Essay

The Document-Based Question, or DBQ, essay is a defining feature of the AP History exam. Of all the essays, this one tends to make students the most anxious. But much of this anxiety is misplaced. Once you understand the DBQ, you will feel less worried about it—and may even come to find it your favorite essay type. Unlike the other two essay types, where you have to call on your memory to provide all the evidence, the documents in the DBQ form the basic evidence you need to use.

To do well on a DBQ, you need to use all, or all but one, of the documents in the question. In addition, you must go beyond the content of the documents in order to set the context, make a clear argument, and analyze the documents properly. Using documents as evidence requires the sophisticated analysis skills we discussed in the section on "Appropriate Use of Relevant Historical Evidence." That means that you have to consider the perspective or point of view of the documents. Every primary source—textual, visual, or statistical—was created for a specific purpose. That doesn't mean the author had an agenda, though sometimes that is the case. But even if the author didn't have an agenda, every document is limited and imperfect in the information it provides. Use the questions included on page xiii to interrogate each document, and then consider the limitations of each document before writing your DBQ. Then be sure to incorporate these insights about document limitations into the essay itself to make your essay more analytical—and therefore stronger.

Consider the example of a photo depicting indentured servants on a nineteenth-century sugar plantation. Students tend to view a document like that as a straightforward factual record. After all, we often hear that "pictures don't lie." But the picture was taken by someone for a particular purpose and the individuals are posed. So it's worth asking *why* someone wanted this picture taken. What purpose would this picture serve? Since it's posed, what's left out of it? How might it misrepresent—or represent in a very limited way—the realities of the indentured experience?

You also need to corroborate your documents. That means bringing the documents into "conversation" with each other. Since the documents in a DBQ don't directly refer to each other, you have to use your deductive skills to see connections. This relates to a distinctive task about the DBQ: You need to organize the evidence from the documents into several categories—usually at least three. The categories are sometimes stated or implied in the prompt, but you'll often have to call on your knowledge of world history and the content of the documents themselves to determine what categories (and how many) make sense. Please note that you can use the same document multiple times, so that often gives you flexibility in coming up with categories.

Finally, as part of the DBQ for AP World History, you will be asked to identify an additional type(s) of document(s) that would help you answer the question. Given that the documents in any DBQ represent a limited sample of the potential primary sources related to the topic of the DBQ, you should always think about a "missing voice"—a type of document that could have been provided but is not. The easiest way to develop this skill is to build off your earlier observations about the limitations of the sources that *are* included in the DBQ. For example, if a factory worker complains about low wages, that might represent a random, disgruntled worker. What kind of document would corroborate the worker's claim? How about a chart of average wages? Obviously, you don't know that such a thing exists, but it's reasonable to assume that such a document could exist—and that if it did, it would provide the evidence you needed. Feel free to mention other sources that you may have encountered previously in your answer, especially if they offer a perspective that is missing. You do not have to identify a specific document as additional evidence, but the type(s) of document(s) you identify must be plausible within the context of the question.

Many students feel anxious about having to write the AP World History essays. But once you become familiar with the elements of each prompt and know how to address these prompts effectively, you'll realize that there's no reason to be stressed about this. In fact, you should feel confident as you approach the writing portion of the test. Unlike the multiple-choice portion of the AP exam, the essay section gives you a lot of freedom to demonstrate what you know in an open-ended way. And if you've been thinking historically, reading the text with that lens, and sharing your ideas in class, you may begin to look forward to the opportunity to show just how developed your historical thinking skills are.

1

Prehistory and the Origins of Patriarchy

Gathering, Agricultural, and Urban Societies, 40,000–1000 B.C.E.

■ HISTORICAL CONTEXT

Men control more of the world's income, wealth, and resources; enjoy more opportunities, freedoms, and positions of power; and exercise greater control over the bodies, wishes, and lives of others than do women. In most of the world, men dominate, parents prefer sons to daughters, and most people—even women—associate maleness with strength, energy, reason, science, and the important public sphere. A system of male rule—"patriarchy"—seems as old as humanity itself. But is it? This chapter will ask if patriarchy is natural or historical. If patriarchy did not always exist, did it have a historical beginning, middle, and, therefore, potentially a historical end? If patriarchy had human causes, can humans also create a more equal world?

The selections in this chapter span the three types of societies known to human history: hunting and gathering (the earliest human lifestyle), agricultural and pastoral (beginning about ten thousand years ago), and urban (beginning about five thousand years ago). Thus, we can speak of the agricultural revolution (8000 B.C.E.) and the urban revolution (3000 B.C.E.) as two of the most important changes in human history. These events drastically transformed the way people earned a living and led to increased populations, greater productivity, and radically changed lifestyles.

As you read, consider how the lives of men and women changed with these revolutions. How did the relationships between men and women change? As people settled in agricultural villages, and later in cities, economic and social differences between groups became more

1

marked. Did differences between the sexes increase as well? Did men and women have relatively equal power before the development of agriculture and the rise of cities? Did patriarchy originate as part of the transition from agricultural to urban society, or did men always have more power?

■ THINKING HISTORICALLY

Thinking about History in Stages

To answer these questions, one must think of early human history in broad periods or stages. However, history does not develop in neat compartments, one clearly distinguished from the other. Historians must organize and analyze disparate events and developments that occur over time to make sense of them. This chapter follows a widely accepted division of early history into the hunting-gathering, agricultural-pastoral, and urban stages. Reflect on how this system of structuring the past makes history more intelligible, and consider the shortcomings of such a system. What challenges to the idea of historical stages do the readings in the chapter pose? On balance, does organizing history into stages make it easier or more difficult to understand complex changes, such as evolving gender roles?

1

NATALIE ANGIER

Furs for Evening, But Cloth Was the Stone Age Standby, 1999

The female "Venus" statues discussed in the following article date back over 20,000 years and are the earliest sculptures of humans. Archaeologists have long considered them symbols of fertility, given their exaggerated depiction of the female anatomy. As New York Times science writer Natalie Angier reports, some archaeologists have recently begun to reinterpret these "Venuses," emphasizing the detailed clothing and reconsidering what these costumes might reveal about the role of women in hunting and gathering societies. What conclusions do archaeologists draw from these new interpretations? What conclusions might you draw from these statues about the roles of women and their relative status in prehistoric society?

Source: Natalie Angier, "Furs for Evening, But Cloth Was the Stone Age Standby," *New York Times*, December 15, 1999, p. F1.

THINKING HISTORICALLY

Grouping prehistory into the hunting-gathering, agricultural-pastoral, and urban stages emphasizes how early people sustained themselves. Archaeologists and historians also divide prehistory into eras defined by the tools that humans developed. They also call the age of hunters and gatherers the Old Stone Age, or Paleolithic Era, because of the rough stone tools and arrow points that humans fashioned in this period. The age of agriculture is called the New Stone Age, or Neolithic Era, because of the use of more sophisticated stone tools. The urban age is often called the Bronze Age because city people began to smelt tin and copper to make bronze tools. Angier's article asks us to reconsider the importance of these designations by highlighting what Dr. Elizabeth Wayland Barber has termed the "string revolution." What is the string revolution, and what was its significance? According to Angier, how might the string revolution prompt us to reconsider stages of prehistory?

Ah, the poor Stone Age woman of our kitschy imagination. When she isn't getting bonked over the head with a club and dragged across the cave floor by her matted hair, she's hunched over a fire, poking at a roasting mammoth thigh while her husband retreats to his cave studio to immortalize the mammoth hunt in fresco. Or she's Raquel Welch, saber-toothed sex kitten, or Wilma Flintstone, the original Soccer Mom. But whatever her form, her garb is the same: some sort of animal pelt, cut nasty, brutish, and short.

Now, according to three anthropologists, it is time to toss such hide-bound clichés of Paleolithic woman on the midden heap of prehistory. In a new analysis of the renowned "Venus" figurines, the handsize statuettes of female bodies carved from 27,000 to 20,000 years ago, the researchers have found evidence that the women of the so-called upper Paleolithic era were far more accomplished, economically powerful, and sartorially gifted than previously believed.

As the researchers see it, subtle but intricate details on a number of the figurines offer the most compelling evidence yet that Paleolithic women had already mastered a revolutionary skill long thought to have arisen much later in human history: the ability to weave plant fibers into cloth, rope, nets, and baskets.

And with a flair for textile production came a novel approach to adorning and flaunting the human form. Far from being restricted to a wardrobe of what Dr. Olga Soffer, one of the researchers, calls "smelly animal hides," Paleolithic people knew how to create fine fabrics that very likely resembled linen. They designed string skirts, slung low on the hips or belted up on the waist, which artfully revealed at least as much

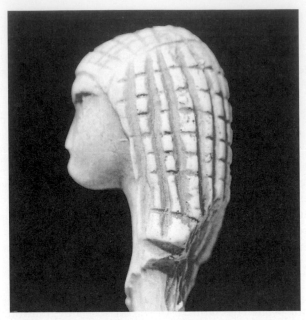

Figure 1.1   The Venus of Brassempouy, France.

Source: Steven Holland, University of Illinois.

as they concealed. They wove elaborate caps and snoods for the head, and bandeaux for the chest—a series of straps that amounted to a cupless brassiere. [See Figure 1.1.]

"Some of the textiles they had must have been incredibly fine, comparable to something from Donna Karan or Calvin Klein," said Dr. Soffer, an archaeologist with the University of Illinois in Urbana-Champaign.

Archaeologists and anthropologists have long been fascinated by the Venus figurines and have theorized endlessly about their origin and purpose. But nearly all of that speculation has centered on the exaggerated body parts of some of the figurines: the huge breasts, the bulging thighs and bellies, the well-defined vulvas. Hence, researchers have suggested that the figurines were fertility fetishes, or prehistoric erotica, or gynecology primers.

"Because they have emotionally charged thingies like breasts and buttocks, the Venus figurines have been the subject of more spilled ink than anything I know of," Dr. Soffer said. "There are as many opinions on them as there are people in the field."

In their new report, which will be published in the spring in the journal *Current Anthropology*, Dr. Soffer and her colleagues, Dr. James M. Adovasio and Dr. David C. Hyland of the Mercyhurst Archaeological Institute at Mercyhurst College in Erie, Pa., point out that voluptuous

Figure 1.2 The Venus of Kostenki (Russia), wearing a woven bandeau.

Source: William Wiegand, Champaign Studio One Photography.

body parts notwithstanding, a number of the figurines are shown wearing items of clothing. And when they zeroed in on the details of those carved garments, the researchers saw proof of considerable textile craftsmanship, an intimate knowledge of how fabric is woven.

"Scholars have been looking at these things for years, but unfortunately, their minds have been elsewhere," Dr. Adovasio said. "Most of them didn't recognize the clothing as clothing. If they noticed anything at all, they misinterpreted what they saw, writing off the bandeaux, for example, as tattoos or body art." [See Figure 1.2.]

Scrutinizing the famed Venus of Willendorf, for example, which was discovered in lower Austria in 1908, the researchers paid particular attention to the statuette's head. The Venus has no face to speak of, but detailed coils surround its scalp. Most scholars have interpreted the coils as a kind of paleo-coiffure, but Dr. Adovasio, an authority on textiles and basketry, recognized the plaiting as what he called a "radially sewn piece of headgear with vertical stem stitches."

Willendorf's haberdashery "might have looked like one of those woven hats you see on Jamaicans on the streets of New York," he said, adding, "These were cool things." [See Figure 1.3.]

Figure 1.3   The Venus of Willendorf.
Source: The Art Gallery Collection / Alamy.

On the Venus of Lespugue, an approximately 25,000-year-old figurine from southwestern France, the anthropologists noticed a "remarkable" degree of detail lavished on the rendering of a string skirt, with the tightness and angle of each individual twist of the fibers carefully delineated. The skirt is attached to a low-slung hip belt and tapers in the back to a tail, the edges of its hem deliberately frayed.

"That skirt is to die for," said Dr. Soffer, who, before she turned to archaeology, was in the fashion business. "Though maybe it's an acquired taste."

To get an idea of what such an outfit might have looked like, she said, imagine a hula dancer wrapping a 1930s-style beaded curtain around her waist. "We're not talking protection from the elements here," Dr. Soffer said. "This would have been ritual wear, if it was worn at all, a way of communicating with higher powers."

Other anthropologists point out that string skirts, which appear in Bronze-Age artifacts and are mentioned by Homer, may have been worn at the equivalent of a debutantes' ball, to advertise a girl's coming of age. In some parts of Eastern Europe, the skirts still survive as lacy elements of folk costumes.

The researchers presented their results earlier this month at a meeting on the importance of perishables in prehistory that was held at the University of Florida in Gainesville. "One of the most common reactions we heard was, 'How could we have missed that stuff all these years?' " Dr. Adovasio said.

Dr. Margaret W. Conkey, a professor of anthropology at the University of California at Berkeley, and co-editor, with Joan Gero, of *Engendering Archaeology* (Blackwell Publishers, 1991) said, "They're helping us to look at old materials in new ways, to which I say bravo!"

Not all scholars had been blinded by the Venusian morphology. Dr. Elizabeth Wayland Barber, a professor of archaeology and linguistics at Occidental College in Los Angeles, included in her 1991 volume *Prehistoric Textiles* a chapter arguing that some Venus figurines were wearing string skirts. The recent work from Dr. Soffer and her colleagues extends and amplifies on Dr. Barber's original observations.

The new work also underscores the often neglected importance of what Dr. Barber has termed the "string revolution." Archaeologists have long emphasized the invention of stone and metal tools in furthering the evolution of human culture. Even the names given to various periods in human history and prehistory are based on heavyweight tools: the word *Paleolithic*—the period extending from about 750,000 years ago to 15,000 years ago—essentially means "Old Stone Age." And duly thudding and clanking after the Paleolithic period were the Mesolithic and Neolithic, or Middle and New Stone Age, the Bronze Age, the Iron Age, the Industrial Age.

But at least as central to the course of human affairs as the invention of stone tools was the realization that plant products could be exploited for purposes other than eating. The fact that some of the Venus figurines are shown wearing string skirts, said Dr. Barber, "means that the people who made them must also have known how to make twisted string."

With the invention of string and the power to weave, people could construct elaborate yet lightweight containers in which to carry, store, and cook food. They could fashion baby slings to secure an infant snugly against its mother's body, thereby freeing up the woman to work and wander. They could braid nets, the better to catch prey animals without the risk of hand-to-tooth combat. They could lash together wooden logs or planks to build a boat.

"The string revolution was a profound event in human history," Dr. Adovasio said. "When people started to fool around with plants and plant byproducts, that opened vast new avenues of human progress."

In the new report, the researchers argue that women are likely to have been the primary weavers and textile experts of prehistory, and may have even initiated the string revolution in the first place—although men undoubtedly did their share of weaving when it came to making hunting and fishing nets, for example. They base that conclusion on modern crosscultural studies, which have found that women constitute the great bulk of the world's weavers, basketry makers, and all-round mistresses of plant goods.

But while vast changes in manufacturing took the luster off the textile business long ago, with the result that such "women's work" is now accorded low status and sweatshop wages, the researchers argue that weaving and other forms of fiber craft once commanded great prestige. By their estimate, the detailing of the stitches shown on some of the Venus figurines was intended to flaunt the value and beauty of the original spinsters' skills. Why else would anybody have bothered etching the stitchery in a permanent medium, if not to boast, whoa! Check out these wefts!

"It's made immortal in stone," Dr. Soffer said. "You don't carve something like this unless it's very important."

The detailing of the Venusian garb also raises the intriguing possibility that the famed little sculptures, which rank right up there with the Lascaux cave paintings in the pantheon of Western art, were hewn by women—moonlighting seamstresses, to be precise. "It's always assumed that the carvers were men, a bunch of guys sitting around making their zaftig Barbie dolls," Dr. Soffer said. "But maybe that wasn't the case, or not always the case. With some of these figurines, the person carving them clearly knew weaving. So either that person was a weaver herself, or he was living with her. He's got an adviser."

Durable though the Venus figurines are, Dr. Adovasio and his co-workers are far more interested in what their carved detailing says about the role of perishables in prehistory. "The vast bulk of what humans made was made in media that hasn't survived," Dr. Adovasio said. Experts estimate the ratio of perishable objects to durable objects generated in the average culture is about 20 to 1.

"We're reconstructing the past based on 5 percent of what was used," Dr. Soffer said.

Because many of the items that have endured over the millennia are things like arrowheads and spear points, archaeologists studying the Paleolithic Era have generally focused on the ways and means of that noble savage, a.k.a. Man the Hunter, to the exclusion of other members of the tribe.

"To this day, in Paleolithic studies we hear about Man the Hunter doing such boldly wonderful things as thrusting spears into woolly mammoths, or battling it out with other men," Dr. Adovasio said. "We've emphasized the activities of a small segment of the population—healthy young men—at the total absence of females, old people of either sex, and children. We've glorified one aspect of Paleolithic life ways at the expense of all the other things that made that life way successful."

Textiles are particularly fleeting. The oldest examples of fabric yet discovered are some carbonate-encrusted swatches from France that are about 18,000 years old, while pieces of cordage and string dating back 19,000 years have been unearthed in the Near East, many thousands of years after the string and textile revolution began.

In an effort to study ancient textiles in the absence of textiles, Dr. Soffer, Dr. Adovasio, and Dr. Hyland have sought indirect signs of textile manufacture. They have pored over thousands of ancient fragments of fired and unfired clay, and have found impressions of early textiles on a number of them, the oldest dating to 29,000 B.C.E. But the researchers believe that textile manufacture far predates this time period, for the sophistication of the stitchery rules out its being, as Dr. Soffer put it, "what you take home from Crafts 101." Dr. Adovasio estimates that weaving and cord-making probably goes back to the year 40,000 B.C.E. "at a minimum," and possibly much further.

Long before people had settled down into towns with domesticated plants and animals, then, while they were still foragers and wanderers, they had, in a sense, tamed nature. The likeliest sort of plants from which they extracted fibers were nettles. "Nettle in folk tales and mythology is said to have magic properties," Dr. Soffer said. "In one story by the Brothers Grimm, a girl whose two brothers have been turned into swans has to weave them nettle shirts by midnight to make them human again." The nettles stung her fingers, but she kept on weaving.

But what didn't make it into Grimms' was that when the girl was done with the shirts, she took out a chisel, and carved herself a Venus figurine.

2

Paleolithic and Neolithic Art from Europe, Africa, Asia, and the Middle East, c. 15,000–2000 B.C.E.

Paleolithic (Old Stone Age) art made by hunters and gatherers was common everywhere before the agricultural revolution. Here we see two examples, from Europe and North Africa. The hunter and bison shown in Figure 1.4 were carved onto the wall of a cave in Lascaux, France around 15,000 B.C.E. Figure 1.5 comes from a

Figure 1.4   Cave drawing from Lascaux, France, c. 15,000 B.C.E.
Source: © AAAC/Topham/The Image Works.

Figure 1.5   Rock carving from Tassili n'Ajjer, Algeria, c. 10,000 B.C.E.
Source: Imagebroker.net/SuperStock.

Figure 1.6   Plaster head from
Ain Ghazal, Jordan, c. 7000 B.C.E.

Source: © Louvre Museum, Paris/Werner
Forman Archive/The Image Works.

large collection of rock art dating from 10,000 B.C.E. in Algeria.
The origins of agriculture led to the creation of a greater range of
art forms and images in what we call the Neolithic or New Stone
Age. We see here examples from Jordan and northern China.
Among the earliest representations of humans are the half-sized
human figures from c. 7000 B.C.E. found near Ain Ghazal in Jordan
(Figure 1.6). Figure 1.7 is a Neolithic ceramic vase from Gansu
province in China. What do these images suggest about the interests of hunters and gatherers? How was Neolithic art different
from Paleolithic art?

THINKING HISTORICALLY

Dating a work of art or any artifact from the past is a complex
process that involves carbon dating (measuring the lost carbon-14
isotopes) of nearby organic remains and other scientific methods.
But, complex as it may be, all historical understanding begins with
reliable dates. The date of an object allows us to place it on a real or
imagined timeline that reveals the relationship of the object to
everything else.

Create a timeline from 40,000 years ago until 2,000 years ago and
place each of these works in its proper place. What, if anything, does

Figure 1.7 Neolithic vase from Gansu
province in China, c. 2000 B.C.E.

Source: DeAgostini/SuperStock.

this visual representation of actual dates suggest to you? Then on the
same timeline mark the beginning of the Neolithic Age and the beginning of the Urban or Bronze Age. This is the difference between raw
dating and organizing the past into technological stages. What
advantages do you see in organizing the past in stages? What might
be the disadvantages?

3

MARJORIE SHOSTAK

Nisa: The Life and Words of a !Kung Woman, 1981

Marjorie Shostak, a writer and photographer, interviewed Nisa, a
woman of the hunting-gathering !Kung people of the Kalahari Desert
of southern Africa. (The exclamation point at the beginning of !Kung

Source: Marjorie Shostak, *Nisa: The Life and Words of a !Kung Woman* (Cambridge:
Harvard University Press, 1981), 51, 56–59, 61–62, 89–90, 132–38.

indicates one of the clicking sounds used in their language.) From these interviews, which took place between 1969 and 1971, Shostak compiled Nisa's story in Nisa's own words.

As you read Nisa's account of her early adulthood, consider how it is similar to, and how it is different from, that of a young woman growing up today in modern society. If Nisa is typical of women in her world, do !Kung women have more or less authority, prestige, or power than women in your own society?

Finally, what does Nisa's story tell us about women in hunting-gathering societies?

THINKING HISTORICALLY

Keep in mind that Nisa exists in the late twentieth century. When we think of stages of history, we are abstracting the human past in a way that vastly oversimplifies what happened but allows us to draw important conclusions. We know hunting and gathering did not end ten thousand years ago when agriculture first began. Hunters and gatherers still live in the world today—in places like the Arctic, the Amazon, and the Kalahari. That is why we use Nisa's account, which we are lucky to have. We have no vivid first-person accounts from those ancient hunters and gatherers—writing was not invented until the first cities developed five thousand years ago. So we generalize from Nisa's experience because we know that in some ways her life is like that of our hunting-gathering ancestors. But there are ways in which it is not. At the very least, the hunters and gatherers in the world today have been pushed by farmers and city people into the most remote parts of the globe—like the Kalahari Desert.

Using a contemporary of ours, like Nisa, as a kind of representative of our most distant ancestors is clearly a strange thing to do. Does it work? What precautions should we take when using a contemporary account as evidence of life in the Paleolithic Era?

One time, my father went hunting with some other men and they took dogs with them. First they saw a baby wildebeest and killed it. Then, they went after the mother wildebeest and killed that too. They also killed a warthog.

As they were coming back, I saw them and shouted out, "Ho, ho, Daddy's bringing home meat! Daddy's coming home with meat!" My mother said, "You're talking nonsense. Your father hasn't even come home yet." Then she turned to where I was looking and said, "Eh-hey, daughter! Your father certainly has killed something. He *is* coming with meat."

I remember another time when my father's younger brother traveled from far away to come and live with us. The day before he arrived he killed an eland. He left it in the bush and continued on to our village. When he arrived, only mother and I were there. He greeted us and asked where his brother was. Mother said, "Eh, he went to look at some tracks he had seen near a porcupine hole. He'll be back when the sun sets." We sat together the rest of the day. When the sun was low in the sky, my father came back. My uncle said, "Yesterday, as I was coming here, there was an eland—perhaps it was just a small one—but I spent a long time tracking it and finally killed it in the thicket beyond the dry water pan. Why don't we get the meat and bring it back to the village?" We packed some things, left others hanging in the trees, and went to where the eland had died. It was a huge animal with plenty of fat. We lived there while they skinned the animal and the meat into strips to dry. A few days later we started home, the men carrying the meat on sticks and the women carrying it in their karosses.

At first my mother carried me on her shoulder. After a long way, she set me down and I started to cry. She was angry, "You're a big girl. You know how to walk." It was true that I was fairly big by then, but I still wanted to be carried. My older brother said, "Stop yelling at her, she's already crying," and he picked me up and carried me. After a long time walking, he also put me down. Eventually, we arrived back at the village.

We lived, eating meat; lived and lived. Then, it was finished. . . .

When adults talked to me, I listened. When I was still a young girl with no breasts, they told me that when a young woman grows up, her parents give her a husband and she continues to grow up next to him.

When they first talked to me about it, I said, "What kind of thing am I that I should take a husband? When I grow up, I won't marry. I'll just lie by myself. If I married, what would I be doing it for?"

My father said, "You don't know what you're saying. I, I am your father and am old; your mother is old, too. When you marry, you will gather food and give it to your husband to eat. He also will do things for you. If you refuse, who will give you food? Who will give you things to wear?"

I said, "There's no question about it, I won't take a husband. Why should I? As I am now, I'm still a child and won't marry." I said to my mother, "You say you have a man for me to marry? Why don't you take him and set him beside Daddy? You marry him and let them be co-husbands. What have I done that you're telling me I should marry?"

My mother said, "Nonsense. When I tell you I'm going to give you a husband, why do you say you want me to marry him? Why are you talking to me like this?"

I said, "Because I'm only a child. When I grow up and you tell me to take a husband, I'll agree. But I haven't passed through my childhood yet and I won't marry!" . . .

When I still had no breasts, when my genitals still weren't developed, when my chest was without anything on it, that was when a man named Bo came from a distant area and people started talking about marriage. Was I not almost a young woman?

One day, my parents and his parents began building our marriage hut. The day we were married, they carried me to it and set me down inside. I cried and cried and cried. Later, I ran back to my parents' hut, lay down beside my little brother, and slept, a deep sleep like death.

The next night, Nukha, an older woman, took me into the hut and stayed with me. She lay down between Bo and myself, because young girls who are still children are afraid of their husbands. So, it is our custom for an older woman to come into the young girl's hut to teach her not to be afraid. The woman is supposed to help the girl learn to like her husband. Once the couple is living nicely together and getting along, the older woman leaves them beside each other.

That's what Nukha was supposed to do. Even the people who saw her come into the hut with me thought she would lay me down and that once I fell asleep, she would leave and go home to her husband.

But Nukha had within her clever deceit. My heart refused Bo because I was a child, but Nukha, she liked him. That was why, when she laid me down in the hut with my husband, she was also laying me down with her lover. She put me in front and Bo was behind. We stayed like that for a very long time. As soon as I was asleep, they started to make love. But as Bo made love to Nukha, they knocked into me. I kept waking up as they bumped me, again and again.

I thought, "I'm just a child. I don't understand about such things. What are people doing when they move around like that? How come Nukha took me into my marriage hut and laid me down beside my husband, but when I started to cry, she changed places with me and lay down next to him? Is he hers? How come he belongs to her yet Mommy and Daddy said I should marry him?"

I lay there, thinking my thoughts. Before dawn broke, Nukha got up and went back to her husband. I lay there, sleeping, and when it started getting light, I went back to my mother's hut.

The next night, when darkness sat, Nukha came for me again. I cried, "He's your man! Yesterday you took me and brought me inside the hut, but after we all lay there, he was with you! Why are you now bringing me to someone who is yours?" She said, "That's not true, he's not mine. He's *your* husband. Now, go to your hut and sit there. Later, we'll lie down."

She brought me to the hut, but once inside, I cried and cried and cried. I was still crying when Nukha lay down with us. After we had been lying there for a very long time, Bo started to make love to her again. I thought, "What is this? What am I? Am I supposed to watch this? Don't they see me? Do they think I'm only a baby?" Later, I got up and told them I had to urinate. I passed by them and went to lie down in mother's hut and stayed there until morning broke.

That day, I went gathering with my mother and father. As we were collecting mongongo nuts and klaru roots, my mother said, "Nisa, as you are, you're already a young woman. Yet, when you go into your marriage hut to lie down, you get up, come back, and lie down with me. Do you think I have married you? No, I'm the one who gave birth to you. Now, take this man as your husband, this strong man who will get food, for you and for me to eat. Is your father the only one who can find food? A husband kills things and gives them to you; a husband works on things that become your things; a husband gets meat that is food for you to eat. Now, you have a husband, Bo; he has married you."

I said, "Mommy, let me stay with you. When night sits, let me sleep next to you. What have you done to me that I'm only a child, yet the first husband you give me belongs to Nukha?" My mother said, "Why are you saying that? Nukha's husband is not your husband. Her husband sits elsewhere, in another hut."

I said, "Well . . . the other night when she took me and put me into the hut, she laid me down in front of her; Bo slept behind. But later, they woke me up, moving around the way they did. It was the same last night. Again, I slept in front and Bo behind and again, they kept bumping into me. I'm not sure exactly what they were doing, but that's why tonight, when night sits, I want to stay with you and sleep next to you. Don't take me over there again."

My mother said, "Yo! My daughter! They were moving about?" I said, "Mm. They woke me while I was sleeping. That's why I got up and came back to you." She said, "Yo! How horny that Bo is! He's screwing Nukha! You are going to leave that man, that's the only thing I will agree to now."

My father said, "I don't like what you've told us. You're only a child, Nisa, and adults are the ones responsible for arranging your marriage. But when an adult gives a husband and that husband makes love to someone else, then that adult hasn't done well. I understand what you have told us and I say that Bo has deceived me. Therefore, when Nukha comes for you tonight, I will refuse to let you go. I will say, 'My daughter won't go into her marriage hut because you, Nukha, you have already taken him for a husband.'"

We continued to talk on our way back. When we arrived at the village, I sat down with my parents. Bo walked over to our marriage hut, then Nukha went over to him. I sat and watched as they talked. I thought, "Those two, they were screwing! That's why they kept bumping into me!"

I sat with Mother and Father while we ate. When evening came, Nukha walked over to us. "Nisa, come, let me take you to your hut." I said, "I won't go." She said, "Get up. Let me take you over there. It's your hut. How come you're already married but today you won't make your hut your home?"

That's when my mother, drinking anger, went over to Nukha and said, "As I'm standing here, I want you to tell me something. Nisa is a child who fears her husband. Yet, when you took her to her hut, you and her husband had sex together. Don't you know her husband should be trying to help bring her up? But that isn't something either of you are thinking about!"

Nukha didn't say anything, but the fire in my mother's words burned. My mother began to yell, cursing her, "Horny, that's what you are! You're no longer going to take Nisa to her husband. And, if you ever have sex with him again, I'll crack your face open. You horny woman! You'd screw your own father!"

That's when my father said, "No, don't do all the talking. You're a woman yet, how come you didn't ask me? I am a man and I will do the talking now. You, you just listen to what I say. Nisa is my child. I also gave birth to her. Now, you are a woman and will be quiet because I am a man."

Then he said, "Nukha, I'm going to tell you something. I am Gau and today I'm going to pull my talk from inside myself and give it to you. We came together here for this marriage, but now something very bad has happened, something I do not agree to at all. Nisa is no longer going to go from here, where I am sitting, to that hut over there, that hut which you have already made your own. She is no longer going to look for anything for herself near that hut."

He continued, "Because, when I agree to give a man to my daughter, then he is only for my daughter. Nisa is a child and her husband isn't there for two to share. So go, take that man, he's already yours. Today my daughter will sit with me; she will sit here and sleep here. Tomorrow I will take her and we will move away. What you have already done to this marriage is the way it will remain."

Nukha didn't say anything. She left and went to the hut without me. Bo said, "Where's Nisa? Why are you empty, returning here alone?" Nukha said, "Nisa's father refused to let her go. She told him that you had made love to me and that's what he just now told me. I don't know what to do about this, but I won't go back to their hut again." Bo said, "I have no use for that kind of talk. Get the girl and come back with her." She said, "I'm not going to Gau's hut. We're finished with that talk now. And when I say I'm finished, I'm saying I won't go back there again."

She left and walked over to her own hut. When her husband saw her, he said, "So, you and Bo are lovers! Nisa said that when you took her to Bo, the two of you . . . how exactly *did* Bo reward you for your help?" But Nukha said, "No, I don't like Bo and he's not my lover. Nisa is just a child and it is just a child's talk she is talking."

Bo walked over to us. He tried to talk but my father said, "You, be quiet. I'm the one who's going to talk about this." So Bo didn't say anything more, and my father talked until it was finished.

The next morning, very early, my father, mother, and aunt packed our things and we all left. We slept in the mongongo groves that night and traveled on until we reached another water hole where we continued to live.

We lived and lived and nothing more happened for a while. After a long time had passed, Bo strung together some trade beads made of wood, put them into a sack with food, and traveled the long distance to the water hole where we were living.

It was late afternoon; the sun had almost left the sky. I had been out gathering with my mother, and we were coming back from the bush. We arrived in the village and my mother saw them, "Eh-hey, Bo's over there. What's he doing here? I long ago refused him. I didn't ask him to come back. I wonder what he thinks he's going to take away from here?"

We put down our gatherings and sat. We greeted Bo and his relatives—his mother, his aunt, Nukha, and Nukha's mother. Bo's mother said, "We have come because we want to take Nisa back with us." Bo said, "I'm again asking for your child. I want to take her back with me."

My father said, "No, I only just took her from you. That was the end. I won't take her and then give her again. Maybe you didn't hear me the first time? I already told you that I refused. Bo is Nukha's husband and my daughter won't be with him again. An adult woman does not make love to the man who marries Nisa."

Then he said, "Today, Nisa will just continue to live with us. Some day, another man will come and marry her. If she stays healthy and her eyes stand strong, if God doesn't kill her and she doesn't die, if God stands beside her and helps, then we will find another man to give to her."

That night, when darkness set, we all slept. I slept beside mother. When morning broke, Bo took Nukha, her mother, and the others and they left. I stayed behind. They were gone, finally gone.

We continued to stay at that water hole, eating things, doing things, and just living. No one talked further about giving me another husband, and we just lived and lived and lived.

4

MARGARET EHRENBERG

Women in Prehistory, 1989

British anthropologist Margaret Ehrenberg argues here that women were likely the first farmers as well as the originators of many of the innovations of the agricultural revolution. What evidence does she offer? What was the importance of the agricultural revolution? When and how, according to Ehrenberg, did men take over?

THINKING HISTORICALLY

In this selection much of the author's evidence is anthropological or ethnographic (rather than archaeological). That is, it comes from our contemporary world, not from digging up the past. How does the use of this kind of evidence depend on the idea of historical stages? From the standpoint of women, was the agricultural revolution a single stage of history, or should we think of it as two stages? If so, what were those stages?

From the point of view of the lives of women, the Neolithic period is perhaps the most important phase of prehistory. . . . It is likely that at the end of the Palaeolithic and Mesolithic, women enjoyed equality with men. They probably collected as much, if not more, of the food eaten by the community and derived equal status from their contribution. But by about four thousand years ago, in the Bronze Age, many of the gender roles and behaviour typical of the world today had probably been established. The implication is that the crucial changes must have taken place during the Neolithic period. . . .

The discovery of farming techniques has usually been assumed to have been made by men, but it is in fact very much more likely to have been made by women. On the basis of anthropological evidence for societies still living traditional foraging lifestyles and those living by simple, non-mechanised farming, taken in conjunction with direct archaeological evidence, it seems probable that it was women who made the first observations of plant behaviour, and worked out, presumably by long trial and error, how to grow and tend crops.

This transition from foraging to farming, which marks the change from the Palaeolithic and Mesolithic or Old and Middle Stone Ages to

---

Source: Margaret Ehrenberg, *Women in Prehistory* (Norman: University of Oklahoma Press, 1989), 77–81, 99–100, 103–7.

the period known to archaeologists as the Neolithic or New Stone Age, seems to have taken place initially in south-west Asia some time after 10,000 BC. By 6000 BC farming was well established throughout that part of the world. . . .

How and why did this change to agriculture take place, and, more particularly, what can we say about the role of women in this process?
. . . Foraging societies still living in the world today . . . gather and hunt food in a way similar to Palaeolithic societies before the invention of agriculture; among these people there is a regularly recurring pattern of food procurement. . . . Women are mainly concerned with gathering plant food, which provides the bulk of the diet of nearly all foragers, while men spend much time hunting animals. Although animal products form an important source of proteins in the diet, meat actually makes up a relatively small proportion of the food intake of these societies. We can also study other groups of people in places such as New Guinea and parts of Africa who still grow crops and keep animals with the aid of only the very simplest technology, in much the same way as we may imagine Neolithic societies would have done. These societies do not use ploughs or artificial irrigation, and they keep few, if any, animals. To distinguish them from people using more mechanised agricultural technologies, anthropologists usually call this type of farming horticulture, and the people using it horticultural societies. . . .

Although present-day horticulturalists live in a wide variety of places around the world, many remarkably regular patterns of behaviour can be observed, and this gives us some degree of confidence in using their lifestyles as a model for the Neolithic, particularly if some of the behaviour patterns can be seen to be reflected in evidence from archaeological sites.
Studies of the roles of women in different types of agricultural communities show a remarkably consistent pattern. In societies where plough agriculture is practised and animals are kept on a significant scale, most of the agricultural work is done by men, with women playing no direct part, or only a very subsidiary role. On the other hand, in horticultural societies, in which hoes or digging sticks are used for making holes or drills in which to plant roots or seeds, women are usually almost wholly responsible for agricultural production. A study of 104 horticultural societies existing today showed that in 50 per cent of them women were exclusively responsible for agriculture, in 33 per cent women and men shared various tasks, and in only 17 per cent were men wholly responsible for farming, and this is after decades or even centuries of contact with societies whose ideology would encourage men to take on greater roles in production. Horticultural societies are still widespread, mainly within the Tropics, in many parts of Africa, central America and Asia. The typical pattern in these areas is one of shifting cultivation, where

patches of land are worked for a few years, and then when soil fertility declines another plot is cleared and cultivated. Although men often help to clear the plots of trees and undergrowth, women usually hoe, sow, tend and harvest the crops. Studies carried out early this century suggest that this pattern of cultivation was more common then than it is today. It also seems very likely that it was even more typical before most parts of the world had contact with European traders and missionaries, with their preconceived ideas about what it was right and proper for women and men to do. . . .

The Secondary Products Revolution, or the Great Male Takeover Bid

In an earlier section it was argued that women almost certainly "invented" or worked out the principles of farming as well as many of the concomitant skills and tools which go to make crop agriculture possible and profitable. As principal food providers they were probably respected and had equal status with men. But between then and now, in all but the most traditional hunter-gatherer and horticultural societies, the status of women has been drastically reduced, and in many areas farming has become a predominantly male preserve. Why the change, and when did it happen? Two facts are certain: Firstly, by the time of the earliest written records, everywhere in Europe farming was primarily a male occupation, and men owned the farmland and the tools. Secondly, in those areas of the world where women are still the main agricultural producers, most of the farming is concerned with crop production, and if animals are kept at all, it is usually on a small farmyard scale, rather than as large herds or flocks. The change to male dominance in agriculture, therefore, took place at some time between the first stages of the Neolithic period and the advent of written records, and may be related to the changing role of animals within the farming economies of prehistoric Europe. It also seems likely that such a drastic shift in lifestyle, whether it took place gradually over millennia or as a sudden "revolution," would have been associated with other changes within society. Anthropologists have shown that in present-day societies a significant (though not 100 per cent) correlation exists between plough agriculture and patrilineal descent and land ownership in the same way as there is a correlation between non-plough agriculture and the heavy involvement, and consequent enhanced status, of women. We can look for evidence of this shift in the archaeological record: for example, changes in family structure, wealth or ownership patterns may show up in settlement sites or in burials. . . .

The crucial changes in farming practice are thought to have taken place around 3000 BC, in the later Neolithic period. This would have been some five millennia after the introduction of farming in the Near

East, and similar economic shifts can be detected in many areas of Europe at about the same time. Andrew Sherratt has suggested that although domesticated animals were kept during the early Neolithic, they were used only as a source of meat; the consumption of milk or milk products was probably not significant, nor were the animals used for pulling ploughs or carts. All these innovations came later and not only revolutionised agricultural productivity, but also reduced the amount of labour involved in farming. Moreover, the greater importance of domesticated animals and their products would have reduced the necessity for hunting wild animals. As the balance of work changed from part hunting, part crop cultivation and tending a small number of animals to an economy dependent on mixed farming, so the roles and duties of women and men may have shifted. Let us examine the evidence and arguments. . . .

Both carts and ploughs first appear in depictions on clay tablets and cylinder seals in Mesopotamia, around the beginning of the fourth millennium BC, and both seem to have spread to Europe fairly rapidly over 500 years or so. One of the earliest depictions of ploughing [Figure 1.8] shows an ox drawing a two-handled plough with a sowing funnel, a device used for sowing seed deeply in the soil and often associated with areas where irrigation is needed. Most significantly the two individuals involved, one guiding the animal from the front, the other guiding the plough, both appear to be men with beards. Early depictions of ploughs in Egypt, from Old Kingdom tombs, also show them being used by men. . . .

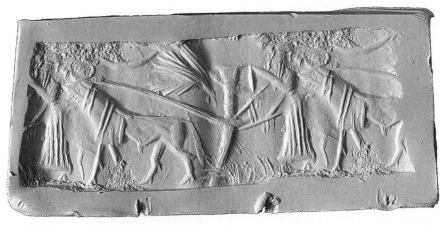

Figure 1.8   Men leading and guiding a two-handled plough, depicted on a cylinder seal from Mesopotamia, late third millennium BC.

Source: Ashmolean Museum, University of Oxford.

In areas of the world where plough agriculture and the herding of animals are the predominant form of farming, men universally play the major role in agricultural tasks. Women either take no part in farming or only a small one. They may sometimes contribute to harvesting, or to the care of domestic animals, if these are kept only in small numbers. An important distinction exists today between Africa, where horticulture predominates, and Asia, where plough agriculture is far more common and where domesticated animals are kept. Even in those areas of Asia, for example, where women are involved to some extent in aspects of plough agriculture, they work fewer hours than men; whereas in Africa, where farming is predominantly carried out without the use of the plough, and primarily by women, they do far more work than men. The other main difference between these two farming regimes is that social and economic stratification is a far more significant factor, with greater extremes of poverty and wealth and of land ownership amongst the Asian plough agriculturalists than amongst the African hoe agricultural-ists or horticulturalists. . . .

Patterns of social organisation in horticultural societies today are quite different from those of intensive agriculturalists: these seem to be linked to the balance of agricultural tasks and to their allocation to each sex. One of the greatest differences is in the position of women. This reinforces the theory that it was in the later Neolithic, when men began to take over most agricultural work, that the social status of women declined.

. . . It is likely that most of the tending of animals was done by men. Large-scale herding often takes place some way from the farm or settlement, as fresh grazing land is continually sought. Raiding by neigh-bouring tribes seems to be an endemic part of most cattle herding—almost a variation on hunting! This has been seen as the origin of warfare, when for the first time people owned a resource which it was both worthwhile and fairly easy to steal.

Secondly, the invention of plough agriculture, too, would probably have resulted in farming becoming predominantly a male activity, while on the basis of ethnographic analogy, at least, women would probably have spent more time in food preparation, child-rearing and textile and perhaps other craft production.

Thirdly, although less land is needed for the same amount of produc-tion, plough agriculture is far more labour-intensive than hoe agricul-ture: where land is poor, ploughing makes agriculture possible. In some areas of prehistoric Europe it had the effect of making large tracts of lighter, sandy soil available, but in other areas it may have allowed an increase in population where there was a real or perceived shortage of land. In the earliest phases of the Neolithic, land shortages would cer-tainly not have been a problem, as witnessed by the rapid population spread discussed in an earlier section. However, in the later Neolithic there may have been a shortage of land perceived to be suitable for agriculture. Women would therefore have been expected to produce more children and thus more labourers. This would have been seen as their major role. Moreover, male children might have been valued most highly, as future farm workers. Women, meanwhile, would have become less valued by men in their own right: as more time was spent in pregnancy and the care of very young infants, so less time could be spent on farming activities. As men took over many of their tasks, they no longer contributed so much to the daily production of food, which had been a crucial factor in maintaining the equal status they had previously enjoyed.

Fourthly, another social change which might have been an indirect result of the secondary products revolution was the switch from matrilocal residence and matrilineal descent to patrilocal residence and patrilineal descent. There is a very strong ethnographic correlation between male-dominated farming and patrilineal descent and patrilocal residence. A male farmer will teach his sons the necessary skills and expect them to tend his land and animals. In a matrilineal system his sister's sons, rather than his own sons, inherit these herds, land and equipment on his death. This is not in the male interest if men are the main agriculturalists. When women were involved in the land-based tasks, they would have learnt the basic skills from their mothers, so it would have been more obvious for them also to inherit their land and equipment. However, it also seems that individual land ownership is less common amongst hoe agriculturalists, and, by definition, less equipment is used. Therefore, at least in terms of material goods, far less is typically at stake in matrilineal than in patrilineal systems.

Finally, the development of agriculture brought with it a large increase, not only in the number of related tasks, including several which are very time-consuming, but also in the range of material possessions such as farming and food-preparation tools and storage vessels. Two consequences would have resulted. On the one hand, this may be seen as the spur to the development of craft specialisation, as some individuals concentrated on the production of one particular item, which they would exchange for other products or services. At first this could have been in addition to normal farming tasks, but increasingly some people might have found that they could acquire enough food and other necessities by producing only their specialised article. In this way exchange must have become more common, and more sophisticated. On the other hand these material possessions, as well as the domesticated animals themselves, would have constituted considerable wealth, which could be accumulated and handed on from one generation to the next. . . .

The wealthy can become powerful by lending to poorer families in return for services, such as farm labour, or support in combat against other groups. By this means the rich are able to become more wealthy, while the poorer become indebted to other families, and have to produce more and more, or spend time on tasks other than directly for their own subsistence. So the vicious circle develops, and it is easy to see how from this point permanent hierarchies not only of wealth, but of power and status come about, in a way which is impossible in forager societies. This is also the context in which a society can begin to think of people, as well as material possessions and land, as objects of value and exchange. A child could be given as labour to a family to whom the child's parents were indebted, or a woman given to work or to produce extra children.

How such fundamental changes actually took place is not clear, even if we assume they were a gradual process in each community. The full consequences which have just been discussed would have developed very slowly, even over millennia, and are difficult to pinpoint chronologically. In any case, as women were increasingly relegated to secondary tasks, by the end of the Neolithic period they had fewer personal resources with which to assert their status. Presumably, as with so many innovations even in the modern world, the social and economic consequences of seemingly minor innovations would not have been apparent until it was too late to return to former *mores*. The discovery of agriculture, which at the beginning of the Neolithic had been such a positive step by women, was by the end of the period to have had unforeseen, and unfortunate, consequences for them.

5

CATHERINE CLAY, CHANDRIKA PAUL, AND CHRISTINE SENECAL

Women in the First Urban Communities, 2009

This selection comes from a text on women in world history. Since world history is full of patriarchal, or male-dominated, societies, one of the thorniest problems is to determine just how widespread patriarchy was. Against the commonly held assumption that patriarchy has always existed, that it is universal or natural, we have seen that male domination was not common in most hunting-gathering and early

Source: Catherine Clay, Chandrika Paul, and Christine Senecal, *Envisioning Women in World History* (New York: McGraw-Hill, 2009), 20–23.

agricultural societies — that is, throughout most of human history. When and how did it come about? What is the answer given in this selection? What kind of evidence best supports the author's conclusion?

THINKING HISTORICALLY

As already mentioned, one of the earliest, and still widely accepted, stage theories of human history posits three important stages: hunter-gatherer, agricultural-pastoral, and city-based or urban. Archaeologists use the corresponding terms of Paleolithic (Old Stone Age), Neolithic (New Stone Age), and Bronze Age. This reading suggests other developments of the urban or Bronze Age that might be better descriptions of the "third" stage than cities or bronze: states, plow agriculture, stratified, slave, and literate and writing-based societies. How does each of these new developments affect the lives of women? If you were to divide only women's history into two, three, or four stages, what would they be?

The world's first cities emerged in Eurasia around 3500 BCE. Fostered by the spread of villages, the urban centers of this continent grew up along major river systems — an environment conducive to planting and harvesting crops with relatively predictable patterns. There were four major regions where urban civilizations developed: in the Fertile Crescent along the Tigris and Euphrates* Rivers (also known as Mesopotamia, "the land between the two rivers"), along the Nile in Egypt, along the Indus River in modern Pakistan, and along the Yellow and Yangtze† Rivers in China.

Eurasia's urban centers brought rapid changes in the organization of populations. Institutional patriarchy probably developed alongside the state, tribute extraction, social stratification, and slavery. The state, especially, was a political institution that organized, disciplined, and enslaved numerous inhabitants in order to provide security and order for itself. Law codes to promote universal standards of behavior, irrigation projects to ensure food supply, and extensive military defense were now possible and deemed necessary. Of course, in order to manage this type of society, institutional governments were needed, and the leaders who ran these growing states exercised a disproportionate share of power. State power transformed everything.

At the same time the world's first urban political institutions were taking shape, a disparity of wealth also grew in urban centers. Gaps between the haves and the have-nots of society appeared in heretofore unseen proportions. Slavery and the slave trade, essential to ancient Eurasian civilizations, are first in evidence. Some have argued that

---

* TY gruhs and yu FRAY teez

† yang zuh

Note: Pronunciations of difficult-to-pronounce terms will be given throughout the book. The emphasis goes on the syllables appearing in all capitals. [Ed.]

men's control and exchange of women's sexuality and reproductive capacity generally became the basis of private property in Mesopotamia between 3100 and 600 BCE. This affected not only female slaves and concubines but also the daughters of elite and free men. A bride's father, representing his family, exchanged her reproductive capacity for wealth and household goods and sometimes less tangible objects, such as status and/or influence. Sometimes payments were made in installments, and after a marriage, when her first child was born, the balance of bridewealth or dowry payments became due. This overall disparity in status, wealth, and power spelled a worsening of women's position.

Another explanation for the worsening of women's position and the emergence of patriarchy focuses on demography and technology, beginning with burgeoning populations of village communities, which, as discussed above, encouraged women's fertility to supply the needed workforce. Populous urban centers could no longer practice *hoe* agriculture, but often needed intensive *plow* agriculture to feed everyone. With more children, urban women had less time for heavier agricultural work and the long, intensive hours needed for cultivation. Women of plow-using cultures may have preferred and chosen to work around the house and to perform lighter agricultural work. This scenario resulted in a gradual loss of women's social power and prestige — sometimes through their own choices that made sense to them at the time, but that accelerated men's control over economic activity and social resources. Ultimately, then, when the communities began using plows and more laborious, intensive methods of cultivation (and the groups prospered materially), women's status changed.

Women's experience in the first urban centers was marked by a general devaluation of their social freedoms, a denial of their claims to the results of their labor, and sometimes even a reshaping of their religious expression. This decline did not affect all women's communities in the same way or at the same time. We notice this in the great variety of women's experiences across Eurasia in all four of the earliest urban areas.

Women and Society in the Earliest Civilizations

Although some villages had begun to experience greater social stratification by 3500 BCE, the difference between the powerful and the powerless was not nearly as marked as it was in the earliest cities. The increased wealth possessed by a small proportion of the urban population led to a growing interest in keeping wealth and power within familial units. And it led in many ways to the constriction of women's lives, whether slave, concubine, free, or elite.

The social experience of many women was shaped by the flourishing Eurasian slave trade. In Mesopotamia as early as 2300 BCE, inscriptions for "slave girl" appear earlier than those translating as "slave male." Female slaves in Mesopotamia often originated as captives of raids and were more plentiful than male slaves. They also seem to have been valued more than male slaves. In Syria, the reward for the return of fleeing females was double that for male fugitive slaves. Enslaved women lived under a wide range of conditions, from the relative comfort of high-level slaves important in the domestic realm, such as concubines (unfree females purchased for reproduction) to female slaves used for their brute physical labor. Thus, although many enslaved women held very low positions in society, the status of some was not as low as slaves in other time periods. For instance, a second-generation slave was often valued more than one that had been recently captured. Furthermore, female slaves could upon occasion be freed from their servitude. In Babylon around 1750 BCE, slave concubines were frequently freed after the demise of their masters. Additionally, the children of freewomen and male slaves were considered to be of free status there. High slave mortality and these legal paths to slave freedom made slave raiding for new supplies a constant imperative.

The situation of free and elite women was shaped by family control. Ensuring the lineage of a family meant keeping ever-closer tabs on women's morality, which could include preserving a woman's virginity until marriage and ensuring that she had only her husband for a sexual partner. This would guarantee that the paternity of family members would be unquestioned. Even a woman's reputation could be of critical interest to her family. We see this in practices such as veiling and seclusion, which marked women's high familial social standing and reputation for chastity (meaning virginity when single and fidelity in marriage), and actually prevented her from any sexual contact with males other than her husband.

As mentioned above, the decrease in women's social influence did not strike equally in all places. For instance, little evidence points to women's morality being constrained in the cities of Harappa and Mohenjo Daro in the Indus River Valley around 2500 BCE. The thousands of written sources from this civilization have yet to be deciphered, and thus it would be hazardous to assume that women's social position never declined there, and yet archaeological evidence suggests that the gap between the haves and the have-nots might not have been terribly significant to the urban population. The façades of the residential buildings in those cities were relatively similar, even though some families possessed much larger storerooms than others. This evidence therefore suggests that maintaining a family's wealth and power, and the corresponding demotion that meant for women, was not as marked there. . . . Similarly, in the less urbanized Egyptian civilization, evidence suggests that women held positions of relative social equality and enjoyed freedom of movement unlike in other ancient societies. Given geographic barriers protecting them from warlike neighbors, Nile and Indus River civilizations were more militarily secure generally than civilizations in Mesopotamia and East Asia, and this may have resulted in fewer constraints on women.

Insight from Law Codes

We can see the inferior social position of urban women in law codes. Although legal texts from Mesopotamia often reflected social guidelines rather than actual practice, they nevertheless give critical insight to the way a society's most powerful people intended to govern. For example, in one Mesopotamian city in 2000 BCE, the murder of a woman was a capital offense. But by the time of Hammurabi‡ (d. 1750 BCE), a Babylonian ruler and famous lawmaker in Mesopotamia, killing a common woman only resulted in a fine according to the law code. (There was a stronger punishment if an elite woman were the victim.)

We can also see the uneven treatment of urban women in the law and practices surrounding marriage and divorce. For instance, wives' positions in Mesopotamia differed from city to city even within the same time frame. Whereas one law code from the urban civilization of Sumer made it legal for a new bride to refuse intercourse without punishment, later, a woman could be drowned if she refused to consummate her marriage. By 2500 BCE a law allowed a man to break his wife's teeth with a burnt brick if she disagreed with him. Divorce laws from Mesopotamian civilizations show that, although women experienced new inequities and constraints, they continued to enjoy some protections also. The cases compiled by the Babylonian ruler Hammurabi about 1700 BCE forbade women from divorcing, yet allowed men to terminate their marriages. Nevertheless, even Hammurabi's law code required divorced men to support their former spouses and any children they had together.

■ REFLECTIONS

A historical stage is a specific example of a larger process that historians call *periodization*. Dividing history into periods is one way historians make the past comprehensible. Without periodization, history would be a vast, unwieldy continuum, lacking points of reference and intelligibility.

One of the earliest forms of historical periodization—years of reign—was a natural system of record keeping in the ancient cities dominated by kings. Each kingdom had its own list of kings, and each

‡ ha muh RAH bee

marked the current date by numbering the years of the king's reign. Some ancient societies periodized their history according to the years of rule of local officials or priesthoods. In the ancient Roman Republic, time was figured according to the terms of the elected consuls. The ancient Greeks used four-year periods called Olympiads, beginning with the first Olympic games in 776 B.C.E.

The ancient Greeks did not use "B.C." or "B.C.E.," of course. The periodization of world history into B.C. ("before Christ") and A.D. (*anno Domini*, "the Year of Our Lord" or "after Christ") did not come until the sixth century A.D., when a Christian monk hit upon a way to center Christ as the major turning point in history. We use a variant of this system in this text, when designating events "B.C.E." for "before the common era" or "C.E." for "of the common era." This translation of "B.C." and "A.D." avoids the Christian bias of the older system but preserves the simplicity of this common dating system, one used worldwide by most people today—even many non-Christians—because of its convenience.

All systems of periodization implicitly claim to designate important transitions in the past. The B.C. periodization inscribed the Christian belief that Christ's life, death, and resurrection fundamentally changed world history. Muslims count the years from a year one A.H. (*anno Hegire*, designating the year of the Prophet Muhammad's escape from Mecca to Medina) in 622 A.D. of the Christian calendar, and Jews date the years from a biblical year one.

Millennia, centuries, and decades are useful periods for societies that count by tens. Although such multiples are only mathematical, some historians use them for rough periodization, to distinguish between the 1950s and the 1960s or between the eighteenth and nineteenth centuries, for example, as if there were a genuine and important transition between one period and the other. Sometimes historians "stretch" the boundaries of centuries or decades to account for earlier or later changes. For example, some historians speak of "the long nineteenth century," embracing the period from the French Revolution in 1789 to the First World War in 1914, on the grounds that peoples' lives were transformed in 1789 rather than in 1800 and in 1914 rather than in 1900. Similarly, the "sixties," as a term for American society and culture during the Vietnam War era, often means the period from about 1963 to about 1975, since civil rights and antiwar activity became significant a few years after the beginning of the decade and the war continued until 1975.

Characterizing and defining a decade or century in chronological terms is only one method of periodization, however. Processes can also be periodized, as we saw in this chapter. All of world history can be divided into three periods: hunting-gathering, agricultural-pastoral, and urban. These are overlapping and continuing periods, and we can date only the beginning of the agricultural-pastoral and the urban periods, at about ten thousand and five thousand years ago, respectively. Further, we found it useful to divide the agricultural-pastoral period into two parts: early hoe agriculture or horticulture, when women still played a primary role, and later plow agriculture and the pastoral "secondary products revolution," when men's work predominated. Thus, our effort to understand the origins of patriarchy benefited from a four-stage periodization in which patriarchy began in an advanced agricultural-pastoral society and subsequent urban societies. These periods began at different times in different places: generally earliest in the Middle East and later in the Americas. To note how processes like plow agriculture or cities change people's lives (so much that we see a new stage of history) is not to say that all societies must take the same route. There may be different historical processes that lead to the same stage, as either plows or irrigation may produce enough food for cities (and lead to patriarchies). All societies do not go through all the same stages. Some today remain at a nonurban stage (making it possible to extrapolate about the past using recent information from anthropologists). Still, some historical processes—the adoption of new technologies or ways of life—can be so powerful that they effect changes almost everywhere. Can you think of other examples of such stage-making processes besides those mentioned in this chapter?

You might also get a sense of how the historian goes about periodizing and a feeling for its value if you periodize something you know a lot about—your own life, for instance. Think of the most important change or changes in your life. How have these changes divided your life into certain periods? Outline your autobiography by marking these periods as parts or chapters of the story of your life so far. To gain a sense of how periodization is imposed on reality and how arbitrary this structuring of the past can be, imagine how a parent or good friend would periodize your life. Would it be different from the way you did it? How and why? How might you periodize your life ten or twenty years from now? How would you have done it five years ago?

2

The Urban Revolution and "Civilization"

Ancient City Societies in Mesopotamia, Egypt, and Peru, 3500–1000 B.C.E.

■ HISTORICAL CONTEXT

The urban revolution that began approximately five thousand years ago produced a vast complex of new inventions, institutions, and ideas in the cities that dominated surrounding farms and pastures. The first selection in this chapter surveys the wide range of innovations in these earliest civilizations.

The term *civilization* has to be used cautiously. Especially when the idea of civilization is used as part of a stage theory of human history, we tend to assume that technological advancement means moral advancement. For instance, one hundred years ago scholars described ancient history as the progression from "savagery" to "barbarism" to "civilization."

It would be a shame to throw out the word *civilization* because it has been written more often with an axe than with a pen. The fact remains that the ancient cities created new ways of life for better or worse that were radically different from the world of agricultural villages. If we discard the word *civilization* as too overburdened with prejudice, we will have to find another one to describe that complex of changes. The term *civilization* comes from the Latin root word for city, *civitas*, from which we also get *civic*, *civilian*, and *citizen*. But, as the first reading argues, cities also created social classes, institutionalized inequalities, and calls to arms; most civilizations created soldiers as well as civilians.

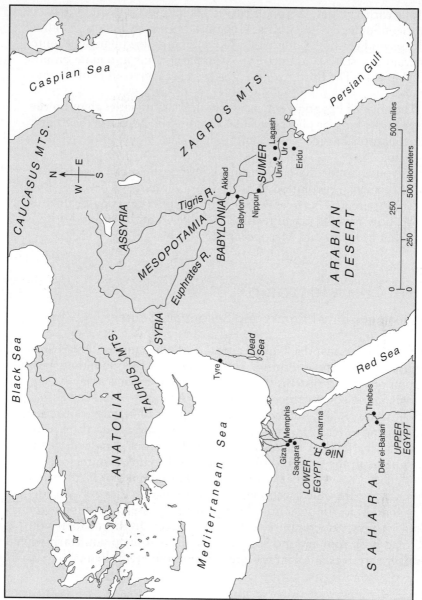

Map 2.1 Early Civilizations: Egypt and Mesopotamia.

33

The earliest cities, the small city-states on the Tigris and Euphrates*
in ancient Sumer, included King Gilgamesh's Uruk, which is recounted
in the second reading. Later cities, like Hammurabi's† Babylon, united
Sumerian city-states and upriver pastoral kingdoms into giant empires
(see Map 2.1). The third reading presents excerpts from Hammurabi's
law code.

The ancient Egyptian empire depended less on cities than on the
power of the king or pharaoh, but life along the Nile was magnified
in the pharaoh's residence city and in his future home in the City of
the Dead.

As you examine these selections, consider the overall transformation of the urban revolution in both Mesopotamia and Egypt. Note
also the differences between Mesopotamian and Egyptian civilizations.
Finally, how was the urban revolution in Peru similar to, and different
from, that in Egypt and Mesopotamia?

■ THINKING HISTORICALLY

Distinguishing Primary and Secondary Sources

For some historians, the "age of cities" is the beginning of history
because cities invented writing. The period before city building and the
creation of writing systems thus is often called "prehistory."

Our knowledge of ancient cities is enormously enhanced by
ancient writings, art, and artifacts, which we call primary sources.
These include literature, law codes, and inscriptions but also sculpture, murals, building remains, tools, and weapons — indeed, virtually
anything from the time and place being studied. Secondary sources
differ: They are written after the fact. History books or historical interpretations are called secondary sources because they rely on primary sources for information. Historians read, study, and interpret
primary sources to compose secondary sources. In this chapter you
will read both primary and secondary sources to help you learn ways
to discern sources and extrapolate information from them.

* TY gruhs and yu FRAY teez
† ha muh RAH bee

1

KEVIN REILLY

Cities and Civilization, 1989

This selection from a college textbook is an obvious secondary source. You know it is a secondary source because it was written long after the events described by a modern historian — me.

This selection does two things. First, it explores the wide range of changes brought about by the urban revolution, from particulars like writing and money and metallurgy to abstractions like social class, visual acuity, and anonymity. After you read the selection, you might make a list of all the inventions and new phenomena of cities. You will likely be surprised by the great number of ideas, institutions, and activities that originated in the first cities. You might also find it interesting to place pluses and minuses next to the items on your list to help you determine whether "civilization" (city life) was, on balance, beneficial or harmful.

Second, the selection compares the "civilizations" of Mesopotamia and Egypt. According to the selection, what are the chief differences between Mesopotamian and Egyptian civilization? What accounts for these differences?

THINKING HISTORICALLY

To get a feel for the differences between a primary source and a secondary source, try to determine what primary sources might lead to some of these interpretations. Choose a sentence or two that appear specific enough to be based on a primary source. What kind of source could lead to such an interpretation? Conversely, find interpretations in this selection that *could not possibly* derive from a primary source and ask yourself, why not? Finally, consider what kind of nonwritten sources and evidence inform this account.

The Urban Revolution: Civilization and Class

The full-scale urban revolution occurred not in the rain-watered lands that first turned some villages into cities, but in the potentially more productive river valleys of Mesopotamia around 3500 B.C.E. Situated along the Tigris and Euphrates rivers, large villages like Eridu, Erech, Lagash, Kish, and later Ur and Babylon built irrigation systems that

Source: Kevin Reilly, *The West and the World: A History of Civilization*, 2nd ed. (New York: Harper & Row, 1989), 48–54, 56, 58, 60.

increased farm production enormously. Settlements like these were able to support five thousand, even ten thousand people, and still allow something like 10 percent of the inhabitants to work full-time at non-farming occupations.

A change of this scale was a revolution, certainly the most important revolution in human living since the invention of agriculture five thousand years earlier. The urban revolution was prepared by a whole series of technological inventions in agricultural society. Between 6000 and 3000 B.C.E. people not only learned how to harness the power of oxen and the wind with the plow, the wheeled cart, and the sailboat; they also discovered the physical properties of metals, learned how to smelt copper and bronze, and began to work out a calendar based on the movements of the sun. River valleys like those of the Tigris and Euphrates were muddy swamps that had to be drained and irrigated to take advantage of the rich soil deposits. The dry land had literally to be built by teams of organized workers.

Therefore, cities required an organizational revolution that was every bit as important as the technological one. This was accomplished under the direction of the new class of rulers and managers—probably from the grasslands—who often treated the emerging cities as a conquered province. The work of irrigation itself allowed the rulers ample opportunity to coerce the inhabitants of these new cities. Rain knows no social distinctions. Irrigated water must be controlled and channeled.

It is no wonder then that the first cities gave us our first kings and our first class societies. In Mesopotamia, along the Nile of Egypt, in China, and later in Middle America the king is usually described as the founder of cities. These kings were able to endow their control with religious sanction. In Egypt and America the king was god. In Mesopotamia a new class of priests carried out the needs of the king's religion of control.

In some cities the new priesthood would appoint the king. In others, the priests were merely his lieutenants. When they were most loyal, their religion served to deify the king. The teachings of the new class of Mesopotamian priests, for instance, were that their god had created the people solely to work for the king and make his life easier. But even when the priesthood attempted to wrest some of the king's power from him, the priests taught the people to accept the divided society, which benefited king and priesthood as providers of a natural god-given order. The priesthood, after all, was responsible for measuring time, bounding space, and predicting seasonal events. The mastery of people was easy for those who controlled time and space.

The priesthood was only one of the new classes that insured the respectability of the warrior-chieftain turned king. Other palace intellectuals—scribes (or writers), doctors, magicians, and diviners—also struggled to maintain the king's prestige and manage his kingdom.

This new class was rewarded, as were the priests, with leisure, status, and magnificent buildings, all of which further exalted the majesty of the king and his city.

Beneath the king, the priesthood, and the new class of intellectuals-managers was another new class charged with maintaining the king's law and order. Soldiers and police were also inventions of the first cities. Like the surrounding city wall, the king's military guard served a double function: It provided defense from outside attack and an obstacle to internal rebellion.

That these were the most important classes of city society can be seen from the physical remains of the first cities. The archeologist's spade has uncovered the monumental buildings of these classes in virtually all of the first cities. The palace, the temple, and the citadel (or fort) are, indeed, the monuments that distinguish cities from villages. Further, the size of these buildings and the permanency of their construction (compared with the small, cheaply built homes of the farmers) attest to the fundamental class divisions of city society.

Civilization: Security and Variety

The most obvious achievements of the first civilizations are the monuments—the pyramids, temples, palaces, statues, and treasures—that were created for the new ruling class of kings, nobles, priests, and their officials. But civilized life is much more than the capacity to create monuments.

Civilized life is secure life. At the most basic level this means security from the sudden destruction that village communities might suffer. Civilized life gives the feeling of permanence. It offers regularity, stability, order, even routine. Plans can be made. Expectations can be realized. People can be expected to act predictably, according to the rules.

The first cities were able to attain stability with walls that shielded the inhabitants from nomads and armies, with the first codes of law that defined human relationships, with police and officials who enforced the laws, and with institutions that functioned beyond the lives of their particular members. City life offered considerably more permanence and security than village life.

Civilization involves more than security, however. A city that provided only order would be more like a prison than a civilization. The first cities provided something that the best-ordered villages lacked. They provided far greater variety: More races and ethnic groups were speaking more languages, engaged in more occupations, and living a greater variety of lifestyles. The abundance of choice, the opportunities for new sensations, new experiences, knowledge—these have always been the appeals of city life. The opportunities for growth and enrichment were far greater than the possibilities of plow and pasture life.

Security plus variety equals creativity. At least the possibility of a more creative, expressive life was available in the protected, semipermanent city enclosures that drew, like magnets, foreign traders and diplomats, new ideas about gods and nature, strange foods and customs, and the magicians, ministers, and mercenaries of the king's court. Civilization is the enriched life that this dynamic urban setting permitted and the human creativity and opportunity that it encouraged. At the very least, cities made even the most common slave think and feel a greater range of things than the tightly knit, clannish agricultural village allowed. That was (and still is) the root of innovation and creativity—of civilization itself.

The variety of people and the complexity of city life required new and more general means of communication. The villager knew everyone personally. Cities brought together people who often did not even speak the same language. Not only law codes but written language itself became a way to bridge the many gaps of human variety. Cities invented writing so that strangers could communicate, and so that those communications could become permanent—remembered publicly, officially recorded. [Writer and philosopher Ralph Waldo] Emerson was right when he said that the city lives by memory, but it was the official memory that enabled the city to carry on its business or religion beyond the lifetime of the village elders. Written symbols that everyone could recognize became the basis of laws, invention, education, taxes, accounting, contracts, and obligations. In short, writing and records made it possible for each generation to begin on the shoulders of its ancestors. Village life and knowledge often seemed to start from scratch. Thus, cities cultivated not only memory and the past, but hope and the future as well. City civilizations invented not only history and record keeping but also prophecy and social planning.

Writing was one city invention that made more general communication possible. Money was another. Money made it possible to deal with anyone just as an agreed-upon public language did. Unnecessary in the village climate of mutual obligations, money was essential in the city society of strangers. Such general media of communication as writing and money vastly increased the number of things that could be said and thought, bought and sold. As a consequence, city life was more impersonal than village life, but also more dynamic and more exciting.

The "Eye" and "I"

[Communication theorist] Marshall McLuhan has written that "civilization gave the barbarian an eye for an ear." We might add that civilization also gave an "I" for an "us." City life made the "eye" and the "I" more important than they had been in the village. The invention of writing made knowledge more visual. The eye had to be trained to recognize the minute differences in letters and words. Eyes took in a greater abundance of detail: laws, prices, the strange cloak of the foreigner, the odd type of shoes made by the new craftsworker from who-knows-where, the colors of the fruit and vegetable market, and elaborate painting in the temple, as well as the written word. In the village one learned by listening. In the city seeing was believing. In the new city courts of law an "eyewitness account" was believed to be more reliable than "hearsay evidence." In some villages even today, the heard and the spoken are thought more reliable than the written and the seen. In the city, even spoken language took on the uniformity and absence of emotion that is unavoidable in the written word. Perhaps emotions themselves became less violent. "Civilized" is always used to mean emotional restraint, control of the more violent passions, and a greater understanding, even tolerance, of the different and foreign.

Perhaps empathy (the capacity to put yourself in someone else's shoes) increased in cities — so full of so many different others that had to be understood. When a Turkish villager was recently asked, "What would you do if you were president of your country?" he stammered: "My God! How can you ask such a thing? How can I . . . I cannot . . . president of Turkey . . . master of the whole world?" He was completely unable to imagine himself as president. It was as removed from his experience as if he were master of the world. Similarly, a Lebanese villager who was asked what he would do if he were editor of a newspaper accused the interviewer of ridiculing him, and frantically waved the interviewer on to another question. Such a life was beyond his comprehension. It was too foreign to imagine. The very variety of city life must have increased the capacity of the lowest commoner to imagine, empathize, sympathize, and criticize.

The oral culture of the village reinforced the accepted by saying and singing it almost monotonously. The elders, the storytellers, and the minstrels must have had prodigious memories. But their stories changed only gradually and slightly. The spoken word was sacred. To say it differently was to change the truth. The written culture of cities taught "point of *view*." An urban individual did not have to remember everything. That was done permanently on paper. Knowledge became a recognition of different interpretations and the capacity to look up things. The awareness of variety meant the possibility of criticism, analysis, and an ever-newer synthesis. It is no wonder that the technical and scientific knowledge of cities increased at a geometric rate compared with the knowledge of villages. The multiplication of knowledge was implicit in the city's demand to recognize difference and variety. Civilization has come to mean that ever-expanding body of knowledge and skill. Its finest achievements have been that knowledge, its writing, and its visual art. The city and civilization (like the child) are to be seen and not heard.

It may seem strange to say that the impersonal life of cities contributed greatly to the development of personality—the "I" as well as the "eye." Village life was in a sense much more personal. Everything was taken personally. Villagers deal with each other not as "the blacksmith," "the baker," "that guy who owes me a goat," or "that no-good bum." They do not even "deal" with each other. They know each other by name and family. They love, hate, support, and murder each other because of who they are, because of personal feelings, because of personal and family responsibility. They have full, varied relationships with each member of the village. They do not merely buy salt from this person, talk about the weather with this other person, and discuss personal matters with only this other person. They share too much with each other to divide up their relationships in that way.

City life is a life of separated, partial relationships. In a city you do not know about the butcher's life, wife, kids, and problems. You do not care. You are in a hurry. You have too many other things to do. You might discuss the weather—but while he's cutting. You came to buy meat. Many urban relationships are like that. There are many business, trading, or "dealing" relationships because there are simply too many people to know them all as relatives.

The impersonality of city life is a shame in a way. (It makes it easier to get mugged by someone who does not even hate you.) But the luxurious variety of impersonal relationships (at least some of the time) provides the freedom for the individual personality to emerge. Maybe that is why people have often dreamed of leaving family and friends (usually for a city) in the hope of "finding themselves." Certainly, the camaraderie and community of village life had a darker side of surveillance and conformity. When everything was known about everyone, it was difficult for the individual to find his or her individuality. Family ties and village custom were often obstacles to asserting self-identity. The city offered its inhabitants a huge variety of possible relationships and personal identities. The urban inhabitant was freer than his village cousin to choose friends, lovers, associates, occupation, housing, and lifestyle. The city was full of choices that the village could not afford or condone. The village probably provided more security in being like everyone else and doing what was expected. But the city provided the variety of possibilities that could allow the individual to follow the "inner self" and cultivate inner gardens.

The class divisions of city society made it difficult for commoners to achieve an effective or creative individuality. But the wealthy and powerful—especially the king—were able to develop models of individuality and personality that were revolutionary. No one before had ever achieved such a sense of the self, and the model of the king's power and freedom became a goal for the rest of the society. The luxury, leisure, and opportunity of the king was a revolutionary force. In contrast to a village elder, the king could do whatever he wanted. Recognizing that, more and more city inhabitants asked, "Why can't we?" City revolutions have continually extended class privilege and opportunities ever since.

Once a society has achieved a level of abundance, once it can offer the technological means, the educational opportunities, the creative outlets necessary for everyone to lead meaningful, happy, healthy lives, then classes may be a hindrance. Class divisions were, however, a definite stimulus to productivity and creativity in the early city civilizations. The democratic villagers preferred stability to improvement. As a result, their horizons were severely limited. They died early, lived precipitously, and suffered without much hope. The rulers of the first cities discovered the possibilities of leisure, creation, and the good life. They invented heaven and utopia—first for themselves. Only very gradually has the invention of civilization, of human potential, sifted down to those beneath the ruling class. In many cases, luxury, leisure, freedom, and opportunity are still the monopolies of the elite. But once the powerful have exploited the poor enough to establish their own paradise on earth and their own immortality after death, the poor also have broader horizons and plans.

Mesopotamian and Egyptian Civilizations: A Tale of Two Rivers

Experts disagree as to whether Mesopotamian or Egyptian civilization is older. Mesopotamian influence in Egypt was considerable enough to suggest slightly earlier origins, but both had evolved distinct civilizations by 3000 B.C.E. Indeed, the difference between the two civilizations attests to the existence of multiple routes to civilized life. In both cases, river valleys provided the necessary water and silt for an agricultural surplus large enough to support classes of specialists who did not have to farm. But the differing nature of the rivers had much to do with the different types of civilization that evolved.

The Egyptians were blessed with the easier and more reliable of the two rivers. The Nile overflowed its banks predictably every year on the parched ground in the summer after August 15, well after the harvest had been gathered, depositing its rich sediment, and withdrawing by early October, leaving little salt or marsh, in time for the sowing of winter crops. Later sowings for summer crops required only simple canals that tapped the river upstream and the natural drainage of the Nile Valley. Further, transportation on the Nile was simplified by the fact that the prevailing winds blew from the north, while the river flowed from the south, making navigation a matter of using sails upstream and dispensing with them coming downstream.

The Euphrates offered none of these advantages as it cut its way through Mesopotamia. The Euphrates flowed high above the flood plain (unlike the neighboring Tigris) so that its waters could be used, but it flooded suddenly and without warning in the late spring, after the summer crops had been sown and before the winter crops could be harvested. Thus, the flooding of the Euphrates offered no natural irrigation. Its waters were needed at other times, and its flooding was destructive. Canals were necessary to drain off water for irrigation when the river was low, and these canals had to be adequately blocked, and the banks reinforced, when the river flooded. Further, since the Euphrates was not as easily navigable as the Nile, the main canals had to serve as major transportation arteries as well.

In Mesopotamia the flood was the enemy. The Mesopotamian deities who ruled the waters, Nin-Girsu and Tiamat, were feared. The forces of nature were often evil. Life was a struggle. In Egypt, on the other hand, life was viewed as a cooperation with nature. Even the Egyptian god of the flood, Hapi, was a helpful deity, who provided the people's daily bread. Egyptian priests and philosophers were much more at ease with their world than were their Mesopotamian counterparts. And, partly because of their different experiences with their rivers, the Mesopotamians developed a civilization based on cities, while the Egyptians did not. From the first Sumerian city-states on the lower Euphrates to the later northern Mesopotamian capital of Babylon, civilization was the product and expression of city life. Egyptian civilization, in contrast, was the creation of the pharaoh's court rather than of cities. Beyond the court, which was moved from one location to another, Egypt remained a country of peasant villages.

A prime reason for Egypt's lack of urbanization was the ease of farming on the banks of the Nile. Canal irrigation was a relatively simple process that did not demand much organization. Small market towns were sufficient for the needs of the countryside. They housed artisans, shopkeepers, the priests of the local temple, and the agents of the pharaoh, but they never swelled with a large middle class and never developed large-scale industry or commerce.

In Sumer, and later in Mesopotamia, the enormous task of fighting the Euphrates required a complex social organization with immediate local needs. Only communal labor could build and maintain the network of subsidiary canals for irrigation and drainage. Constant supervision was necessary to keep the canals free of silt, to remove salt deposits, to maintain the riverbanks at flood-time, and to prevent any farmer from monopolizing the water in periods of drought. Life on the Euphrates required cooperative work and responsibility that never ceased. It encouraged absolute, administrative control over an area larger than the village, and it fostered participation and loyalty to an irrigated area smaller than the imperial state. The city-state was the political answer to the economic problems of Sumer and Mesopotamia.

The religious practices in the Euphrates Valley reflected and supported city organization. Residents of each local area worshiped the local god while recognizing the existence of other local gods in a larger Sumerian, and eventually Mesopotamian, pantheon of gods. The priests of the local temple supervised canal work, the collection of taxes, and the storage of written records, as well as the proper maintenance of religious rituals. Thus, religious loyalty reinforced civic loyalty. Peasant and middle-class Sumerians thought of themselves as citizens of their particular city, worshipers of their particular city god, subjects of their particular god's earthly representative, but not as Sumerian nationals. By contrast, the Egyptian peasant was always an Egyptian, a subject of the pharaoh, but never a citizen.

The local, civic orientation of Mesopotamian cities can be seen in the physical structure of the capital city of Sumer, the city of Ur. Like other cities on the Euphrates, Ur was surrounded by a wall. It was dominated by the temple of Nannar, the moon-god who owned the city, and the palace complex beneath the temple. The residential areas were situated outside of the sacred Temenos, or temple compound, but within the walls, between the river and the main canal. The well-excavated remains of Ur of the seventeenth century B.C.E. show a residential street plan that looks like many Middle Eastern cities of today. A highly congested area of winding alleys and broad streets sheltered one- and two-story houses of merchants, shopkeepers, tradespeople, and occasional priests and scribes that suggest a large, relatively prosperous middle class. Most houses were built around a central courtyard that offered shade throughout the day, with mud-brick, often even plastered, outside walls that protected a number of interior rooms from the sun and the eyes of the tax inspector. The remains of seventeenth-century Ur show both the variety and the density of modern city life. There are specialized districts throughout the city. Certain trades have their special quarters: a bakers' square, probably special areas for the dyers, tanners, potters, and metalworkers. But life is mixed together as well. Subsidiary gods have temples outside the Temenos. Small and large houses are jumbled next to each other. There seems to be a slum area near the Temenos, but there are small houses for workers, tenant farmers, and the poor throughout the city. And no shop or urban professional is more than a short walking distance away. The entire size of the walled city was an oval that extended three-quarters of a mile long and a half a mile wide.

A well-excavated Egyptian city from roughly the same period (the fourteenth century B.C.E.) offers some striking contrasts. Akhetaton, or Tell el Amarna, Pharaoh Akhenaton's capital on the Nile, was not enclosed by walls or canals. It merely straggled down the eastern bank of the Nile for five miles and faded into the desert. Without the need for extensive irrigation or protection, Tell el Amarna shows little of the crowded, vital density of Ur. Its layout lacks any sense of urgency. The

North Palace of the pharaoh is a mile and a half north of the temple complex and offices, which are three and a half miles from the official pleasure garden. The palaces of the court nobility and the large residences of the court's officials front one of the two main roads that parallel the river, or they are situated at random. There is plenty of physical space (and social space) between these and the bunched villages of workers' houses. The remains suggest very little in the way of a middle class or a merchant or professional class beyond the pharaoh's specialists and retainers. Life for the wealthy was, judging from the housing, more luxurious than at Ur, but for the majority of the population, city life was less rich. In many ways, the pharaoh's court at Tell el Amarna was not a city at all.

2

The Epic of Gilgamesh, c. 2700 B.C.E.

The Epic of Gilgamesh is the earliest story written in any language. It also serves as a primary source for the study of ancient Mesopotamia—the land between the two great rivers, the Tigris and Euphrates.

Gilgamesh was an ancient king of Sumer who lived about 2700 B.C.E. Since *The Epic* comes from a thousand years later, we can assume Sumerians kept telling this tale about King Gilgamesh for some time before it was written down. In Sumer, writing was initially used by temple priests to keep track of property and taxes. Soon, however, writing was used to preserve stories and to celebrate kings.

The more you know about the Sumerian people, the more information you will be able to mine from your source. In the previous secondary selection, you read some historical background that will help you make sense of this story. Look in *The Epic* for evidence of the urban revolution discussed in the previous selection. What is the meaning of the story of the taming of Enkidu by the harlot? Does Enkidu also tame Gilgamesh? What two worlds do Enkidu and Gilgamesh represent?

Do the authors or listeners of *The Epic* think city life is better than life in the country? According to *The Epic*, what are the advantages of the city? What problems does it have?

What does the story of the flood tell you about life in ancient Mesopotamia? Would you expect the ancient Egyptians to tell a similar story?

Source: *The Epic of Gilgamesh*, trans. N. K. Sandars (London: Penguin Books, 1972), 61–69, 108–13.

THINKING HISTORICALLY

Reading a primary source differs markedly from reading a secondary source. Primary sources were not written with you or me in mind. It is safe to say that the author of *The Epic of Gilgamesh* never even imagined our existence. For this reason, primary sources are a bit difficult to access. Reading a primary source usually requires some intensive work. You have to keep asking yourself, why was this story told? How would a story like this help or teach people at that time? That is, you must put yourself in the shoes of the original teller and listener.

Primary sources offer us a piece of the past. No historian is in your way explaining things. With your unique perspective, you have an advantage over the intended audience: You can ask questions about the source that the author and original audience never imagined or, possibly, would not have dared ask.

Ask a question for which this primary source can provide an answer, then find the answer.

Prologue: Gilgamesh King in Uruk

I will proclaim to the world the deeds of Gilgamesh. This was the man to whom all things were known; this was the king who knew the countries of the world. He was wise, he saw mysteries and knew secret things, he brought us a tale of the days before the flood. He went on a long journey, was weary, worn-out with labor; returning he rested, he engraved on a stone the whole story.

When the gods created Gilgamesh they gave him a perfect body. Shamash the glorious sun endowed him with beauty, Adad the god of the storm endowed him with courage, the great gods made his beauty perfect, surpassing all others, terrifying like a great wild bull. Two thirds they made him god and one third man.

In Uruk he built walls, a great rampart, and the temple of blessed Eanna for the god of the firmament Anu, and for Ishtar the goddess of love. Look at it still today: the outer wall where the cornice runs, it shines with the brilliance of copper; and the inner wall, it has no equal. Touch the threshold; it is ancient. Approach Eanna the dwelling of Ishtar, our lady of love and war, the like of which no latter-day king, no man alive can equal. Climb upon the wall of Uruk; walk along it, I say; regard the foundation terrace and examine the masonry; is it not burnt brick and good? The seven sages laid the foundations.

The Coming of Enkidu

Gilgamesh went abroad in the world, but he met with none who could withstand his arms till he came to Uruk. But the men of Uruk muttered in their houses, "Gilgamesh sounds the tocsin for his amusement, his arrogance has no bounds by day or night. No son is left with his father, for Gilgamesh takes from all, even the children; yet the king should be a shepherd to his people. His lust leaves no virgin to her lover, neither the warrior's daughter nor the wife of the noble; yet this is the shepherd of the city, wise, comely, and resolute."

The gods heard their lament, the gods of heaven cried to the Lord of Uruk, to Anu the god of Uruk: "A goddess made him, strong as a savage bull, none can withstand his arms. No son is left with his father, for Gilgamesh takes them all; and is this the king, the shepherd of his people? His lust leaves no virgin to her lover, neither the warrior's daughter nor the wife of the noble." When Anu had heard their lamentation the gods cried to Aruru, the goddess of creation, "You made him, O Aruru, now create his equal; let it be as like him as his own reflection, his second self, stormy head for stormy heart. Let them contend together and leave Uruk in quiet."

So the goddess conceived an image in her mind, and it was of the stuff of Anu of the firmament. She dipped her hands in water and pinched off clay, she let it fall in the wilderness, and noble Enkidu* was created. There was virtue in him of the god of war, of Ninurta himself. His body was rough; he had long hair like a woman's; it waved like the hair of Nisaba, the goddess of corn. His body was covered with matted hair like Samuqan's, the god of cattle. He was innocent of mankind; he knew nothing of cultivated land.

Enkidu ate grass in the hills with the gazelle and lurked with wild beasts at the water-holes; he had joy of the water with the herds of wild game. But there was a trapper who met him one day face to face at the drinking-hole, for the wild game had entered his territory. On three days he met him face to face, and the trapper was frozen with fear. He went back to his house with the game that he had caught, and he was dumb, benumbed with terror. His face was altered like that of one who has made a long journey. With awe in his heart he spoke to his father: "Father, there is a man, unlike any other, who comes down from the hills. He is the strongest in the world, he is like an immortal from heaven. He ranges over the hills with wild beasts and eats grass; he ranges through your land and comes down to the wells. I am afraid and dare not go near him. He fills in the pits which I dig and tears up my traps set for the game; he helps the beasts to escape and now they slip through my fingers."

* EHN kee doo

His father opened his mouth and said to the trapper, "My son, in Uruk lives Gilgamesh; no one has ever prevailed against him, he is strong as a star from heaven. Go to Uruk, find Gilgamesh, extol the strength of this wild man. Ask him to give you a harlot, a wanton from the temple of love; return with her, and let her woman's power overpower this man. When next he comes down to drink at the wells she will be there, stripped naked; and when he sees her beckoning he will embrace her, and then the wild beasts will reject him."

So the trapper set out on his journey to Uruk and addressed himself to Gilgamesh saying, "A man unlike any other is roaming now in the pastures; he is as strong as a star from heaven and I am afraid to approach him. He helps the wild game to escape; he fills in my pits and pulls up my traps." Gilgamesh said, "Trapper, go back, take with you a harlot, a child of pleasure. At the drinking-hole she will strip, and when he sees her beckoning he will embrace her and the game of the wilderness will surely reject him."

Now the trapper returned, taking the harlot with him. After a three days' journey they came to the drinking-hole, and there they sat down; the harlot and the trapper sat facing one another and waited for the game to come. For the first day and for the second day the two sat waiting, but on the third day the herds came; they came down to drink and Enkidu was with them. The small wild creatures of the plains were glad of the water, and Enkidu with them, who ate grass with the gazelle and was born in the hills; and she saw him; the savage man, come from far-off in the hills. The trapper spoke to her: "There he is. Now, woman, make your breasts bare, have no shame, do not delay but welcome his love. Let him see you naked, let him possess your body. When he comes near uncover yourself and lie with him; teach him, the savage man, your woman's art, for when he murmurs love to you the wild beasts that shared his life in the hills will reject him."

She was not ashamed to take him, she made herself naked and welcomed his eagerness; as he lay on her murmuring love she taught him the woman's art. For six days and seven nights they lay together, for Enkidu had forgotten his home in the hills; but when he was satisfied he went back to the wild beasts. Then, when the gazelle saw him, they bolted away; when the wild creatures saw him they fled. Enkidu would have followed, but his body was bound as though with a cord, his knees gave way when he started to run, his swiftness was gone. And now the wild creatures had all fled away; Enkidu was grown weak, for wisdom was in him, and the thoughts of a man were in his heart. So he returned and sat down at the woman's feet, and listened intently to what she said. "You are wise, Enkidu, and now you have become like a god. Why do you want to run wild with the beasts in the hills? Come with me. I will take you to strong-walled Uruk, to the blessed temple of Ishtar and of Anu, of love and of heaven: there Gilgamesh lives, who is very strong, and like a wild bull he lords it over men."

When she had spoken Enkidu was pleased; he longed for a comrade, for one who would understand his heart. "Come, woman, and take me to that holy temple, to the house of Anu and of Ishtar, and to the place where Gilgamesh lords it over people. I will challenge him boldly, I will cry out aloud in Uruk, 'I am the strongest here, I have come to change the old order, I am he who was born in the hills, I am he who is strongest of all.'"

She said, "Let us go, and let him see your face. I know very well where Gilgamesh is in great Uruk. O Enkidu, there all the people are dressed in their gorgeous robes, every day is holiday, the young men and the girls are wonderful to see. How sweet they smell! All the great ones are roused from their beds. O Enkidu, you who love life, I will show you Gilgamesh, a man of many moods; you shall look at him well in his radiant manhood. His body is perfect in strength and maturity; he never rests by night or day. He is stronger than you, so leave your boasting. Shamash the glorious sun has given favors to Gilgamesh, and Anu of the heavens, and Enlil, and Ea the wise has given him deep understanding. I tell you, even before you have left the wilderness, Gilgamesh will know in his dreams that you are coming."

Now Gilgamesh got up to tell his dream to his mother, Ninsun, one of the wise gods. "Mother, last night I had a dream. I was full of joy, the young heroes were round me and I walked through the night under the stars of the firmament, and one, a meteor of the stuff of Anu, fell down from heaven. I tried to lift it but it proved too heavy. All the people of Uruk came round to see it, the common people jostled and the nobles thronged to kiss its feet; and to me its attraction was like the love of woman. They helped me, I braced my forehead and I raised it with thongs and brought it to you, and you yourself pronounced it my brother."

Then Ninsun, who is well-beloved and wise, said to Gilgamesh, "This star of heaven which descended like a meteor from the sky; which you tried to lift, but found too heavy, when you tried to move it it would not budge, and so you brought it to my feet; I made it for you, a goad and spur, and you were drawn as though to a woman. This is the strong comrade, the one who brings help to his friend in his need. He is the strongest of wild creatures, the stuff of Anu; born in the grasslands and the wild hills reared him; when you see him you will be glad; you will love him as a woman and he will never forsake you. This is the meaning of the dream."

Gilgamesh said, "Mother, I dreamed a second dream. In the streets of strong-walled Uruk there lay an axe; the shape of it was strange and the people thronged round. I saw it and was glad. I bent down, deeply drawn towards it; I loved it like a woman and wore it at my side." Ninsun answered, "That axe, which you saw, which drew you so powerfully like love of a woman, that is the comrade whom I give you, and he will come in his strength like one of the host of heaven. He is the brave companion who rescues his friend in necessity." Gilgamesh said to his mother, "A friend, a counsellor has come to me from Enlil, and now I shall befriend and counsel him." So Gilgamesh told his dreams; and the harlot retold them to Enkidu.

And now she said to Enkidu, "When I look at you you have become like a god. Why do you yearn to run wild again with the beasts in the hills? Get up from the ground, the bed of a shepherd." He listened to her words with care. It was good advice that she gave. She divided her clothing in two and with the one half she clothed him and with the other herself; and holding his hand she led him like a child to the sheepfolds, into the shepherds' tents. There all the shepherds crowded round to see him, they put down bread in front of him, but Enkidu could only suck the milk of wild animals. He fumbled and gaped, at a loss what to do or how he should eat the bread and drink the strong wine. Then the woman said, "Enkidu, eat bread, it is the staff of life; drink the wine, it is the custom of the land." So he ate till he was full and drank strong wine, seven goblets. He became merry, his heart exulted and his face shone. He rubbed down the matted hair of his body and anointed himself with oil. Enkidu had become a man; but when he had put on man's clothing he appeared like a bridegroom. He took arms to hunt the lion so that the shepherds could rest at night. He caught wolves and lions and the herdsmen lay down in peace; for Enkidu was their watchman, that strong man who had no rival.

He was merry living with the shepherds, till one day lifting his eyes he saw a man approaching. He said to the harlot, "Woman, fetch that man here. Why has he come? I wish to know his name." She went and called the man saying, "Sir, where are you going on this weary journey?" The man answered, saying to Enkidu, "Gilgamesh has gone into the marriage-house and shut out the people. He does strange things in Uruk, the city of great streets. At the roll of the drum work begins for the men, and work for the women. Gilgamesh the king is about to celebrate marriage with the Queen of Love, and he still demands to be first with the bride, the king to be first and the husband to follow, for that was ordained by the gods from his birth, from the time the umbilical cord was cut. But now the drums roll for the choice of the bride and the city groans." At these words Enkidu turned white in the face. "I will go to the place where Gilgamesh lords it over the people, I will challenge him boldly, and I will cry aloud in Uruk, 'I have come to change the old order, for I am the strongest here.'"

Now Enkidu strode in front and the woman followed behind. He entered Uruk, that great market, and all the folk thronged round him where he stood in the street in strong-walled Uruk. The people jostled; speaking of him they said, "He is the spit of Gilgamesh." "He is shorter." "He is bigger of bone." "This is the one who was reared on the milk of wild beasts. His is the greatest strength." The men rejoiced: "Now

Gilgamesh has met his match. This great one, this hero whose beauty is like a god, he is a match even for Gilgamesh."

In Uruk the bridal bed was made, fit for the goddess of love. The bride waited for the bridegroom, but in the night Gilgamesh got up and came to the house. Then Enkidu stepped out, he stood in the street and blocked the way. Mighty Gilgamesh came on and Enkidu met him at the gate. He put out his foot and prevented Gilgamesh from entering the house, so they grappled, holding each other like bulls. They broke the doorposts and the walls shook, they snorted like bulls locked together. They shattered the doorposts and the walls shook. Gilgamesh bent his knee with his foot planted on the ground and with a turn Enkidu was thrown. Then immediately his fury died. When Enkidu was thrown he said to Gilgamesh, "There is not another like you in the world. Ninsun, who is as strong as a wild ox in the byre, she was the mother who bore you, and now you are raised above all men, and Enlil has given you the kingship, for your strength surpasses the strength of men." So Enkidu and Gilgamesh embraced and their friendship was sealed.

The Story of the Flood

[Utnapishtim, the old man, tells the story to Gilgamesh.]

"You know the city Shurrupak, it stands on the banks of Euphrates? That city grew old and the gods that were in it were old. There was Anu, lord of the firmament, their father, and warrior Enlil their counsellor, Ninurta the helper, and Ennugi watcher over canals; and with them also was Ea. In those days the world teemed, the people multiplied, the world bellowed like a wild bull, and the great god was aroused by the clamour. Enlil heard the clamour and he said to the gods in council, 'The uproar of mankind is intolerable and sleep is no longer possible by reason of the babel.' So the gods agreed to exterminate mankind. Enlil did this, but Ea because of his oath warned me in a dream. He whispered their words to my house of reeds, 'Reed-house, reed-house! Wall, O wall, hearken reed-house, wall reflect; O man of Shurrupak, son of Ubara-Tutu; tear down your house and build a boat, abandon possessions and look for life, despise worldly goods and save your soul alive. Tear down your house, I say, and build a boat. These are the measurements of the barque as you shall build her: let her beam equal her length, let her deck be roofed like the vault that covers the abyss; then take up into the boat the seed of all living creatures.'

"When I had understood I said to my lord, 'Behold, what you have commanded I will honour and perform, but how shall I answer the people, the city, the elders?' Then Ea opened his mouth and said to me, his servant, 'Tell them this: I have learnt that Enlil is wrathful against me, I dare no longer walk in his land nor live in his city; I will go down to the Gulf to dwell with Ea my lord. But on you he will rain down abundance, rare fish and shy wild-fowl, a rich harvest-tide. In the evening the rider of the storm will bring you wheat in torrents.'

"In the first light of dawn all my household gathered round me, the children brought pitch and the men whatever was necessary. On the fifth day I laid the keel and the ribs, then I made fast the planking. The ground-space was one acre, each side of the deck measured one hundred and twenty cubits, making a square. I built six decks below, seven in all, I divided them into nine sections with bulkheads between. I drove in wedges where needed, I saw to the punt-poles, and laid in supplies. The carriers brought oil in baskets, I poured pitch into the furnace and asphalt and oil; more oil was consumed in caulking, and more again the master of the boat took into his stores. I slaughtered bullocks for the people and every day I killed sheep. I gave the shipwrights wine to drink as though it were river water, raw wine and red wine and oil and white wine. There was feasting then as there is at the time of the New Year's festival; I myself anointed my head. On the seventh day the boat was complete.

"Then was the launching full of difficulty; there was shifting of ballast above and below till two thirds was submerged. I loaded into her all that I had of gold and of living things, my family, my kin, the beast of the field both wild and tame, and all the craftsmen. I sent them on board, for the time that Shamash had ordained was already fulfilled when he said 'In the evening, when the rider of the storm sends down the destroying rain, enter the boat and batten her down.' The time was fulfilled, the evening came, the rider of the storm sent down the rain. I looked out at the weather and it was terrible, so I too boarded the boat and battened her down. All was now complete, the battening and the caulking; so I handed the tiller to Puzur-Amurri the steersman, with the navigation and the care of the whole boat.

"With the first light of dawn a black cloud came from the horizon; it thundered within where Adad, lord of the storm, was riding. In front over hill and plain Shullat and Hanish, heralds of the storm, led on. Then the gods of the abyss rose up; Nergal pulled out the dams of the nether waters, Ninurta the war-lord threw down the dykes, and the seven judges of hell, the Annunaki, raised their torches, lighting the land with their livid flame. A stupor of despair went up to heaven when the god of the storm turned daylight to darkness, when he smashed the land like a cup. One whole day the tempest raged, gathering fury as it went, it poured over the people like the tides of battle; a man could not see his brother nor the people be seen from heaven. Even the gods were terrified at the flood, they fled to the highest heaven, the firmament of Anu; they crouched against the walls, cowering like curs. . . .

"For six days and six nights the winds blew, torrent and tempest and flood overwhelmed the world, tempest and flood raged together like warring hosts. When the seventh day dawned the storm from the south subsided, the sea grew calm, the flood was stilled; I looked at the face of the world and there was silence, all mankind was turned to clay. The surface of the sea stretched as flat as a roof-top; I opened a hatch and the light fell on my face. Then I bowed low, I sat down and I wept, the tears streamed down my face, for on every side was the waste of water. I looked for land in vain, but fourteen leagues distant there appeared a mountain, and there the boat grounded; on the mountain of Nisir the boat held fast, she held fast and did not budge. One day she held, and a second day on the mountain of Nisir she held fast and did not budge. A third day, and a fourth day she held fast on the mountain and did not budge; a fifth day and a sixth day she held fast on the mountain. When the seventh day dawned I loosed a dove and let her go. She flew away, but finding no resting-place she returned. Then I loosed a swallow, and she flew away but finding no resting-place she returned. I loosed a raven, she saw that the waters had retreated, she ate, she flew around, she cawed, and she did not come back. Then I threw everything open to the four winds, I made a sacrifice and poured out a libation on the mountain top. Seven and again seven cauldrons I set up on their stands, I heaped up wood and cane and cedar and myrtle. When the gods smelled the sweet savour, they gathered like flies over the sacrifice. Then, at last, Ishtar also came, she lifted her necklace with the jewels of heaven that once Anu had made to please her. 'O you gods here present, by the lapis lazuli round my neck I shall remember these days as I remember the jewels of my throat; these last days I shall not forget. Let all the gods gather round the sacrifice, except Enlil. He shall not approach this offering, for without reflection he brought the flood; he consigned my people to destruction.'

"When Enlil had come, when he saw the boat, he was wrath and swelled with anger at the gods, the host of heaven, 'Has any of these mortals escaped? Not one was to have survived the destruction.' Then the god of the wells and canals Ninurta opened his mouth and said to the warrior Enlil, 'Who is there of the gods that devise without Ea? It is Ea alone who knows all things.' Then Ea opened his mouth and spoke to warrior Enlil, 'Wisest of gods, hero Enlil, how could you so senselessly bring down the flood?

> Lay upon the sinner his sin,
> Lay upon the transgressor his transgression,
> Punish him a little when he breaks loose,
> Do not drive him too hard or he perishes;
> Would that a lion had ravaged mankind
> Rather than the flood,
> Would that a wolf had ravaged mankind
> Rather than the flood,
> Would that famine had wasted the world
> Rather than the flood,
> Would that pestilence had wasted mankind
> Rather than the flood.

It was not I that revealed the secret of the gods; the wise man learned it in a dream. Now take your counsel what shall be done with him.'

"Then Enlil went up into the boat, he took me by the hand and my wife and made us enter the boat and kneel down on either side, he standing between us. He touched our foreheads to bless us saying, 'In time past Utnapishtim was a mortal man; henceforth he and his wife shall live in the distance at the mouth of the rivers.' Thus it was that the gods took me and placed me here to live in the distance, at the mouth of the rivers."

3

Hammurabi's Code, c. 1800 B.C.E.

King Hammurabi of Babylon conquered the entire area of Mesopotamia (including Sumer) between 1793 and 1750 B.C.E. His law code provides us with a rare insight into the daily life of ancient urban society.

Law codes give us an idea of a people's sense of justice and notions of proper punishment. This selection includes only parts of Hammurabi's Code, so we cannot conclude that if something is not mentioned here it was not a matter of legal concern. We can, however, deduce much about Babylonian society from the laws mentioned in this selection.

What do these laws tell us about class divisions or social distinctions in Babylonian society? What can we learn from these laws about the roles of women and men? Which laws or punishments seem unusual today? What does that difference suggest to you about ancient Babylon compared to modern society?

THINKING HISTORICALLY

As a primary source, law codes are extremely useful. They zero in on a society's main concerns, revealing minutiae of daily life in great detail. But, for a number of reasons, law codes cannot be viewed as a precise reflection of society.

We cannot assume, for instance, that all of Hammurabi's laws were strictly followed or enforced, anymore than we can assume that for our own society. If there was a law against something, we can safely assume that some people obeyed it and some people did not. (That is, if no one engaged in the behavior, there would be no need for the law.) Therefore, law codes suggest a broad range of behaviors in a society.

While laws tell us something about the concerns of the society that produces them, we cannot presume that all members of society

Source: Martha T. Roth, *Law Collections from Mesopotamia and Asia Minor*, 2nd ed. (Atlanta: Scholar's Press, 1997), 82–128 (selections as numbered).

share the same concerns. Recall that, especially in ancient society, laws were written by the literate, powerful few. What evidence do you see of the upper-class composition of Babylonian law in this code?

Finally, if an ancient law seems similar to our own, we cannot assume that the law reflects motives, intents, or goals similar to our own laws. Laws must be considered within the context of the society in which they were created. Notice, for instance, the laws in Hammurabi's Code that may seem, by our standards, intended to protect women. On closer examination, what appears to be their goal?

Property and Theft[1]

6. If a man steals valuables belonging to the god or to the palace, that man shall be killed, and also he who receives the stolen goods from him shall be killed.

8. If a man steals an ox, a sheep, a donkey, a pig, or a boat — if it belongs either to the god or to the palace, he shall give thirtyfold; if it belongs to a commoner, he shall replace it tenfold; if the thief does not have anything to give, he shall be killed.

14. If a man should kidnap the young child of another man, he shall be killed.

15. If a man should enable a palace slave, a palace slave woman, a commoner's slave, or a commoner's slave woman to leave through the main city-gate, he shall be killed.

17. If a man seizes a fugitive slave or a slave woman in the open country and leads him back to his owner, the slave owner shall give him 2 shekels of silver.

21. If a man breaks into a house, they shall kill him and hang him in front of that very breach.

22. If a man commits a robbery and is then seized, that man shall be killed.

24. If a life (is lost during the robbery), the city and the governor shall weigh and deliver to his kinsmen 60 shekels of silver.

Economics and Contracts

48. If a man has a debt lodged against him, and the storm god Adad devastates his field or a flood sweeps away his crops, or there is no grain grown in the field due to insufficient water — in that year he will not

---

[1] Topical headings added by the editor of this volume are in neither the original nor translated source. [Ed.]

repay grain to his creditor; he shall suspend performance of his contract and he will not give interest payments for that year.

53. If a man neglects to reinforce the embankment of (the irrigation canal of) his field and does not reinforce its embankment and allows the water to carry away the common irrigated area, the man in whose embankment the breach opened shall replace the grain whose loss he caused.

59. If a man cuts down a tree in another man's date orchard without the permission of the owner of the orchard, he shall weigh and deliver 30 shekels of silver.

117. If an obligation is outstanding against a man and he sells or gives into debt service his wife, his son, or his daughter, they shall perform service in the house of their buyer of the one who holds them in debt service for three years; their release shall be secured in the fourth year.

Family and Marriage

128. If a man marries a wife but does not draw up a formal contract for her, that woman is not a wife.

129. If a man's wife should be seized lying with another male, they shall bind them and cast them into the water; if the wife's master allows his wife to live, then the king shall allow his subject (i.e., the other male) to live.

130. If a man pins down another man's virgin wife who is still residing in her father's house, and they seize him lying with her, that man shall be killed; that woman shall be released.

142. If a woman repudiates her husband, and declares, "You will not have marital relations with me"—her circumstances shall be investigated by the authorities of her city quarter, and if she is circumspect and without fault, but her husband is wayward and disparages her greatly, that woman will not be subject to any penalty; she shall take her dowry and she shall depart for her father's house.

143. If she is not circumspect but is wayward, squanders her household possessions, and disparages her husband, they shall cast that woman into the water.

155. If a man selects a bride for his son and his son carnally knows her, after which he himself then lies with her and they seize him in the act, they shall bind that man and cast him into the water.

156. If a man selects a bride for his son and his son does not yet carnally know her, he shall weigh and deliver to her 30 shekels of silver; moreover, he shall restore to her whatever she brought from her father's house, and a husband of her choice shall marry her.

Assault and Personal Injury

195. If a child should strike his father, they shall cut off his hand.

196. If an *awīlu* [highest class] should blind the eye of another *awīlu*, they shall blind his eye.

197. If he should break the bone of another *awīlu*, they shall break his bone.

198. If he should blind the eye of a commoner or break the bone of a commoner, he shall weigh and deliver 60 shekels of silver.

199. If he should blind the eye of an *awīlu*'s slave or break the bone of an *awīlu*'s slave, he shall weigh and deliver one half of his value (in silver).

200. If an *awīlu* should knock out the tooth of another *awīlu* of his own rank, they shall knock out his tooth.

201. If he should knock out the tooth of a commoner, he shall weigh and deliver 20 shekels of silver.

202. If an *awīlu* should strike the cheek of an *awīlu* who is of status higher than his own, he shall be flogged in the public assembly with 60 stripes of an ox whip.

Responsibility and Liability

229. If a builder constructs a house for a man but does not make his work sound, and the house that he constructs collapses and causes the death of the householder, that builder shall be killed.

230. If it should cause the death of a son of the householder, they shall kill a son of that builder.

231. If it should cause the death of a slave of the householder, he shall give to the householder a slave of comparable value for the slave.

232. If it should cause the loss of property, he shall replace anything that is lost; moreover, because he did not make sound the house which he constructed and it collapsed, he shall construct (anew) the house which collapsed at his own expense.

251. If a man's ox is a known gorer, and the authorities of his city quarter notify him that it is a known gorer, but he does not blunt its horns or control his ox, and that ox gores to death a member of the *awīlu* class, he (the owner) shall give 30 shekels of silver.

252. If it is a man's slave (who is fatally gored), he shall give 20 shekels of silver.

4

The Tale of the Eloquent Peasant,
c. 1850 B.C.E.

Archaeologists have yet to discover an equivalent of Hammurabi's Code in the dry sands of Egypt. A few Egyptian Pharaohs were known as law givers, but Egyptian law seems to have emerged more from court cases, the decrees of the Pharaoh, and the decisions of his appointed judges than from law codes. Thanks to an Egyptian tradition that court cases should be written down (and those dry sands), we have a few vivid examples of the workings of Egyptian justice three thousand years ago. "The Tale of the Eloquent Peasant" comes down to us from such a court case, committed to papyrus leaves about 1850 B.C.E. What does this fragment tells us about the life of peasants in ancient Egypt? What makes this peasant different from most others? What do we learn about ancient Egyptian justice?

THINKING HISTORICALLY

Primary sources are not always exactly what they seem. While this source clearly originated in a legal dispute that was transcribed, "The Tale of the Eloquent Peasant" spins a story that appears more entertainment and moral lesson than verbatim court record. What elements of the tale seem to be exaggerations or elaborations intended for dramatic or moral purposes? If you discount these elements as unlikely, what do you think really happened? We cannot be sure, of course, but to read this source as literal truth would lead us to inaccuracies about ancient Egypt. It would be a mistake, for instance, to conclude that the king routinely heard peasant complaints. What other inaccurate conclusions might be drawn from a literal reading of the source? What accurate conclusions about ancient Egypt can you draw from a less literal reading?

There was once a man
called Khunanup;
he was a peasant of the Wadi Natrun,
whose wife was called Meret.
And this peasant said to this wife of his,

Source: "The Tale of the Eloquent Peasant," in The *Tale of Sinuhe and Other Ancient Egyptian Poems 1940–1640 B.C.*, trans. R.B. Parkinson (Oxford: Oxford University Press, 1997), 58–63, 65, 67–68, 73–75. © R.B. Parkinson.

'Look, I am going to Egypt
to buy provisions there for my children.
Go and measure for me
the grain which is left in the storehouse from [yesterday].'
And he measured out for her six gallons of grain.
And this peasant said to this wife of his,
'Look, twenty gallons of grain [are given] to you
and your children for provisions.
But you shall make these six gallons of grain
into bread and beer
for every day, for me to live on.'

This peasant then went down to Egypt,
having loaded his asses with reeds and fan palms,
natron[1] and salt,
sticks . . .
and staffs from Farafra,
leopard skins
and wolf hides,
[pebbles] and [serpentine],
wild mint-plants and *inbi*-fruits,
tebu- and *uben*-plants,
—with all the fair produce of Wadi Natrun.

This peasant then went
south to Heracleopolis.
He then arrived
in the area of Per-Fefi, north of Mednit.
There he met a man, called Nemtinakht,
standing on the riverbank.
He was the son of a gentleman called Isry;
they were liegemen of the High Steward
Meru's son Rensi.
And this Nemtinakht, when he saw this peasant's asses
which tempted his heart, said,
'If only I had some effective charm,
with which to steal this peasant's belongings!'
Now the house of this Nemtinakht was on the water edge,
    which was a path.
It was narrow; it was not broad,
but only as wide as a kilt.
One of its sides was under water,
and the other under grain.
And this Nemtinakht said to his follower,

---

[1] natron: a mineral used for cleaning and mummification. [Ed.]

'Go bring me a sheet from my house!'
It was brought immediately.
Then he spread the sheet on the water-edge pathway.
And its fringe rested on the water,
with its hem on the barley.
And this peasant came on the public path.
And this Nemtinakht said, 'Take care, peasant!
Will you tread on my clothes?'
And this peasant said, 'I'll do as you wish; my way is good.'
He then went upwards.
And this Nemtinakht said, 'Will my barley be your path?'
And this peasant said, 'My way is good,
for the bank is high and the way under barley,
and you block our path with clothes.
Won't you even let us go past the path?'

Then one of the asses took a mouthful
from a clump of barley.
And this Nemtinakht said, 'Look, peasant, I will take your
     ass,
for eating my barley,
and it will tread grain for its offence.'
And this peasant said, 'My way is good;
one clump is destroyed—
one destroying ten!
For ten units I bought my ass
and you seize it for a mouthful
of a clump of grain!
Now, I know the lord of this estate;
it belongs to the High Steward Meru's son Rensi.
Now, he punishes every robber in this entire land.
Am I robbed in his estate?'
And this Nemtinakht said, 'Isn't this
the proverb that people say—
"A wretch's name is uttered only because of his master"?
Even though it's the High Steward you recall,
I'm the one who speaks to you.'

Then he took a stick of fresh tamarisk to him.
Then he beat all his limbs with it,
and his asses were taken, and entered into his estate.
And this peasant now wept very much,
for the pain of what was being done to him.
And this Nemtinakht said, 'Don't raise your voice, peasant,
or, look, you're for the harbour of the Lord of Silence!'
And this peasant said, 'You beat me and steal my belongings?

And then you'll rob my mouth of complaint?
O Lord of Silence, may You give me back my belongings,
so I shan't cry out to Your fearsomeness!'
And this peasant spent a full week
petitioning this Nemtinakht, but he paid no attention.

This peasant then went
to Heracleopolis to petition
the High Steward Meru's son Rensi.
He met him coming out
of the door of his house,
about to board his official barge.
And this peasant said, 'Might I acquaint you with this complaint!
There is a reason to send one of your choice followers
to me, about which I shall send him back to you.'
And the High Steward Meru's son Rensi sent
a choice follower to him,
and this peasant sent him back
about this matter in every detail.
And the High Steward Meru's son Rensi
accused this Nemtinakht to the officials who were with him.

And they said to him, 'Surely it's only a peasant of his
who's run off to someone else.
Look, this is what people do to their peasants
who run off to others.
Is there cause to punish this Nemtinakht
for a little natron,
and a little salt?
Order him to repay it, and he'll repay it.'
The High Steward Meru's son Rensi
was then quiet.
He answered neither the officials,
nor the peasant.

And this peasant came to petition
the High Steward Meru's son Rensi,
and said, 'High Steward, toy lord!
Great of the great,
leader of all that is not and all that is!

If you go down to the Sea of Truth,
you will sail on it with true fair wind;
the bunt will not strip off your sails, not your boat delay;

nor will misfortune come upon your mast, nor your yards
    break;
you will not go headlong, and be grounded;
nor will the flood carry you off;
nor will you taste the river's evil, nor stare in the face of fear.
But to you the fish will come caught;
you will catch fatted fowl.

For you are a father to the orphan
and a husband to the widow,
a brother to the divorced,
an apron to the motherless.
Let me make your name in this land, with every good law:
Leader free from selfishness!
Great one free from baseness!
Destroyer of Falsehood! Creator of Truth!
Who comes at the voice of the caller!

I speak so that you will hear.
Do Truth, praised one whom the praised praise!
Drive off my need—look, I am weighed down!
Examine me—look, I am at a loss!'

Now this peasant made this speech
in the reign of the Majesty of the Dual King Nebkaure, the
    justified.
The High Steward Meru's son Rensi
then went before his Majesty
and said, 'My lord, I have found one of the peasants,
whose speech is truly perfect, and whose goods have been
    stolen.
And, look, he has come to me to appeal about it.'

And his Majesty said, 'As you wish to see me in health
you shall delay him here,
without answering anything he says!
For the sake of his speaking, be quiet
Then we shall be brought it in writing, and we shall hear it.
But provide sustenance for his wife and children!
Look, one of these peasants only comes
to Egypt when his house is all but empty.
Also, provide sustenance for this peasant himself!
You shall have the provisions given to him
without letting him know that you are giving him them!'

And he was given ten loaves of bread,
and two jars of beer daily.
The High Steward Meru's son
Rensi gave them—
gave them to his friend, and his friend gave them to him.
Then the High Steward Meru's son Rensi sent
to the mayor of the Wadi Natrun
about making provisions for this peasant's wife,
three gallons daily.

And this peasant came to appeal to him a second time,
and said, 'High Steward, my lord!
Greatest of the great!
Richest of the rich!
Whose great ones have one greater!
whose rich, one richer!
Helm of heaven!
Beam of earth!
Plumbline bearing the weight!
Helm, drift not!
Beam, tilt not!
Plumbline, go not wrong!
For a lord great through taking what is ownerless
is now robbing someone, while your share is in your
    house.
A jar of beer and three loaves of bread—
what else need you give out to satisfy your dependents?
A mortal must die with his underlings.

Will you then be a man of eternity?
Yet is it not wrong?—the scales tilting,
the weight wandering
the truly upright man turned aside?
Look, Truth flees from under you,
exiled from its place;
the officials are doing evil;
the standard of speech
is now partial,
and the judges snatch when it carries things off—
this means that he who twists speech from its rightness
makes himself go wrong thereby;
the breath-giver is now at a loss on the ground;
he who breathes calmly makes people pant;
the apportioner is greedy,
the dispeller of need is the commander of its making,

and the harbour is its own flood;
the punisher of wrong does evil.' . . .

And this peasant came to appeal to him a third time
and said, 'High Steward, my lord!
You are a Sungod, lord of heaven, with your entourage.
Everyone's portion is with you, like a flood.
You are a Nileflood who revives the water-meadows, and
  restores the ravaged mounds.
Punisher of the robber, protector of the poor—
become not a torrent against the appealer!

Take heed of eternity's approach! Wish to endure,
as is said, "Doing Truth is the breath of life."
Deal punishment to the punishable!
May your standard never be equalled!
Do the scales wander?
Is the balance partial?
And is Thoth lenient? If so, then you should do evil! . . .

And this peasant came to appeal to him a fourth time;
he met him coming out of the gate
of the temple of Herishef,
and said, 'O praised one, may Herishef
from whose temple you have come, praise you!

Destroyed is goodness, it has no unity,
and nothing can hurl Falsehood to the ground.
Has this ferry not gone down? So who can be taken across,
when crossing is made hateful?
Crossing the river on foot—
is that a good crossing? No!
So who now can sleep till dawn?
For destroyed is going by night
and travelling by day,
and making a man attend his good true right.
Look, it is no use to tell you this,
for mercy has passed you by: how miserable is the poor man
  you destroy!

Look, you are a hunter who slakes his desire,
who reaches out and does what he wants,
who harpoons hippopotami and shoots wild bulls,
catches fish and snares fowl.

Yet none hasty-mouthed is free from recklessness;
none light of heart is cautious of intent.
Your heart should be patient, so that you will know Truth!
Suppress your choice for the good of him who would depart
    quietly!
No rapid man cleaves to excellence; no hasty-hearted man
    will exist.

Stretch out to act, now your eyes are opened!
Inform the heart!
Be not harsh because you are powerful, so that evil may
    not reach you!
Pass over a misdeed, and it will be two.
Only the eater tastes;
so the accused replies.
Only the sleeper sees the dream;
so the punishable judge
is an archetype for the evildoer. . . .

If Falsehood sets out, it strays;
it cannot cross in a ferry, and has not altered its course.
He who is rich with it has no children,
and no heirs on earth.
And he who sails with it cannot touch land,
his boat cannot moor in its harbour.

Be heavy no more, you have not yet been light!
Delay no more, you have not yet been swift!
Be not partial! Do not listen to the heart!
Do not disregard one you know!
Do not blind yourself against one who looks to you! Do not
    fend off a supplicator!

You should abandon this negligence, so that your sentence
    will be renowned!
Act for him who acts for you
and listen to none against him,
so that a man will be summoned according to his true right!
There is no yesterday for the negligent,
no friend for him who is deaf to Truth,
no holiday for the selfish.
The accuser becomes wretched,
more wretched than when a pleader,
and the opponent becomes a murderer.

Look, I am pleading to you, and you do not hear—
I will go and plead about you to Anubis.'

And the High Steward Meru's son Rensi
sent two attendants to turn him back.
And this peasant was afraid, thinking this was done
to punish him for the speech he had made.
And this peasant said, 'The thirsty man
approaching water,
the nurseling reaching his mouth
for milk—they die,
while for him who longs to see it come,
death comes slowly.'
And the High Steward Meru's son Rensi said,
'Don't be afraid peasant!
Look, you will be dealing with me.'
And this peasant swore an oath,
'So, shall I live on your bread,
and drink your beer for ever?'
And the High Steward Meru's son Rensi said,
'Now wait here and hear your petitions!'
And he caused every petition to be read out
from a fresh roll according to [its] content.
And the High Steward Meru's son Rensi had them
     presented
before the Majesty of the Dual King Nebkaure, the
     justified.
And they seemed more perfect to his heart
than anything in this entire land.
And his Majesty said, 'Judge yourself, Meru's son!'

And the High Steward Meru's son Rensi
sent two attendants to [bring this Nemtinakht].
Then he was brought, and an inventory made [of his
     household].
Then he found six persons, as well as [his . . .],
his barley, his emmer,
his donkeys, his swine, and his flocks.
And this Nemtinakht [was given] to this peasant,
[with all his property, all his] ser[vants],
[and all the belongings] of this Nemtinakht.

So it ends, [from start to finish,
as found in writing].

5

Images from Hunefer's *Book of the Dead*, c. 1275 B.C.E.

Thanks to the preservative dry climate and the ancient Egyptian interest in illustrating books of papyrus and painting the interiors of pyramids, temples, and tombs, we have excellent visual primary sources
on the daily life of ancient Egypt. These two images are from a papyrus called Hunefer's *Book of the Dead*. Hunefer was a royal official of
the thirteenth century B.C.E. Like other wealthy or powerful Egyptians,
Hunefer had a version of the *Book of the Dead*, with all its prayers and
incantations, prepared especially for him.

In Figure 2.1, Hunefer's mummy is prepared to enter the afterlife.
His wife and daughter dab their heads with dirt. Three priests administer the rituals. The priest on the far left, dressed in a leopard skin,
burns incense and readies the food offerings. Two others prepare the
important ceremony of opening the mummy's mouth so that it can
breathe and eat. Anubis, the jackal-headed god of death, holds the
mummy. Behind him we can read an enlarged version of Hunefer's
tombstone, which will be placed in front of his tomb, a miniature
image of which we see on the far right.

In Figure 2.2 we see Hunefer led by Anubis, about to be judged. In
the center of the frame Hunefer's heart is weighed against a feather. If
his heart is lighter than the feather, he will be admitted to the presence of Osiris and enter the afterlife. If not, his heart will be devoured
by the demon Ammut, whose crocodile head is turned to the ibis-
headed god Thoth, standing to the right of the scales and writing the
verdict. In that case, his existence will end forever. Fortunately, Hunefer's artist assures him of a happy ending. Thoth conducts Hunefer to
Osiris seated on a throne, behind his four sons standing on a lotus
leaf and in front of his wife, the goddess Isis, and her sister. What do
these images tell you about Egyptian society? How do they compare
to your own ideas of death?

THINKING HISTORICALLY

Reading primary sources, whether they be words or images, is always
tricky. Unlike secondary sources, they were not written, painted, or
left for us. The assumptions and intentions of the writer or artist may
be very different from our own, and so we may misunderstand the
meaning or purpose of a work.

Entering an Egyptian tomb today, one cannot help being overwhelmed by the beauty of the paintings. Their vitality can be
breathtaking. To the modern viewer, especially in museums where

Source: *Book of the Dead* of Hunefer, Thebes, Egypt, 19th Dynasty, around 1275 B.C.E.

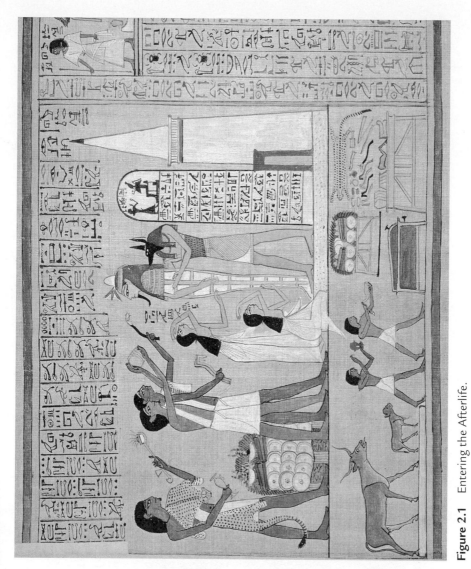

Figure 2.1   Entering the Afterlife.

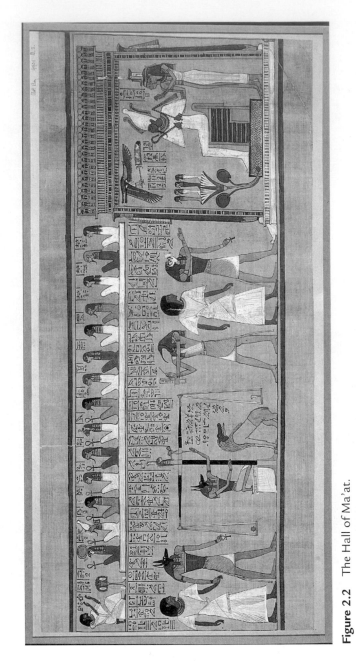

Figure 2.2 The Hall of Ma'at.

68

paintings and papyrus are torn from their original setting, they appear to us as beautiful works of art. And so they are. But for the ancient Egyptians, these images were more than representations, more than art. They were the things depicted. The food that was displayed was food for the deceased in the afterlife; the people painted on the walls were there to provide and serve. The pictures were intended to be more vital than we can imagine. Are visual images more or less reliable as primary sources than written words? What do visuals add to our understanding? How might they mislead us?

Images are different from written words in another way. You are able to make sense of these images from Hunefer's *Book of the Dead* because primary and secondary texts enable us to provide a summary of the story behind them. But the Egyptian artist and viewer knew that story, and hundreds of subplots, by heart. Imagine "reading" the images the way an ancient Egyptian viewer would have. Would the difference between your modern interpretation and the Egyptian viewer's interpretation be similar to the difference between seeing a movie and reading the book? And if "the book" was the wisdom of the ages as everyone knew it, and images could be real, what sort of movie would that be?

6

An Assyrian Law and a Palace Decree, c. 1100 B.C.E.

This selection consists of two official documents from a Mesopotamian city-based empire of about 1100 B.C.E., known today as the Middle Assyrian Empire because it followed the early Assyrian period (twentieth to fifteenth century B.C.E.) and preceded the Neo-Assyrian era (tenth to seventh century B.C.E.). Archaeologists working in Syria and Iraq continue to unearth many laws from all Assyrian eras.

The first document is only one of many laws, and sections are missing. Nevertheless, it provides a rare window onto one urban society at the end of the second millennium B.C.E. What does it tell you about the role of women in this place at this time? What does it tell you about the attitudes of men toward women? What do you think was the purpose of passing this law?

Source: Martha T. Roth, *Law Collections from Mesopotamia and Asia Minor*, 2nd ed. (Atlanta: Scholar's Press, 1997), 167–68 and 205–6.

The second document was a palace regulation meant to apply only to a select group of men and women, not the entire Assyrian society. What does this decree tell you about the lives of men and women in the palace? How were matters at the palace similar to, and different from, those of the larger society?

THINKING HISTORICALLY

Primary sources can be rich repositories of information. They can correct misconceptions and answer questions, even those we never thought to ask. These two Assyrian sources are particularly valuable in telling us about the intersection of gender and social class in 1100 B.C.E. Create two questions that one or both of these documents answers. Then compose two sentences that these documents show as clearly proved errors or misconceptions. For example, if someone believed the practice of veiling women had its origins in Muslim society, how would these documents show that this is a misconception?

Assyrian Law

Wives of a man, or [widows], or any [Assyrian] women who go out into the main thoroughfare [shall not have] their heads [bare]. Daughters of a man . . . [with] either a . . . -cloth or garments or . . . shall be veiled, . . . their heads. . . . When they go about . . . in the main thoroughfare during the daytime, they shall be veiled. A concubine who goes about in the main thoroughfare with her mistress is to be veiled. A married *qadiltu-*woman[1] is to be veiled (when she goes about) in the main thoroughfare, but an unmarried one is to leave her head bare in the main thoroughfare, she shall not veil herself. A prostitute shall not be veiled, her head shall be bare. Whoever sees a veiled prostitute shall seize her, secure witnesses, and bring her to the palace entrance. They shall not take away her jewelry, but he who has seized her takes her clothing; they shall strike her 50 blows with rods; they shall pour hot pitch over her head. And if a man should see a veiled prostitute and release her, and does not bring her to the palace entrance, they shall strike the man 50 blows with rods; the one who informs against him shall take his clothing; they shall pierce his ears, thread them on a cord, tie it at his back; he shall perform the king's service for one full month. Slave women shall not be veiled, and he who should see a veiled slave woman shall seize her and bring her to the palace entrance; they shall cut off her ears; he who seizes her shall take her clothing.

[1] A class of templewomen. [Ed.]

Palace Decree of Tiglath-Pileser I
(r. 1114–1076 B.C.E.)

Tiglath-pileser, king of the universe, king of Assyria, son of Ashur-rēsa-ishi, himself also king of Assyria, issued a decree for the palace commander of the Inner City, the palace herald, the chief of the water sprinklers of the Processional Residence, the physician of the Inner Quarters, and the administrator of all the palaces of the entire extent of the country:

Royal court attendants or dedicatees of the palace personnel who have access to the palace shall not enter the palace without an inspection; if he is not (properly) castrated, they shall turn him into a (castrated) court attendant for a second time.

If either the palace commander of the Inner City, or the palace herald, or the chief of the water sprinklers of the Processional Residence, or the physician of the Inner Quarters, or the administrator of all the palaces of the entire expanse of the country allows an uncastrated court attendant to enter into the palace, and he is later discovered, they shall amputate one foot of each of these officials.

7

SMITHSONIAN MAGAZINE

First City in the New World? 2002

Historians used to think that the urban revolution occurred in the Western Hemisphere much later than in the Eastern. However, as earlier urban sites were uncovered, like Olmec cities in Mexico over 3,000 years old, the origins of civilization in the Americas has been pushed back earlier and earlier. Now archaeologists have dated a site in Peru over a thousand years earlier than the Olmec. That would make the urban revolution in the Americas virtually contemporary with that of the Middle East. What is the evidence for this claim? In what ways was Peru's Caral similar to the cities of Mesopotamia or Egypt? In what ways was it different?

THINKING HISTORICALLY

The author of this secondary source says nothing about written records from this site, but primary sources — pieces of the past — are not limited to writing. We have already seen how historians and

---

Source: *Smithsonian* Magazine, "First City in the New World?" 2002, http://www.smithsonianmag.com/history-archaeology/firstcity.html?c=y&page=1.

Figure 2.3 Part of the excavated temple at Caral, Peru.

Source: © George Steinmetz/Corbis.

archaeologists can interpret the past through the study of physical and organic remains, especially art and artifacts. In fact, one artifact in particular was very important in understanding Caral. What was this, and what was its importance? What other artifacts from the site proved to be useful primary sources for the understanding of Caral?

Six earth-and-rock mounds rise out of the windswept desert of the Supe Valley near the coast of Peru. Dunelike and immense, they appear to be nature's handiwork, forlorn outposts in an arid region squeezed between the Pacific Ocean and the folds of the Andean Cordillera. But looks deceive. These are human-made pyramids, and compelling new evidence indicates they are the remains of a city that flourished nearly 5,000 years ago. If true, it would be the oldest urban center in the Americas and among the most ancient in all the world.

Research developed by Peruvian archaeologist Ruth Shady Solís of San Marcos University suggests that Caral, as the 150-acre complex of pyramids, plazas and residential buildings is known, was a thriving metropolis as Egypt's great pyramids were being built. The energetic archaeologist believes that Caral may also answer nagging questions about the long-mysterious origins of the Inca, the civilization that once stretched from modern-day Ecuador to central Chile and gave rise to such cities as Cuzco and Machu Picchu. Caral may even hold a key to the origins of civilizations everywhere.

Though discovered in 1905, Caral first drew little attention, largely because archaeologists believed the complex structures were fairly recent. But the monumental scale of the pyramids had long tantalized Shady. "When I first arrived in the valley in 1994, I was overwhelmed," she says. "This place is somewhere between the seat of the gods and the home of man." She began excavations two years later, braving primitive conditions on a tight budget. Fourteen miles from the coast and 120 miles north of Peru's capital city of Lima, Caral lies in a desert region that lacks paved roads, electricity and public water. Shady, who enlisted 25 Peruvian soldiers to help with the excavations, often used her own money to advance the work.

For two months she and her crew searched for the broken remains of pots and containers, called potsherds, that most such sites contain. Not finding any only made her more excited; it meant Caral could be what archaeologists term pre-ceramic, or existing before the advent of pot-firing technology in the area. Shady eventually concluded that Caral predated Olmec settlements to the north by 1,000 years. But colleagues remained skeptical. She needed proof.

In 1996, Shady's team began the mammoth task of excavating Pirámide Mayor, the largest of the pyramids. After carefully clearing away several millennia's worth of rubble and sand, they unearthed staircases, circular walls covered with remnants of colored plaster, and squared brickwork. Finally, in the foundation, they found the preserved remains of reeds woven into bags, known as shicras. The original workers, she surmised, must have filled these bags with stones from a hillside quarry a mile away and laid them atop one another inside retaining walls, gradually giving rise to the city of Caral's immense structures.

Shady knew that the reeds were ideal subjects for radiocarbon dating and could make her case. In 1999, she sent samples of them to Jonathan Haas at Chicago's Field Museum and to Winifred Creamer at Northern Illinois University. In December 2000, Shady's suspicions were confirmed: the reeds were 4,600 years old. She took the news calmly, but Haas says he "was virtually in hysterics for three days afterward." In the April 27, 2001, issue of the journal *Science*, the three archaeologists reported that Caral and the other ruins of the Supe Valley are "the locus of some of the earliest population concentrations and corporate architecture in South America." The news stunned other scientists. "It was almost unbelievable," says Betty Meggers, an archaeologist at the Smithsonian Institution. "This data pushed back the oldest known dates for an urban center in the Americas by more than 1,000 years."

What amazed archaeologists was not just the age but the complexity and scope of Caral. Pirámide Mayor alone covers an area nearly the size of four football fields and is 60 feet tall. A 30-foot-wide staircase rises from a sunken circular plaza at the foot of the pyramid, passing over three terraced levels until it reaches the top of the platform, which contains the remains of an atrium and a large fireplace. Thousands of manual laborers would have been needed to build such a mammoth project, not even counting the many architects, craftsmen, supervisors and other managers. Inside a ring of platform pyramids lies a large sunken amphitheater, which could have held many hundreds of people during civic or religious events. Inside the amphitheater, Shady's team found 32 flutes made of pelican and condor bones. And, in April 2002, they uncovered 37 cornets[1] of deer and llama bones. "Clearly, music played an important role in their society," says Shady.

The perimeter of Caral holds a series of smaller mounds, various buildings and residential complexes. Shady discovered a hierarchy in living arrangements: large, well-kept rooms atop the pyramids for the elite, ground-level complexes for craftsmen, and shabbier outlying shantytowns for workers.

But why had Caral been built in the first place? More important, why would people living comfortably in small communities perched on the Pacific Ocean with easy access to abundant marine food choose to move inland to an inhospitable desert? If she could answer this question, Shady believed she might begin to unravel one of the knottiest questions in the field of anthropology today: What causes civilizations to arise? And what was it about the desert landscape of Peru's Supe Valley that caused a complex, hierarchical society to flourish there?

Her excavations convinced Shady that Caral had served as a major trade center for the region, ranging from the rain forests of the Amazon to the high forests of the Andes. She found fragments of the fruit of the *achiote*, a plant still used today in the rain forest as an aphrodisiac. And she found necklaces of snails and the seeds of the coca plant, neither of which was native to Caral. This rich trading environment, Shady believes, gave rise to an elite group that did not take part in the production of food, allowing them to become priests and planners, builders and designers. Thus, the class distinctions elemental to an urban society emerged.

But what sustained such a trading center and drew travelers to it? Was it food? Shady and her team found the remains of sardines and anchovies, which must have come from the coast 14 miles to the west, in the excavations. But they also found evidence that the Caral people ate squash, sweet potatoes and beans. Shady theorized that Caral's early farmers diverted area rivers into trenches and canals, which still crisscross the Supe Valley today, to irrigate their fields. But because she found no traces of maize (corn) or other grains, which can be traded or stored and used to tide a population over in difficult times, she concluded that Caral's trade leverage was not based on stockpiling food supplies.

It was evidence of another crop in the excavations that gave Shady the best clue to the mystery of Caral's success. In nearly every excavated building, her team discovered great quantities of cotton seeds, fibers and

---

[1] Trumpet-like instrument. [Ed.]

textiles. Her theory fell into place when a large fishing net, unearthed at an unrelated dig on Peru's coast, turned out to be as old as Caral. "The farmers of Caral grew the cotton that the fishermen needed to make the nets," Shady speculates. "And the fishermen gave them shellfish and dried fish in exchange for these nets." In essence, the people of Caral enabled fishermen to work with larger and more effective nets, which made the resources of the sea more readily available. The Caral people probably used dried squash as flotation devices for nets and also as containers, thus obviating any need for ceramics.

Eventually Caral would spawn 17 other pyramid complexes scattered across the 35-square-mile area of the Supe Valley. Then, around 1600 B.C., for reasons that may never be answered, the Caral civilization toppled, though it didn't disappear overnight. "They had time to protect some of their architectural structures, burying them discreetly," says Shady. Other nearby areas, such as Chupacigarro, Lurihuasi and Miraya, became centers of power. But based on Caral's size and scope, Shady believes that it is indeed the mother city of the Incan civilization.

She plans to continue excavating Caral and says she would someday like to build a museum on the site. "So many questions still remain," she says. "Who were these people? How did they control the other populations? What was their main god?"

■ REFLECTIONS

To focus our subject in a brief chapter, we have concentrated on Mesopotamia and Egypt almost exclusively. This enabled us to observe the beginnings of the urban revolution in Mesopotamia and one of the most spectacular and best preserved of ancient civilizations in Egypt. The city-states of Mesopotamia and the territorial state of Egypt were the two extremes of ancient civilization. City-states packed most people tightly within their walls. Eighty percent of Mesopotamians lived within city walls by 2800 B.C.E. By contrast, less than 10 percent of Egyptians lived in cities—if we can call their unwalled settlements, palace compounds, and pyramid construction sites "cities" at all. The lesser role of cities in Egypt has led some historians to drop the term *urban revolution* for *the rise of civilization*. Other historians, objecting to the moralistic implications of the term *civilization*, prefer *the rise of complex societies*. *Complex* is not a very precise term, but it would refer to the appearance of social classes; the mixing of different populations; a multilayered governmental structure with rulers, officials, and ordinary people; and numerous specialists who are not full-time farmers or herders. More specifically, we might include kings, priests, writing, wheels, monumental building, markets, and money.

Our addition of early Peruvian civilization widens our lens. The unusually rich anchovy fisheries of Peru enabled the development of complex societies in the desert interior with limited agriculture through irrigation, but without some of the features of civilization in the Eastern Hemisphere. We read that Caral used gourds instead of ceramic containers, but later Peruvians and other Americans fired clay and made ceramics. It used to be said that American Indians lacked writing (as Caral might have), but we can now translate the pictorial writing of Mexico and recognize Peruvian quipus of colored strings as a kind of writing. Wheeled vehicles were absent from the Americas (with the interesting exception of children's toys). Most Americans lacked beasts of burden (though Peruvians used llamas and alpacas). Peruvians and some Mexicans had bronze, but not all were literally "bronze age" and no American Indians had iron.

If we broaden our view to include the "complex societies" of South Asia and China as well as the Americas, similar types of cities pop up like mushrooms after a spring rain. Along the Indus River in Pakistan dozens of small and midsize cities formed independent clones of Harappa and Mohenjo-Daro (see Map 3.1 on page 79). These numerous cities seem to have enjoyed the independence of city-states, linked more by culture and trade than by powerful kings or large armies. A vast web of such cities is still being excavated, stretching from Iran to India and from the coast of East Africa to southern Russia. In China, by contrast, vast territorial states integrated dozens of cities along river valleys and trade routes and throughout the interior, creating a cultural and political unity more like Egypt than Mesopotamia. Thus, a larger lens raises more questions than we have allowed in our brief examination of Mesopotamia and Egypt. How important were such "urban inventions" as kings, soldiers, warfare, wheels, and writing if they did not exist everywhere cities were created? Furthermore, how important were cities in the creation of the complex lives we have lived for the last five thousand years?

We might also ask the larger question: Has the urban revolution improved our lives? The belief that it has lies behind the use of the word *civilization*. Though the root of the word is the same as *city, civil*, and *civilian*, the word *civilization* came into the modern vocabulary of historians and social scientists in the nineteenth century. At this time anthropologists were working to distinguish stages of history and to illustrate the differences between what were then called "primitive" peoples and people of the modern world whom anthropologists considered "civilized." Thus, they contended there had been three stages of history that could be summarized, in chronological order, as savagery, barbarism, and civilization. By the early twentieth century, in the work of the great prehistorian V. Gordon Childe, these terms stood for hunting-gathering, agricultural, and urban societies.

The belief that the world of the anthropologists and the "moderns" of the nineteenth and twentieth centuries was more civilized than the preurban world that they studied was more than a bit presumptuous. But this presumption continues today, in the popular mythology of "country bumpkins" who lack the manners and savoir-faire of their city cousins. Interestingly, it was also the assumption of the earliest founders of cities. *The Epic of Gilgamesh* tells of the need of the city to tame the wild Enkidu so that he can take his place in

> . . . ramparted Uruk,
> Where fellows are resplendent in holiday clothing,
> Where every day is set for celebration.

There are many reasons to be skeptical of the so-called achievements of city life: increased inequality, suppression of women, slavery, organized warfare, conscription, heavy taxation, forced labor, to name some of the most obvious. But our museums are full of the art and artifacts that testify to what the ancients meant by "civilization." The pyramids of Egypt and of South America and the ziggurats of Mesopotamia are among the wonders of the world. Does it matter that the great pyramids of Egypt were built from the forced labor of thousands to provide a resting place for a single person and that people were entombed alive in order to serve him? We can view the pyramids today as a remarkable achievement of engineering and organization while still condemning the manner of their execution. We can admire the art in the tombs, thrill to the revealing detail of ancient Egyptian life, marvel at the persistence of vivid colors mixed almost five thousand years ago, and treasure the art for what it reveals of the world of its creators, while we still detest its purpose.

We can do this because these monuments have become something different for us than what they were for the ancients. They have become testaments to human achievement, regardless of the cost. These ancient city-based societies were the first in which humans produced abundant works of art and architecture, which still astound us in their range, scope, and design.

The significance of the urban revolution was that it produced things that lasted beyond their utility or meaning—thanks to new techniques in cutting and hauling stone; baking brick, tile, and glass; and smelting tin, copper, and bronze—as a legacy for future generations. Even three thousand years ago, Egyptian engineers studied the ancient pyramids to understand a very distant past, 1,500 years before, and to learn, adapt, revive, or revise ancient techniques. In short, the achievement of the urban revolution is that it made knowledge cumulative, so that each generation could stand on the shoulders of its predecessors.

3

Identity in Caste and Territorial Societies

Greece and India, 1000–300 B.C.E.

■ HISTORICAL CONTEXT

Both India and Greece developed ancient city-based civilizations within a thousand years of the urban revolution. In India that civilization was concentrated on the Indus River Valley in what is today Pakistan. (See Map 3.1.) In Greece the Minoan civilization on the island of Crete was followed by the Mycenaean civilization on the mainland. (See Map 3.2.) But both ancient Indian and ancient Greek civilizations were transformed by new peoples from the grasslands of Eurasia, who settled in both areas between 1500 and 1000 B.C.E. Called by later generations the Aryans in India and the Dorians in Greece, these pastoral peoples arrived with horses, different customs, and new technologies. The Aryans came with chariots (as had the early Mycenaeans), while the Dorians, somewhat later, brought iron tools and weapons.

Despite the similar origins of the newcomers and the similar urban experience of the lands in which they settled, Aryan India and Dorian Greece developed in significantly different ways. As William H. McNeill writes in the first selection, by the year 500 B.C.E. Indian and Greek civilizations had found entirely different ways of organizing and administering their societies. And these differences had profound effects on the subsequent history of Indian and European society.

■ THINKING HISTORICALLY

Interpreting Primary Sources in Light of a Secondary Source

In Chapter 2, we distinguished between primary and secondary sources. Similarly, we begin here with a secondary source, or an interpretation. We then turn, as we did in the last chapter, to a series of primary sources. But whereas the last chapter focused on recognizing and distinguishing primary from secondary sources, here we concentrate on the relationship of the primary sources to the secondary interpretation—how one affects our reading of the other.

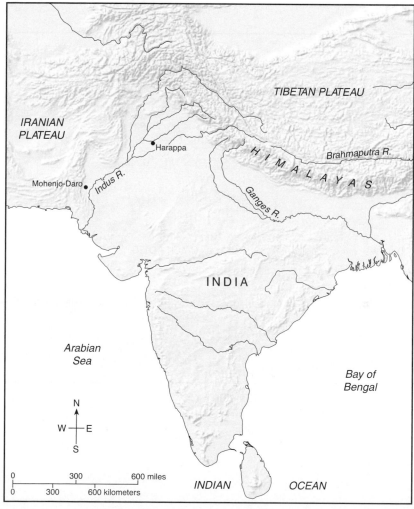

Map 3.1   India and the Indus River Valley, c. 500 B.C.E.

In this chapter, the primary sources were chosen to illustrate points made in the introductory interpretation. This provides an opportunity to understand the interpretation in some detail and with some degree of subtlety. The primary sources do not give you enough material to argue that McNeill is right or wrong, but you will be able to flesh out some of the meaning of his interpretation. You might also reflect more generally on the relationship of sources and interpretations. You will be asked how particular sources support or even contradict the interpretation. You will consider the relevance of sources for other interpretations, and you will imagine what sort of sources you might seek for evidence.

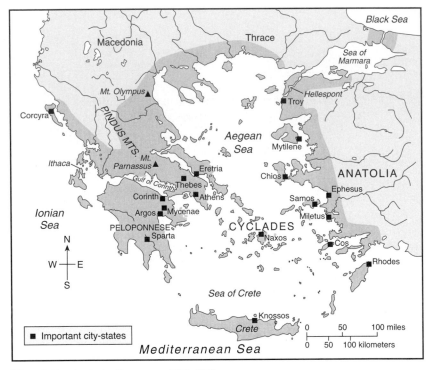

Map 3.2   Archaic Greece, c. 750–500 B.C.E.

1

WILLIAM H. McNEILL
Greek and Indian Civilization, 1971

William H. McNeill is one of the leading world historians in the
United States. In this selection from his college textbook *A World
History*, he compares the different ways in which Indian and Greek
civilizations of the classical age (by around 500 B.C.E.) organized
themselves. He distinguishes between Indian *caste* and Greek
territorial sovereignty. These concepts are complex but useful in
distinguishing between two of the basic ways societies organize
and identify themselves. As you read, try to define what each
term means. McNeill argues that caste and territorial sovereignty
had enormously different effects on the subsequent development
of Indian and European society. What were some of these
different effects?

THINKING HISTORICALLY

As you read this secondary source or historical interpretation, consider what sort of primary sources might have led McNeill to this view
or support his interpretation. Notice especially that in the first half of
the selection, McNeill mentions specific ancient Indian writings:
These are obvious primary sources for his interpretation. Not having
read McNeill's primary sources, can you imagine what in them would
lead to this interpretation?

Less of McNeill's interpretation of Greece is included in this selection; consequently, there is no mention of primary sources. In this
chapter, you will read a number of Greek primary sources, but at this
point can you speculate about what types of sources would demonstrate the Greek idea of territorial sovereignty?

Keep in mind that caste and territorial sovereignty are
modern terms not known or used by the ancients; therefore, you
will not find them in the primary sources that follow. What words
might the ancient Indians or Greeks have used to denote these
concepts?

Source: William H. McNeill, *A World History*, 2nd ed. (New York: Oxford University Press, 1971), 78–83, 88, 90, 95, 99–100.

Caste

A modern caste is a group of persons who will eat with one another and intermarry, while excluding others from these two intimacies. In addition, members of any particular caste must bear some distinguishing mark, so that everyone will know who belongs and who does not belong to it. Definite rules for how to behave in the presence of members of other castes also become necessary in situations where such contacts are frequent. When an entire society comes to be organized on these principles, any group of strangers or intruders automatically becomes another caste, for the exclusive habits of the rest of the population inevitably thrust the newcomers in upon themselves when it comes to eating and marrying. A large caste may easily break into smaller groupings as a result of some dispute, or through mere geographical separation over a period of time. New castes can form around new occupations. Wanderers and displaced individuals who find a new niche in society are automatically compelled to eat together and marry one another by the caste-bound habits of their neighbors.

How or when Indian society came to be organized along these lines remains unclear. Perhaps the Indus civilization itself was built upon something like the caste principle. Or perhaps the antipathy between Aryan invaders and the dark-skinned people whom they attacked lay at the root of the caste system of later India. But whatever the origins of caste, three features of Indian thought and feeling were mobilized to sustain the caste principle in later times. One of these was the idea of ceremonial purity. Fear of contaminating oneself by contact with a member of a lower, "unclean" caste gave Brahmans and others near the top of the pyramid strong reasons for limiting their association with low-caste persons.

From the other end of the scale, too, the poor and humble had strong reasons for clinging to caste. All but the most miserable and marginal could look down upon somebody, a not unimportant psychological feature of the system. In addition, the humbler castes were often groups that had only recently emerged from primitive forest life. They naturally sought to maintain their peculiar customs and habits, even in the context of urban or mixed village life, where men of different backgrounds and different castes lived side by side. Other civilized societies usually persuaded or compelled newcomers to surrender their peculiar ways, and assimilated them in the course of a few generations to the civilized population as a whole. In India, on the contrary, such groups were able to retain their separate identities indefinitely by preserving their own peculiar customs within the caste framework, generation after generation.

The third factor sustaining the caste principle was theoretical: the doctrine of reincarnation and of "varna." The latter declared that all men were naturally divided into four castes: the Brahmans who prayed, the Kshatriyas* who fought, the Vaisyas† who worked, and the Sudras who performed unclean tasks. Official doctrine classified the first three castes as Aryan, the last as non-Aryan, and put much stress on caste rank, from Brahmans at the top to Sudras at the bottom. Reality never corresponded even remotely to this theory. There were hundreds if not thousands of castes in India, rather than the four recognized in Brahmanical teaching. But apparent injustices and anomalies disappeared when the doctrine of reincarnation was combined with the doctrine of varna. The idea of reincarnation, indeed, gave logical explanation and justification to the system by explaining caste as a divinely established institution, hereditary from father to son, and designed to reward and punish souls for their actions in former lives. This undoubtedly helped to stabilize the confused reality. A man of unblemished life, born into the lowest caste, could hope for rebirth higher up the ladder. Conversely, a man of high caste who failed to conform to proper standards could expect rebirth in a lower caste. A man even risked reincarnation as a worm or beetle, if his misbehavior deserved such a punishment.

Clearly, the caste system as observed today did not exist in ancient India. Yet modern castes are the outgrowth of patterns of social organization that are as old as the oldest records. Early Buddhist stories, for instance, reveal many episodes turning upon caste distinctions, and passages in the *Rig Veda*‡ and other ancient writings imply caste-like practices and attitudes. By 500 B.C.E. we can at least be sure that the seeds from which the modern caste organization of society grew had already sprouted luxuriantly on Indian soil.

Caste lessened the significance of political, territorial administration. Everyone identified himself first and foremost with his caste. But a caste ordinarily lacked both definite internal administration and distinct territorial boundaries. Instead, members of a particular caste mingled with men of other castes, observing the necessary precautions to prevent contamination of one by the other. No king or ruler could command the undivided loyalty of people who felt themselves to belong to a caste rather than to a state. Indeed, to all ordinary caste members, rulers, officials, soldiers, and tax collectors were likely to seem mere troublesome outsiders, to be neglected whenever possible and obeyed only as far as necessary. The fragile character of

* KSHAH tree uh
† VYS yuh
‡ rihg VAY dah

most Indian states resulted in large part from this fact. A striking absence of information about war and government is characteristic of all early Indian history; and this, too, presumably reflects Indian peoples' characteristic emotional disengagement from the state and from politics. . . .

The Vedas and Brahmanas

Our knowledge of Aryan religion derives from the Vedas. The Vedas, used as handbooks of religious ritual, consist of songs that were recited aloud during sacrifices, together with other passages instructing the priests what to do during the ceremony. In course of time, the language of the Vedas became more or less unintelligible, even to priests. A great effort was thereupon made to preserve details of accent and pronunciation, by insisting on exact memorization of texts from master to pupil across the generations. Every jot and tittle of the inherited verses was felt to matter, since a misplaced line or mispronounced word could nullify a whole sacrifice and might even provoke divine displeasure.

Preoccupation with correctness of detail speedily shifted emphasis from the gods of the Aryan pantheon to the act of worship and invocation itself. Aryan priests may also have learned about magical powers claimed by priests of the Indus civilization. At any rate, some Brahmans began to argue that by performing rituals correctly they could actually compel the gods to grant what was asked of them. Indeed, proper sacrifice and invocation created the world of gods and men anew, and stabilized afresh the critical relation between natural and supernatural reality. In such a view, the importance and personalities of the separate gods shrank to triviality, while the power and skill of the priesthood was greatly magnified. These extravagant priestly claims were freely put forward in texts called Brahmanas. These were cast in the form of commentaries on the Vedas, purportedly explaining what the older texts really meant, but often changing meanings in the process.

The Upanishads and Mysticism

Priestly claims to exercise authority over gods and men were never widely accepted in ancient India. Chiefs and warriors might be a bit wary of priestly magic, but they were not eager to cede to the priests the primacy claimed by the Brahmanas. Humbler ranks of society also objected to priestly presumption. This is proved by the fact that a rival type of piety took hold in India and soon came to constitute the most distinctive element in the whole religious tradition of the land. Another body of oral literature, the Upanishads,* constitutes our evidence of this religious development. The Upanishads are not systematic treatises nor do they agree in all details. Yet they do express a general consensus on important points.

First of all, the Upanishads conceive the end of religious life in a radically new way. Instead of seeking riches, health, and long life, a wise and holy man strives merely to escape the endless round of rebirth. Success allows his soul to dissolve into the All from whence it had come, triumphantly transcending the suffering, pain, and imperfection of existence.

In the second place, holiness and release from the cycle of rebirths were attained not by obedience to priests nor by observance of ceremonies. The truly holy man had no need of intermediaries and, for that matter, no need of gods. Instead, by a process of self-discipline, meditation, asceticism, and withdrawal from the ordinary concerns of daily life, the successful religious athlete might attain a mystic vision of Truth—a vision which left the seer purged and happy. The nature and content of the mystic vision could never be expressed in words. It revealed Truth by achieving an identity between the individual soul and the Soul of the universe. Such an experience, surpassing human understanding and ordinary language, constituted a foretaste of the ultimate bliss of self-annihilation in the All, which was the final goal of wise and holy life. . . .

While India worked its way toward the definition of a new and distinctive civilization on one flank of the ancient Middle East, on its other flank another new civilization was also emerging: the Greek. The principal stages of early Greek history closely resemble what we know or can surmise about Indian development. But the end product differed fundamentally. The Greeks put political organization into territorial states above all other bases of human association, and attempted to explain the world and man not in terms of mystic illumination but through laws of nature. Thus despite a similar start, when fierce "tamers of horses"—like those of whom Homer[1] later sang—overran priest-led agricultural societies, the Indian and Greek styles of civilization diverged strikingly by 500 B.C.E. . . .

The self-governing city-states created by Greeks on the coast of Asia Minor had . . . great . . . importance in world history. For by inventing the city-state or *polis* (hence our word "politics"), the Greeks of Ionia established the prototype from which the whole Western world derived its penchant for political organization into territorially defined sovereign

---

* oo PAH nee shahdz
[1] Greek poet c. 800 B.C.E.; author of *The Iliad* and *The Odyssey*. [Ed.]

units, i.e., into states. The supremacy of territoriality over all other forms of human association is neither natural nor inevitable, as the Indian caste principle may remind us. . . .

Dominance of the Polis in Greek Culture

So powerful and compelling was the psychological pull of the polis that almost every aspect of Greek cultural activity was speedily caught up in and — as it were — digested by the new master institution of Greek civilization. Religion, art, literature, philosophy, took shape or acquired a new accent through their relationship with the all-engulfing object of the citizens' affection. . . .

Despite the general success of the polis ordering of things, a few individuals fretted over the logical inconsistencies of Greek religion and traditional world view. As trade developed, opportunities to learn about the wisdom of the East multiplied. Inquiring Greeks soon discovered that among the priestly experts of the Middle East there was no agreement about such fundamental questions as how the world was created or why the planets periodically checked their forward movement through the heavens and went backward for a while before resuming their former motion. It was in Ionia that men first confronted this sort of question systematically enough to bother recording their views. These, the first philosophers, sought to explain the phenomena of the world by imaginative exercise of their power of reason. Finding conflicting and unsupported stories about the gods to be unsatisfactory, they took the drastic step of omitting the gods entirely, and boldly substituted natural law instead as the ruling force of the universe. To be sure, the Ionian philosophers did not agree among themselves when they sought to describe how the laws of nature worked, and their naive efforts to explain an ever wider range of phenomena did not meet with much success.

Nevertheless, their attempts at using speculative reason to explain the nature of things marked a major turning point in human intellectual development. The Ionian concept of a universe ruled not by the whim of some divine personality but by an impersonal and unchangeable law has never since been forgotten. Throughout the subsequent history of European and Middle Eastern thought, this distinctively Greek view of the nature of things stood in persistent and fruitful tension with the older, Middle Eastern theistic explanation of the universe. Particular thinkers, reluctant to abandon either position entirely, have sought to reconcile the omnipotence of the divine will with the unchangeability of natural law by means of the most various arguments. Since, however, the two views are as logically incompatible with one another as were the myths from which the Ionian philosophers started, no formulation or reconciliation ever attained lasting and universal consent. Men always had to start over again to reshape for themselves a more satisfactory metaphysic and theology. Here, therefore, lay a growing point for all subsequent European thought which has not yet been exhausted.

Indeed, the recent successes of natural science seem to have vindicated the Ionian concept of natural law in ways and with a complexity that would have utterly amazed Thales* (d. c. 546 B.C.E.) or any of his successors, who merely voiced what turned out to be amazingly lucky guesses. How did they do it? It seems plausible to suggest that the Ionians hit upon the notion of natural law by simply projecting the tight little world of the polis upon the universe. For it was a fact that the polis was regulated by law, not by the personal will or whim of a ruler. If such invisible abstractions could govern human behavior and confine it to certain roughly predictable paths of action, why could not similar laws control the natural world? To such a question, it appears, the Ionians gave an affirmative answer, and in doing so gave a distinctive cast to all subsequent Greek and European thought.

Limitations of the Polis

It would be a mistake to leave the impression that all facets of Greek life fitted smoothly and easily into the polis frame. The busy public world left scant room for the inwardness of personal experience. Striving for purification, for salvation, for holiness, which found such ample expression in the Indian cultural setting, was almost excluded. Yet the Greeks were not immune from such impulses. Through the ancient mystery religions, as well as through such an association as the "Order" founded by Pythagoras,† the famous mathematician and mystic (d. c. 507 B.C.E.), they sought to meet these needs. But when such efforts took organized form, a fundamental incompatibility between the claims of the polis to the unqualified loyalty of every citizen and the pursuit of personal holiness quickly became apparent. This was illustrated by the stormy history of the Pythagorean Order. Either the organized seekers after holiness captured the polis, as happened for a while in the city of Croton in southern Italy, or the magistrates of the polis persecuted the Order, as happened in Pythagoras' old age. There seemed no workable ground of compromise in this, the earliest recorded instance of conflict between church and state in Western history.

* THAY leez
† py THAG uhr ahs

The fundamental difference between Greek and Indian institutions as shaped by about 500 B.C.E. was made apparent by this episode. The loose federation of cultures allowed by the caste principle in India experienced no difficulty at all in accommodating organized seekers after holiness such as the communities of Buddhist monks. By contrast, the exclusive claim upon the citizens' time, effort, and affection which had been staked out by the Greek polis allowed no sort of corporate rival.

Enormous energies were tapped by the polis. A wider segment of the total population was engaged in cultural and political action than had been possible in any earlier civilized society, and the brilliant flowering of classical Greek civilization was the consequence. Yet the very intensity of the political tie excluded ranges of activity and sensitivity that were not compatible with a territorial organization of human groupings, and sowed seeds of civil strife between the Greek cities which soon proved disastrous. But every achievement involves a surrender of alternatives: It is merely that the Greek achievement, by its very magnitude, casts an unusually clear light upon what it also excluded.

2

The Rig Veda: Sacrifice as Creation, c. 1500–500 B.C.E.

As McNeill discusses in the previous selection, the Vedas* are the writings of the ancient Brahman priests in India. They cover a wide variety of religious subjects and concerns: ritual, sacrifice, hymns, healing, incantations, allegories, philosophy, and the problems of everyday life. In general, the earliest Vedas (like the Rig Veda) focus more on the specifics of ritual and sacrifice, reflecting the needs and instructions of the priests more than the Upanishads. The last of the Vedas (like the Upanishads) are more philosophical and speculative.

This selection is from the Rig Veda. What happened when Purusha was sacrificed? What is the meaning of this first sacrifice? How does this story support the role of priests?

THINKING HISTORICALLY

Consider how this primary source supports the division of Indian society into castes, as McNeill discusses in the previous selection. How does this story suggest that the people who wrote the Rig Veda

* VAY duz

Source: "Rig Veda," 10.90, in *Sources of Indian Tradition*, 2nd ed., ed. and rev. Ainslie T. Embree (New York: Columbia University Press, 1988), 18–19.

thought the division of society into four castes was pretty basic? Can you deduce from this source which of the four castes was most likely the originator of the story? Does this support anything else that McNeill said in his interpretation?

Thousand-headed Purusha, thousand-eyed, thousand-footed—he, having pervaded the earth on all sides, still extends ten fingers beyond it.

Purusha alone is all this—whatever has been and whatever is going to be. Further, he is the lord of immortality and also of what grows on account of food.

Such is his greatness; greater, indeed, than this is Purusha. All creatures constitute but one-quarter of him, his three-quarters are the immortal in the heaven.

With his three-quarters did Purusha rise up; one-quarter of him again remains here. With it did he variously spread out on all sides over what eats and what eats not.

From him was Virāj born, from Virāj the evolved Purusha. He, being born, projected himself behind the earth as also before it.

When the gods performed the sacrifice with Purusha as the oblation, then the spring was its clarified butter, the summer the sacrificial fuel, and the autumn the oblation.

The sacrificial victim, namely, Purusha, born at the very beginning, they sprinkled with sacred water upon the sacrificial grass. With him as oblation, the gods performed the sacrifice, and also the Sādhyas [a class of semidivine beings] and the rishis [ancient seers].

From that wholly offered sacrificial oblation were born the verses [ṛc] and the sacred chants; from it were born the meters [chandas]; the sacrificial formula was born from it.

From it horses were born and also those animals who have double rows [i.e., upper and lower] of teeth; cows were born from it, from it were born goats and sheep.

When they divided Purusha, in how many different portions did they arrange him? What became of his mouth, what of his two arms? What were his two thighs and his two feet called?

His mouth became the brāhman; his two arms were made into the rajanya; his two thighs the vaishyas; from his two feet the shūdra was born.

The moon was born from the mind, from the eye the sun was born; from the mouth Indra and Agni, from the breath [prāna] the wind [vāyu] was born.

From the navel was the atmosphere created, from the head the heaven issued forth; from the two feet was born the earth and the quarters (the cardinal directions) from the ear. Thus did they fashion the worlds.

Seven were the enclosing sticks in this sacrifice, thrice seven were the fire-sticks made when the gods, performing the sacrifice, bound down Purusha, the sacrificial victim.

With this sacrificial oblation did the gods offer the sacrifice. These were the first norms [*dharma*] of sacrifice. These greatnesses reached to the sky wherein live the ancient Sādhyas and gods.

3

The Upanishads: Karma and Reincarnation, c. 800–400 B.C.E.

The idea of karma (cause and effect, appropriate consequences) appears in the earliest Upanishads.* Karma meant: "As you sow, so shall you reap." Good karma would be enhanced; bad karma would lead to more bad karma. The universe was a system of complete justice in which all people got what they deserved. The idea that the soul might be reborn in another body may have been an even older idea, but in the Upanishads it combined easily with the idea of karma. That a good soul was reborn in a higher life, or a bad soul in a lower, was perhaps a more material, less subtle, version of the justice of karma. The idea of reincarnation, or the transmigration of souls, united justice with caste.

What effect would these ideas have on people? In what ways would these ideas aid people in gaining a sense of power over their lives? How might these ideas be tools of control? What does "morality" mean in this tradition?

THINKING HISTORICALLY

How does the idea of karma presented in this primary source support McNeill's interpretation of the importance of the caste system in India? Would the idea of reincarnation make caste organization stronger or weaker?

* OO PAH nee shahdz

Source: *Brihad Aranyaka*, IV:4:5–6, in *The Thirteen Principal Upanishads*, ed. and trans. R. E. Hume (Bombay: Oxford University Press, 1954), 140–41. *Chandogya*, V:10:7, in Hume, quoted in *The Hindu Tradition: Readings in Oriental Thought*, ed. Ainslie T. Embree (New York: Vintage, 1966, copyright renewed 1994), 62–63.

According as one acts, according as one conducts himself, so does he become. The doer of good becomes good. The doer of evil becomes evil. One becomes virtuous by virtuous action, bad by bad action.

But people say: "A person is made not of acts, but of desires only." In reply to this I say: As is his desire, such is his resolve; as is his resolve, such the action he performs; what action (*karma*) he performs, that he procures for himself.

On this point there is this verse:—

Where one's mind is attached—the inner self
Goes thereto with action, being attached to it alone.

Obtaining the end of his action,
Whatever he does in this world,
He comes again from that world
To this world of action.

—So the man who desires.

Now the man who does not desire.—He who is without desire, who is freed from desire, whose desire is satisfied, whose desire is the Soul—his breaths do not depart. Being very Brahman, he goes to Brahman.

Accordingly, those who are of pleasant conduct here—the prospect is, indeed, that they will enter a pleasant womb, either the womb of a Brahman, or the womb of a Kshatriya, or the womb of a Vaishya. But those who are of stinking conduct here—the prospect is, indeed, that they will enter a stinking womb, either the womb of a dog, or the womb of a swine, or the womb of an outcaste (*candāla*).

4

The Upanishads: Brahman and Atman, c. 800–400 B.C.E.

In this selection *Brahman* does not refer to priests or to a specific god. In the late Vedas, or Upanishads, Brahman is all divinity, and all is Brahman. Even the individual soul or *atman* can be one with the universal Brahman, "as the Father of Svetaketu demonstrates to his son through the examples of a banyan tree and salt water." How would ideas like these challenge the caste system?

Source: *Chandogya Upanishad*, in *The Upanishads*, trans. Juan Mascaro (Harmondsworth: Penguin Press, 1965), 113–14.

McNeill suggests that the Upanishads expressed a religious vision that challenged the power of priests, sacrifice, and caste. How does this selection from the Upanishads support that interpretation?

Great is the Gayatri, the most sacred verse of the Vedas; but how much greater is the Infinity of Brahman! A quarter of his being is this whole vast universe: the other three quarters are his heaven of Immortality. (3.12.5)

There is a Light that shines beyond all things on earth, beyond us all, beyond the heavens, beyond the highest, the very highest heavens. This is the Light that shines in our heart. (3.13.7)

All this universe is in the truth Brahman. He is the beginning and end and life of all. As such, in silence, give unto him adoration.

Man in truth is made of faith. As his faith is in this life, so he becomes in the beyond: with faith and vision let him work.

There is a Spirit that is mind and life, light and truth and vast spaces. He contains all works and desires and all perfumes and all tastes. He enfolds the whole universe, and in silence is loving to all.

This is the Spirit that is in my heart, smaller than a grain of rice, or a grain of barley, or a grain of mustard-seed, or a grain of canary-seed, or the kernel of a grain of canary-seed. This is the Spirit that is in my heart, greater than the earth, greater than the sky, greater than heaven itself, greater than all these worlds.

He contains all works and desires and all perfumes and all tastes. He enfolds the whole universe and in silence is loving to all. This is the Spirit that is in my heart, this is Brahman. (3.14)

"Bring me a fruit from this banyan tree."

"Here it is, father."

"Break it."

"It is broken, Sir."

"What do you see in it?"

"Very small seeds, Sir."

"Break one of them, my son."

"It is broken, Sir."

"What do you see in it?"

"Nothing at all, Sir."

Then his father spoke to him: "My son, from the very essence in the seed which you cannot see comes in truth this vast banyan tree.

Believe me, my son, an invisible and subtle essence is the Spirit of the whole universe. That is Reality. That is Atman. THOU ART THAT."

"Explain more to me, father," said Svetaketu.

"So be it, my son.

Place this salt in water and come to me tomorrow morning."

Svetaketu did as he was commanded, and in the morning his father said to him: "Bring me the salt you put into the water last night."

Svetaketu looked into the water, but could not find it, for it had dissolved.

His father then said: "Taste the water from this side. How is it?"

"It is salt."

"Taste it from the middle. How is it?"

"It is salt."

"Taste it from that side. How is it?"

"It is salt."

"Look for the salt again and come again to me."

The son did so, saying: "I cannot see the salt. I only see water."

His father then said: "In the same way, O my son, you cannot see the Spirit. But in truth he is here.

An invisible and subtle essence is the Spirit of the whole universe. That is Reality. That is Truth. THOU ART THAT." (6.12–14)

5

The Bhagavad Gita: Caste and Self, c. 1500 B.C.E.

The *Bhagavad Gita** is the best-known work in Hindu religious litera-ture. It is part of a larger epic called the *Mahabharata*,† a story of two feuding families that may have had its origins in India as early as 1500 B.C.E. The *Bhagavad Gita* is a philosophical interlude that inter-rupts the story just before the great battle between the two families. It poses some fundamental questions about the nature of life, death, and proper religious behavior. It begins as the leader of one of the battling armies, Arjuna, asks why he should fight his friends and rela-tives on the other side. The answer comes from none other than the god Krishna, who has taken the form of Arjuna's charioteer.

What is Krishna's answer? What will happen to the people Arjuna kills? What will happen to Arjuna? What would happen to Arjuna if

* BUH guh vahd GEE tuh
† mah hah BAH rah tah

Source: *Bhagavad Gita*, trans. Barbara Stoler Miller (New York: Bantam Books, 1986), 31–34, 52, 86–87.

he refused to fight the battle? What does this selection tell you about
Hindu ideas of life, death, and the self?

THINKING HISTORICALLY

In some ways this work reconciles the conflict in the Upanishads between caste and *atman*. Performing the *dharma*, or duty, of caste is
seen as a liberating act. Would the acceptance of this story support
or challenge the caste system? Does this primary source support
McNeill's interpretation of Indian society?

Lord Krishna

You grieve for those beyond grief,
and you speak words of insight;
but learned men do not grieve
for the dead or the living.

Never have I not existed,
nor you, nor these kings;
and never in the future
shall we cease to exist.

Just as the embodied self
enters childhood, youth, and old age,
so does it enter another body;
this does not confound a steadfast man.

Contacts with matter make us feel
heat and cold, pleasure and pain.
Arjuna, you must learn to endure
fleeting things—they come and go!

When these cannot torment a man,
when suffering and joy are equal
for him and he has courage,
he is fit for immortality.

Nothing of nonbeing comes to be,
nor does being cease to exist;
the boundary between these two
is seen by men who see reality.

Indestructible is the presence
that pervades all this;

no one can destroy
this unchanging reality.

Our bodies are known to end,
but the embodied self is enduring,
indestructible, and immeasurable;
therefore, Arjuna, fight the battle!

He who thinks this self a killer
and he who thinks it killed,
both fail to understand;
it does not kill, nor is it killed.

It is not born,
it does not die;
having been,
it will never not be;
unborn, enduring,
constant, and primordial,
it is not killed
when the body is killed.

Arjuna, when a man knows the self
to be indestructible, enduring, unborn,
unchanging, how does he kill
or cause anyone to kill?

As a man discards
worn-out clothes
to put on new
and different ones,
so the embodied self
discards
its worn-out bodies
to take on other new ones.

Weapons do not cut it,
fire does not burn it,
waters do not wet it,
wind does not wither it.

It cannot be cut or burned;
it cannot be wet or withered;
it is enduring, all-pervasive,
fixed, immovable, and timeless.

It is called unmanifest,
inconceivable, and immutable;
since you know that to be so,
you should not grieve!

If you think of its birth
and death as ever-recurring,
then too, Great Warrior,
you have no cause to grieve!

Death is certain for anyone born,
and birth is certain for the dead;
since the cycle is inevitable,
you have no cause to grieve!

Creatures are unmanifest in origin,
manifest in the midst of life,
and unmanifest again in the end.
Since this is so, why do you lament!

Rarely someone
sees it,
rarely another
speaks it,
rarely anyone
hears it—
even hearing it,
no one really knows it.

The self embodied in the body
of every being is indestructible;
you have no cause to grieve
for all these creatures, Arjuna!

Look to your own duty;
do not tremble before it;
nothing is better for a warrior
than a battle of sacred duty.

The doors of heaven open
for warriors who rejoice
to have a battle like this
thrust on them by chance.

If you fail to wage this war
of sacred duty,
you will abandon your own duty
and fame only to gain evil.

People will tell
of your undying shame,
and for a man of honor
shame is worse than death.

[In this next passage from the *Bhagavad Gita*, Krishna reveals a deeper meaning to his message to Arjuna. Not only must Arjuna act like a warrior because that is his caste, but he must also act without regard to the consequences of his action. What does Krishna seem to mean by this? How does one do "nothing at all even when he engages in action"?]

Abandoning attachment to fruits
of action, always content, independent,
he does nothing at all
even when he engages in action.

He incurs no guilt if he has no hope,
restrains his thought and himself,
abandons possessions,
and performs actions with his body only.

Content with whatever comes by chance,
beyond dualities, free from envy,
impartial to failure and success,
he is not bound even when he acts.

When a man is unattached and free,
his reason deep in knowledge,
acting only in sacrifice,
his action is wholly dissolved.

When devoted men sacrifice
to other deities with faith,
they sacrifice to me, Arjuna,
however aberrant the rites.

I am the enjoyer
and the lord of all sacrifices;
they do not know me in reality,
and so they fail.

Votaries of the gods go to the gods,
ancestor-worshippers go to the ancestors,
those who propitiate ghosts go to them,
and my worshippers go to me.

The leaf or flower or fruit or water
that he offers with devotion,
I take from the man of self-restraint
in response to his devotion.

Whatever you do—what you take,
what you offer, what you give,
what penances you perform—
do as an offering to me, Arjuna!

You will be freed from the bonds of action,
from the fruit of fortune and misfortune;
armed with the discipline of renunciation,
your self liberated, you will join me.

I am impartial to all creatures,
and no one is hateful or dear to me;
but men devoted to me are in me,
and I am within them.

If he is devoted solely to me,
even a violent criminal
must be deemed a man of virtue,
for his resolve is right.

His spirit quickens to sacred duty,
and he finds eternal peace;
Arjuna, know that no one
devoted to me is lost.

If they rely on me, Arjuna,
women, commoners, men of low rank,
even men born in the womb of evil,
reach the highest way.

How easy it is then for holy priests
and devoted royal sages—
in this transient world of sorrow,
devote yourself to me!

Keep me in your mind and devotion,
sacrifice to me, bow to me,
discipline yourself toward me,
and you will reach me!

6

ARISTOTLE

The Athenian Constitution: Territorial Sovereignty, c. 330 B.C.E.

The process of establishing political authority based on the territorial state was not achieved at one particular moment in history. Much of Greek history (indeed, much of world history since the Greeks) witnessed the struggle of territorial authority over family, blood, and kinship ties.

The process of replacing kinship and tribal alliances with a territorial "politics of place" can, however, be seen in the constitutional reforms attributed to the Athenian noble Cleisthenes* in 508 B.C.E. Cleisthenes was not a democrat; his reform of Athenian politics was probably intended to win popular support for himself in his struggle with other noble families. But the inadvertent results of his reforms were to establish the necessary basis for democracy: a territorial state in which commoners as citizens had a stake in government.
A description of those reforms is contained in a document called "The Athenian Constitution," discovered in Egypt only a hundred years ago and thought to have been written by the philosopher Aristotle (384–322 B.C.E.) around 330 B.C.E.

Modern scholars doubt that Cleisthenes created the *demes*† (local neighborhoods) that were the basis of his reforms. Some existed earlier. But by making the *demes* the root of political organization, he undoubtedly undercut the power of dominant families. As *demes* were given real authority, power shifted from relatives to residents. Also, as Cleisthenes expanded the number of citizens, the *deme* structure became more "*deme*-ocratic."

* KLYS thuh neez
† deems

Source: Aristotle, "The Athenian Constitution," in *Aristotle, Politics, and the Athenian Constitution*, trans. John Warrington (London: David Campbell Publishers, 1959).

Notice how the constitutional reform combined a sense of local, residential identity with citizenship in a larger city-state by tying city, country, and coastal *demes* together in each new "tribe." Why were these new tribes less "tribal" than the old ones? What would be the modern equivalent of these new tribes? Was democracy possible without a shift from kinship to territorial or civic identity?

THINKING HISTORICALLY

Territorial sovereignty is something we take for granted. It means the law of the land. Regardless of the beliefs of our parents or ancestors, we obey the law of the territory. In the United States, we are bound to observe the law of the nation and the law of the state and municipal ordinances. We do not take our own family law with us when we move from one town or state or country to another. When we go to Japan, we are bound by Japanese law, even if we are not Japanese. In the modern world, sovereignty, ultimate authority, is tied to territory. Because this is so obvious to us in modern society, it is difficult to imagine that this was not always the case.

Historians have to acknowledge that things they and their societies take for granted may not have always existed; rather, they have developed throughout history. McNeill's interpretation of the essential difference between India and Greece makes such a leap. Many people have pointed out the unique Athenian invention of democracy. But McNeill recognized that the Athenians invented democracy because they had already invented something more fundamental — territorial sovereignty, politics, government, citizenship. How does "The Athenian Constitution" support McNeill's interpretation?

The overthrow of the Peisistratid tyranny left the city split into two factions under Isagoras and Cleisthenes respectively. The former, a son of Tisander, had supported the tyrants; the latter was an Alcmaeonid. Cleisthenes, defeated in the political clubs, won over the people by offering citizen rights to the masses. Thereupon Isagoras, who had fallen behind in the race for power, once more invoked the help of his friend Cleomenes and persuaded him to exorcise the pollution; that is, to expel the Alcmaeonidae, who were believed still to be accursed. Cleisthenes accordingly withdrew from Attica with a small band of adherents, while Cleomenes proceeded to drive out seven hundred Athenian families. The Spartan next attempted to dissolve the Council and to set up Isagoras with three hundred of his supporters as the sovereign authority. The

Council, however, resisted; the populace flew to arms; and Cleomenes with Isagoras and all their forces took refuge in the Acropolis, to which the people laid siege and blockaded them for two days. On the third day it was agreed that Cleomenes and his followers should withdraw. Cleisthenes and his fellow exiles were recalled.

The people were now in control, and Cleisthenes, their leader, was recognized as head of the popular party. This was not surprising; for the Alcmaeonidae were largely responsible for the overthrow of the tyrants, with whom they had been in conflict during most of their rule.

. . . The people, therefore, had every grounds for confidence in Cleisthenes. Accordingly, three years after the destruction of the tyranny, in the archonship of Isagoras, he used his influence as leader of the popular party to carry out a number of reforms. (A) He divided the population into ten tribes instead of the old four. His purpose here was to intermix the members of the tribes so that more persons might have civic rights; and hence the advice "not to notice the tribes," which was tendered to those who would examine the lists of the clans. (B) He increased the membership of the Council from 400 to 500, each tribe now contributing fifty instead of one hundred as before. His reason for not organizing the people into *twelve* tribes was to avoid the necessity of using the existing division into trittyes, which would have meant failing to regroup the population on a satisfactory basis. (C) He divided the country into thirty portions—ten urban and suburban, ten coastal, and ten inland—each containing a certain number of demes. These portions he called trittyes, and assigned three of them by lot to each tribe in such a way that each should have one portion in each of the three localities just mentioned. Furthermore, those who lived in any given deme were to be reckoned fellow demesmen. This arrangement was intended to protect new citizens from being shown up as such by the habitual use of family names. Men were to be officially described by the names of their demes; and it is thus that Athenians still speak of one another. Demes had now supplanted the old naucraries,[1] and Cleisthenes therefore appointed Demarchs whose duties were identical with those of the former Naucrari. He named some of the demes from their localities, and others from their supposed founders; for certain areas no longer corresponded to named localities. On the other hand, he allowed everyone to retain his family and clan and religious rites according to ancestral custom. He also gave the ten tribes names which the Delphic oracle had chosen out of one hundred selected national heroes.

---

[1] Forty-eight subdivisions of the old four tribes, each responsible for one galley of the Athenian navy. [Ed.]

THUCYDIDES

The Funeral Oration of Pericles, 431 B.C.E.

The most famous statement of Greek loyalty to the city-state is the following account of the funeral speech of the Athenian statesman Pericles in the classic *History of the Peloponnesian War* by the ancient historian Thucydides.* The speech eulogized the Athenian soldiers who had died in the war against Sparta in 431 B.C.E.

Notice the high value placed on loyalty to Athens and service to the state. Here is the origin of patriotism. Pericles also insists that Athens is a democratic city-state. He praises Athenian freedom as well as public service. Could there be a conflict between personal freedom and public service? If so, how would Pericles resolve such a conflict? You might also notice that Pericles is praising Athenian citizen-soldiers who died defending not their home but the empire. Could there be a conflict between Athenian democracy and the ambitious empire?

THINKING HISTORICALLY

Are the sentiments that Pericles expresses a consequence of territorial sovereignty? Could such sentiments be expressed in defense of caste? Notice how Pericles speaks of ancestors, family, and parents. Do his words suggest any potential conflict between family ties and loyalty to the state? How is Pericles able to convince his audience of the priority of the state over kinship ties? How does this primary source provide evidence for McNeill's interpretation?

I will speak first of our ancestors, for it is right and seemly that now, when we are lamenting the dead, a tribute should be paid to their memory. There has never been a time when they did not inhabit this land, which by their valour they have handed down from generation to generation, and we have received from them a free state. But if they were worthy of praise, still more were our fathers, who added to their inheritance, and after many a struggle transmitted to us their sons this great empire. And we ourselves assembled here today, who are still most of us in the vigour of life, have carried the work of improvement further, and have richly endowed our city with all things, so that she

* thoo SIH duh deez

Source: *The History of Thucydides*, Book II, trans. Benjamin Jowett (New York: Tandy-Thomas, 1909).

is sufficient for herself both in peace and war. Of the military exploits by which our various possessions were acquired, or of the energy with which we or our fathers drove back the tide of war, Hellenic or Barbarian [non-Greek], I will not speak: for the tale would be long and is familiar to you. But before I praise the dead, I should like to point out by what principles of action we rose to power, and under what institutions and through what manner of life our empire became great. For I conceive that such thoughts are not unsuited to the occasion, and that this numerous assembly of citizens and strangers may profitably listen to them.

Our form of government does not enter into rivalry with the institutions of others. We do not copy our neighbours, but are an example to them. It is true that we are called a democracy, for the administration is in the hands of the many and not of the few. But while the law secures equal justice to all alike in their private disputes, the claim of excellence is also recognised; and when a citizen is in any way distinguished, he is preferred to the public service, not as a matter of privilege, but as the reward of merit. Neither is poverty a bar, but a man may benefit his country whatever be the obscurity of his condition. There is no exclusiveness in our public life, and in our private intercourse we are not suspicious of one another, nor angry with our neighbour if he does what he likes; we do not put on sour looks at him which, though harmless, are not pleasant. While we are thus unconstrained in our private intercourse, a spirit of reverence pervades our public acts; we are prevented from doing wrong by respect for the authorities and for the laws, having an especial regard to those which are ordained for the protection of the injured as well as to those unwritten laws which bring upon the transgressor of them the reprobation of the general sentiment.

And we have not forgotten to provide for our weary spirits many relaxations from toil; we have regular games and sacrifices throughout the year; our homes are beautiful and elegant; and the delight which we daily feel in all these things helps to banish melancholy. Because of the greatness of our city the fruits of the whole earth flow in upon us; so that we enjoy the goods of other countries as freely as of our own.

Then, again, our military training is in many respects superior to that of our adversaries. Our city is thrown open to the world, and we never expel a foreigner or prevent him from seeing or learning anything of which the secret if revealed to an enemy might profit him. We rely not upon management or trickery, but upon our own hearts and hands. And in the matter of education, whereas they from early youth are always undergoing laborious exercises which are to make them brave, we live at ease, and yet are equally ready to face the perils which they face. And here is the proof. . . .

If then we prefer to meet danger with a light heart but without laborious training, and with a courage which is gained by habit and not enforced by law, are we not greatly the gainers? Since we do not anticipate the pain, although, when the hour comes, we can be as brave as those who never allow themselves to rest; and thus too our city is equally admirable in peace and in war. For we are lovers of the beautiful, yet simple in our tastes, and we cultivate the mind without loss of manliness. Wealth we employ, not for talk and ostentation, but when there is a real use for it. To avow poverty with us is no disgrace; the true disgrace is in doing nothing to avoid it. An Athenian citizen does not neglect the state because he takes care of his own household; and even those of us who are engaged in business have a very fair idea of politics. We alone regard a man who takes no interest in public affairs, not as a harmless, but as a useless character; and if few of us are originators, we are all sound judges of policy. The great impediment to action is, in our opinion, not discussion, but the want of that knowledge which is gained by discussion preparatory to action. For we have a peculiar power of thinking before we act and of acting too, whereas other men are courageous from ignorance but hesitate upon reflection. And they are surely to be esteemed the bravest spirits who, having the clearest sense both of the pains and pleasures of life, do not on that account shrink from danger. In doing good, again, we are unlike others; we make our friends by conferring, not by receiving favours. Now he who confers a favour is the firmer friend, because he would fain by kindness keep alive the memory of an obligation; but the recipient is colder in his feelings, because he knows that in requiting another's generosity he will not be winning gratitude but only paying a debt. We alone do good to our neighbours, not upon a calculation of interest, but in the confidence of freedom and in a frank and fearless spirit.

To sum up: I say that Athens is the school of Hellas, and that the individual Athenian in his own person seems to have the power of adapting himself to the most varied forms of action with the utmost versatility and grace. This is no passing and idle word, but truth and fact; and the assertion is verified by the position to which these qualities have raised the state. For in the hour of trial Athens alone among her contemporaries is superior to the report of her. No enemy who comes against her is indignant at the reverses which he sustains at the hands of such a city; no subject complains that his masters are unworthy of him. And we shall assuredly not be without witnesses; there are mighty monuments of our power which will make us the wonder of this and of succeeding ages; we shall not need the praises of Homer or of any other panegyrist whose poetry may please for the moment, although his representation of the facts will not bear the light of day. For we have compelled every land and every sea to open a path for our valour, and have everywhere planted eternal memorials of our friendship and of our enmity. Such is the city of whose sake these men nobly fought and died; they could not bear the thought that she might be taken from them; and every one of us who survive should gladly toil on her behalf.

I have dwelt upon the greatness of Athens because I want to show you that we are contending for a higher prize than those who enjoy none of these privileges, and to establish by manifest proof the merit of these men whom I am now commemorating. Their loftiest praise has been already spoken. For in magnifying the city I have magnified them, and men like them whose virtues made her glorious. And of how few Hellenes can it be said as of them, that their deeds when weighed in the balance have been found equal to their fame! . . . They resigned to hope their unknown chance of happiness; but in the fact of death they resolved to rely upon themselves alone. And when the moment came they were minded to resist and suffer, rather than to fly and save their lives; they ran away from the word of dishonour, but on the battlefield their feet stood fast, and in an instant, at the height of their fortune, they passed away from the scene, not of their fear, but of their glory.

Such was the end of these men; they were worthy of Athens, and the living need not desire to have a more heroic spirit, although they may pray for a less fatal issue. The value of such a spirit is not to be expressed in words. Any one can discourse to you forever about the advantages of a brave defence, which you know already. But instead of listening to him I would have you day by day fix your eyes upon the greatness of Athens, until you become filled with the love of her; and when you are impressed by the spectacle of her glory, reflect that this empire has been acquired by men who knew their duty and had the courage to do it, who in the hour of conflict had the fear of dishonour always present to them, and who, if ever they failed in an enterprise, would not allow their virtues to be lost to their country, but freely gave their lives to her as the fairest offering which they could present at her feast. The sacrifice which they collectively made was individually repaid to them; for they received again each one of himself a praise which grows not old, and the noblest of all sepulchres—I speak not of that in which their remains are laid, but of that in which their glory survives, and is proclaimed always and on every fitting occasion both in word and deed. For the whole earth is the sepulchre of famous men; not only are they commemorated by columns and inscriptions in their own country, but in foreign lands there dwells also an unwritten memorial of them, graven not on stone but in the hearts of men. Make them your examples, and, esteeming courage to be freedom and freedom to be happiness, do not weigh too nicely the perils of war. The unfortunate who has no hope of a change for the better has less reason to throw away his life than the prosperous who, if he survives, is always liable to a change for the worse, and to whom any accidental fall makes the most serious difference. To a man of spirit, cowardice and disaster coming together are far more bitter than death striking him unperceived at a time when he is full of courage and animated by the general hope.

Wherefore I do not now commiserate the parents of the dead who stand here; I would rather comfort them. You know that your life has been passed amid manifold vicissitudes; and that they may be deemed fortunate who have gained most honour, whether an honourable death like theirs, or an honourable sorrow like yours, and whose days have been so ordered that the term of their happiness is likewise the term of their life. I know how hard it is to make you feel this, when the good fortune of others will too often remind you of the gladness which once lightened your hearts. And sorrow is felt at the want of those blessings, not which a man never knew, but which were a part of his life before they were taken from him. Some of you are of an age at which they may hope to have other children, and they ought to bear their sorrow better; not only will the children who may hereafter be born make them forget their own lost ones, but the city will be doubly a gainer. She will not be left desolate, and she will be safer. For a man's counsel cannot have equal weight or worth, when he alone has no children to risk in the general danger. To those of you who have passed their prime, I say: Congratulate yourselves that you have been happy during the greater part of your days; remember that your life of sorrow will not last long, and be comforted by the glory of those who are gone. For the love of honour alone is ever young, and not riches, as some say, but honour is the delight of men when they are old and useless.

To you who are the sons and brothers of the departed, I see that the struggle to emulate them will be an arduous one. For all men praise the dead, and, however pre-eminent your virtue may be, hardly will you be thought, I do not say to equal, but even to approach them. The living have their rivals and detractors, but when a man is out of the way, the honour and good-will which he receives is unalloyed. And, if I am to speak of womanly virtues to those of you who will henceforth be widows, let me sum them up in one short admonition: To a woman not to show more weakness than is natural to her sex is a great glory, and not to be talked about for good or for evil among men.

I have paid the required tribute, in obedience to the law, making use of such fitting words as I had. The tribute of deeds has been paid in part; for the dead have been honourably interred, and it remains only that their children should be maintained at the public charge until they are grown up; this is the solid prize with which, as with a garland, Athens crowns her sons living and dead, after a struggle like theirs. For where the rewards of virtue are greatest, there the noblest citizens are enlisted in the service of the state. And now, when you have duly lamented, everyone his own dead, you may depart.

8

PLATO
The Republic, c. 360 B.C.E.

This selection is from one of the world's most famous books of philosophy. Two events dominated the early life of Plato (428–348 B.C.E.), turning him away from the public life he was expected to lead. Plato was born in the shadow of the Peloponnesian War, which ended with the defeat of Athens in his twenty-third year. Disillusioned with the postwar governments, especially the democracy that condemned his teacher Socrates in 399 B.C.E., Plato forsook the political arena for a life of contemplation.

Plato's philosophical books, called dialogues because of the way they develop ideas from discussion and debate, follow Plato's teacher Socrates around the city-state of Athens. Often they begin, like *The Republic*, with a view of Socrates and other Athenian citizens enjoying the public spaces and festivals of the city. Notice in this introduction how territorial sovereignty creates public places and public activities.

THINKING HISTORICALLY

Plato was neither a democrat nor politically active. Nevertheless, his life and his philosophy exemplify a commitment to the world of what McNeill calls "territorial sovereignty."

A primary source can support a particular viewpoint by espousing it, as Plato espouses the benefits of living in a territorial state or thinking about government. But a source can also provide clues about the society from which it comes. What clues in Plato's text show that his life and the lives of the people around him are shaped by the city-state?

Chapter 1

SOCRATES. I walked down to the Piraeus yesterday with Glaucon, the son of Ariston, to make my prayers to the goddess. As this was the first celebration of her festival, I wished also to see how the ceremony would be conducted. The Thracians, I thought, made as fine a show in the procession as our own people, though they did well enough. The prayers and the spectacle were over, and we were leaving to go back to

Source: Plato, *The Republic of Plato*, trans. F. M. Cornford (London: Oxford University Press, 1941), 2–3, 177–79, 227–35.

the city, when from some way off Polemarchus, the son of Cephalus, caught sight of us starting homewards and sent his slave running to ask us to wait for him. The boy caught my garment from behind and gave me the message.

I turned around and asked where his master was.

There, he answered; coming up behind. Please wait.

Very well, said Glaucon; we will.

A minute later Polemarchus joined us, with Glaucon's brother, Adeimantus, and Niceratus, the son of Nicias, and some others who must have been at the procession.

Socrates, said Polemarchus, I do believe you are starting back to town and leaving us.

You have guessed right, I answered.

Well, he said, you see what a large party we are?

I do.

Unless you are more than a match for us, then, you must stay here.

Isn't there another alternative? said I; we might convince you that you must let us go.

How will you convince us, if we refuse to listen?

We cannot, said Glaucon.

Well, we shall refuse; make up your minds to that.

Here Adeimantus interposed: Don't you even know that in the evening there is going to be a torch-race on horseback in honour of the goddess?

On horseback! I exclaimed; that is something new. How will they do it? Are the riders going to race with torches and hand them on to one another?

Just so, said Polemarchus. Besides, there will be a festival lasting all night, which will be worth seeing. We will go out after dinner and look on. We shall find plenty of young men there and we can have a talk. So please stay, and don't disappoint us.

It looks as if we had better stay, said Glaucon.

Well, said I, if you think so, we will.

Accordingly, we went home with Polemarchus.

[At the home of Polemarchus, the participants meet a number of other old friends. After the usual greetings and gossip, the discussion begins in response to Socrates' question, "What is justice?"

Each of the participants poses an idea of justice that Socrates challenges. Then Socrates outlines an ideal state that would be based on absolute justice. In the following selection he is asked how this ideal could ever come about.

Aside from the specifics of Socrates' argument, notice the way in which public issues, for Socrates, are passionate personal concerns.]

Chapter 18

But really, Socrates, Glaucon continued, if you are allowed to go on like
this, I am afraid you will forget all about the question you thrust aside
some time ago; whether a society so constituted can ever come into
existence, and if so, how. No doubt, if it did exist, all manner of good
things would come about. I can even add some that you have passed
over. Men who acknowledged one another as fathers, sons, or brothers
and always used those names among themselves would never desert one
another; so they would fight with unequalled bravery. And if their
womenfolk went out with them to war, either in the ranks or drawn up
in the rear to intimidate the enemy and act as a reserve in case of need,
I am sure all this would make them invincible. At home, too, I can see
many advantages you have not mentioned. But, since I admit that our
commonwealth would have all these merits and any number more, if
once it came into existence, you need not describe it in further detail.
All we have now to do is to convince ourselves that it can be brought
into being and how.

This is a very sudden onslaught, said I; you have no mercy on my
shillyshallying. Perhaps you do not realize that, after I have barely escaped the first two waves, the third, which you are now bringing down
upon me, is the most formidable of all. When you have seen what it is
like and heard my reply, you will be ready to excuse the very natural
fears which made me shrink from putting forward such a paradox for
discussion.

The more you talk like that, he said, the less we shall be willing to
let you off from telling us how this constitution can come into existence;
so you had better waste no more time.

Well, said I, let me begin by reminding you that what brought us to
this point was our inquiry into the nature of justice and injustice.

True; but what of that?

Merely this: suppose we do find out what justice is, are we going to
demand that a man who is just shall have a character which exactly corresponds in every respect to the ideal of justice? Or shall we be satisfied
if he comes as near to the ideal as possible and has in him a larger measure of that quality than the rest of the world?

That will satisfy me.

If so, when we set out to discover the essential nature of justice and
injustice and what a perfectly just and a perfectly unjust man would be
like, supposing them to exist, our purpose was to use them as ideal patterns: we were to observe the degree of happiness or unhappiness that
each exhibited, and to draw the necessary inference that our own destiny
would be like that of the one we most resembled. We did not set out to
show that these ideals could exist in fact.

That is true.

Then suppose a painter had drawn an ideally beautiful figure complete to the last touch, would you think any the worse of him, if he could not show that a person as beautiful as that could exist?

No, I should not.

Well, we have been constructing in discourse the pattern of an ideal state. Is our theory any the worse, if we cannot prove it possible that a state so organized should be actually founded?

Surely not.

That, then, is the truth of the matter. But if, for your satisfaction, I am to do my best to show under what conditions our ideal would have the best chance of being realized, I must ask you once more to admit that the same principle applies here. Can theory ever be fully realized in practice? Is it not in the nature of things that action should come less close to truth than thought? People may not think so; but do you agree or not?

I do.

Then you must not insist upon my showing that this construction we have traced in thought could be reproduced in fact down to the last detail. You must admit that we shall have found a way to meet your demand for realization, if we can discover how a state might be constituted in the closest accordance with our description. Will not that content you? It would be enough for me.

And for me too.

Then our next attempt, it seems, must be to point out what defect in the working of existing states prevents them from being so organized, and what is the least change that would effect a transformation into this type of government—a single change if possible, or perhaps two; at any rate let us make the changes as few and insignificant as may be.

By all means.

Well, there is one change which, as I believe we can show, would bring about this revolution—not a small change, certainly, nor an easy one, but possible.

What is it?

I have now to confront what we called the third and greatest wave. But I must state my paradox, even though the wave should break in laughter over my head and drown me in ignominy. Now mark what I am going to say.

Go on.

Unless either philosophers become kings in their countries or those who are now called kings and rulers come to be sufficiently inspired with a genuine desire for wisdom; unless, that is to say, political power and philosophy meet together, while the many natures who now go their several ways in the one or the other direction are forcibly debarred from doing so, there can be no rest from troubles, my dear Glaucon, for states, nor yet, as I believe, for all mankind; nor can this commonwealth which we have imagined ever till then see the light of day and grow to its full stature. This it was that I have so long hung back from saying; I knew what a paradox it would be, because it is hard to see that there is no other way of happiness either for the state or for the individual.

Socrates, exclaimed Glaucon, after delivering yourself of such a pronouncement as that, you must expect a whole multitude of by no means contemptible assailants to fling off their coats, snatch up the handiest weapon, and make a rush at you, breathing fire and slaughter. If you cannot find arguments to beat them off and make your escape, you will learn what it means to be the target of scorn and derision.

Well, it was you who got me into this trouble.

Yes, and a good thing too. However, I will not leave you in the lurch. You shall have my friendly encouragement for what it is worth; and perhaps you may find me more complaisant than some would be in answering your questions. With such backing you must try to convince the unbelievers.

I will, now that I have such a powerful ally.

[In arguing that philosophers should be kings, Plato (or Socrates) was parting ways with the democratic tradition of Athens. Like other conservative Athenians, he seems to have believed that democracy degenerated into mob rule. The root of this antidemocratic philosophy was the belief that the mass of people was horribly ignorant and only the rare philosopher had true understanding. Plato expressed this idea in one of the most famous passages in the history of philosophy: the parable of the cave.]

Next, said I, here is a parable to illustrate the degrees in which our nature may be enlightened or unenlightened. Imagine the condition of men living in a sort of cavernous chamber underground, with an entrance open to the light and a long passage all down the cave. Here they have been from childhood, chained by the leg and also by the neck, so that they cannot move and can see only what is in front of them, because the chains will not let them turn their heads. At some distance higher up is the light of a fire burning behind them; and between the prisoners and the fire is a track with a parapet built along it, like the screen at a puppet-show, which hides the performers while they show their puppets over the top.

I see, said he.

Now behind this parapet imagine persons carrying along various artificial objects, including figures of men and animals in wood or stone or other materials, which project above the parapet. Naturally, some of these persons will be talking, others silent.

It is a strange picture, he said, and a strange sort of prisoners.

Like ourselves, I replied; for in the first place prisoners so confined would have seen nothing of themselves or of one another, except the shadows thrown by the firelight on the wall of the Cave facing them, would they?

Not if all their lives they had been prevented from moving their heads.

And they would have seen as little of the objects carried past.

Of course.

Now, if they could talk to one another, would they not suppose that their words referred only to those passing shadows which they saw?

Necessarily.

And suppose their prison had an echo from the wall facing them? When one of the people crossing behind them spoke, they could only suppose that the sound came from the shadow passing before their eyes.

No doubt.

In every way, then, such prisoners would recognize as reality nothing but the shadows of those artificial objects.

Inevitably.

Now consider what would happen if their release from the chains and the healing of their unwisdom should come about in this way. Suppose one of them was set free and forced suddenly to stand up, turn his head, and walk with eyes lifted to the light; all these movements would be painful, and he would be too dazzled to make out the objects whose shadows he had been used to see. What do you think he would say, if someone told him that what he had formerly seen was meaningless illusion, but now, being somewhat nearer to reality and turned towards more real objects, he was getting a truer view? Suppose further that he were shown the various objects being carried by and were made to say, in reply to questions, what each of them was. Would he not be perplexed and believe the objects now shown him to be not so real as what he formerly saw?

Yes, not nearly so real.

And if he were forced to look at the firelight itself, would not his eyes ache, so that he would try to escape and turn back to the things which he could see distinctly, convinced that they really were clearer than these other objects now being shown to him?

Yes.

And suppose someone were to drag him away forcibly up the steep and rugged ascent and not let him go until he had hauled him out into the sunlight, would he not suffer pain and vexation at such treatment, and, when he had come out into the light, find his eyes so full of its radiance that he could not see a single one of the things that he was now told were real?

Certainly he would not see them all at once.

He would need, then, to grow accustomed before he could see things in that upper world. At first it would be easiest to make out shadows, and then the images of men and things reflected in water, and later on the things themselves. After that, it would be easier to watch the heavenly bodies and the sky itself by night, looking at the light of the moon and stars rather than the Sun and the Sun's light in the daytime.

Yes, surely.

Last of all, he would be able to look at the Sun and contemplate its nature, not as it appears when reflected in water or any alien medium, but as it is in itself in its own domain.

No doubt.

And now he would begin to draw the conclusion that it is the Sun that produces the seasons and the course of the year and controls everything in the visible world, and moreover is in a way the cause of all that he and his companions used to see.

Clearly he would come at last to that conclusion.

Then if he called to mind his fellow prisoners and what passed for wisdom in his former dwelling-place, he would surely think himself happy in the change and be sorry for them. They may have had a practice of honouring and commending one another, with prizes for the man who had the keenest eye for the passing shadows and the best memory for the order in which they followed or accompanied one another, so that he could make a good guess as to which was going to come next. Would our released prisoner be likely to covet those prizes or to envy the men exalted to honour and power in the Cave? Would he not feel like Homer's Achilles, that he would far sooner "be on earth as a hired servant in the house of a landless man" or endure anything rather than go back to his old beliefs and live in the old way?

Yes, he would prefer any fate to such a life.

Now imagine what would happen if he went down again to take his former seat in the Cave. Coming suddenly out of the sunlight, his eyes would be filled with darkness. He might be required once more to deliver his opinion on those shadows, in competition with the prisoners who had never been released, while his eyesight was still dim and unsteady; and it might take some time to become used to the darkness. They would laugh at him and say that he had gone up only to come back with his sight ruined; it was worth no one's while even to attempt the ascent. If they could lay hands on the man who was trying to set them free and lead them up, they would kill him.

Yes, they would.

Every feature in this parable, my dear Glaucon, is meant to fit our earlier analysis. The prison dwelling corresponds to the region revealed to us through the sense of sight, and the firelight within it to the power of the Sun. The ascent to see the things in the upper world you may take as standing for the upward journey of the soul into the region of the intelligible; then you will be in possession of what I surmise, since that is what you wish to be told. Heaven knows whether it is true; but this, at any rate, is how it appears to me. In the world of knowledge, the last thing to be perceived and only with great difficulty is the essential Form of Goodness. Once it is perceived, the conclusion must follow that, for all things, this is the cause of whatever is right and good; in the visible world it gives birth to light and to the lord of light, while it is itself sovereign in the intelligible world and the parent of intelligence and truth. Without having had a vision of this Form no one can act with wisdom, either in his own life or in matters of state.

So far as I can understand, I share your belief.

Then you may also agree that it is no wonder if those who have reached their height are reluctant to manage the affairs of men. Their souls long to spend all their time in that upper world—naturally enough, if here once more our parable holds true. Nor, again, is it at all strange that one who comes from the contemplation of divine things to the miseries of human life should appear awkward and ridiculous when, with eyes still dazed and not yet accustomed to the darkness, he is compelled, in a law court or elsewhere, to dispute about the shadows of justice or the images that cast those shadows, and to wrangle over the notions of what is right in the minds of men who have never beheld Justice itself.

It is not at all strange.

No; a sensible man will remember that the eyes may be confused in two ways—by a change from light to darkness or from darkness to light; and he will recognize that the same thing happens to the soul. When he sees it troubled and unable to discern anything clearly, instead of laughing thoughtlessly, he will ask whether, coming from a brighter existence, its unaccustomed vision is obscured by the darkness, in which case he will think its condition enviable and its life a happy one; or whether, emerging from the depths of ignorance, it is dazzled by excess of light. If so, he will rather feel sorry for it; or, if he were inclined to laugh, that would be less ridiculous than to laugh at the soul which has come down from the light.

That is a fair statement.

If this is true, then, we must conclude that education is not what it is said to be by some, who profess to put knowledge into a soul which does not possess it, as if they could put sight into blind eyes. On the contrary, our own account signifies that the soul of every man does possess the power of learning the truth and the organ to see it with; and that, just as one might have to turn the whole body round in order that the eye should see light instead of darkness, so the entire soul must be turned away from this changing world, until its eye can bear to contemplate reality and that supreme splendour which we have called the Good. Hence there may well be an art whose aim would be to effect this very thing, the conversion of the soul, in the readiest way; not to put the power of sight into the soul's eye, which already has it, but to ensure that, instead of looking in the wrong direction, it is turned the way it ought to be.

Yes, it may well be so.

It looks, then, as though wisdom were different from those ordinary virtues, as they are called, which are not far removed from bodily qualities, in that they can be produced by habituation and exercise in a soul which has not possessed them from the first. Wisdom, it seems, is certainly the virtue of some diviner faculty, which never loses its power, though its use for good or harm depends on the direction towards which it is turned. You must have noticed in dishonest men with a reputation for sagacity the shrewd glance of a narrow intelligence piercing the objects to which it is directed. There is nothing wrong with their power of vision, but it has been forced into the service of evil, so that the keener its sight, the more harm it works.

Quite true.

And yet if the growth of a nature like this had been pruned from earliest childhood, cleared of those clinging overgrowths which come of gluttony and all luxurious pleasure and, like leaden weights charged with affinity to this mortal world, hang upon the soul, bending its vision downwards; if, freed from these, the soul were turned round towards true reality, then this same power in these very men would see the truth as keenly as the objects it is turned to now.

Yes, very likely.

Is it not also likely, or indeed certain after what has been said, that a state can never be properly governed either by the uneducated who know nothing of truth or by men who are allowed to spend all their days in the pursuit of culture? The ignorant have no single mark before their eyes at which they must aim in all the conduct of their own lives and of affairs of state; and the others will not engage in action if they can help it, dreaming that, while still alive, they have been translated to the Islands of the Blest.

Quite true.

It is for us, then, as founders of a commonwealth, to bring compulsion to bear on the noblest natures. They must be made to climb the ascent to the vision of Goodness, which we called the highest object of knowledge; and, when they have looked upon it long enough, they must not be allowed, as they now are, to remain on the heights, refusing to come down again to the prisoners or to take any part in their labours and rewards, however much or little these may be worth.

Shall we not be doing them an injustice, if we force on them a worse life than they might have?

You have forgotten again, my friend, that the law is not concerned to make any one class specially happy, but to ensure the welfare of the commonwealth as a whole. By persuasion or constraint it will unite the citizens in harmony, making them share whatever benefits each class can contribute to the common good; and its purpose in forming men of that spirit was not that each should be left to go his own way, but that they should be instrumental in binding the community into one.

True, I had forgotten.

You will see, then, Glaucon, that there will be no real injustice in compelling our philosophers to watch over and care for the other citizens. We can fairly tell them that their compeers in other states may quite reasonably refuse to collaborate: there they have sprung up, like a self-sown plant, in despite of their country's institutions; no one has fostered their growth, and they cannot be expected to show gratitude for a care they have never received. "But," we shall say, "it is not so with you. We have brought you into existence for your country's sake as well as for your own, to be like leaders and king-bees in a hive; you have been better and more thoroughly educated than those others and hence you are more capable of playing your part both as men of thought and as men of action. You must go down, then, each in his turn, to live with the rest and let your eyes grow accustomed to the darkness. You will then see a thousand times better than those who live there always; you will recognize every image for what it is and know what it represents, because you have seen justice, beauty, and goodness in their reality; and so you and we shall find life in our commonwealth no mere dream, as it is in most existing states, where men live fighting one another about shadows and quarrelling for power, as if that were a great prize; whereas in truth government can be at its best and free from dissension only where the destined rulers are least desirous of holding office."

Quite true.

Then will our pupils refuse to listen and to take their turns at sharing in the work of the community, though they may live together for most of their time in a purer air?

No; it is a fair demand, and they are fair-minded men. No doubt, unlike any ruler of the present day, they will think of holding power as an unavoidable necessity.

Yes, my friend; for the truth is that you can have a well-governed society only if you can discover for your future rulers a better way of life than being in office; then only will power be in the hands of men who are rich, not in gold, but in the wealth that brings happiness, a good and wise life. All goes wrong when, starved for lack of anything good in their own lives, men turn to public affairs hoping to snatch from thence the happiness they hunger for. They set about fighting for power, and this internecine conflict ruins them and their country. The life of true philosophy is the only one that looks down upon offices of state; and access to power must be confined to men who are not in love with it; otherwise rivals will start fighting. So whom else can you compel to undertake the guardianship of the commonwealth, if not those who, besides understanding best the principles of government, enjoy a nobler life than the politician's and look for rewards of a different kind?

There is indeed no other choice.

■ REFLECTIONS

Caste and territorial sovereignty were alternate but equally effective systems of social organization in the ancient world. Both worked. Both allocated jobs and rewards, arranged marriages and created families, ensured the peace and fought wars. Neither was necessarily more just, tyrannical, expensive, or arbitrary. Yet each system created its own complex world of ideas and behavior.

Caste and territorial sovereignty were not the only bases for identity in the ancient world. In many societies, a person's identity was based on family ties of a different sort than caste. In China, the family lineage, constituting many generations of relatives, was particularly important. Almost every society in human history organized itself around families to a certain extent, and most societies also had a sense of multiple family units called clans or tribes. The Indian caste system was only one variant of these multifamily systems, and some non-Indian societies had divisions resembling castes.

Family, clan, and tribe are still important determinants of identity in the modern world. In some societies, the authority of a tribal leader, clan elder, or family patriarch rivals that of the state. Nevertheless, the modern world is made up of states. We live according to the law of the land, not that of kinship. In the United States, one obeys the laws of the United States, regardless of who one knows. If the police pull you over for driving through a red light, you do not say that your father gave you permission or your uncle ordered you to drive through red lights. In the territory of the United States, you obey the laws of the United States and the particular state in which you find yourself. When a citizen of the United States goes to Canada, he or she must obey the laws of Canada. This is the world of states, of territorial sovereignty.

One of the major transitions in human history in the last five thousand years has been the rise of territorial sovereignty and the supplanting of the authority of the law of the state over the rule of family, clan, tribe, and caste. This is what developed in ancient Greece twenty-five hundred years ago. It did not occur completely and finally with Cleisthenes or even with the rise of Greek democracy in the fifth century B.C.E. Tribal alliances reasserted themselves periodically in Greece and elsewhere, in the Middle Ages and in modern society. The establishment of territorial sovereignty and ultimately of civil society, where political parties replaced tribes, was gradual and interrupted and is still continuing. Aristotle tells us that after Cleisthenes, Greeks took new surnames based on their new civic "tribes." That would have ended the rule of the old family-based tribes, but we know the old tribal names did not disappear. A thorough transition would mean that political parties would express entirely civic goals without a trace of tribal identity, but that too is a process that still continues. In modern Ireland, for instance, one of the political parties, Finn Gael, means literally the tribe of the Gael. In the wake of the U.S. invasion of Iraq in 2003, many Americans have learned how difficult it is to impose a system of territorial sovereignty on a society where tribal identities are strong.

India today is also a modern state in which the law of the land applies to all regardless of caste, family, or tribe. In fact, recent Indian governments have outlawed discrimination based on caste and created affirmative action programs on behalf of Dalits, the outcastes or untouchables. Nevertheless, Indian newspapers still run matrimonial ads that specify caste, though international Web sites often do not.

Modern society encourages us to be many things. Family and caste can still play a role. Religion, ethnicity, national origin, even race are given an importance in modern society that was often absent or irrelevant in ancient societies. But with the civic society produced by territorial sovereignty comes not only citizenship but also a range of chosen identities based on career, education, job, hobbies, friends, and a wide range of living possibilities. These choices can sometimes overwhelm. Sometimes the indelibility of family, caste, or birth can seem a comfort. But over the long term of history, the range and choice of identities seem likely to increase, and more and more of them will likely be voluntary rather than stamped on the birth certificate.

4

Empire and Government

China and Rome, 300 B.C.E.–300 C.E.

■ HISTORICAL CONTEXT

The Chinese and Roman empires of the classical era were similar in many ways. They were roughly contemporaneous. The Chinese Empire began under the Qin dynasty in 221 B.C.E. and continued in revised form through the Han dynasty until 220 C.E. Rome also reached imperial dimensions after 200 B.C.E., recognizing its first emperor in 27 B.C.E. Like China, the Roman Empire was shaken by invading nomads after 200 C.E. Each empire ruled at least fifty million people over an area of one and a half million square miles. (See Maps 4.1 and 4.2.) Both managed to field and maintain enormous armies and tax, govern, and keep the peace for hundreds of years. How did these empires rule and administer such vast areas for so long? In this chapter we explore the management of both empires by studying the actions of emperors and their governments.

When we think of empire we generally presume two things: the rule of a very large territory by a single power and, usually, that this power is held by a single individual who is the emperor of that territory. These elements were simultaneous in China. After centuries in which six kingdoms struggled for dominance, the king of Qin* conquered the remaining independent kingdoms in China and created a single empire with himself as emperor. Known as the First Emperor, the king of Qin created many of the enduring elements of centralized rule. A sense of his enormous power is apparent today thanks to the 1974 discovery of his tomb near his capital Xianyang† with its thousands of life-size terra cotta soldiers. It was

---

* chin
† shin yong

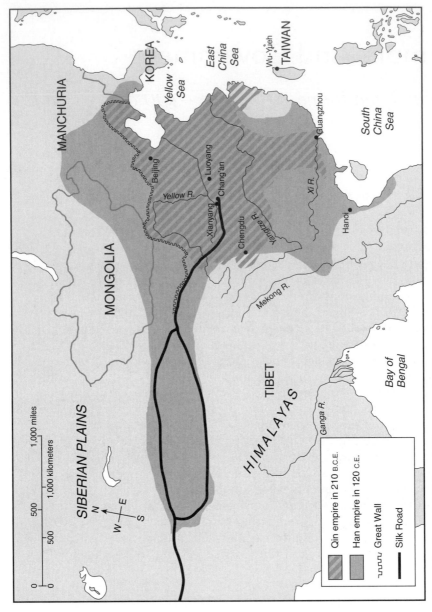

Map 4.1 Imperial China, 210 B.C.E. and 120 C.E.

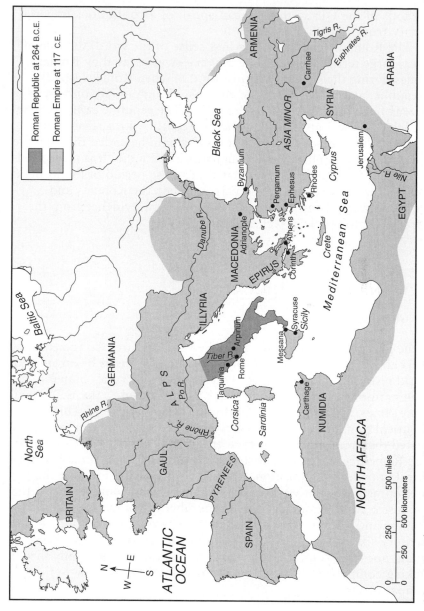

Map 4.2 The Roman Empire, 264 B.C.E. and 117 C.E.

121

built, the ancient sources tell us, by 700,000 workers, all of whom were buried with their emperor so the site would never be revealed. The Qin dynasty did not last long beyond the death of the first emperor, but the successor Han dynasty continued many of the methods of the Qin so that we can speak of a continuous imperial history from 221 B.C.E. to 220 C.E.

The Roman Empire—in the first sense of the word, the rule of a very large territory by a single power—was created by Roman armies during the last two centuries B.C.E. when Rome was still a republic, a government by the citizens, though in fact only by citizens from the wealthiest old families. The republic came to an end after the civil war at the end of the first century B.C.E. Eventually won by Julius Caesar's adopted son Octavian, he ended the republic and declared himself Emperor Augustus in 27 B.C.E. It is the period of the next few hundred years that we call the period of the Roman Empire, but as we compare the way in which the Romans and Chinese governed vast territories, we will draw evidence from the late Roman Republic as well.

■ THINKING HISTORICALLY

Making Comparisons

In the previous chapter, you were asked to compare two societies, India and Greece, on the basis of a comparative thesis by an eminent world historian. In this chapter, you will exercise your comparative imagination without the prompting of someone else's thesis. You will make your own comparisons by thinking comparatively. This is an historical thinking skill that is very different, and much more sophisticated than remembering or even employing someone else's comparison. Remembering a comparison that someone else had made can be useful knowledge acquisition, but it can only be the food for the development of creative thought. The Historical Context section that you just read, for example, offers a number of comparisons of the Chinese and Roman empires—same time period, population, and territory size. We could add more, but memorizing a list of these would not train your ability to think comparatively. It is only through making comparisons of your own that you will learn how to think comparatively.

1

MICHAEL LOEWE

The Government of the Qin and Han Empires, 2006

The government of an empire required a vast array of officials, soldiers, and professional personnel. A new empire like the Qin and then in 202 B.C.E. the first (or "Western") Han also required a plan of organization and administration and a way of controlling old rivals and cementing new loyalties. Michael Loewe, a modern historian of China, highlights how some of these problems were handled in China's Qin and Han empires.

How did the Qin and Han empires structure their governments to deal with the challenge of administering their large territories? What do you see as the strengths and weaknesses of Chinese imperial administration?

THINKING HISTORICALLY

What comparisons does the author make between the Chinese and Roman empires? What other comparative questions come to your mind as you read the selection? What would you have to learn about Rome in order to answer your questions?

The Structure of the Government

Comparison of the ways in which the early Chinese empires operated with those of other pre-modern regimes can be no more than a matter of speculation, but it may nonetheless stimulate valuable enquiry. Although no attempt at such a comparison will be undertaken here, it may be asked whether the governments of Qin and Han were organised in a more systematic and intensive manner than that of the Roman Empire and perhaps of any other regime prior to that of Byzantium. Such a question would involve consideration of a number of features some of which had emerged even from the outset of imperial China, shortly after 221 BCE, and had developed in a marked way by the close of Eastern Han (220 CE).

Qin and Han practice drew on the experience and precedents set in the earlier kingdoms, and many of Qin's and Han's institutions survived

Source: Michael Loewe, *The Government of the Qin and Han Empires, 221 B.C.E.–220 C.E.* (Indianapolis: Hackett Publishing, 2006), 17–18, 37–40, 56–57, 61, 68–69, 71–76, 185, 187–88.

to form characteristic features of government in later times. An established complement of civil servants staffed the organs of administration each one with its defined responsibilities; a senior official who was appointed to such a department and supported by an assistant supervised the work of his subordinates and their clerks. Steps to achieve the purposes of government depended on organising and controlling the population in units of five persons of less. A division of responsibilities could serve to check the growth of a monopoly of power; civil servants advanced in their careers according to a structure that marked their seniority and determined their salary; social privileges and economic advantages separated officials both from the lower orders of humanity who were subject to their instructions and from those whose high status rested on circumstances of birth.

In ideal terms that were by no means always realised, government lay in the hands of men of proven ability, intellect and loyalty who strove to maintain impartiality and to preclude favouritism. There was no concept of basic distinctions between the consultative, administrative and judicial functions of an official, whose duties might embrace the performance of religious rites and the collection of tax, the promotion of education and the conduct of military campaigns. A conscious sense of seniority and hierarchy pervaded the manner of government and the authority reposed in officials, who must needs comply with set procedures in transacting their business and in their relations with their colleagues, senior and junior alike. . . .

The Qin empire had been formed by taking over territories from its neighbouring kingdoms and amalgamating them with lands that were firmly under its existing rule. Such newly acquired lands were administered as units that were termed commanderies or counties, and there was no difficulty in establishing new such units as occasion demanded. From such beginnings and accretions, the whole of the Qin empire was governed as thirty-six, or perhaps as many as forty-six, commanderies under the control of governors, who were appointed by the center. . . .

However, government of China as a single unit was an innovation and a short-lived one at that; there could be no certainty that it would be seen again after the virtual collapse of Qin in 210 BCE. Emerging as apparently the leading protagonist from the ensuing civil warfare, Xiang Yu sought to set up a system of a pre-imperial type; it was to consist of nineteen separate kingdoms over which he would claim to act as overlord. Some of these kingdoms were led by survivors of the royal houses that Qin had destroyed, such an arrangement signifying a rejection of the imperial system. One of the kingdoms, named Han, was placed under the rule of Liu Bang, whom Xiang Yu had relegated to a subordinate position but who had attained a dominant position after some years of warfare. It can only be surmised that, living as he had under pre-imperial, imperial and post-imperial dispensations, and fired by a personal ambition, Liu Bang deliberately chose to re-instate an imperial system under his own control as his chosen way of asserting his authority and governing China. He did so with one major change: the institution of kingdoms as an element in provincial government. . . .

It may be estimated that by the end of Western Han perhaps 100,000 officials were engaged in administering the provinces of the empire. The governors of a highly populated commandery might be responsible for a registered population of two and a half million registered individuals, those of the remote commanderies at the perimeter for less than fifty thousand; they could also be held accountable to some extent for the activities of those persons who had not been registered, living by means of criminal activities or evading apprehension as deserters or vagabonds. The governors were responsible for security, for the maintenance of law and order and, if at the perimeter, for defence. They held judicial powers with which to implement the laws, judge lawsuits and disputes and suppress crime; at times they took command of armed forces. They were enjoined to promote agriculture and education. If posted in regions such as the south (modern Guangdong and Guangxi), they could earn merit by teaching refined habits such as those of wearing clothes or regulated marriages to folk who were as yet unassimilated. They collected revenue which was payable to the centre, and they controlled the registration of the population and the call-up of those members who were due for statutory service as labourers or soldiers. . . .

The Armed Forces

The Qin, Han and Xin dynasties were founded, brought to a close and in the case of Han restored by leaders who attracted supporters and relied on armed forces to achieve their aims. Once established, the rulers of those dynasties could not but have been aware that they lay open to similar action, should their antagonists or rivals resort to the very methods that they had employed, in order to take their place. And before long those rulers needed to face other dangers. Leaders of non-Han peoples whose homes lay beyond the perimeter of their own domains, be they Xiongnu, Qiang, Wuhuan or Xianbei,[1] could all too easily and suddenly disrupt the livelihood of the Han farmers and townspeople. Threats to dynastic continuity or outbreaks of civil fighting led to a call on armed forces on several occasions in Western Han, such as in 180, 154 and

---

[1] Different ethnic groups, many of whom were nomadic. [Ed.]

91 BCE, and they featured in the moves to unseat Wang Mang and to restore the Han dynasty. . . .

By contrast with Rome, no tradition of military heroism developed in China's early empires. On rare occasions successive members of a family followed in one another's footsteps as leaders of armies, as may be seen in the case of Meng Tian. He is best known as the officer who unified Qin's defence system such that it constituted a 'Great Wall'; his father and grandfather had both acted as generals in the kingdoms of the Warring States. . . .

Conscripts, volunteers and convicts on reduced sentences filled the ranks of the forces under a general's command. In Western Han, except for those who enjoyed privileged social status, males aged between twenty-three (or at times twenty) and fifty-six were obliged to serve in the armed forces for two years, one of which was spent in training and one on duty as a guardsman or in the static defence lines of the north. These men formed the bulk of a commander's infantry. In addition to their statutory service, they were subject to recall in times of emergency. . . .

It is open to doubt how far the term 'professional' may be applied to Han concepts of military needs, the means of maintaining armed forces in sufficiency and the use of armies in the field. Records from the orderly rooms of the north-west show clearly that the units stationed there served under a strict command; they were subject to working orders in a manner of which civil officials could be proud. They kept records of letters and documents that they received and sent, together with the times of despatch and delivery; they submitted accounts for the expenditure of money and reports in which officers acknowledged receipt of their pay, either in cash or in textiles. The clerks wrote out scrupulous lists of stores of grain as received and as issued in accordance with the scales laid down according to age and sex. As in services in other cultures, so here some of the records were made out in duplicate. . . .

The Officials

Officials stood apart from other mortals in imperial China. They were members of what may be termed the only profession, admitted thereto thanks to hard-won qualifications, to sponsorship or to favouritism. They received salaries paid by the state. In social terms their distinction from others did not depend on circumstances of birth such as descent from an imperial or royal family, but their degree of dignity and the respect that they received for their authority could rise to be higher than those accorded to princes or nobles. A theoretical classification of the people of the empire according to their occupations placed officials within the *shi*, persons of education and ability with some powers of leadership; these ranked above the farmers, artisans and merchants of the three other types of occupation.

Whereas the society of the early empires did not include other definable groups of persons who could collectively be treated as 'professional,' it did not lack specialists in intellectual proficiency and skills such as medicine, astronomy or mathematics; indeed the complement of officials provided for the inclusion of posts for a few persons with just those gifts. In addition there were men and women who studied the occult and advised how the messages from the supernatural world should best be interpreted and exploited, for the benefit of the emperor or the empire. There were those who sought means that may be described now as irrational with which to bring earthly bliss to individuals in particular or mankind in general. There were physicians who practised independently, treating patients in the highest reaches of society. None of these practitioners, however, attained the same measure of respect as did the specialists in learning and documents who became officials and received the support of the state. . . .

Careers in the civil service, which in time would become highly competitive, could spell long years spent in junior offices before promotion to the most senior posts that carried empire-wide renown. Such eminence reached no more than a fortunate few, and a career could just as easily be cut short with disgrace, owing to a failure to fulfil one's duties or to involvement in political antagonisms. These results were possible because in their higher positions officials would in effect be leading members of a government from whom the emperor requested advice. Their proposals and actions in that capacity might win widespread popular praise; they might equally well excite enmity and hatred among rivals. . . .

We have no means of assessing what proportion of the nearly sixty million registered inhabitants of 1–2 CE were literate. We can surmise that the 130,000 officials who were in post in 5 BCE necessarily had to master the three arts of reading, writing and arithmetic. Possibly such rudimentary skills were also needed by many men of a lower order, such as the constables or watchmen who carried out the basic work of administration as ordered by their superiors up and down the land.

Much of the administration of an empire depended on steady, routine and repetitive work, often in the form of preparing seasonal, monthly or daily reports, perhaps of accountancy or of the receipt and distribution of stores. If daily entries were needed such documents might take the form of a ledger in which the successive days of the calendar were clearly written to await the insertion of the relevant figures. Officials would receive instructions, such as orders to comply with a decree, to call out military forces or to adopt a newly authorised calendar; such instructions came from their superiors whether of the provinces or the central government, and on receipt an official would pass them down to his subordinates for the requisite action. Or officials might receive documents from below, such as the legal dossier of a case that was sub judice; after taking action or recording the opinions and advice such as the limits of their own positions allowed, they would submit such documents to higher authorities for comparable action.

Much of the work of officials concerned taxation, security or criminal proceedings. They would report the action that they had taken to face an abnormal or disastrous situation such as one caused by floods; they might give reasons to explain what could appear to be a failure in their task, for such might be construed as dereliction of duty for which they could face prosecution and trial. With increased seniority an official would find himself governor of a commandery with responsibility for the welfare and control of a registered population of anything between a few hundred thousand and two and a half million. At an even higher level, in the central government, he would supervise a host of specialist offices and their directors and advise the emperor on weighty matters of policy. For such tasks he must be familiar with precedents, good or ill, and he must be aware of the prevailing conditions of the empire. Whether in the provincial or the central government, a senior official must be capable of exercising authority on a wide enough scale to preclude an outbreak of dissidence.

From the outset of empire it may well have been apparent that there was a need to recruit, train and attract persons to join the civil service. We learn that youths of seventeen years could be enrolled to receive instruction, so that they would be able to read documents written in different styles of script and acquire a familiarity with some approved texts of literature. Such arrangements were designed to prepare young men to serve as clerks of a fairly low grade, and after three years they faced a test of their abilities. At the same time other young men were being trained to become prayer reciters, or diviners who operated with the traditional media of turtles' shells; some of those who were at the early stages of training in the mystique of divination might face a test of a practical nature.

Rules for this type of training and testing existed from at least 186 BCE, and different methods of recruitment soon arose. From 165 BCE, or possibly earlier, decrees were ordering senior officials who were installed in the capital city or the provinces to recommend persons of intelligence and fine character, or those able to express themselves cogently, for direct appointment to the service. Sometimes a quota was fixed for the number of men to be recommended. Calls for men of distinction in this way became frequent during Wudi's reign (r. 141–87 BCE), with the introduction of a new criterion, identified as a sense of family responsibility and of known integrity. These steps brought at least two hundred and perhaps as many as three hundred names forward for recommendation annually, and some of the recommended young men entered the service at a higher level than that of those trained according to the rules mentioned above. In Western terms the difference may be compared with that between an officer and gentleman and a non-commissioned officer.

At much the same time (ca. 124 BCE) a further and more advanced style of testing was introduced. A complement of fifty pupils aged eighteen and above were chosen by officials from the provinces for presentation at the Imperial Academy in Chang'an; the lucky few who were chosen were also exempted from the state's obligations of tax and service. Following an assessment of their character and abilities they became pupils of the academicians, scholars who specialised in the interpretation and teaching of approved literary texts. After a year's training they were tested and either posted to a suitable office or dismissed; those officials who had recommended a failure were liable to punishment. . . .

Eunuchs are first seen in powerful positions in the reigns of Xuandi (r. 74–48 BCE) and Yuandi (r. 48–33 BCE), but they were not appointed to senior offices, and it was only between circa 159 and 189 CE that they became a major force in dynastic history. Some offices of a lower level, such as those of the palace writers, were regularly filled by eunuchs while they existed, and eunuchs served in subordinate ways in the Secretariat. As holders of supernumerary titles they could be in a privileged position that was not available to all those appointed to office. . . .

Weaknesses and Problems

The presentation of arguments in China varied greatly from the ways that prevailed in Greece and Rome. For pre-imperial times we may read accounts of encounters between a sovereign and his advisors that are perhaps anecdotal and fictional rather than factual, but they are no less significant for that reason. They tell of incidents in which a roving man of affairs would exert his wits to impress on a ruler the great benefits that would accrue from certain types of action; the arguments that he deployed may not necessarily have been completely free of deception. Or, he might advise against undertaking steps that would appear to lead to immediate gains, but in reality concealed underlying dangers. These tales need not be accepted as veritable records of the ways in which the plans and policies of a kingdom were determined, or how kings might be gullible to persuasion by others, but they take their place in a tradition whereby arguments on the highest matters of state were presented face to face in the secluded safety of audience with a monarch. Neither in pre-imperial nor in early imperial times was there opportunity for the practice of oratory or public declamation either to advance or to denounce a proposed measure of state, as was seen in the assemblies of Athens and in the debates of Rome's senate. Chinese officials were not called upon to defend their decisions in public; nor was there any semblance of following the will expressed by a large number of people.

There was thus no presentation of opposing wills, ideas or arguments in public, and it may be thought that in this way China missed out when compared with the West. Arguments for or against a proposal were first advanced in the form of memorial and counter memorial, or they took place within the narrow confines of a hall in the palace. Exceptionally, the document to which reference has been made, the *Discourses on Salt and Iron*, provides an example of an oral exchange of views that had been expressly ordered by imperial decree. Biased as the account of that exchange is, it illustrates some of the difficulties that faced imperial governments, whether of a practical nature or as matters of principle. In this instance, as we are told, discussion ranged over the whole art of government, the call to increase material prosperity or to give priority to moral precepts.

Called specifically to give advice on the value of the government's monopolies of salt and iron production, spokesmen for the government and its critics argued the case for controlling the population or leaving its members to lead their own lives according to their own devices. They referred to a number of problems that were inherent in a major scheme of economic organisation and to the resulting weaknesses. As against the claim that the monopolies increased the revenue of the government, and that those sources of revenue would be used for the benefit of the people, it was countered that such profits derived from nothing but the people's own goods. The use of coinage, which had perhaps been increasing over the decades, also raised questions: Did the present system allow scope for economic oppression on the part of officials or merchants? Would advantage accrue from raising tax in the form of local products rather than in coin? Money, came the answer, serves to alleviate distress and to equalise prices. The critics of the government drew attention to the failures that could be noticed in the operation of the monopolies and their results; the quality of the iron wares was not necessarily of a high or an even standard, and the goods did not always reach the farmers, who could perhaps not afford to buy them. The spokesman for the government replied that it was the state that could provide a more regular service, with an assured supply of materials and labour, on which private iron masters and commercial magnates could not draw.

2

SIMA QIAN

The Biographies of Harsh Officials, 104–92 B.C.E.

Sima Qian (ca. 145–89 B.C.E.) is often called the father of Chinese historical writing. His own father was one of the important officials of the empire — Prefect of the Grand Scribes of Emperor Wudi, which meant running the imperial library, among other duties. Encouraged by his father to study the past, the young Sima Qian traveled throughout China, collecting and reading historical records. When his father died, Sima Qian vowed to continue his work. Sima Qian's *Records of the Grand Historian* took over a decade to write, and it covered over a thousand years of early Chinese history as well as the history of the Qin and Han empires until his own time. He organized his history as a series of biographies, many of famous kings and emperors, but also of important officials. This brief selection from a chapter on "harsh officials" personalizes the official lives summarized in the previous selection.

As Grand Historian, Sima Qian was as important an official as any he wrote about, and his own life says much about the vulnerability of a high position in the empire. In 99 B.C.E. Sima Qian defended a general who the emperor thought had committed treason. Emperor Wudi then charged Sima Qian with the same crime, punishable by death or castration. In a letter later in life, Sima Qian explained why he chose castration:

It was my obligation to my father to finish his historical work that made me submit to the knife . . . If I had done otherwise, how could I have ever had the face to visit the graves of my parents?

. . . There is no defilement so great as castration. One who has undergone this punishment is nowhere counted as a man. . . . I am fit now for only guarding the palace women's apartments. I can hope for justification only after my death, when my histories become known to the world.

What do our brief selections from his histories — and the Grand Historian's own life — tell you about the government of the Han Empire? How would you characterize Han dynasty government? What does this reading tell you about Han dynasty society?

Source: *Records of the Historian: Chapters from the SHIH CHI of Ssu-ma Ch'ien*, trans. Burton Watson (New York: Columbia University Press, 1969), 300–05.

THINKING HISTORICALLY

It was common for Han dynasty commentators to compare their era favorably with the earlier Qin (*Ch'in* in the following document) dynasty. How does Sima Qian do that? What other comparisons does he make? What comparative question about Rome does this selection suggest to you?

The people scorned agricultural pursuits and turned more and more to deceit, flouting the regulations and thinking up clever ways to evade the law. Good men could not lead them to a life of virtue; only the sternest and most severe treatment had any effect in controlling them. Thus I made The Biographies of the Harsh Officials.

Confucius says, "If you lead the people with laws and control them with punishments, they will try to avoid the punishments but will have no sense of shame. But if you lead them with virtue and control them with rites, they will have a sense of shame and moreover will become good." Lao Tzu states, "The man of superior virtue does not appear to have any virtue; therefore he keeps his virtue. The man of inferior virtue cannot forget his virtue; therefore he has no virtue." He also says, "The more laws are promulgated, the more thieves and bandits there will be."

The Grand Historian remarks: How true these words are! Laws and regulations are only the tools of government; they are not the spring from which flows the purity of good government or the pollution of bad.

Formerly, in the time of the Ch'in, the net of the law was drawn tightly about the empire and yet evil and deceit sprang up on all sides; in the end men thought of nothing but evading their superiors and no one could do anything to save the situation. At that time the law officials worked to bring about order, battling helplessly as though against fire or boiling water. Only the hardiest and cruelest of them were able to bear the strain of office and derive any satisfaction from the task; those who cared for justice and virtue were left to rot in insignificant posts. Therefore Confucius said, "In hearing litigations, I am no better than anyone else. What is necessary is to make it so that there are no more litigations!" And Lao Tzu said, "When the inferior man hears about the Way, he laughs out loud at it." These are no empty words!

When the Han arose, it lopped off the harsh corners of the Ch'in code and returned to an easy roundness, whittled away the embellishments and achieved simplicity; the meshes of the law were spread so far apart that a whale could have passed through. The law officials were honest and simple-hearted and did not indulge in evil, and the common people were orderly and content. So we see that good government depends upon virtue, not harshness.

In the time of Empress Lü we find one instance of a harsh official, a man named Hou Feng who oppressed the members of the imperial family and committed outrages against the high officials, but when the Lü clan was overthrown, he and all his family were arrested and done away with. Again, in the reign of Emperor Ching, we have the case of Ch'ao Ts'o who, combining learning with natural ability, was noted for his sternness. When the leaders of the Seven Kingdoms rose in revolt, however, they used their resentment against Ch'ao Ts'o as an excuse, and in the end Ch'ao Ts'o was executed. After him came such men as Chih Tu and Ning Ch'eng.

Chih Tu

Chih Tu was a native of Yang. He served as a palace attendant under Emperor Wen, and in the time of Emperor Ching was made a general of palace attendants. He had no qualms about voicing his criticisms openly and contradicting the high ministers to their faces at court.

Once he was attending the emperor on an outing to the Shang-lin Park. Madam Chia, one of the emperor's concubines, had retired to the toilet when suddenly a wild boar rushed into the privy. The emperor signaled to Chih Tu to do something, but he refused to move, whereupon the emperor himself seized a weapon and was about to go to her rescue in person. Chih Tu flung himself on the ground before the emperor and said, "If you lose one lady in waiting, we will bring you another! The empire is full of women like Madam Chia. But what about Your Majesty? Though you think lightly of your own safety, what will become of the temples of your ancestors and of the empress dowager?"

With this, the emperor turned back, and the boar also withdrew. When the empress dowager heard of the incident, she rewarded Chih Tu with a gift of a hundred catties of gold. From this time on the emperor treated Chih Tu with great respect.

At this time the Chien clan of Chi-nan, consisting of over three hundred households, was notorious for its power and lawlessness, and none of the two-thousand-picul[1] officials could do anything to control it. Emperor Ching thereupon appointed Chih Tu as governor of Chi-nan. As soon as he reached the province, he executed the worst offenders among the Chien clan, along with the members of their families, and the rest were all overwhelmed with fear. After a year or so under Chih Tu's rule no one in the province dared even to pick up belongings that had been

---

[1] An official rank commanding a 2,000 picul salary. A picul is the weight a man can carry with a shoulder pole. One picul equals 100 catties. [Ed.]

dropped in the road, and the governors of the ten or twelve provinces in the neighborhood looked up to Chih Tu with awe as though he were one of the highest ministers of the court.

Chih Tu was a man of great daring and vigor. He was scrupulously honest and public-minded, and would never deign even to break the seal on letters addressed to him by private individuals. He refused to accept gifts from others or to listen to special requests, but always used to say, "I turned my back on parents and kin when I took office. All that remains for me to do is to fulfill my duties and die, if necessary, to maintain my integrity as an official." To the end of his life he never gave a thought to his wife or family.

Later, Chih Tu was moved to the post of military commander of the capital. The chancellor Chou Ya-fu, the marquis of T'iao, was at the height of his power and behaved with great arrogance, but whenever Chih Tu appeared before Chou Ya-fu, he would only greet Chou Ya-fu with a low bow instead of the customary prostration.

At this time the common people were still simple-hearted and ingenuous; they had a genuine fear of breaking the law and took care to stay out of trouble. Chih Tu alone among the officials put sternness and severity above all other qualities and when it came to applying the letter of the law he made no exception even for the emperor's in-laws. The feudal lords and members of the imperial family all eyed him askance and nicknamed him "The Green Hawk."

Liu Jung, the king of Lin-chiang, was ordered to come to Ch'ang-an and report to the office of the military commander of the capital to answer a list of charges which Chih Tu had drawn up against him. When he arrived, he asked if he might have a brush and scraper to write a letter of apology to the emperor, but Chih Tu forbade the clerks to give him any writing implements. Tou Ying, the marquis of Weioh'i, however, sent someone to slip the writing implements to the king in secret, and so he was able to write his letter of apology, after which he committed suicide. When Empress Dowager Tou heard of this she was furious and managed to have charges brought against Chih Tu. He was obliged to resign his post and retire to his home. Emperor Ching then dispatched an envoy bearing the imperial credentials to honor Chih Tu with the post of governor of Yen-men Province on the northern border. Because of the empress dowager's anger, the emperor did not require Chih Tu to come to the capital to receive the appointment but allowed him to proceed directly from his home to Yen-men and to carry out his new duties as he saw fit.

The Hsiung-nu had long heard of Chih Tu's strict loyalty and integrity, and when he arrived in Yen-men they withdrew their troops from the border; as long as Chih Tu was alive they would not come near the province. The Hsiung-nu leaders even went so far as to fashion a wooden image of Chih Tu which they ordered their mounted archers to use as a target for practice; but none of them were able to hit it, such was the fear that he inspired in them. He was a constant source of worry to the Hsiung-nu.

Empress Dowager Tou, however, finally managed to find some legal pretext for bringing charges against Chih Tu once more. "Chih Tu is a loyal subject," the emperor said to her, "and I would like to pardon him." But the empress dowager replied, "And the king of Lin-chiang—was he not a loyal subject too?" So in the end Chih Tu was executed.

Ning Ch'eng

Ning Ch'eng was a native of Jang. He served under Emperor Ching as a palace attendant and master of guests. He was a man of great spirit. As long as he was a petty official, he thought of nothing but how he could outdo his superiors, and when he himself became a master of others, he treated the men under him like so much soggy firewood to be bound and bundled into shape. By cunning, knavery, and displays of might, he gradually advanced until he had reached the post of chief commandant of Chi-nan.

At this time Chih Tu was the governor of Chi-nan. The men who had previously held the post of chief commandant of Chi-nan had always dismounted from their carriages and entered the governor's office on foot, requesting the clerks to grant them an interview with the governor as though they were no more than magistrates of districts; such was the awe with which they approached Chih Tu. When Ning Ch'eng took over as chief commandant, however, he soon made it clear that he was not only equal to Chih Tu but could outdo him. Chih Tu had long heard of Ning Ch'eng's reputation and was careful to treat him very well, so that the two became fast friends.

Some years later Chih Tu was executed, and the emperor, worried about the large number of outrages and crimes being committed by the members of the imperial family living in the capital, summoned Ning Ch'eng to Ch'ang-an and appointed him as military commander of the capital. In restoring order, he imitated the Ways of Chih Tu, though he was no match for Chih Tu in integrity. It was not long, however, before every member of the imperial family and of the other powerful clans was trembling in awe of him.

When Emperor Wu came to the throne he transferred Ning Ch'eng to the post of prefect of the capital. The emperor's in-laws, however, were assiduous in pointing out Ning Ch'eng's faults and finally managed to have him convicted of some crime. His head was shaved and he was forced to wear a convict's collar about his neck. At this time it was customary for any of the high officials who had been accused of a capital offense to commit suicide; very few of them would ever submit to actual punishment. Ning Ch'eng, however, allowed himself to be subjected to the severest punishment. Considering that he would never again be able to hold public office, he contrived to free himself from his convict's collar, forged the credentials needed to get him through the Pass, and escaped to his home in the east.

"An official who can't advance to a salary of two thousand piculs or a merchant who can't make at least ten million cash is not fit to be called a man!" he declared. With this he bought a thousand or so *ch'ing* of hillside farm land on credit and hired several thousand poor families to work it for him. After a few years a general amnesty was issued, absolving him from his former offenses. By this time he had accumulated a fortune of several thousand pieces of gold. He did any sort of daring feat that took his fancy, since he knew all the faults of the officials in the area. Whenever he went out he was accompanied by twenty or thirty mounted attendants, and he ordered the people of the area about with greater authority than the governor of the province.

3

CONFUCIUS

The Analects, c. 479–221 B.C.E.

Creating and governing an empire requires ideas as much as soldiers and officials. The ideas of Confucius (551–479 B.C.E.), compiled after his death by his disciples in *The Analects*, played a crucial role in the governance of the Chinese Empire from at least the time of the Han dynasty. Notice how the great Han historian Sima Qian began the previous selection with a quote from Confucius. Candidates for official positions in the empire studied the writings attributed to Confucius in order to pass the civil service exams that originated in the Han dynasty. In one sense this might seem a bit strange. Confucius lived long before the Qin establishment of the empire. His world was feudal: Authority was personal, based on family or clan ties, and divided among various competing states. His emphasis on filial piety (duty of sons to fathers, worship of ancestors, and respect of elders) reflects that feudal society. Nevertheless, Confucianism became the bedrock ideology for the governance of the empire. What would be

Source: *The Chinese Classics*, trans. James Legge (New York: John B. Alden, Publisher, 1890), 13–14, 16, 18–19, 64–66, 70–71.

the appeal of these ideas to a Chinese emperor? Which ideas in particular would be useful in governing the empire?

The First Emperor of Qin who unified China was not a follower of Confucius. In fact, at one point he had Confucian writings burned. Why might an empire creator be less attracted to the ideas of Confucius? Which ideas expressed in this selection might bother an aggressive conqueror?

THINKING HISTORICALLY

The set of ideas that serve a particular political interest or function is called an ideology. Based on your reading of the previous chapter, how was the ruling ideology of classical Greece different from that of Han China? How was the dominant Brahman Hindu ideology of classical India different from that of Han China? Is there an equivalent modern American ideology that supports the government of the United States in the world?

On Government by Moral Force

I, 5. The Master [Confucius] said, "To rule a country of a thousand chariots, there must be reverent attention to business, and sincerity; economy in expenditure, and love for men; and the employment of the people at the proper seasons."

II, 3. The Master said, "If the people be led by laws, and uniformity sought to be given them by punishments, they will try to avoid the punishment, but have no sense of shame. If they be led by virtue, and uniformity sought to be given them by the rules of propriety, they will have the sense of shame, and moreover will become good."

XII, 11. The Duke Ching, of Ch'i, asked Confucius about government. Confucius replied, "There is government, when the prince is prince, and the minister is minister; when the father is father, and the son is son." "Good!" said the duke, "If, indeed; the prince be not prince, the minister not minister, the father not father, and the son not son, although I have my revenue, can I enjoy it?"

XII, 19. Chi K'ang asked Confucius about government, saying, "What do you say to killing the unprincipled for the good of the principled?" Confucius replied, "Sir, in carrying on your government, why should you use killing at all? Let your evinced desires be for what is good, and the people will be good. The relation between superiors and inferiors is like that between the wind and the grass. The grass must bend, when the wind blows across it."

XIII, 6. The Master said, "When a prince's personal conduct is correct, his government is effective without the issuing of orders. If his personal conduct is not correct, he may issue orders, but they will not be followed."

XIII, 10. The Master said, "If there were (any of the princes) who would employ me, in the course of twelve months, I should have done something considerable. In three years, the government would be perfected."

XIII, 11. The Master said, "'If good men were to govern a country in succession for a hundred years, they would be able to transform the violently bad, and dispense with capital punishments.' True indeed is this saying!"

On Public Opinion

II, 19. The Duke Ai asked, saying, "What should be done in order to secure the submission of the people?" Confucius replied, "Advance the upright and set aside the crooked, then the people will submit. Advance the crooked and set aside the upright, then the people will not submit."

II, 20. Chi K'ang asked how to cause the people to reverence their ruler, to be faithful to him, and to go on to nerve themselves to virtue. The Master said, "Let him preside over them with gravity;—then they will reverence him. Let him be filial and kind to all;—then they will be faithful to him. Let him advance the good and teach the incompetent;—then they will eagerly seek to be virtuous."

XII, 7. Tsze-kung asked about government. The Master said, "The requisites of government are that there be sufficiency of food, sufficiency of military equipment, and the confidence of the people in their ruler." Tsze-kung said, "If it cannot be helped, and one of these must be dispensed with, which of the three should be foregone first?" "The military equipment," said the Master. Tsze-kung again asked, "If it cannot be helped, and one of the remaining two must be dispensed with, which of them should be foregone?" The Master answered, "Part with the food. From of old, death has been the lot of all men; but if the people have no faith in their rulers, there is no standing for the state."

4

HAN FEI

Legalism, c. 230 B.C.E.

Legalism was the alternative to Confucianism that appealed to the First Emperor of the Qin dynasty. Han Fei (280–233 B.C.E.) had been raised on Confucianism but broke with the tradition as he developed very different ideas about human nature and government. A son of a noble family from the enemy state of Han, Han Fei fell under suspicion

Source: *Sources of Chinese Tradition,* comp. William Theodore de Bary et al. (New York: Columbia University Press, 1963), 1: 127–29, 133–35.

as an advisor of the Qin king Zheng, who became First Emperor. His rival had him arrested and poisoned. The following was taken from the *Han Fei Tzu* (Master Han Fei), as his collected political essays have become known. What is Han Fei's criticism of Confucianism? How would you characterize the ideas of Han Fei? How might these ideas appeal to an empire-builder like the First Emperor?

THINKING HISTORICALLY

To fully understand Han Fei's argument, you need to consider them in relation to those of Confucius. Compare this document to the previous one. Just how different are Han Fei's ideas from those of Confucius? What aspects of Legalism would you expect empire-builders in history to find appealing? Think of two very different rulers from history and compare how they did or did not apply aspects of Legalism to their rule. Do empires require Legalists? Do they require Moralists?

When the sage rules the state, he does not count on people doing good of themselves, but employs such measures as will keep them from doing any evil. If he counts on people doing good of themselves, there will not be enough such people to be numbered by the tens in the whole country. But if he employs such measures as will keep them from doing evil, then the entire state can be brought up to a uniform standard. Inasmuch as the administrator has to consider the many but disregard the few, he does not busy himself with morals but with laws.

Evidently, if one should have to count on arrows which are straight of themselves, there would not be any arrows in a hundred generations; if one should only count on pieces of wood which are circular of themselves, there would not be any wheels in a thousand generations. Though in a hundred generations there is neither an arrow that is straight of itself nor a wheel that is circular of itself, yet people in every generation ride carts and shoot birds. Why is that? It is because the tools for straightening and bending are used. Though without the use of such tools there might happen to be an arrow straight of itself or a wheel circular of itself, the skilled carpenter will not prize it. Why? Because it is not just one person who wishes to ride, or just one shot that the archers wish to shoot. Similarly, though without the use of rewards and punishments there might happen to be an individual good of himself, the intelligent ruler will not prize him. The reason is that the law of the state must not be sidetracked and government is not for one man. Therefore, the capable prince will not be swayed by occasional virtue, but will pursue a course that will assure certainty. . . .

Now, when witches and priests pray for people, they say: "May you live as long as one thousand and ten thousand years!" . . . [T]here is no sign that even a single day has been added to the age of any man. That is the reason why people despise witches and priests. Likewise, when the Confucianists of the present day counsel the rulers they do not discuss the way to bring about order now, but exalt the achievement of good order in the past. They neither study affairs pertaining to law and government nor observe the realities of vice and wickedness, but all exalt the reputed glories of remote antiquity and the achievements of the ancient kings. Sugar-coating their speech, the Confucianists say: "If you listen to our words, you will be able to become the leader of all feudal lords." Such people are but witches and priests among the itinerant counselors, and are not to be accepted by rulers with principles. Therefore, the intelligent ruler upholds solid facts and discards useless frills. He does not speak about deeds of humanity and righteousness, and he does not listen to the words of learned men.

Those who are ignorant about government insistently say: "Win the hearts of the people." If order could be procured by winning the hearts of the people, then even the wise ministers Yi Yin and Kuan Chung would be of no use. For all that the ruler would need to do would be just to listen to the people. Actually, the intelligence of the people is not to be relied upon any more than the mind of a baby. If the baby does not have his head shaved, his sores will recur; if he does not have his boil cut open, his illness will go from bad to worse. However, in order to shave his head or open the boil someone has to hold the baby while the affectionate mother is performing the work, and yet he keeps crying and yelling incessantly. The baby does not understand that suffering a small pain is the way to obtain a great benefit.

Now, the sovereign urges the tillage of land and the cultivation of pastures for the purpose of increasing production for the people, but they think the sovereign is cruel. The sovereign regulates penalties and increases punishments for the purpose of repressing the wicked, but the people think the sovereign is severe. Again, he levies taxes in cash and in grain to fill up the granaries and treasuries in order to relieve famine and provide for the army, but they think the sovereign is greedy. Finally, he insists upon universal military training without personal favoritism, and urges his forces to fight hard in order to take the enemy captive, but the people think the sovereign is violent. These four measures are methods for attaining order and maintaining peace, but the people are too ignorant to appreciate them. . . .

The literati by means of letters upset laws; the cavaliers[1] by means of their prowess transgress prohibitions. Yet the ruler treats them both with decorum. This is actually the cause of all the disorder. Every

---

[1] Horse-mounted soldiers, knights. [Ed.]

departure from the law ought to be apprehended, and yet scholars are nevertheless taken into office on account of their literary learning. Again, the transgression of every prohibition ought to be censured, and yet cavaliers are patronized because of their readiness to draw the sword. Thus, those whom the law reproves turn out to be those whom the ruler employs, and those whom the magistrates suppress are those whom the sovereign patronizes. Thus legal standard and personal inclination as well as ruler and ministers are sharply opposed to each other and all fixed standards are lost. Then, even if there were ten Yellow Emperors,[2] they would not be able to establish any order. Therefore, those who practice humanity and righteousness should not be upheld, for if upheld, they would hinder concrete accomplishments. Again, those who specialize in refinement and learning should not be employed, for if employed, they would disturb the laws. There was in Ch'u an upright man named Kung, who, when his father stole a sheep, reported it to the authorities. The magistrate said: "Put him to death," as he thought the man was faithful to the ruler but disloyal to his father. So the man was apprehended and convicted. From this we can see that the faithful subject of the ruler was an outrageous son to his father. Again, there was a man of Lu who followed his ruler to war, fought three battles, and ran away three times. Confucius interrogated him. The man replied: "I have an old father. Should I die, nobody would take care of him." Confucius regarded him as virtuous in filial piety, commended and exalted him. From this we can see that the dutiful son of the father was a rebellious subject to the ruler. Naturally, following the censure of the honest man by the magistrate, no more culprits in Ch'u were reported to the authorities; and following the reward of the runaway by Confucius, the people of Lu were prone to surrender and run away. The interests of superior and subordinate being so different, it would be hopeless for any ruler to try to exalt the deeds of private individuals and, at the same time, to promote the public welfare of the state. . . .

Today one cannot count even ten men of devotion and faithfulness, yet official posts in the country are counted by the hundreds. If only men of devotion and faithfulness were appointed to office, there would be an insufficiency of candidates, and in that case guardians of order would be few, while disturbers of peace would be many. Therefore the way of the enlightened sovereign consists in making laws uniform and not depending upon the wisdom of men, in making statecraft firm and not yearning after faithful persons, so that the laws do not fail to function and the multitude of officials will commit neither villainy nor deception. . . .

---

[2] Legendary Chinese ruler and culture hero. [Ed.]

5

A Record of the Debate on Salt and Iron, 81 B.C.E.

In 81 B.C.E. the Han emperor Zhao held a debate on the economic policies of the preceding Emperor Wu. The debate centered on the question of whether or not the previous emperor's government monopolies, in salt, iron, and liquor, should be continued or abolished. Those in favor of continuing government control were the Legalists, represented by the Imperial Secretary Sang Hongyang. Those in favor of returning the production and distribution of these products to private hands were the Confucians, called the Literati. The following document records the debates between these two sides. What were the arguments in favor of government monopoly? What were the arguments against? In what ways was this also a debate about empire?

THINKING HISTORICALLY

The question of the proper role of government in the economy has been debated down to the present day. How was this salt and iron debate similar to, and different from, recent debates about the role of government in the American or European economy?

In the sixth year of the era Shiyuan [81 B.C.E.], an imperial edict was issued directing the chancellor and the imperial secretaries to confer with the worthies and literati who had been recommended to the government and to inquire into the grievances and hardships of the people.

The literati responded: We have heard that the way to govern men is to prevent evil and error at their source, to broaden the beginnings of morality, to discourage secondary occupations, and open the way for the exercise of humaneness and rightness. Never should material profit appear as a motive of government. Only then can moral instruction succeed and the customs of the people be reformed. But now in the provinces the salt, iron, and liquor monopolies, and the system of equitable marketing have been established to compete with the people for profit, dispelling rustic generosity and teaching the people greed. Therefore those who pursue primary occupations [farming] have grown few and those following secondary occupations [trading] numerous.

Source: *Sources of Chinese Tradition*, compiled by Wm. Theodore de Bary and Irene Bloom, 2nd ed., vol. 1 (New York: Columbia University Press, 1999), 360–64. © 1999 Columbia University Press.

As artifice increases, basic simplicity declines; and as the secondary occupations flourish, those that are primary suffer. When the secondary
is practiced the people grow decadent, but when the primary is practiced they are simple and sincere. When the people are sincere then
there will be sufficient wealth and goods, but when they become extravagant then famine and cold will follow. We recommend that the
salt, iron, and liquor monopolies and the system of equitable marketing be abolished so that primary pursuits may be advanced and secondary ones suppressed. This will have the advantage of increasing the
profitableness of agriculture.

His Lordship [the Imperial Secretary Sang Hongyang] replied: The
Xiongnu have frequently revolted against our sovereignty and pillaged
our borders. If we are to defend ourselves, then it means the hardships
of war for the soldiers of China, but if we do not defend ourselves properly, then their incursions cannot be stopped. The former emperor [Wu]
took pity upon the people of the border areas who for so long had
suffered disaster and hardship and had been carried off as captives.
Therefore he set up defense stations, established a system of warning
beacons, and garrisoned the outlying areas to ensure their protection.
But the resources of these areas were insufficient, and so he established
the salt, iron, and liquor monopolies and the system of equitable marketing in order to raise more funds for expenditures at the borders. Now
our critics, who desire that these measures be abolished, would empty
the treasuries and deplete the funds used for defense. They would have
the men who are defending our passes and patrolling our walls suffer
hunger and cold. How else can we provide for them? Abolition of these
measures is not expedient!

His Lordship stated: In former times the peers residing in the provinces sent in their respective products as tribute, but there was much
confusion and trouble in transporting them and the goods were often
of such poor quality that they were not worth the cost of transportation. For this reason transportation offices have been set up in each
district to handle delivery and shipping and to facilitate the presentation of tribute from outlying areas. Therefore the system is called
"equitable marketing." Warehouses have been opened in the capital
for the storing of goods, buying when prices are low and selling when
they are high. Thereby the government suffers no loss and the merchants cannot speculate for profit. Therefore this is called the "balanced level" [stabilization]. With the balanced level the people are
protected from unemployment, and with equitable marketing the
burden of labor service is equalized. Thus these measures are designed
to ensure an equal distribution of goods and to benefit the people and
are not intended to open the way to profit or provide the people with
a ladder to crime.

The literati replied: In ancient times taxes and levies took from the people what they were skilled in producing and did not demand what they were poor at. Thus the husbandmen sent in their harvests and the weaving women their goods. Nowadays the government disregards what people have and requires of them what they have not, so that they are forced to sell their goods at a cheap price in order to meet the demands from above. . . . The farmers suffer double hardships and the weaving women are taxed twice. We have not seen that this kind of marketing is "equitable." The government officials go about recklessly opening closed doors and buying everything at will so they can corner all the goods. With goods cornered prices soar, and when prices soar the merchants make their own deals for profit. The officials wink at powerful racketeers, and the rich merchants hoard commodities and wait for an emergency. With slick merchants and corrupt officials buying cheap and selling dear we have not seen that your level is "balanced." The system of equitable marketing of ancient times was designed to equalize the burden of labor upon the people and facilitate the transporting of tribute. It did not mean dealing in all kinds of commodities for the sake of profit.

The Literati Attack Legalist Philosophy

The literati spoke: He who is good with a chisel can shape a round hole without difficulty; he who is good at laying foundations can build to a great height without danger of collapse. The statesman Yi Yin made the ways of Yao and Shun the foundation of the Yin dynasty, and its heirs succeeded to the throne for a hundred generations without break. But Shang Yang made heavy penalties and harsh laws the foundation of the Qin state and with the Second Emperor it was destroyed. Not satisfied with the severity of the laws, he instituted the system of mutual responsibility, made it a crime to criticize the government, and increased corporal punishments until the people were so terrified they did not know where to put their hands and feet. Not content with the manifold taxes and levies, he prohibited the people from using the resources of forests and rivers and made a hundredfold profit on the storage of commodities, while the people were given no chance to voice the slightest objection. Such worship of profit and slight of what is right, such exaltation of power and achievement, lent, it is true, to expansion of land and acquisition of territory. Yet it was like pouring more water upon people who are already suffering from flood and only increasing their distress. You see how Shang Yang opened the way to imperial rule for the Qin, but you fail to see how he also opened for the Qin the road to ruin!

Confucian Literati Ridiculed

His Excellency spoke: . . . Now we have with us over sixty worthy men and literati who cherish the ways of the Six Confucian Arts, fleet in thought and exhaustive in argument. It is proper, gentlemen, that you should pour forth your light and dispel our ignorance. And yet you put all your faith in the past and turn your backs upon the present, tell us of antiquity and give no thought to the state of the times. Perhaps we are not capable of recognizing true scholars. Yet do you really presume with your fancy phrases and attacks upon men of ability to pervert the truth in this manner?

See them [the Confucians] now present us with nothingness and consider it substance, with emptiness and call it plenty! In their coarse gowns and worn shoes they walk gravely along, sunk in meditation as though they had lost something. These are not men who can do great deeds and win fame. They do not even rise above the vulgar masses.

6

NICHOLAS PURCELL

Rome: The Arts of Government, 1988

The evolution of Rome to empire was somewhat different from that of China. In China, the state of Qin formed a unified state by suppressing the independent power of local kings, princes, and nobility. In other words, the First Emperor and the emperors of the Han dynasty brought an end to feudalism.

Conversely, before Rome became an empire, it was a *republic:* a unified state, not a series of competing feudal powers. The Roman Republic inherited Greek ideas of territorial sovereignty and popular government. But as Roman military power spread beyond Italy, a republican form of government became more and more untenable. Governors had to be sent to conquered provinces, soldiers had to be recruited, and taxes had to be collected from non-Romans. The authority of popular institutions of government was eclipsed first by the aristocratic senate and then by warring generals, the dictator Caesar (47–44 B.C.E.), and finally Octavian, Caesar's nephew and

---

Source: Nicholas Purcell, "The Arts of Government," in *The Oxford History of the Classical World: The Roman World,* ed. John Boardman, Jasper Griffin, and Oswyn Murray (Oxford: Oxford University Press, 1988), 154, 155, 156, 170–74, 175–77.

adopted successor, who after 27 B.C.E. declared himself Augustus (Revered) and Imperator (Emperor).

Thus, for at least one hundred years before Rome officially became an empire, it governed vast territories of conquered and allied peoples. The way in which it ruled these subjects after Augustus had been honed by generations of provincial governors and did not change significantly.

In this selection, Nicholas Purcell, a modern historian of Rome, discusses aspects of Roman imperial administration. What does he say about the government of the Roman Empire? What were the strengths and weaknesses of Roman administration?

THINKING HISTORICALLY

How would you compare and contrast Roman administration, as described by Purcell, with Chinese administration of its empire? What are the most important differences? What accounts for these differences? In what respects was Chinese government of its empire superior? In what respects was it not? What other comparative questions does this selection raise in your mind?

"And it came to pass in those days, that there went out a decree from Caesar Augustus, that all the world should be enrolled to be taxed" (Luke 2:1). The evangelist wants to emphasize the centrality in world history of the coming of the Messiah, and accordingly links the birth of Christ to the moment when the power of Rome seemed at its most universal. For him, as often for us, the power of Rome is most potently expressed by reference to its administrative activity. St. Luke, however, was wrong. We know now that no such decree commanded a universal registration of the Roman world, at this time or any other; he exaggerated Roman omnipotence on the basis of the experience of a single province. It remains extremely easy for us too to misunderstand the scope, practice, and effects of Rome's governmental procedures. We mistake patterns of decision-making for policies and take hierarchical sequences of posts for career-structures. When we find the taking of minutes or the accumulation of archives, we immediately see a bureaucracy. Virtuosity in the public service is confused with professionalism. Recent work has been able to show well how far Rome's administration failed, or could be corrupted or subverted, or simply had no effect but oppression on thousands of provincials. There have been fewer examinations of the way in which the arts of government at which the Romans thought themselves that they excelled actually worked—imposing civilization and peace, leniency to the defeated, and war to the last with the proud. . . .

Roman theories of government were not elaborate; the practice too was simple. Two broad categories cover almost all the activities of Roman rule: settling disputes between communities or individuals, and assembling men, goods, or money—jurisdiction and exaction. Antiquity recognized three main types of authority: magistrate, soldier, and master of a household; and all governmental activity in the Roman Empire can be linked with one of these. The first, deriving from the Greek city, covers both the immemorial officers of the city-state which Rome had been and the magistrates of the hundreds of essentially self-governing cities which made up nearly all the Roman Empire. In a *polis* magistrates ran the military; at Rome the usual citizen militia became under the Empire a permanent, institutionally separate army, whose officers played an ever greater part in government culminating in the militarization of the third century. Finally, in a slave-owning society the type of authority exercised within the household was naturally recognizably different, and also came to be of considerable importance in government. . . . [I]t was always through activities which we would hesitate to call governmental that Roman rule was most effectively maintained: through the involvement of the upper classes in public religion, spectacles, impressive patronage of architecture, philosophy, literature, painting; and in civil benefactions all over the Empire. The civilizing and beneficial effects of this should be remembered as we move on to find the actual administrative and executive structure of the Empire erratic and illiberal.

Rome had from the earliest times enjoyed very close contacts with the Greek world, and had, like most ancient cities, a tripartite political structure of magistrates, council (the Senate), and popular assembly. The importance of the last for our purpose is that its early power produced the uniquely Roman and constitutionally vital concept of *imperium*. The Roman people conferred upon its chosen magistrates the right to command it and the sanctions against disobedience—ever more strictly circumscribed—of corporal and capital punishment of its members. . . .

This is why Rome long retained the habit of dealing with her subjects with the respect deserved by the free, and why Roman rule so long remained indirect. To the end of antiquity most of the cities of the Empire and their territories were ruled by local magistrates many of whose domestic executive actions were taken as if they were independent; indeed they often needed to be reminded that there were limits to the licence they were allowed. Similarly Rome also long tolerated local kings and dynasts, and the survival of these dependent kingdoms and free cities contributed much to the fuzzy informality of the power structure of the Empire before the age of the Antonines.[1] . . .

---

[1] 96–192 C.E., period of Roman imperial peace and prosperity; emperors included Trajan (r. 98–117), Hadrian (r. 117–138), and Marcus Aurelius (r. 161–180). [Ed.]

The search for bureaucracy in the Roman world is vain. We should now look a little more closely at the concern with jurisdiction and exaction which Roman administrators really did have. Then, in conclusion, we can consider in general terms the nature of the governmental process and attempt to discover what really held the empire together.

Because Roman officials spent so much time in jurisdiction it was natural that Roman law should become more complicated and more sophisticated. The natural rule that jurisdiction gravitates to the highest available authority operated to increase the workload of governors, the great prefects at Rome, and the Emperor himself, and to hasten the adoption of Roman law. Even in the reign of Augustus,[2] Strabo[3] can already write that Crete, despite its own venerable legal tradition, had come, like all the provinces, to use the laws of Rome (10.4.22). And the bitterest realism about conditions in the Roman Empire cannot overlook the advantages of the existence of a legal framework to imperial rule, which the Hellenistic kingdoms had lacked, and which offered the Empire's subjects at least the theoretical possibility of redress and restrained the arbitrariness of Rome's rule. Law too grew at Rome with the problems first of city and then of Empire, and legal expertise came to provide an entry to the governing class. Professional legal practice was eventually one of the activities which gave many provincials a place in government, and Roman law was one of the most tenacious legacies of imperial rule — its greatest codification was the product of the eastern Empire under Justinian. There is not space here to recount the gradual evolution of Roman law, but the long accumulation of legal interpretations and precedents in the annual edicts of the praetors,[4] which, when codified by Hadrian,[5] formed the foundation of the legal system, and the role of the Emperor as a source of law and patron of the great jurists of the late second and early third centuries need stressing. For our purposes, however, two connected things are important. First, at Rome there was no question of the separation of judiciary and legislature which is so important a liberal principle to modern political thinkers. The law at Rome was on the whole the creation of judges, not lawgivers. The second point follows from this: legal measures show the same variety, casualness, and lack of generality which we find in Roman administrative decisions, and indeed it is difficult to separate the two. There is no proper ancient equivalent of statute law. The result was that the law was not always sufficiently universal, and the underprivileged might well not reap its

[2] Founder of Roman Empire, first of Julio-Claudian line of emperors; ruled as emperor from 27 B.C.E. to 14 C.E. [Ed.]

[3] Greek geographer and historian (63 B.C.E.–21 C.E.). [Ed.]

[4] Roman officials concerned with jurisdiction (law and administration); originally military; magistrates. [Ed.]

[5] Roman emperor (r. 117–138 C.E.). [Ed.]

benefits. Jewish nationalist writers, for example, compare the hypocrisy of Rome to the ambiguous associations of the unclean pig: "Just as a pig lies down and sticks out its trotters as though to say 'I am clean' [because they are cloven], so the evil empire robs and oppresses while pretending to execute justice."

For the burdens of Roman rule on the Empire were heavy and hated, and much of Roman government was devoted to ensuring their efficacy. The collection of tribute, direct and indirect tax, rents, levies in kind, recruits, protection money, requisitioning, and so on in total amounted to a very heavy oppression, even if the amount of tax formally due was not by comparative standards very high. Roman officials from the highest to the most menial were involved with these matters, and finance was a serious administrative concern. Augustus' great catalogue of his achievements is called in full *Res Gestae et Impensae* ("His Deeds and Expenditure"). And this is undoubtedly the view that most provincials had of the way the Empire worked. A prophecy of Rome's fall concentrated on both the exactions of the ruling power and the — less often discussed but equally odious — drain of manpower to Italy via the slave trade: "the wealth that Rome has received from tributary Asia threefold shall Asia receive again from Rome, which will pay in full the price of its insolent pride. And for each of those who labour in the land of the Italians twenty Italians shall toil in Asia as needy slaves" (*Oracula Sibyllina* 3.350 f.). Given this hostility to the harsh realities of the Empire, and given the amateur nature of Roman government, how was stability achieved?

Communications have been described as the nervous system of the body politic. Compared with what had gone before and what followed the rule of Rome, the frequency of movement and the security of roads and harbours was most impressive (though banditry never completely disappeared even from Italy). The imperial posting system, a creation of Augustus refined over the following centuries, became so huge, authoritative, and elaborate that it represented one of the heaviest burdens on the provincials whose food, animals, and dwellings were constantly being requisitioned for passing officials, as inscriptions from a wide range of places and times bear eloquent witness. But there can be no doubt that the roads and harbours of the Empire were one of the most necessary organs of Roman rule.

The transmission, retrieval, and storage of information is a still more basic ingredient of the stability, durability, and effectiveness of government. [German sociologist] Max Weber called documents the bureaucrat's tools of production. The Roman Empire has won a reputation for bureaucratic sophistication. So what of its documents? . . .

The documents were stored in archive rooms, some of which are known archaeologically. But although papers were kept, there were no filing cabinets, card indexes, reference numbers, registration forms.

Collections of documents were made by pasting them together in chronological or—by no means as often as convenience would dictate—in alphabetical order. The codex, the presentation of documents as a book, was occasionally used, but the cartulary, a choice of really important documents for frequent reference, was unknown. Papers were preserved in archives, but it was well known that in most conditions papyrus did not keep well. Why did these things not matter? Because retrieval of documents from the archive was not a particularly urgent consideration in its formation. The tax assessment notice, the letter from the commanding officer, the tax receipt, the birth registration were used only once, in the process of checking a particular tax collection, or implementing a decision. Access to the document *might* be required a second time, but probably only a tiny fraction of all documents was ever looked at twice. The consultation of a document was a serious matter: "for which reason, pious and benevolent Caesar, order that I be given a copy from your *commentarii* as your father intended" says a petitioner to Hadrian. Administrative processes were a favour, a privilege, a wonder, which is why on documents like this, where only what does credit to the purchaser of the inscription appears, what seem to us to be banal details of this kind are recorded in full. So this one actually preserves Hadrian's orders to his secretaries: "Stasimus, Dapenis, publish the decision or opinion from the recorded version (*edite ex forma*)." Authentication was a serious problem, never entirely solved, which helped prevent reliance on documentary authority. The *sardonychus* or imperial signet-ring gave its name to a Palatine department[6]. . . , but there were often rumours that it had fallen into unauthorized hands. The Emperors used codes, but only rather simple ones. One of the principal reasons for the abuse of the public post system was that there was no reliable way of ensuring that only a limited number of people possessed authentic licences to demand hospitality and service. Distribution was another problem. It is very hard for us to imagine how difficult, despite the efficiency of communications, the systematic exchange of documentary information was. A letter of Trajan to Pliny[7] making an important administrative point need never have been known in next door Asia, let alone Germania Inferior. This is perhaps one reason why Pliny's heirs actually published his correspondence. This difficulty no doubt helped to discourage the formation of any monolithic imperial administrative structure.

Documents, once stored, were of surprisingly little use. Governmental acts could not afford to depend on such an unreliable basis. The

---

[6] Department of the palace administration of the Caesars (emperors). [Ed.]

[7] Pliny was an official for the emperor Trajan (r. 98–117 C.E.). The two kept up an extensive correspondence, an example of which is included in selection 8. [Ed.]

archives represented continuity and stability, and were not for regular use. The truth appears well from the story of the disastrous fire of A.D. 192 at Rome, when the central imperial archives of the Palatine were completely destroyed. . . . There is no hint that Roman government was disrupted; but the event was taken as a token that the authority of Rome, embodied in these documents, would weaken. The omen is not so far removed from the association of Rome's universal rule with a census registration at the beginning of the Gospel of St. Luke. . . .

7

CICERO

Letter to His Brother Quintus, 60 B.C.E.

Marcus Tullius Cicero (106–43 B.C.E.) was the most renowned orator and statesman of the late Roman Republic. As a lawyer and champion of the Roman constitution, Cicero fought against tyranny and political corruption, yet he opposed the assassins of Julius Caesar, and in the subsequent civil war he supported Caesar's adopted son, Octavian, against Mark Antony, a move that ultimately cost him his life.

In this selection, Cicero advises his younger brother Quintus (102–43 B.C.E.) who had been re-appointed by the Roman Senate to be Magistrate of the Province of Asia on what to expect and how to behave as a Roman official. What advice does he give his brother? What does this advice tell you about the life of a Roman official in the empire? What does it tell you about Roman administration of the empire?

THINKING HISTORICALLY

In what ways was the professional life of Quintus Cicero different from that of a Chinese official? How was the relationship between a Roman administrator like Quintus and his assistants different from the relationship of a Chinese official and his assistants? What other comparisons or contrasts between the Roman and Chinese empires does this selection raise in your mind?

Source: *The Letters of Cicero, Vol. I, B.C. 68–52,* translated by Evelyn Shuckburgh (London: George Bell and Sons, 1899).

I. . . . I begin by entreating you not to let your soul shrink and be cast down, nor to allow yourself to be overpowered by the magnitude of the business as though by a wave; but, on the contrary, to stand upright and keep your footing, or even advance to meet the flood of affairs. For you are not administering a department of the state, in which fortune reigns supreme, but one in which a well-considered policy and an attention to business are the most important things. But if I had seen you receiving the prolongation of a command in a great and dangerous war, I should have trembled in spirit, because I should have known that the dominion of fortune over us had been at the same time prolonged. As it is, however, a department of the state has been entrusted to you in which fortune occupies no part, or, at any rate, an insignificant one, and which appears to me to depend entirely on your virtue and self-control. We have no reason to fear, as far as I know, any designs of our enemies, any actual fighting in the field, any revolts of allies, any default in the tribute or in the supply of corn, any mutiny in the army: things which have very often befallen the wisest of men in such a way, that they have been no more able to get the better of the assault of fortune than the best of pilots a violent tempest. You have been granted profound peace, a dead calm: yet if the pilot falls asleep, it may even so overwhelm him, though if he keeps awake it may give him positive pleasure. For your province consists, in the first place, of allies of a race which; of all the world, is the most civilized; and, in the second place, of Citizens, who, either as being publicani are very closely connected with me, or, as being traders who have made money, think that they owe the security of their property to my consulship.

II. But it may be said that among even such men as these there occur serious disputes, many wrongful acts are committed, and hotly contested litigation is the result. As though I ever thought that you had no trouble to contend with! I know that the trouble is exceedingly great, and such as demands the very greatest prudence; but remember that it is prudence much more than fortune on which, in my opinion, the result of your trouble depends. For what trouble is it to govern those over whom you are set, if you do but govern yourself? That may be a great and difficult task to others, and indeed it is most difficult: to you it has always been the easiest thing in the world, and indeed ought to be so, for your natural disposition is such that, even without discipline, it appears capable of self-control; whereas a discipline has, in fact, been applied that might educate the most faulty of characters. But while you resist, as you do, money, pleasure, and every kind of desire yourself, there will, I am to be told, be a risk of your not being able to suppress some fraudulent banker or some rather over-extortionate tax-collector! For as to the Greeks, they will think, as they behold the innocence of your life, that one of the heroes of their history, or a demigod from heaven, has come down into the province. And this I say, not to induce you to act thus, but to make you glad that you are acting or have acted so. It is a splendid thing to have been three years in supreme power in Asia without allowing statue, picture, plate, napery, slave, anyone's good looks, or any offer of money—all of which are plentiful in your province—to cause you to swerve from the most absolute honesty and purity of life. What can be imagined so striking or so desirable as that a virtue, a command over the passions, a self-control such as yours, are not remaining in darkness and obscurity, but have been set in the broad daylight of Asia, before the eyes of a famous province, and in the hearing of all nations and peoples? That the inhabitants are not being ruined by your progresses, drained by your charges, agitated by your approach? That there is the liveliest joy, public and private, wheresoever you come, the city regarding you as a protector and not a tyrant, the private house as a guest and not a plunderer?

III. But in these matters I am sure that mere experience has by this time taught you that it is by no means sufficient to have these virtues yourself, but that you must keep your eyes open and vigilant, in order that in the guardianship of your province you may be considered to vouch to the allies, the citizens, and the state, not for yourself alone, but for all the subordinates of your government. However, you have in the persons of your legati men likely to have a regard for their own reputation. Of these in rank, position, and age Tubero is first; who, I think, particularly as he is a writer of history, could select from his own Annals many whom he would like and would be able to imitate. Allienus, again, is ours, as well in heart and affection, as in his conformity to our principles. I need not speak of Gratidius: I am sure that, while taking pains to preserve his own reputation, his fraternal affection for us makes him take pains for ours also. Your quaestor is not of your own selection, but the one assigned you by lot. He is bound both to act with propriety of his own accord, and to conform to the policy and principles which you lay down. But should any one of these adopt a lower standard of conduct, you should tolerate such behaviour, if it goes no farther than a breach, in his private capacity, of the rules by which he was bound, but not if it goes to the extent of employing for gain the authority which you granted him as a promotion. For I am far from thinking, especially since the moral sentiments of the day are so much inclined to excessive laxity and self-seeking, that you should investigate every case of petty misconduct, and thoroughly examine every one of these persons; but that you should regulate your confidence by the trustworthiness of its recipient. And among such persons you will have to vouch for those whom the Republic has itself given you as companions and assistants in public affairs, at least within the limits which I have before laid down.

IV. In the case, however, of those of your personal staff or official attendants whom you have yourself selected to be about you—who are usually spoken of as a kind of praetor's cohort—we must vouch, not only for their acts, but even for their words. But those you have with you are the sort of men of whom you may easily be fond when they are acting rightly, and whom you may very easily check when they show insufficient regard for your reputation. By these, when you were raw to the work, your frank disposition might possibly have been deceived—for the better a man is the less easily does he suspect others of being bad—now, however, let this third year witness an integrity as perfect as the two former, but still more wary and vigilant. Listen to that only which you are supposed to listen to; don't let your ears be open to whispered falsehoods and interested suggestions. Don't let your signet ring be a mere implement, but, as it were, your second self: not the minister of another's will, but a witness of your own. Let your marshal hold the rank which our ancestors wished him to hold, who, looking upon this place as not one of profit, but of labour and duty, scarcely ever conferred it upon any but their freedmen, whom they indeed controlled almost as absolutely as their slaves. Let the lictor be the dispenser of your clemency, not his own; and let the fasces and axes which they carry before you constitute ensigns rather of rank than of power. Let it, in fact, be known to the whole province that the life, children, fame, and fortunes of all over whom you preside are exceedingly dear to you. Finally, let it be believed that you will, if you detect it, be hostile not only to those who have accepted a bribe, but to those also who have given it. And, indeed, no one will give anything, if it is made quite clear that nothing is usually obtained from you through those who pretend to be very influential with you. Not, however, that the object of this discourse is to make you over-harsh or suspicious towards your staff. For if any of them in the course of the last two years has never fallen under suspicion of rapacity, as I am told about Caesius and Chaerippus and Labeo—and think it true, because I know them—there is no authority, I think, which may not be entrusted to them, and no confidence which may not be placed in them with the utmost propriety, and in anyone else like them. But if there is anyone of whom you have already had reason to doubt, or concerning whom you have made some discovery, in such a man place no confidence, intrust him with no particle of your reputation. . . .

And now, considering the caution and care that I would show in matters of this kind—in which I fear I may be somewhat over-severe— what do you suppose my sentiments are in regard to slaves? Upon these we ought to keep a hold in all places, but especially in the provinces. On this head many rules may be laid down, but this is at once the shortest and most easily maintained—that they should behave during your progresses in Asia as though you were travelling on the Appian way, and not suppose that it makes any difference whether they have arrived at

Tralles or Formiae. But if, again, any one of your slaves is conspicuously trustworthy, employ him in your domestic and private affairs; but in affairs pertaining to your office as governor, or in any department of the state, do not let him lay a finger. For many things which may, with perfect propriety, be in-trusted to slaves, must yet not be so entrusted, for the sake of avoiding talk and hostile remark. But my discourse, I know not how, has slipped into the didactic vein, though that is not what I proposed to myself originally. For what right have I to be laying down rules for one who, I am fully aware, in this subject especially, is not my inferior in wisdom, while in experience he is even my superior? Yet, after all, if your actions had the additional weight of my approval, I thought that they would seem more satisfactory to yourself. Wherefore, let these be the foundations on which your public character rests: first and foremost your own honesty and self-control, then the scrupulous conduct of all your staff, the exceedingly cautious and careful selection in regard to intimacies with provincials and Greeks, the strict and unbending government of your slaves. These are creditable even in the conduct of our private and everyday business: in such an important government, where morals are so debased and the province has such a corrupting influence, they must needs seem divine. Such principles and conduct on your part are sufficient to justify the strictness which you have displayed in some acts of administration, owing to which I have encountered certain personal disputes with great satisfaction, unless, indeed, you suppose me to be annoyed by the complaints of a fellow like Paconius—who is not even a Greek, but in reality a Mysian or Phrygian—or by the words of Tuscenius, a madman and a knave, from whose abominable jaws you snatched the fruits of a most infamous piece of extortion with the most complete justice.

VII. These and similar instances of your strict administration in your province we shall find difficulty in justifying, unless they are accompanied by the most perfect integrity: wherefore let there be the greatest strictness in your administration of justice, provided only that it is never varied from favour, but is kept up with impartiality. But it is of little avail that justice is administered by yourself with impartiality and care, unless the same is done by those to whom you have entrusted any portion of this duty. And, indeed, in my view there is no very great variety of business in the government of Asia: the entire province mainly depends on the administration of justice. In it we have the whole theory of government, especially of provincial government, clearly displayed: all that a governor has to do is to show consistency and firmness enough, not only to resist favouritism, but even the suspicion of it. To this also must be added courtesy in listening to pleaders, consideration in pronouncing a decision, and painstaking efforts to convince suitors of its justice, and to answer their arguments.

Correspondence between Pliny and Trajan, c. 112 C.E.

In 112, the Emperor Trajan* appointed Pliny† the Younger, a highly respected author and senator, to be governor of Bithynia, a Roman province in what is today northwestern Turkey. This was the high point of the Roman Empire, in terms of size and governance (see Map 4.2). Unlike the age of Cicero at the end of the Republic, when the Roman Senate retained power, Romans had grown accustomed to the rule of an emperor and institutions of empire.

General religious tolerance prevailed throughout the Roman Empire, and only Rome as the capital of the empire might require worship of a state god, including, at times, the emperor himself. Christians ran afoul of the law and communal practice not only by refusing the demonstration of loyalty to the state but also by aggressively denying the validity of all other gods—an attitude that many found distasteful. A brief correspondence between Pliny and the Emperor Trajan from about the year 112 C.E. has survived, throwing light on official Roman policy toward Christians of that era. What does Pliny's letter to Trajan tell you about the official Roman policy? What do you think of Trajan's answer? What do these letters tell you about Roman government of the empire?

THINKING HISTORICALLY

The period of Trajan's empire more closely resembles the Han dynasty empire than does the age of Cicero. By the end of the first century Roman imperial institutions had been developed and refined. How does Pliny's relationship to Trajan compare with that of a similar official in China to the Chinese emperor? What does this correspondence suggest to you about the difference between Roman and Chinese imperial administration?

Pliny to Trajan

It is my custom, Sire, to refer to you in all cases where I am in doubt, for who can better clear up difficulties and inform me? I have never been present at any legal examination of the Christians, and I do not know, therefore, what are the usual penalties passed upon them, or the limits

---

* TRAY juhn
† PLIH nee

Source: Pliny the Younger: *Letters*, X.25 ff, from William Stearns Davis, ed., *Readings in Ancient History: Illustrative Extracts from the Sources*, 2 vols. (Boston: Allyn and Bacon, 1912–13), Vol. II: *Rome and the West*, 298–300.

of those penalties, or how searching an inquiry should be made. I have hesitated a great deal in considering whether any distinctions should be drawn according to the ages of the accused; whether the weak should be punished as severely as the more robust, or whether the man who has once been a Christian gained anything by recanting? Again, whether the name of being a Christian, even though otherwise innocent of crime, should be punished, or only the crimes that gather around it?

In the meantime, this is the plan which I have adopted in the case of those Christians who have been brought before me. I ask them whether they are Christians, if they say "Yes," then I repeat the question the second time, and also a third—warning them of the penalties involved; and if they persist, I order them away to prison. For I do not doubt that—be their admitted crime what it may—their pertinacity and inflexible obstinacy surely ought to be punished.

There were others who showed similar mad folly, whom I reserved to be sent to Rome, as they were Roman citizens. Later, as is commonly the case, the mere fact of my entertaining the question led to a multiplying of accusations and a variety of cases were brought before me. An anonymous pamphlet was issued, containing a number of names of alleged Christians. Those who denied that they were or had been Christians and called upon the gods with the usual formula, reciting the words after me, and those who offered incense and wine before your image—which I had ordered to be brought forward for this purpose, along with the regular statues of the gods—all such I considered acquitted—especially as they cursed the name of Christ, which it is said *bona fide* Christians cannot be induced to do.

Still others there were, whose names were supplied by an informer. These first said they were Christians, then denied it, insisting they had been, "but were so no longer"; some of them having "recanted many years ago," and more than one "full twenty years back." These all worshiped your image and the god's statues and cursed the name of Christ.

But they declared their guilt or error was simply this—on a fixed day they used to meet before dawn and recite a hymn among themselves to Christ, as though he were a god. So far from binding themselves by oath to commit any crime, they swore to keep from theft, robbery, adultery, breach of faith, and not to deny any trust money deposited with them when called upon to deliver it. This ceremony over, they used to depart and meet again to take food—but it was of no special character, and entirely harmless. They also had ceased from this practice after the edict I issued—by which, in accord with your orders, I forbade all secret societies.

I then thought it the more needful to get at the facts behind their statements. Therefore I placed two women, called "deaconesses," under torture, but I found only a debased superstition carried to great lengths, so I postponed my examination, and immediately consulted you. This seems a matter worthy of your prompt consideration, especially as so many people are endangered. Many of all ages and both sexes are put in peril of their lives by their accusers; and the process will go on, for the contagion of this superstition has spread not merely through the free towns, but into the villages and farms. Still I think it can be halted and things set right. Beyond any doubt, the temples—which were nigh deserted—are beginning again to be thronged with worshipers; the sacred rites, which long have lapsed, are now being renewed, and the food for the sacrificial victims is again finding a sale—though up to recently it had almost no market. So one can safely infer how vast numbers could be reclaimed, if only there were a chance given for repentance.

Trajan to Pliny

You have adopted the right course, my dear Pliny, in examining the cases of those cited before you as Christians; for no hard and fast rule can be laid down covering such a wide question. The Christians are not to be hunted out. If brought before you, and the offense is proved, they are to be punished, but with this reservation—if any one denies he is a Christian, and makes it clear he is not, by offering prayer to our gods, then he is to be pardoned on his recantation, no matter how suspicious his past. As for anonymous pamphlets, they are to be discarded absolutely, whatever crime they may charge, for they are not only a precedent of a very bad type, but they do not accord with the spirit of our age.

9

MARCUS AURELIUS
Meditations, c. 167 c.e.

Marcus Aurelius (121–180 c.e.) was both a Roman emperor (161–180 c.e.) and a philosopher. He is numbered the last of the "five good emperors," a line of emperors that began in 96 c.e. and included Trajan. According to the great historian Edward Gibbon, this was an era in which "the Roman Empire was governed by absolute power, under the guidance of wisdom and virtue."[1]

[1] Edward Gibbon, *The Decline and Fall of the Roman Empire* (New York: Everyman's Library, 1993), vol. 1, chap. 3, p. 90.

Source: Marcus Aurelius, *Meditations*, trans. George Long, bk. 2, *The Internet Classics Archive*, http://classics.mit.edu/Antoninus/meditations.2.two.html.

Although much of his reign was taken up with wars, Marcus
Aurelius also initiated legal reform on behalf of slaves, minors, and
widows. As a philosopher, he was an adherent of Stoicism, a set of
beliefs aptly summarized in this selection from his *Meditations*,
written about 167 c.e. Stoicism originated in Greece in the third
century b.c.e. Stoics believed that negative emotions were the result
of poor judgment and that wisdom made one immune to pain or
misfortune.

In keeping with his Stoic convictions, Marcus Aurelius calls for the
mind to regulate the body. Thus it would seem he meant to lead a
very controlled and contemplative life. And yet, to be the emperor
was to be the most important actor in the Roman world. The
historian Dio Cassius tells us that Marcus Aurelius treated his enemies humanely, but the historian also relates stories of the emperor's
desire to exterminate an entire enemy people. How might Marcus
Aurelius have reconciled his ideas and his actions to produce such
varying results?

The years after 165 c.e. were particularly difficult for the emperor
and the empire. Roman forces had just defeated the Parthian army,
only to return to their homes with a pandemic disease (possibly
smallpox or measles) that lasted until about 180 c.e., claiming the
lives of as many as five million people, including Marcus Aurelius
himself. How might these events have influenced the emperor's
philosophy as recorded in the *Meditations*?

THINKING HISTORICALLY

Compare Marcus Aurelius' personal injunctions on how he should
act with Confucian ideas as expressed in *The Analects* and Han Fei's
Legalist views on government. What sorts of commonalties, if any, do
you detect between these three different philosophies? In what ways
have these philosophies had a lasting influence? Ask two questions
that require you to compare Marcus Aurelius and some aspect of
Chinese history. Ask one question that you can answer from what you
have read in this chapter and another question which would require
research to answer. What sort of research would you have to do in
order to answer the second question?

Begin the morning by saying to thyself, I shall meet with the busy-body,
the ungrateful, arrogant, deceitful, envious, unsocial. All these things
happen to them by reason of their ignorance of what is good and evil.
But I who have seen the nature of the good that it is beautiful, and of the
bad that it is ugly, and the nature of him who does wrong, that it is akin
to me, not only of the same blood or seed, but that it participates in the

same intelligence and the same portion of the divinity, I can neither be injured by any of them, for no one can fix on me what is ugly, nor can I be angry with my kinsman, nor hate him, for we are made for co-operation, like feet, like hands, like eyelids, like the rows of the upper and lower teeth. To act against one another then is contrary to nature; and it is acting against one another to be vexed and to turn away.

Whatever this is that I am, it is a little flesh and breath, and the ruling part. Throw away thy books; no longer distract thyself: it is not allowed; but as if thou wast now dying, despise the flesh; it is blood and bones and a network, a contexture of nerves, veins, and arteries. See the breath also, what kind of a thing it is, air, and not always the same, but every moment sent out and again sucked in. The third then is the ruling part: consider thus: Thou art an old man; no longer let this be a slave, no longer be pulled by the strings like a puppet to unsocial movements, no longer either be dissatisfied with thy present lot, or shrink from the future. . . .

Every moment think steadily as a Roman and a man to do what thou hast in hand with perfect and simple dignity, and feeling of affection, and freedom, and justice; and to give thyself relief from all other thoughts. And thou wilt give thyself relief, if thou doest every act of thy life as if it were the last, laying aside all carelessness and passionate aversion from the commands of reason, and all hypocrisy, and self-love, and discontent with the portion which has been given to thee. Thou seest how few the things are, the which if a man lays hold of, he is able to live a life which flows in quiet, and is like the existence of the gods; for the gods on their part will require nothing more from him who observes these things.

Do wrong to thyself, do wrong to thyself, my soul; but thou wilt no longer have the opportunity of honoring thyself. Every man's life is sufficient. But thine is nearly finished, though thy soul reverences not itself but places thy felicity in the souls of others. . . .

How quickly all things disappear, in the universe the bodies themselves, but in time the remembrance of them; what is the nature of all sensible things, and particularly those which attract with the bait of pleasure or terrify by pain, or are noised abroad by vapoury fame; how worthless, and contemptible, and sordid, and perishable, and dead they are. . . .

Though thou shouldst be going to live three thousand years, and as many times ten thousand years, still remember that no man loses any other life than this which he now lives, nor lives any other than this which he now loses. The longest and shortest are thus brought to the same. For the present is the same to all, though that which perishes is not the same; and so that which is lost appears to be a mere moment. For a man cannot lose either the past or the future: for what a man has not, how can anyone take this from him? These two things then thou must bear in mind; the one, that all things from eternity are of like forms and come round in a circle, and that it makes no difference whether a man shall see the same things during a hundred years or two hundred, or an infinite time; and the second, that the longest liver and he who will die soonest lose just the same. For the present is the only thing of which a man can be deprived, if it is true that this is the only thing which he has, and that a man cannot lose a thing if he has it not. . . .

The soul of man does violence to itself, first of all, when it becomes an abscess and, as it were, a tumour on the universe, so far as it can. For to be vexed at anything which happens is a separation of ourselves from nature, in some part of which the natures of all other things are contained. In the next place, the soul does violence to itself when it turns away from any man, or even moves towards him with the intention of injuring, such as are the souls of those who are angry. In the third place, the soul does violence to itself when it is overpowered by pleasure or by pain. Fourthly, when it plays a part, and does or says anything insincerely and untruly. Fifthly, when it allows any act of its own and any movement to be without an aim, and does anything thoughtlessly and without considering what it is, it being right that even the smallest things be done with reference to an end; and the end of rational animals is to follow the reason and the law of the most ancient city and polity.

Of human life the time is a point, and the substance is in a flux, and the perception dull, and the composition of the whole body subject to putrefaction, and the soul a whirl, and fortune hard to divine, and fame a thing devoid of judgment. And, to say all in a word, everything which belongs to the body is a stream, and what belongs to the soul is a dream and vapor, and life is a warfare and a stranger's sojourn, and after-fame is oblivion. What then is that which is able to conduct a man? One thing and only one, philosophy. But this consists in keeping the daemon[1] within a man free from violence and unharmed, superior to pains and pleasures, doing nothing without purpose, nor yet falsely and with hypocrisy, not feeling the need of another man's doing or not doing anything; and besides, accepting all that happens, and all that is allotted, as coming from thence, wherever it is, from whence he himself came; and, finally, waiting for death with a cheerful mind, as being nothing else than a dissolution of the elements of which every living being is compounded. But if there is no harm to the elements themselves in each continually changing into another, why should a man have any apprehension about the change and dissolution of all the elements? For it is according to nature, and nothing is evil which is according to nature.

[1] Spirit. [Ed.]

■ REFLECTIONS

Stoicism might at first thought seem an odd philosophy for an emperor, stranger still as an ideology to direct the governance of an empire. Yet, the belief that everything is natural or that resistance is always futile, might comfort an emperor, general, or official who feels forced to wage a bloody campaign or annihilate resistant populations. In any case, Stoicism was not the only tool in the armory of Roman rule. Not even the only ideological tool. The great Enlightenment historian Edward Gibbon famously linked Christianity, reputedly a religion of the weak and pacifists, to *The Decline and Fall of the Roman Empire*. If correct, then the martial Roman gods, emperor cults, and state religions might be credited with the growth and maintenance of the empire in its first few hundred years. But the later history of Christianity, the earlier history of Stoicism, and the variable role of Confucianism in China suggest that ideas can be shaped to the needs of different masters and missions.

The more material tools of governance—police, soldiers, officials, laws, forms, and procedures—would seem more practical than the effort to win hearts and minds. So it is striking that Roman officialdom lacked so many of the basic materials of successful administration. Pliny's letter about the Christians is just one example of the many times he found it necessary to refer a minor matter directly to the emperor. Certainly the Chinese emperor was protected from such distractions by layers of bureaucracy and established procedures.

How about the quality of officials? The Chinese made this top priority through competitive civil service exams designed to select the most gifted and well-prepared students, regardless of their wealth or family connections. Indeed the system was an end run around family, clan, and regional ties: an important part of the effort to supplant feudalism with a uniform state. Officials were, for instance, not assigned to serve in their home areas, where personal connections might pull them away from state responsibilities. Cicero's letter to his brother refers to more complex arrangements in the Roman Empire; some assistant officers are appointed by the state, others are personal allies of the new governor. Cicero also reminds us of the numerous private interests in Roman provinces. He tells his brother to watch out for the *publicani*—private citizens who purchased the right to collect taxes, clearly a public function in the Chinese Empire. Did the wide range of private responsibilities in the Roman Empire increase corruption? Or did its more independent judiciary raise the barrier against corruption? As a lawyer, some of Cicero's most famous trials were prosecutions of corrupt officials. The standard of behavior he expresses to his brother reads like a model for any age, but his words also betray the numerous obstacles to attaining them.

These readings might suggest innumerable comparative questions about the Roman and Chinese empires. Some readings discuss the role and status of soldiers: One might ask why their status was higher in Rome. The mention of Chinese eunuchs and of Roman slaves might lead one to ask about Chinese slaves (less common) and Roman eunuchs (rare in the West). The Han debate about salt and iron might lead the reader to ask about Rome (which monopolized salt but not iron) or the role of government monopolies in other times and places.

The study of the Roman Empire has always posed comparative questions about more recent empires, especially the British Empire in the nineteenth century and, for many, the global empire of the United States today. The addition of China, or the history of any other empire, helps us see more patterns and ask more questions that might better help us better understand ourselves.

5

Gender, Sex, and Love in Classical Societies

India, China, and the Mediterranean,
500 B.C.E.–550 C.E.

In the first chapter we saw how male-dominated societies or patriarchies developed, or at the very least strengthened and consolidated, in the wake of plow agriculture, irrigation, and city and state building, beginning about five thousand years ago. In some areas of the world—the Americas, sub-Saharan Africa, and Southeast Asia—patriarchies emerged later or remained less vigorous. Between 500 B.C.E. and 550 C.E. patriarchies flourished in the core areas of early city-societies or "civilizations" in the Mediterranean, India, and China. Historians call this period "classical" because it witnessed the florescence of a number of cultural traditions that are still honored as formative, among them Confucianism, Buddhism, Christianity, and Greco-Roman philosophy. The last chapter illuminated the importance of such philosophical traditions as Confucianism, Legalism, and Stoicism in the period. The next chapter will explore the impact of the great religious traditions of Hinduism, Buddhism, Judaism, and Christianity—all of which were founded or took recognizable form in this period.

This chapter asks about the relationships of men and women in this age of cultural flowering and increasing gender discrimination. What did it mean to be a man or a woman in the classical era? What was the impact of these classical traditions on gender identity? How was being a woman or a man different, and how was it similar, across these classical civilizations? Was it also the classical formative period of our own identities, ideas, and feelings? Or was it ancient history?

164

■ THINKING HISTORICALLY

Asking about Author, Audience, and Agenda

Historical sources, from the simplest laundry list to the most sophisticated work of art, are made by someone for someone to serve a
particular purpose. In other words, each has an author, an audience,
and an agenda. The better we understand who created a source, its
intended reader or viewer, and the reasons it was created, the better we
can make sense of the source and the society or culture in which it was
produced. In many cases much of this information is not available to
us, at least not in the detail we would like. But there are often clues in
the source itself that enable us to determine the author, audience, and
agenda. In this chapter we will interrogate the sources themselves to
find this information.

1

SARAH SHAVER HUGHES AND BRADY HUGHES

Women in the Classical Era, 2005

Sarah and Brady Hughes are modern historians. This selection is part
of their essay on the history of women in the ancient world written for
a book on the history of women. They write here of the classical era in
India, China, Greece, and Rome. All of these were patriarchal societies, but how were they different? The authors also mention Greek
Hellenistic society and pre-Roman Etruscan society. How do these two
societies round out your understanding of women between 500 B.C.E.
and 550 C.E.? What seem to be the conditions or causes that
improved the status of women in some societies and in some periods?

THINKING HISTORICALLY

The authors, audience, and agenda in this selection are fairly
transparent because it is a secondary source written by modern
historians. The authors do not reveal anything of themselves, but
their writing is matter-of-fact and dispassionate and shows an effort

Source: Sarah Shaver Hughes and Brady Hughes, "Women in Ancient Civilizations," in
Women's History in Global Perspective, ed. Bonnie G. Smith (Urbana: University of Illinois
Press, published with the American Historical Association, 2005), 2:26–30, 36–39.

to be thorough. All of this is appropriate in an informative essay written for a college-level audience. Note that this essay is part of a book published with the American Historical Association, the national organization of history teachers and scholars. The original essay carried a considerable number of footnotes (68 notes for a 35-page article), and it lacked the pronunciation and explanatory notes included with this reprinting. Does this suggest a work aimed at scholars, teachers, or students? Does the essay argue a point of scholarship, or does it summarize the scholarly work of others? What other clues in the reading indicate the intended audience and the purpose or agenda of the article?

India

... Women's rights deteriorated after the Vedic* period (1600–800 B.C.E.). No one has been able to prove why this happened. Scholarly interest has focused on women's exclusion from performing Hindu rituals, which was in effect by 500 B.C.E. ... Julia Leslie[1] thinks that women's exclusion resulted from intentional mistranslation of the Vedas[2] by male scholars, as the rituals became more complicated and as the requirement for property ownership was more rigorously enforced at a time when women could not own property.

The falling age of marriage for Indian women is another illustration of their loss of rights. In 400 B.C.E. about sixteen years was a normal age for a bride at marriage; between 400 B.C.E. and 100 C.E. it fell to pre-puberty; and after 100 C.E. pre-puberty was favored. These child marriages also affected women's religious roles. Because girls married before they could finish their education, they were not qualified to perform ritual sacrifices. Furthermore, wives' legal rights eroded. As child wives, they were treated as minors. Then their minority status lengthened until they were lifetime minors as wards of their husbands. Finally, women were prohibited any independence and were always under men's control: their fathers, husbands, or sons. By 100 C.E. Hindu texts defined women with negative characteristics, stating, for example, that women would be promiscuous unless controlled by male relatives. While Indian women were losing their independence, Indian men continued to glorify

---

*VAY dihk

[1] Leslie, "Essence and Existence: Women and Religion in Ancient Indian Text," in *Women's Religious Experience*, ed. Pat Holden (Totawa: Barnes and Noble Books, 1983). Dr. Isobel Julia Leslie (1948–2004), philosopher, historian, and novelist of Indian culture, wrote widely on women in India. [Ed.]

[2] The Vedas (see Chapter 3) were the writings of ancient Indian Hinduism, usually dated as above between 1600 and 800 B.C.E. in origins, though extant texts were written later. [Ed.]

their wives and mothers. A wife was the essence of the home, a man was not complete without a wife, and sons were expected to respect their mothers more than their fathers. As Romila Thapar sums up these contradictions, "The symbol of the woman in Indian culture has been a curious intermeshing of low legal status, ritual contempt, sophisticated sexual partnership, and deification."

One of the causes for this deterioration of women's rights and independence was the increasing rigidity of Hinduism under the influence of the Brahmans.[3] By 600 B.C.E. sects were springing up that opposed Brahman power and ostentatiously omitted some of the Hindu essentials, such as priests, rituals and ceremonies, animal sacrifices, and even caste distinctions.[4] Jainism and Buddhism are two of the sects that have survived. They were especially attractive to women. Jainism, the older religion, gained prominence with the efforts of its last prophet, Mahavira, who lived at the end of the sixth century B.C.E. Jains sought to live without passion and to act "correctly." One could achieve liberation only by living within a monastery or nunnery. Women who sought to join a nunnery found that the Jains had no membership restrictions. Many women entered and found new and exciting roles that were for the first time open to them. . . .

Mahavira's contemporary, Gautama Siddhartha* (the Buddha), began the religion that eventually spread throughout Asia. Among studies of Buddhist women, the early years have been a focus of interest. While Buddhism had no priests, it relied on celibate monks, who were initially homeless, except in the monsoon season, and had to beg for their necessities as they spread their ideas. The Buddha was reluctant to allow women to become nuns. He refused even the women in his family who sought to become nuns until he was reminded repeatedly by his aunt and his disciple Ananda of his stated principle that anyone could attain enlightenment. The Buddha then reluctantly accepted women followers, and they, like monks, eventually lived in their own self-governing celibate monasteries. . . .

China

. . . For Chinese women the ideas of Confucius (551–479 B.C.E.) have been most influential. There is little mention of women in his *Analects.* His neo-Confucian interpreters corrected this omission, however. They made explicit men's desire for a woman's subordination to her family, her husband, and her sons. For example, Lieh Nu Chuan (also known as

---

*GAW tah moh   sih DAHR thah

[3] Brahmans were priests of the Hindu religion. Because the Vedas enshrined priests as the highest caste, early Hinduism is sometimes called Brahminism. *Brahman* is also used to mean the totality of the divine (God). [Ed.]

[4] Some of these "Hindu essentials" may have actually become Hindu essentials in the Brahman encounter with Buddhism and Jainism after 600 B.C.E. [Ed.]

Liu Hsiang, 80–87 B.C.E.) wrote *The Biographies of Eminent Chinese Women,* in which he included 125 biographies of women from the peasant class to the emperor's wife, taken from prehistoric legends to the early years of the Han dynasty.

Although the purpose of these biographical sketches was to provide moral instruction in the passive ideals of Confucian womanhood, translator Albert Richard O'Hara's analysis of the women's actions reveals their influence on events that were important to them. The traditional Chinese interpretation of the genre is evident in one of the best known biographies, that of the widowed mother of Mencius (Meng K'o, or Meng-tzu), whose stern supervision and self-sacrifice were shown to have shaped her son's character and philosophy. This tale drives home the point that a woman's highest ambitions should be fulfilled indirectly through the talents of her sons. Pan Chao,[5] a female scholar in the first century C.E., wrote *The Seven Feminine Virtues* as a Confucian manual for girls' behavior. Its prescriptions of humility, meekness, modesty, and hard work continued to be copied by generations of young women until the twentieth century. . . .

Occasionally, imperial women seized power to govern when acting as regent for an underage emperor. Usually regents exercised this power cautiously behind the scenes because there was much opposition to women's open governance. Two famous empresses ruled openly, however, and sought to transfer royal descent to their own natal families. The first, Empress Lu, violated every canon of Confucian femininity. The widow of Gaodi, the first Han emperor (ruled 202–195 B.C.E.), Empress Lu acted swiftly and brutally to eliminate competitors at court during the near-fifteen years of her rule as regent for her son, her grandson, and another adopted infant grandson. By retaining power until her death in 181 B.C.E., she expected that her own nephews would succeed her. Instead, a civil war over the succession ended the period of peaceful prosperity, low taxes, and lessened punishment for crimes that had made her reign popular with the Chinese people. . . .

Greece

Classical Greece has long been admired for its political theories, philosophy, science, and the arts. Until recently, Greek social history was largely ignored. Slavery, homosexuality, and subordination of women are topics once dismissed as insignificant but now recognized as important to understanding the culture. In the classical period there were actually many "Greeces," with distinct societies developing in the citystates of Athens, Sparta, and Thebes. Gender patterns varied considerably among these cities. Sparta's aristocratic women, for example, were often left alone to acquire wealth and some

---

[5] Ban Zhao in selection 2 in this chapter. [Ed.]

autonomy when their mercenary husbands soldiered elsewhere. To some Athenian men such as Aristotle, Spartan women were thought to be despicable, licentious, greedy, and the reason for Sparta's decline.

Aristotle and other Athenian men dominate the discourse from classical Greece. Their male descriptions tell how Athenian society secluded elite women, denigrated and exploited them, and made them the legal dependents of men. Because no women's writings survive, only indirect evidence suggests how Athenian wives escaped their lives of hard work in the isolated, dark rooms that their husbands imagined necessary to preserve their chastity. But as drawn on vases, groups of Athenian women read to one another, spun and wove, shared child care, or talked. Women are shown in public processions and getting water from wells. Bits of documentary records show respectable married women earning their livings as wet nurses, farm workers, and retail vendors. Most records reveal the lives of privileged women, yet many Athenian women were slaves. Exposure of unwanted female babies was one internal source of slaves, for the rescuer of such an infant became her owner. Athenian enslavement of females was exceptional in its celebration of prostitution in literary and artistic records. One explanation for the large number of slave sex workers may be the Athenians' desire to attract sailors and merchants to their port.

Research on women in the Hellenistic period concentrates on Greek women living in Egypt. These women were much more assertive and influential than their sisters in either contemporary Greece or later Rome. Women in the ruling Ptolemaic[6] family often actually ruled Egypt, some as regents, others as queens. Cleopatra VII (69–30 B.C.E.), one of the best-known women in ancient history, guided her country from a tributary position in the Roman Empire into a partnership with Marc Antony that might have led to Egypt's domination of the eastern Mediterranean. Non-elite women had unusual freedom. They owned property (including land), participated in commerce, produced textiles, were educated, and enjoyed careers as artists, poets, and farmers. But some women were slaves. . . .

Rome

As late as the sixth century B.C.E., Rome was dominated by its northern neighbors, the Etruscans. Although no body of Etruscan literature exists, scholars have sought evidence of women's lives from inscriptions and art found in their tombs. Upper-class Etruscan women were more autonomous and privileged than contemporary Greek women. Paintings of husbands

---

[6] The ruling family of Egypt, descended from Alexander the Great's general, Ptolemy, who took power in 323 B.C.E. The Ptolemies ruled for three hundred years until the Roman conquest. The last of the Ptolemies was Cleopatra VII, who ruled briefly with Marc Antony but was conquered by Octavian in 30 B.C.E. and committed suicide. [Ed.]

and wives feasting together horrified Greek males, who only allowed prostitutes to attend their banquets. Etruscan women were not restricted to their homes as Greek women were and attended the games at gymnasiums. In Italy, all women left votive statues of women in sacred places, probably as a fertility offering, but only Etruscan statues included a nursing child, suggesting an affection for children that paralleled the affectionate touching between couples occasionally shown in their art. Finally, Etruscan women had personal names, in contrast to Greek women, who were known first as their fathers' daughters and later as their husbands' wives.

The Romans did not duplicate the autonomy of women in Etruscan society. Roman women legally were constrained within a highly patriarchal agricultural system organized around clans. A father could kill or sell his children into slavery without fear of legal action. Husbands could kill their wives if they were caught in adultery. Women did not speak in public meetings. They could not buy and sell property without their male relatives' approval. Legally treated as minors, women were first the responsibility of their fathers, then of their husbands, and finally of appointed guardians. Rome was a warrior society and a male republic. Men even dominated the state religion, with the exception of the six Vestal Virgins who served as priestesses. Roman society remained staunchly male until conquests brought wealth to Italy in the second century B.C.E. Changes that accompanied the booty of empire gave women a measure of economic and marital independence that is illustrated by the loosening of legal restrictions against women's property ownership.

The paterfamilias, the oldest male in the family, had complete *manus* (legal control) over his children. In marriage, manus passed from the paterfamilias to the new husband. Among other things, that meant the husband then controlled all of his wife's property. Before the first century B.C.E. some Roman marriages were made without transferring manus to the husband; the wife and her property would remain under her father's control, whose approval was theoretically required for the daughter to buy or sell property. Susan Treggiari explains how this enabled many women to gain control over their property:

> Given ancient expectation of life, it is probable that many women were fatherless for a relatively long period of their married lives. The pattern . . . for the middle ranks of Roman society is that girls married in their late teens and men in their mid- to late twenties. If expectation of life at birth is put between twenty and thirty, then 46 percent of fifteen-year-olds had no father left alive. The percentage grows to 59 percent of twenty-year-olds and 70 percent of twenty-five-year-olds. So there is about a 50 percent chance that a woman was already fatherless at the time of her first marriage.

Upon a father's death, manus was transferred to a guardian, and women began to choose as their guardians men who agreed with them.

By the later years of the Roman Republic, therefore, many women bought and sold land as they pleased. Rome's expansion contributed to this change as it fueled a growing market in real and personal property.

In the third century B.C.E., Rome began two centuries of conquests that eventually placed most of the land surrounding the Mediterranean under Roman administration or in the hands of client states. Roman wives farmed while citizen-soldiers of the Republic were on campaigns, sometimes for more than a decade. Successful wars enriched a Roman elite who accumulated estates worked by male and female slaves as small farmers sold their lands and moved to the city with their wives and children. Elite Romans, both men and women, possessed large estates, luxurious urban houses, much rental property, and many slaves. By 50 B.C.E., Rome had a population of approximately one million. Slaves poured into Italy after successful campaigns, when the defeated enemy was enslaved. As the Romans conquered country after country, they brutalized the captured women, enslaving many. Ruling queens in subdued countries were inevitably replaced with either indigenous male elites or Roman officials. Queen Boudicca of Britain, for example, led a revolt that ended in her death in the first century C.E. Queen Zenobia of Palmyra's invasion of the empire in the third century C.E. was so well organized that Roman authors praised her. Cleopatra of Egypt committed suicide when her plan to make Egypt a regional partner of Rome failed.

Roman women did not publicly speak in the Forum (where men debated civic affairs), with the notable exception of Hortensia in 43 B.C.E. She was the spokesperson for a demonstration of wealthy women who protested taxation without representation for civil wars they did not support. Elite women usually indirectly influenced political decisions through networks of politicians' wives. During the civil wars of the first century B.C.E., wives of some tyrants even made temporary political decisions. On a wider scale, middle-class and elite women took advantage of the turmoil at the end of the Republic[7] to acquire businesses, as analysis of Pompeii[8] shows. Prostitution flowered in Rome with the inflow of slaves, both male and female. A small part of the elite lived in the self-indulgent luxury that became famous in literature. In a brief period of two generations at the end of the first century B.C.E., Roman elite women eschewed children and family responsibilities for a glamorous and self-absorbed life of parties and lovers. In this period men and women were openly adulterous. This "café society" flourished in the chaos of civil wars that nearly destroyed the prestige of the elite and killed or exiled many of them.

[7] In the second half of the first century B.C.E. [Ed.]

[8] The city of Pompeii was buried in the ashes caused by the eruption of Mount Vesuvius (near modern Naples) in 79 C.E. Because of its instant burial, it is a rich source of information and artifacts from the period. [Ed.]

This era of chaos ended during the reign of the emperor Augustus (ruled 27 B.C.E.–14 C.E.), who sought to stabilize Roman society in part by reducing women's freedoms. Women were criticized for adultery, wearing too much makeup, having immodest dress and conduct, and especially for refusing to have children. Augustus procured laws that intended to remove control of marriage and reproduction from the family and allow the state to regulate marriage and reproduction. He attempted to penalize women between the ages of twenty and fifty and men over the age of twenty-five who did not marry and have children by denying them the right to inherit wealth. Furthermore, women were not to be released from male guardianship until they had three children. The Augustan laws made the state the regulator of private behavior and attempted to raise the birthrate of citizens while accepting some of the social changes that had modified the patriarchal society of the old Roman Republic. Augustus sought political support from conservative males by decreasing the autonomy of women who had less political influence than men.

2

BAN ZHAO
Lessons for Women, c. 100 C.E.

The teachings of Confucius (561–479 B.C.E.) provided the Chinese and other Asian peoples with ideals of private and public conduct. Confucius's teachings emphasized the importance of filial piety, or the duty of children to serve and obey their parents, as well as to exercise restraint and treat others as one would like to be treated (see selection 3 in Chapter 4 for excerpts from Confucius's *Analects*). Ban Zhao* (45–116 C.E.) (Pan Chao in the previous selection) was the leading female Confucian scholar of classical China. Born into a literary family and educated by her mother, she was married at the age of fourteen. After her husband's death she finished writing her brother's history of the Han dynasty and served as imperial historian to Emperor Han Hedi (r. 88–105 C.E.) and as an advisor to the Empress-Dowager Deng.

Ban Zhao is best remembered, however, for her *Lessons for Women*, which she wrote to fill a gap in Confucian literature. With their

*bahn ZHOW

Source: *Pan Chao: Foremost Woman Scholar of China*, trans. Nancy Lee Swann (New York: Century Co., 1932), 82–90.

emphasis on the responsibilities of the son to the father and on the moral example of a good ruler, the writings of Confucius virtually ignored women. Ban Zhao sought to rectify that oversight by applying Confucian principles to the moral instruction of women. What does this piece say about the roles of both men and women? In what ways would Ban Zhao's Lessons support Chinese patriarchy? In what ways might they challenge the patriarchy or make it less oppressive for women?

THINKING HISTORICALLY

The author of this primary source provides an unusual bounty of personal autobiographical information in the first section. But why might the modern reader find much of this self-description unconvincing? Similarly, there is a discrepancy between the author's description of her audience and purpose in writing and the modern reader's idea of her audience and agenda. In fact, the introduction (above) and a line by the Hugheses in the previous selection tell you what historians think of the likely audience and agenda for Ban Zhao. What is this discrepancy between the author's presentation and what historians know to be her audience and agenda? How do these discrepancies actually help us better understand the author and, perhaps, Chinese or Confucian classical culture?

I, the unworthy writer, am unsophisticated, unenlightened, and by nature unintelligent, but I am fortunate both to have received not a little favor from my scholarly Father, and to have had a cultured mother and instructresses upon whom to rely for a literary education as well as for training in good manners. More than forty years have passed since at the age of fourteen I took up the dustpan and the broom in the Cao family.[1] During this time with trembling heart I feared constantly that I might disgrace my parents, and that I might multiply difficulties for both the women and the men of my husband's family. Day and night I was distressed in heart, but I labored without confessing weariness. Now and hereafter, however, I know how to escape from such fears.

Being careless, and by nature stupid, I taught and trained my children without system. Consequently I fear that my son Gu may bring disgrace upon the Imperial Dynasty by whose Holy Grace he has unprecedentedly received the extraordinary privilege of wearing the Gold and the Purple,[2] a privilege for the attainment of which by my son, I a humble subject never even hoped. Nevertheless, now that he is a man and able to plan his own life, I need not again have concern for him. But

---

[1] Her husband's family. [Ed.]

[2] Gold seal and purple robe were symbols of high nobility. [Ed.]

I do grieve that you, my daughters, just now at the age for marriage, have not at this time had gradual training and advice; that you still have not learned the proper customs for married women. I fear that by failure in good manners in other families you will humiliate both your ancestors and your clan. I am now seriously ill, life is uncertain. As I have thought of you all in so untrained a state, I have been uneasy many a time for you. At hours of leisure I have composed . . . these instructions under the title, "Lessons for Women." In order that you may have something wherewith to benefit your persons, I wish every one of you, my daughters each to write out a copy for yourself.

From this time on every one of you strive to practice these lessons.

Humility

On the third day after the birth of a girl the ancients observed three customs: first to place the baby below the bed; second to give her a potsherd[3] with which to play; and third to announce her birth to her ancestors by an offering. Now to lay the baby below the bed plainly indicated that she is lowly and weak, and should regard it as her primary duty to humble herself before others. To give her potsherds with which to play indubitably signified that she should practice labor and consider it her primary duty to be industrious. To announce her birth before her ancestors clearly meant that she ought to esteem as her primary duty the continuation of the observance of worship in the home.

These three ancient customs epitomize woman's ordinary way of life and the teachings of the traditional ceremonial rites and regulations. Let a woman modestly yield to others; let her respect others; let her put others first, herself last. Should she do something good, let her not mention it; should she do something bad let her not deny it. Let her bear disgrace; let her even endure when others speak or do evil to her. Always let her seem to tremble and to fear. When a woman follows such maxims as these then she may be said to humble herself before others.

Let a woman retire late to bed, but rise early to duties; let her not dread tasks by day or by night. Let her not refuse to perform domestic duties whether easy or difficult. That which must be done, let her finish completely, tidily, and systematically. When a woman follows such rules as these, then she may be said to be industrious.

Let a woman be correct in manner and upright in character in order to serve her husband. Let her live in purity and quietness of spirit, and attend to her own affairs. Let her love not gossip and silly laughter.

---

[3] A piece of broken pottery. [Ed.]

Let her cleanse and purify and arrange in order the wine and the food for the offerings to the ancestors. When a woman observes such principles as these, then she may be said to continue ancestral worship.

No woman who observes these three fundamentals of life has ever had a bad reputation or has fallen into disgrace. If a woman fails to observe them, how can her name be honored; how can she but bring disgrace upon herself?

Husband and Wife

The Way of husband and wife is intimately connected with Yin and Yang and relates the individual to gods and ancestors. Truly it is the great principle of Heaven and Earth, and the great basis of human relationships. Therefore the "Rites"[4] honor union of man and woman; and in the "Book of Poetry"[5] the "First Ode" manifests the principle of marriage. For these reasons the relationship cannot but be an important one.

If a husband be unworthy, then he possesses nothing by which to control his wife. If a wife be unworthy, then she possesses nothing with which to serve her husband. If a husband does not control his wife, then the rules of conduct manifesting his authority are abandoned and broken. If a wife does not serve her husband, then the proper relationship between men and women and the natural order of things are neglected and destroyed. As a matter of fact the purpose of these two[6] is the same. . . .

Respect and Caution

As Yin and Yang are not of the same nature, so man and woman have different characteristics. The distinctive quality of the Yang is rigidity; the function of the Yin is yielding. Man is honored for strength; a woman is beautiful on account of her gentleness. Hence there arose the common saying: "A man though born like a wolf may, it is feared, become a weak monstrosity; a woman though born like a mouse may, it is feared, become a tiger."

Now for self-culture nothing equals respect for others. To counteract firmness nothing equals compliance. Consequently it can be said that the Way of respect and acquiescence is woman's most important principle of conduct. So respect may be defined as nothing other than holding on to

---

[4] *The Classic of Rites*, one of the five classics of the Confucian canon, believed to be written by Confucius, though the current text dates from the Han dynasty. [Ed.]

[5] *The Classic of Odes*. Also declared one of five classics in the Han dynasty, the *Book of Odes* or *Songs* contains poems from as early as 1000 B.C.E. in the Zhou dynasty, presumed to be edited by Confucius. [Ed.]

[6] The controlling of women by men, and the serving of men by women. [Ed.]

that which is permanent; and acquiescence nothing other than being liberal and generous. Those who are steadfast in devotion know that they should stay in their proper places; those who are liberal and generous esteem others, and honor and serve them.

If husband and wife have the habit of staying together, never leaving one another, and following each other around within the limited space of their own rooms, then they will lust after and take liberties with one another. From such action improper language will arise between the two. This kind of discussion may lead to licentiousness. But of licentiousness will be born a heart of disrespect to the husband. Such a result comes from not knowing that one should stay in one's proper place.

Furthermore, affairs may be either crooked or straight; words may be either right or wrong. Straightforwardness cannot but lead to quarreling; crookedness cannot but lead to accusation. If there are really accusations and quarrels, then undoubtedly there will be angry affairs. Such a result comes from not esteeming others, and not honoring and serving them.

If wives suppress not contempt for husbands, then it follows that such wives rebuke and scold their husbands. If husbands stop not short of anger, then they are certain to beat their wives. The correct relationship between husband and wife is based upon harmony and intimacy, and conjugal love is grounded in proper union. Should actual blows be dealt, how could matrimonial relationship be preserved? Should sharp words be spoken, how could conjugal love exist? If love and proper relationship both be destroyed, then husband and wife are divided.

Womanly Qualifications

A woman ought to have four qualifications: (1) womanly virtue; (2) womanly words; (3) womanly bearing; and (4) womanly work. Now what is called womanly virtue need not be brilliant ability, exceptionally different from others. Womanly words need be neither clever in debate nor keen in conversation. Womanly appearance requires neither a pretty nor a perfect face and form. Womanly work need not be work done more skillfully than that of others.

To guard carefully her chastity; to control circumspectly her behavior; in every motion to exhibit modesty; and to model each act on the best usage, this is womanly virtue.

To choose her words with care; to avoid vulgar language; to speak at appropriate times; and not to weary others with much conversation, may be called the characteristics of womanly words.

To wash and scrub filth away; to keep clothes and ornaments fresh and clean; to wash the head and bathe the body regularly, and to keep the person free from disgraceful filth, may be called the characteristics of womanly bearing.

With whole-hearted devotion to sew and to weave; to love not gossip and silly laughter; in cleanliness and order to prepare the wine and food for serving guests, may be called the characteristics of womanly work.

These four qualifications characterize the greatest virtue of a woman. No woman can afford to be without them. In fact they are very easy to possess if a woman only treasures them in her heart. The ancients had a saying: "Is love afar off? If I desire love, then love is at hand!" So can it be said of these qualifications.

3

VATSYANA

On the Conduct of Wives, Husbands, and Women of the Harem, c. 280–550 c.e.

We know next to nothing about the author of this classic Indian book on *kama* (love, sex, or sensual experience), written between the fourth and sixth centuries c.e. in the Gupta period (c. 280–550 c.e.).[1] What does this selection tell you about classical Indian culture and society, particularly about men, women, and the way they interacted? What does it tell you about sexuality and religion in classical India?

THINKING HISTORICALLY

Vatsyana does not directly tell us anything about himself. Assuming, however, that the translation is faithful to the original, how would you characterize the author's tone and style?

For what kind of people did he write, and what do you think he hoped to accomplish? At the end of the book—a section not included here—the author writes: "The Kama Sutra was composed, according to the precepts of Holy Writ, for the benefit of the world, by Vatsyayana, while leading the life of a religious student, and wholly engaged in the contemplation of the Deity." Does that statement change your idea of the author, his audience, or his agenda in writing the work?

---

[1] The Gupta period was a period not only of cultural flowering, but also of political expansion. The Gupta Empire covered most of north and central India.

Source: Mallanaga Vatsyana, *The Kama Sutra*, trans. Sir Richard F. Burton (1883), *Internet Sacred Texts Archive*, http://www.sacred-texts.com/sex/kama/kama101.htm.

The causes of re-marrying during the lifetime of the wife are as follows:

- The folly or ill-temper of the wife
- Her husband's dislike to her
- The want of offspring
- The continual birth of daughters
- The incontinence of the husband

From the very beginning, a wife should endeavour to attract the heart of her husband, by showing to him continually her devotion, her good temper, and her wisdom. If however she bears him no children, she should herself toilette her husband to marry another woman. And when the second wife is married, and brought to the house, the first wife should give her a position superior to her own, and look upon her as a sister. In the morning the elder wife should forcibly make the younger one decorate herself in the presence of their husband, and should not mind all the husband's favour being given to her. If the younger wife does anything to displease her husband the elder one should not neglect her, but should always be ready to give her most careful advice, and should teach her to do various things in the presence of her husband. Her children she should treat as her own, her attendants she should look upon with more regard, even than on her own servants, her friends she should cherish with love and kindness, and her relations with great honour.

When there are many other wives besides herself, the elder wife should associate with the one who is immediately next to her in rank and age, and should instigate the wife who has recently enjoyed her husband's favour to quarrel with the present favourite. After this she should sympathize with the former, and having collected all the other wives together, should get them to denounce the favourite as a scheming and wicked woman, without however committing herself in any way. If the favourite wife happens to quarrel with the husband, then the elder wife should take her part and give her false encouragement, and thus cause the quarrel to be increased. If there be only a little quarrel between the two, the elder wife should do all she can to work it up into a large quarrel. But if after all this she finds the husband still continues to love his favourite wife she should then change her tactics, and endeavour to bring about a conciliation between them, so as to avoid her husband's displeasure.

Thus ends the conduct of the elder wife.

The younger wife should regard the elder wife of her husband as her mother, and should not give anything away, even to her own relations, without her knowledge. She should tell her everything about herself, and not approach her husband without her permission.

Whatever is told to her by the elder wife she should not reveal to others, and she should take care of the children of the senior even more than of her own. When alone with her husband she should serve him well, but should not tell him of the pain she suffers from the existence of a rival wife. She may also obtain secretly from her husband some marks of his particular regard for her, and may tell him that she lives only for him, and for the regard that he has for her. She should never reveal her love for her husband, nor her husband's love for her to any person, either in pride or in anger, for a wife that reveals the secrets of her husband is despised by him. As for seeking to obtain the regard of her husband, Gonardiya says, that it should always be done in private, for fear of the elder wife. If the elder wife be disliked by her husband, or be childless, she should sympathize with her, and should ask her husband to do the same, but should surpass her in leading the life of a chaste woman.

Thus ends the conduct of the younger wife towards the elder.

A widow in poor circumstances, or of a weak nature, and who allies herself again to a man, is called a widow remarried.

The followers of Babhravya say that a virgin widow should not marry a person whom she may be obliged to leave on account of his bad character, or of his being destitute of the excellent qualities of a man, she thus being obliged to have recourse to another person. Gonardiya is of opinion that as the cause of a widow's marrying again is her desire for happiness, and as happiness is secured by the possession of excellent qualities in her husband, joined to love of enjoyment, it is better therefore to secure a person endowed with such qualities in the first instance. Vatsyayana however thinks that a widow may marry any person that she likes, and that she thinks will suit her.

At the time of her marriage the widow should obtain from her husband the money to pay the cost of drinking parties, and picnics with her relations, and of giving them and her friends kindly gifts and presents; or she may do these things at her own cost if she likes. In the same way she may wear either her husband's ornaments or her own. As to the presents of affection mutually exchanged between the husband and herself there is no fixed rule about them. If she leaves her husband after marriage of her own accord, she should restore to him whatever he may have given her, with the exception of the mutual presents. If however she is driven out of the house by her husband she should not return anything to him.

After her marriage she should live in the house of her husband like one of the chief members of the family, but should treat the other ladies of the family with kindness, the servants with generosity, and all the friends of the house with familiarity and good temper. She should show that she is better acquainted with the sixty-four arts than the other ladies of the house, and in any quarrels with her husband she should not rebuke him severely but in private do everything that he wishes, and make use of the sixty-four ways of enjoyment. She should be obliging to the other wives of her husband, and to their children she should give presents, behave as their mistress, and make ornaments and playthings for their use. In the friends and servants of her husband she should confide more than in his other wives, and finally she should have a liking for drinking parties, going to picnics, attending fairs and festivals, and for carrying out all kinds of games and amusements.

Thus ends the conduct of a virgin widow remarried.

A woman who is disliked by her husband, and annoyed and distressed by his other wives, should associate with the wife who is liked most by her husband, and who serves him more than the others, and should teach her all the arts with which she is acquainted. She should act as the nurse to her husband's children, and having gained over his friends to her side, should through them make him acquainted of her devotion to him. In religious ceremonies she should be a leader, as also in vows and fasts, and should not hold too good an opinion of herself. When her husband is lying on his bed she should only go near him when it is agreeable to him, and should never rebuke him, or show obstinacy in any way. If her husband happens to quarrel with any of his other wives, she should reconcile them to each other, and if he desires to see any woman secretly, she should manage to bring about the meeting between them. She should moreover make herself acquainted with the weak points of her husband's character, but always keep them secret, and on the whole behave herself in such a way as may lead him to look upon her as a good and devoted wife.

Here ends the conduct of a wife disliked by her husband.

The above sections will show how all the women of the king's seraglio are to behave, and therefore we shall now speak separately only about the king.

The female attendants in the harem . . . should bring flowers, ointments and clothes from the king's wives to the king, and he having received these things should give them as presents to the servants, along with the things worn by him the previous day. In the afternoon the king, having dressed and put on his ornaments, should interview the women of the harem, who should also be dressed and decorated with jewels. Then having given to each of them such a place and such respect as may suit the occasion and as they may deserve, he should carry on with them a cheerful conversation. After that he should see such of his wives as may be virgin widows remarried, and after them the concubines and dancing girls. All of these should be visited in their own private rooms.

When the king rises from his noonday sleep, the woman whose duty it is to inform the king regarding the wife who is to spend the night with him should come to him accompanied by the female attendants of that wife whose turn may have arrived in the regular course, and of her who may have been accidentally passed over as her turn arrived, and of her who may have been unwell at the time of her turn. These attendants should place before the king the ointments and unguents sent by each of these wives, marked with the seal of her ring, and their names and their reasons for sending the ointments should be told to the king. After this the king accepts the ointment of one of them, who then is informed that her ointment has been accepted, and that her day has been settled.[2]

At festivals, singing parties and exhibitions, all the wives of the king should be treated with respect and served with drinks.

But the women of the harem should not be allowed to go out alone, neither should any women outside the harem be allowed to enter it except those whose character is well known. And lastly the work which the king's wives have to do should not be too fatiguing.

Thus ends the conduct of the king towards the women of the harem, and of their own conduct.

A man marrying many wives should act fairly towards them all. He should neither disregard nor pass over their faults, and should not reveal to one wife the love, passion, bodily blemishes and confidential reproaches of the other. No opportunity should be given to any one of them of speaking to him about their rivals, and if one of them should begin to speak ill of another, he should chide her and tell her that she has exactly the same blemishes in her character. One of them he should please by secret confidence, another by secret respect, and another by secret flattery, and he should please them all by going to gardens, by amusements, by presents, by honouring their relations, by telling them secrets, and lastly by loving unions. A young woman who is of a good temper, and who conducts herself according to the precepts of the Holy Writ, wins her husband's attachments, and obtains a superiority over her rivals.

Thus ends the conduct of a husband towards many wives.

---

[2] As kings generally had many wives, it was usual for them to enjoy their wives by turns. But as it happened sometimes that some of them lost their turns owing to the king's absence, or to their being unwell, then in such cases the women whose turns had been passed over, and those whose turns had come, used to have a sort of lottery, and the ointments of all the claimants were sent to the king, who accepted the ointment of one of them, and thus settled the question.

4

PLATO
The Symposium, c. 385 B.C.E.

Plato (428–348 B.C.E.) is certainly the most widely read and most influential philosopher of classical Greece. The twentieth-century Platonist A. N. Whitehead famously wrote that all of European philosophy consisted of footnotes to Plato.[1] When we speak of Plato, however, we also mean Socrates, Plato's teacher. In fact, since Plato's writings consist almost entirely of dialogues (discussions) in which Plato is absent but Socrates asks questions and elicits answers and then spells out his own ideas, we have no way of distinguishing the ideas of Plato from those of Socrates. We credit Plato, however, since he is the author of these thirty-five dialogues as well as thirteen letters and was the founder of the Athenian Academy of philosophy.

The Symposium, one of the better-known dialogues, was written about 385 B.C.E. The subject is a symposium or drinking party in which the participants eat, drink, and discuss some philosophical topic — in this case, the meaning of love. This selection contains two views of love before Socrates speaks. What are those views, and what do they tell you about the Greek society of the time — particularly about sexuality and gender? What finally does Socrates say about love? What does his speech tell you about Greek ideas of men, women, love, and sex?

THINKING HISTORICALLY

This dialogue, like the others, is a sort of play with its own author, audience, and agenda. Whose voice is telling the story? What kind of people make up the "audience" of the dinner party? Why have these men come together to discuss this topic? What different agenda might they have had? Of course, even the intended audience of Plato's written dialogue is very much larger than a few men talking. For whom do you think he wrote this? What might have been his purpose? Finally, whose ideas are these? If we know little of the biography of Plato, other than that he was the author of these works and the founder of the Athenian Academy, we know less about Socrates. Indeed, in some dialogues Socrates raises questions as to whether or

---

[1] Alfred North Whitehead, *Process and Reality* (New York: Free Press, 1979), 39.

Source: Plato, *Symposium*, trans. Benjamin Jowett, http://www.ellopos.net/elpenor /greek-texts/ancient-Greece/plato/plato-symposium.asp.

not he expresses his own ideas. How does he suggest that his ideas may not even be his own in this dialogue?

Regarding audience and agenda, we might assume that the dialogues were to be used for teaching purposes at the Academy, but we have no evidence for that assumption either. To what degree do these uncertainties limit our understanding of classical Greek society and culture? Despite these uncertainties, what can we say—from the internal evidence of the dialogue itself—about the likely audience and agenda of this work?

[Our selection begins as the participants have just finished dinner.]

Then, said Eryximachus, as you are all agreed that drinking is to be voluntary, and that there is to be no compulsion, I move, in the next place, that the flute-girl, who has just made her appearance, be told to go away and play to herself, or, if she likes, to the women who are within. Today let us have conversation instead; and, if you will allow me, I will tell you what sort of conversation. . . .

I think that at the present moment we who are here assembled cannot do better than honor the god Love. If you agree with me, there will be no lack of conversation; for I mean to propose that each of us in turn, going from left to right, shall make a speech in honor of Love. Let him give us the best which he can; and Phaedrus, because he is sitting first on the left hand, and because he is the father of the thought,[2] shall begin. . . .

[Phaedrus:]

Numerous are the witnesses who acknowledge Love to be the eldest of the gods. And not only is he the eldest, he is also the source of the greatest benefits to us. For I know not any greater blessing to a young man who is beginning life than a virtuous lover or to the lover than a beloved youth.[3] For the principle which ought to be the guide of men who would nobly live at principle, I say, neither kindred, nor honor, nor wealth, nor any other motive is able to implant so well as love. Of what am I speaking? Of the sense of honor and dishonor, without which neither states nor individuals ever do any good or great work. And I say that a lover who is detected in doing any dishonorable act, or submitting through cowardice when any dishonor is done to him by another, will be more pained at being detected by his beloved than at being seen by his father, or by his companions, or by anyone else. The beloved too, when he is found in any disgraceful situation, has the same feeling about his

[2] Phaedrus had earlier suggested the topic. [Ed.]
[3] Note that this only concerns men and boys. [Ed.]

lover. And if there were only some way of contriving that a state or an army should be made up of lovers and their loves, they would be the very best governors of their own city, abstaining from all dishonor, and emulating one another in honor; and when fighting at each other's side, although a mere handful, they would overcome the world. . . .

[Pausanias:]

If there were only one Love, then what you said would be well enough; but since there are more Loves than one, [we] should have begun by determining which of them was to be the theme of our praises. I will amend this defect; and first of all I would tell you which Love is deserving of praise, and then try to hymn the praiseworthy one in a manner worthy of him. For we all know that Love is inseparable from Aphrodite,[4] and if there were only one Aphrodite there would be only one Love; but as there are two goddesses there must be two Loves.

And am I not right in asserting that there are two goddesses? The elder one, having no mother, who is called the heavenly Aphrodite . . . and the Love who is her fellow-worker is rightly called common, as the other love is called heavenly.[5] . . . The Love who is the offspring of the common Aphrodite is essentially common, and has no discrimination, being such as the meaner sort of men feel, and is apt to be of women as well as of youths, and is of the body rather than of the soul; the most foolish beings are the objects of this love which desires only to gain an end, but never thinks of accomplishing the end nobly, and therefore does good and evil quite indiscriminately. The goddess who is his mother is far younger than the other, and she was born of the union of the male and female, and partakes of both.

But the offspring of the heavenly Aphrodite is derived from a mother in whose birth the female has no part: She is from the male only; this is that love which is of youths, and the goddess being older, there is nothing of wantonness in her. Those who are inspired by this love turn to the male, and delight in him who is the more valiant and intelligent nature; any one may recognize the pure enthusiasts in the very character of their attachments. For they love not boys, but intelligent beings whose reason is beginning to be developed, much about the time at which their beards begin to grow. And in choosing young men to be their companions, they mean to be faithful to them, and pass their whole life in company with them, not to take them in their inexperience, and deceive them, and play the fool

---

[4] The Greek goddess of love and beauty. [Ed.]

[5] Pausanias makes this distinction to account for two Aphrodite origin myths at the time. One is the story of an Aphrodite born in sea foam from her father's discarded genitals—this is the heavenly Aphrodite. Another myth concerns an Aphrodite of common birth. The first accounts for homosexual love, the second for the love between a husband and wife. [Ed.]

with them, or run away from one to another of them. But the love of
young boys should be forbidden by law,[6] because their future is uncertain;
they may turn out good or bad, either in body or soul, and much noble
enthusiasm may be thrown away upon them; in this matter the good are
a law to themselves, and the coarser sort of lovers ought to be restrained
by force; as we restrain or attempt to restrain them from fixing their affections on women of free birth. These are the persons who bring a reproach
on love; and some have been led to deny the lawfulness of such attachments because they see the impropriety and evil of them; for surely nothing that is decorously and lawfully done can justly be censured. . . .

[Finally, it is the turn of Socrates:]

And now, taking my leave of you, I would rehearse a tale of love
which I heard from Diotima of Mantineia, a woman wise in this and in
many other kinds of knowledge, who in the days of old, when the Athenians offered sacrifice before the coming of the plague, delayed the
disease ten years. She was my instructress in the art of love, and I shall
repeat to you what she said to me. . . . "Love," she said, "may be described
generally as the love of the everlasting possession of the good." "That is
most true" [I agreed]. "Then if this be the nature of love, can you tell me
further," she said, "what is the manner of the pursuit? What are they
doing who show all this eagerness and heat which is called love? And
what is the object which they have in view? Answer me." "Nay, Diotima," I replied, "if I had known, I should not have wondered at your
wisdom, neither should I have come to learn from you about this very
matter." "Well," she said, "I will teach you: The object which they have
in view is birth in beauty, whether of body or, soul. . . . And this is the
reason why, when the hour of conception arrives, and the teeming nature is full, there is such a flutter and ecstasy about beauty whose approach is the alleviation of the pain of travail. For love, Socrates, is not,
as you imagine, the love of the beautiful only." "What then?" "The love
of generation and of birth in beauty." "Yes," I said. "Yes, indeed," she
replied. "But why of generation?" "Because to the mortal creature, generation is a sort of eternity and immortality," she replied; "and if, as has
been already admitted, love is of the everlasting possession of the good,
all men will necessarily desire immortality together with good: Wherefore love is of immortality." . . .

". . . [T]he essence of beauty, . . . my dear Socrates, . . . is that life
above all others which man should live, in the contemplation of beauty
absolute; a beauty which if you once beheld, you would see not to be
after the measure of gold, and garments, and fair boys and youths,

---

[6] Such love is only appropriate when expressed toward *ephebos* (boys entering manhood,
roughly eighteen to twenty years old). It should be against the law if boys are younger. [Ed.]

whose presence now entrances you; and you and many a one would be content to live seeing them only and conversing with them without meat or drink, if that were possible—you only want to look at them and to be with them. But what if man had eyes to see the true beauty—the divine beauty, I mean, pure and clear and unalloyed, not clogged with the pollutions of mortality and all the colors and vanities of human life—thither looking, and holding converse with the true beauty simple and divine? Remember how in that communion only, beholding beauty with the eye of the mind, he will be enabled to bring forth, not images of beauty, but realities (for he has hold not of an image but of a reality), and bringing forth and nourishing true virtue to become the friend of God and be immortal, if mortal man may. . . ."

5

OVID

The Art of Love, 1 B.C.E.

Ovid (43 B.C.E.–17 C.E.) was one of the leading poets of the culturally rich age of Augustus, the first Roman emperor. Born into a wealthy family, he socialized in imperial circles and practiced law until he gave it up to write poetry. His first major work, *Amores* (Loves), told love stories of the gods and of his own personal life, having been married three times and divorced twice by the age of thirty. Later, in 1 B.C.E., he began publishing the three volumes of his *Ars Amatoria* (Art of Love), the playful guide to seduction included here. Despite the publication of his more respectable poems about the changing forms of gods and nature, *The Metamorphoses*, Ovid was identified with his poems on love and sexuality at a time when Augustus sought to put an end to the loose morality of Roman nobility, including members of his own family. Because of his poetry and a mistake "more serious than murder," he later wrote, Ovid was exiled by Augustus in 8 C.E. to the coast of the Black Sea, where he lived the last decade of his life, pining for the culture and excitement of Rome.

What does this selection tell you about how men and women could behave in Roman society? What does Ovid think of love? How is Ovid's idea of love different from Plato's? Compare Ovid's *Art of Love* with Vatsyana's *Kama Sutra*. What does this selection suggest about the differences in attitudes toward sexuality between Roman society and Greek, Indian, or Chinese society?

Source: Ovid, *The Art of Love*, trans. A. S. Kline, *Poetry in Translation*, http://www.poetryintranslation.com/klineasartoflove.htm.

THINKING HISTORCALLY

The author appears loud, front, and center in these poems. How would you characterize his voice? He is also fairly explicit about his audience (or audiences), and he suggests various motivations for writing. How would you describe the social class of his intended audience? How does the shift in audience in Book III change your assessment of Ovid's motives? What other reasons might have made him write these poems?

Book I
Part I: His Task

Should anyone here not know the art of love,
read this, and learn by reading how to love.
By art the boat's set gliding, with oar and sail,
by art the chariot's swift: love's ruled by art.

. . .

I sing of safe love, permissible intrigue,
and there'll be nothing sinful in my song.
Now the first task for you who come as a raw recruit
is to find out who you might wish to love.
The next task is to make sure that she likes you:
the third, to see to it that the love will last.
That's my aim, that's the ground my chariot will cover:
that's the post my thundering wheels will scrape.

Part II: How to Find Her

While you're still free, and can roam on a loose rein,
pick one to whom you could say: "You alone please me."
She won't come falling for you out of thin air:
the right girl has to be searched for: use your eyes.

. . .

If you'd catch them very young and not yet grown,
real child-brides will come before your eyes:
if it's young girls you want, thousands will please you.
You'll be forced to be unsure of your desires:
if you delight greatly in older wiser years,
here too, believe me, there's an even greater crowd.

. . .

Part IV: Or at the Theatre

But hunt for them, especially, at the tiered theatre:
that place is the most fruitful for your needs.

There you'll find one to love, or one you can play with,
one to be with just once, or one you might wish to keep.
As ants return home often in long processions,
carrying their favourite food in their mouths,
or as the bees buzz through the flowers and thyme,
among their pastures and fragrant chosen meadows,
so our fashionable ladies crowd to the famous shows:
my choice is often constrained by such richness.
They come to see, they come to be seen as well:
the place is fatal to chaste modesty.

. . .

Part V: Or at the Races, or the Circus

Don't forget the races, those noble stallions:
the Circus holds room for a vast obliging crowd.
No need here for fingers to give secret messages,
nor a nod of the head to tell you she accepts:
You can sit by your lady: nothing's forbidden,
press your thigh to hers, as you can do, all the time:
and it's good the rows force you close, even if you don't like it,
since the girl is touched through the rules of the place.
Now find your reason for friendly conversation,
and first of all engage in casual talk.
Make earnest enquiry whose those horses are:
and rush to back her favourite, whatever it is.
When the crowded procession of ivory gods goes by,
you clap fervently for Lady Venus[1]:
if by chance a speck of dust falls in the girl's lap,
as it may, let it be flicked away by your fingers:
and if there's nothing, flick away the nothing:
let anything be a reason for you to serve her.
If her skirt is trailing too near the ground,
lift it, and raise it carefully from the dusty earth:
Straightaway, the prize for service, if she allows it,
is that your eyes catch a glimpse of her legs.

. . .

Part IX: How to Win Her

So far, riding her unequal wheels, the Muse has taught you
where you might choose your love, where to set your nets.

---

[1] Roman goddess of love; origins in Latin goddess of vegetation and Greek Aphrodite. [Ed.]

Now I'll undertake to tell you what pleases her,
by what arts she's caught, itself a work of highest art.

. . .

Part X: First Secure the Maid

But to get to know your desired-one's maid
is your first care: she'll smooth your way.
See if she's close to her mistress's thoughts,
and has plenty of true knowledge of her secret jests.
Corrupt her with promises, and with prayers:
you'll easily get what you want, if she wishes.
She'll tell the time (the doctors would know it too)
when her mistress's mind is receptive, fit for love.
Her mind will be fit for love when she luxuriates
in fertility,[2] like the crop on some rich soil.

. . .

Part XVII: Tears, Kisses, and Take the Lead

And tears help: tears will move a stone:
let her see your damp cheeks if you can.
If tears (they don't always come at the right time)
fail you, touch your eyes with a wet hand.
What wise man doesn't mingle tears with kisses?
Though she might not give, take what isn't given.
Perhaps she'll struggle, and then say "you're wicked":
struggling she still wants, herself, to be conquered.
Only, take care her lips aren't bruised by snatching,
and that she can't complain that you were harsh.

. . .

Book II
Part XX: The Task's Complete . . . But Now . . .

. . .

I've given you weapons: Vulcan[3] gave Achilles his:
excel with the gifts you're given, as he excelled.
But whoever overcomes an Amazon[4] with my sword,
write on the spoils "Ovid was my master."
Behold, you tender girls ask for rules for yourselves:
well yours then will be the next task for my pen!

---

[2] Recent studies confirm increased desire at the point of ovulation, but Ovid knew only the Roman (and general ancient) association of women and earth, passion and flowering. [Ed.]

[3] Roman god of fire; forged the shield of the warrior Achilles. [Ed.]

[4] Mythic tribe of warrior women. [Ed.]

Book III
Part I: It's Time to Teach You Girls

I've given the Greeks arms, against Amazons: arms remain,
to give to you Penthesilea,[5] and your Amazon troop.
Go equal to the fight: let them win, those who are favoured
by Venus, and her Boy, who flies through all the world.
It's not fair for armed men to battle with naked girls:
that would be shameful, men, even if you win.
Someone will say: "Why add venom to the snake,
and betray the sheepfold to the rabid she-wolf?"
Beware of loading the crime of the many onto the few:
let the merits of each separate girl be seen.

. . .

Only playful passions will be learnt from me:
I'll teach girls the ways of being loved.
Women don't brandish flames or cruel bows:
I rarely see men harmed by their weapons.
Men often cheat: it's seldom tender girls,
and, if you check, they're rarely accused of fraud.

. . .

What destroyed you all, I ask? Not knowing how to love:
your art was lacking: love lasts long through art.
You still might lack it now: but, before my eyes,
stood Venus herself, and ordered me to teach you.
She said to me, then: "What have the poor girls done,
an unarmed crowd betrayed to well-armed men?
Two books of *their* tricks have been composed:
let this lot too be instructed by your warnings." . . .

. . .

Part IV: Make-Up, but in Private

How near I was to warning you, no rankness of the wild goat
under your armpits, no legs bristling with harsh hair!
But I'm not teaching girls from the Caucasian hills,
or those who drink your waters, Mysian Caicus.[6]
So why remind you not to let your teeth get blackened,
by being lazy, and to wash your face each morning in water?

---

[5] In Greek mythology Penthesilea was queen of the Amazons (the warrior women). [Ed.]

[6] Caucasian hills and Mysian Caicus suggest unrefined people from wild areas: the rugged mountains of the Caucusus and the swirling waters of the Caicus River in Roman Asia (northwest Turkey). [Ed.]

You know how to acquire whiteness with a layer of powder:
she who doesn't blush by blood, indeed, blushes by art.
You make good the naked edges of your eyebrows,
and hide your natural cheeks with little patches.

. . .

Still, don't let your lover find cosmetic bottles . . .

. . .

Part XIV: Use Jealousy and Fear

Let all be betrayed: I've unbarred the gates to the enemy:
and let my loyalty be to treacherous betrayal.
What's easily given nourishes love poorly:
mingle the odd rejection with welcome fun.
Let him lie before the door, crying: "Cruel entrance!,"
pleading very humbly, threatening a lot too.
We can't stand sweetness: bitterness renews our taste:

. . .

Also when the lover you've just caught falls into the net,
let him think that only he has access to your room.
Later let him sense a rival, the bed's shared pact:
remove these arts, and love grows old.
The horse runs swiftly from the starting gate,
when he has others to pass, and others follow.
Wrongs relight the dying fires, as you wish:
See (I confess!), I don't love unless I'm hurt.

Part XVIII: And So to Bed

To have been taught more is shameful: but kindly Venus
said: "What's shameful is my particular concern."
Let each girl know herself: adopt a reliable posture
for her body: one layout's not suitable for all.
She who's known for her face, lie there face upwards:
let her back be seen, she whose back delights.

. . .

Woman, feel love, melted to your very bones,
and let both delight equally in the thing.
Don't leave out seductive coos and delightful murmurings,
don't let wild words be silent in the middle of your games.
You to whom nature denies sexual feeling,
pretend to sweet delight with artful sounds.
Unhappy girl, for whom that sluggish place is numb,
which man and woman equally should enjoy.

Only beware when you feign it, lest it shows:
create belief in your movements and your eyes.
When you like it, show it with cries and panting breath:
Ah! I blush, that part has its own secret signs.
She who asks fondly for a gift after love's delights,
can't want her request to carry any weight.
Don't let light into the room through all the windows:
it's fitting for much of your body to be concealed.

The game is done: time to descend, you swans,
you who bent your necks beneath my yoke.
As once the boys, so now my crowd of girls
inscribe on your trophies "Ovid was my master."

6

Depictions of Gender in Classical Societies, c. 500 B.C.E. – 300 C.E.

The images shown here offer examples of how artists and craftsmen depicted gender in classical Greece, China, India, and Egypt. The first image (Figure 5.1) comes from a kouros, which was a freestanding figure of a young man, usually nude and beardless — an art form that developed in Archaic or early Greece. Our image would have appeared on the face of a platform that supported the kouros. It would have stood in a cemetery testifying to the athletic abilities and virility of the deceased. What does this art form tell you about early Greek society?

Figure 5.1 Base of a funerary kouros with six athletes, 510–500 B.C.E.
Source: © BeBa/Iberfoto/The Image Works.

Figure 5.2   Qin Dynasty pottery warrior from tomb of Ch'in Shih-Huang-Ti, 210 B.C.E.

Source: © AAAC/Topham/The Image Works.

Thousands of the full size warriors shown in Figure 5.2, made of baked clay and painted in military uniform but with individual features, were placed in the underground entrance to the tomb of the first Qin emperor and then buried. They were only recently discovered as the location of the tomb was kept secret. It is said that 700,000 workmen constructed the tomb and then were killed to conceal it. In what ways was Qin China like Greece? In what ways was it like the ancient kingdoms of Mesopotamia?

The third image, Figure 5.3, comes from a frieze that most likely decorated a Buddhist temple or monastery in India. It probably would have been one of a number of panels that told stories about the life of the Buddha. This panel tells the story of Sundarananda, the brother of the Buddha, who adored his lovely wife Sundari (Beautiful). Here we see him and a maid help Sundari dress. We see how beautiful she is and how attentive he is. The next panels might have shown the rest of the story: the arrival of the Buddha at Sundarananda's house eager to convert him and take him away from domestic desires; Sundari spitting on the floor saying "you better be back before that dries" as Sundarananda with begging bowl in hand leaves, looking back longingly; the Buddha bringing his brother to heaven to show him the 500 maidens who are waiting his arrival,

Figure 5.3 Sundarananda helping Sundari dress, Kushan period,
first century B.C.E.

Source: DeAgostini/SuperStock.

followed by a trip to hell to show him the boiling pot being prepared
to cook him after his 500 years in heaven. The message of the tale is
that heaven and hell are part of the cycle of life, of desire and loss,
loving and losing. The only solution is release from it all: Even from
beautiful Sundari. How does the image convey this message? What
does it suggest about the roles of men and women?

Figure 5.4 is one of hundreds of excavated portraits of both men
and women from the Fayum or desert oasis area in central Egypt that
were made to adorn the coffin of the mummified individual. The tradition of a portrait on the mummy dates back to Pharaonic Egypt,
but these examples of almost photographic realism stem from the
artistic developments of Hellenistic Greece, some of whose artists
and elite settled in Roman Egypt. What does the look and attire of
this woman suggest to you? How does it reinforce what you have
read about women in Hellenistic Egypt?

THINKING HISTORICALLY

Who would have been the "audience" for these different works of art?
Which works seem to be intended more for men than women? Which
of these reflect patriarchal values? How? What were the purposes of
these different art forms? What message would a cemetery full of

Figure 5.4 Portrait of a Fayum woman with large gold necklace, Roman Egypt, first century B.C.E.– third century C.E.

Source: Detroit Institute of Arts, USA/Gift of Julius H. Haass/ The Bridgeman Art Library International.

figures such as that of the athletes shown in Figure 5.1 convey to Greek men? What would it convey to Greek women? How might a funerary statue for an Athenian woman differ? What do you think viewers were supposed to feel when looking at the Indian frieze shown in Figure 5.3? How does this differ from the message suggested by the warrior figure from the Qin Dynasty? Does this image convey a different message to men than it does to women, and if so, how?

Figure 5.4, like most other Fayum portraits, shows a person who is neither old nor decrepit. They were probably painted when the person was still very much alive. Given the obvious purpose, how would you sit today for your coffin portrait? Would your expression be like that of this woman? How is the agenda of this portrait similar to, or different from, the others here in document 6? How are the audiences similar or different?

■ REFLECTIONS

Over thirty years ago the historian Joan Kelly ignited the study of women's history with an essay that asked: "Did Women Have a Renaissance?" Questioning whether the great eras in men's history were also great eras for women, she found that men's achievements often came at the expense of women. We have seen how the urban revolution fit this pattern. The rise of cities, the creation of territorial states, the invention of writing, and the development of complex societies, all beginning about five thousand years ago, accompanied the development of patriarchal institutions and ideas. Similarly, the rise of classical cultures, cities, and states about twenty-five hundred years ago seems to have cemented patriarchy. The great religious and philosophical traditions of the classical era emerged with the new states. Some, like Chinese Legalism, voiced support for the new order; others, like Confucianism, evoked an older feudal order that was fading. In China neither the statist nor feudal philosophy brought relief to women, though in the hands of someone like Ban Zhao, Confucianism might be shaped to strengthen the bonds between husband and wife as well as the more traditional male-centered bonds. Indian state building of the classical age similarly pitted a renewed patriarchal Brahmanism against emerging Buddhist and other reforming movements for greater social equality. But by the time of the Gupta era, patriarchal Brahmanism had won the day, creating a world for the upper-caste Hindu male secure enough to not require the sexual repression of all women. The upper-class Greek classical patriarchy enjoyed similar assurances.

History is a method of investigation as well as a subject matter. Historians use various methods, some of which we have included in our "Thinking Historically" sections. But beyond these, history is a general method as well. Historians historicize. We make things historical that were previously thought to have no history. We find that some aspects of life that were generally thought to be eternal or unchanging actually have changed over the course of time. They have a history. This chapter shows how ideas of love and gender are historical rather than always and everywhere the same. To see that different cultures have developed or emphasized different ideas of love is not to rule out any role for biology or human nature, but it is to recognize that our emotions are also learned, perhaps more than we thought.

In addition to love, we have learned to historicize gender identity. Male and female stereotypes that held sway into the mid-twentieth century have long been undermined by historical studies of gender, psychological studies, sensitivity training, and public law. We recognize that personality traits stereotypically thought to be "masculine" or "feminine" can be learned or genetically not coded to a male or female anatomy. In this and previous chapters we have also historicized sexuality to the degree that we have seen different ideas about sex and the sacred, and different customs related to sex in different societies. Homosexuality raises the possibility of a more sweeping historicizing of sexuality. Is it possible that the percentage of homosexuals or heterosexuals in society also varies historically? Is same-sex or opposite-sex preference also historical? Are we taught to be "gay" or "straight"? These questions are prompted, of course, by our study of classical Greece, mainly Athens, and, for that matter, a small class of intellectuals in that city-state. Their influence very likely goes far beyond their numbers. We have no way of knowing if Athens contained a higher proportion of homosexuals or bisexuals than other societies. In fact, these may be the wrong questions. It may be that *heterosexuality* and *homosexuality* are also historical constructs. These modern words and the concepts they entail, based as they are on post-Greek religious traditions (Judaic, Christian, and Islamic) that oppose and moralize the difference, may miss what the Greeks meant and felt. For them, these liaisons had more to do with education than lifestyle, they were often more spiritual than physical, and physical penetration had more to do with social standing than gender. For most of these Greeks, it would make more sense to speak of *bisexuality* rather than *homosexuality*, except that bisexuality implies a combination of two extremes they probably did not see. The world has been constantly changing, and so too have the words we use to describe it.

6

From Tribal to Universal Religion

Hindu-Buddhist and Judeo-Christian Traditions, 1000 B.C.E.—100 C.E.

■ HISTORICAL CONTEXT

From 1000 B.C.E. to 100 C.E. two major religious traditions, one centered in the Middle East and the other in northern India, split into at least four major religious traditions, so large that today they are embraced by a majority of the inhabitants of the world. Both of the two original traditions, Hinduism and Judaism, were in 1000 B.C.E. highly restricted in membership. Neither sought converts but instead ministered to members of their own tribe and castes. This chapter explores how these two essentially inward-looking religions created universal religions, open to all. It is a story not only of the emergence of Christianity and Buddhism but also of the development of modern Judaic and Hindu religions.

Remarkably, both of these traditions moved from tribal to universal religions; even more remarkable are the common elements, given their different routes along that path. While Hinduism cultivated a psychological approach to spiritual enlightenment out of a religion based on caste, Brahman priests, and offerings to innumerable deities, Judaism developed an abiding faith in a universal historical providence after the repeated conquest of a local temple administered by a tribal priesthood. In both transitions, traditions of sacrifice, ritual, worldly prosperity, and inherited status diminished, to be replaced by ideas of universal salvation from this world.

Understanding how religions change or evolve is especially diffi-cult because of the tendency of religious adherents to emphasize the timelessness of their truths. Fortunately, religious commitment and belief do not require a denial of historical change. Indeed, many adherents have found strength in all manifestations of the sacred— the specific and historical as well as the universal and eternal.

Whether motives are primarily religious or secular, however, the historical study of religion offers a useful window on understanding large-scale changes in human behavior. Since religions tend to conserve, repeat, and enshrine, change is more gradual than in many other aspects of human thought and behavior: fashion, say, or technology. Thus, when religions develop radically new ideas or institutions, we can learn much about human resistance and innovation by studying the circumstances.

As you read the selections in this chapter, notice over the course of the first millennium B.C.E. how both core religions created new faiths and reformed the old. Notice also the fundamentally different ways these two great religious traditions changed. Finally, observe how the later offspring religions, Buddhism and Christianity, preached ideas that were already current, but not dominant, in the "parental" traditions.

■ THINKING HISTORICALLY

Detecting Change in Primary Sources

Because religions typically prefer conservation over innovation, changes are often grafted onto old formulations. Historians who want to understand when and how change occurred must sometimes look at primary sources to uncover new ideas and ways of doing things that have been assimilated into the tradition.

The easiest way to see change in primary sources is to compare a number of them composed in different historical periods. However, sometimes we are able to see examples of change in a single document. A written source may, for instance, originate in more than one oral account, and the writer may combine them both even though one is later than the other and they represent different ideas. A manuscript might also pick up errors or updates as it is rewritten for the next generation. We will see examples of both of these changes and others in the documents in this chapter.

1

Hinduism: Svetasvatara Upanishad, c. 400 B.C.E.

In Chapter 3 selections from the Hindu Vedas and Upanishads help introduce some basic ideas in Hinduism: the belief that animals and human castes were created out of the primal sacrifice of the god Purusha in the Vedas, the complementary ideas of karma and reincarnation in the Upanishads, and, lastly, the identification of Brahman and *atman* (God and self), also in the Upanishads.

Take a look at the same selections again to understand the changing nature of Hinduism from the earliest Vedas to the latest Upanishads. For example, we see in Chapter 3, selection 2, the interest of the authors of the Vedas in defining and justifying caste differences and the supremacy of the Brahman priests as masters of sacrifice, prayers, rituals, and sacred hymns.

The authors of the Upanishads were less interested in sacrifice and priestly rituals and more absorbed by philosophical questions. Thus, Chapter 3, selection 3, on karma and reincarnation, spells out the idea of justice and a philosophy of nature that reflects the interests of a later settled society. Finally, selection 4 on the identity of Brahman and *atman* reflects an even more meditative Upanishad that virtually ignores the role of priests. This meditative tradition may have existed in early Hinduism, but there is far more evidence of its expression in the Upanishads (after 800 B.C.E.) than in the earlier Vedas.

The *Svetasvatara** Upanishad selection included here reflects an additional step along the path from the religion of priests, sacrifice, and caste obligation to individualized spirituality. Here the idea of the transmigration of souls from one body to another in an endless cycle of reincarnations—an idea that developed after the Vedas—is challenged by the idea that the individual who seeks Brahman might break out of the wheel of life. How would this idea of escaping reincarnation diminish the power of Brahman priests? How does it minimize the importance of caste and karma?

THINKING HISTORICALLY

Recognizing changes in the Hindu tradition is more difficult than in the Judaic tradition. The literature of Judaism is full of historical references: names of historical figures and even dates. Hindu sacred literature, as

* sveh tah SVAH tah ruh

Source: *Svetasvatara* Upanishad in *The Upanishads: The Breath of the Eternal*, trans. Swami Prabhavananda and Frederick Manchester (Hollywood: The Vedanta Society of Southern California, 1948; New York: Mentor Books, 1957), 118–21.

you can tell from this brief introduction, shows virtually no interest in historical names and dates. Because time in India was conceived as cyclical, rather than linear, and the cycles of the Indian time scheme were immense, determining the exact time an event occurred was less important in Hindu thought than understanding its eternal meaning.

Consequently, our analysis of the changes in Hinduism is more logical than chronological. We can therefore speak of a long-term historical process even though we cannot date each step.

The oldest of the thirteen universally recognized Upanishads, all of which were composed between 800 and 400 B.C.E., are the Brihad Aranyaka and the Chandogya (from which selections 3 and 4 in Chapter 3 are taken). The *Svetasvatara* is one of the last of the thirteen, composed closer to 400 B.C.E. What is the idea of time suggested by this Upanishad?

This vast universe is a wheel. Upon it are all creatures that are subject to birth, death, and rebirth. Round and round it turns, and never stops. It is the wheel of Brahman. As long as the individual self thinks it is separate from Brahman, it revolves upon the wheel in bondage to the laws of birth, death, and rebirth. But when through the grace of Brahman it realizes its identity with him, it revolves upon the wheel no longer. It achieves immortality.

He who is realized by transcending the world of cause and effect, in deep contemplation, is expressly declared by the scriptures to be the Supreme Brahman. He is the substance, all else the shadow. He is the imperishable. The knowers of Brahman know him as the one reality behind all that seems. For this reason they are devoted to him. Absorbed in him, they attain freedom from the wheel of birth, death, and rebirth.

The Lord supports this universe, which is made up of the perishable and the imperishable, the manifest and the unmanifest. The individual soul, forgetful of the Lord, attaches itself to pleasure and thus is bound. When it comes to the Lord, it is freed from all its fetters.

Mind and matter, master and servant—both have existed from beginningless time. The Maya which unites them has also existed from beginningless time. When all three—mind, matter, and Maya—are known as one with Brahman, then is it realized that the Self is infinite and has no part in action. Then is it revealed that the Self is all.

Matter is perishable. The Lord, the destroyer of ignorance, is imperishable, immortal. He is the one God, the Lord of the perishable and of all souls. By meditating on him, by uniting oneself with him, by identifying oneself with him, one ceases to be ignorant.

Know God, and all fetters will be loosed. Ignorance will vanish. Birth, death, and rebirth will be no more. Meditate upon him and transcend physical consciousness. Thus will you reach union with the lord of the universe. Thus will you become identified with him who is One without a second. In him all your desires will find fulfillment.

The truth is that you are always united with the Lord. But you must *know* this. Nothing further is there to know. Meditate, and you will realize that mind, matter, and Maya (the power which unites mind and matter) are but three aspects of Brahman, the one reality.

Fire, though present in the firesticks, is not perceived until one stick is rubbed against another. The Self is like that fire: It is realized in the body by meditation on the sacred syllable OM.[1]

Let your body be the stick that is rubbed, the sacred syllable OM the stick that is rubbed against it. Thus shall you realize God, who is hidden within the body as fire is hidden within the wood.

Like oil in sesame seeds, butter in cream, water in the river bed, fire in tinder, the Self dwells within the soul. Realize him through truthfulness and meditation.

Like butter in cream is the Self in everything. Knowledge of the Self is gained through meditation. The Self is Brahman. By Brahman is all ignorance destroyed.

To realize God, first control the outgoing senses and harness the mind. Then meditate upon the light in the heart of the fire—meditate, that is, upon pure consciousness as distinct from the ordinary consciousness of the intellect. Thus the Self, the Inner Reality, may be seen behind physical appearance.

[1] Sacred symbol for God and the sound chanted in meditation. [Ed.]

2

Buddhism: Gotama's Discovery, c. 500–100 B.C.E.

Gotama Siddhartha* (c. 563–483 B.C.E.), known to history as the Buddha, was the son of a Hindu Kshatriya prince in northern India. This selection tells a traditional story about his youth. Because his father was warned by "Brahman soothsayers" that young Gotama would leave his home to live among the seekers in the forest, his father kept the boy distracted in the palace, the sufferings of people outside hidden from him. This selection begins when the prince, or *rāja*, finally agrees to let Gotama tour outside the palace.

*GAH tah mah   sih DAHR thah

Source: "The Life of Gotama the Buddha," trans. E. H. Brewster, in Clarence H. Hamilton, *Buddhism* (1926; reprint, New York: The Bobbs-Merrill Company, 1952), 6–11.

What does Gotama discover? What seems to be the meaning of these discoveries for him? How is his subsequent thought or behavior similar to that of other Hindus in the era? How is the message of this story similar to the lessons of the Upanishads?

THINKING HISTORICALLY

None of the stories we have of the Buddha was written during his lifetime. For some four hundred years, stories of the Buddha were passed by word of mouth before they were put into writing. Can you see any signs in this story that it was memorized and told orally? When the stories were finally written down, some were no doubt more faithful to the Buddha's actual words and experience than others. What elements in this story would most likely reflect the historical experience of Gotama? What parts of the story would most likely be added later by people who worshiped the Buddha?

Now the young lord Gotama, when many days had passed by, bade his charioteer make ready the state carriages, saying: "Get ready the carriages, good charioteer, and let us go through the park to inspect the pleasaunce."[1] "Yes, my lord," replied the charioteer, and harnessed the state carriages and sent word to Gotama: "The carriages are ready, my lord; do now what you deem fit." Then Gotama mounted a state carriage and drove out in state into the park.

Now the young lord saw, as he was driving to the park, an aged man as bent as a roof gable, decrepit, leaning on a staff, tottering as he walked, afflicted and long past his prime. And seeing him Gotama said: "That man, good charioteer, what has he done, that his hair is not like that of other men, nor his body?"

"He is what is called an aged man, my lord."

"But why is he called aged?"

"He is called aged, my lord, because he has not much longer to live."

"But then, good charioteer, am I too subject to old age, one who has not got past old age?"

"You, my lord, and we too, we all are of a kind to grow old; we have not got past old age."

"Why then, good charioteer, enough of the park for today. Drive me back hence to my rooms."

"Yea, my lord," answered the charioteer, and drove him back. And he, going to his rooms, sat brooding sorrowful and depressed, thinking, "Shame then verily be upon this thing called birth, since to one born old age shows itself like that!"

---

[1] A garden. [Ed.]

Thereupon the rāja sent for the charioteer and asked him: "Well, good charioteer, did the boy take pleasure in the park? Was he pleased with it?"

"No, my lord, he was not."

"What then did he see on his drive?"

(And the charioteer told the rāja all.)

Then the rāja thought thus: We must not have Gotama declining to rule. We must not have him going forth from the house into the homeless state. We must not let what the brāhman soothsayers spoke of come true.

So, that these things might not come to pass, he let the youth be still more surrounded by sensuous pleasures. And thus Gotama continued to live amidst the pleasures of sense.

Now after many days had passed by, the young lord again bade his charioteer make ready and drove forth as once before. . . .

And Gotama saw, as he was driving to the park, a sick man, suffering and very ill, fallen and weltering in his own water, by some being lifted up, by others being dressed. Seeing this, Gotama asked: "That man, good charioteer, what has he done that his eyes are not like others' eyes, nor his voice like the voice of other men?"

"He is what is called ill, my lord."

"But what is meant by ill?"

"It means, my lord, that he will hardly recover from his illness."

"But am I too, then, good charioteer, subject to fall ill; have I not got out of reach of illness?"

"You, my lord, and we too, we are all subject to fall ill; we have not got beyond the reach of illness."

"Why then, good charioteer, enough of the park for today. Drive me back hence to my rooms." "Yea, my lord," answered the charioteer, and drove him back. And he, going to his rooms, sat brooding sorrowful and depressed, thinking: Shame then verily be upon this thing called birth, since to one born decay shows itself like that, disease shows itself like that.

Thereupon the rāja sent for the charioteer and asked him: "Well, good charioteer, did the young lord take pleasure in the park and was he pleased with it?"

"No, my lord, he was not."

"What did he see then on his drive?"

(And the charioteer told the rāja all.)

Then the rāja thought thus: We must not have Gotama declining to rule; we must not have him going forth from the house to the homeless state; we must not let what the brāhman soothsayers spoke of come true.

So, that these things might not come to pass, he let the young man be still more abundantly surrounded by sensuous pleasures. And thus Gotama continued to live amidst the pleasures of sense.

Now once again, after many days . . . the young lord Gotama . . . drove forth.

And he saw, as he was driving to the park, a great concourse of people clad in garments of different colours constructing a funeral pyre. And seeing this he asked his charioteer: "Why now are all those people come together in garments of different colours, and making that pile?"

"It is because someone, my lord, has ended his days."

"Then drive the carriage close to him who has ended his days."

"Yea, my lord," answered the charioteer, and did so. And Gotama saw the corpse of him who had ended his days and asked: "What, good charioteer, is ending one's days?"

"It means, my lord, that neither mother, nor father, nor other kinsfolk will now see him, nor will he see them."

"But am I too then subject to death, have I not got beyond reach of death? Will neither the rāja, nor the ranee, nor any other of my kin see me more, or shall I again see them?"

"You, my lord, and we too, we are all subject to death; we have not passed beyond the reach of death. Neither the rāja, nor the ranee, nor any other of your kin will see you any more, nor will you see them."

"Why then, good charioteer, enough of the park for today. Drive me back hence to my rooms."

"Yea, my lord," replied the charioteer, and drove him back.

And he, going to his rooms, sat brooding sorrowful and depressed, thinking: Shame verily be upon this thing called birth, since to one born the decay of life, since disease, since death shows itself like that!

Thereupon the rāja questioned the charioteer as before and as before let Gotama be still more surrounded by sensuous enjoyment. And thus he continued to live amidst the pleasures of sense.

Now once again, after many days . . . the lord Gotama . . . drove forth.

And he saw, as he was driving to the park, a shaven-headed man, a recluse, wearing the yellow robe. And seeing him he asked the charioteer, "That man, good charioteer, what has he done that his head is unlike other men's heads and his clothes too are unlike those of others?"

"That is what they call a recluse, because, my lord, he is one who has gone forth."

"What is that, 'to have gone forth'?"

"To have gone forth, my lord, means being thorough in the religious life, thorough in the peaceful life, thorough in good action, thorough in meritorious conduct, thorough in harmlessness, thorough in kindness to all creatures."

"Excellent indeed, friend charioteer, is what they call a recluse, since so thorough is his conduct in all those respects, wherefore drive me up to that forthgone man."

"Yea, my lord," replied the charioteer and drove up to the recluse. Then Gotama addressed him, saying, "You master, what have you done that your head is not as other men's heads, nor your clothes as those of other men?"

"I, my lord, am one who has gone forth."

"What, master, does that mean?"

"It means, my lord, being thorough in the religious life, thorough in the peaceful life, thorough in good actions, thorough in meritorious conduct, thorough in harmlessness, thorough in kindness to all creatures."

"Excellently indeed, master, are you said to have gone forth since so thorough is your conduct in all those respects." Then the lord Gotama bade his charioteer, saying: "Come then, good charioteer, do you take the carriage and drive it back hence to my rooms. But I will even here cut off my hair, and don the yellow robe, and go forth from the house into the homeless state."

"Yea, my lord," replied the charioteer, and drove back. But the prince Gotama, there and then cutting off his hair and donning the yellow robe, went forth from the house into the homeless state.

Now at Kapilavatthu, the rāja's seat, a great number of persons, some eighty-four thousand souls, heard of what prince Gotama had done and thought: Surely this is no ordinary religious rule, this is no common going forth, in that prince Gotama himself has had his head shaved and has donned the yellow robe and has gone forth from the house into the homeless state. If prince Gotama has done this, why then should not we also? And they all had their heads shaved and donned the yellow robes; and in imitation of the Bodhisat [Buddha][2] they went forth from the house into the homeless state. So the Bodhisat went forth from the house into the homeless state. So the Bodhisat went up on his rounds through the villages, towns, and cities accompanied by that multitude.

Now there arose in the mind of Gotama the Bodhisat, when he was meditating in seclusion, this thought: That indeed is not suitable for me that I should live beset. 'Twere better were I to dwell alone, far from the crowd.

So after a time he dwelt alone, away from the crowd. Those eighty-four thousand recluses went one way, and the Bodhisat went another way.

Now there arose in the mind of Gotama the Bodhisat, when he had gone to his place and was meditating in seclusion, this thought: Verily, this world had fallen upon trouble — one is born, and grows old, and dies, and falls from one state, and springs up in another. And from the suffering, moreover, no one knows of any way to escape, even from decay and death. O, when shall a way of escape from this suffering be made known — from decay and from death?

---

[2] Here the author clearly means the Buddha, but the term *Bodhisat* or *Bodhisattva* came to designate a kind of Buddhist saint who helped others achieve salvation in the later Mahayana school of Buddhism. [Ed.]

3

Buddhism and Caste,
c. 500–100 B.C.E.

This story, part of the Buddhist canon that was written between one hundred and four hundred years after Buddha's death, tells of a confrontation between the Buddha and Brahmans, members of the Hindu priestly caste. Such an encounter would have been common as Brahmans and Buddhists confronted each other during the Maurya Empire (321–184 B.C.E.), which included the great Buddhist convert, King Ashoka (304–232 B.C.E.). (A Brahman reaction set in during the following Shunga dynasty, and Buddhism almost vanished from India.) How would you expect most Brahmans to react to the Buddha's opposition to caste? Would some Brahmans be persuaded by the Buddha's arguments? How and why might Buddhism have a wider appeal than Hinduism?

THINKING HISTORICALLY

What signs do you see in the document that it was not written during the lifetime of the Buddha? Notice the mention of Greece and the dialogue style of this selection. If, as some scholars have suggested, there may be Greek influence here, which Greek writer would they be referring to (see Chapter 3)? How might this Greek influence help us find an approximate date for this writing?

Once when the Lord was staying at Sāvatthī there were five hundred brāhmans from various countries in the city . . . and they thought: "This ascetic Gautama preaches that all four classes are pure. Who can refute him?"

At that time there was a young brāhman named Assalāyana in the city . . . a youth of sixteen, thoroughly versed in the Vedas . . . and in all brāhmanic learning. "He can do it!" thought the brāhmans, and so they asked him to try; surrounded by a crowd of brāhmans, he went to the Lord, and, after greeting him, sat down and said:

"Brāhmans maintain that only they are the highest class, and the others are below them. They are white, the others black; only they are pure, and not the others. Only they are the true sons of Brahmā, born from his mouth, born of Brahmā, creations of Brahmā, heirs of Brahmā. Now what does the worthy Gautama say to that?"

"Do the brāhmans really maintain this, Assalāyana, when they're born of women just like anyone else, of brāhman women who have their periods and conceive, give birth and nurse their children, just like any other women?"

Source: *The Buddhist Tradition in India, China and Japan*, ed. William Theodore de Bary (New York: Random House, 1969), 49–51.

"For all you say, this is what they think. . . ."

"Have you ever heard that in the lands of the Greeks and Kambojas and other peoples on the borders there are only two classes, masters and slaves, and a master can become a slave and vice versa?"

"Yes, I've heard so."

"And what strength or support does that fact give to the brāhmans' claim?"

"Nevertheless, that is what they think."

"Again if a man is a murderer, a thief, or an adulterer, or commits other grave sins, when his body breaks up on death does he pass on to purgatory if he's a kshatriya,[1] vaishya,[2] or shūdra,[3] but not if he's a brāhman?"

"No, Gautama. In such a case the same fate is in store for all men, whatever their class."

"And if he avoids grave sin, will he go to heaven if he's a brāhman, but not if he's a man of the lower classes?"

"No, Gautama. In such a case the same reward awaits all men, whatever their class."

"And is a brāhman capable of developing a mind of love without hate or ill-will, but not a man of the other classes?"

"No, Gautama. All four classes are capable of doing so."

"Can only a brāhman go down to a river and wash away dust and dirt, and not men of the other classes?"

"No, Gautama, all four classes can."

"Now suppose a king were to gather together a hundred men of different classes and to order the brāhmans and kshatriyas to take kindling wood of sāl, pine, lotus, or sandal, and light fires, while the lowclass folk did the same with common wood. What do you think would happen? Would the fires of the high-born men blaze up brightly . . . and those of the humble fail?"

"No, Gautama. It would be alike with high and lowly. . . . Every fire would blaze with the same bright flame." . . .

"Suppose there are two young brāhman brothers, one a scholar and the other uneducated. Which of them would be served first at memorial feasts, festivals, and sacrifices, or when entertained as guests?"

"The scholar, of course; for what great benefit would accrue from entertaining the uneducated one?"

"But suppose the scholar is ill-behaved and wicked, while the uneducated one is well-behaved and virtuous?"

"Then the uneducated one would be served first, for what great benefit would accrue from entertaining an ill-behaved and wicked man?"

---

[1] KSHAH tree uh   Warrior. [Ed.]

[2] VYS yuh   Free peasant, artisan, or producer. [Ed.]

[3] SHOO druh   Serf. [Ed.]

"First, Assalāyana, you based your claim on birth, then you gave up birth for learning, and finally you have come round to my way of thinking, that all four classes are equally pure!"

At this Assalāyana sat silent . . . his shoulders hunched, his eyes cast down, thoughtful in mind, and with no answer at hand.

4

Mahayana Buddhism: The Lotus Sutra, c. 100 C.E.

Written in India in the first or early second century C.E., the Lotus Sutra became one of the favorite Buddhist scriptures in China, Japan, and other Mahayana Buddhist countries. This very brief section from the sutra tells of the Buddha's death ("passing into extinction" or nirvana). The goal of all Buddhists, like the Buddha himself, was a state of consciousness called *bodhi* (enlightenment, or awakening) that brought a release from the suffering of the world and the attainment of ultimate peace, called nirvana. After the Buddha achieved this state, two Buddhist schools developed concerning the issue of how others might attain nirvana. One, the Theravada, said you had to emulate the hard, ascetic life of the Buddha. Another, the Mahayana, said it was easier and open to everyone because you could pray for help.

Mahayana Buddhism developed alongside but in opposition to Theravada (or Orthodox) Buddhism in its home in India. Theravada Buddhism (still practiced in Southeast Asia) was the more exacting and orthodox form of Buddhism; it encouraged all young men to emulate the Buddha by becoming monks, practicing rigorous discipline begging for their food, and studying the classic texts. Mahayana Buddhism means "the Greater Vehicle" because it could appeal to a greater range of people. Central to Mahayana Buddhism is the idea of a Bodhisattva—a Buddha-type who is capable of achieving nirvana but who, instead, helps others reach enlightenment. Thus, one can pray to a Bodhisattva to achieve salvation. Mahayana Buddhism spread through China and North Asia, offering a less demanding avenue to salvation than Theravada Buddhism, because instead of renouncing the everyday world and becoming a monk or a nun, one could continue a normal life while worshiping at temples and making offerings to the Buddha and various Bodhisattvas.

Source: *The Lotus Sutra*, translated by the Buddhist Text Translation Society, Mahayana Buddhists sutras in English at http://www.cttbusa.org/lotus/lotus1_1.asp.

Which ideas of this sutra make Buddhism more universal or offer "salvation" to a broader audience than monks, nuns, and other religious specialists?

THINKING HISTORICALLY

Some words and ideas in this document are "pre-Buddha" and some are "post-Buddha." That is, some words and ideas could be found in a Hindu text before the Buddha was born. Others seem to come from a world after the Buddha has died. Which words or ideas fit into one or the other of these categories? How can you distinguish between what might have happened at the time of the Buddha's death and what was probably added some time later? How are the ideas expressed in this sutra different from the ideas attributed to the Buddha in previous selections from this chapter? What might account for these differences? How did the early Buddhists who composed this sutra transform the Buddha as seeker of enlightenment into the Buddha as object of worship?

I recall that in ages past,
Limitless, countless aeons ago,
There appeared a Buddha, one honored among people
By the name of Brightness of Sun-Moon-Lamp,
That World Honored One[1] proclaimed the Dharma,[2]
Taking limitless living beings across,
Causing countless millions of Bodhisattvas
To enter the wisdom of the Buddhas.

Before that Buddha had left home,
The eight royal sons born to him,
Seeing the Great Sage leave his home,
Also followed him to practice Brahman conduct.

The Buddha then spoke a Great Vehicle[3]
Sutra by the name of Limitless Principles;
Amidst the assembly, and for their sake,
He set it forth in extensive detail.
When the Buddha had finished speaking the Sutra,
Seated in the Dharma-seat,

---

[1] The Buddha. [Ed.]
[2] The Law. [Ed.]
[3] *Mahayana* literally means "Great Vehicle." [Ed.]

He sat in full lotus[4] and entered the Samadhi[5]
Called the Station of Limitless Principles.
From the heavens fell a rain of Mandarava flowers,[6]
And heavenly drums of themselves did sound,
While all the gods, dragons, ghosts and spirits,
Made offerings to the Honored One;
And, within all the Buddha lands,
There occurred a mighty trembling.
The light emitted from between the Buddha's brows
Manifested all these rare events.

The light illumined to the east
Eighteen thousand Buddha lands,
Revealing the places of living beings'
Karmic retributions of birth and death.
Seen, too, were Buddha lands adorned
With a multitude of gems,
The color of lapis lazuli[7] and crystal,
Illumined by the Buddha's light.
Seen as well were gods and people,
Dragons, spirits, and Yaksha[8] Hordes,
Gandharvas and Kinnaras,[9]
Each making offering to the Buddha. . . .

The Buddha, having spoken The Dharma Flower[10]
And caused the assembly to rejoice,
Later, on that very day,
Announced to the host of gods and humans;
"The meaning of the real mark of all Dharmas
Has already been spoken for all of you,
And now at midnight, I
shall enter into Nirvana.
You should single-heartedly advance with vigor,
And avoid laxness, for
Buddhas are difficult indeed to meet,
Encountered but once in a million aeons."

---

[4] Yoga position on folded legs. [Ed.]

[5] Highest state of consciousness reached in meditation. [Ed.]

[6] Bright scarlet flowers associated with the story of an Indian princess. [Ed.]

[7] Rare blue stone. [Ed.]

[8] Indian nature spirits, often tree spirits, imagined in human form. [Ed.]

[9] Ancient tribal peoples or music spirits. [Ed.]

[10] The words that lead to the flowering of the Law; the Buddha's last words; sometimes refers to this Lotus Sutra itself. [Ed.]

All of the disciples of the World Honored One
Hearing of the Buddha's entry into Nirvana,
Each harbored grief and anguish,
"Why must the Buddha take extinction so soon?"
The sagely Lord, the Dharma King,
Then comforted the limitless multitude:
"After my passage into extinction,
None of you should worry or fear,
For the Bodhisattva Virtue Treasury,[11]
With respect to the non-outflow mark of reality,[12]
In heart has penetrated it totally;
He will next become a Buddha,
By the name of Pure Body, and
Will also save uncounted multitudes.

That night the Buddha passed into extinction,
As a flame dies once its fuel has been consumed.
The Sharira[13] were divided up,
And limitless stupas[14] built.
The Bhikshus and Bhikshuni,[15]
Their number like the Ganges' sands,
Redoubled their vigor in advancing
In their quest for the unsurpassed path.

[11] The name of the first Bodhisattva. [Ed.]
[12] He understands the true reality. [Ed.]
[13] The bones of the Buddha after cremation. [Ed.]
[14] Temples, usually built over a bone or other relic of the Buddha. [Ed.]
[15] Ordained nuns and monks. [Ed.]

5

Judaism and the Bible:
History, Laws, and Psalms, c. 850–600 B.C.E.

Just as the caste-based Hinduism of ancient India gave rise to universal Buddhism after 500 B.C.E., so did the Judaism of the Hebrew tribe of Abraham give birth to universalist Christianity. Judaism was already an ancient religion by the time of Jesus and the birth of Christianity. It traced its roots back (perhaps two thousand years) to

Source: Gen. 1:1–31, 2:1–25, 17:1–14; Exod. 19:1–9, 20:1–18; Lev. 1:1–9; Ps. 23:1–6; Amos 5:21–24. All biblical selections are from the New International Version.

Abraham himself, who, according to tradition, made a contract (or covenant) with God to worship him and him alone.

This commitment to one god, and one god only, was a development unique to the history of Judaism. The worship of various ancestral and nature spirits was common practice among hunting-gathering and agricultural peoples. Early cities added numerous local protectors and, in some cases, a pantheon of deities presented in myth and legend. The Bronze Age empires were probably the first to imagine a single ruler of the heavens—an obvious parallel to the role of the emperor on Earth. The Egyptians for a brief moment (around 1300 B.C.E.) preached the singularity of god, in this case the sun god Aton, but that was soon renounced. Persian Zoroastrianism imagined competing gods of light and darkness, each supreme in his realm, an idea that was to leave its mark in Persian-occupied Jerusalem. But the idea of a single creator of the universe—and no other gods—was new to the ancient Hebrews.

Since such a belief was unusual, the descendants of Abraham had difficulty accepting it. In their wanderings throughout the land of the Tigris and Euphrates rivers, from Abraham's native Ur to Egypt and Palestine, the Jews came into contact with many different religious beliefs; some were even tempted by foreign gods. However, by around 1300 B.C.E., Abraham's descendants had escaped Egyptian domination, crossed the Red Sea, and with the help of Moses renewed their covenant with God in the Ten Commandments. Even then, stories were told of Jews who worshiped the Golden Calf and other idols and of the displeasure of the God of Abraham. "I am a jealous God," he told his people. "You shall have no other gods before me."

Such is the story told in the books of the Hebrew Bible,[1] written after the Jews settled in Jerusalem and the surrounding area sometime after 1000 B.C.E. The Hebrew Bible not only recounts the story of the people of Abraham but also takes its story back ages before the patriarch, stretching back to the beginning of the world and forward to the period of Jewish kingdoms after 900 B.C.E., when Kings Saul, David, and Solomon ruled large parts of what is today Israel, Palestine, and Jordan. The Hebrew Bible included their histories, the laws of the two Jewish kingdoms Judah and Israel, and various other writings (songs, poetry called psalms, philosophy, and stories of prophecy).

As you read these first selections from the Bible (Genesis, Exodus, Leviticus, Psalms, Amos), note how they are similar to, and different from, the Vedas and Upanishads of Hinduism. How, for instance, is the Bible's story of the beginning of the world different from the

---

[1] *Hebrew Bible* refers to the books in the Bible that were written in Hebrew. Christians call these books the Old Testament. The first five books of the Bible are called the Torah by Jews. [Ed.]

Hindus' creation story of the sacrifice of Purusha? Why might an understanding of history be more important to the Jews than it was to the Hindus? Compare the role of morality in the religion of Jews and Hindus. In what sense is the morality of Judaism universal and that of Hinduism caste based? How is the Judaic emphasis on morality also different from Buddhist ideas?

THINKING HISTORICALLY

Since the books of the Hebrew Bible were composed over a long period of time, from about 900 B.C.E. to about 165 B.C.E., we might expect to see changes in emphasis, especially since this period was such a tumultuous one in Jewish history. The immediate descendants of Abraham were a nomadic pastoral people — shepherds, Psalm 23 reminds us — though this beautiful psalm attributed to King David was written in an urban, monarchal stage of Jewish history. Leviticus, too, echoes an earlier pastoral life when animal sacrifice, and the worship by shepherds generally, was still practiced.

When did morality replace sacrifice as the sign of respect to the God of Abraham? Was it around 1300 B.C.E., the traditional date for the reception by Moses of the Ten Commandments? Or is the existence of Leviticus, perhaps five hundred years later, a sign that sacrifice was still practiced? The sentiments of Amos (783–743 B.C.E.) suggest that the Jews later rejected not only animal sacrifice but also moral obedience that was not truly felt.

When did monotheism (the belief in one god) become unequivocal, unquestioned? Since this was a new idea, there must have been a time when it wasn't held. Some scholars see signs of an earlier polytheism (belief in many gods) in the book of Genesis itself. For instance, in Genesis 3:5 we find "ye shall be as gods," and Genesis 3:22 reads "And the Lord God said: Behold the man has become like one of us."

Certainly the beginning of Genesis is no-nonsense monotheism, majestically so: "In the beginning God created the heavens and the earth." But scholars have pointed out that this opening is followed by another story of origin, beginning at Chapter 2, Verse 4, that not only tells the story over again, but does so without the intense declarative monotheism. They date this document at about 850 B.C.E. and the section from 1:1 to 2:3 at about 650 B.C.E. Compare the language in Genesis 1 to 2:3 with the section that begins at 2:4. Which selection from Genesis seems more idealized, which more like a report? Which version would probably be closer to the oral storytelling tradition? Which reflects the style of a sophisticated, urban, philosophical culture? Which term is more monotheistic: *God* or *Lord God*?

If we can see increased emphasis on monotheism from 850 to 650 B.C.E., we might also see in these selections the transition from the religion of a tribe of shepherds to that of a political kingdom. What evidence do you see that a pastoral religion of animal sacrifice became a religion of law, or even internalized morality?

Finally, notice that there is no heaven here — no afterlife. God promised Abraham land and prosperity. The ideas of a last judgment, heaven and hell, and salvation became important in Christianity, but we will explore the development of these ideas in Judaism in the second century B.C.E.

Genesis 1

The Beginning

1 In the beginning God created the heavens and the earth.

2 Now the earth was formless and empty, darkness was over the surface of the deep, and the Spirit of God was hovering over the waters.

3 And God said, "Let there be light," and there was light. 4 God saw that the light was good, and He separated the light from the darkness. 5 God called the light "day," and the darkness he called "night." And there was evening, and there was morning—the first day.

6 And God said, "Let there be an expanse between the waters to separate water from water." 7 So God made the expanse and separated the water under the expanse from the water above it. And it was so. 8 God called the expanse "sky." And there was evening, and there was morning—the second day.

9 And God said, "Let the water under the sky be gathered to one place, and let dry ground appear." And it was so. 10 God called the dry ground "land," and the gathered waters he called "seas." And God saw that it was good.

11 Then God said, "Let the land produce vegetation: seed-bearing plants and trees on the land that bear fruit with seed in it, according to their various kinds." And it was so. 12 The land produced vegetation: plants bearing seed according to their kinds and trees bearing fruit with seed in it according to their kinds. And God saw that it was good. 13 And there was evening, and there was morning—the third day.

14 And God said, "Let there be lights in the expanse of the sky to separate the day from the night, and let them serve as signs to mark seasons and days and years, 15 and let them be lights in the expanse of the sky to give light on the earth." And it was so. 16 God made two great lights—the greater light to govern the day and the lesser light to govern the night. He also made the stars. 17 God set them in the expanse of the sky to give light on the earth, 18 to govern the day and the night, and to

separate light from darkness. And God saw that it was good. 19 And there was evening, and there was morning—the fourth day.

20 And God said, "Let the water teem with living creatures, and let birds fly above the earth across the expanse of the sky." 21 So God created the great creatures of the sea and every living and moving thing with which the water teems, according to their kinds, and every winged bird according to its kind. And God saw that it was good. 22 God blessed them and said, "Be fruitful and increase in number and fill the water in the seas, and let the birds increase on the earth." 23 And there was evening, and there was morning—the fifth day.

24 And God said, "Let the land produce living creatures according to their kinds: livestock, creatures that move along the ground, and wild animals, each according to its kind." And it was so. 25 God made the wild animals according to their kinds, the livestock according to their kinds, and all the creatures that move along the ground according to their kinds. And God saw that it was good.

26 Then God said, "Let us make man in our image, in our likeness, and let them rule over the fish of the sea and the birds of the air, over the livestock, over all the earth, and over all the creatures that move along the ground."

27 So God created man in his own image,
in the image of God he created him;
male and female he created them.

28 God blessed them and said to them, "Be fruitful and increase in number; fill the earth and subdue it. Rule over the fish of the sea and the birds of the air and over every living creature that moves on the ground."

29 Then God said, "I give you every seed-bearing plant on the face of the whole earth and every tree that has fruit with seed in it. They will be yours for food. 30 And to all the beasts of the earth and all the birds of the air and all the creatures that move on the ground—everything that has the breath of life in it—I give every green plant for food." And it was so.

31 God saw all that he had made, and it was very good. And there was evening, and there was morning—the sixth day.

Genesis 2

1 Thus the heavens and the earth were completed in all their vast array.

2 By the seventh day God had finished the work he had been doing; so on the seventh day he rested from all his work. 3 And God blessed the seventh day and made it holy, because on it he rested from all the work of creating that he had done.

Adam and Eve

4 This is the account of the heavens and the earth when they were created.

When the LORD God made the earth and the heavens — 5 and no shrub of the field had yet appeared on the earth and no plant of the field had yet sprung up, for the LORD God had not sent rain on the earth and there was no man to work the ground, 6 but streams came up from the earth and watered the whole surface of the ground — 7 the LORD God formed the man from the dust of the ground and breathed into his nostrils the breath of life, and the man became a living being.

8 Now the LORD God had planted a garden in the east, in Eden; and there he put the man he had formed. 9 And the LORD God made all kinds of trees grow out of the ground — trees that were pleasing to the eye and good for food. In the middle of the garden were the tree of life and the tree of the knowledge of good and evil.

10 A river watering the garden flowed from Eden; from there it was separated into four headwaters. 11 The name of the first is the Pishon; it winds through the entire land of Havilah, where there is gold. 12 (The gold of that land is good; aromatic resin and onyx are also there.) 13 The name of the second river is the Gihon; it winds through the entire land of Cush. 14 The name of the third river is the Tigris; it runs along the east side of Asshur. And the fourth river is the Euphrates.

15 The LORD God took the man and put him in the Garden of Eden to work it and take care of it. 16 And the LORD God commanded the man, "You are free to eat from any tree in the garden; 17 but you must not eat from the tree of the knowledge of good and evil, for when you eat of it you will surely die."

18 The LORD God said, "It is not good for the man to be alone. I will make a helper suitable for him."

19 Now the LORD God had formed out of the ground all the beasts of the field and all the birds of the air. He brought them to the man to see what he would name them; and whatever the man called each living creature, that was its name. 20 So the man gave names to all the livestock, the birds of the air and all the beasts of the field.

But for Adam no suitable helper was found. 21 So the LORD God caused the man to fall into a deep sleep; and while he was sleeping, he took one of the man's ribs and closed up the place with flesh. 22 Then the LORD God made a woman from the rib he had taken out of the man, and he brought her to the man.

23 The man said,

"This is now bone of my bones
and flesh of my flesh;
she shall be called 'woman,'
for she was taken out of man."

24 For this reason a man will leave his father and mother and be united to his wife, and they will become one flesh.

25 The man and his wife were both naked, and they felt no shame.

Genesis 17

The Covenant of the Circumcision

1 When Abram was ninety-nine years old, the LORD appeared to him and said, "I am God Almighty; walk before me and be blameless. 2 I will confirm my covenant between me and you and will greatly increase your numbers."

3 Abram fell facedown, and God said to him, 4 "As for me, this is my covenant with you: You will be the father of many nations. 5 No longer will you be called Abram; your name will be Abraham, for I have made you a father of many nations. 6 I will make you very fruitful; I will make nations of you, and kings will come from you. 7 I will establish my covenant as an everlasting covenant between me and you and your descendants after you for the generations to come, to be your God and the God of your descendants after you. 8 The whole land of Canaan, where you are now an alien, I will give as an everlasting possession to you and your descendants after you; and I will be their God."

9 Then God said to Abraham, "As for you, you must keep my covenant, you and your descendants after you for the generations to come. 10 This is my covenant with you and your descendants after you, the covenant you are to keep: Every male among you shall be circumcised. 11 You are to undergo circumcision, and it will be the sign of the covenant between me and you. 12 For the generations to come every male among you who is eight days old must be circumcised, including those born in your household or bought with money from a foreigner—those who are not your offspring. 13 Whether born in your household or bought with your money, they must be circumcised. My covenant in your flesh is to be an everlasting covenant. 14 Any uncircumcised male, who has not been circumcised in the flesh, will be cut off from his people; he has broken my covenant. . . ."

Exodus 19

At Mount Sinai

1 In the third month after the Israelites left Egypt—on the very day—they came to the Desert of Sinai. 2 After they set out from Rephidim, they entered the Desert of Sinai, and Israel camped there in the desert in front of the mountain.

3 Then Moses went up to God, and the LORD called to him from the mountain and said, "This is what you are to say to the house of Jacob and what you are to tell the people of Israel: 4 'You yourselves have seen what I did to Egypt, and how I carried you on eagles' wings and brought you to myself. 5 Now if you obey me fully and keep my covenant, then out of all nations you will be my treasured possession. Although the whole earth is mine, 6 you will be for me a kingdom of priests and a holy nation.' These are the words you are to speak to the Israelites."

7 So Moses went back and summoned the elders of the people and set before them all the words the LORD had commanded him to speak. 8 The people all responded together, "We will do everything the LORD has said." So Moses brought their answer back to the LORD.

9 The LORD said to Moses, "I am going to come to you in a dense cloud, so that the people will hear me speaking with you and will always put their trust in you." Then Moses told the LORD what the people had said.

Exodus 20

The Ten Commandments

1 And God spoke all these words:

2 "I am the LORD your God, who brought you out of Egypt, out of the land of slavery.

3 "You shall have no other gods before me.

4 "You shall not make for yourself an idol in the form of anything in heaven above or on the earth beneath or in the waters below. 5 You shall not bow down to them or worship them; for I, the LORD your God, am a jealous God, punishing the children for the sin of the fathers to the third and fourth generation of those who hate me, 6 but showing love to a thousand [generations] of those who love me and keep my commandments.

7 "You shall not misuse the name of the LORD your God, for the LORD will not hold anyone guiltless who misuses his name.

8 "Remember the Sabbath day by keeping it holy. 9 Six days you shall labor and do all your work, 10 but the seventh day is a Sabbath to the LORD your God. On it you shall not do any work, neither you, nor your son or daughter, nor your manservant or maidservant, nor your animals, nor the alien within your gates. 11 For in six days the LORD made the heavens and the earth, the sea, and all that is in them, but he rested on the seventh day. Therefore the LORD blessed the Sabbath day and made it holy.

12 "Honor your father and your mother, so that you may live long in the land the LORD your God is giving you.

13 "You shall not murder.

14 "You shall not commit adultery.

15 "You shall not steal.

16 "You shall not give false testimony against your neighbor.

17 "You shall not covet your neighbor's house. You shall not covet your neighbor's wife, or his manservant or maidservant, his ox or donkey, or anything that belongs to your neighbor."

18 When the people saw the thunder and lightning and heard the trumpet and saw the mountain in smoke, they trembled with fear.

Leviticus 1

The Burnt Offering

1 The LORD called to Moses and spoke to him from the Tent of Meeting. He said, 2 "Speak to the Israelites and say to them: 'When any of you brings an offering to the LORD, bring as your offering an animal from either the herd or the flock.

3 "'If the offering is a burnt offering from the herd, he is to offer a male without defect. He must present it at the entrance to the Tent of Meeting so that it will be acceptable to the LORD. 4 He is to lay his hand on the head of the burnt offering, and it will be accepted on his behalf to make atonement for him. 5 He is to slaughter the young bull before the LORD, and then Aaron's sons the priests shall bring the blood and sprinkle it against the altar on all sides at the entrance to the Tent of Meeting. 6 He is to skin the burnt offering and cut it into pieces. 7 The sons of Aaron the priest are to put fire on the altar and arrange wood on the fire. 8 Then Aaron's sons the priests shall arrange the pieces, including the head and the fat, on the burning wood that is on the altar. 9 He is to wash the inner parts and the legs with water, and the priest is to burn all of it on the altar. It is a burnt offering, an offering made by fire, an aroma pleasing to the LORD. . . .'"

Psalm 23

A Psalm of David

1 The LORD is my shepherd, I shall not be in want.

2 He makes me lie down in green pastures,
   he leads me beside quiet waters,

3 he restores my soul.
   He guides me in paths of righteousness
   for his name's sake.

4 Even though I walk
  through the valley of the shadow of death,[2]
  I will fear no evil,
  for you are with me;
  your rod and your staff,
  they comfort me.

5 You prepare a table before me
  in the presence of my enemies.
  You anoint my head with oil;
  my cup overflows.

6 Surely goodness and love will follow me
  all the days of my life,
  and I will dwell in the house of the LORD
  forever.

Amos 5

21 "I hate, I despise your religious feasts;
   I cannot stand your assemblies.

22 Even though you bring me burnt offerings and grain offerings,
   I will not accept them.
   Though you bring choice fellowship offerings,
   I will have no regard for them.

23 Away with the noise of your songs!
   I will not listen to the music of your harps.

24 But let justice roll on like a river,
   righteousness like a never-failing stream!"

---

[2] Or *through the darkest valley*. [Ed.]

Judaism and the Bible: Prophecy and the Apocalypse, c. 600–165 B.C.E.

The golden days of Jewish kings were not to last. Powerful empires rose up to challenge and dominate the Jews: the Assyrians in 800 B.C.E., the Babylonians around 600 B.C.E., then the Medes, the Persians, the armies of Alexander the Great, his successor states—ruled by his generals and their descendants—and then the Romans after 64 B.C.E. The Babylonians were among the worst of the invaders. They conquered Jerusalem, destroyed the temple, and brought Jews as hostages to Babylon. In 538 B.C.E. Cyrus, king of the Persians, allowed Jews to return to Jerusalem and even rebuild the temple. But the Jews never regained their kingdom or independence (except for brief periods), and the Greek Seleucid* rulers after Alexander proved to be intolerant of non-Greek forms of worship.

Ironically, it was during this period of conquest and dispersal that Judaism began to develop the elements of a universal religion. The Babylonian destruction of the temple and population transfer made the religion of Yahweh less dependent on place. Virtually all religions of the ancient world were bound to a particular place, usually the sacred temple where the god was thought to reside. Judaism remained a religion of the descendants of Abraham and his son Israel, and the period after 600 B.C.E. was one of intense cultivation of that identity. But much of the Hebrew Bible was composed in exile, as a way of recalling a common history, reaffirming a common identity, and predicting a common destiny. The prophets foresaw a brighter future or explained how the violation of the covenant had brought God's wrath on the people.

One of the great prophets of the exile and the postexile period was Daniel, described as one of the young men who was brought to Babylon by Nebuchadnezzar,† conqueror of Jerusalem in 586 B.C.E. The Book of Daniel begins by recounting that conquest. In Babylon Nebuchadnezzar asked Daniel to reveal the meaning of a dream. You will read his response below.

Daniel is the first to foretell of an apocalyptic end to history and the first to envision personal immortality. Previous prophets had predicted a new independent kingdom of Judah or God's punishment of his people, but Daniel prophesied that God would come down to reign on Earth forever, judging the living and the dead for all eternity. These ideas—an end to history, the Last Judgment, the Kingdom of

*sel OO sihd
†neh boo kuhd NEH zur

Source: Dan. 2:31–45, 11:28–45, 12:1–13. New International Version.

God, eternal life or damnation — became more important later in Christianity than in Judaism, where these notions never entered the mainstream. But their appearance in Daniel shows the way in which Judaic ideas became more universal over the course of the first millennium B.C.E. Why would Daniel's ideas open the Judaic tradition to non-Jews or people not descended from Abraham? How would Daniel's prophecy affect his contemporaries? How would it affect you?

THINKING HISTORICALLY

When did the idea of an afterlife enter Judaism? To answer this question we have to date the Book of Daniel, which is a bit more complex than it would seem. As mentioned, the book is presented as the prophecy of a Daniel who was taken from Jerusalem to Babylon around 586 B.C.E. But the author of the book knows considerably more about the period toward the end of his prophecy (180–165 B.C.E.) than about the third to sixth century B.C.E. This discrepancy and the use of second-century Hebrew and Aramaic have led biblical scholars to conclude that the Book of Daniel is prophecy after the fact, or a book of history presented as prophecy. Detailed footnotes have been added to this selection to show that the author's references to very specific events of the second century, especially the time of Antiochus IV (r. 175–163 B.C.E.), would have been easily recognized by a contemporary audience. So the author lived sometime in this period. He recounts the unhappy story of the conquests of the Jews by successive empires: from the Babylonian (627–550 B.C.E.) and Median (612–550 B.C.E.) to the Persian (550–330 B.C.E.) to the Greek under Alexander (330–323 B.C.E.) to the Seleucids (Alexander's successors), including Antiochus (312–63 B.C.E.). This is the meaning of the gold, silver, bronze, iron, and clay ages. When the author then speaks of the signs of the last days, he distinctly sees the acts of Antiochus IV as the turning point that will bring about God's eternal kingdom. Antiochus pressured the Jews to accept Greek gods. In 168 B.C.E. he polluted the temple in Jerusalem by slaughtering pigs on the altar and then erecting a statue of the Greek god Zeus. This is the event that the author predicts will bring on God's last judgment. Many Jews must have felt that the desecration of the holy temple was such a world-changing event. In fact, the acts of Antiochus also sparked a Jewish revolt under the Macabees, who eventually defeated Antiochus in 163 B.C.E. and restored an independent Jewish state.

What would be the purpose of presenting this prophecy? What would be the advantage of presenting it as the writing of someone who had lived hundreds of years earlier? How can we know that the Book of Daniel was written after 168 but before 163 B.C.E.? When and why would the author of the Book of Daniel have predicted that the end of the world would occur 1,290 days (about 3½ years) after an event in 168 B.C.E.? When and why would the author have written, "Blessed is the one who waits . . . 1,335 days"?

Daniel 2 [Daniel Interprets the Dream of Nebuchadnezzar]

31 "You looked, O king, and there before you stood a large statue—an enormous, dazzling statue, awesome in appearance. 32 The head of the statue was made of pure gold, its chest and arms of silver, its belly and thighs of bronze, 33 its legs of iron, its feet partly of iron and partly of baked clay. 34 While you were watching, a rock was cut out, but not by human hands. It struck the statue on its feet of iron and clay and smashed them. 35 Then the iron, the clay, the bronze, the silver and the gold were broken to pieces at the same time and became like chaff on a threshing floor in the summer. The wind swept them away without leaving a trace. But the rock that struck the statue became a huge mountain and filled the whole earth.

36 "This was the dream, and now we will interpret it to the king. 37 You, O king, are the king of kings. The God of heaven has given you dominion and power and might and glory; 38 in your hands he has placed mankind and the beasts of the field and the birds of the air. Wherever they live, he has made you ruler over them all. You are that head of gold.

39 "After you, another kingdom[1] will rise, inferior to yours. Next, a third kingdom, one of bronze,[2] will rule over the whole earth. 40 Finally, there will be a fourth kingdom,[3] strong as iron—for iron breaks and smashes everything—and as iron breaks things to pieces, so it will crush and break all the others. 41 Just as you saw that the feet and toes were partly of baked clay and partly of iron, so this will be a divided kingdom;[4] yet it will have some of the strength of iron in it, even as you saw iron mixed with clay. 42 As the toes were partly iron and partly clay, so this kingdom will be partly strong and partly brittle. 43 And just as you saw the iron mixed with baked clay, so the people will be a mixture[5] and will not remain united, any more than iron mixes with clay.

[1] Media, or the Mede Empire; Iranians who shared rule with Neo-Babylonians (Chaldeans) and were seen as successors in the Middle East to 550 B.C.E. [Ed.]

[2] Persia, 550–330 B.C.E. [Ed.]

[3] Greek empire of Alexander the Great, 330–323 B.C.E. [Ed.]

[4] The Middle Eastern portion of Alexander's empire was divided after his death in 323 B.C.E. by his generals: Seleucus in Palestine and Syria and Ptolemy in Egypt. The kingdom of the Seleucids (iron) was stronger than that of the Ptolemies (clay). These two dynasties lasted until conquered by Rome and Persian Parthia. [Ed.]

[5] Probably refers to mixing of peoples and cultures in Alexander's and his successors' empire. [Ed.]

44 "In the time of those kings, the God of heaven will set up a kingdom that will never be destroyed, nor will it be left to another people. It will crush all those kingdoms and bring them to an end, but it will itself endure forever. 45 This is the meaning of the vision of the rock cut out of a mountain, but not by human hands—a rock that broke the iron, the bronze, the clay, the silver and the gold to pieces.

"The great God has shown the king what will take place in the future. The dream is true and the interpretation is trustworthy."

Daniel 11 [Daniel Sees the End of the Age of Iron and Clay]

28 "The king[6] of the North will return to his own country[7] with great wealth, but his heart will be set against the holy covenant.[8] He will take action against it and then return to his own country.

29 "At the appointed time he will invade the South again,[9] but this time the outcome will be different from what it was before. 30 Ships of the western coastlands[10] will oppose him, and he will lose heart. Then he will turn back and vent his fury against the holy covenant. He will return and show favor to those who forsake[11] the holy covenant.

31 "His armed forces will rise up to desecrate the temple fortress and will abolish the daily sacrifice. Then they will set up the abomination that causes desolation.[12] 32 With flattery he will corrupt those who have violated the covenant, but the people who know their God will firmly resist him.

33 "Those who are wise will instruct many, though for a time they will fall by the sword or be burned or captured or plundered. 34 When they fall, they will receive a little help,[13] and many who are not sincere will join them.[14] 35 Some of the wise will stumble, so that they may be refined, purified and made spotless until the time of the end, for it will still come at the appointed time.

---

[6] Antiochus IV, the Seleucid emperor from 175 to 164 B.C.E., ruled Palestine, Syria, and Alexander's eastern empire, which included Jerusalem. [Ed.]

[7] Antiochus IV returned to Jerusalem after his first war with Egypt, 170 B.C.E. [Ed.]

[8] Antiochus stole temple treasures and massacred many Jews, 169 B.C.E. [Ed.]

[9] The second war of Antiochus IV with Egypt in 168 B.C.E. was not successful. [Ed.]

[10] Cyprus. Here it means ships of Romans, generally, who blocked him. [Ed.]

[11] Jews like Jason the high priest, who favored Greek customs. [Ed.]

[12] The army of Antiochus broke down the temple walls, desecrated the interior, and installed Greek statues. [Ed.]

[13] While many Jews chose martyrdom, some received the help of Judas Maccabeus, leader of the opposition to Antiochus. [Ed.]

[14] Some of the followers of Judas Maccabeus were insincere. [Ed.]

The King Who Exalts Himself

36 "The king will do as he pleases. He will exalt and magnify himself above every god[15] and will say unheard-of things against the God of gods. He will be successful until the time of wrath is completed, for what has been determined must take place. 37 He will show no regard for the gods of his fathers or for the one desired by women, nor will he regard any god, but will exalt himself above them all. 38 Instead of them, he will honor a god of fortresses; a god unknown to his fathers he will honor with gold and silver, with precious stones and costly gifts. 39 He will attack the mightiest fortresses with the help of a foreign god and will greatly honor those who acknowledge him. He will make them rulers over many people and will distribute the land at a price.

40 "At the time of the end the king of the South[16] will engage him in battle, and the king of the North will storm out against him with chariots and cavalry and a great fleet of ships. He will invade many countries and sweep through them like a flood. 41 He will also invade the Beautiful Land. Many countries will fall, but Edom, Moab and the leaders of Ammon will be delivered from his hand. 42 He will extend his power over many countries; Egypt will not escape. 43 He will gain control of the treasures of gold and silver and all the riches of Egypt, with the Libyans and Nubians in submission. 44 But reports from the east and the north[17] will alarm him, and he will set out in a great rage to destroy and annihilate many. 45 He will pitch his royal tents between the seas at the beautiful holy mountain.[18] Yet he will come to his end,[19] and no one will help him."

Daniel 12

The End Times

1 "At that time Michael,[20] the great prince who protects your people, will arise. There will be a time of distress such as has not happened from the beginning of nations until then. But at that time your people — everyone whose name is found written in the book — will be delivered. 2 Multitudes who sleep in the dust of the earth will awake: some to everlasting life, others to shame and everlasting contempt. 3 Those who are wise will shine like the brightness of the heavens, and

---

[15] Antiochus had himself declared "Epiphanes," or God Manifest. [Ed.]
[16] Ptolemy VI Philometor (Egypt) initiated the third Egyptian war, against Antiochus. [Ed.]
[17] Antiochus spent his last year in war with Armenia and Parthia (Persia). [Ed.]
[18] In Palestine. [Ed.]
[19] Antiochus IV died at Tabae in Persia in 163 B.C.E. [Ed.]
[20] Protective angel of Israel. [Ed.]

those who lead many to righteousness, like the stars for ever and ever. 4 But you, Daniel, close up and seal the words of the scroll until the time of the end. Many will go here and there to increase knowledge."

5 Then I, Daniel, looked, and there before me stood two others, one on this bank of the river and one on the opposite bank. 6 One of them said to the man clothed in linen, who was above the waters of the river, "How long will it be before these astonishing things are fulfilled?"

7 The man clothed in linen, who was above the waters of the river, lifted his right hand and his left hand toward heaven, and I heard him swear by him who lives forever, saying, "It will be for a time, times and half a time. When the power of the holy people has been finally broken, all these things will be completed."

8 I heard, but I did not understand. So I asked, "My lord, what will the outcome of all this be?"

9 He replied, "Go your way, Daniel, because the words are closed up and sealed until the time of the end. 10 Many will be purified, made spotless and refined, but the wicked will continue to be wicked. None of the wicked will understand, but those who are wise will understand.

11 "From the time that the daily sacrifice is abolished and the abomination that causes desolation is set up, there will be 1,290 days. 12 Blessed is the one who waits for and reaches the end of the 1,335 days.

13 "As for you, go your way till the end. You will rest, and then at the end of the days you will rise to receive your allotted inheritance."

7

The Christian Bible: Jesus According to Matthew, c. 70 C.E.

The ideas first enunciated in Daniel — the coming end of the world or the Kingdom of God, the Last Judgment, individual immortality or life after death — were to become central to the branch of Judaism that produced Christianity. Along with Judaic monotheism and the insistence of the prophets (like Amos) on internalized morality, the idea of personal responsibility and eternal salvation or damnation gave Christianity an appeal that would eventually reach far beyond the children of Abraham.

In this selection from the Christian New Testament, the evangelist Matthew recounts Jesus speaking of the apocalypse with a note of urgency. Like Daniel, Jesus speaks of the signs that the end is at hand.

Source: Matt. 24:1–41. New International Version.

Yet, in the same chapter, sometimes in the same paragraph, Matthew recounts Jesus telling his listeners that there is plenty of time before the end.

What accounts for this apparent contradiction? If you were in the audience listening to Jesus, which idea would motivate you more — that the end of the world is rapidly approaching or that it is generations away? If you were taking notes for the daily newspaper, which message would get the headline? If you were writing a history of Jesus for future generations, which message would you emphasize?

THINKING HISTORICALLY

Matthew wrote his gospel about forty years after Jesus died. If he had been among those who heard Jesus speak, he took a long time to write it down. It is more likely that the author of this gospel is a second-generation evangelist, drawing on an earlier source, now lost. He may have had access to an earlier eyewitness account or to a collection of sayings of Jesus.

We know that Matthew updated the words of Jesus for the benefit of those Christians living after 70 C.E. Notice, for example, Matthew's reference to Daniel in 24:15: Jesus tells his listeners that when they see the abomination of the temple of which Daniel spoke, they should flee into the mountains to prepare for the end. But we know today that Daniel was speaking of the desecration of the temple by Antiochus IV in 168 B.C.E. Matthew, unaware of the historical context of Daniel and writing after the Roman destruction of the temple in 70 C.E., believed that Roman destruction was the event Daniel was predicting. So Matthew updates the message of Jesus for future generations by including the temple destruction for the readers of his gospel ("let the reader understand"). This is one of the ways we know that Matthew's text was written after 70 C.E. Jesus would not have referred to an event that was for his audience forty years into the future and expect his audience to understand his reference. In addition to the Daniel reference, which parts of this selection are most likely the written updates of Matthew? Which statements are most likely the actual spoken words of Jesus?

Matthew 24

Signs of the End of the Age

1 Jesus left the temple and was walking away when his disciples came up to him to call his attention to its buildings. 2 "Do you see all these things?" he asked. "I tell you the truth, not one stone here will be left on another; every one will be thrown down."

3 As Jesus was sitting on the Mount of Olives, the disciples came to him privately. "Tell us," they said, "when will this happen, and what will be the sign of your coming and of the end of the age?"

4 Jesus answered: "Watch out that no one deceives you. 5 For many will come in my name, claiming, 'I am the Christ,' and will deceive many. 6 You will hear of wars and rumors of wars, but see to it that you are not alarmed. Such things must happen, but the end is still to come. 7 Nation will rise against nation, and kingdom against kingdom. There will be famines and earthquakes in various places. 8 All these are the beginning of birth pains.

9 "Then you will be handed over to be persecuted and put to death, and you will be hated by all nations because of me. 10 At that time many will turn away from the faith and will betray and hate each other, 11 and many false prophets will appear and deceive many people. 12 Because of the increase of wickedness, the love of most will grow cold, 13 but he who stands firm to the end will be saved. 14 And this gospel of the kingdom will be preached in the whole world as a testimony to all nations, and then the end will come.

15 "So when you see standing in the holy place 'the abomination that causes desolation,' spoken of through the prophet Daniel—let the reader understand—16 then let those who are in Judea flee to the mountains. 17 Let no one on the roof of his house go down to take anything out of the house. 18 Let no one in the field go back to get his cloak. 19 How dreadful it will be in those days for pregnant women and nursing mothers! 20 Pray that your flight will not take place in winter or on the Sabbath. 21 For then there will be great distress, unequaled from the beginning of the world until now—and never to be equaled again. 22 If those days had not been cut short, no one would survive, but for the sake of the elect those days will be shortened. 23 At that time if anyone says to you, 'Look, here is the Christ!' or, 'There he is!' do not believe it. 24 For false Christs and false prophets will appear and perform great signs and miracles to deceive even the elect—if that were possible. 25 See, I have told you ahead of time.

26 "So if anyone tells you, 'There he is, out in the desert,' do not go out; or, 'Here he is, in the inner rooms,' do not believe it. 27 For as lightning that comes from the east is visible even in the west, so will be the coming of the Son of Man. 28 Wherever there is a carcass, there the vultures will gather.

29 "Immediately after the distress of those days
　'the sun will be darkened,
　and the moon will not give its light;
　the stars will fall from the sky,
　and the heavenly bodies will be shaken.'

30 "At that time the sign of the Son of Man will appear in the sky, and all the nations of the earth will mourn. They will see the Son of Man

coming on the clouds of the sky, with power and great glory. 31And he will send his angels with a loud trumpet call, and they will gather his elect from the four winds, from one end of the heavens to the other.

32 "Now learn this lesson from the fig tree: As soon as its twigs get tender and its leaves come out, you know that summer is near. 33 Even so, when you see all these things, you know that it is near, right at the door. 34 I tell you the truth, this generation will certainly not pass away until all these things have happened. 35 Heaven and earth will pass away, but my words will never pass away.

The Day and Hour Unknown

36 "No one knows about that day or hour, not even the angels in heaven, nor the Son, but only the Father. 37 As it was in the days of Noah, so it will be at the coming of the Son of Man. 38 For in the days before the flood, people were eating and drinking, marrying and giving in marriage, up to the day Noah entered the ark; 39 and they knew nothing about what would happen until the flood came and took them all away. That is how it will be at the coming of the Son of Man. 40 Two men will be in the field; one will be taken and the other left. 41 Two women will be grinding with a hand mill; one will be taken and the other left."

8

Paul, Letters, c. 50 C.E.

Paul of Tarsus (d. c. 65 C.E.), born with the name Saul in a Jewish community in what is today southeastern Turkey, was educated in the Hellenistic Greek culture of his time. As a young man, according to his testimony, he persecuted the followers of Jesus until, about the year 33, on the road to Damascus he was thrown from his horse, blinded, and reprimanded by God for his actions. From then on, Paul became the most vigorous missionary of Jesus, traveling throughout the Mediterranean converting nonbelievers and corresponding with communities of fellow followers. In contrast to the followers of Jesus in Jerusalem, Paul spread his gospel to others who were neither Jewish nor had known Jesus, believing that the message of the life, death, and resurrection of Jesus transcended any particular national community. In these selections from his letters to communities of Jesus followers throughout the Mediterranean, Paul emphasizes certain

---

Source: Rom. 2:25–29; 1 Cor. 15:1–8; Eph. 1:1–10, 2:1–10. New International Version.

ideas that opened up the religion to non-Jews and aided its spread to new communities. What are these ideas? How would these new ideas or emphases make the early church of Jesus universal in its appeal and potential membership?

THINKING HISTORICALLY

As a Jew, Paul would have been familiar with the Hebrew Bible in Greek translation, though it had not yet been codified in its present form. He would also have had access to stories about Jesus, though the gospels that we have in Greek had not yet been written. How different is Paul's message about Jesus from the message that later appeared in the gospel according to Matthew? How similar is it? Is Paul more interested in presenting the message *of* Jesus or the message *about* Jesus?

Romans 2

25 Circumcision has value if you observe the law, but if you break the law, you have become as though you had not been circumcised. 26 If those who are not circumcised keep the law's requirements, will they not be regarded as though they were circumcised? 27 The one who is not circumcised physically and yet obeys the law will condemn you who, even though you have the written code and circumcision, are a lawbreaker.

28 A man is not a Jew if he is only one outwardly, nor is circumcision merely outward and physical. 29 No, a man is a Jew if he is one inwardly; and circumcision is circumcision of the heart, by the Spirit, not by the written code. Such a man's praise is not from men, but from God.

1 Corinthians 15

The Resurrection of Christ

1 Now, brothers, I want to remind you of the gospel I preached to you, which you received and on which you have taken your stand. 2 By this gospel you are saved, if you hold firmly to the word I preached to you. Otherwise, you have believed in vain.

3 For what I received I passed on to you as of first importance: that Christ died for our sins according to the Scriptures, 4 that he was buried, that he was raised on the third day according to the Scriptures, 5 and that he appeared to Peter, and then to the Twelve. 6 After that, he appeared to more than five hundred of the brothers at the same time, most

of whom are still living, though some have fallen asleep. 7 Then he appeared to James, then to all the apostles, 8 and last of all he appeared to me also, as to one abnormally born.[1]

Ephesians 1

1 Paul, an apostle of Christ Jesus by the will of God,
   To the saints in Ephesus, the faithful in Christ Jesus:
2 Grace and peace to you from God our Father and the Lord Jesus Christ.

Spiritual Blessings in Christ

3 Praise be to the God and Father of our Lord Jesus Christ, who has blessed us in the heavenly realms with every spiritual blessing in Christ. 4 For he chose us in him before the creation of the world to be holy and blameless in his sight. In love 5 he predestined us to be adopted as his sons through Jesus Christ, in accordance with his pleasure and will — 6 to the praise of his glorious grace, which he has freely given us in the One he loves. 7 In him we have redemption through his blood, the forgiveness of sins, in accordance with the riches of God's grace 8 that he lavished on us with all wisdom and understanding. 9 And he made known to us the mystery of his will according to his good pleasure, which he purposed in Christ, 10 to be put into effect when the times will have reached their fulfillment — to bring all things in heaven and on earth together under one head, even Christ. . . .

Ephesians 2

Made Alive in Christ

1 As for you, you were dead in your transgressions and sins, 2 in which you used to live when you followed the ways of this world and of the ruler of the kingdom of the air, the spirit who is now at work in those who are disobedient. 3 All of us also lived among them at one time, gratifying the cravings of our sinful nature and following its desires and thoughts. Like the rest, we were by nature objects of wrath. 4 But because of his great love for us, God, who is rich in mercy, 5 made us alive with Christ even when we were dead in transgressions — it is by grace you have been saved. 6 And God raised us up with Christ and seated us

[1] Refers to vision on road to Damascus after death of Jesus — an event out of normal time. [Ed.]

with him in the heavenly realms in Christ Jesus, 7 in order that in the coming ages he might show the incomparable riches of his grace, expressed in his kindness to us in Christ Jesus. 8 For it is by grace you have been saved, through faith—and this not from yourselves, it is the gift of God—9 not by works, so that no one can boast. 10 For we are God's workmanship, created in Christ Jesus to do good works, which God prepared in advance for us to do.

■ REFLECTIONS

The layers of revision are etched more sharply in the book of Daniel in the Hebrew Bible and Matthew in the New Testament of the Bible than in the Hindu and Buddhist documents because dates, chronology, and time sequences were far more important to the Judeo-Christian tradition. It was, and is, a tradition committed to the belief that God works in time; that there is a beginning, middle, and end to things; and that it is crucially important for humans to know where they are in the providential timeline. A modern skeptic might be bothered by the way the author or authors of Daniel turn history into prophecy. But for the Jews of the 160s B.C.E., the need to get the dates right and be ready for the end of days was far more important than checking who predicted what when.

Ironically, the precise prophecy of Daniel transcended its historical moorings when it was used by the author of Matthew in an effort to update the prophecy of Jesus, and it has been used regularly by every generation since with a different "king of the south" and new supporting cast. But if the Judeo-Christian tradition has left a legacy of apocalyptic warnings and millennial musings, it has also given us the interest and the tools that have shaped this chapter. The need to date, to find the actual words, to peel away the layers of rust that obfuscate an authentic past—that is a fine legacy indeed.

We have seen how Hinduism produced Buddhism and how Judaism generated Christianity, but neither Hinduism nor Judaism ended two thousand years ago. In fact, both "parental" religions underwent profound changes as well. Both became more universal, less dependent on particular places or people, and less limited to caste, region, or tribe.

We saw in the Upanishads how, around 500 B.C.E., Hinduism became almost monotheistic in its worship of Brahman. Similarly, about three hundred years later, Hindu devotional cults that centered on two of the other deities of the Hindu pantheon (Vishnu—especially in his incarnation as Krishna—and Shiva) developed. Reread the last eight stanzas of the *Bhagavad Gita* (written about 200 B.C.E.) in

Chapter 3 to see how the worship of Vishnu/Krishna became enormously appealing to masses of Indian people.

At about the time of Jesus, Judaism also underwent a transformation that has continued until this day. A process that began with the destruction of the first temple and the captivity in Babylon in the sixth century B.C.E.—the development of a Judaism independent of a particular temple or place—was revived after the Romans destroyed the second temple in 70 C.E. The Roman conquest created a more global Judaism than the Babylonian conquest. Judaism became a religion of rabbis (teachers) rather than of temple priests and guardians. So great was this transformation of Judaism that one might argue, with Alan Segal in *Rebecca's Children*, that "the time of Jesus marks the birth of not one but two great religions in the West, Judaism and Christianity. . . . So great is the contrast between previous Jewish religious systems and rabbinism."[1]

[1] Alan F. Segal, *Rebecca's Children: Judaism and Christianity in the Roman World* (Cambridge: Harvard University Press, 1986), 1.

7

The Spread of Universal Religions

Afro-Eurasia, 100–1000 C.E.

■ HISTORICAL CONTEXT

From their beginnings, Buddhism and Christianity were less tribal and more universal than their parental religions, Hinduism and Judaism, because they offered universal salvation to their followers. The teachings of Jesus and the Buddha emphasized personal religious experience over the dictates of caste, ancestry, and formal law, making their ideas more likely to spread beyond their cultures of origin. Both religions, however, had relatively small followings at the deaths of their founders. How, then, did they win millions of converts within the next few hundred years? Similarly, how did Islam, founded in 622, spread from the Arabian peninsula to embrace the Berbers of North Africa, the Visigoths of Spain, Syrians, Persians, Turks, Central Asians, Indians, and even the western Chinese by 750? What was happening throughout Eurasia that explained these successes? In this chapter we explore how both an array of powerful and charismatic individuals and specific economic, political, and social conditions helped to broaden the appeal of the salvation religions and find larger audiences for their gospels.

The previous chapter explored the rise of universal religions. Paul of Tarsus almost singlehandedly separated Jesus from his Jewish roots, presenting him as the Son of God who was sacrificed for the sins of humankind, not just a prophet or messiah (king) of the Jewish people. Similarly, Mahayana Buddhists taught that Buddha was more than a teacher and spiritual guide whom one could imitate; he was a savior, responsive to prayer and worship. In addition, the devout could appeal to numerous Christian saints or Buddhist Bodhisattvas for help in achieving salvation.

Religious leaders weren't the only ones spreading faith; merchants and traders (occupations of the Prophet Muhammad) also played a crucial role. The spread of universal faiths and common cultures over great distances owed much to the expansive roads and maritime transport of the Roman and Chinese empires, as well as the Persian, Central Asian, and Indian states in between (see Map 7.1 on p. 237). But it was also a product of the Silk Road, or Roads, that connected China with Rome by land and sea after 100 B.C.E. The expansion of the great religious traditions was the work of merchants as well as monks; statues of gods traveled in camel caravans, and holy images were carried on rolls of silk.

Contact alone, however, is not enough to explain why people converted to Christianity, Buddhism, and Islam. The appeals to salvation beyond this world testified to difficult times. Nomadic pastoral peoples undermined the stability of empires already weakened by public debt, class antagonisms, dwindling crop yields, and disease. Populations declined from 200 to 800 C.E. and did not reach earlier levels again until about 1000 C.E. in Europe and China. People sought spiritual reassurance as well as economic alliances that would protect them in uncertain times. When those in power adopted new religions, it often benefited others to follow their lead, and thus a network of influence for new religious movements was secured.

■ THINKING HISTORICALLY

Understanding Continuity and Change

Thinking historically involves thinking about the way things do and do not change over time. In this chapter we will be looking at Christianity, Buddhism, and Islam as they expand, and we will ask how they bring change to the regions, people, and customs where they make converts. We will also ask how the religions themselves change as they expand. Only when we can see exactly what has changed, and what has remained constant—known as continuities—can we begin to understand the causes of change.

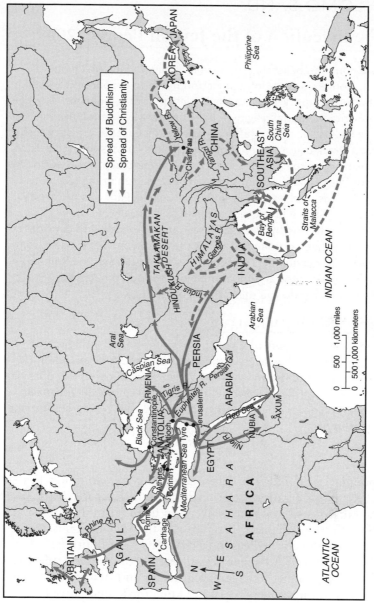

Map 7.1 The Spread of Early Christianity and Buddhism.

1

SHLOMO SAND

The Invention of the Jewish People, 2009

It is a common belief that Judaism is a religion into which one is born. Conversions are infrequent and not even encouraged by some orthodox groups. We saw in the last chapter that Judaism was indeed an inherited national religion for the people of ancient Palestine. But in the Hellenistic period (after Alexander the Great and his successors spread Greek culture throughout the Middle East), some schools of Judaism embraced a more global view of their place in the world. We saw different manifestations of such universalism in the teachings of Daniel, Jesus, and, especially, Paul. But maybe Paul was neither as unique nor such a break with Judaism as is usually maintained.

In this selection by an Israeli historian we are asked to consider the possibility that Christianity was not the only branch of Judaism that converted large numbers of people in the centuries of the Roman Empire. What is the argument of Shlomo Sand? What is his evidence? What do you think of his conclusion?

THINKING HISTORICALLY

Sand makes a number of startling claims for both continuity and change. What claims of change does he make for the spread of the Jewish and Christian religions? What claim of continuity does he make for both religions? Why is a religion based on belief that one chooses to convert to more open to changes than a religion that one is born into?

The popularity of Judaism before and after the Common Era spread beyond the Mediterranean region. In *Antiquities of the Jews*, Josephus tells the fabulous story of the conversion to Judaism in the first century CE of the rulers of Adiabene (Hadyab). As this conversion is described in other sources, there is no reason to doubt its broad outline.

The kingdom of Adiabene was in the north of the Fertile Crescent, roughly corresponding to today's Kurdistan and Armenia. Jewish proselytizing led to the conversion of the kingdom's much-loved heir to the throne, Izates, as well as his mother Helena, herself an important personage in the kingdom. They were persuaded to convert by a merchant named Hananiah, who assured the prince that it was enough to observe the precepts without being circumcised. However, when the prince

Source: Shlomo Sand, *The Invention of the Jewish People*, trans. Yael Lotan (London: Verso, 2009), 165–73, 176.

ascended the throne, a stricter Jewish preacher, a Galilean named Eleazar, demanded that he circumcise himself in order to complete his conversion, and Izates complied. Josephus reports that the ruling dynasty's conversion annoyed Adiabene's nobility, some of whom tried to rebel. But Izates succeeded in suppressing and eliminating his pagan enemies, and when his brother Monobazus II (Monobaz) succeeded him, he too converted to Judaism, along with the rest of the royal family. Queen Helena, accompanied by her son, went on a pilgrimage to Jerusalem, where she helped the Judeans to survive a severe drought, and she was buried in the holy city in a grand "royal tomb" built for her. The sons of Izates also went to the holy city in the center of Judea to be educated in the faith. . . .

The kingdom of Adiabene was the first political entity outside Judea to convert to Judaism, but it was not the last. Nor was it the only one to give rise to an important Jewish community that would survive until modern times.

If Alexander's conquests created an open Hellenistic sphere, Rome's expansion and her enormous empire completed the process. Henceforth, all the cultural centers around the Mediterranean basin would undergo the dynamism of blending and the forging of new phenomena. The littorals[1] grew closer, and the passage from the eastern to the western end became easier and faster. This emerging world opened a fresh perspective for the spread of Judaism; at its high point there, Judaism was professed by 7 to 8 percent of all the empire's inhabitants. The word "Jew" ceased to denote the people of Judea, and now included the masses of proselytes and their descendants.

At the height of Judaism's expansion, in the early third century CE, Cassius Dio described this significant historical development, asserting: "I do not know how this title [Jews] came to be given to them, but it applies also to all the rest of mankind, although of alien race, who affect their customs." His near contemporary, the Christian theologian Origen, wrote: "The noun *ioudaios* is not the name of an *ethnos*, but of a choice [in the manner of life]. For if there be someone not from the nation of the Jews, a gentile, who accepts the ways of the Jews and becomes a proselyte, this person would properly be called a *Ioudaios*."* . . .

As the rate of conversion to Judaism intensified, so did the government's disquiet and the resentment on the part of many Latin intellectuals.

---

* ee oo DAH yos
[1] Coasts. [Ed.]

The great Roman poet Horace made a humorous reference to the Jewish missionary drive in one of his poems: "like the Jews, we [the poets] will force you to come over to our numerous party." The philosopher Seneca thought the Jews were a damned people, because "the customs of this accursed race have gained such influence that they are now received throughout all the world. The vanquished have given laws to their victors." The historian Tacitus, no lover of Jews, was even more acerbic about the converts to Judaism:

> The most degraded out of other races, scorning their national beliefs, brought to them their contributions and presents. This augmented the wealth of the Jews . . . Circumcision was adopted by them as a mark of difference from other men. Those who come over to their religion adopt the practice, and have this lesson first instilled into them, to despise all gods, to disown their country, and set at nought parents, children, and brethren.

Juvenal, the author of the *Satires*, written in the early second century CE, was especially sarcastic. He did not hide his disgust at the wave of Judaization sweeping over many good Romans, and ridiculed the process of conversion that had become popular in his time:

> Some who have had a father who reveres the Sabbath, worship nothing but the clouds, and the divinity of the heavens, and see no difference between eating swine's flesh, from which their father abstained, and that of man; and in time they take to circumcision. Having been wont to flout the laws of Rome, they learn and practise and revere the Jewish law, and all that Moses committed to his secret tome, forbidding to point out the way to any not worshipping the same rites, and conducting none but the circumcised to the desired fountain. For all which the father was to blame, who gave up every seventh day to idleness, keeping it apart from all the concerns of life.

At the end of the second century, Celsus, a philosopher known for his dislike of the Christians, was much less hostile to the Jews. But as the conversions grew apace, and the old religions were abandoned, he became openly antagonistic toward the proselytized masses, stating, "If, then, in these respects the Jews were carefully to preserve their own law, they are not to be blamed for so doing, but those persons rather who have forsaken their own usages, and adopted those of the Jews."

This mass phenomenon annoyed the authorities in Rome and upset a good many of the capital's prominent literati. It upset them because Judaism became seductive to broad circles. All the conceptual and intellectual elements that would make for the future appeal of Christianity and its eventual triumph were present in this transient success of Judaism; traditional, conservative Romans felt the danger and voiced their concern in various ways.

The crisis of the hedonistic culture, the absence of an integrating belief in collective values, and the corruption infecting the administration of the imperial government appeared to call for tighter normative systems and a firmer ritual framework—and the Jewish religion met those needs. The Sabbath rest, the concept of reward and punishment, the belief in an afterlife, and above all the transcendent hope of resurrection were enticing features that persuaded many people to adopt the Jewish faith.

Furthermore, Judaism also offered a rare communal feeling that the spreading imperial world, with its corrosive effects on old identities and traditions, seemed to lack. It was not easy to follow the new set of commandments, but joining the chosen people, the holy nation, also conferred a precious sense of distinction, a fair compensation for the effort. The most intriguing element of this process was its gender aspect—it was the women who led the large-scale movement of Judaization.

Josephus's story about Damascus noted that Judaism was especially popular among the city's women, and as we have seen, Queen Helena of Adiabene had a decisive role in the conversion of the royal family. In the New Testament, we are told, Saul of Tarsus, known as Paul, had a disciple who was "the son of a certain woman which was a Jewess and believed, but his father *was* a Greek" (Acts 16:1). In Rome, too, the women were drawn more readily to Judaism. The poet Martial, who came from Iberia, made fun of the women who observed the Sabbath. Epigraphic material[2] from the Jewish catacombs names as many female converts as male. Especially notable is the inscription about Veturia Paulla, who was renamed Sarah after her conversion and became the "mother" of two synagogues. Fulvia (wife of Saturninus)—on whose account, according to Josephus, Jews were expelled in the year 19 CE — was a full convert. Pomponia Graecina, the wife of the famous commander Aulus Plautius, who conquered Britain, was put on trial and divorced by her husband for her devotion to the Jewish (or possibly the Christian) faith. Poppaea Sabina, the emperor Nero's second wife, made no secret of her tendency to Judaism. These women and many other matrons spread the Jewish faith in Rome's upper classes. There is evidence that Judaism was also becoming popular among the lower urban classes, as well as among the soldiers and freed slaves. From Rome, Judaism spilled over to parts of Europe annexed by the Roman Empire, such as the Slavic and Germanic lands, southern Gaul and Spain.

The pivotal role of women in proselytization might indicate a particular female interest in the religion's personal laws, such as the early

[2] Inscriptions. [Ed.]

rules of personal purification, which were preferred to the common pagan customs. Possibly it was also due to the fact that women did not have to undergo circumcision, which was a difficult requirement that deterred many would-be male converts. In the second century CE, after Hadrian prohibited all circumcision, the emperor Antoninus Pius permitted the Jews to circumcise their sons, but forbade males who were not children of Jews to do it. This was another reason that, parallel with the increase of converts, there was a growing category of "God-fearers"—probably an adaptation of the biblical term "fearers of Yahweh" (*sebomenoi* in Greek; *metuentes* in Latin).

These were semi-converts—people who formed broad peripheries around the Jewish community, took part in its ceremonies, attended the synagogues, but did not keep all the commandments. Josephus mentions them several times, and describes Nero's wife as God-fearing. The term is also found in many extant synagogue inscriptions as well as Roman catacombs. The New Testament confirms their massive presence. For example: "And there were dwelling at Jerusalem Jews, devout men, out of every nation under heaven" (Acts 2:5). When Paul reached Antioch, he entered a synagogue on the Sabbath and began his sermon with the words, "Men of Israel, and ye that fear God, give audience" (Acts 13:16). In case some of his hearers were puzzled by this address, he said further: "Men *and* brethren, children of the stock of Abraham, and whosoever among you feareth God, to you is the word of this salvation sent" (13:26). The text goes on: "Now when the congregation was broken up, many of the Jews and religious proselytes followed Paul and Barnabas" (13:43). The next week, a row broke out between zealous Jews and the two successful preachers—"But the Jews stirred up the devout and honourable women, and the chief men of the city, and raised persecution against Paul and Barnabas, and expelled them out of their coasts" (13:50). The two missionaries went on their way and reached the city of Philippi in Macedonia. There, "we sat down, and spake unto the women which resorted *thither*. And a certain woman . . . whose heart the Lord opened . . . was baptized, and her household" (Acts 16:13–15).

It was precisely in these gray areas, between troubled paganism and partial or full conversion to Judaism, that Christianity made headway. Carried by the momentum of proliferating Judaism and the flourishing varieties of religious syncretism, an open and more flexible belief system arose that skillfully adapted to those who accepted it. It is amazing to what extent the followers of Jesus, the authors of the New Testament, were conscious of the two competing marketing policies. The Gospel of Matthew offers additional testimony to outright Jewish missionizing as well as its limitation: "Woe unto you, scribes and Pharisees, hypocrites! for ye compass sea and land to make one proselyte; and when he is made, ye make him twofold more the child of hell than yourselves" (Matt. 23:15).

This was, of course, the criticism of experienced, professional preachers about the strict commandments from which they were distancing themselves. These new preachers were better at interpreting the sensitivities of the shaky polytheistic world, and knew how to offer it a more sophisticated, user-friendly approach to the monotheistic deity. . . .

In this lively culture of God-fearers, partial converts, full converts, Christian Jews, and born Jews, canceling commandments while preserving the belief in the one god was a revolutionary move of liberation and alleviation. For the spreading monotheism to withstand persecution and external opposition, it had to loosen the exclusivist tendency that lingered in it from the time of Ezra and Nehemiah.[3] In the rising Christian world, there was greater equality between new and established members, and there was even some preference for the "poor in spirit," namely the newcomers. The young religion discarded the element of privileged genealogy—now limited to Jesus as the son of God—and opted for a more sublime genealogy, that of the messianic-universal telos: "There is neither Jew nor Greek, there is neither bond nor free, there is neither male nor female: for ye are all one in Christ Jesus. And if ye *be* Christ's, then are ye Abraham's seed and heirs according to the promise" (Gal. 3: 28–9)

It was Paul who completed the transformation of "Israel in the flesh" into "Israel in the spirit," an idea that conformed with the open and flexible policy of identities that increasingly characterized the Roman Empire. It was not surprising that this dynamic monotheistic movement, which introduced the idea of charity and compassion for all (and the resurrection of at least one person), eventually triumphed over paganism, and cast it into the rubbish bin of history throughout Europe.

[3] Fifth Century B.C.E. [Ed.]

2

EUSEBIUS

Life of Constantine, c. 339

Christians in the Roman Empire were generally subject to greater persecution than Jews. Judaism in Palestine was considered a national religion, and thus free from Roman interference, but

Source: P. Schaff and H. Wace, eds., *The Library of Nicene and Post-Nicene Fathers*, vol. I, *Church History, Life of Constantine, Oration in Praise of Constantine* (New York: The Christian Literature Company, 1890), 489–91.

monotheists, whether Jews or Christians, who flouted Roman state religion and sought converts to do the same, were to be challenged. The degree that challenge should take was not always clear to Roman administrators, as Pliny's letter to the Emperor Trajan demonstrates (see document 4.8). Nevertheless, state persecution was the standard response during the first three centuries, occurring first and perhaps most viciously under Emperor Nero (37–68 C.E.) and then continuing intermittently thereafter.

If Christians were persecuted by Roman officials and emperors, and despised by the thoughtful and powerful elite of Roman society, how then did Christianity ever succeed? Part of the answer lies in the location of these Christians. They were more concentrated in urban than rural areas (the Latin word *pagan* meant "rural" before it meant "unchristian") and managed to gain significant advocates among the powerful elite.

Perhaps the most powerful urban, elite advocate for Christianity was the Roman emperor Constantine (288–337 C.E.). The emperor's historian Eusebius* (260–339 C.E.) recognized both the importance of the emperor and the role of the empire in the success of Christianity in winning the Roman Empire:

> At the same time one universal power, the Roman Empire arose and flourished, while the enduring and implacable hatred of nation against nation was now removed; and as the knowledge of one god and one way of religion and salvation, even the doctrine of Christ, was made known to all mankind; so at the same time the entire dominion of the Roman Empire being invested in a single sovereign, profound peace reigned throughout the world. And thus, by the express appointment of the same God, two roots of blessing, the Roman Empire and the doctrine of Christian piety, sprang up together for the benefit of men.[1]

Prior to his rule as emperor, Constantine ruled the imperial lands of Gaul and Britain as a Caesar. In 312 C.E., Constantine (r. 306–337) was about to invade Italy and try to gain the throne of the western empire by defeating Maxentius, who ruled Rome. In his *Life of Constantine*, Eusebius, who knew the emperor, tells a story about events prior to the invasion that must have circulated at the time to explain Constantine's support of Christianity. What reasons does Eusebius give for Constantine's adoption of Christianity? What does this story suggest about Constantine's knowledge of Christianity before his conversion? What does it suggest about the way people chose religions at this time?

---

* yoo SAY bee uhs
[1] Eusebius, *Oration in Praise of Constantine*, xv, 4. [Ed.]

THINKING HISTORICALLY

We think of conversion as a transforming experience. However, a close reading of this selection shows little change in Constantine himself. Other sources confirm this. Constantine continued the gladiator displays that had been so offensive to Christians, left memorials to other deities, and ruled brutally. But if adopting Christianity was more of a political than spiritual mission for Constantine, he nevertheless carried it out forcefully. He styled himself an Old Testament King David, rebuilt Jerusalem, unified the eastern and western halves of the Roman Empire (which had been split under the previous emperor for administrative purposes), and commandeered the church by holding councils, persecuting "heresies," and enforcing a uniform dogma that transformed the church from a marginalized cult protest to prominence in the governance of the empire. How was the Christianity that Constantine embraced different from that known to Paul or Pliny?

Being convinced, however, that he needed some more powerful aid than his military forces could afford him, on account of the wicked and magical enchantments which were so diligently practiced by the tyrant [Maxentius], he sought Divine assistance, deeming the possession of arms and a numerous soldiery of secondary importance, but believing the cooperating power of Deity invincible and not to be shaken. He considered, therefore, on what God he might rely for protection and assistance. While engaged in this enquiry, the thought occurred to him, that, of the many emperors who had preceded him, those who had rested their hopes in a multitude of gods, and served them with sacrifices and offerings, had in the first place been deceived by flattering predictions, and oracles which promised them all prosperity, and at last had met with an unhappy end, while not one of their gods had stood by to warn them of the impending wrath of heaven; while one alone [Constantine's father][2] who had pursued an entirely opposite course, who had condemned their error, and honored the Supreme God during his whole life, had found him to be the Saviour and Protector of his empire, and the Giver of every good thing. Reflecting on this, and well weighing the fact that they who had trusted in many gods had also fallen by manifold forms of death, without leaving behind them either family or offspring, stock, name, or memorial among men: while the God of his father had given to him, on the other hand, manifestations of his power

---

[2] Eusebius claims that Constantine's father, Constantius, was a Christian, though he appeared to be pagan. [Ed.]

and very many tokens: and considering farther that those who had already taken arms against the tyrant, and had marched to the battle-field under the protection of a multitude of gods, had met with a dishonorable end (for one of them had shamefully retreated from the contest without a blow, and the other, being slain in the midst of his own troops, became, as it were, the mere sport of death); reviewing, I say, all these considerations, he judged it to be folly indeed to join in the idle worship of those who were no gods, and after such convincing evidence, to err from the truth; and therefore felt it incumbent on him to honor his father's God alone.

Accordingly he called on Him with earnest prayer and supplications that he would reveal to him who He was, and stretch forth His right hand to help him in his present difficulties. And while he was thus praying with fervent entreaty, a most marvelous sign appeared to him from heaven, the account of which it might have been hard to believe had it been related by any other person. But since the victorious emperor himself long afterwards declared it to the writer of this history, when he was honored with his acquaintance and society, and confirmed his statement by an oath, who could hesitate to accredit the relation, especially since the testimony of after-time has established its truth? He said that about noon, when the day was already beginning to decline, he saw with his own eyes the trophy of a cross of light in the heavens, above the sun, and bearing the inscription, CONQUER BY THIS. At this sight he himself was struck with amazement, and his whole army also, which followed him on this expedition, and witnessed the miracle.

He said, moreover, that he doubted within himself what the import of this apparition could be. And while he continued to ponder and reason on its meaning, night suddenly came on; then in his sleep the Christ of God appeared to him with the same sign which he had seen in the heavens, and commanded him to make a likeness of that sign which he had seen in the heavens, and to use it as a safeguard in all engagements with his enemies.

At the dawn of day he arose, and communicated the marvel to his friends: and then, calling together the workers in gold and precious stones, he sat in the midst of them, and described to them the figure of the sign he had seen, bidding them represent it in gold and precious stones. And this representation I myself have had an opportunity of seeing. . . .

The emperor constantly made use of this sign of salvation as a safeguard against every adverse and hostile power, and commanded that others similar to it should be carried at the head of all his armies.

These things were done shortly afterwards. But at the time above specified, being struck with amazement at the extraordinary vision, and resolving to worship no other God save Him who had appeared to him, he sent for those who were acquainted with the mysteries of His doctrines, and enquired who that God was, and what was intended by the sign of the vision he had seen.

They affirmed that He was God, the only begotten Son of the one and only God: that the sign which had appeared was the symbol of immortality, and the trophy of that victory over death which He had gained in time past when sojourning on earth. They taught him also the causes of His advent, and explained to him the true account of His incarnation. Thus he was instructed in these matters, and was impressed with wonder at the divine manifestation which had been presented to his sight. Comparing, therefore, the heavenly vision with the interpretation given, he found his judgment confirmed; and, in the persuasion that the knowledge of these things had been imparted to him by Divine teaching, he determined thenceforth to devote himself to the reading of the inspired writings.

3

Christianity in China: The Nestorian Monument, 781

This selection is part of an inscription found on a ten-foot stone in China. It was inscribed in Aramaic and Chinese in 781 by Nestorian Christian missionaries in China who came from Syria. In Syria, Nestorian Christian beliefs were not very different from those of other Christians. They believed that Jesus had both a human and divine nature but emphasized the human side of Jesus more than other Christians. From Syria, Nestorians brought Christianity to Persia and Central Asia, reaching China by at least 635. What does the emperor's proclamation suggest about the way Christianity came to China? Why did the emperor support it?

THINKING HISTORICALLY

How is the message of this inscription different from that of Jesus, Paul, or other early Christians (see Chapter 6)? What words or ideas in this document show the influence of Confucian or Daoist thought? What expected Christian words or ideas are missing from this document? What do these changes tell you about Christianity in China? What seems to have remained constant, and what seems to have changed?

Source: Charles F. Horne, ed., *The Sacred Books and Early Literature of the East*, vol. XII, *Medieval China* (New York: Parke, Austin, & Lipscomb, 1917), 381–92. Modernized by Jerome S. Arkenberg. Internet East Asian History Sourcebook. http://www.fordham.edu /halsall/eastasia/781nestorian.html.

"Behold the unchangeably true and invisible, who existed through all eternity without origin; the far-seeing perfect intelligence, whose mysterious existence is everlasting; operating on primordial substance he created the universe, being more excellent than all holy intelligences, inasmuch as he is the source of all that is honorable. This is our eternal true lord God, triune[1] and mysterious in substance. He appointed the cross as the means for determining the four cardinal points,[2] he moved the original spirit, and produced the two principles of nature;[3] the somber void[4] was changed, and heaven and earth were opened out; the sun and moon revolved, and day and night commenced; having perfected all inferior objects, he then made the first man; upon him he bestowed an excellent disposition, giving him in charge the government of all created beings; man, acting out the original principles of his nature, was pure and unostentatious;[5] his unsullied and expansive mind was free from the least inordinate desire; until Satan introduced the seeds of falsehood,[6] to deteriorate his purity of principle; the opening thus commenced in his virtue gradually enlarged, and by this crevice in his nature was obscured and rendered vicious; hence three hundred and sixty-five sects followed each other in continuous track,[7] inventing every species of doctrinal complexity; while some pointed to material objects as the source of their faith,[8] others reduced all to vacancy, even to the annihilation of the two primeval principles,[9] some sought to call down blessings by prayers and supplications,[10] while others by an assumption of excellence held themselves

[1] The idea of the Trinity, that God consisted of three persons—Father, Son, and Holy Spirit—became orthodox in the fourth century, after the Council at Nicaea (325) declared that the Father and Son were of the same substance. Ironically, this council defeated the Arian emphasis on the humanity of Jesus, which was closer to the view of Nestorian Christianity. The Council of Nicaea was called by Constantine to unify Christian belief; Nicaea (modern Iznik, Turkey) was the capital of Bithnia, where Pliny governed, attempted urban renewal, and met Christians in the first century. [Ed.]

[2] The Chinese character for the number 10 is a cross. So this could be translated as "he appointed the Chinese figure for 10 as the means for determining the four cardinal points" of the compass: north, east, south, and west. One translator suggests that this is a whimsical way of saying that this God created all the universe; that is, he is not just a god of a mountain or stream. [Ed.]

[3] Probably refers to the Nestorian idea that the two natures of Christ, human and divine, were conjoined. A church council at Ephesus in 431 held that they became one nature, causing some Nestorians to split and move eastward. The Chinese may have thought of two natures as yin and yang. [Ed.]

[4] This void may be closer to Daoism or Buddhism. [Ed.]

[5] Compare this sentence to Genesis. [Ed.]

[6] May refer to the temptation of Adam. [Ed.]

[7] May refer to mankind cast out of paradise. [Ed.]

[8] Possibly a criticism of the Buddhist idea of the world as maya, or illusion. [Ed.]

[9] May refer to the Daoist idea of emptiness. [Ed.]

[10] May refer to ancestor worship. [Ed.]

up as superior to their fellows;[11] their intellects and thoughts continually wavering, their minds and affections incessantly on the move, they never obtained their vast desires, but being exhausted and distressed they revolved in their own heated atmosphere; till by an accumulation of obscurity they lost their path, and after long groping in darkness they were unable to return. Thereupon, our Trinity being divided in nature, the illustrious and honorable Messiah,[12] veiling his true dignity, appeared in the world as a man; angelic powers promulgated the glad tidings, a virgin gave birth to the Holy One in Syria; a bright star announced the felicitous event, and Persians observing the splendor came to present tribute; the ancient dispensation, as declared by the twenty-four holy men [the writers of the Old Testament], was then fulfilled, and he laid down great principles for the government of families and kingdoms; he established the new religion of the silent[13] operation of the pure spirit of the Triune; he rendered virtue subservient to direct faith; he fixed the extent of the eight boundaries,[14] thus completing the truth and freeing it from dross; he opened the gate of the three constant principles,[15] introducing life and destroying death; he suspended the bright sun[16] to invade the chambers of darkness, and the falsehoods of the devil were thereupon defeated; he set in motion the vessel of mercy[17] by which to ascend to the bright mansions, whereupon rational beings were then released, having thus completed the manifestation of his power, in clear day he ascended to his true station.[18]

Twenty-seven sacred books [the number in the New Testament] have been left, which disseminate intelligence by unfolding the original transforming principles. By the rule for admission, it is the custom to apply the water of baptism,[19] to wash away all superficial show and to cleanse and purify the neophytes. As a seal, they hold the cross, whose influence is reflected in every direction, uniting all without distinction. As they strike the wood, the fame of their benevolence is diffused

[11] May refer to Confucians. [Ed.]

[12] "Second Person of the Trinity" may be a better translation, since there is no Chinese for "Messiah." [Ed.]

[13] Recalls the Daoist idea that the sage conveys wisdom without words. [Ed.]

[14] Perhaps the eight beatitudes in Matthew ("Blessed are the . . . ," etc.), as opposed to the Buddha's eight-fold path. [Ed.]

[15] Some translate this as three virtues: faith, hope, and charity. Followers of Persian Manichaenism would understand it as the three Permanences of the Almighty: his Light, Strength, and Goodness. [Ed.]

[16] Possible reference to crucifixion (though, if so, very veiled). Probable intent is that followers will recognize meaning but nonbelievers won't be put off by the idea of a God who was executed and died. [Ed.]

[17] Christ's death on the cross, like the sacrifice of a Bodhisattva (a vessel of mercy). [Ed.]

[18] Reference to Christ ascending into heaven. [Ed.]

[19] Baptism, or immersion in water as a rite of purification, was practiced in Judaism, but in early Christianity it became associated with being a Christian. [Ed.]

abroad; worshiping toward the east, they hasten on the way to life and glory; they preserve the beard to symbolize their outward actions, they shave the crown to indicate the absence of inward affections; they do not keep slaves, but put noble and mean all on an equality; they do not amass wealth, but cast all their property into the common stock; they fast, in order to perfect themselves by self-inspection; they submit to restraints, in order to strengthen themselves by silent watchfulness; seven times a day they have worship and praise for the benefit of the living and the dead; once in seven days they sacrifice, to cleanse the heart and return to purity.

It is difficult to find a name to express the excellence of the true and unchangeable doctrine; but as its meritorious operations are manifestly displayed, by accommodation it is named the Illustrious Religion.[20] Now without holy men,[21] principles cannot become expanded; without principles, holy men cannot become magnified; but with holy men and right principles, united as the two parts of a signet, the world becomes civilized and enlightened.

In the time of the accomplished Emperor Tai-tsung, the illustrious and magnificent founder of the dynasty, among the enlightened and holy men who arrived was the most-virtuous Olopun,[22] from the country of Syria. Observing the azure clouds, he bore the true sacred books; beholding the direction of the winds,[23] he braved difficulties and dangers. In the year of our Lord 635 he arrived at Chang-an; the Emperor sent his Prime Minister, Duke Fang Hiuen-ling; who, carrying the official staff to the west border, conducted his guest into the interior; the sacred books were translated in the imperial library, the sovereign investigated the subject in his private apartments; when becoming deeply impressed with the rectitude and truth of the religion, he gave special orders for its dissemination.

In the seventh month of the year A.D. 638 the following imperial proclamation was issued:

"Right principles have no invariable name, holy men have no invariable station; instruction is established in accordance with the locality, with the object of benefiting the people at large. The greatly virtuous Olopun, of the kingdom of Syria, has brought his sacred

[20] This sentence is full of phrases from the *Tao Te Ching*. [Ed.]

[21] Some translators prefer "ruler" to "holy men," suggesting that this was a flattering call for the Chinese emperor to help spread the religion. [Ed.]

[22] Identified as Raban in some translations, the Nestorian monk who brought Christianity. [Ed.]

[23] Reference (not translated here) to the sound of winds in musical tubes refers to the Chinese form of divination. [Ed.]

books and images from that distant part, and has presented them at our chief capital. Having examined the principles of this religion, we find them to be purely excellent and natural; investigating its originating source, we find it has taken its rise from the establishment of important truths; its ritual is free from perplexing expressions, its principles will survive when the framework is forgot; it is beneficial to all creatures; it is advantageous to mankind. Let it be published throughout the Empire, and let the proper authority build a Syrian church in the capital in the I-ning May,[24] which shall be governed by twenty-one priests. When the virtue of the Chau Dynasty declined, the rider on the azure ox ascended to the west;[25] the principles of the great Tang becoming resplendent, the Illustrious breezes have come to fan the East."

Orders were then issued to the authorities to have a true portrait of the Emperor taken; when it was transferred to the wall of the church, the dazzling splendor of the celestial visage irradiated the Illustrious portals. The sacred traces emitted a felicitous influence, and shed a perpetual splendor over the holy precincts. According to the Illustrated Memoir of the Western Regions, and the historical books of the Han and Wei dynasties, the kingdom of Syria reaches south to the Coral Sea; on the north it joins the Gem Mountains; on the west it extends toward the borders of the immortals and the flowery forests; on the east it lies open to the violent winds and tideless waters. The country produces fire-proof cloth,[26] life-restoring incense,[27] bright moon-pearls,[28] and night-luster gems. Brigands and robbers are unknown, but the people enjoy happiness and peace. None but Illustrious laws prevail; none but the virtuous are raised to sovereign power. The land is broad and ample, and its literary productions are perspicuous and clear. . . .

[The following is in Syriac at the foot of the stone.]

"In the year of the Greeks one thousand and ninety-two [781 C.E.], the Lord Jazedbuzid, Priest and Vicar-episcopal of Cumdan the royal city, son of the enlightened Mailas, Priest of Balkh a city of Turkestan, set up this tablet, whereon is inscribed the Dispensation of our Redeemer, and the preaching of the apostolic missionaries to the King of China."

---

[24] I-ning quarter of Chang-an was west where Persian and Central Asian merchants were concentrated. [Ed.]

[25] Evokes story told of Lao Tze riding an ox into the west at the end of his life. The point of this sentence, which was probably not part of the imperial proclamation, is that the Nestorian faith prospered after the end of the dynasty. [Ed.]

[26] Probably asbestos. [Ed.]

[27] Probably a balsam said to revive plague victims; used medicinally and in mummification. [Ed.]

[28] Likely oysters. [Ed.]

4

Buddhism in China:
The Disposition of Error, Fifth or Sixth Century

When Buddhist monks traveled from India to China, they came to a culture with different philosophical and religious traditions. In China, ancestor worship, which did not exist for Indians who believed in reincarnation, was a very important religious tradition. The leading Chinese philosopher Confucius said very little about religion but stressed the need for respect: sons to fathers (filial piety), wives to husbands, children to parents, students to teachers, youngsters to elders, everyone to the emperor, the living to the deceased. More spiritual and meditative was the religion developed by the followers of a contemporary of Confucius, Lao Tze,* whose *Dao De Jing* (The Book of the Way) prescribed the peace that came from an acceptance of natural flows and rhythms. "Practice nonaction" was the Daoist method.

The Disposition of Error is a Buddhist guide for converting the Chinese. While the author and date are uncertain, this kind of tract was common under the Southern Dynasties (420–589 c.e.). The author uses a frequently-asked-questions (FAQ) format that enables us to see what the Chinese — mainly Confucian — objections were to Buddhism, as well as what they considered good Buddhist answers.

What were the main Chinese objections to Buddhism? Why were Buddhist ideas of death and rebirth such a stumbling block for Chinese Confucians? Were Confucian ideas about care of the body and hair only superficial concerns, or did they reflect basic differences between Confucianism and Buddhism? What did the Buddhists expect to be the main appeal of their religion?

THINKING HISTORICALLY

This Buddhist missionary's guide to converting the Chinese offers a unique window on both the continuities of Chinese tradition and the possibilities of change. We can see continuities in those Chinese beliefs and styles that the Buddhist monks accept, adopt, or attempt to work within. Note the style of presentation in this guide, for instance. Compare it to the *Analects* of Confucius and the Buddhist documents you have read. Is an FAQ format closer to Confucian or

---

*low TSAY

Source: Hung-ming Chi, in Taishō daizōkyō, LII, 1–7, quoted in William Theodore de Bary, ed., *The Buddhist Tradition in India, China and Japan* (New York: Random House, 1969), 132–37.

Buddhist style? Note also the different ways in which Confucian and Buddhist documents refer to an authority to solve a problem. Does this document follow Confucian or Buddhist style?

Why Is Buddhism Not Mentioned in the Chinese Classics?

The questioner said: If the way of the Buddha is the greatest and most venerable of ways, why did Yao, Shun, the Duke of Chou, and Confucius not practice it? In the Five Classics one sees no mention of it. You, sir, are fond of the *Book of Odes* and the *Book of History*, and you take pleasure in rites and music. Why, then, do you love the way of the Buddha and rejoice in outlandish arts? Can they exceed the Classics and commentaries and beautify the accomplishments of the sages? Permit me the liberty, sir, of advising you to reject them.

Mou Tzu said: All written works need not necessarily be the words of Confucius, and all medicine does not necessarily consist of the formulae of [the famous physician] P'ien-ch'üeh. What accords with principle is to be followed, what heals the sick is good. The gentleman-scholar draws widely on all forms of good, and thereby benefits his character. Tzu-kung [a disciple of Confucius] said, "Did the Master have a permanent teacher?" Yao served Yin Shou, Shun served Wuch'eng, the Duke of Chou learned from Lü Wang, and Confucius learned from Lao Tzu. And none of these teachers is mentioned in the Five Classics. Although these four teachers were sages, to compare them to the Buddha would be like comparing a white deer to a unicorn, or a swallow to a phoenix. Yao, Shun, the Duke of Chou, and Confucius learned even from such teachers as these. How much less, then, may one reject the Buddha, whose distinguishing marks are extraordinary and whose superhuman powers know no bounds! How may one reject him and refuse to learn from him? The records and teachings of the Five Classics do not contain everything. Even if the Buddha is not mentioned in them, what occasion is there for suspicion?

Why Do Buddhist Monks Do Injury to Their Bodies?

The questioner said: The *Classic of Filial Piety* says, "Our torso, limbs, hair, and skin we receive from our fathers and mothers. We dare not do them injury." When Tseng Tzu was about to die, he bared his hands and feet.[1] But now the monks shave their heads. How this violates the sayings of the sages and is out of keeping with the way of the filially pious! . . .

[1] To show he had preserved them intact from all harm.

Mou Tzu said: . . . Confucius has said, "He with whom one may follow a course is not necessarily he with whom one may weigh its merits." This is what is meant by doing what is best at the time. Furthermore, the *Classic of Filial Piety* says, "The kings of yore possessed the ultimate virtue and the essential Way." T'ai-po cut his hair short and tattooed his body, thus following of his own accord the customs of Wu and Yüeh and going against the spirit of the "torso, limbs, hair, and skin" passage.[2] And yet Confucius praised him, saying that his might well be called the ultimate virtue.

Why Do Monks Not Marry?

The questioner said: Now of felicities there is none greater than the continuation of one's line, of unfilial conduct there is none worse than childlessness. The monks forsake wife and children, reject property and wealth. Some do not marry all their lives. How opposed this conduct is to felicity and filial piety! . . .

Mou Tzu said: . . . Wives, children, and property are the luxuries of the world, but simple living and inaction are the wonders of the Way. Lao Tzu has said, "Of reputation and life, which is dearer? Of life and property, which is worth more?" . . . Hsü Yu and Ch'ao-fu dwelt in a tree. Po I and Shu Ch'i starved in Shou-yang, but Confucius praised their worth, saying, "They sought to act in accordance with humanity and they succeeded in acting so." One does not hear of their being illspoken of because they were childless and propertyless. The monk practices the Way and substitutes that for the pleasures of disporting himself in the world. He accumulates goodness and wisdom in exchange for the joys of wife and children.

Death and Rebirth

The questioner said: The Buddhists say that after a man dies he will be reborn. I do not believe in the truth of these words. . . .

Mou Tzu said: . . . The spirit never perishes. Only the body decays. The body is like the roots and leaves of the five grains, the spirit is like the seeds and kernels of the five grains. When the roots and leaves come forth they inevitably die. But do the seeds and kernels perish? Only the body of one who has achieved the Way perishes. . . .

Someone said: If one follows the Way one dies. If one does not follow the Way one dies. What difference is there?

---

[2] Uncle of King Wen of the Chou who retired to the barbarian land of Wu and cut his hair and tattooed his body in barbarian fashion, thus yielding his claim to the throne to King Wen.

Mou Tzu said: You are the sort of person who, having not a single day of goodness, yet seeks a lifetime of fame. If one has the Way, even if one dies one's soul goes to an abode of happiness. If one does not have the Way, when one is dead one's soul suffers misfortune.

Why Should a Chinese Allow Himself to Be Influenced by Indian Ways?

The questioner said: Confucius said, "The barbarians with a ruler are not so good as the Chinese without one." Mencius criticized Ch'en Hsiang for rejecting his own education to adopt the ways of [the foreign teacher] Hsü Hsing, saying, "I have heard of using what is Chinese to change what is barbarian, but I have never heard of using what is barbarian to change what is Chinese." You, sir, at the age of twenty learned the way of Yao, Shun, Confucius, and the Duke of Chou. But now you have rejected them, and instead have taken up the arts of the barbarians. Is this not a great error?

Mou Tzu said: . . . What Confucius said was meant to rectify the way of the world, and what Mencius said was meant to deplore one-sidedness. Of old, when Confucius was thinking of taking residence among the nine barbarian nations, he said, "If a gentleman-scholar dwells in their midst, what baseness can there be among them?" . . . The Commentary says, "The north polar star is in the center of heaven and to the north of man." From this one can see that the land of China is not necessarily situated under the center of heaven. According to the Buddhist scriptures, above, below, and all around, all beings containing blood belong to the Buddha-clan. Therefore I revere and study these scriptures. Why should I reject the Way of Yao, Shun, Confucius, and the Duke of Chou? Gold and jade do not harm each other, crystal and amber do not cheapen each other. You say that another is in error when it is you yourself who err.

Why Must a Monk Renounce Worldly Pleasures?

The questioner said: Of those who live in the world, there is none who does not love wealth and position and hate poverty and baseness, none who does not enjoy pleasure and idleness and shrink from labor and fatigue. . . . But now the monks wear red cloth, they eat one meal a day, they bottle up the six emotions, and thus they live out their lives. What value is there in such an existence?

Mou Tzu said: Wealth and rank are what man desires, but if he cannot obtain them in a moral way, he should not enjoy them. Poverty and meanness are what man hates, but if he can only avoid them by departing from the Way, he should not avoid them. Lao Tzu has said, "The five colors make men's eyes blind, the five sounds make men's ears deaf, the five flavors dull the palate, chasing about and hunting make men's minds mad, possessions difficult to acquire bring men's conduct to an impasse. The sage acts for his belly, not for his eyes." Can these words possibly be vain? Liu-hsia Hui would not exchange his way of life for the rank of the three highest princes of the realm. Tuankan Mu would not exchange his for the wealth of Prince Wen of Wei. . . . All of them followed their ideas, and cared for nothing more. Is there no value in such an existence?

Does Buddhism Have No Recipe for Immortality?

The questioner said: The Taoists say that Yao, Shun, the Duke of Chou, and Confucius and his seventy-two disciples did not die, but became immortals. The Buddhists say that men must all die, and that none can escape. What does this mean?

Mou Tzu said: Talk of immortality is superstitious and unfounded; it is not the word of the sages. Lao Tzu says, "Even Heaven and earth cannot be eternal. How much the less can man!" Confucius says, "The wise man leaves the world, but humanity and filial piety last forever." I have observed the six arts and examined the commentaries and records. According to them, Yao died, Shun had his [death place at] Mount Ts'ang-wu, Yü has his tomb on K'uai-chi, Po I and Shu Ch'i have their grave in Shou-yang. King Wen died before he could chastise Chou, King Wu died without waiting for King Ch'eng to grow up. We read of the Duke of Chou that he was reburied, and of Confucius that [shortly before his death] he dreamed of two pillars. [As for the disciples of Confucius], Po-yü died before his father, of Tzu Lu it is said that his flesh was chopped up and pickled.

5

Selections from the Quran, Seventh Century

In the centuries following the expansion of Christianity and Buddhism, a new monotheistic salvation religion, Islam, originated in Arabia and spread rapidly among Arab polytheists as well as to many Jews and Christians along ancient trade routes (see Map 7.2). The new faith centered on the Quran (or Koran), which is said by Islamic believers, or Muslims, to be the word of God as spoken by the Angel Gabriel to the Prophet Muhammad about 610. Muhammad then

Source: Chapters 1, 91, 109, and 112: *Approaching the Qur'an: The Early Revelations*, trans. Michael Sells (Ashland, OR: White Cloud Press, 1999), 42, 108, 128, 136. Chapters 2 and 4: *The New On-Line Translation of the Qur'an*, the Noor Foundation, http://islamusa.org/.

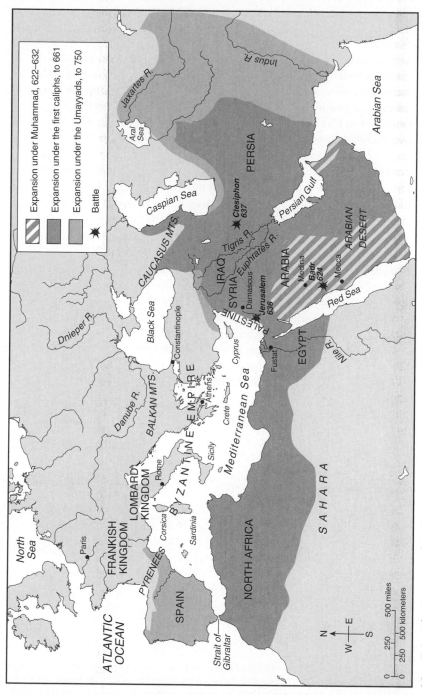

Map 7.2 The Expansion of Islam to 750 C.E.

257

recited these words so that others could memorize them or write them down. After Muhammad's death (632), these writings and memories were gathered together to form the Quran (literally "Recitation").

The chapters (or *surahs*) of the Quran, 114 in all, are organized primarily by length, with the longest first, and in reverse chronological order. This means that the earliest pieces, which are among the shortest, are found at the end of the book. We begin with the first, an exception to this length rule, *surah* 1, "The Opening," followed in rough chronology by a few of the earliest *surahs*: numbers 99, 109, and 112. We conclude with excerpts from the later *surahs*, number 2, "The Cow,"[1] and number 4, "Women." What beliefs do these *surahs* convey? How are they similar to, and different from, the beliefs of Judaism and Christianity? Which messages of the Quran would be effective in aiding the expansion of the religion?

THINKING HISTORICALLY

The early *surahs* (those with higher numbers) almost certainly reflect the concerns of early Islam. What are these concerns? The later *surahs* (such as 2 and 4) were probably written after Muhammad, threatened by the ruling tribes, had fled Mecca and taken control of the government of Medina. They may even have been written after Muhammad's death when his successors struggled with problems of governance. Judging from these later chapters, what kinds of issues most concerned leaders of the Muslim community? How did the message or emphasis change from the early to the later *surahs*? What would account for such a change?

Surah 1
The Opening

In the name of God
  the Compassionate the Caring
Praise be to God
  lord sustainer of the worlds
the Compassionate the Caring
master of the day of reckoning
To you we turn to worship
  and to you we turn in time of need

---

[1] The title "The Cow" refers to verses 67–73 in *surah* 2 of the Quran (not included here), which tell of a dispute between Moses and the Israelites. After Moses tells the Israelites that God wants them to sacrifice a cow, they hesitate by asking a number of questions as to what kind of cow. The Muslim meaning is that one should submit to God, not debate his commands. [Ed.]

Guide us along the road straight
the road of those to whom you are giving
   not those with anger upon them
   not those who have lost the way

Surah 99
The Quaking

In the Name of God the Compassionate the Caring

When the earth is shaken, quaking
When the earth bears forth her burdens
And someone says "What is with her?"
At that time she will tell her news
As her lord revealed her
At that time people will straggle forth
   to be shown what they have done
Whoever does a mote's weight good will see it
Whoever does a mote's weight wrong will see it

Surah 109
Those Who Reject the Faith

In the Name of God the Compassionate the Caring

Say: You who reject the faith
I do not worship what you worship
and you do not worship what I worship
I am not a worshipper of what you worship
You are not a worshipper of what I worship
A reckoning for you and a reckoning for me

Surah 112
Sincerity / Unity

In the Name of God the Compassionate the Caring

Version 1
   Say he is God, one
   God forever
   Not begetting, unbegotten,
     and having as an equal none

Version 2
   Say he is God, one
   God the refuge

Not begetting, unbegotten,
    and having as an equal none

Version 3
    Say he is God, one
    God the rock
    Not begetting, unbegotten,
        and having as an equal none

Surah 2
The Cow

Section 22

177. It is not the sole virtue that you turn your faces to the east or the west but true virtue is theirs, who believe in Allâh, the Last Day, the angels, the Book, and in the Prophets, and who give away their wealth (and substance) out of love for Him, to the near of kin, the orphans, the needy, the wayfarer and to those who ask (in charity) and in ransoming the slaves; and who observe the Prayer, who go on presenting the *Zakât* (the purifying alms) and those who always fulfill their pledges and agreements when they have made one, and those who are patiently persevering in adversity and distress and (steadfast) in times of war. It is these who have proved truthful (in their promises and in their faith) and it is these who are strictly guarded against evil.

178. O you who believe! equitable retaliation has been ordained for you in (the matter of) the slain. (Everyone shall pay for his own crime), the freeman (murderer) for the freeman (murdered), and the slave (murderer) for the slave (murdered), and the female (murderer) for the female (murdered), but who has been granted any remission by his (aggrieved) brother (or family) then pursuing (of the matter) shall be done with equity and fairness, and the payment (of the blood money) to him (the heir) should be made in a handsome manner. This is an alleviation from your Lord and a mercy. But he who exceeds the limits after this (commandment), for him is a grievous punishment.

179. O people of pure and clear wisdom! your very life lies in (the law of) equitable retaliation, (you have been so commanded) so that you may enjoy security.

180. It has been prescribed for you at the time of death to any one of you, that if the (dying) person is leaving considerable wealth behind, to make a will to his parents and the near of kin to act with equity and fairness. This is an obligation incumbent on those who guard against evil.

181. He who alters it (the will) after he has heard it, (should know that) it is those that alter it who shall bear the burden of sin. Allâh indeed is All-Hearing, All-Knowing.

182. If anyone apprehends that the testator is partial or follows a sinful course there will be no blame on him provided he sets things right (and so brings about reconciliation) between them (the parties concerned under the will). Surely, Allâh is Great Protector, Ever Merciful.

Section 23

183. O you who believe! you are bound to observe fasting as those before you (followers of the Prophets) were bound, so that you may guard against evil.

184. (You are required to fast) for a prescribed number of days. But if anyone of you is sick or is on a journey he shall fast (to make up) the prescribed number in other days. And for those who are able to fast is an expiation (as thanksgiving) the feeding of a poor person (daily for the days of fasting). And he who volunteers (extra) good, (will find that) it is even better for him. And that you observe fasting is better for you, if you only know.

185. The (lunar) month of *Ramadzân* is that in which the Qur'ân (started to be) revealed as a guidance for the whole of mankind with its clear evidences (providing comprehensive) guidance and the Discrimination (between right and wrong). Therefore he who shall witness the month, should fast (for full month) during it, but he who is sick or is on a journey shall fast (to make up) the prescribed number in other days. Allâh wishes facility for you and does not wish hardship for you. (This facility is given to you) that you may complete the number (of required fasts) and you may exalt the greatness of Allâh for His having guided you, and that you may render thanks (to Him). . . .

187. (Though during Fasting you must abstain from all the urges of nature including the sexual urge) it is made lawful for you on the nights of the fasts to approach and lie with your wives (for sexual relationship). They are (a sort of) garment for you and you are (a sort of) garment for them. Allâh knows that you have been doing injustice to yourselves (by restricting conjugal relations with your wives even at night), so He turned to you with mercy and provided you relief; now enjoy their company (at night during *Ramadzân*) and seek what Allâh has ordained for you. Eat and drink till the white streak of the dawn becomes distinct to you from the black streak (of the darkness), then complete the fast till nightfall. And you shall not lie with them (your wives) while you perform *I'tikâf* (while you are secluding in the mosque for prayer and devotion to God). These are the limits (imposed) by Allâh so do not approach these (limits). Thus does Allâh explain His commandments for people that they may become secure against evil. . . .

Section 24

190. And fight in the cause of Allâh those who fight and persecute you, but commit no aggression. Surely, Allâh does not love the aggressors.

191. And slay them (the aggressors against whom fighting is made incumbent) when and where you get the better of them, in disciplinary way, and turn them out whence they have turned you out. (Killing is bad but) lawlessness is even worse than carnage. But do not fight them in the precincts of *Masjid al-Harâm* (the Holy Mosque at Makkah) unless they fight you therein. Should they attack you (there) then slay them. This indeed is the recompense of such disbelievers.

192. But if they desist (from aggression) then, behold, Allâh is indeed Great Protector, Ever Merciful.

193. And fight them until persecution is no more and religion is (freely professed) for Allâh. But if they desist (from hostilities) then (re-member) there is no punishment except against the unjust (who still persist in persecution). . . .

195. And spend in the cause of Allâh and do not cast yourselves into ruin with your own hands, and do good to others, and verily Allâh loves the doers of good to others.

196. Accomplish the *Hajj** (the Greater Pilgrimage to Makkah) and the *'Umrah* (the minor pilgrimage) for the sake of Allâh. But if you are kept back, then (offer) whatever sacrifice is easily available, and do not shave your heads (as is prescribed for the Pilgrims) till the offering reaches its destination (in time, or place). And whosoever of you is sick and has an ailment of his head (necessitating shaving before time) then he should make an expiation either by fasting or alms-giving or by making a sacrifice. When you are in peaceful conditions then he, who would avail himself of the *'Umrah* (a visit to the *Ka'bah* or a minor *Hajj*) together with the *Hajj* (the Greater Pilgrimage and thus performs *Tammattu'*) should make whatever offering is easily available; and whosoever finds none (for an offering) should fast for three days during (the days of) the pilgrimage and (for) seven (days) when he returns (home)—these are ten complete (days of fasting in all). This is for him whose family does not reside near the *Masjid al-Harâm* (the Holy Mosque at Makkah). Take Allâh as a shield, and know that Allâh is Severe in retribution (if you neglect your duties).

Section 25

197. The months of performing the *Hajj* are well Known; so who-ever undertakes to perform the *Hajj* in them (should remember that) there is (to be) no obscenity, nor abusing, nor any wrangling during the (time of) *Hajj*. And whatever good you do Allâh knows it. And take provisions for yourselves. Surely, the good of taking provision is guarding (yourselves) against the evil (of committing sin and begging). Take Me alone as (your) shield, O people of pure and clear wisdom!

*HAH juh

198. There is no blame on you that you seek munificence from your Lord (by trading during the time of _Hajj_). When you pour forth (in large numbers) from 'Arafât then glorify Allâh (with still more praises) near Mash'aral-Harâm (Holy Mosque in _Muzdalifah_), and remember Him (with gratitude) as He has guided you, though formerly you were certainly amongst the astray. . . .

Surah 4
Women

Section 1

1. O you people! take as a shield your Lord Who created you from a single being. The same stock from which He created the man He created his spouse, and through them both He caused to spread a large number of men and women. O people! regard Allâh with reverence in Whose name you appeal to one another, and (be regardful to) the ties of relationship (particularly from the female side). Verily, Allâh ever keeps watch over you.

2. And give the orphans their property and substitute not (your) worthless things for (their) good ones, nor consume their property mingling it along with your own property, for this indeed is a great sin.

3. And if (you wish to marry them and) you fear that you will not be able to do justice to the orphan girls then (marry them not, rather) marry of women (other than these) as may be agreeable to you, (you may marry) two or three or four (provided you do justice to them), but if you fear that you will not be able to deal (with all of them) equitably then (confine yourselves only to) one, or (you may marry) that whom your right hands possess (your female captives of war). That is the best way to avoid doing injustice.

4. And give the women their dowers unasked, willingly and as agreed gift. But if they be pleased to remit you a portion thereof, of their own free will, then take it with grace and pleasure.

Section 2

11. Allâh prescribes (the following) law (of inheritance) for your children. For male is the equal of the portion of two females; but if they be all females (two or) more than two, for them is two thirds of what he (the deceased) has left; and if there be only one, for her is the half and for his parents, for each one of the two is a sixth of what he has left, if he (the deceased) has a child; but if he has no child and his parents only be his heirs, then for the mother is one third (and the rest two thirds is for the father); but if there be (in addition to his parents) his brothers (and sisters) then there is one sixth for the mother after (the payment of)

any bequest he may have bequeathed or (still more important) of any debt (bequests made by the testator and his debts shall however be satisfied first). Your fathers and your children, you do not know which of them deserve better to benefit from you. (This) fixing (of portions) is from Allâh. Surely, Allâh is All-Knowing, All-Wise.

12. And for you is half of that which your wives leave behind, if they have no child; but if they have a child, then for you is one fourth of what they leave behind, after (the payment of) any bequest they may have bequeathed or (still more important) of any (of their) debt. And for them (your wives) is one fourth of what you leave behind if you have no child; but if you leave a child, then, for them is an eighth of what you leave after (the payment of) any bequest you have bequeathed or (still more important) of any debt. And if there be a man or a woman whose heritage is to be divided and he (or she—the deceased) has no child and he (or she) has (left behind) a brother or a sister then for each one of the twain is a sixth; but if they be more than one then they are (equal) sharers in one third after the payment of any bequest bequeathed or (still more important) of any debt (provided such bequest made by the testator and the debt) shall be without (any intent of) being harmful (to the interests of the heirs). This is an injunction from Allâh, and Allâh is All-Knowing, Most Forbearing.

13. These are the limits (of the law imposed) by Allâh, and who obeys Allâh and His Messenger He will admit them into Gardens served with running streams; therein they shall abide for ever; and that is a great achievement.

14. But whoso disobeys Allâh and His Messenger and transgresses the limits imposed by Him He will make him enter Fire where he shall abide long, and for him is a humiliating punishment.

15. As to those of your women who commit sexual perversity, call in four of you to witness against them, and if they bear witness then confine them to their houses, until death overtakes them or Allâh makes for them a way out.

16. And if two of your males commit the same (act of indecency), then punish them both, so if they repent and amend (keeping their conduct good) then turn aside from them, verily Allâh is Oft-Returning (with compassion), Ever Merciful.

6

RICHARD C. FOLTZ

The Islamization of the Silk Road, 1999

In the following selection Foltz, a modern historian of religion,
explores the early history of Islam and its spread east of the Mediterranean. Placing the rise of Islam solidly within the Arab traditions of trading and raiding, Foltz distinguishes between the initial
development of unified Arab rule and the subsequent spread of
Islamic religious culture. He argues that the "convert or die" idea
that pervades the history of Islam is largely mythic and that early
Muslim rulers actually discouraged conversion. According to Foltz,
what role did economics play in early Muslim expansion? How did
Islam spread so widely and so quickly, and what was the nature of
this early growth? How did non-Arabs who converted to Islam
change it?

THINKING HISTORICALLY

What economic and political forces does Foltz emphasize? What
continuities does Foltz suggest? What roles did individuals play in the
conversion process? What similarities were there between the spread
of Buddhism, Christianity, and Islam?

No religious tradition in world history favored trade as much as did
Islam. The Prophet Muhammad himself was a businessman by profession.
While in his twenties he became employed by a wealthy merchant woman
of Mecca, Khadija, and made his reputation by successfully carrying out
a trade mission to Syria; Khadija married him soon after.

Sometime around 610 of the common era, Muhammad, who liked
to spend time alone meditating in the mountains outside Mecca, began
hearing voices during the course of these retreats. At first he began to
doubt his own sanity, but Khadija persuaded him that these voices might
be divine in nature and should be listened to. Gradually Muhammad
came to believe he was receiving revelations from God, calling upon him
to "rise and warn" his fellow Meccans that the time had come to mend
their ways.

Source: Richard C. Foltz, *Religions of the Silk Road: Overland Trade and Cultural
Exchange from Antiquity to the Fifteenth Century* (New York: St. Martin's Press, 1999),
89–93, 95–97.

Mecca was a desert town with little to subsist on apart from its trade. Successful merchants must have been its wealthiest inhabitants. Many of the revelations Muhammad received dealt with social injustice, which was clearly a problem in Mecca at that time. His message found a growing audience of sympathetic ears, while it increasingly alienated the social classes who were the target of his criticism. Before long certain powerful residents of Mecca were making life difficult for Muhammad and his followers.

In 622 the citizens of Yathrib, a town some two hundred twenty miles to the north of Mecca, were involved in factional disputes they could not resolve. Hearing of Muhammad's reputation for fairness and piety, they invited him to come and arbitrate. He accepted. Sending most of his followers ahead of him, the Prophet of Islam put his affairs in order and finally left his hometown, an event known to Muslims as the *hijra*, or migration, which marks the beginning of the Islamic calendar.

Once in Yathrib, the Muslims were not only no longer persecuted, they enjoyed special status. From their new power base they launched raids (Ar. *Razzia*) on Meccan-bound caravans, at the same time enriching their own treasury while inflicting damage on their former persecutors. After several battles with the Meccans, the Muslims were able to negotiate the right to return to Mecca for the traditional Arabian pilgrimage to the sacred *ka' ba* stone; by 628 Mecca was under Muslim control.

Raiding caravans was an established part of the economic life of Arabia. The only rule was that one couldn't raid clan members or groups with whom one had made a nonaggression pact. With the successes of the Muslims growing from year to year, eventually all the tribes of the Arabian peninsula sent emissaries to Muhammad in order to seek such pacts. Their professions of loyalty were described by later Muslim writers as "submission," which in Arabic is *islam*. Small wonder that these sources, and the non-Muslim histories based on them, interpret this as meaning all the Arabian tribes had accepted the new religion.

Understanding this term "submission" in its more restricted literal sense, however, more easily explains what happened upon the Prophet's death in 632: Most of the Arabian tribes rebelled. Later Muslim sources refer to these as rebellions of "apostasy." A simpler interpretation would be that the rebel parties simply saw their nonaggression pacts as having been rendered null and void by the Prophet's passing.

The Muslims immediately chose a successor, or caliph (from Middle Pers. *Khalifa*), Abu Bakr, under whose leadership the various Arab tribes were forced to resubmit. Since the Arabian economy required the component of raiding, and since according to the nonaggression pacts no one in Arabia could legitimately be raided, the Muslims were forced to launch forays beyond the Arabian peninsula into Byzantine and

Persian territory. Their success in defeating the armies of both empires probably surprised many of the Muslims as much as it did their imperial enemies.

It is important to recognize the economic aspect of Muslim expansion, driven by the ancient Arabian tradition of raiding. While in hindsight both Muslims and non-Muslims have read into this early expansion a large element of religious zeal, the Arab armies of the time were simply doing what they were naturaly acculturated to do, what the economic conditions of their homeland had always constrained them to do. What had changed was that, for the first time, all the Arab groups of the peninsula had excluded for themselves the possibility of raiding other Arab groups. They were forced, therefore, to raid elsewhere. Their new religious self-concept may indeed have inspired them by giving divine meaning to their increasing successes, but other factors were at work as well.

Iranians, in the form of Medes, Achemenians, Parthians, and Sasanians, had been vying with Athenian, Seleucid, and Roman Greeks for hegemony in western Asia for over a millennium. By the seventh century both the Sasanian Persian and Byzantine Greek empires were exhausted and decadent. Neither treated their subject peoples in Mesopotamia, Syria, or Egypt with anything that could be called benevolence. In many locations townspeople threw open the gates to the Arabs and welcomed them as liberators. The Muslims were, in fact, no more foreign in most of the lands they conquered than had been the previous rulers, and at first they were less exploitative.

By the 660s, however, the ruling Arab family, the Umayyads, had set themselves up in Damascus in very much the mold of the Byzantine governors they had dislodged. Throughout the subsequent decades non-Muslims came to chafe under the new regime. Many Arab Muslims, furthermore, resented the imperial manner and "un-Islamic" lifestyles of the Umayyads, many of whom had taken to drinking and debauchery in the best Roman tradition.

But the group which was to bring about the Umayyads' downfall and, in doing so, forever change the very nature of Islam as a cultural tradition was the non-Arabs who chose to adopt the Islamic religion.

Initially and throughout the Umayyad period, the Arabs had seen Islam as a religion belonging to them; their subjects, likewise, referred to Islam as "the Arab religion" (al-din al-'arab). The Quran enjoined Muslims to spread Muslim *rule* throughout the world but laid down no requirement to spread the faith itself. The original impulse of holy war (*jihad*) was that no Muslim should be constrained to live under the rule of infidels. Once a given locality agreed to submit to Muslim authority and pay the poll tax (*jizya*) levied on protected communities (*dhimmis*, usually "peoples of the Book," i.e., Christians and Jews), there was no further need for coercion on either side.

In fact, Arab Muslims had strong reasons *not* to want non-Arabs to join the faith, since conversion directly affected both their sources of income and the spread of its distribution among Muslims. Conversely, there were numerous reasons why non-Muslims might wish to join the ruling group, which could most obviously be symbolized by adopting their faith. Despite some apparent resistance from the Arab elite, by the early eighth century non-Arab converts were probably beginning to outnumber Arab Muslims.

Islam had attempted to eliminate class and racial distinctions, but even during the Prophet's lifetime this goal was never met. Early converts and their descendants often felt entitled to greater status and privilege than later converts, and members of aristocratic families never forgot who came from humble ones. Tribal and clan loyalties affected government appointments and led to rivalries.

Often these rivalries developed power bases in garrison towns where particular factions were dominant. Local governors, therefore, usually had more or less personal armies at their ready disposal. In areas where the Arabs were quartered among non-Arab majority populations, there was increasing pressure from converts to be treated on equal footing with Arab Muslims.

The problem was that a non-Arab, even after converting to Islam, had no tribal affiliation which could provide him an identity within Arab society. A solution to this was devised whereby an Arab Muslim could take a non-Arab convert under his wing as a "client" (*mawla*), making the convert a sort of honorary tribal member. Of course, such clients were at the mercy of the individual who sponsored them.

Over time this inequality between Arab and non-Arab Muslims became a major pretext for various parties disaffected with Umayyad rule. Not surprisingly it was in eastern Iran, at the fringes of Umayyad power, that a rebel movement capable of overthrowing the central government and completely reshaping Muslim society took place.

In addition to complaints about the un-Islamic character of the Umayyad elite and the inequalities between Arab and non-Arab Muslims, the anti-Umayyad movement could draw on the issue of the very legitimacy of Umayyad rule. The first Umayyad caliph, Mu'awiya, had assumed power by refusing to recognize the selection of the Prophet's nephew and son-in-law, Ali, as fourth caliph. A significant minority of Muslims felt that leadership should be sought in charismatic authority passed down through the Prophet's line. For the "partisans of Ali" (*shi' at Ali*), the Umayyads (and indeed the first three caliphs) had been usurpers from the outset.

All of these antigovernment impulses came together in the so-called Abbasid revolution of 749 to 751, in which a Khurasan-based Muslim army rallied behind an Iranian general, Abu Muslim, in the name of an Arab descendant of the Prophet's uncle Abbas. The rebels succeeded in wresting power from the Umayyads, moved the capital to Mesopotamia, and began setting up a new Islamic administration on the Sasanian imperial model. . . .

As with any case of mass cultural conversion, the Islamization of Central Asia was a complex process which occurred on more than one level. The first, and most visible, level was the spread of political power. It is worth noting that the spread of a particular religion's rule is not identical with the spread of faith, although historians have often written as if it were.

Muslim rule over the western half of the Silk Road came fairly early and was established, albeit through a period of false starts and occasional reversals, by the mid-eighth century. Muslims thereafter controlled much of trans-Asian trade, which became the second major factor in the Islamization of Central Asian culture. Gradually a third factor, the influence of charismatic Muslim preachers, entered into the process.

The reality of Muslim rule could no longer be reasonably ignored once the numerous eighth-century attempts to rally behind local, non-Islamic religious figures had all failed. Politics was therefore an initial influence encouraging Central Asians to abandon their native cultural traditions and join the growing world culture of Islamic civilization. It appears, however, that the only local rulers, especially those who had raised arms against the Muslims, were ever subjected to the convert-or-die alternative that has so long been the stereotype characterizing the spread of Islam. Other people, at least at first, would have embraced the faith of their new rulers for other reasons, in certain cases no doubt spiritual ones.

One of the most commonly cited incentives to religio-cultural conversion is the pursuit of patronage. Anyone directly dependent on the government for his livelihood might sense advantages in joining the cultural group of his patrons and accepting the norms and values of that ruling group. To a large extent, converts to Islam do appear to have held onto their preconquest positions, and being a Muslim increased one's chances of attaining a new or better one.

A second and probably greater influence affecting Islamization was the Muslim domination of commercial activity. A businessman could feel that becoming a Muslim would facilitate contacts and cooperation with other Muslim businessmen both at home and abroad; he would also benefit from favorable conditions extended by Muslim officials and from the Islamic laws governing commerce.

The presence of Muslim rule and the increasing Muslim dominance of trade meant that Islamization came first in the urban areas along the Silk Road and only in later centuries spread to the countryside. The gradual Islamization of the nomadic Turkic peoples of Central and Inner Asia was at first directly tied to their increasing participation in the oasis-based Silk Road trade in the tenth century, accelerated by the political activities of three Turkic Muslim dynasties—the Qarakhanids, the Ghaznavids, and the Seljuks—and supplemented by the proselytizing efforts of Muslim missionaries.

The third major factor accounting for the Islamization of the Silk Road, which follows those of politics and economics, is assimilation. Whatever the reasons for one's converting to Islam, Islamization occurs most profoundly (and irrevocably) among the succeeding generation, since the convert's children in principle will be raised within the father's new community, not his original one. Furthermore, although a Muslim man may marry a non-Muslim woman, Islamic law requires that the children of a mixed marriage be raised as Muslims. However, . . . it may be safe to assume that aspects of pre-Islamic local religion survived through transmission by non-Muslim wives of Muslims.

7

Peace Terms with Jerusalem, 636

The early expansion of Islam was far more rapid and more forceful than the expansion of Christianity and Buddhism. By 636, Arab armies had conquered many of the lands previously held by the Byzantine and Persian empires. Merchants and holy men would spread the faith even farther afield at a later stage. But by 750 an Arab-dominated Muslim government controlled North Africa, the Arabian peninsula, and significant portions of Eurasia from the Strait of Gibraltar to the western borders of India and China. (See Map 7.2 on page 257.)

How much of this early expansion was military conquest and how much religious conversion? To help us answer this question, we look at an early peace treaty after the conquest of Jerusalem from the Byzantine Empire (known then as the Roman Empire, but ruled from Constantinople).

As the Arabian force for Judeo-Christian monotheism, Muslims had a strong sentimental attachment to Jerusalem. In the first years of the faith, Muhammad and his followers prayed facing Jerusalem, Al Quds

---

Source: "Peace Terms with Jerusalem (636)," in *Islam from the Prophet Muhammad to the Conquest of Constantinople*, ed. and trans. Bernard Lewis, vol. I, *Politics and War* (New York: Harper & Row, 1974), 235–36. Originally published in Al Tabari, *Tarik al-Rusulcwa'l muluk*, vol. I (Leiden: Brill), 2405–6.

(the Holy City, as it is still called in Arabic). In 624, after only modest Jewish conversions, Mecca was substituted as the *qibla* or direction to face for prayer. At the time of Muhammad's death (632), his followers controlled most of Arabia. His successor (or *caliph*), Abu Bakr (r. 632–634), regained control of the tribes that tried to withdraw from the alliance after the Prophet's death and turned to the conquest of Iraq and Syria. The second caliph, Umar (r. 634–644), negotiated the surrender of the Byzantine forces that controlled Jerusalem after the defeat of Byzantine armies in 636. This document, written by the caliph and directed to the Christian community of Jerusalem, set the terms for continued Christian presence in the city. Many of these terms were continuations of past practice. One of the terms included *jizya*, which was a tax or tribute that non-Muslims paid Muslim governments for protection. This document also reinstates the expulsion of Jews from Jerusalem, a policy first instated under Roman administration and later continued under the Byzantine Christian administration, though Umar later allowed Jews to reside in the city.

Other Muslim sources tell us that the inhabitants of Jerusalem appealed to Umar to take control of Jerusalem. What evidence do you see in these terms that would make that story plausible? What would both sides, Muslim and Christian, seem to gain by these terms?

THINKING HISTORICALLY

If this peace treaty were observed as written, what would have changed in Jerusalem? What would have remained the same? Are these changes mainly religious or political? To what extent, if any, does Muslim control of Jerusalem suggest Jewish or Christian conversions to Islam?

In the name of God the Merciful and the Compassionate.

This is the safe-conduct accorded by the servant of God Umar, the Commander of the Faithful, to the people of Aelia [Jerusalem].[1]

He accords them safe-conduct for their persons, their property, their churches, their crosses, their sound and their sick, and the rest of their worship.

---

[1] Aelia Capitolina was the name given to Jerusalem by Roman emperor Hadrian after he suppressed the second Jewish revolt in 132–135 (the first revolt was 66–70). He also expelled Jews from the city and banned them from living there. The Christian Byzantines continued this policy. Thus, this was a concession to Christians. Umar later let the Jews return to Jerusalem. In the seventh century one could be both a Jew and a Muslim. [Ed.]

Their churches shall neither be used as dwellings nor destroyed. They shall not suffer any impairment, nor shall their dependencies, their crosses, nor any of their property.

No constraint shall be exercised against them in religion nor shall any harm be done to any among them.

No Jew shall live with them in Aelia.

The people of Aelia must pay the *jizya*[2] in the same way as the people of other cities.

They must expel the Romans[3] and the brigands from the city. Those who leave shall have safe-conduct for their persons and property until they reach safety. Those who stay shall have safe-conduct and must pay the *jizya* like the people of Aelia.

Those of the people of Aelia who wish to remove their persons and effects and depart with the Romans and abandon their churches and their crosses shall have safe-conduct for their persons, their churches, and their crosses, until they reach safety.

The country people who were already in the city before the killing of so-and-so may, as they wish, remain and pay the *jizya* the same way as the people of Aelia or leave with the Romans or return to their families. Nothing shall be taken from them until they have gathered their harvest.

This document is placed under the surety of God and the protection [*dhimma*] of the Prophet, the Caliphs and the believers, on condition that the inhabitants of Aelia pay the *jizya* that is due from them.

Witnessed by Khālid ibn al-Wald, 'Amr ibn al-Āṣ, 'Abd al-Raḥmān ibn 'Awf, Muāwiya ibn Abī Sufyān, the last of whom wrote this document in the year 15 [636].

[2] A tax on non-Muslims in return for exemption from the *zakat* tax on Muslims and military service. [Ed.]

[3] Byzantine soldiers and officials. [Ed.]

8

Epic of Sundiata, Thirteenth Century

This is a brief selection from one of the great epics of West Africa. In a culture without a system of written notation, stories like this were told by griots — specialists with prodigious memories. Most of these griots worked in the courts of kings, learning, like their fathers before

Source: *Sunjata: A West African Epic of the Mande Peoples*, trans. David C. Conrad and narrated by Djanka Tassey Condé (Indianapolis, IN: Hackett, 2004), 17–19 (lines 420–93).

them, to tell the story of their patron's family. The *Epic of Sundiata* is the account of one of the great families of the Mande people. The *Epic* centers on Sundiata Keita (c. 1217–1255), who founded the Mali Empire. Our selection is drawn from the story of Maghan Konfara, Sundiata's father, and tells of his conversion to Islam. It begins with the declaration of a visitor, Manjan Bereté, after Maghan Konfara has asked to marry his sister. What does this story add to your understanding of religious conversions and the spread of salvation religions?

THINKING HISTORICALLY

A single conversion would seem to bring far less change than the conquest of a city. Yet, as we have seen, the conversion of a king might have consequences as profound as the conquest of a kingdom. What sort of changes would you expect to occur after this conversion? We are also used to thinking of religious conversion as a momentous change for the individual who experiences it, not the casual affair depicted here. What, if anything, does this story tell you about the history of internal or psychological change?

[The visitor declares:]

"We are Bereté.
It was our ancestor who planted a date farm for the Prophet
        at Mecca
That was the beginning of our family identity.
When the date farm was planted for the Prophet,
He blessed our ancestor.
He said everyone should leave us alone:
Bè anu to yè, and that is why they call us Bereté.
No man of Manden will tell you
That we originated the Bereté family identity.
It was the Prophet who said we should be set apart,
That nobody's foolishness should trouble us.
Bè anu to yè, everyone should leave us alone.
Thus we became the Bereté.
From that time up to today,
We have not done anything other than the Prophet's business.
This place[1] has already become impious

---

[1] Maghan Konfara's place, Konfara, Farakoro, or more generally the land of the Mande (modern southwest Mali). [Ed.]

Because of your lack of attention to Islam.
So how can I give you my little sister?
I did not come from Farisi[2] for that purpose,
So I will not give you my little sister."
"Aaah," said Simbon,[3] "Give her to me.
If you want wealth, I will give you wealth."
(You heard it?)
"If you not give her to me,
I will take her for myself,
Because you are not in your home, you are in my home."
When Manjan Bereté was told this, he said,
"If you take my sister for yourself, I will go back to Farisi.
I will go and get Suraka[4] warriors to come and destroy Manden
If you take my little sister by force."
Simbon said, "You just do that.
If you go back to Farisi to get warriors,
You might come and destroy Manden.
But by then your sister will be pregnant,
I will have a child by then.
Even if I die, it will still be my child."
(You heard it?)
He said, "I have taken her."
He took her.
"If you call for wealth, I will give you wealth.
If you call for the sword, I will agree to that.
I have the power, you have no power, you are in my place."

Manjan Bereté packed up his books and went back to Farisi.
He went and told his fathers and brothers,
"The Mande *mansa*[5] that I went to visit,
He has used his chiefly power to take my little sister from me."
His fathers and brothers said, "Ah, Manjan Bereté,
Your youth has betrayed you.
You carry the sacred book.
Go back and tell the Mande people,
Tell Simbon,
That if he is in love with your younger sister,
You will give him both her and the book.

[2] Fars, Persia. [Ed.]
[3] Speaks for Maghan Konfara. [Ed.]
[4] Arab, Moor, or North African warriors. [Ed.]
[5] King. [Ed.]

Tell him 'If you convert, and become another like me,
So that we can proselytize together,
I will give you my younger sister,
But if you refuse to convert, I will go for my warriors.'
If he does not convert, come back and we will give you warriors.
If he agrees to convert, that is what you went for."

Manjan Bereté returned to Farakoro.
After he explained to Simbon,
Maghan Konfara said, "What your father said,
That your youth betrayed you, is true.
If you had done what he said in the first place,
You would not have returned to Farisi.
All I want is a child, no matter what the cost.
I agree to what you propose.
Since you have requested that I convert,
I agree."
They shaved his head, and together they read the Koran.
After reading the Koran,
Manjan Bereté gave his little sister to Maghan Konfara.

■ REFLECTIONS

The expansion of the great universal religions continued well beyond 1000. In fact, it continues today. We live in a world of about two hundred nation-states, but two-thirds of the world's people follow only three religions: Christianity, Islam, and Buddhism. We return to the question that opened this chapter: What enabled these particular religions to convert so many?

We noted here, and in the previous chapter, that many of the religions of this period were book or text based. The Bible and Quran were said by many to be given by God. The stories of the Buddha also took on an aura of authority that must have enhanced their appeal. Most people could not read or write, of course, but the great religions created writing-based bureaucracies, educators, and thinkers who ensured the dissemination of the sacred scripture, eternal truths, and revered tales. The stories of the life of Jesus were carved into the walls of the Christian churches, etched into the colored glass of the windows, and told and reenacted in the religious rite of the Eucharist, which celebrated the last supper of Jesus. Statues of the Buddha of every size and description were carved and placed for worship in temples throughout Asia. Five times a day, the Muslim call to prayer reverberated from the minarets that spiked the skyline from Morocco to Malacca, and from Tashkent to Timbuktu. One did not have to be able to read in order to pray.

The learned devised, collected, or correlated these texts, often insisting they were the words of the founder, spoken by God or engraved in stone. Then they and their successors explained and interpreted them, often turning intractable prose into metaphor, amending failed prophecies, and inventing myths to suit current politics.

Our readings suggest that the decision to adopt a particular religion was often more political than theological. Kings and emperors made the decision, often with the same degree of calculation whether they were defending state cults, like Trajan (document 4.8), embracing radical challenges, like Constantine, or simply negotiating a marriage, like Sundiata's father. Universal religions and imperial systems fit well together because it was easier for the emir or emperor to work with a unified set of religious values and only universal religions allowed new converts. Example and influence probably played a greater role than conquest. The spread of Islam was the most obvious conquest in this period (as Christianity was later), but the image of Muslims forcing others to convert or die was largely a projection of later Christian crusaders. Recent historical research reveals a rapid military conquest by traditional Arab raiding armies followed later by a gradual process of conversion. Many conquered people, like the Jews of Jerusalem, viewed the Arab armies as liberators. In general, Arab rule was remote and indirect. Normally, the Arabs left earlier structures in control, sometimes making the collection of tribute more efficient, even more lenient. Arab Muslim conquerors were not highly motivated in winning converts because mass conversions would limit the *jizya*, the head tax that only non-Muslims paid. A study by the historian Richard Bulliet shows that Iranians adopted Muslim names (a sign of conversion) gradually a hundred years after the conquest of 648 and that the number of Iranian Muslims increased over the next few hundred years at rates that can be charted on a standard bell curve, the same way any new style or technology rises and then levels off close to saturation.

Distinguishing change and continuity is a historical skill useful in understanding any historical document, period, process, or place. It helps us pose questions, not give simplistic answers like "religion x was continuous, but religion y changed." Everything changes to some degree. It is relative change or constancy that we are after. How fast, how sudden, what specifically changed, and what continued pretty much as before? And what can we learn from asking these questions?

If Judaism was a universal religion that converted large populations from North Africa to Central Asia in the years before and after the fall of Rome, then its continuity, like that of the other universal religions, is in belief and tradition, not ethnicity or place. If the continuity of Islam stretches back to a more widespread Judaism than previously thought, then it makes sense to think of a Judeo-Christian-Islamic tradition, to recognize the apocalyptic theme that pulses through it, and to see the continuity between Islam and Nestorian Christianity, as well as the seal of a new prophecy. On the other hand, a post-Nestorian Christianity in Tang China that neither mentions Jesus nor explains the symbolism of the cross, but instead speaks in the metaphors of the Dao, may tell us more about the continuity of Chinese cultural traditions than of Christianity. Lessons like these are not only interesting in their own right. They might have also been useful for later generations of empire builders, colonial settlers, missionaries, and diplomats.

8

Migrations, Trade, and Travel

The Movement of People, Goods, and Ideas in Eurasia, Africa, and the Pacific, 3000 B.C.E.—1350 C.E.

■ HISTORICAL CONTEXT

We tend to think of immigration issues as very current, and indeed they are. But human migration is an old story. In fact, the movement of peoples is the oldest story of human history, going back to the migrations of early humans out of Africa two million to a hundred thousand years ago.

By 3000 B.C.E. all of the continents except Antarctica had been occupied by humans for at least 10,000 years, agriculture had spread in parts of all of those areas, and many were dotted by cities and organized into states. However, over the course of the next thousand years, three major migrations began to reshape the core of Eurasia, most of sub-Saharan Africa, and much of Southeast Asia and the Pacific. These were the formative population movements of the last five thousand years: the Indo-European impact on Eurasia, the Bantu expansion of central and southern Africa, and the Austronesian migration to Southeast Asia and later Polynesian settlement of the Pacific.

After considering these long-term migrations, two of which—the Bantu and Polynesian—continued into the Middle Ages, we will refocus on the Medieval era. Here we will look at a process of migration of people, plants, technologies, and ideas from Southeast Asia northward through Eurasia, a process our author and historian, Lynda Shaffer, calls "Southernization." This was a process not only of migrations but also the establishment of trading networks and religious missions that often developed hand in hand.

278

Finally we will read some of the travel accounts of two of the great travelers of the Medieval era. The first, from about 400 C.E., is the Chinese monk Faxian who traveled to India to obtain writings and relics of the Buddha. The other, from about 1350, is the great Muslim traveler Ibn Battuta who traveled from Morocco to China. Together they provide close-ups of travel and trade at the beginning and end of the Middle Ages. We will also read one of the great tools consulted by traders.

■ THINKING HISTORICALLY

Sifting Factors

By "sifting factors," I mean distinguishing political, economic, social, and cultural features of sources, facts, events, or subjects. These four aspects of life, paralleling four major specialties of historians, don't cover everything under the Sun. But if we use them broadly enough, we have a useful model for bringing order to the past. In the context of this chapter the political will also include diplomatic (a field of history that is sometimes independent); economic will include the study of trade, business, money, poverty, and similar subjects; and social will include demography or demographic history, the study of peoples—as in migrations. Other subjects of social history are family, gender, education, marriage, social class, and status. Under culture, we will include religion, ideas, styles, music, art, philosophy, science, literature, and popular culture.

From the preceding, you can see that these are not hard-and-fast categories. Some might say religious history, for example, should be separate from cultural history because religion includes social behavior as much as ideas. Others might like a separate category for technology; otherwise do we place it under science and, therefore, culture? And what about work, war, or marriage? How would you categorize these conditions? The problem is that human behavior is too complex to put everything in four neat boxes. But like historians, we have to organize the chaos of information in order to make any sense of it. Therefore, we will be systematic in categorizing the material in this chapter by political, economic, social, and cultural factors. The best way to proceed might be to mark a page with four columns labeled P, E, S, and C, and then list items mentioned in the readings in one, or more if appropriate, of these columns.

1

PATRICK MANNING

Austronesian, Indo-European, and Bantu Migrations, 2005

In this selection, a modern world historian who is a specialist in African and migration history, sketches out the three great long migrations between 3000 B.C.E. and the first millennium C.E. The Austronesians of Southeast Asia and Oceania were themselves descended from people who migrated from Yunan in southwest China to Taiwan. From there the Austronesians brought their culture to Southeast Asia and the islands of New Guinea and the Bismarck Archipelago of the southwestern Pacific. There assimilation eventually produced the people we call Polynesians who settled the islands of the Pacific in the first millennium C.E. The Indo-Europeans, or Aryans, traveled with their horses and chariots from the grasslands north of the Black Sea and Caspian Sea in what is today southern Russia eastward through Europe to the Atlantic and southwestward to India over the period from 3000 B.C.E. to 1500 B.C.E. The Bantu people migrated south and east from Cameroon in West Africa, assimilating with forest dwellers in the south and East Africans before settling much of southern Africa.

What are the different ways in which these migrations occurred? In what ways were they similar? How might these migrations be considered early steps of globalization?

THINKING HISTORICALLY

Historians normally consider migration to be part of the study of demography, the study of human populations—a part of social history. In these three cases, however, much of the evidence for the movement of people comes from the study of language. Such terms as *Austronesian, Polynesian, Indo-European*, and *Bantu* are names for related languages. Thus, the evidence for the movement or changes in language usage is dependent on the work of philologists who study literary sources and linguists who study language. In terms of our distinction between political, social, economic, and cultural history, which factor(s) would be most appropriate in studying this aspect of the historical record?

Notice how Manning's migration history also contains evidence of foods and other subjects. What are these subjects? Under which of the four categories would you classify them?

Source: Patrick Manning, *Migrations in World History* (New York: Routledge, 2005), 80–84.

The human habit of migration, by small and large groups, made itself felt in this era [after 3000 B.C.E.] as in previous times. The difference is that after 3000 BCE migrations are easier to document in detail because of the availability of written records. Still, some of the most significant migratory movements of this era are documented by linguistic and archaeological evidence rather than through written records. In this section I will describe migrations that linked rural areas to each other, and which in so doing led to significant change in world population distribution, and to opening of new linkages among populations.

Migrations in Southeast Asia, in this period as in earlier times, set trends affecting much of the eastern hemisphere. Sino-Tibetan-speakers, with an ancestral homeland in the deep valleys to the east of the Himalayas, had periodically sent migrants out in various directions. . . . In the period leading up to 3000 BCE, the Tibetan plateau yielded to new technology, including domestication of the yak (a high-altitude relative of cattle), and the Tibetan population and language took shape. In the same period, Burmese-speakers moved south along the Salween and Irrawaddy valleys and occupied lands up to the shores of the Indian Ocean.

Meanwhile the neighboring Austric family of languages, with an ancestral homeland only slightly further lower in the same valleys, also spread from Yunnan in various directions, especially to the south and the east. The Austric languages, spoken in an area overlapping Sino-Tibetan languages, were nonetheless distinct. Most speakers of these languages remained on the Southeast Asian mainland, where today they predominate in the nations of Vietnam, Thailand, Laos, and Cambodia. The northern range of the Austric homeland, over time, came to be shared with southward-moving groups of Chinese-speakers.

Best documented, however, are the migrations of those among the speakers of Austric languages who left the mainland and populated the islands of Southeast Asia and the Pacific. [See Map 8.1.] The ancestors of Austronesian-speakers had developed a homeland downriver from Yunnan, with advanced rice production, but also with boats. These canoes with outriggers for stability may have been developed in the inland rivers, but when fitted with sails they proved to have special benefits for oceanic travel. [See Figure 8.1.] After crossing the strait of over 100 kilometers to Taiwan, the developing Austronesian populations were then able to sail with shorter crossings north along the chain of islands leading to Okinawa and toward Japan, and south to the Philippines. This migration began in about 3000 BCE, or perhaps somewhat before that time. Setting up farms of rice, yams, chickens, and pigs as well as harvesting the sea, Austronesian-speakers settled throughout the Indonesian archipelago and even moved northwest to the Malayan mainland.

Some of the Austronesians headed further west, and their languages survive in Madagascar—where languages are most closely

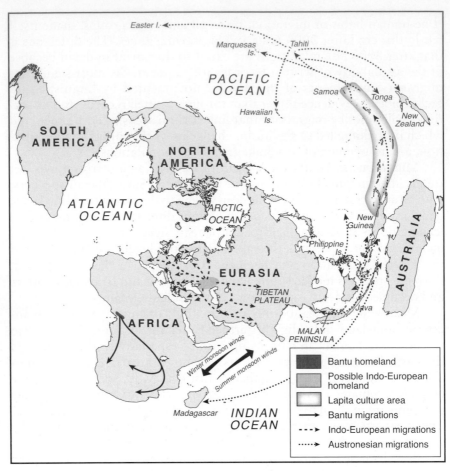

Map 8.1   Bantu, Indo-European, and Austronesian Migrations.

related to languages of Borneo. These mariners appear to have made their travels at the beginning of the Common Era or perhaps even earlier. They thus appear to have been sailing the Indian Ocean at the same time as Greek, Roman, Indian, and Persian ships were sailing the same waters. This is also the era that Lynda Shaffer has called "Southernization," in which Indonesian and Indian mariners knit together the whole Indian Ocean.

Austronesian-speakers spreading into Taiwan, the Philippines, and the Indonesian archipelago encountered local populations who, presumably, spoke Indo-Pacific languages and lived by fishing, hunting, and gathering. (Language-distribution studies indicate that the Indo-Pacific languages once covered a huge area, including most of Indonesia and areas of the eastern Indian Ocean, as well as islands surrounding New Guinea, and Tasmania as well.) The Austronesian-speakers, with their

Figure 8.1 Polynesian double-hulled canoe from Captain James Cook's
A Voyage to the Pacific Ocean, c. 1784.

Source: The Granger Collection, New York.

economy relying on rice and yams, became more populous and absorbed the Indo-Pacific-speakers until they got to Papua New Guinea and the Bismarck Archipelago, where Indo-Pacific-speakers had long since developed agriculture relying on taro, bananas, sugar cane, and other crops. The Papuans were too numerous to be absorbed by the visitors. The incoming Austronesian-speakers, however, were able to establish a firm presence in the coastal areas of New Guinea and neighboring islands. The stage was set for intermarriage, an exchange of traditions, and development of a new tradition.

Out of this social crucible came populations that occupied lands across the far reaches of the Pacific. These populations were the sole groups to inhabit the area now known as Polynesia, and they shared with other groups the lands of Micronesia and Melanesia. They speak Austronesian languages, but their culture and their genetic composition rely substantially on the Indo-Pacific-speaking peoples of New Guinea. This culture thrived beginning about 3000 BCE along the northern coast of New Guinea and the neighboring Bismarck Islands. By 1000 BCE these settlers had reached Tonga and Samoa, thousands of kilometers to the southeast. Rice lost its importance among these farmers, but Southeast Asian yams, chickens, and pigs combined with Papuan taro and bananas and with seafood to provide a varied cuisine. The development of a characteristic style of pottery known as Lapita marks the archaeological remains of these peoples. Equally important was the double-hulled sailing craft developed by the Lapita peoples, which eased the sailing of the high seas. The Polynesian double-hulled vessels had stability, speed, maneuverability, and the capacity to hold large numbers of sailors and supplies for long voyages. With these vessels, navigation skills could be developed to a high level. Without writing or instruments, but with intensive observation of stars, winds, the currents, and the patterns of birds, mariners of the Pacific were able to develop pinpoint navigation.

From their homeland, Polynesian mariners reached the Marquesas Islands, from which they were able to carry out voyages of discovery north to Hawaii, east to Easter Island, and south to New Zealand. It is likely even that these mariners reached and settled on the coast of South America. The evidence is indirect but, I find, convincing. There they learned to cultivate sweet potatoes from the peoples of the Peruvian coast, and brought cuttings with them to the islands. Ultimately, the sweet potato made possible the development of a large Polynesian population on the islands of New Zealand—a region where the normal Polynesian crops, especially taro, could not thrive. These Lapita societies maintained an active trade network until about 500 CE, then allowed it to decline. In the western Pacific, however, the network of rapid connection among islands through double-hulled and outrigger canoes continued to the nineteenth century.

Meanwhile, at the opposite, western fringe of the Austronesian diaspora, the occupation of Madagascar and the Comoros may have been parallel to that of Polynesia and Micronesia in two fashions. First, Austronesian-speaking mariners led in the settlement. Second, it may be that Austronesian connection with East African populations led to a social and biological synthesis that distinguished this stage of migration from those before it. That is, we may seek an East African equivalent to the Lapita homeland of the Pacific. In each case, the argument is that cross-community exchanges may have been important even in migrations that appear from a distance to be a massive colonization effort.

At about the time when the Austronesian mariners began their voyages, Indo-European-speakers in the steppes north of the Black Sea took steps beyond their practice of hunting horses and were able to domesticate them. The result soon led to horse-drawn chariots and then to mounted warriors, especially among Indo-European speakers but also among neighboring groups speaking Altaic or Semitic languages. Horses, harnessed to two-wheeled chariots, became a potent military force, and were associated with the expansion of several Indo-European-speaking groups, including the Hittites of the Anatolian peninsula. Among the eastern groups of Indo-European languages were the Indo-Iranian languages. [See Map 8.1.]

This expansion of Indo-European horse-keepers was a development subsequent to the spread of agriculture throughout Eurasia, which had begun several thousand years earlier. The Indo-Iranian subgroup of Indo-Europeans filtered into Iran and, in a related movement, into north India. Those in Iran gave rise to the religious tradition of Zoroaster and then to the Achaemenid dynasty that created the first large empire. Those in India brought the religious poetry known as the Vedas.

Horses spread beyond Indo-European-speakers soon enough. Speakers of Altaic languages, also reliant on horses (and, in the opinion of some, the first to domesticate them), moved periodically from the East and Central Asian homelands far to the west and somewhat to the south. The Avars and Scythians were such groups in the first millennium BCE, and were followed in the fifth century CE by the Xiongnu in the east and the Huns in the west. Domestication of camels—both in Central Asia and in Arabia—took place in the first millennium CE.

At much the same time as the Aryan migrations into Iran and India, another set of movements remade the map of a similarly sized region of Africa. This was the dispersal of Bantu-speakers into Central and eastern Africa. [See Map 8.1.] Their style of movement, however, was on foot rather than by chariot, and warfare appears to have been less important than farming in their expansion. They were farmers like the Aryans, but lacked horses. They slowly advanced into the forests that are now Cameroon and Congo, displacing and absorbing previous inhabitants in a fashion parallel to that of the Austronesians and the Aryans. When Bantu migrants reached the highland areas of East Africa late in the first millennium BCE, they encountered other farming groups. There, as had been the case in Melanesia, a more complex set of interactions and a new set of innovations developed. Through combination with peoples from Afroasiatic and perhaps Nilo-Saharan language groups, the Bantu-speakers adopted cattle, sheep, and millet, and expanded more rapidly into eastern and southern Africa.

To show that these three stories of rural migration were not only similar but connected, we need only return to the Austronesian voyages to the western Indian Ocean. On the eastern coast of Africa, Austronesian-speakers introduced bananas, Asian yams, the music of xylophones, and outrigger canoes. The first three of these innovations spread across the African continent from hand to hand; bananas were of particular importance in the valleys and highlands of Bantu-speaking Central Africa, where they became a crop of first importance.

By the same token, the Austronesian migrants had to pass through Indian waters on their way to East Africa, and surely camped and settled at several points along the coast, probably as merchants. Along the coasts of north India and Iran, they would therefore have encountered Indo-Iranian-speakers whose ancestors had entered the region over a thousand years earlier.

LYNDA NORENE SHAFFER

Southernization, 1994

The author of this selection began her career as a historian of China, but she is currently a world historian, having published books on Native American, Southeast Asian, and Chinese history. Shaffer coins the term *Southernization* to suggest that *Westernization* was preceded by an earlier "southern" process of technological expansion that eventually made Westernization possible. Which of her examples of Southernization do you find most important in changing the world? Which least significant? Did India and Indian Ocean societies of the early Middle Ages play a role like that of the West today?

THINKING HISTORICALLY

The mark of an excellent piece of scholarship in world history is the way the author integrates various states, empires, regions, even continents into a single narrative. At its best, this integration allows us to see patterns that were not visible from the viewpoint of a single state, region, or area. Notice the range of political entities (from cities to dynasties) that Shaffer mentions. Plot the political entities that Shaffer mentions on a timeline of your own creation and then survey them in an historical atlas.

Good historical writing also makes connections of another kind: connections between different aspects of life, often using the broad categories of politics, economics, society, and culture. Specialists often address these topics individually, and such specialized study is often the best way to approach an enormous body of source material. A historian of science or mathematics, for example, has enough to do just focusing on his or her area of specialization. But once some of this specialist work is done, it becomes possible for a generalist to see if there are connections that might be made between different branches of study, be it Indian mathematical innovation and the spread of pomegranates or mastering the monsoon winds. A work of historical integration like Shaffer's has jumped the boundaries not only of political, economic, social, and cultural history but also the boundaries of numerous subgroups: the history of food, technology, science, climate, and religion, to name a few. The best way to see what factors an author has used is to deconstruct her analysis: List all of these categories and sub-categories that Shaffer uses and note the examples of each she gives in the text.

Source: Lynda Norene Shaffer, "Southernization," *Journal of World History* 5 (Spring 1994): 1–21.

The term *Southernization* is a new one. It is used here to refer to a multifaceted process that began in Southern Asia and spread from there to various other places around the globe. The process included so many interrelated strands of development that it is impossible to do more here than sketch out the general outlines of a few of them. Among the most important that will be omitted from this discussion are the metallurgical, the medical, and the literary. Those included are the development of mathematics; the production and marketing of subtropical or tropical spices; the pioneering of new trade routes; the cultivation, processing, and marketing of southern crops such as sugar and cotton; and the development of various related technologies.

The term *Southernization* is meant to be analogous to *Westernization*. Westernization refers to certain developments that first occurred in western Europe. Those developments changed Europe and eventually spread to other places and changed them as well. In the same way, southernization changed Southern Asia and later spread to other areas, which then underwent a process of change.

Southernization was well under way in Southern Asia by the fifth century C.E., during the reign of India's Gupta kings (320–535 C.E.). It was by that time already spreading to China. In the eighth century various elements characteristic of Southernization began spreading through the lands of the Muslim caliphates. Both in China and in the lands of the caliphate, the process led to dramatic changes, and by the year 1200 it was beginning to have an impact on the Christian Mediterranean. One could argue that within the Northern Hemisphere, by this time the process of Southernization had created an Eastern Hemisphere characterized by a rich south and a north that was poor in comparison. And one might even go so far as to suggest that in Europe and its colonies, the process of Southernization laid the foundation for Westernization.

The Indian Beginning

Southernization was the result of developments that took place in many parts of southern Asia, both on the Indian subcontinent and in Southeast Asia. By the time of the Gupta kings, several of its constituent parts already had a long history in India. Perhaps the oldest strand in the process was the cultivation of cotton and the production of cotton textiles for export. Cotton was first domesticated in the Indus River valley some time between 2300 and 1760 B.C.E., and by the second millennium B.C.E., the Indians had begun to develop sophisticated dyeing techniques. During these early millennia Indus River valley merchants are known to have lived in Mesopotamia, where they sold cotton textiles.

In the first century C.E. Egypt became an important overseas market for Indian cottons. By the next century there was a strong demand for these textiles both in the Mediterranean and in East Africa, and by the fifth century they were being traded in Southeast Asia. The Indian textile trade continued to grow throughout the next millennium. Even after the arrival of European ships in Asian ports at the turn of the sixteenth century, it continued unscathed. According to one textile expert, "India virtually clothed the world" by the mid-eighteenth century. The subcontinent's position was not undermined until Britain's Industrial Revolution, when steam engines began to power the production of cotton textiles.

Another strand in the process of Southernization, the search for new sources of bullion, can be traced back in India to the end of the Mauryan Empire (321–185 B.C.E.). During Mauryan rule Siberia had been India's main source of gold, but nomadic disturbances in Central Asia disrupted the traffic between Siberia and India at about the time that the Mauryans fell. Indian sailors then began to travel to the Malay peninsula and the islands of Indonesia in search of an alternative source, which they most likely "discovered" with the help of local peoples who knew the sites. (This is generally the case with bullion discoveries, including those made by Arabs and Europeans.) What the Indians (and others later on) did do was introduce this gold to international trade routes.

The Indians' search for gold may also have led them to the shores of Africa. Although its interpretation is controversial, some archaeological evidence suggests the existence of Indian influence on parts of East Africa as early as 300 C.E. There is also one report that gold was being sought in East Africa by Ethiopian merchants, who were among India's most important trading partners.

The sixth-century Byzantine geographer Cosmas Indicopleustes described Ethiopian merchants who went to some location inland from the East African coast to obtain gold. "Every other year they would sail far to the south, then march inland, and in return for various made-up articles they would come back laden with ingots of gold." The fact that the expeditions left every other year suggests that it took two years to get to their destination and return. If so, their destination, even at this early date, may have been Zimbabwe. The wind patterns are such that sailors who ride the monsoon south as far as Kilwa can catch the return monsoon to the Red Sea area within the same year. But if they go beyond Kilwa to the Zambezi River, from which they might go inland to Zimbabwe, they cannot return until the following year.

Indian voyages on the Indian Ocean were part of a more general development, more or less contemporary with the Mauryan Empire, in which sailors of various nationalities began to knit together the shores of the "Southern Ocean," a Chinese term referring to all the waters from the South China Sea to the eastern coast of Africa. During this period there is no doubt that the most intrepid sailors were the Malays, peoples who lived in what is now Malaysia, Indonesia, the southeastern coast of Vietnam, and the Philippines.

Sometime before 300 B.C.E. Malay sailors began to ride the monsoons, the seasonal winds that blow off the continent of Asia in the colder months and onto its shores in the warmer months. Chinese records indicate that by the third century B.C.E. "Kunlun" sailors, the Chinese term for the Malay seamen, were sailing north to the southern coasts of China. They may also have been sailing west to India, through the straits now called Malacca and Sunda. If so they may have been the first to establish contact between India and Southeast Asia.

Malay sailors had reached the eastern coast of Africa at least by the first century B.C.E., if not earlier. Their presence in East African waters is testified to by the peoples of Madagascar, who still speak a Malayo-Polynesian language. Some evidence also suggests that Malay sailors had settled in the Red Sea area. Indeed, it appears that they were the first to develop a long-distance trade in a southern spice. In the last centuries B.C.E., if not earlier, Malay sailors were delivering cinnamon from South China Sea ports to East Africa and the Red Sea.

By about 400 C.E. Malay sailors [Polynesians] could be found two-thirds of the way around the world, from Easter Island to East Africa. They rode the monsoons without a compass, out of sight of land, and often at latitudes below the equator where the northern pole star cannot be seen. They navigated by the wind and the stars, by cloud formations, the color of the water, and swell and wave patterns on the ocean's surface. They could discern the presence of an island some thirty miles from its shores by noting the behavior of birds, the animal and plant life in the water, and the swell and wave patterns. Given their manner of sailing, their most likely route to Africa and the Red Sea would have been by way of the island clusters, the Maldives, the Chagos, the Seychelles, and the Comoros.

Malay ships used balance lug sails, which were square in shape and mounted so that they could pivot. This made it possible for sailors to tack against the wind, that is, to sail into the wind by going diagonally against it, first one way and then the other. Due to the way the sails were mounted, they appeared somewhat triangular in shape, and thus the Malays' balance lug sail may well be the prototype of the triangular lateen, which can also be used to tack against the wind. The latter was invented by both the Polynesians to the Malays' east and by the Arabs to their west, both of whom had ample opportunity to see the Malays' ships in action.

It appears that the pepper trade developed after the cinnamon trade. In the first century C.E. Southern India began supplying the Mediterranean with large quantities of pepper. Thereafter, Indian merchants could be found living on the island of Socotra, near the mouth of the Red Sea, and Greek-speaking sailors, including the anonymous author of the *Periplus of the Erythraean Sea*,[1] could be found sailing in the Red Sea and riding the monsoons from there to India.

Indian traders and shippers and Malay sailors were also responsible for opening up an all-sea route to China. The traders' desire for silk drew them out into dangerous waters in search of a more direct way to its source. By the second century C.E. Indian merchants could make the trip by sea, but the route was slow, and it took at least two years to make a round trip. Merchants leaving from India's eastern coast rounded the shores of the Bay of Bengal. When they came to the Isthmus of Kra, the narrowest part of the Malay peninsula, the ships were unloaded, and the goods were portaged across to the Gulf of Thailand. The cargo was then reloaded on ships that rounded the gulf until they reached Funan, a kingdom on what is now the Kampuchea [Cambodia]-Vietnam border. There they had to wait for the winds to shift, before embarking upon a ship that rode the monsoon to China.

Some time before 400 C.E. travelers began to use a new all-sea route to China, a route that went around the Malay peninsula and thus avoided the Isthmus of Kra portage. The ships left from Sri Lanka and sailed before the monsoon, far from any coasts, through either the Strait of Malacca or the Strait of Sunda into the Java Sea. After waiting in the Java Sea port for the winds to shift, they rode the monsoon to southern China. The most likely developers of this route were Malay sailors, since the new stopover ports were located within their territories.

Not until the latter part of the fourth century, at about the same time as the new all-sea route began to direct commercial traffic through the Java Sea, did the fine spices—cloves, nutmeg, and mace—begin to assume importance on international markets. These rare and expensive spices came from the Moluccas, several island groups about a thousand miles east of Java. Cloves were produced on about five minuscule islands off the western coast of Halmahera; nutmeg and mace came from only a few of the Banda Islands, some ten islands with a total area of seventeen square miles, located in the middle of the Banda Sea. Until 1621 these Moluccan islands were the only places in the world able to produce cloves, nutmeg, and mace in commercial quantities. The Moluccan producers themselves brought their spices to the international markets of the Java Sea ports and created the market for them.

It was also during the time of the Gupta kings, around 350 C.E., that the Indians discovered how to crystallize sugar. There is considerable disagreement about where sugar was first domesticated. Some believe that the plant was native to New Guinea and domesticated there, and others argue that it was domesticated by Southeast Asian peoples living in what is now southern China. In any case, sugar cultivation spread to

[1] Written about 60 C.E. [Ed.]

the Indian subcontinent. Sugar, however, did not become an important item of trade until the Indians discovered how to turn sugarcane juice into granulated crystals that could be easily stored and transported. This was a momentous development, and it may have been encouraged by Indian sailing, for sugar and clarified butter (ghee) were among the dietary mainstays of Indian sailors.

The Indians also laid the foundation for modern mathematics during the time of the Guptas. Western numerals, which the Europeans called Arabic since they acquired them from the Arabs, actually come from India. (The Arabs call them Hindi numbers.) The most significant feature of the Indian system was the invention of the zero as a number concept. The oldest extant treatise that uses the zero in the modern way is a mathematical appendix attached to Aryabhata's text on astronomy, which is dated 499 C.E.

The Indian zero made the place-value system of writing numbers superior to all others. Without it, the use of this system, base ten or otherwise, was fraught with difficulties and did not seem any better than alternative systems. With the zero the Indians were able to perform calculations rapidly and accurately, to perform much more complicated calculations, and to discern mathematical relationships more aptly. These numerals and the mathematics that the Indians developed with them are now universal—just one indication of the global significance of Southernization.

As a result of these developments India acquired a reputation as a place of marvels, a reputation that was maintained for many centuries after the Gupta dynasty fell. As late as the ninth century Amr ibn Bahr al Jahiz (c. 776–868), one of the most influential writers of Arabic, had the following to say about India:

> As regards the Indians, they are among the leaders in astronomy, mathematics—in particular, they have Indian numerals—and medicine; they alone possess the secrets of the latter, and use them to practice some remarkable forms of treatment. They have the art of carving statues and painted figures. They possess the game of chess, which is the noblest of games and requires more judgment and intelligence than any other. They make Kedah swords, and excel in their use. They have splendid music. . . . They possess a script capable of expressing the sounds of all languages, as well as many numerals. They have a great deal of poetry, many long treatises, and a deep understanding of philosophy and letters; the book *Kalila wa-Dimna* originated with them. They are intelligent and courageous. . . . Their sound judgment and sensible habits led them to invent pins, cork, toothpicks, the drape of clothes, and the dyeing of hair. They are handsome, attractive, and forbearing; their women are proverbial; and their country produces the matchless

Indian aloes which are supplied to kings. They were the originators of the science of *fikr*, by which a poison can be counteracted after it has been used, and of astronomical reckoning, subsequently adopted by the rest of the world. When Adam descended from Paradise, it was to their land that he made his way.

The Southernization of China

These Southern Asian developments began to have a significant impact on China after 350 C.E. The Han dynasty had fallen in 221 C.E., and for more than 350 years thereafter China was ruled by an ever-changing collection of regional kingdoms. During these centuries Buddhism became increasingly important in China, Buddhist monasteries spread throughout the disunited realm, and cultural exchange between India and China grew accordingly. By 581, when the Sui dynasty reunited the empire, processes associated with Southernization had already had a major impact on China. The influence of Southernization continued during the T'ang (618–906) and Sung (960–1279) dynasties. One might even go so far as to suggest that the process of Southernization underlay the revolutionary social, political, economic, and technological developments of the T'ang and Sung.

The Chinese reformed their mathematics, incorporating the advantages of the Indian system, even though they did not adopt the Indian numerals at that time. They then went on to develop an advanced mathematics, which was flourishing by the time of the Sung dynasty. Cotton and indigo became well established, giving rise to the blueblack peasant garb that is still omnipresent in China. Also in the Sung period the Chinese first developed cotton canvas, which they used to make a more efficient sail for ocean-going ships.

Although sugar had long been grown in some parts of southern China it did not become an important crop in this region until the process of Southernization was well under way. The process also introduced new varieties of rice. The most important of these was what the Chinese called Champa rice, since it came to China from Champa, a Malay kingdom located on what is now the southeastern coast of Vietnam. Champa rice was a drought-resistant, early ripening variety that made it possible to extend cultivation up well-watered hillsides, thereby doubling the area of rice cultivation in China. . . .

In southern China the further development of rice production brought significant changes in the landscape. Before the introduction of Champa rice, rice cultivation had been confined to lowlands, deltas, basins, and river valleys. Once Champa rice was introduced and rice cultivation spread up the hillsides, the Chinese began systematic terracing and made use of sophisticated techniques of water control on mountain slopes. Between the mid-eighth and the early twelfth century the population of southern China tripled, and the total Chinese population doubled. According to Sung dynasty household registration figures for 1102 and 1110—figures that Sung dynasty specialists have shown to be reliable— there were 100 million people in China by the first decade of the twelfth century.

Before the process of Southernization, northern China had always been predominant, intellectually, socially, and politically. The imperial center of gravity was clearly in the north, and the southern part of China was perceived as a frontier area. But Southernization changed this situation dramatically. By 600, southern China was well on its way to becoming the most prosperous and most commercial part of the empire. The most telling evidence for this is the construction of the Grand Canal, which was completed around 610, during the Sui dynasty. Even though the rulers of the Sui had managed to put the pieces of the empire back together in 581 and rule the whole of China again from a single northern capital, they were dependent on the new southern crops. Thus it is no coincidence that this dynasty felt the need to build a canal that could deliver southern rice to northern cities.

The T'ang dynasty, when Buddhist influence in China was especially strong, saw two exceedingly important technological innovations—the invention of printing and gunpowder. These developments may also be linked to Southernization. Printing seems to have developed within the walls of Buddhist monasteries between 700 and 750, and subtropical Sichuan was one of the earliest centers of the art. The invention of gunpowder in China by Taoist alchemists in the ninth century may also be related to the linkages between India and China created by Buddhism. In 644 an Indian monk identified soils in China that contained saltpeter and demonstrated the purple flame that results from its ignition. As early as 919 C.E. gunpowder was used as an igniter in a flamethrower, and the tenth century also saw the use of flaming arrows, rockets, and bombs thrown by catapults. The earliest evidence of a cannon or bombard (1127) has been found in Sichuan, quite near the Tibetan border, across the Himalayas from India.

By the time of the Sung the Chinese also had perfected the "south-pointing needle," otherwise known as the compass. Various prototypes of the compass had existed in China from the third century B.C.E., but the new version developed during the Sung was particularly well suited for navigation. Soon Chinese mariners were using the south-pointing needle on the oceans, publishing "needle charts" for the benefit of sea captains, and following "needle routes" on the Southern Ocean.

Once the Chinese had the compass they, like Columbus, set out to find a direct route to the spice markets of Java and ultimately to the Spice Islands in the Moluccas. Unlike Columbus, they found them. They did not bump into an obstacle, now known as the Western Hemisphere, on their way, since it was not located between China and the Spice Islands. If it had been so situated, the Chinese would have found it some 500 years before Columbus.

Cities on China's southern coasts became centers of overseas commerce. Silk remained an important export, and by the T'ang dynasty it had been joined by a true porcelain, which was developed in China sometime before 400 C.E. China and its East Asian neighbors had a monopoly on the manufacture of true porcelain until the early eighteenth century. Many attempts were made to imitate it, and some of the resulting imitations were economically and stylistically important. China's southern ports were also exporting to Southeast Asia large quantities of ordinary consumer goods, including iron hardware, such as needles, scissors, and cooking pots. Although iron manufacturing was concentrated in the north, the large quantity of goods produced was a direct result of the size of the market in southern China and overseas. Until the British Industrial Revolution of the eighteenth century, no other place ever equaled the iron production of Sung China.

The Muslim Caliphates

In the seventh century C.E., Arab cavalries, recently converted to the new religion of Islam, conquered eastern and southern Mediterranean shores that had been Byzantine (and Christian), as well as the [Persian] Sassanian empire (Zoroastrian) in what is now Iraq and Iran. In the eighth century they went on to conquer Spain and Turko-Iranian areas of Central Asia, as well as northwestern India. Once established on the Indian frontier, they became acquainted with many of the elements of Southernization.

The Arabs were responsible for the spread of many important crops, developed or improved in India, to the Middle East, North Africa, and Islamic Spain. Among the most important were sugar, cotton, and citrus fruits. Although sugarcane and cotton cultivation may have spread to Iraq and Ethiopia before the Arab conquests, only after the establishment of the caliphates did these southern crops have a major impact throughout the Middle East and North Africa.

The Arabs were the first to import large numbers of enslaved Africans in order to produce sugar. Fields in the vicinity of Basra, at the northern end of the Persian Gulf, were the most important sugar-producing areas within the caliphates, but before this land could be used, it had to be desalinated. To accomplish this task, the Arabs imported East African (Zanj) slaves. This African community remained in the area, where they worked as agricultural laborers. The famous writer al Jahiz, whose essay on India was quoted earlier, was a descendant of

Zanj slaves. In 869, one year after his death, the Zanj slaves in Iraq re-belled. It took the caliphate fifteen years of hard fighting to defeat them, and thereafter Muslim owners rarely used slaves for purposes that would require their concentration in large numbers.

The Arabs were responsible for moving sugarcane cultivation and sugar manufacturing westward from southern Iraq into other relatively arid lands. Growers had to adapt the plant to new conditions, and they had to develop more efficient irrigation technologies. By 1000 or so sug-arcane had become an important crop in the Yemen; in Arabian oases; in irrigated areas of Syria, Lebanon, Palestine, Egypt, and the Mahgrib; in Spain; and on Mediterranean islands controlled by Muslims. By the tenth century cotton also had become a major crop in the lands of the caliphate, from Iran and Central Asia to Spain and the Mediterranean islands. Cotton industries sprang up wherever the plant was cultivated, producing for both local and distant markets. . . .

Under Arab auspices, Indian mathematics followed the same routes as the crops. Al-Kharazmi (c. 780–847) introduced Indian mathematics to the Arabic-reading world in his *Treatise on Calculation with the Hindu Numerals*, written around 825. Mathematicians within the ca-liphates then could draw upon the Indian tradition, as well as the Greek and Persian. On this foundation Muslim scientists of many nationalities, including al-Battani (d. 929), who came from the northern reaches of the Mesopotamian plain, and the Persian Omar Khayyám (d. 1123), made remarkable advances in both algebra and trigonometry.

The Arab conquests also led to an increase in long-distance com-merce and the "discovery" of new sources of bullion. Soon after the Abbasid caliphate established its capital at Baghdad, the caliph al-Mansur (r. 745–75) reportedly remarked, "This is the Tigris; there is no obstacle between us and China; everything on the sea can come to us." By this time Arab ships were plying the maritime routes from the Persian Gulf to China, and they soon outnumbered all others using these routes. By the ninth century they had acquired the compass (in China, most likely), and they may well have been the first to use it for marine navigation, since the Chinese do not seem to have used it for this purpose until after the tenth century.

. . . [Similarly,] the Arabs "pioneered" or improved an existing long-distance route across the Sahara, an ocean of sand rather than water. Routes across this desert had always existed, and trade and other con-tacts between West Africa and the Mediterranean date back at least to the Phoenician period. Still, the numbers of people and animals crossing this great ocean of sand were limited until the eighth century when Arabs, desiring to go directly to the source of the gold,[2] prompted an

---

[2] One of the sources of gold was the area called the "gold coast" of Africa, south of the Sahara centered in what is today Ghana. [Ed.]

expansion of trade across the Sahara. Also during the eighth century Abdul al-Rahman, an Arab ruler of Morocco, sponsored the construction of wells on the trans-Saharan route from Sijilmasa to Wadidara to facilitate this traffic. This Arab "discovery" of West African gold eventually doubled the amount of gold in international circulation. East Africa, too, became a source of gold for the Arabs. By the tenth century Kilwa had become an important source of Zimbabwean gold.

Developments after 1200: The Mongolian Conquest and the Southernization of the European Mediterranean

By 1200 the process of Southernization had created a prosperous south from China to the Muslim Mediterranean. Although mathematics, the pioneering of new ocean routes, and "discoveries" of bullion are not inextricably connected to locations within forty degrees of the equator, several crucial elements in the process of Southernization were closely linked to latitude. Cotton generally does not grow above the fortieth parallel. Sugar, cinnamon, and pepper are tropical or subtropical crops, and the fine spices will grow only on particular tropical islands. Thus for many centuries the more southern parts of Asia and the Muslim Mediterranean enjoyed the profits that these developments brought, while locations that were too far north to grow these southern crops were unable to participate in such lucrative agricultural enterprises.

The process of Southernization reached its zenith after 1200, in large part because of the tumultuous events of the thirteenth century. During that century in both hemispheres there were major transformations in the distribution of power, wealth, and prestige. In the Western Hemisphere several great powers went down. Cahokia (near East St. Louis, Illinois), which for three centuries had been the largest and most influential of the Mississippian mound-building centers, declined after 1200, and in Mexico Toltec power collapsed. In the Mediterranean the prestige of the Byzantine empire was destroyed when Venetians seized its capital in 1204. From 1212 to 1270 the Christians conquered southern Spain, except for Granada. In West Africa, Ghana fell to Sosso, and so did Mali, one of Ghana's allies. But by about 1230 Mali, in the process of seeking its own revenge, had created an empire even larger than Ghana's. At the same time Zimbabwe was also becoming a major power in southern Africa.

The grandest conquerors of the thirteenth century were the Central Asians. Turkish invaders established the Delhi sultanate in India. Mongolian cavalries devastated Baghdad, the seat of the Abbasid caliphate since the eighth century, and they captured Kiev, further weakening Byzantium. By the end of the century they had captured China, Korea, and parts of mainland Southeast Asia as well.

Because the Mongols were pagans at the time of their conquests, the western Europeans cheered them on as they laid waste to one after another Muslim center of power in the Middle East. The Mongols were stopped only when they encountered the Mamluks of Egypt at Damascus. In East Asia and Southeast Asia only the Japanese and the Javanese were able to defeat them. The victors in Java went on to found Majapahit, whose power and prestige then spread through maritime Southeast Asia.

Both hemispheres were reorganized profoundly during this turmoil. Many places that had flourished were toppled, and power gravitated to new locales. In the Eastern Hemisphere the Central Asian conquerors had done great damage to traditional southern centers just about everywhere, except in Africa, southern China, southern India, and maritime Southeast Asia. At the same time the Mongols' control of overland routes between Europe and Asia in the thirteenth and early fourteenth centuries fostered unprecedented contacts between Europeans and peoples from those areas that had long been southernized. Marco Polo's long sojourn in Yüan Dynasty China is just one example of such interaction.

Under the Mongols overland trade routes in Asia shifted north and converged on the Black Sea. After the Genoese helped the Byzantines to retake Constantinople from the Venetians in 1261, the Genoese were granted special privileges of trade in the Black Sea. Italy then became directly linked to the Mongolian routes. Genoese traders were among the first and were certainly the most numerous to open up trade with the Mongolian states in southern Russia and Iran. In the words of one Western historian, in their Black Sea colonies they "admitted to citizenship" people of many nationalities, including those of "strange background and questionable belief," and they "wound up christening children of the best ancestry with such uncanny names as Saladin, Hethum, or Hulugu."

Such contacts contributed to the Southernization of the Christian Mediterranean during this period of Mongolian hegemony. Although European conquerors sometimes had taken over sugar and cotton lands in the Middle East during the Crusades, not until some time after 1200 did the European-held Mediterranean islands become important exporters. Also after 1200 Indian mathematics began to have a significant impact in Europe. Before that time a few western European scholars had become acquainted with Indian numerals in Spain, where the works of al-Kharazmi, al-Battani, and other mathematicians had been translated into Latin. Nevertheless, Indian numerals and mathematics did not become important in western Europe until the thirteenth century after the book *Liber abaci* (1202), written by Leonardo Fibonacci of Pisa (c. 1170–1250), introduced them to the commercial centers of Italy. Leonardo had grown up in North Africa (in what is now Bejala, Algeria), where his father, consul over the Pisan merchants in that port, had sent him to study calculation with an Arab master.

In the seventeenth century, when Francis Bacon observed the "force and virtue and consequences of discoveries," he singled out three technologies in particular that "have changed the whole face and state of things throughout the world." These were all Chinese inventions—the compass, printing, and gunpowder. All three were first acquired by Europeans during this time of hemispheric reorganization.

It was most likely the Arabs who introduced the compass to Mediterranean waters, either at the end of the twelfth or in the thirteenth century. Block printing, gunpowder, and cannon appeared first in Italy in the fourteenth century, apparently after making a single great leap from Mongolian-held regions of East Asia to Italy. How this great leap was accomplished is not known, but the most likely scenario is one suggested by Lynn White Jr., in an article concerning how various other Southern (rather than Eastern) Asian technologies reached western Europe at about this time. He thought it most likely that they were introduced by "Tatar" slaves, Lama Buddhists from the frontiers of China whom the Genoese purchased in Black Sea marts and delivered to Italy. By 1450 when this trade reached its peak, there were thousands of these Asian slaves in every major Italian city. . . .

The Rise of Europe's North

The rise of the north, or more precisely, the rise of Europe's northwest, began with the appropriation of those elements of Southernization that were not confined by geography. In the wake of their southern European neighbors, they became partially southernized, but they could not engage in all aspects of the process due to their distance from the equator. Full Southernization and the wealth that we now associate with northwestern Europe came about only after their outright seizure of tropical and subtropical territories and their rounding of Africa and participation in Southern Ocean trade. . . .

Even though the significance of indigenous developments in the rise of northwestern Europe should not be minimized, it should be emphasized that many of the most important causes of the rise of the West are not to be found within the bounds of Europe. Rather, they are the result of the transformation of western Europe's relationships with other regions of the Eastern Hemisphere. Europe began its rise only after the thirteenth-century reorganization of the Eastern Hemisphere facilitated its Southernization, and Europe's northwest did not rise until it too was reaping the profits of Southernization. Thus the rise of the North Atlantic powers should not be oversimplified so that it appears to be an isolated and solely European phenomenon, with roots that spread no farther afield than Greece. Rather, it should be portrayed as one part of a hemisphere-wide process, in which a northwestern Europe ran to catch up with a more developed south—a race not completed until the eighteenth century.

3

FAXIAN

Travel on the Silk Road and Seas, c. 400

Faxian (or Fa-Hien as rendered here) was a Chinese Buddhist monk who traveled from Chang'an China to India beginning in 399 in search of holy books and relics of the Buddha. He did not return until 414. It took him six years to reach central India and he spent another six years in India, visiting places where the Buddha had lived, collecting stories about the Buddha, and gathering holy books and art.

This selection comes from Faxian's account of his travels. The first four chapters describe his travel on the Silk Road from Chang'an to Khotan in far Western China; the last chapter describes his sea voyages home from Sri Lanka to Java and from Java to China. This sea route was sometimes called a southern silk road.

The Silk Road proper was a land route from Eastern China — Chang'an or Xian or Beijing — to Western China, and then on to Central Asia and the Mediterranean. It developed in the early Han Empire, the story goes, as a way for the Chinese to secure Central Asian horses in exchange for silk. Faxian's interests have nothing to do with horses or silk, and we can tell from his description that the route had as much to do with religion as trade. What does this selection tell you about Faxian and Chinese Buddhism? What does it tell you about travel at the beginning of the fifth century?

THINKING HISTORICALLY

This is a source that can be read for many different purposes. It is crucial to an understanding of the history of Buddhism in China, an important topic of religious and cultural history. Some of that, especially Faxian's description of the Buddhist kingdom of Khotan, is included here. But, for the most part, we have excluded Faxian's thoughts on Buddhism. This is because we are reading this source for a different purpose — to understand travel, especially long-distance travel in this period. Historians do this all of the time. We comb sources for information that might have been incidental to the author. Choose a few topics that you would like to know more about: food, social class, or something else that appears in the text. Then sift through the text to find mentions of this subject. Gather the information, sort it according to the four key factors of political, economic, social, and cultural history, and then see if you can use it to draw some conclusion or make some statement.

Source: *A Record of Buddhist Kingdoms: Being an Account of the Chinese Monk Fa-Hien of His Travels in India and Ceylon* (A.D. *399–414*) *in Search of the Buddhist Books of Discipline*, trans. James Legge (Oxford at the Clarendon Press, 1886), 10–22, 111–16.

Chapter I: From Ch'ang-Gan to the Sandy Desert

After starting from Ch'ang-gan, they passed through Lung, and came to the kingdom of K'een-kwei, where they stopped for the summer retreat. When that was over, they went forward to the kingdom of Now-t'an, crossed the mountain of Yang-low, and reached the emporium of Chang-yih. There they found the country so much disturbed that travelling on the roads was impossible for them. Its king, however, was very attentive to them, kept them (in his capital), and acted the part of their danapati.[1]

Here they met with Che-yen, Hwuy-keen, Sang-shao, Pao-yun, and Sang-king; and in pleasant association with them, as bound on the same journey with themselves, they passed the summer retreat (of that year) together, resuming after it their travelling, and going on to T'un-hwang, (the chief town) in the frontier territory of defence extending for about 80 le from east to west, and about 40 from north to south. Their company, increased as it had been, halted there for some days more than a month, after which Fa-hien and his four friends started first in the suite of an envoy, having separated (for a time) from Pao-yun and his associates.

Le Hao, the prefect of T'un-hwang, had supplied them with the means of crossing the desert (before them), in which there are many evil demons and hot winds. (Travelers) who encounter them perish all to a man. There is not a bird to be seen in the air above, nor an animal on the ground below. Though you look all round most earnestly to find where you can cross, you know not where to make your choice, the only mark and indication being the dry bones of the dead (left upon the sand).

Chapter II: On to Shen-Shen and Thence to Khoten

After travelling for seventeen days, a distance we may calculate of about 1500 le, (the pilgrims) reached the kingdom of Shen-shen, a country rugged and hilly, with a thin and barren soil. The clothes of the common people are coarse, and like those worn in our land of Han, some wearing felt and others coarse serge or cloth of hair;—this was the only difference seen among them. The king professed (our) Law, and there might be in the country more than four thousand monks, who were all students of the hinayana.[2] The common people of this and other kingdoms (in that region), as well as the sramans, all practice the rules of India, only that the latter do so more exactly, and the former more loosely. So (the travellers) found it in all the kingdoms through which they went on

[1] Patron. [Ed.]
[2] Orthodox; strictly followed asceticism of the Buddha. [Ed.]

their way from this to the west, only that each had its own peculiar barbarous speech. (The monks), however, who had (given up the worldly
life) and quitted their families, were all students of Indian books and the
Indian language. Here they stayed for about a month, and then proceeded on their journey, fifteen days walking to the north-west bringing
them to the country of Woo-e. In this also there were more than four
thousand monks, all students of the hinayana. They were very strict in
their rules, so that sramans[3] from the territory of Ts'in were all unprepared for their regulations. Fa-hien, through the management of Foo
Kung-sun, /maitre d'hotellerie/, was able to remain (with his company in
the monastery where they were received) for more than two months, and
here they were rejoined by Pao-yun and his friends. (At the end of that
time) the people of Woo-e neglected the duties of propriety and righteousness, and treated the strangers in so niggardly a manner that Che-
yen, Hwuy-keen, and Hwuy-wei went back towards Kao-ch'ang, hoping
to obtain there the means of continuing their journey. Fa-hien and the
rest, however, through the liberality of Foo Kung-sun, managed to go
straight forward in a south-west direction. They found the country uninhabited as they went along. The difficulties which they encountered in
crossing the streams and on their route, and the sufferings which they
endured, were unparalleled in human experience, but in the course of a
month and five days they succeeded in reaching Yu-teen.[4]

Chapter III: Khoten. Processions of Images.
The King's New Monastery

Yu-teen is a pleasant and prosperous kingdom, with a numerous and
flourishing population. The inhabitants all profess our Law, and join together in its religious music for their enjoyment. The monks amount to
several myriads, most of whom are students of the mahayana.[5] They all
receive their food from the common store. Throughout the country the
houses of the people stand apart like (separate) stars, and each family has
a small tope[6] reared in front of its door. The smallest of these may be
twenty cubits high, or rather more. They make (in the monasteries) rooms
for monks from all quarters, the use of which is given to travelling monks
who may arrive, and who are provided with whatever else they require.

---

[3] Monks or nuns. [Ed.]

[4] Yu-teen, here also called Khoten, is now called the ancient Buddhist kingdom of Khotan.
Conquered by Tibet in 670 and by Muslims in 1006. It is now the largely Muslim city of
Hotan. [Ed.]

[5] Less orthodox and more open to public participation and worship than Hinayana. While
Hinayana was more successful in Southeast Asia, Mahayana won over Tibet, China, Mongolia,
Japan, Korea, and northern Vietnam. [Ed.]

[6] Bell-shaped dome structure similar to a miniature stupa or Buddhist temple. [Ed.]

The lord of the country lodged Fa-hien and the others comfortably, and supplied their wants, in a monastery called Gomati, of the mahayana school. Attached to it there are three thousand monks, who are called to their meals by the sound of a bell. When they enter the refectory, their demeanour is marked by a reverent gravity, and they take their seats in regular order, all maintaining a perfect silence. No sound is heard from their alms-bowls and other utensils. When any of these pure men require food, they are not allowed to call out (to the attendants) for it, but only make signs with their hands.

Hwuy-king, Tao-ching, and Hwuy-tah set out in advance towards the country of K'eeh-ch'a; but Fa-hien and the others, wishing to see the procession of images, remained behind for three months. There are in this country four great monasteries, not counting the smaller ones. Beginning on the first day of the fourth month, they sweep and water the streets inside the city, making a grand display in the lanes and byways. Over the city gate they pitch a large tent, grandly adorned in all possible ways, in which the king and queen, with their ladies brilliantly arrayed, take up their residence (for the time).

The monks of the Gomati monastery, being mahayana students, and held in great reverence by the king, took precedence of all others in the procession. At a distance of three or four le from the city, they made a four-wheeled image car, more than thirty cubits high, which looked like the great hall (of a monastery) moving along. The seven precious substances[7] were grandly displayed about it, with silken streamers and canopies hanging all around. The (chief) image[8] stood in the middle of the car, with two Bodhisattvas[9] in attendance upon it, while devas[10] were made to follow in waiting, all brilliantly carved in gold and silver, and hanging in the air. When (the car) was a hundred paces from the gate, the king put off his crown of state, changed his dress for a fresh suit, and with bare feet, carrying in his hands flowers and incense, and with two rows of attending followers, went out at the gate to meet the image; and, with his head and face (bowed to the ground), he did homage at its feet, and then scattered the flowers and burnt the incense. When the image was entering the gate, the queen and the brilliant ladies with her in the gallery above scattered far and wide all kinds of flowers, which floated about and fell promiscuously to the ground. In this way everything was done to promote the dignity of the occasion. The carriages of the monasteries were all different, and each one had its own day for the procession. (The ceremony) began on the first day of the fourth month, and

[7] Sanskrit phrase translated by Chinese to mean precious stones: usually gold, silver, lapis lazuli, rock crystal, rubies, diamonds, or emeralds, and agate. [Ed.]

[8] The Buddha. [Ed.]

[9] Buddhist saints of the Mahayana tradition. People who postponed their own nirvana to help others. [Ed.]

[10] Spirits. [Ed.]

ended on the fourteenth, after which the king and queen returned to the palace.

Seven or eight le to the west of the city there is what is called the King's New Monastery, the building of which took eighty years, and extended over three reigns. It may be 250 cubits in height, rich in elegant carving and inlaid work, covered above with gold and silver, and finished throughout with a combination of all the precious substances. Behind the tope there has been built a Hall of Buddha, of the utmost magnificence and beauty, the beams, pillars, venetianed doors, and windows being all overlaid with gold-leaf. Besides this, the apartments for the monks are imposingly and elegantly decorated, beyond the power of words to express. Of whatever things of highest value and preciousness the kings in the six countries on the east of the (Ts'ung) range of mountains are possessed, they contribute the greater portion (to this monastery), using but a small portion of them themselves.

Chapter IV: Through the Ts'ung or "Onion" Mountains to K'eeh-Ch'a

When the processions of images in the fourth month were over, Sangshao, by himself alone, followed a Tartar who was an earnest follower of the Law, and proceeded towards Kophene. Fa-hien and the others went forward to the kingdom of Tsze-hoh, which it took them twenty-five days to reach. Its king was a strenuous follower of our Law, and had (around him) more than a thousand monks, mostly students of the mahayana. Here (the travellers) abode fifteen days, and then went south for four days, when they found themselves among the Ts'ung-ling mountains, and reached the country of Yu-hwuy, where they halted and kept their retreat. When this was over, they went on among the hills for twenty-five days, and got to K'eeh-ch'a[11] there rejoining Hwuy-king and his two companions. . . .

Chapter XL: Disastrous Passage to Java; and Thence to China

Fa-hien abode in this country two years; and, in addition (to his acquisitions in Patna), succeeded in getting a copy of the Vinaya-pitaka of the Mahisasakah (school); the Dirghagama and Samyuktagama (Sutras); and also the Samyukta-sanchaya-pitaka;—all being works unknown in the land of Han. Having obtained these Sanskrit works, he took passage

[11] Probably in Ladak, northwest India. [Ed.]

in a large merchantman, on board of which there were more than 200 men, and to which was attached by a rope a smaller vessel, as a provision against damage or injury to the large one from the perils of the navigation. With a favourable wind, they proceeded eastwards for three days, and then they encountered a great wind. The vessel sprang a leak and the water came in. The merchants wished to go to the small vessel; but the men on board it, fearing that too many would come, cut the connecting rope. The merchants were greatly alarmed, feeling their risk of instant death. Afraid that the vessel would fill, they took their bulky goods and threw them into the water. Fa-hien also took his pitcher and washing-basin, with some other articles, and cast them into the sea; but fearing that the merchants would cast overboard his books and images, he could only think with all his heart of Kwan-she-yin,[12] and commit his life to (the protection of) the church of the land of Han,[13] (saying in effect), "I have travelled far in search of our Law. Let me, by your dread and supernatural (power), return from my wanderings, and reach my resting-place!"

In this way the tempest continued day and night, till on the thirteenth day the ship was carried to the side of an island, where, on the ebbing of the tide, the place of the leak was discovered, and it was stopped, on which the voyage was resumed. On the sea (hereabouts) there are many pirates, to meet with whom is speedy death. The great ocean spreads out, a boundless expanse. There is no knowing east or west; only by observing the sun, moon, and stars was it possible to go forward. If the weather were dark and rainy, (the ship) went as she was carried by the wind, without any definite course. In the darkness of the night, only the great waves were to be seen, breaking on one another, and emitting a brightness like that of fire, with huge turtles and other monsters of the deep (all about). The merchants were full of terror, not knowing where they were going. The sea was deep and bottomless, and there was no place where they could drop anchor and stop. But when the sky became clear, they could tell east and west, and (the ship) again went forward in the right direction. If she had come on any hidden rock, there would have been no way of escape.

After proceeding in this way for rather more than ninety days, they arrived at a country called Java-dvipa,[14] where various forms of error and Brahmanism are flourishing, while Buddhism in it is not worth speaking of. After staying there for five months, (Fa-hien) again embarked in another large merchantman, which also had on board more than 200 men. They carried provisions for fifty days, and commenced the voyage on the sixteenth day of the fourth month. Fa-hien kept his

---

[12] Chinese goddess of compassion and mercy. [Ed.]
[13] China. [Ed.]
[14] India established first kingdom in Java c. 78. [Ed.]

retreat on board the ship. They took a course to the north-east, intending to fetch Kwang-chow. After more than a month, when the night-drum had sounded the second watch, they encountered a black wind and tempestuous rain, which threw the merchants and passengers into consternation. Fa-hien again with all his heart directed his thoughts to Kwan-she-yin and the monkish communities of the land of Han; and, through their dread and mysterious protection, was preserved to day-break. After day-break, the Brahmans deliberated together and said, "It is having this Sramana on board which has occasioned our misfortune and brought us this great and bitter suffering. Let us land the bhikshu[15] and place him on some island-shore. We must not for the sake of one man allow ourselves to be exposed to such imminent peril." A patron of Fa-hien, however, said to them, "If you land the bhikshu, you must at the same time land me; and if you do not, then you must kill me. If you land this Sramana, when I get to the land of Han, I will go to the king, and inform against you. The king also reveres and believes the Law of Buddha, and honours the bhikshus." The merchants hereupon were perplexed, and did not dare immediately to land (Fa-hien).

At this time the sky continued very dark and gloomy, and the sailing-masters looked at one another and made mistakes. More than seventy days passed (from their leaving Java), and the provisions and water were nearly exhausted. They used the salt-water of the sea for cooking, and carefully divided the (fresh) water, each man getting two pints. Soon the whole was nearly gone, and the merchants took counsel and said, "At the ordinary rate of sailing we ought to have reached Kwang-chow, and now the time is passed by many days;—must we not have held a wrong course?" Immediately they directed the ship to the north-west, looking out for land; and after sailing day and night for twelve days, they reached the shore on the south of mount Lao,[16] on the borders of the prefecture of Ch'ang-kwang, and immediately got good water and vegetables. They had passed through many perils and hardships, and had been in a state of anxious apprehension for many days together; and now suddenly arriving at this shore, and seeing those (well-known) vegetables, the lei and kwoh, they knew indeed that it was the land of Han. Not seeing, however, any inhabitants nor any traces of them, they did not know whereabouts they were. Some said that they had not yet got to Kwang-chow, and others that they had passed it. Unable to come to a definite conclusion, (some of them) got into a small boat and entered a creek, to look for some one of whom they might ask what the place was. They found two hunters, whom they brought back with them, and then called on Fa-hien to act as interpreter and question them. Fa-hien first spoke

---

[15] Buddhist monk. [Ed.]
[16] Near modern Qingdao. [Ed.]

assuringly to them, and then slowly and distinctly asked them, "Who are you?" They replied, "We are disciples of Buddha?" He then asked, "What are you looking for among these hills?" They began to lie, and said, "To-morrow is the fifteenth day of the seventh month. We wanted to get some peaches to present[17] to Buddha." He asked further, "What country is this?" They replied, "This is the border of the prefecture of Ch'ang-kwang, a part of Ts'ing-chow under the (ruling) House of Tsin." When they heard this, the merchants were glad, immediately asked for (a portion of) their money and goods, and sent men to Ch'ang-kwang city.

The prefect Le E was a reverent believer in the Law of Buddha. When he heard that a Sramana had arrived in a ship across the sea, bringing with him books and images, he immediately came to the sea-shore with an escort to meet (the traveller), and receive the books and images, and took them back with him to the seat of his government. On this the merchants went back in the direction of Yang-chow; (but) when (Fa-hien) arrived at Ts'ing-chow, (the prefect there) begged him (to remain with him) for a winter and a summer. After the summer retreat was ended, Fa-hien, having been separated for a long time from his (fellow-) masters, wished to hurry to Ch'ang-gan; but as the business which he had in hand was important, he went south to the Capital;[18] and at an interview with the masters (there) exhibited the Sutras and the collection of the Vinaya (which he had procured).

After Fa-hien set out from Ch'ang-gan, it took him six years to reach Central India; stoppages there extended over (other) six years; and on his return it took him three years to reach Ts'ing-chow. The countries through which he passed were a few under thirty. From the sandy desert westwards on to India, the beauty of the dignified demeanour of the monkhood and of the transforming influence of the Law was beyond the power of language fully to describe; and reflecting how our masters had not heard any complete account of them, he therefore (went on) without regarding his own poor life, or (the dangers to be encountered) on the sea upon his return, thus incurring hardships and difficulties in a double form. He was fortunate enough, through the dread power of the three Honoured Ones,[19] to receive help and protection in his perils; and therefore he wrote out an account of his experiences, that worthy readers might share with him in what he had heard and said.

---

[17] They probably said they were Buddhists to please the monk, Faxian, but realizing that Buddhists don't hunt they said they were looking for peaches. [Ed.]

[18] Probably not Chang'an, but Nanjing, the capital of the southern Jin/Tsin under a different name.

[19] Buddha, Law, and Monkhood. [Ed.]

4

IBN BATTUTA
Travels, 1354

Ibn Battuta (1304–1369), a Muslim Berber from Tangier Morocco left to make the pilgrimage to Mecca at the age of twenty-one, a journey of sixteen months. He did not return for another twenty-four years. Instead he joined a caravan of returning pilgrims to Iraq and continued on over the years to Persia, Afghanistan, India, and China. Including later travels to sub-Saharan Africa, he covered about 75,000 miles, probably more than anyone else had ever done before the age of steam.

In this selection from his account of his travels, the *Rihla* or *Journey*, he describes his entry into India and some of his experiences in the city of Delhi (here rendered as Dilhi) under the Muslim ruler, Muhammad bin Tughluq in 1334. What does this selection tell you about travel in India at the time? What does it tell you about Ibn Battuta? In what ways has travel changed? In what ways is it similar?

THINKING HISTORICALLY

This selection from the *Rihla* was chosen because of what it tells us about travel, usually classified as a sub-category of social history. Even this selection, however, could be read for information about political, economic, or cultural history. Explain how.

North-Western India

Banj Ab is one of the greatest rivers on earth. It rises in flood in the hot season, and the inhabitants of that country sow at the time of its flood, just as the people of Egypt do during the Nile flood. This river is the frontier of the territories of the exalted Sultan Muhammad Shah, king of Hind and Sind.

When we reached this river the officials of the intelligence service came to us and wrote a report about us. From the province of Sind to the sultan's capital, the city of Dihli, it is fifty days' journey, but when the intelligence officers write to the sultan from Sind the letter reaches him in five days by the postal service.

Source: *The Travels of Ibn Battutah*, abridged, introduced, and annotated by Tim Mackintosh-Smith (New York: Picador, 2002), 149–51, 155–57, 187–90, 199; translated by Sir Hamilton Gibb and C. F. Beckinham (Hakluyt Society, 1958, 2000).

Description of the Barid[1]

The service of couriers on foot has within the space of each mile three relays. The manner of its organization is as follows. At every third of a mile there is an inhabited village, outside which there are three pavilions. In these sit men girded up ready to move off, each of whom has a rod two cubits long with copper bells at the top. When a courier leaves the town he takes the letter in the fingers of one hand and the rod with the bells in the other, and runs with all his might. The men in the pavilions, on hearing the sound of the bells, get ready to meet him and when he reaches them one of them takes the letter in his hand and passes on, running with all his might and shaking his rod until he reaches the next relay, and so they continue until the letter reaches its destination. This post is quicker than the mounted post, and they often use it to transport fruits from Khurasan which are regarded as great luxuries in India; the couriers put them on woven baskets like plates and carry them with great speed to the sultan. In the same way they transport the principal criminals; they place each man on a stretcher and run carrying the stretcher on their heads. Likewise they bring the sultan's drinking water when he resides at Dawlat Abad, carrying it from the river Gang [Ganges], to which the Hindus go on pilgrimage and which is at a distance of forty days' journey from there.

When the intelligence officials write to the sultan informing him of those who arrive in his country, the letter is written with the utmost precision and fulness of description. They report to him that a certain man has arrived of such-and-such appearance and dress, and note the number of his party, slaves and servants and beasts, his behaviour both on the move and at rest, and all his doings, omitting no details relating to all of these. When the newcomer reaches the town of Multan, which is the capital of Sind, he stays there until the sultan's order is received regarding his entry and the degree of hospitality to be extended to him. A man is honoured in that country only according to what may be seen of his actions, conduct, and zeal, since no one there knows anything of his family or parentage. The king of India, the Sultan Abu'l-Mujahid Muhammad Shah, makes a practice of honouring strangers and showing affection to them and singling them out for governorships or high dignities of state. The majority of his courtiers, palace officials, ministers of state, judges, and relatives by marriage are foreigners, and he has issued a decree that foreigners are to be called in his country by the title of Aziz [Honourable], so that this has become a proper name for them.

Every person proceeding to the court of this king must needs have a gift ready to present to him in person, in order to gain his favour. The sultan requites him for it by a gift many times its value. We shall have

[1] Postal service. [Ed.]

much to tell later on about the presents made to him by foreigners. When people became familiar with this habit of his, the merchants in Sind and India began to furnish each person who came to visit the sultan with thousands of dinars as a loan, and to supply him with whatever he might desire to offer as a gift or for his own use, such as riding animals, camels and goods. They place both their money and their persons at his service, and stand before him like attendants. When he reaches the sultan, he receives a magnificent gift from him and pays off his debts and his dues to them in full. So they ran a flourishing trade and made vast profits, and it became an established usage amongst them. On reaching Sind I followed this practice and bought horses, camels, white slaves and other goods from the merchants. I had already bought in Ghaznah from an Iraqi merchant about thirty horses and a camel with a load of arrows, for this is one of the things presented to the sultan. This merchant went off to Khurasan and on returning later to India received his money from me. He made an enormous profit through me and became one of the principal merchants. I met him many years later, in the city of Aleppo, when the infidels had robbed me of everything I possessed, but I received no kindness from him. . . .

From Ujah I travelled to the city Multan, the capital of the land of Sind and residence of its ruling amir. On the road to Multan and ten miles distant from it is the river called Khusru Abad, a large river that cannot be crossed except by boat. At this point the goods of all who pass are subjected to a rigorous examination and their baggage searched. Their practice at the time of our arrival was to take a quarter of everything brought in by the merchants, and to exact a duty of seven dinars for every horse. When we set about the crossing of this river and the baggage was examined, the idea of having my baggage searched was very disagreeable to me, for though there was nothing much in it, it seemed a great deal in the eyes of the people, and I did not like having it looked into. By the grace of God Most High there arrived on the scene one of the principal officers on behalf of Qutb al-Mulk, the governor of Multan, who gave orders that I should not be subjected to examination or search. And so it happened, and I gave thanks to God for the mercies which He had vouchsafed me. We spent that night on the bank of the river and next morning were visited by the postmaster. I was introduced to him and went in his company to visit the governor of Multan.

The Governor of Multan and the Ordering of Affairs at His Court

The Governor of Multan is Qutb al-Mulk, one of the greatest and most excellent of the amirs. When I entered his presence, he rose to greet me, shook my hand, and bade me sit beside him. I presented him with a white slave, a horse, and some raisins and almonds. These are among the greatest gifts that can be made to them, since they do not grow in their land but are imported from Khurasan. This governor in his public audience sat on a large carpeted dais, having the qadi and the preacher beside him. To right and left of him were ranged the commanders of the troops, and armed men stood at his back, while the troops were passed in review before him. They had a number of bows there, and when anyone comes desiring to be enrolled in the army as an archer he is given one of the bows to draw. They differ in stiffness and his pay is graduated according to the strength he shows in drawing them. For anyone desiring to be enrolled as a trooper there is a target set up; he puts his horse into a run and tries to hit it with his lance. There is a ring there too, suspended to a low wall; the candidate puts his horse into a run until he comes level with the ring, and if he lifts it off with his lance he is accounted among them a good horseman. For those wishing to be enrolled as mounted archers, there is a ball placed on the ground; each man gallops towards it and shoots at it, and his pay is proportioned to his accuracy in hitting it.

Two months after we reached Multan two of the sultan's chamberlains arrived in the town. They had instructions to arrange for the journey to Dihli of all those who had come on one mission or another. They came to me together and asked me why I had come to India. I told them that I had come to enter permanently the service of Khund Alam ['Master of the World'], namely the sultan, this being how he is called in his dominions. He had given orders that no one coming from Khurasan should be allowed to enter India unless he came with the intention of staying there. So when I told them that I had come to stay they summoned the qadi and notaries and drew up a contract binding me and those of my company who wished to remain in India, but some of them refused to take this engagement.

We then set out on the journey to the capital, which is forty days' march from Multan through continuously inhabited country. The first town we entered was the city of Abuhar, which is the first of these lands of Hind, a small but pretty place with a large population, and with flowing streams and trees. . . .

We continued our journey from the city of Abuhar across open country extending for a day's journey. On its borders are formidable mountains, inhabited by Hindu infidels who frequently hold up parties of travellers. Of the inhabitants of India the majority are infidels. Some of them are subjects under Muslim rule; others of them are rebels and warriors, who maintain themselves in the fastness of the mountains and plunder travelers. . . .

Account of the Sultan's Arrival and Our Meeting with Him

On the fourth of Shawwal [8th June 1334] the sultan alighted at a castle called Tilbat, seven miles from the capital, and the vizier ordered us to go out to him. We set out, each man with his present of horses, camels, fruits of Khurasan, Egyptian swords, mamluks, and sheep brought from the land of the Turks, and came to the gate of the castle where all the newcomers were assembled. They were then introduced before the sultan in order of precedence and were given robes of linen, embroidered in gold. When my turn came I entered and found the sultan seated on a chair. At first I took him to be one of the chamberlains until I saw him with the chief of the royal intimates, whom I had come to know during the sultan's absence. The chamberlain made obeisance and I did so too. After this the chief of the intimate courtiers said to me, '*Bismillah*, Mawlana Badr al-Din,' for in India they used to call me Badr al-Din, and *mawlana* [Our Master] is a title given to all scholars. I approached the sultan, who took my hand and shook it, and continuing to hold it addressed me most affably, saying in Persian, 'This is a blessing; your arrival is blessed; be at ease, I shall be compassionate to you and give you such favours that your fellow-countrymen will hear of it and come to join you.' Then he asked me where I came from and I said to him, 'From the land of the Maghrib.' He said to me, 'The land of Abd al-Mu'min?' and I said, 'Yes.' Every time he said any encouraging word to me I kissed his hand, until I had kissed it seven times, and after he had given me a robe of honour I withdrew.

Account of the Sultan's Entry into His Capital

On the day following that on which we went out to the sultan each one of us was given a horse from the sultan's stables, with a richly ornamented saddle and bridle, and when the sultan mounted for the entry into his capital we rode in the front part of the procession together with the Grand Qadi Sadr al-Jahan. The elephants were decorated and paraded in front of the sultan, with standards fixed on them and sixteen parasols, some of them gilded and some set with precious stones. Over the sultan's head there was displayed a parasol of the same kind and in front of him was carried the *ghashiyah*, which is a saddle-cloth studded with gems. On some of the elephants there were mounted small military catapults, and when the sultan came near the city parcels of gold and silver coins mixed together were thrown from these machines. The men on foot in front of the sultan and the other persons present scrambled for the money, and they kept on scattering it until the procession reached the palace. There marched before him thousands of foot-soldiers, and wooden pavilions covered with silk fabrics were constructed with singing girls in them, as we have already related.

After his entry into the city the sultan used to summon us to eat in his presence and would enquire how we fared and address us most affably. He said to us one day, 'You have honoured as by your coming and we cannot sufficiently reward you. The elder amongst you is in the place of my father, the man of mature age is my brother, and the young man like my son. There is in my kingdom nothing greater than this city of mine and I give it to you,' whereupon we thanked him and invoked blessings upon him.

One day he sent two of his high officers to us to say, 'The Master of the World says to you, "Whoever amongst you is capable of undertaking the function of vizier or secretary or commander or judge or professor or shaikh, I shall appoint to that office."' Everyone was silent at first, for what they were wanting was to gain riches and return to their countries. Then one of the officers said to me in Arabic, 'What do you say, *ya say-yidi?*' (The people of that country never address an Arab except by the title of sayyid, and it is by this title that the sultan himself addresses him, out of respect for the Arabs.) I replied, 'Vizierships and secretaryships are not my business, but as to qadis and shaikhs, that is my occupation, and the occupation of my fathers before me. And as for military commands, you know that the non-Arabs were converted to Islam only at the point of the sword of the Arabs.' The sultan was pleased when he heard what I said.

He was at the time in the Thousand Columns eating a meal, and he sent for us and we are in his presence as he was eating. We then withdrew to the outside of the Thousand Columns and my companions sat down, while I retired on account of a boil which prevented me from sitting. When the sultan summoned us a second time my companions presented themselves and made excuses to him on my behalf. I came back after the afternoon prayer and I performed the sunset and night prayers in the audience hall. The chamberlain then came out and summoned us. I went in and found the sultan of the terrace of the palace with his back leaning on the royal couch, the Vizier Khwajah Jahan before him, and the 'great king' Qabulah standing there upright. When I saluted him the 'great king' said to me, 'Do homage, for the Master of the World has appointed you qadi of the royal city of Dihli and has fixed your stipend at 12,000 dinars a year, and assigned to you village to that amount, and commanded for you 12,000 dinars in cash, which you shall draw from the treasury tomorrow (if God will), and has given you a horse with its saddle and bridle and has ordered you to be invested with a *maharibi* robe of honour,' that is, a robe which has on its breast and on its back the figure of a *mihrab*. So I did homage and when he had taken me by the hand and presented me before the sultan, the sultan said to me, 'Do not think that the office of qadi of Dihli is one of the minor functions; it is the highest of functions in our estimation.' I understood what he said though I could not speak in Persian fluently, but the sultan understood Arabic although he could not speak it fluently, so I said to him, 'O Master, I belong to the school of Malik and these people are Hanafis, and I do not know the language.' He replied, 'I have appointed two substitutes for you; they will be guided by your advice and you will be the one who signs all the documents, for you are in the place of a son to us,' to which I replied, 'Nay, but your slave and your servant.' He said to me in Arabic with humility and friendly kindness, 'No, but you are our lord and master.' . . .

Account of His Command to Me to Proceed to China on Embassy

When I had completed forty days the sultan sent me saddled horses, slave girls and boys, robes and a sum of money, so I put on the robes and went to him. I had a quilted tunic of blue cotton which I wore during my retreat, and as I put it off and dressed in the sultan's robes I upbraided myself. Ever after, when I looked at that tunic, I felt a light within me, and it remained in my possession until the infidels despoiled me of it on the sea. When I presented myself before the sultan, he showed me greater favour than before, and said to me, 'I have expressly sent for you to go as my ambassador to the king of China, for I know your love of travel and sightseeing.' He then provided me with everything I required, and appointed certain other persons to accompany me, as I shall relate presently.

5

FRANCESCO BALDUCCI PEGOLOTTI
Merchant Handbook, 1343

Francesco Balducci Pegolotti (c. 1290–1347) was a businessman employed by the Bardi Company of Florence. In that capacity, he worked in London, Antwerp, and Cyprus. While he did not travel to China himself, he learned much about the routes and terms of trade in Asia from those who did travel there for the merchant companies of Florence, Genoa, and Venice. Between 1335 and 1343 he compiled that information for the *Merchant Handbook* that is excerpted here. The route he discusses leads from north of the Black Sea to northwest of the Caspian Sea, north into the Khanate of the Golden Horde, and then across to what is today Uzbekistan and Kazakhstan into China along one of the silk roads.

Notice that this is the period of Mongol supremacy in Asia. What does this selection tell you about business travel in this period? What does it tell you about trade on the silk roads? What role did the Mongols play?

Source: Henry Yule and Henri Cordier, tr. and ed., *Cathay and the Way Thither, Being a Collection of Medieval Notices of China*, Vol. III (London: Hakluyt Society, 1866), 287–95. Spelling modernized and Americanized.

THINKING HISTORICALLY

Most of this, like the previous selections, might be broadly classified as social history. But trade is also economic history. What could an economic historian learn from this selection? If you were writing a cultural history, what might you draw from this account?

Information Regarding the Journey to Cathay, for Such As Will Go by Tana and Come Back with Goods

In the first place, from Tana to Gintarchan may be twenty-five days with an ox-wagon, and from ten to twelve days with a horse-wagon. On the road you will find plenty of Mongols, that is to say, of armed men. And from Gittarchan to Sara may be a day by river, and from Sara to Saracanco, also by river, eight days. You can do this either by land or by water; but by water you will be at less charge for your merchandize.

From Saracanco to Organci may be twenty days journey in camel-wagon. It will be well for anyone travelling with merchandize to go to Organci, for in that city there is a ready sale for goods. From Organci to Oltrarre is thirty-five to forty days in camel-wagons. But if when you leave Saracanco you go direct to Oltrarre, it is a journey of fifty days only, and if you have no merchandize it will be better to go this way than to go by Organci.

From Oltrarre to Armalec is forty-five days' journey with pack-asses, and every day you find Mongols. And from Armalec to Camexu is seventy days with asses, and from Camexu until you come to a river called [Grand Canal?] . . . is forty-five days on horseback; and then you can go down the river to Cassai, and there you can dispose of the *sommi* of silver that you have with you, for that is a most active place of business. After getting to Cassai you carry on with the money which you get for the *sommi* of silver which you sell there; and this money is made of paper, and is called *balishi*. And four pieces of this money are worth one *sommo* of silver in the province of Cathay. And from Cassai to Garnalec [Beijing], which is the capital city of the country of Cathay, is thirty days' journey.

Things Needful for Merchants Who Desire to Make the Journey to Cathay Above Described

In the first place, you must let your beard grow long and not shave. And at Tana you should furnish yourself with a dragoman [translator/guide]. And you must not try to save money in the matter of dragomen by taking a bad one instead of a good one. For the additional wages of the good one will not cost you so much as you will save by having him. And besides the dragoman it will be well to take at least two good men servants, who are acquainted with the Cumanian [Central Asian] tongue. And if the merchant likes to take a woman with him from Tana, he can do so; if he does not like to take one there is no obligation, only if he does take one he will be kept much more comfortably than if he does not take one. Howbeit, if he do take one, it will be well that she be acquainted with the Cumanian tongue as well as the men.

And from Tana travelling to Gittarchan you should take with you twenty-five days' provisions, that is to say, flour and salt fish, for as to meat you will find enough of it at all the places along the road. And so also at all the chief stations noted in going from one country to another in the route, according to the number of days set down above, you should furnish yourself with flour and salt fish; other things you will find in sufficiency, and especially meat.

The road you travel from Tana to Cathay is perfectly safe, whether by day or by night, according to what the merchants say who have used it. Only if the merchant, in going or coming, should die upon the road, everything belonging to him will become the perquisite of the lord of the country in which he dies, and the officers of the lord will take possession of all. And in like manner if he die in Cathay. But if his brother be with him, or an intimate friend and comrade calling himself his brother, then to such an one they will surrender the property of the deceased, and so it will be rescued.

And there is another danger: this is when the lord of the country dies, and before the new lord who is to have the lordship is proclaimed; during such intervals there have sometimes been irregularities practiced on the Franks, and other foreigners. (They call *Franks* all the Christians of these parts from Romania westward.) And neither will the roads be safe to travel until the other lord be proclaimed who is to reign in room of him who is deceased.

Cathay is a province which contained a multitude of cities and towns. Among others there is one in particular, that is to say the capital city, to which is great resort of merchants, and in which there is a vast amount of trade; and this city is called Cambalec. And the said city hath a circuit of one hundred miles, and is all full of people and bourses [markets] and of dwellers in the said city.

You may calculate that a merchant with a dragoman, and with two men servants, and with goods to the value of twenty-five thousand golden florins, should spend on his way to Cathay from sixty to eighty *sommi* of silver, and not more if he manage well; and for all the road back again from Cathay to Tana, including the expenses of living and the pay of servants, and all other charges, the cost will be about five *sommi* per head of pack animals, or something less. And you may reckon the *sommo* to be worth five golden florins. You may reckon also that each ox-wagon will require one ox, and will carry ten cantars Genoese weight; and the camel-wagon will require three camels, and will carry thirty cantars Genoese weight; and the horse-wagon will require one horse, and will commonly carry six and half cantars of silk, at 250 Genoese pounds to the cantar [a Genoese pound was apparently about 12 ounces]. And a bale of silk may be reckoned at between 110 and 115 Genoese pounds.

You may reckon also that from Tana to Sara the road is less safe than on any other part of the journey; and yet even when this part of the road is at its worst, if you are some sixty men in the company you will go as safely as if you were in your own house.

Anyone from Genoa or from Venice, wishing to go to the places above-named, and to make the journey to Cathay, should carry linens with him, and if he visit Organci he will dispose of these well. In Organci he should purchase *sommi* of silver, and with these he should proceed without making any further investment, unless it be some bales of the very finest stuffs which go in small bulk, and cost no more for carriage than coarser stuffs would do.

Merchants who travel this road can ride on horseback or on asses, or mounted in any way that they list to be mounted.

Whatever silver the merchants may carry with them as far as Cathay the lord of Cathay will take from them and put into his treasury. And to merchants who thus bring silver they give that paper money of theirs in exchange. This is of yellow paper, stamped with the seal of the lord aforesaid. And this money is called *balishi*; and with this money you can readily buy silk and all other merchandize that you have a desire to buy. And all the people of the country are bound to receive it. And yet you shall not pay a higher price for your goods because your money is of paper. And of the said paper money there are three kinds, one being worth more than another, according to the value which has been established for each by that lord.

And you may reckon that you can buy for one *sommo* of silver nineteen or twenty pounds of Cathay silk, when reduced to Genoese weight, and that the *sommo* should weigh eight and a half ounces of Genoa, and should be of the alloy of eleven ounces and seventeen deniers to the pound.

You may reckon also that in Cathay you should get three or three and a half pieces of damasked silk for a *sommo*; and from three and a half to five pieces of *nacchetti* of silk and gold, likewise for a *sommo* of silver.

■ REFLECTIONS

The Greek philosopher Heraclitus famously said that you can't step into the same river twice. (He could have said you can't step into the *same* river once!) The waters are always changing so no two trips are the same. Travel is always to some degree a step into the unknown. Our selection from Ibn Battuta only hinted at the many adventures and misadventures that awaited him: the escapes from bandits, ambush, drowning, and public execution; the number of times he was robbed of everything but his prayer rug or the clothes he wore, the loss of the royal treasures with which he had been entrusted. We also only touched on the wide range of his positive experiences: the prestigious offices and responsibilities, the wives and fortunes that were given him as he traveled from one world to another. The long title of the *Rihla* captures the positive: *A Gift to Those Who Contemplate the Wonders of Cities and the Marvels of Travelling*. A devout Muslim who begins his journey on a pilgrimage to Mecca and makes detours throughout to visit "great saints," and holy men, Ibn Battuta is also the first modern traveler. Whether traveling alone, surrounded by an entourage, or escorted by a sultan's cavalry, Ibn Battuta is on his own, following his nose, looking for new wonders and marvels. He tries on new identities, sires families, administers kingdoms, and then discards them, traveling on as the winds change.

A thousand years earlier Faxian also began a pilgrimage. He too suffered dangerous terrain, bandit-infested roads, overcrowded leaky ships, bone-crushing accommodations, and life-threatening attacks. He too rejoiced in his travels—at the discovery of the Buddhist kingdom of Khotan and, in pages we did not include, of marvelous discoveries of Buddhist texts, encounters at Buddhist monasteries and hospitals, and immersion in the Buddha's world. Unlike Ibn Battuta, Faxian remained a pilgrim throughout. The long title of his *Record* underlines his single-mindedness: *A Record of Buddhist Kingdoms, Being an Account by the Chinese Monk Faxian of his Travels in India and Ceylon in Search of the Buddhist Books of Discipline*. There was no room in Faxian's travels for diversion or a change of plans. He might spend another month to witness a Buddhist festival, but he was not about to choose a different home, occupation, or identity. For Faxian, travel was a necessary path to his goal. For Ibn Battuta and innumerable travelers since, the path was the goal.

Were the paths of the fourteenth century safer, smoother, or better tended than they had been a thousand years before? In some places they were, but changes were likely more a consequence of local or recent circumstances than long-term improvement. The Sultan's fleet-footed postal service may have been the envy of some, but, except for the shorter runs, it was no more advanced than the first marathon almost two thousand years before. The roads of India were as dangerous as they had ever been, in part because the rule of the Sultan was recently unraveling. They had been better under the Guptas a thousand years before. If there were technological changes occurring that would eventually nurture the modern independent traveler, it is hard to see them in the dirt roads or pirate-infested open seas of the fourteenth century.

In what ways were the travelers of the Middle Ages different from the individuals who took part in the great migrations of the previous millennia? We have virtually no information to reconstruct the lives of individual Indo-European or Bantu travelers. Evidence suggests movement of families, clans, or tribes, not individuals. Migrations were also normally gradual, measurable in miles per generation. The great Polynesian migrations often spanned great distances and each colonization of a new island began with a small group. But this too was a process of gradual settlement over the course of many generations. In one respect Polynesian colonization into the Pacific was unique: Since the deep Pacific islands were empty of human inhabitants, colonization was essentially a one-way process. By contrast, the Indo-European, Bantu, and even early Austronesian migrations created assimilated and hybrid cultures and societies.

Lynda Shaffer's essay on "Southernization" reminds us that all of these movements involved more than people. Languages and cultures, even seeds and technologies, could move while some people stayed in place. In fact, as Patrick Manning explains, much of our evidence for the movement of people is based on the evidence of the movement of language. In modern India, Hindu nationalists have made much of this fact in an attempt to preserve an ancestry free of West Asian foreigners. But prior to the modern era of telegraph, radio, television, and the Internet no cultural expansion occurred without the physical movement of people. The process of Southernization created a zone of intercommunication that included Brahmin priests who brought the Vedas to Cambodia, Arab merchants in East Africa, mace planters in the Moluccas, and Chinese monks who followed the footsteps of Faxian. In some respects, Ibn Battuta was also part of that process, aiding the spread of Islam, six hundred years after it had conquered Silk Road cities like Faxian's paradise of Buddhist Khotan, and at the moment that it was extending the faith to the islands that would become Indonesia, the world's most populous Muslim-majority nation today, and the place from which Faxian took the summer southern winds back to China.

9

Love, Sex, and Marriage
Medieval Europe and Asia, 400–1350

Most people in modern society share a common ideal about love, sex, and marriage. That ideal is that love, sex, and marriage are, and should be, a unified and exclusive experience. We might boil this down to a set of simple injunctions: You should marry the one you love, and love the one you marry; you should not love others more; you should have sex only with the one you love and marry. To say this is our ideal is not to say we always live up to it; rather, it is to say that we feel we ought to, and when we do not, we feel guilt, remorse, or disappointment with ourselves. In some parts of modern society, this ideal has recently been rejected, replaced by a culture of "hook-ups" or casual sex, but even then the rejected ideal casts a long shadow. A postlove culture is not a nonlove culture: It bears the marks of what it seeks to replace.

Historically, this love-culture ideal is relatively new. The idea that marriage should be based on love was hardly viable in societies where parents arranged marriages (as they did until very recently in most societies). Nor was sexual pleasure an intrinsic element. Most societies regulated women's sexual activity, but not men's. Patriarchal societies often made little association between sexuality and either marriage or love.

The modern idea of romantic love owes much to the idea of romance that developed in Europe in the Middle Ages. We have other ideas of love, to be sure: friendship, religious love, parental love, among others. But when we read love stories, watch romantic films or plays, or listen to love songs, we draw on the ideas and images of medieval romance. We begin this chapter by studying this European set of ideas because it is the origin of much of what we mean when we use the word *love* today. We might be surprised, however, to see how little such love had to do with marriage or even sex. Next we look at two cultures of love—in India and Japan, about the same time period—that are in some ways similar and in some ways different. Finally, for another perspective, we read ideas about sex from a Chinese visitor to medieval Cambodia.

■ THINKING HISTORICALLY

Analyzing Cultural Differences

In the previous chapter, we distinguished among the economic, social, political, and cultural aspects of a society. In this chapter we will examine cultural aspects alone. Actually, culture is never alone, any more than is economics, politics, or social behavior. Culture is nothing less than all our thoughts and feelings and the way we express them by the way we walk, talk, dream, and read history books. Every culture encompasses a wide variety of ideas and behavior at any one time, making it difficult to argue that a certain idea or behavior defines the culture as a whole. Nevertheless, if there were no commonalities there could be no culture.

Initially our focus is on love, the idea of romantic love or courtly love, that was "cultivated" in medieval Europe (and perhaps also in India and Japan). This is preeminently a cultural product. Sex we think of as biological, and marriage is certainly a social institution, but we will look at sex as driven as much by the psyche as the body, and we will touch on the way people thought about marriage. Therefore, we will be making cultural comparisons. We will ask how each culture thought about love, sex, and marriage, and how each culture did or did not put them together. You may be struck by how varied cultures can be. For some, a conclusion of human relativity is disconcerting; but it might also be seen as a testament to human invention and capacity. In any case, the exercise in making comparisons is a fundamental skill in navigating any of our worlds.

1

KEVIN REILLY

Love in Medieval Europe, India, and Japan, 1997

We hesitantly introduce this piece as a secondary source. It might be better called a tertiary source because it is based so much on the work of others and is part of a chapter in a college textbook. Nevertheless, it sets the stage for our discussion about love. The selection begins with the classic argument that romantic love was a product of medieval Europe, originating in the troubadour tradition of southern France around the twelfth century. The story of Ulrich von Liechtenstein, although probably not typical, details all the facets of the new idea of love, as well as the courts of chivalry that developed its code of behavior. What, according to this interpretation, are the elements of romantic love? How is it similar to, or different from, other kinds of love? How does it relate to sex and marriage? How is the medieval Indian tradition of *bhakti* different from European romantic love? How were medieval Hindu ideas of sex different from Christian ideas of sex? How was the Japanese idea of love during the Heian* period (794–1185) different from European romantic love? How was it similar?

THINKING HISTORICALLY

One way to understand what makes one culture different from another is to discount the extreme behavior at the fringes and focus on what most people think or do. But another way is to compare the extremes of one culture with the extremes of another, on the assumption that the extremists of any culture will magnify the culture's main trait. You might think of Ulrich von Liechtenstein as an extreme example of medieval European ideas of romantic love. A question to ask after you read about other societies is: Could there have been an Ulrich elsewhere? Could medieval India or Japan have produced an Ulrich? If not, why not?

Notice also that this selection highlights particular social classes as well as particular cultures. How do cultures and classes interact to form the ideal of romantic love in Europe and something both similar and different in Japan?

* hay AHN

Source: Kevin Reilly, *The West and the World*, 3rd ed. (Princeton, NJ: Markus Wiener, 1997), 279–80, 282–83, 287–92.

In the Service of Woman

In the twelfth century the courtly love tradition of the troubadours traveled north into France and Germany, and it became a guide to behavior for many young knights.

We are lucky to have the autobiography of one of these romantic knights, a minor noble who was born in Austria about 1200. His name was Ulrich von Liechtenstein, and he called his autobiography, appropriately enough, *In the Service of Woman*.[1]

At an early age Ulrich learned that the greatest honor and happiness for a knight lay in the service of a beautiful and noble woman. He seems to have realized, at least subconsciously, that true love had to be full of obstacles and frustrations in order to be spiritually ennobling. So at the age of twelve Ulrich chose as the love of his life a princess. She was a perfect choice: Far above him socially, she was also older than Ulrich and already married. Ulrich managed to become a page in her court so that he could see her and touch the same things that she touched. Sometimes he was even able to steal away to his room with the very water that she had just washed her hands in, and he would secretly drink it.

By the age of seventeen Ulrich had become a knight and took to the countryside to joust in the tournaments wearing the lady's colors. Finally after a number of victories, Ulrich gained the courage to ask his niece to call on the lady and tell her that he wanted to be a distant, respectful admirer. The princess would have none of it. She told Ulrich's niece that she was repulsed by Ulrich's mere presence, that he was low class and ugly—especially with that harelip of his. On hearing her reply Ulrich was overjoyed that she had noticed him. He went to have his harelip removed, recuperated for six weeks, and wrote a song to the princess. When the lady heard of this she finally consented to let Ulrich attend a riding party she was having, suggesting even that he might exchange a word with her if the opportunity arose. Ulrich had his chance. He was next to her horse as she was about to dismount, but he was so tongue-tied that he couldn't say a word. The princess thought him such a boor that she pulled out a lock of his hair as she got off her horse.

Ulrich returned to the field for the next three years. Finally the lady allowed him to joust in her name, but she wouldn't part with as much as a ribbon for him to carry. He sent her passionate letters and songs that he had composed. She answered with insults and derision. In one letter the princess derided Ulrich for implying that he had lost a finger while fighting for her when he had actually only wounded it slightly. Ulrich responded by having a friend hack off the finger and send it to the lady in a green velvet case. The princess was evidently so impressed with the

---

[1] Paraphrased from Morton Hunt, *The Natural History of Love* (New York: Alfred A. Knopf, 1959), 132–39. Quotations from Hunt.

power that she had over Ulrich that she sent back a message that she would look at it every day—a message that Ulrich received as he had the others—"on his knees, with bowed head and folded hands."

More determined than ever to win his lady's love, Ulrich devised a plan for a spectacular series of jousts, in which he challenged all comers on a five-week trip. He broke eight lances a day in the service of his princess. After such a showing, the princess sent word that Ulrich might at last visit her, but that he was to come disguised as a leper and sit with the other lepers who would be there begging. The princess passed him, said nothing, and let him sleep that night out in the rain. The following day she sent a message to Ulrich that he could climb a rope to her bedroom window. There she told him that she would grant no favors until he waded across the lake; then she dropped the rope so that he fell into the stinking moat.

Finally, after all of this, the princess said that she would grant Ulrich her love if he went on a Crusade in her name. When she learned that he was making preparations to go, she called it off and offered her love. After almost fifteen years Ulrich had proved himself to the princess.

What was the love that she offered? Ulrich doesn't say, but it probably consisted of kisses, an embrace, and possibly even a certain amount of fondling. Possibly more, but probably not. That was not the point. Ulrich had not spent fifteen years for sex. In fact, Ulrich had not spent fifteen years to win. The quest is what kept him going. His real reward was in the suffering and yearning. Within two years Ulrich was after another perfect lady.

Oh yes. We forgot one thing. Ulrich mentions that in the middle of his spectacular five-week joust, he stopped off for three days to visit the wife and kids. He was married? He was married. He speaks of his wife with a certain amount of affection. She was evidently quite good at managing the estate and bringing up the children. But what were these mundane talents next to the raptures of serving the ideal woman? Love was certainly not a part of the "details of crops, and cattle, fleas and fireplaces, serfs and swamp drainage."[2] In fact, Ulrich might expect that his wife would be proud of him if she knew what he was up to. The love of the princess should make Ulrich so much more noble and esteemed in his wife's eyes.

Courtly Love

The behavior of Ulrich von Liechtenstein reflected in exaggerated form a new idea of love in the West. Historians have called it "courtly love" because it developed in the courts of Europe, where noble ladies and knights of "quality" came together. For the first time since the Greeks a man could idealize a woman, but only if he minimized her sexuality. The evidence is overwhelming that these spiritual affairs would ideally never be consummated.

[2] Morton Hunt.

It is difficult for us to understand how these mature lords and ladies could torture themselves with passionate oaths, feats of endurance, and fainting spells when they heard their lover's name or voice, in short the whole repertoire of romance, and then refrain from actually consummating that love. Why did they insist on an ideal of "pure love" that allowed even naked embraces but drew the line at intercourse, which they called "false love"? No doubt the Christian antipathy for sex was part of the problem. Earlier Christian monks had practiced a similar type of *agape*;[3] Christianity had always taught that there was a world of difference between love and lust. The tendency of these Christian men to think of their ladies as replicas of the Virgin Mother also made sex inappropriate, if not outright incestuous.

But these lords and ladies were also making a statement about their "class" or good breeding. They were saying (as did Sigmund Freud almost a thousand years later) that civilized people repress their animal lust. They were distinguishing themselves from the crude peasants and soldiers around them who knew only fornication and whoring and raping. They were cultivating their emotions and their sensitivity, and priding themselves on their self-control. They were privileged (as members of the upper class) to know that human beings were capable of loyalty and love and enjoying beauty without behaving like animals. They were telling each other that they were refined, that they had "class." . . .

Further, despite the new romanticized view of the woman (maybe because of it), wives were just as excluded as they had always been. Noble, uplifting love, genuine romantic love, could not be felt for someone who swept the floor any more than it could be felt *by* someone whose life was preoccupied with such trivia. The lords and one of their special ladies, Marie, the countess of Champagne, issued the following declaration in 1174:

> We declare and we hold as firmly established that love cannot exert its power between two people who are married to each other. For lovers give each other everything freely, under no compulsion of necessity, but married people are in duty bound to give in to each other's desires and deny themselves to each other in nothing.[4]

The Court of Love

The proclamation was one of many that were made by the "courts of love" that these lords and ladies established in order to settle lovers' quarrels—and to decide for themselves the specifics of the new morality. . . .

No one did more to formulate these rules than Andreas Capellanus. Andreas not only summarized the numerous cases that came before the court, but he used these decisions to write a manual of polite, courtly

---

[3] Greek for a spiritual love. [Ed.]

[4] Andreas Capellanus, *Tractatus de Amore*, 1:6, 7th Dialogue. Quoted in Hunt, 143–44.

love. He called his influential book *A Treatise on Love and Its Remedy*, a title that indicated his debt to Sappho and the Greek romantic idea of love as a sickness. Andreas, however, did not think that he was advocating a "romantic" idea of love. The word was not even used in his day. He considered himself to be a modern twelfth-century Ovid—merely updating the Roman's *Art of Love*. He called himself Andreas the Lover and, like Ovid, considered himself an expert on all aspects of love.

But Andreas only used the same word as Ovid. The similarity ended there. The "aspects" of love that Andreas taught concerned the loyalty of the lovers, courteous behavior, the spiritual benefits of "pure love," the importance of gentleness, the subservience of the man to his lover, and the duties of courtship. There is none of Ovid's preoccupation with the techniques of seduction. Andreas is not talking about sex. In fact, he clearly advises against consummating the relationship.

Ovid made fun of infatuation and silly emotional behavior, but urged his readers to imitate such sickness in order to get the woman in bed. Andreas valued the passionate emotional attachment that Ovid mocked. Sincerity and honesty were too important to Andreas to dream of trickery, deceit, or pretense. Love, for Andreas, was too noble an emotion, too worthy a pursuit, to be put on like a mask. In short, the Roman had been after sexual gratification; the Christian wanted to refine lives and cleanse souls. They both called it love, but Andreas never seemed to realize that they were not talking the same language.

A Medieval Indian Alternative: Mystical Eroticism

Sometimes the best way to understand our own traditions is to study those of a different culture. It is difficult, for instance, for us to see Christian sexual morality as unusual because it has shaped our culture to such a great extent.

There have been alternatives, however. One of the most remarkable was the Indian ecstatic religion of the Middle Ages. Some medieval temple sculpture was erotic. The temples at Khajuraho and Orissa are full of sexual imagery: sensuous nudes and embracing couples. Similarly, the popular story *Gita Govinda* of the twelfth century tells of the loves of the god Krishna. He is shown scandalizing young women, dancing deliriously, and bathing with scores of admirers. Krishna's erotic appeal is a testament to his charisma. He is

> divine in proportion to his superiority as a great lover. . . . Worshippers were encouraged to commit excesses during festivals as the surest way to achieve . . . ecstasy, the purging climax of the orgiastic feast, the surmounting of duality.[5]

[5] Richard Lannoy, *The Speaking Tree: A Study of Indian Culture and Society* (Oxford: Oxford University Press, 1971), 64.

Among the most popular forms of medieval Hindu worship were the *bhakti* cults, which originated in devotion to Krishna in the *Bhagavad Gita*. *Bhakti* cults underline the difference between Indian and European devotion. While the Christian church discouraged spiritual love that might easily lead to "carnal love," the Indian *bhakti* sects encouraged rituals of ecstasy and sensual love precisely because they obliterated moral distinctions. The ecstatic union with the divine Krishna, Vishnu, or Shiva enabled the worshiper to transcend the limitations of self and confining definitions of good and evil.

Thus, Indian ecstatic religion sought sexual expression as a path to spiritual fulfillment. It is interesting that the word *bhakti* meant sex as well as worship, while we use the word "devotion" to mean worship and love. Hindu eroticism had nothing to do with the private expression of romantic love. In fact, it was the opposite. While romantic love depended on the development of the individual personality and the cultivation of individual feelings, *bhakti* depended on the loss of self in the sexual act.

Bhakti cults differed from the European courtly love tradition in one other important respect. They were not expressions of upper-class control. They were popular expressions of religious feeling. In essence they were directed against the dominating *brahman* and *kshatriya* castes because they challenged the importance of caste distinctions altogether. The ecstatic communion with the deity that they preached was open to all, regardless of caste. They appealed even to women and untouchables, as well as to farmers and artisans.

As Christianity did in Europe, popular Hinduism of the Middle Ages replaced a classical formal tradition with a spiritual passion. Ovid's *Art of Love* and the *Kama Sutra* were mechanical, passionless exercises for tired ruling classes. Both India and Europe turned to more emotionally intense religious experiences in the Middle Ages. . . . But the differences between Christian courtly love and *bhakti* cults were also profound. In India, sexual passion was an avenue to spiritual salvation. In Christian Europe sexual passion was at best a dead end, and at worst a road to hell.

Polygamy, Sexuality, and Style: A Japanese Alternative

At the same time that feudal Europe was developing a code of chivalry that romanticized love and almost desexualized marriage, the aristocracy of feudal Japan was evolving a code of polygamous sexuality without chivalry and almost without passion. We know about the sexual lives of Japanese aristocrats between 950 and 1050—the apex of the Heian period—through a series of remarkable novels and diaries, almost all of which were written by women. These first classics of Japanese literature, like *The Tale of Genji* and *The Pillow Book*, were written by women because Japanese men were still writing the "more important" but less-informative laws and theological studies in Chinese (just as Europeans still wrote in a Latin that was very different from the everyday spoken language).

When well-born Japanese in the Heian court spoke of "the world" they were referring to a love affair, and the novels that aristocratic women like Murasaki Shikibu or Sei Shonagon had time to compose in the spoken language were full of stories of "the world."

In *The World of the Shining Prince* Ivan Morris distinguishes three types of sexual relationships between men and women of the Heian aristocracy. (Homosexuality among the court ladies was "probably quite common," he writes, "as in any society where women were obliged to live in continuous and close proximity," but male homosexuality among "warriors, priests, and actors" probably became prevalent in later centuries.) The first type of heterosexual relationship was between the male aristocrat and his "principal wife." She was often several years older than her boy-husband and frequently served more as a guardian than as a bride. She was always chosen for her social standing, usually to cement a political alliance between ruling families. Although the match must frequently have been loveless, her status was inviolate; it was strictly forbidden, for instance, for a prince to exalt a secondary wife to principal wife. Upon marriage the principal wife would normally continue to live with her family, visited by her husband at night, until he became the head of his own household on the death or retirement of his father. Then the principal wife would be installed with all of her servants and aides as the head of the north wing of her husband's residence. An aristocratic woman (but never a peasant woman) might also become a secondary wife or official concubine. If she were officially recognized as such (much to the pleasure of her family), she might be moved into another wing of the official residence (leading to inevitable conflicts with the principal wife and other past and future secondary wives), or she might be set up in her own house. The arrangements were virtually limitless. The third and most frequent type of sexual relationship between men and women was the simple (or complex) affair—with a lady at court, another man's wife or concubine, but usually with a woman of a far lower class than the man. Ivan Morris writes of this kind of relationship:

> Few cultured societies in history can have been as tolerant about sexual relations as was the world of *The Tale of Genji*. Whether or not a gentleman was married, it redounded to his prestige to have as many affairs as possible; and the palaces and great mansions were full of ladies who were only too ready to accommodate him if approached in the proper style. From reading the *Pillow Book* we can tell how extremely commonplace these casual affairs had become in court circles, the man usually visiting the girl at night behind her screen of state and leaving her at the crack of dawn.[6]

[6] Ivan Morris, *The World of the Shining Prince: Court Life in Ancient Japan* (Baltimore: Penguin Books, 1969), 237.

That emphasis on "the proper style" is what distinguishes the sexuality of medieval Japan from that of ancient Rome, and reminds us of the medieval European's display of form—the aristocracy's mark of "class." Perhaps because the sexuality of the Heian aristocracy was potentially more explosive than the repressed rituals of European chivalry, style was that much more important. Polygamous sexuality could be practiced without tearing the society apart (and destroying aristocratic dominance in the process) only if every attention were given to style. Listen, for instance, to what the lady of *The Pillow Book* expected from a good lover:

> A good lover will behave as elegantly at dawn as at any other time. He drags himself out of bed with a look of dismay on his face. The lady urges him on: "Come, my friend, it's getting light. You don't want anyone to find you here." He gives a deep sigh, as if to say that the night has not been nearly long enough and that it is agony to leave. Once up, he does not instantly pull on his trousers. Instead he comes close to the lady and whispers whatever was left unsaid during the night. Even when he is dressed, he still lingers, vaguely pretending to be fastening his sash.
>
> Presently he raises the lattice, and the two lovers stand together by the side door while he tells her how he dreads the coming day, which will keep them apart; then he slips away. The lady watches him go, and this moment of parting will remain among her most charming memories.
>
> Indeed, one's attachment to a man depends largely on the elegance of his leave-taking. When he jumps out of bed, scurries about the room, tightly fastens his trouser-sash, rolls up the sleeves of his Court cloak, over-robe, or hunting costume, stuffs his belongings into the breast of his robe and then briskly secures the outer sash—one really begins to hate him.[7]

The stylistic elegance of the lover's departure was one of the principal themes of Heian literature. Perhaps no situation better expressed the mood of the Japanese word *aware** (a word that was used over a thousand times in *The Tale of Genji*), which meant the poignant or the stylishly, even artistically, sorrowful—a style of elegant resignation. The word also suggests the mood of "the lady in waiting" and even the underlying anguish and jealousy of a precariously polygamous existence for the women consorts and writers of the Japanese feudal age. . . .

---

* ah wa ray
[7] *The Pillow Book of Sei Shonagon*, trans. Ivan Morris (Baltimore: Penguin Books, 1971), 49–50.

Aristocracies have behaved in similar ways throughout the world, and throughout history. They demonstrate their "class" or "good breeding" with elaborate rituals that differentiate their world from the ordinary. But the example of aristocratic Heian Japan a thousand years ago points to some of the differences between Japanese and Christian culture. The Japanese developed rituals of courtship and seduction for the leisured few that were sexually satisfying and posed no threat to marriage. They were rituals that showed artistic refinement rather than sexual "purity" or chastity. They could be sexual because Japanese culture did not disparage sexuality. Rather it disparaged lack of "taste." The affair did not threaten marriage because the culture did not insist on monogamy. The new sexual interest could be carried on outside or inside the polygamous estate of the Japanese aristocrat. Perhaps the main difference, then, is that the Japanese aristocrat invented stylized sex rather than romantic love.

2

ULRICH VON LIECHTENSTEIN

The Service of Ladies, 1255

This selection is drawn from Ulrich von Liechtenstein's own account of his adventures. After over ten years of service, as a page and then a distant admirer, in 1226, von Liechtenstein undertook a spectacular series of jousts to impress and win his lady, the princess. In the course of a five-week itinerary in northern Italy and southern German-speaking areas in which he took on all comers, he claims to have broken 307 lances. In the first part of this selection he details his preparation for the traveling tournament. In the second part, he tells of a brief interruption in his jousting for a stop at home. What does this selection tell you about von Liechtenstein's ideas of love and marriage?

THINKING HISTORICALLY

Sometimes the best entry point for analyzing cultural differences is to begin with the surprising or incomprehensible. If we can refrain from merely dismissing what seems beyond the pale, this can be an opportunity to understand how cultures can be truly different from our own.

Source: Ulrich von Liechtenstein, *The Service of Ladies*, trans. J. W. Thomas (Suffolk, England and Rochester, NY: The Boydell Press, 2004; published by arrangement with University of North Carolina Press, Chapel Hill, 1969), 46–49, 85–86.

Even a moderately careful reading of the two selections from von Liechtenstein's autobiography should evoke some surprise. In the first selection, von Liechtenstein sketches a visual image of himself on horseback that is far from our expectations. Imagine what he must have looked like. Imagine how others must have seen him. Recognizing that this was not some Halloween prank, that others proceeded to joust with him rather than laugh him out of town, we are forced to rethink what his outfit and presentation meant to him and those in his society. The recognition that the meaning of an act (like donning women's clothing) could be vastly different in Europe of the thirteenth century from what it is today offers the entry to comparative analysis.

We may also note that there are many things in von Liechtenstein's description of love that are not at all surprising. This may be because they have become second nature to our own society. Certainly some of the elements of romantic love, which were fresh in von Liechtenstein's day, have become clichés in modern film and television. What do you make of the elements of this story that are familiar? What do you make of those that surprise you?

"My service must be God's command.
Now let me tell you what I've planned.
I'll take on woman's dress and name
and thus disguised will strive for fame.
Sweet God protect me and sustain!
I'll travel with a knightly train
up to Bohemia from the sea.
A host of knights shall fight with me.

"This very winter I shall steal
out of the land and shall conceal
my goal from everyone but you.
I'll travel as a pilgrim who
to honor God is bound for Rome
(no one will question this at home).
I'll stop in Venice and shall stay
in hiding till the first of May.

"I'll carefully remain unseen
but deck myself out like a queen;
it should be easy to acquire
some lovely feminine attire
which I'll put on—now hear this last—
and when St. George's day is past,
the morning afterwards, I'll ride
(I pray that God is on my side)

"from the sea to Mestre, near
by Venice. He who breaks a spear
with me to serve, by tourneying,
his lady fair will get a ring
of gold and it will be quite nice.
I'll give it to him with this advice,
that he present it to his love,
the one he's in the service of.

"Messenger, I'll make the trip
so there will never be a slip
and no one possibly can guess
whose form is hid beneath the dress.
For I'll be clad from head to toe
in woman's garb where'er I go,
fully concealed from people's eyes.
They'll see me only in disguise.

"If you would please me, messenger,
then travel once again to her.
Just tell her what I have in mind
and ask if she will be so kind
as to permit that I should fight
throughout this journey as her knight.
It's something she will not repent
and I'll be glad of her assent."

He rode at once to tell her this
and swore upon his hope of bliss
my loyalty would never falter,
that I was true and would not alter.
He told my plan in full detail
and said, "My lady, should you fail
to let him serve and show your trust
in him, it wouldn't seem quite just."

"Messenger," she spoke, "just let
him have this message, don't forget.
This trip, if I have understood
you right, will surely do him good
and he will win a rich reward
in praise from many a lady and lord.
Whether it helps with me or not,
from others he will gain a lot."

The messenger was pleased and sure.
He found me by the river Mur
at Liechtenstein where I was then.
'T was nice to have him there again.
I spoke, "O courtly youth, now tell
me if the lady's feeling well.
For, if my darling's doing fine,
then shall rejoice this heart of mine."

He spoke, "She's fair and happy too;
she bade me bring this word to you
about your journey. If you should
go through with it 't will do you good
and, whether it helps with her or not,
from others you will gain a lot.
She certainly supports your aim
and says that you'll be rich in fame."

. . .

I got to Venice without delay
and found a house in which to stay,
right on the edge of town, a place
where none would ever see my face
who might have recognized me there.
I was as cautious everywhere
and all the winter long I hid.
But let me tell you what I did:

I had some woman's clothing made
to wear throughout the masquerade.
They cut and sewed for me twelve skirts
and thirty fancy lady's shirts.
I bought two braids for my disguise,
the prettiest they could devise,
and wound them with some pearls I got
which didn't cost an awful lot.

I bade the tailors then prepare
three velvet cloaks for me to wear,
all white. The saddles too on which
the master labored, stitch by stitch,
were silver white. As for a king
was made the saddle covering,
long and broad and gleaming white.
The bridles all were rich and bright.

The tailors sewed for every squire
(there were a dozen) white attire.
A hundred spears were made for me
and all as white as they could be.
But I need not continue so,
for all I wore was white as snow
and everything the squires had on
was just as white as any swan.

My shield was white, the helmet too.
I had them make ere they were through
a velvet cover for each steed
as armor. These were white, indeed,
as was the battle cape which I
should wear for jousting by and by,
the cloth of which was very fine.
I was quite pleased to call it mine.

At last I had my horses sent
to me (none knew just where they went)
and got some servants, as I'd planned,
each native to a foreign land.
They carefully did not let slip
a thing about my coming trip
and I took heed that those who came
to serve me never learned my name.

· · ·

They rode toward me with armor on;
I had not waited long to don
a rich and splendid battle dress.
Von Ringenberg with full success
broke off a spear on me. The one
I jousted with when this was done
I knocked down backwards off his horse,
which made him feel ashamed, of course.

The spears I broke then numbered four.
On the field had come no more
with armor on and lance in hand
and so I stopped. At my command
the servants gave six rings away.
I sought the inn where I should stay
and found a pretty hostel there;
I got some other things to wear.

I changed my clothing under guard,
and then the hostel door was barred.
I took with me a servant who
would not say anything, I knew.
We stole away without a sound
and rode with joy to where I found
my dearest wife whom I adore;
I could not ever love her more.

She greeted me just as a good
and loving woman always should
receive a husband she holds dear.
That I had come to see her here
had made her really very pleased.
My visit stilled her grief and eased
her loneliness. We shared our bliss,
my sweet and I, with many a kiss.

She was so glad to see her knight,
and I had comfort and delight
till finally the third day came;
to give me joy was her sole aim.
When dawn appeared it was the third.
I dressed, an early mass was heard,
I prayed God keep me from transgressing,
and then received a friendly blessing.

Right after that I took my leave,
lovingly, you may believe,
and rode with joyful heart to where
I'd left my servants unaware.
I entered Gloggnitz hastily
and found them waiting there for me,
prepared to journey on again.
At once we left the city then.

We rode to Neunkirchen gaily decked
and were received as I'd expect
of those whose manners are refined.
Each knight was courteous and kind
who waited there with spear and shield.
When I came riding on the field
I found them all prepared, adorned
with trappings no one would have scorned.

Nine waited there, not more nor less,
to joust with me, in battle dress.
I saw them and it wasn't long
till I'd donned armor, bright and strong.
The first to come I'd heard much of;
his great desire was ladies' love.
It was Sir Ortold von Graz, a name
already widely known to fame.

All that he wore was of the best.
The good man cut me in the chest
so strong and skilful was his joust;
through shield and armor went the thrust.
When I beheld the wound indeed
and saw that it began to bleed
I hid it quickly with my coat
before the other knights took note.

I broke nine lances there in haste
and found my inn. I dared not waste
much time before I got in bed.
I sent nine rings of golden red
to each of them who with his spear
had earned from me a present here.
My injuries were deftly bound
by a doctor whom my servants found.

3

ANDREAS CAPELLANUS

The Art of Courtly Love, 1184–1186

Andreas Capellanus (Andreas the Chaplain) compiled this guide to
courtly love between 1184 and 1186. He probably intended his book
to update Ovid's *Art of Love*, as discussed in selection 1, but his
approach reflects many of the new ideas of love circulating among
the upper classes of Europe in the twelfth century. Andreas says that
love is suffering, but also that it is wonderful. What does he mean?

Source: Andreas Capellanus, *The Art of Courtly Love*, trans. John J. Parry (New York:
Columbia University Press, 1990), 28–30, 31–32, 159, 161–62, 163–64, 177, 184–86.

Compare his ideas about sex and marriage to those of Ulrich von Liechtenstein. The bishop of Paris condemned Andreas's ideas in 1277, but do they seem religious or Christian in any way? Notice the author's attention to passion and proper behavior. What does Andreas think is the proper relationship between passionate love and marriage? What is his attitude toward sexuality? Homosexuality?

THINKING HISTORICALLY

Compare this idea of "character" with that of the Japanese (discussed in the first selection). What does Andreas think of multiple partners? Compare this attitude with those of other cultures. How do the ideas of Andreas the Chaplain on love and marriage compare to those of a modern Christian chaplain?

Introduction to the Treatise on Love

We must first consider what love is, whence it gets its name, what the effect of love is, between what persons love may exist, how it may be acquired, retained, increased, decreased, and ended, what are the signs that one's love is returned, and what one of the lovers ought to do if the other is unfaithful.

What Love Is

Love is a certain inborn suffering derived from the sight of and excessive meditation upon the beauty of the opposite sex, which causes each one to wish above all things the embraces of the other and by common desire to carry out all of love's precepts in the other's embrace.

That love is suffering is easy to see, for before the love becomes equally balanced on both sides there is no torment greater, since the lover is always in fear that his love may not gain its desire and that he is wasting his efforts. He fears, too, that rumors of it may get abroad, and he fears everything that might harm it in any way, for before things are perfected a slight disturbance often spoils them. If he is a poor man, he also fears that the woman may scorn his poverty; if he is ugly, he fears that she may despise his lack of beauty or may give her love to a more handsome man; if he is rich, he fears that his parsimony in the past may stand in his way. To tell the truth, no one can number the fears of one single lover. This kind of love, then, is a suffering which is felt by only one of the persons and may be called "single love." But even after both are in love the fears that arise are just as great, for each of the lovers fears that what he has acquired with so much effort may be lost through the effort of someone else, which is certainly much worse for a man than if, having no hope, he sees that his efforts are accomplishing nothing, for it is worse to lose the things you are seeking than to be deprived of a gain you merely hope for. The lover fears, too, that he may offend his loved one in some way; indeed he fears so many things that it would be difficult to tell them.

That this suffering is inborn I shall show you clearly, because if you will look at the truth and distinguish carefully you will see that it does not arise out of any action; only from the reflection of the mind upon what it sees does this suffering come. For when a man sees some woman fit for love and shaped according to his taste, he begins at once to lust after her in his heart; then the more he thinks about her the more he burns with love, until he comes to a fuller meditation. Presently he begins to think about the fashioning of the woman and to differentiate her limbs, to think about what she does, and to pry into the secrets of her body, and he desires to put each part of it to the fullest use. Then after he has come to this complete meditation, love cannot hold the reins, but he proceeds at once to action; straightway he strives to get a helper to find an intermediary. He begins to plan how he may find favor with her, and he begins to seek a place and a time opportune for talking; he looks upon a brief hour as a very long year, because he cannot do anything fast enough to suit his eager mind. It is well known that many things happen to him in this manner. This inborn suffering comes, therefore, from seeing and meditating. Not every kind of meditation can be the cause of love, an excessive one is required; for a restrained thought does not, as a rule, return to the mind, and so love cannot arise from it.

Between What Persons Love May Exist

Now, in love you should note first of all that love cannot exist except between persons of opposite sexes. Between two men or two women love can find no place, for we see that two persons of the same sex are not at all fitted for giving each other the exchanges of love or for practicing the acts natural to it. Whatever nature forbids, love is ashamed to accept. . . .

What the Effect of Love Is

Now it is the effect of love that a true lover cannot be degraded with any avarice. Love causes a rough and uncouth man to be distinguished for his handsomeness; it can endow a man even of the humblest birth with nobility of character; it blesses the proud with humility; and the man in love becomes accustomed to performing many services gracefully for everyone. O what a wonderful thing is love, which makes a man shine with so many virtues and teaches everyone, no matter who he is, so many good traits of character! There is another thing about love that we should not praise in few words: it adorns a man, so to speak, with the virtue of chastity, because he who shines with the light of one love can hardly think of embracing another woman, even a beautiful one. For when he thinks deeply of his beloved the sight of any other woman seems to his mind rough and rude. . . .

If One of the Lovers Is Unfaithful to the Other

If one of the lovers should be unfaithful to the other, and the offender is the man, and he has an eye to a new love affair, he renders himself wholly unworthy of his former love, and she ought to deprive him completely of her embraces. . . .

But what if he should be unfaithful to his beloved—not with the idea of finding a new love, but because he has been driven to it by an irresistible passion for another woman? What, for instance, if chance should present to him an unknown woman in a convenient place or what if at a time when Venus is urging him on to that which I am talking about he should meet with a little strumpet or somebody's servant girl? Should he, just because he played with her in the grass, lose the love of his beloved? We can say without fear of contradiction that just for this a lover is not considered unworthy of the love of his beloved unless he indulges in so many excesses with a number of women that we may conclude that he is overpassionate. But if whenever he becomes acquainted with a woman he pesters her to gain his end, or if he attains his object as a result of his efforts, then rightly he does deserve to be deprived of his former love, because there is strong presumption that he has acted in this way with an eye toward a new one, especially where he has strayed with a woman of the nobility or otherwise of an honorable estate. . . .

But I know that once when I sought advice I got the answer that a true lover can never desire a new love unless he knows that for some definite and sufficient reason the old love is dead; we know from our own experience that this rule is very true. We have fallen in love with a woman of the most admirable character, although we have never had, or hope to have, any fruit of this love. For we are compelled to pine away for love of a woman of such lofty station that we dare not say one word about it, nor dare we throw ourself upon her mercy, and so at length we are forced to find our body shipwrecked. But although rashly and without foresight we have fallen into such great waves in this tempest, still we cannot think about a new love or look for any other way to free ourself.

But since you are making a special study of the subject of love, you may well ask whether a man can have a pure love for one woman and a mixed or common love with another. We will show you, by an unanswerable argument, that no one can feel affection for two women in this fashion. For although pure love and mixed love may seem to be very different things, if you will look at the matter properly you will see that pure love, so far as its substance goes, is the same as mixed love and comes from the same feeling of the heart. The substance of the love is the same in each case, and only the manner and form of loving are different, as this illustration will make clear to you. Sometimes we see a man with a desire to drink his wine unmixed, and at another time his appetite prompts him to drink only water or wine and water mixed; although his appetite manifests itself differently, the substance of it is the same and unchanged. So likewise when two people have long been united by pure love and afterwards desire to practice mixed love, the substance of the love remains the same in them, although the manner and form and the way of practicing it are different. . . .

The Rules of Love

Let us come now to the rules of love, and I shall try to present to you very briefly those rules which the King of Love[1] is said to have proclaimed with his own mouth and to have given in writing to all lovers. . . .

I. Marriage is no real excuse for not loving.
II. He who is not jealous cannot love.
III. No one can be bound by a double love.
IV. It is well known that love is always increasing or decreasing.
V. That which a lover takes against the will of his beloved has no relish.
VI. Boys do not love until they arrive at the age of maturity.
VII. When one lover dies, a widowhood of two years is required of the survivor.
VIII. No one should be deprived of love without the very best of reasons.
IX. No one can love unless he is impelled by the persuasion of love.
X. Love is always a stranger in the home of avarice.
XI. It is not proper to love any woman whom one should be ashamed to seek to marry.
XII. A true lover does not desire to embrace in love anyone except his beloved.
XIII. When made public love rarely endures.
XIV. The easy attainment of love makes it of little value; difficulty of attainment makes it prized.
XV. Every lover regularly turns pale in the presence of his beloved.
XVI. When a lover suddenly catches sight of his beloved his heart palpitates.

[1] King Arthur of Britain. [Ed.]

XVII.   A new love puts to flight an old one.

XVIII.   Good character alone makes any man worthy of love.

XIX.   If love diminishes, it quickly fails and rarely revives.

XX.   A man in love is always apprehensive.

XXI.   Real jealousy always increases the feeling of love.

XXII.   Jealousy, and therefore love, are increased when one suspects his beloved.

XXIII.   He whom the thought of love vexes, eats and sleeps very little.

XXIV.   Every act of a lover ends in the thought of his beloved.

XXV.   A true lover considers nothing good except what he thinks will please his beloved.

XXVI.   Love can deny nothing to love.

XXVII.   A lover can never have enough of the solaces of his beloved.

XXVIII.   A slight presumption causes a lover to suspect his beloved.

XXIX.   A man who is vexed by too much passion usually does not love.

XXX.   A true lover is constantly and without intermission possessed by the thought of his beloved.

XXXI.   Nothing forbids one woman being loved by two men or one man by two women.

4

PROCOPIUS

The Secret History, c. 550–560

Our attention now shifts from medieval Western Europe to the Byzantine Empire, in this case the early Byzantine Empire of the sixth century. The author of the following document, Procopius (500–565), was an historian who wrote about his own time. In addition to *The Secret History*, which was not published in his lifetime, he published a seven-volume history of Byzantine wars and a short volume praising the vast architectural achievements of the emperor Justinian (482–565). Justinian's long reign was crucial in defining the Byzantine Empire, a process the emperor saw as reviving the Roman Empire after the fall of Rome in 465. Among Justinian's accomplishments were codifying Roman law and restoring control of Italy from his

Source: Procopius, *Secret History*, translated by Richard Atwater (New York: Covicii Friede; Chicago: P. Covicii, 1927), (repr. Ann Arbor, Michigan: University of Michigan Press, 1961).

capital at Constantinople. In the 540s, however, the empire was wracked by a devastating bubonic plague from which it did not truly recover until the ninth century.

The tone of *The Secret History* is in sharp contrast to the author's works that were published in his lifetime. Its critique of Justinian may have been an attempt by the author to balance the effusive praise of Justinian that appeared in his published works, and certainly explains why it was never published. Perhaps Justinian surprised his historian by waiting him out, living until he was eighty-two and dying in the same year as Procopius.

In this selection, Procopius writes of Justinian and Theodora, the woman he married shortly before becoming emperor. In what way is this a love story? In what way is it not?

THINKING HISTORICALLY

How would you compare attitudes toward sex, love, and marriage in Justinian's Byzantium with the Western European societies in the previous readings? How would you account for their differences in cultural attitudes and practices?

[Justinian] took a wife: and in what manner she was born and bred, and, wedded to this man, tore up the Roman Empire by the very roots, I shall now relate.

Acacius was the keeper of wild beasts used in the amphitheater in Constantinople; he belonged to the Green faction and was nicknamed the Bearkeeper. This man, during the rule of Anastasius, fell sick and died, leaving three daughters named Comito, Theodora and Anastasia: of whom the eldest was not yet seven years old. His widow took a second husband, who with her undertook to keep up Acacius's family and profession. But Asterius, the dancing master of the Greens, on being bribed by another removed this office from them and assigned it to the man who gave him the money. For the dancing masters had the power of distributing such positions as they wished.

When this woman saw the populace assembled in the amphitheater, she placed laurel wreaths on her daughters' heads and in their hands, and sent them out to sit on the ground in the attitude of suppliants. The Greens eyed this mute appeal with indifference; but the Blues[1] were moved to bestow on the children an equal office, since their own animal-keeper had just died.

---

[1] The Blues and Greens were fans of two chariot racing teams that acted like gangs and fought in politics. [Ed.]

When these children reached the age of girlhood, their mother put them on the local stage, for they were fair to look upon; she sent them forth, however, not all at the same time, but as each one seemed to her to have reached a suitable age. Comito, indeed, had already become one of the leading hetaerae[2] of the day.

Theodora, the second sister, dressed in a little tunic with sleeves, like a slave girl, waited on Comito and used to follow her about carrying on her shoulders the bench on which her favored sister was wont to sit at public gatherings. Now Theodora was still too young to know the normal relation of man with maid, but consented to the unnatural violence of villainous slaves who, following their masters to the theater, employed their leisure in this infamous manner. And for some time in a brothel she suffered such misuse.

But as soon as she arrived at the age of youth, and was now ready for the world, her mother put her on the stage. Forthwith, she became a courtesan, and such as the ancient Greeks used to call a common one, at that: for she was not a flute or harp player, nor was she even trained to dance, but only gave her youth to anyone she met, in utter abandonment. Her general favors included, of course, the actors in the theater; and in their productions she took part in the low comedy scenes. For she was very funny and a good mimic, and immediately became popular in this art. There was no shame in the girl, and no one ever saw her dismayed: no role was too scandalous for her to accept without a blush.

She was the kind of comedienne who delights the audience by letting herself be cuffed and slapped on the cheeks, and makes them guffaw by raising her skirts to reveal to the spectators those feminine secrets here and there which custom veils from the eyes of the opposite sex. With pretended laziness she mocked her lovers, and coquettishly adopting ever new ways of embracing, was able to keep in a constant turmoil the hearts of the sophisticated. And she did not wait to be asked by anyone she met, but on the contrary, with inviting jests and a comic flaunting of her skirts herself tempted all men who passed by, especially those who were adolescent.

On the field of pleasure she was never defeated. Often she would go picnicking with ten young men or more, in the flower of their strength and virility, and dallied with them all, the whole night through. When they wearied of the sport, she would approach their servants, perhaps thirty in number, and fight a duel with each of these; and even thus found no allayment of her craving. Once, visiting the house of an illustrious gentleman, they say she mounted the projecting corner of her dining couch, pulled up the front of her dress, without a blush, and thus carelessly showed her wantonness. . . . Often, even in the theater, in the sight of all the people, she removed her costume and stood nude in their midst,

---

[2] Hetaerae: prostitute. [Ed.]

except for a girdle about the groin: not that she was abashed at revealing that, too, to the audience, but because there was a law against appearing altogether naked on the stage, without at least this much of a fig-leaf. Covered thus with a ribbon, she would sink down to the stage floor and recline on her back. Slaves to whom the duty was entrusted would then scatter grains of barley from above into the calyx of this passion flower, whence geese, trained for the purpose, would next pick the grains one by one with their bills and eat. When she rose, it was not with a blush, but she seemed rather to glory in the performance. . . .

So perverse was her wantonness that she should have hid not only the customary part of her person, as other women do, but her face as well. Thus those who were intimate with her were straightway recognized from that very fact to be perverts, and any more respectable man who chanced upon her in the Forum avoided her and withdrew in haste, lest the hem of his mantle, touching such a creature, might be thought to share in her pollution. For to those who saw her, especially at dawn, she was a bird of ill omen. And toward her fellow actresses she was as savage as a scorpion: for she was very malicious.

Later, she followed Hecebolus, a Tyrian who had been made governor of Pentapolis, serving him in the basest of ways; but finally she quarreled with him and was sent summarily away. Consequently, she found herself destitute of the means of life, which she proceeded to earn by prostitution, as she had done before this adventure. She came thus to Alexandria, and then traversing all the East, worked her way to Constantinople; in every city plying a trade (which it is safer, I fancy, in the sight of God not to name too clearly) as if the Devil were determined there be no land on earth that should not know the sins of Theodora.

Thus was this woman born and bred, and her name was a byword beyond that of other common wenches on the tongues of all men.

But when she came back to Constantinople, Justinian fell violently in love with her. At first he kept her only as a mistress, though he raised her to patrician rank. Through him Theodora was able immediately to acquire an unholy power and exceedingly great riches. She seemed to him the sweetest thing in the world, and like all lovers, he desired to please his charmer with every possible favor and requite her with all his wealth. The extravagance added fuel to the flames of passion. With her now to help spend his money he plundered the people more than ever, not only in the capital, but throughout the Roman Empire. . . .

Now as long as the former Empress was alive, Justinian was unable to find a way to make Theodora his wedded wife. In this one matter she opposed him as in nothing else: for the lady abhorred vice, being a rustic and of barbarian descent, as I have shown. She was never able to do any real good, because of her continued ignorance of the affairs of state. She dropped her original name, for fear people would think it ridiculous, and adopted the name of Euphemia when she came to the palace. But finally her death removed this obstacle to Justinian's desire.

Justin, doting and utterly senile, was now the laughing stock of his subjects; he was disregarded by everyone because of his inability to oversee state affairs; but Justinian they all served with considerable awe. His hand was in everything, and his passion for turmoil created universal consternation.

It was then that he undertook to complete his marriage with Theodora. But as it was impossible for a man of senatorial rank to make a courtesan his wife, this being forbidden by ancient law, he made the Emperor nullify this ordinance by creating a new one, permitting him to wed Theodora, and consequently making it possible for anyone else to marry a courtesan. Immediately after this he seized the power of the Emperor, veiling his usurpation with a transparent pretext: for he was proclaimed colleague of his uncle as Emperor of the Romans by the questionable legality of an election inspired by terror.

So Justinian and Theodora ascended the imperial throne three days before Easter, a time, indeed, when even making visits or greeting one's friends is forbidden. And not many days later Justin died of an illness, after a reign of nine years. Justinian was now sole monarch, together, of course, with Theodora.

Thus it was that Theodora, though born and brought up as I have related, rose to royal dignity over all obstacles. For no thought of shame came to Justinian in marrying her, though he might have taken his pick of the noblest born, most highly educated, most modest, carefully nurtured, virtuous and beautiful virgins of all the ladies in the whole Roman Empire: a maiden, as they say, with upstanding breasts. Instead, he preferred to make his own: what, had been common to all men, alike, careless of all her revealed history, took in wedlock a woman who was not only guilty of every other contamination but boasted of her many abortions.

I need hardly mention any other proof of the character of this man: for all the perversity of his soul was completely displayed in this union; which alone was ample interpreter, witness, and historian of his shamelessness. For when a man once disregards the disgrace of his actions and is willing to brave the contempt of society, no path of lawlessness is thereafter taboo to him; but with unflinching countenance he advances, easily and without a scruple, to acts of the deepest infamy.

However, not a single member of even the Senate, seeing this disgrace befalling the State, dared to complain or forbid the event; but all of them bowed down before her as if she were a goddess. Nor was there a priest who showed any resentment, but all hastened to greet her as Highness. And the populace who had seen her before on the stage, directly raised its hands to proclaim itself her slave in fact and in name. Nor did any soldier grumble at being ordered to risk the perils of war for the benefit of Theodora: nor was there any man on earth who ventured to oppose her.

Confronted with this disgrace, they all yielded, I suppose, to necessity, for it was as if Fate were giving proof of its power to control mortal affairs as malignantly as it pleases: showing that its decrees need not always be according to reason or human propriety. Thus does Destiny sometimes raise mortals suddenly to lofty heights in defiance of reason, in challenge to all out cries of injustice; but admits no obstacle, urging on his favorites to the appointed goal without let or hindrance. But as this is the will of God, so let it befall and be written.

Now Theodora was fair of face and of a very graceful, though small, person; her complexion was moderately colorful, if somewhat pale; and her eyes were dazzling and vivacious. All eternity would not be long enough to allow one to tell her escapades while she was on the stage, but the few details I have mentioned above should be sufficient to demonstrate the woman's character to future generations.

What she and her husband did together must now be briefly described: for neither did anything without the consent of the other. For some time it was generally supposed they were totally different in mind and action; but later it was revealed that their apparent disagreement had been arranged so that their subjects might not unanimously revolt against them, but instead be divided in opinion.

Thus they split the Christians into two parties, each pretending to take the part of one side, thus confusing both . . . ; and then they ruined both political factions. Theodora feigned to support the Blues with all her power, encouraging them to take the offensive against the opposing party and perform the most outrageous deeds of violence; while Justinian, affecting to be vexed and secretly jealous of her, also pretended he could not openly oppose her orders. And thus they gave the impression often that they were acting in opposition. Then he would rule that the Blues must be punished for their crimes, and she would angrily complain that against her will she was defeated by her husband. . . .

And in legal disputes each of the two would pretend to favor one of the litigants, and compel the man with the worse case to win: and so they robbed both disputants of most of the property at issue.

In the same way, the Emperor, taking many persons into his intimacy, gave them offices by power of which they could defraud the State to the limits of their ambition. And as soon as they had collected enough plunder, they would fall out of favor with Theodora, and straightway be ruined. At first he would affect great sympathy in their behalf, but soon he would somehow lose his confidence in them, and an air of doubt would darken his zeal in their behalf. Then Theodora would use them shamefully, while he, unconscious as it were of what was being done to them, confiscated their properties and boldly enjoyed their wealth. By such well-planned hypocrisies they confused the public and, pretending to be at variance with each other, were able to establish a firm and mutual tyranny.

5

KALIDASA
Shakuntala, c. 400

In addition to ideas of eroticized devotion discussed in the first selection, Indian culture even earlier developed an idea of love that resembled the European romantic idea. We see this idea in the plays of Kalidasa (c. 400 C.E.), one of the greatest Indian dramatists. His play *Shakuntala*, a classic of the Hindu literary tradition, tells the story of a love between a king and a hermit girl. The two fall passionately in love with each other although they have barely exchanged words. Despite their different stations in life, they are equally overcome by *kama*, one of the four great forces in the Hindu culture — the force of love and physical attraction.

In this selection from Act 3 (of seven acts), Shakuntalā, who says she loves the king, is urged by her friends, Priyamvadā and Anasūyā, who say they "don't know what it is to be in love," to write a letter to the king, who overhears their conversation. The love of two people from radically different social backgrounds is a common theme in romantic stories. How is this theme developed here? How does such a "socially imbalanced" love threaten social stability? How does it raise questions about passion and power that help distinguish love from sex or marriage? How does an idea of propriety (proper behavior) balance the threat of passion?

THINKING HISTORICALLY

Compare the author's attention to physical signs of love with Ulrich's love story. In what ways is this story of love similar to European ideas of romantic love? In what ways is it different?

PRIYAMVADĀ   Compose a love letter and I'll hide it in a flower. I'll deliver it to his hand on the pretext of bringing a gift from our offering to the deity.
ANASŪYĀ   This subtle plan pleases me. What does Shakuntalā say?
SHAKUNTALĀ   I'll try my friend's plan.
PRIYAMVADĀ   Then compose a poem to declare your love!
SHAKUNTALĀ   I'm thinking, but my heart trembles with fear that he'll reject me.

Source: Kalidasa, *Shakuntala*, Act III, trans. Barbara Stoler Miller, in *Theater of Memory: The Plays of Kalidasa*, ed. Barbara Stoler Miller (New York: Columbia University Press, 1984), 114–18.

KING [IN HIDING]   (*delighted*)
> The man whom you fear will reject you
> waits longing to love you, timid girl—
> a suitor may be lucky or cursed,
> but his goodness of fortune always wins.

BOTH FRIENDS   Why do you devalue your own virtues? Who would keep autumn moonlight from cooling the body by covering it with a bit of cloth?

SHAKUNTALĀ (*smiling*)   I'm following your advice. (*She sits thinking*)

KING   As I stare at her, my eyes forget to blink.
> She arches an eyebrow
> struggling to compose the verse—
> the down rises on her cheek,
> showing the passion she feels.

SHAKUNTALĀ   I have thought of a song, but there's nothing I can write it on.

PRIYAMVADĀ   Engrave the letters with your nails on this lotus leaf! It's as delicate as a parrot's breast.

SHAKUNTALĀ   (*miming what Priyamvadā described*) Listen and tell me if this makes sense!

BOTH FRIENDS   We're both paying attention.

SHAKUNTALĀ (*sings*)
> I don't know your heart,
> but day and night Love
> violently burns my limbs
> with desire for you, cruel man.

KING (*having been listening to them, entering suddenly*)
> Love torments you, slender girl,
> but he utterly consumes me—
> daylight makes the moon fade
> when it folds the white lotus.

BOTH FRIENDS (*looking, rising with delight*)   Welcome to the swift success of love's desire! (*Shakuntalā tries to rise.*)

KING   Don't strain yourself!
> Limbs on a couch of crushed flowers
> and fragrant tips of lotus stalks
> are too frail from suffering
> to perform ceremonial acts . . .

ANASŪYĀ   We've heard that kings have many loves. Will our beloved friend become a sorrow to her relatives after you've spent your time with her?

KING   Noble lady, enough of this! I may have many wives, but my royal line rests on two foundations: the sea-bound earth and this friend of yours!

BOTH FRIENDS   We are assured.

PRIYAMVADĀ   (*casting a glance*) Anasūyā this fawn is looking for its mother. Let's take it to her! (*They both begin to leave.*)

SHAKUNTALĀ   Come back! Don't leave me unprotected!

BOTH FRIENDS   The protector of the earth is at your side.

SHAKUNTALĀ   Why have they gone?

KING   Don't be alarmed! A servant worships at your side.
   Shall I set moist winds in motion
   with lotus-leaf fans to cool your pain,
   or put your pale red lotus feet on my lap
   and stroke them, voluptuous girl?

SHAKUNTALĀ   I cannot sin against those I respect! (*standing as if she wants to leave*)

KING   Beautiful Shakuntalā, the day is still hot.
   Why leave this couch of flowers
   and its shield of lotus leaves
   to venture into the heat
   with your frail wan limbs?
   (*Saying this, he forces her to turn around.*)

SHAKUNTALĀ   Puru king, control yourself! Though I'm burning with love I'm not free to give myself to you.

KING   Don't fear your elders! The father of your family knows the law. When he finds out, he will not fault you. Many kings' daughters first marry in secret and their fathers bless them.

SHAKUNTALĀ   Release me! I must ask my friends' advice!

KING   Yes, I shall release you.

SHAKUNTALĀ   When?

KING
   Only let my thirsting mouth
   gently drink from your lips,
   the way a bee sips nectar
   from a fragile virgin blossom.

6

MURASAKI SHIKIBU

The Tale of Genji, c. 1000

The *Tale of Genji* is, by some measures, the world's first novel. It was written by Murasaki Shikibu, a woman at the Japanese court, probably in the first decade after the year 1000. During the Heian period (794–1185) of Japanese history, women in the Japanese aristocracy differentiated their culture from the Chinese one that had dominated it since the seventh century.

Source: Murasaki Shikibu, *The Tale of Genji*, trans. Royall Tyler (New York: Penguin Books, 2001), 155–61.

In *The Tale of Genji* we also see signs of multiple marriages and numerous lovers, consorts, and courtesans among the Heian aristocracy. The emperor had been married but preferred a lower-class courtesan, Lady Kiritsubo, who died shortly after giving birth to Genji. Lady Kokiden, a more powerful mistress of the emperor, ensured that her son, Suzku, would outrank Genji as the next emperor. She forced the emperor to make Genji a commoner and to make him go into exile. After Lady Kiritsubo's death, the despondent emperor met a princess, Fujitsubo, who reminded him of Kiritsubo. She became the emperor's favorite as well as the love of her stepson, Genji, who returned from exile. Fujitsubo bore the emperor a son whom everyone but she and Genji knew to be the emperor's, and that son became the Heir Apparent. Genji, cut off from intimate contact with Fujitsubo, and uninterested in his wife, played lover and patron to the young Murasaki, who bore him a future emperor, and carried out various affairs and liaisons—one of which is described in this selection. What does this relationship between Genji and one of the younger sisters of Kokiden tell you about sex, love, and marriage in upper-class Heian society?

This selection also reveals much about the culture of the Japanese court. Notice the cultivation of music, dance, and poetry among the court nobility. What, if anything, does this display of sensitivity have to do with ideas of love and marriage? What signs do you see here of the persistence of Chinese culture in Heian Japan?

Also, notice the absence of monogamy in the court. The emperor is married but has taken in turn three consorts: Kokiden, Kiritsubo, and now Fujitsubo. What is the relationship between marriage and sex in this society? What does that tell you about the mores of the time?

THINKING HISTORICALLY

Would you call this a story of romantic love? In what ways is the love Lady Murasaki describes similar to, or different from, the love Andreas Capellanus describes in selection 3? What aspects of Heian Japanese culture are different from the culture of medieval Europe? Is the dominant upper-class idea of love in Japan during this period different from that of Europe? How is this Japanese idea of love and marriage different from that of India?

A little past the twentieth of the second month, His Majesty held a party to honor the cherry tree before the Shishinden.[1] To his left and right were enclosures for the Empress and the Heir Apparent, whose pleasure it was to be present according to his wishes. The Kokiden

[1] The main hall at the Kyoto Imperial Palace. [Ed.]

Consort took offense whenever Her Majesty received such respect, but she came, for she would not have missed the event.

It was a lovely day, with a bright sky and birdsong to gladden the heart, when those who prided themselves on their skill—Princes, senior nobles, and all—drew their rhymes and began composing Chinese verses. As usual, Genji's very voice announcing, "I have received the character 'spring,'" resembled no other. The Secretary Captain came next. He was nervous about how he might look, after Genji, but he maintained a pleasing composure, and his voice rang out with impressive dignity. Most of the rest appeared tense and self-conscious. Naturally, those belonging to the lesser ranks were even more in awe of the genius of His Majesty and the Heir Apparent, which stood out even then, when so many others excelled at that sort of thing. They advanced in dread across the immaculate expanse of the broad court, only to make a painful labor of their simple task. . . .

When the time came to declaim the poems, the Reader could not get on with Genji's because the gathering repeated and commented admiringly on every line. Even the Doctors were impressed. His Majesty was undoubtedly pleased, since to him Genji was the glory of every such occasion.

The Empress wondered while she contemplated Genji's figure how the Heir Apparent's mother could dislike him so, and she lamented that she herself liked him all too well.

"If with common gaze I could look upon that flower just as others do,
why should it occur to me to find in him any flaw?"

she murmured. One wonders how anyone could have passed on words meant only for herself.

The festival ended late that night. Once the senior nobles had withdrawn, once the Empress and the Heir Apparent were gone and all lay quiet in the beauty of brilliant moonlight, Genji remained drunkenly unwilling to grant that the night was over. His Majesty's gentlewomen all being asleep, he stole off toward the Fujitsubo, in case fortune should favor him at this odd hour, but the door through which he might have approached her was locked, and so he went on, sighing but undeterred, to the long aisle of the Kokiden, where he found the third door open. Hardly anyone seemed to be about, since the Consort had gone straight to wait on His Majesty. The door to the inner rooms was open, too. There was no sound.

This is how people get themselves into trouble, he thought, stepping silently up into the hall. Everyone must be asleep. But could it be? He heard a young and pretty voice, surely no common gentlewoman's, coming his way and singing, "Peerless the night with a misty moon . . ." He happily caught her sleeve.

"Oh, don't! Who are you?" She was obviously frightened.
"You need not be afraid.

That you know so well the beauty of the deep night leads me to assume
you have with the setting moon nothing like a casual bond!"

With this he put his arms around her, lay her down, and closed the door.
Her outrage and dismay gave her delicious appeal.

"A man—there is a man here!" she cried, trembling.

"I may do as I please, and calling for help will not save you. Just
be still!"

She knew his voice and felt a little better. She did not want to seem
cold or standoffish, despite her shock. He must have been quite drunk,
because he felt he must have her, and she was young and pliant enough
that she probably never thought seriously of resisting him.

She pleased him very much, and he was upset to find daybreak soon
upon them. She herself seemed torn. "Do tell me your name!" he pleaded.
"How can I keep in touch with you? Surely you do not want this to
be all!"

With sweet grace she replied,

"If with my sad fate I were just now to vanish, would you really
come—ah, I wonder!—seeking me over grassy wastes of moor?"

"I understand. Please forgive me.

While I strove to learn in what quarter I should seek my
dewdrop's dwelling, wind, I fear, would be blowing out across
the rustling moors.

We might be frank with each other. Or would you prefer to evade me?"

He had no sooner spoken than gentlewomen began rising noisily,
and there was much coming and going between the Kokiden and His
Majesty's apartments. They were both in peril. He merely gave her his
fan as a token, took hers, and went away.

Some of the many women at the Kiritsubo were awake. "He certainly keeps up his secret exploring, doesn't he!" they whispered, poking
each other and pretending all the while to be asleep.

He came in and lay down, but he stayed awake. What a lovely girl!
She must be one of the Consort's younger sisters—the fifth or sixth, I
suppose, since she had not known a man before.[2] . . . It was all very
difficult, and he was unlikely to find out which one she was even if he
tried. She did not seem eager to break it off, though—so why did she
not leave me any way to correspond with her? These ruminations of his
no doubt confirmed his interest in her, but still, when he thought of *her,*

---

[2] Genji's brother. [Ed.]

he could not help admiring how superbly inaccessible she was in comparison.

The second party was to be today, and he was busy from morning to night. He played the *sō no koto*. The event was more elegant and amusing than the one the day before. Dawn was near when Fujitsubo went to wait on His Majesty.

Desperate to know whether she of the moon at dawn would now be leaving the palace, he set the boundlessly vigilant Yoshikiyo and Koremitsu to keep watch. When he withdrew from His Majesty's presence, they gave him their report. "Several carriages have just left from the north gate, where they were waiting discreetly," they said. "Relatives of His Majesty's ladies were there, and when the Fourth Rank Lieutenant and the Right Controller rushed out to see the party off, we gathered that it must have been the Kokiden Consort who was leaving. Several other quite distinguished ladies were obviously in the party, too. There were three carriages in all."

Genji's heart beat fast. How was he to learn which one she was? What if His Excellency her father found out and made a great fuss over him? That would be highly unwelcome, as long as he still knew so little about her. At any rate, he could not endure his present ignorance, and he lay in an agony of frustration about what to do. He thought fondly of his young lady. How bored she must be, and probably dejected as well, since he had not seen her for days!

The keepsake fan was a triple cherry blossom layered one with a misty moon reflected in water painted on its colored side—not an original piece of work but welcome because so clearly favored by its owner. Her talk of "grassy wastes of moor" troubled him, and he wrote on the fan, which he then kept with him,

> "All that I now feel, I have never felt before, as the moon at dawn
> melts away before my eyes into the boundless heavens." . . .

The lady of the misty moon remembered that fragile dream with great sadness. Her father had decided that her presentation to the Heir Apparent was to take place in the fourth month, and the prospect filled her with despair. Meanwhile her lover, who thought he knew how to pursue her if he wished, had not yet actually found out which sister she was, and besides, he hesitated to associate himself with a family from which he had nothing but censure. Then, a little after the twentieth of the third month, the Minister of the Right held an archery contest attended by many senior nobles and Princes and followed immediately by a party for the wisteria blossoms.

The cherry blossom season was over, but two of His Excellency's trees must have consented to wait, for they were in late and glorious bloom. He had had his recently rebuilt residence specially decorated for the Princesses' donning of the train. Everything was in the latest style, in consonance with His Excellency's own florid taste.

His Excellency had extended an invitation to Genji as well, one day when they met at court, and Genji's failure to appear disappointed him greatly, for to his mind this absence cast a pall over the gathering. . . .

Genji dressed with great care, and the sun had set by the time he arrived to claim his welcome.

He wore a grape-colored train-robe under a cherry blossom dress cloak of sheer figured silk. Among the formal cloaks worn by everyone else, his costume displayed the extravagant elegance of a Prince, and his grand entry was a sensation. The very blossoms were abashed, and the gathering took some time to regain its animation.

He played beautifully, and it was quite late by the time he left again, on the pretext of having drunk so much that he was not well. The First and Third Princesses were in the main house, and he went to sit by the door that opened from there toward the east. The lattice shutters were up, and all the women were near the veranda, since this was the corner where the wisteria was blooming. Their sleeves spilled showily under the blinds as though for the New Year's mumming, but Genji disapproved and only found his thoughts going to Fujitsubo.

"I felt unwell to begin with," he said, "and then I was obliged to drink until now I am quite ill. May I be allowed to hide in Their Highnesses' company, if it is not too forward of me to ask?" He thrust himself halfway through the blind in the double doorway.

"Oh, no, please!" one cried. "Surely it is for little people like us to claim protection from the great!"

Genji saw that these ladies, although not of commanding rank, were not ordinary young gentlewomen either. Their stylish distinction was clear. The fragrance of incense hung thickly in the air, and the rustling of silks conveyed ostentatious wealth, for this was a household that preferred modish display to the deeper appeal of discreet good taste. The younger sister had no doubt taken possession of the doorway because Their Highnesses wished to look out from there.

He should not have accepted the challenge, but it pleased him, and he wondered with beating heart which one she was. "Alas," he sang as innocently as could be, still leaning against a pillar, "my fan is mine no more, for I have met with woe . . ."

"What a very odd man from Koma!" The one who answered seemed not to understand him.

Another said nothing but only sighed and sighed. He leaned toward her, took her hand through her standing curtain, and said at a guess,

*"How sadly I haunt the slope of Mount Irusa, where the crescent
sets, yearning just to see again the faint moon that I saw then!*

Why should that be?"

This must have been too much for her, because she replied,

"Were it really so that your heart goes straight and true, would you lose your way even in the dark of night, when no moon is in the sky?"

Yes, it was her voice. He was delighted, though at the same time . . .

7

ZHOU DAGUAN

Sex in the City of Angkor, 1297

Angkor, the great Kymer or Cambodian civilization of the Middle Ages, originated in the early ninth century. At its zenith in the twelfth and thirteenth centuries, its empire included the southern halves of modern Laos and Thailand as well as all of modern Cambodia. In 1296 Zhou Daguan was sent on a mission to Cambodia by the Mongol emperor of China, Temur Khan, the grandson and successor of Kubilai Khan. He stayed in the recently completed capital, which still stands today as Angkor Thom, and wrote his record of the country and its people. This is a brief selection from what remains of that account. What does it tell you about family life and attitudes toward sex and sexuality in Angkor?

THINKING HISTORICALLY

Zhou Daguan makes no comparisons with other cultures, but implicit in almost every statement is a comparison with his own Chinese culture. What surprises him? What does he find strange or even offensive? What do his responses tell us about the differences between Chinese and Cambodian customs or ideas regarding sex and love? Compare Cambodian ideas about sex with those in Europe, Japan, and India. What do you think explains these differences? What seems to be the impact of different religions on a culture's attitudes toward sex and sexuality?

Source: Zhou Daguan, *A Record of Cambodia: The Land and Its People*, trans. Peter Harris (Chiang Mai, Thailand: Silkworm Books, 2007), 54–59.

6
The People

The one thing people know about southern barbarians is that they are coarse, ugly, and very black. I know nothing at all about those living on islands in the sea or in remote villages, but this is certainly true of those in the ordinary localities. When it comes to the women of the palace and women from the *nanpeng*—that is, the great houses—there are many who are as white as jade, but that is because they do not see the light of the sun.

Generally, men and women alike wrap a cloth around their waist, but apart from that they leave their smooth chests and breasts uncovered. They wear their hair in a topknot and go barefoot. This is the case even with the wives of the king.

The king has five wives, one principal wife and one for each of the four cardinal points. Below them, I have heard, there are four or five thousand concubines and other women of the palace. They also divide themselves up by rank. They only go out of the palace on rare occasions.

Every time I went inside the palace to see the king, he always came out with his principal wife, and sat at the gold window in the main room. The palace women lined up by rank in two galleries below the window. They moved to and fro to steal looks at us, and I got a very full view of them. Any family with a female beauty is bound to have her summoned into the palace.

At the lower level there are also the so-called *chenjialan*, servant women who come and go providing services inside the palace and number at least a thousand or two. In their case they all have husbands and live mixed in among ordinary people. They shave back the hair on the top of their head, which gives them the look of northerners with their "open canal" partings.[1] They paint the area with vermilion, which they also paint on to either side of their temples. In this way they mark themselves out as being *chenjialan*. They are the only women who can go into the palace; no one else below them gets to go in. There is a continuous stream of them on the roads in front of and behind the inner palace.

Apart from wearing their hair in a topknot, ordinary women do not have ornaments in their hair like pins or combs. They just wear gold bracelets on their arms and gold rings on their fingers. The *chenjialan* and the women in the palace all wear them too. Men and women usually perfume themselves with scents made up of a mixture of sandalwood, musk, and other fragrances.

Every family practices Buddhism.

There are a lot of effeminate men in the country who go round the markets every day in groups of a dozen or so. They frequently solicit the attentions of Chinese in return for generous gifts. It is shameful and wicked.

---

[1] Hair pulled back to show a wide part, which is then painted red. [Ed.]

7
Childbirth

As soon as they give birth the local women prepare some hot rice, mix it with salt, and put it into the entrance of the vagina. They usually take it out after a day and a night. Because of this, women do not fall sick when they are giving birth, and usually contract so as to be like young girls again.

When I first heard this I was surprised by it, and seriously doubted whether it was true. Then a girl in the family I was staying with gave birth to a child, and I got a full picture of what happened to her. The day after the birth, she took up the baby right away and went to bathe in the river with it. It was a truly amazing thing to see.

Then again, I have often heard people say that the local women are very lascivious, so that a day or two after giving birth they are immediately coupling with their husbands. If a husband doesn't meet his wife's wishes he will be abandoned right away, as Zhu Maichen[2] was. If the husband happens to have work to do far away, if it is only for a few nights that is all right, but if it is for more than ten nights or so the wife will say, "I'm not a ghost — why am I sleeping alone?" This is how strong their sexual feelings are. That said, I have heard that there are some who exercise self-restraint.

The women age very quickly indeed, the reason being that they marry and have children young. A twenty- or thirty-year-old woman is like a Chinese woman of forty or fifty.

8
Young Girls

When a family is bringing up a daughter, her father and mother are sure to wish her well by saying, "May you have what really matters — in future may you marry thousands and thousands of husbands!"

When they are seven to nine years old — if they are girls from wealthy homes — or only when they are eleven — if they come from the poorest families — girls have to get a Buddhist monk or a Daoist to take away their virginity, in what is called *zhentan*.

So every year, in the fourth month of the Chinese calendar, the authorities select a day and announce it countrywide. The families whose daughters should be ready for *zhentan* let the authorities know in advance. The authorities first give them a huge candle. They make a mark

---

[2] A Han dynasty folktale of a poor scholar, Zhu Maichen, whose wife left him for another man. [Ed.]

on it, and arrange for it to be lit at dusk on the day in question. When the mark is reached the time for *zhentan* has come.

A month, fifteen days, or ten days beforehand, the parents have to choose a Buddhist monk or a Daoist. This depends on where the Buddhist and Daoist temples are. The temples often also have their own clients. Officials' families and wealthy homes all get the good, saintly Buddhist monks in advance, while the poor do not have the leisure to choose.

Wealthy and noble families give the monks wine, rice, silk and other cloth, betel nuts, silverware, and the like, goods weighing as much as a hundred piculs and worth two or three hundred ounces of Chinese silver. The smallest amount a family gives weighs ten to forty piculs, depending on how thrifty the family is.

The reason poor families only start dealing with the matter when their girls reach eleven is simply that it is hard for them to manage these things. Some wealthy families do also give money for poor girls' *zhentan*, which they call doing good work. Moreover in any one year a monk can only take charge of one girl, and once he has agreed to and accepted the benefits, he cannot make another commitment.

On the night in question a big banquet with drums and music is laid on for relatives and neighbors. A tall canopy is put up outside the entrance to the house, and various clay figurines of people and animals are laid out on top of it. There can be ten or more of these, or just three or four—or none at all in the case of poor families. They all have to do with events long ago, and they usually stay up for seven days before people start taking them down.

At dusk the monk is met with palanquin, parasol, drums, and music and brought back to the house. Two pavilions are put up, made of colorful silk. The girl sits inside one, and the monk inside the other. You can't understand what he's saying because the drums and music are making so much noise—on that night the night curfew is lifted. I have heard that when the time comes the monk goes into a room with the girl and takes away her virginity with his hand, which he then puts into some wine. Some say the parents, relatives and neighbors mark their foreheads with it, others say they all taste it. Some say the monk and the girl have sex together, others say they don't. They don't let Chinese see this, though, so I don't really know.

Toward dawn the monk is seen off again with palanquin, parasol, drums, and music. Afterward silk, cloth, and the like have to be given to the monk to redeem the body of the girl. If this is not done the girl will be the property of the monk for her whole life and won't be able to marry anyone else.

The instance of this that I saw took place early on the sixth night of the fourth month of the year *dingyou* in the Dade reign period (1297).

Before this happens, the parents always sleep together with their daughter; afterward, she is excluded from the room and goes wherever she wants without restraint or precaution. When it comes to marriage, there is a ceremony with the giving of gifts, but it is just a simple, easygoing affair. There are many who get married only after leading a dissolute life, something local custom regards as neither shameful nor odd.

On a *zhentan* night up to ten or more families from a single alley may be involved. On the city streets people are out meeting Buddhist monks and Daoists, going this way and that, and the sounds of drums and music are everywhere.

9
Slaves

Family slaves are all savages purchased to work as servants. Most families have a hundred or more of them; a few have ten or twenty; only the very poorest have none at all. The savages are people from the mountains. They have their own way of categorizing themselves, but are commonly called "thieving Zhuang." When they come to the city, none of them dares go in and out of people's homes. They are so despised that if there is a quarrel between two city dwellers, it only takes one of them to be called a Zhuang for hatred to enter into the marrow of his bones. . . .

The males and females mate together, but the master would never have reason to have intercourse with them. Sometimes a Chinese who comes to Cambodia and has long been single will act carelessly, but as soon as he has had relations with one of them the master will hear of it, and the following day he will refuse to sit with the Chinese, on the grounds that he has come into contact with a savage.

Sometimes one of them will have intercourse with an outsider, to the point of becoming pregnant and having a baby. But the master won't try and find out where it is from, since the mother has no status and he will profit from the child, who can eventually become his slave.

■ REFLECTIONS

Cultural comparisons, formerly a staple of historical studies, have come under harsh criticism in recent years, and for good reason. The ambitious general histories and philosophical anthropologies written at the beginning of the twentieth century were full of gross generalizations about the "essence" of various cultures and the advantages of one civilization over another. These grand overviews, predating serious empirical studies of African, Asian, and Latin American societies, invariably argued that such "premodern," or "traditional," societies lacked some critical cultural attribute honed in Europe that enabled Europeans to conquer the world after 1500. It goes without saying that these sweeping interpretations were written by Europeans and their North American descendants.

The comparative history of love got caught up in the academic whirlwind of historians and anthropologists, who, in seeking to explain European expansion, industrialization, and modernization, argued that conjugal love—the nonromantic familial variety—created family units in Europe and America that were different from those in other parts of the world. They saw the Western family as the stimulus of modern society. Some also found the Western practices of dating, mate choosing, and individual decision making unique.

Toward the end of the twentieth century, in a postcolonial age that had grown skeptical of Western claims of objectivity, cultural comparisons were seen for what they often were—thinly veiled exercises in self-aggrandizement and implicit rationales for Western domination. For example, Western scientific racism, in which some Western anthropologists and scientists divided the world by cranial sizes, nose width, or culture-bound intelligence tests (always putting themselves on top), lost favor after its rationale was exposed as the foundation for the horrific genocides of World War II.

There is a growing debate about the strategy of explaining Western growth and dominance by looking for Western traits that non-Western cultures lacked. But whether or not such a strategy is wise, we would be foolish to stop trying to compare cultures. Cultures are rich repositories of human thought and behavior; they differ over time and across the globe; and the process of comparison is essential to learning and creating knowledge. In any case, historical comparisons should not be about establishing which culture is better or worse. Culture, almost by definition, is good for the particular society in which it arises. That people in different parts of the world have found different ways of dealing with the same human conditions should not surprise us. To call some better than others is meaningless.

What we can learn from cultural comparison is something about the malleability of human nature and the range of options available to us. We also learn much about ourselves when we peer at another face in the mirror. The differences leap out at us over time as well as space. In some ways, Ulrich's mirror is as foreign as Genji's. In other ways, it is not. In response to an age of prejudice and cultural stereotyping, many well-intentioned people choose to deny or celebrate cultural differences. A far wiser course is to understand what these differences reveal about our world and us.

10

The First Crusade

*Muslims, Christians, and Jews during the
First Crusade, 1095–1099*

■ HISTORICAL CONTEXT

In the eleventh century the Seljuk Turks, recently converted to Islam,
emerged from the grasslands of Central Asia to conquer much of the
land held by the weakened caliphate at Baghdad, the Egyptian Fatimid
Caliphate, and the Byzantine Empire. By 1095 the Seljuks controlled
the important cities of Baghdad and Jerusalem and threatened to take
Constantinople.

Alexius, the Byzantine emperor, appealed to the Roman pope for
help and found a receptive audience. Pope Urban II was continuing
recent papal efforts to strengthen the Roman church's power over the
scattered nobles and princes of European feudal society. He sought to
free the church of abuses such as the sale of church offices and to bring
peace to the fractious countryside, riddled with private armies of knights
that fought each other or preyed on Christian peasants.

Urban II's efforts to revitalize Christendom found a mission in the
Seljuk occupation of Jerusalem, and in 1095 the First Crusade began
with his urgent call for Christians to rout the new Muslim occupiers
of the Holy Land. (See Map 10.1.)

The Crusades were an important chapter in the religious and military history—or more broadly, the cultural and political history—of
both European and Islamic civilizations. They brought large numbers
of European Christians and Muslims into contact with each other in a
struggle and dialogue that would last for centuries.

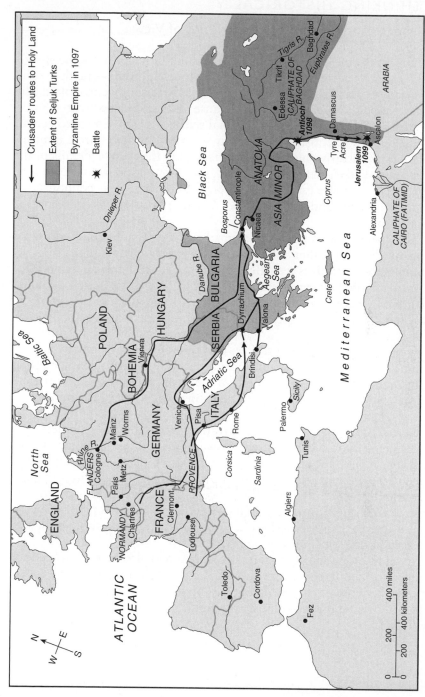

Map 10.1 The First Crusade, 1095–1099.

Crusaders' routes to Holy Land

Extent of Seljuk Turks

Byzantine Empire in 1097

Battle

ATLANTIC OCEAN

North Sea

Baltic Sea

ENGLAND

FLANDERS

NORMANDY

Paris

Chartres

FRANCE

Clermont

Toulouse

PROVENCE

GERMANY

Cologne

Rhine R.

Mainz

Worms

Metz

BOHEMIA

POLAND

Vienna

HUNGARY

Danube R.

Venice

Pisa

ITALY

Rome

Brindisi

Adriatic Sea

SERBIA

BULGARIA

Dyrrachium

Valona

Aegean Sea

Corsica

Sardinia

Palermo

Sicily

Tunis

Algiers

Fez

Toledo

Cordova

Mediterranean Sea

Crete

Dnieper R.

Kiev

Black Sea

Bosporus

Constantinople

Nicaea

ASIA MINOR

ANATOLIA

Cyprus

Alexandria

CALIPHATE OF CAIRO (FATIMID)

Tyre

Acre

Jerusalem 1099

Ascalon

Damascus

Antioch 1098

Edessa

Tikrit

CALIPHATE OF BAGHDAD

Baghdad

Tigris R.

Euphrates R.

ARABIA

0   200   400 miles

0   200   400 kilometers

N

E

S

W

361

■ THINKING HISTORICALLY

Understanding Narrative and Point of View

When most people think of history, they think of narrative—the story itself. Narrative settles on specific details—one at a time—neither indiscriminately nor as examples of general laws, but usually chronologically, as they happen, woven in a chain of cause and effect. The "truth" of narrative is different from that of social science, which aspires to generality. The social scientist writes, "Holy wars among states are a dime a dozen." The narrative historian immerses us in the specific details of the battle: "The Duke's trumpets sounded, the shimmering line swayed forward, the long lances came down to point at the foe, their pennons shadowing the ground before them." A good narrative has the appeal of a good story.

The problem with narrative stems from the same factors that make it so appealing. By telling a believable story, narrative bypasses our critical faculties. It gives us little if any room to stop and question. We are carried along, sometimes enthralled, by a story that seems to build its truth one incontrovertible fact at a time. If we accept the legitimacy of the narrator, we have little basis for opening the story to analysis. Of course, not all narrators are interested in telling the truth, and even those who are may make mistakes. But even when they hope to be truthful and get their facts right (as do the authors in this chapter), they are invariably telling one truth out of many possible truths, and the one they tell has much to do with their own knowledge, assumptions, interests, and perspectives.

In this chapter you will read narratives from different perspectives. Consequently, you will gain greater awareness of other possible views the further you read. But there is always more to learn about any subject, and we will not presume any knowledge beyond this chapter. Therefore, we will only begin the process of analyzing narrative by asking you what questions you might ask about an author's point of view, bias, or interest. You should build on the attention to author, audience, and agenda developed in Chapter 5.

In addition to analyzing narratives, you will also be encouraged to write your own. In this way you will gain a better understanding of perhaps the most important, and certainly the most popular, form of historical presentation, both by examining its structure and by doing it yourself.

1

FULCHER OF CHARTRES

An Account of Pope Urban's Speech at Clermont, c. 1100–1127

The Chronicle of Fulcher of Chartres is one of the few firsthand accounts of the First Crusade. Born in 1059, Fulcher was likely present at the Council of Clermont, where Pope Urban II issued his call for the First Crusade in 1095. In response to Urban's plea, Fulcher joined the army of Robert of Normandy, Stephen of Blois, and Robert of Flanders. He then joined Baldwin of Boulogne in Edessa (see Map 10.1, p. 361), the first of a number of feudal Crusader states along the eastern Mediterranean, and later visited Jerusalem after its capture by the Crusaders. In 1100, when Baldwin became king of Jerusalem, Fulcher returned to Jerusalem to continue as Baldwin's chaplain. There he wrote his history from 1101 until about 1128. The reliability of Fulcher's Chronicles, therefore, depends on his important contacts as well as his own observations. In addition, Fulcher had access to at least two important collections of letters and documents in Jerusalem.

Why, according to Fulcher, did Pope Urban II call the Council of Clermont? What did he hope to accomplish? How important among the pope's concerns was the capture of Jerusalem? How important was strengthening the church?

THINKING HISTORICALLY

What indications do you see in Urban's speech that the capture of Jerusalem was only part of his agenda, perhaps even an afterthought? Fulcher's account of the speech and his section on "events after the council" mainly address the issue of Jerusalem. That emphasis is appropriate in a history of the crusade, since historical narrative must follow a particular thread. If Fulcher had written a history of church reforms rather than of the First Crusade, what "events after the council" might he have included?

A narrative, or story, is different from an explanation. What do you think were the causes of the First Crusade, based on what you have read so far? How is your answer an explanation rather than a narrative? How would you make your answer more of a narrative?

Source: *The First Crusade: The Chronicle of Fulcher of Chartres and Other Source Materials*, 2nd ed., ed. Edward Peters (Philadelphia: University of Pennsylvania Press, 1998), 49–55.

I. The Council of Clermont

1. In the year 1095 from the Lord's Incarnation, with Henry reigning in Germany as so-called emperor,[1] and with Philip as king in France, manifold evils were growing in all parts of Europe because of wavering faith. In Rome ruled Pope Urban II, a man distinguished in life and character, who always strove wisely and actively to raise the status of the Holy Church above all things.

2. He saw that the faith of Christianity was being destroyed to excess by everybody, by the clergy as well as by the laity. He saw that peace was altogether discarded by the princes of the world, who were engaged in incessant warlike contention and quarreling among themselves. He saw the wealth of the land being pillaged continuously. He saw many of the vanquished, wrongfully taken prisoner and very cruelly thrown into foulest dungeons, either ransomed for a high price or, tortured by the triple torments of hunger, thirst, and cold, blotted out by a death hidden from the world. He saw holy places violated; monasteries and villas burned. He saw that no one was spared of any human suffering, and that things divine and human alike were held in derision.

3. He heard, too, that the interior regions of Romania, where the Turks ruled over the Christians, had been perniciously subjected in a savage attack.[2] Moved by long-suffering compassion and by love of God's will, he descended the mountains to Gaul, and in Auvergne he called for a council to congregate from all sides at a suitable time at a city called Clermont. Three hundred and ten bishops and abbots, who had been advised beforehand by messengers, were present.

4. Then, on the day set aside for it, he called them together to himself and, in an eloquent address, carefully made the cause of the meeting known to them. In the plaintive voice of an aggrieved Church, he expressed great lamentation, and held a long discourse with them about the raging tempests of the world, which have been mentioned, because faith was undermined.

5. One after another, he beseechingly exhorted them all, with renewed faith, to spur themselves in great earnestness to overcome the Devil's devices and to try to restore the Holy Church, most unmercifully weakened by the wicked, to its former honorable status.

---

[1] Henry IV (1056–1106). Fulcher uses the term "so-called emperor," since Henry was not recognized as rightful emperor by adherents of Gregory VII and Urban II.

[2] This refers to the Seljuk conquest of Anatolia, probably to Manzikert, 1071.

II. The Decree of Pope Urban in the Council

1. "Most beloved brethren," he said, "by God's permission placed over the whole world with the papal crown, I, Urban, as the messenger of divine admonition, have been compelled by an unavoidable occasion to come here to you servants of God. I desired those whom I judged to be stewards of God's ministries to be true stewards and faithful, with all hypocrisy rejected.

2. "But with temperance in reason and justice being remote, I, with divine aid, shall strive carefully to root out any crookedness or distortion which might obstruct God's law. For the Lord appointed you temporarily as stewards over His family to serve it nourishment seasoned with a modest savor. Moreover, blessed will you be if at last the Overseer find you faithful.

3. "You are also called shepherds; see that you are not occupied after the manner of mercenaries. Be true shepherds, always holding your crooks in your hands; and sleeping not, guard on every side the flock entrusted to you.

4. "For if through your carelessness or negligence, some wolf seizes a sheep, you doubtless will lose the reward prepared for you by our Lord. Nay, first most cruelly beaten by the whips of the lictors,[3] you afterwards will be angrily cast into the keeping of a deadly place.

5. "Likewise, according to the evangelical sermon, you are the 'salt of the earth.' But if you fail, it will be disputed wherewith it was salted. O how much saltiness, indeed, is necessary for you to salt the people in correcting them with the salt of wisdom, people who are ignorant and panting with desire after the wantonness of the world; so that, unsalted, they might not be rotten with sins and stink whenever the Lord might wish to exhort them.

6. "For if because of the sloth of your management, He should find in them worms, that is, sin, straightway, He will order that they, despised, be cast into the dungheap. And because you could not make restoration for such a great loss, He will banish you, utterly condemned in judgment, from the familiarity of His love.

7. "It behooves saltiness of this kind to be wise, provident, temperate, learned, peace-making, truth-seeking, pious, just, equitable, pure. For how will the unlearned be able to make men learned, the intemperate make temperate, the impure make them pure? If one despises peace, how will he appease? Or if one has dirty hands, how will he be able to wipe the filth off another one defiled? For it is read, 'If the blind lead the blind, both shall fall into a ditch.'[4]

[3] Enforcers. Latin term for imperial bodyguards. [Ed.]
[4] Matthew 15:14.

8. "Set yourselves right before you do others, so that you can blame-lessly correct your subjects. If you wish to be friends of God, gladly practice those things which you feel will please Him.

9. "Especially establish ecclesiastical affairs firm in their own right, so that no simoniac[5] heresy will take root among you. Take care lest the vendors and moneychangers, flayed by the scourges of the Lord, be mis-erably driven out into the narrow streets of destruction.

10. "Uphold the Church in its own ranks altogether free from all secular power. See that the tithes of all those who cultivate the earth are given faithfully to God; let them not be sold or held back.

11. "Let him who has seized a bishop be considered an outlaw. Let him who has seized or robbed monks, clerics, nuns and their servants, pilgrims, or merchants, be excommunicated. Let the robbers and burn-ers of homes and their accomplices, banished from the Church, be smitten with excommunication.

12. "It must be considered very carefully, as Gregory says, by what penalty he must be punished who seizes other men's property, if he who does not bestow his own liberally is condemned to Hell. For so it hap-pened to the rich man in the well-known Gospel, who on that account was not punished because he had taken away the property of others, but because he had misused that which he had received.

13. "And so by these iniquities, most beloved, you have seen the world disturbed too long; so long, as it was told to us by those reporting, that perhaps because of the weakness of your justice in some parts of your provinces, no one dares to walk in the streets with safety, lest he be kidnapped by robbers by day or thieves by night, either by force or trick-ery, at home or outside.

14. "Wherefore the Truce,[6] as it is commonly called, now for a long time established by the Holy Fathers, must be renewed. In admonition, I entreat you to adhere to it most firmly in your own bishopric. But if anyone affected by avarice or pride breaks it of his own free will, let him be excommunicated by God's authority and by the sanction of the de-crees of this Holy Council."

III. The Pope's Exhortation Concerning the Expedition to Jerusalem

1. These and many other things having been suitably disposed of, all those present, both clergy and people, at the words of Lord Urban, the Pope, voluntarily gave thanks to God and confirmed by a faithful

---

[5] Buying or selling church offices. [Ed.]

[6] Truce of God—Cessation of all feuds from Wednesday evening to Monday morning in every week and during church festivals, ordered by the Church in 1041. This was proclaimed anew at the Council of Clermont.

promise that his decrees would be well kept. But straightway he added that another thing not less than the tribulation already spoken of, but even greater and more oppressive, was injuring Christianity in another part of the world, saying:

2. "Now that you, O sons of God, have consecrated yourselves to God to maintain peace among yourselves more vigorously and to uphold the laws of the Church faithfully, there is work to do, for you must turn the strength of your sincerity, now that you are aroused by divine correction, to another affair that concerns you and God. Hastening to the way, you must help your brothers living in the Orient, who need your aid for which they have already cried out many times.

3. "For, as most of you have been told, the Turks, a race of Persians,[7] who have penetrated within the boundaries of Romania[8] even to the Mediterranean to that point which they call the Arm of Saint George[9] in occupying more and more of the lands of the Christians, have overcome them, already victims of seven battles, and have killed and captured them, have overthrown churches, and have laid waste God's kingdom. If you permit this supinely for very long, God's faithful ones will be still further subjected.

4. "Concerning this affair, I, with suppliant prayer—not I, but the Lord—exhort you, heralds of Christ, to persuade all of whatever class, both knights and footmen, both rich and poor, in numerous edicts, to strive to help expel that wicked race from our Christian lands before it is too late.

5. "I speak to those present, I send word to those not here; moreover, Christ commands it. Remission of sins will be granted for those going thither, if they end a shackled life either on land or in crossing the sea, or in struggling against the heathen. I, being vested with that gift from God, grant this to those who go.

6. "O what a shame, if a people, so despised, degenerate, and enslaved by demons would thus overcome a people endowed with the trust of almighty God, and shining in the name of Christ! O how many evils will be imputed to you by the Lord Himself, if you do not help those who, like you, profess Christianity!

7. "Let those," he said, "who are accustomed to wage private wars wastefully even against Believers, go forth against the Infidels in a battle worthy to be undertaken now and to be finished in victory. Now, let those, who until recently existed as plunderers, be soldiers of Christ; now, let those, who formerly contended against brothers and relations,

---

[7] Really Seljuk Turks who conquered lands from east to west by way of Persia.

[8] Fulcher uses the term *Romania* to refer to the Anatolian as well as to the European provinces of the Byzantine Empire, but here, of course, he means the Anatolian. The Seljuks called the state which they founded here *Rum*.

[9] An eleventh-century term for the Bosporus, since it ran by St. George's monastery near Byzantium. [Ed.]

rightly fight barbarians; now, let those, who recently were hired for a few pieces of silver, win their eternal reward. Let those, who wearied themselves to the detriment of body and soul, labor for a twofold honor. Nay, more, the sorrowful here will be glad there, the poor here will be rich there, and the enemies of the Lord here will be His friends there.

8. "Let no delay postpone the journey of those about to go, but when they have collected the money owed to them and the expenses for the journey, and when winter has ended and spring has come, let them enter the crossroads courageously with the Lord going on before."

IV. The Bishop of Puy and the Events after the Council

1. After these words were spoken, the hearers were fervently inspired. Thinking nothing more worthy than such an undertaking, many in the audience solemnly promised to go, and to urge diligently those who were absent. There was among them one Bishop of Puy, Ademar by name, who afterwards, acting as vicar-apostolic, ruled the whole army of God wisely and thoughtfully, and spurred them to complete their undertaking vigorously.

2. So, the things that we have told you were well established and confirmed by everybody in the Council. With the blessing of absolution given, they departed; and after returning to their homes, they disclosed to those not knowing, what had taken place. As it was decreed far and wide throughout the provinces, they established the peace, which they call the Truce, to be upheld mutually by oath.

3. Many, one after another, of any and every occupation, after confession of their sins and with purified spirits, consecrated themselves to go where they were bidden.

4. Oh, how worthy and delightful to all of us who saw those beautiful crosses, either silken or woven of gold, or of any material, which the pilgrims sewed on the shoulders of their woolen cloaks or cassocks by the command of the Pope, after taking the vow to go. To be sure, God's soldiers, who were making themselves ready to battle for His honor, ought to have been marked and fortified with a sign of victory. And so by embroidering the symbol [of the cross] on their clothing in recognition of their faith, in the end they won the True Cross itself. They imprinted the ideal so that they might attain the reality of the ideal.

5. It is plain that good meditation leads to doing good work and that good work wins salvation of the soul. But, if it is good to mean well, it is better, after reflection, to carry out the good intention. So, it is best to win salvation through action worthy of the soul to be saved. Let each and everyone, therefore, reflect upon the good, that he makes better in fulfillment, so that, deserving it, he might finally receive the best, which does not diminish in eternity.

6. In such a manner Urban, a wise man and reverenced,
   Meditated a labor, whereby the world florescenced.[10]

For he renewed peace and restored the laws of the Church to their former standards; also he tried with vigorous instigation to expel the heathen from the lands of the Christians. And since he strove to exalt all things of God in every way, almost everyone gladly surrendered in obedience to his paternal care.

[10] Blossomed. [Ed.]

2

Chronicle of Solomon bar Simson, c. 1140

Solomon bar Simson (who is known only from this chronicle) provides a Hebrew chronicle of the First Crusade that takes up the story after Pope Urban II's appeal. In early 1096, a few French and German crusaders led their followers in attacks on Jews in the cities of Speyer, Worms, and Mainz. Solomon bar Simson tells the story of these massacres from the viewpoint of the survivors. What seems to have been the reason for the attacks on Jews? What role was played by the common people, the officials of the church, and the government?

THINKING HISTORICALLY

Little is known about the author of this chronicle. Simson may have written this a generation after 1096: If so, he probably based it on earlier versions. Those who survived by converting to Christianity may have helped to shape the story, even if they later returned to Judaism. Some scholars see traces of Christian culture in the accounts of martyrdom, which was not a common theme in Hebrew writing until this time. What signs do you see of the Jewish author's knowledge of Christianity?

This narrative, like the previous selection, includes quotations from speeches. How can you tell that some of these quotations do not contain the exact words that were spoken?

Source: "Chronicle of Solomon bar Simson," in *The Jews and the Crusaders: The Hebrew Chronicles of the First and Second Crusades*, ed. and trans. Shlomo Eidelberg (Madison: University of Wisconsin Press, 1977), 21–26.

Solomon bar Simson's narrative contains another element that, although absent from modern histories, is found in other narratives of the Crusades and is especially pronounced here. This is not just a narrative of human action and intention, but also an interpretation of divine action and intention. Why is this narrative strategy necessary for this author? If you were writing a narrative of the Crusades today, would you want to tell both of these stories, or only the human one? Why?

I will now recount the event of this persecution in other martyred communities as well—the extent to which they clung to the Lord, God of their fathers, bearing witness to His Oneness to their last breath.

In the year four thousand eight hundred and fifty-six, the year one thousand twenty-eight of our exile, in the eleventh year of the cycle Ranu, the year in which we anticipated salvation and solace, in accordance with the prophecy of Jeremiah: "Sing with gladness for Jacob, and shout at the head of the nations," etc.—this year turned instead to sorrow and groaning, weeping and outcry. Inflicted upon the Jewish People were the many evils related in all the admonitions; those enumerated in Scripture as well as those unwritten were visited upon us.

At this time arrogant people, a people of strange speech, a nation bitter and impetuous, Frenchmen and Germans, set out for the Holy City, which had been desecrated by barbaric nations, there to seek their house of idolatry and banish the Ishmaelites and other denizens of the land and conquer the land for themselves. They decorated themselves prominently with their signs, placing a profane symbol—a horizontal line over a vertical one—on the vestments of every man and woman whose heart yearned to go on the stray path to the grave of their Messiah. Their ranks swelled until the number of men, women, and children exceeded a locust horde covering the earth; of them it was said: "The locusts have no king [yet go they forth all of them by bands]."[1] Now it came to pass that as they passed through the towns where Jews dwelled, they said to one another: "Look now, we are going a long way to seek out the profane shrine and to avenge ourselves on the Ishmaelites, when here, in our very midst, are the Jews—they whose forefathers murdered and crucified him for no reason. Let us first avenge ourselves on them and exterminate them from among the nations so that the name of Israel will no longer be remembered, or let them adopt our faith and acknowledge the offspring of promiscuity."

When the Jewish communities became aware of their intentions, they resorted to the custom of our ancestors, repentance, prayer, and charity. The hands of the Holy Nation turned faint at this time, their

[1] Proverbs 30:27. [Ed.]

hearts melted, and their strength flagged. They hid in their innermost rooms to escape the swirling sword. They subjected themselves to great endurance, abstaining from food and drink for three consecutive days and nights, and then fasting many days from sunrise to sunset, until their skin was shriveled and dry as wood upon their bones. And they cried out loudly and bitterly to God.

But their Father did not answer them; He obstructed their prayers, concealing Himself in a cloud through which their prayers could not pass, and He abhorred their tent, and He removed them out of His sight—all of this having been decreed by Him to take place "in the day when I visit"; and this was the generation that had been chosen by Him to be His portion, for they had the strength and the fortitude to stand in His Sanctuary, and fulfill His word, and sanctify His Great Name in His world. It is of such as these that King David said: "Bless the Lord, ye angels of His, ye almighty in strength, that fulfil His word," etc.

That year, Passover fell on Thursday, and the New Moon of the following month, Iyar, fell on Friday and the Sabbath. On the eighth day of Iyar, on the Sabbath, the foe attacked the community of Speyer and murdered eleven holy souls who sanctified their Creator on the holy Sabbath and refused to defile themselves by adopting the faith of their foe. There was a distinguished, pious woman there who slaughtered herself in sanctification of God's Name. She was the first among all the communities of those who were slaughtered. The remainder were saved by the local bishop without defilement [i.e., baptism], as described above.

On the twenty-third of Iyar they attacked the community of Worms.[2] The community was then divided into two groups; some remained in their homes and others fled to the local bishop seeking refuge. Those who remained in their homes were set upon by the steppe-wolves who pillaged men, women, and infants, children, and old people. They pulled down the stairways and destroyed the houses, looting and plundering; and they took the Torah Scroll, trampled it in the mud, and tore and burned it. The enemy devoured the children of Israel with open maw.

Seven days later, on the New Moon of Sivan—the very day on which the Children of Israel arrived at Mount Sinai to receive the Torah—those Jews who were still in the court of the bishop were subjected to great anguish. The enemy dealt them the same cruelty as the first group and put them to the sword. The Jews, inspired by the valor of their brethren, similarly chose to be slain in order to sanctify the Name before the eyes of all, and exposed their throats for their heads to be severed for the glory of the Creator. There were also those who took their own lives, thus fulfilling the verse: "The mother was dashed in pieces with her children."[3] Fathers fell upon their sons, being slaughtered upon one another,

---

[2] Town in the Holy Roman Empire (now Germany). [Ed.]
[3] Hosea 10:14. [Ed.]

and they slew one another—each man his kin, his wife and children; bridegrooms slew their betrothed, and merciful women their only children. They all accepted the divine decree wholeheartedly and, as they yielded up their souls to the Creator, cried out: "Hear, O Israel, the Lord is our God, the Lord is One." The enemy stripped them naked, dragged them along, and then cast them off, sparing only a small number whom they forcibly baptized in their profane waters. The number of those slain during the two days was approximately eight hundred—and they were all buried naked. It is of these that the Prophet Jeremiah lamented: "They that were brought up in scarlet embrace dunghills."[4] I have already cited their names above. May God remember them for good.

[4] Lamentations 4:5. [Ed.]

3

IBN AL-ATHIR
Causes of the Crusade, c. 1231

Ibn al-Athir* (1160–1233) was one of the great Muslim historians. His most important work was a multivolume history that was for all intents a world history, from the time of Adam to his present. An ethnic Kurd, he spent most of his life in Mosul, Iraq, but also lived in Aleppo and Damascus in Syria, where he fought for the army of Saladin. For the early period of his multivolume history he borrowed heavily from the works of earlier Muslim historians.

Ibn al-Athir offers two possible explanations for the causes of the First Crusade. What are these, and how are they different from Fulcher's explanation? What does the author's account suggest about Muslim attitudes toward Christians? How according to the author did the Christians conquer Antioch?

THINKING HISTORICALLY

Periodization is an important issue that must be addressed when writing a narrative account of something. Especially when we are asking about the causes of something, we must decide when that something began. Notice how we have dated this chapter. How is Ibn al-Athir's periodization different from ours and that of Fulcher? If we

* IH buhn   ahl AH tuhr

Source: Francesco Gabrieli, *Arab Historians of the Crusades*, trans. E. J. Costello (Berkeley: University of California Press, 1969), 3–7.

begin the history of the crusade when Ibn al-Athir does, how does that change the story? Is it possible to combine both his and Fulcher's story into the same narrative? Why or why not?

The power of the Franks first became apparent when in the year 478/1085–86 they invaded the territories of Islām and took Toledo and other parts of Andalusia, as was mentioned earlier. Then in 484/1091 they attacked and conquered the island of Sicily and turned their attention to the African coast. Certain of their conquests there were won back again but they had other successes, as you will see.

In 490/1097 the Franks attacked Syria. This is how it all began: Baldwin, their King,[1] a kinsman of Roger the Frank who had conquered Sicily, assembled a great army and sent word to Roger saying: 'I have assembled a great army and now I am on my way to you, to use your bases for my conquest of the African coast. Thus you and I shall become neighbours.'

Roger called together his companions and consulted them about these proposals. 'This will be a fine thing both for them and for us!' they declared, 'for by this means these lands will be converted to the Faith!' At this Roger raised one leg and farted loudly, and swore that it was of more use than their advice. 'Why?' 'Because if this army comes here it will need quantities of provisions and fleets of ships to transport it to Africa, as well as reinforcements from my own troops. Then, if the Franks succeed in conquering this territory they will take it over and will need provisioning from Sicily. This will cost me my annual profit from the harvest. If they fail they will return here and be an embarrassment to me here in my own domain. As well as all this Tamīm[2] will say that I have broken faith with him and violated our treaty, and friendly relations and communications between us will be disrupted. As far as we are concerned, Africa is always there. When we are strong enough, we will take it.'

He summoned Baldwin's messenger and said to him: 'If you have decided to make war on the Muslims your best course will be to free Jerusalem from their rule and thereby win great honour. I am bound by certain promises and treaties of allegiance with the rulers of Africa.' So the Franks made ready and set out to attack Syria.

Another story is that the Fatimids of Egypt were afraid when they saw the Seljuqids extending their empire through Syria as far as Gaza, until they reached the Egyptian border and Atsiz[3] invaded Egypt itself.

---

[1] Baldwin is a mythical character, compounded of the various Baldwins of Flanders and Jerusalem; or else the first Baldwin is mistakenly thought to have been already a king in the West.

[2] The Zirid amīr of Tunisia Tamīm ibn Mu'izz.

[3] A general of the Seljuqid Sultan Malikshāh, who in 1076 attacked Egypt from Palestine.

They therefore sent to invite the Franks to invade Syria and so protect Egypt from the Muslims.[4] But God knows best.

When the Franks decided to attack Syria they marched east to Constantinople, so that they could cross the straits and advance into Muslim territory by the easier, land route. When they reached Constantinople, the Emperor of the East refused them permission to pass through his domains. He said: 'Unless you first promise me Antioch, I shall not allow you to cross into the Muslim empire.' His real intention was to incite them to attack the Muslims, for he was convinced that the Turks, whose invincible control over Asia Minor he had observed, would exterminate every one of them. They accepted his conditions and in 490/1097 they crossed the Bosphorus at Constantinople. Iconium and the rest of the area into which they now advanced belonged to Qilij Arslān ibn Sulaimān ibn Qutlumísh, who barred their way with his troops. They broke through in rajab 490/July 1097, crossed Cilicia, and finally reached Antioch, which they besieged.

When Yaghi Siyān, the ruler of Antioch, heard of their approach, he was not sure how the Christian people of the city would react, so he made the Muslims go outside the city on their own to dig trenches, and the next day sent the Christians out alone to continue the task. When they were ready to return home at the end of the day he refused to allow them. 'Antioch is yours,' he said, 'but you will have to leave it to me until I see what happens between us and the Franks.' 'Who will protect our children and our wives?' they said. 'I shall look after them for you.' So they resigned themselves to their fate, and lived in the Frankish camp for nine months, while the city was under siege.

Yaghi Siyān showed unparalleled courage and wisdom, strength and judgment. If all the Franks who died had survived they would have overrun all the lands of Islām. He protected the families of the Christians in Antioch and would not allow a hair of their heads to be touched.

After the siege had been going on for a long time the Franks made a deal with one of the men who were responsible for the towers. He was a cuirass-maker called Ruzbih whom they bribed with a fortune in money and lands. He worked in the tower that stood over the river-bed, where the river flowed out of the city into the valley. The Franks sealed their pact with the cuirass-maker, God damn him! and made their way to the water-gate. They opened it and entered the city. Another gang of them climbed the tower with ropes. At dawn, when more than 500 of them were in the city and the defenders were worn out after the night watch, they sounded their trumpets. Yaghi Siyān woke up and asked what the noise meant. He was told that trumpets had sounded from the citadel and that it must have been taken. In fact the sound came not from the citadel but from the tower. Panic seized Yaghi Siyān and he opened the

[4] Of course the Fatimids were also Muslims, but they were heretics and so opposed to the rest of *sunni* Islām.

city gates and fled in terror, with an escort of thirty pages. His army commander arrived, but when he discovered on enquiry that Yaghi Siyān had fled, he made his escape by another gate. This was of great help to the Franks, for if he had stood firm for an hour, they would have been wiped out. They entered the city by the gates and sacked it, slaughtering all the Muslims they found there. This happened in jumada I (491/April/May 1098). As for Yaghi Siyān, when the sun rose he recovered his self control and realized that his flight had taken him several *farsakh*[5] from the city. He asked his companions where he was, and on hearing that he was four *farsakh* from Antioch he repented of having rushed to safety instead of staying to fight to the death. He began to groan and weep for his desertion of his household and children. Overcome by the violence of his grief he fell fainting from his horse. His companions tried to lift him back into the saddle, but they could not get him to sit up, and so left him for dead while they escaped. He was at his last gasp when an Armenian shepherd came past, killed him, cut off his head and took it to the Franks at Antioch.

The Franks had written to the rulers of Aleppo and Damascus to say that they had no interest in any cities but those that had once belonged to Byzantium. This was a piece of deceit calculated to dissuade these rulers from going to the help of Antioch.

[5] One *farsakh* is about four miles.

4

ANNA COMNENA
The Alexiad, c. 1148

Anna Comnena was the daughter of Emperor Alexius
(r. 1081–1118) of Byzantium. Threatened on three sides — by the
Seljuk Turks to the east, the Norman kingdom of southern Italy
to the west, and rebellions to the north — Alexius appealed for
aid to Pope Urban II of Rome in 1095. He expected a mercenary
army, but because the pope saw a chance to send a massive force
against Muslim occupiers of Jerusalem as well as against those
threatening Constantinople, Alexius instead received an uncontrollable ragtag force of Christians and Crusaders that included his
Norman enemies, led by Bohemond.

Source: Anna Comnena, *The Alexiad of the Princess Anna Comnena*, trans. Elizabeth A. S. Dawes (London: Routledge & Kegan Paul Ltd., 1967), 247–52. Reprinted in William H. McNeill and Schuyler O. Houser, *Medieval Europe* (Oxford: Oxford University Press, 1971), 135–40.

Princess Anna recalled the story of the First Crusade's appearance in Byzantium some forty years later in her history titled *The Alexiad* after her father. According to Anna, how did Alexius respond to the approach of the Crusader army? Did Alexius fear the Franks more than he feared the Turks?

THINKING HISTORICALLY

This is a fourth perspective on the history of the First Crusade — the view of a Christian ally of Rome, more directly threatened than the Roman church by the Muslim armies. Yet, Byzantium and Rome were also at odds. Since 1054, they had accepted a parting of the ways, theologically and institutionally, with Byzantium now the center of the Eastern Orthodox Church. And with the advancing Frankish armies, Anna and Alexius were not sure whether they were facing friend or foe. How does Anna view the Franks? How does Anna's critical perspective change our idea of the Crusaders? How might her idea of the Franks change our narrative of the early stage of the crusade?

Notice how this narrative combines a sequence of events with generalizations (often about the "race" or nature of the Franks) to explain specific events. Does a narrative history have to include generalizations as well as a sequence of specific events? Can the events alone provide sufficient explanation?

Before he [the Emperor Alexius] had enjoyed even a short rest, he heard a report of the approach of innumerable Frankish[1] armies. Now he dreaded their arrival for he knew their irresistible manner of attack, their unstable and mobile character and all the peculiar natural and concomitant characteristics which the Frank retains throughout; and he also knew that they were always agape for money, and seemed to disregard their truces readily for any reason that cropped up. For he had always heard this reported of them, and found it very true. However, he did not lose heart, but prepared himself in every way so that, when the occasion called, he would be ready for battle. And indeed the actual facts were far greater and more terrible than rumour made them. For the whole of the West and all the barbarian tribes which dwell between the further side of the Adriatic[2] and the pillars of Heracles,[3] had all migrated in a body and were marching into Asia through the intervening Europe, and were making the journey with all their household. The reason of this upheaval was

[1] Term generalizes from Franks (mainly French) to refer to all Western Europeans. [Ed.]
[2] Italy. [Ed.]
[3] Gibraltar, at the meeting of the Mediterranean and the Atlantic Ocean. [Ed.]

more or less the following. A certain Frank, Peter by name, nicknamed Cucupeter,[4] had gone to worship at the Holy Sepulchre[5] and after suffering many things at the hands of the Turks and Saracens who were ravaging Asia, he got back to his own country with difficulty. But he was angry at having failed in his object, and wanted to undertake the same journey again. However, he saw that he ought not to make the journey to the Holy Sepulchre alone again, lest worse things befall him, so he worked out a cunning plan. This was to preach in all the Latin countries that "the voice of God bids me announce to all the Counts in France" that they should all leave their homes and set out to worship at the Holy Sepulchre, and to endeavour wholeheartedly with hand and mind to deliver Jerusalem from the hand of Hagarenes.[6] And he really succeeded. For after inspiring the souls of all with this quasi-divine command he contrived to assemble the Franks from all sides, one after the other, with arms, horses and all the other paraphernalia of war. And they were all so zealous and eager that every highroad was full of them. And those Frankish soldiers were accompanied by an unarmed host more numerous than the sand or the stars, carrying palms and crosses on their shoulders, women and children, too, came away from their countries and the sight of them was like many rivers streaming from all sides, and they were advancing towards us through Dacia[7] generally with all their hosts. Now the coming of these many peoples was preceded by a locust which did not touch the wheat, but made a terrible attack on the vines. This was really a presage as the diviners of the time interpreted it, and meant that this enormous Frankish army would, when it came, refrain from interference in Christian affairs, but fall very heavily upon the barbarian Ishmaelites[8] who were slaves to drunkenness, wine, and Dionysus.[9] For this race is under the sway of Dionysus and Eros,[10] rushes headlong into all kind of sexual intercourse, and is not circumcised either in the flesh or in their passions. It is nothing but a slave, nay triply enslaved, to the ills wrought by Aphrodite. For this reason they worship and adore Astarte and Ashtaroth[11] too and value above all the image of the moon,

---

[4] Peter the Hermit, an effective lay preacher who raised an unruly army (far more peasants than knights) that Anna Comnena saw as the first army of Crusaders. [Ed.]

[5] The Church of the Holy Sepulchre in Jerusalem is said to hold the tomb where Jesus was buried. [Ed.]

[6] Muslims, who were considered "children of Hagar" (Gen. 16). [Ed.]

[7] Modern Romania.

[8] Muslims. Descended from Abraham's son Ishmael (and servant Hagar), whereas Jews were thought descended from Isaac, son of Abraham and wife Sarah. [Ed.]

[9] Anna's account of the beliefs of the Muslims was highly biased. Muhammad forbade his followers to drink intoxicating liquors.

[10] Dionysus was the Greek god associated with wine and revelry; Eros was the patron of lovers, and son of Aphrodite, goddess of love.

[11] Names of the Semitic goddess of fertility.

and the golden figure of Hobar[12] in their country. Now in these symbols Christianity was taken to be the corn because of its wineless and very nutritive qualities; in this manner the diviners interpreted the vines and the wheat. However let the matter of the prophecy rest.

The incidents of the barbarians' approach followed in the order I have described, and persons of intelligence could feel that they were witnessing a strange occurrence. The arrival of these multitudes did not take place at the same time nor by the same road (for how indeed could such masses starting from different places have crossed the straits of Lombardy all together?). Some first, some next, others after them and thus successively all accomplished the transit, and then marched through the Continent. Each army was preceded, as we said, by an unspeakable number of locusts; and all who saw this more than once recognized them as forerunners of the Frankish armies. When the first of them began crossing the straits of Lombardy sporadically the Emperor summoned certain leaders of the Roman forces, and sent them to the parts of Dyrrachium and Valona[13] with instructions to offer a courteous welcome to the Franks who had crossed, and to collect abundant supplies from all the countries along their route; then to follow and watch them covertly all the time, and if they saw them making any foraging-excursions, they were to come out from under cover and check them by light skirmishing. These captains were accompanied by some men who knew the Latin tongue, so that they might settle any disputes that arose between them.

Let me, however, give an account of this subject more clearly and in due order. According to universal rumour Godfrey,[14] who sold his country, was the first to start on the appointed road; this man was very rich and very proud of his bravery, courage and conspicuous lineage; for every Frank is anxious to outdo the others. And such an upheaval of both men and women took place then as had never occurred within human memory, the simpler-minded were urged on by the real desire of worshipping at our Lord's Sepulchre, and visiting the sacred places; but the more astute, especially men like Bohemund and those of like mind, had another secret reason, namely, the hope that while on their travels they might by some means be able to seize the capital [Constantinople] itself,[15] looking upon this as a kind of corollary. And Bohemund disturbed the minds of many nobler men by thus cherishing his old grudge

---

[12] I.e., Hathor, the Egyptian goddess of love, usually depicted with the head of a cow. (N.B. Idol worship was strictly forbidden by Islamic law.)

[13] Ports on the Adriatic, directly opposite the heel of Italy in modern Albania.

[14] Godfrey of Bouillon, the duke of Lower Lorraine (c. 1060–1100). To raise money for the Crusade, he sold two of his estates, and pledged his castle at Bouillon to the bishop of Liège.

[15] Bohemund and his father, Robert Guiscard, had already led Norman armies against Byzantium. [Ed.]

against the Emperor. Meanwhile Peter, after he had delivered his message, crossed the straits of Lombardy before anybody else with eighty thousand men on foot, and one hundred thousand on horseback, and reached the capital by way of Hungary.[16] For the Frankish race, as one may conjecture, is always very hotheaded and eager, but when once it has espoused a cause, it is uncontrollable.

The Emperor, knowing what Peter had suffered before from the Turks, advised him to wait for the arrival of the other Counts, but Peter would not listen for he trusted the multitude of his followers, so he crossed and pitched his camp near a small town called Helenopolis.[17] After him followed the Normans[18] numbering ten thousand, who separated themselves from the rest of the army and devastated the country round Nicaea, and behaved most cruelly to all. For they dismembered some of the children and fixed others on wooden spits and roasted them at the fire, and on persons advanced in age they inflicted every kind of torture. But when the inhabitants of Nicaea became aware of these doings, they threw open their gates and marched out upon them, and after a violent conflict had taken place they had to dash back inside their citadel as the Normans fought so bravely. And thus the latter recovered all the booty and returned to Helenopolis. Then a dispute arose between them and the others who had not gone out with them, as is usual in such cases, for the minds of those who stayed behind were aflame with envy, and thus caused a skirmish after which the headstrong Normans drew apart again, marched to Xerigordus[19] and took it by assault. When the Sultan[20] heard what had happened, he dispatched Elchanes[21] against them with a substantial force. He came, and recaptured Xerigordus and sacrificed some of the Normans to the sword, and took others captive, at the same time laid plans to catch those who had remained behind with Cucupeter. He placed ambushes in suitable spots so that any coming from the camp in the direction of Nicaea would fall into them unexpectedly and be killed. Besides this, as he knew the Franks' love of money, he sent for two active-minded men and ordered them to go to Cucupeter's camp and proclaim there that the Normans had gained possession of Nicaea, and were now dividing everything in it. When this report was circulated among Peter's followers, it upset them terribly. Directly [when] they heard the words "partition" and "money" they started in a disorderly crowd along the road to Nicaea, all but

[16] Peter's contingent probably numbered about twenty thousand including noncombatants.

[17] I.e., Peter moved his forces across the Bosporus and into Asia Minor.

[18] Bohemund's army. Normans, descended from Viking "Northmen" and Franks, had conquered Sicily and southern Italy. [Ed.]

[19] A castle held by the Turks.

[20] Qilij Arslan I, ruled 1092–1106.

[21] An important Turkish military commander.

unmindful of their military experience and the discipline which is essential for those starting out to battle. For, as I remarked above, the Latin race is always very fond of money, but more especially when it is bent on raiding a country; it then loses its reason and gets beyond control. As they journeyed neither in ranks nor in squadrons, they fell foul of the Turkish ambuscades near the river Dracon and perished miserably. And such a large number of Franks and Normans were the victims of the Ishmaelite sword, that when they piled up the corpses of the slaughtered men which were lying on either side they formed, I say, not a very large hill or mound or a peak, but a high mountain as it were, of very considerable depth and breadth—so great was the pyramid of bones. And later men of the same tribe as the slaughtered barbarians built a wall and used the bones of the dead to fill the interstices as if they were pebbles, and thus made the city their tomb in a way. This fortified city is still standing today with its walls built of a mixture of stones and bones. When they had all in this way fallen prey to the sword, Peter alone with a few others escaped and reentered Helenopolis,[22] and the Turks, who wanted to capture him, set fresh ambushes for him. But when the Emperor received reliable information of all this, and the terrible massacre, he was very worried lest Peter should have been captured. He therefore summoned Constantine Catacalon Euphorbenus (who has already been mentioned many times in this history), and gave him a large force which was embarked on ships of war and sent him across the straits to Peter's succour. Directly [when] the Turks saw him land they fled. Constantine, without the slightest delay, picked up Peter and his followers, who were but few, and brought them safe and sound to the Emperor. On the Emperor's reminding him of his original thoughtlessness and saying that it was due to his not having obeyed his, the Emperor's, advice that he had incurred such disasters, Peter, being a haughty Latin, would not admit that he himself was the cause of the trouble, but said it was the others who did not listen to him, but followed their own will, and he denounced them as robbers and plunderers who, for that reason, were not allowed by the Saviour to worship at His Holy Sepulchre. Others of the Latins, such as Bohemund and men of like mind, who had long cherished a desire for the Roman Empire,[23] and wished to win it for themselves, found a pretext in Peter's preaching, as I have said, deceived the more single-minded, caused this great upheaval and were selling their own estates under the pretence that they were marching against the Turks to redeem the Holy Sepulchre.

---

[22] According to other accounts of the battle, Peter was in Constantinople at the time.
[23] Byzantine Empire. [Ed.]

5

FULCHER OF CHARTRES

The Siege of Antioch, c. 1100–1127

We return here to Fulcher's Chronicles (Book I, Chapters 16 and 17). Antioch, in northern Syria, was the largest and most formidable Muslim-controlled city on the Crusaders' route to Jerusalem. After laying siege to the city for more than two years, the Crusader forces had suffered losses that seriously reduced their strength and morale. After their initial success, what events seem to have caused these reversals? What were the strengths and weaknesses of the Crusader armies? Compare Fulcher's account of the fall of Antioch with that of Ibn al-Athir. How do they differ?

THINKING HISTORICALLY

Like the narrative of Solomon bar Simson, this narrative operates on two levels: the human and the divine. Notice how Fulcher attempts to interpret both of these narrative lines, separately and in their interaction. How much of Fulcher's narrative recounts God's work? How much recounts the work of the Crusaders? How does he combine these two threads? Of course, modern historians are normally limited to the human thread. Try to write a narrative that shows how the human Crusaders conquered Antioch. How might the account of Ibn al-Athir help you do this?

XVI. The Wretched Poverty of the Christians and the Flight of the Count of Blois

1. In the year of the Lord 1098, after the region all around Antioch had been wholly devastated by the multitude of our people, the strong as well as the weak were more and more harassed by famine.

2. At that time, the famished ate the shoots of beanseeds growing in the fields and many kinds of herbs unseasoned with salt; also thistles, which, being not well cooked because of the deficiency of firewood, pricked the tongues of those eating them; also horses, asses, and camels, and dogs and rats. The poorer ones ate even the skins of the beasts and seeds of grain found in manure.

3. They endured winter's cold, summer's heat, and heavy rains for God. Their tents became old and torn and rotten from the continuation of rains. Because of this, many of them were covered by only the sky.

Source: *The First Crusade: The Chronicle of Fulcher of Chartres and Other Source Materials,* 2nd ed., ed. Edward Peters (Philadelphia: University of Pennsylvania Press, 1998), 73–75.

4. So like gold thrice proved and purified sevenfold by fire, long pre-destined by God, I believe, and weighed by such a great calamity, they were cleansed of their sins. For even if the assassin's sword had not failed, many, long agonizing, would have voluntarily completed a martyr's course. Perhaps they borrowed the grace of such a great ex-ample from Saint Job, who, purifying his soul by the torments of his body, ever held God fast in mind. Those who fight with the heathen, labor because of God.

5. Granting that God—who creates everything, regulates everything created, sustains everything regulated, and rules by virtue—can destroy or renew whatsoever He wishes, I feel that He assented to the destruc-tion of the heathen after the scourging of the Christians. He permitted it, and the people deserved it, because so many times they cheaply destroyed all things of God. He permitted the Christians to be killed by the Turks, so that the Christians would have the assurance of salvation; the Turks, the perdition of their souls. It pleased God that certain Turks, already predestined for salvation, were baptized by priests. "For those whom He predestined, He also called and glorified."

6. So what then? There were some of our men, as you heard before, who left the siege because it brought so much anguish; others, because of poverty; others, because of cowardice; others, because of fear of death; first the poor and then the rich.

7. Stephen, Count of Blois, withdrew from the siege and returned home to France by sea. Therefore all of us grieved, since he was a very noble man and valiant in arms. On the day following his departure, the city of Antioch was surrendered to the Franks. If he had persevered, he would have rejoiced much in the victory with the rest. This act disgraced him. For a good beginning is not beneficial to anyone unless it be well consummated. I shall cut short many things in the Lord's affairs lest I wander from the truth, because lying about them must be especially guarded against.

8. The siege lasted continuously from this same month of October, as it was mentioned, through the following winter and spring until June. The Turks and Franks alternately staged many attacks and counter-attacks; they overcame and were overcome. Our men, however, tri-umphed more often than theirs. Once it happened that many of the fleeing Turks fell into the Fernus River, and being submerged in it, they drowned. On the near side of the river, and on the far side, both forces often waged war alternately.

9. Our leaders constructed castles before the city, from which they often rushed forth vigorously to keep the Turks from coming out [of the city]. By this means, the Franks took the pastures from their animals. Nor did they get any help from Armenians outside the city, although these Armenians often did injury to our men.

XVII. The Surrender of the City of Antioch

1. When it pleased God that the labor of His people should be consummated, perhaps pleased by the prayers of those who daily poured out supplications and entreaties to Him, out of His compassion He granted that through a fraud of the Turks the city be returned to the Christians in a secret surrender. Hear, therefore, of a fraud, and yet not a fraud.

2. Our Lord appeared to a certain Turk, chosen beforehand by His grace, and said to him: "Arise, thou who sleepest! I command thee to return the city to the Christians." The astonished man concealed that vision in silence.

3. However, a second time, the Lord appeared to him: "Return the city to the Christians," He said, "for I am Christ who command this of thee." Meditating what to do, he went away to his ruler, the prince of Antioch, and made that vision known to him. To him the ruler responded: "You do not wish to obey the phantom, do you, stupid?" Returning, he was afterwards silent.

4. The Lord again appeared to him, saying: "Why hast thou not fulfilled what I ordered thee? Thou must not hesitate, for I, who command this, am Lord of all." No longer doubting, he discreetly negotiated with our men, so that by his zealous plotting they might receive the city.

5. He finished speaking, and gave his son as hostage to Lord Bohemond, to whom he first directed that discourse, and whom he first persuaded. On a certain night, he sent twenty of our men over the wall by means of ladders made of ropes. Without delay, the gate was opened. The Franks, already prepared, entered the city. Forty of our soldiers, who had previously entered by ropes, killed sixty Turks found there, guards of the tower. In a loud voice, altogether the Franks shouted: "God wills it! God wills it!" For this was our signal cry, when we were about to press forward on any enterprise.

6. After hearing this, all the Turks were extremely terrified. Then, when the redness of dawn had paled, the Franks began to go forward to attack the city. When the Turks had first seen Bohemond's red banner on high, furling and unfurling, and the great tumult aroused on all sides, and the Franks running far and wide through the streets with their naked swords and wildly killing people, and had heard their horns sounding on the top of the wall, they began to flee here and there, bewildered. From this scene, many who were able fled into the citadel situated on a cliff.

7. Our rabble wildly seized everything that they found in the streets and houses. But the proved soldiers kept to warfare, in following and killing the Turks.

6

IBN AL-QALANISI
The Damascus Chronicle, 1159

Here we switch to a Muslim view of the Crusades, especially of the
battles of Antioch, Jerusalem, and Ascalon (modern Ashkelon, Israel).
Ibn al-Qalanisi* (c. 1070–1160) was a scholar in Damascus, Syria.
How does his account of the battle for Antioch differ from the previous
selection by Fulcher of Chartres? How do you resolve these differences?

THINKING HISTORICALLY

We noticed how the medieval Christian historian provided two historical threads—the human and divine. How does this Muslim account integrate the threads of human action and divine will?

Modern historians restrict their accounts to human action but
seek to include the views of both sides in a conflict. How do you integrate both sides into your narrative? Also, what signs do you see here
of a possible second conflict, this one between Muslims?

A.H. 491[1]

[9th December, 1097, to 27th November, 1098]

At the end of First Jumādā [beginning of June, 1098] the report arrived
that certain of the men of Antioch among the armourers in the train of
the amīr Yāghī Siyān had entered into a conspiracy against Antioch and
had come to an agreement with the Franks to deliver the city up to them,
because of some ill-usage and confiscations which they had formerly suffered at his hands. They found an opportunity of seizing one of the city
bastions adjoining the Jabal, which they sold to the Franks, and thence
admitted them into the city during the night. At daybreak they raised the
battle cry, whereupon Yāghī Siyān took to flight and went out with a
large body, but not one person amongst them escaped to safety. When he
reached the neighbourhood of Armanāz, an estate near Ma'arrat Masrīn,
he fell from his horse to the ground. One of his companions raised him

---

*IH buhn ahl kahl ah NEE see

[1] "A.H." centers the Muslim calendar like B.C. and A.D. center the Christian calendar. A.H.
means the year of the Hegira, the year Muhammad fled Mecca for Medina and established the
first Muslim society there. This was in 622 of the Christian calendar. But the lunar years of
the Muslim calendar are shorter than the Christian by about 1/20. Thus, the corresponding
year to A.H. 491 is 1098. [Ed.]

Source: H. A. R. Gibb, *The Damascus Chronicle of the Crusades*, extracted and translated
from the *Chronicle of Ibn al-Qalanisi* (Mineola, NY: Dover Publications, 2002), 44–49.

up and remounted him, but he could not maintain his balance on the back of the horse, and after falling repeatedly he died. As for Antioch, the number of men, women, and children, killed, taken prisoner, and enslaved from its population is beyond computation. About three thousand men fled to the citadel and fortified themselves in it, and some few escaped for whom God had decreed escape.

In Sha'bān [July] news was received that al-Afdal, the commander-in-chief (amīr al-juyūsh), had come up from Egypt to Syria at the head of a strong 'askar.[2] He encamped before Jerusalem, where at that time were the two amīrs Sukmān and Il-Ghāzī, sons of Ortuq, together with a number of their kinsmen and followers and a large body of Turks, and sent letters to them, demanding that they should surrender Jerusalem to him without warfare or shedding of blood. When they refused his demand, he opened an attack on the town, and having set up mangonels[3] against it, which effected a breach in the wall, he captured it and received the surrender of the Sanctuary of David[4] from Sukmān. On his entry into it, he shewed kindness and generosity to the two amīrs, and set both them and their supporters free. They arrived in Damascus during the first ten days of Shawwāl [September], and al-Afdal returned with his 'askar to Egypt.

In this year also the Franks set out with all their forces to Ma'arrat al-Nu'mān,[5] and having encamped over against it on 29th Dhu'l-Hijja [27th November], they opened an attack on the town and brought up a tower and scaling-ladders against it.

Now after the Franks had captured the city of Antioch through the devices of the armourer, who was an Armenian named Fīrūz,[6] on the eve of Friday, 1st Rajab [night of Thursday 3rd June], and a series of reports were received confirming this news, the armies of Syria assembled in uncountable force and proceeded to the province of Antioch, in order to inflict a crushing blow upon the armies of the Franks. They besieged the Franks until their supplies of food were exhausted and they were reduced to eating carrion; but thereafter the Franks, though they were in the extremity of weakness, advanced in battle order against the armies of Islām, which were at the height of strength and numbers, and they broke the ranks of the Muslims and scattered their multitudes. The lords of the

---

[2] Small military force of slaves and freed men, under Muslim amirs. [Ed.]

[3] A catapult that could hurl large stones as far as four hundred feet to break down a wall. [Ed.]

[4] The Citadel of Jerusalem.

[5] Ma'arrat al-Numān or Ma'arat al-Numān: Syrian city south of Antioch. The conquest of Antioch did not provide enough food, so the Crusaders marched on to this next city on route to Jerusalem. There they massacred the population of 10,000–20,000 and by some accounts cannibalized some of them. [Ed.]

[6] In the text Nairūz.

pedigree steeds[7] were put to flight, and the sword was unsheathed upon the footsoldiers who had volunteered for the cause of God, who had girt themselves for the Holy War, and were vehement in their desire to strike a blow for the Faith and for the protection of the Muslims. This befel on Tuesday, the [twenty] sixth of Rajab, in this year [29th June, 1098].

A.H. 492

[28th November, 1098, to 16th November, 1099]

In Muharram of this year [December, 1098], the Franks made an assault on the wall of Ma'arrat al-Nu'mān from the east and north. They pushed up the tower until it rested against the wall, and as it was higher, they deprived the Muslims of the shelter of the wall. The fighting raged round this point until sunset on 14th Muharram [11th December], when the Franks scaled the wall, and the townsfolk were driven off it and took to flight. Prior to this, messengers had repeatedly come to them from the Franks with proposals for a settlement by negotiation and the surrender of the city, promising in return security for their lives and property, and the establishment of a [Frankish] governor amongst them, but dissension among the citizens and the fore-ordained decree of God prevented acceptance of these terms. So they captured the city after the hour of the sunset prayer, and a great number from both sides were killed in it. The townsfolk fled to the houses of al-Ma'arra, to defend themselves in them, and the Franks, after promising them safety, dealt treacherously with them. They erected crosses over the town, exacted indemnities from the townsfolk, and did not carry out any of the terms upon which they had agreed, but plundered everything that they found, and demanded of the people sums which they could not pay. On Thursday 17th Safar [13th January, 1099] they set out for Kafr Tāb.

Thereafter they proceeded towards Jerusalem, at the end of Rajab [middle of June] of this year, and the people fled in panic from their abodes before them. They descended first upon al-Ramla, and captured it after the ripening of the crops. Thence they marched to Jerusalem, the inhabitants of which they engaged and blockaded, and having set up the tower against the city they brought it forward to the wall. At length news reached them that al-Afdal was on his way from Egypt with a mighty army to engage in the Holy War against them, and to destroy them, and to succour and protect the city against them. They therefore attacked the city with increased vigour, and prolonged the battle that day until the daylight faded, then withdrew from it, after promising the inhabitants to renew the attack upon them on the morrow. The townsfolk descended from the wall at sunset, whereupon the Franks renewed their assault upon it, climbed up the tower, and gained a footing on the city wall. The

---

[7] Literally "of the short-haired and swift-paced."

defenders were driven down, and the Franks stormed the town and gained possession of it. A number of the townsfolk fled to the sanctuary [of David], and a great host were killed. The Jews assembled in the synagogue, and the Franks burned it over their heads. The sanctuary was surrendered to them on guarantee of safety on the 22nd of Sha'bān [14th July] of this year, and they destroyed the shrines and the tomb of Abraham. Al-Afdal arrived with the Egyptian armies, but found himself forestalled, and having been reinforced by the troops from the Sāhil,[8] encamped outside Ascalon on 14th Ramadān [4th August], to await the arrival of the fleet by sea and of the Arab levies. The army of the Franks advanced against him and attacked him in great force. The Egyptian army was thrown back towards Ascalon, al-Afdal himself taking refuge in the city. The swords of the Franks were given mastery over the Muslims, and death was meted out to the footmen, volunteers, and townsfolk, about ten thousand souls, and the camp was plundered. Al-Afdal set out for Egypt with his officers, and the Franks besieged Ascalon, until at length the townsmen agreed to pay them twenty thousand dinars as protection money, and to deliver this sum to them forthwith. They therefore set about collecting this amount from the inhabitants of the town, but it befel that a quarrel broke out between the [Frankish] leaders, and they retired without having received any of the money. It is said that the number of the people of Ascalon who were killed in this campaign—that is to say of the witnesses, men of substance, merchants, and youths, exclusive of the regular levies—amounted to two thousand seven hundred souls.

[8] The Sāhil was the general name given to the coastal plain and the maritime towns, from Ascalon to Bairūt.

7

RAYMOND OF ST. GILES, COUNT OF TOULOUSE

The Capture of Jerusalem by the Crusaders, 1099

The author of this letter or proclamation was the secular military leader chosen by Pope Urban II to lead the crusade. By the time of the capture of Jerusalem in 1099, he was certainly—with the Norman Bohemond and a couple other nobles—among the top military

Source: Raymond of St. Giles, Count of Toulouse, "The Capture of Jerusalem by the Crusaders," *Translations and Reprints from the Original Sources of European History*, 4th ed., ed. D. C. Munro, vol. 1, bk. 4 (New York: AMC Press, Inc., 1971), 8–12.

leaders. How does he account for their capture of Jerusalem? How would you explain it? Raymond tells how immediately after conquering Jerusalem, the Crusaders went to meet an Egyptian army (mistakenly identified as Babylonian) at Ascalon. How does Raymond explain their success? How did Ibn al-Qalanisi explain it? How might you explain it?

THINKING HISTORICALLY

What seems to be the purpose of this letter? How might Raymond's purpose color what he says? A letter can read much like a historical narrative, as does this one by Raymond of St. Giles. The author clearly wants to tell his readers what has happened. But this letter addressed to the pope, his bishops, and "the whole Christian people" is as much a testament to God's work as it is a history. Why does this make it difficult to construct the human narrative? Which events could you confidently include in your history of the crusade?

To lord Paschal, pope of the Roman church,[1] to all the bishops, and to the whole Christian people, from the archbishop of Pisa, duke Godfrey, now, by the grace of God, defender of the church of the Holy Sepulchre, Raymond, count of St. Giles, and the whole army of God, which is in the land of Israel, greeting.

Multiply your supplications and prayers in the sight of God with joy and thanksgiving, since God has manifested His mercy in fulfilling by our hands what He had promised in ancient times. For after the capture of Nicaea, the whole army, made up of more than three hundred thousand soldiers, departed thence. And, although this army was so great that it could have in a single day covered all Romania and drunk up all the rivers and eaten up all the growing things, yet the Lord conducted them amid so great abundance that a ram was sold for a penny and an ox for twelve pennies or less. Moreover, although the princes and kings of the Saracens rose up against us, yet, by God's will, they were easily conquered and overcome. Because, indeed, some were puffed up by these successes, God opposed to us Antioch, impregnable to human strength. And there He detained us for nine months and so humbled us in the siege that there were scarcely a hundred good horses in our whole army. God opened to us the abundance of His blessing and mercy and led us into the city, and delivered the Turks and all of their possessions into our power.

Inasmuch as we thought that these had been acquired by our own strength and did not worthily magnify God who had done this, we were

[1] Pope Paschal II (r. 1099–1118). [Ed.]

beset by so great a multitude of Turks that no one dared to venture forth at any point from the city. Moreover, hunger so weakened us that some could scarcely refrain from eating human flesh. It would be tedious to narrate all the miseries which we suffered in that city. But God looked down upon His people whom He had so long chastised and mercifully consoled them. Therefore, He at first revealed to us, as a recompense for our tribulation and as a pledge of victory, His lance which had lain hidden since the days of the apostles. Next, He so fortified the hearts of the men, that they who from sickness or hunger had been unable to walk, now were endued with strength to seize their weapons and manfully to fight against the enemy.

After we had triumphed over the enemy, as our army was wasting away at Antioch from sickness and weariness and was especially hindered by the dissensions among the leaders, we proceeded into Syria, stormed Barra and Marra, cities of the Saracens, and captured the fortresses in that country. And while we were delaying there, there was so great a famine in the army that the Christian people now ate the putrid bodies of the Saracens.[2] Finally, by the divine admonition, we entered into the interior of Hispania,[3] and the most bountiful, merciful and victorious hand of the omnipotent Father was with us. For the cities and fortresses of the country through which we were proceeding sent ambassadors to us with many gifts and offered to aid us and to surrender their walled places. But because our army was not large and it was the unanimous wish to hasten to Jerusalem, we accepted their pledges and made them tributaries. One of the cities forsooth, which was on the sea-coast, had more men than there were in our whole army. And when those at Antioch and Laodicea and Archas heard how the hand of the Lord was with us, many from the army who had remained in those cities followed us to Tyre. Therefore, with the Lord's companionship and aid, we proceeded thus as far as Jerusalem.

And after the army had suffered greatly in the siege, especially on account of the lack of water, a council was held and the bishops and princes ordered that all with bare feet should march around the walls of the city, in order that He who entered it humbly in our behalf might be moved by our humility to open it to us and to exercise judgment upon His enemies. God was appeased by this humility and on the eighth day after the humiliation He delivered the city and His enemies to us. It was the day indeed on which the primitive church was driven thence, and on which the festival of the dispersion of the apostles is celebrated. And if you desire to know what was done with the enemy who were found

---

[2] Radulph of Caen, another Crusader chronicler, wrote, "In Ma'arra our troops boiled pagan adults alive in cooking-pots; they impaled children on spits and devoured them grilled." [Ed.]

[3] Probably a metaphor for an extremely fertile Muslim land, as Muslim Spain was known to be. [Ed.]

there, know that in Solomon's Porch and in his temple our men rode in the blood of the Saracens up to the knees of their horses.

Then, when we were considering who ought to hold the city, and some moved by love for their country and kinsmen wished to return home, it was announced to us that the king of Babylon had come to Ascalon with an innumerable multitude of soldiers. His purpose was, as he said, to lead the Franks, who were in Jerusalem, into captivity, and to take Antioch by storm. But God had determined otherwise in regard to us.

Therefore, when we learned that the army of the Babylonians was at Ascalon, we went down to meet them, leaving our baggage and the sick in Jerusalem with a garrison. When our army was in sight of the enemy, upon our knees we invoked the aid of the Lord, that He who in our other adversities had strengthened the Christian faith, might in the present battle break the strength of the Saracens and of the devil and extend the kingdom of the church of Christ from sea to sea, over the whole world. There was no delay; God was present when we cried for His aid, and furnished us with so great boldness, that one who saw us rush upon the enemy would have taken us for a herd of deer hastening to quench their thirst in running water. It was wonderful, indeed, since there were in our army not more than 5,000 horsemen and 15,000 foot-soldiers, and there were probably in the enemy's army 100,000 horsemen and 400,000 foot-soldiers. Then God appeared wonderful to His servants. For before we engaged in fighting, by our very onset alone, He turned this multitude in flight and scattered all their weapons, so that if they wished afterwards to attack us, they did not have the weapons in which they trusted. There can be no question how great the spoils were, since the treasures of the king of Babylon were captured. More than 100,000 Moors perished there by the sword. Moreover, their panic was so great that about 2,000 were suffocated at the gate of the city. Those who perished in the sea were innumerable. Many were entangled in the thickets. The whole world was certainly fighting for us, and if many of ours had not been detained in plundering the camp, few of the great multitude of the enemy would have been able to escape from the battle.

And although it may be tedious, the following must not be omitted: On the day preceding the battle the army captured many thousands of camels, oxen, and sheep. By the command of the princes these were divided among the people. When we advanced to battle, wonderful to relate, the camels formed in many squadrons and the sheep and oxen did the same. Moreover, these animals accompanied us, halting when we halted, advancing when we advanced, and charging when we charged. The clouds protected us from the heat of the sun and cooled us.

Accordingly, after celebrating the victory, the army returned to Jerusalem. Duke Godfrey remained there; the count of St. Giles, Robert, count of Normandy, and Robert, count of Flanders, returned to Laodicea. There they found the fleet belonging to the Pisans and to Bohemond.

After the archbishop of Pisa had established peace between Bohemond and our leaders, Raymond prepared to return to Jerusalem for the sake of God and his brethren.

Therefore, we call upon you of the Catholic Church of Christ and of the whole Latin church to exult in the so admirable bravery and devotion of your brethren, in the so glorious and very desirable retribution of the omnipotent God, and in the so devoutly hoped-for remission of all our sins through the grace of God. And we pray that He may make you—namely, all bishops, clerks, and monks who are leading devout lives, and all the laity—to sit down at the right hand of God, who liveth and reigneth God for ever and ever. And we ask and beseech you in the name of our Lord Jesus, who has ever been with us and aided us and freed us from all our tribulations, to be mindful of your brethren who return to you, by doing them kindnesses and by paying their debts, in order that God may recompense you and absolve you from all your sins and grant you a share in all the blessings which either we or they have deserved in the sight of the Lord. Amen.

8

IBN AL-ATHIR

The Conquest of Jerusalem, c. 1231

In this selection we return to the history of Ibn al-Athir (1160–1233). The following excerpt, taken from his work *The Perfect History*, is one of the most authoritative, roughly contemporaneous histories of the First Crusade from the Muslim perspective. What reason does al-Athir give for the Egyptian capture of Jerusalem from the Turks? Why were the Franks successful in wresting Jerusalem and other lands from Muslim control? What is the significance of the poem at the end of the selection?

THINKING HISTORICALLY

There are always more than two sides to a story, but it is certainly useful to have battle descriptions from two sides of a conflict. In constructing your own narrative of the battle of Jerusalem, you might first look for points of agreement. On what points does Ibn al-Athir agree with other accounts you have read? How else would you decide which elements from each account to include in your narrative?

Source: Francesco Gabrieli, ed., *Arab Historians of the Crusades: Selected and Translated from the Arabic Sources*, ed. and trans. E. J. Costello. Islamic World Series (Berkeley: University of California Press, 1969), 10–12.

Taj ad-Daula Tutūsh was the Lord of Jerusalem but had given it as a feoff to the amīr Suqmān ibn Artūq the Turcoman. When the Franks defeated the Turks at Antioch the massacre demoralized them, and the Egyptians, who saw that the Turkish armies were being weakened by desertion, besieged Jerusalem under the command of al-Afdal ibn Badr al-Jamali. Inside the city were Artūq's sons, Suqmān and Ilghazi, their cousin Sunij and their nephew Yaquti. The Egyptians brought more than forty siege engines to attack Jerusalem and broke down the walls at several points. The inhabitants put up a defense, and the siege and fighting went on for more than six weeks. In the end the Egyptians forced the city to capitulate, in Sha'bān 491 [August 1098]. Suqmān, Ilghazi, and their friends were well treated by al-Afdal, who gave them large gifts of money and let them go free. They made for Damascus and then crossed the Euphrates. Suqmān settled in Edessa and Ilghazi went on into Iraq. The Egyptian governor of Jerusalem was a certain Iftikhār ad-Daula, who was still there at the time of which we are speaking.

After their vain attempt to take Acre by siege, the Franks moved on to Jerusalem and besieged it for more than six weeks. They built two towers, one of which, near Sion, the Muslims burnt down, killing everyone inside it. It had scarcely ceased to burn before a messenger arrived to ask for help and to bring the news that the other side of the city had fallen. In fact Jerusalem was taken from the north on the morning of Friday 22 Sha'bān 492 [July 15, 1099]. The population was put to the sword by the Franks, who pillaged the area for a week. A band of Muslims barricaded themselves into the Oratory of David and fought on for several days. They were granted their lives in return for surrendering. The Franks honoured their word, and the group left by night for Ascalon. In the Masjid al-Aqsa the Franks slaughtered more than 70,000 people, among them a large number of Imams and Muslim scholars, devout and ascetic men who had left their homelands to live lives of pious seclusion in the Holy Place. The Franks stripped the Dome of the Rock of more than forty silver candelabra, each of them weighing 3,600 drams, and a great silver lamp weighing forty-four Syrian pounds, as well as a hundred and fifty smaller silver candelabra and more than twenty gold ones, and a great deal more booty. Refugees from Syria reached Baghdād in Ramadan,[1] among them the qadi Abu Sa'd al-Hárawi. They told the Caliph's ministers a story that wrung their hearts and brought tears to their eyes. On Friday they went to the Cathedral Mosque and begged for help, weeping so that their hearers wept with them as they described the sufferings of the Muslims in that Holy City:

---

[1] The holy month of Ramadan, the month of fasting. [Ed.]

the men killed, the women and children taken prisoner, the homes pillaged. Because of the terrible hardships they had suffered, they were allowed to break the fast. . . .

It was the discord between the Muslim princes, as we shall describe, that enabled the Franks to overrun the country. Abu l-Muzaffar al-Abiwardi composed several poems on this subject, in one of which he says:

> We have mingled blood with flowing tears, and there is no room
>   left in us for Pity.
> To shed tears is a man's worst weapon when the swords stir up the
>   embers of war.
> Sons of Islām, behind you are battles in which heads rolled at
>   your feet.
> Dare you slumber in the blessed shade of safety, where life is as
>   soft as an orchard flower?
> How can the eye sleep between the lids at a time of disasters that
>   would waken any sleeper?
> While your Syrian brothers can only sleep on the backs of their
>   chargers, or in vultures' bellies!
> Must the foreigners feed on our ignominy, while you trail behind
>   you the train of a pleasant life, like men whose world is at peace?
> When blood has been spilt, when sweet girls must for shame hide
>   their lovely faces in their hands!
> When the white swords' points are red with blood, and the iron of
>   the brown lances is stained with gore!
> At the sound of sword hammering on lance young children's hair
>   turns white.
> This is war, and the man who shuns the whirlpool to save his life
>   shall grind his teeth in penitence.
> This is war, and the infidel's sword is naked in his hand, ready to
>   be sheathed again in men's necks and skulls.
> This is war, and he who lies in the tomb at Medina seems to raise
>   his voice and cry: "O sons of Hashim!
> I see my people slow to raise the lance against the enemy: I see the
>   Faith resting on feeble pillars.
> For fear of death the Muslims are evading the fire of battle, refus-
>   ing to believe that death will surely strike them."
> Must the Arab champions then suffer with resignation, while the
>   gallant Persians shut their eyes to their dishonour?

9

Letter from a Jewish Pilgrim in Egypt, 1100

The following letter was written in 1100 by an anonymous Jewish pilgrim from Alexandria, unable to make his pilgrimage to Jerusalem because of the ongoing war. How does the letter's author regard the Egyptian sultan? How does he view the struggle between the sultan and the Franks? What does this suggest about the lives of Jews under Muslim rule during this time period?

THINKING HISTORICALLY

What does this letter add to your understanding of the Crusaders' capture of Jerusalem? How would you write a narrative of the First Crusade that took advantage of Christian, Muslim, and Jewish sources?

In Your Name, You Merciful.

If I attempted to describe my longing for you, my Lord, my brother *and cousin*, — may God prolong your days and make permanent your honour, success, happiness, health, and welfare; and . . . subdue your enemies — all the paper in the world would not suffice. My longing will but increase and double, just as the days will grow and double. May *the Creator of the World* presently make us meet together in joy when I return under His guidance to my homeland *and to the inheritance of my Fathers* in complete happiness, *so that we rejoice and be happy through His great mercy and His vast bounty; and thus may be His will*!

You may remember, my Lord, that many years ago I left our country to seek God's mercy and help in my poverty, to behold Jerusalem and return thereupon. However, when I was in Alexandria God brought about circumstances which caused a slight delay. Afterwards, however, "the sea grew stormy," and many armed bands made their appearance in Palestine; *"and he who went forth and he who came had no peace,"* so that hardly one survivor out of a whole group came back to us from Palestine and told us that scarcely anyone could save himself from those armed bands, since they were so numerous and were gathered round . . . every town. There was further the journey through the desert, among [the bedouins] and whoever escaped from the one, fell into the hands of the other. Moreover, mutinies [spread throughout the country and reached] even Alexandria, so that we ourselves were besieged several times and the city was ruined; . . . the end however *was good*, for the Sultan — may God bestow glory upon his victories — conquered the city

---

Source: S. D. Goitein, trans., "Contemporary Letters on the Capture of Jerusalem by the Crusaders," *Journal of Jewish Studies* 3, no. 4 (1952): 162–77.

and caused justice to abound in it in a manner unprecedented in the history of any king in the world; not even a dirham was looted from anyone. Thus I had come to hope that because of his justice and strength God would give the land into his hands, and I should thereupon go to Jerusalem in safety and tranquility. For this reason I proceeded from Alexandria to Cairo, in order to start [my journey] from there.

When, however, God had given Jerusalem, the blessed, into his hands this state of affairs continued for too short a time to allow for making a journey there. The Franks arrived and killed everybody in the city, whether of *Ishmael or of Israel*; and the few who survived the slaughter were made prisoners. Some of these have been ransomed since, while others are still in captivity in all parts of the world.

Now, all of us had anticipated that our Sultan—may God bestow glory upon his victories—would set out against them [the Franks] with his troops and chase them away. But time after time our hope failed. Yet, to this very present moment we do hope that God will give his [the Sultan's] enemies into his hands. For it is inevitable that the armies will join in battle this year; and, if God grants us victory through him [the Sultan] and he conquers Jerusalem—and so it may be, with God's will—I for one shall not be amongst those who will linger, but shall go there to behold the city; and shall afterwards return straight to you—if God wills it. My salvation is in God, for this [is unlike] the other previous occasions [of making a pilgrimage to Jerusalem]. God, indeed, will exonerate me, since at my age I cannot afford to delay and wait any longer; I want to return home under any circumstances, if I still remain alive—whether I shall have seen Jerusalem or have given up the hope of doing it—both of which are possible.

You know, of course, my Lord, what has happened to us in the course of the last five years: the plague, the illnesses, and ailments have continued unabated for four successive years. As a result of this the wealthy became impoverished and a great number of people died *of the plague*, so that entire families perished in it. I, too, was affected with a grave illness, from which I recovered only about a year ago; then I was taken ill the following year so that (on the margin) for four years I have remained. . . . He who has said: *The evil diseases of Egypt* . . . he who hiccups does not live . . . ailments and will die . . . otherwise . . . will remain alive.

■ REFLECTIONS

The First Crusade (1095–1099) marks only the beginning of a protracted conflict between Christians and Muslims that continued until, perhaps, the eighteenth century. In the Holy Land there were intermittent conflicts over the next forty years culminating in what was called the Second Crusade, from 1147 to 1149. Meanwhile, the conquest of Muslims in Spain, which had been equated with the crusade by Pope Urban II, continued, as did frequent crusades into Eastern Europe.

The establishment of Latin kingdoms in Palestine could not be maintained without continual reinforcements, and they were vulnerable to Muslim attack. It was the loss of the Crusader state of Edessa that launched the Second Crusade. Instead the Crusaders conquered formerly friendly Damascus. A Muslim power struggle resulted in the rise of Saladin (c. 1138–1193), who united Egypt, Syria, and Iraq and conquered Jerusalem. This led to the Third Crusade (1189–1192), in which the kings of England, France, and Germany attempted to recapture Jerusalem. Their failure led to a German Crusade (1197–1198) that took Beirut and Sidon on the Mediterranean coast but was otherwise a failure. Then a large, mainly French Fourth Crusade (1202–1204) was mounted from Venice, but it resulted in the sacking of Constantinople in 1204, dealing an irreparable blow to the Byzantine Empire. A Fifth Crusade (1217–1229) recovered Jerusalem, which was retaken by the Muslims in 1244, leading to crusades initiated by King Louis IX of France. Other crusading armies invaded Egypt, Tunisia, Muslim Spain, northwest Africa, southern France, Poland, Latvia, Germany, Russia, the Mongol Empire, Finland, Bosnia, and Italy, against papal enemies and Eastern Orthodox Christians as well as Muslims. Recent histories of the Crusades have ended their narratives in 1521, 1560, 1588, and 1798, according to Jonathan Riley-Smith, who ends the recent *Oxford History of the Crusades* with images of the Crusades in twentieth-century wars. Does the imagery of the Crusades still animate our wars?

Americans like former president George W. Bush have learned the effects of using the term *crusade* in the context of American aspirations in the Middle East, and the interference of Western forces in the region has been a constant reminder to Muslims of a long history of Western intervention that began with the First Crusade. In Syria, Lebanon, Jordan, Palestine, and Israel, one can still see Crusader castles looming over the landscape and meet the descendants and coreligionists of the founders of Crusader states. From the perspective of many Muslims, unquestioned U.S. support of Israel, especially in Jerusalem, is a direct continuation of the Crusades. On more than one occasion, leaders of Middle Eastern countries have pictured themselves as a modern-day Saladin rising to battle invading Christian Crusaders.

Writing a narrative of the First Crusade is difficult enough given the many sides to the conflict. Anna Comnena and the Orthodox Christians of Byzantium had a very different perspective than the Franks or Roman Christian Crusaders of Western Europe. Nor were Muslims a single force of opposition. The Seljuk Turks had different interests than the caliph of Baghdad, and, contrary to the opinion of

Raymond St. Giles, the Fatimid Egyptian forces at Ascalon were neither biblical Babylonians nor Abbasids from Baghdad. Then, too, there
were Jews, and those in Germany may have had different interests than
those in Egypt, despite an agreement about Christian crusading. There
are more sources than we have been able to explore here, and more interpretations than we have been able to include.

After trying your hand at writing a narrative of the First Crusade,
you might think of how narratives are constructed. Each story leaves
out some information to include other information, lest it read like a
phone book. How do you decide whose "numbers" to include? To
stimulate your thoughts about narrative choices, you might choose a
subject a little closer to home so that you have greater knowledge of
the primary sources. Try a narrative of your own life up to now. If you
dare, ask someone close to you to point out what you missed or
overemphasized.

11

Raiders of Steppe and Sea: Vikings and Mongols

Eurasia and the Atlantic, 900–1350

■ HISTORICAL CONTEXT

Ever since the first urban settlements emerged five thousand years ago, they have been at risk of attack. The domestication of the horse and the development of sailing ships about four thousand years ago increased that risk. Much of ancient history is the story of the conflict between settled peoples and raiders on horseback or sailors on fleet ships. Eventually — between the third and fifth centuries C.E. — the great empires of Rome and Han dynasty China succumbed to raiding nomadic tribes from Central Asia. As nomadic peoples settled themselves, new waves of raiders appeared.

In the previous chapter, we explored the impact of the Seljuk Turks who conquered cities in the Middle East that had been taken hundreds of years earlier by Arab armies on horseback. At about the same time as the Turks emerged from Central Asia to threaten settlements south of the great Eurasian steppe grasslands, a new force from the north, Viking raiders on sailing ships, burst across the northern seas to attack the coastal enclaves and river cities of Europe and what came to be known in their wake as Russia. As generations oscillated between raiding and trading, new waves of Norsemen explored the edges of known waters to plant new settlements as far west as Iceland, Greenland, and North America. (See Map 11.1.) Who were these people? What did they hope to accomplish? How were they different from the land-raiders who preceded them?

At about the time that the Vikings were becoming farmers and settlers in their conquered lands, around the year 1200, the Eurasian steppe exploded with its last and largest force of nomadic tribesmen

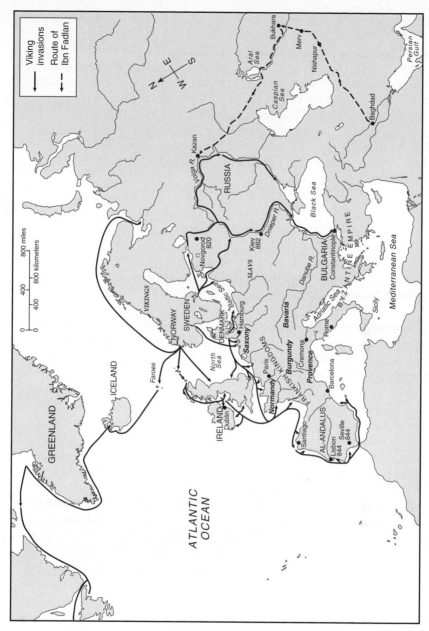

Map 11.1 Viking Invasions and Voyages of the Ninth and Tenth Centuries.

on horseback: the Mongols. Between the election of Genghis Khan*
(c. 1162–1227) as the Khan of Khans in 1206 and the pandemic
plague known as the Black Death of 1346–1350 (or the end of the
Mongol Yuan dynasty in China in 1368), the Mongols swept across
Eurasia and created the largest empire the world had ever seen. (See
Map 11.2.) Who were the Mongols? What made them so successful?
How were they similar to, and different from, the Norsemen?

What was the impact of these raiding peoples on settled societies?
How did they change each other? How did they change themselves? How
did they create some of the conditions necessary for the modern world to
come into being?

■ THINKING HISTORICALLY

Distinguishing Historical Understanding from Moral Judgments

The ancient Greeks called non-Greeks "barbarians" (because their
languages contained "bar-bar"-like sounds that seemed foreign, untu-
tored, and, thus, uncivilized). Since then the terms *barbarian* and
civilized have been weighted with the same combination of descriptive
and moral meaning. In the nineteenth century it was even fashionable
among historians and anthropologists to use these terms to distinguish
between nomadic peoples and settled, urban peoples. As our first
reading (and perhaps modern common sense) makes clear, rural or
nomadic people are not necessarily less "moral" than city people;
technological development is hardly the same thing as moral
development (or the opposite).

What connection, if any, is there between history and morality?
Stories of the past are frequently used to celebrate or condemn past
individuals or groups. Sometimes we find past behavior shocking or
reprehensible. Is it logical or proper to make moral judgments about
the past? Can historians find answers to moral questions by studying
the past?

Perhaps the place to begin is by recognizing that just as the "is" is
different from the "ought," so too the "was" is different from the
"should have been." Historians must begin by finding out what was.
Our own moral values may lead us to ask certain questions about the
past, but the historian's job is only to find out what happened. We will
see in the following selections how difficult it has been for past observers
to keep their own moral judgments from coloring their descriptions of

* geng GIHZ kahn

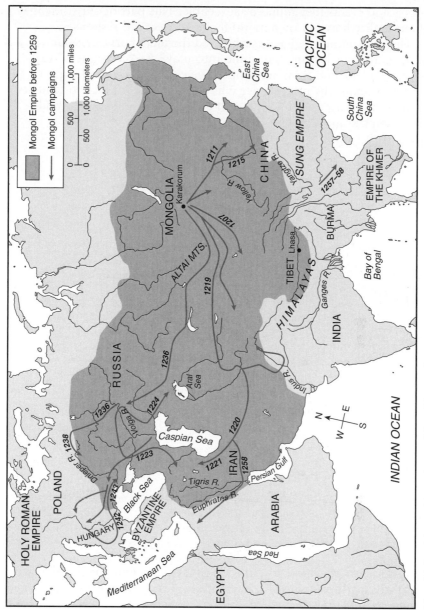

Map 11.2   Mongol Invasions of the Thirteenth Century.

peoples and events they found disagreeable. This part of our study may help us realize how our own moral feelings affect our responses.

Then, assuming we have established the facts fairly, can our moral sentiments legitimately come into play? As "consumers" of history, readers, and thinking people, we cannot avoid making judgments about the past. Under what conditions are such judgments fair, helpful, or appropriate? We will explore this much larger and more complex question in this chapter.

1

GREGORY GUZMAN

Were the Barbarians a Negative or Positive Factor in Ancient and Medieval History? 1988

Gregory Guzman is a modern world historian. In this essay he asks some questions about the peoples who have been called "barbarians." How were the lives of pastoral nomads different from those of settled people? How did the horse shape life on the steppe? How effective were these herders as rulers of settled societies? What were the achievements of the pastoral nomads?

THINKING HISTORICALLY

Why, according to Guzman, have most histories of the barbarians made them look bad? How have city people or historians let their own prejudices block an appreciation of the achievements of pastoralists?

According to the general surveys of ancient and medieval history found in most textbooks, barbarian peoples and/or primitive savages repeatedly invaded the early Eurasian civilized centers in Europe, the Middle East, India, and China. All accounts of the early history of these four civilizations contain recurrent references to attacks by such familiar and famous barbarians as the Hittites, Hyksos, Kassites,

Source: Gregory Guzman, "Were the Barbarians a Negative or Positive Factor in Ancient and Medieval History?" *The Historian* 50 (August 1988): 558–72.

Aryans, Scythians, Sarmatians, Hsiung-nu, Huns, Germans, Turks, and Mongols, and they also record the absorption and assimilation of these Inner Asian barbarian hordes into the respective cultures and lifestyles of the more advanced coastal civilizations. The early sources generally equate the barbarians with chaos and destruction. The barbarians are presented as evil and despicable intruders, associated only with burning, pillaging, and slaughtering, while the civilized peoples are portrayed as the good and righteous forces of stability, order, and progress.

But it must be remembered that most of these early sources are not objective; they are blatantly one-sided, biased accounts written by members of the civilized societies. Thus, throughout recorded history, barbarians have consistently received bad press — bad PR to use the modern terminology. By definition, barbarians were illiterate, and thus they could not write their own version of events. All written records covering barbarian-civilized interaction came from the civilized peoples at war with the barbarians — often the sedentary peoples recently defeated and overwhelmed by those same barbarians. Irritated and angered coastal historians tended to record and emphasize only the negative aspects of their recent interaction with the barbarians. These authors tended to condemn and denigrate the way their barbarian opponents looked and to associate them with the devil and evil, rather than to report with objectivity what actually happened. For example, the Roman historian Ammianus Marcellinus, whose description is distorted by hatred and fear, described the barbarians as "two-footed beasts, seemingly chained to their horses from which they take their meat and drink, never touching a plough and having no houses." While living in Jerusalem, St. Jerome also left a vivid description of the Huns who ". . . filled the whole earth with slaughter and panic alike as they flittered hither and thither on their swift horses. . . . They were at hand everywhere before they were expected; by their speed they outstripped rumor, and they took pity neither upon religion nor rank nor age nor wailing childhood. Those who had just begun to live were compelled to die. . . ."

Such reports obviously made the barbarians look bad, while their nomadic habits and practices, which differed from those of the sedentary coastal peoples, were clearly portrayed as inferior and less advanced: the incarnation of evil itself. These horror-filled and biased descriptions were not the accounts of weak and defenseless peoples. Rather, they were written by the citizens of the most advanced and powerful states and empires in Europe, the Middle East, India, and China. The individual barbarian tribes were, nevertheless, able to attack and invade these strong and well-organized civilized states with relative impunity — pillaging and killing almost at will.

Several important questions, not addressed by the ancient and medieval historians, need to be answered here. Who were these barbarians? Why and how did they manage to repeatedly defeat and overwhelm so easily the wealthiest and most advanced civilizations of the day? And why were they so vehemently condemned and hated in recorded history, if these barbarian Davids were able to consistently defeat such mighty Goliath civilized centers? Since the rich and populous civilized states enjoyed tremendous advantages in the confrontations, why have the barbarians so often been denied the popular role of the underdog?

In the process of answering those questions, this study would like to suggest that maybe the barbarians were not really the "bad guys." While they may not deserve to be called the "good guys," they made a much more positive contribution to human civilization than presented in the grossly distorted written sources. The barbarians deserve much more credit than they have been given, for they created a complex pastoral lifestyle as an alternative to sedentary agriculture, and in that achievement they were not subhuman savages only out to loot, pillage, and destroy. As this study will show, the barbarians played a much more positive and constructive role in the development and diffusion of early human history than that with which they are usually credited.

Before proceeding further, it is necessary to identify these much-maligned barbarians and describe how their way of life and their basic practices differed from those of the sedentary coastal peoples in order to better evaluate the barbarian role and its impact on the history of humanity.

In terms of identity, the barbarians were the steppe nomads of Inner Asia or Central Eurasia. This area represents one of the toughest and most inhospitable places in the world in which to survive. The climate of the interior of the large Eurasian landmass is not moderated by the distant seas, resulting in extremes of climate, of hot and cold, wet and dry. It is an area of ice, forest, desert, and mountains—with bitter winds, dust, and poor soil. Unlike the coastal regions with their dependable moisture and warmth, the soil of Inner Asia was too cold, poor, and dry for agriculture; thus the sedentary urban lifestyle of the coastal civilized centers was not an option in the Eurasian heartland. The people living there had to be tough to endure such a hostile environment, where they constantly fought both nature and other people for survival.

Due to necessity, the people of Inner Asia were nomads, wandering in search of food and pasture, and they became herdsmen, shepherds, and warriors. These steppe nomads, the barbarians of recorded history, were frequently nothing more than migrants looking for new homes; these people needed little encouragement to seek safety, security, and better living conditions in the warm, rich, and fertile coastal civilization centers. Thus the steppe barbarians were not always savage marauders coming only to loot and pillage. Many of the so-called barbarian invaders constituted a surplus population which harsh Inner Asia could not support, or they represented whole tribes being pushed out of their ancestral homeland by stronger tribes behind them. At any rate, these repeated waves of nomadic peoples leaving the steppes soon encountered the coastal civilizations.

These Inner Asian barbarians were more or less harmless outsiders until the horse dramatically changed their lifestyle on the vast steppes. They adopted the pastoral system as the best way of providing for basic needs. The natural pasture provided by the steppe grassland proved ideal for grazing large herds and flocks of animals. Soon their whole life revolved around their animals; they became shepherds, herders, and keepers of beasts. . . .

The dominant feature of this emerging barbarian pastoralism was its mounted nature; it was essentially a horse culture by 1000 B.C. At first small horses were kept only for food and milk, but bigger horses eventually led to riding. Once an accomplished fact, mounted practices dramatically changed the lifestyle of the barbarian steppe peoples. Horseback riding made the tending of scattered herds faster and less tiring, and it enlarged the size of herds while increasing the range of pastoral movement. It also made possible, when necessary, the total migration of entire tribes and clans. Mastery of the horse reduced the vast expanses of steppe pasturage to more manageable proportions. Steppe nomads moved twice a year between traditional winter and summer pastures; the spring and fall were spent moving between the necessary grazing grounds. All peoples and possessions moved with regularity; the nomads became used to living in the saddle, so to speak.

The horse thus became the center of pastoral life on the steppes. The barbarian nomads could literally live off their animals which provided meat, milk, and hides for clothing, coverings, boots, etc. Tools and weapons were made from the bones and sinews, and dried dung was used as fuel. The barbarians ate, sold, negotiated, slept, and took care of body functions in the saddle. . . . These mounted practices led to the emergence of the centaur motif in Middle Eastern art, as the civilized people tended to view the horse and rider as one inseparable unit.

Military action also became an integral part of nomadic steppe life. Warfare was simply cavalry action by the pastoral herdsmen who served as soldiers for the duration of the conflict. Steppe military service differed little from the normal, on-the-move pastoral life. Large-scale steppe alliances were hard to organize and even harder to hold together among the independent nomads. Such temporary alliances, called hordes, rose swiftly to great strength and power, but they usually declined and disintegrated just as quickly.

At any rate, these barbarian nomads were tough and hardy war-riors. The horse gave them speed and mobility over both the light and heavily armed infantry of the civilized centers, but for this speed and mobility the barbarians gave up any type of defensive armor. They learned to guide their horses with their knees, since both arms needed to be free for the bow and arrow, their primary offensive weapon. . . .

Early civilized armies had no cavalry. The famous Macedonian pha-lanx and the formidable Roman legions contained only light and heav-ily armed infantry. At first these brave foot soldiers had no tactical maneuvers to face and contain a barbarian cavalry charge. Even more devastating was the storm of arrows raining down upon them long be-fore they could engage in the traditional hand-to-hand combat. The formidable steppe cavalry thus subjected civilized defenses to continu-ous pressure. Every nomad with a horse and bow was a potential front-line soldier who was tough, resourceful, and ferocious, whereas only a small percentage of the civilized population was equipped and trained for war. The nomadic lifestyle and the speed of the horse eliminated the need for expensive and heavy metal armor and its accompanying tech-nological skills. Cavalry tactics gave an initial military advantage to the barbarians and the mounted horsemen won most of the early battles. The best defense against barbarian cavalry was an insurmount-able obstacle, a wall. . . .

Since they had the military advantage of cavalry tactics, the steppe nomads attacked and conquered various coastal civilizations with regu-larity. In a typical conquest, the victorious barbarians were the new military/political rulers. These new rulers possessed strengths obvious to all. The barbarians had vigorous and dynamic leadership; good, able, and char-ismatic leadership had been needed to organize the independent nomads into an effective horde in the first place. The new rulers had the complete loyalty of their followers; their group identity based on common blood and ancestors resulted in an intense personal and individual allegiance and commitment.

The first century after the initial conquest was usually an era of dynamic leadership, good government, and economic prosperity, as nomadic strengths mixed with the local advances and practices of that civilization. The new ruling family was often a fusion of the best of both sides as the barbarian victors married into the previous ruling dynasty. This brought forth an age of powerful and successful rulers, and pro-duced an era of energetic leadership, good government, low taxes, agri-cultural revival, and peace. . . .

After this early period of revitalized and dynamic rule, slow decline usually set in. Royal vigor and ability sank as the rulers became soft, both mentally and physically. Without physical exercise and self-discipline, the rulers became overindulgent, instantly acquiring everything they wanted—excessive amounts of food or drink, harems, puppets, and yes-men as advisers. At the same time court rivalries and internal divisiveness began to emerge once the strong unity required for the conquest was no longer needed. A rivalry that often arose was between the ruler and various groups of his followers. . . . His steppe horsemen began to give first loyalty to their new family land rather than to their individual leader who was now weak, impaired, and soft. Such internal rivalries weakened the central government and led to chaos and civil wars. Thus, a civilized center was ripe for the next series of invasions and conquest. . . .

The barbarians can and should be viewed as representing a dynamic and vital element in human history for they periodically revived many stagnating coastal civilizations. Many of these sedentary centers flourished, growing rich and powerful. In the process they also became conservative, settled into a fixed routine. Preferring the status quo, they tended to use old answers and ways to face new problems and issues, and as a consequence they lost the vitality and flexibility required for healthy and progressive growth.

The barbarians were active and dynamic. In their conquests of civilized centers, they frequently destroyed and eliminated the old and outdated and preserved and passed on only the good and useful elements. Sometimes, the mounted invaders also introduced new ideas and practices. Some of these new barbarian innovations (horseback riding, archery, trousers, and boots, etc.) fused with the good and useful practices of the sedentary peoples. . . . The ongoing encounters with barbarian strangers inevitably fostered innovation and progress in the civilized centers. . . .

It can be argued that barbarians also played a positive role in the spread and diffusion of civilization itself. The four major Eurasian civilization centers were separated from each other by deserts, mountains, and the vast expanses of the steppe heartland of Inner Asia. In its early stages each civilization was somewhat isolated from the others. Overland trade and contact was possible only through the barbarian steppe highway which stretched over five thousand miles across Eurasia, from Hungary to Manchuria. There was little early sea contact between the four sedentary centers, as naval travel was longer and more dangerous than the overland routes.

Thus the steppe barbarians were the chief agency through which the ideas and practices of one civilization were spread to another before 1500 A.D. According to [historian] William H. McNeill, there was much conceptual diffusion carried along the steppe highway by the barbarians. Writing originated in the ancient Middle East. The concept, not the form, of writing then spread eastward from the Middle East, as the Indian and Chinese forms and characters were significantly different than Middle Eastern cuneiform. The making and use of bronze and chariots also spread from the Middle East to Europe, India, and China. Chariots were introduced to China, on the eastern end of the steppe highway, a few centuries after their appearance in the Middle East. Needless to say, this type of early cultural diffusion is difficult to document with any degree of certainty, but enough evidence exists to make it highly probable, even if not scientifically provable.

The late medieval period provides even more examples of cultural diffusion via the movement of barbarians along the Inner Asian steppe highway. The great Eurasian *Pax Mongolica*[1] opened the way for much cultural cross-fertilization in the late-thirteenth and early-fourteenth centuries. Chinese inventions like gunpowder and printing made their way to the Middle East and Europe in this period. Records show that Chinese artillerymen accompanied the Mongol armies into the Middle East. Papal envoys like John of Plano Carpini and William of Rubruck traveled to the Mongol capital of Karakorum in the 1240s and 1250s. In the 1280s, Marco Polo brought with him from Kublai Khan's court in China a Mongol princess to be the bride of the Mongol Khan of Persia. . . .

This cultural interaction and exchange between Eurasian coastal civilizations ended with the collapse of the Mongol Khanates in Persia and China in the mid-fourteenth century. The barbarian Mongols, therefore, provided the last period of great cultural cross-fertilization before the modern age.

Historical evidence that exists enables one to argue that the barbarian nomads played an active and positive role in the history of mankind. The barbarian invaders revitalized stagnant and decaying civilizations and were responsible for a certain amount of cultural diffusion between emerging ancient and medieval civilizations. The traditional portrayal of barbarians as mere marauders and destroyers is misleading and incorrect. Unfortunately this is the usual role they are given when historians center their study of the past narrowly on the civilized centers and the biased written sources produced by those peoples. All too often historians tend to adopt and reflect the biases and values of their subjects under study, and thus continue to denigrate and condemn all barbarians without objectively evaluating their real contributions to human development. The study of the steppe nomads, the barbarians, is just as valid a topic for historical analysis as the traditional study of coastal sedentary civilizations. Only by knowing and understanding the pastoral barbarian can historians accurately evaluate the constant interaction between the two lifestyles and come to understand the full picture of humanity's early growth and development in the ancient and medieval periods of Eurasian history.

---

[1] Mongolian Peace, after the *Pax Romana*, or Roman Peace. [Ed.]

2

IBN FADLAN
The Viking Rus, 922

In 921 the Muslim caliph of Baghdad sent Ibn Fadlan* on a mission to the king of the Bulgars.[1] The Muslim king of the Bulgars may have been looking for an alliance with the caliph of Baghdad against the Khazars, sandwiched between them just west of the Caspian Sea. North and west of the Bulgars was the area that became Ukraine and Russia. The Volga River, which had its source in the Ural Mountains, flowed south through this land into the Caspian Sea. In the eighth and ninth centuries this area was inhabited by various tribes, many of which spoke early Slavic languages. At some point these tribes were united under the command of a people called the Rus. The origins of the Rus are disputed, but most experts believe that they were either Vikings or the descendants of Vikings and Slavs.

Ibn Fadlan provides our earliest description of these Rus (or Northmen, as he calls them here), whom he encountered on the Volga near the modern city of Kazan during his trip to the Bulgar king. (See Map 11.1 on page 399 for his route.) They or their ancestors had sailed downriver from the Baltic Sea on raiding and trading expeditions. What does Ibn Fadlan tell us about these Scandinavian raiders who gave their name to Russia?

THINKING HISTORICALLY

Notice Ibn Fadlan's moral judgments about the Viking Rus. Notice your own moral judgments. How are Ibn Fadlan's judgments different from your own? What do you think accounts for those differences?

I saw how the Northmen had arrived with their wares, and pitched their camp beside the Volga. Never did I see people so gigantic; they are tall as palm trees, and florid and ruddy of complexion. They wear neither camisoles nor *chaftans*,[2] but the men among them wear a garment of

---

* IH buhn fahd LAHN

[1] These Bulgars, with a Muslim king, had recently been forced north of the Caspian Sea (while other Bulgars moved west to what is today Bulgaria where they were converted to Christianity by Byzantium). [Ed.]

[2] Probably means no fine or fitted tops or robes; but see later description of funeral. [Ed.]

Source: Albert Stanborough Cook, "Ibn Fadlan's Account of Scandinavian Merchants on the Volga in 922," *Journal of English and Germanic Philology* 22, no. 1 (1923): 56–63.

rough cloth, which is thrown over one side, so that one hand remains free. Every one carries an axe, a dagger, and a sword, and without these weapons they are never seen. Their swords are broad, with wavy lines, and of Frankish make. From the tip of the finger-nails to the neck, each man of them is tattooed with pictures of trees, living beings, and other things. The women carry, fastened to their breast, a little case of iron, copper, silver, or gold, according to the wealth and resources, of their husbands. Fastened to the case they wear a ring, and upon that a dagger, all attached to their breast. About their necks they wear gold and silver chains. If the husband possesses ten thousand dirhems, he has one chain made for his wife; if twenty thousand, two; and for every ten thousand, one is added. Hence it often happens that a Scandinavian woman has a large number of chains about her neck. Their most highly prized ornaments consist of small green shells, of one of the varieties which are found in [the bottoms of] ships. They make great efforts to obtain these, paying as much as a dirhem for such a shell, and stringing them as a necklace for their wives.

They are the filthiest race that God ever created. They do not wipe themselves after going to stool, nor wash themselves after a nocturnal pollution, any more than if they were wild asses.

They come from their own country, anchor their ships in the Volga, which is a great river, and build large wooden houses on its banks. In every such house there live ten or twenty, more or fewer. Each man has a couch, where he sits with the beautiful girls he has for sale. Here he is as likely as not to enjoy one of them while a friend looks on. At times several of them will be thus engaged at the same moment, each in full view of the others. Now and again a merchant will resort to a house to purchase a girl, and find her master thus embracing her, and not giving over until he has fully had his will.

Every morning a girl comes and brings a tub of water, and places it before her master. In this he proceeds to wash his face and hands, and then his hair, combing it out over the vessel. Thereupon he blows his nose, and spits into the tub, and, leaving no dirt behind, conveys it all into this water. When he has finished, the girl carries the tub to the man next [to] him, who does the same. Thus she continues carrying the tub from one to another till each of those who are in the house has blown his nose and spit into the tub, and washed his face and hair.

As soon as their ships have reached the anchorage, every one goes ashore, having at hand bread, meat, onions, milk, and strong drink, and betakes himself to a high, upright piece of wood, bearing the likeness of a human face; this is surrounded by smaller statues, and behind these there are still other tall pieces of wood driven into the ground. He advances to the large wooden figure, prostrates himself before it, and thus addresses it: "O my Lord, I am come from a far country, bringing with me so and so many girls, and so and so many pelts of sable" [or, marten]; and when he has thus enumerated all his merchandise, he continues, "I have brought thee this present," laying before the wooden statue what he has brought, and saying: "I desire thee to bestow upon me a purchaser who has gold and silver coins, who will buy from me to my heart's content, and who will refuse none of my demands." Having so said, he departs. If his trade then goes ill, he returns and brings a second, or even a third present. If he still continues to have difficulty in obtaining what he desires, he brings a present to one of the small statues, and implores its intercession, saying: "These are the wives and daughters of our lord." Continuing thus, he goes to each statue in turn, invokes it, beseeches its intercession, and bows humbly before it. If it then chances that his trade goes swimmingly, and he disposes of all his merchandise, he reports: "My lord has fulfilled my desire; now it is my duty to repay him." Upon this, he takes a number of cattle and sheep, slaughters them, gives a portion of the meat to the poor, and carries the rest before the large statue and the smaller ones that surround it, hanging the heads of the sheep and cattle on the large piece of wood which is planted in the earth. When night falls, dogs come and devour it all. Then he who has so placed it exclaims: "I am well pleasing to my lord; he has consumed my present."

If one of their number falls sick, they set up a tent at a distance, in which they place him, leaving bread and water at hand. Thereafter they never approach nor speak to him, nor visit him the whole time, especially if he is a poor person or a slave. If he recovers and rises from his sick bed, he returns to his own. If he dies, they cremate him; but if he is a slave they leave him as he is till at length he becomes the food of dogs and birds of prey.

If they catch a thief or a robber, they lead him to a thick and lofty tree, fasten a strong rope round him, string him up, and let him hang until he drops to pieces by the action of wind and rain.

I was told that the least of what they do for their chiefs when they die, is to consume them with fire. When I was finally informed of the death of one of their magnates, I sought to witness what befell. First they laid him in his grave—over which a roof was erected—for the space of ten days, until they had completed the cutting and sewing of his clothes. In the case of a poor man, however, they merely build for him a boat, in which they place him, and consume it with fire. At the death of a rich man, they bring together his goods, and divide them into three parts. The first of these is for his family; the second is expended for the garments they make; and with the third they purchase strong drink, against the day when the girl resigns herself to death, and is burned with her master. To the use of wine they abandon themselves in mad fashion, drinking it day and night; and not seldom does one die with the cup in his hand.

When one of their chiefs dies, his family asks his girls and pages: "Which one of you will die with him?" Then one of them answers, "I."

From the time that he [or she] utters this word, he is no longer free: should he wish to draw back, he is not permitted. For the most part, however, it is the girls that offer themselves. So, when the man of whom I spoke had died, they asked his girls, "Who will die with him?" One of them answered, "I." She was then committed to two girls, who were to keep watch over her, accompany her wherever she went, and even, on occasion, wash her feet. The people now began to occupy themselves with the dead man — to cut out the clothes for him, and to prepare whatever else was needful. During the whole of this period, the girl gave herself over to drinking and singing, and was cheerful and gay.

When the day was now come that the dead man and the girl were to be committed to the flames, I went to the river in which his ship lay, but found that it had already been drawn ashore. Four corner-blocks of birch and other woods had been placed in position for it, while around were stationed large wooden figures in the semblance of human beings. Thereupon the ship was brought up, and placed on the timbers above mentioned. In the mean time the people began to walk to and fro, uttering words which I did not understand. The dead man, meanwhile, lay at a distance in his grave, from which they had not yet removed him. Next they brought a couch, placed it in the ship, and covered it with Greek cloth of gold, wadded and quilted, with pillows of the same material. There came an old crone, whom they call the angel of death, and spread the articles mentioned on the couch. It was she who attended to the sewing of the garments, and to all the equipment; it was she, also, who was to slay the girl. I saw her; she was dark, . . . thickset, with a lowering countenance.

When they came to the grave, they removed the earth from the wooden roof, set the latter aside, and drew out the dead man in the loose wrapper in which he had died. Then I saw that he had turned quite black, by reason of the coldness of that country. Near him in the grave they had placed strong drink, fruits, and a lute; and these they now took out. Except for his color, the dead man had not changed. They now clothed him in drawers, leggings, boots, and a *kurtak* and *chaftan* of cloth of gold, with golden buttons, placing on his head a cap made of cloth of gold, trimmed with sable! Then they carried him into a tent placed in the ship, seated him on the wadded and quilted covering, supported him with the pillows, and, bringing strong drink, fruits, and basil, placed them all beside him. Then they brought a dog, which they cut in two, and threw into the ship; laid all his weapons beside him; and led up two horses which they chased until they were dripping with sweat, whereupon they cut them in pieces with their swords, and threw the flesh into the ship. Two oxen were then brought forward, cut in pieces, and flung into the ship. Finally they brought a cock and a hen, killed them, and threw them in also.

The girl who had devoted herself to death meanwhile walked to and fro, entering one after another of the tents which they had there. The occupant of each tent lay with her, saying, "Tell your master, 'I [the man] did this only for love of you.'"

When it was now Friday afternoon, they led the girl to an object which they had constructed, and which looked like the framework of a door. She then placed her feet on the extended hands of the men, was raised up above the framework, and uttered something in her language, whereupon they let her down. Then again they raised her, and she did as at first. Once more they let her down, and then lifted her a third time, while she did as at the previous times. They then handed her a hen, whose head she cut off and threw away; but the hen itself they cast into the ship. I inquired of the interpreter what it was that she had done. He replied: "The first time she said, 'Lo, I see here my father and mother'; the second time, 'Lo, now I see all my deceased relatives sitting'; the third time, 'Lo, there is my master, who is sitting in Paradise. Paradise is so beautiful, so green. With him are his men and boys. He calls me, so bring me to him.'" Then they led her away to the ship.

Here she took off her two bracelets, and gave them to the old woman who was called the angel of death, and who was to murder her. She also drew off her two anklets, and passed them to the two servingmaids, who were the daughters of the so-called angel of death. Then they lifted her into the ship, but did not yet admit her to the tent. Now men came up with shields and staves, and handed her a cup of strong drink. This she took, sang over it, and emptied it. "With this," so the interpreter told me, "she is taking leave of those who are dear to her." Then another cup was handed her, which she also took, and began a lengthy song. The crone admonished her to drain the cup without lingering, and to enter the tent where her master lay. By this time, as it seemed to me, the girl had become dazed [or, possibly, crazed]; she made as though she would enter the tent, and had brought her head forward between the tent and the ship, when the hag seized her by the head, and dragged her in. At this moment the men began to beat upon their shields with the staves, in order to drown the noise of her outcries, which might have terrified the other girls, and deterred them from seeking death with their masters in the future. Then six men followed into the tent, and each and every one had carnal companionship with her. Then they laid her down by her master's side, while two of the men seized her by the feet and two by the hands. The old woman known as the angel of death now knotted a rope around her neck, and handed the ends to two of the men to pull. Then with a broad-bladed dagger she smote her between the ribs, and drew the blade forth while the two men strangled her with the rope till she died.

The next of kin to the dead man now drew near, and, taking a piece of wood, lighted it, and walked backwards toward the ship holding the stick in one hand, with the other placed upon his buttocks (he being naked), until the wood which had been piled under the ship was ignited. Then the others came up with staves and firewood, each one carrying a stick already lighted at the upper end, and threw it all on the pyre. The pile was soon aflame, then the ship, finally the tent, the man, and the girl, and everything else in the ship. A terrible storm began to blow up, and thus intensified the flames, and gave wings to the blaze.

At my side stood one of the Northmen, and I heard him talking with the interpreter, who stood near him. I asked the interpreter what the Northman had said, and received this answer: "'You Arabs,' he said, 'must be a stupid set! You take him who is to you the most revered and beloved of men, and cast him into the ground, to be devoured by creeping things and worms. We, on the other hand, burn him in a twinkling, so that he instantly, without a moment's delay, enters into Paradise.' At this he burst out into uncontrollable laughter, and then continued: 'It is the love of the Master [God] that causes the wind to blow and snatch him away in an instant.'" And, in very truth, before an hour had passed, ship, wood, and girl had with the man, turned to ashes.

Thereupon they heaped over the place where the ship had stood something like a rounded hill, and erecting on the centre of it a large birchen post, wrote on it the name of the deceased, along with that of the king of the Northmen. Having done this, they left the spot.

3

BARRY CUNLIFFE

The Western Vikings, 2001

The Vikings who sailed down the rivers of Russia to raid, trade, and settle came mainly from eastern Scandinavia — what is today Sweden and Finland. Their cousins in western Scandinavia sailed to the south and west. In this selection from a wide-ranging history of the European Atlantic world, the author, a modern archaeologist, discusses the expansion of Western Vikings — mainly Danes and Norwegians — into the Atlantic. How would you compare the expansion of the Western Vikings with that of the Eastern Vikings into what became Russia?

Source: Barry Cunliffe, *Facing the Ocean: The Atlantic and Its Peoples* (Oxford: Oxford University Press, 2001), 482–83, 488–95, 499, 514–16.

THINKING HISTORICALLY

The modern historian lets us hear enough from the medieval victims of the Vikings for us to feel their fear, and his list of destroyed cities and massacred peoples registers the horror they must have unleashed in their era. But Cunliffe also puts the Viking attacks in a longer-term historical perspective. How does that longer-term perspective change your reaction to the Viking raids?

The Coming of the Northmen

About 790 Beaduheard, the king's reeve[1] at Dorchester in southern Britain, got news that three foreign ships had landed at Portland and, assuming them to be traders, he went to welcome them. He was wrong. They were raiders from Scandinavia and he died for his mistake. The Dorset landing was a foretaste. A few years later, in 793, the raiding began in earnest with the attack on the monastery of St. Cuthbert on Lindisfarne:[2] "Never before has such terror appeared in Britain as we have now suffered from a pagan race, nor was it thought that such an inroad from the sea could be made. Behold, the church of St. Cuthbert spattered with the blood of the priests of God, despoiled of all its ornaments; a place more venerable than all in Britain is given as prey to pagan people." So wrote the English cleric Alcuin at the court of Charlemagne. Many more raids followed around the coasts of Britain and Ireland. The Franks were soon to suffer, so too the Bretons.[3] By the 840s Viking war bands were exploring further south along the Atlantic coasts. A vast fleet of 150 ships sailed up the Garonne and plundered almost to Toulouse.[4] Then it moved onwards to attack Galicia and Lisbon before sailing into the Guadalquivir.[5] Here, from their base on the Isla Menor, the Vikings pillaged Seville but were severely mauled by the Moors. Those captured were hanged from the city's palm trees, and two hundred Viking heads were sent by the Emir to his allies in Tangier as an effective witness to his military prowess. Undeterred, the Viking force continued through the Straits of Gibraltar harassing the coasts as they sailed to the mouth of the Rhône where, on an island in the Camargue,[6] a base was established for raiding upriver into the heart of France and across the sea to the coasts of Italy. In 861 they returned to their base on the Loire. The expedition had been "at once profitable and honourable."

[1] Representative. [Ed.]
[2] Island off the northwest coast of Britain. [Ed.]
[3] People of Brittany, northwest France. [Ed.]
[4] City in south central France. [Ed.]
[5] River in southern Spain. [Ed.]
[6] Marshland in Rhône River delta. [Ed.]

The Mediterranean venture, while a notable feat, was of little lasting consequence. But meanwhile, in the north, raids and settlement had reached significant proportions. Some indication of what was going on is given by the pained lamentation of Ermentarius, a monk at Noir-moutier,[7] writing in the 860s:

> The number of ships increases, the endless flood of Vikings never ceases to grow bigger. Everywhere Christ's people are the victims of massacre, burning, and plunder. The Vikings overrun all that lies before them, and no one can withstand them. They seize Bordeaux, Périgueux, Limoges, Angoulême, Toulouse; Angers, Tours, and Orleans are made deserts. Ships past counting voyage up the Seine . . . Rouen is laid waste, looted, and burnt; Paris, Beauvais, Meaux are taken, Melun's stronghold is razed to the ground, Chartres occupied, Evreux and Bayeux looted, and every town invested. . . .

Why the Raids of the Northmen Began

The raids of the Danes and Norwegians began in the last decade of the eighth century, and over the next seventy years rose to a devastating crescendo. No single factor was responsible for unleashing the fury, but there can be little doubt that the overseas ventures became possible only after the longship had reached its peak of excellence by the middle of the eighth century. The Scandinavian landscape demanded good shipping. The long Atlantic coastline of Norway, with its deeply indented fjords, was accessible with ease only by sea, while the sounds and islands of Denmark had, for millennia, been bound together by boat. The Baltic, too, was a cradle for navigation—a great inland sea providing ease of access between the extensive littorals[8] and their productive hinterlands, and to the river routes penetrating far south across the North European Plain. Throughout Scandinavia settlements favoured the sea coasts and the inland lakes and waterways. They faced the open water and kept their backs to the forest. Thus communities depended upon ships for their livelihood, their rulers able to maintain their power only by command of the sea. In such a world it is easy to see how the ship became a symbol of authority, honed to perfection to reflect the status of the elite. A ship, either real or symbolic, might also accompany its owner in his burial. . . . By the early years of the ninth century, all the features characteristic of the classic Viking ship had been brought together, creating fast and highly efficient seagoing vessels suitable for carrying men across the ocean in search of land and plunder.

---

[7] Atlantic island off France. [Ed.]
[8] Coasts. [Ed.]

. . . In the course of the eighth century, trade between continental Europe and England developed apace, with well-established links leading northwards to the Baltic. In this way the volume of mercantile traffic in the southern North Sea increased dramatically, while the rulers of Denmark became increasingly aware of the wealth to be had to the south. Through the various traders who visited the Scandinavian ports they would also have learnt the political geography of western Europe — most notably the whereabouts of its rich, isolated monasteries and the distracting factional disputes endemic among its ruling households. To the Scandinavian elite there was much prestige to be had in leading a successful raid: the spoils would enrich the begetters and would bind followers closer to their leader. In the competitive emulation which accompanied the early raiding expeditions the number, intensity, and duration of the raids inevitably escalated.

Another, quite different, factor at work was the desire for new land to settle. With a growing population the narrow coastal zone of Norway was too restricted a territory to provide the social space needed for enterprising sons to establish themselves. The only solution was to find new territories overseas in Britain and Ireland, and further afield on the more remote islands of the north Atlantic. For the most part what was sought was new farmland, like the home territories, where families could set up new farms with plenty of space around for expansion by successive generations. It was this that the north Atlantic could supply in plenty. What England had to offer was rather different but no less acceptable — well-run estates which new Scandinavian lords could leave largely undisturbed, simply taking the profits.

Another incentive to moving overseas was the possibility of setting up merchant colonies emulating those that were so successful in the Baltic and along the eastern coasts of the North Sea. York, already a developing English market, was taken over by the Northmen in 866 and rapidly expanded to become the principal entrepôt[9] in northern Britain, while an entirely new port-of-trade was established at Dublin and soon became a centre for Irish Sea commerce. In all of these ventures the ship was vital.

It would be wrong to give the impression that overseas activities were narrowly focused: trading could soon turn into raiding, while raiding could dissipate itself into settlement. One was never exclusive of the other. This is evocatively summed up in an account of the lifestyle of Svein Asleifarson recorded in the twelfth-century *Orkneyinga Saga*, no doubt referring wistfully to a long-gone era when Vikings behaved like Vikings:

> In the spring he had more than enough to occupy him, with a great deal of seed to sow which he saw to carefully himself. Then when the job was done, he would go off plundering in the Hebrides

[9] Storage site for trade goods. [Ed.]

and in Ireland on what he called his "spring-trip," then back home just after midsummer where he stayed till the cornfields had been reaped and the grain was safely in. After that he would go off raiding again, and never came back till the first month of winter was ended. This he used to call his "autumn trip."

The Vikings in the West: A Brief Progress

... *Viking* is the word frequently used by the English sources to describe raiders and settlers from Scandinavia, while the Carolingian sources prefer *Northmen*. Both words include, without differentiation, Danes and Norwegians. Until the mid-ninth century it is possible to make a broad distinction between Norwegians, who settled northern and western Scotland and the Northern and Western Isles and were active in the Irish Sea, and Danes, who raided the North Sea and Channel coasts, but thereafter the distinction becomes blurred.

The progress of the settlement of north-western Britain by the Norwegians is unrecorded, but contact began as early as the seventh century and it is quite likely that the colonization was largely completed during the course of the eighth century. The newly settled areas provided the springboard for attacks on Ireland and the Irish Sea coasts, becoming increasingly widespread and frequent in the period 795–840. The rich and unprotected monasteries were the target. Iona[10] was attacked three times, in 795, 802, and 806, in the first flush of activity. Thereafter raids thrust further and further south — 821 Wexford, 822 Cork, and 824 the isolated monastery of Skelling Michael in the Atlantic off the Kerry coast.[11] Having picked off the vulnerable coastal communities the attacks then began to penetrate inland, but usually no more than 30 kilometres or so from the safety of navigable water. These early attacks were opportunistic hit-and-run affairs, meeting no significant organized opposition.

Meanwhile in the North Sea the Danes adopted similar tactics. In 820 a massive Danish fleet of two hundred vessels threatened Saxony, and in three successive years, beginning in 834, the great trading port of Dorestad[12] was devastated. Frisia[13] became the immediate focus of contention. In 838 the Danish king Harik demanded of the Frankish king Louis that "The Frisians be given over to him" — a request that was roundly refused. The vulnerability of the coast was vividly brought home

---

[10] Island off Scotland. [Ed.]

[11] These are places in modern Ireland. [Ed.]

[12] City in modern Netherlands. [Ed.]

[13] North Sea coast from modern Netherlands to Germany; people spoke Frisian (close to English). [Ed.]

when, in 835, the monastery of St. Philibert on the island of Noirmoutier south of the Loire estuary was attacked. England suffered only sporadic raids at first, but these intensified in the 830s. . . .

The events of 840–865 saw the Scandinavians working the full length of the Atlantic zone from the Rhine to Gibraltar and beyond, but they were at their most active and most persistent along the major rivers — the Seine, the Thames, the Loire, and the Garonne — feeding off the cities that owed their wealth and well-being to their command of the river routes. The rivers that brought them their commercial advantage through access to the sea now brought men who sought to take it for themselves.

The 860s saw a change of pace from raid to settlement, accompanied by intensified and co-ordinated opposition by those whose land the Northmen were intent on taking. The Franks were the first to come to terms with the new reality by building fortified bridges across the rivers Seine and Loire, by fortifying towns and monasteries, and by paying tribute to groups of Vikings in return for protection or military services. These tactics protected the heart of the kingdom while leaving the lower reaches of the two rivers to the roving bands of invaders who had now taken up residence in the areas. The strategy kept Frankia free from further incursions until a new wave of attacks began on Paris in 885. . . .

Towards the end of the tenth century, with the rise of a strong dynasty in Denmark under Harald Bluetooth and his son, Sven Forkbeard, a new phase of Viking raiding was initiated, and once more it was the Atlantic coastal regions as far south as Iberia that took the brunt of the attack. England was particularly vulnerable. In 991 Sven Forkbeard led his first raid against the English, his activities culminating in the conquest of the kingdom in 1013. Three years later, after his death, his son Knut was formally recognized as king of England. Dynastic squabbles and claims and counter-claims to the English throne rumbled on throughout the eleventh century, but the failure of the threatened Danish conquest of England to materialize in 1085 was the effective end of the Viking episode. Occasional Norwegian expeditions to the Northern and Western Isles were the last ripples, three centuries after the Viking wave first struck.

The Northmen and the Atlantic Communities

That the impact of the Scandinavians on the Atlantic communities was profound and lasting there can be no doubt, but sufficient will have been said to show that it varied significantly from region to region.

In lightly inhabited or empty lands like the Northern and Western Isles, the Faroes, Iceland, and Greenland, Scandinavian culture was directly transplanted in its entirety and flourished much in the style of the Norwegian homeland, but elsewhere the Scandinavian component fused with indigenous culture. In regions where the local systems were well established and comparatively stable, as in eastern England and the maritime region of France (soon to become Normandy), the new order emerged imperceptibly from the old with little disruption to the social or economic balance, but in other areas, like Ireland, where warfare between rival factions of the elite was endemic, the Scandinavian presence was a catalyst for widespread change. Here the ferocity of the Irish warlords matched their own. For this reason the small enclaves established at harbours around the coast remained small, developing as isolated trading colonies in an otherwise hostile landscape. Apart from certain areas of the north-east, large-scale land-taking and settlement was not possible. Much the same pattern can be seen in south-west Wales.

The Scandinavian settlements of the Irish Sea zone chose good docking facilities, initially to serve as protected anchorages for the vessels of the early raiders, but these quickly developed as trading centres, making the Irish Sea the major focus of exchange in the Scandinavian maritime system. From here ships might go south to Andalucía, north to Iceland and beyond, or around Britain eastwards to the Baltic. In this way the Irish Sea became the hub of a complex network of communications built upon the long-distance exchange systems which had already been established in the preceding centuries.

In Brittany a rather different pattern of interaction emerged. Here the long-term hostility between the Bretons and the Franks provided a situation in which raiding and mercenary activity could profitably be maintained, while the internecine warfare that broke out in both kingdoms in the painful periods when succession was being contested offered the raiders further opportunities for easy intervention. Throughout this time the Loire formed the focus of Scandinavian activity and Nantes was often in their control, but there is, as yet, little evidence that a major trading enclave developed here. It may simply have been that the political turmoil in the region allowed warfare in its various modes to provide the necessary economic underpinning to sustain Viking society. From the Breton point of view the Scandinavian presence, disruptive though it was, was an important factor in helping to maintain their independence from the Franks.

South of the Loire, Viking military activity was sporadic and superficial, at least in so far as the historical record allows us to judge, but given their interest in trade it is difficult to believe that there were not regular visits by merchants to the Gironde and Garonne and along the Atlantic seaboard of Iberia. In this they would simply have been following the routes plied by their predecessors.

Some measure of the integration of the multifaceted maritime system that emerged is provided by a wreck excavated at Skuldelev in the Danish fjord of Roskilde. It was one of six that had been sunk to block the fjord from seaward attack some time in the late eleventh or early twelfth century. The vessel was a typical Viking longship suitable for carrying fifty to sixty warriors. Dendrochronology has shown that the ship had been built about 1060 at, or in the vicinity of, Dublin. What service it saw as a raiding vessel in the seas around Britain and France we will never know, but its final resting place 2,200 kilometres from the yard in which it had been built is a vivid reminder of the capacity of the sea in bringing the communities of Atlantic Europe ever closer together.

4

Eirik's Saga, c. 1260

Scandinavian seafarers spread out in all directions in the tenth century. While Swedes and Finns sailed down the rivers of Russia to the Black and Caspian seas, Danes conquered and colonized from England down the coast of France into the Mediterranean as far as Italy, North Africa, and Arabia. The Vikings of Norway sailed mainly westward, colonizing Iceland, Greenland, and North America (certainly Newfoundland but likely farther south). The Norsemen discovered Iceland in about 860 and began settlement some fourteen years later. By 930, Iceland contained the families and retainers of many lords who fled western Norway to escape the conquering Harald Fairhair.

Eirik the Red (950–1003) came to Iceland with his family in 960 after his father had to flee Norway because of "some killings." In turn, Eirik was exiled from Iceland in 982 after he committed murder in the heat of two quarrels. Exile meant searching for a settlement even farther west, leading Eirik to Greenland. Although not the first to see or land in Greenland, Eirik established the first colony there.

Insofar as it captures the oral tradition, this excerpt from "Eirik's Saga," written about 1260, gives us an idea of Viking thought in the tenth century. What kind of world does it portray? How does it contribute to your understanding of the Viking expansion?

THINKING HISTORICALLY

How does this internal view of Viking society inevitably change our moral perspective from that of an outsider? How might the differences between Ibn Fadlan and this author lead to different moral perspectives?

Source: "Eirik's Saga," in *The Vinland Sagas: The Norse Discovery of America*, trans. and introduction by Magnus Magnusson and Hermann Palsson (Harmondsworth, Middlesex, England: Penguin Books, 1965), 75–78.

There was a warrior king called Olaf the White, who was the son of King Ingjald. Olaf went on a Viking expedition to the British Isles, where he conquered Dublin and the adjoining territory and made himself king over them. He married Aud the Deep-Minded, the daughter of Ketil Flat-Nose; they had a son called Thorstein the Red.

Olaf was killed in battle in Ireland, and Aud and Thorstein the Red then went to the Hebrides. There Thorstein married Thurid, the daughter of Eyvind the Easterner; they had many children.

Thorstein the Red became a warrior king, and joined forces with Earl Sigurd the Powerful, together they conquered Caithness, Sutherland, Ross, and Moray, and more than half of Argyll. Thorstein ruled over these territories as king until he was betrayed by the Scots and killed in battle.

Aud the Deep-Minded was in Caithness when she learned of Thorstein's death; she had a ship built secretly in a forest, and when it was ready she sailed away to Orkney. There she gave away in marriage Groa, daughter of Thorstein the Red.

After that, Aud set out for Iceland; she had twenty freeborn men aboard her ship. She reached Iceland and spent the first winter with her brother Bjorn at Bjarnarhaven. Then she took possession of the entire Dales district between Dogurdar River and Skraumuhlaups River, and made her home at Hvamm. She used to say prayers at Kross Hills; she had crosses erected there, for she had been baptized and was a devout Christian.

Many well-born men, who had been taken captive in the British Isles by Vikings and were now slaves, came to Iceland with her. One of them was called Vifil; he was of noble descent. He had been taken prisoner in the British Isles and was a slave until Aud gave him his freedom.

When Aud gave land to members of her crew, Vifil asked her why she did not give him some land like the others. Aud replied that it was of no importance, and said that he would be considered a man of quality wherever he was. She gave him Vifilsdale, and he settled there. He married, and had two sons called Thorbjorn and Thorgeir; they were both promising men, and grew up with their father.

Eirik Explores Greenland

There was a man called Thorvald, who was the father of Eirik the Red. He and Eirik left their home in Jaederen because of some killings and went to Iceland. They took possession of land in Hornstrands, and made their home at Drangar. Thorvald died there, and Eirik the Red then married Thjodhild, and moved south to Haukadale; he cleared land there and made his home at Eirikstead, near Vatnshorn.

Eirik's slaves started a landslide that destroyed the farm of a man called Valthjof, at Valthjofstead; so Eyjolf Saur, one of Valthjof's kinsmen, killed the slaves at Skeidsbrekkur, above Vatnshorn. For this, Eirik killed Eyjolf Saur; he also killed Hrafn the Dueller, at Leikskalar. Geirstein and Odd of Jorvi, who were Eyjolf's kinsmen, took action over his killing, and Eirik was banished from Haukadale.

Eirik then took possession of Brok Island and Oxen Island, and spent the first winter at Tradir, in South Island. He lent his benchboards to Thorgest of Breidabolstead. After that, Eirik moved to Oxen Island, and made his home at Eirikstead. He then asked for his benchboards back, but they were not returned; so Eirik went to Breidabolstead and seized them. Thorgest pursued him, and they fought a battle near the farmstead at Drangar. Two of Thorgest's sons and several other men were killed there.

After this, both Eirik and Thorgest maintained a force of fightingmen at home. Eirik was supported by Styr Thorgrimsson, Eyjolf of Svin Island, Thorbjorn Vifilsson, and the sons of Thorbrand of Alptafjord; Thorgest was supported by Thorgeir of Hitardale, Aslak of Langadale and his son Illugi, and the sons of Thord Gellir.

Eirik and his men were sentenced to outlawry at the Thorsness Assembly. He made his ship ready in Eiriksbay, and Eyjolf of Svin Island hid him in Dimunarbay while Thorgest and his men were scouring the islands for him.

Thorbjorn Vifilsson and Styr and Eyjolf accompanied Eirik out beyond the islands, and they parted in great friendship; Eirik said he would return their help as far as it lay within his power, if ever they had need of it. He told them he was going to search for the land that Gunnbjorn, the son of Ulf Crow, had sighted when he was driven westwards off course and discovered the Gunnbjarnar Skerries; he added that he would come back to visit his friends if he found this country.

Eirik put out to sea past Snæfells Glacier, and made land near the glacier that is known as Blaserk. From there he sailed south to find out if the country were habitable there. He spent the first winter on Eiriks Island, which lies near the middle of the Eastern Settlement. In the spring he went to Eiriksfjord, where he decided to make his home. That summer he explored the wilderness to the west and gave names to many landmarks there. He spent the second winter on Eiriks Holms, off Hvarfs Peak. The third summer he sailed all the way north to Snæfell and into Hrafnsfjord, where he reckoned he was farther inland than the head of Eiriksfjord. Then he turned back and spent the third winter on Eiriks Island, off the mouth of Eiriksfjord.

He sailed back to Iceland the following summer and put in at Breidafjord. He stayed the winter with Ingolf of Holmlatur. In the spring he fought a battle with Thorgest of Breidabolstead and was defeated. After that a reconciliation was arranged between them.

That summer Eirik set off to colonize the country he had discovered; he named it *Greenland*, for he said that people would be much more tempted to go there if it had an attractive name.

5

YVO OF NARBONA

The Mongols, 1243

Within a couple of generations after 1206, a nomadic tribe of herders from the grasslands of Central Asia created a mounted army that conquered an expanse from the Pacific coast of Asia to Eastern Europe. With the conquest of the Islamic caliphate at Baghdad in 1258 and Song dynasty China by 1276, Mongols ruled about a hundred million people, having killed about thirty million others. They ruled almost a third of the human population and the largest land empire the world had ever known. Who were they? How did they manage such a feat? What were its costs?

To help answer some of those questions, we have a selection from a letter written in 1243 from one Yvo of Narbona[1] (we know nothing else about him) to the archbishop of Bordeaux, France. Yvo has just witnessed the conquest of Hungary by a Mongol army. He describes what he saw and also relates the account of an Englishman (also unknown, even by name) who worked for the Mongols as an interpreter before he escaped amidst the Mongol withdrawal from Hungary. What does this document tell us about the Mongols? What does it suggest about the reasons for their rapid expansion? What does it suggest about their impact?

THINKING HISTORICALLY

No people before modern times received greater condemnation than the Mongols. Their negative reputation originated in the writings of their victims almost immediately after Genghis Khan expanded

---

[1] Narbona, or Narbonne, was a Mediterranean port city in what is today southern France.

Source: Samuel Purchas, *Hakluytus Posthumus or Purchas His Pilgrimes: Contayning a History of the World, in Sea voyages & lande-Trauells, by Englishmen & others* [*with* Purchas his Pilgrimage or Relations of the world] (London: William Stanley for Henrie Featherstone 1625–26) 5 vols., 183–87. Spelling modernized and Americanized.

Mongol power into China and Central Asia in the 1210s and 1220s. The second-generation Mongol onslaught on Russia and Europe had a similar impact. Here we get an eyewitness account of the Mongol invasion of Hungary in 1241. Actually, we have two accounts: The tale of an Englishman who served as interpreter for the Mongols is contained within the letter of Yvo, who was also a witness. Which of these two witnesses is more objective, or less moralistic? What examples do you see of either witness judging rather than describing? What descriptions do not seem factually based? What examples do you see of either witness interpreting Mongol behavior in a favorable light?

Part of an Epistle written by one Yvo of Narbona unto the Archbishop of Bordeaux, containing the confession of an Englishman as touching the barbarous demeanor of the Tartars,[2] *which had lived long among them, and was drawn along perforce with them in their expedition against Hungary: Recorded by Mathew Paris in the year of our Lord 1243.*

The Lord therefore being provoked to indignation, by reason of this and other sins committed among us Christians, is become, as it were, a destroying enemy, and a dreadful avenger.[3] This I may justly affirm to be true, because a huge nation, and a barbarous and inhumane people, whose law is lawless, whose wrath is furious, even the rod of God's anger, overruns and utterly wastes infinite countries, cruelly abolishing all things where they come, with fire and sword. And this present summer, the foresaid nation, being called Tartars, departing out of Hungary,[4] which they had surprised by treason, laid siege unto the very same town, wherein I myself abode, with many thousands of soldiers: neither were there in the said town on our part above 50 men of war, whom, together with 20 crossbows, the captain had left in garrison. All these, out of certain high places, beholding the enemies vast army, and abhorring the beastly cruelty of Anti-Christ his accomplices, signified forthwith unto their governor, the hideous lamentations of his Christian subjects, who suddenly being surprised in all the province adjoining, without any difference or respect of condition, fortune, sex, or age, were

[2] The Mongols were misidentified as "Tatars" (another central Asian people), which then became "Tartars," probably to suggest people of "Tartarus," the underground place of punishment in Greek mythology, that is, devils. [Ed.]

[3] Like the prophets of ancient Israel, Christians interpreted invasions as God's punishment for their sins. [Ed.]

[4] The Mongols invaded Hungary in 1241 under Batu Khan, the grandson of Genghis Khan. They withdrew in the spring of 1242 because of the death of Ogodei, the successor to Genghis, to return to Mongolia to choose the next Great Khan. [Ed.]

by manifold cruelties, all of them destroyed:[5] with whose carcasses, the Tartarian chieftains, and their brutish and savage followers, glutting themselves, as with delicious cakes, left nothing for vultures but the bare bones. And a strange thing it is to consider, that the greedy and ravenous vultures disdained to prey upon any of the relics, which remained. Old and deformed women they gave, as it were for daily sustenance, unto their Cannibals:[6] the beautiful devoured they not, but smothered them lamenting and scratching, with forced and unnatural ravishments. Like barbarous miscreants, they quelled virgins unto death, and cutting off their tender paps[7] to present for dainties unto their magistrates, they engorged themselves with their bodies.[8]

. . . In the meantime crying from the top of a high mountain, the Duke of Austria, the King of Bohemia, the Patriarch of Aquileia, the Duke of Carinthia, and (as some report) the Earl of Baden, with a mighty power, and in battle array, approaching towards them, that accursed crew immediately vanished,[9] and all those Tartarian vagabonds retired themselves into the distressed and vanquished land of Hungary; who as they came suddenly, so they departed also on the sudden: which their celerity[10] caused all men to stand in horror and astonishment of them. But of the said fugitives, the prince of Dalmatia took eight: one of which number the Duke of Austria knew to be an English man, who was perpetually banished out of the Realm of England, in regard of certain notorious crimes by him committed. This fellow, on the behalf of the most tyrannical king of the Tartars, had been twice, as a messenger and interpreter, with the king of Hungary, menacing and plainly foretelling the mischief which afterward happened, unless he would submit himself and his kingdom unto the Tartars yoke. Well, being allured by our Princes to confess the truth, he made such oaths and protestations, as (I think) the devil himself would have been trusted for. First therefore he reported of himself, that presently after the time of his banishment, namely about the 30th year of his age, having lost all that he had in the city of Acon[11] at dice, even in the midst of Winter, being compelled by ignominious hunger, wearing nothing about

---

[5] The Mongols normally spared women and children. In this case they killed all the captives before returning to Mongolia. [Ed.]

[6] The charge of cannibalism is contested by modern historians. The Mongols would sometimes eat horse meat, mice, lice, and the afterbirth of foals, but the eating of human flesh was a rare occurrence, confined to threats of starvation. [Ed.]

[7] Breasts. [Ed.]

[8] Rape was common among all medieval armies, as was the selection of young women for slaves or harems, but the charges of cutting off their breasts are almost certainly fictional since that would make captured women less valuable. [Ed.]

[9] A classic Mongol tactic was a pretended retreat followed by an ambush, but this may refer to the return to Mongolia. [Ed.]

[10] Speed. [Ed.]

[11] Acre, in modern north-coastal Israel. Captured by the Crusaders in 1104 and again in 1191. Stronghold of Crusader state until 1291 fall to Mamluks. [Ed.]

him but a shirt of sack, a pair of shoes, and a hair cap only, being shaven like a fool, and uttering an uncouth noise as if he had been dumb, he took his journey, and so travelling many countries, and finding in divers places friendly entertainment, he prolonged his life in this manner for a season, albeit every day by rashness of speech, and inconstancy of heart, he endangered himself to the devil. At length, by reason of extreme travail, and continual change of air and of meats in Chaldea,[12] he fell into a grievous sickness insomuch that he was weary of his life. Not being able therefore to go forward or backward, and staying there a while to refresh himself, he began (being somewhat learned) to commend to writing those words which he heard spoken, and within a short space, so aptly to pronounce, and to utter them himself, that he was reputed for a native member of that country: and by the same dexterity he attained to many languages. This man the Tartars having intelligence of by their spies, drew him perforce into their society: and being admonished by an oracle or vision, to challenge dominion over the whole earth, they allured him by many rewards to their faithful service, by reason that they wanted Interpreters. But concerning their manners and superstitions, of the disposition and stature of their bodies, of their country and manner of fighting etc., he protested the particulars following to be true: namely, that they were above all men, covetous, hasty, deceitful, and merciless: notwithstanding, by reason of the rigor and extremity of punishments to be inflicted upon them by their superiors, they are restrained from brawling, and from mutual strife and contention. The ancient founders and fathers of their tribes, they call by the name of gods,[13] and at certain set times they do celebrate solemn feasts unto them, many of them being particular, and but four only general. They think that all things are created for themselves alone. They esteem it no offense to exercise cruelty against rebels. They are hardy and strong in the breast, lean and pale-faced, rough and hug-shouldered, having flat and short noses, long and sharp chins, their upper jaws are low and declining, their teeth long and thin, their eye-brows extending from their foreheads down to their noses, their eyes inconstant and black, their countenances writhen and terrible, their extreme joints strong with bones and sinews, having thick and great thighs, and short legs, and yet being equal unto us in stature: for that length which is wanting in their legs, is supplied in the upper parts of their bodies. Their country in old time was a land utterly desert and waste,[14] situated far beyond Chaldea, from whence they have expelled lions, bears, and such like untamed beasts, with their bows, and

---

[12] Mesopotamia; modern Iraq. [Ed.]

[13] Might refer to elements of ancestor worship in traditional Mongol belief system of Tengriism, which also included elements of shamanism, animism, and totenism, but Genghis Khan recognized the numerous religions of Central Asia (including Christianity, Buddhism, and Islam) and so maintained religious tolerance. [Ed.]

[14] Bordered by desert in the south and forests in the north, the steppe is relatively treeless and dry but with ample grass for grazing. [Ed.]

other engines. Of the hides of beasts being tanned, they use to shape for themselves light but yet impenetrable armor. They ride fast bound unto their horses, which are not very great in stature, but exceedingly strong, and maintained with little provender.[15] They used to fight constantly and valiantly with javelins, maces, battle-axes, and swords. But especially they are excellent archers, and cunning warriors with their bows. Their backs are slightly armed, that they may not flee. They withdraw not themselves from the combat till they see the chief standard of their general give back. Vanquished, they ask no favor, and vanquishing, they show no compassion. They all persist in their purpose of subduing the whole world under their own subjection, as if they were but one man, and yet they are more than millions in number.[16] They have 60,000 couriers, who being sent before upon light horses to prepare a place for the army to encamp in, will in the space of one night gallop three days journey. And suddenly diffusing themselves over a whole province, and surprising all the people thereof unarmed, unprovided, dispersed, they make such horrible slaughters, that the king or prince of the land invaded, cannot find people sufficient to wage battle against them, and to withstand them. They delude all people and princes of regions in time of peace, pretending that for a cause, which indeed is no cause. Sometimes they say that they will make a voyage to Cologne to fetch home the three wise kings into their own country;[17] sometimes to punish the avarice and pride of the Romans,[18] who oppressed them in times past;[19] sometimes to conquer barbarous and Northern nations; sometimes to moderate the fury of the Germans[20] with their own meek mildness; sometimes to learn warlike feats and stratagems of the French; sometimes for the finding out of fertile ground to suffice their huge multitudes; sometimes again in derision they say that they intend to go on pilgrimage to St. James of Galicia.[21] In regard of which slights and collusions certain indiscreet governors concluding a league with them, have granted them free passage through their territories, which leagues notwithstanding being violated, were an occasion of ruin and destruction unto the governors, etc.

[15] Food. [Ed.]

[16] A likely exaggeration. Probably more like a million. Individual armies like Batu's probably numbered something like 30,000. Total forces of 500,000 might have been possible. All Mongol men rode in battle. All enemies were killed or enslaved. At its height the Mongol Empire might have ruled 100 million people. On the other hand, Mongol rule depleted the population of that empire by tens of millions. [Ed.]

[17] Cologne, in modern Germany. A medieval legend told of how the three kings who visited Jesus were reburied together in St. Peter's church in Cologne. [Ed.]

[18] "Romans" is a general term for Christians of Western Europe. [Ed.]

[19] May refer to the Roman Empire or to Christian Crusades, or it may conflate both. [Ed.]

[20] The German Teutonic Knights fought Crusades to Christianize the Baltic, Poland, and Hungary in the thirteenth century. [Ed.]

[21] Santiago De Compostela, in northwest Spain; a pilgrimage site, said to be the burial place of St. James. [Ed.]

6

The Secret History of the Mongols, c. 1240

This Mongol account records the early years of Mongol expansion under Genghis Khan, the founder of the empire. Born Temujin in 1155 or 1167, this son of a minor tribal chieftain attracted the support of Mongol princes in the years between 1187 and 1206 through a series of decisive military victories over other tribes and competing Mongol claimants to the title of Great Khan.

The Mongols were illiterate before the time of Genghis Khan, who adopted the script of the Uighurs,* one of the more literate peoples of the steppe. Thus *The Secret History* was written in Mongolian with Uighur letters. The only surviving version is a fourteenth-century Chinese translation. The author is unknown, but the book provides detailed accounts of the early years of Temujin and ends with the reign of his son and successor, Ogodei, in 1228 — only a year after his father's death.

Because so much about the Mongols was written by their literate enemies, *The Secret History* is an invaluable resource: It is clearly an "insider's" account of the early years of Mongol expansion. Although it includes mythic elements — it begins with the augury of the birth of a blue wolf to introduce Genghis Khan — *The Secret History* is, without doubt, an authentic representation of a Mongol point of view.

In this selection, you will read the Mongol account of an important Mongol victory over the Naiman, a neighboring Turkic- or Mongol-speaking people, in 1204. What does the account tell you about the lives of steppe nomads like the Naiman and Mongols? What does this selection tell you about the sources of Mongol military strength?

THINKING HISTORICALLY

What moral values does this selection reveal? Do the Mongols think of themselves as "moral" people? Is the author-historian interested in describing what happened objectively or in presenting an unblemished, sanitized view?

In what ways does this written Mongol history make you more sympathetic to the Mongols? Notice that the selection begins with

* WEE gurs

Source: Adapted by K. Reilly from R. P. Lister, *Genghis Khan* (New York: Barnes & Noble, 1993), 166–76. While this volume is a retelling of the almost indecipherable *The Secret History of the Mongols* in Lister's own words, the selections that follow simplify without contextualizing or explaining the original work. More scholarly editions, trans. and ed. Francis Woodman Cleaves (Cambridge, MA: Harvard University Press, 1982) and Paul Kahn (San Francisco: North Point Press, 1984), are less accessible.

an "inside" view of the Mongol's enemy, the Naiman. How informed
and fair does the Mongol author seem to be toward the Naiman? Do
you think the Mongol authors described the Naiman more accurately
than Chinese or Europeans described the Mongols?

Tayang Khan of the Naiman

When the news was brought to [the Naiman] Tayang Khan that
someone claiming to be Ong Khan had been slain at the Neikun watercourse, his mother, Gurbesu, said: "Ong Khan was the great Khan
of former days. Bring his head here! If it is really he, we will sacrifice
to him."

She sent a message to Khorisu, commanding him to cut the head off
and bring it in. When it was brought to her, she recognised it as that of
Ong Khan. She placed it on a white cloth, and her daughter-in-law carried out the appropriate rites. . . . A wine-feast was held and stringed
instruments were played. Gurbesu, taking up a drinking-bowl, made an
offering to the head of Ong Khan.

When the sacrifice was made to it, the head grinned.

"He laughs!" Tayang Khan cried. Overcome by religious awe, he
flung the head on the floor and trampled on it until it was mangled
beyond recognition.

The great general Kokse'u Sabrakh was present at these ceremonies,
and observed them without enthusiasm. It was he who had been the only
Naiman general to offer resistance to Temujin and Ong Khan on their
expedition against Tayang Khan's brother Buyiruk.

"First of all," he remarked, "you cut off the head of a dead ruler,
and then you trample it into the dust. What kind of behaviour is this?
Listen to the baying of those dogs: It has an evil sound. The Khan your
father, Inancha Bilgei, once said: 'My wife is young, and I, her husband,
am old. Only the power of prayer has enabled me to beget my son, this
same Tayang. But will my son, born a weakling, be able to guard and
hold fast my common and evil-minded people?'

"Now the baying of the dogs seems to announce that some disaster
is at hand. The rule of our queen, Gurbesu, is firm; but you, my Khan,
Torlukh Tayang, are weak. It is truly said of you that you have no
thought for anything but the two activities of hawking and driving game,
and no capacity for anything but these."

Tayang Khan was accustomed to the disrespect of his powerful general, but he was stung into making a rash decision.

"There are a few Mongols in the east. From the earliest days this old
and great Ong Khan feared them, with their quivers; now they have
made war on him and driven him to death. No doubt they would like to
be rulers themselves. There are indeed in Heaven two shining lights, the

sun and the moon, and both can exist there; but how can there be two rulers here on earth? Let us go and gather those Mongols in."

His mother Gurbesu said: "Why should we start making trouble with them? The Mongols have a bad smell; they wear black clothes. They are far away, out there; let them stay there. Though it is true," she added, "that we could have the daughters of their chieftains brought here; when we had washed their hands and feet, they could milk our cows and sheep for us."

Tayang Khan said: "What is there so terrible about them? Let us go to these Mongols and take away their quivers."

"What big words you are speaking," Kokse'u Sabrakh said. "Is Tayang Khan the right man for it? Let us keep the peace."

Despite these warnings, Tayang Khan decided to attack the Mongols. It was a justifiable decision; his armies were stronger, but time was on Temujin's side. Tayang sought allies, sending a messenger to Alakhu Shidigichuri of the Onggut, in the south, the guardians of the ramparts between Qashin and the Khingan. "I am told that there are a few Mongols in the east," he said. "Be my right hand! I will ride against them from here, and we will take their quivers away from them."

Alakhu's reply was brief: "I cannot be your right hand." He in his turn sent a message to Temujin. "Tayang Khan of the Naiman wants to come and take away your quivers. He sent to me and asked me to be his right hand. I refused. I make you aware of this, so that when he comes your quivers will not be taken away."[1]

War against the Naiman

When he received Alakhu's message Temujin, having wintered near Guralgu, was holding one of his immense roundups of game on the camel-steppes of Tulkinche'ut, in the east. The beasts had been encircled by the clansmen and warriors; the chieftains were gathered together, about to begin the great hunt.

"What shall we do now?" some of them said to each other. "Our horses are lean at this season."

. . . The snow had only lately left the steppe; the horses had found nothing to graze on during these recent months. Their ribs stuck out and they lacked strength.

The Khan's youngest brother, Temuga, spoke up. . . .

"How can that serve as an excuse," he said, "that the horses are lean? My horses are quite fat enough. How can we stay sitting here, when we receive a message like that?"

---

[1] Temujin, grateful for this warning, sent him five hundred horses and a thousand sheep. His friendship with Alakhu was valuable to him at a later time.

Prince Belgutai spoke. . . .

"If a man allows his quivers to be taken away during his lifetime, what kind of an existence does he have? For a man who is born a man, it is a good enough end to be slain by another man, and lie on the steppe with his quiver and bow beside him. The Naiman make fine speeches, with their many men and their great kingdom. But suppose, having heard their fine speeches, we ride against them, would it be so difficult to take their quivers away from them? We must mount and ride; it is the only thing to do."

Temujin was wholly disposed to agree with these sentiments. He broke off the hunt, set the army in motion, and camped near Ornu'u on the Khalkha. Here he paused for a time while he carried out a swift reorganization of the army. A count was held of the people; they were divided up into thousands, hundreds, and tens, and commanders of these units were appointed. Also at this time he chose his personal bodyguards, the seventy day-guards and eighty night-guards.

Having reorganised the army, he marched away from the mountainside of Ornu'u on the Khalkha, and took the way of war against the Naiman.

The spring of the Year of the Rat [1204] was by now well advanced. During this westward march came the Day of the Red Disc, the sixteenth day of the first moon of summer. On this day, the moon being at the full, the Khan caused the great yak's-tail banner to be consecrated, letting it be sprinkled with fermented mare's milk, with the proper observances.

They continued the march up the Kerulen, with Jebe and Khubilai in the van. When they came on to the Saari steppes, they met with the first scouts of the Naiman. There were a few skirmishes between the Naiman and Mongol scouts; in one of these, a Mongol scout was captured, a man riding a grey horse with a worn saddle. The Naiman studied this horse with critical eyes, and thought little of it. "The Mongols' horses are inordinately lean," they said to each other.

The Mongol army rode out on to the Saari steppes, and began to deploy themselves for the forthcoming battle. . . . Dodai Cherbi, one of the newly appointed captains, put a proposal before the Khan.

"We are short in numbers compared to the enemy; besides this, we are exhausted after the long march, our horses in particular. It would be a good idea to settle in this camp, so that our horses can graze on the steppe, until they have had as much to eat as they need. Meanwhile, we can deceive the enemy by making puppets and lighting innumerable fires. For every man, we will make at least one puppet, and we will burn fires in five places. It is said that the Naiman people are very numerous, but it is rumored also that their king is a weakling, who has never left his tents. If we keep them in a state of uncertainty about our numbers, with our puppets and our fires, our geldings can stuff themselves till they are fat."

The suggestion pleased Temujin, who had the order passed on to the soldiers to light fires immediately. Puppets were constructed and placed all over the steppe, some sitting or lying by the fires, some of them even mounted on horses.

At night, the watchers of the Naiman saw, from the flanks of the mountain, fires twinkling all over the steppe. They said to each other: "Did they not say that the Mongols were very few? Yet they have more fires than there are stars in Heaven."

Having previously sent to Tayang Khan news of the lean grey horse with the shabby saddle, they now sent him the message: "The warriors of the Mongols are camped out all over the Saari steppes. They seem to grow more numerous every day; their fires outnumber the stars."

When this news was brought to him from the scouts, Tayang Khan was at the watercourse of Khachir. He sent a message to his son Guchuluk.

"I am told that the geldings of the Mongols are lean, but the Mongols are, it seems, numerous. Once we start fighting them, it will be difficult to draw back. They are such hard warriors that when several men at once come up against one of them, he does not move an eyelid; even if he is wounded, so that the black blood flows out, he does not flinch. I do not know whether it is a good thing to come up against such men.

"I suggest that we should assemble our people and lead them back to the west, across the Altai; and all the time, during this retreat, we will fight off the Mongols as dogs do, by running in on them from either side as they advance. Our geldings are too fat; in this march we shall make them lean and fit. But the Mongols' lean geldings will be brought to such a state of exhaustion they will vomit in the Mongols' faces."

On receiving this message, Guchuluk Khan, who was more warlike than his father, said: "That woman Tayang has lost all his courage, to speak such words. Where does this great multitude of Mongols come from? Most of the Mongols are with Jamukha, who is here with us. Tayang speaks like this because fear has overcome him. He has never been farther from his tent than his pregnant wife goes to urinate. He has never dared to go so far as the inner pastures where the knee-high calves are kept." So he expressed himself on the subject of his father, in the most injurious and wounding terms.

When he heard these words, Tayang Khan said: "I hope the pride of this powerful Guchuluk will not weaken on the day when the clash of arms is heard and the slaughter begins. Because once we are committed to battle against the foe, it will be hard to disengage again."

Khorisu Beki, a general who commanded under Tayang Khan, said: "Your father, Inancha Bilgei, never showed the back of a man or the haunch of a horse to opponents who were just as worthy as these. How can you lose your courage so early in the day? We would have done better to summon your mother Gurbesu to command over us. It is a pity that Kokse'u Sabrakh has grown too old to lead us. Our army's discipline has become lax. For the Mongols, their hour has come. It is finished! Tayang, you have failed us." He belted on his quiver and galloped off.

Tayang Khan grew angry. "All men must die," he said. "Their bodies must suffer. It is the same for all men. Let us fight, then."

So, having created doubt and dismay, and lost the support of some of his best leaders, he decided to give battle. He broke away from the watercourse of Khachir, marched down the Tamir, crossed the Orkhon and skirted the eastern flanks of the mountain Nakhu. When they came to Chakirma'ut, Temujin's scouts caught sight of them and brought back the message: "The Naiman are coming!"

The Battle of Chakirma'ut

When the news was brought to Temujin he said: "Sometimes too many men are just as big a handicap as too few."

Then he issued his general battle orders. "We will march in the order 'thick grass,' take up positions in the 'lake' battle order, and fight in the manner called 'gimlet.'"[2] He gave Kasar the command of the main army, and appointed Prince Otchigin to the command of the reserve horses, a special formation of great importance in Mongol warfare.

The Naiman, having advanced as far as Chakirma'ut, drew themselves up in a defensive position on the foothills of Nakhu, with the mountain behind them. . . . The Mongols forced their scouts back on to the forward lines, and then their forward lines back on to the main army, and drove tightly knit formations of horsemen again and again into the Naiman ranks. The Naiman, pressed back on themselves, could do nothing but retreat gradually up the mountain. Many of their men . . . hardly had the chance to fight at all, but were cut down in an immobile mass of men as soon as the Mongols reached them.

Tayang Khan, with his advisers, also retreated up the mountain as the day advanced. From the successive spurs to which they climbed, each one higher than the last, they could see the whole of this dreadful disaster as it took place below them.

Jamukha was with Tayang Khan. . . .

"Who are those people over there," Tayang Khan asked him, "who throw my warriors back as if they were sheep frightened by a wolf, who come huddling back to the sheepfold?"

Jamukha said: "My *anda*[3] Temujin has four hounds whom he brought up on human flesh, and kept in chains. They have brows of copper, snouts like chisels, tongues like bradawls, hearts of iron, and

---

[2] These were the names of various tactical disciplines in which he had drilled his army.
[3] Sworn brother, blood brother, declared ally.

tails that cut like swords. They can live on dew, and ride like the wind. On the day of battle they eat the flesh of men. You see how, being set loose, they come forward slavering for joy. Those two are Jebe and Khubilai; those two are Jelmei and Subetai. That is who those four hounds are.". . .

"Who is it coming up there in the rear," Tayang Khan asked him, "who swoops down on our troops like a ravening falcon?"

"That is my *anda* Temujin. His entire body is made of sounding copper; there is no gap through which even a bodkin could penetrate. There he is, you see him? He advances like an eagle about to seize his prey. You said formerly that if you once set eyes on the Mongols you would not leave so much of them as the skin of a lamb's foot. What do you think of them now?"

By this time the chieftains were standing on a high spur. Below them, the great army of the Naiman, Jamukha's men with them, were retreating in confusion, fighting desperately as the Mongols hemmed them in.

"Who is that other chieftain," Tayang asked Jamukha, "who draws ever nearer us, in a dense crowd of men?"

"Mother Hoelun brought up one of her own sons on human flesh. He is nine feet tall; he eats a three-year-old cow every day. If he swallows an armed man whole, it makes no difference to his appetite. When he is roused to anger, and lets fly with one of his *angqu'a* [forked] arrows, it will go through ten or twenty men. His normal range is a thousand yards; when he draws his bow to its fullest extent, he shoots over eighteen hundred yards. He is mortal, but he is not like other mortals; he is more than a match for the serpents of Guralgu. He is called Kasar."

They were climbing high up the mountain now, to regroup below its summit. Tayang Khan saw a new figure among the Mongols.

"Who is that coming up from the rear?" he asked Jamukha.

"That is the youngest son of Mother Hoelun. He is called Otchigin [Odeigin] the Phlegmatic. He is one of those people who go to bed early and get up late. But when he is behind the army, with the reserves, he does not linger; he never comes too late to the battle lines."

"We will climb to the peak of the mountain," Tayang Khan said.

Jamukha, seeing that the battle was lost, slipped away to the rear and descended the mountain, with a small body of men. One of these he sent to Temujin with a message. "Say this to my *anda*. Tayang Khan, terrified by what I have told him, has completely lost his senses. He has retreated up the mountain as far as he can. He could be killed by one harsh word. Let my *anda* take note of this: They have climbed to the top of the mountain, and are in no state to defend themselves any more. I myself have left the Naiman."

Since the evening was drawing on, Temujin commanded his troops in the forefront of the attack to draw back. Bodies of men were sent forward on the wings, east and west, to encircle the summit of Mount Nakhu.

There they stood to arms during the night. During the night, the Naiman army tried to break out of the encircling ring. Bodies of horsemen plunged down the mountainside in desperate charges; many fell and were trampled to death, the others were slain. In the first light they were seen lying about the mountain in droves, like fallen trees. Few were left defending the peak; they put up little resistance to the force sent up against them.

7

IBN AL-ATHIR
The Mongols, c. 1231

The great Muslim historian Ibn al-Athir (1160–1233), whose history of the First Crusade we excerpted in the previous chapter, actually lived through the early period of the Mongol invasion. Like many of his contemporaries he saw these events in biblical terms. In this selection he refers to the Mongols as Tatars, a common word at the time for the Turkic-speaking people subjugated by the Mongols and a word that evoked classical Tartarus, a realm of Hades, or Hell.

If you peel away the biblical allusions, what did the Mongols actually do, according to the author? How would you compare their conquests to those of the Vikings or others you have read about?

THINKING HISTORICALLY

How might Ibn al-Athir's use of biblical language be unfair to the Mongols? Does it make his writing less objective? Can you point to places in the text where he is too moralistic or judgmental regarding the Mongols?

For some years I continued averse from mentioning this event, deeming it so horrible that I shrank from recording it and ever withdrawing one foot as I advanced the other. To whom, indeed, can it be easy to write the announcement of the death-blow of Islam and the Muslims, or who is he on whom the remembrance thereof can weigh lightly? O would that my mother had not born me or that I had died and become a forgotten thing ere this befell! Yet, withal a number of my friends urged me to set it

Source: Edward G. Browne, *A Literary History of Persia* (Cambridge: Cambridge University Press, 1902), Vol. II, 427–31.

down in writing, and I hesitated long, but at last came to the conclusion that to omit this matter could serve no useful purpose.

I say, therefore, that this thing involves the description of the greatest catastrophe and the most dire calamity (of the like of which days and nights are innocent) which befell all men generally, and the Muslims in particular; so that, should one say that the world, since God Almighty created Adam until now, has not been afflicted with the like thereof, he would but speak the truth. For indeed history does not contain anything which approaches or comes near unto it. For of the most grievous calamities recorded was what Nebuchadnezzar inflicted on the children of Israel by his slaughter of them and his destruction of Jerusalem; and what was Jerusalem in comparison to the countries which these accursed miscreants destroyed, each city of which was double the size of Jerusalem? Or what were the children of Israel compared to those whom these slew? For verily those whom they massacred in a single city exceeded all the children of Israel. Nay, it is unlikely that mankind will see the like of this calamity, until the world comes to an end and perishes, except the final outbreak of Gog and Magog.[1]

For even Antichrist will spare such as follow him, though he destroy those who oppose him, but these Tatars spared none, slaying women and men and children, ripping open pregnant women and killing unborn babes. Verily to God do we belong, and unto Him do we return, and there is no strength and no power save in God, the High, the Almighty, in face of this catastrophe, whereof the sparks flew far and wide, and the hurt was universal; and which passed over the lands like clouds driven by the wind. For these were a people who emerged from the confines of China, and attacked the cities of Turkestan, like Kashghar and Balasaghun, and thence advanced on the cities of Transoxiana, such as Samarqand, Bukhara and the like, taking possession of them, and treating their inhabitants in such wise as we shall mention; and of them one division then passed on into Khurasan, until they had made an end of taking possession, and destroying, and slaying, and plundering, and thence passing on to Ray, Hamadan and the Highlands, and the cities contained therein, even to the limits of Iraq, whence they marched on the towns of Adharbayjan and Arraniyya, destroying them and slaying most of their inhabitants, of whom none escaped save a small remnant; and all this in less than a year; this is a thing whereof the like has not been heard. And when they had finished with Adharbayjan and Arraniyya, they passed on to Darband-i-Shirwan, and occupied its cities, none of which escaped save the fortress wherein was their King; wherefore they passed by it to the countries of the Lan and the Lakiz and the various nationalities which dwell in that region, and plundered, slew, and destroyed them to the full. And thence they made their way to the lands of Qipchaq, who are the

---

[1] From Book of Ezekiel associated with idea of apocalypse.

most numerous of the Turks, and slew all such as withstood them, while the survivors fled to the fords and mountain-tops, and abandoned their country, which these Tatars overran. All this they did in the briefest space of time, remaining only for so long as their march required and no more.

Another division, distinct from that mentioned above, marched on Ghazna and its dependencies, and those parts of India, Sistan and Kirman which border thereon, and wrought therein deeds like unto the other, nay, yet more grievous. Now this is a thing the like of which ear has not heard; for Alexander, concerning whom historians agree that he conquered the world, did not do so with such swiftness, but only in the space of about ten years; neither did he slay, but was satisfied that men should be subject to him. But these Tatars conquered most of the habitable globe, and the best, the most flourishing and most populous part thereof, and that whereof the inhabitants were the most advanced in character and conduct, in about a year; nor did any country escape their devastations which did not fearfully expect them and dread their arrival.

Moreover they need no commissariat, nor the conveyance of supplies, for they have with them sheep, cows, horses, and the like quadrupeds, the flesh of which they eat, naught else. As for their beasts which they ride, these dig into the earth with their hoofs and eat the roots of plants, knowing naught of barley. And so, when they alight anywhere, they have need of nothing from without. As for their religion, they worship the sun when it rises, and regard nothing as unlawful, for they eat all beasts, even dogs, pigs, and the like; nor do they recognize the marriage-tie, for several men are in marital relations with one woman, and if a child is born, it knows not who is its father.

Therefore Islam and the Muslims have been afflicted during this period with calamities wherewith no people hath been visited. These Tatars (may God confound them!) came from the East, and wrought deeds which horrify all who hear of them, and which you shall, please God, see set forth in full detail in their proper connection. And of these was the invasion of Syria by the Franks (may God curse them!) out of the West, and their attack on Egypt, and occupation of the port of Damietta therein, so that Egypt and Syria were like to be conquered by them, but for the grace of God and the help which He vouchsafed us against them, as we have mentioned under the year 614 (A.D. 1217–1218). Of these, moreover, was that the sword was drawn between those who escaped from these two foes, and strife was rampant, as we have also mentioned: and verily unto God do we belong and unto Him do we return! We ask God to vouchsafe victory to Islam and the Muslims, for there is none other to aid, help, or defend the True Faith. But if God intends evil to any people, naught can avert it, nor have they any ruler save Him. As for these Tatars, their achievements were only rendered possible by the absence of any effective obstacle; and the cause of this absence was that Muhammad Khwarazmshah had overrun the lands, slaying and destroying their Kings, so that he remained alone ruling over all these countries; wherefore, when he was defeated by the Tatars, none was left in the lands to check those or protect these, that so God might accomplish a thing which was to be done.

It is now time for us to describe how they first burst forth into the lands. Stories have been related to me, which the hearer can scarcely credit, as to the terror of the Tatars, which God Almighty cast into men's hearts; so that it is said that a single one of them would enter a village or a quarter wherein were many people, and would continue to slay them one after another, none daring to stretch forth his hand against this horseman. And I have heard that one of them took a man captive, but had not with him any weapon wherewith to kill him; and he said to his prisoner, "Lay your head on the ground and do not move," and he did so, and the Tatar went and fetched his sword and slew him therewith. Another man related to me as follows: "I was going," said he, "with seventeen others along a road, and there met us a Tatar horseman, and bade us bind one another's arms. My companions began to do as he bade them, but I said to them, 'He is but one man; wherefore, then, should we not kill him and flee?' They replied, 'We are afraid.' I said, 'This man intends to kill you immediately; let us therefore rather kill him, that perhaps God may deliver us.' But I swear by God that not one of them dared to do this, so I took a knife and slew him, and we fled and escaped." And such occurrences were many.

8

JOHN OF PLANO CARPINI

History of the Mongols, 1245–1250

Genghis Khan united the tribes of the steppe and conquered northern China, capturing Peking by 1215. He then turned his armies against the West, conquering the tribes of Turkestan and the Khorezmian Empire, the great Muslim power of Central Asia, by 1222 and sending an army around the Caspian Sea into Russia. In 1226, he turned again to the East, subduing and destroying the kingdom of Tibet before he died in 1227. One historian, Christopher Dawson, summarizes the career of Genghis Khan this way:

Source: John of Plano Carpini, "History of the Mongols," in *Mission to Asia: Narratives and Letters of the Franciscan Missionaries in Mongolia and China in the Thirteenth and Fourteenth Centuries*, trans. a nun of Stanbrook Abbey, ed. Christopher Dawson (1955; reprint, New York: Harper & Row, 1966), 60–69.

In spite of the primitive means at his disposal, it is possible that [Genghis Khan] succeeded in destroying a larger portion of the human race than any modern expert in total warfare. Within a dozen years from the opening of his campaign against China, the Mongol armies had reached the Pacific, the Indus, and the Black Sea, and had destroyed many of the great cities in India. For Europe especially, the shock was overwhelming.[1]

European fears intensified in 1237 as the principal Mongol armies under Batu Khan systematically destroyed one Russian city after another. In April 1241, one Mongol army destroyed a combined force of Polish and German armies, while another defeated the Hungarian army and threatened Austria. In 1245, desperate to learn as much as possible about Mongol intentions, Pope Innocent IV sent a mission to the Mongols. For this important task, he sent two Franciscan monks — one of whom was John of Plano Carpini — with two letters addressed to the Emperor of the Tartars (a compounded error that changed the Tatars, the Mongols' enemy, into the denizens of Tartarus, or Hell).

In May, the barefoot sixty-five-year-old Friar John reached Batu's camp on the Volga River, from which he was relayed to Mongolia by five fresh horses a day in order to reach the capital at Karakorum in time for the installation of the third Great Khan, Guyuk (r. 1246–1248) in July and August.

In this selection from his *History of the Mongols*, John writes of his arrival in Mongolia for the installation of Guyuk (here written as Cuyuc). In what ways does John's account change or expand your understanding of the Mongols? Was John a good observer? How does he compensate for his ignorance (as an outside observer) of Mongol society and culture? In what ways does he remain a victim of his outsider status?

How was Mongol society similar to, and different from, Viking society? Compare the role of women in Mongol and Viking societies.

THINKING HISTORICALLY

How would you characterize John's moral stance toward the Mongols? How is his judgment of the Mongols different from that of Yvo of Narbona, and what might account for that difference? Consider your own moral judgment, if any, of the Mongols. How is it related to your historical understanding?

---

[1] From Christopher Dawson, ed., *Mission to Asia*, p. xii.

. . . On our arrival Cuyuc had us given a tent and provisions, such as it is the custom for the Tartars to give, but they treated us better than other envoys. Nevertheless we were not invited to visit him for he had not yet been elected, nor did he yet concern himself with the government. The translation of the Lord Pope's letter, however, and the things I had said had been sent to him by Bati. After we had stayed there for five or six days he sent us to his mother where the solemn court was assembling. By the time we got there a large pavilion had already been put up made of white velvet, and in my opinion it was so big that more than two thousand men could have got into it. Around it had been erected a wooden palisade, on which various designs were painted. On the second or third day we went with the Tartars who had been appointed to look after us and there all the chiefs were assembled and each one was riding with his followers among the hills and over the plains round about.

On the first day they were all clothed in white velvet, on the second in red—that day Cuyuc came to the tent—on the third day they were all in blue velvet, and on the fourth in the finest brocade. In the palisade round the pavilion were two large gates, through one of which the Emperor alone had the right to enter and there were no guards placed at it although it was open, for no one dare enter or leave by it; through the other gate all those who were granted admittance entered and there were guards there with swords and bows and arrows. . . . The chiefs went about everywhere armed and accompanied by a number of their men, but none, unless their group of ten was complete, could go as far as the horses; indeed those who attempted to do so were severely beaten. There were many of them who had, as far as I could judge, about twenty marks' worth of gold on their bits, breastplates, saddles, and cruppers. The chiefs held their conference inside the tent and, so I believe, conducted the election. All the other people however were a long way away outside the aforementioned palisade. There they remained until almost midday and then they began to drink mare's milk and they drank until the evening, so much that it was amazing to see. We were invited inside and they gave us mead as we would not take mare's milk. They did this to show us great honour, but they kept on plying us with drinks to such an extent that we could not possibly stand it, not being used to it, so we gave them to understand that it was disagreeable to us and they left off pressing us.

Outside were Duke Jerozlaus of Susdal in Russia and several chiefs of the Kitayans and Solangi, also two sons of the King of Georgia, the ambassador of the Caliph of Baghdad, who was a Sultan, and more than ten other Sultans of the Saracens, so I believe and so we were told by the stewards. There were more than four thousand envoys there, counting those who were carrying tribute, those who were bringing gifts, the Sultans and other chiefs who were coming to submit to them, those summoned by the Tartars and the governors of territories. All these were put together outside the palisade and they were given drinks at the same time, but when we were outside with them we and Duke Jerozlaus were always given the best places. I think, if I remember rightly, that we had been there a good four weeks when, as I believe, the election took place; the result however was not made public at that time; the chief ground for my supposition was that whenever Cuyuc left the tent they sang before him and as long as he remained outside they dipped to him beautiful rods on the top of which was scarlet wool, which they did not do for any of the other chiefs. They call this court the Sira Orda.

Leaving there we rode all together for three or four leagues to another place, where on a pleasant plain near a river among the mountains another tent had been set up, which is called by them the Golden Orda, it was here that Cuyuc was to be enthroned on the feast of the Assumption of Our Lady. . . .

At that place we were summoned into the presence of the Emperor, and Chingay the protonotary wrote down our names and the names of those who had sent us, also the names of the chief of the Solangi and of others, and then calling out in a loud voice he recited them before the Emperor and all the chiefs. When this was finished each one of us genuflected four times on the left knee and they warned us not to touch the lower part of the threshold. After we had been most thoroughly searched for knives and they had found nothing at all, we entered by a door on the east side, for no one dare enter from the west with the sole exception of the Emperor or, if it is a chief's tent, the chief; those of lower rank do not pay much attention to such things. This was the first time since Cuyuc had been made Emperor that we had entered his tent in his presence. He also received all the envoys in that place, but very few entered his tent.

So many gifts were bestowed by the envoys there that it was marvellous to behold—gifts of silk, samite, velvet, brocade, girdles of silk threaded with gold, choice furs, and other presents. The Emperor was also given a sunshade or little awning such as is carried over his head, and it was all decorated with precious stones. . . .

Leaving there we went to another place where a wonderful tent had been set up all of red velvet, and this had been given by the Kitayans; there also we were taken inside. Whenever we went in we were given mead and wine to drink, and cooked meat was offered us if we wished to have it. A lofty platform of boards had been erected, on which the Emperor's throne was placed. The throne, which was of ivory, was wonderfully carved and there was also gold on it, and precious stones, if I remember rightly, and pearls. Steps led up to it and it was rounded behind. Benches were also placed round the throne, and here the ladies sat in their seats on the left; nobody, however, sat on the right, but the chiefs were on benches in the middle and the rest of the people sat beyond them. Every day a great crowd of ladies came.

Finally, after some time, John was to be brought again before the Emperor. When he heard from them that we had come to him he ordered us to go back to his mother, the reason being that he wished on the following day to raise his banner against the whole of the Western world—we were told this definitely by men who knew . . .—and he wanted us to be kept in ignorance of this. On our return we stayed for a few days, then we went back to him again and remained with him for a good month, enduring such hunger and thirst that we could scarcely keep alive, for the food provided for four was barely sufficient for one, moreover, we were unable to find anything to buy, for the market was a very long way off. If the Lord had not sent us a certain Russian, by name Cosmas, a goldsmith and a great favourite of the Emperor, who supported us to some extent, we would, I believe, have died, unless the Lord had helped us in some other way. . . .

After this the Emperor sent for us, and through Chingay his protonotary told us to write down what we had to say and our business, and give it to him. We did this and wrote out for him all that we said earlier to Bati. . . . A few days passed by; then he had us summoned again and told us through Kadac, the procurator of the whole empire, in the presence of Bala and Chingay his protonotaries and many other scribes, to say all we had to say: We did this willingly and gladly. Our interpreter on this as on the previous occasion was Temer, a knight of Jerozlaus': and there were also present a cleric who was with him and another cleric who was with the Emperor. On this occasion we were asked if there were any people with the Lord Pope who understood the writing of the Russians or Saracens or even of the Tartars. We gave answer that we used neither the Ruthenian nor Saracen writing; there were however Saracens in the country but they were a long way from the Lord Pope; but we said that it seemed to us that the most expedient course would be for them to write in Tartar and translate it for us, and we would write it down carefully in our own script and we would take both the letter and the translation to the Lord Pope. Thereupon they left us to go to the Emperor.

On St. Martin's day we were again summoned, and Kadac, Chingay, and Bala, the aforementioned secretaries, came to us and translated the letter for us word by word. When we had written it in Latin, they had it translated so that they might hear a phrase at a time, for they wanted to know if we had made a mistake in any word. When both letters were written, they made us read it once and a second time in case we had left out anything. . . .

It is the custom for the Emperor of the Tartars never to speak to a foreigner, however important he may be, except through an intermediary, and he listens and gives his answer, also through the intermediary. Whenever his subjects have any business to bring before Kadac, or while they are listening to the Emperor's reply, they stay on their knees until the end of the conversation, however important they may be. It is not possible nor indeed is it the custom for anyone to say anything about any matter after the Emperor has declared his decision. This Emperor not only has a procurator and protonotaries and secretaries, but all officials for dealing with both public and private matters, except that he has no advocates, for everything is settled according to the decision of the Emperor without the turmoil of legal trials. The other princes of the Tartars do the same in those matters concerning them.

The present Emperor may be forty or forty-five years old or more; he is of medium height, very intelligent, and extremely shrewd, and most serious and grave in his manner. He is never seen to laugh for a slight cause nor to indulge in any frivolity, so we were told by the Christians who are constantly with him. The Christians of his household also told us that they firmly believed he was about to become a Christian, and they have clear evidence of this, for he maintains Christian clerics and provides them with supplies of Christian things; in addition he always has a chapel before his chief tent and they sing openly and in public and beat the board for services after the Greek fashion like other Christians, however big a crowd of Tartars or other men be there. The other chiefs do not behave like this.

. . . on the feast of St. Brice [November 13th], they gave us a permit to depart and a letter sealed with the Emperor's seal, and sent us to the Emperor's mother. She gave each of us a fox-skin cloak, which had the fur outside and was lined inside, and a length of velvet; our Tartars stole a good yard from each of the pieces of velvet and from the piece given to our servant they stole more than half. This did not escape our notice, but we preferred not to make a fuss about it.

We then set out on the return journey.

■ REFLECTIONS

The great Chinese artist Zheng Sixiao (1241–1318) continued to paint his delicate Chinese orchids in the years after the Mongol defeat of the Sung dynasty, under the alien rule of Kublai Khan (r. 1260–1294), the fifth Great Khan and the founder of the Mongol Yuan dynasty of China. But when Zheng was asked why he always painted the orchids without earth around their roots, he replied that the earth had been stolen by the barbarians.

Just as it would be a mistake to see a fifth-generation Mongol ruler like Kublai as a barbarian, it would also be a mistake to assume that Zheng's hardened resistance remained the norm. In fact, a younger generation of artists found opportunity and even freedom in Kublai's China. Kublai appointed some of the most famous Chinese painters of his era to positions of government—Ministries of War, Public Works, Justice, Personnel, Imperial Sacrifices—actively recruiting the bright young men, artists and intellectuals, for his government. While some painters catered to the Mongol elite's inclination for paintings of horses, others relished the wider range of subjects allowed by a regime free of highly cultivated prejudices.

If conquest invariably brings charges of barbarism, it also eventually turns to issues of government and administration. Administrators need officials. Though Kublai Khan abolished the Chinese civil service examination system because it would have forced him to rely on Chinese officials, the Chinese language, and an educational system based on the Chinese classics, he actively sought ways of governing that were neither too Chinese nor too Mongolian. Typically, he promulgated a Chinese alphabet that was based on Tibetan, hoping that its phonetic symbols would make communication easier and less classical. Many of his achievements were unintended. While his officials continued to use Chinese characters and the Uighur script, the Yuan dynasty witnessed a flowering of literary culture, including theater and novels. For some, no doubt, the wind from the steppe blew away the dust and cobwebs that had accumulated for too long.

Our judgment of the Mongols depends to a great extent on the period of Mongol history we consider. But while it is easy to condemn Genghis Khan and the initial conquests and praise the later enlightened governance, two considerations come to mind. First, in the great sweep of history, many "barbarians" became benign, even indulgent, administrators. Second, the Mongols were not unique in making that transition.

Before the Mongols, the Vikings had already made the transition from raiding to trading and from conquering to colonizing. In fact, as Cunliffe points out, the Vikings had always been farmer-sailors who were as hungry for land as for plunder. Unlike the Mongols who were born on horses, continually picking up and remaking camp in new pastureland, the Vikings became nomadic in emergencies when a search for new settlements was necessary.

The memory of Viking assaults also faded faster than that of the Mongols. The Viking Rus had the Mongols to thank. The Rus of Viking cities like Novgorod became the national heroes of anti-Mongol Russian legend, eventually becoming the Russians. In Europe, too, the descendants of Vikings helped establish new national identities. The last great Viking king, Harald the Hard Ruler, "Thunderbolt of the North," won back his father's crown as king of Norway in 1047, after preparing himself in Russian trading cities and Byzantine courts. He had married a Russian princess and fought for the Byzantines in Asia Minor, Jerusalem, and the Caucasus Mountains. In 1066, this king of

Norway lost his control of England when he was killed by an English earl. A few days later the new English king was killed by William Duke of Normandy, a Viking son who had previously conquered much of France. Norman rule was to last over a hundred years, from 1066 to 1215, and create a new English identity.

At the end of the day, history is neither moral nor immoral. History is what happened, for better or worse, and moralistic history is generally bad history. The Vikings and Mongols of our period were no more morally frozen in time than were the Christian and Muslim Crusaders of the same era who visited such violence upon each other.

Just as the role of nomads and settlers changes over time, so does the degree to which a people are particularly aggressive or peaceful. It is hard to imagine a more fearful people than the Mongols of the thirteenth century or the Vikings of the tenth century. Yet modern Scandinavia, Iceland, and Mongolia are among the most peaceful places on the planet.

12

The Black Death

Afro-Eurasia, 1346–1350

■ HISTORICAL CONTEXT

The Mongol peace that made the Persian Ilkhanid dynasty (1256–1353) and the Chinese Yuan dynasty (1279–1368) sister empires nurtured a level of economic exchange and artistic communication greater than in the most cosmopolitan days of the early Roman/Han Silk Road. But the new caravan routes that spanned Central Asia could carry microbes as well as people. The plague that had long been endemic in country rats spread by fleas to city rats and other animals, including humans. As early as 1346, travelers reported millions killed in China, Central Asia, and the Middle East. In Europe and Egypt, approximately a third of the population perished. In some cities, the death toll was greater than half. This pandemic plague of 1346–1350 is sometimes called the Black Death, after the discolored wounds it caused.

■ THINKING HISTORICALLY
Considering Cause and Effect

The study of history, like the practice of medicine, is a process of understanding the causes of certain effects. In medicine the effects are diseases or good health; in history they are more varied events. Nevertheless, understanding the causes of things is central to both disciplines. For medical specialists the goal of understanding causes is implicitly a part of the process of improving health or finding a cure. Historians rarely envision "cures" for social ills, but many believe that an understanding of cause and effect can improve society's chances of avoiding undesirable outcomes in favor of more helpful ones.

Still, the most hopeful medical researcher or historian would agree that the process of relating cause and effect, of finding causes and explaining effects, is fraught with difficulties. There is first the problem of precisely defining the effect to be explained. Next there is the need to find possible causes in past events (though medical specialists often have the advantage of replicating the past by experiment). Then there is the need to establish a connection between the past event and the current condition (avoiding the logical fallacy *post hoc ergo propter hoc:* "after this, therefore because of this"). We will explore some of those difficulties in this chapter.

1

MARK WHEELIS

Biological Warfare at the 1346 Siege of Caffa, 2002

We are used to thinking of biological warfare as a recently developed threat. This article, published in a journal for public health professionals, suggests a longer history. According to the author, how and where did the Black Death originate? What was the significance of the Mongol siege of the northern Black Sea port of Caffa in 1346? The author draws on the contemporary account of the Black Death by Gabriele de' Mussis. On what points does he agree and disagree with de' Mussis?

THINKING HISTORICALLY

The author of this selection, a professor of microbiology at the University of California, was trained as a bacterial physiologist and geneticist, but for more than the last ten years his research has concentrated on the history and control of biological weapons. Notice how he uses both medical and historical ways of explaining causes. In medicine and science, the study of causes is called etiology. Give an example from the reading of an etiological explanation of the Black Death. The author also offers historical explanations of causes. Give examples of these. How are the etiological and historical similar and different?

Source: Mark Wheelis, "Biological Warfare at the 1346 Siege of Caffa," *Emerging Infectious Diseases* 8, no. 9 (September 2002): 971–75. The journal is published by the U.S. Centers for Disease Control and Prevention (C.D.C.), Atlanta, and is also available online at http://www.cdc.gov/ncidod/EID/vol8no9/01-0536.htm.

The Black Death, which swept through Europe, the Near East, and North Africa in the mid-fourteenth century, was probably the greatest public health disaster in recorded history and one of the most dramatic examples ever of emerging or reemerging disease. Europe lost an esti- mated one-quarter to one-third of its population, and the mortality in North Africa and the Near East was comparable. China, India, and the rest of the Far East are commonly believed to have also been severely affected, but little evidence supports that belief.

A principal source on the origin of the Black Death is a memoir by the Italian Gabriele de' Mussis. This memoir has been published several times in its original Latin and has recently been translated into English (although brief passages have been previously published in translation). This narrative contains some startling assertions: that the Mongol army hurled plague-infected cadavers into the besieged Crimean city of Caffa, thereby transmitting the disease to the inhabitants; and that fleeing survi- vors of the siege spread plague from Caffa to the Mediterranean Basin. If this account is correct, Caffa should be recognized as the site of the most spectacular incident of biological warfare ever, with the Black Death as its disastrous consequence. After analyzing these claims, I have concluded that it is plausible that the biological attack took place as described and was responsible for infecting the inhabitants of Caffa; however, the event was unimportant in the spread of the plague pandemic.

Origin of the Fourteenth-Century Pandemic

The disease that caused this catastrophic pandemic has, since Hecker,[1] generally been considered to have been a plague, a zoonotic disease caused by the gram-negative bacterium *Yersinia pestis*, the principal reservoir for which is wild rodents. The ultimate origin of the Black Death is uncertain—China, Mongolia, India, central Asia, and southern Russia have all been suggested. Known fourteenth-century sources are of little help; they refer repeatedly to an eastern origin, but none of the reports is firsthand. Historians generally agree that the outbreak moved west out of the steppes north of the Black and Caspian Seas, and its spread through Europe and the Middle East is fairly well documented. [See Map 12.1.] However, despite more than a century of speculation about an ultimate origin further east, the requisite scholarship using Chinese and central Asian sources has yet to be done. In any event, the Crimea[2] clearly played a pivotal role as the proximal source from which the Mediterranean Basin was infected.

---

[1] Justus Friedrich Karl Hecker (1795–1850), German physician who founded the study of disease in history. See *The Black Death: The Dancing Mania*. [Ed.]

[2] The peninsula that juts into the Black Sea from the north (modern Ukraine); Caffa was one of its port cities. [Ed.]

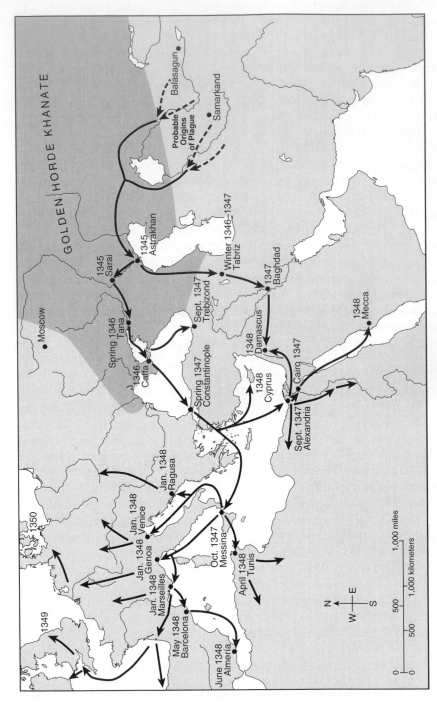

Map 12.1 Tentative Chronology of the Initial Spread of Plague in the Mid-Fourteenth Century.

Historical Background to the Siege of Caffa

Caffa (now Feodosija, Ukraine) was established by Genoa in 1266 by agreement with the Kahn of the Golden Horde. It was the main port for the great Genoese merchant ships, which connected there to a coastal shipping industry to Tana (now Azov, Russia) on the Don River. Trade along the Don connected Tana to Central Russia, and overland caravan routes linked it to Sarai and thence to the Far East.

Relations between Italian traders and their Mongol hosts were uneasy, and in 1307 Toqtai, Kahn of the Golden Horde, arrested the Italian residents of Sarai, and besieged Caffa. The cause was apparently Toqtai's displeasure at the Italian trade in Turkic slaves (sold for soldiers to the Mameluke Sultanate). The Genoese resisted for a year, but in 1308 set fire to their city and abandoned it. Relations between the Italians and the Golden Horde remained tense until Toqtai's death in 1312.

Toqtai's successor, Özbeg, welcomed the Genoese back, and also ceded land at Tana to the Italians for the expansion of their trading enterprise. By the 1340s, Caffa was again a thriving city, heavily fortified within two concentric walls. The inner wall enclosed 6,000 houses, the outer 11,000. The city's population was highly cosmopolitan, including Genoese, Venetian, Greeks, Armenians, Jews, Mongols, and Turkic peoples.

In 1343 the Mongols under Janibeg (who succeeded Özbeg in 1340) besieged Caffa and the Italian enclave at Tana following a brawl between Italians and Muslims in Tana. The Italian merchants in Tana fled to Caffa (which, by virtue of its location directly on the coast, maintained maritime access despite the siege). The siege of Caffa lasted until February 1344, when it was lifted after an Italian relief force killed 15,000 Mongol troops and destroyed their siege machines. Janibeg renewed the siege in 1345 but was again forced to lift it after a year, this time by an epidemic of plague that devastated his forces. The Italians blockaded Mongol ports, forcing Janibeg to negotiate, and in 1347 the Italians were allowed to reestablish their colony in Tana.

Gabriele de' Mussis

Gabriele de' Mussis, born circa 1280, practiced as a notary in the town of Piacenza, over the mountains just north of Genoa. [Nineteenth-century Italian historian] Tononi summarizes the little we know of him. His practice was active in the years 1300–1349. He is thought to have died in approximately 1356.

Although [the German historian] Henschel thought de' Mussis was present at the siege of Caffa, Tononi asserts that the Piacenza archives contain deeds signed by de' Mussis spanning the period 1344 through the first half of 1346. While this does not rule out travel to Caffa in late

1346, textual evidence suggests that he did not. He does not claim to have witnessed any of the Asian events he describes and often uses a passive voice for descriptions. After describing the siege of Caffa, de' Mussis goes on to say, "Now it is time that we passed from east to west to discuss all the things which we ourselves have seen. . . ."

The Narrative of Gabriele de' Mussis

The de' Mussis account is presumed to have been written in 1348 or early 1349 because of its immediacy and the narrow time period described. The original is lost, but a copy is included in a compilation of historical and geographic accounts by various authors, dating from approximately 1367. The account begins with an introductory comment by the scribe who copied the documents: "In the name of God, Amen. Here begins an account of the disease or mortality which occurred in 1348, put together by Gabrielem de Mussis of Piacenza."

The narrative begins with an apocalyptic speech by God, lamenting the depravity into which humanity has fallen and describing the retribution intended. It goes on:

". . . In 1346, in the countries of the East, countless numbers of Tartars and Saracens were struck down by a mysterious illness which brought sudden death. Within these countries broad regions, far-spreading provinces, magnificent kingdoms, cities, towns and settlements, ground down by illness and devoured by dreadful death, were soon stripped of their inhabitants. An eastern settlement under the rule of the Tartars called Tana, which lay to the north of Constantinople and was much frequented by Italian merchants, was totally abandoned after an incident there which led to its being besieged and attacked by hordes of Tartars who gathered in a short space of time. The Christian merchants, who had been driven out by force, were so terrified of the power of the Tartars that, to save themselves and their belongings, they fled in an armed ship to Caffa, a settlement in the same part of the world which had been founded long ago by the Genoese.

"Oh God! See how the heathen Tartar races, pouring together from all sides, suddenly invested the city of Caffa and besieged the trapped Christians there for almost three years. There, hemmed in by an immense army, they could hardly draw breath, although food could be shipped in, which offered them some hope. But behold, the whole army was affected by a disease which overran the Tartars and killed thousands upon thousands every day. It was as though arrows were raining down from heaven to strike and crush the Tartars' arrogance. All medical advice and attention was useless; the Tartars died as soon as the signs of disease appeared on their bodies: swellings in the armpit or groin caused by coagulating humours, followed by a putrid fever.

"The dying Tartars, stunned and stupefied by the immensity of the disaster brought about by the disease, and realizing that they had no hope of escape, lost interest in the siege. But they ordered corpses to be placed in catapults[3] and lobbed into the city in the hope that the intolerable stench would kill everyone inside.[4] What seemed like mountains of dead were thrown into the city, and the Christians could not hide or flee or escape from them, although they dumped as many of the bodies as they could in the sea. And soon the rotting corpses tainted the air and poisoned the water supply, and the stench was so overwhelming that hardly one in several thousand was in a position to flee the remains of the Tartar army. Moreover one infected man could carry the poison to others, and infect people and places with the disease by look alone. No one knew, or could discover, a means of defense.

"Thus almost everyone who had been in the East, or in the regions to the south and north, fell victim to sudden death after contracting this pestilential disease, as if struck by a lethal arrow which raised a tumor on their bodies. The scale of the mortality and the form which it took persuaded those who lived, weeping and lamenting, through the bitter events of 1346 to 1348 — the Chinese, Indians, Persians, Medes, Kurds, Armenians, Cilicians, Georgians, Mesopotamians, Nubians, Ethiopians, Turks, Egyptians, Arabs, Saracens, and Greeks (for almost all the East has been affected) — that the last judgement had come.

". . . As it happened, among those who escaped from Caffa by boat were a few sailors who had been infected with the poisonous disease. Some boats were bound for Genoa, others went to Venice and to other Christian areas. When the sailors reached these places and mixed with the people there, it was as if they had brought evil spirits with them: every city, every settlement, every place was poisoned by the contagious pestilence, and their inhabitants, both men and women, died suddenly. And when one person had contracted the illness, he poisoned his whole family even as he fell and died, so that those preparing to bury his body were seized by death in the same way. Thus death entered through the windows, and as cities and towns were depopulated their inhabitants mourned their dead neighbours."

The account closes with an extended description of the plague in Piacenza, and a reprise of the apocalyptic vision with which it begins.

---

[3] Technically trebuchets, not catapults. Catapults hurl objects by the release of tension on twisted cordage; they are not capable of hurling loads over a few dozen kilograms. Trebuchets are counter-weight-driven hurling machines, very effective for throwing ammunition weighing a hundred kilos or more.

[4] Medieval society lacked a coherent theory of disease causation. Three notions coexisted in a somewhat contradictory mixture: 1) disease was a divine punishment for individual or collective transgression; 2) disease was the result of "miasma," or the stench of decay; and 3) disease was the result of person-to-person contagion.

Commentary

In this narrative, de' Mussis makes two important claims about the siege of Caffa and the Black Death: that plague was transmitted to Europeans by the hurling of diseased cadavers into the besieged city of Caffa and that Italians fleeing from Caffa brought it to the Mediterranean ports.

Biological Warfare at Caffa

De' Mussis's account is probably secondhand and is uncorroborated; however, he seems, in general, to be a reliable source, and as a Piacenzian he would have had access to eyewitnesses of the siege. Several considerations incline me to trust his account: this was probably not the only, nor the first, instance of apparent attempts to transmit disease by hurling biological material into besieged cities; it was within the technical capabilities of besieging armies of the time; and it is consistent with medieval notions of disease causality.

Tentatively accepting that the attack took place as described, we can consider two principal hypotheses for the entry of plague into the city: it might, as de' Mussis asserts, have been transmitted by the hurling of plague cadavers; or it might have entered by rodent-to-rodent transmission from the Mongol encampments into the city.

Diseased cadavers hurled into the city could easily have transmitted plague, as defenders handled the cadavers during disposal. Contact with infected material is a known mechanism of transmission; for instance, among 284 cases of plague in the United States in 1970–1995 for which a mechanism of transmission could be reasonably inferred, 20 percent were thought to be by direct contact. Such transmission would have been especially likely at Caffa, where cadavers would have been badly mangled by being hurled, and many of the defenders probably had cut or abraded hands from coping with the bombardment. Very large numbers of cadavers were possibly involved, greatly increasing the opportunity for disease transmission. Since disposal of the bodies of victims in a major outbreak of lethal disease is always a problem, the Mongol forces may have used their hurling machines as a solution to their mortuary problem, in which case many thousands of cadavers could have been involved. De' Mussis's description of "mountains of dead" might have been quite literally true.

Thus it seems plausible that the events recounted by de' Mussis could have been an effective means of transmission of plague into the city. The alternative, rodent-to-rodent transmission from the Mongol encampments into the city, is less likely. Besieging forces must have camped at least a kilometer away from the city walls. This distance is necessary to have a healthy margin of safety from arrows and artillery and to provide space for logistical support and other military activities between the encampments and the front lines. Front-line location must have been approximately 250–300 m from the walls; trebuchets are known from modern reconstruction to be capable of hurling 100 kg more than 200 m, and historical sources claim 300 m as the working range of large machines. Thus, the bulk of rodent nests associated with the besieging armies would have been located a kilometer or more away from the cities, and none would have likely been closer than 250 m. Rats are quite sedentary and rarely venture more than a few tens of meters from their nest. It is thus unlikely that there was any contact between the rat populations within and outside the walls.

Given the many uncertainties, any conclusion must remain tentative. However, the considerations above suggest that the hurling of plague cadavers might well have occurred as de' Mussis claimed, and if so, that this biological attack was probably responsible for the transmission of the disease from the besiegers to the besieged. Thus, this early act of biological warfare, if such it were, appears to have been spectacularly successful in producing casualties, although of no strategic importance (the city remained in Italian hands, and the Mongols abandoned the siege).

Crimea as the Source of European and Near Eastern Plague

There has never been any doubt that plague entered the Mediterranean from the Crimea, following established maritime trade routes. Rat infestations in the holds of cargo ships would have been highly susceptible to the rapid spread of plague, and even if most rats died during the voyage, they would have left abundant hungry fleas that would infect humans unpacking the holds. Shore rats foraging on board recently arrived ships would also become infected, transmitting plague to city rat populations.

Plague appears to have been spread in a stepwise fashion, on many ships rather than on a few [see Map 12.1], taking over a year to reach Europe from the Crimea. This conclusion seems fairly firm, as the dates for the arrival of plague in Constantinople and more westerly cities are reasonably certain. Thus de' Mussis was probably mistaken in attributing the Black Death to fleeing survivors of Caffa, who should not have needed more than a few months to return to Italy.

Furthermore, a number of other Crimean ports were under Mongol control, making it unlikely that Caffa was the only source of infected ships heading west. And the overland caravan routes to the Middle East from Serai and Astrakhan insured that plague was also spreading south (Map 12.1), whence it would have entered Europe in any case. The siege of Caffa and its gruesome finale thus are unlikely to have been seriously implicated in the transmission of plague from the Black Sea to Europe.

Conclusion

Gabriele de' Mussis's account of the origin and spread of plague appears to be consistent with most known facts, although mistaken in its claim that plague arrived in Italy directly from the Crimea. His account of biological attack is plausible, consistent with the technology of the time, and it provides the best explanation of disease transmission into besieged Caffa. This thus appears to be one of the first biological attacks recorded and among the most successful of all time.

However, it is unlikely that the attack had a decisive role in the spread of plague to Europe. Much maritime commerce probably continued throughout this period from other Crimean ports. Overland caravan routes to the Middle East were also unaffected. Thus, refugees from Caffa would most likely have constituted only one of several streams of infected ships and caravans leaving the region. The siege of Caffa, for all of its dramatic appeal, probably had no more than anecdotal importance in the spread of plague, a macabre incident in terrifying times.

Despite its historical unimportance, the siege of Caffa is a powerful reminder of the horrific consequences when disease is successfully used as a weapon. The Japanese use of plague as a weapon in World War II and the huge Soviet stockpiles of *Y. pestis* prepared for use in an all-out war further remind us that plague remains a very real problem for modern arms control, six and a half centuries later.

2

GABRIELE DE' MUSSIS
Origins of the Black Death, c. 1348

Gabriele de' Mussis (d. 1356) was a lawyer who lived in the northern Italian city of Piacenza. The previous reading introduced you to de' Mussis and the importance of his history of the Black Death. Since Wheelis quoted abundantly from the story of the siege of Caffa, we pick up the story in de' Mussis's words regarding the spread of the plague to Europe, where, as he wrote, he had direct evidence. How would you rate de' Mussis as an eyewitness observer? According to his evidence, how did the Black Death spread in Italy? How deadly was it?

Source: *The Black Death*, trans. and ed. Rosemary Horrox (Manchester, England: Manchester University Press, 1994), 18–26.

THINKING HISTORICALLY

As in the previous selection, there are two causal chains in this account, but in this case they are not medical and historical. Rather, reminiscent of the readings on the First Crusade, they are divine and human chains of causation. What, according to the author, were the divine or religious causes of the Black Death? What were the human, physical, or scientific causes? What remedies does each type of cause call for?

Now it is time that we passed from east to west, to discuss all the things which we ourselves have seen, or known, or consider likely on the basis of the evidence, and, by so doing, to show forth the terrifying judgements of God. Listen everybody, and it will set tears pouring from your eyes. For the Almighty has said: "I shall wipe man, whom I created, off the face of the earth. Because he is flesh and blood, let him be turned to dust and ashes. My spirit shall not remain among man."

— "What are you thinking of, merciful God, thus to destroy your creation and the human race; to order and command its sudden annihilation in this way? What has become of your mercy; the faith of our fathers; the blessed virgin, who holds sinners in her lap; the precious blood of the martyrs; the worthy army of confessors and virgins; the whole host of paradise, who pray ceaselessly for sinners; the most precious death of Christ on the cross and our wonderful redemption? Kind God, I beg that your anger may cease, that you do not destroy sinners in this way, and, because you desire mercy rather than sacrifice, that you turn away all evil from the penitent, and do not allow the just to be condemned with the unjust."

— "I hear you, sinner, dropping words into my ears. I bid you weep. The time for mercy has passed. I, God, am called to vengeance. It is my pleasure to take revenge on sin and wickedness. I shall give my signs to the dying, let them take steps to provide for the health of their souls."

As it happened, among those who escaped from Caffa by boat were a few sailors who had been infected with the poisonous disease. Some boats were bound for Genoa, others went to Venice and to other Christian areas. . . .

— "We Genoese and Venetians bear the responsibility for revealing the judgements of God. Alas, once our ships had brought us to port we went to our homes. And because we had been delayed by tragic events, and because among us there were scarcely ten survivors from a thousand sailors, relations, kinsmen and neighbours flocked to us from all sides. But, to our anguish, we were carrying the darts of death. While they hugged and kissed us we were spreading poison from our lips even as we spoke."

When they returned to their own folk, these people speedily poisoned the whole family, and within three days the afflicted family would succumb to the dart of death. Mass funerals had to be held and there was not enough room to bury the growing numbers of dead. Priests and doctors, upon whom most of the care of the sick devolved, had their hands full in visiting the sick and, alas, by the time they left they too had been infected and followed the dead immediately to the grave. Oh fathers! Oh mothers! Oh children and wives! For a long time prosperity preserved you from harm, but one grave now covers you and the unfortunate alike. You who enjoyed the world and upon whom pleasure and prosperity smiled, who mingled joys with follies, the same tomb receives you and you are handed over as food for worms. Oh hard death, impious death, bitter death, cruel death, who divides parents, divorces spouses, parts children, separates brothers and sisters. We bewail our wretched plight. The past has devoured us, the present is gnawing our entrails, the future threatens yet greater dangers. What we laboured to amass with feverish activity, we have lost in one hour.

Where are the fine clothes of gilded youth? Where is nobility and the courage of fighters, where the mature wisdom of elders and the regal throng of great ladies, where the piles of treasure and precious stones? Alas! All have been destroyed; thrust aside by death. To whom shall we turn, who can help us? To flee is impossible, to hide futile. Cities, fortresses, fields, woods, highways and rivers are ringed by thieves — which is to say by evil spirits, the executioners of the supreme Judge, preparing endless punishments for us all.

We can unfold a terrifying event which happened when an army was camped near Genoa. Four of the soldiers left the force in search of plunder and made their way to Rivarolo on the coast, where the disease had killed all the inhabitants. Finding the houses shut up, and no one about, they broke into one of the houses and stole a fleece which they found on a bed. They then rejoined the army and on the following night the four of them bedded down under the fleece. When morning comes it finds them dead. As a result everyone panicked, and thereafter nobody would use the goods and clothes of the dead, or even handle them, but rejected them outright.

Scarcely one in seven of the Genoese survived. In Venice, where an inquiry was held into the mortality, it was found that more than 70 percent of the people had died, and that within a short period 20 out of 24 excellent physicians had died. The rest of Italy, Sicily, and Apulia and the neighbouring regions maintain that they have been virtually emptied of inhabitants. The people of Florence, Pisa, and Lucca, finding themselves bereft of their fellow residents, emphasise their losses. The Roman Curia at Avignon, the provinces on both sides of the Rhône, Spain, France, and the Empire cry up their griefs and disasters — all of which makes it extraordinarily difficult for me to give an accurate picture.

By contrast, what befell the Saracens can be established from trustworthy accounts. In the city of Babylon alone (the heart of the Sultan's power), 480,000 of his subjects are said to have been carried off by disease in less than three months in 1348—and this is known from the Sultan's register which records the names of the dead, because he receives a gold bezant for each person buried. I am silent about Damascus and his other cities, where the number of dead was infinite. In the other countries of the East, which are so vast that it takes three years to ride across them and which have a population of 10,000 for every one inhabitant of the west, it is credibly reported that countless people have died.

Everyone has a responsibility to keep some record of the disease and the deaths, and because I am myself from Piacenza I have been urged to write more about what happened there in 1348. . . .

I don't know where to begin. Cries and laments arise on all sides. Day after day one sees the Cross and the Host[1] being carried about the city, and countless dead being buried. The ensuing mortality was so great that people could scarcely snatch breath. The living made preparations for their burial, and because there was not enough room for individual graves, pits had to be dug in colonnades and piazzas, where nobody had ever been buried before. It often happened that man and wife, father and son, mother and daughter, and soon the whole household and many neighbours, were buried together in one place. The same thing happened in Castell' Arquato and Viguzzolo and in the other towns, villages, cities, and settlements, and last of all in the Val Tidone, where they had hitherto escaped the plague.

Very many people died. One Oberto de Sasso, who had come from the infected neighbourhood around the church of the Franciscans, wished to make his will and accordingly summoned a notary and his neighbours as witnesses, all of whom, more than sixty of them, died soon after. At this time the Dominican friar Syfredo de Bardis, a man of prudence and great learning who had visited the Holy Sepulchre, also died, along with 23 brothers of the same house. There also died within a short time the Franciscan friar Bertolino Coxadocha of Piacenza, renowned for his learning and many virtues, along with 24 brothers of the same house, nine of them on one day; seven of the Augustinians; the Carmelite friar Francesco Todischi with six of his brethren; four of the order of Mary; more than sixty prelates and parish priests from the city and district of Piacenza; many nobles; countless young people; numberless women, particularly those who were pregnant. It is too distressing to recite any more, or to lay bare the wounds inflicted by so great a disaster.

---

[1] The consecrated Eucharistic wafer. The reference is to priests taking the last sacrament to the dying. [Ed.]

Let all creation tremble with fear before the judgement of God. Let human frailty submit to its creator. May a greater grief be kindled in all hearts, and tears well up in all eyes as future ages hear what happened in this disaster. When one person lay sick in a house no one would come near. Even dear friends would hide themselves away, weeping. The physician would not visit. The priest, panic-stricken, administered the sacraments with fear and trembling.

Listen to the tearful voices of the sick: "Have pity, have pity, my friends. At least say something, now that the hand of God has touched me."

"Oh father, why have you abandoned me? Do you forget that I am your child?"

"Mother, where have you gone? Why are you now so cruel to me when only yesterday you were so kind? You fed me at your breast and carried me within your womb for nine months."

"My children, whom I brought up with toil and sweat, why have you run away?"

Man and wife reached out to each other, "Alas, once we slept happily together but now are separated and wretched."

And when the sick were in the throes of death, they still called out piteously to their family and neighbours, "Come here. I'm thirsty, bring me a drink of water. I'm still alive. Don't be frightened. Perhaps I won't die. Please hold me tight, hug my wasted body. You ought to be holding me in your arms."

At this, as everyone else kept their distance, somebody might take pity and leave a candle burning by the bed head as he fled. And when the victim had breathed his last, it was often the mother who shrouded her son and placed him in the coffin, or the husband who did the same for his wife, for everybody else refused to touch the dead body. . . .

I am overwhelmed, I can't go on. Everywhere one turns there is death and bitterness to be described. The hand of the Almighty strikes repeatedly, to greater and greater effect. The terrible judgement gains in power as time goes by.

—What shall we do? Kind Jesus, receive the souls of the dead, avert your gaze from our sins and blot out all our iniquities.

We know that whatever we suffer is the just reward of our sins. Now, therefore, when the Lord is enraged, embrace acts of penance, so that you do not stray from the right path and perish. Let the proud be humbled. Let misers, who withheld alms from the poor, blush for shame. Let the envious become zealous in almsgiving. Let lechers put aside their filthy habits and distinguish themselves in honest living. Let the raging and wrathful restrain themselves from violence. Let gluttons temper their appetites by fasting. Let the slaves of sloth arise and dress themselves in good works. Let adolescents and youths abandon their present delight in following fashion. Let there be good faith and equity among judges, and respect for the law among merchants. Let pettifogging lawyers study and grow wise before they put pen to paper. Let members of religious orders abandon hypocrisy. Let the dignity of prelates be put to better use. Let all of you hurry to set your feet on the way of salvation. And let the overweening vanity of great ladies, which so easily turns into voluptuousness, be bridled. It was against their arrogance that Isaiah inveighed: "Because the daughters of Sion are haughty, and have walked with stretched out necks and wanton glances of their eyes, and made a noise as they walked with their feet, and moved in a set pace. . . . Thy fairest men also shall fall by the sword: and thy valiant ones in battle. And her gates shall lament and mourn: and she shall sit desolate on the ground" [Isaiah 3.16–26]. This was directed against the pride of ladies and young people.

For the rest, so that the conditions, causes, and symptoms of this pestilential disease should be made plain to all, I have decided to set them out in writing. Those of both sexes who were in health, and in no fear of death, were struck by four savage blows to the flesh. First, out of the blue, a kind of chilly stiffness troubled their bodies. They felt a tingling sensation, as if they were being pricked by the points of arrows. The next stage was a fearsome attack which took the form of an extremely hard, solid boil. In some people this developed under the armpit and in others in the groin between the scrotum and the body. As it grew more solid, its burning heat caused the patients to fall into an acute and putrid fever, with severe headaches. As it intensified its extreme bitterness could have various effects. In some cases it gave rise to an intolerable stench. In others it brought vomiting of blood, or swellings near the place from which the corrupt humour arose: on the back, across the chest, near the thigh. Some people lay as if in a drunken stupor and could not be roused. Behold the swellings, the warning signs sent by the Lord.[2] All these people were in danger of dying. Some died on the very day the illness took possession of them, others on the next day, others—the majority—between the third and fifth day. There was no known remedy for the vomiting of blood. Those who fell into a coma, or suffered a swelling or the stink of corruption very rarely escaped. But from the fever it was sometimes possible to make a recovery. . . .

Truly, then was a time of bitterness and grief, which served to turn men to the Lord. I shall recount what happened. A warning was given by a certain holy person, who received it in a vision, that in cities, towns and other settlements, everyone, male and female alike, should gather in their parish church on three consecutive days and, each with a lighted candle in their hand, hear with great devotion the mass of the Blessed Anastasia, which is normally performed at dawn on Christmas day, and they should humbly beg for mercy, so that they might be delivered from the disease through the merits of the holy mass. Other people sought deliverance through the mediation of a blessed martyr; and

---

[2] A pun: *bulla* is a swelling, but it is also the word for the papal seal, and hence for a papal document (or bull). De' Mussis is playing on the idea of the swelling characteristic of the plague being God's seal, notifying the victim of his imminent fate. [Ed.]

others humbly turned to other saints, so that they might escape the abomination of disease. For among the aforesaid martyrs, some, as stories relate, are said to have died from repeated blows, and it was therefore the general opinion that they would be able to protect people against the arrows of death. Finally, in 1350, the most holy Pope Clement ordained a general indulgence, to be valid for a year, which remitted penance and guilt to all who were truly penitent and confessed. And as a result a numberless multitude of people made the pilgrimage to Rome, to visit with great reverence and devotion the basilicas of the blessed apostles Peter and Paul and St John.

Oh, most dearly beloved, let us therefore not be like vipers, growing ever more wicked, but let us rather hold up our hands to heaven to beg for mercy on us all, for who but God shall have mercy on us? With this, I make an end. May the heavenly physician heal our wounds—our spiritual rather than our bodily wounds. To whom be the blessing and the praise and the glory for ever and ever, Amen.

3

GIOVANNI BOCCACCIO

The Plague in Florence:
From the *Decameron*, c. 1350

Giovanni Boccaccio* (1313–1375) was a poet in Florence, Italy, when the plague struck in 1348. His *Decameron*† is a collection of a hundred tales based on his experiences during the plague years. This selection is drawn from the Introduction. What does Boccaccio add to your understanding of the Black Death?

THINKING HISTORICALLY

Compare Boccaccio's treatment of divine and human causes of the plague. Boccaccio not only muses on the causes of the plague; he also sees the plague as the cause of new forms of behavior. What were the behavioral effects of the plague according to Boccaccio?

* boh KAH chee oh
† deh KAM uh rahn

Source: Giovanni Boccaccio, *Decameron*, trans. G. H. McWilliam (Harmondsworth, England: Penguin, 1972), 50–58.

I say, then, that the sum of thirteen hundred and forty-eight years had elapsed since the fruitful Incarnation of the Son of God, when the noble city of Florence, which for its great beauty excels all others in Italy, was visited by the deadly pestilence. Some say that it descended upon the human race through the influence of the heavenly bodies, others that it was a punishment signifying God's righteous anger at our iniquitous way of life. But whatever its cause, it had originated some years earlier in the East, where it had claimed countless lives before it unhappily spread westward, growing in strength as it swept relentlessly on from one place to the next.

In the face of its onrush, all the wisdom and ingenuity of man were unavailing. Large quantities of refuse were cleared out of the city by officials specially appointed for the purpose, all sick persons were forbidden entry, and numerous instructions were issued for safeguarding the people's health, but all to no avail. Nor were the countless petitions humbly directed to God by the pious, whether by means of formal processions or in any other guise, any less ineffectual. For in the early spring of the year we have mentioned, the plague began, in a terrifying and extraordinary manner, to make its disastrous effects apparent. It did not take the form it had assumed in the East, where if anyone bled from the nose it was an obvious portent of certain death. On the contrary, its earliest symptom, in men and women alike, was the appearance of certain swellings in the groin or the armpit, some of which were egg-shaped whilst others were roughly the size of the common apple. Sometimes the swellings were large, sometimes not so large, and they were referred to by the populace as *gavòccioli*. From the two areas already mentioned, this deadly *gavòcciolo* would begin to spread, and within a short time it would appear at random all over the body. Later on, the symptoms of the disease changed, and many people began to find dark blotches and bruises on their arms, thighs, and other parts of the body, sometimes large and few in number, at other times tiny and closely spaced. These, to anyone unfortunate enough to contract them, were just as infallible a sign that he would die as the *gavòcciolo* had been earlier, and as indeed it still was.

Against these maladies, it seemed that all the advice of physicians and all the power of medicine were profitless and unavailing. Perhaps the nature of the illness was such that it allowed no remedy; or perhaps those people who were treating the illness (whose numbers had increased enormously because the ranks of the qualified were invaded by people, both men and women, who had never received any training in medicine), being ignorant of its causes, were not prescribing the appropriate cure. At all events, few of those who caught it ever recovered, and in most cases death occurred within three days from the appearance of the symptoms we have described, some people dying more rapidly than others, the majority without any fever or other complications.

But what made this pestilence even more severe was that whenever those suffering from it mixed with people who were still unaffected, it would rush upon these with the speed of a fire racing through dry or oily substances that happened to be placed within its reach. Nor was this the full extent of its evil, for not only did it infect healthy persons who conversed or had any dealings with the sick, making them ill or visiting an equally horrible death upon them, but it also seemed to transfer the sickness to anyone touching the clothes or other objects which had been handled or used by its victims. . . .

Some people were of the opinion that a sober and abstemious mode of living considerably reduced the risk of infection. They therefore formed themselves into groups and lived in isolation from everyone else. Having withdrawn to a comfortable abode where there were no sick persons, they locked themselves in and settled down to a peaceable existence, consuming modest quantities of delicate foods and precious wines and avoiding all excesses. They refrained from speaking to outsiders, refused to receive news of the dead or sick, and entertained themselves with music and whatever other amusements they were able to devise.

Others took the opposite view, and maintained that an infallible way of warding off this appalling evil was to drink heavily, enjoy life to the full, go round singing and merrymaking, gratify all of one's cravings whenever the opportunity offered, and shrug the whole thing off as one enormous joke. Moreover, they practised what they preached to the best of their ability, for they would visit one tavern after another, drinking all day and night to immoderate excess; or alternatively (and this was their more frequent custom), they would do their drinking in various private houses, but only in the ones where the conversation was restricted to subjects that were pleasant or entertaining. Such places were easy to find, for people behaved as though their days were numbered, and treated their belongings and their own persons with equal abandon. Hence most houses had become common property, and any passing stranger could make himself at home as naturally as though he were the rightful owner. But for all their riotous manner of living, these people always took good care to avoid any contact with the sick.

In the face of so much affliction and misery, all respect for the laws of God and man had virtually broken down and been extinguished in our city. For like everybody else, those ministers and executors of the laws who were not either dead or ill were left with so few subordinates that they were unable to discharge any of their duties. Hence everyone was free to behave as he pleased.

There were many other people who steered a middle course between the two already mentioned, neither restricting their diet to the same degree as the first group, nor indulging so freely as the second in drinking and other forms of wantonness, but simply doing no more than satisfy their appetite. Instead of incarcerating themselves, these people moved about freely, holding in their hands a posy of flowers, or fragrant herbs, or one of a wide range of spices, which they applied at frequent intervals to their nostrils, thinking it an excellent idea to fortify the brain with smells of that particular sort; for the stench of dead bodies, sickness, and medicines seemed to fill and pollute the whole of the atmosphere.

Some people, pursuing what was possibly the safer alternative, callously maintained that there was no better or more efficacious remedy against a plague than to run away from it. Swayed by this argument, and sparing no thought for anyone but themselves, large numbers of men and women abandoned their city, their homes, their relatives, their estates, and their belongings, and headed for the countryside, either in Florentine territory or, better still, abroad. It was as though they imagined that the wrath of God would not unleash this plague against men for their iniquities irrespective of where they happened to be, but would only be aroused against those who found themselves within the city walls; or possibly they assumed that the whole of the population would be exterminated and that the city's last hour had come.

Of the people who held these various opinions, not all of them died. Nor, however, did they all survive. On the contrary, many of each different persuasion fell ill here, there, and everywhere, and having themselves, when they were fit and well, set an example to those who were as yet unaffected, they languished away with virtually no one to nurse them. It was not merely a question of one citizen avoiding another, and of people almost invariably neglecting their neighbours and rarely or never visiting their relatives, addressing them only from a distance; this scourge had implanted so great a terror in the hearts of men and women that brothers abandoned brothers, uncles their nephews, sisters their brothers, and in many cases wives deserted their husbands. But even worse, and almost incredible, was the fact that fathers and mothers refused to nurse and assist their own children, as though they did not belong to them.

Hence the countless numbers of people who fell ill, both male and female, were entirely dependent upon either the charity of friends (who were few and far between) or the greed of servants, who remained in short supply despite the attraction of high wages out of all proportion to the services they performed. Furthermore, these latter were men and women of coarse intellect and the majority were unused to such duties, and they did little more than hand things to the invalid when asked to do so and watch over him when he was dying. And in performing this kind of service, they frequently lost their lives as well as their earnings.

As a result of this wholesale desertion of the sick by neighbours, relatives, and friends, and in view of the scarcity of servants, there grew up a practice almost never previously heard of, whereby when a woman fell ill, no matter how gracious or beautiful or gently bred she might be, she raised no objection to being attended by a male servant, whether he was young or not. Nor did she have any scruples about showing him every part of her body as freely as she would have displayed it to a woman, provided that the nature of her infirmity required her to do so; and this explains why those women who recovered were possibly less chaste in the period that followed.

Moreover a great many people died who would perhaps have survived had they received some assistance. And hence, what with the lack of appropriate means for tending the sick, and the virulence of the plague, the number of deaths reported in the city whether by day or night was so enormous that it astonished all who heard tell of it, to say nothing of the people who actually witnessed the carnage. . . .

As for the common people and a large proportion of the bourgeoisie, they presented a much more pathetic spectacle, for the majority of them were constrained, either by their poverty or the hope of survival, to remain in their houses. Being confined to their own parts of the city, they fell ill daily in their thousands, and since they had no one to assist them or attend to their needs, they inevitably perished almost without exception. Many dropped dead in the open streets, both by day and by night, whilst a great many others, though dying in their own houses, drew their neighbours' attention to the fact more by the smell of their rotting corpses than by any other means. And what with these, and the others who were dying all over the city, bodies were here, there, and everywhere. . . .

[T]here were no tears or candles or mourners to honour the dead; in fact, no more respect was accorded to dead people than would nowadays be shown towards dead goats. For it was quite apparent that the one thing which, in normal times, no wise man had ever learned to accept with patient resignation (even though it struck so seldom and unobtrusively), had now been brought home to the feeble-minded as well, but the scale of the calamity caused them to regard it with indifference.

Such was the multitude of corpses (of which further consignments were arriving every day and almost by the hour at each of the churches), that there was not sufficient consecrated ground for them to be buried in, especially if each was to have its own plot in accordance with long-established custom. So when all the graves were full, huge trenches were excavated in the churchyards, into which new arrivals were placed in their hundreds, stowed tier upon tier like ships' cargo, each layer of corpses being covered over with a thin layer of soil till the trench was filled to the top.

But rather than describe in elaborate detail the calamities we experienced in the city at that time, I must mention that, whilst an ill wind was blowing through Florence itself, the surrounding region was no less badly affected. In the fortified towns, conditions were similar to those in the city itself on a minor scale; but in the scattered hamlets and the countryside proper, the poor unfortunate peasants and their families had no physicians or servants whatever to assist them, and collapsed by the wayside, in their fields, and in their cottages at all hours of the day and night, dying more like animals than human beings. Like the townspeople, they too grew apathetic in their ways, disregarded their affairs, and neglected their possessions. Moreover, they all behaved as though each day was to be their last, and far from making provision for the future by tilling their lands, tending their flocks, and adding to their previous labours, they tried in every way they could think of to squander the assets already in their possession. Thus it came about that oxen, asses, sheep, goats, pigs, chickens, and even dogs (for all their deep fidelity to man) were driven away and allowed to roam freely through the fields, where the crops lay abandoned and had not even been reaped, let alone gathered in. And after a whole day's feasting, many of these animals, as though possessing the power of reason, would return glutted in the evening to their own quarters without any shepherd to guide them.

But let us leave the countryside and return to the city. What more remains to be said, except that the cruelty of heaven (and possibly, in some measure, also that of man) was so immense and so devastating that between March and July of the year in question, what with the fury of the pestilence and the fact that so many of the sick were inadequately cared for or abandoned in their hour of need because the healthy were too terrified to approach them, it is reliably thought that over a hundred thousand human lives were extinguished within the walls of the city of Florence? Yet before this lethal catastrophe fell upon the city, it is doubtful whether anyone would have guessed it contained so many inhabitants.

4

Images of the Black Death, Fourteenth and Fifteenth Centuries

Contemporary accounts testify to the plague's terrifying physical, social, and psychological impact. Images from the period document the ravages of the epidemic as well, sometimes in gruesome detail. The engraving in Figure 12.1, for example, shows a plague victim covered in the dark blotches characteristic of the disease. The town in the background appears to be going up in flames while lightning flares in the sky above. What else do you think is going on in this image?

Figure 12.1 The Black Death, 1348.

Source: The Bridgeman Art Library.

Figures 12.2 and 12.3 show two well-documented phenomena of the plague years: The first depicts a group of flagellants, members of a movement who wandered from town to town beating themselves with whips studded with iron nails in an effort to do penance for the sins they believed had brought on the plague. Written accounts confirm many elements in this picture: Flagellants usually carried crosses or banners with crosses on them, wore long pleated skirts, and went around bare-chested, the better to make their scourging as painful as possible. Figure 12.3 illustrates a similar impulse toward punishment as a means of coping with the plague, but this time the violence is directed outward, against Jews, so often the scapegoats in troubled times. Baseless accusations that Jews poisoned wells to spread the plague resulted in many such attacks against them during the period.

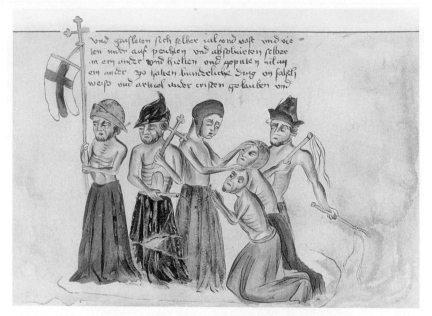

Figure 12.2 Flagellants, from a fifteenth-century chronicle from Constance, Switzerland.

Source: © Bettmann/CORBIS.

Figure 12.3 The burning of Jews in an early printed woodcut.

Source: Mary Evans Picture Library/Alamy.

Figure 12.4 François de la Sarra, tomb at La Sarraz, Switzerland, c. 1390.

Source: Musée de l'Elysée, Lausanne.

The final image, Figure 12.4, is one of a transi tomb from 1390. Transi tombs, which emerged during and after the plague era, were a major departure from standard funerary monuments that typically offered an idealized depiction of the deceased. Instead these tombs showed decaying or skeletal corpses covered with worms and other emblems of bodily corruption. Scholars differ over their meaning. How might you explain them?

THINKING HISTORICALLY

What can these images tell us about fourteenth-century people's beliefs about the possible causes — medical or religious — of the plague? Do the images suggest a greater belief in medical or religious causes? Think about the social and religious changes wrought by the plague recounted in the de' Mussis and Boccaccio readings. What evidence, if any, do you see in these images of these changes?

5

AHMAD AL-MAQRIZI

The Plague in Cairo, Fifteenth Century

Ahmad al-Maqrizi* (1364–1442) became a historian after pursuing a
career as an administrator in post-plague Cairo. Although he wrote
his history of the plague period more than fifty years after the event,
he probably had access to contemporary sources that are now lost to
us. Compare al-Maqrizi's account of the plague in Cairo with the
prior accounts of the plague in Italy. How was the experience of the
Black Death in Cairo similar to, and different from, the experience
in Florence?

THINKING HISTORICALLY

Like Boccaccio, al-Maqrizi devotes more attention to the effects than to
the causes of the Black Death. What effects were similar in Florence and
Cairo? Al-Maqrizi discusses certain effects that were not mentioned in
the Italian accounts. Which, if any, of these effects do you think also
probably occurred in Italy?

In January 1349, there appeared new symptoms that consisted of
spitting up of blood. The disease caused one to experience an internal
fever, followed by an uncontrollable desire to vomit; then one spat up
blood and died. The inhabitants of a house were stricken one after the
other, and in one night or two, the dwelling became deserted. Each
individual lived with this fixed idea that he was going to die in this
way. He prepared for himself a good death by distributing alms;
he arranged for scenes of reconciliation and his acts of devotion
multiplied. . . .

By January 21, Cairo had become an abandoned desert, and one did
not see anyone walking along the streets. A man could go from
the Port Zuwayla to Bāb al-Nasr[1] without encountering a living soul.
The dead were very numerous, and all the world could think of nothing
else. Debris piled up in the streets. People went around with worried
faces. Everywhere one heard lamentations, and one could not pass by
any house without being overwhelmed by the howling. Cadavers formed

---

* ahk MAHD ahl mah KREE zee
[1] This was apparently the busiest boulevard in medieval Cairo.

Source: John Aberth, *The Black Death: The Great Mortality of 1348–1350, A Brief History
with Documents* (Boston: Bedford/St. Martin's, 2005), 84–87.

a heap on the public highway, funeral processions were so many that they could not file past without bumping into each other, and the dead were transported in some confusion. . . .

One began to have to search for readers of the Koran for funeral ceremonies, and a number of individuals quit their usual occupations in order to recite prayers at the head of funeral processions. In the same way, some people devoted themselves to smearing crypts with plaster; others presented themselves as volunteers to wash the dead or carry them. These latter folk earned substantial salaries. For example, a reader of the Koran took ten *dirhams*.[2] Also, hardly had he reached the oratory when he slipped away very quickly in order to go officiate at a new [funeral]. Porters demanded 6 *dirhams* at the time they were engaged, and then it was necessary to match it [at the grave]. The gravedigger demanded fifty *dirhams* per grave. Most of the rest of these people died without having taken any profit from their gains. . . . Also families kept their dead on the bare ground, due to the impossibility of having them interred. The inhabitants of a house died by the tens and, since there wasn't a litter ready to hand, one had to carry them away in stages. Moreover, some people appropriated for themselves without scruple the immovable and movable goods and cash of their former owners after their demise. But very few lived long enough to profit thereby, and those who remained alive would have been able to do without. . . .

Family festivities and weddings had no more place [in life]. No one issued an invitation to a feast during the whole time of the epidemic, and one did not hear any concert. The *vizier*[3] lifted a third of what he was owed from the woman responsible [for collecting] the tax on singers. The call to prayer was canceled in various places, and in the exact same way, those places [where prayer] was most frequent subsisted on a *muezzin*[4] alone. . . .

The men of the [military] troop and the cultivators took a world of trouble to finish their sowing [of fields]. The plague emerged at the end of the season when the fields were becoming green. How many times did one see a laborer, at Gaza, at Ramleh, and along other points of the Syrian littoral,[5] guide his plow being pulled by oxen suddenly fall down dead, still holding in his hands his plow, while the oxen stood at their place without a conductor.

It was the same in Egypt: When the harvest time came, there remained only a very small number of *fellahs*.[6] The soldiers and their valets left for the

---

[2] A silver coin used in the Muslim world.

[3] The chief minister of the caliph, or leader of the Muslim community.

[4] An official of the mosque who called the faithful to prayer from the minaret.

[5] The coastal plain of southern Palestine, where the most fertile land was located.

[6] Arabic word for ploughman or tiller, which also denoted the peasantry of Egypt and is the origin of the modern term *fellahin*.

harvest and attempted to hire workers, promising them half of the crop, but they could not find anyone to help them reap it. They loaded the grain on their horses, did the mowing themselves, but, being powerless to carry out the greatest portion of the work, they abandoned this enterprise.

The endowments[7] passed rapidly from hand to hand as a consequence of the multiplicity of deaths in the army. Such a concession passed from one to the other until the seventh or eighth holder, to fall finally [into the hands] of artisans, such as tailors, shoemakers, or public criers, and these mounted the horse, donned the [military] headdress, and dressed in military tunics.

Actually, no one collected the whole revenue of his endowment, and a number of holders harvested absolutely nothing. During the flooding of the Nile[8] and the time of the sprouting of vegetation, one could procure a laborer only with difficulty: On half the lands only did the harvest reach maturity. Moreover, there was no one to buy the green clover [as feed] and no one sent their horses to graze over the field. This was the ruin of royal properties in the suburbs of Cairo, like Matarieh, Hums, Siryaqus, and Bahtit. In the canton [administrative district] of Nay and Tanan, 1,500 *feddans*[9] of clover were abandoned where it stood: No one came to buy it, either to pasture their beasts on the place or to gather it into barns and use it as fodder.

The province of Upper Egypt was deserted, in spite of the vast abundance of cultivable terrain. It used to be that, after the land surface was cultivated in the territory of Asyūt,[10] 6,000 individuals were subject to payment of the property tax; now, in the year of the epidemic [1348–1349], one could not count on more than 106 contributors. Nevertheless, during this period, the price of wheat did not rise past fifteen *dirhams* per *ardeb*.[11]

Most of the trades disappeared, for a number of artisans devoted themselves to handling the dead, while the others, no less numerous, occupied themselves in selling off to bidders [the dead's] movable goods and clothing, so well that the price of linen and similar objects fell by a fifth of their real value, at the very least, and still further until one found customers. . . .

Thus the trades disappeared: One could no longer find either a water carrier, or a laundress, or a domestic. The monthly salary of a groom rose from thirty *dirhams* to eighty. A proclamation made in Cairo invited the artisans to take up their old trades, and some of the recalcitrants reformed themselves. Because of the shortage of men and camels, a goatskin of water reached the price of eight *dirhams*, and in order to grind an *ardeb* of wheat, one paid fifteen *dirhams*.

---

[7] Mamluk commanders and elite soldiers, like their Ayyubid predecessors, were paid out of the revenues of land grants, known as *iqtas* (similar to fiefs in Europe). With the dearth of labor caused by the Black Death, it became far more difficult to extract income from these estates.

[8] This usually took place between September and November of every year.

[9] A *feddan* is equivalent to 1.038 acres.

[10] Located along the Nile in Upper Egypt, about midway between Cairo and Aswan.

[11] An *ardeb* is equivalent to 5.62 bushels.

MICHAEL W. DOLS

The Comparative Communal Responses to the Black Death in Muslim and Christian Societies, 1974

Here a modern historian compares the impact of the Black Death in Christian Europe and the Muslim Middle East. He is particularly interested in how Christian and Muslim communities had different group responses. What similarities or differences does he see in the actual disease and its death toll? How is his description of the disease similar to, or different from, those in the previous selections? How might you account for any differences in the descriptions? How would you summarize the author's thesis or argument? How were the responses to the plague different in Christian and Muslim societies? What is his explanation for these differences?

THINKING HISTORICALLY

In modern society, we tend to give greater credence to scientific and medical explanations of disease. We are even inclined to dismiss the religious explanations of our medieval forbears. But Dols suggests that the religious ideas of the fourteenth century caused the different responses to the plague. Thus, the consequences of the Black Death were different in Europe and the Middle East. What sort of argument could be made to dispute Dols's idea of causes and consequences?

In the middle of the fourteenth century a devastating pandemic of plague, commonly known in European history as the Black Death, swept through the entire Mediterranean world. This cataclysmic event caused a dramatic demographic decline in Muslim and Christian countries and provoked definable communal responses. . . .

The pandemic was transmitted from central Asia and spread throughout the Middle East, North Africa, and Europe. Based on contemporary Arabic and Latin sources, we can be certain of the existence of the three

Source: Michael W. Dols, "The Comparative Communal Responses to the Black Death in Muslim and Christian Societies," *Viator* 5 (1974): 269–87.

major forms of plague (bubonic, pneumonic, and septicaemic)[1] in these regions. In any historical comparison of the role of the pandemic in Muslim and Christian societies we can assume as a constant the medical nature of the disease itself. In addition, almost all of the medieval physicians believed that the immediate cause of this disease was a pestilential miasma or corruption of the air; this belief was broadly accepted in both societies due to their common reliance on the theory of epidemics found in Hippocrates and elaborated by Galen and Ibn Sina (Avicenna), the greatest medical authorities for the fourteenth century physicians. Therefore, in the Oriental and Western plague treatises there is similar advice for improving or changing the air in a plague-stricken community. . . .

The Black Death was variously interpreted by contemporary European writers. The pandemic was considered, however, by most European observers to result directly from the pestilential miasma, and it was believed that the disease was contagious, which accounts for the important protective measures taken by the Italian cities and the widespread advocacy of flight as the best means of escaping the epidemic. The physicians mention natural causations of the disease (such as an unfavorable conjunction of the planets, or earthquakes) among the remote causes of the miasma. Yet only one European treatise gives a concrete remedy against the astrological causes of plague; the customary recommendations were flight and prayer.

The most commonly held opinion about the ultimate cause of the plague pandemic was religious: the European Christian viewed the Black Death as an overwhelming punishment from God for his sins and those of his fellow Christians. Despite the other interpretations of the disease, this view is the only one that satisfactorily explains the extraordinary forms of communal behavior that took place in many parts of Europe during the Black Death. This supernatural solution was propagated by the Church and is reflected in contemporary European art and literature. The chronicles of the fourteenth century almost always attribute the affliction to divine retribution for the wickedness of European society. [William] Langland[2] summarizes the common view succinctly: "These pestilences were for pure sin."

Based directly on biblical and classical precedents, a conviction of personal guilt and a need for individual and collective expiation were engendered in the faithful Christian. His attitude to the Black Death is well illustrated by the European communal response. This response took the forms of the flagellant movement, the persecution of alien groups (particularly the Jews), and a pessimistic preoccupation with imminent death.[3]

[1] All three are produced by the virus *Yersinia pestis*; *bubonic* is named for "buboes" or lesions on the skin (see Figure 12.1), *pneumonic* (like pneumonia) is in the lungs, and *septicaemic* is in the blood. [Ed.]

[2] Contemporary author (c. 1330–c. 1400). [Ed.]

[3] See Figures 12.2, 12.3, and 12.4. [Ed.]

The flagellant movement was based on a belief in the mortification of the flesh as suitable penance for men's sins. Beginning in mid-thirteenth-century Italy, a series of natural disasters convinced many that God's wrath was visiting men as a punishment for their sinfulness. This concept was acted out in expiatory pilgrimages and processions in an attempt to divert or allay God's chastisement. The processions recurred continually during the later Middle Ages. From their inception, an implicit element of the flagellant movement was its participation in the millennial ideas that Professor Cohn[4] has shown to be a significant theme of late medieval Christendom, stemming especially from the millennial scheme of Joachim of Fiore.[5] Self-flagellation was "a collective *imitatio Christi*,[6] a redemptive sacrifice which protected the world from final overwhelming catastrophe, and by virtue of which they themselves [the flagellants] became a holy elite.". . .

The flagellant movement was a complex social phenomenon. Its apocalyptic ambitions proved to be an incentive to personal mysticism, anticlericalism, and social revolutionary ideas such as the destruction of private wealth. The flagellants were also intimately associated with the second major feature of the European reaction to the pandemic: the persecution of the Jews.

The massacres of the Jews during the Black Death were unprecedented in their extent and ferocity until the twentieth century. The first attacks on the Jews resulted from the accusation that this inassimilable community had caused the pestilence by poisoning wells; this was neither new (Jews had been accused and massacred in southern France and Spain during the . . . epidemics of 1320 and 1333), nor confined to the Jews alone. Lepers, gravediggers and other social outcasts, Muslims in Spain, or any foreigners were liable to attack. . . . But in September 1348 the forced confessions from ten Jews in Chillon[7] were adduced to support this fantasy and to implicate all European Jews. A second wave of massacres from the middle of 1349 was instigated by the propaganda of the flagellants. In many cities of Germany and the Low Countries (Frankfort, Maine, Cologne, Brussels) the destruction of the Jewish population was led by the flagellants, aided by the masses of the poor. Pope Clement VI finally condemned the flagellants in 1349 after two bulls in the same year against the persecution of the Jews had been ineffectual. . . .

In the complex psychological response to the Black Death, the natural preoccupation with death was therefore not inconsistent with

---

[4] Norman Cohn, *The Pursuit of the Millennium.* [Ed.]

[5] Twelfth-century theologian; predicted New Age of universal harmony based on Book of Revelations. [Ed.]

[6] Imitation of Christ, in suffering. [Ed.]

[7] A castle on Lake Geneva in modern Switzerland. [Ed.]

a vision of the biblical Apocalypse.[8] Many believed that the end of the world had come, plague being the apocalyptic rider on the white horse. In an account of the island of Cyprus during the pandemic, an Arabic chronicler testifies to the Christian belief by his remark that the Christian Cypriots "feared that it was the end of the world." The Black Death did not create these forms of reaction or the ideology that lay behind them; it was a stimulus, despite its irregularity of attack, which exposed the nerve system of late medieval Christian society.

The Middle Eastern interpretations of the Black Death display a diversity of opinions similar to that of the European accounts. Yet, the dominant Muslim view of plague was set forth in the formulation of three religio-legal principles, which directly affected communal behavior: (1) plague was a mercy from God and a martyrdom for the faithful Muslim; (2) a Muslim should not enter nor flee from a plague-stricken land; and (3) there was no contagion of plague since disease came directly from God. . . .

All three traditions were attributed to the Prophet. Muhammad was reputed to have prohibited flight from a plague-stricken community. . . . Accordingly, Muhammad was understood to have denied the pre-Islamic Arab belief in contagion. Consistent with this idea that plague was a divine selection is the principle that plague was a mercy from God for the faithful Muslim but a punishment for the infidel. . . .

The importance of these three principles to Muslim society was in what they did *not* affirm: they did not declare that plague was God's punishment; they did not encourage flight; and they did not support a belief in the contagious nature of plague—all of which were prevalent in Christian Europe. These principles appear to be borne out by the reports of the general communal responses to the Black Death in the major cities in the Middle East.

The Muslim reaction to the Black Death was characterized by organized communal supplication that included processions through the cities and mass funerals in the mosques. There is no indication of the abandonment of religious rites and services for the dead but rather an increased emphasis on personal piety and ritual purity. . . .

It is reported that pious men were stationed at various places of worship in Cairo and Fustat[9] in order to recite the funeral prayers. Many men left their normal occupations to profit from the funerals, as by chanting the funeral prayers at the head of processions. These processions from the mosques or homes to the cemeteries filled the streets of Cairo during the Black Death. They were so numerous that they could not pass in the roadways without disturbing one another. Moreover,

[8]The end of the world. See Chapter 6, Book of Daniel, for origins of idea. Also see Book of Revelations. [Ed.]

[9]Old Cairo. [Ed.]

there were pious visitations to the graves in the common belief that the souls of the deceased resided in the tombs. . . .

An important part of urban activity in response to the Black Death was the communal prayers for the lifting of the disease. During the greatest severity of the pandemic, orders were given in Cairo to assemble in the mosques and to recite the recommended prayers in common. Fasting and processions took place in the cities during the Black Death and later plague epidemics; the supplicatory[10] processions followed the traditional form of prayer for rain. . . . As the Black Death worsened, a proclamation was made in Damascus inviting the population to fast for three days and to go out on the fourth day (Friday) to the Mosque of the Foot, in order to supplicate God for the removing of this scourge. Most of the Damascenes were reported to have fasted, and several spent the night in the Umayyad Mosque[11] performing the acts of faith as in the ritual during Ramadan and reading al-Bukhari.[12] On Friday morning the inhabitants of Damascus came out from all sides, including Jews, Christians, Samaritans, old men and women, young infants, the poor, amirs, notables, and magistrates. Before the morning prayer, they marched from the Umayyad Mosque to the Mosque of the Foot and did not cease chanting the prayers throughout the day. . . .

The plague treatises also attest to a large number of popular magical beliefs and practices concerning plague, which should be interpreted as a significant element in the total religious response of Muslim society. The amulets and talismans, incantations, and magical inscriptions that were directed against plague were not unique phenomena; they were only part of a vast body of magical beliefs and practices that are more familiarly associated with the "evil eye." . . .

The comparison of Christian and Muslim societies during the Black Death points to the significant disparity in their general communal responses. . . . [In Christian Europe] mass communal funeral services, processions, and journeys to the cemeteries were greatly limited by the common European belief in contagion. . . . Conversely, the Arabic sources do not attest to the "striking manifestations of abnormal collective psychology, of dissociation of the group mind," which occurred in Christian Europe. Fear and trepidation of the Black Death in Europe activated what Professor Trevor-Roper has called, in a different context,[13] a European "stereotype of fear"; the collective emotion played upon a mythology of messianism, anti-Semitism, and man's culpability for his sins.

[10] Pleading, begging. [Ed.]
[11] The great mosque in Damascus, the capital of the Umayyad Caliphate. [Ed.]
[12] Compiler of *hadiths* (sayings of the Prophet). [Ed.]
[13] *The European Witch-Craze of the Sixteenth and Seventeenth Centuries* (1978). [Ed.]

Why are the corresponding phenomena not found in the Muslim reaction to the Black Death? The stereotypes did not exist. There is no evidence for the appearance of messianic movements in Muslim society at this time which might have associated the Black Death with an apocalypse. . . . Furthermore, the fact that there was no certainty that plague was a divine punishment for sin removed the impetus for a cohesive puritanical and revivalist popular movement.

The impact of the Black Death poses the question of the Muslim attitude toward minorities. The unassimilated communities were tolerated in medieval Muslim society and, in this instance, were not held responsible for the ravages of the pandemic. However theoretical, the legal tenet against contagion of plague would have militated against the accusation of the minorities. In no case is there a direct causal relationship to be found between the Black Death (and subsequent plague epidemics) and the active persecution of minorities as in Europe.

The Christian belief in plague as a divine punishment for men's sins was preached by clergymen deeply committed to the idea of original sin and man's guilt arising from his essential depravity, as well as to a fundamental contempt—both Christian and Stoic—for this world. The Black Death was the occasion for the vigorous realization of these ideas. However, there is no doctrine of original sin and of man's insuperable guilt in Islamic theology. The Muslim writers on plague did not dwell on the guilt of their co-religionists even if they did admit that plague was a divine warning against sin. Prayer was supplication and not expiation.

In contrast, the general reaction of Muslim society to the Black Death was governed by its interpretation as only another common natural disaster. . . . Further, obedience to the decision of the communal leader (*mukhldr*) with regard to moving away or remaining must be preserved. If changing the air by flight cannot be undertaken because: (1) the epidemic is universal; (2) the fear that the plague victims would be neglected; or (3) the need to preserve the commonweal of the community (which is an essential tenet of Islam) from disruption and disorder, the people are simply to remain and improve their circumstances by cleaning their houses and fumigating the air with various scents and fresh fruits.

The prescriptions . . . for a Muslim community at the time of a plague epidemic bring into focus the contrasting orientations of the two religions. The Black Death touched upon the central theme of Christian teaching concerning evil and human suffering; Western man took the plague epidemic as an individual trial more than a collective, social calamity. The Islamic tradition, however, has not concerned itself to the same degree with personal suffering; the central problem for the Muslim is the solemn responsibility for his decisions that affect other men's lives and fortunes within a purposeful creation. The cosmic settings of the two faiths are wide apart in their emphasis: where the Muslim's primary duty was toward the correct behavior of the total community based on the sacred law, the Christian's was with personal redemption. Where the Qur'an supplied guidance, the Bible furnished consolation. For the Muslim the Black Death was part of a God-ordered, natural universe; for the Christian it was an irruption of the profane world of sin and misery.

In sum, it would be as great an error to discount the religious interpretations of plague as motives and limits to communal behavior as to discount the classical medical theories of plague which underlay most of the medical remedies and treatments in both the East and West. Taken together, the medieval Christian ideas of punishment and guilt, militancy toward alien communities, and millennialism are raised to crucial significance in contrast to the Muslim understanding of the Black Death. The operative European Christian concepts were lacking in Muslim society as were their unattractive consequences of religious fanaticism, persecution, and desperation. The predominant theological views of the two societies set the framework for normative attitudes and the prescriptions for communal behavior in which human nature found expression and form when confronted by the Black Death.

■ REFLECTIONS

It might seem that there would be little more we could learn about a plague that occurred over 650 years ago. But that is not the case. Historians are constantly asking new questions about the past, sometimes armed with new sources of information or new techniques of investigation. One recent line of inquiry has centered on the causes of the disease. In *The Black Death and the Transformation of the West* (Harvard University Press, 1997), David Herlihy questions whether the Black Death was in fact the plague. His student, Samuel K. Cohn Jr., answers a vigorous "no." Cohn's *The Black Death Transformed: Disease and Culture in Early Renaissance Europe* (Arnold, 2003) argues that the disease resembled a viral infection rather than the bacterium *Yersinia pestis* that causes the plague. Cohn writes that the Black Death, like the flu pandemic of 1918, was highly contagious, moved very rapidly, apparently on droplets in the air, taking enormous casualties. By contrast, the last wave of plague, which originated in Hong Kong in 1894 (and from which *Y. pestis* was identified), traveled slowly as it was transferred by fleas from rats to humans, infecting only those who were bitten, and killing only about 3 percent of those exposed. Further, Cohn points out, we do not hear of rats and fleas in the accounts of the Black Death. He adds that twentieth-century plague deaths in India and Manchuria continued year after year, providing no immunity from exposure, whereas the Black Death occurred only in the summer of 1348 (when incidentally the hot, dry weather meant few fleas) and then again for about one year every decade, causing fewer and fewer fatalities, except for children—who had no immunity. This would seem to be a good case for DNA testing. In fact, a disputed test of a bone from a possible Black Death victim in France revealed the existence of *Y. pestis*, but other samples have not, leaving the issue still in doubt.

Scholars have also explored the dimensions of the Black Death beyond Europe. Until recently, the subject was a virtual monopoly of European historians, but we can now ask about the Black Death in Egypt and the Middle East, as we do here with Michael W. Dols's comparison of the consequences of Christian and Muslim beliefs. Stuart J. Borsch, in *The Black Death in Egypt and England: A Comparative Study* (University of Texas Press, 2005), asks about longer-term consequences: Why did Europe recover and thrive after 1350 whereas the economy of Egypt began a long decline? He finds the answer in the differences between the landholding systems of English peasants, who prospered as their numbers declined, and the disinterested absentee landlords of the Egyptian Mamluk regime (1250–1517), who just cut their losses and left. Other factors may account for the long-term economic decline of Egypt and other Muslim regimes in contrast to the revival of Christian Europe. Whereas Michael Dols emphasizes the role of religious ideas, others have commented on the changing balance of religious and secular explanations in both cultures. Religious explanations were, in fact, more common in Christian Europe in 1348 than they were in Muslim Egypt, where secular explanations outnumbered religious ones. Yet this imbalance was reversed in later years. After 1350 Europeans increasingly described the event in secular terms, crediting individual doctors and medical treatments rather than supernatural factors for their survival. The Islamic world of the Middle East moved in the opposite direction after 1350, becoming less secular and more religious. Cohn offers the rise of secular humanism in the European Renaissance as further evidence that the Black Death was like a flu that abated as people developed immunity and therefore felt more confident about human effort; but a similar response to the same disease did not occur in Egypt or the Middle East, more generally.

We still do not know how global the Black Death was. We trace its origins to Central Asia because we have no anecdotal or literary evidence for China or India. But we know that the population of China declined drastically from about 1200 to 1400[1] and that India was part of the Eurasian zone of shared diseases and immunities. We also do not know if the Black Death penetrated beyond the Sahara or up the Nile to sub-Saharan Africa. So there is still a lot more to learn, even to answer today's questions.

---

[1] In 1400 the Chinese population was actually about the same as it had been in 1200, but in both the previous and the subsequent 200-year period, it increased by 40–50 percent. A continuous population increase between 1200 and 1400 would have added about 150 million people. But this was also the period of the Mongol conquest and the revolt against the Mongols that issued in the Ming dynasty, both extraordinary killers.

13

On Cities

European, Chinese, Islamic, and Mexican Cities, 1000–1550

■ HISTORICAL CONTEXT

During the last five thousand years, cities have grown and multiplied, with the world becoming increasingly urbanized. There have been interruptions in this process, however: the period of the Mongol invasions in the first half of the thirteenth century and the era of the Black Death, the plague that wiped out urban populations in the middle of the fourteenth century, for instance. But, by and large, the general course of world history has promoted the rise and expansion of cities and of urban over rural populations.

In this chapter, we ask what this increasing urbanization meant for those who lived in the cities and for those who did not. We compare cities in various parts of the world between 1000 and 1550. We will study primary and secondary sources, and you will be asked to note the ways in which these cities are similar and different.

■ THINKING HISTORICALLY

Evaluating a Comparative Thesis

Many of the chapters, even individual readings, in this volume have been comparative. Making comparisons is a critical skill in any disciplined thinking process. In the study of world history, comparisons are particularly important and potentially fruitful, since until recently the historical profession tended to study different nations' histories somewhat in isolation from each other or without reference to a broader comparative context.

However, comparisons are not useful in and of themselves. They are merely a first step toward a thesis that attempts to explain the differences or similarities noticed. To say that something is bigger or smaller, hotter or colder, than something else, that one country is more densely populated or more religious than another, may be obvious or interesting, but the observation takes on meaning with the application of a theory or thesis that explains the difference. In history, there are many comparative theses. An example of one might run something like this: Canada has a more universal health care system than the United States because it has a longer tradition of mutual aid and trust in government. Now, one might agree or disagree with either the comparison or the explanation. If one disagrees with the comparison there is no need to go further. But if one agrees with the comparison, then one has to evaluate the comparative thesis.

In this chapter you will be asked to consider a comparative thesis about cities that is offered in the first reading. The other readings in the chapter will enable you to consider what evidence they offer for or against the initial comparison and its explanatory thesis.

1

FERNAND BRAUDEL

Towns and Cities, 1983

Fernand Braudel* (1902–1985) was one of the great historians of the twentieth century, and the following selection, which provides a broad overview of medieval towns and cities throughout the world, is from one of his interpretative works of world history. According to Braudel, what were some of the distinctive characteristics of Western, or European, towns? Why did Western towns acquire these characteristics? How does Braudel describe Chinese and Islamic cities? Why and how did these towns develop differently?

THINKING HISTORICALLY

Braudel begins with a comparative judgment — that European towns "were marked by an unparalleled freedom." How does he explain this supposed difference between European towns and those of

* broh DELL

Source: Fernand Braudel, *The Structures of Everyday Life: The Limits of the Possible* (London: Collins, 1983), 509–14, 524–25.

other societies? He offers a thesis about the development of European towns. He says that because the European state was weak,
these towns developed autonomous, self-governing bodies of largely
middle-class citizens who thought of themselves as a community.
They were not governed by a king, emperor, or territorial state, but,
rather, governed themselves through a number of organizations. In
addition to governing councils and militaries, these organizations
included guilds, church groups, and various other voluntary societies
in which citizens exercised real power over their lives. Braudel attributes these differences to the long history of European feudalism
and weak states, and to the rise of capitalism and a middle class in
these independent towns.

As you read Braudel, try to weigh his evidence for both the comparison and his explanation. Does it appear from the reading that
inhabitants of European towns had greater freedom than the people
of other towns? If you agree with his comparison, try to evaluate his
explanation. Was there a complex of features in Western society that
did not occur elsewhere? What is his evidence for that comparative
thesis? What else would you want to learn to challenge or confirm
his thesis?

The Originality of Western Towns

. . . What were Europe's differences and original features? Its towns
were marked by an unparalleled freedom. They had developed as autonomous worlds and according to their own propensities. They had
outwitted the territorial state, which was established slowly and then
only grew with their interested co-operation—and was moreover
only an enlarged and often insipid copy of their development. They
ruled their countrysides autocratically, regarding them exactly as later
powers regarded their colonies, and treating them as such. They pursued an economic policy of their own via their satellites and the nervous system of urban relay points; they were capable of breaking
down obstacles and creating or recreating protective privileges. Imagine what would happen if modern states were suppressed so that the
Chambers of Commerce of the large towns were free to act as they
pleased!

Even without resort to doubtful comparisons these long-standing
realities leap to the eye. And they lead us to a key problem which can be
formulated in two or three different ways: What stopped the other cities
of the world from enjoying the same relative freedom? Or to take another
aspect of the same problem, why was change a striking feature of the
destiny of Western towns (even their physical existence was transformed)
while the other cities have no history by comparison and seem to have

been shut in long periods of immobility? Why were some cities like steam-engines while the others were like clocks, to parody Lévi-Strauss?[1] Comparative history compels us to look for the reason for these differences and to attempt to establish a dynamic "model" of the turbulent urban evolution of the West, whereas a model representing city life in the rest of the world would run in a straight and scarcely broken line across time.

Free Worlds

Urban freedom in Europe is a classic and fairly well documented subject; let us start with it.

In a simplified form we can say:

1. The West well and truly lost its urban framework with the end of the Roman Empire. Moreover the towns in the Empire had been gradually declining since before the arrival of the barbarians. The very relative animation of the Merovingian period[2] was followed, slightly earlier in some places, slightly later in others, by a complete halt.

2. The urban renaissance from the eleventh century was precipitated by and superimposed on a rise in rural vigour, a growth of fields, vineyards, and orchards. Towns grew in harmony with villages and clearly outlined urban law often emerged from the communal privileges of village groups. The town was often simply the country revived and remodeled. . . .

This rural rearrangement naturally brought to the nascent city the representatives of political and social authority: nobles, lay princes, and ecclesiastics.

3. None of this would have been possible without a general return to health and a growing monetary economy.[3] . . .

Thousands of towns were founded at this time, but few of them went on to brilliant futures. Only certain regions, therefore, were urbanized in depth, thus distinguishing themselves from the rest and playing a vitalizing role: such was the region between the Loire and the Rhine, for instance, or northern and central Italy, and certain key points on Mediterranean coasts. Merchants, craft guilds, industries, long-distance trade, and banks were quick to appear there, as well as a certain kind of bourgeoisie[4] and even

---

[1] Claude Lévi-Strauss (1908–2009), anthropologist who in 1962 compared primitive societies to clocks (controlled change returning to order) and modern societies to steam engines (dynamic, unpredictable change). [Ed.]

[2] 450–751. [Ed.]

[3] He means the reappearance of money and markets, especially in towns. [Ed.]

[4] A middle class in the sense that they were in the middle between aristocrats and peasants. A property-owning city-based class who made their living in the new money economy (from bankers and lawyers to merchants, store owners, and writers). [Ed.]

some sort of capitalism.[5] The destinies of these very special cities were linked not only to the progress of the surrounding countryside but to international trade. Indeed, they often broke free of rural society and former political ties. The break might be achieved violently or amicably, but it was always a sign of strength, plentiful money, and real power.

Soon there were no states around these privileged towns. This was the case in Italy and Germany, with the political collapses of the thirteenth century. The hare beat the tortoise for once. Elsewhere—in France, England, Castile, even in Aragon—the earlier rebirth of the territorial state restricted the development of the towns, which in addition were not situated in particularly lively economic areas. They grew less rapidly than elsewhere. . . .

In fact the miracle in the West was not so much that everything sprang up again from the eleventh century, after having been almost annihilated with the disaster of the fifth. History is full of examples of secular revivals, of urban expansion, of births and rebirths: Greece from the fifth to the second century B.C.E.; Rome perhaps; Islam from the ninth century; China under the Sungs. But these revivals always featured two runners, the state and the city. The state usually won and the city then remained subject and under a heavy yoke. The miracle of the first great urban centuries in Europe was that the city won hands down, at least in Italy, Flanders, and Germany. It was able to try the experiment of leading a completely separate life for quite a long time. This was a colossal event. Its genesis cannot be pinpointed with certainty, but its enormous consequences are visible.

Towns as Outposts of Modernity

It was on the basis of this liberty that the great Western cities, and other towns they influenced and to which they served as examples, built up a distinctive civilization and spread techniques which were new, or had been revived or rediscovered after centuries—it matters little which. The important thing is that these cities had the rare privilege of following through an unusual political, social, and economic experience.

In the financial sphere, the towns organized taxation, finances, public credit, customs, and excise. They invented public loans: the first issues of the Monte Vecchio[6] in Venice could be said to go back to 1167, the first formulation of the Casa di San Giorgio[7] to 1407. One after another, they

---

[5] There are many definitions of capitalism: a money-based economic system; a system where everything (land, labor, and capital) is for sale; the modern economic system in which society is based on the market; a system in which capital (productive resources, money, companies) is privately rather than publicly owned. [Ed.]

[6] The Republic of Venice's first bonds. [Ed.]

[7] Genoa's first public bank. In 1407 Genoa was bankrupt after wars with Venice. The governing Council of Ancients authorized the House of St. George to raise money by selling city debt (at 7 percent interest) and collecting taxes and custom duties owed to the city. [Ed.]

[the towns] reinvented gold money, following Genoa which may have minted the *genovino* as early as the late twelfth century. They organized industry and the guilds; they invented long-distance trade, bills of exchange, the first forms of trading companies and accountancy. They also quickly became the scene of class struggles: . . . nobles against bourgeois; poor against rich ("thin people" *popolo magro* against "fat people" *popolo grosso*). . . .

This society divided from within also faced enemies from without— . . . everybody who was not a citizen. The cities were the West's first focus for patriotism—and the patriotism they inspired was long to be more coherent and much more conscious than the territorial kind, which emerged only slowly in the first states. . . .

A new state of mind was established, broadly that of an early, still faltering, Western capitalism—a collection of rules, possibilities, calculations, the art both of getting rich and of living. It also included gambling and risk: the key words of commercial language, *fortuna, ventura, ragione, prudenza, sicurta,*[8] define the risks to be guarded against. No question now of living from day to day as noblemen did, always putting up their revenues to try to meet the level of their expenditure, which invariably came first—and letting the future take care of itself. The merchant was economical with his money, calculated his expenditure according to his returns, his investments according to their yield. . . . He would also be economical with his time: . . . "time is money."

Capitalism and towns were basically the same thing in the West. Lewis Mumford humorously claimed that capitalism was the cuckoo's egg laid in the confined nests of the medieval towns. By this he meant to convey that the bird was destined to grow inordinately and burst its tight framework (which was true), and then link up with the state, the conqueror of towns but heir to their institutions and way of thinking and completely incapable of dispensing with them. The important thing was that even when it had declined as a city the town continued to rule the roost all the time it was passing into the actual or apparent service of the prince. The wealth of the state would still be the wealth of the town: Portugal converged on Lisbon, the Netherlands on Amsterdam, and English primacy was London's primacy (the capital modelled England in its own image after the peaceful revolution of 1688). The latent defect in the Spanish imperial economy was that it was based on Seville—a controlled town rotten with dishonest officials and long dominated by foreign capitalists—and not on a powerful free town capable of producing and carrying through a really individual economic policy. . . .

---

[8] Luck, business venture, reason, prudence, security. [Ed.]

Towns similar to those in medieval Europe—masters of their fate for a brief moment—only arose in Islam when the empires collapsed. They marked some outstanding moments in Islamic civilization. But they only lasted for a time and the main beneficiaries were certain marginal towns like Cordoba, or the cities which were urban republics by the fifteenth century, like Ceuta before the Portuguese occupation in 1415, or Oran before the Spanish occupation in 1509. The usual pattern was the huge city under the rule of a prince or a Caliph: a Baghdad or a Cairo.

Towns in distant Asia were of the same type: imperial or royal cities, enormous, parasitical, soft, and luxurious—Delhi and Vijayanagar, Peking and to some extent Nanking, though this was rather different. The great prestige enjoyed by the prince comes as no surprise to us. And if one ruler was swallowed up by the city or more likely by his palace, another immediately took his place and the subjection continued. Neither will it surprise us to learn that these towns were incapable of taking over the artisanal trades from the countryside: They were both open towns and subject towns simultaneously. Besides, in India as in China, social structures already existing hampered the free movement of the towns. If the town did not win its independence, it was not only because of the bastinadoes[9] ordered by the mandarins[10] or the cruelty of the prince to merchants and ordinary citizens. It was because society was prematurely fixed, crystallized in a certain mould.

In India, the caste system automatically divided and broke up every urban community. In China, the cult of the *gentes*[11] on the one hand was confronted on the other by a mixture comparable to that which created the Western town: Like the latter it acted as a melting-pot, breaking old bonds and placing individuals on the same level. The arrival of immigrants created an "American" environment, where those already settled set the tone and the way of life. In addition, there was no independent authority representing the Chinese town as a unit, in its dealings with the State or with the very powerful countryside. The rural areas were the real heart of living, active, and thinking China.

The town, residence of officials and nobles, was not the property of either guilds or merchants. There was no gradual "rise of the bourgeoisie" here. No sooner did a bourgeoisie appear than it was tempted by class betrayal, fascinated by the luxurious life of the mandarins. The towns might have lived their own lives, filled in the contours of their own destiny, if individual initiative and capitalism had had a clear field. But the tutelary State hardly lent itself to this. . . .

[9] Beatings (often on the soles of the feet). [Ed.]
[10] Chinese bureaucrats. [Ed.]
[11] People. [Ed.]

Only the West swung completely over in favor of its towns. The towns caused the West to advance. It was, let us repeat, an enormous event, but the deep-seated reasons behind it are still inadequately explained. What would the Chinese towns have become if the junks[12] had discovered the Cape of Good Hope at the beginning of the fifteenth century, and had made full use of such a chance of world conquest?

[12] Chinese flat-bottomed ships with battened sails. [Ed.]

2

Organizing Self-Government in Ipswich, 1200

On May 25, 1200, King John of England granted the town of Ipswich on the English Channel a charter of self-government, declaring it a "free borough." This selection is a contemporary account of what the townspeople of Ipswich did to implement that charter. What did they do? How would you describe the government they created? What were the capital portmen to do? How well would they have represented the population of the town?

THINKING HISTORICALLY

In what ways does this selection support what Fernand Braudel said about the development of European towns in the previous selection? What signs do you see that might indicate that the king still played a role in the government of the town? What indications are there that self-government was not democratic?

On Thursday following the festival of the Nativity of St. John the Baptist in the second year of the reign of King John [29 June, 1200], the whole town of the borough of Ipswich gathered in the churchyard of St. Mary at Tower to elect two bailiffs [managers] and four coroners [judges] for the town, according to the specifications of the charter of the King, which that king recently granted to the borough. On which day the townsmen, by common assent and with one voice, elected two upright and law-abiding men, of their town, viz., John fitz Norman

Source: Translated from the Latin in Charles Gross, *The Gild Merchant; A Contribution to British Municipal History*, Vol. II (Oxford: At the Clarendon Press, 1890), 116–18.

and William de Beaumes, who were sworn to the administration as bailiffs of the town and that they shall behave well and faithfully to both poor and rich.

They also unanimously elected on that day four coroners, viz. John fitz Norman, William de Beaumes, Philip de Porta, and Roger Lew, who were sworn to the administration of pleas of the crown and to doing other things which concern the crown in the borough, and to supervise the bailiffs in the just and legal treatment of poor as well as rich.

On the same day it was ordained by common counsel of the town that henceforth there ought to be in the borough twelve sworn capital portmen, such as there are in other free boroughs of England, and that they should have full power on behalf of themselves and the whole town to govern and maintain the borough and all its liberties, and to render judgments of the town; and also to take care of, ordain and do in the borough whatever may need to be done to maintain the status and reputation of the town. And on this matter the bailiffs and coroners declared that the whole town should come to the churchyard on Sunday following the festival of the Apostles Peter and Paul, to elect 12 capital portmen, according to the intent of this ordinance.

On Sunday following the festival of the Apostles Peter and Paul [2 July], the whole town of Ipswich gathered before the bailiffs and coroners to elect 12 capital portmen for the town, as was previously decided. By consent of the town, the bailiffs and coroners elected four upright and law-abiding men from each parish of the town, who were sworn to elect 12 capital portmen from the better, wiser and more able townsmen to make ordinances for the well-being of the town, as was already said. And those sworn men of the parishes came and elected, on behalf of themselves and the whole town, these 12 names written below, viz. John fitz Norman, William de Beaumes, Philip de Porta, Roger Lew, Peter Everard, William Goscalk, Amise Bolle, John de Saint George, John le Mayster, Sayer fitz Thurstan, Robert Parys and Andrew Peper. Who took oath before the whole town that they would govern the borough of Ipswich well and faithfully, maintain as best they could all the liberties recently granted to the townsmen of the borough by the charter of the King, maintain all liberties and free customs of the town, render just judgments in the town court without discrimination towards any individual, and moreover ordain and do all things touching the status and reputation of the town, and to deal lawfully and justly with poor as well as rich.

On the same day as the 12 capital portmen were sworn in this fashion, they required the whole town to raise its hands over the book and in one voice to solemnly swear that from that hour forth they would obey, attend, counsel and support the bailiffs, coroners, and each and every of the 12 capital portmen, with their bodies and their properties for the purpose of preserving and maintaining the reputation, liberties and free customs of the town in whatever location necessary (excepting against the lord King or his power), with all their might, insofar as they ought to do within justice and reason.

On the same day it was agreed that the new charter of the King be handed over to two upright and law-abiding townsmen for safekeeping, viz. John fitz Norman and Philip de Porta, who were sworn to faithfully keep the charter and deliver it to the town when it shall be necessary and when they shall be warned and required to do so by the town. And because as much had been ordained and done for the status and reputation of the town as could be that day, it was agreed that the bailiffs, coroners and all capital portmen should come together on Thursday next after the festival of the Translation of St. Thomas the Martyr to ordain and do whatever might be required for the status and reputation of the town.

3

GREGORIO DATI

Corporations and Community in Florence, Fourteenth Century

This is an account of the Italian city of Florence and its inhabitants from 1380 to 1405. While family identity was primary, residents of Florence were also members of many corporate organizations that served to channel their loyalty to the larger urban community. Among these were guilds and parish churches, as well as political, welfare, and religious organizations. On public holidays like the feast day of St. John the Baptist, the patron saint of Florence, these various groups would come together in a display of communal solidarity that was often more fraternal than the deliberations in the political arena. What seems to motivate people to participate in public acts and parades in Florence?

THINKING HISTORICALLY

Are events like those described here signs of urban autonomy, or are they likely to encourage it? What aspects of this account support Braudel's thesis?

Source: Gregorio Dati, *"Istoria di Firenze dall'anno MCCCLXXX all'anno MCCCCV"* (History of Florence from 1380 to 1405) (Florence, 1735), in *The Society of Renaissance Florence*, ed. and trans. Gene Brucker (New York: Harper & Row, 1971), 75–78.

When springtime comes and the whole world rejoices, every Florentine begins to think about organizing a magnificent celebration on the feast day of St. John the Baptist [June 24]. . . . For two months in advance, everyone is planning marriage feasts or other celebrations in honor of the day. There are preparations for the horse races, the costumes of the retinues, the flags, and the trumpets; there are the pennants and the wax candles and other things which the subject territories offer to the Commune. Messengers are sent to obtain provisions for the banquets, and horses come from everywhere to run in the races. The whole city is engaged in preparing for the feast, and the spirits of the young people and the women [are animated] by these preparations. . . . Everyone is filled with gaiety; there are dances and concerts and songfests and tournaments and other joyous activities. Up to the eve of the holiday, no one thinks about anything else.

Early on the morning of the day before the holiday, each guild has a display outside of its shops of its fine wares, its ornaments, and jewels. There are cloths of gold and silk sufficient to adorn ten kingdoms. . . . Then at the third hour, there is a solemn procession of clerics, priests, monks, and friars, and there are so many [religious] orders, and so many relics of saints, that the procession seems endless. [It is a manifestation] of great devotion, on account of the marvelous richness of the adornments . . . and clothing of gold and silk with embroidered figures. There are many confraternities of men who assemble at the place where their meetings are held, dressed as angels, and with musical instruments of every kind and marvelous singing. They stage the most beautiful representations of the saints, and of those relics in whose honor they perform. They leave from S. Maria del Fiore [the cathedral] and march through the city and then return.

Then, after midday, when the heat has abated before sunset, all of the citizens assemble under [the banner of] their district, of which there are sixteen. Each goes in the procession in turn, the first, then the second, and so on with one district following the other, and in each group the citizens march two by two, with the oldest and most distinguished at the head, and proceeding down to the young men in rich garments. They march to the church of St. John [the Baptistery] to offer, one by one, a wax candle weighing one pound. . . . The walls along the streets through which they pass are all decorated, and there are . . . benches on which are seated young ladies and girls dressed in silk and adorned with jewels, pearls, and precious stones. This procession continues until sunset, and after each citizen has made his offering, he returns home with his wife to prepare for the next morning.

Whoever goes to the Piazza della Signoria on the morning of St. John's Day witnesses a magnificent, marvelous, and triumphant sight, which the mind can scarcely grasp. Around the great piazza are a hundred towers which appear to be made of gold. Some were brought on carts and others by porters. . . . [These towers] are made of wood, paper, and wax [and decorated] with gold, colored paints, and with figures. . . . Next to the rostrum of the palace [of the Signoria] are standards . . . which belong to the most important towns which are subject to the Commune: Pisa, Arezzo, Pistoia, Volterra, Cortona, Lucignano. . . .

First to present their offering, in the morning, are the captains of the Parte Guelfa, together with all of the knights, lords, ambassadors, and foreign knights. They are accompanied by a large number of the most honorable citizens, and before them, riding on a charger covered with a cloth . . . is one of their pages carrying a banner with the insignia of the Parte Guelfa. Then there follow the above-mentioned standards, each one carried by men on horseback . . . and they all go to make their offerings at the Baptistery. And these standards are given a tribute by the districts which have been acquired by the Commune of Florence. . . . The wax candles, which have the appearance of golden towers, are the tribute of the regions which in most ancient times were subject to the Florentines. In order of dignity, they are brought, one by one, to be offered to St. John, and on the following day, they are hung inside the church and there they remain for the entire year until the next feast day. . . . Then come . . . an infinite number of large wax candles, some weighing one hundred pounds and others fifty, some more and some less . . . carried by the residents of the villages [in the *contado*[1]] which offer them. . . .

Then the lord priors and their colleges come to make their offerings, accompanied by their rectors, that is, the podestà, the captain [of the *popolo*[2]], and the executor. . . . And after the lord [priors] come those who are participating in the horse race, and they are followed by the Flemings and the residents of Brabant who are weavers of woolen cloth in Florence. Then there are offerings by twelve prisoners who, as an act of mercy, have been released from prison . . . in honor of St. John, and these are poor people. . . . After all of these offerings have been made, men and women return home to dine. . . .

[1] Countryside. [Ed.]
[2] People. [Ed.]

4

MARCO POLO
On the City of Hangzhou, 1299

In *The Travels of Marco Polo*, the Venetian merchant recounted his travels across the Silk Road to Mongolia and China. According to his account, he stayed in China from 1275 to 1292 before returning to Venice. In 1275, the Chinese Southern Song capital of Hangzhou had just been conquered by Kublai Khan, the grandson of Genghis Khan.

Source: Marco Polo, *The Travels of Marco Polo*, the Complete Yule-Currier ed. (New York: Dover, 1993), 2:185–206.

The Mongols were able to conquer China, but they could not radically change it. The structure and organization of towns and cities remained very much the way it had been under the Song. In addition to Hangzhou, which Marco Polo calls Kinsay, he had been to the Mongol capital at Karakorum and to the Chinese cities of Peking and Chang'an. Why does he consider the city of Hangzhou "the finest and the noblest in the world"? How does his description support that characterization?

THINKING HISTORICALLY

In what ways does the Hangzhou that emerges from this document resemble Florence? In what ways was Hangzhou significantly different? Does Marco Polo's description show signs that Chinese cities were autonomous or that they were not? What do you see in this account of Hangzhou that supports or challenges Braudel's comparison and thesis?

When you have left the city of Changan and have travelled for three days through a splendid country, passing a number of towns and villages, you arrive at the most noble city of Kinsay,[1] a name which is as much as to say in our tongue "The City of Heaven," as I told you before.

And since we have got thither I will enter into particulars about its magnificence; and these are well worth the telling, for the city is beyond dispute the finest and the noblest in the world. In this we shall speak according to the written statement which the Queen of this Realm sent to Bayan the conqueror of the country for transmission to the Great Kaan, in order that he might be aware of the surpassing grandeur of the city and might be moved to save it from destruction or injury. I will tell you all the truth as it was set down in that document. For truth it was, as the said Messer Marco Polo at a later date was able to witness with his own eyes. And now we shall rehearse those particulars.

First and foremost, then, the document stated the city of Kinsay to be so great that it hath an hundred miles of compass. And there are in it twelve thousand bridges of stone,[2] for the most part so lofty that a great fleet could pass beneath them. And let no man marvel that there are so many bridges, for you see the whole city stands as it were in the water and surrounded by water, so that a great many bridges are required to give free passage about it. [And though the bridges be so high, the approaches are so well contrived that carts and horses do cross them.]

The document aforesaid also went on to state that there were in this city twelve guilds of the different crafts, and that each guild had twelve thousand houses in the occupation of its workmen. Each of these houses contains at

---

[1] *Kinsay* simply means "capital." The current name is Hangzhou. [Ed.]
[2] Generally assumed to be an exaggeration; one thousand would have been a lot. [Ed.]

least twelve men, whilst some contain twenty and some forty,—not that these are all masters, but inclusive of the journeymen who work under the masters. And yet all these craftsmen had full occupation, for many other cities of the kingdom are supplied from this city with what they require.

The document aforesaid also stated that the number and wealth of the merchants, and the amount of goods that passed through their hands, was so enormous that no man could form a just estimate thereof. And I should have told you with regard to those masters of the different crafts who are at the head of such houses as I have mentioned, that neither they nor their wives ever touch a piece of work with their own hands, but live as nicely and delicately as if they were kings and queens. The wives indeed are most dainty and angelical creatures! Moreover it was an ordinance laid down by the King that every man should follow his father's business and no other, no matter if he possessed 100,000 bezants.[3]

Inside the city there is a Lake which has a compass of some thirty miles:[4] and all round it are erected beautiful palaces and mansions, of the richest and most exquisite structure that you can imagine, belonging to the nobles of the city. There are also on its shores many abbeys and churches of the Idolaters. In the middle of the Lake are two Islands, on each of which stands a rich, beautiful, and spacious edifice, furnished in such style as to seem fit for the palace of an Emperor. And when any one of the citizens desired to hold a marriage feast, or to give any other entertainment, it used to be done at one of these palaces. And everything would be found there ready to order, such as silver plate, trenchers, and dishes [napkins and tablecloths], and whatever else was needful. The King made this provision for the gratification of his people, and the place was open to every one who desired to give an entertainment. . . .

The people are Idolaters; and since they were conquered by the Great Kaan they use paper money. [Both men and women are fair and comely, and for the most part clothe themselves in silk, so vast is the supply of that material, both from the whole district of Kinsay, and from the imports by traders from other provinces.] And you must know they eat every kind of flesh, even that of dogs and other unclean beasts, which nothing would induce a Christian to eat.

Since the Great Kaan occupied the city he has ordained that each of the twelve thousand bridges should be provided with a guard of ten men, in case of any disturbance, or of any being so rash as to plot treason or insurrection against him. [Each guard is provided with a hollow instrument of wood and with a metal basin, and with a timekeeper to enable them to know the hour of the day or night. . . .]

---

[3] A gold coin struck at Byzantium (or Constantinople) and used throughout Europe from the ninth century on. [Ed.]

[4] The circumference of the lake was more probably 30 li. A li was about a third of a mile, but it was sometimes used to mean a hundredth of a day's march. The entire circumference of the city could not have been more than 100 li. [Ed.]

Part of the watch patrols the quarter, to see if any light or fire is burning after the lawful hours; if they find any they mark the door, and in the morning the owner is summoned before the magistrates, and unless he can plead a good excuse he is punished. Also if they find any one going about the streets at unlawful hours they arrest him, and in the morning they bring him before the magistrates. Likewise if in the day-time they find any poor cripple unable to work for his livelihood, they take him to one of the hospitals, of which there are many, founded by the ancient kings, and endowed with great revenues. Or if he be capable of work they oblige him to take up some trade. . . .

The Kaan watches this city with especial diligence because it forms the head of all Manzi;[5] and because he has an immense revenue from the duties levied on the transactions of trade therein, the amount of which is such that no one would credit it on mere hearsay.

All the streets of the city are paved with stone or brick, as indeed are all the highways throughout Manzi, so that you ride and travel in every direction without inconvenience. . . .

You must know also that the city of Kinsay has some three thousand baths, the water of which is supplied by springs. They are hot baths, and the people take great delight in them, frequenting them several times a month, for they are very cleanly in their persons. They are the finest and largest baths in the world; large enough for one hundred persons to bathe together.

And the Ocean Sea comes within twenty-five miles of the city at a place called Ganfu, where there is a town and an excellent haven, with a vast amount of shipping which is engaged in the traffic to and from India and other foreign parts, exporting and importing many kinds of wares, by which the city benefits. And a great river flows from the city of Kinsay to that sea-haven, by which vessels can come up to the city itself. This river extends also to other places further inland.

Know also that the Great Kaan hath distributed the territory of Manzi into nine parts, which he hath constituted into nine kingdoms. To each of these kingdoms a king is appointed who is subordinate to the Great Kaan, and every year renders the accounts of his kingdom to the fiscal office at the capital. This city of Kinsay is the seat of one of these kings, who rules over one hundred forty great and wealthy cities. For in the whole of this vast country of Manzi there are more than twelve hundred great and wealthy cities, without counting the towns and villages, which are in great numbers. And you may receive it for certain that in each of those twelve hundred cities the Great Kaan has a garrison, and that the smallest of such garrisons musters one thousand men; whilst there are some of ten thousand, twenty thousand, and thirty thousand; so that the total number of troops is something scarcely calculable. . . . And all of them belong to the army of the Great Kaan.

[5] Southern China. [Ed.]

I repeat that everything appertaining to this city is on so vast a scale, and the Great Kaan's yearly revenues therefrom are so immense, that it is not easy even to put it in writing, and it seems past belief to one who merely hears it told. But I *will* write it down for you. . . .

I must tell you that in this city there are 160 *tomans*[6] of fires, or in other words 160 *tomans* of houses. Now I should tell you that the *toman* is 10,000, so that you can reckon the total as altogether 1,600,000 houses, among which are a great number of rich palaces. There is one church only, belonging to the Nestorian Christians.

There is another thing I must tell you. It is the custom for every burgess of this city, and in fact for every description of person in it, to write over his door his own name, the name of his wife, and those of his children, his slaves, and all the inmates of his house, and also the number of animals that he keeps. And if any one dies in the house then the name of that person is erased, and if any child is born its name is added. So in this way the sovereign is able to know exactly the population of the city. And this is the practice also throughout all Manzi and Cathay.

And I must tell you that every hosteler who keeps an hostel for travellers is bound to register their names and surnames, as well as the day and month of their arrival and departure. And thus the sovereign hath the means of knowing, whenever it pleases him, who come and go throughout his dominions. And certes this is a wise order and a provident [one].

The position of the city is such that it has on one side a lake of fresh and exquisitely clear water (already spoken of), and on the other a very large river. The waters of the latter fill a number of canals of all sizes which run through the different quarters of the city, carry away all impurities, and then enter the Lake; whence they issue again and flow to the Ocean, thus producing a most excellent atmosphere. By means of these channels, as well as by the streets, you can go all about the city. Both streets and canals are so wide and spacious that carts on the one and boats on the other can readily pass to and fro, conveying necessary supplies to the inhabitants.

At the opposite side the city is shut in by a channel, perhaps forty miles in length, very wide, and full of water derived from the river aforesaid, which was made by the ancient kings of the country in order to relieve the river when flooding its banks. This serves also as a defence to the city, and the earth dug from it has been thrown inward, forming a kind of mound enclosing the city.

In this part are the ten principal markets, though besides these there are a vast number of others in the different parts of the town. The former are all squares of half a mile to the side, and along their front passes the main street, which is forty paces in width, and runs straight from end to end of the city, crossing many bridges of easy and commodious approach. At every four miles of its length comes one of those great squares of

[6] A *toman* is a Mongol measurement of ten thousand. [Ed.]

two miles (as we have mentioned) in compass. So also parallel to this great street, but at the back of the marketplaces, there runs a very large canal, on the bank of which toward the squares are built great houses of stone, in which the merchants from India and other foreign parts store their wares, to be handy for the markets. In each of the squares is held a market three days in the week, frequented by forty thousand or fifty thousand persons, who bring thither for sale every possible necessary of life, so that there is always an ample supply of every kind of meat and game, as of roebuck, red-deer, fallow-deer, hares, rabbits, partridges, pheasants, francolins, quails, fowls, capons, and of ducks and geese an infinite quantity; for so many are bred on the Lake that for a Venice groat of silver [7] you can have a couple of geese and two couple of ducks. Then there are the shambles where the larger animals are slaughtered, such as calves, beeves, kids, and lambs, the flesh of which is eaten by the rich and the great dignitaries.

Those markets make a daily display of every kind of vegetables and fruits; and among the latter there are in particular certain pears of enormous size, weighing as much as ten pounds apiece, and the pulp of which is white and fragrant like a confection; besides peaches in their season both yellow and white, of every delicate flavour. . . .

All the ten marketplaces are encompassed by lofty houses, and below these are shops where all sorts of crafts are carried on, and all sorts of wares are on sale, including spices and jewels and pearls. Some of these shops are entirely devoted to the sale of wine made from rice and spices, which is constantly made fresh, and is sold very cheap.

Certain of the streets are occupied by the women of the town, who are in such a number that I dare not say what it is. They are found not only in the vicinity of the marketplaces, where usually a quarter is assigned to them, but all over the city. They exhibit themselves splendidly attired and abundantly perfumed, in finely garnished houses, with trains of waiting-women. These women are extremely accomplished in all the arts of allurement, and readily adapt their conversation to all sorts of persons, insomuch that strangers who have once tasted their attractions seem to get bewitched, and are so taken with their blandishments and their fascinating ways that they never can get these out of their heads. Hence it comes to pass that when they return home they say they have been to Kinsay or the City of Heaven, and their only desire is to get back thither as soon as possible.

Other streets are occupied by the Physicians, and by the Astrologers, who are also teachers of reading and writing; and an infinity of other professions have their places round about those squares. In each of the squares there are two great palaces facing one another, in which are established the officers appointed by the King to decide differences arising between merchants, or other inhabitants of the quarter. It is the daily duty of these officers to see that the guards are at their posts on the neighbouring bridges, and to punish them at their discretion if they are absent. . . .

[7] A small coin. Point is that because there are so many, they are very cheap. [Ed.]

The natives of the city are men of peaceful character, both from education and from the example of their kings, whose disposition was the same. They know nothing of handling arms, and keep none in their houses. You hear of no feuds or noisy quarrels or dissensions of any kind among them. Both in their commercial dealings and in their manufactures they are thoroughly honest and truthful, and there is such a degree of good will and neighbourly attachment among both men and women that you would take the people who live in the same street to be all one family.

And this familiar intimacy is free from all jealousy or suspicion of the conduct of their women. These they treat with the greatest respect, and a man who should presume to make loose proposals to a married woman would be regarded as an infamous rascal. They also treat the foreigners who visit them for the sake of trade with great cordiality, and entertain them in the most winning manner, affording them every help and advice on their business. But on the other hand they hate to see soldiers, and not least those of the Great Kaan's garrisons, regarding them as the cause of their having lost their native kings and lords.

5

S. D. GOITEIN

Cairo: An Islamic City in Light of the Geniza, 1969

The author of this selection provides an especially detailed picture of medieval Cairo due to an unusual discovery of documents. "The Geniza" refers to a treasure trove of documents maintained by a Jewish synagogue in Cairo from the tenth to thirteenth centuries. It contains correspondence, legal documents, receipts, inventories, prescriptions, and notes—written in Hebrew characters in the Arabic language—and offers a rare opportunity to review virtually everything a community wrote over a long period of time. It is an extremely valuable resource that can answer most questions about medieval society in Cairo.

In this selection, S. D. Goitein studies the documents for the insight they provide into city life in Cairo. What do the Geniza documents tell us about city life in Cairo? What would it have been like to live in medieval Cairo? In what ways would life in medieval Cairo have been similar to, or different from, life in a city

Source: S. D. Goitein, "Cairo: An Islamic City in Light of the Geniza," in *Middle Eastern Cities*, ed. Ira M. Lapidus (Berkeley and Los Angeles: University of California Press, 1969), 90–95.

of medieval Europe or medieval China? What is the significance of the lack of public buildings and guilds in Cairo? In what ways was the Muslim identity larger or more cosmopolitan than European urban identities?

THINKING HISTORICALLY

How does this support or challenge Braudel's thesis? Is Cairo more like a European city or a Chinese city? How is it different from each?

. . . It is astounding how rarely government buildings are mentioned in the Geniza documents. There were the local police stations and prisons, as well as the offices where one received the licenses occasionally needed, but even these are seldom referred to. The Mint and the Exchange are frequently referred to, but at least the latter was only semi-public in character, since the persons working there were not on the government payroll. Taxes were normally collected by tax farmers.[1] Thus there was little direct contact between the government and the populace and consequently not much need for public buildings. The imperial palace and its barracks formed a city by itself, occasionally mentioned in Ayyūbid times, but almost never in the Fāṭimid period.

Government, although not conspicuous by many public buildings, was present in the city in many other ways. A city was governed by a military commander called *amīr*, who was assisted by the *wālī* or superintendent of the police. Smaller towns had only a *wālī* and no *amīr*. Very powerful, sometimes more powerful than the *amīr*, was the *qāḍī*, or judge, who had administrative duties in addition to his substantial judicial functions. The chief *qāḍī* often held other functions such as the control of the taxes or of a port, as we read with regard to Alexandria or Tyre. The city was divided into small administrative units called *rab'* (which is not the classical *rub*, meaning quarter, but instead designates an area, or rather a compound). Each *rab'* had a superintendent called *ṣāḥib rab'* (pronounced rub), very often referred to in the Geniza papers. In addition to regular and mounted police there were plain clothesmen, or secret service men, called *aṣḥāb al-khabar*, "informants" who formed a government agency independent even of the *qāḍī*, a state of affairs for which there seem to exist parallels in more modern times.

An ancient source tells us that the vizier[2] al-Ma'mūn, mentioned above, instructed the two superintendents of the police of Fusṭāṭ[3] and

---

[1] Private collectors who bought or were given authority to collect taxes and keep all or a percentage of proceeds. Common practice in ancient world. [Ed.]

[2] Prime minister. [Ed.]

[3] Old Cairo. [Ed.]

Cairo, respectively, to draw up exact lists of the inhabitants showing their occupations and other circumstances and to permit no one to move from one house to another without notification of the police. This is described as an extraordinary measure aimed at locating any would-be assassins who might have been sent to the Egyptian capital by the Bāṭiniyya, an Ismāʿīlī group using murder as a political weapon. Such lists, probably with fewer details, no doubt were in regular use for the needs of taxation. In a letter from Sicily, either from its capital Palermo or from Mazara on its southwestern tip, the writer, an immigrant from Tunisia around 1063, informs his business friend in Egypt that he is going to buy a house and that he has already registered for the purpose in the *qānūn* (Greek *canon*) which must have designated an official list of inhabitants. With regard to non-Muslims, a differentiation was made between permanent residents and newcomers. Whether the same practice existed with respect to Muslims is not evident from the Geniza papers.

What were the dues that a town dweller had to pay to the government in his capacity as the inhabitant of a city, and what were the benefits that he derived from such payments? By right of conquest, the ground on which Fusṭāṭ stood belonged to the Muslims, that is, to the government (the same was the case in many other Islamic cities), and a ground rent, called *ḥikr*, had to be paid for each building. A great many deeds of sale, gift, and rent refer to this imposition. . . .

Besides the ground rent, every month a *ḥarāsa*, or "due for protection," had to be paid to the government. The protection was partly in the hands of a police force, partly in those of the superintendents of the compounds, and partly was entrusted to nightwatchmen, usually referred to as *ṭawwāfūn*, literally, "those that make the round," but known also by other designations. As we learn expressly from a Geniza source, the nightwatchmen, like the regular police, were appointed by the government (and not by a municipality or local body which did not exist). The amounts of the *ḥarāsa* in the communal accounts cannot be related to the value of the properties for which they were paid, but it is evident that they were moderate.

In a responsum[4] written around 1165, Rabbi Maimon, the father of Moses Maimonides,[5] states that the markets of Fusṭāṭ used to remain open during the nights, in contrast of course to what the writer was accustomed from having lived in other Islamic cities. In Fusṭāṭ, too, this had not been always the case. In a description of the festival of Epiphany from the year 941 in which all parts of the population took part, it is mentioned as exceptional that the streets were not closed during that particular night.

[4] A legal document. [Ed.]
[5] (1135–1204), a Jewish rabbi, physician, and philosopher in Spain and Egypt. [Ed.]

Sanitation must have been another great concern of the government, for the items "removal of rubbish" (called "throwing out of dust") and "cleaning of pipes" appear with great regularity in the monthly accounts preserved in the Geniza. One gets the impression that these hygienic measures were not left to the discretion of each individual proprietor of a house. The clay tubes bringing water (for washing purposes) to a house and those connecting it with a cesspool constantly needed clearing, and there are also many references to their construction. The amounts paid for both operations were considerable. The Geniza has preserved an autograph note by Maimonides permitting a beadle[6] to spend a certain sum on "throwing out of dust" (presumably from a synagogue). This may serve as an illustration for the fact that landlords may have found the payment of these dues not always easy.

In this context we may also draw attention to the new insights gained through the study of the documents from the Geniza about the social life of Cairo. Massignon[7] had asserted, and he was followed by many, that the life-unit in the Islamic city was the professional corporation, the guilds of the merchants, artisans, and scholars which had professional, as well as social and religious functions. No one would deny that this was true to a large extent for the sixteenth through the nineteenth centuries. However, there is not a shred of evidence that this was true for the ninth through the thirteenth centuries. . . .

Further, we have stated before that no formal citizenship existed. The question is, however, how far did people feel a personal attachment to their native towns. "Homesickness," says Professor Gibb in his translation of the famous traveler Ibn Baṭṭūṭa, "was hardly to be expected in a society so cosmopolitan as that of medieval Islam." Indeed the extent of travel and migration reflected in the Geniza is astounding. No less remarkable, however, is the frequency of expressions of longing for one's native city and the wish to return to it, as well as the fervor with which compatriots stuck together when they were abroad. On the other hand, I cannot find much of neighborhood factionalism or professional *esprit de corps*, both of which were so prominent in the later Middle Ages. Under an ever more oppressive military feudalism and government-regimented economy, life became miserable and insecure, and people looked for protection and assistance in their immediate neighborhood. In an earlier period, in a free-enterprise, competitive society, there was no place for such factionalism. A man felt himself to be the son of a city which provided him with the security, the economic possibilities, and the spiritual amenities which he needed.

---

[6] A minor official. [Ed.]
[7] Louis Massignon (1883–1962), a French scholar of Islam. [Ed.]

6

BERNAL DÍAZ
Cities of Mexico, c. 1568

Bernal Díaz (1492–1580) accompanied Hernando Cortés* and
the band of Spanish conquistadors who were the first Europeans
to see the cities of the central Mexican plateau, dominated by the
Aztec capital of Tenochtitlan,† or Mexico, in 1519. Later in life,
he recalled what he saw in this account of *The Conquest of New
Spain*. The cities of Mexico provide the best example of how much
cities could differ. Unlike the cities of Eurasia, or even Islamic
Africa, the development of Mexican cities was entirely separate
from and uninfluenced by the other cultures we have studied.
Therefore, this description of Mexico, and the other cities of the
Mexican plateau, like Iztapalapa and Coyoacan, is enormously
useful to us.

What impressed Díaz about the cities of Mexico? How, according
to Díaz, were they different from the cities of Europe?

THINKING HISTORICALLY

In what respects were these cities different from others you have
read about? What other cities do they most resemble? How
does this selection support or challenge Braudel's comparison
and thesis?

Next morning, we came to a broad causeway¹ and continued our march
towards Iztapalapa. And when we saw all those cities and villages built
in the water, and other great towns on dry land, and that straight and
level causeway leading to Mexico, we were astounded. These great towns
and *cues*² and buildings rising from the water, all made of stone, seemed
like an enchanted vision from the tale of Amadis. Indeed, some of our
soldiers asked whether it was not all a dream. It is not surprising therefore that I should write in this vein. It was all so wonderful that I do not
know how to describe this first glimpse of things never heard of, seen, or
dreamed of before.

* kohr TEHZ
† the NOHCH teet LAHN
¹ The causeway of Cuitlahuac, which separated the lakes of Chalco and Xochimilco. [Ed.]
² Spanish for temple; probably refers to pyramids. [Ed.]

Source: Bernal Díaz, *The Conquest of New Spain*, trans. J. M. Cohen (London: Penguin
Books, 1963), 214–20, 230–35.

503

When we arrived near Iztapalapa we beheld the splendour of the other *Caciques*[3] who came out to meet us, the lord of that city whose name was Cuitlahuac, and the lord of Culuacan, both of them close relations of Montezuma. And when we entered the city of Iztapalapa, the sight of the palaces in which they lodged us! They were very spacious and well built, of magnificent stone, cedar wood, and the wood of other sweet-smelling trees, with great rooms and courts, which were a wonderful sight, and all covered with awnings of woven cotton.

When we had taken a good look at all this, we went to the orchard and garden, which was a marvelous place both to see and walk in. I was never tired of noticing the diversity of trees and the various scents given off by each, and the paths choked with roses and other flowers, and the many local fruit-trees and rose-bushes, and the pond of fresh water. Another remarkable thing was that large canoes could come into the garden from the lake, through a channel they had cut, and their crews did not have to disembark. Everything was shining with lime and decorated with different kinds of stonework and paintings which were a marvel to gaze on. Then there were birds of many breeds and varieties which came to the pond. I say again that I stood looking at it, and thought that no land like it would ever be discovered in the whole world, because at that time Peru was neither known nor thought of.[4] But today all that I then saw is overthrown and destroyed; nothing is left standing.

The Entrance into Mexico

Early next day we left Iztapalapa with a large escort of these great *Caciques*, and followed the causeway, which is eight yards wide and goes so straight to the city of Mexico that I do not think it curves at all. Wide though it was, it was so crowded with people that there was hardly room for them all. Some were going to Mexico and others coming away, besides those who had come out to see us, and we could hardly get through the crowds that were there. For the towers and the *cues* were full, and they came in canoes from all parts of the lake. No wonder, since they had never seen horses or men like us before!

With such wonderful sights to gaze on we did not know what to say, or if this was real that we saw before our eyes. On the land side there were great cities, and on the lake many more. The lake was crowded

---

[3] ka SEEK ehs   Word for rulers in the language of the Taino, a Native American people of the Caribbean. [Ed.]

[4] Spanish arrived about 1527; Díaz began writing of 1521 conquest of Mexico in 1568. [Ed.]

with canoes. At intervals along the causeway there were many bridges, and before us was the great city of Mexico [Tenochtitlan]. . . .

We marched along our causeway to a point where another small causeway branches off to another city called Coyoacan, and there, beside some towerlike buildings, which were their shrines, we were met by many more *Caciques* and dignitaries in very rich cloaks. The different chieftains wore different brilliant liveries, and the causeways were full of them. Montezuma[5] had sent these great *Caciques* in advance to receive us, and as soon as they came before Cortes they told him in their language that we were welcome, and as a sign of peace they touched the ground with their hands and kissed it. . . .

They led us to our quarters, which were in some large houses capable of accommodating us all and had formerly belonged to the great Montezuma's father, who was called Axayacatl. Here Montezuma now kept the great shrines of his gods, and a secret chamber containing gold bars and jewels. This was the treasure he had inherited from his father, which he never touched. Perhaps their reason for lodging us here was that, since they called us *Teules*[6] and considered us as such, they wished to have us near their idols. In any case they took us to this place, where there were many great halls, and a dais hung with the cloth of their country for our Captain, and matting beds with canopies over them for each of us.

On our arrival we entered the large court, where the great Montezuma was awaiting our Captain. Taking him by the hand, the prince led him to his apartment in the hall where he was to lodge, which was very richly furnished in their manner. . . .

We divided our lodgings by companies, and placed our artillery in a convenient spot. Then the order we were to keep was clearly explained to us, and we were warned to be very much on the alert, both the horsemen and the rest of us soldiers. We then ate a sumptuous dinner which they had prepared for us in their native style.

So, with luck on our side, we boldly entered the city of Tenochtitlan or Mexico on 8 November in the year of our Lord 1519. . . .

I must now speak of the skilled workmen whom Montezuma employed in all the crafts they practised, beginning with the jewellers and workers in silver and gold and various kinds of hollowed objects, which excited the admiration of our great silversmiths at home. Many of the best of them lived in a town called Atzcapotzalco, three miles from Mexico. There were other skilled craftsmen who worked with precious stones and *chalchihuites*,* and specialists in feather-work, and very fine painters and carvers. We can form some judgement of

---

* chal chee WEE tes
[5] Montezuma or Moctezuma II (c. 1480–1520), the Aztec emperor. [Ed.]
[6] Gods. [Ed.]

what they did then from what we can see of their work today. There are three Indians now living in the city of Mexico, named Marcos de Aquino, Juan de la Cruz, and El Crespillo, who are such magnificent painters and carvers that, had they lived in the age of the Apelles of old,[7] or of Michael Angelo,[8] or Berruguete[9] in our own day, they would be counted in the same rank.

Let us go on to the women, the weavers and sempstresses, who made such a huge quantity of fine robes with very elaborate feather designs. These things were generally brought from some towns in the province of Cotaxtla, which is on the north coast, quite near San Juan de Ulua. In Montezuma's own palaces very fine cloths were woven by those chieftains' daughters whom he kept as mistresses; and the daughters of other dignitaries, who lived in a kind of retirement like nuns in some houses close to the great *cue* of Huichilobos,[10] wore robes entirely of feather-work. Out of devotion for that god and a female deity who was said to preside over marriage, their fathers would place them in religious retirement until they found husbands. They would then take them out to be married.

Now to speak of the great number of performers whom Montezuma kept to entertain him. There were dancers and stilt-walkers, and some who seemed to fly as they leapt through the air, and men rather like clowns to make him laugh. There was a whole quarter full of these people who had no other occupation. He had as many workmen as he needed, too, stonecutters, masons, and carpenters, to keep his houses in repair. . . .

When we had already been in Mexico for four days, . . . Cortés said it would be a good thing to visit the large square of Tlatelolco and see the great *cue* of Huichilobos. So he sent Aguilar, Doña Marina,[11] and his own young page Orteguilla, who by now knew something of the language, to ask for Montezuma's approval of this plan. On receiving his request, the prince replied that we were welcome to go, but for fear that we might offer some offence to his idols he would himself accompany us with many of his chieftains. Leaving the

---

[7] Famous Ancient Greek painter. [Ed.]

[8] Michelangelo (1476–1564), Renaissance master painter and sculptor. [Ed.]

[9] Berruguete is either Pedro (1450–1504) or his son, Alonso (1488–1561), both famous Spanish painters. [Ed.]

[10] Huitzilopochtli, Aztec god of sun and war; required human sacrifice. [Ed.]

[11] Also known as Malinche (mah LEEN cheh). According to Díaz, she was the daughter of a cacique, who was given away after her mother remarried. She had learned Nahuatl as a youth and Yucatec Mayan as a slave. Thus, with the help of a Spanish sailor who learned Mayan, Cortéz could translate between Nahuatl and Spanish. Dona Marina also learned Spanish and became Cortéz's translator and mistress, eventually giving birth to Cortéz's son, Martin. [Ed.]

palace in his fine litter, when he had gone about half way, he dismounted beside some shrines, since he considered it an insult to his gods to visit their dwelling in a litter. Some of the great chieftains then supported him by the arms, and his principal vassals walked before him, carrying two staves, like sceptres raised on high as a sign that the great Montezuma was approaching. When riding in his litter he had carried a rod, partly of gold and partly of wood, held up like a wand of justice. The prince now climbed the steps of the great *cue*, escorted by many *papas*,[12] and began to burn incense and perform other ceremonies for Huichilobos. . . .

On reaching the market-place, escorted by the many *Caciques* whom Montezuma had assigned to us, we were astounded at the great number of people and the quantities of merchandise, and at the orderliness and good arrangements that prevailed, for we had never seen such a thing before. The chieftains who accompanied us pointed everything out. Every kind of merchandise was kept separate and had its fixed place marked for it.

Let us begin with the dealers in gold, silver, and precious stones, feathers, cloaks, and embroidered goods, and male and female slaves who are also sold there. They bring as many slaves to be sold in that market as the Portuguese bring Negroes from Guinea. Some are brought there attached to long poles by means of collars round their necks to prevent them from escaping, but others are left loose. Next there were those who sold coarser cloth, and cotton goods and fabrics made of twisted thread, and there were chocolate merchants with their chocolate. In this way you could see every kind of merchandise to be found anywhere in New Spain, laid out in the same way as goods are laid out in my own district of Medina del Campo, a centre for fairs, where each line of stalls has its own particular sort. So it was in this great market. There were those who sold sisal cloth and ropes and the sandals they wear on their feet, which are made from the same plant. All these were kept in one part of the market, in the place assigned to them, and in another part were skins of tigers and lions, otters, jackals, and deer, badgers, mountain cats, and other wild animals, some tanned and some untanned, and other classes of merchandise.

There were sellers of kidney-beans and sage and other vegetables and herbs in another place, and in yet another they were selling fowls, and birds with great dewlaps,[13] also rabbits, hares, deer, young ducks, little dogs, and other such creatures. Then there were the fruiterers; and the women who sold cooked food, flour and honey cake, and

[12] Aztec priests. [Ed.]
[13] Turkeys.

tripe, had their part of the market. Then came pottery of all kinds, from big water-jars to little jugs, displayed in its own place, also honey, honeypaste, and other sweets like nougat. Elsewhere they sold timber too, boards, cradles, beams, blocks, and benches, all in a quarter of their own.

Then there were the sellers of pitch-pine for torches, and other things of that kind, and I must also mention, with all apologies, that they sold many canoe-loads of human excrement, which they kept in the creeks near the market. This was for the manufacture of salt and the curing of skins, which they say cannot be done without it. I know that many gentlemen will laugh at this, but I assure them it is true. I may add that on all the roads they have shelters made of reeds or straw or grass so that they can retire when they wish to do so, and purge their bowels unseen by passers-by, and also in order that their excrement shall not be lost. . . .

We went on to the great *cue*, and as we approached its wide courts, before leaving the market-place itself, we saw many more merchants who, so I was told, brought gold to sell in grains, just as they extract it from the mines. This gold is placed in the thin quills of the large geese of that country, which are so white as to be transparent. They used to reckon their accounts with one another by the length and thickness of these little quills, how much so many cloaks or so many gourds of chocolate or so many slaves were worth, or anything else they were bartering.

Now let us leave the market, having given it a final glance, and come to the courts and enclosures in which their great *cue* stood. Before reaching it you passed through a series of large courts, bigger I think than the Plaza at Salamanca. These courts were surrounded by a double masonry wall and paved, like the whole place, with very large smooth white flagstones. Where these stones were absent everything was whitened and polished, indeed the whole place was so clean that there was not a straw or a grain of dust to be found there.

When we arrived near the great temple and before we had climbed a single step, the great Montezuma sent six *papas* and two chieftains down from the top, where he was making his sacrifices, to escort our Captain; and as he climbed the steps, of which there were one hundred and fourteen, they tried to take him by the arms to help him up in the same way as they helped Montezuma, thinking he might be tired, but he would not let them near him.

The top of the *cue* formed an open square on which stood something like a platform, and it was here that the great stones stood on which they placed the poor Indians for sacrifice. Here also was a massive image like a dragon, and other hideous figures, and a great deal of blood that had been spilled that day. Emerging in the company of two *papas* from the shrine which houses his accursed images, Montezuma made a deep bow to us all and said: "My lord Malinche, you must be tired after climbing this great *cue* of ours." And Cortés replied that none of us was ever exhausted by anything. Then Montezuma took him by the hand, and told him to look at his great city and all the other cities standing in the water, and the many others on the land round the lake; and he said that if Cortés had not had a good view of the great market-place he could see it better from where he now was. So we stood there looking, because that huge accursed *cue* stood so high that it dominated everything. We saw the three causeways that led into Mexico: the causeway of Iztapalapa by which we had entered four days before. . . . We saw the fresh water which came from Chapultepec to supply the city, and the bridges that were constructed at intervals on the causeways so that the water could flow in and out from one part of the lake to another. We saw a great number of canoes, some coming with provisions and others returning with cargo and merchandise; and we saw too that one could not pass from one house to another of that great city and the other cities that were built on the water except over wooden drawbridges or by canoe. We saw *cues* and shrines in these cities that looked like gleaming white towers and castles: a marvellous sight. All the houses had flat roofs, and on the causeways were other small towers and shrines built like fortresses.

Having examined and considered all that we had seen, we turned back to the great market and the swarm of people buying and selling. The mere murmur of their voices talking was loud enough to be heard more than three miles away. Some of our soldiers who had been in many parts of the world, in Constantinople, in Rome, and all over Italy, said that they had never seen a market so well laid out, so large, so orderly, and so full of people.

7

Map of Aztec Capital and Gulf of Mexico, 1524

This double map was made in the German city of Nuremburg to accompany the printing of the letters from Cortez to the Hapsburg Emperor Charles V, King of Spain (Figure 13.1). The map on the left is of the Gulf of Mexico. The south is at the top, the Caribbean Sea entering from the east on the left, and Mexico City on the right. Note Cuba, the Yucatan peninsula, and Florida. Why do you suppose most of the named places are on the south (top) side of the map? What would have been Cortez's route to Mexico City?

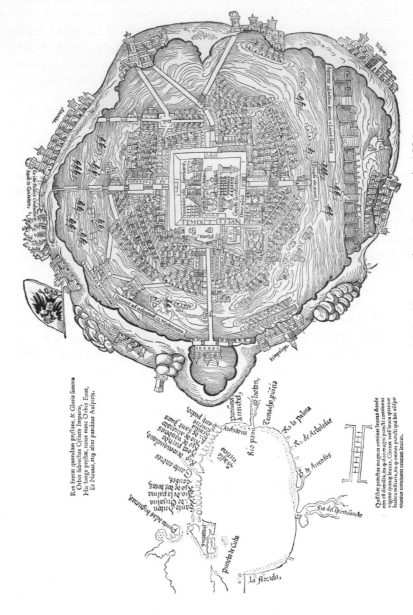

Figure 13.1 Cortés' map of Tenochtitlan, published in Nuremberg, Germany in 1524.

Source: Beinecke Rare Book and Manuscript Library, Yale University.

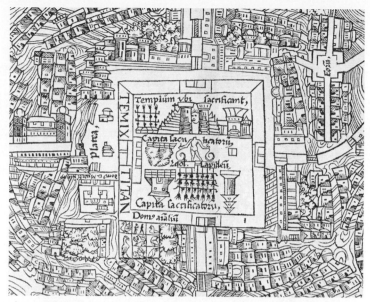

Figure 13.2 Detail of 1524 Nuremberg map of Tenochtitlan.
Source: Beinecke Rare Book and Manuscript Library, Yale University.

On the right of the Gulf of Mexico is a map of the Aztec capital of Tenochtitlan (modern Mexico City), shown in the center of the lake Texcoco, with the many causeways crossing the lake to the city. Notice how the artist (it's unknown if the artist was Spanish or German) imagines the look of Mexico's buildings. The styling of the buildings throughout the map is similar, except for the central square. That particular square is magnified on the map, symbolizing its importance in Aztec religion. The scholar Barbara E. Mundy[1] suggests that in contrast to the European styling of the rest of the map, the image of the central square very likely came from an earlier Aztec map that has since been lost. Her evidence includes the following:

1. The resemblance of the square on the Nuremberg map (Figure 13.2) to an Aztec map reproduced in the *Primeros Memoriales* (Figure 13.3).
2. The awareness by the artist of both these maps that the two temples in the center of the city were joined by a connecting line at the top and the bottom (roof and ground).

[1] Barbara E. Mundy, "Mapping the Aztec Capital: The 1524 Nuremberg Map of Tenochtitlan, Its Sources and Meanings," *Imago Mundi*, 50 (1998): 11–33.)

Figure 13.3 Map of the temple precinct of Tenochtitlan that draws on firsthand Aztec information, published in the *Primeros Memoriales*, c. 1561.

Source: © Patrimonio Nacional.

3. The importance both artists give to the Aztec ritual of human sacrifice, rather than Spanish concerns (look for the skulls in both figures, the blood on the steps in Figure 13.3, and the decapitated body in Figure 13.2).

4. The absence of other buildings in the square that the Spanish would have thought worth noting, but the Mexicans did not because they were not important to Aztec religion. The Sun pictured as a human face with hair suggesting fire in Equinox position between the two temples.

What do you make of this argument? Which, if any, evidence do you find convincing?

THINKING HISTORICALLY

Compare this map to the images of the cities shown in the following document. How does the image of Tenochtitlan compare to the Asian, Islamic, and European cities shown there? Does the large central square on this map resemble Asian or Islamic cities more than European ones? Excluding the central square, and ignoring the European architecture and perspective of the rest of this map, how would Tenochtitlan be more like a European city?

8

Images of Medieval Cities, Fifteenth and Sixteenth Centuries

The first two images, of Florence and Cairo, are bird's-eye illustrations that might function as maps. They are both done by European artists. In what ways were the two cities similar? In what ways were they different? The second set of images shows a Chinese city (probably Kaifeng, capital of the Song dynasty), attributed to the Chinese artist Zhang Zeduan (1085–1145) and the Italian city of Siena about 1339. In what ways are the Italian and Chinese cities similar and different?

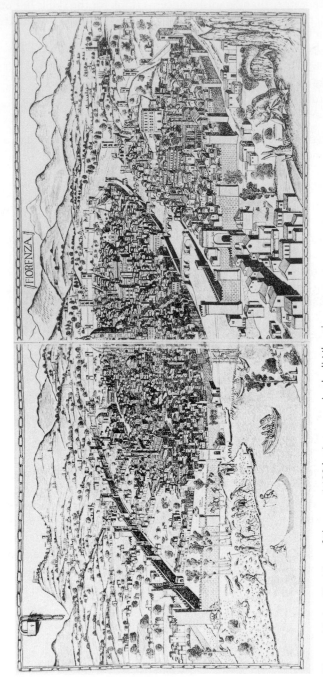

Figure 13.4 *City View of Florence, 1482* by Lucantonio degli Uberti.
Source: The Granger Collection, New York.

514

Figure 13.5 Cairo, 1549.

Figure 13.6 A Chinese city in *Along the River during the Qingming Festival* by Zhang Zeduan (detail).

Source: Werner Forman/Art Resource, NY.

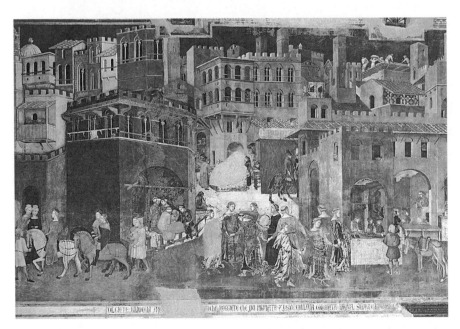

Figure 13.7 Siena in *Effects of Good Government* by Ambrogio Lorenzetti. Fresco in Hall of Nine, Siena.

Source: Palazzo Pubblico, Siena, Italy/The Bridgeman Art Library.

■ REFLECTIONS

Our selections certainly offer support for Braudel's thesis on the European city. The chartering of cities as independent corporations with their own laws, courts, and independent citizenry was a phenomenon repeated throughout Europe, especially in the West and the Mediterranean from the eleventh to the fifteenth centuries. The Florentine festival demonstrates how citizens came together in so many groups to celebrate their collective identity as citizens. Europe was a world without emperors, in which kings and lords were forced to bargain freedoms for favors.

Marco Polo unwittingly points to the power of the emperor, Song or Mongol, in imperial China. The capital city especially is designed and maintained according to his specifications. City life may be vibrant. There may even be enormous markets and wealthy merchants, but it is the emperor's city, not the merchants'. Rich merchants might train their sons to govern, but only as officials of the emperor.

Neither Chinese nor Muslim urban dwellers find their primary identities as citizens or even as residents of a particular city. They may be Cairenes, but they are Muslims first. Muslims had no need for self-governing cities when they could travel and work anywhere in the vast world of Islam.

Braudel struggled with American cities. North American towns, he thought, were re-creations of European towns. In Latin America, he classified Mexico City as similar to the imperial capitals of other parts of the world. Like Hangzhou, Mexico City could be astonishingly rich, but it was not an autonomous entity under Aztecs or Spaniards. The readings were selected not to stack the deck, but to show what Braudel meant. Consequently, some qualifications of Braudel's thesis might be in order.

First, we should not assume that autonomous or communal cities were limited to Europe. Rather, they were a product of a feudal, or politically weak and decentralized, society, where urban populations could bargain for special privileges. We could find similar examples of urban autonomy among, for example, Japanese port cities during the Japanese feudal era of the fourteenth to sixteenth centuries. One of these, Sakai, was called the Venice of Japan. Not until after 1600 and the recentralization of Japan under the Tokugawa administration were these independent cities brought to heel. In many ways, Tokugawa developments paralleled those of Europe, where centralized states also subordinated the independence of commercial cities after 1700.

Second, the absence of a movement for urban autonomy in Islamic and Chinese cities — important as it was in the time and places discussed in this chapter — was not universal. Chinese cities before the Mongol Yuan dynasty, especially in the earlier Sung dynasty, had developed an extremely prosperous commercial class. And while it is true that they did not gain (or seek) urban independence, they were content to exercise sufficient influence on the local representatives of the emperor. No appointed official could think lightly of ignoring the advice of Chinese merchants, the uniquely Chinese class of civil-service exam graduates, and the many Chinese guilds (one of the more important forces for self-government in Europe).

Third, while medieval Muslim cities encouraged little urban autonomy or identity, a prosperous class of merchants—always at the core of Islam—were nourished by more enlightened sultans and emirs. The Turkish historian Halil Inalcik writes that it was "the deliberate policy" of the Ottoman government, as it founded its successive capitals at Bursa in 1326, Edirne in 1402, and Istanbul in 1453, to create commercial and industrial centers, and that it consequently used every means—from tax exemptions to force—to attract and settle merchants and artisans in the new capitals. With the same end in view, Mehmed II encouraged the Jews of Europe to migrate to his new capital at Istanbul as they were being expelled from Spain and Portugal.

Braudel's thesis emphasizes the differences among cities, but as he well knew, one could emphasize the similarities as well. All cities distinguished themselves from the countryside that they controlled and exploited. All cities built and concentrated the wealth, achievements, and opportunities of the culture within their walls. All cities were greater engines of change than were villages, farms, and pastures. And some have argued that all cities promote patriarchy and class stratification.

Today about half the world's people live in cities. In 1800 only 3 percent of the world's population lived in cities. It is expected that by 2030, 60 percent of the world's population will be urban. Does that mean the lives of so many people will change in a similar way? Does it mean increasing patriarchy? Increasing exploitation of the countryside? Increasing inequality? Do significant choices need to be made about the types of cities we inhabit? Can we find ways to make our cities of the future our own?

14

Environment, Culture, and Technology

Europe, Asia, Oceania, and South America, 500–1500

■ HISTORICAL CONTEXT

Everyone knows that the world has changed drastically since the Middle Ages. And most people would agree that the most important and far-reaching changes have occurred in the fields of ecology, technology, and science. Global population has grown tenfold. The world has become a single ecological unit where microbes, migrants, and money travel everywhere at jet speed. In most parts of the world, average life expectancy has doubled; cities have mushroomed, supplanting farm and pasture. Machines have replaced the labor of humans and animals. Powers that were only imagined in the Middle Ages—elixirs to cure disease, energy to harness rivers, machines that could fly—are now commonplace. Other aspects of life—among them religion, political behavior, music, and art—have also evolved, but even these were affected significantly by advances in modern science and technology.

Have the changes been for good or ill? The signs of environmental stress are visible everywhere. The North Pole floats in the summer. Ten-thousand-year-old glaciers are disappearing. The oceans are rising two to four inches every ten years. Our atmosphere contains more carbon gasses than it has for at least 650,000 years. The stored energy of millions of years burns to service the richest members of a couple of generations. Ancient aquifers are drained to water the lawns of desert cities.

Precisely what change or changes occurred? When did the cycle of change begin, and what caused it? We will examine these questions here. You will read some substantial answers. These explanations of long-term change differ most markedly in how they explain the roots of the transformation. Lynn White Jr. defines the transformation to modernity in largely technological and ecological terms but emphasizes the role of cultural causes. Though a historian of medieval European technology, he focuses on the role of medieval European religion: Christianity. Jared Diamond writes of cultural failures to meet new natural and technological crises. Diamond, a professor of geography with numerous specializations in fields like physiology, evolutionary biology, and biogeography, warns that our contemporary ecological problems are very similar to earlier tragedies that ended in a failure of will. Terry Hunt and J. R. McNeill challenge this assessment and in the process, offer alternative explanations of our environmental problems. The final selection raises new questions about an environment we thought we knew—the Amazon.

■ THINKING HISTORICALLY

Evaluating Grand Theories

Big questions deserve big answers—or at least grand theories. Here we consider grand theories about the origins of our technological transformation and ecological difficulties, the links between environmental decline and the growth of technology and science, and the role of Western (European and American) economic growth in undermining the environment. Grand theories are especially speculative. They give us much to question and challenge. But their scope and freshness can often suggest new insights. Grand theories almost inevitably have elements that seem partly wrong and partly right. You will be encouraged to weigh some of the many elements in these theories. After reading the first essay, you will view visual sources and then read essays that offer support and criticism of the grand theories raised here. Then you can evaluate the theories, decide where you agree and disagree, and, perhaps, begin to develop your own grand theory as well.

1

LYNN WHITE JR.

The Historical Roots of Our Ecological Crisis, 1967

This classic essay first appeared in the magazine *Science* in 1967 and has since been reprinted and commented on many times. What do you think of White's linkage of ecological crisis and Christianity? Which of White's arguments and evidence do you find most persuasive? Which do you find least convincing? Imagine a continuum that includes all of the world's people, from the most ecologically minded "tree-huggers" on one end to the most damaging polluters and destroyers of the environment on the other end. Where on that continuum would you place the historical majority of Christians? Buddhists? Why?

THINKING HISTORICALLY

A grand theory like this—that Christianity is responsible for our environmental problems—argues far more than can be proven in such a brief essay. White concentrates on making certain kinds of connections and marshaling certain kinds of evidence. In addition to weighing the arguments he makes, consider the gaps in his argument. What sorts of evidence would you seek to make White's theory more convincing?

A conversation with Aldous Huxley[1] not infrequently put one at the receiving end of an unforgettable monologue. About a year before his lamented death he was discoursing on a favorite topic: man's unnatural treatment of nature and its sad results. To illustrate his point he told how, during the previous summer, he had returned to a little valley in England where he had spent many happy months as a child. Once it had been composed of delightful grassy glades; now it was becoming overgrown with unsightly brush because the rabbits that formerly kept such growth under control had largely succumbed to a disease, myxomatosis, that was deliberately introduced by the local farmers to reduce the rabbits' destruction of crops. Being something of a Philistine,[2] I could be silent no longer, even in the interests of great rhetoric. I interrupted to point out that the rabbit itself had been brought as a domestic animal to England in 1176, presumably to improve the protein diet of the peasantry.

[1] Aldous Huxley (1894–1963), British author of novels, short stories, travel books, biography, and essays. Best known for *Brave New World* (1932). [Ed.]

[2] An anti-intellectual (though obviously White is not; he was only impatient with Huxley's pedantry). [Ed.]

Source: Lynn White Jr., "The Historical Roots of Our Ecological Crisis," *Science* 155 (March 1967): 1203–7.

All forms of life modify their contexts. The most spectacular and benign instance is doubtless the coral polyp. By serving its own ends, it has created a vast undersea world favorable to thousands of other kinds of animals and plants. Ever since man became a numerous species he has affected his environment notably. The hypothesis that his firedrive[3] method of hunting created the world's great grasslands and helped to exterminate the monster mammals of the Pleistocene from much of the globe is plausible, if not proved. For six millennia at least, the banks of the lower Nile have been a human artifact rather than the swampy African jungle which nature, apart from man, would have made it. The Aswan Dam, flooding five thousand square miles, is only the latest stage in a long process. In many regions terracing or irrigation, overgrazing, and the cutting of forests by Romans to build ships to fight Carthaginians or by Crusaders to solve the logistics problems of their expeditions have profoundly changed some ecologies. Observation that the French landscape falls into two basic types, the open fields of the north and the *bocage*[4] of the south and west, inspired Marc Bloch to undertake his classic study of medieval agricultural methods. Quite unintentionally, changes in human ways often affect nonhuman nature. It has been noted, for example, that the advent of the automobile eliminated huge flocks of sparrows that once fed on the horse manure littering every street.

The history of ecologic change is still so rudimentary that we know little about what really happened, or what the results were. The extinction of the European aurochs[5] as late as 1627 would seem to have been a simple case of overenthusiastic hunting. On more intricate matters it often is impossible to find solid information. For a thousand years or more the Frisians and Hollanders have been pushing back the North Sea, and the process is culminating in our own time in the reclamation of the Zuider Zee.[6] What, if any, species of animals, birds, fish, shore life, or plants have died out in the process? In their epic combat with Neptune have the Netherlanders overlooked ecological values in such a way that the quality of human life in the Netherlands has suffered? I cannot discover that the questions have ever been asked, much less answered.

---

[3] Paleolithic hunters used fires to drive animals to their deaths. [Ed.]

[4] Full of groves or woodlands. Marc Bloch reasoned that the open fields north of the Loire River in France must have been plowed by teams of oxen and heavy plows because of the hard soil. In the south farmers could use scratch plows on the softer soil and therefore did not clear large fields, preserving more woodlands. [Ed.]

[5] A now extinct European wild ox believed to be the ancestor of European domestic cattle. [Ed.]

[6] Once a Dutch lake, it was joined to the North Sea by a flood in the thirteenth century but has since been reclaimed by the building of a dam. [Ed.]

People, then, have often been a dynamic element in their own environment, but in the present state of historical scholarship we usually do not know exactly when, where, or with what effects man-induced changes came. . . . But it was not until about four generations ago that Western Europe and North America arranged a marriage between science and technology, a union of the theoretical and the empirical approaches to our natural environment. The emergence in widespread practice of the Baconian creed that scientific knowledge means technological power over nature can scarcely be dated before about 1850, save in the chemical industries, where it is anticipated in the eighteenth century. Its acceptance as a normal pattern of action may mark the greatest event in human history since the invention of agriculture, and perhaps in nonhuman terrestrial history as well.

Almost at once the new situation forced the crystallization of the novel concept of ecology; indeed, the word *ecology* first appeared in the English language in 1873. Today, less than a century later, the impact of our race upon the environment has so increased in force that it has changed in essence. When the first cannons were fired, in the early fourteenth century, they affected ecology by sending workers scrambling to the forests and mountains for more potash, sulfur, iron ore, and charcoal, with some resulting erosion and deforestation. Hydrogen bombs are of a different order: A war fought with them might alter the genetics of all life on this planet. By 1285 London had a smog problem arising from the burning of soft coal, but our present combustion of fossil fuels threatens to change the chemistry of the globe's atmosphere as a whole, with consequences which we are only beginning to guess. With the population explosion, the carcinoma of planless urbanism, the now geological deposits of sewage and garbage, surely no creature other than man has ever managed to foul its nest in such short order. . . .

What shall we do? No one yet knows. Unless we think about fundamentals, our specific measures may produce new backlashes more serious than those they are designed to remedy.

As a beginning we should try to clarify our thinking by looking, in some historical depth, at the presuppositions that underlie modern technology and science. Science was traditionally aristocratic, speculative, intellectual in intent; technology was lower-class, empirical, action-oriented. The quite sudden fusion of these two, toward the middle of the nineteenth century, is surely related to the slightly prior and contemporary democratic revolutions which, by reducing social barriers, tended to assert a functional unity of brain and hand. Our ecologic crisis is the product of an emerging, entirely novel, democratic culture. The issue is whether a democratized world can survive its own implications. Presumably we cannot unless we rethink our axioms.

The Western Traditions of Technology and Science

One thing is so certain that it seems stupid to verbalize it: Both modern technology and modern science are distinctively *Occidental*. Our technology has absorbed elements from all over the world, notably from China; yet everywhere today, whether in Japan or in Nigeria, successful technology is Western. Our science is the heir to all the sciences of the past, especially perhaps to the work of the great Islamic scientists of the Middle Ages, who so often outdid the ancient Greeks in skill and perspicacity: al-Rāzī in medicine, for example; or ibn-al-Haytham in optics; or Omar Khayyám in mathematics. . . .

The leadership of the West, both in technology and in science, is far older than the so-called Scientific Revolution of the seventeenth century or the so-called Industrial Revolution of the eighteenth century. These terms are in fact outmoded and obscure the true nature of what they try to describe—significant stages in two long and separate developments. By A.D. 1000 at the latest—and perhaps, feebly, as much as two hundred years earlier—the West began to apply water power to industrial processes other than milling grain. This was followed in the late twelfth century by the harnessing of wind power. From simple beginnings, but with remarkable consistency of style, the West rapidly expanded its skills in the development of power machinery, labor-saving devices, and automation. Those who doubt should contemplate that most monumental achievement in the history of automation: the weight-driven mechanical clock, which appeared in two forms in the early fourteenth century. Not in craftsmanship but in basic technological capacity, the Latin West of the later Middle Ages far outstripped its elaborate, sophisticated, and esthetically magnificent sister cultures, Byzantium and Islam. In 1444 a great Greek ecclesiastic, Bessarion, who had gone to Italy, wrote a letter to a prince in Greece. He is amazed by the superiority of Western ships, arms, textiles, glass. But above all he is astonished by the spectacle of waterwheels sawing timbers and pumping the bellows of blast furnaces. Clearly, he had seen nothing of the sort in the Near East.

By the end of the fifteenth century the technological superiority of Europe was such that its small, mutually hostile nations could spill out over all the rest of the world, conquering, looting, and colonizing. The symbol of this technological superiority is the fact that Portugal, one of the weakest states of the Occident, was able to become, and to remain for a century, mistress of the East Indies. . . .

In the present-day vernacular understanding, modern science is supposed to have begun in 1543, when both Copernicus and Vesalius published their great works. It is no derogation of their accomplishments, however, to point out that such structures as the *Fabrica*[7] and the *De revolutionibus*[8] do not appear overnight. The distinctive Western tradition of science, in fact, began in the late eleventh century with a massive movement of translation of Arabic and Greek scientific works into Latin. . . . [W]ithin less than two hundred years effectively the entire corpus of Greek and Muslim science was available in Latin, and was being eagerly read and criticized in the new European universities. Out of criticism arose new observation, speculation, and increasing distrust of ancient authorities. By the late thirteenth century Europe had seized global scientific leadership from the faltering hands of Islam. . . .

Since both our technological and our scientific movements got their start, acquired their character, and achieved world dominance in the Middle Ages, it would seem that we cannot understand their nature or their present impact upon ecology without examining fundamental medieval assumptions and developments.

Medieval View of Man and Nature

Until recently, agriculture has been the chief occupation even in "advanced" societies; hence, any change in methods of tillage has much importance. Early plows, drawn by two oxen, did not normally turn the sod but merely scratched it. Thus, cross-plowing was needed and fields tended to be squarish. In the fairly light soils and semiarid climates of the Near East and Mediterranean, this worked well. But such a plow was inappropriate to the wet climate and often sticky soils of northern Europe. By the latter part of the seventh century after Christ, however, following obscure beginnings, certain northern peasants were using an entirely new kind of plow, equipped with a vertical knife to cut the line of the furrow, a horizontal share to slice under the sod, and a moldboard to turn it over. The friction of this plow with the soil was so great that it normally required not two but eight oxen. It attacked the land with such violence that cross-plowing was not needed, and fields tended to be shaped in long strips.

In the days of the scratch-plow, fields were distributed generally in units capable of supporting a single family. Subsistence farming was the presupposition. But no peasant owned eight oxen: to use the new and more efficient plow, peasants pooled their oxen to form large plowteams,

[7] *De Humani Corporis Fabrica* (1543), an illustrated work on human anatomy based on dissections, was produced by Andreas Vesalius (1514–1564), a Flemish anatomist, at the University of Padua in Italy. [Ed.]

[8] *De revolutionibus orbium coelestium* (1543; On the Revolution of Heavenly Bodies) was published by Nicolas Copernicus (1473–1543); it showed the sun as the center of a system around which the Earth revolved. [Ed.]

originally receiving (it would appear) plowed strips in proportion to their contribution. Thus, distribution of land was based no longer on the needs of a family but, rather, on the capacity of a power machine to till the earth. Man's relation to the soil was profoundly changed. Formerly man had been part of nature; now he was the exploiter of nature. Nowhere else in the world did farmers develop any analogous agricultural implement. Is it coincidence that modern technology, with its ruthlessness toward nature, has so largely been produced by descendants of these peasants of northern Europe?

This same exploitive attitude appears slightly before A.D. 830 in Western illustrated calendars. In older calendars the months were shown as passive personifications. The new Frankish calendars, which set the style for the Middle Ages, are very different: They show men coercing the world around them—plowing, harvesting, chopping trees, butchering pigs. Man and nature are two things, and man is master.

These novelties seem to be in harmony with larger intellectual patterns. What people do about their ecology depends on what they think about themselves in relation to things around them. Human ecology is deeply conditioned by beliefs about our nature and destiny—that is, by religion. . . .

The victory of Christianity over paganism was the greatest psychic revolution in the history of our culture. It has become fashionable today to say that, for better or worse, we live in "the post-Christian age." Certainly the forms of our thinking and language have largely ceased to be Christian, but to my eye the substance often remains amazingly akin to that of the past. Our daily habits of action, for example, are dominated by an implicit faith in perpetual progress which was unknown either to Greco-Roman antiquity or to the Orient. It is rooted in, and is indefensible apart from, Judeo-Christian teleology.[9] The fact that Communists share it merely helps to show what can be demonstrated on many other grounds: that Marxism, like Islam, is a Judeo-Christian heresy. We continue today to live, as we have lived for about seventeen hundred years, very largely in a context of Christian axioms.

What did Christianity tell people about their relations with the environment?

. . . Christianity inherited from Judaism not only a concept of time as nonrepetitive and linear but also a striking story of creation. By gradual stages a loving and all-powerful God had created light and darkness, the heavenly bodies, the earth and all its plants, animals, birds, and fishes. Finally, God had created Adam and, as an afterthought,

---

[9] The biblical idea that God's purpose is revealed in his creation, that human history can be seen as the result of God's intentions. [Ed.]

Eve to keep man from being lonely. Man named all the animals, thus establishing his dominance over them. God planned all of this explicitly for man's benefit and rule: No item in the physical creation had any purpose save to serve man's purposes. And, although man's body is made of clay, he is not simply part of nature: He is made in God's image.

Especially in its Western form, Christianity is the most anthropocentric religion the world has seen. As early as the second century both Tertullian and Saint Irenaeus of Lyons were insisting that when God shaped Adam he was foreshadowing the image of the incarnate Christ, the Second Adam. Man shares, in great measure, God's transcendence of nature. Christianity, in absolute contrast to ancient paganism and Asia's religions (except, perhaps, Zoroastrianism), not only established a dualism of man and nature but also insisted that it is God's will that man exploit nature for his proper ends.

At the level of the common people this worked out in an interesting way. In Antiquity every tree, every spring, every stream, every hill had its own *genius loci*, its guardian spirit. These spirits were accessible to men, but were very unlike men; centaurs, fauns, and mermaids show their ambivalence. Before one cut a tree, mined a mountain, or dammed a brook, it was important to placate the spirit in charge of that particular situation, and to keep it placated. By destroying pagan animism, Christianity made it possible to exploit nature in a mood of indifference to the feelings of natural objects. . . .

When one speaks in such sweeping terms, a note of caution is in order. Christianity is a complex faith, and its consequences differ in differing contexts. What I have said may well apply to the medieval West, where in fact technology made spectacular advances. But the Greek East, a highly civilized realm of equal Christian devotion, seems to have produced no marked technological innovation after the late seventh century, when Greek fire[10] was invented. The key to the contrast may perhaps be found in a difference in the tonality of piety and thought which students of comparative theology find between the Greek and the Latin Churches. The Greeks believed that sin was intellectual blindness, and that salvation was found in illumination, orthodoxy—that is, clear thinking. The Latins, on the other hand, felt that sin was moral evil, and that salvation was to be found in right conduct. Eastern theology has been intellectualist. Western theology has been voluntarist. The Greek saint contemplates; the Western saint acts. The implications of Christianity for the conquest of nature would emerge more easily in the Western atmosphere.

---

[10] Byzantine incendiary weapon developed about seventh century. Siphon tube spewed fire on enemy. Used especially against Arab ships (material continued to burn on water). [Ed.]

The Christian dogma of creation, which is found in the first clause of all the Creeds, has another meaning for our comprehension of today's ecologic crisis. By revelation, God had given man the Bible, the Book of Scripture. But since God had made nature, nature also must reveal the divine mentality. The religious study of nature for the better understanding of God was known as natural theology. In the early Church, and always in the Greek East, nature was conceived primarily as a symbolic system through which God speaks to men: The ant is a sermon to sluggards; rising flames are the symbol of the soul's aspiration. This view of nature was essentially artistic rather than scientific. . . .

However, in the Latin West by the early thirteenth century natural theology was following a very different bent. It was ceasing to be the decoding of the physical symbols of God's communication with man and was becoming the effort to understand God's mind by discovering how his creation operates. The rainbow was no longer simply a symbol of hope first sent to Noah after the Deluge: Robert Grosseteste, Friar Roger Bacon, and Theodoric of Freiberg produced startlingly sophisticated work on the optics of the rainbow, but they did it as a venture in religious understanding. From the thirteenth century onward, up to and including Leibnitz and Newton, every major scientist, in effect, explained his motivations in religious terms. Indeed, if Galileo had not been so expert an amateur theologian he would have got into far less trouble: The professionals resented his intrusion. And Newton seems to have regarded himself more as a theologian than as a scientist. It was not until the late eighteenth century that the hypothesis of God became unnecessary to many scientists.

It is often hard for the historian to judge, when men explain why they are doing what they want to do, whether they are offering real reasons or merely culturally acceptable reasons. The consistency with which scientists during the long formative centuries of Western science said that the task and the reward of the scientist was "to think God's thoughts after him" leads one to believe that this was their real motivation. If so, then modern Western science was cast in a matrix of Christian theology. The dynamism of religious devotion, shaped by the Judeo-Christian dogma of creation, gave it impetus.

An Alternative Christian View

We would seem to be headed toward conclusions unpalatable to many Christians. Since both *science* and *technology* are blessed words in our contemporary vocabulary, some may be happy at the notions, first, that, viewed historically, modern science is an extrapolation of natural theology and, second, that modern technology is at least partly to be explained as an Occidental, voluntarist realization of the Christian dogma of man's transcendence of, and rightful mastery over, nature. But, as we now recognize, somewhat over a century ago science and technology—hitherto quite separate activities—joined to give mankind powers which, to judge by many of the ecologic effects, are out of control. If so, Christianity bears a huge burden of guilt.

I personally doubt that disastrous ecologic backlash can be avoided simply by applying to our problems more science and more technology. Our science and technology have grown out of Christian attitudes toward man's relation to nature which are almost universally held not only by Christians and neo-Christians but also by those who fondly regard themselves as post-Christians. Despite Copernicus, all the cosmos rotates around our little globe. Despite Darwin, we are *not*, in our hearts, part of the natural process. We are superior to nature, contemptuous of it, willing to use it for our slightest whim. . . .

What we do about ecology depends on our ideas of the man-nature relationship. More science and more technology are not going to get us out of the present ecologic crisis until we find a new religion, or rethink our old one. . . .

Possibly we should ponder the greatest radical in Christian history since Christ: Saint Francis of Assisi. The prime miracle of Saint Francis is the fact that he did not end at the stake, as many of his left-wing followers did. He was so clearly heretical that a General of the Franciscan Order, Saint Bonaventura, a great and perceptive Christian, tried to suppress the early accounts of Franciscanism. The key to an understanding of Francis is his belief in the virtue of humility—not merely for the individual but for man as a species. Francis tried to depose man from his monarchy over creation and set up a democracy of all God's creatures. With him the ant is no longer simply a homily for the lazy, flames a sign of the thrust of the soul toward union with God; now they are Brother Ant and Sister Fire, praising the Creator in their own ways as Brother Man does in his.

Later commentators have said that Francis preached to the birds as a rebuke to men who would not listen. The records do not read so: He urged the little birds to praise God, and in spiritual ecstasy they flapped their wings and chirped rejoicing. Legends of saints, especially the Irish saints, had long told of their dealings with animals but always, I believe, to show their human dominance over creatures. With Francis it is different. The land around Gubbio in the Apennines was being ravaged by a fierce wolf. Saint Francis, says the legend, talked to the wolf and persuaded him of the error of his ways. The wolf repented, died in the odor of sanctity, and was buried in consecrated ground.

What Sir Steven Ruciman calls "the Franciscan doctrine of the animal soul" was quickly stamped out. . . . [St. Francis's] view of nature and of man rested on a unique sort of pan-psychism of all things animate and inanimate, designed for the glorification of their transcendent Creator, who, in the ultimate gesture of cosmic humility, assumed flesh, lay helpless in a manger, and hung dying on a scaffold.

I am not suggesting that many contemporary Americans who are concerned about our ecologic crisis will be either able or willing to counsel with wolves or exhort birds. However, the present increasing disruption of the global environment is the product of a dynamic technology and science which were originating in the Western medieval world against which Saint Francis was rebelling in so original a way. Their growth cannot be understood historically apart from distinctive attitudes toward nature which are deeply grounded in Christian dogma. The fact that most people do not think of these attitudes as Christian is irrelevant. No new set of basic values has been accepted in our society to displace those of Christianity. Hence we shall continue to have a worsening ecologic crisis until we reject the Christian axiom that nature has no reason for existence save to serve man.

The greatest spiritual revolutionary in Western history, Saint Francis, proposed what he thought was an alternative Christian view of nature and man's relation to it: He tried to substitute the idea of the equality of all creatures, including man, for the idea of man's limitless rule of creation. He failed. Both our present science and our present technology are so tinctured with orthodox Christian arrogance toward nature that no solution for our ecologic crisis can be expected from them alone. Since the roots of our trouble are so largely religious, the remedy must also be essentially religious, whether we call it that or not. We must rethink and refeel our nature and destiny. The profoundly religious, but heretical, sense of the primitive Franciscans for the spiritual autonomy of all parts of nature may point a direction. I propose Francis as a patron saint for ecologists.

2

Image from a Cistercian Manuscript, Twelfth Century

This image of a Christian monk chopping down a tree while his lay servant prunes the branches is from a manuscript of the Cistercian order of monks, from the twelfth century. The Cistercians, more than other orders, spoke out in favor of conserving forest resources, but they also celebrated manual labor. Does this image indicate that the monks were in favor of forest clearance?

Source: Image from a Cistercian manuscript, twelfth century, monk chopping tree (Dijon, Bibliothèque municipale, MS 173), duplicated in *Cambridge Illustrated History of the Middle Ages*, ed. Robert Fossier (Cambridge: Cambridge University Press, 1997), 72.

Figure 14.1 Twelfth-century manuscript.

Source: Bibliotheque municipale de Dijon, ms 173, f41.

THINKING HISTORICALLY

Does this image lend support to White's argument? Why or why not? If there were many such images, would visual evidence like this convince you of White's argument? Would it be more convincing if almost all European images of trees showed someone chopping them down and virtually no Chinese tree images showed that? In other words, how much visual evidence would convince you of White's interpretation?

3

Image from a French Calendar, Fifteenth Century

This French calendar scene for March is from the early fifteenth century. What sorts of activities does it show? How does it relate specifically to White's argument about the changing images of European calendars? (See p. 526.) The top half of the calendar shows an astrological zodiac. In what ways are these images of nature different from those in the bottom half?

THINKING HISTORICALLY

What technologies are shown here? Were any of these technologies particularly recent or European? Does this image merely illustrate White's argument, or does it support it to some extent? What other visual evidence would you want to see to be persuaded by White's argument?

Source: From *Les trés riches heures du duc de Berry*, Giraudon, Musée de Condé.

Figure 14.2 French calendar scene for March.

Source: Réunion des Musées Nationaux/Art Resource, N.Y.

4

Image of a Chinese *Feng-Shui* Master, Nineteenth Century

Although the Chinese celebrated the natural landscape in their paintings, they also created drawings that showcased their advanced technologies. The Chinese made and used the compass (as well as paper, printing, and gunpowder) long before Europeans. Instead of using it to subdue the natural world, however, they used it to find harmony with nature, specifically through the practice of *feng-shui*.* *Feng-shui*, which literally means wind over water, is the Chinese art of determining the best position and placement of structures such as houses within the natural environment. In the following image we see a type of compass used in the work of a Chinese *feng-shui* master. Before building, the *feng-shui* master would use instruments like this to ascertain the flow of energy (*chi*) on the site, resulting in new buildings that would be in harmony with, rather than obstruct, this flow. How might a compass detect energy? How was the Chinese use of a compass-like device different from the modern scientific use of the compass?

THINKING HISTORICALLY

An image has many elements to read. What information is revealed about Chinese society in this image, in addition to the scientific devices? What significance do you attach to the artist's depiction of humans and the natural setting? In what ways does this image support Lynn White Jr.'s argument? In what ways does it challenge his interpretation? On balance, do you find it more supportive or critical of White's position?

* fung SHWEE

Source: Joseph Needham, *Science and Civilization in China* (Cambridge: Cambridge University Press, 1956), 2:362.

Figure 14.3 Chinese *feng-shui* master.

5

Image of European Surveying Instruments, c. 1600

Europeans used a wide range of instruments for surveying and gunnery by 1600. Here we see various instruments for figuring the height or depth of an object by making it the third side of a triangle. What does this image show us about European ideas of the Earth and the heavens? How would this knowledge be useful in war as well as surveying? What does it suggest about European ideas of nature?

THINKING HISTORICALLY

Compare this European image with the previous Chinese image. If these images are at all representative of their cultures, what does the comparison suggest about European and Chinese attitudes toward nature? How do these images support or challenge Lynn White Jr.'s thesis?

Figure 14.4   European surveying, c. 1600.

Source: The Granger Collection, New York.

Source: Kevin Reilly, *The West and the World: A History of Civilization*, 2nd ed. (New York: Harper & Row, 1989), 344.

6

JARED DIAMOND
Easter Island's End, 1995

In comparison with the grand theory of White, an essay on a small island in the Pacific might seem to be an exercise in the recent vogue of
small-bore "micro-history." It is not. Jared Diamond, author of *Guns,
Germs, and Steel,* uses small examples to big effect. In this selection
and in his larger book-length treatment, *Collapse: How Societies Choose
to Fail or Succeed,* Diamond teases a global lesson from the history of
tiny Easter Island. What is that lesson? What does Diamond's essay
suggest about the causes of environmental decline? Are we in danger
of duplicating the fate of Easter Island? How can we avoid the fate of
Easter Island?

THINKING HISTORICALLY

How does Diamond's essay challenge the thesis of Lynn White Jr.? Do
you see in this essay an alternative grand theory for understanding
our environmental problems? If so, what is that theory? Do you agree
or disagree with it? Why or why not?

In just a few centuries, the people of Easter Island wiped out their
forest, drove their plants and animals to extinction, and saw their complex society spiral into chaos and cannibalism. Are we about to follow
their lead?

Among the most riveting mysteries of human history are those posed
by vanished civilizations. Everyone who has seen the abandoned buildings of the Khmer, the Maya, or the Anasazi is immediately moved to
ask the same question: Why did the societies that erected those structures disappear? . . .

Among all such vanished civilizations, that of the former Polynesian
society on Easter Island remains unsurpassed in mystery and isolation.
The mystery stems especially from the island's gigantic stone statues and
its impoverished landscape, but it is enhanced by our associations with
the specific people involved: Polynesians represent for us the ultimate in
exotic romance. . . .

But my interest has been revived recently by . . . painstaking research
and analysis. My friend David Steadman, a paleontologist, has been
working with a number of other researchers who are carrying out the
first systematic excavations on Easter intended to identify the animals

Source: Jared Diamond, "Easter Island's End," *Discover* 16, no. 8 (August 1995).

and plants that once lived there. Their work is contributing to a new interpretation of the island's history that makes it a tale not only of wonder but of warning as well.

Easter Island, with an area of only 64 square miles, is the world's most isolated scrap of habitable land. It lies in the Pacific Ocean more than 2,000 miles west of the nearest continent (South America), 1,400 miles from even the nearest habitable island (Pitcairn). Its subtropical location and latitude—at 27 degrees south, it is approximately as far below the equator as Houston is north of it—help give it a rather mild climate, while its volcanic origins make its soil fertile. In theory, this combination of blessings should have made Easter a miniature paradise, remote from problems that beset the rest of the world.

The island derives its name from its "discovery" by the Dutch explorer Jacob Roggeveen, on Easter (April 5) in 1722. Roggeveen's first impression was not of a paradise but of a wasteland: "We originally, from a further distance, have considered the said Easter Island as sandy; the reason for that is this, that we counted as sand the withered grass, hay, or other scorched and burnt vegetation, because its wasted appearance could give no other impression than of a singular poverty and barrenness."

The island Roggeveen saw was a grassland without a single tree or bush over ten feet high. Modern botanists have identified only 47 species of higher plants native to Easter, most of them grasses, sedges, and ferns. The list includes just two species of small trees and two of woody shrubs. With such flora, the islanders Roggeveen encountered had no source of real firewood to warm themselves during Easter's cool, wet, windy winters. Their native animals included nothing larger than insects, not even a single species of native bat, land bird, land snail, or lizard. For domestic animals, they had only chickens. European visitors throughout the eighteenth and early nineteenth centuries estimated Easter's human population at about 2,000, a modest number considering the island's fertility. As Captain James Cook recognized during his brief visit in 1774, the islanders were Polynesians (a Tahitian man accompanying Cook was able to converse with them). Yet despite the Polynesians' well-deserved fame as a great seafaring people, the Easter Islanders who came out to Roggeveen's and Cook's ships did so by swimming or paddling canoes that Roggeveen described as "bad and frail." Their craft, he wrote, were "put together with manifold small planks and light inner timbers, which they cleverly stitched together with very fine twisted threads. . . . But as they lack the knowledge and particularly the materials for caulking and making tight the great number of seams of the canoes, these are accordingly very leaky, for which reason they are compelled to spend half the time in bailing." The canoes, only ten feet long, held at most two people, and only three or four canoes were observed on the entire island.

Figure 14.5   Easter Island statues.

Source: © Westend 61 GmbH/Alamy.

With such flimsy craft, Polynesians could never have colonized Easter from even the nearest island, nor could they have traveled far offshore to fish. The islanders Roggeveen met were totally isolated, unaware that other people existed. Investigators in all the years since his visit have discovered no trace of the islanders' having any outside contacts: not a single Easter Island rock or product has turned up elsewhere, nor has anything been found on the island that could have been brought by anyone other than the original settlers or the Europeans. Yet the people living on Easter claimed memories of visiting the uninhabited Sala y Gomez reef 260 miles away, far beyond the range of the leaky canoes seen by Roggeveen. How did the islanders' ancestors reach that reef from Easter, or reach Easter from anywhere else?

Easter Island's most famous feature is its huge stone statues, more than 200 of which once stood on massive stone platforms lining the coast. [See Figure 14.5.] At least 700 more, in all stages of completion, were abandoned in quarries or on ancient roads between the quarries and the coast, as if the carvers and moving crews had thrown down their tools and walked off the job. Most of the erected statues were carved in a single quarry and then somehow transported as far as six miles — despite heights as great as 33 feet and weights up to 82 tons. The abandoned statues, meanwhile, were as much as 65 feet tall and weighed up to 270 tons. The stone platforms were equally gigantic: up to 500 feet long and 10 feet high, with facing slabs weighing up to 10 tons.

Roggeveen himself quickly recognized the problem the statues posed: "The stone images at first caused us to be struck with astonishment," he wrote, "because we could not comprehend how it was possible that these people, who are devoid of heavy thick timber for making any machines, as well as strong ropes, nevertheless had been able to erect such images." Roggeveen might have added that the islanders had no wheels, no draft animals, and no source of power except their own muscles. How did they transport the giant statues for miles, even before erecting them? To deepen the mystery, the statues were still standing in 1770, but by 1864 all of them had been pulled down, by the islanders themselves. Why then did they carve them in the first place? And why did they stop?

The statues imply a society very different from the one Roggeveen saw in 1722. Their sheer number and size suggest a population much larger than 2,000 people. What became of everyone? Furthermore, that society must have been highly organized. Easter's resources were scattered across the island: the best stone for the statues was quarried at Rano Raraku near Easter's northeast end; red stone, used for large crowns adorning some of the statues, was quarried at Puna Pau, inland in the southwest; stone carving tools came mostly from Aroi in the northwest. Meanwhile, the best farmland lay in the south and east, and the best fishing grounds on the north and west coasts. Extracting and redistributing all those goods required complex political organization. What happened to that organization, and how could it ever have arisen in such a barren landscape? . . .

[There is] overwhelming evidence that the Easter Islanders were typical Polynesians derived from Asia rather than from the Americas and that their culture (including their statues) grew out of Polynesian culture. Their language was Polynesian, as Cook had already concluded. Specifically, they spoke an eastern Polynesian dialect related to Hawaiian and Marquesan, a dialect isolated since about A.D. 400, as estimated from slight differences in vocabulary. Their fishhooks and stone adzes resembled early Marquesan models. Last year DNA extracted from 12 Easter Island skeletons was also shown to be Polynesian. The islanders grew bananas, taro, sweet potatoes, sugarcane, and paper mulberry—typical Polynesian crops, mostly of Southeast Asian origin. Their sole domestic animal, the chicken, was also typically Polynesian and ultimately Asian, as were the rats that arrived as stowaways in the canoes of the first settlers.

What happened to those settlers? The fanciful theories of the past must give way to evidence gathered by hardworking practitioners in three fields: archeology, pollen analysis, and paleontology. Modern archeological excavations on Easter have continued since Heyerdahl's 1955 expedition. The earliest radiocarbon dates associated with human activities are around A.D. 400 to 700, in reasonable agreement with the approximate settlement date of 400 estimated by linguists. The period of statue construction peaked around 1200 to 1500, with few if any statues erected thereafter. Densities of archeological sites suggest a large population; an estimate of 7,000 people is widely quoted by archeologists, but other estimates range up to 20,000, which does not seem implausible for an island of Easter's area and fertility.

Archeologists have also enlisted surviving islanders in experiments aimed at figuring out how the statues might have been carved and erected. Twenty people, using only stone chisels, could have carved even the largest completed statue within a year. Given enough timber and fiber for making ropes, teams of at most a few hundred people could have loaded the statues onto wooden sleds, dragged them over lubricated wooden tracks or rollers, and used logs as levers to maneuver them into a standing position. Rope could have been made from the fiber of a small native tree, related to the linden, called the hauhau. However, that tree is now extremely scarce on Easter, and hauling one statue would have required hundreds of yards of rope. Did Easter's now barren landscape once support the necessary trees? . . .

. . . [Pollen analysis reveals that for] at least 30,000 years before human arrival and during the early years of Polynesian settlement, Easter was not a wasteland at all. Instead, a subtropical forest of trees and woody bushes towered over a ground layer of shrubs, herbs, ferns, and grasses. . . . The tall, unbranched trunks of the Easter Island palm would have been ideal for transporting and erecting statues and constructing large canoes. The palm would also have been a valuable food source, since its [still-surviving] Chilean relative yields edible nuts as well as sap from which Chileans make sugar, syrup, honey, and wine.

What did the first settlers of Easter Island eat when they were not glutting themselves on the local equivalent of maple syrup? Recent excavations by David Steadman, of the New York State Museum at Albany, have yielded a picture of Easter's original animal world as surprising as Flenley and King's picture of its plant world. . . . Less than a quarter of the bones in its early garbage heaps (from the period 900 to 1300) belonged to fish; instead, nearly one-third of all bones came from porpoises.

Nowhere else in Polynesia do porpoises account for even 1 percent of discarded food bones. But most other Polynesian islands offered animal food in the form of birds and mammals. . . . The porpoise species identified at Easter, the common dolphin, weighs up to 165 pounds. It generally lives out at sea, so it could not have been hunted by line fishing or spearfishing from shore. Instead, it must have been harpooned far offshore, in big seaworthy canoes built from the extinct palm tree.

In addition to porpoise meat, Steadman found, the early Polynesian settlers were feasting on seabirds. For those birds, Easter's remoteness and lack of predators made it an ideal haven as a breeding site, at least until humans arrived. Among the prodigious numbers of seabirds that bred on Easter were albatross, boobies, frigate birds, fulmars, petrels, prions, shearwaters, storm petrels, terns, and tropic birds. With at least 25 nesting species, Easter was the richest seabird breeding site in Polynesia and probably in the whole Pacific. Land birds as well went into early Easter Island cooking pots. . . .

Porpoises, seabirds, land birds, and rats did not complete the list of meat sources formerly available on Easter. A few bones hint at the possibility of breeding seal colonies as well. All these delicacies were cooked in ovens fired by wood from the island's forests.

Such evidence lets us imagine the island onto which Easter's first Polynesian colonists stepped ashore some 1,600 years ago, after a long canoe voyage from eastern Polynesia. They found themselves in a pristine paradise. What then happened to it? The pollen grains and the bones yield a grim answer.

Pollen records show that destruction of Easter's forests was well under way by the year 800, just a few centuries after the start of human settlement. Then charcoal from wood fires came to fill the sediment cores, while pollen of palms and other trees and woody shrubs decreased or disappeared, and pollen of the grasses that replaced the forest became more abundant. Not long after 1400 the palm finally became extinct, not only as a result of being chopped down but also because the now ubiquitous rats prevented its regeneration: of the dozens of preserved palm nuts discovered in caves on Easter, all had been chewed by rats and could no longer germinate. While the hauhau tree did not become extinct in Polynesian times, its numbers declined drastically until there weren't enough left to make ropes from. By the time Heyerdahl visited Easter, only a single, nearly dead toromiro tree remained on the island, and even that lone survivor has now disappeared. (Fortunately, the toromiro still grows in botanical gardens elsewhere.)

The fifteenth century marked the end not only for Easter's palm but for the forest itself. Its doom had been approaching as people cleared land to plant gardens; as they felled trees to build canoes, to transport and erect statues, and to burn; as rats devoured seeds; and probably as the native birds died out that had pollinated the trees' flowers and dispersed their fruit. The overall picture is among the most extreme examples of forest destruction anywhere in the world: the whole forest gone, and most of its tree species extinct.

The destruction of the island's animals was as extreme as that of the forest: without exception, every species of native land bird became extinct. Even shellfish were overexploited, until people had to settle for small sea snails instead of larger cowries. Porpoise bones disappeared abruptly from garbage heaps around 1500; no one could harpoon porpoises anymore, since the trees used for constructing the big seagoing canoes no longer existed. The colonies of more than half of the seabird species breeding on Easter or on its offshore islets were wiped out.

In place of these meat supplies, the Easter Islanders intensified their production of chickens, which had been only an occasional food item. They also turned to the largest remaining meat source available: humans, whose bones became common in late Easter Island garbage heaps. Oral traditions of the islanders are rife with cannibalism; the most inflammatory taunt that could be snarled at an enemy was "The flesh of your mother sticks between my teeth." With no wood available to cook these new goodies, the islanders resorted to sugarcane scraps, grass, and sedges to fuel their fires.

All these strands of evidence can be wound into a coherent narrative of a society's decline and fall. The first Polynesian colonists found themselves on an island with fertile soil, abundant food, bountiful building materials, ample lebensraum,[1] and all the prerequisites for comfortable living. They prospered and multiplied.

After a few centuries, they began erecting stone statues on platforms, like the ones their Polynesian forebears had carved. With passing years, the statues and platforms became larger and larger, and the statues began sporting ten-ton red crowns — probably in an escalating spiral of one-upmanship, as rival clans tried to surpass each other with shows of wealth and power. . . .

Eventually Easter's growing population was cutting the forest more rapidly than the forest was regenerating. The people used the land for gardens and the wood for fuel, canoes, and houses — and, of course, for lugging statues. As forest disappeared, the islanders ran out of timber and rope to transport and erect their statues. Life became more uncomfortable — springs and streams dried up, and wood was no longer available for fires.

People also found it harder to fill their stomachs, as land birds, large sea snails, and many seabirds disappeared. Because timber for building seagoing canoes vanished, fish catches declined and porpoises disappeared from the table. Crop yields also declined, since deforestation allowed the soil to be eroded by rain and wind, dried by the sun, and its nutrients to be leeched from it. Intensified chicken production and cannibalism replaced only part of all those lost foods. Preserved statuettes with sunken cheeks and visible ribs suggest that people were starving.

With the disappearance of food surpluses, Easter Island could no longer feed the chiefs, bureaucrats, and priests who had kept a complex society running. Surviving islanders described to early European visitors how local chaos replaced centralized government and a warrior class took over from the hereditary chiefs. The stone points of spears and daggers, made by the warriors during their heyday in the 1600s and 1700s, still litter the ground of Easter today. By around 1700, the population began to crash toward between one-quarter and one-tenth of its former number. People took to living in caves for protection against their enemies. Around 1770 rival clans started to topple each other's statues, breaking the heads off. By 1864 the last statue had been thrown down and desecrated.

[1] Room to live. [Ed.]

As we try to imagine the decline of Easter's civilization, we ask ourselves, "Why didn't they look around, realize what they were doing, and stop before it was too late? What were they thinking when they cut down the last palm tree?"

I suspect, though, that the disaster happened not with a bang but with a whimper. After all, there are those hundreds of abandoned statues to consider. The forest the islanders depended on for rollers and rope didn't simply disappear one day — it vanished slowly, over decades. Perhaps war interrupted the moving teams; perhaps by the time the carvers had finished their work, the last rope snapped. In the meantime, any islander who tried to warn about the dangers of progressive deforestation would have been overridden by vested interests of carvers, bureaucrats, and chiefs, whose jobs depended on continued deforestation. Our Pacific Northwest loggers are only the latest in a long line of loggers to cry, "Jobs over trees!" The changes in forest cover from year to year would have been hard to detect: yes, this year we cleared those woods over there, but trees are starting to grow back again on this abandoned garden site here. . . .

Gradually trees became fewer, smaller, and less important. By the time the last fruit-bearing adult palm tree was cut, palms had long since ceased to be of economic significance. That left only smaller and smaller palm saplings to clear each year, along with other bushes and treelets. No one would have noticed the felling of the last small palm.

By now the meaning of Easter Island for us should be chillingly obvious. Easter Island is Earth writ small. Today, again, a rising population confronts shrinking resources. We too have no emigration valve, because all human societies are linked by international transport, and we can no more escape into space than the Easter Islanders could flee into the ocean. If we continue to follow our present course, we shall have exhausted the world's major fisheries, tropical rain forests, fossil fuels, and much of our soil by the time my sons reach my current age.

. . . Our risk now is of winding down, slowly, in a whimper. Corrective action is blocked by vested interests, by well-intentioned political and business leaders, and by their electorates, all of whom are perfectly correct in not noticing big changes from year to year. Instead, each year there are just somewhat more people, and somewhat fewer resources, on Earth. It would be easy to close our eyes or to give up in despair. If mere thousands of Easter Islanders with only stone tools and their own muscle power sufficed to destroy their society, how can billions of people with metal tools and machine power fail to do worse? But there is one crucial difference. The Easter Islanders had no books and no histories of other doomed societies. Unlike the Easter Islanders, we have histories of the past — information that can save us. My main hope for my sons' generation is that we may now choose to learn from the fates of societies like Easter's.

7

TERRY HUNT

Rethinking the Fall of Easter Island, 2006

The author, an anthropologist specializing in Polynesia, thinks research on Easter Island shows different causes for the collapse of the Rapanui culture than those put forth by Jared Diamond in the previous selection. What are these different causes? How persuasive is Hunt's argument and evidence?

THINKING HISTORICALLY

This is an article that challenges a grand theory; it does not propose one. What is the grand theory that Hunt challenges? What is his challenge? How persuasive do you find his challenge? What, if anything, remains of Diamond's grand theory that is still convincing to you? What parts of Hunt's essay could be used to construct an alternative grand theory about ecological change? What would that theory be?

Every year, thousands of tourists from around the world take a long flight across the South Pacific to see the famous stone statues of Easter Island. Since 1722, when the first Europeans arrived, these megalithic figures, or *moai*, have intrigued visitors. Interest in how these artifacts were built and moved led to another puzzling question: What happened to the people who created them?

In the prevailing account of the island's past, the native inhabitants — who refer to themselves as the Rapanui and to the island as Rapa Nui — once had a large and thriving society, but they doomed themselves by degrading their environment. According to this version of events, a small group of Polynesian settlers arrived around 800 to 900 A.D., and the island's population grew slowly at first. Around 1200 A.D., their growing numbers and an obsession with building moai led to increased pressure on the environment. By the end of the 17th century, the Rapanui had deforested the island, triggering war, famine and cultural collapse.

Jared Diamond, a geographer and physiologist at the University of California, Los Angeles, has used Rapa Nui as a parable of the dangers of environmental destruction. "In just a few centuries," he wrote in a 1995 article for *Discover* magazine, "the people of Easter Island wiped out their forest, drove their plants and animals to extinction, and saw

Source: Terry Hunt, "Rethinking the Fall of Easter Island," *American Scientist* 94 (May 2006): 412–19.

their complex society spiral into chaos and cannibalism. Are we about to follow their lead?" In his 2005 book *Collapse*, Diamond described Rapa Nui as "the clearest example of a society that destroyed itself by overexploiting its own resources."

Two key elements of Diamond's account are the large number of Polynesians living on the island and their propensity for felling trees. He reviews estimates of the island's native population and says that he would not be surprised if it exceeded 15,000 at its peak. Once the large stands of palm trees were all cut down, the result was "starvation, a population crash, and a descent into cannibalism." When Europeans arrived in the 18th century, they found only a small remnant of this civilization.

Diamond is certainly not alone in seeing Rapa Nui as an environmental morality tale. In their book *Easter Island, Earth Island*, authors John R. Flenley of Massey University in New Zealand and Paul G. Bahn worried about what the fate of Rapa Nui means for the rest of human civilization: "Humankind's covetousness is boundless. Its selfishness appears to be genetically inborn. . . . But in a limited ecosystem, selfishness leads to increasing population imbalance, population crash, and ultimately extinction."

When I first went to Rapa Nui to conduct archaeological research, I expected to help confirm this story. Instead, I found evidence that just didn't fit the underlying timeline. As I looked more closely at data from earlier archaeological excavations and at some similar work on other Pacific islands, I realized that much of what was claimed about Rapa Nui's prehistory was speculation. I am now convinced that self-induced environmental collapse simply does not explain the fall of the Rapanui.

Radiocarbon dates from work I conducted with a colleague and a number of students over the past several years and related paleoenvironmental data point to a different explanation for what happened on this small isle. The story is more complex than usually depicted.

The first colonists may not have arrived until centuries later than has been thought, and they did not travel alone. They brought along chickens and rats, both of which served as sources of food. More important, however, was what the rats ate. These prolific rodents may have been the primary cause of the island's environmental degradation. Using Rapa Nui as an example of "ecocide," as Diamond has called it, makes for a compelling narrative, but the reality of the island's tragic history is no less meaningful.

Early Investigations

More than 3,000 kilometers of ocean separate Rapa Nui from South America, the nearest continent. The closest habitable island is Pitcairn (settled by the infamous *Bounty* mutineers in the 18th century), which lies more than 2,000 kilometers to the west. Rapa Nui is small, only about 171 square kilometers, and it lies just south of the tropics, so its climate is somewhat less inviting than many tropical Pacific islands. Strong winds bearing salt spray and wide fluctuations in rainfall can make agriculture difficult.

The flora and fauna of Rapa Nui are limited. Other than chickens and rats, there are few land vertebrates. Many of the species of birds that once inhabited the island are now locally extinct. Large palm trees from the genus *Jubaea* long covered much of the island, but they, too, eventually disappeared. A recent survey of the island found only 48 different kinds of native plants, including 14 introduced by the Rapanui.

Accounts by European visitors to Rapa Nui have been used to argue that by the time of European discovery in 1722 the Rapanui were in a state of decline, but the reports are sometimes contradictory. In his log, Dutch explorer Jacob Roggeveen, who led the first Europeans to set foot on Rapa Nui, portrayed the island as impoverished and treeless. After they left, however, Roggeveen and the commanders of his three ships described it as "exceedingly fruitful, producing bananas, potatoes, sugar-cane of remarkable thickness, and many other kinds of the fruits of the earth. . . . This land, as far as its rich soil and good climate are concerned is such that it might be made into an earthly Paradise, if it were properly worked and cultivated." In his own account of the voyage, one of Roggeveen's commanders later wrote that he had spotted "whole tracts of woodland" in the distance.

A 19th-century European visitor, J. L. Palmer, stated in the *Journal of the Royal Geographic Society* that he had seen "boles of large trees, Edwardsia, coco palm, and hibiscus." Coconut trees are a recent introduction to the island, so Palmer might have seen the now-extinct *Jubaea* palm. . . .

Rats in Paradise

For thousands of years, most of Rapa Nui was covered with palm trees. Pollen records show that the *Jubaea* palm became established at least 35,000 years ago and survived a number of climatic and environmental changes. But by the time Roggeveen arrived in 1722, most of these large stands of forest had disappeared.

It is not a new observation that virtually all of the shells housing palm seeds found in caves or archaeological excavations of Rapa Nui show evidence of having been gnawed on by rats, but the impact of rats on the island's fate may have been underestimated. Evidence from elsewhere in the Pacific shows that rats have often contributed to deforestation, and they may have played a major role in Rapa Nui's environmental degradation as well. . . .

Whether rats were stowaways or a source of protein for the Polynesian voyagers, they would have found a welcoming environment on Rapa Nui—an almost unlimited supply of high-quality food and, other than people, no predators. In such an ideal setting, rats can reproduce so quickly that their population doubles about every six or seven weeks. A single mating pair could thus reach a population of almost 17 million in just over three years. On Kure Atoll in the Hawaiian Islands, at a latitude similar to Rapa Nui but with a smaller supply of food, the population density of the Polynesian rat was reported in the 1970s to have reached 45 per acre. On Rapa Nui, that would equate to a rat population of more than 1.9 million. At a density of 75 per acre, which would not be unreasonable given the past abundance of food, the rat population could have exceeded 3.1 million.

The evidence from elsewhere in the Pacific makes it hard to believe that rats would not have caused rapid and widespread environmental degradation. But there is still the question of how much of an effect rats had relative to the changes caused by humans, who cut down trees for a number of uses and practiced slash-and-burn agriculture. I believe that there is substantial evidence that it was rats, more so than humans, that led to deforestation. . . .

A Misplaced Metaphor?

. . . The first settlers arrived from other Polynesian islands around 1200 A.D. Their numbers grew quickly, perhaps at about three percent annually, which would be similar to the rapid growth shown to have taken place elsewhere in the Pacific. On Pitcairn Island, for example, the population increased by about 3.4 percent per year following the appearance of the *Bounty* mutineers in 1790. For Rapa Nui, three percent annual growth would mean that a colonizing population of 50 would have grown to more than a thousand in about a century. The rat population would have exploded even more quickly, and the combination of humans cutting down trees and rats eating the seeds would have led to rapid deforestation. Thus, in my view, there was no extended period during which the human population lived in some sort of idyllic balance with the fragile environment.

It also appears that the islanders began building moai and ahu soon after reaching the island. The human population probably reached a maximum of about 3,000, perhaps a bit higher, around 1350 A.D. and remained fairly stable until the arrival of Europeans. The environmental limitations of Rapa Nui would have kept the population from growing much larger. By the time Roggeveen arrived in 1722, most of the island's trees were gone, but deforestation did not trigger societal collapse, as Diamond and others have argued.

There is no reliable evidence that the island's population ever grew as large as 15,000 or more, and the actual downfall of the Rapanui resulted not from internal strife but from contact with Europeans. When Roggeveen landed on Rapa Nui's shores in 1722, a few days after Easter (hence the island's name), he took more than 100 of his men with him, and all were armed with muskets, pistols and cutlasses. Before he had advanced very far, Roggeveen heard shots from the rear of the party. He turned to find 10 or 12 islanders dead and a number of others wounded. His sailors claimed that some of the Rapanui had made threatening gestures. Whatever the provocation, the result did not bode well for the island's inhabitants.

Newly introduced diseases, conflict with European invaders and enslavement followed over the next century and a half, and these were the chief causes of the collapse. In the early 1860s, more than a thousand Rapanui were taken from the island as slaves, and by the late 1870s the number of native islanders numbered only around 100. In 1888, the island was annexed by Chile. It remains part of that country today.

In the 1930s, French ethnographer Alfred Metraux visited the island. He later described the demise of Rapa Nui as "one of the most hideous atrocities committed by white men in the South Seas." It was genocide, not ecocide, that caused the demise of the Rapanui. An ecological catastrophe did occur on Rapa Nui, but it was the result of a number of factors, not just human short-sightedness. . . .

8

J. R. McNEILL

Sustainable Survival, 2010

Like the previous selection, this article begins with an evaluation of Jared Diamond's *Collapse: How Societies Choose to Fail or Succeed*. But as an environmental historian, McNeill turns to his own broad view of environmental history in order to frame his own theory about ecologically sustainable societies. What is that view? How is it different from Diamond's?

Source: J. R. McNeill, "Sustainable Survival," in Patricia A. McAnany and Norman Yoffee, eds., *Questioning Collapse: Human Resilience, Ecological Vulnerability, and the Aftermath of Empire* (Cambridge: Cambridge University Press, 2010), 360–65.

THINKING HISTORICALLY

McNeill writes that our environmental problems today are too different from those of Easter Island (or the other historical cases Diamond discusses) for them to be of use to us today. If he is right, what sort of history would be useful to us today? Does McNeill's own grand survey of environmental history offer useful lessons to solve our problems? If so, what are those lessons?

Judgments of success or failure, survival or collapse, are often more difficult to make than we might wish. Perspective and context matter. Can a society that survived a century be counted a success whereas one that lasted 450 years count as a failure? Can one that responds to environmental stresses by migration be judged a failure whereas one that responds by conquering neighboring lands, or enlisting resources from other continents, be judged a success?

Simplicity has its virtues, especially when trying to stir an audience to action. In *Collapse,* Diamond appears motivated by a deep concern for the environmental state of the earth. I find this prudent, appropriate, and laudable. Many environmentalists face choices between what is most intellectually rigorous (which usually involves admitting to legions of uncertainties) and what is most likely to rally people to action (which usually involves skating over uncertainties). Different authors will make different choices when confronted with this dilemma, and careful readers will be interested in them. Diamond many times acknowledges uncertainties, especially with archeological evidence. But he nevertheless has chosen to rally readers as best he can even when it leads him into intellectual difficulties.

Sustained Survival

Diamond's laudable concern for the avoidance of collapse, for sustained survival, raises the question of what that might mean. To Diamond it apparently means the maintenance of levels of population and social complexity in a given place. But there are other ways to see it. One, which is of particular interest to many anthropologists, is the maintenance of a culture. In this view survival consists of the maintenance of whatever the preferred markers of a culture may be, such as language or religion. Whether a million people share this culture or only a few thousand is less important, so long as the culture survives. Whether those sharing this culture live in cities, with complex social hierarchies, or in villages, is less important. Whether those sharing this culture live where their ancestors did, or have migrated elsewhere, is less important. What is important is that the culture survives. This is also often important to bearers of a given culture, especially if they are migrants, not just to anthropologists. The indefinite survival of Chinese culture means a lot to many Chinese, whether they live in China or in California. As chapters in this book emphasize, the same is true for some cultural (and biological) descendants of the ancient Maya and Anasazi today.

Another way to look at sustained survival is through a political lens. For some people what matters most is the survival of a specific polity, rather than a culture, or certain levels of population and complexity. This is especially true in times and places where people identify, via nationalism or some other mechanism, with their state. One thousand or 3,000 years ago almost no one aside from royalty cared about the survival of a given state. But royalty and their allies went to great lengths to try to perpetuate their own states, not least by doing all within their power to encourage ethnic, tribal, nationalist, or religious identification of the population with the state. More recently broader segments of societies have identified with their states and often have made great efforts, through voluntary military service, for example, to advance the interests of their states.

The boundary between cultural survival and political survival is, of course, often permeable. Sometimes it seems that the best way to perpetuate one's preferred culture is through the perpetuation of the state that most embodies it. Many Jews presumably feel this way about Israel, Finns about Finland, and Vietnamese about Vietnam.

In the end, of course, no culture or polity lasts forever. Survival is provisional. None of the states in existence 1,500 years ago exist today. Only with the most flexible of definitions could one say that any of the cultures in existence 1,500 years ago exist today. But for most people, this does not matter. Political or cultural survival in the short term is often worth, for most people, considerable sacrifice, even if, when seen in the long run, it is all in vain.

A third way to look at sustained survival is through an ecological lens. Diamond does this himself, emphasizing environmental factors in his analyses of various collapses. But are there any enduring ecological success stories, any cases of sustainable survival that lasted longer than the Tokugawa regime or the Dominican Republic? The answer, I think, is that there are, but they are not many, and none of them are of much use as a direct example to help us resolve the problems of today.

The most enduring ecologically sustainable societies in human history have been those that did not practice agriculture. For the great majority of the human time on earth, our ancestors foraged for food and other materials they needed. They had local environmental impacts, often unhelpful from the point of view of ensuring their own survival.

But because they were few in number and the earth large, they could always walk somewhere else and find more of what they needed. The key was mobility and sparse population. It was probably a demanding life in several respects, but it was ecologically sustainable.

With the emergence of agriculture, which happened several times in several places but for the first time probably around 11,000 years ago, sustainability became a potential problem. All farming is a struggle against the depletion of soil nutrients. Crops absorb nutrients; these are eaten by people or animals; then they spend shorter or longer periods of time in human or animal bodies, before returning to the soil. If these nutrients in one manner or another return to farmers' fields, then a nutrient cycle can last indefinitely. If they do not, then those fields gradually lose nutrients and over time produce less and less food—unless some intervention such as fertilizer counteracts nutrient loss. In most farming systems, some nutrients were returned to farmers' fields as manure, "night soil," or ashes, but some was lost. In systems of shifting agriculture, where farmers raise a crop for a few years and then abandon plots for a decade or more, nutrient loss is checked. But in farming systems that supplied cities, many more nutrients were lost, because they were exported, as food, to distant places and never returned as night soil or manure. In places where soils were deep and rich, the nutrient problem might safely be ignored for centuries. But not forever.

In a few important situations, farming societies overcame this fundamental nutrient problem. Perhaps the most durable, the gold-medal winner for ecological sustainability, was Egypt. For 7,500 years people have been farming in Egypt. Until 1971 they did so in an ecologically sustainable manner. The source of Egypt's success and ecological continuity is not that elites chose to succeed in recognition of their broader interests. Rather, it is, or was, the silt carried by the Nile flood. Every year, except in the worst droughts, the Nile flooded and deposited on its banks and throughout its delta a nutrient-rich silt from the volcanic highlands of Ethiopia. In effect, Ethiopia's erosion subsidized Egyptian farmers, allowing them to sidestep problems of nutrient loss and sustainability. The annual flood also carried plenty of organic matter from the wetlands of southern Sudan (the Sudd), further enriching the silt that settled on Egyptian fields. This happy situation came to an end only when the Aswan High Dam was completed in 1971, and the Nile's silt began to accumulate in the dam's reservoir instead of spreading over farmers' fields. Nowadays Egypt is one of the world's greatest importers of artificial fertilizers—and of food—and is as far from ecological sustainability as a society can be.

Between the introduction of farming in Egypt and 1971 tremendous changes took place. One political regime followed another. The culture of the earliest Egyptians disappeared under layers of Pharaonic Egyptian,

Greek, Roman, Byzantine, and Arab cultures, marbled with numerous other influences. Through it all, farmers won their daily bread from the banks of the Nile by combining seed and silt with the sweat of their brows.

Southern China and Medieval Europe also developed more or less sustainable agricultural systems as long as 1,000 to 1,500 years ago. In China it involved an interlocking system of paddy rice, fish ponds, and mulberry trees (for silkworm cultivation), which kept nutrients cycling within an almost closed system. Medieval European agriculture, if not supporting cities, was also very nearly sustainable, as livestock browsed in woodlands and in "outfields" and brought their manure to "infields," thereby constantly topping up the nutrient supply. As one sixteenth-century Polish nobleman put it, "manure is worth more than a man with a doctorate."

Like Egypt, these systems were ecologically successful over long periods of time, far longer than any of the successes offered by Diamond. States, rulers, and — in Europe if not in China — cultures came and went, but these farming systems endured. As in Egypt, their success did not result from wise leadership, but instead from centuries of trial and error and some favorable circumstances. This means that they cannot serve Diamond's hortatory purposes. He could scarcely offer them as hopeful examples for humankind today, even if they proved far more durable than, say, the ecological systems of the twentieth-century Dominican Republic or Tokugawa Japan.

Sustained survival can come in different forms, depending on what one most values. If it is ecological sustainability one prizes above other forms of continuity, then Egypt before 1971 deserves the highest marks. But it is well to remember Egypt was a unique case, the gift of the Nile.

The environmental problems that bedevil the world today are, for better or for worse, vastly different from those that beset Tokugawa Japan or Easter Island. They are different in scale, as Diamond recognizes. They do not, for the most part, readily lend themselves to solution via wise decisions by enlightened leaders, because they are all complicated, and many of them derive in large measure from the energy system that has gradually come to prevail over the past 200 years: a fossil fuel energy system.

Fossil fuels function as an Ethiopian highlands for the modern world: they represent an enormous subsidy, not from a distant place, but from a distant time, the carboniferous era. They make it possible for 6.5 billion people to eat. Fossil fuels are the fertilizer of modern agriculture. They pump up groundwater and power tractors. They serve as the feedstocks for pesticides and herbicides. They make nitrogenous fertilizers practical. And they power the vehicles that move crops to kitchens. They sustain us.

But they also make us unsustainable. First and most obviously, they exist in limited supply. Predictions of the imminent exhaustion of coal and oil go back at least to the 1860s and have always proved wrong so far. But they are not fundamentally wrong. A time will come when all that is left is too difficult to extract at reasonable cost. For oil this might be ten years off or 100. For coal it will be longer. But it will come—unless we abandon fossil fuels first. Second, fossil fuels make our global society unsustainable because of climate change. Roughly three-quarters of the carbon dioxide emitted into the atmosphere derives from the combustion of fossil fuels (most of the rest comes from the burning of biomass and destruction of forests). This has been warming the earth's atmosphere for at least the last few decades, and probably the last 150 years. If we were to use fossil fuels for the next 200 years as we have used them for the last 200, we are likely to raise temperature and sea level (through thermal expansion) to levels not experienced on earth at any time in the human career, indeed, not in many millions of years.

Our ways are radically unsustainable. Diamond is right to be concerned by that. He is right to prefer hope to despair, and admirable in that he has used his fame to draw attention to issues of sustainability. But he is, as often as not, wrong in his judgments about successes and failures among societies of the past.

9

SIMON ROMERO

Once Hidden by Forest, Carvings in Land Attest to Amazon's Lost World, 2012

We have already noted the growth of cities in the Western Hemisphere almost contemporaneously with the earliest cities in the Middle East. But the largest cities of the Americas were situated on the Pacific Coast of the Andes in what is now Peru (see Document 2.7) and in what is today Guatemala and Mexico (see Documents 13.6 and 13.7). In recent decades historians have also recognized the role of cities in the Mississippi valley, the Eastern woodlands, and the southwest of what is now the United States. But few specialists have paid any attention to what is today the vast Amazon rain forest—except to see it as a perpetual natural resource, untouched by

Source: Simon Romero, "Once Hidden by Forest, Carvings in Land Attest to Amazon's Lost World," *New York Times*, January 15, 2012, A6.

urbanites until very recently. How does this article challenge that idea? How does it change your understanding of environmental history?

THINKING HISTORICALLY

How would you compare this history of the Amazon with the history of Easter Island?

"I know that this will not sit well with ardent environmentalists," one of the scientists quoted in this article says. Why wouldn't it? Do the discoveries discussed in this article challenge any of our grand theories about the environment? If so, what? How can we use this information to construct a better grand theory of historical change? How can we use this new information to make us better protectors of our natural environment?

Edmar Araújo still remembers the awe.

As he cleared trees on his family's land decades ago near Rio Branco, an outpost in the far western reaches of the Brazilian Amazon, a series of deep earthen avenues carved into the soil came into focus.

"These lines were too perfect not to have been made by man," said Mr. Araújo, a 62-year-old cattleman. "The only explanation I had was that they must have been trenches for the war against the Bolivians."

But these were no foxholes, at least not for any conflict waged here at the dawn of the 20th century. According to stunning archaeological discoveries here in recent years, the earthworks on Mr. Araújo's land and hundreds like them nearby are much, much older — potentially upending the conventional understanding of the world's largest tropical rain forest.

The deforestation that has stripped the Amazon since the 1970s has also exposed a long-hidden secret lurking underneath thick rain forest: flawlessly designed geometric shapes spanning hundreds of yards in diameter.

Alceu Ranzi, a Brazilian scholar who helped discover the squares, octagons, circles, rectangles and ovals that make up the land carvings, said these geoglyphs found on deforested land were as significant as the famous Nazca lines, the enigmatic animal symbols visible from the air in southern Peru.

"What impressed me the most about these geoglyphs was their geometric precision, and how they emerged from forest we had all been taught was untouched except by a few nomadic tribes," said Mr. Ranzi, a paleontologist who first saw the geoglyphs in the 1970s and, years later, surveyed them by plane.

For some scholars of human history in Amazonia, the geoglyphs in the Brazilian state of Acre and other archaeological sites suggest that the forests of the western Amazon, previously considered uninhabitable for sophisticated societies partly because of the quality of their soils, may not have been as "Edenic" as some environmentalists contend.

Instead of being pristine forests, barely inhabited by people, parts of the Amazon may have been home for centuries to large populations numbering well into the thousands and living in dozens of towns connected by road networks, explains the American writer Charles C. Mann. In fact, according to Mr. Mann, the British explorer Percy Fawcett vanished on his 1925 quest to find the lost "City of Z" in the Xingu, one area with such urban settlements.

In addition to parts of the Amazon being "much more thickly populated than previously thought," Mr. Mann, the author of "1491," a groundbreaking book about the Americas before the arrival of Columbus, said, "these people purposefully modified their environment in long-lasting ways."

As a result of long stretches of such human habitation, South America's colossal forests may have been a lot smaller at times, with big areas resembling relatively empty savannas.

Such revelations do not fit comfortably into today's politically charged debate over razing parts of the forests, with some environmentalists opposed to allowing any large-scale agriculture, like cattle ranching and soybean cultivation, to advance further into Amazonia.

Scientists here say they, too, oppose wholesale burning of the forests, even if research suggests that the Amazon supported intensive agriculture in the past. Indeed, they say other swaths of the tropics, notably in Africa, could potentially benefit from strategies once used in the Amazon to overcome soil constraints.

"If one wants to recreate pre-Columbian Amazonia, most of the forest needs to be removed, with many people and a managed, highly productive landscape replacing it," said William Woods, a geographer at the University of Kansas who is part of a team studying the Acre geoglyphs.

"I know that this will not sit well with ardent environmentalists," Mr. Woods said, "but what else can one say?"

While researchers piece together the Amazon's ecological history, mystery still shrouds the origins of the geoglyphs and the people who made them. So far, 290 such earthworks have been found in Acre, along with about 70 others in Bolivia and 30 in the Brazilian states of Amazonas and Rondônia.

Researchers first viewed the geoglyphs in the 1970s, after Brazil's military dictatorship encouraged settlers to move to Acre and other parts of the Amazon, using the nationalist slogan "occupy to avoid surrendering" to justify the settlement that resulted in deforestation.

But little scientific attention was paid to the discovery until Mr. Ranzi, the Brazilian scientist, began his surveys in the late 1990s, and Brazilian, Finnish and American researchers began finding more geoglyphs by using high-resolution satellite imagery and small planes to fly over the Amazon.

Denise Schaan, an archaeologist at the Federal University of Pará in Brazil who now leads research on the geoglyphs, said radiocarbon testing indicated that they were built 1,000 to 2,000 years ago, and might have been rebuilt several times during that period.

Initially, Ms. Schaan said, researchers, pondering the 20-foot depth of some of the trenches, thought they were used to defend against attacks. But a lack of signs of human settlement within and around the earthworks, like vestiges of housing and trash piles, as well as soil modification for farming, discounted that theory.

Researchers now believe that the geoglyphs may have held ceremonial importance, similar, perhaps, to the medieval cathedrals in Europe. This spiritual role, said William Balée, an anthropologist at Tulane University, could have been one that involved "geometry and gigantism."

Still, the geoglyphs, located at a crossroads between Andean and Amazonian cultures, remain an enigma.

They are far from pre-Columbian settlements discovered elsewhere in the Amazon. Big gaps also remain in what is known about indigenous people in this part of the Amazon, after thousands were enslaved, killed or forced from their lands during the rubber boom that began in the late 19th century.

For Brazil's scientists and researchers, Ms. Schaan said, the earthworks are "one of the most important discoveries of our time." But the repopulation of this part of the Amazon threatens the survival of the geoglyghs after being hidden for centuries.

Forests still cover most of Acre, but in cleared areas where the geoglyphs are found, dirt roads already cut through some of the earthworks. People live in wooden shacks inside others. Electricity poles dot the geoglyphs. Some ranchers use their trenches as watering holes for cattle.

"It's a disgrace that our patrimony is treated this way," said Tiago Juruá, the author of a new book here about protecting archaeological sites including the earthworks.

Mr. Juruá, a biologist, and other researchers say the geoglyphs found so far are probably just a sampling of what Acre's forests still guard under their canopies. After all, they contend that outside of modern cities, fewer people live today in the Amazon than did before the arrival of Europeans five centuries ago.

"This is a new frontier for exploration and science," Mr. Juruá said. "The challenge now is to make more discoveries in forests that are still standing, with the hope that they won't soon be destroyed."

■ REFLECTIONS

Grand theories are difficult to evaluate, as are these. In part the difficulty is that they cover so much. How many images or primary sources could ever establish that a particular set of Christian ideas affected the way Christians actually behaved? And yet we know, or believe, that ideas matter. How many histories of societal collapse do we need to understand the threats to our own? And yet, we know that the more knowledge we possess of how others have struggled and failed or succeeded, the better our own chances for survival.

At least two issues lie beneath the surface of the debate in this chapter. One is the issue of culture, specifically the importance of cultural or religious ideas in shaping human behavior. White argues that religious ideas have a profound impact on how societies behave. Diamond, however see culture as adaptive rather than formative. For the others, not only are Christian or monotheistic ideas irrelevant, but historical processes leave precious little room for thoughtful intervention. The micro view of Hunt gives center stage to rats and a walk-on role to European settlers. The macro view of McNeill is a useful reminder of basic technological constraints that cry out for cultural and political intervention.

Historians are always working between ideas and things. Historians of ideas may have a tendency to see ideas shaping history, and historians of things (economic historians, for instance) may see ideas as mere rationalizations. But good historians are not predictable. Lynn White Jr. is perhaps best known for his book *Medieval Technology and Social Change* in which he argued, among other things, that the introduction of the stirrup into medieval Europe was the cause of the society and culture we call feudalism. While this idea is much debated today, one would have a hard time finding an example of a stronger argument of how a thing created a culture. Nor does Diamond, a professor of geography and physiology, ignore the role of ideas. In addition to the case of Easter Island, he surveys the example of Viking collapse in Greenland in his recent book, *Collapse: How Societies Choose to Fail or Succeed* (a title that suggests the power of will and ideas). The Vikings, he suggests, failed in Greenland because they were unable to change their culture in ways necessary to adapt to the new environment. For Diamond, ideas and political will offer the only hope against the blind destructiveness of entrenched interests and seemingly unstoppable historical processes.

Another issue below the surface of this debate is the relationship between ecology and economic development. We tend to think that one comes at the expense of the other. White criticizes Western (Christian) environmental behavior with the same lens that has allowed others to celebrate Western (Christian) economic development. This is a reason, by the way, why many contemporary world historians find both views too centered on the West or Europe. But if Europe was not the source of modern technology, it was also not a source of our modern ecological predicament. Diamond is also critical of approaches that start and end in Europe. (His area of specialty is New Guinea.) Since he eliminated religious or cultural motives, his story of Easter Island can be read as an indictment of economic growth as the cause of ecological collapse. But the villain in Diamond's essay is not any kind of economic growth; it is the competitive economic exploitation of different tribes without any common plan or restraint. His message for our own predicament is to correct the anarchy of competing greedy corporations and interest groups with a common agenda and control.

Are not genuine economic growth and ecological balance mutually supportive? It is difficult to imagine long-term, healthy economic growth continuing while wrecking the environment. Similarly with environmental movements: White has us imagine that the true environmentalists are Buddhist mendicants and Hindu tree-huggers. But Buddhist monks might be content to cultivate their own gardens and ignore the rest of the world. After all, modern ecological political movements are largely products of rich societies with threatened environments. Might the most precarious ecologies display—by necessity—the greatest ecological concern? If that is the case, is the renewed popularity of environmental movements in our own age at least a sign of hope?

We can do nothing effective, however, without the guidance of historical knowledge. Romero's article reminds us that we cannot assume that any part of the world is what it always was. Nothing remains the same. The better we understand how the world is changing, the better world we can make it.

15

Overseas Expansion in the Early Modern Period

Asia, Africa, Europe, and the Americas, 1400–1600

■ HISTORICAL CONTEXT

Between 1400 and 1500, the balance between Chinese and European sea power changed drastically. Before 1434, Chinese shipbuilding was the envy of the world. Chinese ships were larger, more numerous, safer, and better outfitted than European ships. The Chinese navy made frequent trips through the South China Sea to the Spice Islands, through the Indian Ocean, and as far as East Africa and the Persian Gulf (see Map 15.1). Every island, port, and kingdom along the route was integrated into the Chinese system of tributaries. Goods were exchanged, marriages arranged, and princes taken to visit the Chinese emperor.

In the second half of the fifteenth century, the Chinese navy virtually disappeared. At the same time, the Portuguese began a series of explorations down the coast of Africa and into the Atlantic Ocean. In 1434 Portuguese ships rounded the treacherous Cape Bojador, just south of Morocco, and in 1498 Bartolomeu Dias rounded the Cape of Good Hope. Vasco da Gama sailed into the Indian Ocean, arriving in Calicut the following year. And in 1500 a fortuitous landfall in Brazil by Pedro Cabral gave the Portuguese a claim from the western Atlantic to the Indian Ocean. By 1512 Portuguese ships had reached the Bandas and Moluccas — the Spice Islands of what is today eastern Indonesia.

Beginning in 1492, after the defeat of the Moors (Muslims) and the voyages of Columbus, the Spanish claimed most of the Western Hemisphere until challenged by the Dutch, English, and French. European control in the Americas penetrated far deeper than in Asia, where it was limited to enclaves on the coast and where European nations were in an almost

560

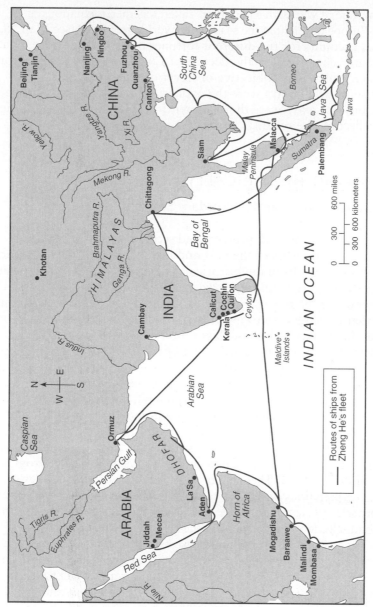

Map 15.1 Chinese Naval Expeditions, 1405–1433.

561

perpetual state of war with each other. Taken together, the nations of Western Europe dominated the seas of the world after 1500 (see Map 15.2).

What accounts for the different fortunes of China and Europe in the fifteenth century? Were the decline of China and the rise of Europe inevitable? Probably no objective observer of the time would have thought so. In what ways were the expansions of China and Europe similar? In what ways were they different? Think about these questions as you reflect on the readings in this chapter.

■ THINKING HISTORICALLY

Reading Primary and Secondary Sources

This chapter contains both primary and secondary sources. *Primary sources* are actual pieces of the past and include anything—art, letters, essays, and so on—from the historical period being studied. If a future historian were to study and research students in American colleges at the beginning of the twenty-first century, some primary sources might include diaries, letters, cartoons, music videos, posters, paintings, e-mail messages, blogs and Web sites, class notes, school newspapers, tests, and official and unofficial records. *Secondary sources* are usually books and articles *about* the past—interpretations of the past. These sources are "secondary" because they must be based on primary sources; therefore, a history written after an event occurs is a secondary source.

In your studies, you will be expected to distinguish primary from secondary sources. A quick glance at the introductions to this chapter's selections tells you that the first article is written by a modern journalist in 1999 and the last is written by a modern environmentalist, taken from his book published in 1991. These are both secondary sources since they are modern interpretations of the past rather than documents from the past. The other selections in this chapter are such documents, or primary sources. The second selection is an account of the great fifteenth-century Chinese admiral Zheng He's* voyage to Southeast Asia written by someone who was there, Ma Huan, a member of the crew. The third selection is similarly a participant's account of the voyage of the first European fleet to reach South Asia, that of Vasco da Gama at the end of the fifteenth century. These and the fourth selection, a letter penned by Christopher Columbus more than five hundred years ago, are firsthand accounts of worlds long past.

Having determined whether selections are primary or secondary sources, we also explore some of the subtle complexities that are overlooked by such designations.

* jung HUH

Note: Pronunciations of difficult-to-pronounce terms will be given throughout the book. The emphasis goes on the syllable appearing in all capitals. [Ed.]

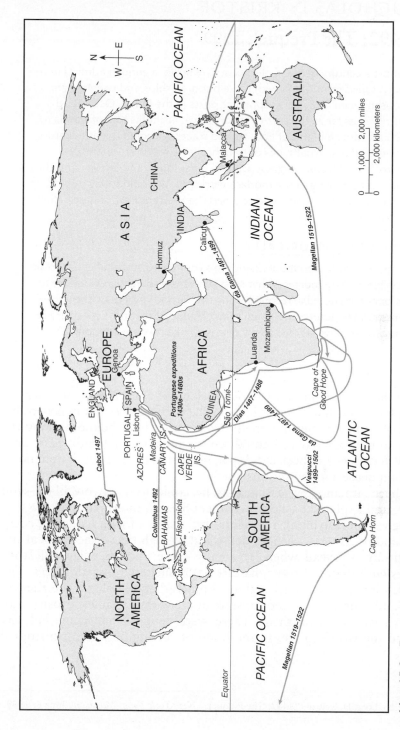

Map 15.2 European Overseas Exploration, 1430s–1530s.

NICHOLAS D. KRISTOF

1492: The Prequel, 1999

Almost a century before Columbus, Zheng He, a eunuch admiral in the court, sailed from China with three hundred ships and twenty-eight thousand men. His fleet stopped at ports in the Indian Ocean and journeyed as far as the east coast of Africa. Nicholas Kristof travels to the East African island of Pate to find traces of these fifteenth-century Chinese sailors. What types of evidence is he seeking? What does Kristof's brief history suggest about China, India, and Europe and their roles in the making of the modern world? How would today's world be different if Chinese ships had reached the Western Hemisphere before Columbus?

THINKING HISTORICALLY

In his secondary account of Zheng He's voyages, Kristof alludes to certain possible primary sources. What sorts of primary sources are available to historians interested in reconstructing the life and voyages of Zheng He? What primary sources are not available? Why are they not available? Has Kristof's recent voyage led to the discovery of a new primary source?

From the sea, the tiny East African island of Pate, just off the Kenyan coast, looks much as it must have in the 15th century: an impenetrable shore of endless mangrove trees. As my little boat bounced along the waves in the gray dawn, I could see no antennae or buildings or even gaps where trees had been cut down, no sign of human habitation, nothing but a dense and mysterious jungle.

The boatman drew as close as he could to a narrow black-sand beach, and I splashed ashore. My local Swahili interpreter led the way through the forest, along a winding trail scattered with mangoes, coconuts, and occasional seashells deposited by high tides. The tropical sun was firmly overhead when we finally came upon a village of stone houses with thatched roofs, its dirt paths sheltered by palm trees. The village's inhabitants, much lighter-skinned than people on the Kenyan mainland, emerged barefoot to stare at me with the same curiosity with which I was studying them. These were people I had come halfway around the world to see, in the hope of solving an ancient historical puzzle.

Source: Nicholas D. Kristof, "1492: The Prequel," *New York Times Magazine*, June 6, 1999, 6, 80:1.

"Tell me," I asked the first group I encountered, "where did the people here come from? Long ago, did foreign sailors ever settle here?" The answer was a series of shrugs. "I've never heard about that," one said. "You'll have to ask the elders."

I tried several old men and women without success. Finally the villagers led me to the patriarch of the village, Bwana Mkuu Al-Bauri, the keeper of oral traditions. He was a frail old man with gray stubble on his cheeks, head, and chest. He wore a yellow sarong around his waist; his ribs pressed through the taut skin on his bare torso. Al-Bauri hobbled out of his bed, resting on a cane and the arm of a grandson. He claimed to be 121 years old; a pineapple-size tumor jutted from the left side of his chest.

"I know this from my grandfather, who himself was the keeper of history here," the patriarch told me in an unexpectedly clear voice. "Many, many years ago, there was a ship from China that wrecked on the rocks off the coast near here. The sailors swam ashore near the village of Shanga—my ancestors were there and saw it themselves.

"The Chinese were visitors, so we helped those Chinese men and gave them food and shelter, and then they married our women. Although they do not live in this village, I believe their descendants still can be found somewhere else on this island."

I almost felt like hugging Bwana Al-Bauri. For months I had been poking around obscure documents and research reports, trying to track down a legend of an ancient Chinese shipwreck that had led to a settlement on the African coast. My interest arose from a fascination with what to me is a central enigma of the millennium: Why did the West triumph over the East?

For most of the last several thousand years, it would have seemed far likelier that Chinese or Indians, not Europeans, would dominate the world by the year 2000, and that America and Australia would be settled by Chinese rather than by the inhabitants of a backward island called Britain. The reversal of fortunes of East and West strikes me as the biggest news story of the millennium, and one of its most unexpected as well.

As a resident of Asia for most of the past thirteen years, I've been searching for an explanation. It has always seemed to me that the turning point came in the early 1400s, when Admiral Zheng He sailed from China to conquer the world. Zheng He (pronounced JUNG HUH) was an improbable commander of a great Chinese fleet, in that he was a Muslim from a rebel family and had been seized by the Chinese Army when he was still a boy. Like many other prisoners of the time, he was castrated, his sexual organs completely hacked off, a process that killed many of those who suffered it. But he was a brilliant and tenacious boy who grew up to be physically imposing. A natural leader, he had the good fortune to be assigned, as a houseboy, to the household of a great prince, Zhu Di.

In time, the prince and Zheng He grew close, and they conspired to overthrow the prince's nephew, the Emperor of China. With Zheng He as one of the prince's military commanders, the revolt succeeded and the prince became China's Yongle Emperor. One of the emperor's first acts (after torturing to death those who had opposed him) was to reward Zheng He with the command of a great fleet that was to sail off and assert China's pre-eminence in the world.

Between 1405 and 1433, Zheng He led seven major expeditions, commanding the largest armada the world would see for the next five centuries. Not until World War I did the West mount anything comparable. Zheng He's fleet included twenty-eight thousand sailors on three hundred ships, the longest of which were four hundred feet. By comparison, Columbus in 1492 had ninety sailors on three ships, the biggest of which was eighty-five feet long. Zheng He's ships also had advanced design elements that would not be introduced in Europe for another 350 years, including balanced rudders and watertight bulwark compartments.

The sophistication of Zheng He's fleet underscores just how far ahead of the West the East once was. Indeed, except for the period of the Roman Empire, China had been wealthier, more advanced, and more cosmopolitan than any place in Europe for several thousand years. Hangzhou, for example, had a population in excess of a million during the time it was China's capital (in the twelfth century), and records suggest that as early as the seventh century, the city of Guangzhou had 200,000 foreign residents: Arabs, Persians, Malays, Indians, Africans, and Turks. By contrast, the largest city in Europe in 1400 was probably Paris, with a total population of slightly more than 100,000.

A half-century before Columbus, Zheng He had reached East Africa and learned about Europe from Arab traders. The Chinese could easily have continued around the Cape of Good Hope and established direct trade with Europe. But as they saw it, Europe was a backward region, and China had little interest in the wood, beads, and wine Europe had to trade. Africa had what China wanted—ivory, medicines, spices, exotic woods, even specimens of native wildlife.

In Zheng He's time, China and India together accounted for more than half of the world's gross national product, as they have for most of human history. Even as recently as 1820, China accounted for 29 percent of the global economy and India another 16 percent, according to the calculations of Angus Maddison, a leading British economic historian.

Asia's retreat into relative isolation after the expeditions of Zheng He amounted to a catastrophic missed opportunity, one that laid the groundwork for the rise of Europe and, eventually, America. Westerners often attribute their economic advantage today to the intelligence, democratic habits, or hard work of their forebears, but a more important reason may well have been the folly of fifteenth-century Chinese rulers. That is why I came to be fascinated with Zheng He and set out earlier this year to retrace his journeys. I wanted to see what legacy, if any, remained of his achievement, and to figure out why his travels did not remake the world in the way that Columbus's did.

Zheng He lived in Nanjing, the old capital, where I arrived one day in February. Nanjing is a grimy metropolis on the Yangtze River in the heart of China. It has been five centuries since Zheng He's death, and his marks on the city have grown faint. The shipyards that built his fleet are still busy, and the courtyard of what had been his splendid seventy-two-room mansion is now the Zheng He Memorial Park, where children roller-skate and old couples totter around for exercise. But though the park has a small Zheng He museum, it was closed—for renovation, a caretaker told me, though he knew of no plans to reopen it.

I'd heard that Zheng He's tomb is on a hillside outside the city, and I set out to find it. It wasn't long before the road petered out, from asphalt to gravel to dirt to nothing. No tomb was in sight, so I approached an old man weeding a vegetable garden behind his house. Tang Yiming, seventy-two, was still lithe and strong. His hair was gray and ragged where he had cut it himself, disastrously, in front of a mirror. Evidently lonely, he was delighted to talk, and offered to show me the path to the tomb. As we walked, I mentioned that I had read that there used to be an old Ming Dynasty tablet on Zheng He's grave.

"Oh, yeah, the old tablet," he said nonchalantly. "When I was a boy, there was a Ming Dynasty tablet here. When it disappeared, the Government offered a huge reward to anyone who would return it—a reward big enough to build a new house. Seemed like a lot of money. But the problem was that we couldn't give it back. People around here are poor. We'd smashed it up to use as building materials."

A second mystery concerned what, if anything, is actually buried in Zheng He's tomb, since he is believed to have died on his last voyage and been buried at sea. So I said in passing that I'd heard tell the tomb is empty, and let my voice trail off.

"Oh, there's nothing in there," Tang said, a bit sadly. "No bones, nothing. That's for sure."

"How do you know?"

"In 1962, people dug up the grave, looking for anything to sell. We dug up the ground to one and a half times the height of a man. But there was absolutely nothing in there. It's empty."

The absence of impressive monuments to Zheng He in China today should probably come as no surprise, since his achievement was ultimately renounced. Curiously, it is not in China but in Indonesia where his memory has been most actively kept alive. Zheng He's expeditions led directly to the wave of Chinese immigration to Southeast Asia, and in some countries he is regarded today as a deity. In the Indonesia city of Semarang, for example, there is a large temple honoring Zheng He, located near a cave where he once nursed a sick friend. Indonesians still pray to Zheng He for a cure or good luck.

Not so in his native land. Zheng He was viewed with deep suspicion by China's traditional elite, the Confucian scholars, who made sure to destroy the archives of his journey. Even so, it is possible to learn something about his story from Chinese sources—from imperial archives and even the memoirs of crewmen. The historical record makes clear, for example, that it was not some sudden impulse of extroversion that led to Zheng He's achievement. It grew, rather, out of a long sailing tradition. Chinese accounts suggest that in the fifth century a Chinese monk sailed to a mysterious "far east country" that sounds very much like Mayan Mexico, and Mayan art at that time suddenly began to include Buddhist symbols. By the thirteenth century, Chinese ships regularly traveled to India and occasionally to East Africa.

Zheng He's armada was far grander, of course, than anything that came before. His grandest vessels were the "treasure ships," 400 feet long and 160 feet wide, with nine masts raising red silk sails to the wind, as well as multiple decks and luxury cabins with balconies. His armada included supply ships to carry horses, troop transports, warships, patrol boats, and as many as twenty tankers to carry fresh water. The full contingent of 28,000 crew members included interpreters for Arabic and other languages, astrologers to forecast the weather, astronomers to study the stars, pharmacologists to collect medicinal plants, ship-repair specialists, doctors, and even two protocol officers to help organize official receptions.

In the aftermath of such an incredible undertaking, you somehow expect to find a deeper mark on Chinese history, a greater legacy. But perhaps the faintness of Zheng He's trace in contemporary China is itself a lesson. In the end, an explorer makes history but does not necessarily change it, for his impact depends less on the trail he blazes than on the willingness of others to follow. The daring of a great expedition ultimately is hostage to the national will of those who remain behind.

In February I traveled to Calicut, a port town in southwestern India that was (and still is) the pepper capital of the world. The evening I arrived, I went down to the beach in the center of town to look at the coastline where Zheng He once had berthed his ships. In the fourteenth and fifteenth centuries, Calicut was one of the world's great ports, known to the Chinese as "the great country of the Western ocean." In the early fifteenth century, the sight of Zheng He's fleet riding anchor in Calicut harbor symbolized the strength of the world's two greatest powers, China and India.

On this sultry evening, the beach, framed by long piers jutting out to sea, was crowded with young lovers and ice-cream vendors. Those piers are all that remain of the port of Calicut, and you can see at a glance that they are no longer usable. The following day I visited the port offices, musty with handwritten ledgers of ship visits dating back nearly a century. The administrator of the port, Captain E. G. Mohanan, explained matter-of-factly what had happened. "The piers got old and no proper maintenance was ever carried out," he said, as a ceiling fan whirred tiredly overhead. "By the time we thought of it, it was not economical to fix it up." So in 1989, trade was halted, and one of the great ports of the world became no port at all.

The disappearance of a great Chinese fleet from a great Indian port symbolized one of history's biggest lost opportunities—Asia's failure to dominate the second half of this millennium. So how did this happen?

While Zheng He was crossing the Indian Ocean, the Confucian scholar-officials who dominated the upper echelons of the Chinese Government were at political war with the eunuchs, a group they regarded as corrupt and immoral. The eunuchs' role at court involved looking after the concubines, but they also served as palace administrators, often doling out contracts in exchange for kickbacks. Partly as a result of their legendary greed, they promoted commerce. Unlike the scholars—who owed their position to their mastery of two thousand-year-old texts—the eunuchs, lacking any such roots in a classical past, were sometimes outward-looking and progressive. Indeed, one can argue that it was the virtuous, incorruptible scholars who in the mid-fifteenth century set China on its disastrous course.

After the Yongle Emperor died in 1424, China endured a series of brutal power struggles; a successor emperor died under suspicious circumstances and ultimately the scholars emerged triumphant. They ended the voyages of Zheng He's successors, halted construction of new ships, and imposed curbs on private shipping. To prevent any backsliding, they destroyed Zheng He's sailing records and, with the backing of the new emperor, set about dismantling China's navy.

By 1500 the Government had made it a capital offense to build a boat with more than two masts, and in 1525 the Government ordered the destruction of all oceangoing ships. The greatest navy in history, which a century earlier had 3,500 ships (by comparison, the United States Navy today has 324), had been extinguished, and China set a course for itself that would lead to poverty, defeat, and decline.

Still, it was not the outcome of a single power struggle in the 1440s that cost China its worldly influence. Historians offer a host of reasons for why Asia eventually lost its way economically and was late to industrialize; two and a half reasons seem most convincing.

The first is that Asia was simply not greedy enough. The dominant social ethos in ancient China was Confucianism and in India it was caste, with the result that the elites in both nations looked down their noses at business. Ancient China cared about many things—prestige, honor, culture, arts, education, ancestors, religion, filial piety—but making money came far down the list. Confucius had specifically declared that it was wrong for a man to make a distant voyage while his parents were alive, and he had condemned profit as the concern of "a little man." As it was, Zheng He's ships were built on such a grand scale and carried such lavish gifts to foreign leaders that the voyages were not the huge money spinners they could have been.

In contrast to Asia, Europe was consumed with greed. Portugal led the age of discovery in the fifteenth century largely because it wanted spices, a precious commodity; it was the hope of profits that drove its ships steadily farther down the African coast and eventually around the Horn to Asia. The profits of this trade could be vast: Magellan's crew once sold a cargo of twenty-six tons of cloves for ten thousand times the cost.

A second reason for Asia's economic stagnation is more difficult to articulate but has to do with what might be called a culture of complacency. China and India shared a tendency to look inward, a devotion to past ideals and methods, a respect for authority, and a suspicion of new ideas. David S. Landes, a Harvard economist, has written of ancient China's "intelligent xenophobia"; the former Indian Prime Minister Jawaharlal Nehru referred to the "petrification of classes" and the "static nature" of Indian society. These are all different ways of describing the same economic and intellectual complacency.

Chinese elites regarded their country as the "Middle Kingdom" and believed they had nothing to learn from barbarians abroad. India exhibited much of the same self-satisfaction. "Indians didn't go to Portugal not because they couldn't but because they didn't want to," mused M. P. Sridharan, a historian, as we sat talking on the porch of his home in Calicut.

The fifteenth-century Portuguese were the opposite. Because of its coastline and fishing industry, Portugal always looked to the sea, yet rivalries with Spain and other countries shut it out of the Mediterranean trade. So the only way for Portugal to get at the wealth of the East was by conquering the oceans.

The half reason is simply that China was a single nation while Europe was many. When the Confucian scholars reasserted control in Beijing and banned shipping, their policy mistake condemned all of China. In contrast, European countries committed economic suicide selectively. So when Portugal slipped into a quasi-Chinese mind-set in the sixteenth century, slaughtering Jews and burning heretics, and driving astronomers and scientists abroad, Holland and England were free to take up the slack.

When I first began researching Zheng He, I never thought I'd be traveling all the way to Africa to look for traces of his voyages. Then I came across a few intriguing references to the possibility of an ancient Chinese shipwreck that might have left some Chinese stranded on the island of Pate (pronounced PAH-tay). One was a skeptical reference in a scholarly journal, another was a casual conversation with a Kenyan I met a few years ago, and the third was the epilogue of Louise Levathes's wonderful 1994 book about China's maritime adventures, "When China Ruled the Seas." Levathes had traveled to Kenya and found people who believed they were descended from survivors of a Chinese shipwreck. So, on a whim and an expense account, I flew to Lamu, an island off northern Kenya, and hired a boat and an interpreter to go to Pate and see for myself.

Pate is off in its own world, without electricity or roads or vehicles. Mostly jungle, it has been shielded from the twentieth century largely because it is accessible from the Kenyan mainland only by taking a boat through a narrow tidal channel that is passable only at high tide. Initially I was disappointed by what I found there. In the first villages I visited, I saw people who were light-skinned and had hair that was not tightly curled, but they could have been part Arab or European rather than part Chinese. The remote villages of Chundwa and Faza were more promising, for there I found people whose eyes, hair, and complexion hinted at Asian ancestry, though their background was ambiguous.

And then on a still and sweltering afternoon I strolled through the coconut palms into the village of Siyu, where I met a fisherman in his forties named Abdullah Mohammed Badui. I stopped and stared at the man in astonishment, for he had light skin and narrow eyes. Fortunately, he was as rude as I was, and we stared at each other in mutual surprise before venturing a word. Eventually I asked him about his background and appearance.

"I am in the Famao clan," he said. "There are fifty or one hundred of us Famao left here. Legend has it that we are descended from Chinese and others.

"A Chinese ship was coming along and it hit rocks and wrecked," Badui continued. "The sailors swam ashore to the village that we now call Shanga, and they married the local women, and that is why we Famao look so different."

Another Famao, with the same light complexion and vaguely Asian features, approached to listen. His name was Athman Mohammed Mzee, and he, too, told of hearing of the Chinese shipwreck from the elders. He volunteered an intriguing detail: The Africans had given giraffes to the Chinese.

Salim Bonaheri, a fifty-five-year-old Famao man I met the next day, proudly declared, "My ancestors were Chinese or Vietnamese or something like that." I asked how they had got to Pate.

"I don't know," Bonaheri said with a shrug. Most of my conversations were like that, intriguing but frustrating dead ends. I was surrounded by people whose appearance seemed tantalizingly Asian, but who had only the vaguest notions of why that might be. I kept at it, though, and eventually found people like Khalifa Mohammed Omar, a fifty-five-year-old Famao fisherman who looked somewhat Chinese and who also clearly remembered the stories passed down by his grandfather. From him and others, a tale emerged.

Countless generations ago, they said, Chinese sailors traded with local African kings. The local kings gave them giraffes to take back to China. One of the Chinese ships struck rocks off the eastern coast of Pate, and the sailors swam ashore, carrying with them porcelain and other goods from the ship. In time they married local women, converted to Islam, and named the village Shanga, after Shanghai. Later, fighting erupted among Pate's clans, Shanga was destroyed, and the Famao fled, some to the mainland, others to the village of Siyu.

Every time I heard the story about the giraffes my pulse began to race. Chinese records indicate that Zheng He had brought the first giraffes to China, a fact that is not widely known. The giraffe caused an enormous stir in China because it was believed to be the mythical qilin, or Chinese unicorn. It is difficult to imagine how African villagers on an island as remote as Pate would know about the giraffes unless the tale had been handed down to them by the Chinese sailors.

Chinese ceramics are found in many places along the east African coast, and their presence on Pate could be the result of purchases from Arab traders. But the porcelain on Pate was overwhelmingly concentrated among the Famao clan, which could mean that it had been inherited rather than purchased. I also visited some ancient Famao graves that looked less like traditional Kenyan graves than what the Chinese call "turtle-shell graves," with rounded tops.

Researchers have turned up other equally tantalizing clues. Craftsmen on Pate and the other islands of Lamu practice a kind of basket-weaving that is common in southern China but unknown on the Kenyan mainland. On Pate, drums are more often played in the Chinese than the African style, and the local dialect has a few words that may be Chinese in origin. More startling, in 1569 a Portuguese priest named Monclaro wrote that Pate had a flourishing silk-making industry—Pate, and no other place in the region. Elders in several villages on Pate confirmed to me that their island had produced silk until about half a century ago.

When I asked my boatman, Bakari Muhaji Ali, if he thought it was possible that a ship could have wrecked off the coast near Shanga, he laughed. "There are undersea rocks all over there," he said. "If you don't know exactly where you're going, you'll wreck your ship for sure."

If indeed there was a Chinese shipwreck off Pate, there is reason to think it happened in Zheng He's time. For if the shipwreck had predated him, surviving sailors would not have passed down stories of the giraffes. And if the wreck didn't occur until after Zheng He, its survivors could not have settled in Shanga, since British archeological digs indicate that the village was sacked, burned, and abandoned in about 1440—very soon after Zheng He's last voyage.

Still, there is no hard proof for the shipwreck theory, and there are plenty of holes in it. No ancient Chinese characters have been found on tombs in Pate, no nautical instruments have ever turned up on the island, and there are no Chinese accounts of an African shipwreck. This last lacuna might be explained by the destruction of the fleet's records. Yet if one of Zheng He's ships did founder on the rocks off Pate, then why didn't some other ships in the fleet come to the sailors' rescue?

As I made my way back through the jungle for the return trip, I pondered the significance of what I'd seen on Pate. In the faces of the Famao, in those bits of pottery and tantalizing hints of Chinese culture, I felt as though I'd glimpsed the shadowy outlines of one of the greatest might-have-beens of the millennium now ending. I thought about the Columbian Exchange, the swap of animals, plants, genes, germs, weapons, and peoples that utterly remade both the New World and the Old, and I couldn't help wondering about another exchange—Zheng He's—that never took place, yet could have.

If ancient China had been greedier and more outward-looking, if other traders had followed in Zheng He's wake and then continued on, Asia might well have dominated Africa and even Europe. Chinese might have settled in not only Malaysia and Singapore, but also in East Africa, the Pacific Islands, even in America. Perhaps the Famao show us what the mestizos of such a world might have looked like, the children of a hybrid culture that was never born. What I'd glimpsed in Pate was the highwater mark of an Asian push that simply stopped—not for want of ships or know-how, but strictly for want of national will.

All this might seem fanciful, and yet in Zheng He's time the prospect of a New World settled by the Spanish or English would have seemed infinitely more remote than a New World made by the Chinese. How different would history have been had Zheng He continued on to America? The mind rebels; the ramifications are almost too overwhelming to contemplate. So consider just one: This magazine would have been published in Chinese.

2

MA HUAN
On Calicut, India, 1433

Ma Huan was a Chinese Muslim who acted as an aide and interpreter on Zheng He's expeditions to Southeast Asia. In 1433 he wrote *The Overall Survey of the Ocean Shores,* a travel account of the lands he visited. This selection, taken from that account, describes his visit to Calicut on the Malabar, or southwest, coast of India. Note that Ma Huan is not always an accurate observer. More familiar with Buddhists than Hindus, for example, he mistakes the latter for the former. Nevertheless, he provides some useful information about

Source: Ma Huan, "On Calicut, India," in *Ma Huan, Ying-yai Sheng-lan: The Overall Survey of the Ocean's Shores,* ed. and trans. by Feng Ch'eng-Chun with an introduction by J. V. G. Mills (Bangkok: The White Lotus Press, 1970), 137–44.

Hindu-Muslim relations, the spread of the Abrahamic religions (note the story about Moses), the vitality of Indian trade, and the variety of Indian plants, animals, and manufactures. In addition to describing Calicut, what does Ma Huan tell us about the reasons for these expeditions?

THINKING HISTORICALLY

Ma Huan's account of Zheng He's expedition does not seem to have had an official purpose, but it was probably published instead to satisfy the growing interests of a Chinese public hungry for information about foreign lands and peoples. What sorts of things are of interest to Ma Huan? What does this tell us about his audience? How are his interests similar to, or different from, those of a modern traveler? What might be Ma Huan's strengths and weaknesses as a primary source?

The Country of Ku-Li
[Calicut]

[This is] the great country of the Western Ocean.

Setting sail from the anchorage in the country of Ko-chih,[1] you travel north-west, and arrive [here] after three days. The country lies beside the sea. [Travelling] east from the mountains for five hundred, or seven hundred, *li*, you make a long journey through to the country of K'an-pa-i.[2] On the west [the country of Ku-li] abuts on the great sea; on the south it joins the boundary of the country of Ko-chih; [and] on the north side it adjoins the territory of the country of Hen-nu-erh.[3]

"The great country of the Western Ocean" is precisely this country.

In the fifth year of the Yung-lo [period] the court ordered[4] the principal envoy the grand eunuch Cheng Ho and others to deliver an imperial mandate to the king[5] of this country and to bestow on him a patent conferring a title of honour, and the grant of a silver seal, [also] to

---

[1] Cochin, a city in southwest India along the Arabian Sea, 80 miles south of Calicut; Ma Huan made a very slow voyage.

[2] Koyampadi, modern Coimbatore, situated in about 11° N, 77° E, 76 miles nearly due east of Calicut. In giving the distance as 500 *li*, nearly 200 miles, Ma Huan was guilty of an exaggeration.

[3] Now called Honavar, situated in 14° 16′ N, 74° 27′ E; it is on the coast, 199 miles northward from Calicut.

[4] The order was made in October 1407; but, although in nominal command of this, the second expedition, Cheng Ho did not accompany it.

[5] A new king, Mana Vikraman, had evidently succeeded since Cheng Ho was at Calicut in 1406–7 during the course of his first expedition.

promote all the chiefs and award them hats and girdles of various grades.

[So Cheng Ho] went there in command of a large fleet of treasure-ships, and he erected a tablet with a pavilion over it and set up a stone which said "Though the journey from this country to the Central Country is more than a hundred thousand *li*, yet the people are very similar, happy and prosperous, with identical customs. We have here engraved a stone, a perpetual declaration for ten thousand ages." [6]

The king of the country is a Nan-k'un[7] man; he is a firm believer in the Buddhist religion;[8] [and] he venerates the elephant and the ox.

The population of the country includes five classes, the Muslim people, the Nan-K'un people, the Che-ti people, the Ko-ling people, and the Mu-kua people.

The king of the country and the people of the country all refrain from eating the flesh of the ox.[9] The great chiefs are Muslim people; [and] they all refrain from eating the flesh of the pig.[10] Formerly there was a king who made a sworn compact with the Muslim people, [saying] "You do not eat the ox; I do not eat the pig; we will reciprocally respect the taboo,"[11] [and this compact] has been honoured right down to the present day.

The king has cast an image of Buddha in brass; it is named Nai-na-erh;[12] he has erected a temple of Buddha and has cast tiles of brass and covered the dais of Buddha with them; [and] beside [the dais] a well has been dug. Every day at dawn the king goes to [the well], draws water, and washes [the image of] Buddha; after worshipping, he orders men to collect the pure dung of yellow oxen; this is stirred with water in a brass basin [until it is] like paste; [then] it is smeared all over the surface of the ground and walls inside the temple. Moreover, he has given orders that the chiefs and wealthy personages shall also smear and scour themselves with ox-dung every morning.

He also takes ox-dung, burns it till it is reduced to a white ash, and grinds it to a fine powder; using a fair cloth as a small bag, he fills it with the ash, and regularly carries it on his person. Every day at dawn, after he has finished washing his face, he takes the ox-dung ash, stirs it up with water, and smears it on his forehead and between his two

---

[6] Translated "May the period Yung-lo last for ever."

[7] Probably Ma Huan wrote "Nan-p'i" and meant the upper classes consisting of Brahmans and Kshatriyas.

[8] Ma Huan is mistaken; the king was a Hindu.

[9] Detestation of cow-slaughter is the most prominent outward mark of Hinduism.

[10] It is noteworthy that a Hindu ruler was employing Muslims as great officers.

[11] Since it was the king who made the compact, it would seem reasonable to prefer, "You do not eat the pig; I do not eat the ox"; thus, they agreed to respect each others' convictions in the matter of diet. It scarcely needs to be said that the pig is anathema to Muslims.

[12] The name might be a corruption of Narayana, a name for Vishnu. All these references to Buddha, then, must be construed as references to a Hindu deity.

thighs—thrice in each [place]. This denotes his sincerity in venerating Buddha[13] and in venerating the ox.

There is a traditional story that in olden times there was a holy man named Mou-hsieh,[14] who established a religious cult; the people knew that he was a true [man of] Heaven, and all men revered and followed him. Later the holy man went away with [others] to another place, and ordered his younger brother named Sa-mo-li[15] to govern and teach the people.

[But] his younger brother began to have depraved ideas; he made a casting of a golden calf and said "This is the holy lord; everyone who worships it will have his expectations fulfilled." He taught the people to listen to his bidding and to adore the golden ox, saying "It always excretes gold." The people got the gold, and their hearts rejoiced; and they forgot the way of Heaven; all took the ox to be the true lord.

Later Mou-hsieh the holy man returned; he saw that the multitude, misled by his younger brother Sa-mo-li, were corrupting the holy way; thereupon he destroyed the ox and wished to punish his younger brother; [and] his younger brother mounted a large elephant and vanished.

Afterwards, the people thought of him and hoped anxiously for his return. Moreover, if it was the beginning of the moon, they would say "In the middle of the moon he will certainly come," and when the middle of the moon arrived, they would say once more "At the end of the moon he will certainly come"; right down to the present day they have never ceased to hope for his return.

This is the reason why the Nan-k'un[16] people venerate the elephant and the ox.

The king has two great chiefs who administer the affairs of the country; both are Muslims.

The majority of the people in the country all profess the Muslim religion. There are twenty or thirty temples of worship, and once in seven days they go to worship. When the day arrives, the whole family fast and bathe, and attend to nothing else. In the *ssu* and *wu* periods,[17] the menfolk, old and young, go to the temple to worship. When the *wei* period[18] arrives, they disperse and return home; thereupon they carry on with their trading, and transact their household affairs.

---

[13] Again, a Hindu deity.

[14] "Musa" (Moses). Ma Huan alleges that the incidents occurred at Calicut. Presumably he learnt the story of Aaron and the golden calf from Arab informants. A number of Old Testament characters, including Moses, figure prominently in the Koran.

[15] "Al-Sameri" (the Samaritan), the name appearing in the Koran.

[16] Probably Ma Huan wrote "Nan-p'i," and referred to the upper classes of Brahmans and Kshatriyas.

[17] 9 A.M. to 11 A.M., and 11 A.M. to 1 P.M., respectively.

[18] 1 P.M. to 3 P.M.

The people are very honest and trustworthy. Their appearance is smart, fine, and distinguished.

Their two great chiefs received promotion and awards from the court of the Central Country.

If a treasure-ship goes there, it is left entirely to the two men to superintend the buying and selling; the king sends a chief and a Che-ti Wei-no-chi[19] to examine the account books in the official bureau; a broker comes and joins them; [and] a high officer who commands the ships discusses the choice of a certain date for fixing prices. When the day arrives, they first of all take the silk embroideries and the openwork silks, and other such goods which have been brought there, and discuss the price of them one by one; [and] when [the price] has been fixed, they write out an agreement stating the amount of the price; [this agreement] is retained by these persons.

The chief and the Che-ti, with his excellency the eunuch, all join hands together, and the broker then says "In such and such a moon on such and such a day, we have all joined hands and sealed our agreement with a hand-clasp; whether [the price] be dear or cheap, we will never repudiate it or change it."

After that, the Che-ti and the men of wealth then come bringing precious stones, pearls, corals, and other such things, so that they may be examined and the price discussed; [this] cannot be settled in a day; [if done] quickly, [it takes] one moon; [if done] slowly, [it takes] two or three moons.[20]

Once the money-price has been fixed after examination and discussion, if a pearl or other such article is purchased, the price which must be paid for it is calculated by the chief and the Wei-no-chi who carried out the original transaction; [and] as to the quantity of the hemp-silk or other such article which must be given in exchange for it, goods are given in exchange according to [the price fixed by] the original hand-clasp—there is not the slightest deviation.[21]

In their method of calculation, they do not use a calculating-plate;[22] for calculating, they use only the two hands and two feet and the twenty digits on them; and they do not make the slightest mistake; [this is] very extraordinary.

[19] Another observer, Kung Chen, translates "accountant," and adds that the man in question was a broker; Kung Chen further notes that "they wrote out a contract in duplicate, and each [party] kept one [document]."

[20] Presumably the goods were unloaded, unless the Chinese left one or two ships behind; at any rate, on the seventh expedition the Chinese stayed only 4 days, from 10 to 14 December 1432, at Calicut.

[21] This instructive disquisition on administrative procedure illustrates the meticulous care taken to fix the rate of exchange in times prior to the advent of the Europeans.

[22] The abacus, a wooden frame in which are fixed a number of beads strung on parallel wires; used by the Chinese for all kinds of arithmetic calculations upon the decimal system; it came into use in late Sung times.

The king uses gold of sixty per cent [purity] to cast a coin for current use; it is named a *pa-nan*;[23] the diameter of the face of each coin is three *fen* eight *li* [in terms of] our official *ts'un*;[24] it has lines[25] on the face and on the reverse; [and] it weighs one *fen* on our official steelyard.[26] He also makes a coin of silver; it is named a *ta-erh*;[27] each coin weighs about three *li*;[28] [and] this coin is used for petty transactions. . . .

The people of the country also take the silk of the silk-worm, soften it by boiling, dye it in all colours, and weave it into kerchiefs with decorative stripes at intervals; the breadth is four or five *ch'ih*, and the length one *chang* two or three *ch'ih*;[29] [and] each length is sold for one hundred gold coins.[30]

As to the pepper: the inhabitants of the mountainous countryside have established gardens, and it is extensively cultivated. When the period of the tenth moon arrives, the pepper ripens; [and] it is collected, dried in the sun, and sold. Of course, big pepper-collectors come and collect it, and take it up to the official storehouse to be stored; if there is a buyer, an official gives permission for the sale; the duty is calculated according to the amount [of the purchase price] and is paid in to the authorities. Each one *po-ho* of pepper is sold for two hundred gold coins.[31]

The Che-ti mostly purchase all kinds of precious stones and pearls, and they manufacture coral beads and other such things.

Foreign ships from every place come there; and the king of the country also sends a chief and a writer and others to watch the sales; thereupon they collect the duty and pay it in to the authorities.

The wealthy people mostly cultivate coconut trees—sometimes a thousand trees, sometimes two thousand or three thousand—; this constitutes their property.

The coconut has ten different uses. The young tree has a syrup, very sweet, and good to drink; [and] it can be made into wine by fermentation, The old coconut has flesh, from which they express oil, and make sugar, and make a foodstuff for eating. From the fibre which envelops the outside [of the nut] they make ropes for ship-building. The shell of the coconut makes bowls and makes cups; it is also good for burning to

---

[23] Representing the sound *fanam*. The king was an independent sovereign minting his own coinage; but doubtless, as in 1443, he "lived in great fear" of Vijayanagar (Abdul Razzak).

[24] The diameter of the *fanam*, being 0.38 of the Chinese *ts'un* of 1.22 inches, equalled 0.46 of an English inch.

[25] Or "characters."

[26] The gold content weighed 3.45 grains or 0.00719 ounce troy.

[27] Representing the sound *tar* or *tare* (*tara*).

[28] If the silver was pure, the silver content weighed 0.00359 ounce troy.

[29] The equivalent of 4 *ch'ih* was 48.9 inches; 1 *chang* 2 *ch'ih* equaled 12 feet 2.9 inches.

[30] The gold content weighed 345.375 grains or 0.7195 ounce troy.

[31] The gold content of 200 *fanam* weighed 690.751 grains or 1.439 ounces troy.

ash for the delicate operation of inlaying[32] gold or silver. The trees are good for building houses, and the leaves are good for roofing houses.

For vegetables they have mustard plants, green ginger, turnips, caraway seeds, onions, garlic, bottle-gourds, egg-plants, cucumbers, and gourd-melons[33]—all these they have in [all] the four seasons [of the year]. They also have a kind of small gourd which is as large as [one's] finger, about two *ts'un*[34] long, and tastes like a green cucumber. Their onions have a purple skin; they resemble garlic; they have a large head and small leaves; [and] they are sold by the *chin*[35] weight.

The *mu-pieb-tzu*[36] tree is more than ten *chang* high; it forms a fruit which resembles a green persimmon and contains thirty or forty seeds; it falls of its own accord when ripe; [and] the bats, as large as hawks, all hang upside-down and rest on this tree.

They have both red and white rice, [but] barley and wheat are both absent; [and] their wheat-flour all comes from other places as merchandise for sale [here].

Fowls and ducks exist in profusion, [but] there are no geese. Their goats have tall legs and an ashen hue; they resemble donkey-foals. The water-buffaloes are not very large. Some of the yellow oxen weigh three or four hundred *chin*;[37] the people do not eat their flesh; [but] consume only the milk and cream. The people never eat rice without butter. Their oxen are cared for until they are old; [and] when they die, they are buried. The price of all kinds of sea-fish is very cheap. Deer and hares [from up] in the mountains are also for sale.

Many of the people rear peafowl. As to their other birds: they have crows, green hawks, egrets, and swallows; [but] of other kinds of birds besides these they have not a single one, great or small. The people of the country can also play and sing; they use the shell of a calabash to make a musical instrument, and copper wires to make the strings; and they play [this instrument] to accompany the singing of their foreign songs; the melodies are worth hearing.[38]

---

[32] *Hsiang*, "a box," used for *hsiang*, "side rooms," which in turn is used for *hsiang*, "to inlay."

[33] *Tung kua*, "eastern gourd," the same vegetable as *tung kua*, "winter gourd."

[34] That is, 2.4 inches.

[35] That is, 1.3 pounds avoirdupois.

[36] The tree is *Momordica cochinchinensis*. The editor is indebted to Dr. J. Needham, F.R.S., for the information that *Momordica* seeds were prescribed in the form of paste for abscesses, ulcers, and wounds, as well as in other ways for other affections. The equivalent of 10 *chang* was 102 feet.

[37] The equivalent of 300 *chin* was 394.6 pounds avoirdupois.

[38] Music was cultivated at the royal courts, and numbers of musicians were employed in the temples. Conti, in his account of Vijayanagar city, records solemn singing at religious festivals, and the celebration of weddings with "banquets, songs, trumpets, and instruments muche like unto ours." The instrument referred to by Ma Huan was probably the vina, a fretted instrument of the guitar kind, which was particularly favoured by Indian musicians.

As to the popular customs and the marriage- and funeral-rites, the So-li people and the Muslim people each follow the ritual forms of their own class, and these are different.

The king's throne does not descend to his son, but descends to his sister's son; descent is to the sister's son [because] they consider that the offspring of the women's body alone constitutes the legal family. If the king has no elder or younger sister, [the throne] descends to his younger brother; [and] if he has no younger brother, [the throne] is yielded up to some man of merit. Such is the succession from one generation to another.

3

Journal of the First Voyage of Vasco da Gama, 1498

In 1497 the Portuguese seaman Vasco da Gama left Portugal with a fleet of four ships, arriving in India ten months later. He benefited from the experience of Bartolomeu Dias, who ten years before had negotiated the rough waters of the South African Cape. But Dias had returned to Portugal. Da Gama continued up the African coast and sailed across the Indian Ocean to the port of Calicut, the center of a kingdom that encompassed much of the modern state of Kerala in southwest India. What seem to have been the motives of Portugal and da Gama in sailing to South Asia? How were the Portuguese intentions similar to, and different from, those of China earlier in the century? How would you compare the preparation and behavior of Chinese and Portuguese crews? How would you explain the differences between Chinese and Portuguese voyages?

THINKING HISTORICALLY

We do not know the identity of the author of this document. He was one of the officers or crewmen who sailed on this voyage, however, and many of their names are known to us. What indications do you have that they spanned a wide range of Portuguese society?

The fact that the author was a witness does not mean that he gets everything right. What does he miss? What might have caused him to be misled? Generally, primary sources get more things right than wrong. How do you know this is true for this selection? How do we determine where a primary source is reliable and where it is not?

Source: *A Journal of the First Voyage of Vasco da Gama, 1497–1499,* trans. and ed. E. G. Ravenstein (London: Hakluyt Society, 1898), 48–59, 60–63.

Calicut

[*Arrival.*][1] That night[2] [May 20] we anchored two leagues from the city of Calicut, and we did so because our pilot mistook *Capua,*[3] a town at that place, for Calicut. Still further there is another town called *Panda-rani.*[4] We anchored about a league and a half from the shore. After we were at anchor, four boats (*almadias*) approached us from the land, who asked of what nation we were. We told them, and they then pointed out Calicut to us.

On the following day [May 21] these same boats came again alongside, when the captain-major[5] sent one of the convicts[6] to Calicut, and those with whom he went took him to two Moors from Tunis,[7] who could speak Castilian and Genoese. The first greeting that he received was in these words: "May the Devil take thee! What brought you hither?" They asked what he sought so far away from home, and he told them that we came in search of Christians and of spices. They said: "Why does not the King of Castile, the King of France, or the Signoria of Venice send thither?" He said that the King of Portugal would not consent to their doing so, and they said he did the right thing. After this conversation they took him to their lodgings and gave him wheaten bread and honey. When he had eaten he returned to the ships, accompanied by one of the Moors, who was no sooner on board, than he said these words: "A lucky venture, a lucky venture! Plenty of rubies, plenty of emeralds! You owe great thanks to God, for having brought you to a country holding such riches!" We were greatly astonished to hear his talk, for we never expected to hear our language spoken so far away from Portugal.

[*A description of Calicut.*] The city of Calicut is inhabited by Christians.[8] They are of tawny complexion. Some of them have big beards and long hair, whilst others clip their hair short or shave the head, merely allowing a tuft to remain on the crown as a sign that they are Christians.

---

[1] Brackets enclose editorial additions of translator, Ravenstein, unless otherwise indicated. [Ed.]

[2] Afternoon (*a tarde*), according to Glenn J. Ames, *Em Nome de Deus* (Leiden: Brill, 2009), 70. [Ed.]

[3] Kappatt, a village about 7 miles north of Calicut. [Ed.]

[4] About 14 miles north of Calicut. [Ed.]

[5] Da Gama. [Ed.]

[6] The crew included a number of "convict-exiles," men who had been convicted of a crime punishable by death who were pardoned by the king to sail as adventurers and live out their lives overseas. Da Gama wanted such people in his crew to create a permanent presence overseas. [Ed.]

[7] Likely Muslim exiles from Spain after the defeat of the last Muslim stronghold in Granada by Christians in 1492. [Ed.]

[8] There were Christians in southern India, but the population was overwhelmingly Hindu. [Ed.]

They also wear moustaches. They pierce the ears and wear much gold in them. They go naked down to the waist, covering their lower extremities with very fine cotton stuffs. But it is only the most respectable who do this, for the others manage as best they are able.

The women of this country, as a rule, are ugly and of small stature. They wear many jewels of gold round the neck, numerous bracelets on their arms, and rings set with precious stones on their toes. All these people are well-disposed and apparently of mild temper. At first sight they seem covetous and ignorant.

[*A messenger sent to the King.*] When we arrived at Calicut the king was fifteen leagues away. The captain-major sent two men to him with a message, informing him that an ambassador had arrived from the King of Portugal with letters, and that if he desired it he would take them to where the king then was.

The king presented the bearers of this message with much fine cloth. He sent word to the captain-major bidding him welcome, saying that he was about to proceed to Calicut. As a matter of fact, he started at once with a large retinue.

[*At Anchor at Pandarani, May 27.*] A pilot accompanied our two men, with orders to take us to a place called Pandarani, below the place [Capua] where we anchored at first. At this time we were actually in front of the city of Calicut. We were told that the anchorage at the place to which we were to go was good, whilst at the place we were then it was bad, with a stony bottom, which was quite true; and, moreover, that it was customary for the ships which came to this country to anchor there for the sake of safety. We ourselves did not feel comfortable, and the captain-major had no sooner received this royal message than he ordered the sails to be set, and we departed. We did not, however, anchor as near the shore as the king's pilot desired.

When we were at anchor, a message arrived informing the captain-major that the king was already in the city. At the same time the king sent a *bale*,[9] with other men of distinction, to Pandarani, to conduct the captain-major to where the king awaited him. This *bale* is like an *alcaide*,[10] and is always attended by two hundred men armed with swords and bucklers. As it was late when this message arrived, the captain-major deferred going.

[*Gama goes to Calicut.*] On the following morning, which was Monday, May 28th, the captain-major set out to speak to the king, and took with him thirteen men, of which I was one.[11] On landing, the captain-major was received by the *alcaide*, with whom were many men,

---

[9] Governor. [Ed.]

[10] Mayor. [Ed.]

[11] We know the names of about half of the thirteen, but not which of them is the author. [Ed.]

armed and unarmed. The reception was friendly, as if the people were pleased to see us, though at first appearances looked threatening, for they carried naked swords in their hands. A palanquin[12] was provided for the captain-major, such as is used by men of distinction in that country, as also by some of the merchants, who pay something to the king for this privilege. The captain-major entered the palanquin, which was carried by six men by turns. Attended by all these people we took the road of Calicut, and came first to another town, called Capua. The captain-major was there deposited at the house of a man of rank, whilst we others were provided with food, consisting of rice, with much butter, and excellent boiled fish. The captain-major did not wish to eat, and as we had done so, we embarked on a river close by, which flows between the sea and the mainland, close to the coast. The two boats in which we embarked were lashed together, so that we were not separated. There were numerous other boats, all crowded with people. As to those who were on the banks I say nothing; their number was infinite, and they had all come to see us. We went up that river for about a league, and saw many large ships drawn up high and dry on its banks, for there is no port here.

When we disembarked, the captain-major once more entered his palanquin. The road was crowded with a countless multitude anxious to see us. Even the women came out of their houses with children in their arms and followed us.

[*A Christian Church.*][13] When we arrived [at Calicut] they took us to a large church, and this is what we saw: —

The body of the church is as large as a monastery, all built of hewn stone and covered with tiles. At the main entrance rises a pillar of bronze as high as a mast, on the top of which was perched a bird, apparently a cock.[14] In addition to this, there was another pillar as high as a man, and very stout. In the center of the body of the church rose a chapel, all built of hewn stone, with a bronze door sufficiently wide for a man to pass, and stone steps leading up to it. Within this sanctuary stood a small image which they said represented Our Lady.[15] Along the walls, by the main entrance, hung seven small bells. In this church the captain-major said his prayers, and we with him.[16]

---

[12] An enclosed chair carried on poles front and rear. [Ed.]

[13] The translator, Ravenstein, who supplied this heading, added a note: "This 'church' was, of course, a pagoda or temple." [Ed.]

[14] Ravenstein (1898) believes the bird to be a Hindu war-god. Ames (2009) suggests it was an image of Garuda, the bird-god who carried Vishnu, the creator-god of the Hindu trinity. [Ed.]

[15] Possibly Mari, a local deity, protector from smallpox. [Ed.]

[16] Another source reports that at least one of the crew did not believe it was a Christian church. He is said to have knelt next to Vasco da Gama and said: "If this is the devil, I worship the True God" (Ames, 2009, 76). [Ed.]

We did not go within the chapel, for it is the custom that only certain servants of the church, called *quafees*,[17] should enter. These *quafees* wore some threads passing over the left shoulder and under the right arm, in the same manner as our deacons wear the stole. They threw holy water over us, and gave us some white earth,[18] which the Christians of this country are in the habit of putting on their foreheads, breasts, around the neck, and on the forearms. They threw holy water upon the captain-major and gave him some of the earth, which he gave in charge of someone, giving them to understand that he would put it on later.[19]

Many other saints were painted on the walls of the church, wearing crowns. They were painted variously, with teeth protruding an inch from the mouth, and four or five arms.

Below this church there was a large masonry tank, similar to many others which we had seen along the road.

[*Progress through the Town.*] After we had left that place, and had arrived at the entrance to the city [of Calicut] we were shown another church, where we saw things like those described above. Here the crowd grew so dense that progress along the street became next to impossible, and for this reason they put the captain-major into a house, and us with him.

The king sent a brother of the *bale*, who was a lord of this country, to accompany the captain-major, and he was attended by men beating drums, blowing *anafils* and bagpipes, and firing off matchlocks. In conducting the captain-major they showed us much respect, more than is shown in Spain to a king. The number of people was countless, for in addition to those who surrounded us, and among whom there were two thousand armed men, they crowded the roofs and houses.

[*The King's Palace.*] The further we advanced in the direction of the king's palace, the more did they increase in number. And when we arrived there, men of much distinction and great lords came out to meet the captain-major, and joined those who were already in attendance upon him. It was then an hour before sunset. When we reached the palace we passed through a gate into a courtyard of great size, and before we arrived at where the king was, we passed four doors, through which we had to force our way, giving many blows to the people. When, at last, we reached the door where the king was, there came forth from it a little old man, who holds a position resembling that of a bishop, and whose advice the king acts upon in all affairs of the church. This man embraced the captain-major when he entered the door. Several men were wounded at this door, and we only got in by the use of much force.

---

[17] Ames (2009) suggests that this term for Brahman priests was either the Arabic *quadi* (judge) or *kafir* (unbeliever). [Ed.]

[18] Possibly ash from burnt cow dung. [Ed.]

[19] Did da Gama's refusal to anoint himself with ash mean he questioned the legitimacy of ritual or church? [Ed.]

[*A Royal Audience, May 28.*] The king[20] was in a small court, reclining upon a couch covered with a cloth of green velvet, above which was a good mattress, and upon this again a sheet of cotton stuff, very white and fine, more so than any linen. The cushions were after the same fashion. In his left hand the king held a very large golden cup [spittoon], having a capacity of half an almude [8 pints]. At its mouth this cup was two palmas [16 inches] wide, and apparently it was massive. Into this cup the king threw the husks of a certain herb which is chewed by the people of this country because of its soothing effects, and which they call *atambor*.[21] On the right side of the king stood a basin of gold, so large that a man might just encircle it with his arms: this contained the herbs. There were likewise many silver jugs. The canopy above the couch was all gilt.

The captain, on entering, saluted in the manner of the country: by putting the hands together, then raising them towards Heaven, as is done by Christians when addressing God, and immediately afterwards opening them and shutting fists quickly. The king beckoned to the captain with his right hand to come nearer, but the captain did not approach him, for it is the custom of the country for no man to approach the king except only the servant who hands him the herbs, and when anyone addresses the king he holds his hand before the mouth, and remains at a distance. When the king beckoned to the captain he looked at us others, and ordered us to be seated on a stone bench near him, where he could see us. He ordered that water for our hands should be given us, as also some fruit, one kind of which resembled a melon, except that its outside was rough and the inside sweet, whilst another kind of fruit resembled a fig, and tasted very nice. There were men who prepared these fruits for them; and the king looked at them eating, and smiled; and talked to the servant who stood near him supplying him with the herbs referred to.

Then, throwing his eyes on the captain, who sat facing him, he invited him to address himself to the courtiers present, saying they were men of much distinction, that he could tell them whatever he desired to say, and they would repeat it to him (the king). The captain-major replied that he was the ambassador of the King of Portugal, and the bearer of a message which he could only deliver to him personally. The king said this was good, and immediately asked him to be conducted to a chamber. When the captain had entered, the king, too, rose and joined him, whilst we remained where we were. All this happened about sunset. An old man who was in the court took away the couch as soon as the king rose, but allowed the plate to remain. The king, when he joined

[20] Manivikraman Raja. [Ed.]
[21] Betel-nut. [Ed.]

the captain, threw himself upon another couch, covered with various stuffs embroidered in gold, and asked the captain what he wanted.

And the captain told him he was the ambassador of a King of Portugal, who was Lord of many countries and the possessor of great wealth of every description, exceeding that of any king of these parts; that for a period of sixty years his ancestors had annually sent out vessels to make discoveries in the direction of India, as they knew that there were Christian kings there like themselves. This, he said, was the reason which induced them to order this country to be discovered, not because they sought for gold or silver, for of this they had such abundance that they needed not what was to be found in this country. He further stated that the captains sent out traveled for a year or two, until their provisions were exhausted, and then returned to Portugal, without having succeeded in making the desired discovery. There reigned a king now whose name was Dom Manuel, who had ordered him to build three vessels, of which he had been appointed captain-major, and who had ordered him not to return to Portugal until he should have discovered this King of the Christians, on pain of having his head cut off. That two letters had been intrusted to him to be presented in case he succeeded in discovering him, and that he would do so on the ensuing day; and, finally, he had been instructed to say by word of mouth that he [the King of Portugal] desired to be his friend and brother.

In reply to this the king said that he was welcome; that, on his part, he held him as a friend and brother, and would send ambassadors with him to Portugal. This latter had been asked as a favor, the captain pretending that he would not dare to present himself before his king and master unless he was able to present, at the same time, some men of this country.

These and many other things passed between the two in this chamber, and as it was already late in the night, the king asked the captain with whom he desired to lodge, with Christians or with Moors? And the captain replied, neither with Christians nor with Moors, and begged as a favor that he be given a lodging by himself. The king said he would order it thus, upon which the captain took leave of the king and came to where the men were, that is, to a veranda lit up by a huge candlestick. By that time four hours of the night had already gone.[22] . . .

[*Presents for the King.*] On Tuesday, May 29, the captain-major got ready the following things to be sent to the king, viz., twelve pieces of *lambel*,[23] four scarlet hoods, six hats, four strings of coral, a case containing six wash-hand basins, a case of sugar, two casks of oil, and two of honey.[24] And as it is the custom not to send anything to the king

---

[22] Four hours after sunset, or about 10 P.M. [Ed.]

[23] Striped cloth. [Ed.]

[24] The ships had been loaded by Bartolomeu Dias (1451–1500), who used such goods effectively in trading with Africans. [Ed.]

without the knowledge of the Moor, his factor, and of the *bale*, the captain informed them of his intention. They came, and when they saw the present they laughed at it, saying that it was not a thing to offer to a king, that the poorest merchant from Mecca, or any other part of India, gave more, and that if he wanted to make a present it should be in gold, as the king would not accept such things. When the captain heard this he grew sad, and said that he had brought no gold, that, moreover, he was no merchant, but an ambassador; that he gave of that which he had, which was his own [private gift] and not the king's; that if the King of Portugal ordered him to return he would intrust him with far richer presents; and that if King Camolim[25] would not accept these things he would send them back to the ships. Upon this they declared that they would not forward his presents, nor consent to his forwarding them himself. When they had gone there came certain Moorish merchants, and they all depreciated the present which the captain desired to be sent to the king.

When the captain saw that they were determined not to forward his present, he said, that as they would not allow him to send his present to the palace he would go to speak to the king, and would then return to the ships. They approved of this, and told him that if he would wait a short time they would return and accompany him to the palace. And the captain waited all day, but they never came back. The captain was very wroth at being among so phlegmatic and unreliable a people, and intended, at first, to go to the palace without them. On further consideration, however, he thought it best to wait until the following day. The men diverted themselves, singing and dancing to the sound of trumpets, and enjoyed themselves much.

[*A Second Audience, May 30.*] On Wednesday morning the Moors returned, and took the captain to the palace, and others with him. The palace was crowded with armed men. Our captain was kept waiting with his conductors for fully four long hours, outside a door, which was only opened when the king sent word to admit him, attended by two men only, whom he might select. The captain-major said that he desired to have Fernao Martins with him, who could interpret, and his secretary. It seemed to him, as it did to us, that this separation portended no good.

When he had entered, the king said that he had expected him on Tuesday. The captain-major said that the long road had tired him, and that for this reason he had not come to see him. The king then said that he had told him that he came from a very rich kingdom, and yet had brought him nothing; that he had also told him that he was the bearer of

---

[25] Camorim (with a soft *c*) is a version of the king's title, more often written as Zamorin or Samorin, meaning ruler of the coasts or king of the seas. [Ed.]

a letter, which had not yet been delivered. To this the captain rejoined that he had brought nothing, because the object of his voyage was merely to make discoveries, but that when other ships came he would then see what they brought him; as to the letter, it was true that he had brought one, and would deliver it immediately.

The king then asked what it was he had come to discover: stones or men? If he came to discover men, as he said, why had he brought nothing? Moreover, he had been told that he carried with him the golden image of a Santa Maria. The captain-major said that the Santa Maria was not of gold, and that even if she were he would not part with her, as she had guided him across the ocean, and would guide him back to his own country. The king then asked for the letter. The captain said that he begged as a favor, that as the Moors wished him ill and might misinterpret him, a Christian able to speak Arabic should be sent for. The king said this was well, and at once sent for a young man, of small stature, whose name was Quaram. The captain-major then said that he had two letters, one written in his own language and the other in that of the Moors;[26] that he was able to read the former, and knew that it contained nothing but what would prove acceptable; but that as to the other he was unable to read it, and it might be good, or contain something that was erroneous. As the Christian was unable to *read* Moorish, four Moors took the letter and read it between them, after which they translated it to the king, who was well satisfied with its contents.

The king then asked what kind of merchandise was to be found in his country. The captain said there was much corn,[27] cloth, iron, bronze, and many other things. The king asked whether he had any merchandise with him. The captain-major replied that he had a little of each sort, as samples, and that if permitted to return to the ships he would order it to be landed, and that meantime four or five men would remain at the lodgings assigned them. The king said no! He might take all his people with him, securely moor his ships, land his merchandise, and sell it to the best advantage. Having taken leave of the king the captain-major returned to his lodgings, and we with him. As it was already late no attempt was made to depart that night.

[26] Arabic. [Ed.]

[27] Corn had already been transplanted from the Americas by this time, but the author more likely meant wheat (Ames, 2009, 83). [Ed.]

4

CHRISTOPHER COLUMBUS

Letter to King Ferdinand and Queen Isabella, 1493

Christopher Columbus sent this letter to his royal backers, King Ferdinand and Queen Isabella of Spain, on his return in March 1493 from his first voyage across the Atlantic. (See Map 15.3.)

An Italian sailor from Genoa, Columbus, in 1483–1484, tried to convince King John II of Portugal to underwrite his plan to sail across the western ocean to the spice-rich East Indies. Relying on a Florentine map that used Marco Polo's overstated distance from Venice to Japan across Asia and an understated estimate of the circumference of the globe, Columbus believed that Japan lay only 2,500 miles west of the Portuguese Azores. King John II rejected the proposal because he had more accurate estimates indicating that sailing around Africa was the shorter route, as the voyages of Bartolomeu Dias in 1488 and Vasco da Gama in 1497–1499 proved.

Less knowledgeable about navigation, the new Spanish monarchs, Ferdinand and Isabella, supported Columbus and financed his plan to sail west to Asia. In four voyages, Columbus touched a number of Caribbean islands and the coast of Central America, settled Spaniards on Hispaniola (Española), and began to create one of the largest empires in world history for Spain — all the while thinking he was near China and Japan, in the realm of the Great Khan whom Marco Polo had met and who had died hundreds of years earlier.

In what ways was the voyage of Columbus similar to that of da Gama? In what ways was it similar to that of Zheng He? In what ways was it different from both of these voyages? Taking the voyages of da Gama and Columbus together, what were the differences between Chinese and European expansion?

THINKING HISTORICALLY

Because this document comes from the period we are studying and is written by Columbus himself, it is a primary source. Primary sources have a great sense of immediacy and can often seem to transport us directly into the past. However, involvement when reading does not always lead to understanding, so it is important to

---

Source: "First Voyage of Columbus," in *The Four Voyages of Columbus*, ed. Cecil Jane (New York: Dover, 1988), 1–18.

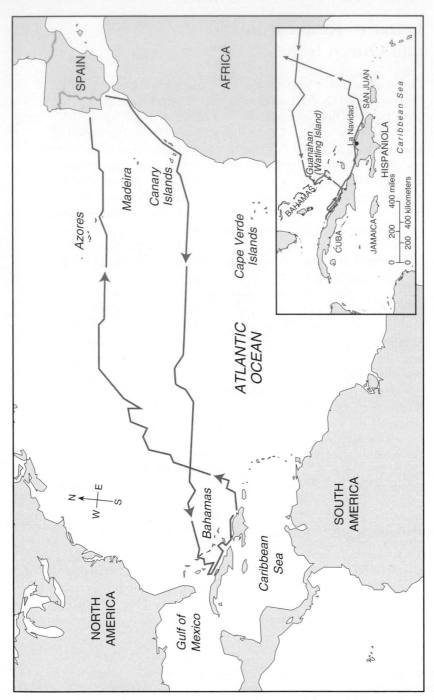

Map 15.3 Columbus's First Voyage, 1492–1493.

590

think critically about the source and the writer's intended audience as we read. First we must determine the source of the document. Where does it come from? Is it original? If not, is it a copy or a translation? Next, we must determine who wrote it, when it was written, and for what purpose. After answering these questions, we are able to read the document with a critical eye, which leads to greater understanding.

The original letter by Columbus has been lost. This selection is an English translation based on three different printed Spanish versions of the letter. So this text is a reconstruction, not an original, though it is believed to be quite close to the original.

The original letter was probably composed during a relaxed time on the return voyage before its date of February 15, 1493 — possibly as early as the middle of January — and sent to the Spanish monarchs from Lisbon in order to reach them by the time Columbus arrived in Barcelona.

What does Columbus want to impart to Ferdinand and Isabella? First and foremost, he wants them to know that he reached the Indies, that the voyage was a success. And so, the letter's opening sentence tells us something that Columbus certainly did not intend or know. We learn that on his return in 1493, Columbus thought he had been to the Indies when in fact he had not. (It is due to Columbus's confusion that we call the islands he visited the West Indies and Native Americans "Indians.")

Knowing what the author wants a reader to believe is useful information because it serves as a point of reference for other statements the author makes. The success of Columbus's voyage is a case in point. Columbus does not admit to the loss of one of his ships in his letter, nor does he explain fully why he had to build a fort at Navidad and leave some of his crew there, returning home without them. Clearly, Columbus had reason to worry that his voyage would be viewed as a failure. He had not found the gold mines he sought or the Asian cities described by Marco Polo. He thought he had discovered many spices, though only the chili peppers were new. Notice, as you read this letter, how Columbus presents his voyage in the best light.

Aside from what Columbus intends, what facts do you learn from the letter about Columbus, his first voyage, and his encounter with the New World? What seems to drive Columbus to do what he does? What is Columbus's attitude toward the "Indians"? What does Columbus's letter tell us about the society and culture of the Taino* — the people he met in the Caribbean?

* TY noh

Sir, As I know that you will be pleased at the great victory with which Our Lord has crowned my voyage, I write this to you, from which you will learn how in thirty-three days, I passed from the Canary Islands to the Indies with the fleet which the most illustrious king and queen, our sovereigns, gave to me. And there I found very many islands filled with people innumerable, and of them all I have taken possession for their highnesses, by proclamation made and with the royal standard unfurled, and no opposition was offered to me. To the first island which I found, I gave the name *San Salvador*, in remembrance of the Divine Majesty, Who has marvellously bestowed all this; the Indians call it "Guanahani."* To the second, I gave the name *Isla de Santa María de Concepción*; to the third, *Fernandina*; to the fourth, *Isabella*; to the fifth, *Isla Juana*, and so to each one I gave a new name.

When I reached Juana, I followed its coast to the westward, and I found it to be so extensive that I thought that it must be the mainland, the province of Catayo. And since there were neither towns nor villages on the seashore, but only small hamlets, with the people which I could not have speech, because they all fled immediately, I went forward on the same course, thinking that I should not fail to find great cities and towns. And, at the end of many leagues, seeing that there was no change and that the coast was bearing me northwards, which I wished to avoid, since winter was already beginning and I proposed to make from it to the south, and as moreover the wind was carrying me forward, I determined not to wait for a change in the weather and retraced my path as far as a certain harbour known to me. And from that point, I sent two men inland to learn if there were a king or great cities. They travelled three days' journey and found an infinity of small hamlets and people without number, but nothing of importance. For this reason, they returned.

I understood sufficiently from other Indians, whom I had already taken, that this land was nothing but an island. And therefore I followed its coast eastwards for one hundred and seven leagues to the point where it ended. And from that cape, I saw another island, distant eighteen leagues from the former, to the east, to which I at once gave the name "Española." And I went there and followed its northern coast, as I had in the case of Juana, to the eastward for one hundred and eighty-eight great leagues in a straight line. This island and all the others are very fertile to a limitless degree, and this island is extremely so. In it there are many harbours on the coast of the sea, beyond comparison with others which I know in Christendom, and many rivers, good and large, which is marvellous. Its lands are high, and there are in it very many sierras and very lofty mountains, beyond comparison with the island of Teneriffe. All are most beautiful, of a thousand shapes, and all are accessible and

---

* gwah nah HAH nee

filled with trees of a thousand kinds and tall, and they seem to touch the sky. And I am told that they never lose their foliage, as I can understand, for I saw them as green and as lovely as they are in Spain in May, and some of them were flowering, some bearing fruit, and some in another stage, according to their nature. And the nightingale was singing and other birds of a thousand kinds in the month of November there where I went. There are six or eight kinds of palm, which are a wonder to behold on account of their beautiful variety, but so are the other trees and fruits and plants. In it are marvellous pine groves, and there are very large tracts of cultivatable lands, and there is honey, and there are birds of many kinds and fruits in great diversity. In the interior are mines of metals, and the population is without number. Española is a marvel.

The sierras and mountains, the plains and arable lands and pastures, are so lovely and rich for planting and sowing, for breeding cattle of every kind, for building towns and villages. The harbours of the sea here are such as cannot be believed to exist unless they have been seen, and so with the rivers, many and great, and good waters, the majority of which contain gold. In the trees and fruits and plants, there is a great difference from those of Juana. In this island, there are many spices and great mines of gold and of other metals.

The people of this island, and of all the other islands which I have found and of which I have information, all go naked, men and women, as their mothers bore them, although some women cover a single place with the leaf of a plant or with a net of cotton which they make for the purpose. They have no iron or steel or weapons, nor are they fitted to use them, not because they are not well built men and of handsome stature, but because they are very marvellously timorous. They have no other arms than weapons made of canes, cut in seeding time, to the ends of which they fix a small sharpened stick. And they do not dare to make use of these, for many times it has happened that I have sent ashore two or three men to some town to have speech, and countless people have come out to them, and as soon as they have seen my men approaching they have fled, even a father not waiting for his son. And this, not because ill has been done to anyone; on the contrary, at every point where I have been and have been able to have speech, I have given to them of all that I had, such as cloth and many other things, without receiving anything for it; but so they are, incurably timid. It is true that, after they have been reassured and have lost their fear, they are so guileless and so generous with all they possess, that no one would believe it who has not seen it. They never refuse anything which they possess, if it be asked of them; on the contrary, they invite anyone to share it, and display as much love as if they would give their hearts, and whether the thing be of value or whether it be of small price, at once with whatever trifle of whatever kind it may be that is given to them, with that they are content. I forbade that they should be given things so worthless as fragments of broken crockery and scraps of broken glass, and ends of straps, although when they were able to get them, they fancied that they possessed the best jewel in the world. So it was found that a sailor for a strap received gold to the weight of two and a half *castellanos*, and others much more for other things which were worth much less. As for new *blancas*,[1] for them they would give everything which they had, although it might be two or three *castellanos*' weight of gold or an *arroba*[2] or two of spun cotton. . . . They took even the pieces of the broken hoops of the wine barrels and, like savages, gave what they had, so that it seemed to me to be wrong and I forbade it. And I gave a thousand handsome good things, which I had brought, in order that they might conceive affection, and more than that, might become Christians and be inclined to the love and service of their highnesses and of the whole Castilian nation, and strive to aid us and to give us of the things which they have in abundance and which are necessary to us. And they do not know any creed and are not idolaters; only they all believe that power and good are in the heavens, and they are very firmly convinced that I, with these ships and men, came from the heavens, and in this belief they everywhere received me, after they had overcome their fear. And this does not come because they are ignorant; on the contrary, they are of a very acute intelligence and are men who navigate all those seas, so that it is amazing how good an account they give of everything, but it is because they have never seen people clothed or ships of such a kind.

And as soon as I arrived in the Indies, in the first island which I found, I took by force some of them, in order that they might learn and give me information of that which there is in those parts, and so it was that they soon understood us, and we them, either by speech or signs, and they have been very serviceable. I still take them with me, and they are always assured that I come from Heaven, for all the intercourse which they have had with me; and they were the first to announce this wherever I went, and the others went running from house to house and to the neighbouring towns, with loud cries of, "Come! Come to see the people from Heaven!" So all, men and women alike, when their minds were set at rest concerning us, came, so that not one, great or small, remained behind, and all brought something to eat and drink, which they gave with extraordinary affection. In all the island, they have very many canoes, like rowing *fustas*,[3] some larger, some smaller, and some are larger than a *fusta* of eighteen benches. They are not so broad, because they are made of a single log of wood, but a *fusta* would not keep up with them in rowing, since their speed is a thing incredible. And in these they navigate among all those islands, which are innumerable,

---

[1] Spanish copper coins. [Ed.]
[2] A unit of weight (about 25 pounds) indicated by the @ symbol. [Ed.]
[3] Fast ships with oars and sails, probably of Arab origin. [Ed.]

and carry their goods. One of these canoes I have seen with seventy and eighty men in her, and each one with his oar.

In all these islands, I saw no great diversity in the appearance of the people or in their manners and language. On the contrary, they all understand one another, which is a very curious thing, on account of which I hope that their highnesses will determine upon their conversion to our holy faith, towards which they are very inclined.

I have already said how I have gone one hundred and seven leagues in a straight line from west to east along the seashore of the island Juana, and as a result of that voyage, I can say that this island is larger than England and Scotland together, for, beyond these one hundred and seven leagues, there remain to the westward two provinces to which I have not gone. One of these provinces they call "Avan," and there the people are born with tails; and these provinces cannot have a length of less than fifty or sixty leagues, as I could understand from those Indians whom I have and who know all the islands.

The other, Española, has a circumference greater than all Spain, from Colibre, by the sea-coast, to Fuenterabia in Vizcaya, since I voyaged along one side one hundred and eighty-eight great leagues in a straight line from west to east. It is a land to be desired and, seen, it is never to be left. And in it, although of all I have taken possession for their highnesses and all are more richly endowed than I know how, or am able, to say, and I hold them all for their highnesses, so that they may dispose of them as, and as absolutely as, of the kingdoms of Castile, in this Española, in the situation most convenient and in the best position for the mines of gold and for all intercourse as well with the mainland here as with that there, belonging to the Grand Khan, where will be great trade and gain, I have taken possession of a large town, to which I gave the name *Villa de Navidad*, and in it I have made fortifications and a fort, which now will by this time be entirely finished, and I have left in it sufficient men for such a purpose with arms and artillery and provisions for more than a year, and a *fusta*, and one, a master of all seacraft, to build others, and great friendship with the king of that land, so much so, that he was proud to call me, and to treat me as, a brother. And even if he were to change his attitude to one of hostility towards these men, he and his do not know what arms are and they go naked, as I have already said, and are the most timorous people that there are in the world, so that the men whom I have left there alone would suffice to destroy all that land, and the island is without danger for their persons, if they know how to govern themselves.

In all these islands, it seems to me that all men are content with one woman, and to their chief or king they give as many as twenty. It appears to me that the women work more than the men. And I have not been able to learn if they hold private property; what seemed to me to appear was that, in that which one had, all took a share, especially of eatable things.

In these islands I have so far found no human monstrosities, as many expected, but on the contrary the whole population is very well-formed, nor are they negros as in Guinea, but their hair is flowing, and they are not born where there is intense force in the rays of the sun; it is true that the sun has there great power, although it is distant from the equinoctial line twenty-six degrees. In these islands, where there are high mountains, the cold was severe this winter, but they endure it, being used to it and with the help of meats which they eat with many and extremely hot spices. As I have found no monsters, so I have had no report of any, except in an island "Quaris," the second at the coming into the Indies, which is inhabited by a people who are regarded in all the islands as very fierce and who eat human flesh. They have many canoes with which they range through all the islands of India and pillage and take as many as they can. They are no more malformed than the others, except that they have the custom of wearing their hair long like women, and they use bows and arrows of the same cane stems, with a small piece of wood at the end, owing to lack of iron which they do not possess. They are ferocious among these other people who are cowardly to an excessive degree, but I make no more account of them than of the rest. These are those who have intercourse with the women of "Matinino," which is the first island met on the way from Spain to the Indies, in which there is not a man. These women engage in no feminine occupation, but use bows and arrows of cane, like those already mentioned, and they arm and protect themselves with plates of copper, of which they have much.

In another island, which they assure me is larger than Española, the people have no hair. In it, there is gold incalculable, and from it and from the other islands, I bring with me Indians as evidence.

In conclusion, to speak only of that which has been accomplished on this voyage, which was so hasty, their highnesses can see that I will give them as much gold as they may need, if their highnesses will render me very slight assistance; moreover, spice and cotton, as much as their highnesses shall command; and mastic, as much as they shall order to be shipped and which, up to now, has been found only in Greece, in the island of Chios, and the Seignory sells it for what it pleases; and aloe wood, as much as they shall order to be shipped, and slaves, as many as they shall order to be shipped and who will be from the idolaters. And I believe that I have found rhubarb and cinnamon, and I shall find a thousand other things of value, which the people whom I have left there will have discovered, for I have not delayed at any point, so far as the wind allowed me to sail, except in the town of Navidad, in order to leave it secured and well established, and in truth, I should have done much more, if the ships had served me, as reason demanded.

This is enough . . . and the eternal God, our Lord, Who gives to all those who walk in His way triumph over things which appear to be impossible, and this was notably one; for, although men have talked or have written of these lands, all was conjectural, without suggestion of ocular evidence, but amounted only to this, that those who heard for the most part listened and judged it to be rather a fable than as having any vestige of truth. So that, since Our Redeemer has given this victory to our most illustrious king and queen, and to their renowned kingdoms, in so great a matter, for this all Christendom ought to feel delight and make great feasts and give solemn thanks to the Holy Trinity with many solemn prayers for the great exaltation which they shall have, in the turning of so many peoples to our holy faith, and afterwards for temporal benefits, for not only Spain but all Christians will have hence refreshment and gain.

This, in accordance with that which has been accomplished, thus briefly.

Done in the caravel,[4] off the Canary Islands, on the fifteenth of February, in the year one thousand four hundred and ninety-three.

At your orders.   El Almirante.

After having written this, and being in the sea of Castile, there came on me so great a south-south-west wind, that I was obliged to lighten ship. But I ran here to-day into this port of Lisbon, which was the greatest marvel in the world, whence I decided to write to their highnesses. In all the Indies, I have always found weather like May; where I went in thirty-three days and I had returned in twenty-eight, save for these storms which have detained me for fourteen days, beating about in this sea. Here all the sailors say that never has there been so bad a winter nor so many ships lost.

Done on the fourth day of March.

[4] Sailing ship, in this case the *Santa Maria*. [Ed.]

5

KIRKPATRICK SALE

The Conquest of Paradise, 1991

In this selection from his popular study of Columbus, Sale is concerned with Columbus's attitude toward nature in the New World. Sale regards Columbus as a symbol of European expansion. If Columbus is distinctly European, what is Sale saying about European expansion? How and what does Sale add to your understanding of the similarities and differences between Chinese and European expansion?

Source: Kirkpatrick Sale, *The Conquest of Paradise* (New York: Penguin, 1991), 92–104.

Was Columbus much different from Zheng He? Or were the areas and peoples they visited causes for different responses? Vasco da Gama visited the same areas as Zheng He. How similar, or different, was da Gama from Zheng He? If da Gama was a better symbol of European expansion, how different was the European experience from the Chinese?

THINKING HISTORICALLY

Clearly, this selection is a secondary source; Sale is a modern writer, not a fifteenth-century contemporary of Columbus. Still, you will not have to read very far into the selection to realize that Sale has a distinct point of view. Secondary sources, like primary ones, should be analyzed for bias and perspective, and the author's interpretation should be identified.

Sale is an environmentalist and a cultural critic. Do his beliefs and values hinder his understanding of Columbus, or do they inform and illuminate aspects of Columbus that might otherwise be missed? Does Sale help you recognize things you would not have seen on your own, or does he persuade you to see things that might not truly be there?

Notice how Sale uses primary sources in his text. He quotes from Columbus's journal and his letter to King Ferdinand and Queen Isabella. Do these quotes help you understand Columbus, or do they simply support Sale's argument? What do you think about Sale's use of the Spanish *Colón** for *Columbus*? Does Sale "take possession" of Columbus by, in effect, "renaming" him for modern readers? Is the effect humanizing or debunking?

Notice how Sale sometimes calls attention to what the primary source did *not* say rather than what it did say. Is this a legitimate way to understand someone, or is Sale projecting a twentieth-century perspective on Columbus to make a point?

Toward the end of the selection, Sale extends his criticism beyond Columbus to include others. Who are the others? What is the effect of this larger criticism?

Admiral Colón spent a total of ninety-six days exploring the lands he encountered on the far side of the Ocean Sea—four rather small coralline islands in the Bahamian chain and two substantial coastlines of what he finally acknowledged were larger islands—every one of which he "took possession of" in the name of his Sovereigns.

The first he named San Salvador, no doubt as much in thanksgiving for its welcome presence after more than a month at sea as for the Son

* koh LOHN

of God whom it honored; the second he called Santa María de la Concepcíon, after the Virgin whose name his flagship bore; and the third and fourth he called Fernandina and Isabela, for his patrons, honoring Aragon before Castile for reasons never explained (possibly protocol, possibly in recognition of the chief sources of backing for the voyage). The first of the two large and very fertile islands he called Juana, which Fernando [Columbus's son] says was done in honor of Prince Juan, heir to the Castilian throne, but just as plausibly might have been done in recognition of Princess Juana, the unstable child who eventually carried on the line; the second he named la Ysla Española, the "Spanish Island," because it resembled (though he felt it surpassed in beauty) the lands of Castile.

It was not that the islands were in need of names, mind you, nor indeed that Colón was ignorant of the names that native peoples had already given them, for he frequently used those original names before endowing them with his own. Rather, the process of bestowing new names went along with "taking possession of" those parts of the world he deemed suitable for Spanish ownership, showing the royal banners, erecting various crosses, and pronouncing certain oaths and pledges. If this was presumption, it had an honored heritage: It was Adam who was charged by his Creator with the task of naming "every living creature," including the product of his own rib, in the course of establishing "dominion over" them.

Colón went on to assign no fewer than sixty-two other names on the geography of the islands—capes, points, mountains, ports—with a blithe assurance suggesting that in his (and Europe's) perception the act of name-giving was in some sense a talisman of conquest, a rite that changed raw neutral stretches of far-off earth into extensions of Europe. The process began slowly, even haltingly—he forgot to record, for example, until four days afterward that he named the landfall island San Salvador—but by the time he came to Española at the end he went on a naming spree, using more than two-thirds of all the titles he concocted on that one coastline. On certain days it became almost a frenzy: on December 6 he named six places, on the nineteenth six more, and on January 11 no fewer than ten—eight capes, a point, and a mountain. It is almost as if, as he sailed along the last of the islands, he was determined to leave his mark on it the only way he knew how, and thus to establish his authority—and by extension Spain's—even, as with baptism, to make it thus sanctified, and real, and official. . . .

This business of naming and "possessing" foreign islands was by no means casual. The Admiral took it very seriously, pointing out that "it was my wish to bypass no island without taking possession" (October 15) and that "in all regions [I] always left a cross standing" (November 16) as a mark of Christian dominance. There even seem to have been certain prescriptions for it (the instructions from the Sovereigns speak of "the administering of the oath and the performing of the rites prescribed in such cases"), and Rodrigo de Escobedo was sent along as secretary of the fleet explicitly to witness and record these events in detail.

But consider the implications of this act and the questions it raises again about what was in the Sovereigns' minds, what in Colón's. Why would the Admiral assume that these territories were in some way *un*possessed—even by those clearly inhabiting them—and thus available for Spain to claim? Why would he not think twice about the possibility that some considerable potentate—the Grand Khan of China, for example, whom he later acknowledged (November 6) "must be" the ruler of Española—might descend upon him at any moment with a greater military force than his three vessels commanded and punish him for his territorial presumption? Why would he make the ceremony of possession his very first act on shore, even before meeting the inhabitants or exploring the environs, or finding out if anybody there objected to being thus possessed—particularly if they actually owned the great treasures he hoped would be there? No European would have imagined that anyone—three small boatloads of Indians, say—could come up to a European shore or island and "take possession" of it, nor would a European imagine marching up to some part of North Africa or the Middle East and claiming sovereignty there with impunity. Why were these lands thought to be different?

Could there be any reason for the Admiral to assume he had reached "unclaimed" shores, new lands that lay far from the domains of any of the potentates of the East? Can that really have been in his mind—or can it all be explained as simple Eurocentrism, or Eurosuperiority, mixed with cupidity and naiveté? . . .

Once safely "possessed,"[1] San Salvador was open for inspection. Now the Admiral turned his attention for the first time to the "naked people" staring at him on the beach—he did not automatically give them a name, interestingly enough, and it would be another six days before he decided what he might call them—and tried to win their favor with his trinkets.

> They all go around as naked as their mothers bore them; and also the women, although I didn't see more than one really young girl. All that I saw were young people [*mancebos*], none of them more than 30 years old. They are very well built, with very handsome bodies and very good faces; their hair [is] coarse, almost like the silk of a horse's tail, and short. They wear their hair over their eyebrows, except for a little in the back that they wear long and never cut. Some of them paint themselves black (and they are the color of the Canary Islanders, neither black nor white), and some paint themselves white, and some red, and some with what they find. And some paint their faces, and some of them the whole body, and some the eyes only, and some of them only the nose.

It may fairly be called the birth of American anthropology.

---

[1] Given Spanish names. [Ed.]

A crude anthropology, of course, as superficial as Colón's descriptions always were when his interest was limited, but simple and straightforward enough, with none of the fable and fantasy that characterized many earlier (and even some later) accounts of new-found peoples. There was no pretense to objectivity, or any sense that these people might be representatives of a culture equal to, or in any way a model for, Europe's. Colón immediately presumed the inferiority of the natives, not merely because (a sure enough sign) they were naked, but because (his society could have no surer measure) they seemed so technologically backward. "It appeared to me that these people were very poor in everything," he wrote on that first day, and, worse still, "they have no iron." And they went on to prove their inferiority to the Admiral by being ignorant of even such a basic artifact of European life as a sword: "They bear no arms, nor are they acquainted with them," he wrote, "for I showed them swords and they grasped them by the blade and cut themselves through ignorance." Thus did European arms spill the first drops of native blood on the sands of the New World, accompanied not with a gasp of compassion but with a smirk of superiority.

Then, just six sentences further on, Colón clarified what this inferiority meant in his eyes:

> They ought to be good servants and of good intelligence [*ingenio*]. . . . I believe that they would easily be made Christians, because it seemed to me that they had no religion. Our Lord pleasing, I will carry off six of them at my departure to Your Highnesses, in order that they may learn to speak.

No clothes, no arms, no possessions, no iron, and now no religion—not even speech: hence they were fit to be servants, and captives. It may fairly be called the birth of American slavery.

Whether or not the idea of slavery was in Colón's mind all along is uncertain, although he did suggest he had had experience as a slave trader in Africa (November 12) and he certainly knew of Portuguese plantation slavery in the Madeiras and Spanish slavery of Guanches in the Canaries. But it seems to have taken shape early and grown ever firmer as the weeks went on and as he captured more and more of the helpless natives. At one point he even sent his crew ashore to kidnap "seven head of women, young ones and adults, and three small children"; the expression of such callousness led the Spanish historian Salvador de Madariaga to remark, "It would be difficult to find a starker utterance of utilitarian subjection of man by man than this passage [whose] form is no less devoid of human feeling than its substance."

To be sure, Colón knew nothing about these people he encountered and considered enslaving, and he was hardly trained to find out very much, even if he was moved to care. But they were in fact members of an extensive, populous, and successful people whom Europe, using its own peculiar taxonomy, subsequently called "Taino" (or "Taíno"), their own word for "good" or "noble," and their response when asked who they were. They were related distantly by both language and culture to the Arawak people of the South American mainland, but it is misleading (and needlessly imprecise) to call them Arawaks, as historians are wont to do, when the term "Taino" better establishes their ethnic and historical distinctiveness. They had migrated to the islands from the mainland at about the time of the birth of Christ, occupying the three large islands we now call the Greater Antilles and arriving at Guanahani (Colón's San Salvador) and the end of the Bahamian chain probably sometime around A.D. 900. There they displaced an earlier people, the Guanahacabibes (sometimes called Guanahatabeys), who by the time of the European discovery occupied only the western third of Cuba and possibly remote corners of Española; and there, probably in the early fifteenth century, they eventually confronted another people moving up the islands from the mainland, the Caribs, whose culture eventually occupied a dozen small islands of what are called the Lesser Antilles.

The Tainos were not nearly so backward as Colón assumed from their lack of dress. (It might be said that it was the Europeans, who generally kept clothed head to foot during the day despite temperatures regularly in the eighties, who were the more unsophisticated in garmenture—especially since the Tainos, as Colón later noted, also used their body paint to prevent sunburn.) Indeed, they had achieved a means of living in a balanced and fruitful harmony with their natural surroundings that any society might well have envied. They had, to begin with, a not unsophisticated technology that made exact use of their available resources, two parts of which were so impressive that they were picked up and adopted by the European invaders: *canoa* (canoes) that were carved and fire-burned from large silk-cotton trees, "all in one piece, and wonderfully made" (October 13), some of which were capable of carrying up to 150 passengers; and *hamaca* (hammocks) that were "like nets of cotton" (October 17) and may have been a staple item of trade with Indian tribes as far away as the Florida mainland. Their houses were not only spacious and clean—as the Europeans noted with surprise and appreciation, used as they were to the generally crowded and slovenly hovels and huts of south European peasantry—but more apropos, remarkably resistant to hurricanes; the circular walls were made of strong cane poles set deep and close together ("as close as the fingers of a hand," Colón noted), the conical roofs of branches and vines tightly interwoven on a frame of smaller poles and covered with heavy palm leaves. Their artifacts and jewelry, with the exception of a few gold trinkets and ornaments, were based largely on renewable materials, including bracelets and necklaces of coral, shells, bone, and stone, embroidered cotton belts, woven baskets, carved statues and chairs, wooden and shell utensils, and pottery of variously intricate decoration depending on period and place.

Perhaps the most sophisticated, and most carefully integrated, part of their technology was their agricultural system, extraordinarily productive and perfectly adapted to the conditions of the island environment. It was based primarily on fields of knee-high mounds, called *conucos*, planted with *yuca* (sometimes called manioc), *batata* (sweet potato), and various squashes and beans grown all together in multi-crop harmony: The root crops were excellent in resisting erosion and producing minerals and potash, the leaf crops effective in providing shade and moisture, and the mound configurations largely resistant to erosion and flooding and adaptable to almost all topographic conditions including steep hillsides. Not only was the *conuco* system environmentally appropriate — "conuco agriculture seems to have provided an exceptionally ecologically well-balanced and protective form of land use," according to David Watts's recent and authoritative *West Indies* — but it was also highly productive, surpassing in yields anything known in Europe at the time, with labor that amounted to hardly more than two or three hours a week, and in continuous yearlong harvest. The pioneering American geographical scholar Carl Sauer calls Taino agriculture "productive as few parts of the world," giving the "highest returns of food in continuous supply by the simplest methods and modest labor," and adds, with a touch of regret, "The white man never fully appreciated the excellent combination of plants that were grown in conucos."

In their arts of government the Tainos seem to have achieved a parallel sort of harmony. Most villages were small (ten to fifteen families) and autonomous, although many apparently recognized loose allegiances with neighboring villages, and they were governed by a hereditary official called a *kaseke* (*cacique,** in the Spanish form), something of a cross between an arbiter and a prolocutor, supported by advisers and elders. So little a part did violence play in their system that they seem, remarkably, to have been a society without war (at least we know of no war music or signals or artifacts, and no evidence of intertribal combats) and even without overt conflict (Las Casas reports that no Spaniard ever saw two Tainos fighting). And here we come to what was obviously the Tainos' outstanding cultural achievement, a proficiency in the social arts that led those who first met them to comment unfailingly on their friendliness, their warmth, their openness, and above all — so striking to those of an acquisitive culture — their generosity.

"They are the best people in the world and above all the gentlest," Colón recorded in his *Journal* (December 16), and from first to last he was astonished at their kindness:

* kah SEEK

They became so much our friends that it was a marvel. . . . They traded and gave everything they had, with good will [October 12].

I sent the ship's boat ashore for water, and they very willingly showed my people where the water was, and they themselves carried the full barrels to the boat, and took great delight in pleasing us [October 16].

They are very gentle and without knowledge of what is evil; nor do they murder or steal [November 12].

Your Highnesses may believe that in all the world there can be no better or gentler people . . . for neither better people nor land can there be. . . . All the people show the most singular loving behavior and they speak pleasantly [December 24].

I assure Your Highnesses that I believe that in all the world there is no better people nor better country. They love their neighbors as themselves, and they have the sweetest talk in the world, and are gentle and always laughing [December 25].

Even if one allows for some exaggeration—Colón was clearly trying to convince Ferdinand and Isabella that his Indians could be easily conquered and converted, should that be the Sovereigns' wish—it is obvious that the Tainos exhibited a manner of social discourse that quite impressed the rough Europeans. But that was not high among the traits of "civilized" nations, as Colón and Europe understood it, and it counted for little in the Admiral's assessment of these people. However struck he was with such behavior, he would not have thought that it was the mark of a benign and harmonious society, or that from it another culture might learn. For him it was something like the wondrous behavior of children, the naive guilelessness of prelapsarian[2] creatures who knew no better how to bargain and chaffer and cheat than they did to dress themselves: "For a lacepoint they gave good pieces of gold the size of two fingers" (January 6), and "They even took pieces of the broken hoops of the wine casks and, like beasts [como besti], gave what they had" (Santangel Letter).[3] Like beasts; such innocence was not human.

It is to be regretted that the Admiral, unable to see past their nakedness, as it were, knew not the real virtues of the people he confronted. For the Tainos' lives were in many ways as idyllic as their surroundings, into which they fit with such skill and comfort. They were well fed and well housed, without poverty or serious disease. They enjoyed considerable leisure, given over to dancing, singing, ballgames, and sex, and expressed themselves artistically in basketry, woodworking, pottery, and

---

[2] Before the Fall. In other words, before the time, according to the Old Testament, when Adam and Eve sinned and were banished by God from the Garden of Eden. [Ed.]

[3] Santangel was the minister of Ferdinand and Isabella who received the letter. [Ed.]

jewelry. They lived in general harmony and peace, without greed or covetousness or theft. . . .

It is perhaps only natural that Colón should devote his initial attention to the handsome, naked, naive islanders, but it does seem peculiar that he pays almost no attention, especially in the early days, to the spectacular scenery around them. Here he was, in the middle of an old-growth tropical forest the likes of which he could not have imagined before, its trees reaching sixty or seventy feet into the sky, more varieties than he knew how to count much less name, exhibiting a lushness that stood in sharp contrast to the sparse and denuded lands he had known in the Mediterranean, hearing a melodious multiplicity of bird songs and parrot calls—why was it not an occasion of wonder, excitement, and the sheer joy at nature in its full, arrogant abundance? But there is not a word of that: He actually said nothing about the physical surroundings on the first day, aside from a single phrase about "very green trees" and "many streams," and on the second managed only that short sentence about a big island with a big lake and green trees. Indeed, for the whole two weeks of the first leg of his voyage through the Bahamas to Cuba, he devoted only a third of the lines of description to the phenomena around him. And there are some natural sights he seems not to have noticed at all: He did not mention (except in terms of navigation) the nighttime heavens, the sharp, glorious configurations of stars that he must have seen virtually every night of his journey, many for the first time.

Eventually Colón succumbed to the islands' natural charms as he sailed on—how could he not?—and began to wax warmly about how "these islands are very green and fertile and the air very sweet" (October 15), with "trees which were more beautiful to see than any other thing that has ever been seen" (October 17), and "so good and sweet a smell of flowers or trees from the land" (October 19). But his descriptions are curiously vapid and vague, the language opaque and lifeless:

> The other island, which is very big [October 15] . . . this island is very large [October 16] . . . these islands are very green and fertile [October 15] . . . this land is the best and most fertile [October 17] . . . in it many plants and trees . . . if the others are very beautiful, this is more so [October 19] . . . here are some great lagoons . . . big and little birds of all sorts . . . if the others already seen are very beautiful and green and fertile, this one is much more so [October 21] . . . full of very good harbors and deep rivers [October 28].

You begin to see the Admiral's problem: He cares little about the features of nature, at least the ones he doesn't use for sailing, and even when he admires them he has little experience in assessing them and less acquaintance with a vocabulary to describe them. To convey the lush density and stately grandeur of those tropical forests, for example, he had little more than the modifiers "green" and "very": "very green trees" (October 12), "trees very green" (October 13), "trees . . . so green and with leaves like those of Castile" (October 14), "very green and very big trees" (October 19), "large groves are very green" (October 21), "trees . . . beautiful and green" (October 28). And when he began to be aware of the diversity among those trees, he was still unable to make meaningful distinctions: "All the trees are as different from ours as day from night" (October 17), "trees of a thousand kinds" (October 21), "a thousand sorts of trees" (October 23), "trees . . . different from ours" (October 28), "trees of a thousand sorts" (November 14), "trees of a thousand kinds" (December 6).

Such was his ignorance—a failing he repeatedly bemoaned ("I don't recognize them, which gives me great grief," October 19)—that when he did stop to examine a species he often had no idea what he was looking at. "I saw many trees very different from ours," he wrote on October 16, "and many of them have branches of many kinds, and all on one trunk, and one twig is of one kind and another of another, and so different that it is the greatest wonder in the world how much diversity there is of one kind from the other. That is to say, one branch has leaves like a cane, and another like mastic, and thus on one tree five or six kinds, and all so different." There is no such tree in existence, much less "many of them," and never was: Why would anyone imagine, or so contrive, such a thing to be?

Colón's attempts to identify species were likewise frequently wrong-headed, usually imputing to them commercial worth that they did not have, as with the worthless "aloes" he loaded such quantities of. The "amaranth" he identified on October 28 and the "oaks" and "arbutus" of November 25 are species that do not grow in the Caribbean; the "mastic" he found on November 5 and loaded on board to sell in Spain was gumbo-limbo, commercially worthless. (On the other hand, one of the species of flora he deemed of no marketable interest— "weeds [*tizon*] in their hands to drink in the fragrant smoke" [November 6]—was tobacco.) Similarly, the "whales" he spotted on October 16 must have been simply large fish, the "geese" he saw on November 6 and again on December 22 were ducks, the "nightingales" that kept delighting him (November 6; December 7, 13) do not exist in the Americas, and the skulls of "cows" he identified on October 29 were probably not those of land animals but of manatees.

This all seems a little sad, revealing a man rather lost in a world that he cannot come to know, a man with a "geographic and naturalistic knowledge that doesn't turn out to be very deep or nearly complete," and "a limited imagination and a capacity for comparisons conditioned by a not very broad geographic culture," in the words of Gaetano Ferro, a Columbus scholar and professor of geography at the University of Genoa. One could not of course have expected that an adventurer and sailor of this era would also be a naturalist, or necessarily even have some genuine interest in or curiosity about the natural world, but it is a disappointment nonetheless that the Discoverer of the New World turns out to be quite so simple, quite so inexperienced, in the ways of discovering his environment.

Colón's limitations, I hasten to say, were not his alone; they were of his culture, and they would be found in the descriptions of many others — Vespucci, Cortés, Hawkins, Juet, Cartier, Champlain, Raleigh — in the century of discovery to follow. They are the source of what the distinguished English historian J. H. Elliott has called "the problem of description" faced by Europeans confronting the uniqueness of the New World: "So often the physical appearance of the New World is either totally ignored or else described in the flattest and most conventional phraseology. This off-hand treatment of nature contrasts strikingly with the many precise and acute descriptions of the native inhabitants. It is as if the American landscape is seen as no more than a backcloth against which the strange and perennially fascinating peoples of the New World are dutifully grouped." The reason, Elliott thinks, and this is telling, may be "a lack of interest among sixteenth-century Europeans, and especially those of the Mediterranean world, in landscape and in nature." This lack of interest was reflected in the lack of vocabulary, the lack of that facility common to nature-based peoples whose cultures are steeped in natural imagery. Oviedo, for example, setting out to write descriptions for his *Historia General* in the next century, continually threw his hands up in the air: "Of all the things I have seen," he said at one point, "this is the one which has most left me without hope of being able to describe it in words"; or at another, "It needs to be painted by the hand of a Berruguete or some other excellent painter like him, or by Leonardo da Vinci or Andrea Mantegna, famous painters whom I knew in Italy." Like Colón, visitor after visitor to the New World seemed mind-boggled and tongue-tied trying to convey the wonders before them, and about the only color they seem to have eyes for is green — and not very many shades of that, either. . . .

■ REFLECTIONS

It is difficult to ignore moral issues when considering explorations and explorers. The prefix *great* is used liberally, and words like *discovery* and *courage* readily fit when describing "firsts" and "unknowns." However, celebratory images, national myths, and heroic biographies inevitably breed skepticism. Sometimes the result is an opposite assessment. Kirkpatrick Sale charges Columbus with arrogance, ignorance, and insufficient curiosity. Chinese historians of the last twenty years have swung from ignoring to celebrating the voyages of Zheng He, and some more recently have criticized Zheng He for military suppression of those in the lands his fleet visited.

On the matter of preparation, the difference between the Chinese and European voyages is especially striking. Da Gama at least brought an Arabic interpreter, though the absence of valuable gifts undermined the success of the voyage. The floating Chinese scientific laboratories, traveling experts, sages, and interpreters contrast starkly with the lack of a single artist or naturalist on board Columbus's ships. But the inability to distinguish shades of green is not a moral failure. We might say that Columbus's voyage was premature, Zheng He's meticulously planned and prepared. Like the designers of a modern aircraft, the Chinese built in redundancies: separate compartments that could fill with water without sinking the ship, more rice and fresh water than they would need, experts to find plants that might cure diseases yet unknown. By contrast, Columbus seems like a loose cannon, unaware of where he was going or where he had been, capable of lighting a match inside a dark powder shed.

These were, and in many ways still are, the differences between Chinese and European (now Western) scientific innovation. No European king could organize an enterprise on the scale of Zhu Di, Zheng He's emperor. No Chinese emperor had reason to sanction an experimental voyage into the unknown. The domain of the emperor was the known world, of which he was the center. In the Europe of closely competing princes, a Columbus could hatch a personal scheme with minimal supervision and barely sufficient funding and the consequences could still be—indeed, were—momentous. (See Chapter 16.) Was such a system irresponsible? Today, as we begin to probe the heavens around us, even as we tamper with technologies that change the balance of natural forces on Earth, we might consider whether the Confucian scholars of six hundred years ago were on to something when they burned the ships and destroyed all the records of their age of great discovery.

Primary sources are not limited to artifacts, images, and old written records, however. In the recent phase of celebrating the memory of Zheng He, the Chinese claimed as their own a young woman from Kenya, Mwamaka Sharifu, who looked like some of the people Kristof saw in 1999. Chinese-African faces on the coast of East Africa are evidence of contact, but not of contact in 1421. Combined, however, with family stories, DNA tests, local histories, and archaeological finds, a single living primary source may become the basis for a new interpretation of a broader history. In the case of Mwamaka Sharifu, members of her family, and other residents of coastal Somalia and Kenya, the evidence has proved convincing.

16

Atlantic World Encounters

Europeans, Americans, and Africans,
1500–1850

■ HISTORICAL CONTEXT

European expansion in the Atlantic that began with Portuguese voyages along the African coast in the 1440s and Columbus's discovery of the Americas in 1492 created a new Atlantic zone of human contact and communication that embraced four continents and one ocean. Nothing prior—neither the Chinese contacts with Africa in the early fifteenth century, nor the expansion of Islam throughout Eurasia in the almost thousand years since the Prophet Muhammad's death in 632—had so thoroughly and so permanently changed the human and ecological balance of the world.

Sub-Saharan Africa had already been integrated into the world of Eurasia by 1450. African populations became more mixed as peoples from the Niger River area migrated east and south throughout the continent during the fifteen hundred years before the arrival of the Portuguese. Muslims from North Africa and the Middle East aided or established Muslim states and trading ports south of the Sahara in East and West Africa after 1000. Cultural and technical innovations of the Middle East, like the literacy that came with Islam, penetrated slowly, and the spread of the many plants and animals of the Northern Hemisphere was slowed by the Sahara and equator. However, microbes traveled swiftly and easily from Eurasia to Africa, creating a single set of diseases and immunities for the peoples of the Afro-Eurasian Old World.

The peoples of the Americas, having been isolated ecologically for more than ten thousand years, were not so fortunate. The arrival of Europeans and Africans in the Americas after 1492 had devastating consequences for Native American populations. Old World diseases like

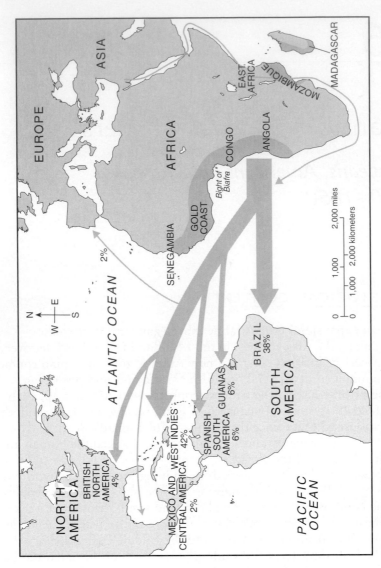

Map 16.1 The Atlantic Slave Trade.

smallpox were responsible for millions of Native American deaths—a tragedy of far greater scope than the casualties caused by wars. To work the mines and plantations of the New World, Europeans used Indian labor, but increasingly, especially for lowland plantations, they used African slaves (see Map 16.1). By 1850 the combination of Indian "die-off" and African and European migration resulted in vastly different populations in the Americas. On some Caribbean islands and in plantation areas like northeastern Brazil, Indian populations were entirely replaced by Africans. At the same time, European animals (for example, goats, cattle, horses) multiplied in the absence of natural predators.

The new Atlantic ecological system was not a uniform zone, however. Coastal regions in Western Europe and towns on the eastern seaboard of the Americas prospered, while American interiors and African populations in Africa stagnated or declined. The Atlantic Ocean became a vast lake that united port cities and plantations with sailing ships that carried African slaves to the Caribbean, Caribbean sugar and rum to North American and European industrial ports, and guns, pots, and liquor to the African "Slave Coast."

Thus, the Atlantic world was integrated with the Old World. Trade routes that began in Boston or Bahia, Brazil, stretched across Eurasia and around southern Africa into the Indian Ocean and the China Sea. Crops that had previously been known only to Native Americans—corn, potatoes, and tomatoes—fueled population explosions from Ireland to China and graced the tables of peasants and princes in between. What began as an effort by European merchants to import Asian spices directly became after 1650 (as European tastes for pepper and Asian spices moderated) a new global pantry of possibilities.

In this chapter, we will read selections that describe this new global dynamic. We will read of Europeans in the Americas and in West Africa and examine European depictions of natives from both North and South America. We will also explore some of the African and American responses to this European expansion. When studying these accounts and images, notice how individuals at the frontier of a new age understood and treated each other. Consider how these exchanges, so apparently fortuitous and transitory at the time, changed the face of the world.

▪ THINKING HISTORICALLY

Comparing Primary Sources

By comparing and contrasting one thing with another, we learn more about each, and by examining related works in their proper context, we learn more about the whole of which they are part. In the first chapter we compared China and Europe or Chinese and European expansion in the fifteenth century. In this chapter we look at the Atlantic world, specifically at Europeans in Africa and the Americas. We begin with three views of the Spanish conquest of Mexico — separate accounts by the Spanish conquistadors, by the Mexicans, and by a Dominican friar. The fourth selection juxtaposes two European depictions of Native Americans.

The final five selections examine encounters between Europeans and Africans and the development of the Atlantic slave trade. Did Europeans treat Africans differently from the way they treated Native Americans? If so, why? How were the African reactions to Europeans different from the Native American reactions? What accounts for those differences?

1

BERNAL DÍAZ

The Conquest of New Spain, c. 1560

Bernal Díaz del Castillo was born in Spain in 1492, the year Columbus sailed to America. After participating in two explorations of the Mexican coast, Díaz joined the expedition of Hernán Cortés to Mexico City in 1519. He wrote this history of the conquest much later, when he was in his seventies; he died circa 1580, a municipal official with a small estate in Guatemala.

The conquest of Mexico did not automatically follow from the first Spanish settlements in Santo Domingo, Hispaniola, and then Cuba in the West Indies. The Spanish crown had given permission for trade and exploration, not colonization. But many Spaniards, from fortune-seeking peasant-soldiers to minor nobility, were eager to conquer their own lands and exploit the populations of dependent Indians.

Cortés, of minor noble descent, at the age of nineteen sailed to the Indies, where he established a sizeable estate on the island of Hispaniola. When he heard stories of Montezuma's gold, he was determined to find the fabled capital of the Aztec Empire, Tenochtitlán* (modern Mexico City). He gathered more than five hundred amateur soldiers, eleven ships, sixteen horses, and several pieces of artillery, then sailed across the Caribbean and Gulf of Mexico and there began the long march from the coast up to the high central plateau of Mexico.

---

* teh NOHCH teet LAHN

Source: Bernal Díaz, *The Conquest of New Spain*, trans. J. M. Cohen (Baltimore: Penguin Books, 1963), 217–19, 221–25, 228–38, 241–43.

The Aztecs were new to central Mexico, arriving from the North American desert only about two hundred years before the Spanish, around 1325. By 1500 they had established dominion over almost all other city-states of Mexico, ruling an empire that stretched as far south as Guatemala and as far east as the Maya lands of the Yucatan Peninsula.

Aztec power relied on a combination of old and new religious ideas and a military system that conquered through terror. The older religious tradition that the Aztecs adopted from Toltec culture centered on Quetzalcoatl* — the feathered serpent, god of creation and brotherhood, whose nurturing forces continued in Aztec society in a system of universal education and in festivals dedicated to life, creativity, and procreation. But the Aztecs also worshiped Huitzilopochtli,† a warrior-god primed for death and sacrifice, who was given dominant status in the Aztec pantheon. Huitzilopochtli (rendered "Huichilobos"‡ in this selection) was a force for building a powerful Aztec Empire. Drawing on the god's need for human sacrifice — a need not unknown among religions of central Mexico (or Christians) — Montezuma's predecessors built altars to Huitzilopochtli at Tenochtitlán, Cholula, and other sites. The war-god required a never-ending supply of human hearts, a need that prompted armies to ever-more remote sections of Central America in search of sacrificial victims and that created an endless supply of enemies of the Aztecs, among them, the Tlaxcalans.

With the help of his Indian captive and companion Doña Marina — called La Malinche§ by some of the Indians (thus, Montezuma sometimes calls Cortés "Lord Malinche" in the selection) — Cortés was able to communicate with the Tlaxcalans and other Indians who were tired of Aztec domination. On his march toward Tenochtitlán, Cortés stopped to join forces with the Tlaxcalans, perhaps cementing the relationship and demonstrating his resolve through a brutal massacre of the people of Cholula, an Aztec ally and archenemy of the Tlaxcalans. By the time Cortés arrived at Tenochtitlán, Montezuma knew of the defeat of his allies at Cholula.

This selection from Bernal Díaz begins with the Spanish entry into Tenochtitlán. What impresses Díaz, and presumably other Spanish conquistadors, about the Mexican capital city? What parts of the city attract his attention the most? What conclusions does he draw about Mexican (or Aztec) civilization? Does he think Spanish civilization is equal, inferior, or superior to that of Mexico?

* keht zahl koh AH tuhl
† wheat zee loh po ACHT lee
‡ wee chee LOH bohs
§ lah mah LEEN cheh   A variation on "Marina." In contemporary Mexico a traitor is often called a "Malinchisto."

Díaz gives us a dramatic account of the meeting of Cortés and Montezuma. What do you think each is thinking and feeling? Do you see any signs of tension in their elaborate greetings? Why are both behaving so politely? What do they want from each other?

Notice how the initial hospitality turns tense. What causes this? Is either side more to blame for what happens next? Was conflict inevitable? Could the encounter have ended in some sort of peaceful resolution?

THINKING HISTORICALLY

Remember, we are going to compare Díaz's view with a Mexican view of these events. From your reading of Díaz, does he seem able to understand the Mexican point of view? Would you call him a sympathetic observer?

When Cortes saw, heard, and was told that the great Montezuma was approaching, he dismounted from his horse, and when he came near to Montezuma each bowed deeply to the other. Montezuma welcomed our Captain, and Cortes, speaking through Doña Marina, answered by wishing him very good health. Cortes, I think, offered Montezuma his right hand, but Montezuma refused it and extended his own. Then Cortes brought out a necklace which he had been holding. It was made of those elaborately worked and coloured glass beads called *margaritas*, . . . and was strung on a gold cord and dipped in musk to give it a good odour. This he hung round the great Montezuma's neck, and as he did so attempted to embrace him. But the great princes who stood round Montezuma grasped Cortes' arm to prevent him, for they considered this an indignity.

Then Cortes told Montezuma that it rejoiced his heart to have seen such a great prince, and that he took his coming in person to receive him and the repeated favours he had done him as a high honour. After this Montezuma made him another complimentary speech, and ordered two of his nephews who were supporting him, the lords of Texcoco and Coyoacan, to go with us and show us our quarters. Montezuma returned to the city with the other two kinsmen of his escort, the lords of Cuitlahuac and Tacuba; and all those grand companies of *Caciques*[1] and dignitaries who had come with him returned also in his train. . . .

On our arrival we entered the large court, where the great Montezuma was awaiting our Captain. Taking him by the hand, the prince led him

---

[1] kah SEEK   Chiefs. [Ed.]

to his apartment in the hall where he was to lodge, which was very richly furnished in their manner. Montezuma had ready for him a very rich necklace, made of golden crabs, a marvellous piece of work, which he hung round Cortes' neck. His captains were greatly astonished at this sign of honour.

After this ceremony, for which Cortes thanked him through our interpreters, Montezuma said: "Malinche, you and your brothers are in your own house. Rest a while." He then returned to his palace, which was not far off.

We divided our lodgings by companies, and placed our artillery in a convenient spot. Then the order we were to keep was clearly explained to us, and we were warned to be very much on the alert, both the horsemen and the rest of us soldiers. We then ate a sumptuous dinner which they had prepared for us in their native style.

So, with luck on our side, we boldly entered the city of Tenochtitlán or Mexico on 8 November in the year of our Lord 1519.

The Stay in Mexico

. . . Montezuma had ordered his stewards to provide us with everything we needed for our way of living: maize, grindstones, women to make our bread, fowls, fruit, and plenty of fodder for the horses. He then took leave of us all with the greatest courtesy, and we accompanied him to the street. However, Cortes ordered us not to go far from our quarters for the present until we knew better what conduct to observe.

Next day Cortes decided to go to Montezuma's palace. But first he sent to know whether the prince was busy and to inform him of our coming. He took four captains with him: Pedro de Alvarado, Juan Velazquez de Leon, Diego de Ordaz, and Gonzalo de Sandoval, and five of us soldiers.

When Montezuma was informed of our coming, he advanced into the middle of the hall to receive us, closely surrounded by his nephews, for no other chiefs were allowed to enter his palace or communicate with him except upon important business. Cortes and Montezuma exchanged bows, and clasped hands. Then Montezuma led Cortes to his own dais, and setting him down on his right, called for more seats, on which he ordered us all to sit also.

Cortes began to make a speech through our interpreters, saying that we were all now rested, and that in coming to see and speak with such a great prince we had fulfilled the purpose of our voyage and the orders of our lord the King. The principal things he had come to say on behalf of our Lord God had already been communicated to Montezuma through his three ambassadors, on that occasion in the sandhills when he did us the favour of sending us the golden moon and sun. We had then told him that we were Christians and worshipped one God alone, named

Jesus Christ, who had suffered His passion and death to save us; and
that what they worshipped as gods were not gods but devils, which were
evil things, and if they were ugly to look at, their deeds were uglier. But
he had proved to them how evil and ineffectual their gods were, as both
the prince and his people would observe in the course of time, since,
where we had put up crosses such as their ambassadors had seen, they
had been too frightened to appear before them.

The favour he now begged of the great Montezuma was that he
should listen to the words he now wished to speak. Then he very carefully expounded the creation of the world, how we are all brothers, the
children of one mother and father called Adam and Eve; and how such
a brother as our great Emperor, grieving for the perdition of so many
souls as their idols were leading to hell, where they burnt in living flame,
had sent us to tell him this, so that he might put a stop to it, and so that
they might give up the worship of idols and make no more human
sacrifices—for all men are brothers—and commit no more robbery or
sodomy. He also promised that in the course of time the King would
send some men who lead holy lives among us, much better than our
own, to explain this more fully, for we had only come to give them
warning. Therefore he begged Montezuma to do as he was asked.

As Montezuma seemed about to reply, Cortes broke off his speech,
saying to those of us who were with him: "Since this is only the first
attempt, we have now done our duty."

"My lord Malinche," Montezuma replied, "these arguments of
yours have been familiar to me for some time. I understand what you
said to my ambassadors on the sandhills about the three gods and the
cross, also what you preached in the various towns through which you
passed. We have given you no answer, since we have worshipped our
own gods here from the beginning and know them to be good. No doubt
yours are good also, but do not trouble to tell us any more about them
at present. Regarding the creation of the world, we have held the same
belief for many ages, and for this reason are certain that you are those
who our ancestors predicted would come from the direction of the sunrise. As for your great King, I am in his debt and will give him of what I
possess. For, as I have already said, two years ago I had news of the
Captains who came in ships, by the road that you came, and said they
were servants of this great king of yours. I should like to know if you are
all the same people."

Cortes answered that we were all brothers and servants of the
Emperor, and that they had come to discover a route and explore the
seas and ports, so that when they knew them well we could follow, as
we had done. Montezuma was referring to the expeditions of Francisco
Hernandez de Cordoba and of Grijalva, the first voyages of discovery.
He said that ever since that time he had wanted to invite some of these
men to visit the cities of his kingdom, where he would receive them and

do them honour, and that now his gods had fulfilled his desire, for we were in his house, which we might call our own. Here we might rest and enjoy ourselves, for we should receive good treatment. If on other occasions he had sent to forbid our entrance into his city, it was not of his own free will, but because his vassals were afraid. For they told him we shot out flashes of lightning, and killed many Indians with our horses, and that we were angry *Teules*,[2] and other such childish stories. But now that he had seen us, he knew that we were of flesh and blood and very intelligent, also very brave. Therefore he had a far greater esteem for us than these reports had given him, and would share with us what he had.

We all thanked him heartily for his . . . good will, and Montezuma replied with a laugh, because in his princely manner he spoke very gaily: "Malinche, I know that these people of Tlascala with whom you are so friendly have told you that I am a sort of god or *Teule*, and keep nothing in any of my houses that is not made of silver and gold and precious stones. But I know very well that you are too intelligent to believe this and will take it as a joke. See now, Malinche, my body is made of flesh and blood like yours, and my houses and palaces are of stone, wood, and plaster. It is true that I am a great king, and have inherited the riches of my ancestors, but the lies and nonsense you have heard of us are not true. You must take them as a joke, as I take the story of your thunders and lightnings."

Cortes answered also with a laugh that enemies always speak evil and tell lies about the people they hate, but he knew he could not hope to find a more magnificent prince in that land, and there was good reason why his fame should have reached our Emperor.

While this conversation was going on, Montezuma quietly sent one of his nephews, a great *Cacique*, to order his stewards to bring certain pieces of gold, which had apparently been set aside as a gift for Cortes, and ten loads of fine cloaks which he divided: the gold and cloaks between Cortes and the four captains, and for each of us soldiers two gold necklaces, each worth ten pesos, and two loads of cloaks. The gold that he then gave us was worth in all more than a thousand pesos, and he gave it all cheerfully, like a great and valiant prince.

As it was now past midday and he did not wish to be importunate, Cortes said to Montezuma: "My lord, the favours you do us increase, load by load, every day, and it is now the hour of your dinner." Montezuma answered that he thanked us for visiting him. We then took our leave with the greatest courtesy, and returned to our quarters, talking as we went of the prince's fine breeding and manners and deciding to show him the greatest respect in every way, and to remove our quilted caps in his presence, which we always did.

[2] Gods. [Ed.]

The great Montezuma was about forty years old, of good height, well proportioned, spare and slight, and not very dark, though of the usual Indian complexion. He did not wear his hair long but just over his ears, and he had a short black beard, well-shaped and thin. His face was rather long and cheerful, he had fine eyes, and in his appearance and manner could express geniality or, when necessary, a serious composure. He was very neat and clean, and took a bath every afternoon. He had many women as his mistresses, the daughters of chieftains, but two legitimate wives who were *Caciques* in their own right, and when he had intercourse with any of them it was so secret that only some of his servants knew of it. He was quite free from sodomy. The clothes he wore one day he did not wear again till three or four days later. He had a guard of two hundred chieftains lodged in rooms beside his own, only some of whom were permitted to speak to him. When they entered his presence they were compelled to take off their rich cloaks and put on others of little value. They had to be clean and walk barefoot, with their eyes downcast, for they were not allowed to look him in the face, and as they approached they had to make three obeisances, saying as they did so, "Lord, my lord, my great lord!" Then, when they had said what they had come to say, he would dismiss them with a few words. They did not turn their backs on him as they went out, but kept their faces towards him and their eyes downcast, only turning round when they had left the room. Another thing I noticed was that when other great chiefs came from distant lands about disputes or on business, they too had to take off their shoes and put on poor cloaks before entering Montezuma's apartments; and they were not allowed to enter the palace immediately but had to linger for a while near the door, since to enter hurriedly was considered disrespectful. . . .

Montezuma had two houses stocked with every sort of weapon; many of them were richly adorned with gold and precious stones. There were shields large and small, and a sort of broadsword, and two-handed swords set with flint blades that cut much better than our swords, and lances longer than ours, with five-foot blades consisting of many knives. Even when these are driven at a buckler or a shield they are not deflected. In fact they cut like razors, and the Indians can shave their heads with them. They had very good bows and arrows, and double and single-pointed javelins as well as their throwing-sticks and many slings and round stones shaped by hand, and another sort of shield that can be rolled up when they are not fighting, so that it does not get in the way, but which can be opened when they need it in battle and covers their bodies from head to foot. There was also a great deal of cotton armour richly worked on the outside with different coloured feathers, which they used as devices and distinguishing marks, and they had casques and helmets made of wood and bone which were also highly decorated with feathers on the outside. They had other arms of different kinds which I will not mention through fear of prolixity, and workmen skilled in the manufacture of such things, and stewards who were in charge of these arms. . . .

I have already described the manner of their sacrifices. They strike open the wretched Indian's chest with flint knives and hastily tear out the palpitating heart which, with the blood, they present to the idols in whose name they have performed the sacrifice. Then they cut off the arms, thighs, and head, eating the arms and thighs at their ceremonial banquets. The head they hang up on a beam, and the body of the sacrificed man is not eaten but given to the beasts of prey. They also had many vipers in this accursed house, and poisonous snakes which have something that sounds like a bell in their tails. These, which are the deadliest snakes of all, they kept in jars and great pottery vessels full of feathers, in which they laid their eggs and reared their young. They were fed on the bodies of sacrificed Indians and the flesh of the dogs that they bred. We know for certain, too, that when they drove us out of Mexico and killed over eight hundred and fifty of our soldiers, they fed those beasts and snakes on their bodies for many days, as I shall relate in due course. These snakes and wild beasts were dedicated to their fierce idols, and kept them company. As for the horrible noise when the lions and tigers roared, and the jackals and foxes howled, and the serpents hissed, it was so appalling that one seemed to be in hell. . . .

When our Captain and the Mercedarian friar realized that Montezuma would not allow us to set up a cross at Huichilobos' *cue*[3] or build a church there, it was decided that we should ask his stewards for masons so that we could put up a church in our own quarters. For every time we had said mass since entering the city of Mexico we had had to erect an altar on tables and dismantle it again.

The stewards promised to tell Montezuma of our wishes, and Cortes also sent our interpreters to ask him in person. Montezuma granted our request and ordered that we should be supplied with all the necessary material. We had our church finished in two days, and a cross erected in front of our lodgings, and mass was said there each day until the wine gave out. For as Cortes and some other captains and a friar had been ill during the Tlascalan campaign, there had been a run on the wine that we kept for mass. Still, though it was finished, we still went to church every day and prayed on our knees before the altar and images, firstly because it was our obligation as Christians and a good habit, and secondly so that Montezuma and all his captains should observe us and, seeing us worshipping on our knees before the cross—especially when we intoned the Ave Maria—might be inclined to imitate us.

It being our habit to examine and inquire into everything, when we were all assembled in our lodging and considering which was the best place for an altar, two of our men, one of whom was the carpenter

---

[3] The temple of the sun-god, who demanded human sacrifice. [Ed.]

Alonso Yañez, called attention to some marks on one of the walls which showed that there had once been a door, though it had been well plastered up and painted. Now as we had heard that Montezuma kept his father's treasure in this building, we immediately suspected that it must be in this room, which had been closed up only a few days before. Yañez made the suggestion to Juan Velazquez de Leon and Francisco de Lugo, both relatives of mine, to whom he had attached himself as a servant; and they mentioned the matter to Cortes. So the door was secretly opened, and Cortes went in first with certain captains. When they saw the quantity of golden objects—jewels and plates and ingots—which lay in that chamber they were quite transported. They did not know what to think of such riches. The news soon spread to the other captains and soldiers, and very secretly we all went in to see. The sight of all that wealth dumbfounded me. Being only a youth at the time and never having seen such riches before, I felt certain that there could not be a store like it in the whole world. We unanimously decided that we could not think of touching a particle of it, and that the stones should immediately be replaced in the doorway, which should be blocked again and cemented just as we had found it. We resolved also that not a word should be said about this until times changed, for fear Montezuma might hear of our discovery.

Let us leave this subject of the treasure and tell how four of our most valiant captains took Cortes aside in the church, with a dozen soldiers who were in his trust and confidence, myself among them, and asked him to consider the net or trap in which we were caught, to look at the great strength of the city and observe the causeways and bridges, and remember the warnings we had received in every town we had passed through that Huichilobos had counselled Montezuma to let us into the city and kill us there. We reminded him that the hearts of men are very fickle, especially among the Indians, and begged him not to trust the good will and affection that Montezuma was showing us, because from one hour to another it might change. If he should take it into his head to attack us, we said, the stoppage of our supplies of food and water, or the raising of any of the bridges, would render us helpless. Then, considering the vast army of warriors he possessed, we should be incapable of attacking or defending ourselves. And since all the houses stood in the water, how could our Tlascalan allies come in to help us? We asked him to think over all that we had said, for if we wanted to preserve our lives we must seize Montezuma immediately, without even a day's delay. We pointed out that all the gold Montezuma had given us, and all that we had seen in the treasury of his father Axayacatl, and all the food we ate was turning to poison in our bodies, for we could not sleep by night or day or take any rest while these thoughts were in our minds. If any of our soldiers gave him less drastic advice, we concluded, they would be senseless beasts charmed by the gold and incapable of looking death in the eye.

When he had heard our opinion, Cortes answered: "Do not imagine, gentlemen, that I am asleep or that I do not share your anxiety. You must have seen that I do. But what strength have we got for so bold a course as to take this great lord in his own palace, surrounded as he is by warriors and guards? What scheme or trick can we devise to prevent him from summoning his soldiers to attack us at once?"

Our captains (Juan Velazquez de Leon, Diego de Ordaz, Gonzalo de Sandoval, and Pedro de Alvarado) replied that Montezuma must be got out of his palace by smooth words and brought to our quarters. Once there, he must be told that he must remain as a prisoner, and that if he called out or made any disturbance he would pay for it with his life. If Cortes was unwilling to take this course at once, they begged him for permission to do it themselves. With two very dangerous alternatives before us, the better and more profitable thing, they said, would be to seize Montezuma rather than wait for him to attack us. Once he did so, what chance would we have? Some of us soldiers also remarked that Montezuma's stewards who brought us our food seemed to be growing insolent, and did not serve us as politely as they had at first. Two of our Tlascalan allies had, moreover, secretly observed to Jeronimo de Aguilar that for the last two days the Mexicans had appeared less well disposed to us. We spent a good hour discussing whether or not to take Montezuma prisoner, and how it should be done. But our final advice, that at all costs we should take him prisoner, was approved by our Captain, and we then left the matter till next day. All night we prayed God to direct events in the interests of His holy service. . . .

2

The Broken Spears: The Aztec Account of the Conquest of Mexico, c. 1540s

This Aztec account, one of several written by native priests and wise men of the encounter between the Spanish and the Indians of Mexico, was written some years after the events described. Spanish Christian monks helped a postconquest generation of Aztec Nahuatl* speakers translate the illustrated manuscripts of the conquest period. According to this account, how did Montezuma respond to Cortés?

*nah WAH tuhl

Source: *The Broken Spears: The Aztec Account of the Conquest of Mexico*, ed. Miguel Leon-Portilla (Boston: Beacon Press, 1990), 64–76.

Was Montezuma's attitude toward the Spanish shared by other Aztecs? How reliable is this account, do you think, in describing Montezuma's thoughts, motives, and behavior?

THINKING HISTORICALLY

How does the Aztec account of the conquest differ from that of the Spanish, written by Díaz? Is this difference merely a matter of perspective, or do the authors disagree about what happened? To the extent to which there are differences, how do you decide which account to believe and accept?

Speeches of Motecuhzoma and Cortes

When Motecuhzoma[1] had given necklaces to each one, Cortes asked him: "Are you Motecuhzoma? Are you the king? Is it true that you are the king Motecuhzoma?"

And the king said: "Yes, I am Motecuhzoma." Then he stood up to welcome Cortes; he came forward, bowed his head low and addressed him in these words: "Our lord, you are weary. The journey has tired you, but now you have arrived on the earth. You have come to your city, Mexico. You have come here to sit on your throne, to sit under its canopy.

"The kings who have gone before, your representatives, guarded it and preserved it for your coming. The kings Itzcoatl, Motecuhzoma the Elder, Axayacatl, Tizoc, and Ahuitzol ruled for you in the City of Mexico. The people were protected by their swords and sheltered by their shields.

"Do the kings know the destiny of those they left behind, their posterity? If only they are watching! If only they can see what I see!

"No, it is not a dream. I am not walking in my sleep. I am not seeing you in my dreams. . . . I have seen you at last! I have met you face to face! I was in agony for five days, for ten days, with my eyes fixed on the Region of the Mystery. And now you have come out of the clouds and mists to sit on your throne again.

"This was foretold by the kings who governed your city, and now it has taken place. You have come back to us; you have come down from the sky. Rest now, and take possession of your royal houses. Welcome to your land, my lords!"

When Motecuhzoma had finished, La Malinche translated his address into Spanish so that the Captain could understand it. Cortes replied in his strange and savage tongue, speaking first to La Malinche: "Tell

---

[1] Montezuma (earlier spelling). [Ed.]

Motecuhzoma that we are his friends. There is nothing to fear. We have wanted to see him for a long time, and now we have seen his face and heard his words. Tell him that we love him well and that our hearts are contented."

Then he said to Motecuhzoma: "We have come to your house in Mexico as friends. There is nothing to fear."

La Malinche translated this speech and the Spaniards grasped Motecuhzoma's hands and patted his back to show their affection for him.

Attitudes of the Spaniards and the Native Lords

The Spaniards examined everything they saw. They dismounted from their horses, and mounted them again, and dismounted again, so as not to miss anything of interest.

The chiefs who accompanied Motecuhzoma were: Cacama, king of Tezcoco; Tetlepanquetzaltzin, king of Tlacopan; Itzcuauhtzin the Tlacochcalcatl, lord of Tlatelolco; and Topantemoc, Motecuhzoma's treasurer in Tlatelolco. These four chiefs were standing in a file.

The other princes were: Atlixcatzin [chief who has taken captives];[2] Tepeoatzin, the Tlacochcalcatl; Quetzalaztatzin, the keeper of the chalk; Totomotzin; Hecateupatiltzin; and Cuappiatzin.

When Motecuhzoma was imprisoned, they all went into hiding. They ran away to hide and treacherously abandoned him!

The Spaniards Take Possession of the City

When the Spaniards entered the Royal House, they placed Motecuhzoma under guard and kept him under their vigilance. They also placed a guard over Itzcuauhtzin, but the other lords were permitted to depart.

Then the Spaniards fired one of their cannons, and this caused great confusion in the city. The people scattered in every direction; they fled without rhyme or reason; they ran off as if they were being pursued. It was as if they had eaten the mushrooms that confuse the mind, or had seen some dreadful apparition. They were all overcome by terror, as if their hearts had fainted. And when night fell, the panic spread through the city and their fears would not let them sleep.

In the morning the Spaniards told Motecuhzoma what they needed in the way of supplies: tortillas, fried chickens, hens' eggs, pure water, firewood, and charcoal. Also: large, clean cooking pots, water jars, pitchers, dishes, and other pottery. Motecuhzoma ordered that it be sent to them.

---

[2] Military title given to a warrior who had captured four enemies.

The chiefs who received this order were angry with the king and no longer revered or respected him. But they furnished the Spaniards with all the provisions they needed—food, beverages, and water, and fodder for the horses.

The Spaniards Reveal Their Greed

When the Spaniards were installed in the palace, they asked Motecuhzoma about the city's resources and reserves and about the warriors' ensigns and shields. They questioned him closely and then demanded gold.

Motecuhzoma guided them to it. They surrounded him and crowded close with their weapons. He walked in the center, while they formed a circle around him.

When they arrived at the treasure house called Teucalco, the riches of gold and feathers were brought out to them: ornaments made of quetzal feathers, richly worked shields, disks of gold, the necklaces of the idols, gold nose plugs, gold greaves,[3] and bracelets and crowns.

The Spaniards immediately stripped the feathers from the gold shields and ensigns. They gathered all the gold into a great mound and set fire to everything else, regardless of its value. Then they melted down the gold into ingots. As for the precious green stones, they took only the best of them; the rest were snatched up by the Tlaxcaltecas. The Spaniards searched through the whole treasure house, questioning and quarreling, and seized every object they thought was beautiful.

The Seizure of Motecuhzoma's Treasures

Next they went to Motecuhzoma's storehouse, in the place called Totocalco [Place of the Palace of the Birds],[4] where his personal treasures were kept. The Spaniards grinned like little beasts and patted each other with delight.

When they entered the hall of treasures, it was as if they had arrived in Paradise. They searched everywhere and coveted everything; they were slaves to their own greed. All of Motecuhzoma's possessions were brought out: fine bracelets, necklaces with large stones, ankle rings with little gold bells, the royal crowns, and all the royal finery—everything that belonged to the king and was reserved to him only. They seized these treasures as if they were their own, as if this plunder were merely a stroke of good luck. And when they had taken all the gold, they heaped up everything else in the middle of the patio.

---

[3] Leg armour. [Ed.]
[4] The zoological garden attached to the royal palaces.

La Malinche called the nobles together. She climbed up to the palace roof and cried: "Mexicanos, come forward! The Spaniards need your help! Bring them food and pure water. They are tired and hungry; they are almost fainting from exhaustion! Why do you not come forward? Are you angry with them?"

The Mexicans were too frightened to approach. They were crushed by terror and would not risk coming forward. They shied away as if the Spaniards were wild beasts, as if the hour were midnight on the blackest night of the year. Yet they did not abandon the Spaniards to hunger and thirst. They brought them whatever they needed, but shook with fear as they did so. They delivered the supplies to the Spaniards with trembling hands, then turned and hurried away.

The Preparations for the Fiesta

The Aztecs begged permission of their king to hold the fiesta of Huitzilopochtli.[5] The Spaniards wanted to see this fiesta to learn how it was celebrated. A delegation of the celebrants came to the palace where Motecuhzoma was a prisoner, and when their spokesman asked his permission, he granted it to them.

As soon as the delegation returned, the women began to grind seeds of the *chicalote*.[6] These women had fasted for a whole year. They ground the seeds in the patio of the temple.

The Spaniards came out of the palace together, dressed in armor and carrying their weapons with them. They stalked among the women and looked at them one by one; they stared into the faces of the women who were grinding seeds. After this cold inspection, they went back into the palace. It is said that they planned to kill the celebrants if the men entered the patio.

The Statue of Huitzilopochtli

On the evening before the fiesta of Toxcatl, the celebrants began to model a statue of Huitzilopochtli. They gave it such a human appearance that it seemed the body of a living man. Yet they made the statue with nothing but a paste made of the ground seeds of the chicalote, which they shaped over an armature of sticks.

When the statue was finished, they dressed it in rich feathers, and they painted crossbars over and under its eyes. They also clipped on its

---

[5] Aztec war-god. See Introduction to selections. [Ed.]
[6] Edible plants also used in medicines. [Ed.]

earrings of turquoise mosaic; these were in the shape of serpents, with gold rings hanging from them. Its nose plug, in the shape of an arrow, was made of gold and was inlaid with fine stones.

They placed the magic headdress of hummingbird feathers on its head. They also adorned it with an *anecuyotl*, which was a belt made of feathers, with a cone at the back. Then they hung around its neck an ornament of yellow parrot feathers, fringed like the locks of a young boy. Over this they put its nettle-leaf cape, which was painted black and decorated with five clusters of eagle feathers.

Next they wrapped it in its cloak, which was painted with skull and bones, and over this they fastened its vest. The vest was painted with dismembered human parts: skulls, ears, hearts, intestines, torsos, breasts, hands, and feet. They also put on its *maxtlatl*, or loincloth, which was decorated with images of dissevered limbs and fringed with amate paper. This *maxtlatl* was painted with vertical stripes of bright blue.

They fastened a red paper flag at its shoulder and placed on its head what looked like a sacrificial flint knife. This too was made of red paper; it seemed to have been steeped in blood.

The statue carried a *tehuehuelli*, a bamboo shield decorated with four clusters of fine eagle feathers. The pendant of this shield was blood-red, like the knife and the shoulder flag. The statue also carried four arrows.

Finally, they put the wristbands on its arms. These bands, made of coyote skin, were fringed with paper cut into little strips.

The Beginning of the Fiesta

Early the next morning, the statue's face was uncovered by those who had been chosen for that ceremony. They gathered in front of the idol in single file and offered it gifts of food, such as round seedcakes or perhaps human flesh. But they did not carry it up to its temple on top of the pyramid.

All the young warriors were eager for the fiesta to begin. They had sworn to dance and sing with all their hearts, so that the Spaniards would marvel at the beauty of the rituals.

The procession began, and the celebrants filed into the temple patio to dance the Dance of the Serpent. When they were all together in the patio, the songs and the dance began. Those who had fasted for twenty days and those who had fasted for a year were in command of the others; they kept the dancers in file with their pine wands. (If anyone wished to urinate, he did not stop dancing, but simply opened his clothing at the hips and separated his clusters of heron feathers.)

If anyone disobeyed the leaders or was not in his proper place they struck him on the hips and shoulders. Then they drove him out of the patio, beating him and shoving him from behind. They pushed him so hard that he sprawled to the ground, and they dragged him outside by the ears. No one dared to say a word about this punishment, for those who had fasted during the year were feared and venerated; they had earned the exclusive title "Brothers of Huitzilopochtli."

The great captains, the bravest warriors, danced at the head of the files to guide the others. The youths followed at a slight distance. Some of the youths wore their hair gathered into large locks, a sign that they had never taken any captives. Others carried their headdresses on their shoulders; they had taken captives, but only with help.

Then came the recruits, who were called "the young warriors." They had each captured an enemy or two. The others called to them: "Come, comrades, show us how brave you are! Dance with all your hearts!"

The Spaniards Attack the Celebrants

At this moment in the fiesta, when the dance was loveliest and when song was linked to song, the Spaniards were seized with an urge to kill the celebrants. They all ran forward, armed as if for battle. They closed the entrances and passageways, all the gates of the patio: the Eagle Gate in the lesser palace, the Gate of the Canestalk and the Gate of the Serpent of Mirrors. They posted guards so that no one could escape, and then rushed into the Sacred Patio to slaughter the celebrants. They came on foot, carrying their swords and their wooden or metal shields.

They ran in among the dancers, forcing their way to the place where the drums were played. They attacked the man who was drumming and cut off his arms. Then they cut off his head, and it rolled across the floor.

They attacked all the celebrants, stabbing them, spearing them, striking them with their swords. They attacked some of them from behind, and these fell instantly to the ground with their entrails hanging out. Others they beheaded: they cut off their heads, or split their heads to pieces.

They struck others in the shoulders, and their arms were torn from their bodies. They wounded some in the thigh and some in the calf.

They slashed others in the abdomen, and their entrails all spilled to the ground. Some attempted to run away, but their intestines dragged as they ran; they seemed to tangle their feet in their own entrails. No matter how they tried to save themselves, they could find no escape.

Some attempted to force their way out, but the Spaniards murdered them at the gates. Others climbed the walls, but they could not save themselves. Those who ran into the communal houses were safe there for a while; so were those who lay down among the victims and pretended to be dead. But if they stood up again, the Spaniards saw them and killed them.

The blood of the warriors flowed like water and gathered into pools. The pools widened, and the stench of blood and entrails filled the air. The Spaniards ran into the communal houses to kill those who were hiding. They ran everywhere and searched everywhere; they invaded every room, hunting and killing.

3

BARTOLOMÉ DE LAS CASAS

The Devastation of the Indies, 1555

Las Casas (1484–1566) emigrated with his father from Spain to the island of Hispaniola in 1502. Eight years later he became a priest, served as a missionary to the Taino of Cuba (1512), attempted to create a utopian society for the Indians of Venezuela, and became a Dominican friar in 1522. Repelled by his early experience among the conquistadors, Las Casas the priest and friar devoted his adult life to aiding the Indians in the Americas and defending their rights in the Spanish court. This selection is drawn from his brief history, *The Devastation of the Indies*, published in 1555. The work for this book and a larger volume, *In Defense of the Indians*, presented his case against Indian slavery in the great debate at the Spanish court at Valladolid in 1550. Along with his monumental *History of the Indies*, published after his death, the writings of Las Casas constituted such an indictment of Spanish colonialism that Protestant enemies were able to argue that Catholic slavery and exploitation of the "New World" was worse than their own, a dubious proposition that became known as "the Black Legend." What do you make of this account by Las Casas? Does he exaggerate, or is it likely that these events happened?

THINKING HISTORICALLY

Compare this account with the two previous selections. Do you think the Spanish treated the people of Hispaniola and Mexico differently? Do these three readings offer different interpretations of the role of Christianity in the Americas?

Source: Bartolomé de Las Casas, *The Devastation of the Indies: A Brief Account*, trans. Herma Briffault (Baltimore: Johns Hopkins University Press, 1992), 32–35, 40–41.

This [Hispaniola][1] was the first land in the New World to be destroyed and depopulated by the Christians, and here they began their subjection of the women and children, taking them away from the Indians to use them and ill use them, eating the food they provided with their sweat and toil. The Spaniards did not content themselves with what the Indians gave them of their own free will, according to their ability, which was always too little to satisfy enormous appetites, for a Christian eats and consumes in one day an amount of food that would suffice to feed three houses inhabited by ten Indians for one month. And they committed other acts of force and violence and oppression which made the Indians realize that these men had not come from Heaven. And some of the Indians concealed their foods while others concealed their wives and children and still others fled to the mountains to avoid the terrible transactions of the Christians.

And the Christians attacked them with buffets and beatings, until finally they laid hands on the nobles of the villages. Then they behaved with such temerity and shamelessness that the most powerful ruler of the islands had to see his own wife raped by a Christian officer.

From that time onward the Indians began to seek ways to throw the Christians out of their lands. They took up arms, but their weapons were very weak and of little service in offense and still less in defense. (Because of this, the wars of the Indians against each other are little more than games played by children.) And the Christians, with their horses and swords and pikes began to carry out massacres and strange cruelties against them. They attacked the towns and spared neither the children nor the aged nor pregnant women nor women in childbed, not only stabbing them and dismembering them but cutting them to pieces as if dealing with sheep in the slaughter house. They laid bets as to who, with one stroke of the sword, could split a man in two or could cut off his head or spill out his entrails with a single stroke of the pike. They took infants from their mothers' breasts, snatching them by the legs and pitching them headfirst against the crags or snatched them by the arms and threw them into the rivers, roaring with laughter and saying as the babies fell into the water, "Boil there, you offspring of the devil!" Other infants they put to the sword along with their mothers and anyone else who happened to be nearby. They made some low wide gallows on which the hanged victim's feet almost touched the ground, stringing up their victims in lots of thirteen, in memory of Our Redeemer and His twelve Apostles, then set burning wood at their feet and thus burned them alive. To others they attached straw or wrapped their whole bodies in straw and set them afire. With still others, all those they wanted to capture alive, they cut off their hands and hung them round the victim's neck, saying, "Go now, carry the message," meaning, Take the news to the Indians who have fled to the

---

[1] The island that today includes the Dominican Republic and Haiti. [Ed.]

mountains. They usually dealt with the chieftains and nobles in the following way: they made a grid of rods which they placed on forked sticks, then lashed the victims to the grid and lighted a smoldering fire underneath, so that little by little, as those captives screamed in despair and torment, their souls would leave them.

I once saw this, when there were four or five nobles lashed on grids and burning; I seem even to recall that there were two or three pairs of grids where others were burning, and because they uttered such loud screams that they disturbed the captain's sleep, he ordered them to be strangled. And the constable, who was worse than an executioner, did not want to obey that order (and I know the name of that constable and know his relatives in Seville), but instead put a stick over the victims' tongues, so they could not make a sound, and he stirred up the fire, but not too much, so that they roasted slowly, as he liked. I saw all these things I have described, and countless others.

And because all the people who could do so fled to the mountains to escape these inhuman, ruthless, and ferocious acts, the Spanish captains, enemies of the human race, pursued them with the fierce dogs they kept which attacked the Indians, tearing them to pieces and devouring them. And because on few and far between occasions, the Indians justifiably killed some Christians, the Spaniards made a rule among themselves that for every Christian slain by the Indians, they would slay a hundred Indians. . . .

Because the particulars that enter into these outrages are so numerous they could not be contained in the scope of much writing, for in truth I believe that in the great deal I have set down here I have not revealed the thousandth part of the sufferings endured by the Indians, I now want only to add that, in the matter of these unprovoked and destructive wars, and God is my witness, all these acts of wickedness I have described, as well as those I have omitted, were perpetrated against the Indians without cause, without any more cause than could give a community of good monks living together in a monastery. And still more strongly I affirm that until the multitude of people on this island of Hispaniola were killed and their lands devastated, they committed no sin against the Christians that would be punishable by man's laws, and as to those sins punishable by God's law, such as vengeful feelings against such powerful enemies as the Christians have been, those sins would be committed by the very few Indians who are hardhearted and impetuous. And I can say this from my great experience with them: their hardness and impetuosity would be that of children, of boys ten or twelve years old. I know by certain infallible signs that the wars waged by the Indians against the Christians have been justifiable wars and that all the wars waged by the Christians against the Indians have been unjust wars, more diabolical than any wars ever waged anywhere in the world. This I declare to be so of all the many wars they have waged against the peoples throughout the Indies.

After the wars and the killings had ended, when usually there survived only some boys, some women, and children, these survivors were distributed among the Christians to be slaves. The *repartimiento* or distribution was made according to the rank and importance of the Christian to whom the Indians were allocated, one of them being given thirty, another forty, still another, one or two hundred, and besides the rank of the Christian there was also to be considered in what favor he stood with the tyrant they called Governor. The pretext was that these allocated Indians were to be instructed in the articles of the Christian Faith. As if those Christians who were as a rule foolish and cruel and greedy and vicious could be caretakers of souls! And the care they took was to send the men to the mines to dig for gold, which is intolerable labor, and to send the women into the fields of the big ranches to hoe and till the land, work suitable for strong men. Nor to either the men or the women did they give any food except herbs and legumes, things of little substance. The milk in the breasts of the women with infants dried up and thus in a short while the infants perished.

4

European Views of Native Americans, Sixteenth and Seventeenth Centuries

Las Casas's sympathetic view of the Indians was hardly one shared by the average Frenchman, Italian, or Scot. Indeed, many Europeans harbored fantastical and negative notions about the inhabitants of the "New World," envisioning them as wild and cannibalistic, savage and ruthless toward their enemies. Reinforcing this impression were images that circulated throughout Europe during the sixteenth and seventeenth centuries, such as this engraving from 1564, part of a series by Flemish engraver Theodore de Bry, based on paintings by an artist who had accompanied a French expedition to Florida a few decades earlier. Figure 16.1 shows the alleged cannibalistic practices by natives supposedly witnessed by the explorers. What is going on in this picture? It is likely that de Bry made adjustments to his engravings from the originals to please potential buyers. If so, what does this tell us about the expectations of European audiences about the Americas and their inhabitants?

Almost seventy-five years later, a very different set of no less remarkable images emerged from a Dutch colony in northeastern Brazil. Count Johan Maurits, the humanist governor general of the colony from 1636 to 1644, brought several artists and scientists with him to observe and record the region's flora and fauna as well as its

Figure 16.1   Cannibalism, engraving by Theodore de Bry.

Source: Scene of Cannibalism, from 'Brevis Narratio,' engraved by Theodore de Bry (1528–98) 1564 (coloured engraving), Le Moyne, Jacques (de Morgues) (1533–88) (after)/ Service Historique de la Marine, Vincennes, France/Giraudon/The Bridgeman Art Library.

inhabitants. Johan Maurits, who was fascinated by the local peoples and their cultures, commissioned from artist Albert Eckhout a number of still-lifes and group and individual portraits, including one showing a female Tapuya Indian (see Figure 16.2). According to Dutch accounts, the Tapuya were more warlike and less "civilized" than some of the other local peoples—for example, they sometimes consumed their dead instead of burying them. Aside from the body parts this woman carries in her hand and in her bag, what other signs of this warlike tendency do you see in Figure 16.2? Look closely at the many interesting details in this painting. What does the artist seem to be interested in showing?

THINKING HISTORICALLY

What are the differences in style and content between Figures 16.1 and 16.2, and how do you account for them? Which of the following factors do you think is most important in explaining their differences: chronology, agenda of the artist, the potential audience for the image, the

Figure 16.2 Tapuya Indian, by Albert Eckhout.
Source: The Granger Collection, New York.

setting in which they were produced? What might be the pitfalls for students of history in comparing these two images? How do you reconcile Las Casas's account in the previous source with the scene portrayed in Figure 16.1? Which source would you consider more reliable, and why? Which source would a sixteenth-century Spaniard have considered more reliable, and why? Consider how women are depicted in these works. What differences and similarities do you see? What might that tell us about European notions of women and gender in the New World?

NZINGA MBEMBA

Appeal to the King of Portugal, 1526

Although Europeans conquered the Americas beginning in the fifteenth century, they were unable to conquer the African continent until the nineteenth and twentieth centuries. Rivers that fell steeply to the sea, military defenses, and diseases like malaria proved insurmountable to Europeans before the age of the steamship, the machine gun, and antimalarial quinine. Before the last half of the nineteenth century, Europeans had to be content with alliances with African kings and rulers. The Portuguese had been the first to meet Africans in the towns and villages along the Atlantic coast, and they became the first European missionaries and trading partners.

Nzinga Mbemba, whose Christian name was Affonso, was king of the West African state of Congo (comprising what is today parts of Angola as well as the two Congo states) from about 1506 to 1543. He succeeded his father, King Nzinga, a Kuwu who, shortly after his first contact with the Portuguese in 1483, sent officials to Lisbon to learn European ways. In 1491 father and son were baptized, and Portuguese priests, merchants, artisans, and soldiers were provided with a coastal settlement.

What exactly is the complaint of the king of Congo? What seems to be the impact of Portuguese traders (called "factors") in the Congo? What does King Affonso want the king of Portugal to do?

THINKING HISTORICALLY

This selection offers an opportunity to compare European expansion in the Americas and Africa. Portuguese contact with Nzinga Mbemba of the Congo was roughly contemporaneous with Spanish colonialism in the Americas. What differences do you see between these two cases of early European expansion? Can you think of any reasons that Congo kings converted to Christianity whereas Mexican kings did not?

Compare the Europeans' treatment of Africans with their treatment of Native Americans. Why did Europeans enslave Africans and not, for the most part, American Indians?

Sir, Your Highness [of Portugal] should know how our Kingdom is being lost in so many ways that it is convenient to provide for the necessary remedy, since this is caused by the excessive freedom given by

Source: Basil Davidson, *The African Past* (Boston: Little, Brown, and Company, 1964), 191–94.

your factors and officials to the men and merchants who are allowed to come to this Kingdom to set up shops with goods and many things which have been prohibited by us, and which they spread throughout our Kingdoms and Domains in such an abundance that many of our vassals, whom we had in obedience, do not comply because they have the things in greater abundance than we ourselves; and it was with these things that we had them content and subjected under our vassalage and jurisdiction, so it is doing a great harm not only to the service of God, but to the security and peace of our Kingdoms and State as well.

And we cannot reckon how great the damage is, since the mentioned merchants are taking every day our natives, sons of the land and the sons of our noblemen and vassals and our relatives, because the thieves and men of bad conscience grab them wishing to have the things and wares of this Kingdom which they are ambitious of; they grab them and get them to be sold; and so great, Sir, is the corruption and licentiousness that our country is being completely depopulated, and Your Highness should not agree with this nor accept it as in your service. And to avoid it we need from those [your] Kingdoms no more than some priests and a few people to teach in schools, and no other goods except wine and flour for the holy sacrament. That is why we beg of Your Highness to help and assist us in this matter, commanding your factors that they should not send here either merchants or wares, because it is *our will that in these Kingdoms there should not be any trade of slaves nor outlet for them*.[1] Concerning what is referred above, again we beg of Your Highness to agree with it, since otherwise we cannot remedy such an obvious damage. Pray Our Lord in His mercy to have Your Highness under His guard and let you do for ever the things of His service. I kiss your hands many times.

> At our town of Congo, written on the sixth day of July.
> João Teixeira did it in 1526.
> The King. Dom Affonso.
> [On the back of this letter the following can be read:
> To the most powerful and excellent prince Dom João, King our Brother.]

Moreover, Sir, in our Kingdoms there is another great inconvenience which is of little service to God, and this is that many of our people [*naturaes*], keenly desirous as they are of the wares and things of your Kingdoms, which are brought here by your people, and in order to satisfy their voracious appetite, seize many of our people, freed and exempt men; and very often it happens that they kidnap even noblemen and the

---

[1] Emphasis in the original.

sons of noblemen, and our relatives, and take them to be sold to the white men who are in our Kingdoms; and for this purpose they have concealed them; and others are brought during the night so that they might not be recognized.

And as soon as they are taken by the white men they are immediately ironed and branded with fire, and when they are carried to be embarked, if they are caught by our guards' men the whites allege that they have bought them but they cannot say from whom, so that it is our duty to do justice and to restore to the freemen their freedom, but it cannot be done if your subjects feel offended, as they claim to be.

And to avoid such a great evil we passed a law so that any white man living in our Kingdoms and wanting to purchase goods in any way should first inform three of our noblemen and officials of our court whom we rely upon in this matter, and these are Dom Pedro Manipanza and Dom Manuel Manissaba, our chief usher, and Gonçalo Pires our chief freighter, who should investigate if the mentioned goods are captives or free men, and if cleared by them there will be no further doubt nor embargo for them to be taken and embarked. But if the white men do not comply with it they will lose the aforementioned goods. And if we do them this favor and concession it is for the part Your Highness has in it, since we know that it is in your service too that these goods are taken from our Kingdom, otherwise we should not consent to this. . . .

Sir, Your Highness has been kind enough to write to us saying that we should ask in our letters for anything we need, and that we shall be provided with everything, and as the peace and the health of our Kingdom depend on us, and as there are among us old folks and people who have lived for many days, it happens that we have continuously many and different diseases which put us very often in such a weakness that we reach almost the last extreme; and the same happens to our children, relatives, and natives owing to the lack in this country of physicians and surgeons who might know how to cure properly such diseases. And as we have got neither dispensaries nor drugs which might help us in this forlornness, many of those who had been already confirmed and instructed in the holy faith of Our Lord Jesus Christ perish and die; and the rest of the people in their majority cure themselves with herbs and breads and other ancient methods, so that they put all their faith in the mentioned herbs and ceremonies if they live, and believe that they are saved if they die; and this is not much in the service of God.

And to avoid such a great error and inconvenience, since it is from God in the first place and then from your Kingdoms and from Your Highness that all the goods and drugs and medicines have come to save us, we beg of you to be agreeable and kind enough to send us two physicians and two apothecaries and one surgeon, so that they may come with their drug-stores and all the necessary things to stay in our kingdoms, because we are in extreme need of them all and each of them. We shall do them all good and shall benefit them by all means, since they are sent by Your Highness, whom we thank for your work in their coming. We beg of Your Highness as a great favor to do this for us, because besides being good in itself it is in the service of God as we have said above.

6

CAPTAIN THOMAS PHILLIPS

Buying Slaves in 1693

Phillips, the captain of the English ship *Hannibal*, arrived at the African port of Ouidah (Whydah) in what is today Benin to purchase slaves for transport and sale in the West Indian islands of St. Thomas and Barbados. From this part of his journal, we can see that the Captain is well versed in the procedures for buying slaves on the African coast. What sorts of preparations has he made for the purchase? How does he go about making the purchase? What does this selection tell you about the African slave trade?

THINKING HISTORICALLY

The circumstances by which Europeans encountered Africans were clearly different from those by which they encountered Native Americans. What are these differences, and how do they account for differences in their attitudes toward Africans and Indians?

This day got our canoos and all things else ready, in order to go ashore to-morrow to purchase our slaves.

May the 21st. This morning I went ashore at Whidaw, accompany'd by my doctor and purser, Mr. Clay, the present captain of the *East India Merchant*, his doctor and purser, and about a dozen of our seamen for our guard, arm'd, in order here to reside till we could purchase 1300 negro slaves, which was the number we both wanted, to compleat 700 for the *Hannibal*, and 650 for the *East India Merchant*, according to our agreement in our charter-parties with the Royal African Company; in

Source: Capt. Thomas Phillips' Journal, in *Churchill's Collection of Voyages*, vol. 6, London, 1746. Reprinted in George Francis Dow, *Slave Ships and Slaving*, originally published by the Marine Research Society, Salem, MA, 1927. Reprinted by Dover Press, 2002, 58–64.

procuring which quantity of slaves we spent about nine weeks, during which time what observations my indisposition with convulsions in my head, &c. would permit me to make on this country, its trade, manners, &c. are as follows, viz. . . .

Our factory, built by Captain Wiburne, Sir John Wiburne's brother, stands low near the marshes, which renders it a very unhealthy place to live in; the white men the African Company send there, seldom returning to tell their tale; 'tis compass'd round with a mud wall, about six foot high, and on the south-side is the gate; within is a large yard, a mud thatch'd house, where the factor[1] lives, with the white men; also a store-house, a trunk for slaves, and a place where they bury their dead white men, call'd, very improperly, the hog-yard; there is also a good forge, and some other small houses: To the east are two small flankers of mud, with a few popguns and harquebusses,[2] which serve more to terrify the poor ignorant negroes than to do any execution. . . .

This factory, feared as 'tis, proved very beneficial to us, by housing our goods which came ashore late, and could not arrive at the king's town where I kept my warehouse, ere it was dark, when they would be very incident to be pilfer'd by the negro porters which carry them, at which they are most exquisite; for in the day-time they would steal the cowries,[3] altho' our white men that attended the goods from the marine watched them, they having instruments like wedges, made on purpose to force asunder the staves of the barrels, that contain'd the cowries, whereby the shells dropt out; and when any of our seamen that watch'd the goods came near such porters, they would take out their machine, and the staves would insensibly close again, so that no hole did appear, having always their wives and children running by them to carry off the plunder; which with all our threats and complaints made to the king, we could not prevent, tho' we often beat them cruelly, and piniar'd some, but it was all one, what was bred in the bone, &c. whatever we could do would not make them forbear.

The factory prov'd beneficial to us in another kind; for after we had procured a parcel of slaves, and sent them down to the sea-side to be carry'd off, it sometimes proved bad weather, and so great a sea, that the canoos could not come ashore to fetch them, so that they returned to the factory, where they were secured and provided for till good weather presented, and then were near to embrace the opportunity, we some-times shipping off a hundred of both sexes at a time.

We had our cook ashore, and eat as well as we could, provisions being plenty and cheap; but we soon lost our stomachs by sickness, most of my men having fevers, and myself such convulsions and aches in my

---

[1] Manager or agent. [Ed.]
[2] Firearms with a long barrel and a cord to ignite powder. [Ed.]
[3] Shells used as currency. [Ed.]

head, that I could hardly stand or go to the trunk without assistance, and there often fainted with the horrid stink of the negroes, it being an old house where all the slaves are kept together, and evacuate nature where they lie, so that no jakes[4] can stink worse; there being forced to sit three or four hours at a time, quite ruin'd my health, but there was no help.

When we were at the trunk, the king's slaves, if he had any, were the first offer'd to sale, which the cappasheirs[5] would be very urgent with us to buy, and would in a manner force us to it ere they would shew us any other, saying they were the Reys Cosa,[6] and we must not refuse them, tho' as I observed they were generally the worst slaves in the trunk, and we paid more for them than any others, which we could not remedy, it being one of his majesty's prerogatives. Then the cappasheirs each brought out his slaves according to his degree and quality, the greatest first, &c. and our surgeon examined them well in all kinds, to see that they were sound wind and limb, making them jump, stretch out their arms swiftly, looking in their mouths to judge of their age; for the cappasheirs are so cunning, that they shave them all close before we see them, so that let them be never so old we can see no grey hairs in their heads or beards; and then having liquor'd them well and sleeked with palm oil, 'tis no easy matter to know an old one from a middle-aged one, but by the teeths decay. But our greatest care of all is to buy none that are pox'd, lest they should infect the rest aboard; for tho' we separate the men and women aboard by partitions and bulk-heads, to prevent quarrels and wranglings among them, yet do what we can they will come together, and that distemper which they call the yaws, is very common here, and discovers itself by almost the same symptoms as the *Lues Venerea*[7] or clap does with us; therefore our surgeon is forc'd to examine the privities of both men and women with the nicest scrutiny, which is a great slavery, but what can't be omitted. When we had selected from the rest such as we liked, we agreed in what goods to pay for them, the prices being already stated before the king, how much of each sort of merchandize we were to give for a man, woman, and child, which gave us much ease, and saved abundance of disputes and wranglings, and gave the owner a note, signifying our agreement of the sorts of goods; upon delivery of which the next day he receiv'd them; then we mark'd the slaves we had bought in the breast, or shoulder, with a hot iron, having the letter of the ship's name on it, the place being before anointed with a little palm oil, which caused but little pain, the mark being usually well in four or five days, appearing very plain and white after.

When we had purchased to the number of 50 or 60, we would send them aboard, there being a cappasheir, intitled the captain of the slaves, whose care it was to secure them to the waterside, and see them all

---

[4] British slang for a latrine. [Ed.]
[5] Slave handlers appointed by the African king. [Ed.]
[6] The African king's special slaves. [Ed.]
[7] Venereal disease (STD). [Ed.]

off; and if in carrying to the marine any were lost, he was bound to make them good to us, the captain of the trunk being oblig'd to do the like, if any run away while under his care, for after we buy them we give him charge of them till the captain of the slaves comes to carry them away: There are two officers appointed by the king for this purpose, to each of which every ship pays the value of a slave in what goods they like best for their trouble, when they have done trading. . . .

There is likewise a captain of the sand, who is appointed to take care of the merchandise we have come ashore to trade with, that the negroes do not plunder them. . . .

When our slaves were come to the sea-side, our canoos were ready to carry them off to the longboat, if the sea permitted, and he convey'd them aboard ship, where the men were all put in irons, two and two shackl'd together, to prevent their mutiny, or swimming ashore.

The negroes are so wilful and loth to leave their own country, that they have often leap'd out of the canoos, boat and ship, into the sea, and kept under water till they were drowned, to avoid being taken up and saved by our boats, which pursued them; they having a more dreadful apprehension of Barbadoes than we can have of hell, tho' in reality they live much better there than in their own country; but home is home, &c. . . . We had about 12 negroes did wilfully drown themselves, and others starv'd themselves to death; for 'tis their belief that when they die they return home to their own country and friends again.

The best goods to purchase slaves here are cowries, the smaller the more esteemed; for they pay them all by tale, the smallest being as valuable as the biggest, but take them from us by measure or weight, of which about 100 pounds for a good man-slave. The next in demand are brass neptunes or basons, very large, thin, and flat; for after they have bought them they cut them in pieces to make anilias or bracelets, and collars for their arms, legs and necks. The other preferable goods are blue paper sletias, cambricks or lawns, caddy chints, broad ditto, coral, large, smooth, and of a deep red, rangoes large and red, iron bars, powder and brandy.[8]

With the above goods a ship cannot want slaves here, and may purchase them for about three pounds fifteen shillings a head, but near half the cargo value must be cowries or booges, and brass basons, to set off the other goods that we buy cheaper, as coral, rangoes, iron, &c. else they will not take them; for if a cappasheir sells five slaves, he will have two of them paid for in cowries, and one in brass, which are dear slaves; for a slave in cowries costs us above four pounds in England; whereas a slave in coral, rangoes, or iron, does not cost fifty shillings; but without

[8] Sletias were cloths, also called silesias, after their probable origin; cambricks were fine white linens from Cambray, Flanders; chints referred to chintz, an Indian cotton with brightly-colored design, usually flowers; broad referred to broad cloths; lawns were linens from Laorn, France; rangoes were beads. [Ed.]

the cowries and brass they will take none of the last goods, and but small quantities at best, especially, if they can discover that you have good store of cowries and brass aboard . . . therefore every man that comes here, ought to be very cautious in making his report to the king at first, of what sorts and quantities of goods he has, and be sure to say his cargo consists mostly in iron, coral, rangoes, chints, &c. so that he may dispose of those goods as soon as he can. . . .

7

J. B. ROMAIGNE

Journal of a Slave Ship Voyage, 1819

The French slave ship *Le Rodeur* sailed from the Guinea coast of Africa to the French Caribbean island of Guadeloupe in April, 1819. The ship carried twenty-two crewmen and a cargo of 160 African slaves. J. B. Romaigne, the twelve-year-old son of a Guadeloupe planter, was a passenger under the special care of the captain. This is his journal of the voyage, written for his mother. What happened on that voyage? How were the slaves treated? What does this account tell you about the transatlantic slave trade?

THINKING HISTORICALLY

Both this and the previous selection are taken from journals, or diaries. What unique characteristics and common elements of diaries should enhance their reliability for the historian? Is the journal of a twelve-year-old likely to be more or less reliable than that of a sea captain like Phillips? What aspects of this document make it seem more, or less, reliable to you?

I

"It is now just a week since we sailed; but, indeed, it is not my fault that I have not sooner sat down to write. The first two days I was sick, and the other five were so stormy that I could not sit at the table without holding. Even now we are rolling like a great porpoise yet I can sit very well and keep the pen steady. Since I am to send you what I do without

Source: Capt. Ernest H. Pentecost, RNR, "Introduction" to George Francis Dow, *Slave Ships and Slaving*, originally published by the Marine Research Society, Salem, MA, 1927. Reprinted by Dover Press, 2002, xxvii–xxxv.

copying it over again at the end of the voyage, I shall take what pains I can; but I hope, my dear mother, you will consider that my fingers are grown hard and tarry with hauling all day on the ropes, the Captain being determined, as he says, to make me a sailor. The Captain is very fond of me and is very good-tempered; he drinks a great deal of brandy; he is a fine, handsome man and I am sure I shall like him very much.

II

"I enquired of the Captain today, how long it would be before we should get to Guadaloupe; and he told me we had a great distance to go before we should steer that way at all. He asked how I should like to have a little black slave and I said very well; that I was to have plenty of them at Guadaloupe. He asked me what I could do with them. 'Feed them,' I said. 'That is right,' said the Captain; 'it will make them strong. But you will make them work won't you?' added he. 'Yes, to be sure,' said I. 'Then I can tell you you must flog them as well as feed them.' 'I will,' said I, 'it is what I intend, but I must not hurt them very much.' 'Of course not maim them,' returned he, 'for then they could not work; but if you do not make them feel to the marrow, you might as well throw them into the sea.'

III

"Since we have been at this place, Bonny Town in the Bonny river, on the coast of Africa, I have become more accustomed to the howling of these negroes. At first, it alarmed me, and I could not sleep. The Captain says that if they behave well they will be much better off at Guadaloupe; and I am sure, I wish the ignorant creatures would come quietly and have it over. Today, one of the blacks whom they were forcing into the hold, suddenly knocked down a sailor and attempted to leap overboard. He was caught, however, by the leg by another of the crew, and the sailor, rising up in a passion, hamstrung him with a cutlass. The Captain, see-ing this, knocked the butcher flat upon the deck with a handspike. 'I will teach you to keep your temper,' said he, with an oath. 'He was the best slave in the lot.' I ran to the main chains and looked over; for they had dropped the black into the sea when they saw that he was useless. He continued to swim, even after he had sunk under water, for I saw the red track extending shoreward; but by and by, it stopped, widened, faded, and I saw it no more.

IV

"We are now fairly at sea again, and I am sure my dear Mother, I am heartily glad of it. The Captain is in the best temper in the world; he walks the deck, rubbing his hands and humming a tune. He says he has six dozen slaves on board, men, women and children, and all in prime marketable condition. I have not seen them, however, since we set sail. Their cries are so terrible that I do not like to go and look down into the hold. . . .

V

"Today, word was brought to the Captain, while we were at breakfast, that two of the slaves were dead, suffocated, as was supposed, by the closeness of the hold; and he immediately ordered the rest should be brought up, gang by gang, to the forecastle, to give them air. I ran up on deck to see them. They did not appear to me to be very unwell; but these blacks, who are not distinguished from one another by dress, are so much alike one can hardly tell.

"However, they had no sooner reached the ship's side, than first one, then another, then a third, sprang up on the gunwale, and darted into the sea, before the astonished sailors could tell what they were about. Many more made the attempt, but without success; they were all knocked flat to the deck, and the crew kept watch over them with handspikes and cutlasses till the Captain's pleasure should be known with regard to the revolt.

"The negroes, in the meantime, who had got off, continued dancing about among the waves, yelling with all their might, what seemed to me a song of triumph, in the burden of which they were joined by some of their companions on deck. Our ship speedily left the ignorant creatures behind; their voices came fainter and fainter upon the wind; the black head, first of one, then of another, disappeared; and then the sea was without a spot; and the air without a sound.

"When the Captain came up on deck, having finished his breakfast, and was told of the revolt, his face grew pale, and he gnashed his teeth. 'We must make an example,' said he, 'or our labour will be lost.' He then ordered the whole of the slaves in the ship to be tied together in gangs and placed upon the forecastle, and having selected six, who were known to have joined in the chorus of the revolters and might thus be considered as the ringleaders, he caused three of them to be shot, and the other three hanged, before the eyes of their comrades. . . .

VII

"The negroes, ever since the revolt, were confined closely to the lower hold and this brought on a disease called ophthalmia, which produced blindness. The sailors, who sling down the provisions from the upper hold, report that the disease is spreading frightfully and today, at dinner, the Captain and the surgeon held a conference on the subject. The surgeon declared that, from all he could learn, the cases were already so numerous as to be beyond his management; but the Captain insisted that every slave cured was worth his value and that it was better to lose a part than all. The disease, it seems, although generally fatal to the negro, is not always so. The patient is at first blind; but some escape, eventually, with the loss of one eye or a mere dimness of vision. The result of the conversation was, that the infected slaves were to be transferred to the upper hold and attended by the surgeon the same as if they were white men.

VIII

"All the slaves and some of the crew are blind. The Captain, the surgeon, and the mate are blind. There is hardly enough men left, out of our twenty-two, to work the ship. The Captain preserves what order he can and the surgeon still attempts to do his duty, but our situation is frightful.

IX

"All the crew are now blind but one man. The rest work under his orders like unconscious machines; the Captain standing by with a thick rope, which he sometimes applies, when led to any recreant by the man who can see. My own eyes begin to be affected; in a little while, I shall see nothing but death. I asked the Captain if he would not allow the blacks to come up on deck. He said it was of no use; that the crew, who were always on deck, were as blind as they; that if brought up, they would only drown themselves, whereas, if they remained where they were, there would, in all probability, be at least a portion of them salable, if we had ever the good fortune to reach Guadaloupe. . . .

X

"Mother, your son was blind for ten days, although now so well as to be able to write. I can tell you hardly anything of our history during that period. Each of us lived in a little dark world of his own, peopled by shadows and phantasms. . . .

"Then there came a storm. No hand was upon the helm, not a reef upon the sails. On we flew like a phantom ship of old, that cared not for wind or weather, our masts straining and cracking; . . . the furious sea one moment devouring us up, stem and stern, and the next casting us forth again, as if with loathing and disgust. . . . The wind, at last, died moaningly away, and we found ourselves rocking, without progressive motion, on the sullen deep. We at length heard a sound upon the waters, unlike that of the smooth swell which remained after the storm, and our hearts beat with a hope which was painful from its suddenness and intensity. We held our breath. The sound was continued; it was like the splashing of a heavy body in smooth water; and a simultaneous cry arose from every lip on deck and was echoed by the men in their hammocks below and by the slaves in the hold. . . .

"The Captain was the first to recover his self-possession, and our voices sank into silence when we heard him speak the approaching vessel with the usual challenge.

" 'Ship Ahoy! Ahoy! What ship?'

" 'The *Saint Leon* of Spain. Help us for God's sake!'

" 'We want help ourselves,' replied our Captain.

" 'We are dying of hunger and thirst. Send us on board some provisions and a few hands to work the ship and name your own terms.'

" 'We can give you food, but we are in want of hands. Come on board of us and we will exchange provisions with you for men,' answered our Captain.

" 'Dollars! dollars! We will pay you in money, a thousand fold; but we cannot send. We have negroes on board; they have infected us with ophthalmia, and we are all stone-blind.'

"At the announcement of this horrible coincidence, there was a silence among us, for some moments, like that of death. It was broken by a fit of laughter, in which I joined myself; and, before our awful merriment was over, we could hear, by the sound of the curses which the Spaniards shouted against us, that the *St. Leon* had drifted away.

"This vessel, in all probability, foundered at sea, as she never reached any port.

XI

"The man who preserved his sight the longest, recovered the soonest; and to his exertions alone, under the providence of God and the mercy of the blessed saints, is it owing that we are now within a few leagues of Guadaloupe, this twenty-first day of June 1819. I am myself almost well. The surgeon and eleven more are irrecoverably blind; the Captain has lost one eye; four others have met with the same calamity; and five are able to see, though dimly, with both. Among the slaves, thirty-nine are completely blind and the rest blind of one eye or their sight otherwise injured.

"This morning the Captain called all hands on deck, negroes and all. The shores of Guadaloupe were in sight. I thought he was going to return God thanks publicly for our miraculous escape.

" 'Are you quite certain," said the mate, 'that the cargo is insured?'

" 'I am,' said the Captain. 'Every slave that is lost must be made good by the underwriters. Besides, would you have me turn my ship into a hospital for the support of blind negroes? They have cost us enough already. Do your duty.'

"The mate picked out thirty-nine negroes who were completely blind, and, with the assistance of the rest of the crew, tied a piece of ballast to the legs of each. The miserable wretches were then thrown into the sea."

8

Images of African-American Slavery,
Eighteenth and Nineteenth Centuries

The visual record of slavery in the Americas is dominated by images rendered by members of the slave-owning societies; few images by slaves themselves exist. Nevertheless, much can be learned about the circumstances of slavery from the illustrations that do exist. Figure 16.3 shows a sale of slaves in Africa that was not atypical. Who are the slaves? Who is selling them? Who is buying them?

The work and living conditions of slaves varied among countries and slaveholders. Many slaves were put to work on large plantations to help with large-scale production, while others worked in smaller operations or as house servants and were sometimes hired out to work in other locations by their masters. A fortunate few were eventually granted their freedom after years of dedicated labor. Figure 16.4 depicts plantation work in Martinique in the early nineteenth century. Published in a traveler's account of the Americas, the text accompanying this image reads: "The slaves are called to work by the plantation bell at 6 in the morning, each person takes his hoe to the field under the supervision of overseers, either European or Creole; in a single line, they work in unison while chanting some African work song; the overseers occasionally use the whip to increase the work pace; at 11 the bell sounds, they take a meal, then resume their work until 6 in the evening." What does this image tell you that you might not have known about slavery?

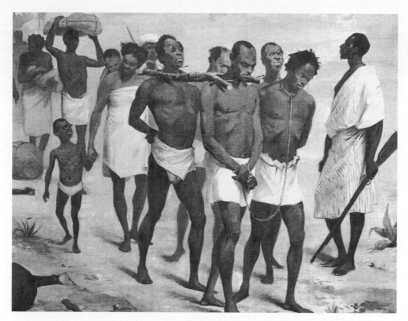

Figure 16.3 Buying slaves in Africa, late 1700s or early 1800s.

Source: The Granger Collection, New York.

Figure 16.4 Plantation work, Martinique, 1826.

Source: *Voyage pittoresque dans les deux Amériques*, Albert and Shirley Small Special Collections Library, University of Virginia.

Figure 16.5   Slave market, Rio de Janeiro, Brazil, 1830s.
Source: Snark/Art Resource, NY.

Slaves were sold at auction both upon arrival from Africa and sometimes when being sold by their owners. Figure 16.5 illustrates a slave
auction in Brazil in the 1830s. Do slaves appear to be in high demand
here? What does this image suggest to you about the cost and care of
slaves in Brazil? Figure 16.6 offers a contrasting scene from a British
newspaper of slaves awaiting sale in the United States. The article from
the *Illustrated London News* reads: "The accompanying engraving represents a gang of Negroes exhibited in the city of New Orleans, previous
to an auction, from a sketch made on the spot by our artist. The men
and women are well clothed, in their Sunday best—the men in blue
cloth... with beaver hats; and the women in calico dresses, of more or
less brilliancy, with silk bandana handkerchiefs bound round their
heads. . . . they stand through a good part of the day, subject to the
inspection of the purchasing or non-purchasing passing crowd. . . .
An orderly silence is preserved as a general rule at these sales, although
conversation does not seem to be altogether prohibited." What does
this image suggest to you about slavery in New Orleans in 1861?

THINKING HISTORICALLY

These four images of African slavery in the Americas are selected out of
thousands of paintings, engravings, and drawings, almost all done by
Europeans who held varying attitudes toward slavery. Even if they accurately depict what the European artist saw at a particular moment in a

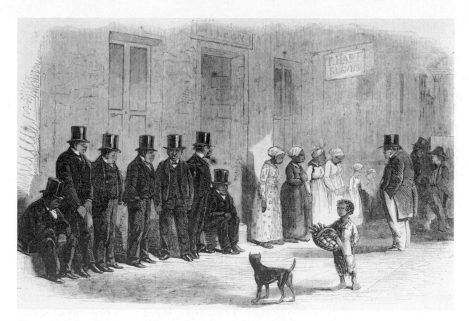

Figure 16.6 Slaves awaiting sale, New Orleans, 1861.

Source: A Slave-Pen at New Orleans—Before the Auction, from *Harper's Weekly*, 24th January 1863 (engraving) (b&w photo), American School (19th century)/Private Collection/The Bridgeman Art Library.

particular place, we should be careful to avoid making generalizations based on a single image. Nevertheless, often a primary source, written or visual, prompts new questions rather than answers to old ones. What questions occur to you when you view these images?

9

HARRIET JACOBS

Incidents in the Life of a Slave Girl, Written by Herself, 1861

Harriet Jacobs (1813–1897) was born a slave in North Carolina. In 1835, after the events described in this selection, she escaped her owner and managed to hide until fleeing to the North in 1842. Hers was one of the first accounts of slavery by a woman who had lived the

Source: Harriet Jacobs, *Incidents in the Life of a Slave Girl, Written by Herself* with Related Documents, ed. Jennifer Fleischner (Boston: Bedford/St. Martin's, 2010), 39–41, 52–53, 55–61.

experience. The book was published under the pseudonym of Linda Brent in 1861, the first year of the Civil War. Popular among Northern abolitionists, it was greeted as a major work of literature in England. What does her story tell you about slavery in the United States?

THINKING HISTORICALLY

This is the only one of our selections on slavery that was written by a former slave. It is also the only one written by a woman. How do these factors shape the narrative? In what ways do they make her account more or less reliable?

III. The Slaves' New Year's Day

Dr. Flint owned a fine residence in town, several farms, and about fifty slaves, besides hiring a number by the year.

Hiring-day at the south takes place on the 1st of January. On the 2d, the slaves are expected to go to their new masters. On a farm, they work until the corn and cotton are laid. They then have two holidays. Some masters give them a good dinner under the trees. This over, they work until Christmas eve. If no heavy charges are meantime brought against them, they are given four or five holidays, whichever the master or overseer may think proper. Then comes New Year's eve; and they gather together their little alls, or more properly speaking, their little nothings, and wait anxiously for the dawning of day. At the appointed hour the grounds are thronged with men, women, and children, waiting, like criminals, to hear their doom pronounced. The slave is sure to know who is the most humane, or cruel master, within forty miles of him.

It is easy to find out, on that day, who clothes and feeds his slaves well; for he is surrounded by a crowd, begging, "Please, massa, hire me this year. I will work *very* hard, massa."

If a slave is unwilling to go with his new master, he is whipped, or locked up in jail, until he consents to go, and promises not to run away during the year. Should he chance to change his mind, thinking it justifiable to violate an extorted promise, woe unto him if he is caught! The whip is used till the blood flows at his feet; and his stiffened limbs are put in chains, to be dragged in the field for days and days!

If he lives until the next year, perhaps the same man will hire him again, without even giving him an opportunity of going to the hiring-ground. After those for hire are disposed of, those for sale are called up.

O, you happy free women, contrast *your* New Year's day with that of the poor bond-woman! With you it is a pleasant season, and the light of the day is blessed. Friendly wishes meet you every where, and gifts are showered upon you. Even hearts that have been estranged from you soften at this season, and lips that have been silent echo back, "I wish you a happy New Year." Children bring their little offerings, and raise their rosy lips for a caress. They are your own, and no hand but that of death can take them from you.

But to the slave mother New Year's day comes laden with peculiar sorrows. She sits on her cold cabin floor, watching the children who may all be torn from her the next morning; and often does she wish that she and they might die before the day dawns. She may be an ignorant creature, degraded by the system that has brutalized her from childhood; but she has a mother's instincts, and is capable of feeling a mother's agonies.

On one of these sale days, I saw a mother lead seven children to the auction-block. She knew that *some* of them would be taken from her; but they took *all*. The children were sold to a slave-trader, and their mother was bought by a man in her own town. Before night her children were all far away. She begged the trader to tell her where he intended to take them; this he refused to do: How *could* he, when he knew he would sell them, one by one, wherever he could command the highest price? I met that mother in the street, and her wild, haggard face lives to-day in my mind. She wrung her hands in anguish, and exclaimed, "Gone! All gone! Why *don't* God kill me?" I had no words wherewith to comfort her. Instances of this kind are of daily, yea, of hourly occurrence.

Slaveholders have a method, peculiar to their institution, of getting rid of *old* slaves, whose lives have been worn out in their service. I knew an old woman, who for seventy years faithfully served her master. She had become almost helpless, from hard labor and disease. Her owners moved to Alabama, and the old black woman was left to be sold to any body who would give twenty dollars for her. . . .

V. The Trials of Girlhood

During the first years of my service in Dr. Flint's family, I was accustomed to share some indulgences with the children of my mistress. Though this seemed to me no more than right, I was grateful for it, and tried to merit the kindness by the faithful discharge of my duties. But I now entered on my fifteenth year — a sad epoch in the life of a slave girl. My master began to whisper foul words in my ear. Young as I was, I could not remain ignorant of their import. I tried to treat them with indifference or contempt. The master's age, my extreme youth, and the fear that his conduct would be reported to my grandmother, made him bear this treatment for many months. He was a crafty man, and resorted to many means to accomplish his purposes. Sometimes he had stormy, terrific ways, that made his victims tremble; sometimes he assumed a gentleness that he thought must surely subdue. Of the two, I preferred his stormy moods, although they left me trembling. He tried his utmost to corrupt the pure principles my grandmother had instilled. He peopled my young mind with unclean images, such as only a vile monster could think of. I turned from him with disgust and hatred. But he was my master. I was compelled to live under the same roof with him—where I saw a man forty years my senior daily violating the most sacred commandments of nature. He told me I was his property; that I must be subject to his will in all things. My soul revolted against the mean tyranny. But where could I turn for protection? . . .

I longed for some one to confide in. I would have given the world to have laid my head on my grandmother's faithful bosom, and told her all my troubles. But Dr. Flint swore he would kill me, if I was not as silent as the grave.

VI. The Jealous Mistress

. . . Mrs. Flint possessed the key to her husband's character before I was born. She might have used this knowledge to counsel and to screen the young and the innocent among her slaves; but for them she had no sympathy. They were the objects of her constant suspicion and malevolence. She watched her husband with unceasing vigilance; but he was well practised in means to evade it. . . .

I had entered my sixteenth year, and every day it became more apparent that my presence was intolerable to Mrs. Flint. Angry words frequently passed between her and her husband. He had never punished me himself, and he would not allow any body else to punish me. In that respect, she was never satisfied; but, in her angry moods, no terms were too vile for her to bestow upon me. Yet I, whom she detested so bitterly, had far more pity for her than he had, whose duty it was to make her life happy. I never wronged her, or wished to wrong her, and one word of kindness from her would have brought me to her feet.

After repeated quarrels between the doctor and his wife, he announced his intention to take his youngest daughter, then four years old, to sleep in his apartment. It was necessary that a servant should sleep in the same room, to be on hand if the child stirred. I was selected for that office, and informed for what purpose that arrangement had been made. By managing to keep within sight of people, as much as possible, during the day time, I had hitherto succeeded in eluding my master, though a razor was often held to my throat to force me to change this line of policy. At night I slept by the side of my great aunt, where I felt safe. He was too prudent to come into her room. She was an old woman, and had been in the family many years. Moreover, as a married man, and a professional man, he deemed it necessary to save appearances in some degree. But he resolved to remove the obstacle in the way of his scheme; and he thought he had planned it so that he should evade suspicion. He was well aware how much I prized my refuge by the side of my old aunt, and he determined to dispossess me of it. The first night the doctor had the little child in his room alone. The next morning, I was ordered to take my station as nurse the following night. A kind Providence interposed in my favor. During the day Mrs. Flint heard of this new arrangement, and a storm followed. I rejoiced to hear it rage.

After a while my mistress sent for me to come to her room. Her first question was, "Did you know you were to sleep in the doctor's room?"

"Yes, ma'am."

"Who told you?"

"My master."

"Will you answer truly all the questions I ask?"

"Yes, ma'am."

"Tell me, then, as you hope to be forgiven, are you innocent of what I have accused you?"

"I am."

She handed me a Bible, and said, "Lay your hand on your heart, kiss this holy book, and swear before God that you tell me the truth."

I took the oath she required, and I did it with a clear conscience.

"You have taken God's holy word to testify your innocence," said she. "If you have deceived me, beware! Now take this stool, sit down, look me directly in the face, and tell me all that has passed between your master and you."

I did as she ordered. As I went on with my account her color changed frequently, she wept, and sometimes groaned. She spoke in tones so sad, that I was touched by her grief. The tears came to my eyes; but I was soon convinced that her emotions arose from anger and wounded pride. She felt that her marriage vows were desecrated, her dignity insulted; but she had no compassion for the poor victim of her husband's perfidy. She pitied herself as a martyr; but she was incapable of feeling for the condition of shame and misery in which her unfortunate, helpless slave was placed.

Yet perhaps she had some touch of feeling for me; for when the conference was ended, she spoke kindly, and promised to protect me. I should have been much comforted by this assurance if I could have had confidence in it; but my experiences in slavery had filled me with distrust. She was not a very refined woman, and had not much control over her passions. I was an object of her jealousy, and, consequently, of her hatred; and I knew I could not expect kindness or confidence from her under the circumstances in which I was placed. I could not blame her. Slaveholders' wives feel as other women would under similar circumstances. The fire of her temper kindled from small sparks, and now the flame became so intense that the doctor was obliged to give up his intended arrangement.

I knew I had ignited the torch, and I expected to suffer for it afterwards; but I felt too thankful to my mistress for the timely aid she rendered me to care much about that. She now took me to sleep in a room adjoining her own. There I was an object of her especial care, though not of her especial comfort, for she spent many a sleepless night to watch over me. . . .

. . . I pitied Mrs. Flint. She was a second wife, many years the junior of her husband; and the hoary-headed miscreant was enough to try the patience of a wiser and better woman. She was completely foiled, and knew not how to proceed. She would gladly have had me flogged for my supposed false oath; but, as I have already stated, the doctor never allowed any one to whip me. The old sinner was politic. The application of the lash might have led to remarks that would have exposed him in the eyes of his children and grandchildren. How often did I rejoice that I lived in a town where all the inhabitants knew each other! If had been on a remote plantation, or lost among the multitude of a crowded city, I should not be a living woman at this day.

The secrets of slavery are concealed like those of the Inquisition. My master was, to my knowledge, the father of eleven slaves. But did the mothers dare to tell who was the father of their children? Did the other slaves dare to allude to it, except in whispers among themselves? No, indeed! They knew too well the terrible consequences. . . .

Reader, I draw no imaginary pictures of southern homes. I am telling you the plain truth. Yet when victims make their escape from this wild beast of Slavery, northerners consent to act the part of bloodhounds, and hunt the poor fugitive back into his den, "full of dead men's bones, and all uncleanness."[1] Nay, more, they are not only willing, but proud, to give their daughters in marriage to slaveholders. . . . The young wife soon learns that the husband in whose hands she has placed her happiness pays no regard to his marriage vows. Children of every shade of complexion play with her own fair babies, and too well she knows that they are born unto him of his own household. . . .

Southern women often marry a man knowing that he is the father of many little slaves. They do not trouble themselves about it. They regard such children as property, as marketable as the pigs on the plantation; and it is seldom that they do not make them aware of this by passing them into the slave-trader's hands as soon as possible, and thus getting them out of their sight.

[1] Biblical reference to Matthew 23:27. [Ed.]

■ REFLECTIONS

This chapter asks you to compare European encounters with Native Americans and Africans. Why did Europeans enslave Africans and not, for the most part, American Indians? Because so many Africans were brought to the Americas to work on plantations, this topic is especially compelling.

Initially, of course, Indians *were* enslaved. Recall the letter of Columbus (Chapter 15, selection 4). Part of the reason this enslavement did not continue was the high mortality of Native Americans exposed to smallpox and other Old World diseases. In addition, Native Americans who survived the bacterial onslaught had the "local knowledge" and support needed to escape from slavery.

Above and beyond this were the humanitarian objections of Spanish priests like Bartolomeo de Las Casas and the concerns of the Spanish monarchy that slavery would increase the power of the conquistadors at the expense of the Crown. In 1542 the enslavement of Indians was out-lawed in Spanish dominions of the New World. Clearly, these "New Laws" were not always obeyed by Spaniards in the Americas or by the Portuguese subjects of the unified Spanish-Portuguese crown between 1580 and 1640. Still, the different legal positions of Africans and Indians in the minds of Europeans require further explanation.

Some scholars have suggested that the difference in treatment lies in the differing needs of the main European powers involved in the encounter. The anthropologist Marvin Harris makes the argument this way:

> The most plausible explanation of the New Laws [of 1542] is that they represented the intersection of the interests of three power groups: the Church, the Crown, and the colonists. All three of these interests sought to maximize their respective control over the aboriginal populations. Outright enslavement of the Indians was the method preferred by the colonists. But neither the Crown nor the Church could permit this to happen without surrendering their own vested and potential interests in the greatest resource of the New World—its manpower.[1]

Why then did Europeans permit and even encourage the enslave-ment of Africans? In this matter all three power groups stood to gain. Africans who remained in Africa were of no use to anybody, since effective military and political domination of that continent by Europeans was not achieved until the middle of the nineteenth century. To make use of African manpower, Africans had to be removed from their homelands. The only way to accomplish this was

[1] Marvin Harris, *Patterns of Race in the Americas* (New York: W. W. Norton, 1964), 17.

to buy them as slaves from dealers on the coast. For both the Crown and the church, it was better to have Africans under the control of the New World colonists than to leave Africans under the control of Africans.

But of course the Atlantic world slave trade was just one of the lasting outcomes of Atlantic world encounters. Toward the end of his dramatic account of the Spanish conquest of Mexico (selection 1), Bernal Díaz describes a grizzly discovery made by the victorious conquistadors:

> I solemnly swear that all the houses and stockades in the lake were full of heads and corpses. I do not know how to describe it but it was the same in the streets and courts of Tlatelolco. We could not walk without treading on the bodies and heads of dead Indians. (Díaz, 1963, 405)

After two years of continual and heavy warfare, the fortunes of the Spanish turned in their favor and they seized a ravaged city where, according to Bernal Díaz, "the stench was so bad, no one could endure it." Díaz assumed that the Mexicans had been starved and denied fresh water, but we now know that at least part of the cause was the spread of smallpox, a disease that the Spanish carried from the Old World and for which the Native Americans had no immunities. Because of thousands of years of contact, Africans shared many of the same immunities as Europeans, but Native Americans, having inhabited a separate biological realm for over ten thousand years, were completely vulnerable to the new diseases and perished in droves.

Ultimately, slavery came to an end, even if in some cases—the work of Italians on Brazilian sugar plantations, Chinese rail workers, or free African day laborers—it was hard to see a difference in working conditions. In any case, the long-term impact of the "Columbian exchange" was more ecological than economic. The potatoes of South America and the corn of Mexico fed more families in Afro-Eurasia than had ever existed in the Americas. Conversely, the flora and fauna of the Americas were transformed through the introduction of the grasses, trees, fruits, grains, horses, cattle, pigs, and chickens that had nourished the ancestors of the conquistadors.

17

State and Religion
Asian, Islamic, and Christian States, 1500–1800

■ HISTORICAL CONTEXT

The relationship between state and religion is a matter of concern and debate almost everywhere in the modern world. In the United States, the issue of the separation of church and state engenders conflicts about the legality of abortion, prayer in the schools, government vouchers for religious schools, and the public display of religious symbols like the Ten Commandments, Nativity scenes, and Chanukah menorahs. Governments in countries as diverse as France and Turkey have recently debated the wearing of headscarves and the display of religious symbols in public schools and other public spaces.

Few states in the world today are dedicated to a single religion as are Saudi Arabia, Israel, and the Vatican. Yet even such places where religious devotion is extreme allow citizenship, residence, and rights in some measure for people of other religions. A few other states have official religions: Brazil is officially Roman Catholic, as was Italy until 1984; Iran is officially Muslim. But, with some notable exceptions, these types of designations often have little effect on what people believe or how they behave.

Although the role of religion in public life and the relationship between church and state are important current issues, from the long-term historical view, the state has become more important in peoples' lives while religion has become less influential. In the period before 1500, with the notable exception of China, many religious organizations were more important than political entities. But, in much of the world, the story of the last five hundred years has been the replacement of religious authority by that of the state. With the increased power of the state, secularism has become more pervasive, often triggering revivals of religious fundamentalism in reaction.

In this chapter, we look at religion and the state in various parts of the world two to five hundred years ago to see how different things were, but also to locate the roots of present church-state conflicts. We look first at China, where state formation began over two thousand years ago and official Confucianism supported the authority of the emperor. Japan, by contrast, emerged from feudalism to state formation after 1600. Both East Asian societies struggled with the claims of Buddhists, Christians, Muslims, and popular religious sects. Next we look at India, conquered by the Muslim Mughals after 1500, many of whom were remarkably tolerant of Hindus and Hinduism. Similarly, the Ottoman Empire protected a wide range of minority religions despite its Muslim majority. We conclude with the West (Europe and colonial America) to understand how Christian states struggled with some of the challenges posed by religion. Ultimately, we will be looking for the roots of religious toleration.

Kings and political leaders are almost all more comfortable with some kind of orthodoxy (conventional belief and practice) than with heterodoxy (dissident or heretical belief and practice). But one person's orthodox belief is another's heterodoxy. Most Islamic states, for instance, see Iran's Shi'ism as heterodox, but Shi'ism has been the orthodox norm for most Iranians for centuries. Orthodoxy frequently undermines religious toleration. In modern society, we often see toleration as a product of secularism. In fact, the history of church and state suggests something very different.

■ THINKING HISTORICALLY

Appreciating Context

Normally a quote taken "out of context" refers to a quote separated out from other words, which, if included, would qualify or change the meaning. For instance if you quoted Martin Luther as saying "A Christian is a perfectly free lord of all, subject to none"[1] in order to establish the Protestant Reformer as a proponent of individual freedom, but you failed to quote Luther's next sentence, which is "A Christian is a perfectly dutiful servant of all, subject to all," then you would be guilty of taking the first quote out of context. You would have misconstrued Luther's meaning and failed to understand his complexity.

That is the simple meaning of context: the surrounding words of a quotation that must be included to grasp its full meaning. Context can mean much more than that, however. It can mean not only words, but actions too, that are not only adjacent, but close enough to be relevant.

---

[1] Martin Luther, "The Freedom of a Christian" (1520), in *Luther-Selected Political Writings*, ed. J.M. Porter (Philadelphia: Fortress Press, 1974), 25.

Context helps us understand any words or event. Your mother shouts at you with uncharacteristic anger for a simple thing like not taking out the garbage. You might try to put it in context by recalling she's had a bad day. For her, the context might be that you have been negligent about other responsibilities. There can be many different contextual explanations. The job of an historian is to discover the context or contexts that increase the meaning of something. Was a strongly anti-war letter written just after a devastating battle? Did a religious conversion occur in a mass revival, or after a near-death experience?

As we examine the following primary sources, we will see that sometimes an important context is apparent in the document and sometimes it is not. When it is not, we will have to look beyond the source.

1

JONATHAN SPENCE
Emperor Kangxi on Religion, 1661–1722

Kangxi[1] was emperor of China from 1661 to 1722. A descendant of conquering Manchu warriors, Kangxi overcame the last resistance of the previous Ming dynasty and, during his reign, which was the longest of any Chinese emperor, brought the Qing (or Manchu) dynasty to its greatest size and strength. In this selection, the modern historian Jonathan Spence presents the emperor in his own voice, drawn from innumerable primary sources and often the emperor's own words. How would you describe Kangxi's attitude toward religion? What do you think he would say if asked about the proper relationship between religion and the state? What characteristics of Chinese society might explain these ideas?

THINKING HISTORICALLY

Kangxi's reflections on religion and the state developed not in a vacuum, but in the context of the recent arrival of Roman Catholic Christians in China, especially Jesuit missionaries. China encountered Nestorian Christians from Syria as early as the seventh century (see document 7.3), but they assimilated into Chinese culture and practically disappeared before the Mongols came in the thirteenth century (some Mongols, incidentally, with their Nestorian Christian wives). After the Mongols, the Ming dynasty banned Christians in China,

[1] Cong SHE   Spelled K'ang Hsi in older Wade-Giles system of Romanization.

Source: Jonathan D. Spence, *Emperor of China: Self-Portrait of K'ang-Hsi* (New York: Vintage Books, 1975), 80–85.

while allowing Jews and Muslims to remain. So Kangxi was ruling at a pivotal moment when the new Jesuit order was attempting to convert the Chinese to Christianity. Matteo Ricci, the founder of the Jesuit mission to China, taught fellow Jesuits to impress the emperor with clocks and scientific instruments and offers to share their knowledge, while at the same time demonstrating humility toward traditional Chinese Confucianism. They learned Chinese, wore Chinese clothing, and accepted Confucianism as a moral code rather than a competing religion. As you read the selection, note Kangxi's references to Christians. How are his concerns about Christians different from concerns about followers of other religions? How might Christians pose a greater or different threat to Kangxi? How much of Kangxi's attitude toward religion seems based on his encounter with Christians? How different do you think it would be if the Christians never arrived?

Every country must have some spirits that it reveres. This is true for our dynasty, as for Mongols or Mohammedans, Miao or Lolo, or other foreigners. Just as everyone fears something, some snakes but not toads, some toads but not snakes; and as all countries have different pronunciations and different alphabets. But in this Catholic religion, the Society of Peter quarrels with the Jesuits, Bouvet[2] quarrels with Mariani, and among the Jesuits the Portuguese want only their own nationals in their church while the French want only French in theirs. This violates the principles of religion. Such dissension cannot be inspired by the Lord of Heaven but by the Devil, who, I have heard the Westerners say, leads men to do evil since he can't do otherwise. . . .

Since I discovered on the Southern Tour of 1703 that there were missionaries wandering at will over China, I had grown cautious and determined to control them more tightly: to bunch them in the larger cities and in groups that included men from several different countries, to catalogue their names and residences, and to permit no new establishments without my express permission. For with so many Westerners coming to China it has been hard to distinguish the real missionaries from other white men pretending to be missionaries. As I clarified it for de Tournon[3]: "Hereafter we will permit residence in China to all those who come from the West

---

[2] Joachim Bouvet (1656–1730) was a French Jesuit who taught Kangxi astronomy and mathematics and, according to the emperor, understood Chinese better than other Westerners. As a leading "Figurist," Bouvet believed that all of Christianity could be found in the ancient Chinese religious text, the *I Ching*. This idea was criticized by other missionaries who thought it understated the importance of the Bible. [Ed.]

[3] Charles-Thomas Maillard de Tournon (1668–1710) was a papal legate to China to control missionaries and end the acceptance of some Chinese phrases and Confucian rites by Chinese Christians; this led to his imprisonment by Kangxi. [Ed.]

and will not return there. Residence permission will not be granted to those who come one year expecting to go home the next—because such people are like those who stand outside the main gate and discuss what people are doing inside the house. Besides these meddlers there are also those out for profit, greedy traders, who should not be allowed to live here." After the arguments with de Tournon and Maigrot[4] I made all missionaries who wanted to stay on in China sign a certificate, stating that they would remain here for life and follow Ricci on the Rites.[5] Forty or fifty who refused were exiled to Canton; de Tournon was sent to Macao, his secretary, Appiani, we kept in prison in Peking.

Despite these sterner restrictions, the Westerners continued to cause me anxiety. Our ships were being sold overseas; reports came of ironwood for keel blocks being shipped out of Kwangtung; Luzon and Batavia became havens for Chinese outlaws; and the Dutch were strong in the Southern Seas. I ordered a general inquiry among residents of Peking who had once lived on the coast, and called a conference of the coastal governors-general. "I fear that some time in the future China is going to get into difficulties with these various Western countries," I said. "That is my prediction." Similarly I had warned earlier that China must be strong to forestall a possible threat from Russia. General Ch'en Mao insisted even more strongly on the dangers from Holland and France, Spain and England, and of missionaries and merchants conniving together. I did not agree with him that we should disarm all their ships, but I did agree to reiterate the 1669 edict that banned Westerners from preaching in the provinces.

Three of the Peking Jesuits—Suares, Parrenin, and Mourao—came to protest: "We learn that the Boards have pronounced a strict sentence and the Christian religion is proscribed."

I reassured them: "No. The sentence is not strict, and the Christian religion is not proscribed. Only Westerners without the certificate are forbidden to preach. This prohibition does not affect those who have the certificate."

"This distinction as made by the Emperor is not clearly expressed in the sentence."

"It is clearly expressed. I have read the sentence with care. If you were hoping that those without certificates might be permitted to preach your laws, then that hope is no longer possible."

"But at the beginning of the sentence the 1669 edict is cited."

---

[4] Charles Maigrot (1652–1730) was administrator of Christian missions in China after 1684. In 1692 Kangxi issued an Edict of Toleration that formally allowed Chinese to become Christians. The following year Maigrot condemned the rites honoring Confucius and rituals associated with ancestor worship. [Ed.]

[5] Refers to the position of Matteo Ricci (1552–1610), a founder of the Jesuit mission to China, and later of Joachim Bouvet that the rites of Confucius were moral and civic rather than religious and that therefore they could be practiced by Chinese Christians. [Ed.]

"That is true, but the point of it is to prevent those without certificates from preaching."

"We are just afraid that the provincial officials will treat us all alike, and that they will not permit even those of us who have certificates to preach the holy law."

"If that occurs, those who have certificates have only to produce them. The officials will see that permission to preach your laws is granted. You can preach the law, and it's up to the Chinese to listen—if they so choose. As for those without a certificate, let them come here, and I will give them one." (I smiled during these last words.) "Anyway, even those with the certificate are only being permitted to preach for a time. Later on we'll see what decision to take in their case."

"But if they cause trouble to those with certificates, we will come to the Emperor for help."

"Take care to inform me if such is the case."

"There is one thing that causes us particular anguish—namely, that the Boards treat us as rebels."

"Don't worry about that. It's just a conventional formula that the Boards use."

"As soon as this edict is published, the officials will search out the missionaries and Christians and stir up trouble."

"As far as this searching out goes, it's essential. When I sent Li Ping-chung to Canton I gave him an order for the Governor-General, telling him to search out and to assemble in one place all those without certificates. And I've just given similar orders to Governor-General Yang Lin on his return to Canton, and am awaiting his reply."

The Westerners in China were only as drops of rain in the immensity of the ocean, said de Tournon in our audience, and I had to laugh. Yet some of their words were no different from the wild or improper teachings of Buddhists and Taoists, and why should they be treated differently? One of my censors wrote that the Western god fashioned a man with a human soul from the blood of a virgin, Mary; and they claimed that Jesus was born in the reign of Han Ai-ti [reigned 6 B.C.–A.D. 1], that he was killed on a cross for man's sins, and that they had meetings in which slaves and masters, men and women, mixed together and drank some holy substance. I had asked Verbiest[6] why God had not forgiven his son without making him die, but though he had tried to answer I had not understood him. Also, though in China there had been a flood at about the same time as that reported for Noah, those on the Chinese plains had been drowned, while those who escaped to the mountains were saved. And I told Fontaney[7] that I would gladly witness some of the miracles they talked about, but none was forthcoming.

[6] Ferdinand Verbiest (1623–1688), Flemish Jesuit missionary in China; mathematician and astronomer. [Ed.]

[7] Baptist de Fontenay (1643–1710), missionary, mathematician, and astronomer. [Ed.]

In the past, both Buddhists and Taoists had been made to fill out certificates, and the superiors in the various temples have to register their monks—they are not allowed to chant or beg for alms or set out their sacred images in the streets of Peking, and may not act as exorcists for patients suffering from seizures without getting official permission. Certainly there are more Buddhists and Taoists—the census of 1667 listed 140,193 monks divided among 79,622 temples of various sizes—but there were many Christians also. When I asked Verbiest for exact figures in 1688 he said there were 15,758 Christians just in Peking. Even though I realized it was quite impractical to close down temples, and order people to return to secular life, there was no harm in following the principle of "preparing for trouble before trouble comes." So I strictly banned all the sects[8] such as the "non-action," "white lotus," "incense smelling," "origin of the dragon," and "all-submerging Yang," and stiffened the penalties for all officials who failed to report heterodox teachers in their localities. Also I banned the so-called "incense associations," where men and women mixed together and sold erotic works and special medicines; I ordered the printing blocks of certain mystical and magical books burned; and I continued to enforce the prohibitions against the private ownership of forbidden books—though I allowed exceptions for those working at home in astronomy and mathematics.

[8] These were Daoist and Buddhist sects. [Ed.]

2

Japanese Edicts Regulating Religion, 1645 and 1665

The history of the state in Japan was very different from that of China. Between 1200 and 1600 Japan went through a period in which the state was eclipsed by aristocratic, warrior, and religious groups. When the Tokugawa Shogunate reasserted the authority of a central state in 1600, the memory of monk-soldiers and numerous independent armies called for a series of measures directed at controlling religious institutions and other independent powers. In one measure, all farmers were forbidden to have swords. Another regulated all religious temples. Between 1633 and 1639 the Tokugawa government took the further step of closing the country to all foreign religions, a move directed mainly at the influence previously enjoyed by Portuguese Catholic missionaries.

Source: Yosaburo Takekoshi, *The Economic Aspects of the History of the Civilization of Japan* (New York: Macmillan, 1930), 2:88–89. Reprinted in *Japan: A Documentary History*, ed. David J. Lu (Armonk, NY: M. E. Sharpe, 2005), 1:224–25.

The first of the two documents in this selection is a vow by which
Japanese Christians renounced their faith in 1645. The second document is a government edict regulating temples, mainly Buddhist, in
1665. What do these documents tell you about the relationship
between the state and religion in Tokugawa Japan?

THINKING HISTORICALLY

The first document, from 1645, in which a group of Japanese swear
they are renouncing Christianity is full of contradictions that cry out for
contextual explanation. The Japanese history of Christianity was similar
to the Chinese. Whether or not there was a Nestorian Christian presence by 500 C.E. as some argue, Roman Catholic Christianity came to
Japan with the first Jesuits, including Francis Xavier in 1549. At the end
of the sixteenth century and the beginning of the seventeenth century,
Christians were persecuted and the church was banned. In response
some Japanese Christians went underground, disguising their religion
with the appearance of a return to Japanese culture, including Buddha-
like images of Jesus and Mary. They were called *Kakure Kirishitans* ("hidden Christians"). What are the contradictions in this document that
suggest these people had been or continued to be hidden Christians?
What parts of the document suggest a false renunciation? What might
account for the difference in the last paragraph?

The second Japanese document was written in the time of the
Chinese Emperor Kangxi. How might Kangxi's meditations on religion
provide a context that might also help us understand this document?

Renouncing the Kirishitan[1] Faith, 1645

Vow of Namban (Southern Barbarians): We have been Kirishitans for
many years. But the more we learn of the Kirishitan doctrines the greater
becomes our conviction that they are evil. In the first place, we who received instructions from the padre regarding the future life were threatened with excommunication which would keep us away from association
with the rest of humanity in all things in the present world, and would
cast us into hell in the next world. We were also taught that, unless a
person committing a sin confesses it to the padre and secures his pardon,
he shall not be saved in the world beyond. In that way the people were
led into believing in the padres. All that was for the purpose of taking
the lands of others.

When we learned of it, we "shifted" from Kirishitan and became
adherents of Hokkekyō[2] while our wives became adherents of Ikkōshō.[3]

---

[1] Christian. [Ed.]
[2] Buddhist sect based on the Lotus Sutra sermon of the Buddha. [Ed.]
[3] Pure Land Buddhism. [Ed.]

We hereby present a statement in writing to you, worshipful Magistrate, as a testimony.

Hereafter we shall not harbor any thought of the Kirishitan in our heart. Should we entertain any thought of it at all, we shall be punished by Deus Paternus (God the Father), Jesus (His Son), Spirito Santo (the Holy Ghost), as well as by Santa Maria (St. Mary), various angels, and saints.

The grace of God will be lost altogether. Like Judas Iscariot, we shall be without hope, and shall be mere objects of ridicule to the people. We shall never rise. The foregoing is our Kirishitan vow.

Japanese Pledge: We have no thought of the Kirishitan in our hearts. We have certainly "shifted" our faith. If any falsehood be noted in our declaration now or in the future, we shall be subject to divine punishment by Bonten, Taishaku, the four deva kings, the great or little gods in all the sixty or more provinces of Japan, especially the Mishima Daimyōjin, the representatives of the god of Izu and Hakone, Hachiman Daibosatsu, Temman Daijizai Tenjin, especially our own family gods, Suwa Daimyōjin, the village people, and our relatives. This is to certify to the foregoing.

The second year of Shōhō [1645]
Endorsement.

Regulations for Buddhist Temples, 1665

1. The doctrines and rituals established for different sects must not be mixed and disarranged. If there is anyone who does not behave in accordance with this injunction, an appropriate measure must be taken expeditiously.

2. No one who does not understand the basic doctrines or rituals of a given sect is permitted to become the chief priest of a temple. Addendum: If a new rite is established, it must not preach strange doctrines.

3. The regulations which govern relationships between the main temple and branch temples must not be violated. However, even the main temple cannot take measures against branch temples in an unreasonable manner.

4. Parishioners of the temples can choose to which temple they wish to belong and make contributions. Therefore priests must not compete against one another for parishioners.

5. Priests are enjoined from engaging in activities unbecoming of priests, such as forming groups or planning to fight one another.

6. If there is anyone who has violated the law of the land, and that fact is communicated to a temple, it must turn him away without question.

7. When making repairs to a temple or a monastery, do not make them ostentatiously. Addendum: Temples must be kept clean without fail.

8. The estate belonging to a temple is not subject to sale, nor can it be mortgaged.

9. Do not allow anyone who has expressed a desire to become a disciple but is not of good lineage to enter the priesthood freely. If there is a particular candidate who has an improper and questionable background, the judgment of the domanial lord or magistrate of his domicile must be sought and then act accordingly.

The above articles must be strictly observed by all the sects. . . .

Fifth year of Kanbun [1665], seventh month, 11th day.

3

BADA'UNI
Akbar and Religion, 1595

At the same time the Chinese and Japanese were confronting Christian missionaries, the descendants of Muslim Turkic and Mongol peoples of Central Asia were conquering the Hindu kingdoms of northern India. Babur (1483–1530), the first of these Mughal rulers, swept into India from Afghanistan in 1525. Successive Mughal emperors enlarged the empire, so that by the time of Akbar (r. 1556–1605) it included all of northern India. Like his contemporaries Philip II of Spain (r. 1556–1598) and Elizabeth of England (r. 1558–1603), Akbar created an elaborate and enduring administrative bureaucracy. But unlike Philip and Elizabeth, who waged religious wars against each other and forcibly converted their domestic subjects and newly conquered peoples, Akbar reached out to his Hindu subjects in ways that would have astonished his European contemporaries. In fact, he angered many of his own Muslim advisors, including Bada'uni, the author of the following memoir. What bothered Bada'uni about Akbar? What does this selection tell you about Akbar's rule? What factors might have motivated his toleration of heterodoxy?

Source: 'Abdul Qadir Bada'uni, *Muntakhab ut-Tawarikh*, trans. G. S. A. Ranking and W. H. Lowe (Calcutta: Asiatic Society of Bengal, 1895–1925), 2:200–201, 255–61 *passim*, 324. Edited and reprinted in *Sources of Indian Tradition*, ed. Ainslie T. Embree (New York: Columbia University Press, 1988), 465–68.

THINKING HISTORICALLY

We know from other sources that Akbar made special efforts to include Hindus in his administration. About a third of his governing bureaucracy was Hindu, and he gave Hindu-governed territories a large degree of self-rule, allowing them to retain their own law and courts. Various taxes normally paid by non-Muslims were abolished. Among Akbar's five thousand wives, many were Hindus including his favorite, the mother of his successor, Jahangir (r. 1605–1628). Akbar's policy of toleration continued under his son and grandson, Jahangir and Shah Jahan (r. 1628–1658), but was largely reversed by his great grandson, Aurangzeb (r. 1658–1707). How does this understanding of a particular past provide context?

Context can also help us understand our distance from the past. Our contemporary mind-set can blind us to those differences. To give a small example, Bada'uni writes in this selection of people who behaved "like Jews and Egyptians for hatred of each other." The modern reader may take this as a reference to the modern conflict between Jews and Muslims, especially that between Israel and Egypt: an idea that reinforces the conviction that Jews and Muslims are eternal enemies. But Bada'uni is not thinking of Egypt as Muslim, even though it was Muslim in the seventeenth century and had been for a thousand years. If he had, there would be no reason to single out Egypt, then under Ottoman rule, since so many other states were Muslim and contained Jews. Bada'uni had to be referring to the biblical account of Moses in Pharoah's Egypt, pre-Muslim by two thousand years. Consequently, rather than suggest Muslim antipathy to Jews, Bada'uni's reference shows us how Muslims were familiar with the Hebrew Bible, and how they understood Judaism and the Bible as part of their Muslim heritage.

Modern ideas might distort the meaning not only of a minor reference like the above, but the meaning, impact, or uniqueness of the entire text. For instance, most of us in modern society believe in toleration and religious freedom. But did Bada'uni? How is Bada'uni's attitude toward his subject different from ours? How might that difference lead us to misunderstand what Bada'uni is trying to convey? What is the value of keeping Bada'uni's ideas in mind alongside Akbar's?

In the year nine hundred and eighty-three [1605] the buildings of the 'Ibādatkhāna[1] were completed. The cause was this. For many years previously the emperor had gained in succession remarkable and decisive victories. The empire had grown in extent from day to day; everything

[1] Hall of Religious Discussions. [Ed.]

turned out well, and no opponent was left in the whole world. His Majesty had thus leisure to come into nearer contact with ascetics and the disciples of his reverence [the late] Mucīn, and passed much of his time in discussing the word of God and the word of the Prophet. Questions of Sufism,[2] scientific discussions, inquiries into philosophy and law, were the order of the day.

And later that day the emperor came to Fatehpur. There he used to spend much time in the Hall of Worship in the company of learned men and shaikhs and especially on Friday nights, when he would sit up there the whole night continually occupied in discussing questions of religion, whether fundamental or collateral. The learned men used to draw the sword of the tongue on the battlefield of mutual contradiction and opposition, and the antagonism of the sects reached such a pitch that they would call one another fools and heretics. The controversies used to pass beyond the differences of Sunni, and Shī'a, of Hanafī and Shā fi'ī, of lawyer and divine, and they would attack the very bases of belief. And Makhdūm-ul-Mulk wrote a treatise to the effect that Shaikh 'Abd-al-Nabī had unjustly killed Khizr Khān Sarwānī, who had been suspected of blaspheming the Prophet [peace be upon him!], and Mīr Habsh, who had been suspected of being a Shī'a, and saying that it was not right to repeat the prayers after him, because he was undutiful toward his father, and was himself afflicted with hemorrhoids. Shaikh 'Abd-al-Nabī replied to him that he was a fool and a heretic. Then the mullās [Muslim theologians] became divided into two parties, and one party took one side and one the other, and became very [much like] Jews and Egyptians for hatred of each other. And persons of novel and whimsical opinions, in accordance with their pernicious ideas and vain doubts, coming out of ambush, decked the false in the garb of the true, and wrong in the dress of right, and cast the emperor, who was possessed of an excellent disposition, and was an earnest searcher after truth, but very ignorant and a mere tyro,[3] and used to the company of infidels and base persons, into perplexity, till doubt was heaped upon doubt, and he lost all definite aim, and the straight wall of the clear law and of firm religion was broken down, so that after five or six years not a trace of Islam was left in him: and everything was turned topsy-turvy. . . .

And samanas [Hindu or Buddhist ascetics] and brāhmans (who as far as the matter of private interviews is concerned gained the advantage over everyone in attaining the honor of interviews with His Majesty, and in associating with him, and were in every way superior in reputation to all learned and trained men for their treatises on morals, and on physical and religious sciences, and in religious ecstasies, and stages of spiritual

---

[2] Mystical, poetic Islamic tradition. [Ed.]
[3] Beginner. [Ed.]

progress and human perfections) brought forward proofs, based on reason and traditional testimony, for the truth of their own, and the fallacy of our religion, and inculcated their doctrine with such firmness and assurance, that they affirmed mere imaginations as though they were self-evident facts, the truth of which the doubts of the sceptic could no more shake "Than the mountains crumble, and the heavens be cleft!" And the Resurrection, and Judgment, and other details and traditions, of which the Prophet was the repository, he laid all aside. And he made his courtiers continually listen to those revilings and attacks against our pure and easy, bright and holy faith. . . .

Some time before this a brāhman, named Puruk'hotam, who had written a commentary on the Book, *Increase of Wisdom* (Khirad-afzā), had had private interviews with him, and he had asked him to invent particular Sanskrit names for all things in existence. And at one time a brāhman, named Debi, who was one of the interpreters of the *Mahābhā rata*,[4] was pulled up the wall of the castle sitting on a bedstead till he arrived near a balcony, which the emperor had made his bedchamber. Whilst thus suspended he instructed His Majesty in the secrets and legends of Hinduism, in the manner of worshiping idols, the fire, the sun and stars, and of revering the chief gods of these unbelievers, such as Brahma, Mahadev [Shiva], Bishn [Vishnu], Kishn [Krishna], Ram, and Mahama (whose existence as sons of the human race is a supposition, but whose nonexistence is a certainty, though in their idle belief they look on some of them as gods, and some as angels). His Majesty, on hearing further how much the people of the country prized their institutions, began to look upon them with affection. . . .

Sometimes again it was Shaikh Tā j ud-dīn whom he sent for. This shaikh was son of Shaikh Zakarīya of Ajodhan. . . . He had been a pupil of Rashīd Shaikh Zamān of Panipat, author of a commentary on the *Paths* (Lawā'ih), and of other excellent works, was most excellent in Sufism, and in the knowledge of theology second only to Shaikh Ibn 'Arabī and had written a comprehensive commentary on the *Joy of the Souls* (Nuzhat ul-Arwāh). Like the preceding he was drawn up the wall of the castle in a blanket, and His Majesty listened the whole night to his Sufic obscenities and follies. The shaikh, since he did not in any great degree feel himself bound by the injunctions of the law, introduced arguments concerning the unity of existence, such as idle Sufis discuss, and which eventually lead to license and open heresy. . . .

Learned monks also from Europe, who are called *Padre*, and have an infallible head, called *Papa*,[5] who is able to change religious ordinances as he may deem advisable for the moment, and to whose authority kings must submit, brought the Gospel, and advanced proofs for the

---

[4] Classical Indian epic; source of Hinduism. See Volume 1, selection 5 in Chapter 3. [Ed.]
[5] The Roman Catholic pope. [Ed.]

Trinity. His Majesty firmly believed in the truth of the Christian religion, and wishing to spread the doctrines of Jesus, ordered Prince Murād to take a few lessons in Christianity under good auspices, and charged Abū'l Fazl to translate the Gospel. . . .

Fire worshipers also came from Nousarīn Gujarat, proclaimed the religion of Zardusht [Zarathustra] as the true one, and declared reverence to fire to be superior to every other kind of worship. They also attracted the emperor's regard, and taught him the peculiar terms, the ordinances, the rites and ceremonies of the Kaianians [a pre-Muslim Persian dynasty]. At last he ordered that the sacred fire should be made over to the charge of Abū'l Fazl, and that after the manner of the kings of Persia, in whose temples blazed perpetual fires, he should take care it was never extinguished night or day, for that it is one of the signs of God, and one light from His lights. . . .

His Majesty also called some of the yogis, and gave them at night private interviews, inquiring into abstract truths; their articles of faith; their occupation; the influence of pensiveness; their several practices and usages; the power of being absent from the body; or into alchemy, physiognomy, and the power of omnipresence of the soul.

4

MARTIN LUTHER

Sermon on Religion and the State, 1528–1540

Martin Luther (1483–1546), the iconic father of the Protestant Reformation, was a Catholic monk, priest, and then professor of theology in Germany when in 1517 he challenged the papacy, first on the issue of the church selling indulgences that were said to speed a soul to heaven and then, increasingly, over issues of corruption and church power. Luther believed that the church had gone astray, becoming materialistic and out of touch with its original mission. He sought a return to the origins of Christianity, quoting Paul on the need for faith alone. He translated the Bible from Latin into German so that anyone could understand their religion, without the intervention of priests, pope, or all of the trappings of what he viewed as a bloated church. According to Luther, every believer was a priest, and

Source: Martin Luther, *The Sermons of Martin Luther,* vol. 5 (Grand Rapids, MI: Baker Book House, 1983), 294–306.

therefore priests could marry. The Catholic hierarchy, ceremony, even most of the sacraments were unnecessary. After an effort to defend his beliefs, Luther was summoned by the Church to recant. He refused and in 1521 was excommunicated from the Catholic Church. By then he had fled capture by the Catholic Holy Roman Emperor and the Roman papacy, receiving the protection of the German princes, splitting Roman Christianity into Catholicism and Protestantism and creating a new church and doctrine, Lutheranism, with a German national identity.

Luther's writings, including the German Bible, theological treatises, weekly hymns and sermons, periodic tracts, thoughts, and musings, fill over sixty volumes. This selection comes from one of his sermons. Luther began by quoting Matthew 22:15–22, the best known Christian statement about the relationship between the state and religion. What is that position? Would you call it a belief in the separation of church and state? How would you compare it to Akbar's position on church and state?

THINKING HISTORICALLY

In this sermon, Luther tries to define the relationship between church and state in a way that he believes is most true to the account of Matthew and, therefore, most true for his time. But his time was different from that of Matthew, with two different political contexts. How was the relationship of Luther to the state different from that of Jesus as described in the sermon? Which of the two was more dependent on state support? What evidence do you see in Luther's sermon that would suggest greater trust in the state than Jesus expressed?

Another context is suggested at the very end of this selection. Luther refers to the peasant revolt of 1523–1524, when peasants rebelled against their landlords, feudal obligations, and even the German princes. Some believed that Luther's ideas of individual justification by faith and the freedom of a Christian fomented the rebellion. Why might the revolt and accusations make Luther more inclined to frame the question of church and state the way he did here?

Sermon for 23rd Sunday after Trinity: Matthew 22:15–22

Then the Pharisees went out and laid plans to trap him in his words. They sent their disciples to him along with the Herodians. "Teacher," they said, "we know that you are a man of integrity and that you teach the way of God in accordance with the truth. You aren't swayed by others, because you pay no attention to who they are. Tell us then, what is your opinion? Is it right to pay the imperial tax to Caesar or not?"

But Jesus, knowing their evil intent, said, "You hypocrites, why are you trying to trap me? Show me the coin used for paying the tax." They brought him a denarius, and he asked them, "Whose image is this? And whose inscription?"

"Caesar's," they replied.

Then he said to them, "So give back to Caesar what is Caesar's, and to God what is God's."

When they heard this, they were amazed. So they left him and went away.

"Give back to Caesar what is Caesar's, and to God what is God's."

Although the Pharisees did not deserve it, the Lord teaches them the right way. And with these words he also confirms the worldly sword or government. They had hoped he would condemn it and speak against it; he does not do it, however, but praises earthly government and commands to render unto it what is due to it. It is therefore his desire that there should be magistrates, princes and masters, whom we are to obey, be they what they may and what they list; neither should we ask whether they possess and exercise government and authority justly or unjustly. We should only pay heed to that power and authority which is good, for it is ordered and instituted by God, Rom. 13, 1: You are not allowed to upbraid the government, when at times you are oppressed by princes and tyrants, who abuse the power they have from God: some day they will surely have to answer for it. The abuse of a thing does not make it bad, if it was good in itself. A golden chain is good, and it is not made worse by being worn around a whore's neck; or if someone were to destroy one of my eyes with it, should I therefore blame the chain? Truly nay.

Thus one must also bear the authority of the ruler. If he abuses it, I am not therefore to bear him a grudge, nor take revenge of and punish him with my hands. One must obey him solely for God's sake, for he stands in God's stead. Let them impose taxes as intolerable as they may: one must obey them and, suffer everything patiently, for God's sake. Whether they do right or not, that will be taken care of in due time. If therefore your possessions, aye, your life and whatsoever you have, be taken from you by those in power, then you are to say: I give it to you willingly, I acknowledge you as my masters, gladly will I be obedient to you. Whether you use the power given to you by God well or ill, that is your affair.

But what if they would take the Gospel from us or forbid us to preach it? Then you are to say: The Gospel and Word of God, I will not give up to you. This is not within your power, for your rule is a temporal rule, over worldly matters; but the Gospel is a spiritual, heavenly treasure, and therefore your authority does not extend over the Gospel and God's Word. We recognize the emperor as a master of temporal affairs, not of God's Word; this we shall not suffer to be torn from us, for it is the power of God, Rom. 1, 16, against which not even the gates of hell shall prevail.

Therefore, the Lord beautifully summarizes these two things, and in one saying distinguishes them from each other: "Render unto Caesar the things that are Caesar's, and unto God the things that are God's." This honor is due to God, that we are to hold him as a true, almighty and wise God, and attribute to him all the good things that can be named. And even if I do not render him this honor, he still keeps it; nothing is added to or subtracted from it. But in me he is true, almighty and wise, if I consider him as such, and believe him to be such as he proclaims himself. To the emperor, however, and to all in power, are due reverence, taxes, revenue and obedience. God will have the heart; body and possessions are the government's, which is to rule over them in God's stead. This St. Paul says to the Romans in round and clear words, Rom. 13, 1–7: "Let every soul be in subjection to the higher powers: for there is no power but of God; and the powers that be are ordained of God. Therefore he that resisteth the power, withstandeth the ordinance of God: and they that withstand shall receive to themselves judgment. For rulers are not a terror to the good work, but to the evil. And wouldest thou have no fear of the power? do that which is good, and thou shalt have praise from the same: for he is a minister of God to thee for good. But if thou do that which is evil, be afraid; for he beareth not the sword in vain: for he is a minister of God, an avenger for wrath to him that doeth evil. Wherefore ye must needs be in subjection, not only because of the wrath, but also for conscience' sake. Hence for this cause ye pay tribute also, for they are ministers of God's service, attending continually upon this very thing. Render to all their dues: tribute to whom tribute is due; custom to whom custom; fear to whom fear; honor to whom honor."

And for this reason also has government been ordained by God, that it may uphold general peace, which thing alone cannot be paid for by all the money in the world. We just noticed a few things in the uprising of the peasant, what damage, misery and woe are caused by rebellion and the breaking of peace. God grant that things do not go further and that we experience no more. Enough is said on this Gospel. Of temporal government we have written a special booklet. Whoever desires to read it may do so. There he will find more on this subject.

5

BENJAMIN J. KAPLAN
European Faiths and States, 2007

In Europe the state emerged as a major force after 1500. But the rise
of the European state was accompanied by a cultural revolution.
That revolution was the creation of self-conscious faith-based communities, spurred by the Protestant Reformation and the Catholic
response. In this selection, Benjamin J. Kaplan, a modern historian,
shows the novelty and intolerance of this combination of confessional community and state power. Why was this combination so
volatile? Did it make European society and European governments
more intolerant than were other societies like China, Japan, or India?
How were these changes in Europe similar to, and different from,
those in the other societies during the same period?

THINKING HISTORICALLY

If we were reading Benjamin Kaplan as a primary source, we might
ask about the context of someone writing in the first decade of the
present century (notice publication was 2007) about religious intolerance. But we are reading Kaplan as a secondary source. So instead,
let us consider how he provides context that helps us understand
sources from the period he discusses. How does he help you understand Martin Luther? In what ways does his work change your view of
Luther? Does he put Luther in a different context?

No religion is static, and over its two millennia of existence the Roman
Catholic Church has transformed itself several times. The so-called In-
vestiture Controversy[1] of the eleventh century precipitated one such
transformation; in the 1960s, Vatican II[2] decreed another. So too in the
sixteenth century, partly in response to the Protestant challenge, partly
driven by internal impulses for renewal and reform, the Catholic Church
initiated sweeping changes in everything from ecclesiastic administration and the training of priests to liturgy and forms of private devotion.

---

[1] A struggle in Europe in the eleventh and twelfth centuries over whether kings or the pope
had authority to appoint church officials. [Ed.]
[2] An important series of changes under Pope John XXIII said to modernize the Catholic
Church (1962–1965). [Ed.]

Source: Benjamin J. Kaplan, *Divided by Faith: Religious Conflict and the Practice of Toleration
in Early Modern Europe* (Cambridge: Harvard University Press, 2007), 28–32, 100–03.

Conventionally, the drive to enact these changes is referred to as either the Counter-Reformation or the Catholic Reformation, the first term emphasizing its reactive quality, the second its self-generation. Both terms, however, obscure a crucial fact: that changes in Catholicism resembled in some respects the reforms instituted by Protestants. That is, for all the differences and points of contention that bitterly divided them, in some respects the churches of early modern Europe were developing in parallel to one another. Christianity was changing, irrespective of church. The new type of Christianity that resulted from this process is known as "confessional." Its emergence, also called the "rise of confessionalism" or the "formation of confessions," can be charted beginning in the sixteenth century and continuing through the seventeenth.

To dispel any confusion, it must be explained that the term *confession* and its derivatives do not refer in this context to the Catholic sacrament of penance. Rather they refer to a type of document, the "confession of faith," a declaration of the fundamental doctrines held by a church. Perhaps the most famous was the Augsburg Confession of 1530, which came to define Lutheran orthodoxy. All early modern churches issued such documents, which embodied three of the most basic trends then in Christianity: the internalization of church teaching, the drawing of sharp dichotomies, and the quest for "holy uniformity." Each fueled intolerance.

The timing and modalities of these trends varied greatly by church and by region, and in Ireland they had hardly affected the vast majority of peasants (who remained loyal to Catholicism) by the 1660s. According to Englishman Jeremy Taylor, the Irish peasantry could "give no account of their religion what it is: only they believe as their priest bids them and go to mass which they understand not, and reckon their beads to tell the number and the tale of their prayers, and abstain from eggs and flesh in Lent, and visit St. Patrick's well, and leave pins and ribbons, yarn or thread in their holy wells, and pray to God, S. Mary and S. Patrick, S. Columbanus and S. Bridget, and desire to be buried with S. Francis cord about them, and to fast on Saturdays in honour of our Lady."[3]

Granted that Taylor was a hostile outsider, his description not only matches what we know about seventeeth-century Ireland, it captures a state of affairs that was quite the norm across Europe prior to the Reformation. For medieval Christians, religion was as much a set of ritual practices as a set of beliefs. It entailed feasting and fasting on prescribed days; attending mass; reciting prayers in a language (Latin) they scarcely understood; making pilgrimages to holy places, where they offered sacrifices to wonder-working saints; and a wide array of other "works."

---

[3] Keith Thomas, *Religion and the Decline of Magic* (New York, 1971), pp. 76–77.

These had merit, according to theologians, only if performed in a devout frame of mind. In practice, though, priests and laity attributed to them an efficacy as reliable as transubstantiation, the miracle of the mass whereby wafer and wine became Christ's body and blood. The more frequently they were performed, it was said, the more divine grace they conveyed and the better your chances of going to heaven. Many religious acts, in any event, were directed less toward attaining salvation after death than toward escaping misfortune in life. Making the sign of the cross, wearing an amulet containing the words from the Gospel of John, parading images of saints through parish streets: such acts were believed to ward off evil, offering protection from disease, accident, war, and famine.

In medieval Europe, ordinary laypeople knew little church doctrine. They received no formal religious instruction, and their pastors rarely preached. Like Taylor's peasants, they could establish their orthodoxy simply by declaring they "believe as their priest bids them." Such ignorance did not matter greatly in a world where everyone was by default Catholic. It did after Europe split into competing "confessions," each propounding a rival truth. As each church began to define its identity in terms of its unique teachings, doctrine took on an unprecedented importance, and the expectation, echoed in Taylor's disdain, began to build that church members know what their church taught and how it differed from other churches. For Protestants, this expectation was built into the very definition of their religion, which taught that salvation is "by faith alone." All the Protestant churches accepted it as their mission to teach Christians what they needed to believe to be saved. At the same time, a more general dynamic operated: the very existence of alternatives created pressure for Christians to be better informed and more self-conscious in their commitments. Catholic reformers too began to demand that ordinary church members internalize the teachings of their church. Religion itself thus came increasingly to mean belief in a particular creed, and a life lived in accordance with it.

It was easy for churches to enunciate such dramatically raised standards. Implementing them required decades, in some regions as much as two centuries, of strenuous effort. The churches had to undertake massive pedagogic campaigns, which they conducted via preaching, education, printed propaganda, church discipline, and revamped rituals. In all these areas Protestant reformers broke new ground. They made the sermon the centerpiece of Protestant worship. They required that children receive elementary religious instruction, either at school or through special catechism[4] classes. They released torrents of printed propaganda and encouraged ordinary Christians to read scripture. They established new institutions and procedures to supervise parish life. . . .

---

[4] Indoctrination; memorizing doctrine. [Ed.]

Facing many of the same challenges as Protestant reformers, Catholic reformers had no qualms about adopting the former's pedagogic methods (and vice versa). The Jesuits in particular engaged in a range of activities that show striking parallels to those of their enemies. They became renowned preachers, wrote catechisms (that of Peter Canisius was the most popular in Catholic Europe), and founded hundreds of new schools, mostly at the secondary and college level. Using the *Spiritual Exercises* written by their founder, Ignatius of Loyola, they taught people how to examine their own consciences and achieve pious goals through a remarkable self-discipline. As confessors, chaplains, and organizers of a new type of club, the Marian sodality, they encouraged frequent confession and Communion. This disciplinary routine encouraged the internalization of norms even as it provided an external mechanism for enforcing them. . . .

Just as the welfare of towns and villages depended on God's favor, Europeans believed, so did that of countries. . . . In 1663, when Ottoman armies launched an offensive into central Europe, prayers went up across the Continent. One pietist preacher warned his Dutch congregation that the Turks would conquer all unless lax, indifferent Christians put into practice the teachings they mouthed. Two decades later the Turks attacked again, this time reaching the walls of Vienna. At this critical juncture, Pope Innocent XI marshaled an international alliance to relieve the imperial capital. Protestant as well as Catholic princes of Germany sent troops to fight alongside Poles and Austrians. After the combined Christian army broke the Turks' siege, Innocent organized a "Holy League" whose forces drove the Turks once and for all back to the Balkans. This crusade was the last hurrah for the medieval concept of a united Christendom led by pope and emperor.

By then, two developments had made the concept almost completely anachronistic. One we have already examined: the division of Christendom into competing confessions. The other was the emergence of political units resembling modern nation-states. Particularism[5] did not disappear, either as a set of power relationships or as a mentality. Increasingly, though, Europe's rulers asserted an impersonal authority that can be called sovereignty, rather than (or, perhaps better, in addition to) the personal suzerainty[6] of the feudal Middle Ages. They codified laws, issued regulations, raised taxes, formalized institutions, and mobilized networks of officials, casting in this way a tighter net of control over society. One must not exaggerate the control rulers achieved, for early modern governments never had the tools of law enforcement modern ones take for granted. More than is often realized, their

[5] Local, personal, and decentralized politics, as in medieval feudalism. [Ed.]
[6] Dependence. [Ed.]

authority depended on the consent of the governed. Nevertheless, by the late seventeenth century some princes had achieved what at the time was called "absolute" authority: they could wage war, issue laws, and impose taxes without the approval of representative institutions, or with sure knowledge of their rubber stamp. "Absolutism" vested all sovereign power in a single individual, but even in polities that remained fragmented, like those of the Dutch and Swiss, there developed "a more encompassing, more systematic, and more literate articulation of power and authority."[7] The development took as many forms as there were forms of polity, but across Europe it was clear: the state grew stronger as an institution and more cohesive as a political community.

The fusion of these two developments, confessionalism and state formation, was explosive. The fictional Irishman Dooley, creation of modern humorist Finley Peter Dunne, once observed: "Rellijon is a quare thing. Be itself it's all right. But sprinkle a little pollyticks into it an' dinnymit is bran flour compared with it. Alone it prepares a man f'r a better life. Combined with polyticks it hurries him to it."[8] The observation has a special ring of truth in the mouth of an Irishman, for in modern Ireland, religious and political causes—Protestantism and Union with Britain, Catholicism and Irish Nationalism—have become inseparable. In the sixteenth century, religion and politics combined similarly across Europe. Religious enemies, their hatreds fanned by confessional ideology, became political enemies, and vice versa, as people at odds with one another for social or political reasons tended to choose opposing sides religiously as well. In this way, Europe's religious divisions not only created new conflicts, they threw ideological fuel on the fires of existing ones. Competitions for power, wealth, or land became cosmic struggles between the forces of God and Satan. Inversely, the bonds of a common confession brought people together in equally powerful ways. When they cut across social or political lines, they could make friends of strangers or even former enemies. On every level, from the local to the international, co-religionists felt an impulse to make common cause with one another.

To Europe's rulers, then, the rise of confessionalism held out both perils and promises. A difference in religion could alienate their subjects from them and undermine their authority. As the French Wars of Religion demonstrated, to the horror of contemporaries, it could set citizen against fellow citizen and tear states apart in civil war. A shared religion, on the other hand, could bolster rulers' authority, binding their subjects

---

[7] So characterized by Randolph C. Head in "Fragmented Dominion, Fragmented Churches: The Institutionalization of the *Landfrieden* in the Thurgau, 1531–1610," *Archiv fur Reformationsgeschichte* 96 (205): 119.

[8] Leonard W. Levy, *The Establishment Clause: Religion and the First Amendment* (New York, 1986), ix.

to them and to one another more firmly. Given these starkly contrasting possibilities, it is no wonder rulers tried to impose religious uniformity on their territories. Their personal piety impelled many to do the same. Since the thirteenth century, the Catholic Church had asked them to swear they would "strive in good faith and to the best of their ability to exterminate in the territories subject to their jurisdiction all heretics pointed out by the Church."[9] The division of Western Christendom gave them compelling new reasons to do so.

In its wake, Europe's rulers tried to make their personal choice of faith official for their state. Most succeeded, though, as we shall see, not all. Either way, the resulting confessional allegiance eventually became a defining aspect of political identity. Whether or not it initially had wide support, the allegiance was institutionalized and sank popular roots. In some essential and irreversible way, England became a Protestant country, Poland a Catholic one, Sweden Lutheran, the Dutch Republic Calvinist, and so forth. This fusion of religious and political identity, piety and patriotism, was (after confessionalism and the communal quest for holiness) the third great cause of religious intolerance in early modern Europe. Forged in the course of Europe's religious wars, it led both rulers and ordinary people to equate orthodoxy with loyalty and religious dissent with sedition. It gave national politics and even foreign affairs the power to spark waves of religious riots as well as official persecution.

[9] Robert I. Moore, *The Formation of a Persecuting Society: Power and Deviance in Western Europe, 950–1250* (Oxford, 1987), 7.

6

Remonstrance of the Inhabitants of the Town of Flushing to Governor Stuyvesant, December 27, 1657

A guiding principle in Europe after 1555 was that the religion of the prince would be the religion of the people. Thus, religious freedom meant moving somewhere else. Many did, including the Pilgrims, Puritans, Catholics, and later, Quakers, Baptists, and Methodists who came to the Americas. But those who sought religious freedom for themselves rarely sought it for others. In New England, it took the voice of Roger Williams (1603–1683), a religious fundamentalist in a colony

Source: http://www.queensbp.org/remonstrance/index.html.

of more establishment Protestantism, to demand the separation of church and state. The principle of religious freedom originated to protect the conscience of a minority against the state, though Williams retained the principle in his own colony of Providence, which became Rhode Island.

The colony of New Netherland (comprising settlements in today's New York, New Jersey, Delaware, and Connecticut), with its capital, New Amsterdam, on the southern tip of Manhattan, was founded by the Dutch. Less to save souls than to make money, the colony was to be a center of trade, very much like its parent, the Netherlands. The Netherlands enshrined freedom of religion from its origins in 1579, declaring "no one shall be persecuted or investigated because of his religion." In 1625 the same principle was to hold in the Dutch West India Company colony. To a great extent freedom of conscience did prevail. The first Jews in North America were welcomed in New Amsterdam in 1654, refugees from a New Holland, Brazil, recently conquered by Portugal.

Nevertheless, the official religion of New Netherland was the Dutch Reformed Church and Peter Stuyvesant, the Dutch General Director of the colony from 1647 to 1664, drew the line at Quakers, who he thought to be particularly troublesome. In 1657 Stuyvesant made it a crime for anyone in the colony to harbor Quakers. Citizens of Flushing (now Queens) directed the following response to Stuyvesant. What did they declare? What reasons did they give? What was the significance of their action?

THINKING HISTORICALLY

Sometimes, knowing the context of a document enhances its impact. To the modern ear, the sentiments expressed in the Flushing Remonstrance are admirable, but quite familiar. In the modern context, it might not seem like such a courageous act. But in the context of the time, the stakes were quite high. Earlier in1657 Stuyvesant had publicly tortured a Quaker preacher. The signers could certainly expect retribution. In fact, many of the signers were imprisoned or exiled. By scanning the names of the signers, you cannot tell that none of them were Quakers, but you can tell something of their nationality and social standing (at least as indicated by education). Were they all the same nationality: Was it Dutch or English? Were they powerful legal adversaries of the Governor General or ordinary men? How do these contexts make their statement more impressive?

Right Honourable [Governor Stuyvesant]

You have been pleased to send unto us a certain prohibition or command that we should not receive or entertain any of those people called

Quakers because they are supposed to be, by some, seducers of the people. For our part we cannot condemn them in this case, neither can we stretch out our hands against them, for out of Christ God is a consuming fire, and it is a fearful thing to fall into the hands of the living God.

Wee desire therefore in this case not to judge least we be judged, neither to condemn least we be condemned, but rather let every man stand or fall to his own Master. Wee are bounde by the law to do good unto all men, especially to those of the household of faith. And though for the present we seem to be unsensible for the law and the Law giver, yet when death and the Law assault us, if wee have our advocate to seeke, who shall plead for us in this case of conscience betwixt God and our own souls; the powers of this world can neither attach us, neither excuse us, for if God justifye who can condemn and if God condemn there is none can justifye.

And for those jealousies and suspicions which some have of them, that they are destructive unto Magistracy and Ministerye, that cannot bee, for the Magistrate hath his sword in his hand and the Minister hath the sword in his hand, as witnesse those two great examples, which all Magistrates and Ministers are to follow, Moses and Christ, whom God raised up maintained and defended against all enemies both of flesh and spirit; and therefore that of God will stand, and that which is of man will come to nothing. And as the Lord hath taught Moses or the civil power to give an outward liberty in the state, by the law written in his heart designed for the good of all, and can truly judge who is good, who is evil, who is true and who is false, and can pass definitive sentence of life or death against that man which arises up against the fundamental law of the States General; soe he hath made his ministers a savor of life unto life and a savor of death unto death.

The law of love, peace and liberty in the states extending to Jews, Turks and Egyptians, as they are considered sons of Adam, which is the glory of the outward state of Holland, soe love, peace and liberty, extending to all in Christ Jesus, condemns hatred, war and bondage. And because our Saviour sayeth it is impossible but that offences will come, but woe unto him by whom they cometh, our desire is not to offend one of his little ones, in whatsoever form, name or title hee appears in, whether Presbyterian, Independent, Baptist or Quaker, but shall be glad to see anything of God in any of them, desiring to doe unto all men as we desire all men should doe unto us, which is the true law both of Church and State; for our Saviour sayeth this is the law and the prophets.

Therefore if any of these said persons come in love unto us, we cannot in conscience lay violent hands upon them, but give them free egresse and regresse unto our Town, and houses, as God shall persuade our consciences, for we are bounde by the law of God and man to doe good unto all men and evil to noe man. And this is according to the patent and charter of our Towne, given unto us in the name of the States General, which we are not willing to infringe, and violate, but shall houlde to our patent and shall remaine, your humble subjects, the inhabitants of Vlishing.

Written this 27th of December in the year 1657, by mee.

Edward Hart, Clericus

Additional Signers

Tobias Feake	Nathaniell Tue
The marke of William Noble	Nicholas Blackford
William Thorne, Seignior	The marke of Micah Tue
The marke of William Thorne, Jr.	The marke of Philip Ud
Edward Tarne	Robert Field, senior
John Store	Robert Field, junior
Nathaniel Hefferd	Nich Colas Parsell
Benjamin Hubbard	Michael Milner
The marke of William Pidgion	Henry Townsend
The marke of George Clere	George Wright
Elias Doughtie	John Foard
Antonie Feild	Henry Semtell
Richard Stocton	Edward Hart
Edward Griffine	John Mastine
John Townesend	Edward Farrington

■ REFLECTIONS

Religious hospitals, school choice, abortion, the public display of religious symbols—what is the proper relationship of government and religion? The North American colonies of the seventeenth century evolved a principle of the separation of church and state, largely out of religious, not secular motives. It was an idea that had recent roots in Europe, originating in the formation of the Dutch Republic in 1579, but its roots ran deep in Christianity. Christians in the Middle Ages talked about the two swords of power (clerical and secular), St Augustine wrote about the two cities (of God and man) and Jesus distinguished between the responsibilities to God and Caesar. In the sixteenth century, Luther reaffirmed this distinction, but he gave German princes far greater authority over religious matters than most Christians would allow today.

Luther, John Calvin, Henry VIII, and most early Protestants were vigorous proponents of state religions, the legislation of Christian morality, and the censorship and proscription of contrary beliefs and behavior. Benjamin Kaplan shows how both the Protestant Reformation and the similar Catholic Counter-Reformation created robustly intolerant religious communities. New kings and parliaments put religious doctrines into the service of national states as if they were badges of identity or flags to be saluted.

It is a modern conceit that tolerance must have gradually increased since the "dark ages." Kaplan shows us how intolerance increased in Europe with the rise of confessional faiths and the state. A similar transition occurred in India from Akbar to Aurangzeb. In both cases, the religious fundamentalists made government less tolerant of diversity or heterodoxy. The religious leaders who suffered most under the Mughals were not Hindus, but reformers who attempted to unite Hinduism and Islam under a new monotheism, the Sikhs. As often happens, the reformers closest to home smelled the foulest.

Neither the Chinese nor Japanese traditions held religious orthodoxies. But both required proper observance of certain social and political proprieties. Strong governments, as in most of Chinese history, turned principles like Confucian filial piety into virtual religions but they had the force of law and made little appeal to conscience or individual choice. Daoism and Buddhism appealed to the inner lives of Chinese and Japanese devotees, but normally posed no conflict to state power. Only in periods of unrest, feudalism, or the breakdown of the state did Buddhist or Daoist priests and monks exercise political power. Even then, however, they did not challenge the state as much as they filled the vacuum left by its disappearance. In both Japan and Europe, the post-feudal age was one in which the state's rise depended, in part, on the reclamation and monopolization of powers previously exercised by religious institutions.

Many pasts, but increasingly one present. As cultural differences meld with the force of rockets and the speed of the Internet, one might well ask what separate histories matter to a common present. Increasingly principles of toleration are enshrined by international organizations in declarations of human rights and the proceedings of international tribunals. Whether we see the roots of modern principles of tolerance in Confucian secularism, Christian separation of church and state, or Muslim cosmopolitanism, we live in a world where intolerance is widely condemned and legitimately prosecuted.

And yet, fanaticism and intolerance have not disappeared. Religious fundamentalists of various stripes declare their missions to take over governments, convert populations, and bring about the rule of God. History has shown that tolerance need not be secular. Indeed even the aggressively secular regimes of the twentieth and twenty-first centuries have demonstrated and continue to demonstrate a capacity for brutal persecution of dissidents, religious and otherwise.

18

Women, Marriage, and Family

China and Europe, 1550–1700

■ HISTORICAL CONTEXT

The family is the oldest and most important social institution. For those who marry, marriage can be one of the most important passages in one's life. Yet up until the last few decades these subjects rarely registered as important topics in world history. There were at least three reasons for this: One was the tendency to think of history as the story of public events only—the actions of political officials, governments, and their representatives—instead of the private and domestic sphere. The second was the assumption that the private or domestic sphere had no history, that it had always been the same. As the documents in this chapter will show, nothing could be further from the truth. The third is that most history was written by men until about forty years ago.

Since the urban revolution five thousand years ago, most societies have been patriarchal. The laws, social codes, and dominant ideas have enshrined the power and prestige of men over women, husbands over wives, fathers over children, gods over goddesses, even brothers over sisters. Double standards for adultery, inheritance laws that favor sons, and laws that deny women property or political rights all attest to the power of patriarchal culture and norms. Almost everywhere patriarchies have limited women to the domestic sphere while granting men public and political power.

To better focus our investigation, we will concentrate on two of the important patriarchal civilizations of the Early Modern period: China and Europe. We will study a variety of sources from each, including laws, diaries, and fiction. Our goal will be to notice and characterize customs and ideas about marriage and family life in these two civilizations.

■ THINKING HISTORICALLY

Making Comparisons

We learn by making comparisons. Every new piece of knowledge we acquire leads to a comparison with what we already know. For example, we arrive in a new town and we are struck by something that we have not seen before. The town has odd street lamps, flowerpots on the sidewalks, or lots of trucks on the street. We start to formulate a theory about the differences between what we observe in the new town and what we already know about our old town. We think we're on to something, but our theory falls apart when we make more observations by staying in the new town another day, or traveling on to the next town, or going halfway across the world. As we gain more experience and make more observations, our original theory explaining an observed difference is supplanted by a much more complex theory about *types* of towns.

History is very much like travel. We learn by comparison, one step at a time, and the journey is never ending. On this trip we begin in China and then move on to Europe. We begin with primary sources and then conclude with a secondary source that will allow us to draw upon our previous readings to make increasingly informed and complex comparisons. Welcome aboard. Next stop, China.

1

Family Instructions for the Miu Lineage, Late Sixteenth Century

Chinese families in Ming times (1368–1644) often organized themselves into groups by male lineage. These groups often shared common land, built ancestral halls, published genealogies, honored their common ancestors, and ensured the success and well-being of future generations. To accomplish the last of these, lineage groups frequently compiled lists of family rules or instructions. This particular example, from the various lines of the Miu family of the Guangdong province in the south, shows how extensive these instructions could be. What values did these family instructions encourage? What activities did the Miu lineage regulate? What kind of families, and what kind of individuals, were these rules intended to produce? How would these rules have had a different impact on women and men?

Source: "Family Instructions for the Miu Lineage, Late Sixteenth Century," trans. Clara Yu, in *Chinese Civilization: A Sourcebook*, 2nd ed., ed. Patricia Ebrey (New York: Free Press, 1993), 238–40, 241–43.

THINKING HISTORICALLY

It is difficult to read this selection without thinking of one's own family and of families in one's own society. How many of the Miu lineage's concerns are concerns of families you know? Family instructions and lineage organizations are not common features of modern American society, even among Chinese Americans who may have a sense of their lineage and family identity. What institutions in modern American society regulate the activities addressed by these family instructions? Or are these activities left for self-regulation or no regulation at all? From reading this document, what do you think are some of the differences between Ming-era Chinese families and modern American families?

Work Hard at One of the Principal Occupations

1. To be filial to one's parents, to be loving to one's brothers, to be diligent and frugal—these are the first tenets of a person of good character. They must be thoroughly understood and faithfully carried out.

One's conscience should be followed like a strict teacher and insight should be sought through introspection. One should study the words and deeds of the ancients to find out their ultimate meanings. One should always remember the principles followed by the ancients, and should not become overwhelmed by current customs. For if one gives in to cruelty, pride, or extravagance, all virtues will be undermined, and nothing will be achieved.

Parents have special responsibilities. *The Book of Changes*[1] says: "The members of a family have strict sovereigns." The "sovereigns" are the parents. Their position in a family is one of unique authority, and they should utilize their authority to dictate matters to maintain order, and to inspire respect, so that the members of the family will all be obedient. If the parents are lenient and indulgent, there will be many troubles which in turn will give rise to even more troubles. Who is to blame for all this? The elders in a family must demand discipline of themselves, following all rules and regulations to the letter, so that the younger members emulate their good behavior and exhort each other to abide by the teachings of the ancient sages. Only in this way can the family hope to last for generations. If, however, the elders of a family should find it difficult to abide by these regulations, the virtuous youngsters of the family should help them along. Because the purpose of my work is to make such work easier, I am not afraid of giving many small details. . . .

2. Those youngsters who have taken Confucian scholarship as their hereditary occupation should be sincere and hard-working, and try to

[1] The *I Ching*, a Chinese classic. [Ed.]

achieve learning naturally while studying under a teacher. Confucianism is the only thing to follow if they wish to bring glory to their family. Those who know how to keep what they have but do not study are as useless as puppets made of clay or wood. Those who study, even if they do not succeed in the examinations, can hope to become teachers or to gain personal benefit. However, there are people who study not for learning's sake, but as a vulgar means of gaining profit. These people are better off doing nothing.

Youngsters who are incapable of concentrating on studying should devote themselves to farming; they should personally grasp the ploughs and eat the fruit of their own labor. In this way they will be able to support their families. If they fold their hands and do nothing, they will soon have to worry about hunger and cold. If, however, they realize that their forefathers also worked hard and that farming is a difficult way of life, they will not be inferior to anyone. In earlier dynasties, officials were all selected because they were filial sons, loving brothers, and diligent farmers. This was to set an example for all people to devote themselves to their professions, and to ensure that the officials were familiar with the hardships of the common people, thereby preventing them from exploiting the commoners for their own profit.

3. Farmers should personally attend to the inspection, measurement, and management of the fields, noting the soil as well as the terrain. The early harvest as well as the grain taxes and the labor service obligations should be carefully calculated. Anyone who indulges in indolence and entrusts these matters to others will not be able to distinguish one kind of crop from another and will certainly be cheated by others. I do not believe such a person could escape bankruptcy.

4. The usual occupations of the people are farming and commerce. If one tries by every possible means to make a great profit from these occupations, it usually leads to loss of capital. Therefore it is more profitable to put one's energy into farming the land; only when the fields are too far away to be tilled by oneself should they be leased to others. One should solicit advice from old farmers as to one's own capacity in farming.

Those who do not follow the usual occupations of farming or business should be taught a skill. Being an artisan is a good way of life and will also shelter a person from hunger and cold. All in all, it is important to remember that one should work hard when young, for when youth expires one can no longer achieve anything. Many people learn this lesson only after it is too late. We should guard against this mistake.

5. Fish can be raised in ponds by supplying them with grass and manure. Vegetables need water. In empty plots one can plant fruit trees such as the pear, persimmon, peach, prune, and plum, and also beans, wheat, hemp, peas, potatoes, and melons. When harvested, these vegetables and fruits can sustain life. During their growth, one should give

them constant care, nourishing them and weeding them. In this way, no labor is wasted and no fertile land is left uncultivated. On the contrary, to purchase everything needed for the morning and evening meals means the members of the family will merely sit and eat. Is this the way things should be?

6. Housewives should take full charge of the kitchen. They should make sure that the store of firewood is sufficient, so that even if it rains several days in succession, they will not be forced to use silver or rice to pay for firewood, thereby impoverishing the family. Housewives should also closely calculate the daily grocery expenses, and make sure there is no undue extravagance. Those who simply sit and wait to be fed only are treating themselves like pigs and dogs, but also are leading their whole households to ruin. . . .

Exercise Restraint

1. Our young people should know their place and observe correct manners. They are not permitted to gamble, to fight, to engage in lawsuits, or to deal in salt[2] privately. Such unlawful acts will only lead to their own downfall.

2. If land or property is not obtained by righteous means, descendants will not be able to enjoy it. When the ancients invented characters, they put gold next to two spears to mean "money," indicating that the danger of plunder or robbery is associated with it. If money is not accumulated by good means, it will disperse like overflowing water; how could it be put to any good? The result is misfortune for oneself as well as for one's posterity. This is the meaning of the saying: "The way of Heaven detests fullness, and only the humble gain." Therefore, accumulation of great wealth inevitably leads to great loss. How true are the words of Laozi![3]

A person's fortune and rank are predestined. One can only do one's best according to propriety and one's own ability; the rest is up to Heaven. If one is easily contented, then a diet of vegetables and soups provides a lifetime of joy. If one does not know one's limitations and tries to accumulate wealth by immoral and dishonest means, how can one avoid disaster? To be able to support oneself through life and not leave one's sons and grandsons in hunger and cold is enough; why should one toil so much?

3. Pride is a dangerous trait. Those who pride themselves on wealth, rank, or learning are inviting evil consequences. Even if one's accomplishments

---

[2] Get involved in the salt trade, a state monopoly. Salt was used as a preservative for fish, meat, and other foods. [Ed.]

[3] Lao Tzu, legendary Chinese philosopher and author of the *Dao de Jing,* the Daoist classic. [Ed.]

are indeed unique, there is no need to press them on anyone else. "The way of Heaven detests fullness, and only the humble gain." I have seen the truth of this saying many times.

4. Taking concubines in order to beget heirs should be a last resort, for the sons of the legal wife and the sons of the concubine are never of one mind, causing innumerable conflicts between half brothers. If the parents are in the least partial, problems will multiply, creating misfortune in later generations. Since families have been ruined because of this, it should not be taken lightly.

5. Just as diseases are caused by what goes into one's mouth, misfortunes are caused by what comes out of one's mouth. Those who are immoderate in eating and unrestrained in speaking have no one else to blame for their own ruin.

6. Most men lack resolve and listen to what their women say. As a result, blood relatives become estranged and competitiveness, suspicion, and distance arise between them. Therefore, when a wife first comes into a family, it should be made clear to her that such things are prohibited. "Start teaching one's son when he is a baby; start teaching one's daughter-in-law when she first arrives." That is to say, preventive measures should be taken early.

7. "A family's fortune can be foretold from whether its members are early risers" is a maxim of our ancient sages. Everyone, male and female, should rise before dawn and should not go to bed until after the first drum. Never should they indulge themselves in a false sense of security and leisure, for such behavior will eventually lead them to poverty.

8. Young family members who deliberately violate family regulations should be taken to the family temple, have their offenses reported to the ancestors, and be severely punished. They should then be taught to improve themselves. Those who do not accept punishment or persist in their wrongdoings will bring harm to themselves.

9. As a preventive measure against the unpredictable, the gates should be closed at dusk, and no one should be allowed to go out. Even when there are visitors, dinner parties should end early, so that there will be no need for lighting lamps and candles. On very hot or very cold days, one should be especially considerate of the kitchen servants.

10. For generations this family had dwelt in the country, and everyone has had a set profession; therefore, our descendants should not be allowed to change their place of residence. After living in the city for three years, a person forgets everything about farming; after ten years, he does not even know his lineage. Extravagance and leisure transform people, and it is hard for anyone to remain unaffected. I once remarked that the only legitimate excuse to live in a city temporarily is to flee from bandits.

11. The inner and outer rooms, halls, doorways, and furniture should be swept and dusted every morning at dawn. Dirty doorways and courtyards and haphazardly placed furniture are sure signs of a

declining family. Therefore, a schedule should be followed for cleaning them, with no excuses allowed.

12. Those in charge of cooking and kitchen work should make sure that breakfast is served before nine o'clock in the morning and dinner before five o'clock in the afternoon. Every evening the iron wok and other utensils should be washed and put away, so that the next morning, after rising at dawn, one can expect tea and breakfast to be prepared immediately and served on time. In the kitchen no lamps are allowed in the morning or at night. This is not only to save the expense, but also to avoid harmful contamination of food. Although this is a small matter, it has a great effect on health. Furthermore, since all members of the family have their regular work to do, letting them toil all day without giving them meals at regular hours is no way to provide comfort and relief for them. If these rules are deliberately violated, the person in charge will be punished as an example to the rest.

13. On the tenth and twenty-fifth days of every month, all the members of this branch, from the honored aged members to the youngsters, should gather at dusk for a meeting. Each will give an account of what he has learned, by either calling attention to examples of good and evil, or encouraging diligence, or expounding his obligations, or pointing out tasks to be completed. Each member will take turns presenting his own opinions and listening attentively to others. He should examine himself in the matters being discussed and make efforts to improve himself. The purpose of these meetings is to encourage one another in virtue and to correct each other's mistakes.

The members of the family will take turns being the chairman of these meetings, according to schedule. If someone is unable to chair a meeting on a certain day, he should ask the next person in line to take his place. The chairman should provide tea, but never wine. The meetings may be canceled on days of ancestor worship, parties, or other such occasions, or if the weather is severe. Those who are absent from these meetings for no reason are only doing themselves harm.

There are no set rules for where the meeting should be held, but the place should be convenient for group discussions. The time of the meeting should always be early evening, for this is when people have free time. As a general precaution the meeting should never last until late at night.

14. Women from lower-class families who stop at our houses tend to gossip, create conflicts, peek into the kitchens, or induce our women to believe in prayer and fortune-telling, thereby cheating them out of their money and possessions. Consequently, one should question these women often and punish those who come for no reason, so as to put a stop to the traffic.

15. Blood relatives are as close as the branches of a tree, yet their relationships can still be differentiated according to importance and

priority: Parents should be considered before brothers, and brothers should be considered before wives and children. Each person should fulfill his own duties and share with others profit and loss, joy and sorrow, life and death. In this way, the family will get along well and be blessed by Heaven. Should family members fight over property or end up treating each other like enemies, then when death or misfortune strikes they will be of even less use than strangers. If our ancestors have consciousness, they will not tolerate these unprincipled descendants who are but animals in man's clothing. Heaven responds to human vices with punishments as surely as an echo follows a sound. I hope my sons and grandsons take my words seriously.

16. To get along with patrilineal relatives, fellow villages, and relatives through marriage, one should be gentle in speech and mild in manners. When one is opposed by others, one may remonstrate with them; but when others fall short because of their limitations, one should be tolerant. If one's youngsters or servants get into fights with others, one should look into oneself to find the blame. It is better to be wronged than to wrong others. Those who take affront and become enraged, who conceal their own shortcomings and seek to defeat others, are courting immediate misfortune. Even if the other party is unbearably unreasonable, one should contemplate the fact that the ancient sages had to endure much more. If one remains tolerant and forgiving, one will be able to curb the other party's violence.

2

PU SONGLING

The Lady Knight-Errant, 1679

Born into a poor landlord-merchant family in Qing China, Pu Songling (1640–1715) succeeded in passing a low-level civil service exam but not the higher level exam until he was seventy-one. He spent most of his life tutoring and gathering stories for *Strange Stories from a Chinese Studio*, a collection of supernatural tales that made him famous. The following tale from this collection is a story of a courtship but not a marriage, and it is a story of a woman who is more than she seems.

What core values does this story celebrate?

Source: P'u Sung-ling, "The Lady Knight-Errant," ed. & trans. Lorraine S. Y. Lieu, Ma Yau-Woon, and Joseph S. M. Lau, *Traditional Chinese Stories: Themes and Variations* (New York: Columbia University Press, 1978), 77–81.

THINKING HISTORICALLY

All cultures tell stories related to courtship or marriage. How is the world described here similar to, and different from, that of the previous selection? In what ways is this "boy meets girl story" similar to those of your own culture? In what ways is it different? How might a North American version of this go? How would the moral of the story be different?

There was once a young man by the name of Ku, born of a poor family in Chin-ling.[1] He was talented and skilled in a variety of arts and crafts. However, since he could not bear to leave his aging mother, he made a simple living by selling calligraphy and paintings. He was single even at the age of twenty-five.

Opposite to where he lived was an empty house. One day, an old woman and a young girl came by to rent the place, but since there was no man in their family, Ku did not feel that it was appropriate for him to make a courtesy call.

One day when he returned home he saw the young girl coming out of his mother's room. She was about eighteen or nineteen, and of rare beauty and gracefulness. She made no attempt to hide when she saw Ku. There was an air of awe-inspiring composure about her. Ku went inside and questioned his mother. Mrs. Ku said, "That is the girl across the street. She came to borrow my scissors and ruler. She told me that only her mother lived with her. She doesn't seem to come from a poor family. When I asked why she isn't married, she said that she has to take care of her aged mother. I shall pay her mother a visit tomorrow, and sound her out. If they don't ask for too much, perhaps you can take care of her mother for her."

The next day, she went over to the young girl's house. She found the mother hard of hearing, and when she looked around the house, there did not seem to be enough food there for the following day. She asked the old woman how they managed to get by, and the latter replied that they depended solely on the young girl's needlework. Finally, Mrs. Ku brought up the question of a possible marriage between the two families. The old woman seemed agreeable and turned around to seek the opinion of her daughter. Though the girl did not say anything, she was apparently not too happy about it. So Mrs. Ku returned home.

Later, as she thought about the girl's reaction, she said to her son, "Do you think we've been turned down because we're too poor?

---

[1] Nanking, China. [Ed.]

What a strange girl! So quiet and so straight-faced. Just as the saying goes, 'As beautiful as the peach and pear blossoms, but cold as the frost and snow.'" Mother and son exchanged their views on the matter for a good while and then ended their discussion with a sigh.

One day, Ku was at his studio when a young man came to buy paintings. He looked handsome enough, but his manner was rather frivolous. Ku asked where he came from, and the young man replied that he came from the neighboring village. From then on, he came over every two or three days, and became fairly close to Ku. Later, they started to tease and joke with each other; and when Ku embraced the young man, he made no more than a show of refusing. Thus they carried on a secretive relationship which was to become more intimate by the day.

One day, as the girl happened to pass by, the young man gazed at her for a while and asked Ku who she was. Ku told him what he knew about her and the young man said, "What a beautiful and fearsome girl she is!"

Later, when Ku went inside, his mother said, "The young girl just came over to borrow some rice. She said that they haven't eaten for one whole day. This girl is devoted to her mother; what a pity that she should be in such circumstances. We should try to help her."

Ku agreed with what his mother said, and carried a peck of rice over to the girl's house, conveying his mother's goodwill. The girl accepted the rice but did not say a word of thanks to him.

After that, she often went over to Ku's house, helping with his mother's sewing and other needlework. She took care of all the household chores like a housewife. So Ku held her in even higher esteem. Whenever he had some delicacies, he would bring a portion over to her mother. The girl never thanked him. Once, when Ku's mother got an abscess on her private parts which caused her to cry out day and night in pain, the girl frequently stayed by her bedside, looking after her, washing the wound, and applying medicine to it three or four times a day. Mrs. Ku felt uneasy, but the girl did not seem to mind the task at all. Ku's mother sighed and said to her, "Ah, where can I find a daughter-in-law such as you to see me through the end of my days?" As she said that, her voice was choked with tears.

"Your son is devoted to you," the girl comforted her, "so you're much better off than my mother, who has only a helpless girl to look after her."

"But surely even a devoted son can't do bedside chores like these! Anyhow, I'm old and could die any day. What I'm worried about is an heir for the family."

As she spoke, Ku came in. Mrs. Ku wept and said, "I'm grateful for all that this young lady has done for us. Don't you forget to repay her kindness."

Ku bowed deeply, but the girl said, "You were kind to my mother and I didn't thank you, so why should you thank me now?"

Ku's respect and love for her grew deeper; yet she remained just as cold and aloof to him as before.

One day, Ku had his gaze fixed on the girl as she walked out the door. Suddenly she turned around and smiled bewitchingly at Ku. Ku was overjoyed and followed her to her house. When he flirted with her, she did not rebuke him, so they went to bed happily and made love. Afterward, she cautioned Ku, "I hope you understand that this is a one-time thing." Ku returned home without saying anything.

The next day, he approached the girl again, but she flatly refused him and left. However, she went to Ku's place as frequently as before and met him quite often; but she did not give him the slightest encouragement. Any effort on his part to exchange pleasantries with her was met with unyielding sternness.

One day, when they had a moment to themselves, she abruptly asked Ku, "Who is that young man you were talking to the other day?" Ku told her and she said, "He has taken liberties with me several times. Seeing that you're quite close to him. I didn't want to mention it earlier. But please tell him this time: if he doesn't mend his ways, he won't live to see another day."

Ku relayed her message to the young man when he came in the evening, adding, "You must be careful. Don't offend her again!"

"If she's so chaste," the young man said, "how come the two of you are on such good terms?" Ku protested his innocence, but the young man retorted, "If there is nothing between the two of you, then why would she tell you improper things like these?" Ku could not answer, whereupon the young man said, "Well, tell her this for me, too. Tell her, don't be so self-righteous and try to put up such a chaste appearance; otherwise, I shall certainly spread this whole thing far and wide!"

Ku was extremely angry and his face showed it, so the young man left.

One night, when Ku was sitting alone at home, the girl came in unexpectedly and greeted him with a smile. "It seems that our love hasn't ended yet."

Ku was overwhelmed with joy and held the girl tightly in his arms. Suddenly they heard footsteps and both jumped up. The door was pushed open and the young man walked in. Startled, Ku asked him, "What are you doing here?"

The young man laughed. "I've come to watch the show of some virtuous and chaste people!" Then he looked at the girl and said, "You can't blame anyone now, can you?"

The girl scowled and flushed with anger. Without a word, she pulled up her topcoat and took out a shiny foot-long dagger from a leather bag, the sight of which frightened the young man so much that he immediately took to his heels. The girl gave chase, but there was no one in sight outside. She flung the dagger into the air; it rose with a loud twang and was as bright as a rainbow. Then something fell to the ground with a loud thud. Ku hurried to look at it by candlelight. It was a white fox with a severed head. Ku was terrified.

"This is your Boy Charmer!" the girl told him. "I've spared him time and again, only he didn't seem to care enough for his life."

As she was replacing the dagger in the leather bag, Ku pulled her toward the house, but she said, "I don't feel like it anymore. Your Boy Charmer has spoiled the game. Wait until tomorrow night." And she left immediately without looking back.

The next evening, the girl came as promised and they spent the night together. When Ku asked her about her magic, she said, "This is something you shouldn't know about. Also, keep what you saw last night to yourself; otherwise it will bring you only trouble."

Ku then brought up the subject of marriage again, and in reply she said, "I sleep with you in the same bed, and I do all the housework here; what am I if not a wife to you? Since we live like husband and wife already, why talk about marriage?"

"Is it because I'm poor?"

"If you're poor, I'm not any better off. It's only because I feel for you in your poverty that I'm here with you tonight."

Before she left, she reminded Ku again, "Meetings such as this can't be repeated too often. If I can come, I will; but if I cannot, it's no use forcing me."

Afterward, whenever they ran into each other and Ku wanted to talk privately with her, she avoided him. Yet she kept doing all the housework and needlework in Ku's house, as before.

Several months later, the girl's mother died. Ku exhausted all his resources to help the girl bury her. From then on, the girl lived alone. Ku thought that he could take advantage of the situation, so one day he climbed over the wall and called to her from outside the window. When there was no answer, he looked through the doorway and found the house empty. He suspected that the girl had gone out to meet someone else. He returned at night but again the girl was not there. He left his jade pendant by the window and departed.

The next day, they met in his mother's room. When Ku came out, the girl followed him out and said, "You seem to have doubts about me, am I right? Everyone has his own secrets that can't be shared with others. How can I make you believe me? Anyway, there is something urgent which I must discuss with you right now." Ku asked her what it was, and she said, "I'm already eight months pregnant and I'm afraid that the child might come any time. Since I have no legitimate position in your family, I can only give you a child; I can't raise it for you. You can tell your mother secretly to look for a wet nurse, under the pretext that she herself wants to adopt a child. Don't tell anyone that the child is mine."

Ku agreed and relayed her wish to his mother. She smiled and said, "What a strange girl! She refused to marry you and yet she has no qualms at carrying on an affair with you!"

She carried out the girl's plan happily and waited for her delivery.

More than a month had passed, and when the girl failed to show up for several days in a row, Mrs. Ku became suspicious and went over to have a look. The door was tightly shut and all was quiet inside. She knocked for a long time before the girl came out, with her hair all disheveled and her face soiled. She opened the door for Ku's mother and closed it immediately. Inside her room, Mrs. Ku found a baby crying on the bed. The old woman was surprised and asked, "When was he born?"

"Three days ago," she replied.

Mrs. Ku unwrapped the baby and found it to be a chubby boy with a wide forehead. Overjoyed, she said, "You have given me a grandson, but what is a single girl like you going to do all alone in the world?"

"This is my secret, and I'm afraid I can't explain it to you," the girl replied. "You can carry the baby home at night when there is no one around."

The old lady returned and told her son, and both of them were puzzled. They went over and took the baby home at night.

Several nights later, the girl suddenly came over around midnight, carrying a leather bag in her hand. She smiled and said, "I've accomplished my goal. It's time for me to say good-bye."

Ku immediately pressed her for a reason, to which she answered, "I've always remembered your kindness in helping me to support my mother. I once told you that our bedding together was a one-time affair because one should not repay one's debt in bed. But since you're so poor and could not afford to get married, I tried to give you an heir. I was hoping to bear you a boy by taking you just once, but unfortunately my period came as usual afterward so I had to break my rules and do it again. Now that I have repaid your kindness, my wish is fulfilled and I have no regrets."

"What is inside that bag?"

"The head of my enemy."

Ku picked it up and looked inside. He saw a bearded head, all smashed and smeared with blood. Though frightened out of his wits, he managed to get the story from the girl, who finally took him into her confidence. "I've never mentioned it to you before because I was afraid that you might let the secret out inadvertently. Now that my work is finished, I can tell you about it freely. I'm originally from Chekiang Province. My father was a prefect. He was falsely charged and killed by his enemy, and our house was confiscated. I took my mother away and we lived quiet for three whole years under concealed identities. The reason why I waited so long before avenging my father was that my mother was still alive. And after my mother died, I was held up by my pregnancy.

Remember the night you came by and I was out? Well, I went out to better acquaint myself with the ways in and out of the enemy's house. I didn't want to take chances." As she was leaving, she said these parting words to Ku: "Please take good care of my son. You yourself will not be blessed with long life, but this son of yours can bring fame and great honor to your family. Since it's so late, I don't want to wake your mother. Good-bye!"

Grief-stricken, Ku was about to ask her where she was going when, quick as a lightning flash, the girl disappeared. Ku sighed and stood there petrified for a long time.

He told his mother everything the next morning, but they could do no more than express their sorrow and admiration for her.

Three years later, just as was predicted by the girl, Ku died a premature death. His son later became a *chin-shih*[2] at the age of eighteen, and he took care of his grandmother throughout her old age.

[2] The highest academic degree. [Ed.]

3

Qing Law Code on Marriage, 1644–1810

The Chinese law code of the Qing dynasty was essentially the same as the preceding Ming dynasty. The entire code covered no more than about 600 pages. Implementation was left up to judges who seemed to have based decisions more on the facts of the case than legal precedent. This selection contains sections from the code on the subject of marriage. Keep in mind that these are only selections from the code, so the absence of an issue does not mean that the code did not cover it.

Try to determine the reasons for these laws. What purpose did each of these serve? What do these laws tell you about Qing China?

THINKING HISTORICALLY

How would you compare this document with the previous two selections? Which of these laws are similar to those in your own society? Which are not? For those that are not similar, does your society have a different way of solving the problem or is the issue not a problem?

Source: Ta Tsing leu lee, *Being the Fundamental Laws, and a Selection from the Supplementary Statutes, of the Penal Code of China,* trans. George Thomas Staunton (London: T. Cadell & W. Davies, 1810), 107–08, 110–12, 116–18, 120. Spelling modernized.

Section 101

Marriages: How Regulated

When a marriage is intended to be contracted, it shall be, in the first instance reciprocally explained to, and clearly understood by, the families interested, whether the parties who design to marry are or are not, diseased, infirm, aged, or under age; and whether they are the children of their parents by blood, or only by adoption; if either of the contracting families then object, the proceedings shall be carried no further; if they still approve, they shall then in conjunction with the negotiators of the marriage, if such there be, draw up the marriage-articles.

If, after the woman is thus regularly affianced by the recognition of the marriage-articles, or by a personal interview and agreement between the families, the family of the intended bride should repent having entered into the contract, and refuse to execute it, the person amongst them who had authority to give her away shall be punished with 50 blows, and the marriage shall be completed agreeably to the original contract.—Although the marriage-articles should not have been drawn up in writing, the acceptance of the marriage-presents shall be sufficient evidence of the agreement between the parties. . . .

Section 102

Lending Wives or Daughters on Hire

Whoever lends any one of his wives, to be hired as a temporary wife, shall be punished with 80 blows,—whoever lends his daughter in like manner, shall be punished with 60 blows; the wife or daughter in such cases, shall not be held responsible.

Whoever, falsely representing any of his wives as his sister, gives her away in marriage, shall receive 100 blows, and the wife consenting thereto, shall be punished with 80 blows.

Those who knowingly receive in marriage the wives, or hire for a limited time the wives or daughters of others, shall participate equally in the aforesaid punishment, and the parties thus unlawfully connected, shall be separated; the daughter shall be returned to her parents, and the wife to the family to which she originally belonged; the pecuniary confederation in each case shall be forfeited to government. Those who ignorantly receive such persons in marriage, contrary to the laws, shall be excused, and recover the amount of the marriage-presents.

Section 103

Regard to Rank and Priority among Wives

Whoever degrades his first or principal wife to the condition of an inferior wife or concubine, shall be punished with 100 blows. Whoever, during the life-time of his first wife, raises an inferior wife to the rank and condition of a first wife, shall be punished with 90 blows, and in both the cases, each of the several wives shall be replaced in the rank to which she was originally entitled upon her marriage.

Whoever, having a first wife living, enters into marriage with another female as a first wife, shall likewise be punished with 90 blows; and the marriage being considered null and void, the parties shall be separated, and the woman returned to her parents.

Section 105

Marriage During the Legal Period of Mourning

If any man or woman enters into an equal marriage during the legal period of mourning for a deceased parent, or any widow enters into a second and equal marriage within the legal period of mourning for her deceased husband, the offending party shall be punished with 100 blows.

If it is not an equal match, that is to say, if a man takes an inferior wife from a subordinate rank, or a woman connects herself in marriage as one of the inferior wives of her husband, the punishment attending a breach of this law shall be less by two degrees.

If a widow who, during the life of her husband, had received honorary rank from the Emperor, ever marries again, she shall suffer punishment as above described, and moreover lose her rank, as well as be separated from her second husband. . . .

Section 110

Marriage of Officers of Government into Families Subject to Their Jurisdiction

If any officer belonging to the government of a city of the first, second, or third order, marries, while in office, the wife or daughter of any inhabitant of the country under his jurisdiction, he shall be punished with 8o blows.

If any officer of government marries the wife or daughter of any person having an interest in the legal proceedings at the same time under his investigation, he shall be punished with 100 blows, and the member of the family of the bride, who gave her away, shall be equally punishable. The woman, whether previously married or not, shall be restored to her parents, and the marriage-present forfeited in every case to government.

If the officer of government accomplishes the marriage by the force or influence of his authority, his punishment shall be increased two degrees, and the family of the female, being in such a case exempt from responsibility, she shall, if previously single, be restored to her parents; and if previously married, to her former husband; the marriage-present shall, not in either case be forfeited. . . .

Section 113

Marriage with Female Musicians and Comedians

If any officer or clerk of government, either in the civil or military department, marries, as his first or other wife, a female musician or comedian, he shall be punished with 60 blows, and the marriage being null and void, the female shall be sent back to her parents and rendered incapable of returning to her profession. The marriage-present shall be forfeited to government.

If the son or grand-son, being the heir of any officer of government having hereditary rank, commits this offence; he shall suffer the same punishment, and whenever he succeeds to the inheritance, his parental honours shall descend to him under a reduction of one degree.

Section 116

Law of Divorce

If a husband repudiates his first wife, without her having broken the matrimonial connection by the crime of adultery, or otherwise; and without her having furnished him with any of the seven justifying causes of divorce, he shall in every such case be punished with 80 blows. Moreover, although one of the seven justifying causes of divorce should be chargeable upon the wife, namely, (1) barrenness; (2) lasciviousness;. (3) disregard of her husband's parents; (4) talkativeness; (5) thievish propensities; (6) envious and suspicious temper; and, lastly, (7) inveterate infirmity; yet, if any of the three reasons against a divorce should exist, namely, (1) the wife's having mourned three years for her husband's parents; (2) the family's having become rich after having been poor previous to, and at the time of, marriage; and, (3) the wife's having no parents living to receive her back again; in these cases, none of the seven aforementioned causes will justify a divorce, and the husband who puts away his wife upon such grounds, shall suffer punishment two degrees less than that last stated, and be obliged to receive her again.

If the wife shall have broken the matrimonial connection by an act of adultery, or by any other act, which by law not only authorizes but requires that the parties should be separated, the husband shall receive a punishment of 80 blows, if he retains her.

When the husband and wife do not agree, and both parties are desirous of separation, the law limiting the right of divorce shall not be enforced to prevent it. . . .

4

ANNA BIJNS

"Unyoked Is Best! Happy the Woman without a Man," 1567

Anna Bijns* (1494–1575) was a Flemish nun and poet who lived in Antwerp, taught in a Catholic school in that city, wrote biting criticism of Martin Luther and the Protestant Reformation, and in her many works helped shape the Dutch language. The impact of Luther, and Protestantism more generally, on the lives of women has been the subject of much debate. Luther opposed nunneries and monasticism, believing that it was the natural duty of all women to marry and bear children. At the same time, he encouraged a level of reciprocal love and respect in marriage that was less emphasized in Catholicism. The Protestant translations of the Bible from Latin also opened a pathway for individuals, including educated women, to participate in the religious life, though not as nuns. Whether or not the sentiments of this poem are more Catholic than Protestant, are they more European than Chinese? Why or why not?

THINKING HISTORICALLY

No one should imagine that the ideas conveyed in this poem were typical or representative of European thought in the sixteenth century. This was obviously an extreme view that ran counter to traditional and commonly accepted ideas. Note how some phrases of the

* bynz

Source: Anna Bijns, "Unyoked Is Best," trans. Kristiaan P. G. Aercke, in *Women and Writers of the Renaissance and Reformation*, ed. Katharina M. Wilson (Athens: The University of Georgia Press, 1987), 382–83.

poem convey the recognition that most people will disagree with the sentiments being expressed.

When we are comparing documents from different cultures, we must always try to understand how representative they are of the views of the larger population. The Miu family document (selection 1) expresses the views of a single family, but lineage regulations were common in sixteenth-century China, and their ubiquity reflected an even greater consensus on the importance of the family. Anna Bijns's poem is a personal view that expresses a minority opinion. But in what sense is this a European, rather than Chinese, minority view? Do you think Anna Bijns's view might appeal to more people today than it did in the sixteenth century? If so, why?

How good to be a woman, how much better to be a man!
Maidens and wenches, remember the lesson you're about to hear.
Don't hurtle yourself into marriage far too soon.
The saying goes: "Where's your spouse? Where's your honor?"
But one who earns her board and clothes
Shouldn't scurry to suffer a man's rod.
So much for my advice, because I suspect—
Nay, see it sadly proven day by day—
'T happens all the time!
However rich in goods a girl might be,
Her marriage ring will shackle her for life.
If however she stays single
With purity and spotlessness foremost,
Then she is lord as well as lady, Fantastic, not?
Though wedlock I do not decry:
Unyoked is best! Happy the woman without a man.

Fine girls turning into loathly hags—
'Tis true! Poor sluts! Poor tramps! Cruel marriage!
Which makes me deaf to wedding bells.
Huh! First they marry the guy, luckless dears,
Thinking their love just too hot to cool.
Well, they're sorry and sad within a single year.
Wedlock's burden is far too heavy.
They know best whom it harnessed.
So often is a wife distressed, afraid.
When after troubles hither and thither he goes
In search of dice and liquor, night and day,
She'll curse herself for that initial "yes."
So, beware ere you begin.
Just listen, don't get yourself into it.
Unyoked is best! Happy the woman without a man.

A man oft comes home all drunk and pissed
Just when his wife had worked her fingers to the bone
(So many chores to keep a decent house!),
But if she wants to get in a word or two,
She gets to taste his fist—no more.
And that besotted keg she is supposed to obey?
Why, yelling and scolding is all she gets,
Such are his ways—and hapless his victim.
And if the nymphs of Venus he chooses to frequent,
What hearty welcome will await him home.
Maidens, young ladies: learn from another's doom,
Ere you, too, end up in fetters and chains,
Please don't argue with me on this,
No matter who contradicts, I stick to it:
Unyoked is best! Happy the woman without a man.

A single lady has a single income,
But likewise, isn't bothered by another's whims.
And I think: that freedom is worth a lot.
Who'll scoff at her, regardless what she does,
And though every penny she makes herself,
Just think of how much less she spends!
An independent lady is an extraordinary prize—
All right, of a man's boon she is deprived,
But she's lord and lady of her very own hearth.
To do one's business and no explaining sure is lots of fun!
Go to bed when she list,[1] rise when she list, all as she will,
And no one to comment! Grab tight your independence then.
Freedom is such a blessed thing.
To all girls: though the right Guy might come along:
Unyoked is best! Happy the woman without a man.

Regardless of the fortune a woman might bring,
Many men consider her a slave, that's all.
Don't let a honeyed tongue catch you off guard,
Refrain from gulping it all down. Let them rave,
For, I guess, decent men resemble white ravens.
Abandon the airy castles they will build for you.
Once their tongue has limed[2] a bird:
Bye bye love—and love just flies away.
To women marriage comes to mean betrayal
And the condemnation to a very awful fate.

---

[1] Wants. [Ed.]
[2] Caught. [Ed.]

All her own is spent, her lord impossible to bear.
It's *peine forte et dure*[3] instead of fun and games.
Oft it was the money, and not the man
Which goaded so many into their fate.
Unyoked is best! Happy the woman without a man.

[3] Long and forceful punishment; a form of torture whereby the victim was slowly crushed
by heaping rocks on a board laid over his or her body. [Ed.]

5

The Autobiography of Mrs. Alice Thornton, 1645–1657

Alice Thornton (1626–1706/7) had a comfortable childhood in Ireland where her father was Lord Deputy, the king's representative. After her father's death in 1640, family circumstances declined, but despite the eruption of the English Civil War and the family's loyalty to the deposed King Charles and the Church of England, they managed an upper-middle-class standard of living in England.

Our selections from Alice Thornton's autobiography are drawn from events that occurred between 1645 and 1657. What happened in 1645 that might have influenced her idea of marriage? How did she feel about marriage when the idea was proposed in 1651? How would you characterize her married life?

THINKING HISTORICALLY

How were the author's family circumstances different from those of a woman born into the Miu lineage? How would you compare the author's relationship with her mother to that of the characters to their mothers in Pu Songling's story? What differences between European and Chinese marriage is revealed in this account?

The Death of My Sister Danby, Sept. 30, 1645

About this year, my dear and only sister, the Lady Danby, drew near her time for delivery of her sixteenth child. Ten whereof had been baptized, the other six were stillborn, when she was above half gone with them,

Source: *The Autobiography of Mrs. Alice Thornton, of East Norton, Co., York* (London: The Surtees Society, 1875), 49–50, 75–77, 81–88, 91, 94–95. For ease of reading the spelling has been modernized in some instances. [Ed.]

she having miscarried of them all upon frights by fire in her chamber, falls, and such like accidents happening. . . .

She had been very ill long time before her delivery, and much altered in the heat of her body, being feverish. After exceeding sore travail she was delivered of a goodly son about August 3rd, by one dame Sworre. This boy was named Francis, after another of that name, a sweet child that died that summer of the smallpox. This child came double into the world, with such extremity that she was exceedingly tormented with pains, so that she was deprived of the benefit of sleep for fourteen days, except a few frightful slumbers; neither could she eat anything for her nourishment as usual. Yet still did she spend her time in discourse of goodness excellently pious, godly, and religious, instructing her children and servants, and preparing her soul for her dear Redeemer, as it was her saying she should not be long from Him. . . .

The Marriage of Alice Wandesforde, December 15, 1651

After many troubles and afflictions under which it pleased God to exercise my mother and self in since the death of my father, she was desirous to see me comfortably settled in the estate of marriage, in which she hoped to receive some satisfaction, finding age and weakness to seize more each year, which added a spur to her desires for the future well-being of her children, according to every one of their capacities. As to myself, I was exceedingly satisfied in that happy and free condition, wherein I enjoyed my time with delight abundantly in the service of my God, and the obedience I owed to such an excellent parent, in whose enjoyment I accounted my days spent with great content and comfort; the only fears which possessed me was least I should be deprived of that great blessing I had in her life. Nor could I, without much reluctance, draw my thoughts to the change of my single life, knowing too much of the cares of this world sufficiently without the addition of such incident to the married estate. As to the fortune left by my father, it was fair, and more then competent, so that I needed not fear (by God's blessing) to have been troublesome to my friends, but to be rather in a condition to assist them if need had required. . . .

Nevertheless, such was my dear mother's affection to the family for it's preservation, that she harkened to the proposal made for Mr. Thornton's marriage, albeit therein she disobliged some persons of very good worth and quality which had solicited her earnestly in my behalf, and such as were of large and considerable estates of her neighbors about her. And, after the first and second view betwixt us, she closed so far with him that she was willing he should proceed in his suit, and that cordially, if I should see cause to accept. For my own particular, I was not hasty to change my free estate without much consideration, both as to my present and future, the first inclining me rather to continue so still, wherein none could be more satisfied. The second would contract much more trouble, twisted inseparably with those comforts God gave in that estate. Yet might I be hopeful to serve God in those duties incumbent on a wife, a mother, a mistress, and governess in a family. And if it pleased God so to dispose of me in marriage, making me a more public instrument of good to those several relations, I thought it rather duty in me to accept my friends' desires for a joint benefit, then my own single retired content, so that Almighty God might receive the glory of my change, and I more capacitated to serve Him in this generation, in what He thus called me unto. Therefore it highly concerned me to enter into this greatest change of my life with abundance of fear and caution, not lightly, nor unadvisedly, nor, as I may take my God to witness that knows the secrets of hearts, I did it not to fulfill the lusts of the flesh, but in chastity and singleness of heart, as marrying in the Lord. And to that end that I might have a blessing upon me, in all my undertakings, I powered out my petitions before the God of my life to direct, strengthen, lead, and counsel me what to do in this concern, which so much tended to my future comfort or discomfort. . . . After which petitions to my God, I was the more inclined to accept of this proposition of my friends' finding; also that the gentleman seemed to be a very godly, sober, and discreet person, free from all manner of vice, and of a good conversation. . . .

Alice Wandesforde, the daughter of Christopher Wandesford, Esq., late Lord Deputy of Ireland, was married to William Thornton, esquire, of Easte Newton, at my mother's house in Hipswell, by Mr. Siddall, December the 15th, 1651. Mr. Siddall made a most pious and profitable exhortation to us, showing our duties, and teaching us the fear of the Lord in this our new estate of life, with many zealous prayers for us. My dear and honored mother gave me in marriage, in the presence of my own brother John Wandesforde; my uncle Norton, my uncle Darley (Francis), my cousin Dodsworth of Wattlosse, George Lightfoote, and Dafeny, Robert Webster, Martha Richison, Ralfe Ianson, Robert Loftus the elder. . . .

A Deliverance from Death That Day on Which I Was Married, December 15th, 1651

That very day on which I was married, having been in health and strength for many years before, I fell suddenly so ill and sick after two o'clock in the afternoon that I thought, and all that saw me did believe, it would have been my last night, being surprised with a violent pain in my head and stomach, causing a great vomiting and sickness at my heart, which lasted eight hours before I had any intermission; but, blessed be the Lord our God, the Father of mercies, Which had compassion on me, and by the means that was used I was strengthened wonderfully beyond expectation, being pretty well about ten o'clock at night. My dear husband, with my mother, was exceeding tender over me, which was a great comfort to my spirits. What the cause of this fit was I could not conjecture, save that I might have brought it upon me by cold taken the night before, when I sat up late in preparing for the next day, and washing my feet at that time of the year, which my mother did believe was the cause of that dangerous fit the next day. But, however it was, or from what cause it proceeded, I received a great mercy in my preservation from God, and shall ever acknowledge the same in humble gratitude for His infinite loving kindness forever. I looked upon this first business of my new condition to be a little discouragement, although God was able to turn all things for the best and to my good, that I might not build too much hopes of happiness in things of this world, nor in the comforts of a loving husband, whom God had given me, but set my desires more upon the love of my Lord and God.

Meditations upon My Deliverance of My First Child, and of the Great Sickness Followed for Three-Quarters of a Year; August 6, 1652, Lasted til May 12, 1653

About seven weeks after I married it pleased God to give me the blessing of conception. The first quarter I was exceeding sickly in breeding, till I was with quick childe; after which I was very strong and healthy, I bless God, only much hotter than formerly, as is usual in such cases from a natural cause, insomuch that my nose bled much when I was about half gone, by reason of the increase of heat. Mr. Thornton had a desire that I should visit his friends, in which I freely joined, his mother living about fifty miles from Hipswell, and all at Newton and Buttercrambe. In my passage thither I sweat exceedingly, and was much inclining to be feverish, wanting not eight weeks of my time, so that Dr. Wittie said that I should go near to fall into a fever, or some desperate sickness, if I did not cool my blood, by taking some away, and if I had stayed but two days longer, I had followed his advice. In his return home from Newton, his own estate, I was carried over Hambleton towards Sir William Askough's house, where I passed down on foot a very high wall betwixt Hudhill and Whitsoncliffe, which is above a mile steep down, and indeed so bad that I could not scarce tread the narrow steps, which was exceeding bad for me in that condition, and sore to endure, the way so straight and none to lead me but my maid [Susan Gosling], which could scarce make shift to get down herself, all our company being gone down before. Each step did very much strain me, being so big with child, nor could I have got down if I had not then been in my full strength and nimble on foot. But, I bless God, I got down safe at last, though much tired, and hot and weary, finding myself not well, but troubled with pains after my walk. Mr. Thornton would not have brought me that way if he had known it so dangerous, and I was a stranger in that place; but he was advised by some to go that way before we came down the hill. This was the first occasion which brought me a great deal of misery, and killed my sweet infant in my womb. . . . The doctor came post the next day, when he found me very weak, and durst not let me blood that night, but gave me cordials, etc., till the next day, and if I got but one hour's rest that night, he would do it the morning following. That night the two doctors had a dispute about the letting me bleed. Mr. Mahum was against it, and Dr. Wittie for it; but I soon decided that dispute, and told them, if they would save my life, I must bleed. So the next day I had six or seven ounces taken which was turned very bad by my sickness, but I found a change immediately in my sight, which was exceeding dim before, and then I see as well as ever clearly, and my strength began a little to return; these things I relate that I may set forth the mercy of my ever gracious God, Who had blessed the means in such manner. Who can sufficiently extol His Majesty for His boundless mercies to me His weak creature, for from that time I was better, and he had hopes of my life. The doctor stayed with me seven days during my sickness; my poor infant within me was greatly forced with violent motions perpetually, till it grew so weak that it had left stirring, and about the 27th of August I found myself in great pains as it were the colic, after which I began to be in travail, and about the next day at night I was delivered of a goodly daughter, who lived not so long as that we could get a minister to baptize it, though we presently sent for one. This my sweet babe and first child departed this life half an hour after its birth, being received, I hope, into the arms of Him that gave it. She was buried that night, being Friday, the 27th of August, 1652, at Easby church. The effects of this fever remained by several distempers successively, first, after the miscarriage I fell into a most terrible shaking ague, lasting one quarter of a year, by fits each day twice, in much violence, so that the sweat was great with faintings, being thereby weakened till I could not stand or go. The hair on my head came off, my nails of my fingers and toes came off, my teeth did shake, and ready to come out and grew black. After the ague left me, upon a medicine of London treacle, I fell into the jaundice, which vexed me very hardly one full quarter and a half more. I finding Dr. Wittie's judgment true, that it would prove a chronic distemper; but blessed be the Lord, upon great and many means used and all remedies, I was at length cured of all distempers and weaknesses, which, from its beginning, had lasted three-quarters of a year full out. Thus had I a sad entertainment and beginning of my change of life, the comforts thereof being turned into much discomforts and weaknesses, but still I was upheld by an Almighty Power, therefore will I praise the Lord my God. Amen. . . .

Upon the Birth of My Second Child and Daughter, Born at Hipswell on the 3rd of January in the Year 1654

Alice Thornton, my second child, was born at Hipswell near Richmond in Yorkshire the 3rd day of January, 1654, baptized the 5th of the same. Witnesses, my mother the Lady Wandesforde, my uncle Mr. Major Norton, and my cousin Yorke his daughter, at Hipswell, by Mr. Michell Siddall, minister then of Caterick.

It was the pleasure of God to give me but a week time after my daughter Alice her birth, and she had many preservations from death in the first year, being one night delivered from being overlaid by her nurse, who laid in my dear mother's chamber a good while. One night my mother was writing pretty late, and she heard my dear child make a groaning troublesomely, and stepping immediately to nurse's bedside she saw the nurse fallen asleep, with her breast in the child's mouth, and lying over the child; at which she, being affrighted, pulled the nurse suddenly off from her, and so preserved my dear child from being smothered. . . .

Elizabeth Thornton's Death, the 5th of September, 1656

It pleased God to take from me my dear child Betty, which had been long in the rickets and consumption, gotten at first by an ague, and much gone in the rickets, which I conceived was caused by ill milk at two nurses. And notwithstanding all the means I used, and had her with Naly at St. Mungno's Well for it, she grew weaker, and at the last, in a most desperate cough that destroyed her lungs, she died. . . .

Elizabeth Thornton, my third child, died the 5th of September, 1656, betwixt the hours of five and six in the morning. Her age was one year six months and twenty-one days. Was buried the same day at Catterick by Mr. Siddall.

Meditations on the Deliverance of My First Son and Fifth Child at Hipswell the 10th of December, 1657

It pleased God, in much mercy, to restore me to strength to go to my full time, my labor beginning three days; but upon the Wednesday, the ninth of December, I fell into exceeding sharp travail in great extremity, so that the midwife did believe I should be delivered soon. But lo! it fell out contrary, for the child stayed in the birth, and came cross with his feet first, and in this condition continued till Thursday morning between two and three o'clock, at which time I was upon the rack in bearing my child with such exquisite torment, as if each lime were divided from other, for the space of two hours; when at length, being speechless and breathless, I was, by the infinite providence of God, in great mercy delivered. But I having had such sore travail in danger of my life so long, and the child coming into the world with his feet first, caused the child to be almost strangled in the birth, only living about half an hour, so died before we could get a minister to baptize him, although he was sent for.

6

Diary of the Countess de Rochefort, 1689

The Countess de Rochefort was an aristocrat in the court of Louis XIV. She lived on an estate in Avignon in the south of France. A good deal of the time, her husband[1] was away on military campaigns. To do so in 1689 he needed most of the family's available cash for expenses, leaving the countess to manage the estate under financial pressure. These selections from her diary for 1689 give us an idea of the daily life of a woman of the aristocracy who still is quite busy.

How does she spend her days? How dependent or independent does she seem? Does this source tell you anything about the lives of aristocratic women in Europe? If so, what?

THINKING HISTORICALLY

In both China and Europe, aristocrats lived very different lives from the middle classes. How different was the world of the countess from that of Alice Thornton? In what ways might the author's life have been different from a noble's wife in China? What would account for those differences?

25 May, 1689. I wrote to M. Carretier, my attorney at the Court of Toulouse, to ask for news. . . . I wrote to M. Penaut, my attorney at

---

[1] Comte de Rochefort (1630–1712), younger son of Louis de Rohan, duc de Montbazon.

Source: Julia O'Faolain and Lauro Martines, eds., *Not in God's Image: Women in History from the Greeks to the Victorians* (New York: Harper & Row, 1973), 234–37. From *Une Grande Dame dans son ménage au temps de Louis XIV, D'apres le journal de la comtesse de Rochefort* (1689).

Montpellier, to proceed with our suit against the community of Beaucaire. The same day I wrote also to M. Belot, attorney at the Court of Toloze, for news of M. Brocardy's case.

M. Odoacre, the community's arbiter arrived today. He and the royal attorney began discussing things after dinner. It does not look to me as though we can hope for an amicable settlement. . . . Today I also went to Mormont to look at the woods. I found that far too much had been cut, but what is left is growing back very well. The part that is for sale is worth more than 40 écus, for the wood is thicker there. . . .

1 June. I ordered that on all our lands prayers be offered for M. de Rochefort until he returns.

The butcher from Roche paid me 34 livres, 10 sols of what he owes me, plus 71 pounds of mutton at 2 sols and 4 deniers per pound, and 15 pounds of beef at 18 deniers. Adding it all up, he has paid off 43 livres, 10 sols of his debt. . . .

Toward evening, being at Bégude, I inspected my crops and found them very fine. However, the tenant tells me that if he had sowed earlier the wheat would be finer and more plentiful. I decided therefore to let him follow his own judgment as to when he should sow. He also told me that the ditches need scouring, and I admitted that they did.

I got the carders in today to work on a hundredweight of washed wool from which I aim to make 8 cannes [1 canne = between 2 and 3 meters] of crépon, 14 of light wool, 13 of floss serge, and 30 of caddis.

3 June. I forgot to note that on the first of the month I had work started on one of the two mill stones at the Rochefort mill. It was very urgent because the wheat was coming out unground. I am giving the mason his food while he works on it.

10 June. M. Jean Artaud came to see me to offer to lease the small farm house at Beaujeu. . . .

13 June. We began reeling the silk today. . . . Nine pounds of cocoons produced fifteen ounces of fine silk.

14 June. I got up early to supervise the storing of the casks in the cellar. I had the vats made and the small cellars got ready for the fair. I'm having a large wooden vat made for pressing the grapes. . . .

A small pewter carafe I had made has been delivered. I have also had dishes and two dozen plates remade. All my pewter has been reworked and I have had it marked as well.

I sent 4 lbs. of soap to Pernes, where I'm having thread bleached. . . .

The same day I sent to M. Patron, the trimmer, to ask how much braid would be needed for my livery. He said I would need 80 cannes [160 meters] of the wide and 30 [60 meters] of the narrow and that to make that much would take 10 lbs. of heavy silk and 8 lbs. of fine floss silk. . . . I sent 2 cannes of red caddis to T. to make the footmen's jackets. . . .

Catin came from Rochefort today where she had been supervising the carders. She brought 100 chickens which were left of those I had bought; adding the 28 I had here, that makes 128. I have over 40 hens as well, one cock and 10 turkeys. . . .

15 June. I ordered the guard at Rochefort to sell my wine. He sold two casks to the butcher and is keeping the third one for the harvest.

I have arranged to have the Gazette sent and held for me twice a week at Tarascon.

20 June. I got up early and heard Mass, then went to see my meadow at Maubuisson. I have had all the wines in my cellar tasted; they were pronounced to be excellent. There are 22 casks altogether. I have decided to keep three and sell the rest.

I spent the rest of the day cutting out and having underclothes made up for my children.

21 June. I got up early as usual to write to M. de Rochefort and to M. Sicard. After Mass, I had the attics prepared for the new wheat; what's left of the old will be ground into flour for the servants. Next I gave orders to have my old skirts cut up to make dresses for my son, the chevalier.

M. Treven de Villeneuve came to see me to tell me that . . . he was obliged to ask me for money owed for two pensions, which amounts to 733 livres, 6 sols, 8 deniers. I answered that it was not too good a time to ask me for money, that M. de Rochefort had taken all I had to pay for his campaign and that I even had letters from the government dispensing me from paying any money out before his return. . . .

27 June. I got up early to prepare for the bleeding I am to have done on my ankle because of the bad headaches I have been suffering for some time. . . .

5 July . . . the Sisters of Mercy wrote from Avignon asking for their pension and back payments. I wrote asking them to wait until the harvest, when I would pay them; otherwise I would use my *lettres d'Etat* to stop their suit.

6 July . . . I spent the rest of the day making an inventory of the furniture, beds, chairs and so forth to make sure that nothing gets damaged during the fair.

I had good news from M. de Rochefort.

12 July. I spent the morning having beds made up in the rooms that are to be let during the fair.

I wrote to my attorney. . . .

I went down to the cellar and tasted my wines. I had the three best casks marked; they will be kept for Monsieur, and three others for the commonalty.

27 July. I spent the day doing my accounts. . . .

17 September. I sent M. Trevenin the rest of what I owed him. . . . The tenant at Jonquieres says . . . the owner of a neighboring farmhouse has been encroaching on our land. This will have to be looked into at once. . . .

26 September. M. de Rochefort came home. . . .

30 May, 1690. From November 10 until February I was so depressed with melancholy at the bad state in which I saw my business that I was neither eating nor sleeping; . . . melancholy is good for neither the body nor the soul. . . . Now I'm partly over it. . . . I am getting back to work. . . . God has remedied my affairs when I was least expecting it. With His grace, I hope to get things into shape in a few years. But the house will have to be carefully run; I must economize all I can or else in a bad year it is impossible to make ends meet. And then we must deprive ourselves of a lot so as to be able to help the poor. . . .

7

Court Case on Marriage in High Court of Aix, 1689

At the same time as the Countess of Rochefort was managing her estate in Avignon without the help of her husband, Joseph Cabassol and his wife, Anne Geniere, were called to the High Court of Aix, France, 42 miles away. The couple's marriage was being challenged by some of the members of Cabassol's family. Who were these people? What was the reason for the suit? What was the reasoning of the court? What does this case tell you about social class and marriage in France at this time?

THINKING HISTORICALLY

Compare this document to the Qing law code (document 3). How do you think judges in Qing China might have handled a case like this? To what extent were the Chinese interests in this sort of case similar to, and different from, those of Louis XIV's France? How is our U.S. law similar or different?

Case tried before the High Court of Aix in 1689. Joseph Cabassol . . . was the eldest of the seven children of a lawyer at the High Court of Aix. . . . [After his parent's death he succeeded to his inheritance. Then some years later] he fell in love with the woman Anne Geniere, a widow [who] had been brought before the Provost of Marseille because of her

Source: Julia O'Faolain and Lauro Martines, eds., *Not in God's Image: Women in History from the Greeks to the Victorians* (New York: Harper & Row, 1973), 222–24.

scandalous life. Convicted of prostitution and pimping, she had been sentenced by the judge to three years' banishment. . . . This sentence was confirmed, after appeal, by a decision of the High Court of Aix in 1683.

On 19 April 1688, Joseph Cabassol and Anne Geniere appeared before the bishop of Avignon, told him they were inhabitants of that town, that they wanted to get married, and that there was no canonical impediment. In proof of this, they brought three witnesses . . . and asked to be dispensed from publishing banns [request granted]. . . . They were married the following day . . . and returned to Aix on the following fourth of May. . . .

On the fourteenth of that same month of May, Joseph Cabassol's family, hearing of his marriage, his uncle, two brothers, and a sister put in a petition to have it annulled.

In Joseph Cabassol's defense, it was said that an adult of thirty years of age is free according to all the laws of God and man to choose his own wife. . . . Joseph Cabassol said that neither his uncle nor his brothers and sister were entitled to attack his marriage.

Monsieur de Saint-Martin, Director of Public Prosecutions . . . admitted that the consent of brothers and uncles is not necessary in the case of the marriage of an adult. . . .

One could not, however, conclude that such persons are never entitled to oppose the marriage of an adult. . . . The grounds for attacking this marriage were essentially two: that it was celebrated without publishing the banns and that it was not celebrated by the parties' own parish priest. . . . It was claimed that Anne Geniere had rented two furnished rooms, paying for three years rent in advance, in the town of Avignon. But we can state right away that this pretended domicile is not of the sort required by the holy decretals and the statutes . . . [which demand] that one should have lived a year or the best part of a year in a parish before one becomes really a parishioner. But the defendants had lived neither a year nor anything like it in Avignon when they got married there. . . . And so they did not satisfy the first condition. . . . If it were enough to change house for a while in order to establish domicile in order to get married, then the forethought of the Council of Trent would be illusory and that of the Royal Statute would be useless. One could make a parish priest for oneself according to one's needs, and where then could parents turn to get their authority respected? . . . Would this not be authorizing the worst license and covering it with a specious veil of marriage? . . . In order to determine whether the plaintiffs are entitled to petition for the invalidation of the marriage we must decide whether . . . the defendants' marriage is prejudicial to their honor. . . . If Anne Geniere had no other faults but those of her low rank and fortune, we would find the plaintiffs too fastidious. . . . But this is a woman who, over and above the inequality. . . . has led a scandalous life. She has been stigmatized by a sentence which is a perpetual monument to her infamy. . . . If a man who wastes his patrimony can be declared incapable of managing his affairs, does it not seem that since Cabassol is wasting his honor, and managing his true interests so badly, we should listen to the voice of his relatives? . . . When the vapors with which mad passion have confused his mind withdraw . . . he will approve what he condemns today. . . .

For these reasons we believe that the petition to invalidate the marriage should be allowed . . . and that the defendants be condemned to give alms to the amount of ten pounds each to the hospitals of this town and forbidden to frequent each other, yet that they be allowed the recourse of taking any steps they think fit toward lodging an appeal in an ecclesiastical court. . . . Judgment given in conformity with these conclusions on the 14th March, 1689.

8

MARY JO MAYNES AND ANN WALTNER
Women and Marriage in Europe and China, 2001

This article is the product of a rich collaboration between historians of China and Europe who show us how a study of women and marriage is anything but peripheral to a study of these areas. What is their thesis about European and Chinese marriage patterns? What do marriage patterns tell us about a society? How do the other readings in this chapter support or challenge their thesis?

THINKING HISTORICALLY

The authors begin by comparing the role of religion, the state, and the family in setting marriage patterns in both China and Europe. Did Christianity allow European women more independence than Confucianism allowed women in China? In which society was the patriarchal family more powerful, and what was the relative impact of patriarchy on women in both societies? How did the age and rate at which people married in each society compare? What was the importance of Chinese concubinage and Christian ideals of chastity?

Source: Mary Jo Maynes and Ann Waltner, "Childhood, Youth, and the Female Life Cycle: Women's Life-Cycle Transitions in a World-Historical Perspective: Comparing Marriage in China and Europe," *Journal of Women's History* 12, no. 4 (Winter 2001): 11–19.

The authors' questions about marriage in Europe and China lead finally to a consideration of one of the most frequently asked comparative questions: Why did Europe industrialize before China? Do the different European and Chinese marriage patterns answer this question? What other comparative questions would we have to ask to arrive at a full answer?

Comparing Marriage Cross-Culturally

. . . Beginning in the late 1500s, women in northern Italy began to appeal to legal courts run by the Catholic Church when they got into disputes with their families over arranged marriages. Within the early modern Italy family system the father held a great deal of authority over his children and it was usual for the parents to determine when and whom sons and daughters married. Women and children held little power in comparison with adult men. But the Catholic Church's insistence that both parties enter into the marriage willingly gave some women an out—namely, an appeal to the Church court, claiming that the marriage their family wanted was being forced upon them without their consent. Surprisingly, these young women often won their cases against their fathers. In early modern China, by way of contrast, state, religion, and family were bound together under the veil of Confucianism. Paternal authority echoed and reinforced the political and the moral order. Religious institutions could rarely be called upon to intervene in family disputes. Therefore, young women (or young men, for that matter) had no clearly established institutional recourse in situations of unwanted marriage. So, despite the fact that paternal power was very strong in both early modern Italy and early modern China, specific institutional differences put young women at the moment of marriage in somewhat different positions.

We began with the presumption that however different the institution of "marriage" was in Italy and China, it nevertheless offered enough similarities that it made sense to speak comparatively about a category called "marriage." Parallels in the two cultures between the institution of marriage and the moment in the woman's life course that it represented make comparison useful. Nevertheless, this particular comparison also isolates some of the variable features of marriage systems that are especially significant in addressing gender relations in a world-historical context. In China, the rules of family formation and family governance were generally enforced within the bounds of each extended family group. State and religious influences were felt only indirectly through family leaders as mediators or enforcers of state and religious law. Throughout Europe, beginning in the Middle Ages, the institution of marriage was altered first by the effort of the Catholic Church to wrest some control over marriage from the family by defining it as a sacrament, and then eventually by the struggle between churches and state authorities to regulate families.

This contest among church, state, and family authorities over marriage decisions turns out to have been a particular feature of European history that had consequences for many aspects of social life. A focus on the moment of marriage presents special opportunities for understanding connections between the operation of gender relations in everyday life and in the realm of broader political developments. Marriage is a familial institution, of course, but, to varying degrees, political authorities also have a stake in it because of its implications for property transfer, reproduction, religion, and morality—in short, significant aspects of the social order. In this essay, we compare one dimension of marriage—its timing in a woman's life cycle—in two contexts, Europe and China. We argue that variations in marriage timing have world-historical implications. We examine how a woman's status and situation shifted at marriage and then suggest some implications of comparative differences in the timing and circumstances of this change of status.

The Moment of Marriage in European History

One striking peculiarity of Central and Western European history between 1600 and 1850 was the relatively late age at first marriage for men and women compared with other regions of the world. The so-called "Western European marriage pattern" was marked by relatively late marriage—that is, relative to other regions of the world where some form of marriage usually occurred around the time of puberty. In much of Europe, in contrast, men did not typically marry until their late twenties and women their mid-twenties. This practice of relatively late marriage was closely connected with the custom of delaying marriage until the couple commanded sufficient resources to raise a family. For artisans this traditionally meant having a shop and master status. For merchants it entailed saving capital to begin a business. In the case of peasant couples, this meant having a house and land and basic farming equipment. It was the responsibility of the family and the community to oversee courtship, betrothal, and marriage to assure that these conditions were met. This phenomenon was also rooted in the common practice of neolocality—the expectation that a bride and groom would set up their own household at or soon after marriage. This "delayed" marriage has attracted the attention of European historical demographers. The delay of marriage meant, quite significantly, that most European women did not begin to have children until their twenties. But this marriage pattern also has significance in other realms as well. In particular, young people of both sexes experienced a relatively long hiatus between puberty and marriage.

Unmarried European youth played a distinctive role in economic, social, cultural, and political life through such institutions as guilds, village youth groups, and universities. For the most part, historians' attention to European youth has centered on young men. Major works on the history of youth in Europe, like theories of adolescent development, tend to center on the male experience as normative. Only when gender differences in youth are recognized and the history of young women is written will the broad historical significance of the European marriage pattern become clear. Contrast between European demographic history and that of other world regions suggests a comparative pattern of particular significance for girls: Delayed marriage and childbearing meant that teenage girls were available for employment outside the familial household (either natal or marital) to a degree uncommon elsewhere. Household divisions of labor according to age and gender created constant demand for servants on larger farms; typically, unmarried youth who could be hired in from neighboring farms as servants filled this role. A period of service in a farm household, as an apprentice, or as a domestic servant in an urban household characterized male and female European youth in the life-cycle phase preceding marriage. Historians have noted but never fully explored the role young women played in European economic development, and in particular their role in the early industrial labor force.

Late marriage had gender-specific cultural ramifications as well. Whereas it was considered normal and even appropriate for teenage men to be initiated into heterosexual intercourse at brothels, in most regions of Europe, young women were expected to remain chaste until marriage. Delay of marriage heightened anxiety over unmarried women's sexuality, especially the dangers to which young women were increasingly exposed as the locus of their labor shifted from home and village to factory and city. Premarital or extramarital sexuality was uncommon, and was rigorously policed especially in the period following the religious upheavals of the Reformation in the sixteenth century. In rural areas, church and community, in addition to the family, exerted control over sexuality. Moreover, the unmarried male youth cohort of many village communities often served, in effect, as "morals police," enforcing local customs. These young men regulated courtship rituals, organized dances that young people went to, and oversaw the formation of couples. Sometimes, judging and public shaming by the youth group was the fate of couples who were mismatched by age or wealth or who violated sexual taboos. Some customs, at least symbolically, punished young men from far away who married local women, removing them from the marriage pool. Often, such a bridegroom had to pay for drinks in each village that the bridal couple passed through as they moved from the bride's parish church to their new abode—the longer the distance, the more expensive his bill.

Once married, a couple would usually begin having children immediately. Demographic evidence suggests that for most of Central and
Western Europe there was virtually no practice of contraception among
lower classes prior to the middle of the nineteenth century. Women had
babies about every two years (more or less frequently according to region and depending on such local customs as breast-feeding length and
intercourse taboos). Even though completed family sizes could be large
by modern standards, the number of children most women bore was
still less than if they had married in their teens. And prevailing high mortality rates further reduced the number of children who survived to
adulthood.

The Moment of Marriage in Chinese History

The Chinese marriage system was traditionally characterized by early
age at marriage, nearly universal marriage for women, virilocal residence (a newly married couple resided with the groom's parents), concubinage for elite men, and norms that discouraged widow remarriage.
From the sixteenth through twentieth centuries, Chinese men and
women married much younger on average than did their European
counterparts—late teens or early twenties for women and a bit later for
men. A bride typically moved to her husband's family home, which was
often in a different village from her own. The moment of marriage not
only meant that a girl would leave her parents but that she would also
leave her network of kin and friends, all that was familiar. Families chose
marriage partners, and a matchmaker negotiated the arrangements.
Nothing resembling courtship existed; the bride and groom would often
first meet on their wedding day.

Because a newly married Chinese couple would typically reside in an
already-existing household, it was not necessary for an artisan to become established, a merchant to accumulate capital, or a peasant to own
a farm before marrying. Newly married couples participated in ongoing
domestic and economic enterprises that already supported the groom's
family. New households were eventually established by a process of
household division, which typically happened at the death of the father
rather than the moment of marriage (although it could happen at other
points in the family cycle as well).

Daughters were groomed from birth for marriage. They were
taught skills appropriate to their social class or the social class into
which their parents aspired to marry them. (In the ideal Chinese marriage, the groom was in fact supposed to be of slightly higher social
status than the bride.) The feet of upper-class girls (and some who were
not upper class) were bound, since Chinese men found this erotic.
Bound feet also symbolically, if not actually, restricted upper-class

women's movement. Thus bound feet simultaneously enhanced the sexual desirability of upper-class women and served to contain their sexuality within domestic bounds.

Virtually all Chinese girls became brides, though not all of them married as principal wives. (This contrasts with the European pattern where a substantial minority of women in most regions never married.) Upper-class men might take one or more concubines in addition to a principal wife. The relationship between a man and his concubine was recognized legally and ritually, and children born of these unions were legitimate. A wife had very secure status: divorce was almost nonexistent. A concubine's status, in contrast, was much more tenuous. She could be expelled at the whim of her "husband"; her only real protection was community sentiment. Although only a small percentage of Chinese marriages (no more than 5 percent) involved concubines, the practice remained an important structural feature of the Chinese marriage system until the twentieth century. Concubinage also provides a partial explanation of why, despite the fact that marriage was nearly universal for women, a substantial proportion of men (perhaps as high as 10 percent) never married. Also contributing to this apparent anomaly was the practice of sex-selective infanticide, a common practice that discriminated against girl babies and, ultimately, reduced the number of potential brides.

Once married, Chinese couples began to have children almost immediately, generally spacing births at longer intervals than did European couples. The reasons for this are not yet completely understood, although infanticide, extended breast-feeding, and the fairly large number of days on which sexual intercourse was forbidden all seem to have played a role in lowering Chinese family size.

Early marriage in China meant that the category of "youth," which has been so significant for European social and economic history, has no precise counterpart in Chinese history. Young Chinese women labored, to be sure, but the location of their work was domestic—either in the household of their father or husband. Female servants existed in China, but their servitude was normally of longer duration than the life-cycle servitude common in Europe. The domestic location of young women's labor in the Chinese context also had implications for the particular ways in which Chinese industries were organized, as we suggest below.

Patterns of Marriage in Europe and China

To sum up, then, there are differences of both timing of and residency before and after marriage that are particularly germane to the comparative history of young women. As demographic historians James Z. Lee and Wang Feng also have argued, "in China, females have always married universally and early . . . in contrast to female marriage in Western Europe, which occurred late or not at all." Whereas, in the nineteenth century, all but 20 percent of young Chinese women were married by age twenty, among European populations, between 60 and 80 percent of young women remained single at this age. In traditional China, only 1 or 2 percent of women remained unmarried at age thirty, whereas between 15 and 25 percent of thirty-year-old Western European women were still single. (For men, the differences though in the same direction are far less stark.) As for residence, in the Western European neolocal pattern, norms and practices in many regions resulted in a pattern whereby newly married couples moved into a separate household at marriage; but concomitant with this was their delaying marriage until they could afford a new household. In China, newly married couples generally resided in the groom's father's household. In Western Europe, the majority of postpubescent young men and many young women left home in their teenage years for a period of employment. In the early modern era, such employment was often as a servant or apprentice in either a craft or a farm household, but, over time, that employment was increasingly likely to be in a nondomestic work setting, such as a factory, store, or other urban enterprise. "Youth" was a distinctive phase in the life course of young men and increasingly of young women in Europe, although there were important gender distinctions. Such a period of postpubescent semiautonomy from parental households did not exist for Chinese youth, especially not for young women in traditional China. Young men more typically remained in their father's household and young women moved at marriage in their late teens from their own father's household to that of their husband's father.

Comparing the Moment of Marriage: Implications and Cautions

We would now like to discuss some of the world-historical implications of this important (if crude) comparison in the marriage systems of China and Western Europe. There are obviously many possible realms for investigation. For example, these patterns imply differences in young women's education, intergenerational relationships among women (especially between mothers and daughters and mothers-in-law and daughters-in-law), and household power relations. Here, we restrict our discussion to two areas of undoubted world-historical significance, namely economic development, on the one hand, and sexuality and reproduction, on the other.

The question of why the Industrial Revolution, or, alternatively, the emergence of industrial capitalism, occurred first in Europe, has been and remains salient for both European and world historians. R. Bin Wong explores this question in his innovative comparative study of economic development in Europe and China. Wong argues that there were rough parallels in the dynamics linking demographic expansion and economic growth in China and Europe until the nineteenth century. Both economies were expanding on the basis of growth of rural industrial enterprises in which peasant families supplemented agricultural work and income with part-time industrial production. What the Chinese case demonstrates, Wong argues, is that this so-called protoindustrial form of development may be viewed as an alternative route to industrialization rather than merely a precursor of factory production. Indeed, Charles Tilly has suggested that a prescient contemporary observer of the European economy in 1750 would likely have predicted such a future—that is "a countryside with a growing proletariat working in both agriculture and manufacturing."

While Wong's study is devoted to comparative examination of the economic roots and implications of varying paths to industrial development, he also connects economic and demographic growth. In particular, Wong mentions the link between marriage and economic opportunity: "in both China and Europe, rural industry supported lower age at marriage and higher proportions of ever married than would have been plausible in its absence. This does not mean that ages at marriage dropped in Europe when rural industry appeared, but the possibility was present. For China, the development of rural industry may not have lowered ages at marriage or raised proportions married as much as it allowed previous practices of relatively low ages at marriage and high proportions of women ever married to continue." What Wong does not explore is the way in which these "previous practices" that connected the low age at marriage with both virilocality and a relatively high commitment to the domestic containment of daughters and wives also had implications for patterns of economic development. In a comparative account of why Chinese industrial development relied heavily on domestic production, the fact that the young female labor force in China was to an extent far greater than that of Europe both married and "tied" to the male-headed household needs to be part of the story. This pattern of female marriage and residency held implications for entrepreneurial choice that helped to determine the different paths toward industrialization in Europe and China. World-historical comparison, taking into account aspects of gender relations and marriage and kinship systems, highlights their possible significance for economic development, a significance that has not been given proper attention by economic historians. Indeed, it is arguable that the family and marital status of the young women who played so significant a role in the workforce (especially those employed in the textile industry, which was key to early industrial development in both Europe and China) were major factors in the varying paths to development followed in China and Europe in the centuries of protoindustrial growth and industrialization.

A second set of implications concerns sexuality and reproduction. Again, we are aided by another recent study, which, in a fashion parallel to Wong's, uses Chinese historical evidence to call into question generalizations about historical development based on a European model. In their book on Chinese demographic history, Lee and Wang argue against the hegemonic Malthusian (mis)understandings according to which the family and population history to China has been seen as an example of a society's failure to curb population growth by any means other than recurrent disaster (by "positive" rather than "preventive" checks in Malthusian terms). They note the important difference in marriage systems that we have just described, but they dispute conclusions too often drawn from the Chinese historical pattern concerning overpopulation. Instead, according to Lee and Wang "persistently high nuptiality . . . did not inflate Chinese fertility, because of . . . the low level of fertility within marriage."

This second example points to another important realm for which the age at which women marry has great consequences. But the findings reported by Lee and Wang also caution scholars against leaping to comparative conclusions about one society on the basis of models established in another, even while their claims still suggest the value of comparison. We should not presume that since Chinese women were married universally and young, they therefore had more children or devoted a greater proportion of their time and energy to childbearing and child rearing than did their later married counterparts in Europe. Although the evidence is far from definitive, it nevertheless indicates that total marital fertility may have been somewhat lower in China than in Europe until the late nineteenth or early twentieth centuries. The factors in China that produced this pattern included relatively high rates of infanticide, especially of female infants, as well as different beliefs and practices about child care and sexuality. For example, babies were apparently breast-fed longer in China than in Europe (a pattern in turn related to the domestic location of women's work), which would have both increased infants' chances of survival and also lengthened the intervals between births.[1] In the realm of sexuality, pertinent factors include both prescriptions for men against overly frequent intercourse, and coresidence with a parental generation whose vigilance included policing young couples' sexual behavior.

These two examples are meant to suggest how looking at women's life cycles comparatively both enhances our understanding of the implications of varying patterns for women's history and also suggests the very broad ramifications, indeed world-historical significance, of different ways of institutionalizing the female life cycle.

---

[1] Breastfeeding temporarily lowers female fertility. [Ed.]

■ REFLECTIONS

Women's history has entered the mainstream during the last few decades. An older view, still pervasive in the academic world forty years ago, assumed that women's history was adequately covered by general history, which was largely the story of the exploits of men. Political, military, and diplomatic history took precedence over historical fields seen as less resolutely masculine, such as social and cultural history.

Today, women's history not only stands independently in college and university curriculums but has also helped open doors to a wide range of new fields in social history—gender, family, childhood, sexuality, domesticity, and health, to name but a few. These new research fields have contributed significantly to issues of general history, as the authors of the last reading show. In fact, the growth and development of new fields of research and teaching in social and cultural history have had the effect of relegating the study of presidents, wars, and treaties to the periphery of the profession. A recent meeting of the American Historical Association, where historians came together to talk about their work, had more sessions on women, gender, and sexuality than on politics, diplomacy, military, war, World War I, World War II, and the American Civil War combined.

Some more traditional historians complain that this is a fad, and that sooner or later the profession will get back to the more "important" topics. But others respond that it is hard to think of anything more important than the history of half of humanity. This debate leads to questions about the importance of particular individuals in history. Who had a greater impact, for instance, thirtieth U.S. president Calvin Coolidge (1872–1933) or Marie Curie (1867–1934), who won the Nobel Prize for isolating radium for therapeutic purposes?

What role do individuals play on the historical canvas anyway? A president or Nobel laureate works according to social norms, available resources, supporting institutions, and the work of hundreds or thousands of others, living and dead. Forty years ago, historians put greater stress on institutions, movements, and perceived forces than they do today. In recent years, historians have looked for the "agency" of individuals and groups, perhaps in an effort to see how people can have an impact on their world. The power of slavery and the impact of imperialism have been balanced with the tales of slave revolts, the stories of successful collaborators, adapters, and resisters, and the voices of slaves and indigenous and colonized peoples. We see this in the study of women's history as well.

We began this chapter with the observation that we live in a patriarchy. Even if we are dismantling it in the twenty-first century, it was a powerful force between 1500 and 1800: a historical force, not natural, but a product of the urban revolution, perhaps, beginning about five thousand years ago. It is useful to understand its causes, describe its workings, and relate its history. But does doing so only hamper our capacity for change? Does it ignore the stories of women who have made a difference? Conversely, are women empowered, humanity enriched, by knowing how individual women were able to work within the system, secure their needs, engage, negotiate, compromise? Do the stories of a Pu Songling or the poems of an Anna Bijns inspire us? Or do they misrepresent the past and, by consequence, delude us?

Perhaps there are no easy answers to those questions, but our exercise in comparison might come in handy. The rich and varied detail of the human past should warn us against absolute declarations. We may emphasize patriarchy or emphasize women's power, but we would be foolish to deny either. In consequence, it may be most useful to ask more specific questions and to compare. Can women own property here? Is there more restriction on women's movement in this society or that? Only then can we begin to understand why here and not there, why then and not now. And only then can we use our understanding of the past to improve the present.

19

The Scientific Revolution

Europe, the Ottoman Empire, China, Japan, and the Americas, 1600–1800

■ HISTORICAL CONTEXT

Modern life is unthinkable apart from science. We surround ourselves with its products, from cars and computers to telephones and televisions; we are dependent on its institutions—hospitals, universities, and research laboratories; and we have internalized the methods and procedures of science in every aspect of our daily lives, from balancing checkbooks to counting calories. Even on social and humanitarian questions, the scientific method has become almost the exclusive model of knowledge in modern society.

We can trace the scientific focus of modern society to what is often called the "scientific revolution" of the seventeenth century. The seventeenth-century scientific revolution was a European phenomenon, marked by the work of such notables as Nicolas Copernicus (1473–1543) in Poland, Galileo Galilei (1564–1642) in Tuscany, and Isaac Newton (1642–1727) in England. But it was also a global event, prompted initially by Europe's new knowledge from Asia, Africa, and the Americas, and ultimately spread as a universal method for understanding and manipulating the world.

What was the scientific revolution? How revolutionary was it? How similar, or different, was European science from that practiced elsewhere in the world? And how much did the European revolution affect scientific traditions elsewhere? These are some of the issues we will study in this chapter.

■ THINKING HISTORICALLY

Distinguishing Change from Revolution

The world is always changing; it always has been changing. Sometimes, however, the change seems so formidable, extensive, important, or quick that we use the term *revolution*. In fact, we will use the term in this and the next two chapters. In this chapter we will examine what historians call the scientific revolution. The next chapter will deal with political revolutions and the chapter following with the industrial revolution. In each of these cases there are some historians who object that the changes were not really revolutionary, that they were more gradual or limited. Thus, we ask the question, how do we distinguish between mere change and revolutionary change?

In this chapter you will be asked, how revolutionary were the changes that are often called the scientific revolution? The point, however, is not to get your vote, pro or con, but to get you to think about how you might answer such a question. Do we, for instance, compare "the before" with "the after" and then somehow divide by the time it took to get from one to the other? Do we look at what people said at the time about how things were changing? Are we gauging speed of change or extent of change? What makes things change at different speeds? What constitutes a revolution?

1

JACK GOLDSTONE

Why Europe? 2009

This selection is drawn from a book by a modern historian who asks one of the enduring questions of modern history: Why was it that people in Europe pioneered the breakthroughs in modern scientific thought in the seventeenth century that led to an industrial revolution? This is a particularly intriguing question when you realize, as Goldstone points out, that between 1000 and 1500 China, India, and the Muslim world made far greater strides in science than Europe. What were the obstacles to advancement in scientific thought in most societies before 1500? What happened in Europe between 1500 and 1650 to change the way people thought about

Source: Jack Goldstone, *Why Europe? The Rise of the West in World History 1500–1850* (New York: McGraw-Hill, 2009), 144–53.

nature, and how did that thinking change? How did rationalism and empiricism change European science after 1650? How does a combination of rationalism and empiricism produce better science than either separately or than the other two sources of authority: tradition and religion?

THINKING HISTORICALLY

Goldstone does not use the term *scientific revolution* in this selection, but he discusses a number of changes in European society, politics, and beliefs that might be called revolutionary. What are these changes? What would make them revolutionary changes? Is it a matter of how fast they occurred, how widespread they were, what impact they had, or how unusual or uniquely European they were? Which of these measures makes them more revolutionary?

One must ask, given the glorious achievements of Islamic and other scientific traditions that were sustained over many centuries: Why did they not develop the same kind of advances leading to industrialization as did the modern European sciences?

Varieties of World Science and Different Approaches to Understanding Nature

Approaches to natural science varied across time and across different civilizations. Some traditions, such as that of China, made enormous advances in herbal medicine but remained weak in basic anatomy. Other traditions, like that of the Mayan Indians of Central America, were extremely accurate in observational astronomy but very weak in physics and chemistry.

Nonetheless, most premodern scientific traditions shared several common elements. First, their scientific understanding of nature was generally embedded in the framework for understanding the universe laid out in their society's major religious or philosophical traditions. Although there was potential for great conflict if scientific studies of nature should contradict elements of religion, this was usually avoided by making the religious views dominant, so that scientific findings would have to be reconciled with or subordinated to religious beliefs. This does *not* mean that religions were opposed to science—quite the opposite! Most political and religious leaders sponsored both scientific and religious studies, believing that each supported the other. Many distinguished Confucian scholars, Islamic judges, and Catholic priests were also outstanding mathematicians and scientists. For the most part, detailed observations of nature, including accurate measurements of planetary motions and natural phenomena, were considered valuable as privileged knowledge to political and religious elites or socially useful for improving architecture, farming, and medicine.

However, science generally remained intermingled with religious and philosophical beliefs, and any inconsistencies were generally resolved in favor of preserving the established religion. This meant that truly novel work risked being suppressed by political and religious authorities, especially during periods of religious conservatism or state enforcement of orthodox religious views.

Second, most premodern sciences maintained a separation between mathematics and natural philosophy (the study of nature). Mathematics was considered useful for exploring the properties of numbers (arithmetic) and relationships in space (geometry). It was also useful for a host of practical problems, such as surveying; compiling tables of planetary positions in the skies for navigation, calendars, and astrology; and accounting. But most premodern scientific traditions—including those of the ancient Greeks, medieval Europeans, Arabs, and the Chinese—held that mathematics was *not* useful for studying the basic constitution of the universe. This was the main subject matter of natural philosophy (the study of the natural world) and theology (the study of religious issues, including the relationship of humans and the natural world to the creator).

If one wanted to know the nature of God or the soul, or the relations between humankind and God, or the purpose of animals, or the nature of the stuff that composed the world—plants, stones, fire, air, liquids, gases, crystals—well, these were problems for reasoning based on experience and logic, not on mathematical equations. The task of philosophy was to comprehend the essential nature of things and their relationships. Measurement was a practical matter, useful but best left to surveyors, craftspeople, moneylenders, and other practical folks.

Thus the Chinese and Indian traditions believed in a basic hidden force of nature—*qi* in China and *prana* in India—that animated and infused the world. For Chinese scientists, the world was always changing, and these changes formed complex cycles and flows of opposing forces that operated to maintain an overall harmony. Thus despite their enormous skill and use of detailed mathematics and observation in areas from canals and irrigation works to astronomy and clocks, it never occurred to orthodox Chinese scientists to regard the universe as a mechanical clockwork or to apply mathematical equations to understand why natural processes occurred. What mattered was understanding signs of the ever-shifting flows of *qi* between opposing conditions—*yin* and *yang*—to avoid excesses and to maintain the harmony of the whole.

The Greeks too, since the time of Aristotle, similarly maintained a separation of mathematics from natural philosophy. Aristotle's philosophy of nature, which by the Middle Ages had become the dominant natural philosophy in Europe, analyzed nature by identifying the basic elements that composed all things. For Aristotle, there were four basic elements—earth, fire, air, and water—which were defined in terms of how they behaved. Things made of earth are solid and naturally tend to fall to the center of the universe, which is why the solid earth beneath us consists of a sphere, and all solid things fall toward it. Fire naturally rises, so things infused with fire rise. Air is transparent and moves across the surface of the Earth as winds; water flows and moves in currents and puddles and fills the seas and oceans. Since the Moon and Sun and stars and planets neither move up nor down but remain in the heavens, moving in circles in the skies, they must be composed of yet another, distinct element that was perfect and unchanging, which the Greeks called the "aether."

The way these principles were discovered and proved was through logic and argument based on experience, not through mathematics. Although mathematical forms and principles could help identify and measure relationships in nature, the true "essence" of reality was set by philosophy. For example, even though the planets actually move at varying speeds in elliptical orbits around the Sun, for over 1,000 years Islamic and European astronomers sought to describe their orbits solely in terms of combinations of uniform and circular motions, because Aristotle's natural philosophy had decreed that this was the only way that heavenly bodies could move.

In the Middle Ages, European scholars continued to treat mathematics as mainly a practical field, while focusing their attention on logic and argument as the keys to advancing knowledge. Although medieval scholars in Europe did make significant advances in the study of motion and absorbed much of the critical commentary on Greek science and philosophy from the Islamic world, they did not reject or replace the major tenets of classical Greek science or their own religious theology. Rather, much of the effort of European thought in the Middle Ages consisted of efforts to reconcile and synthesize the writings of the Greek authors on science and politics with the precepts of the Christian Bible and other religious texts, culminating in the work of St. Thomas Aquinas.

The Islamic scientific tradition went further than any other in using experiments and mathematical reasoning to challenge the arguments of Ptolemy, Galen, and others of the ancient Greeks, creating new advances in medicine, chemistry, physics, and astronomy. Yet within Islam, the discussion of the fundamental relationships and characteristics of nature was separated into the teachings of the Islamic sciences, based on classical religious texts, and the teachings of the foreign sciences, including all the works of Greek and Indian authors. After the writings of the philosophical critic Al-Ghazali in the eleventh century, who championed the value of the Islamic sciences on truly fundamental issues, this division was generally maintained, and even the most remarkable advances and findings with regard to revisions of Greek learning were not permitted to challenge the fundamental views of the universe as expressed in Islamic religious works.

Thus in all the major scientific traditions, whereas precise measurement and sophisticated mathematics were widely used, mathematical reasoning was not used to challenge the fundamental understanding of nature that was expressed in natural philosophy and religious thought.

Third, in most places, the dominant assumptions and traditions of science were so distinctive and so well established that they could hardly be shaken even by encounters with different notions and ideas. These scientific traditions tended to grow incrementally, with each successive generation modifying yet building on the works of their predecessors, so that over time a rich and longstanding tradition of scientific methods and findings grew up, intertwined with an established religious tradition. These structures of thought tended to resist wholesale change or replacement and to marginalize heterodox or conflicting views.

Thus by 1500, there were many different varieties of science in the world, each with their own strengths and distinctive characteristics. Most had developed precise observations of the Earth and heavens and had systematized a great number and variety of discoveries about nature. Most had developed a classification of essential relationships or characteristics of natural things. Most were linked in some fashion to one of the great axial age religions and over many centuries had worked to accumulate knowledge while building frameworks that were compatible with those religions. And in the next century or two, most scientific traditions would be driven to greater subordination to classical and religious orthodoxy by rulers who were responding to the political and social conflicts that struck over almost all of Europe and Asia.

How then was it possible that any culture could develop . . . technical innovations, based on new instruments and mathematical natural science . . . ? To understand this, we have to grasp the unusual events and discoveries that led to unexpected changes in Europe's approach to science.

Europe's Unusual Trajectory: From Embracing to Escaping Its Classical Tradition, 1500–1650

The study of ancient schools of thought was given a new direction by the realization, by the early 1500s, that the Spanish voyages to the west had discovered not just an alternate route to India, but in fact a whole new continent, a "New World" unknown to ancient geographers and scientists. Navigators came to realize that practically all of Greek geography was badly mistaken. Also in the early 1500s, the research of the Belgian anatomist Andreas Vesalius (who was building on the prior work of Arab scholars) demonstrated to Europeans that Galen's knowledge of human anatomy was, in many respects, inaccurate or deficient because it was based on deductions from animal dissections rather than on empirical study of human cadavers. Vesalius showed that many of Galen's (and Aristotle's) statements about the heart, the liver, the blood vessels, and the skeleton were wrong.

Then in 1543, Copernicus published his new methods for calculating the movements of the planets based on a solar system with a moving Earth circling the Sun. Although some supporters, trying to avoid conflict with the church, argued that his work should only be taken as a new method of predicting planetary positions, Copernicus argued quite forcefully that the structure and dynamics of the solar system made more sense, logically and aesthetically, if the Earth and all other planets revolved around the Sun. If so, then the system of Ptolemy and Aristotle, with the Earth as the center of all motion, was in error.

In 1573, the Danish astronomer Tycho Brahe published his account of the supernova that had suddenly appeared near the constellation of Cassiopeia in 1572. This was a phenomenon that had never been recorded in European astronomy. Indeed, since the time of Aristotle, it was assumed that the skies were unchanging and constant in their perfection. Comets and meteors were known, of course, but they were considered weather phenomena, like lightning that occurred close to the Earth rather than in the celestial heavens. But the supernova was not a comet or meteorite, because it showed no motion: It was a new body that behaved like a fixed star—something that was, according to Aristotle's philosophy, impossible.

Five years later, Brahe showed by careful observation of the movements of the great comet of 1577 that this comet must be farther away from the Earth than the Moon and thus was moving through the celestial heavens, not the atmosphere, striking yet another blow against Aristotle's cosmic system. Supernovae that can be observed from Earth by the naked eye are rare, but as chance would have it, in 1604, yet another supernova made its appearance, thus showing conclusively that the heavens were not unchanging after all.

By the late 1500s and early 1600s, therefore, the wisdom of Aristotle, Galen, and Ptolemy, which had been accepted for over 1,000 years, was coming under widespread attack. European scholars sought out new observations and new instruments for studying nature that could help determine who was correct, or incorrect, in their description of nature and the universe.

In 1609, Galileo used the new spyglass or telescope—invented by Dutch lens-grinders and then improved by Galileo himself—to observe the heavens. Looking at the Moon through a telescope rather than only the unaided eye, Galileo saw what looked like giant mountains and craters on the surface, which through the telescope looked positively Earthlike! Jupiter was found to have its own moons circling it, implying that the Earth could not be the center of all celestial motions. In every direction were previously unknown stars, and even the Milky Way was revealed to consist of thousands of tiny stars. Though many critics at first dismissed the views through the telescope as false magic, enough people acquired their own telescopes and confirmed Galileo's discoveries that they were widely accepted. People came to realize that the universe in which they lived was nothing like that described by the ancient Greek authorities.

Copernicus was not the first astronomer to suggest that the Earth revolved on its axis and moved around the Sun, instead of being the fixed center of the universe; a few ancient Greek and Islamic astronomers had also suggested that this was possible. However, until telescopic observations of the moons of Jupiter demonstrated the fact of motion around a body other than the Earth, there was no evidence on which to base a successful overthrow of Aristotle's views. It was only after 1600, with so many new observations that contradicted the ancient Greeks' knowledge—of geography, of anatomy, and of astronomy—piling up in all directions, that it became possible, even imperative, to adopt alternatives to Aristotle in particular and to Greek science and philosophy as a whole.

From 1600 to 1638, a series of books presenting new knowledge or proclaiming the need for a "new science" made a compelling case that the knowledge of the ancients was seriously flawed.

1600: William Gilbert, *On the Magnet*
1620: Francis Bacon, *The New Organon, or True Directions Concerning the Interpretation of Nature*
1620: Johannes Kepler, *The New Astronomy*
1626: Francis Bacon, *The New Atlantis*
1628: William Harvey, *On the Motion of the Heart and Blood*
1638: Galileo, *Discourses on Two New Sciences*

Gilbert argued that compass needles pointed north because the whole earth acted as a giant magnet. Francis Bacon argued that Aristotle's mainly deductive logic (collected under the title *Organon*—which means "instrument or tool") could not be trusted as a guide to understanding nature; instead Bacon argued for the use of inductive logic, based on a program of experiment and observation, as a superior method for discovering knowledge of the world. Kepler showed that the planets actually traveled in elliptical orbits around the sun, not in circles. And William Harvey showed that, contrary to Galen's teachings, the supposedly separate veins and arteries were in fact one system through which the blood was circulated by the beating of the heart.

By the mid-1600s, therefore, European philosophers and scientists found themselves in a world where the authority of ancient texts was clearly no longer a secure foundation for knowledge. Other major civilizations did not suffer such blows. For the Chinese, Indians, and Muslims—accustomed to operating in a vast intercontinental trade sphere from China to Europe and generally seeing themselves at the center of all that mattered—the discovery of new, lightly peopled lands far to the west made little difference. But for Europeans—who had long seen themselves on the literal edge of the civilized world with all that mattered lying to the east—the discovery of new and wholly unknown lands to the west changed their fundamental position in the world.

Similarly, Chinese and Indian astronomers had observed supernovae before (accurately recording observations of the heavens for thousands of years) and had long ago developed philosophies of nature that were built around ideas of continuous change as the normal course of things in the universe. Unlike the Greeks and Europeans, they had no rigid notions of perfect and unchanging heavens, separate from the Earth, that would cause their classical traditions to be fundamentally challenged by new observations of comets and stars.

Moreover, just when Europeans started their impassioned debates over these new observations and put forth their alternative ideas, the Ottoman, Mughal, and Chinese Empires were focused on internal concerns, seeking to recover from internal rebellions by closing off outside influences and strengthening traditional orthodox beliefs.

Thus the Europeans, more than any other major civilization, suddenly found that the classical tradition that they had sought to embrace now had to be escaped if they were going to understand the true nature of their world and their universe. This led Europeans to undertake a search for new systems of philosophy and new ways of studying and describing nature.

Searching for New Directions in European Science: Cartesian Reasoning and British Empiricism, 1650–1750

Prior to 1650, all major civilizations drew on four basic sources to justify knowledge and authority (which were generally closely connected). These were

1. Tradition—knowledge that was revered for its age and long use
2. Religion or revelation—knowledge that was based on sacred texts or the sayings of prophets, saints, and other spiritual leaders
3. Reason—knowledge that was obtained from logical demonstration, either in arithmetic and geometry or by deductive reasoning from basic premises

4. Repeated observation and experience—knowledge that was
    confirmed by widely shared and repeated observations and
    everyday experience, such as that day follows night, the sun
    rises in the east, objects fall, heat rises. This also includes various
    agricultural and manufacturing techniques that were proven
    in use.

We have noted that in Europe by the early 1600s new discoveries,
observations, and concepts about the Earth and the universe had already
started to chip away at tradition and religious belief as guides to knowledge about the natural world. In addition, the seventeenth century was
a period of sharp religious schism and conflict in Europe, capped by the
Thirty Years' War (1618–1648). During these years Catholics, Lutherans,
Calvinists, and other sects all claimed to be correcting the errors of
others' interpretation of Christian faith, and various religious groups
rebelled and embroiled Europe in massive civil and international wars.
The lack of accepted religious authority and of any way to choose
between competing claims seemed to offer nothing but the prospect of
endless conflict.

The same problems, as we have noted, led Asian empires to promote
a return to their traditional orthodox beliefs to suppress these conflicts.
Some European states tried to do the same thing. In Spain and Italy and
part of Germany and Poland, the counter-Reformation led to the suppression of heresies and unorthodox views and enforcement of traditional Catholic beliefs. These states banned books that threatened
Catholic orthodoxy and sought to curtail the actions of "dangerous"
authors, such as Giordano Bruno and Galileo (Bruno was burned at the
stake for his heresies; Galileo, more prudent and better connected, was
allowed to live under house arrest). France and the Netherlands, though
less severe, and Britain through 1640, also tried to restore uniform state
religions and force dissenters underground or into exile. However, in a
few states—including Britain after 1689, Denmark, and Prussia—
religious tolerance remained, and throughout western Europe, there
was a checkerboard of different states following different varieties of
religion—Catholic, Calvinist, Lutheran. Throughout Europe, the result
of the rise and spread of Protestantism in the sixteenth and seventeenth
centuries was that the authority of the Catholic Church—and of the
philosophical and scientific work that was closely associated with the
church's teachings—was seriously weakened. This provided an additional
reason for philosophers to struggle to find a new basis for more certain
knowledge.

European thinkers therefore turned away from the first and second
major sources of knowledge and authority—tradition and religion—to
seek new systems of knowledge. After 1650, two major directions were
proposed to deal with this dilemma—rationalism and empiricism.

One way to set aside traditional and revelation-based assumptions was to try to get down to bedrock conclusions by reasoning purely from logic. The critical figure leading this approach was the French philosopher and mathematician René Descartes, who resolved to begin by doubting everything—the teaching of the ancients, the teachings of the church, and even his own experience. He extended his doubt until only one thing remained certain—the fact of his own doubt! This fact could then be the basis for logical deductions. After all, if Descartes could not escape the fact of his own doubt, he—as a doubting, thinking entity—must exist! This conclusion was rendered in his famous statement "I think, therefore I am."

Descartes continued this argument further. If he doubted, he could not be perfect. But if he was aware of his imperfection, this could only be because a perfect entity existed, thus there must be a perfect being, or God. And because we can only conceive of God as perfect, and hence perfectly logical, the universe constructed by God must also follow perfect logic. Descartes further argued that we can only logically perceive space if something is there, extending through space (empty space, Descartes argued, was a logical contradiction). What must fill space, then, are invisible particles whose motions and interactions must cause all that we see.

In this fashion, Descartes built up a logically consistent model of a mechanical universe in which all phenomena are to be explained by the movements and collisions of moving particles. This led Descartes to numerous valuable insights, such as the notion that we see things because invisible particles of light move from the objects we see to strike our eyes. But it also led him to deduce things that we now know are simply not true, such as the idea that the planets travel around the Sun because they are caught up in vortexes or whirlpools of swirling invisible particles.

This Cartesian rationalism provided a very attractive alternative to Aristotelian philosophy, which was now in disrepute. It seemed to have the power of purely logical demonstration behind its ideas. Also, because all phenomena were reduced to the motions of particles, it held the promise of applying mathematical principles—already worked out by Galileo for many kinds of particle motion—to all of nature. Finally, it allowed one to explain almost anything by coming up with some characteristics of particles. For example, one could suggest that spicy or sweet flavors were the respective results of sharp or smooth particles hitting the tongue or that different colors of light were produced by particles of light spinning at different speeds.

However, Cartesian rationalism also had its defects. In putting reason above experience, Cartesians disdained experiments. This limited what could be learned or discovered and often led to significant errors. Descartes' assumptions led him to misjudge the way bodies acted in collisions and turned his followers away from studying the properties of vacuums (since empty space could not exist, they must be tricks or errors by experimenters). Descartes also flatly ruled out the possibility of forces acting directly across space between objects, such as gravity. For all of its virtues, Cartesian rationalism therefore saddled its followers with a variety of errors and false explanations of the mechanics of motion in nature.

The motion of the Earth, the weight of the atmosphere, and the properties of vacuums were all discoveries whose proof rested on the use of scientific instruments (telescopes, barometers, vacuum pumps) to capture information not ordinarily available to the senses. The use of such instruments was a prime feature of the Baconian plan of developing scientific knowledge by experiments.

The experimental program reached its most systematic organization in the work of the Royal Society of London, led by Robert Boyle and later by Isaac Newton. The Royal Society based its research on experiments with scientific instruments and apparatus publicly performed at meetings of the society, and accounts of those experiments were widely published. The Royal Society used air pumps, telescopes, microscopes, electrostatic generators, prisms, lenses, and a variety of other tools to carry out its investigations. Indeed, the society came to rely on specially trained craftspeople to supply the growing demand for scientific instruments for its members.

The fame of the Royal Society in Britain skyrocketed with the achievements of Isaac Newton. Newton was the first to demonstrate that both motion on the Earth—whether the movement of falling apples, cannonballs, or the tides—and the motions of the planets through the heavens could *all* be explained by the action of a universal force of gravity. This force acted to attract objects to each other with a strength that increased with their mass but decreased with the inverse square of the distance between them. Newton's theory of gravity made it possible, for the first time, to explain the precise path and speed that the planets followed through the skies, as well as the movement of the Moon and the tides.

Newton also discovered the correct laws of mechanical force—that force was needed for all changes in the direction or speed of motion of an object, in proportion to the mass of the object and the magnitude of the change. Newton's laws of force made it possible to easily figure out the amount of work provided by, for example, a volume of falling water based on the height that it fell, or the amount of work it would take to raise a certain weight a desired distance. Newton further discovered the key principle of optics: that white light was composed of a number of different colors of light, each of which bent slightly differently when moving through water or a glass lens, thus creating rainbows in the sky and color patterns in prisms and lenses. . . .

2

Images of Anatomy, Fourteenth and Sixteenth Centuries

Andreas Vesalius (1514–1564), like generations of physicians before him, learned anatomy from the writings of Galen (129–216 c.e.), a Greek-born Roman. Because of Galen's authority, and subsequent Christian and Muslim strictures against conducting dissections, very little was learned about human anatomy for the next thousand years. Only gradually after 1200 were dissections performed again, and yet most physicians still read Galen while surgeons (formerly barbers) did the cutting. Vesalius himself began as a defender of Galen, until he moved from his native Belgium to teach at the University of Padua in Italy in 1537. There he was able to secure enough cadavers of executed criminals to perform multiple dissections and discover that Galen (who had only been able to dissect animals) had been wrong about elements of human anatomy. A facile artist himself, Vesalius engaged leading Italian draftsmen for the publication of his findings in *De humani corporis fabrica* (On the Structure of the Human Body), published in 1543.

Two images from the fourteenth century (Figures 19.1 and 19.2) are followed by two images from the *Fabrica*, one showing muscles (Figure 19.3) and another showing bones of the human skeleton (Figure 19.4). How would you describe the differences between the drawings in the *Fabrica* and those of the fourteenth century?

THINKING HISTORICALLY

The actual mistakes that Vesalius found in Galen might seem relatively trivial. For instance, Vesalius realized that the human jaw was one bone, not two as Galen claimed after dissecting monkeys. He also saw that the sternum (which protects the chest) is three bones instead of seven and that, also contrary to Galen, the fibula and tibia of the human leg were longer than the arm. In this regard we might think of his work as evolutionary rather than revolutionary. Yet when we compare the images of the fourteenth century with those of Vesalius, barely more than a hundred years later, the differences strike us as revolutionary. Why do you think that is? Was this a revolution? If so, in what?

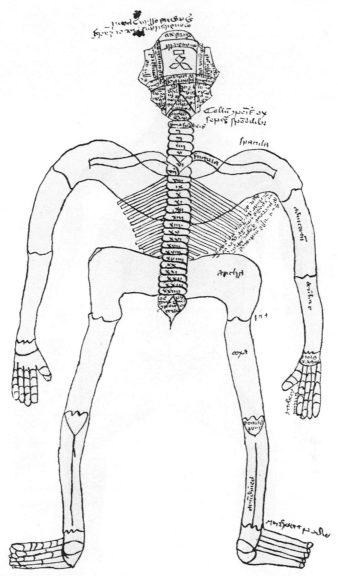

Figure 19.1 Skeleton drawing, from the Latin Munich MS Codex, fourteenth century.

Source: Wellcome Library, London.

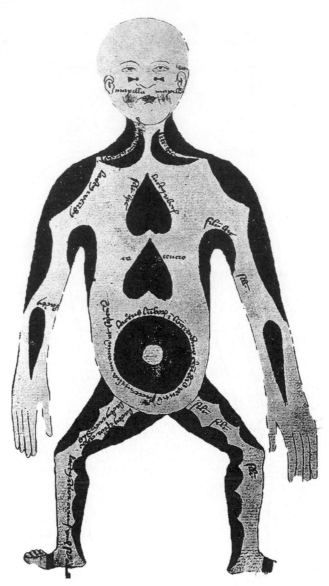

Figure 19.2   Muscular system of a man, from the Rudnitz
Five-Figure Series, 1399.

Source: Wellcome Library, London.

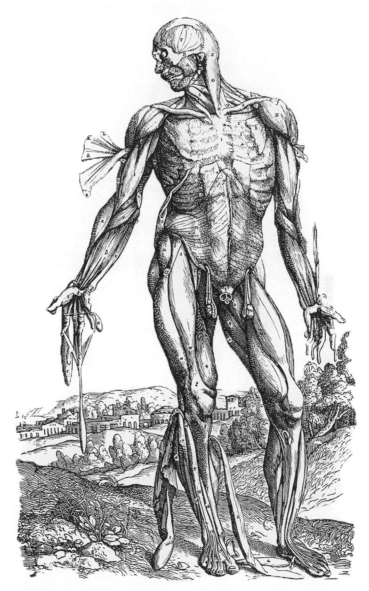

Figure 19.3 Woodcut of muscles, from Vesalius, *De humani corporis fabrica*, 1543.

Source: The Granger Collection, New York.

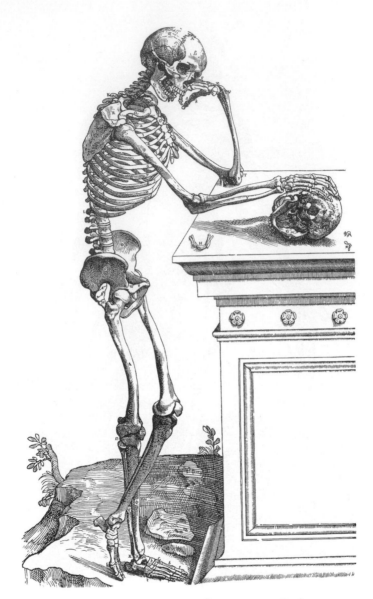

Figure 19.4 Woodcut of a skeleton, from Vesalius, *De humani corporis fabrica*, 1543.

Source: The Granger Collection, New York.

3

ISAAC NEWTON

The Mathematical Principles of Natural Philosophy, 1687

Isaac Newton (1643–1727) was probably the most influential scientist in world history. His range was breathtaking, covering optics, astronomy, mathematics, and physics. He invented calculus, discovered the relationship between light and color, and devised laws of motion and gravity that provided the framework of modern science for the next two hundred years. *The Mathematical Principles of Natural Philosophy* (1687) was his most influential work. We include here only the four "Rules of Reasoning in Philosophy."[1] Try to put each one in your own words. Why do you think he called them general rules of reasoning rather than specific rules for science?

In the first selection, Jack Goldstone underlined the importance of the European method of applying mathematics to the study of nature and the British empirical or experimental method of creating knowledge. How do these passages in Newton's writing emphasize both of these approaches?

THINKING HISTORICALLY

When we look at *The Mathematical Principles of Natural Philosophy,* or the *Principia,* as it is called in abbreviated Latin form, and once we cut through the seventeenth-century language, we come upon ideas that seem fairly obvious to us today. That they were not obvious then is a measure of how revolutionary they were. Try to imagine what people believed before Newton established these principles. For example, before Newton established the law of gravity, people did not believe that objects flew around at will; so what exactly is new here? Give examples of thinking that ignores these rules of reasoning.

Rule I

We are to admit no more causes of natural things, than such as are both true and sufficient to explain their appearances.

To this purpose the philosophers say, that Nature does nothing in vain, and more is in vain, when less will serve; for Nature is pleased with simplicity, and affects not the pomp of superfluous causes.

---

[1] As they were revised in a later edition (1726).

Source: Isaac Newton, *The Mathematical Principles of Natural Philosophy*, trans. A. Motte (London, 1729). Available on the American Libraries website at http://www.archive.org /details/newtonspmathema00newtrich (accessed October 25, 2009).

Rule II

Therefore to the same natural effects we must, as far as possible, assign the same causes.

As to respiration in a man, and in a beast; the descent of stones in Europe and in America; the light of our culinary fire and of the sun; the reflection of light in the earth, and in the planets.

Rule III

The qualities of bodies, which admit neither intension nor remission of degrees,[2] and which are found to belong to all bodies within reach of our experiments, are to be esteemed the universal qualities of all bodies whatsoever.

For since the qualities of bodies are only known to us by experiments, we are to hold for universal, all such as universally agree with experiments; and such as are not liable to diminution, can never be quite taken away. We are certainly not to relinquish the evidence of experiments for the sake of dreams and vain fictions of our own devising; nor are we to recede from the analogy of Nature, which is wont to be simple, and always consonant to itself. We no other way know the extension of bodies, than by our senses, nor do these reach it in all bodies; but because we perceive extension in all that are sensible, therefore we ascribe it universally to all others, also. That abundance of bodies are hard we learn by experience. And because the hardness of the whole arises from the hardness of the parts, we therefore justly infer the hardness of the undivided particles not only of the bodies we feel but of all others. That all bodies are impenetrable we gather not from reason, but from sensation. The bodies which we handle we find impenetrable and thence conclude impenetrability to be a universal property of all bodies whatsoever. That all bodies are moveable, and endowed with certain powers (which we call the forces of inertia) of persevering in their motion or in their rest, we only infer from the like properties observed in the bodies which we have seen. The extension, hardness, impenetrability, mobility, and force of inertia of the whole result from the extension, hardness, impenetrability, mobility, and forces of inertia of the parts: and thence we conclude that the least particles of all bodies to be also all extended, and hard, and impenetrable, and moveable, and endowed with their proper forces of inertia. And this is the foundation of

---

[2] Qualities of bodies that do not get larger or smaller, harder or softer, etc. Refers to permanent qualities of bodies: their extension, hardness, movability. The point is that we can assume these qualities are universal, and that they will be found in similar bodies, even those that are in the heavens (and therefore not measurable). [Ed.]

all philosophy. Moreover, that the divided but contiguous particles of bodies may be separated from one another, is a matter of observation; and, in the particles that remain undivided, our minds are able to distinguish yet lesser parts, as is mathematically demonstrated. But whether the parts so distinguished, and not yet divided, may, by the powers of nature, be actually divided and separated from one another, we cannot certainly determine. Yet had we the proof of but one experiment, that any undivided particle, in breaking a hard and solid body, suffered a division, we might by virtue of this rule, conclude, that the undivided as well as the divided particles, may be divided and actually separated into infinity.

Lastly, if it universally appears, by experiments and astronomical observations, that all bodies about the earth, gravitate toward the earth; and that in proportion to the quantity of matter which they severally contain; that the moon likewise, according to the quantity of its matter, gravitates toward the earth; that on the other hand our sea gravitates toward the moon; and all the planets mutually one toward another; and the comets in like manner towards the sun; we must, in consequence of this rule, universally allow, that all bodies whatsoever are endowed with a principle of mutual gravitation. For the argument from the appearances concludes with more force for the universal gravitation of all bodies, than for their impenetrability, of which among those in the celestial regions, we have no experiments, nor any manner of observation. Not that I affirm gravity to be essential to all bodies. By their inherent force I mean nothing but their force of inertia. This is immutable. Their gravity is diminished as they recede from the earth.

Rule IV

In experimental philosophy we are to look upon propositions collected by general induction[3] from phenomena as accurately or very nearly true, notwithstanding any contrary hypotheses that may be imagined, till such time as other phenomena occur, by which they may either be made more accurate, or liable to exceptions.

This rule we must follow to ensure that the argument of induction may not be evaded by hypotheses.

---

[3] Induction is reasoning from the specific to the general: deriving a general principle from specific examples or instances. For example: This, that, and the other frog are gray, so frogs must be gray. [Ed.]

4

BONNIE S. ANDERSON AND
JUDITH P. ZINSSER

Women and Science, 1988

This selection from a history of European women shows how some
women, especially the better educated, could participate in the scientific
revolution of the seventeenth and eighteenth centuries. But Anderson
and Zinsser also demonstrate how much of the scientific revolution endowed male prejudices with false scientific respectability. What factors
seem to have enabled women to participate in the scientific revolution?
In what ways was the scientific revolution a new bondage for women?

THINKING HISTORICALLY

What do the authors mean when they say that for women "there was
no Scientific Revolution"? In what ways were women's lives different
after the scientific revolution? In what ways were they the same? Were
the differences caused by the scientific revolution?

Women Scientists

In the same way that women responded to and participated in
Humanism,[1] so they were drawn to the intellectual movement known
as the Scientific Revolution. The excitement of the new discoveries of
the seventeenth and eighteenth centuries, in particular, inspired a few
gifted women scientists to formulate their own theories about the natural world, to perform their own experiments, and to publish their findings. In contrast to those educated strictly and formally according to
Humanist precepts, these women had little formal training, and chose
for themselves what they read and studied. Rather than encouraging
them, their families at best left them to their excitement with the
wonders of the "Scientific Revolution"; at worst, parents criticized
their daughters' absorption in such inappropriate, inelegant, and
unfeminine endeavors.

All across Europe from the sixteenth to the eighteenth centuries
these women found fascination in the natural sciences. They corresponded and studied with the male scientists of their day. They observed,

---

[1] A faith in the capacities of humans that reached religious dimensions in the sixteenth
century. Renaissance humanism valued reason, classical culture and literature, and civic
engagement. [Ed.]

Source: Bonnie S. Anderson and Judith P. Zinsser, *A History of Their Own: Women in Europe
from Prehistory to the Present* (New York: Harper & Row, 1988) 2:87–89, 96–99.

and they formulated practical applications from their new knowledge of botany, horticulture, and chemistry. The Countess of Chinchon, wife of the Viceroy to Peru, brought quinine bark to Spain from Latin America because it had cured her malaria. Some noblewomen, like the German Anna of Saxony (1532–1582), found medical uses for the plants they studied. The most gifted of these early naturalists is remembered not as a scientist but as an artist. Maria Sibylla Merian (1647–1717) learned drawing and probably acquired her interest in plants and insects from her stepfather, a Flemish still-life artist. As a little girl she went with him into the fields to collect specimens. Though she married, bore two daughters, and ran a household, between 1679 and her death in 1717 she also managed to complete and have published six collections of engravings of European flowers and insects. These were more than artist's renderings. For example, her study of caterpillars was unique for the day. Unlike the still life done by her contemporaries, the drawings show the insect at every stage of development as observed from the specimens that she collected and nursed to maturity. She explained:

> From my youth I have been interested in insects, first I started with silkworms in my native Frankfurt-am-Main. After that . . . I started to collect all the caterpillars I could find to observe their changes.

Merian's enthusiasm, patience, and skill brought her to the attention of the director of the Amsterdam Botanical Gardens and other male collectors. When her daughter married and moved to the Dutch colony of Surinam, their support was important when she wanted to raise the money for a new scientific project. In 1699, at the age of fifty-two, Maria Sibylla Merian set off on what became a two-year expedition into the interior of South America. She collected, made notations and sketches. Only yellow fever finally forced her to return to Amsterdam in 1701. The resulting book of sixty engravings established her contemporary reputation as a naturalist.

Mathematics, astronomy, and studies of the universe also interested these self-taught women scientists. In 1566 in Paris Marie de Coste Blanche published *The Nature of the Sun and Earth*. Margaret Cavendish (1617–1673), the seventeenth-century Duchess of Newcastle, though haphazard in her approach to science, produced fourteen books on everything from natural history to atomic physics.

Even more exceptional in the eighteenth century was the French noblewoman and courtier, Emilie du Châtelet (1706–1749). She gained admission to the discussions of the foremost mathematicians and scientists of Paris, earned a reputation as a physicist and as an interpreter of the theories of Leibnitz and Newton. Emilie du Châtelet showed unusual intellectual abilities even as a child. By the age of ten she had read Cicero, studied mathematics and metaphysics. At twelve she could speak English, Italian, Spanish, and German and translated Greek and Latin texts like

Aristotle and Virgil. Presentation at court and life as a courtier changed none of her scientific interests and hardly modified her studious habits. She seemed to need no sleep, read incredibly fast, and was said to appear in public with ink stains on her fingers from her notetaking and writing. When she took up the study of Descartes, her father complained to her uncle: "I argued with her in vain; she would not understand that no great lord will marry a woman who is seen reading every day." Her mother despaired of a proper future for such a daughter who "flaunts her mind, and frightens away the suitors her other excesses have not driven off." It was her lover and lifelong friend, the Duke de Richelieu, who encouraged her to continue and to formalize her studies by hiring professors in mathematics and physics from the Sorbonne to tutor her. In 1733 she stormed her way into the Café Gradot, the Parisian coffee-house where the scientists, mathematicians, and philosophers regularly met. Barred because she was a woman, she simply had a suit of men's clothes made for herself and reappeared, her long legs now in breeches and hose, to the delight of cheering colleagues and the consternation of the management. . . .

Châtelet made her reputation as a scientist with her three-volume work on the German mathematician and philosopher Leibnitz, *The Institutions of Physics,* published in 1740. Contemporaries also knew of her work from her translation of Newton's *Principles of Mathematics,* her book on algebra, and her collaboration with Voltaire on his treatise about Newton.

From the fifteenth to the eighteenth centuries privileged women participated in the new intellectual movements. Like the men of their class, they became humanist scholars, naturalists, and scientists. Unfortunately, many of these women found themselves in conflict with their families and their society. A life devoted to scholarship conflicted with the roles that women, however learned, were still expected to fulfill.

Science Affirms Tradition

In the sixteenth and seventeenth centuries Europe's learned men questioned, altered, and dismissed some of the most hallowed precepts of Europe's inherited wisdom. The intellectual upheaval of the Scientific Revolution caused them to examine and describe anew the nature of the universe and its forces, the nature of the human body and its functions. Men used telescopes and rejected the traditional insistence on the smooth surface of the moon. Galileo, Leibnitz, and Newton studied and charted the movement of the planets, discovered gravity and the true relationship between the earth and the sun. Fallopio dissected the human body, Harvey discovered the circulation of the blood, and Leeuwenhoek found spermatozoa with his microscope.

For women, however, there was no Scientific Revolution. When men studied female anatomy, when they spoke of female physiology, of women's reproductive organs, of the female role in procreation, they ceased to be scientific. They suspended reason and did not accept the evidence of their senses. Tradition, prejudice, and imagination, not scientific observation, governed their conclusions about women. The writings of the classical authors like Aristotle and Galen continued to carry the same authority as they had when first written, long after they had been discarded in other areas. Men spoke in the name of the new "science" but mouthed words and phrases from the old misogyny. In the name of "science" they gave a supposed physiological basis to the traditional views of women's nature, function, and role. Science affirmed what men had always known, what custom, law, and religion had postulated and justified. With the authority of their "objective," "rational" inquiry they restated ancient premises and arrived at the same traditional conclusions: the innate superiority of the male and the justifiable subordination of the female.

In the face of such certainty, the challenges of women like Lucrezia Marinella and María de Zayas had little effect. As Marie de Gournay, the French essayist, had discovered at the beginning of the seventeenth century, those engaged in the scientific study of humanity viewed the female as if she were of a different species—less than human, at best; nature's mistake, fit only to "play the fool and serve [the male]."

The standard medical reference work, *Gynaecea*, reprinted throughout the last decades of the sixteenth century, included the old authorities like Aristotle and Galen, and thus the old premises about women's innate physical inferiority. A seventeenth-century examination for a doctor in Paris asked the rhetorical question "Is woman an imperfect work of nature?" All of the Aristotelian ideals about the different "humors" of the female and male survived in the popular press even after they had been rejected by the medical elite. The colder and moister humors of the female meant that women had a passive nature and thus took longer to develop in the womb. Once grown to maturity, they were better able to withstand the pain of childbirth.

Even without reference to the humors, medical and scientific texts supported the limited domestic role for women. Malebranche, a French seventeenth-century philosopher, noted that the delicate fibers of the woman's brain made her overly sensitive to all that came to it; thus she could not deal with ideas or form abstractions. Her body and mind were so relatively weak that she must stay within the protective confines of the home to be safe.

No amount of anatomical dissection dispelled old bits of misinformation or changed the old misconceptions about women's reproductive organs. Illustrations continued to show the uterus shaped like a flask with two horns, and guides for midwives gave the principal role in labor to the fetus. As in Greek and Roman medical texts these new "scientific" works assumed that women's bodies dictated their principal function, procreation. Yet even this role was devalued. All of the evidence of dissection and deductive reasoning reaffirmed the superiority of the male's role in reproduction. Men discovered the spermatazoon, but not the ovum. They believed that semen was the single active agent. Much as Aristotle had done almost two millennia earlier, seventeenth-century scientific study hypothesized that the female supplied the "matter," while the life and essence of the embryo came from the sperm alone.

These denigrating and erroneous conclusions were reaffirmed by the work of the seventeenth-century English scientist William Harvey. Having discovered the circulation of the blood, Harvey turned his considerable talents to the study of human reproduction and published his conclusions in 1651. He dissected female deer at all stages of their cycle, when pregnant and when not. He studied chickens and roosters. With all of this dissection and all of this observation he hypothesized an explanation for procreation and a rhapsody to male semen far more extreme than anything Aristotle had reasoned. The woman, like the hen with her unfertilized egg, supplies the matter, the man gives it form and life. The semen, he explained, had almost magical power to "elaborate, concoct"; it was "vivifying" . . . endowed with force and spirit and generative influence," coming as it did from "vessels so elaborate, and endowed with such vital energy." So powerful was this fluid that it did not even have to reach the woman's uterus or remain in the vagina. Rather he believed it gave off a "fecundating power," leaving the woman's body to play a passive, or secondary, role. Simple contact with this magical elixir of life worked like lightning, or—drawing on another set of his experiments—"in the same way as iron touched by the magnet is endowed with its powers and can attract other iron to it." The woman was but the receiver and the receptacle.

Anatomy and physiology confirmed the innate inferiority of woman and her limited reproductive function. They also proved as "scientific truth" all of the traditional negative images of the female nature. A sixteenth-century Italian anatomist accepted Galen's view and believed the ovaries to be internal testicles. He explained their strange placement so "as to keep her from perceiving and ascertaining her sufficient perfection," and to humble her "continual desire to dominate." An early-seventeenth-century French book on childbirth instructed the midwife to tie the umbilical cord far from the body to assure a long penis and a well-spoken young man for a male child and close to the body to give the female a straighter form and to ensure that she would talk less.

No one questioned the equally ancient and traditional connection between physiology and nature: the role of the uterus in determining a woman's behavior. The organ's potential influence confirmed the female's irrationality and her need to accept a subordinate role to the male. The sixteenth-century Italian anatomist Fallopio repeated Aristotle's idea that the womb lusted for the male in its desire to procreate. The French sixteenth-century doctor and writer Rabelais took Plato's view of the womb as insatiable, like an animal out of control when denied sexual intercourse, the cause of that singularly female ailment, "hysteria." Other sixteenth- and seventeenth-century writers on women and their health adopted all of the most misogynistic explanations of the traditional Greek and Roman authorities. No menstruation meant a diseased womb, an organ suffocating in a kind of female excrement. Only intercourse with a man could prevent or cure the condition. Left untreated the uterus would put pressure on other organs, cause convulsions, or drive the woman crazy. Thus, the male remained the key agent in the woman's life. She was innately inferior, potentially irrational, and lost to ill-health and madness without his timely intervention.

So much changed from the fifteenth to the eighteenth centuries in the ways in which women and men perceived their world, its institutions and attitudes. The Renaissance offered the exhilaration of a society in which the individual could be freed from traditional limitations. In the spirit of Humanistic and scientific inquiry men questioned and reformulated assumptions about the mind's capabilities and the description of the natural universe. New methods of reasoning and discourse, of observation and experimentation, evolved and led to the reorientation of the natural universe and more accurate descriptions of the physical world, including man's own body. Yet when it came to questions and assumptions about women's function and role and to descriptions of her nature and her body, no new answers were formulated. Instead, inspired by the intellectual excitement of the times and the increasing confidence in their own perceptions of the spiritual and material world, men argued even more strongly from traditional premises, embellishing and revitalizing the ancient beliefs. Instead of breaking with tradition, descriptions of the female accumulated traditions: the classical, the religious, the literary, the customary, and the legal—all stated afresh in the secular language of the new age. Instead of being freed, women were ringed with yet more binding and seemingly incontrovertible versions of the traditional attitudes about their inferior nature, their proper function and role, and their subordinate relationship to men.

With the advent of printing, men were able to disseminate these negative conclusions about women as they never could before. From the sixteenth century on the printing presses brought the new tracts, pamphlets, treatises, broadsides, and engravings to increasing numbers of Europeans: pictures of the sperm as a tiny, fully formed infant; works by scholars and jurists explaining the female's "natural" physical and legal incapacity; romances and ballads telling of unchaste damsels and vengeful wives set to plague man.

Although these misogynistic attitudes about women flourished and spread, the defense of women had also begun. In her *Book of the City of Ladies* Christine de Pizan, the fifteenth-century writer, asks why no one had spoken on their behalf before, why the "accusations and slanders" had gone uncontradicted for so long? Her allegorical mentor, "Rectitude," replies, "Let me tell you that in the long run, everything comes to a head at the right time."

The world of the courts had widened the perimeters of women's expectations and given some women increased opportunities. However, for the vast majority of women, still not conscious of their disadvantaged and subordinate status, changes in material circumstances had a far greater impact. From the seventeenth to the twentieth centuries more women were able to live the life restricted in previous ages to the few. In Europe's salons and parlors they found increased comfort, greater security, and new ways to value their traditional roles and functions. For these women, "the right time"—the moment for questioning and rejecting the ancient premises of European society—lay in the future.

5

LADY MARY WORTLEY MONTAGUE

Letter on Turkish Smallpox Inoculation, 1717

Lady Mary Wortley Montague, an English aristocrat, came down with smallpox in 1715. She survived, but was badly scarred by the rash that accompanied the often-fatal disease. Her younger brother died from smallpox, one of the tens of thousands who succumbed in epidemics across Europe and around the world in the eighteenth and nineteenth centuries. Two years after her recovery Montague traveled to Istanbul with her husband, who was the British ambassador to the Ottoman Empire. There, she witnessed a new approach to warding off smallpox infections, as she described in the following letter to a friend in England. What process does Montague describe in her letter? What was her response to the events she witnessed in Turkey?

Source: *Letters of Lady Mary Wortley Montague, written during her travels in Europe, Asia, and Africa, to which are added poems by the same author* (Bordeaux: J. Pinard, 1805). The UCLA Louis M. Darling Biomedical Library, History and Special Collections Division. Also available from Gutenberg E-Books at Lady Mary Wortley Montague, Her Life and Letters (1689–1762). Author: Lewis Melville. Release Date: January 4, 2004 [EBook #10590].

THINKING HISTORICALLY

This letter provides a clear example of how scientific observation can change the material world in which we live. After observing the Turkish smallpox inoculation, Montague had her son and daughter inoculated. In fact, she became an advocate for smallpox inoculation in England and played an important role in persuading the English medical profession to support the innovative procedure. Montague paved the way for a safer vaccine, developed by Edward Jenner in 1796, that would eventually eradicate the disease from the planet.

Despite her admirable efforts, it was difficult to convince Europeans to embrace smallpox inoculation, which had been practiced in Asia for centuries. Even though the effectiveness of this technology came to be recognized in England during Montague's lifetime, the French and other Europeans, according to Voltaire, thought that the English were "fools and madmen" for experimenting with inoculation. What does this suggest about the nature of scientific discovery? Besides lack of knowledge, what other obstacles need to be overcome? What does this resistance say about how revolutionary the "scientific revolution" was?

To Mrs. S. C., Adrianople, April 1, O.S.

A Propos of distempers, I am going to tell you a thing, that will make you wish yourself here. The small pox, so fatal, and so general amongst us, is here entirely harmless, by the invention of ingrafting, which is the term they give it. There is a set of old women, who make it their business to perform the operation, every autumn, in the month of September, when the great heat is abated. People send to one another to know if any of their family has a mind to have the small-pox; they make parties for this purpose, and when they are met (commonly fifteen or sixteen together) the old woman comes with a nut-shell full of the matter of the best sort of small pox, and asks what vein you please to have opened. She immediately rips open that you offer to her, with a large needle (which gives you no more pain than a common scratch), and puts into the vein as much matter as can lie upon the head of her needle, and after that, binds up the little wound with a hollow bit of shell, and in this manner opens four or five veins. The Grecians have commonly the superstition of opening one in the middle of the forehead, one in each arm, and one in the breast, to mark the sign of the cross; but this has a very ill effect, all these wounds leaving little scars, and is not done by those that are not superstitious, who choose to have them in the legs, or that part of the arm that is concealed. The children or young patients play together all the rest of the day, and are in perfect health to the eighth.

Then the fever begins to seize them, and they keep their beds two days, very seldom three. They have very rarely above twenty or thirty in their faces, which never mark, and in eight days time they are as well as before their illness. Where they are wounded, there remains running sores during the distemper, which I don't doubt is a great relief to it. Every year thousands undergo this operation, and the French ambassador says pleasantly that they take the small-pox here by way of diversion, as they take the waters in other countries. There is no example of any one that has died in it, and you may believe I am well satisfied of the safety of this experiment, since I intend to try it on my dear little son. I am patriot enough to take pains to bring this useful invention into fashion in England, and I should not fail to write to some of our doctors very particularly about it, if I knew any one of them that I thought had virtue enough to destroy such a considerable branch of their revenue, for the good of mankind. But that distemper is too beneficial to them, not to expose to all their resentment the hardy wight[1] that should undertake to put an end to it. Perhaps if I live to return, I may, however have the courage to war with them. Upon this occasion, admire the heroism in the heart of

Your friend, etc. etc.

[1] Creature. [Ed.]

6

LYNDA NORENE SHAFFER

China, Technology, and Change, 1986–1987

In this essay an important contemporary world historian asks us to compare the revolutionary consequences of scientific and technological changes that occurred in China and Europe before the seventeenth century. What is Shaffer's argument? In what ways was the European scientific revolution different from the changes in China she describes here?

THINKING HISTORICALLY

What exactly was the impact of printing, the compass, and gunpowder in Europe? What was the "before" and "after" for each of these innovations? What, according to Shaffer, was the situation in China before and after each of these innovations? Were these innovations as revolutionary in China as they were in Europe?

Source: Lynda Norene Shaffer, "China, Technology, and Change," *World History Bulletin* 4, no. 1 (Fall/Winter 1986–1987): 1–6.

Francis Bacon (1561–1626), an early advocate of the empirical method, upon which the scientific revolution was based, attributed Western Europe's early modern take-off to three things in particular: printing, the compass, and gunpowder. Bacon had no idea where these things had come from, but historians now know that all three were invented in China. Since, unlike Europe, China did not take off onto a path leading from the scientific to the Industrial Revolution, some historians are now asking why these inventions were so revolutionary in Western Europe and, apparently, so unrevolutionary in China.

In fact, the question has been posed by none other than Joseph Needham, the foremost English-language scholar of Chinese science and technology. It is only because of Needham's work that the Western academic community has become aware that until Europe's take-off, China was the unrivaled world leader in technological development. That is why it is so disturbing that Needham himself has posed this apparent puzzle. The English-speaking academic world relies upon him and repeats him; soon this question and the vision of China that it implies will become dogma. Traditional China will take on supersociety qualities — able to contain the power of printing, to rein in the potential of the compass, even to muffle the blast of gunpowder.

The impact of these inventions on Western Europe is well known. Printing not only eliminated much of the opportunity for human copying errors, it also encouraged the production of more copies of old books and an increasing number of new books. As written material became both cheaper and more easily available, intellectual activity increased. Printing would eventually be held responsible, at least in part, for the spread of classical humanism and other ideas from the Renaissance. It is also said to have stimulated the Protestant Reformation, which urged a return to the Bible as the primary religious authority.

The introduction of gunpowder in Europe made castles and other medieval fortifications obsolete (since it could be used to blow holes in their walls) and thus helped to liberate Western Europe from feudal aristocratic power. As an aid to navigation the compass facilitated the Portuguese- and Spanish-sponsored voyages that led to Atlantic Europe's sole possession of the Western Hemisphere, as well as the Portuguese circumnavigation of Africa, which opened up the first all-sea route from Western Europe to the long-established ports of East Africa and Asia.

Needham's question can thus be understood to mean, Why didn't China use gunpowder to destroy feudal walls? Why didn't China use the compass to cross the Pacific and discover America, or to find an all-sea route to Western Europe? Why didn't China undergo a Renaissance or Reformation? The implication is that even though China possessed these technologies, it did not change much. Essentially Needham's question is asking, What was wrong with China?

Actually, there was nothing wrong with China. China was changed fundamentally by these inventions. But in order to see the changes, one must abandon the search for peculiarly European events in Chinese history, and look instead at China itself before and after these breakthroughs.

To begin, one should note that China possessed all three of these technologies by the latter part of the Tang dynasty (618–906)—between four and six hundred years before they appeared in Europe. And it was during just that time, from about 850, when the Tang dynasty began to falter, until 960, when the Song dynasty (960–1279) was established, that China underwent fundamental changes in all spheres. In fact, historians are now beginning to use the term *revolution* when referring to technological and commercial changes that culminated in the Song dynasty, in the same way that they refer to the changes in eighteenth- and nineteenth-century England as the Industrial Revolution. And the word might well be applied to other sorts of changes in China during this period.

For example, the Tang dynasty elite was aristocratic, but that of the Song was not. No one has ever considered whether the invention of gunpowder contributed to the demise of China's aristocrats, which occurred between 750 and 960, shortly after its invention. Gunpowder may, indeed, have been a factor although it is unlikely that its importance lay in blowing up feudal walls. Tang China enjoyed such internal peace that its aristocratic lineages did not engage in castle-building of the sort typical in Europe. Thus, China did not have many feudal fortifications to blow up.

The only wall of significance in this respect was the Great Wall, which was designed to keep steppe nomads from invading China. In fact, gunpowder may have played a role in blowing holes in this wall, for the Chinese could not monopolize the terrible new weapon, and their nomadic enemies to the north soon learned to use it against them. The Song dynasty ultimately fell to the Mongols, the most formidable force ever to emerge from the Eurasian steppe. Gunpowder may have had a profound effect on China—exposing a united empire to foreign invasion and terrible devastation—but an effect quite opposite to the one it had on Western Europe.

On the other hand, the impact of printing on China was in some ways very similar to its later impact on Europe. For example, printing contributed to a rebirth of classical (that is, preceding the third century A.D.) Confucian learning, helping to revive a fundamentally humanistic outlook that had been pushed aside for several centuries.

After the fall of the Han dynasty (206 B.C.–A.D. 220), Confucianism had lost much of its credibility as a world view, and it eventually lost its central place in the scholarly world. It was replaced by Buddhism, which had come from India. Buddhists believed that much human pain and confusion resulted from the pursuit of illusory pleasures and dubious ambitions: Enlightenment and, ultimately, salvation would come from a progressive disengagement from the real world, which they also believed to be illusory. This point of view dominated Chinese intellectual life until the ninth century. Thus the academic and intellectual comeback of classical Confucianism was in essence a return to a more optimistic literature that affirmed the world as humans had made it.

The resurgence of Confucianism within the scholarly community was due to many factors, but printing was certainly one of the most important. Although it was invented by Buddhist monks in China, and at first benefited Buddhism, by the middle of the tenth century, printers were turning out innumerable copies of the classical Confucian corpus. This return of scholars to classical learning was part of a more general movement that shared not only its humanistic features with the later Western European Renaissance, but certain artistic trends as well.

Furthermore, the Protestant Reformation in Western Europe was in some ways reminiscent of the emergence and eventual triumph of Neo-Confucian philosophy. Although the roots of Neo-Confucianism can be found in the ninth century, the man who created what would become its most orthodox synthesis was Zhu Xi (Chu Hsi, 1130–1200). Neo-Confucianism was significantly different from classical Confucianism, for it had undergone an intellectual (and political) confrontation with Buddhism and had emerged profoundly changed. It is of the utmost importance to understand that not only was Neo-Confucianism new, it was also heresy, even during Zhu Xi's lifetime. It did not triumph until the thirteenth century, and it was not until 1313 (when Mongol conquerors ruled China) that Zhu Xi's commentaries on the classics became the single authoritative text against which all academic opinion was judged.

In the same way that Protestantism emerged out of a confrontation with the Roman Catholic establishment and asserted the individual Christian's autonomy, Neo-Confucianism emerged as a critique of Buddhist ideas that had taken hold in China, and it asserted an individual moral capacity totally unrelated to the ascetic practices and prayers of the Buddhist priesthood. In the twelfth century Neo-Confucianists lifted the work of Mencius (Meng Zi, 370–290 B.C.) out of obscurity and assigned it a place in the corpus second only to that of the *Analects of Confucius*. Many facets of Mencius appealed to the Neo-Confucianists, but one of the most important was his argument that humans by nature are fundamentally good. Within the context of the Song dynasty, this was an assertion that morality could be pursued through an engagement in human affairs, and that the Buddhist monks' withdrawal from life's mainstream did not bestow upon them any special virtue.

The importance of these philosophical developments notwith-standing, printing probably had its greatest impact on the Chinese political system. The origin of the civil service examination system in China can be traced back to the Han dynasty, but in the Song dynasty government-administered examinations became the most important route to political power in China. For almost a thousand years (except the early period of Mongol rule), China was governed by men who had come to power simply because they had done exceedingly well in examinations on the Neo-Confucian canon. At any one time thousands of students were studying for the exams, and thousands of inexpensive books were required. Without printing such a system would not have been possible.

The development of this alternative to aristocratic rule was one of the most radical changes in world history. Since the examinations were ultimately open to 98 percent of all males (actors were one of the few groups excluded), it was the most democratic system in the world prior to the development of representative democracy and popular suffrage in Western Europe in the eighteenth and nineteenth centuries. (There were some small-scale systems, such as the classical Greek city-states, which might be considered more democratic, but nothing comparable in size to Song China or even the modern nation-states of Europe.)

Finally we come to the compass. Suffice it to say that during the Song dynasty, China developed the world's largest and most technologi-cally sophisticated merchant marine and navy. By the fifteenth century its ships were sailing from the north Pacific to the east coast of Africa. They could have made the arduous journey around the tip of Africa and on into Portuguese ports; however, they had no reason to do so. Although the Western European economy was prospering, it offered nothing that China could not acquire much closer to home at much less cost. In par-ticular, wool, Western Europe's most important export, could easily be obtained along China's northern frontier.

Certainly, the Portuguese and the Spanish did not make their un-precedented voyages out of idle curiosity. They were trying to go to the Spice Islands, in what is now Indonesia, in order to acquire the most valuable commercial items of the time. In the fifteenth century these is-lands were the world's sole suppliers of the fine spices, such as cloves, nutmeg, and mace, as well as a source for the more generally available pepper. It was this spice market that lured Columbus westward from Spain and drew Vasco Da Gama around Africa and across the Indian Ocean.

After the invention of the compass, China also wanted to go to the Spice Islands and, in fact, did go, regularly—but Chinese ships did not have to go around the world to get there. The Atlantic nations of Western Europe, on the other hand, had to buy spices from Venice (which con-trolled the Mediterranean trade routes) or from other Italian city-states;

or they had to find a new way to the Spice Islands. It was necessity that mothered those revolutionary routes that ultimately changed the world.

Gunpowder, printing, the compass—clearly these three inventions changed China as much as they changed Europe. And it should come as no surprise that changes wrought in China between the eighth and tenth centuries were different from changes wrought in Western Europe between the thirteenth and fifteenth centuries. It would, of course, be unfair and ahistorical to imply that something was wrong with Western Europe because the technologies appeared there later. It is equally unfair to ask why the Chinese did not accidentally bump into the Western Hemisphere while sailing east across the Pacific to find the wool markets of Spain.

7

SUGITA GEMPAKU

A Dutch Anatomy Lesson in Japan, 1771

Sugita Gempaku* (1733–1817) was a Japanese physician who, as he tells us here in his memoir, suddenly discovered the value of Western medical science when he chanced to witness a dissection shortly after he obtained a Dutch anatomy book.

What was it that Sugita Gempaku learned on that day in 1771? What were the differences between the treatments of anatomy in the Chinese *Book of Medicine* and the Dutch medical book? What accounts for these differences?

THINKING HISTORICALLY

How might the Dutch book have changed the way the author practiced medicine? How did it change his knowledge of the human body? How did it change the relevance of his knowledge of the human body to the medicine he practiced? How revolutionary was the new knowledge for Sugita Gempaku?

* SOO gee tah   gehm PAH koo

Source: Sugita Gempaku, *Ranto Kotohajime* (The Beginning of Dutch Studies in the East), in *Japan: A Documentary History*, ed. David J. Lu (Armonk, NY: M. E. Sharpe, 2005), 1:264–66. Iwanami Shoten, *Nihon Koten Bunka Taikei* (Major Compilation of Japanese Classics) (Tokyo: Iwanami Shoten, 1969), 95:487–93.

Whenever I met Hiraga Gennai (1729–1779), we talked to each other on this matter: "As we have learned, the Dutch method of scholarly investigation through field work and surveys is truly amazing. If we can directly understand books written by them, we will benefit greatly. However, it is pitiful that there has been no one who has set his mind on working in this field. Can we somehow blaze this trail? It is impossible to do it in Edo. Perhaps it is best if we ask translators in Nagasaki to make some translations. If one book can be completely translated, there will be an immeasurable benefit to the country." Every time we spoke in this manner, we deplored the impossibility of imple-menting our desires. However, we did not vainly lament the matter for long.

Somehow, miraculously I obtained a book on anatomy written in that country. It may well be that Dutch studies in this country began when I thought of comparing the illustrations in the book with real things. It was a strange and even miraculous happening that I was able to obtain that book in that particular spring of 1771. Then at the night of the third day of the third month, I received a letter from a man by the name of Tokuno Bambei, who was in the service of the then Town Commissioner, Magaribuchi Kai-no-kami. Tokuno stated in his letter that "A post-mortem examination of the body of a condemned criminal by a resident physician will be held tomorrow at Senjukotsukahara. You are welcome to witness it if you so desire." At one time my colleague by the name of Kosugi Genteki had an occasion to witness a post-mortem dissection of a body when he studied under Dr. Yamawaki Tōyō of Kyoto. After seeing the dissection firsthand, Kosugi remarked that what was said by the people of old was false and simply could not be trusted. "The people of old spoke of nine internal organs, and nowadays, people divide them into five viscera and six internal organs. That [perpetuates] inaccuracy," Kosugi once said. Around that time (1759) Dr. Tōyō published a book entitled *Zōshi* (*On Internal Organs*). Having read that book, I had hoped that some day I could witness a dissection. When I also acquired a Dutch book on anatomy, I wanted above all to compare the two to find out which one accurately described the truth. I rejoiced at this unusually fortunate circumstance, and my mind could not entertain any other thought. However, a thought occurred to me that I should not monopolize this good fortune, and decided to share it with those of my colleagues who were diligent in the pursuit of their medicine. . . . Among those I invited was one [Maeno] Ryōtaku (1723–1803). . . .

The next day, when we arrived at the location . . . Ryōtaku reached under his kimono to produce a Dutch book and showed it to us. "This is a Dutch book of anatomy called *Tabulae Anatomicae*. I bought this a few years ago when I went to Nagasaki, and kept it." As I examined it, it was the same book I had and was of the same edition. We held each other's hands and exclaimed: "What a coincidence!" Ryōtaku continued by saying: "When I went to Nagasaki, I learned and heard," and opened his book. "These are called *long* in Dutch, they are lungs," he taught us. "This is *hart*, or the heart. When it says *maag* it is the stomach, and when it says *milt* it is the spleen." However, they did not look like the heart given in the Chinese medical books, and none of us were sure until we could actually see the dissection.

Thereafter we went together to the place which was especially set for us to observe the dissection in Kotsukahara. . . . The regular man who performed the chore of dissection was ill, and his grandfather, who was ninety years of age, came in his place. He was a healthy old man. He had experienced many dissections since his youth, and boasted that he dissected a number of bodies. Those dissections were performed in those days by men of the *eta*[1] class. . . . That day, the old butcher pointed to this and that organ. After the heart, liver, gall bladder, and stomach were identified, he pointed to other parts for which there were no names. "I don't know their names. But I have dissected quite a few bodies from my youthful days. Inside of everyone's abdomen there were these parts and those parts." Later, after consulting the anatomy chart, it became clear to me that I saw an arterial tube, a vein, and the suprarenal gland. The old butcher again said, "Every time I had a dissection, I pointed out to those physicians many of these parts, but not a single one of them questioned 'what was this?' or 'what was that?'" We compared the body as dissected against the charts both Ryōtaku and I had, and could not find a single variance from the charts. The Chinese *Book of Medicine* (*Yi Jing*) says that the lungs are like the eight petals of the lotus flower, with three petals hanging in front, three in back, and two petals forming like two ears and that the liver has three petals to the left and four petals to the right. There were no such divisions, and the positions and shapes of intestines and gastric organs were all different from those taught by the old theories. The official physicians, Dr. Okada Yōsen and Dr. Fujimoto Rissen, have witnessed dissection seven or eight times. Whenever they witnessed the dissection, they found that the old theories contradicted reality. Each time they were perplexed and could not resolve their doubts. Every time they wrote down what they thought was strange. They wrote in their books. "The more we think of it, there must be fundamental differences in the bodies of Chinese and of the eastern barbarians [i.e., Japanese]." I could see why they wrote this way.

---

[1] The *eta* were an untouchable caste in Japan, defined by their restriction to certain occupations associated with death: tanning or working with hides, cremating the dead, butchering meat, and, thus, doing autopsies. They could not be physicians. The term is derogatory. Their descendants today are called Burakumin. [Ed.]

That day, after the dissection was over, we decided that we also should examine the shape of the skeletons left exposed on the execution ground. We collected the bones, and examined a number of them. Again, we were struck by the fact that they all differed from the old theories while conforming to the Dutch charts.

The three of us, Ryōtaku, [Nakagawa] Junan (1739–1786), and I went home together. On the way home we spoke to each other and felt the same way. "How marvelous was our actual experience today. It is a shame that we were ignorant of these things until now. As physicians who serve their masters through medicine, we performed our duties in complete ignorance of the true form of the human body. How disgraceful it is. Somehow, through this experience, let us investigate further the truth about the human body. If we practice medicine with this knowledge behind us, we can make contributions for people under heaven and on this earth." Ryōtaku spoke to us. "Indeed, I agree with you wholeheartedly." Then I spoke to my two companions. "Somehow if we can translate anew this book called *Tabulae Anatomicae*, we can get a clear notion of the human body inside out. It will have great benefit in the treatment of our patients. Let us do our best to read it and understand it without the help of translators." Ryōtaku responded: "I have been wanting to read Dutch books for some time, but there has been no friend who would share my ambitions. I have spent days lamenting it. If both of you wish, I have been in Nagasaki before and have retained some Dutch. Let us use it as a beginning to tackle the book together." After hearing it, I answered, "This is simply wonderful. If we are to join our efforts, I shall also resolve to do my very best." . . .

The next day, we assembled at the house of Ryōtaku and recalled the happenings of the previous day. When we faced that *Tabulae Anatomicae*, we felt as if we were setting sail on a great ocean in a ship without oars or a rudder. With the magnitude of the work before us, we were dumbfounded by our own ignorance. However, Ryōtaku had been thinking of this for some time, and he had been in Nagasaki. He knew some Dutch through studying and hearing, and knew some sentence patterns and words. He was also ten years older than I, and we decided to make him head of our group and our teacher. At that time I did not know the twenty-five letters of the Dutch alphabet. I decided to study the language with firm determination, but I had to acquaint myself with letters and words gradually.

BENJAMIN FRANKLIN

Letter on a Balloon Experiment in 1783

Benjamin Franklin (1706–1790) was the preeminent statesman, diplomat, and spokesman for the British colonies that became the United States during his long lifetime. Trained as a candle maker and printer, he became a journalist, publisher, merchant, homespun philosopher, and inveterate inventor. He invented the lightning rod, the Franklin stove, bifocals, and the medical catheter, among other things. His inventions sprang from a gift of immense curiosity and an exhaustive reading in the science of his day.

Franklin, sometimes called "the first American," represented the fledging Republic in France during the Revolution, ensuring French participation against the British. In 1783 he signed the second Treaty of Paris, by which the British recognized the independence of the United States. Franklin was the only founding father to sign the Declaration of Independence (1776), the Treaty of Paris (1783), and the Constitution of the United States (1789). Throughout his life Franklin furthered his interest in scientific experiment and invention. In December of 1783, he wrote to a friend in England about a recent invention that he had witnessed in Paris: an early experiment in air travel in a balloon. What did Franklin see, and what did it mean to him?

THINKING HISTORICALLY

What evidence do you see in this letter that the scientific revolution was a genuinely revolutionary change? What was revolutionary about it? What evidence do you see that the people of the time thought they were living in a revolutionary age? How would you compare their attitudes with those of people today toward modern technological innovations?

To Sir Joseph Banks[1]

Passy, Dec. 1, 1783.

Dear Sir:—

In mine of yesterday I promised to give you an account of Messrs. Charles & Robert's experiment, which was to have been made this day,

[1] Banks (1743–1820) was a leading British botanist and naturalist. He sailed to the South Pacific with Captain James Cook and served as president of the Royal Society, trustee of the British Museum, and advisor to George III, whom he encouraged to fund numerous scientific expeditions. (He was also an early British recipient of a smallpox vaccination, in 1760.) [Ed.]

Source: Nathan G. Goodman, ed., *The Ingenious Dr. Franklin, Selected Scientific Letters of Benjamin Franklin* (Philadelphia: University of Pennsylvania Press, 1931), 99–102.

and at which I intended to be present. Being a little indisposed, and the air cool, and the ground damp, I declined going into the garden of the Tuileries, where the balloon was placed, not knowing how long I might be obliged to wait there before it was ready to depart, and chose to stay in my carriage near the statue of Louis XV, from whence I could well see it rise, and have an extensive view of the region of air through which, as the wind sat, it was likely to pass. The morning was foggy, but about one o'clock the air became tolerably clear, to the great satisfaction of the spectators, who were infinite, notice having been given of the intended experiment several days before in the papers, so that all Paris was out, either about the Tuileries, on the quays and bridges, in the fields, the streets, at the windows, or on the tops of houses, besides the inhabitants of all the towns and villages of the environs. Never before was a philosophical experiment so magnificently attended. Some guns were fired to give notice that the departure of the balloon was near, and a small one was discharged, which went to an amazing height, there being but little wind to make it deviate from its perpendicular course, and at length the sight of it was lost. Means were used, I am told, to prevent the great balloon's rising so high as might endanger its bursting. Several bags of sand were taken on board before the cord that held it down was cut, and the whole weight being then too much to be lifted, such a quantity was discharged as to permit its rising slowly. Thus it would sooner arrive at that region where it would be in equilibrio with the surrounding air, and by discharging more sand afterwards, it might go higher if desired. Between one and two o'clock, all eyes were gratified with seeing it rise majestically from among the trees, and ascend gradually above the buildings, a most beautiful spectacle. When it was about two hundred feet high, the brave adventurers held out and waved a little white pennant, on both sides [of] their car, to salute the spectators, who returned loud claps of applause. The wind was very little, so that the object though moving to the northward, continued long in view; and it was a great while before the admiring people began to disperse. The persons embarked were Mr. Charles, professor of experimental philosophy, and a zealous promoter of that science; and one of the Messieurs Robert, the very ingenious constructors of the machine. When it arrived at its height, which I suppose might be three or four hundred toises,[2] it appeared to have only horizontal motion. I had a pocket-glass, with which I followed it, till I lost sight first of the men, then of the car, and when I last saw the balloon, it appeared no bigger than a walnut. I write this at seven in the evening. What became of them is not yet known here. I hope they descended by daylight, so as to see and avoid falling among trees or on houses, and that the experiment was completed without any mischievous accident, which the novelty of it and the want of experience might

---

[2] twaz   A height rod equal to 1.949 meters (or about 2 yards). [Ed.]

well occasion. I am the more anxious for the event, because I am not well informed of the means provided for letting themselves down, and the loss of these very ingenious men would not only be a discouragement to the progress of the art, but be a sensible loss to science and society.

I shall inclose one of the tickets of admission, on which the globe was represented, as originally intended, but is altered by the pen to show its real state when it went off. When the tickets were engraved the car was to have been hung to the neck of the globe, as represented by a little drawing I have made in the corner.

I suppose it may have been an apprehension of danger in straining too much the balloon or tearing the silk, that induced the constructors to throw a net over it, fixed to a hoop which went round its middle, and to hang the car to that hoop.

Tuesday morning, December 2d.—I am relieved from my anxiety by hearing that the adventurers descended well near L'Isle Adam before sunset. This place is near seven leagues from Paris. Had the wind blown fresh they might have gone much farther.

If I receive any further particulars of importance, I shall communicate them hereafter.

With great esteem, I am, dear sir, your most obedient and most humble servant,

FRANKLIN

P.S. *Tuesday evening.*—Since writing the above I have received the printed paper and the manuscript containing some particulars of the experiment, which I enclose. I hear further that the travellers had perfect command of their carriage, descending as they pleased by letting some of the inflammable air escape, and rising again by discharging some sand; that they descended over a field so low as to talk with the labourers in passing, and mounted again to pass a hill. The little balloon falling at Vincennes shows that mounting higher it met with a current of air in a contrary direction, an observation that may be of use to future aerial voyagers.

■ REFLECTIONS

Was there a scientific revolution in the seventeenth and eighteenth centuries? By most measures we would have to say "yes." There were new polished-glass instruments with which to observe and measure; books, theories, diagrams, debates, and discoveries emerged at a dizzying pace. Age-old authorities—Aristotle, Ptolemy, even the Bible—were called into question. The wisdom of the ages was interrogated for evidence and forced to submit to tests by experiment.

There was a revolution in the way Europeans looked at their surroundings. In the words of Shakespeare, the great English dramatist, the world became a stage, a spectacle apart that could be viewed and analyzed by objective observers. Nature no longer displayed its forces as omens or metaphors. The rainbow was no longer a sign of hope, the comet a harbinger of divine disapproval. Heavenly events might be explained in the same way as were events on Earth. Newton's rules underline the simplicity of assumptions that nature is uniform and not unnecessarily complex. We can assume that the fire in the fireplace has the same qualities as the fire of the sun, that unchanging qualities of hardness, mobility, or gravity would apply to objects too distant to measure as they do to those within our grasp. Nature follows laws that humans can derive by experiment and induction.

Goldstone reminds us that many of the scientific developments in Europe sprang from foreign innovations, and in some fields Europe was not as advanced as other societies. Lady Mary Montague provides a dramatic example of that fact. Yet the scientific revolution's unique combination of observation and generalization, experimentation and mathematics, induction and deduction established a body of knowledge and a method for research that proved lasting and irreversible.

Why was it that China, so scientifically and technologically adept during the Sung dynasty, pictured hearts and lungs as flower petals in the late-Ming and early-Qing seventeenth century? Was it that Chinese science lost momentum or changed direction? Or does such a question, as Lynda Shaffer warns, judge China unfairly by Western standards? Do the petal hearts reflect a different set of interests rather than a failure of Chinese science?

Chinese scientists excelled in acupuncture, massage, and herbal medicine, while European scientists excelled in surgery. It turned out that the inner workings of the human body were better revealed in surgical dissection than in muscle manipulation or pharmacology. And, as Sugita Gempaku reminds us, the Europeans not only cut and removed, but they also named what they found and tried to understand how it worked. Perhaps the major difference between science in Europe and that in India, China, and Japan in the seventeenth century was one of perspective: Europeans were beginning to imagine the human body as a machine and asking how it worked. In some respects, the metaphor of man as a machine proved more fruitful than organic metaphors of humans as plants or animals.

Asking probing questions and testing the answers also changed our understanding of the heavens. If mathematical calculations indicated that a star would appear at a particular spot in the heavens and it did not, Galileo might just as soon have questioned the observation as the math. From the seventeenth century on, scientists would check one or the other on the assumption that observation and mathematics could be brought together to understand the same event, that they would have to be in agreement, and that such agreement could lead to laws that could then be tested and proved or disproved.

It is this method of inquiry, not the discoveries, that was new. For the scientific method that emerged during this period constituted a systematic means of inquiry based on agreed-upon rules of hypothesis, experimentation, theory testing, law, and dissemination. This scientific inquiry was a social process in two important ways: First, any scientific discovery had to be reproducible and recognized by other scientists to gain credence. Second, a community of scientists was needed to question, dismiss, or validate the work of its members.

Europe in the seventeenth century saw the proliferation of numerous scientific associations, academies, institutes, and public experiments. These numerous organizations testified not only to a growing interest in science but also to a continuing public conversation. Science in Europe thus became a matter of public concern, a popular endeavor. Compare the masses of Parisians Ben Franklin described who turned out to view the balloon experiment with the few physicians gathered around Sugita Gempaku who could learn from the expertise of outcast butchers.

Ultimately, then, the difference between European science and that of India or China in the seventeenth century may have had more to do with society than with culture. The development of modern scientific methods relied on the numerous debates and discussions of a self-conscious class of gentlemen scientists in a Europe where news traveled quickly and ideas could be translated and tested with confidence across numerous borders. To what extent does science everywhere today demonstrate the hallmarks of the seventeenth-century scientific revolution?

20

Enlightenment and Revolution

Europe, the Americas, and India, 1650–1850

■ HISTORICAL CONTEXT

Much of the modern world puts its faith in science, reason, and democracy. The seventeenth-century scientific revolution established reason as the key to understanding nature. During the eighteenth century, philosophy, social organization, and government all came under the critical light of reason. Historians call this movement the "Enlightenment," and its consequences were revolutionary. Most— though, as we shall see, not all—people believed that reason would eventually lead to freedom. Freedom of thought, religion, and association, and political liberties and representative governments were hailed as hallmarks of the Age of Enlightenment.

For some, enlightened society meant a more controlled rather than a more democratic society. Philosophers like Immanuel Kant and Jean Jacques Rousseau wanted people to become free but thought most people were incapable of achieving such a state. Rulers who were called "enlightened despots" believed that the application of reason to society would make people happier, but not necessarily freer.

Ultimately, however, the Enlightenment's faith in reason led to calls for political revolution as well as for schemes of order. In England in the seventeenth century, in America and France at the end of the eighteenth century, and in Latin America shortly thereafter, revolutionary governments were created according to rational principles of liberty and equality that dispatched monarchs and enshrined the rule of the people. In this chapter we will concentrate on the heritage of the Enlightenment, examining competing tendencies toward order and revolution, stability and liberty, equality and freedom. We will also compare the American and the French Revolutions, and these with the later revolutions in Latin America. Finally, we will extend our understanding of the global nature of the Enlightenment by looking at similar developments in India.

768

Map 20.1 Latin American Independence, 1804–1830.

■ THINKING HISTORICALLY

Close Reading and Interpretation of Texts

At the core of the Enlightenment was a trust in reasoned discussion, a belief that people could understand each other, even if they were not in agreement. Such understanding demanded clear and concise communication in a world where the masses were often swayed by fiery sermons and flamboyant rhetoric. But the Enlightenment also put its faith in the written word and a literate public. Ideas were debated face-to-face in the salons and coffeehouses of Europe and its colonies, but it was through letters, diaries, the new world of newspapers, and the burgeoning spread of printed books that the people of the Enlightenment learned what they and their neighbors thought.

It is appropriate, then, for us to read the selections in this chapter—most primary sources—in the spirit in which they were written. We will pay special attention to the words and language that the authors use and will attempt to understand exactly what they meant, even why they chose the words they did. Such explication is a twofold process; we must understand the words first and foremost; then we must strive to understand the words in their proper context, as they were intended by the author. To achieve our first goal, we will paraphrase, a difficult task because the eighteenth-century writing style differs greatly from our own: Sentences are longer and arguments are often complex. Vocabularies were broad during this period, and we may encounter words that are used in ways unknown to us and out of usage today. As to our latter goal, we must try to make the vocabulary and perspective of the authors our own. Grappling with what makes the least sense to us and trying to understand why it was said is the challenge.

1

DAVID HUME

On Miracles, 1748

The European Enlightenment of the eighteenth century was the expression of a new class of intellectuals, independent of the clergy but allied with the rising middle class. Their favorite words were *reason, nature,* and *progress.* They applied the systematic doubt of René Descartes (1596–1650) and the reasoning method of the scientific revolution to human affairs, including religion and politics. With caustic wit and good humor, they asked new questions and popularized new points of view that would eventually revolutionize Western politics and culture. While the French *philosophes* and Voltaire (1694–1778) may be the best known, the Scottish philosopher David Hume (1711–1776) may have been the most brilliant. What does Hume argue in this selection? Does he prove his point to your satisfaction? How does he use reason and nature to make his case? Is reason incompatible with religion?

THINKING HISTORICALLY

The first step in understanding what Hume means in this essay must come from a careful reading—a sentence-by-sentence exploration. Try to paraphrase each sentence, putting it into your own words. For example, you might paraphrase the first sentence like this: "I've found a way to disprove superstition; this method should be useful as long as superstition exists, which may be forever." Notice the content of such words as *just* and *check.* What does Hume mean by these words and by *prodigies?*

Source: *The Philosophical Works of David Hume* (Edinburgh: A. Black and W. Tait, 1826).

The second sentence is a concise definition of the scientific method. How would you paraphrase it? The second and third sentences summarize the method Hume has discovered to counter superstition. What is the meaning of the third sentence?

In the rest of the essay, Hume offers four proofs, or reasons, why miracles do not exist. How would you paraphrase each of these? Do you find these more or less convincing than his more general opening and closing arguments? What does Hume mean by *miracles*?

I flatter myself that I have discovered an argument . . . , which, if just, will, with the wise and learned, be an everlasting check to all kinds of superstitious delusion, and consequently will be useful as long as the world endures; for so long, I presume, will the accounts of miracles and prodigies be found in all history, sacred and profane. . . .

A wise man proportions his belief to the evidence. . . .

A miracle is a violation of the laws of nature; and as a firm and unalterable experience has established these laws, the proof against a miracle, from the very nature of the fact, is as entire as any argument from experience can possibly be imagined. . . . Nothing is esteemed a miracle, if it ever happens in the common course of nature. It is no miracle that a man, seemingly in good health, should die on a sudden; because such a kind of death, though more unusual than any other, has yet been frequently observed to happen. But it is a miracle that a dead man should come to life; because that has never been observed in any age or country. There must, therefore, be an uniform experience against every miraculous event, otherwise the event would not merit that appellation. And as an uniform experience amounts to a proof, there is here a direct and full *proof*, from the nature of the fact, against the existence of any miracle. . . .

(Further) there is not to be found, in all history, any miracle attested by a sufficient number of men, of such unquestioned good sense, education, and learning, as to secure us against all delusion in themselves; of such undoubted integrity, as to place them beyond all suspicion of any design to deceive others; of such credit and reputation in the eyes of mankind, as to have a great deal to lose in case of their being detected in any falsehood. . . .

Secondly, We may observe in human nature a principle which, if strictly examined, will be found to diminish extremely the assurance, which we might, from human testimony, have in any kind of prodigy. . . . The passion of *surprise* and *wonder*, arising from miracles, being an agreeable emotion, gives a sensible tendency towards the belief of those events from which it is derived. . . .

With what greediness are the miraculous accounts of travellers received, their descriptions of sea and land monsters, their relations of wonderful adventures, strange men, and uncouth manners? But if the spirit of religion join itself to the love of wonder, there is an end of common sense; and human testimony, in these circumstances, loses all pretensions to authority. A religionist may be an enthusiast, and imagine he sees what has no reality: He may know his narrative to be false, and yet persevere in it, with the best intentions in the world, for the sake of promoting so holy a cause: Or even where this delusion has not place, vanity, excited by so strong a temptation, operates on him more powerfully than on the rest of mankind in any other circumstances; and self-interest with equal force. . . .

The many instances of forged miracles and prophecies and supernatural events, which, in all ages, have either been detected by contrary evidence, or which detect themselves by their absurdity, prove sufficiently the strong propensity of mankind to the extraordinary and marvellous, and ought reasonably to beget a suspicion against all relations of this kind.[1] . . .

Thirdly, It forms a strong presumption against all supernatural and miraculous relations, that they are observed chiefly to abound among ignorant and barbarous nations; or if a civilized people has ever given admission to any of them, that people will be found to have received them from ignorant and barbarous ancestors, who transmitted them with that inviolable sanction and authority which always attend received opinions. . . .

I may add, as a *fourth* reason, which diminishes the authority of prodigies, that there is no testimony for any, even those which have not been expressly detected, that is not opposed by any infinite number of witnesses; so that not only the miracle destroys the credit of testimony, but the testimony destroys itself. To make this the better understood, let us consider, that in matters of religion, whatever is different is contrary; and that it is impossible the religions of ancient Rome, of Turkey, of Siam, and of China, should all of them be established on any solid foundation. Every miracle, therefore, pretended to have been wrought in any of these religions (and all of them abound in miracles), as its direct scope is to establish the particular system to which it is attributed; so has it the same force, though more indirectly, to overthrow every other system. In destroying a rival system, it likewise destroys the credit of those miracles on which that system was established, so that all the prodigies of different religions are to be regarded as contrary facts, and the evidences of these prodigies, whether weak or strong, as opposite to each other. . . .

Upon the whole, then, it appears, that no testimony for any kind of miracle has ever amounted to a probability, much less to a proof; and that, even supposing it amounted to proof, it would be opposed by another proof, derived from the very nature of the fact which it would endeavour to establish. It is experience only which gives authority to human testimony; and it is the same experience which assures us of the

[1] Accounts of miracles. [Ed.]

laws of nature. When, therefore, these two kinds of experience are contrary, we have nothing to do but to subtract the one from the other, and embrace an opinion either on one side or the other, with that assurance which arises from the remainder. But according to the principle here explained, this subtraction with regard to all popular religions amounts to an entire annihilation; and therefore we may establish it as a maxim, that no human testimony can have such force as to prove a miracle, and make it a just foundation for any such system of religion.

2

JEAN JACQUES ROUSSEAU
The Social Contract, 1762

Jean Jacques Rousseau (1712–1778) was one of the leading thinkers of the Enlightenment, whose ideas were as central as those of Diderot (with whom he studied and quarreled), Voltaire (next to whom he is buried in the Pantheon), and Hume (who sheltered him in England toward the end of his life). Rousseau's indifference to formal religion both reflected and influenced French Enlightenment thought, and his political ideas affected the radicals of the French Revolution, though he died eleven years before its outbreak. In both his native Geneva and France, where he spent most of his life, Rousseau's work was often banned. In fact, most of his work was not published until after his death.

The Social Contract, Or Principles of Political Right (1762) challenged the monarchy and called for a government of the people, a force Rousseau saw not in individuals or the competing classes of a society of unequals, but in a "general will" that was greater than any institution or the sum of the people. Which ideas expressed here would be a threat to the French monarchy or establishment? Why would Rousseau's writing appeal to people who wanted to overthrow the regime?

THINKING HISTORICALLY

The power of Enlightenment thought was its radical willingness to ask, and try to answer, fundamental questions. What are some of the fundamental questions this selection grapples with? What does Rousseau mean by such phrases as the "state of nature," the "social compact," and the "general will"?

Source: Jean Jacques Rousseau, *The Social Contract, Or Principles of Political Right*, trans. G. D. H. Cole. Rendered into HTML and text by Jon Roland of the Constitution Society. Available at www. constitution.org/jjr/socon.htm.

Book I

I mean to inquire if, in the civil order,[1] there can be any sure and legitimate rule of administration, men being taken as they are and laws as they might be. In this inquiry I shall endeavor always to unite what right sanctions with what is prescribed by interest, in order that justice and utility may in no case be divided.

I enter upon my task without proving the importance of the subject. I shall be asked if I am a prince or a legislator, to write on politics. I answer that I am neither, and that is why I do so. If I were a prince or a legislator, I should not waste time in saying what wants doing; I should do it, or hold my peace.

As I was born a citizen of a free State, and a member of the Sovereign,[2] I feel that, however feeble the influence my voice can have on public affairs, the right of voting on them makes it my duty to study them: and I am happy, when I reflect upon governments, to find my inquiries always furnish me with new reasons for loving that of my own country.

1. Subject of the First Book

Man is born free; and everywhere he is in chains. One thinks himself the master of others, and still remains a greater slave than they. How did this change come about? I do not know. What can make it legitimate? That question I think I can answer.

If I took into account only force, and the effects derived from it, I should say: "As long as a people is compelled to obey, and obeys, it does well; as soon as it can shake off the yoke, and shakes it off, it does still better; for, regaining its liberty by the same right as took it away, either it is justified in resuming it, or there was no justification for those who took it away." But the social order is a sacred right which is the basis of all other rights. Nevertheless, this right does not come from nature, and must therefore be founded on conventions. . . .

4. Slavery

Since no man has a natural authority over his fellow, and force creates no right, we must conclude that conventions[3] form the basis of all legitimate authority among men. . . .

So, from whatever aspect we regard the question, the right of slavery is null and void, not only as being illegitimate, but also because it is

---

[1] Civil order: opposed to the state of nature; civic society, the world of citizens. [Ed.]
[2] The ultimate authority, which Rousseau says should be the General Will. [Ed.]
[3] Agreements, compacts. [Ed.]

absurd and meaningless. The words *slave* and *right* contradict each other, and are mutually exclusive. It will always be equally foolish for a man to say to a man or to a people: "I make with you a convention wholly at your expense and wholly to my advantage; I shall keep it as long as I like, and you will keep it as long as I like."

6. *The Social Compact*

I suppose men to have reached the point at which the obstacles in the way of their preservation in the state of nature[4] show their power of resistance to be greater than the resources at the disposal of each individual for his maintenance in that state. That primitive condition can then subsist no longer; and the human race would perish unless it changed its manner of existence.

But, as men cannot engender new forces, but only unite and direct existing ones, they have no other means of preserving themselves than the formation, by aggregation, of a sum of forces great enough to overcome the resistance. These they have to bring into play by means of a single motive power, and cause to act in concert.

This sum of forces can arise only where several persons come together: but, as the force and liberty of each man are the chief instruments of his self-preservation, how can he pledge them without harming his own interests, and neglecting the care he owes to himself? This difficulty, in its bearing on my present subject, may be stated in the following terms:

"*The problem is to find a form of association which will defend and protect with the whole common force the person and goods of each associate, and in which each, while uniting himself with all, may still obey himself alone, and remain as free as before.*" This is the fundamental problem of which the *Social Contract* provides the solution. . . .

. . . [F]or, in the first place, as each gives himself absolutely, the conditions are the same for all; and, this being so, no one has any interest in making them burdensome to others. Moreover, the alienation being without reserve,[5] the union is as perfect as it can be, and no associate has anything more to demand: for, if the individuals retained certain rights, as there would be no common superior to decide between them and the public, each, being on one point his own judge, would ask to be so on all; the state of nature would thus continue, and the association would necessarily become inoperative or tyrannical.

Finally, each man, in giving himself to all, gives himself to nobody; and as there is no associate over whom he does not acquire the same right as he yields others over himself, he gains an equivalent for everything he loses, and an increase of force for the preservation of what he has.

---

[4] A hypothetical or primitive existence before government; a frequent starting point in Enlightenment thinking about government. [Ed.]

[5] Each gives his freedom to the whole freely and completely. [Ed.]

If then we discard from the social compact what is not of its essence, we shall find that it reduces itself to the following terms:

"Each of us puts his person and all his power in common under the supreme direction of the general will, and, in our corporate capacity, we receive each member as an indivisible part of the whole."

3

The American Declaration of Independence, 1776

If anyone had taken a poll of Americans in the thirteen colonies as late as 1775, independence would not have won a majority vote anywhere. Massachusetts might have come close, perhaps, but nowhere in the land was there a definitive urge to separate from the British Empire. Still, three thousand miles was a long way for news, views, appointees, and petitions to travel, and tensions between the colonies and Britain had been growing.

Of course, each side looked at the cost of colonial administration differently. The British believed that they had carried a large part of the costs of migration, administration of trade, and control of the sea, while the colonists resented the humiliation resulting from their lack of political representation and the often inept royal officials and punitive legislation imposed on them from afar by the Parliament and the king.

By the spring of 1775, events were rapidly pushing the colonies toward independence. In April, British troops engaged colonial forces at Lexington and Concord, instigating a land war that was to last until 1781. In the midst of other urgent business, most notably raising an army, the Continental Congress asked a committee that included Thomas Jefferson, Benjamin Franklin, and John Adams to compose a statement outlining these and other reasons for separation from Britain. Jefferson wrote the first draft, the bulk of which became the final version accepted by the Continental Congress on July 4, 1776.

The Declaration of Independence was preeminently a document of the Enlightenment. Its principal author, Thomas Jefferson, exemplified the Enlightenment intellectual. Conversant in European literature, law, and political thought, he made significant contributions to

---

Source: *A Documentary History of the United States*, ed. Richard D. Heffner (New York: Penguin Books, 1991), 15–18.

eighteenth-century knowledge in natural science and architecture. Benjamin Franklin and other delegates to the Congress in Philadelphia were similarly accomplished.

It is no wonder, then, that the Declaration and the establishment of an independent United States of America should strike the world as the realization of the Enlightenment's basic tenets. That a wholly new country could be created by people with intelligence and foresight, according to principles of reason, and to realize human liberty, was heady stuff.

What were the goals of the authors of this document? In what ways was the Declaration a call for democracy? In what ways was it not?

THINKING HISTORICALLY

Before interpreting any document, we must read it carefully and put it into context—that is, determine the what, where, and why. Some of this information may be available in the text itself. For instance, to whom is the Declaration addressed? What is the reason given for writing it?

The urgency and immediate purpose of the Declaration of Independence separate it from the more theoretical *Social Contract* by Rousseau. But the age of Enlightenment enshrined similar concerns, and therefore similar ideas and language. What words or phrases are similar in both documents? How is their meaning similar or different?

Consider also the disparity between the lofty sentiments of liberty and independence and the existence of slavery in the Americas. How is Rousseau's treatment of slavery different from Jefferson's? How is it possible that Jefferson and some of the signers of the Declaration could own slaves while declaring it "self-evident that all men are created equal"? To whom did this statement apply?

In Congress, July 4, 1776, the Unanimous Declaration of the Thirteen United States of America

When in the course of human events, it becomes necessary for one people to dissolve the political bands which have connected them with another, and to assume among the powers of the earth, the separate and equal station to which the Laws of Nature and of Nature's God entitle them, a decent respect to the opinions of mankind requires that they should declare the causes which impel them to the separation.

We hold these truths to be self-evident, that all men are created equal, that they are endowed by their Creator with certain unalienable rights, that among these are life, liberty, and the pursuit of happiness. That to secure these rights, governments are instituted among men, deriving their just powers from the consent of the governed. That whenever any form of government becomes destructive of these ends, it is the right of the people to alter or to abolish it, and to institute new government, laying its foundation on such principles and organizing its powers in such form, as to them shall seem most likely to effect their safety and happiness. Prudence, indeed, will dictate that governments long established should not be changed for light and transient causes; and accordingly all experience hath shown, that mankind are more disposed to suffer, while evils are sufferable, than to right themselves by abolishing the forms to which they are accustomed. But when a long train of abuses and usurpations, pursuing invariably the same object evinces a design to reduce them under absolute despotism, it is their right, it is their duty, to throw off such government, and to provide new guards for their future security. Such has been the patient sufferance of these Colonies; and such is now the necessity which constrains them to alter their former systems of government. The history of the present King of Great Britain is a history of repeated injuries and usurpations, all having in direct object the establishment of an absolute tyranny over these States. To prove this, let facts be submitted to a candid world.

He has refused his assent to laws, the most wholesome and necessary for the public good.

He has forbidden his Governors to pass laws of immediate and pressing importance, unless suspended in their operation till his assent should be obtained; and when so suspended, he has utterly neglected to attend to them.

He has refused to pass other laws for the accommodation of large districts of people, unless those people would relinquish the right of representation in the Legislature, a right inestimable to them and formidable to tyrants only.

He has called together legislative bodies at places unusual, uncomfortable, and distant from the depository of their public records, for the sole purpose of fatiguing them into compliance with his measures.

He has dissolved representative houses repeatedly, for opposing with manly firmness his invasions on the rights of the people.

He has refused for a long time, after such dissolutions, to cause others to be elected; whereby the legislative powers, incapable of annihilation, have returned to the people at large for their exercise; the State remaining in the meantime exposed to all the dangers of invasion from without and convulsions within.

He has endeavoured to prevent the population of these states; for that purpose obstructing the laws of naturalization of foreigners; refusing to pass others to encourage their migration hither, and raising the conditions of new appropriations of lands.

He has obstructed the administration of justice, by refusing his assent to laws for establishing judiciary powers.

He has made judges dependent on his will alone, for the tenure of their offices, and the amount and payment of their salaries.

He has erected a multitude of new offices, and sent hither swarms of officers to harass our people, and eat out their substance.

He has kept among us, in times of peace, standing armies without the consent of our legislatures.

He has affected to render the military independent of and superior to the civil power.

He has combined with others to subject us to a jurisdiction foreign to our constitution, and unacknowledged by our laws; giving his assent to their acts of pretended legislation:

For quartering large bodies of armed troops among us:

For protecting them, by a mock trial, from punishment for any murders which they should commit on the inhabitants of these States:

For cutting off our trade with all parts of the world:

For imposing taxes on us without our consent:

For depriving us in many cases, of the benefits of trial by jury:

For transporting us beyond seas to be tried for pretended offences:

For abolishing the free system of English laws in a neighbouring Province, establishing therein an arbitrary government, and enlarging its boundaries so as to render it at once an example and fit instrument for introducing the same absolute rule into these Colonies:

For taking away our Charters, abolishing our most valuable laws, and altering fundamentally the forms of our governments:

For suspending our own Legislatures, and declaring themselves invested with power to legislate for us in all cases whatsoever.

He has abdicated government here, by declaring us out of his protection and waging war against us.

He has plundered our seas, ravaged our coasts, burnt our towns, and destroyed the lives of our people.

He is at this time transporting large armies of foreign mercenaries to complete the works of death, desolation, and tyranny, already begun with circumstances of cruelty and perfidy scarcely paralleled in the most barbarous ages, and totally unworthy the head of a civilized nation.

He has constrained our fellow citizens taken captive on the high seas to bear arms against their country, to become the executioners of their friends and brethren, or to fall themselves by their hands.

He has excited domestic insurrections amongst us, and has endeavoured to bring on the inhabitants of our frontiers, the merciless Indian savages, whose known rule of warfare, is an undistinguished destruction of all ages, sexes, and conditions.

In every state of these oppressions we have petitioned for redress in the most humble terms: our repeated petitions have been answered only by repeated injury. A prince whose character is thus marked by every act which may define a tyrant is unfit to be the ruler of a free people.

Nor have we been wanting in attention to our British brethren. We have warned them from time to time of attempts by their legislature to extend an unwarrantable jurisdiction over us. We have reminded them of the circumstances of our emigration and settlement here. We have appealed to their native justice and magnanimity, and we have conjured them by the ties of our common kindred to disavow these usurpations, which would inevitably interrupt our connections and correspondence. They too have been deaf to the voice of justice and of consanguinity. We must, therefore, acquiesce in the necessity, which denounces our separation, and hold them, as we hold the rest of mankind, enemies in war, in peace friends.

We, therefore, the Representatives of the United States of America, in General Congress assembled, appealing to the Supreme Judge of the world for the rectitude of our intentions, do, in the name, and by authority of the good people of these Colonies, solemnly publish and declare, That these United Colonies are, and of right ought to be Free and Independent States; that they are absolved from all allegiance to the British Crown, and that all political connection between them and the State of Great Britain, is and ought to be totally dissolved; and that as Free and Independent States, they have full power to levy war, conclude peace, contract alliances, establish commerce, and to do all other acts and things which Independent States may of right do. And for the support of this declaration, with a firm reliance on the protection of Divine Province, we mutually pledge to each other our lives, our fortunes, and our sacred honor.

4

ABIGAIL ADAMS AND JOHN ADAMS

Remember the Ladies, 1776

As a delegate to the Second Continental Congress, future American president John Adams was in Philadelphia in the spring of 1776, collaborating on writing the Declaration of Independence. In the meantime his wife, Abigail, assumed the role of the head of the household, caring for their children and managing the family farm in Braintree,

Source: Letters from Abigail Adams to John Adams, 31 March–5 April 1776, John Adams to Abigail Adams, 14 April 1776, Abigail Adams to John Adams, 7–9 May 1776 [electronic editions]. *Adams Family Papers: An Electronic Archive* (Boston: Massachusetts Historical Society, 2002), http://www.masshist.org/digitaladams/.

Massachusetts. Their relationship had always been characterized by robust intellectual debate, and John even referred to his wife as "Sister Delegate." In their famous correspondence during this period, Abigail urged her husband to "remember the ladies" as he and his fellow revolutionaries constructed the basis for the new American government. What did she mean by this? How did her husband respond? What did she think of his response?

THINKING HISTORICALLY

Enlightenment thinkers often employed grand abstractions like "all men are created equal" for both their rational simplicity and their dramatic revolutionary claim. As a consequence, such abstractions were often more sweeping in their implications than even the revolutionaries of the era intended. For example, John and Abigail Adams, both of whom opposed slavery, did not intend for "all men" to include blacks, either enslaved or free. But men like Adams might not have seriously considered how women would respond to the proclamation of universal equality. What in Adams's response to his wife reveals that he did not intend to extend universal equality to women? Does his response somehow undermine the Declaration of Independence?

Letter from Abigail Adams to John Adams, 31 March–5 April 1776

. . . I long to hear that you have declared an independency—and by the way in the new Code of Laws which I suppose it will be necessary for you to make I desire you would Remember the Ladies, and be more generous and favourable to them than your ancestors. Do not put such unlimited power into the hands of the Husbands. Remember all Men would be tyrants if they could. If perticuliar care and attention is not paid to the Ladies we are determined to foment a Rebellion, and will not hold ourselves bound by any Laws in which we have no voice, or Representation.

That your Sex is Naturally Tyrannical is a Truth so thoroughly established as to admit of no dispute, but such of you as wish to be happy willingly give up the harsh title of Master for the more tender and endearing one of Friend. Why then, not put it out of the power of the vicious and the Lawless to use us with cruelty and indignity [with impunity]. Men of Sense in all Ages abhor those customs which treat us only as the vassals of your Sex. Regard us then as Beings placed by providence under your protection and in imitation of the Supreme Being make use of the power only for our happiness.

Letter from John Adams to Abigail Adams, 14 April 1776

. . . As to Declarations of Independency, be patient. Read our Privateering Laws, and our Commercial Laws. What signifies a Word.

As to your extraordinary Code of Laws, I cannot but laugh. We have been told that our Struggle has loosened the bands of Government every where. That Children and Apprentices were disobedient—that schools and Colleges were grown turbulent—that Indians slighted their Guardians and Negroes grew insolent to their Masters.

But your Letter was the first Intimation that another Tribe more numerous and powerfull than all the rest were grown discontented.—This is rather too coarse a Compliment but you are so saucy, I wont blot it out.

Depend upon it, We know better than to repeal our Masculine systems. Altho they are in full Force, you know they are little more than Theory. We dare not exert our Power in its full Latitude. We are obliged to go fair, and softly, and in Practice you know We are the subjects. We have only the Name of Masters, and rather than give up this, which would compleatly subject Us to the Despotism of the Peticoat, I hope General Washington, and all our brave Heroes would fight. I am sure every good Politician would plot, as long as he would against Despotism, Empire, Monarchy, Aristocracy, Oligarchy, or Ochlocracy. . . .

Letter from Abigail Adams to John Adams, 7–9 May 1776

. . . I can not say that I think you very generous to the Ladies, for whilst you are proclaiming peace and good will to Men, Emancipating all Nations, you insist upon retaining an absolute power over Wives. But you must remember that Arbitary power is like most other things which are very hard, very liable to be broken—and notwithstanding all your wise Laws and Maxims we have it in our power not only to free ourselves but to subdue our Masters, and without violence throw both your natural and legal authority at our feet. . . .

5

The French Declaration of the Rights of Man and Citizen, 1789

The founding of the Republic of the United States of America provided a model for other peoples chafing under oppressive rule to emulate. Not surprisingly then, when the French movement to end political injustices turned to revolution in 1789 and the revolutionaries convened at the National Assembly, the Marquis de Lafayette (1757–1834), hero of the American Revolution, proposed a Declaration of the Rights of Man and Citizen. Lafayette had the American Declaration in mind, and he had the assistance of Thomas Jefferson, present in Paris as the first United States ambassador to France.

While the resulting document appealed to the French revolutionaries, the French were not able to start afresh as the Americans had done. In 1789 Louis XVI was still king of France: He could not be made to leave by a turn of phrase. Nor were men created equal in France in 1789. Those born into the nobility led lives different from those born into the Third Estate (the 99 percent of the population who were not nobility or clergy), and they had different legal rights as well. This disparity was precisely what the revolutionaries and the Declaration sought to change. Inevitably, though, such change would prove to be a more violent and revolutionary proposition than it had been in the American colonies.

In what ways did the Declaration of the Rights of Man and Citizen resemble the American Declaration of Independence? In what ways was it different? Which was more democratic?

THINKING HISTORICALLY

Compare the language of the Declaration of the Rights of Man and Citizen with that of Rousseau and that of Jefferson. In what ways does it borrow from each? Like both prior documents, the French Declaration is full of abstract, universal principles. But notice how such abstractions can claim our consent by their rationality without informing us as to how they will be implemented. What is meant by the first right, for instance? What does it mean to say that men are "born free"? Why is it necessary to distinguish between "born" and "remain"? What is meant by the phrase "general usefulness"? Do statements like these increase people's liberties, or are they intentionally vague so they can be interpreted at will?

The slogan of the French Revolution was "Liberty, Equality, Fraternity." Which of the rights in the French Declaration emphasize liberty, which equality? Can these two goals be opposed to each other? Explain how.

Source: *A Documentary History of the French Revolution*, ed. John Hall Stewart (London: Macmillan, 1979), 113–15.

The representatives of the French people, organized in National Assembly, considering that ignorance, forgetfulness, or contempt of the rights of man are the sole causes of public misfortunes and of the corruption of governments, have resolved to set forth in a solemn declaration the natural, inalienable, and sacred rights of man, in order that such declaration, continually before all members of the social body, may be a perpetual reminder of their rights and duties; in order that the acts of the legislative power and those of the executive power may constantly be compared with the aim of every political institution and may accordingly be more respected; in order that the demands of the citizens, founded henceforth upon simple and incontestable principles, may always be directed towards the maintenance of the Constitution and the welfare of all.

Accordingly, the National Assembly recognizes and proclaims, in the presence and under the auspices of the Supreme Being, the following rights of man and citizen.

1. Men are born and remain free and equal in rights; social distinctions may be based only upon general usefulness.

2. The aim of every political association is the preservation of the natural and inalienable rights of man; these rights are liberty, property, security, and resistance to oppression.

3. The source of all sovereignty resides essentially in the nation; no group, no individual may exercise authority not emanating expressly therefrom.

4. Liberty consists of the power to do whatever is not injurious to others; thus the enjoyment of the natural rights of every man has for its limits only those that assure other members of society the enjoyment of those same rights; such limits may be determined only by law.

5. The law has the right to forbid only actions which are injurious to society. Whatever is not forbidden by law may not be prevented, and no one may be constrained to do what it does not prescribe.

6. Law is the expression of the general will; all citizens have the right to concur personally, or through their representatives, in its formation; it must be the same for all, whether it protects or punishes. All citizens, being equal before it, are equally admissible to all public offices, positions, and employments, according to their capacity, and without other distinction than that of virtues and talents.

7. No man may be accused, arrested, or detained except in the cases determined by law, and according to the forms prescribed thereby. Whoever solicit, expedite, or execute arbitrary orders, or have them executed, must be punished; but every citizen summoned or apprehended in pursuance of the law must obey immediately; he renders himself culpable by resistance.

8. The law is to establish only penalties that are absolutely and obviously necessary; and no one may be punished except by virtue of a law established and promulgated prior to the offence and legally applied.

9. Since every man is presumed innocent until declared guilty, if arrest be deemed indispensable, all unnecessary severity for securing the person of the accused must be severely repressed by law.

10. No one is to be disquieted because of his opinions, even religious, provided their manifestation does not disturb the public order established by law.

11. Free communication of ideas and opinions is one of the most precious of the rights of man. Consequently, every citizen may speak, write, and print freely, subject to responsibility for the abuse of such liberty in the cases determined by law.

12. The guarantee of the rights of man and citizen necessitates a public force; therefore, is instituted for the advantage of all and not for the particular benefit of those to whom it is entrusted.

13. For the maintenance of the public force and for the expenses of administration a common tax is indispensable; it must be assessed equally on all citizens in proportion to their means.

14. Citizens have the right to ascertain, by themselves or through their representatives, the necessity of the public tax, to consent to it freely, to supervise its use, and to determine its quota, assessment, payment, and duration.

15. Society has the right to require of every public agent an accounting of his administration.

16. Every society in which the guarantee of rights is not assured or the separation of powers not determined has no constitution at all.

17. Since property is a sacred and inviolate right, no one may be deprived thereof unless a legally established public necessity obviously requires it, and upon condition of a just and previous indemnity.

6

OLYMPE DE GOUGES

French Declaration of Rights for Women, 1791

Olympe de Gouges (1748–1793) was a French playwright whose writings became increasingly political as the French Revolution progressed after 1789. When the revolutionary government of the National Assembly passed a new constitution in 1791 with the Declaration of the Rights of Man and Citizen of 1789 as the preamble, and still did not give women the vote, de Gouges wrote the following document.

Source: http://fr.wikisource.org/wiki/D%C3%A9claration_des_droits_de_la_femme_et_de_la_citoyenne. Translated from the French by the editor.

What was Olympe de Gouges's argument? What specific rights for women was she seeking?

THINKING HISTORICALLY

Compare this document with the Declaration of the Rights of Man and Citizen. What are the similarities and differences? What is the purpose of the similarities? What is the significance of the differences?

Mankind, are you capable of being just? It is a woman who asks the question; you will not deprive her of that right at least. Tell me? Who has given you the soverign empire to oppress my sex? Your strength? Your talents? Observe the creator in his wisdom; survey nature in all its grandeur, with which you seem to want to be in harmony, and give me, if you dare, an example of this tryanical empire.

Go back to animals. Consult the elements, study plants, finally glance at all the modifications of organic matter; and surrender to the evidence as I offer you the means; search, probe, and distinguish, if you can, the sexes in the administration of nature. Everywhere you will find them mingled, everywhere they cooperate in the harmonious unity of this immortal masterpiece.

Man alone has raised his exception to a principle. Bizarre, blind, bloated with science and degenerated, in a century of enlightenment and wisdom, in the crassest ignorance, he wants to command as a despot a sex which has received all intellectual faculties; he pretends to be revolutionary, and claims his rights to equality, in order to say nothing more about it.

Preamble

Mothers, daughters, sisters, representatives of the nation, demand to be constituted a national assembly. Considering that ignorance, forgetfulness or contempt of the rights of women are the only causes of public misfortunes and government corruption, they resolve to expose in a solemn declaration, the natural, inalienable, and sacred rights of women, so that this declaration, being constantly before the public, reminds them constantly of their rights and their duties, so that the authoritative acts of men and women are always comparable to the goals of every political institution, and deserving of respect, so that citizens' demands, from now on based on simple and incontestable principles, will always support the constitution, good morals, and the happiness of all.

Consequently, the sex that is as superior in beauty as in the courage of maternity recognizes and declares, in the presence and under the auspices of the Supreme Being, the following Rights of Woman as Citizen.

I. Woman is born free and remains equal to man in rights. Social distinctions may be founded only on general usefulness.

II. The aim of every political association is the preservation of the natural and inalienable rights of Women and Men: these are the rights to liberty, property, security, and especially the resistance to oppression.

III. The source of all sovereignty resides essentially in the Nation, which is the meeting of women and men: no body, no individual, may exercise authority not emanating expressly therefrom.

IV. Liberty and Justice consist of restoring the rights of others; since the exercise of the rights of women has no limits other than those imposed by perpetual male tyranny, these limits must be made to conform to natural law and reason.

V. Laws of nature and reason forbid all acts harmful to society; everything which is not prohibited by these wise and divine laws cannot be prevented, and no one can be constrained to do what they do not prescribe.

VI. Law is be the expression of the general will; all citizens, male and female, have the right to concur personally or through their representatives in its formation; it must be the same for all; all citizens being equal before it, are equally admissable to all public offices, positions, and employments, according to their capacity and without other distinction than that of virtues and talents. . . .

X. No one is to be disquieted because of his opinions; woman has the right to mount the scaffold; she must equally have the right to mount the rostrum, provided that her demonstrations do not disturb the legally established public order.

XI. The free communication of thoughts and opinions is one of the most precious rights of woman, since that liberty assures recognition of children by their fathers. Any female citizen thus may say freely, I am the mother of a child which belongs to you, without being forced by a barbarous prejudice to hide the truth; subject to responsibility for the abuse of this liberty in cases determined by law. . . .

XIII. For the maintenance of the public force and the expenses of administration, the contributions of woman and man are equal; she shares all the duties and all the painful tasks; therefore, she must have the same share in the distribution of positions, employment, offices, honors, and jobs. . . .

XVI. Every society in which the guarantee of rights is not assured or the separation of powers not determined has no constitution at all; the constitution is void if the majority of individuals comprising the nation have not cooperated in drafting it.

XVII. Property belongs to both sexes whether united or separate; for each it is an inviolable and sacred right; no one may be deprived thereof unless a legally established public necessity obviously requires it, and upon condition of a just and previous indemnity.

7

TOUSSAINT L'OUVERTURE
Letter to the Directory, 1797

When the French revolutionaries proclaimed the Declaration of the Rights of Man and Citizen in 1789, the French colony of Saint-Domingue[1] (now Haiti) contained a half million African slaves, most of whom worked on the sugar plantations that made France one of the richest countries in the world. Thus, the French were confronted with the difficult problem of reconciling their enlightened principles with the extremely profitable, but fundamentally unequal, institution of slavery.

French revolutionaries remained locked in debate about this issue when in 1791, the slaves of Saint-Domingue organized a revolt that culminated in establishing Haiti's national independence twelve years later. François Dominique Toussaint L'Ouverture,* a self-educated Haitian slave, led the revolt and the subsequent battles against the French planter class and French armies, as well as the Spanish forces of neighboring Santo Domingo—the eastern side of the island now known as the Dominican Republic—and the antirevolutionary forces of Britain, all of whom vied for control of the island at the end of the eighteenth century.

---

* too SAN   loo vehr TUR

[1] san doh MANG   *Santo Domingo* was the Spanish name for the eastern half of Hispaniola (now the Dominican Republic). *Saint-Domingue* was the French name for the western half of the island, now Haiti. *San Domingo*, which is used in the text, is a nineteenth-century abbreviation for *Saint-Domingue*. To further complicate matters, both the Spanish and French sometimes used their term for the whole island of Hispaniola. Spain controlled the entire island until 1697, when the Spanish recognized French control of the west.

Source: Toussaint L'Ouverture, "Letter to the Directory, November 5, 1797," in *The Black Jacobins*, ed. C. L. R. James (New York: Vintage Books, 1989), 195–97.

At first Toussaint enjoyed the support of the revolutionary government in Paris; in the Decree of 16 Pluviôse[2] (1794) the National Convention abolished slavery in the colonies. But after 1795 the revolution turned on itself, and Toussaint feared that the new conservative government, called the Directory, might send troops to restore slavery on the island.

In 1797 he wrote the Directory the letter that follows. Notice how Toussaint negotiated a difficult situation. How did he try to reassure the government of his allegiance to France? At the same time, how did he attempt to convince the Directory that a return to slavery was unthinkable?

THINKING HISTORICALLY

Notice how Toussaint defines different groups of people. What does he mean, for instance, by "the proprietors of San Domingo" as opposed to "the people of San Domingo"? What does he mean by "the colonists" and "our common enemies"? How does the use of these terms aid his cause?

... The impolitic and incendiary discourse of Vaublanc[3] has not affected the blacks nearly so much as their certainty of the projects which the proprietors of San Domingo are planning: insidious declarations should not have any effect in the eyes of wise legislators who have decreed liberty for the nations. But the attempts on that liberty which the colonists propose are all the more to be feared because it is with the veil of patriotism that they cover their detestable plans. We know that they seek to impose some of them on you by illusory and specious promises, in order to see renewed in this colony its former scenes of horror. Already perfidious emissaries have stepped in among us to ferment the destructive leaven prepared by the hands of liberticides. But they will not succeed. I swear it by all that liberty holds most sacred. My attachment to France, my knowledge of the blacks, make it my duty not to leave you ignorant either of the crimes which they meditate or the oath that we renew, to bury ourselves under the ruins of a country revived by liberty rather than suffer the return of slavery.

It is for you, Citizens Directors, to turn from over our heads the storm which the eternal enemies of our liberty are preparing in the shades

---

[2] PLOO vee ohs   Rainy; the name of the second winter month according to the revolutionary calendar.

[3] Vincent-Marie Viénot, Count of Vaublanc (1756–1845). Born into an aristocratic family in San Domingo, he was a French royalist politician. In Paris in September 1797, he gave a speech intended to impeach republican Directors and trigger a royalist coup. [Ed.]

of silence. It is for you to enlighten the legislature, it is for you to prevent the enemies of the present system from spreading themselves on our unfortunate shores to sully it with new crimes. Do not allow our brothers, our friends, to be sacrificed to men who wish to reign over the ruins of the human species. But no, your wisdom will enable you to avoid the dangerous snares which our common enemies hold out for you. . . .

I send you with this letter a declaration which will acquaint you with the unity that exists between the proprietors of San Domingo who are in France, those in the United States, and those who serve under the English banner. You will see there a resolution, unequivocal and carefully constructed, for the restoration of slavery; you will see there that their determination to succeed has led them to envelop themselves in the mantle of liberty in order to strike it more deadly blows. You will see that they are counting heavily on my complacency in lending myself to their perfidious views by my fear for my children. It is not astonishing that these men who sacrifice their country to their interests are unable to conceive how many sacrifices a true love of country can support in a better father than they, since I unhesitatingly base the happiness of my children on that of my country, which they and they alone wish to destroy.

I shall never hesitate between the safety of San Domingo and my personal happiness; but I have nothing to fear. It is to the solicitude of the French Government that I have confided my children. . . . I would tremble with horror if it was into the hands of the colonists that I had sent them as hostages; but even if it were so, let them know that in punishing them for the fidelity of their father, they would only add one degree more to their barbarism, without any hope of ever making me fail in my duty. . . . Blind as they are! They cannot see how this odious conduct on their part can become the signal of new disasters and irreparable misfortunes, and that far from making them regain what in their eyes liberty for all has made them lose, they expose themselves to a total ruin and the colony to its inevitable destruction. Do they think that men who have been able to enjoy the blessing of liberty will calmly see it snatched away? They supported their chains only so long as they did not know any condition of life more happy than that of slavery. But to-day when they have left it, if they had a thousand lives they would sacrifice them all rather than be forced into slavery again. But no, the same hand which has broken our chains will not enslave us anew. France will not revoke her principles, she will not withdraw from us the greatest of her benefits. She will protect us against all our enemies; she will not permit her sublime morality to be perverted, those principles which do her most honour to be destroyed, her most beautiful achievement to be degraded, and her Decree of 16 Pluviôse which so honours humanity to be revoked. *But if, to re-establish slavery in San Domingo, this was done, then I declare to you it would be to attempt the impossible: we have known how to face dangers to obtain our liberty, we shall know how to brave death to maintain it.*

This, Citizens Directors, is the morale of the people of San Domingo, those are the principles that they transmit to you by me.

My own you know. It is sufficient to renew, my hand in yours, the oath that I have made, to cease to live before gratitude dies in my heart, before I cease to be faithful to France and to my duty, before the god of liberty is profaned and sullied by the liberticides, before they can snatch from my hands that sword, those arms, which France confided to me for the defence of its rights and those of humanity, for the triumph of liberty and equality.

8

DIPESH CHAKRABARTY

Compassion and the Enlightenment, 2000

In this essay, a modern historian argues that the Enlightenment was not confined to Europe and was more profound than is often thought. Here Chakrabarty demonstrates an Indian Enlightenment in the northeastern region of Bengal. He further reveals the profound way in which the Enlightenment changed not only peoples' ideas but also their feelings, signaling the beginning of the modern self. What does he mean by "the modern self"? What, according to the author, is the role of reason and compassion in creating the modern self? How did the Enlightenment change human feelings?

Compare the ideas noted in this essay of the Bengali Indian authors, Rammohun Roy and Iswarchandra Vidyasagar, with the ideas of European Enlightenment thinkers that you have read in this chapter. How is Roy's compassion for women similar to, or different from, that of Abigail Adams and Olympe de Gouges? How is it like the compassion of Toussaint?

THINKING HISTORICALLY

Chakrabarty underscores the use of some key Enlightenment concepts by these Bengali authors. What does he mean by "compassion in general"? What are the connections, according to Chakrabarty, among such concepts as suffering, compassion, reason, natural sentiments, universality, and custom?

Source: Dipesh Chakrabarty, *Provincializing Europe: Postcolonial Thought and Historical Difference*, Princeton Studies in Culture/Power/History (Princeton: Princeton University Press, 2000), 119–24.

The capacity to notice and document suffering (even if it be one's own suffering) from the position of a generalized and necessarily disembodied observer is what marks the beginnings of the modern self. This self has to be generalizable in principle; in other words, it should be such that it signifies a position available for occupation by anybody with proper training. If it were said, for instance, that only a particular type of person—such as a Budhha or a Christ—was capable of noticing suffering and of being moved by it, one would not be talking of a generalized subject position. To be a Budhha or Christ is not within the reach of everybody through simple education and training. So the capacity for sympathy must be seen as a potential inherent in the nature of man in general and not in the uniqueness of a particular person. Such a "natural theory of sentiments," as we shall see, was indeed argued by Enlightenment philosophers such as David Hume and Adam Smith.

A critical distinction also has to be made between the act of displaying suffering and that of observing or facing the sufferer. To display suffering in order to elicit sympathy and assistance is a very old—and perhaps universal and still current—practice. The deformed beggars of medieval Europe or of contemporary Indian or U.S. cities are subjects of suffering, but they are not disembodied subjects. The sufferer here is an embodied self, which is always a particular self, grounded in this or that body. Nor would the sympathy felt for only a particular sufferer (such as a kin or a friend) be "modern" in my sense. The person who is not an immediate sufferer but who has the capacity to become a secondary sufferer through sympathy for a generalized picture of suffering, and who documents this suffering in the interest of eventual social intervention—such a person occupies the position of the modern subject. In other words, the moment of the modern observation of suffering is a certain moment of self-recognition on the part of an abstract, general human being. It is as though a person who is able to see in himself or herself the general human also recognizes the same figure in the particular sufferer, so that the moment of recognition is a moment when the general human splits into the two mutually recognizing and mutually constitutive figures of the sufferer and the observer of suffering. It was argued, however, in the early part of the nineteenth century that this could not happen without the aid of reason, for habit and custom— unopposed by reason—could blunt the natural human capacity for sympathy. Reason, that is, education in rational argumentation, was seen as a critical factor in helping to realize in the modern person this capacity for seeing the general.

Something like such a natural theory of sentiments was argued, in effect, by the two most important nineteenth-century Bengali social reformers who exerted themselves on questions concerning the plight of widows: Rammohun Roy (1772/4–1833) and Iswarchandra Vidyasagar (1820–1901). Roy was instrumental in the passing of the act that made *sati* illegal in 1829, and Vidyasagar successfully agitated for widows to have the legal right to remarry, a right enshrined in the Act for the Remarriage of Hindu Widows, 1856. These legal interventions also allow us to make a further distinction between suffering as viewed by religions such as Buddhism and suffering as a subject of modern social thought. In religious thought, suffering is existential. It shadows man in his life. In social thought, however, suffering is not an existential category. It is specific and hence open to secular interventions.

Rammohun Roy's well-known tract entitled *Brief Remarks Regarding Modern Encroachments on the Ancient Right of Females*, was one of the first written arguments in modern India in favor of women's right to property. This document on property rights also discusses the place of sentiments such as cruelty, distress, wounding feelings, misery, and so on, in human relations. Both strands—rights and sentiments—were intertwined in Roy's argument connecting the question of property with the issue of sentiments, and both saw suffering as an historical and eradicable problem in society:

> In short a widow, according to the [current] exposition of the law, can receive nothing . . . [unless her husband dies] leaving two or more sons, and all of them survive and be inclined to allot a share to their mother. . . . The consequence is, that a woman who is looked upon as the sole mistress of a family one day, on the next becomes dependent on her sons, and subject to the slights of her daughters-in-law. . . . Cruel sons often wound the feelings of their dependent mothers. . . . Step-mothers, who are often numerous on account of polygamy, are still more shamefully neglected in general by their step-sons, and sometimes dreadfully treated by their sisters-in-law. . . . [The] restraints on female inheritance encourage, in a great degree, polygamy, a frequent source of the greatest misery in native families.[1]

There are two interesting features of this document that make it the work of a modern observer of suffering. First, in observing this cruelty to widows and women, Roy put himself in the transcendental position of the modern subject. This becomes clear if we look closely at the following sentence of his text: "How distressing it must be to the female community and to those who interest themselves in their behalf, to

[1] Rammohun Roy, "Brief Remarks Regarding Modern Encroachments on the Ancient Rights of Females," in Ajitkumar Ghosh, ed., *Rammohan rachanabali* (Calcutta: Haraf Prakashani, 1973), pp. 496–497.

observe daily that several daughters in a rich family can prefer no claim to any portion of the property . . . left by their deceased father . . . ; while they . . . are exposed to be given in marriage to individuals who already have several wives and have no means of maintaining them."[2] Roy presents himself here both as a subject experiencing affect — "distress" — as well as a representative subject, one who "interests [himself] in their [women's] behalf." The capacity for sympathy is what unites the representative person with those who are represented; they share the same "distress." The second clause in the sentence refers to a new type of representation: people who took an interest in women's condition on behalf of women. But who were these women? They were not particular, specific women marked by their belonging to particular families or particular networks of kinship. Women here are a collective subject; the expression "female community" connotes a general community. It is this "general community" that shares the distress of a Rammohun Roy, the observer who observes on behalf of this collective community. And therefore the feeling of "distress" that Rammohun Roy speaks of refers to a new kind of compassion, something one could feel for suffering beyond one's immediate family. Compassion in general, we could call it.

But from where would such compassion or sympathy spring? What made it possible for a Rammohun or Vidyasagar to feel this "compassion in general" that most members of their community (presumably) did not yet feel? How would society train itself to make this compassion a part of the comportment of every person, so that compassion became a generally present sentiment in society? It is on this point that both Rammohun and Vidyasagar gave an answer remarkable for its affiliation to the European Enlightenment. Reason, they argued in effect, was what could release the flow of the compassion that was naturally present in all human beings, for only reason could dispel the blindness induced by custom and habit. Reasonable human beings would see suffering and that would put to work the natural human capacity for sympathy, compassion, and pity.

Rammohun raised the question of compassion in a pointed manner in his 1819 answer to Kashinath Tarkabagish's polemical tract *Bidhayak nishedhak shombad* directed against his own position on *sati*. "What is a matter of regret," he said, "is that the fact of witnessing with your own eyes women who have thus suffered much sadness and domination, does not arouse even a small amount of compassion in you so that the forcible burning [of widows] may be stopped."[3] Why was this so? Why did the act of seeing not result in sympathy? Rammohun's answer is clearly given in his 1818 tract

---

[2] Ibid., pp. 496–497, 500–501.
[3] "Prabartak o nibartaker dvitiyo shombad," in *Rammohun rachanabali*, p. 203.

called *Views on Burning Widows Alive*, which targeted the advocates of the practice. Here Rammohun refers to the forcible way in which widows were "fastened" to the funeral pyre in the course of the performance of *sati*, and directly raises the question of mercy or compassion (*daya*): "you are unmercifully resolved to commit the sin of female murder." His opponent, the "advocate" of *sati*, replies: "You have repeatedly asserted that from want of feeling we promote female destruction. This is incorrect. For it is declared in our Veda and codes of law, that mercy is the root of virtue, and from our practice of hospitality, &c., our compassionate dispositions are well known."[4]

Rammohun's response to this introduces an argument for which he presents no scriptural authority and which went largely unanswered in the debates of the time. This is the argument about "habits of insensibility." Much like the Enlightenment thinkers of Europe, and perhaps influenced by them, Rammohun argued that it was because the practice of *sati* had become a custom — a matter of blind repetition — that people were prevented from experiencing sympathy even when they watched somebody being forced to become a *sati*. The natural connection between their vision and feelings of pity was blocked by habit. If this habit could be corrected or removed, the sheer act of seeing a woman being forced to die would evoke compassion. Roy said:

> That in other cases you show charitable dispositions is acknowledged. But by witnessing from your youth the voluntary burning of women amongst your elder relatives, your neighbours and the inhabitants of the surrounding villages, and by observing the indifference at the time when the women are writhing under the torture of the flames, habits of insensibility are produced. For the same reason, when men or women are suffering the pains of death, you feel for them no sense of compassion, like worshippers of female deities who, witnessing from their infancy the slaughter of kids and buffaloes, feel no compassion for them in the time of their suffering death.[5]

We encounter the same argument about the relationship between sight and compassion in the writings of Iswarchandra Vidyasagar, the

---

[4] *Rammohan rachanabali*, p. 575. This is Rammohun's own translation of his 1818 text "sahamaran bishaye prabartak o nibartaker shombad," ibid., p. 175.

[5] Ibid. Distinguishing between "custom" and "reason," Hume equated the former with "habit." David Hume, *Enquiries Concerning Human Understanding and Concerning the Principles of Morals* (1777), introduction by L. A. Sigby-Bigge (Oxford: Clarendon Press, 1990), p. 43. In his *Treatise*, he argues that it is "custom or repetition" that can convert "pain into pleasure." See idem, *A Treatise of Human Nature* (1739–1740), edited by L. A. Selby-Bigge, revised by P. H. Nidditch (Oxford: Clarendon, 1978), p. 422.

Bengali reformer responsible for the act that in 1856 permitted Hindu widows to remarry. Vidyasagar's fundamental reasoning as to the solution of widows' problems had some critical differences from the position of Rammohun Roy but like the latter, he too argued that it was custom and habit that stymied the otherwise natural relationship between the sight and compassion:[6]

> People of India! . . . Habit has so darkened and overwhelmed your intellect and good sense that it is hard for the juice of compassion to flow in the ever-dry hearts of yours even when you see the plight of hapless widows. . . . Let no woman be born in a country where men have no compassion, no feelings of duty and justice, no sense of good and bad, no consideration, where only the preservation of custom is the main and supreme religion—let the ill-fated women not take birth in such a country.
>
> Women! I cannot tell what sins [of past lives] cause you to be born in India![7]

Both Rammohun and Vidyasagar thus espoused a natural theory of compassion, the idea that compassion was a sentiment universally present in something called "human nature," however blocked its expression might be in a particular situation. This recalls Adam Smith, explaining his theory of sympathy: "How selfish soever man may be supposed, there are some principles in his nature which interest him in the fortune of others. . . . Of this kind is pity or compassion, the emotion we feel for the misery of others."[8] Hume also defined "pity" as a general sentiment, as "a concern for . . . the misery of others, without any friendship . . . to occasion this concern," and connected it to the general human capacity for sympathy. He wrote: "No quality of human nature is more remarkable . . . than that propensity we have to sympathize with others."[9] It is only on the basis of this kind of an understanding that Roy and Vidyasagar assigned to reason a critical role in fighting the effects of custom. Reason did not produce the sentiment of compassion; it simply helped in letting sentiments take their natural course by removing the obstacle of mindless custom. Needless to say, the underlying vision of the human being was truly a universal one.

---

[6] Vidyasagar's intellectual positions are discussed with insight and critical sympathy in Asok Sen, *Iswarchandra Vidyasagar and His Elusive Milestones* (Calcutta: Ridhhi, 1975).

[7] I have followed and modified the translation provided in Isvarchandra Vidyasagar, *Marriage of Hindu Widows*, edited by Arabindo Poddar (Calcutta, 1976), pp. 107–108.

[8] Adam Smith, *The Theory of Moral Sentiments*, edited by D. D. Raphael and A. L. Macfie (Indianapolis: Liberty Fund, 1984), p. 9. See also p. 22. Raphael and Macfie explain (p. 14n) that Smith's theories were in part a refutation of Hobbes's and Mandeville's contention that all sentiments arose from self-love.

[9] Hume, *Treatise*, pp. 316, 369.

■ REFLECTIONS

The Enlightenment and its political legacies—secular order and revolutionary republicanism—were European in origin but global in impact. In this chapter, we have touched on just a few of the crosscurrents of what some historians call an "Atlantic Revolution." A tide of revolutionary fervor swept through France, the United States, and Latin America, found sympathy in Russia in 1825, and echoed in the Muslim heartland, resulting in secular, modernizing regimes in Turkey and Egypt in the next century. Chakrabarty helps us ask if there may have been independent roots of reasoned compassion in India as well.

The political appeal of the Enlightenment, of rationally ordered society, and of democratic government continues. Some elements of this eighteenth-century revolution—the rule of law; regular, popular elections of representatives; the separation of church and state, of government and politics, and of civil and military authority—are widely recognized ideals and emerging global realities. Like science, the principles of the Enlightenment are universal in their claims and often seem universal in their appeal. Nothing is simpler, more rational, or easier to follow than a call to reason, law, liberty, justice, or equality. And yet every society has evolved its own guidelines under different circumstances, often with lasting results. France had its king and still has a relatively centralized state. The United States began with slavery and still suffers from racism. South American states became free of Europe only to dominate Native Americans, and they continue to do so. None of the enlightened or revolutionary societies of the eighteenth century extended the "rights of man" to women. One democratic society had a king, another a House of Lords, another a national church. Are these different adaptations of the Enlightenment ideal? Or are these examples of incomplete revolution, cases of special interests allowing their governments to fall short of principle?

The debate continues today as more societies seek to realize responsive, representative government and the rule of law while oftentimes respecting conflicting traditions. Muslim countries and Israel struggle with the competing demands of secular law and religion, citizenship and communalism. Former communist countries adopt market economies and struggle with traditions of collective support and the appeal of individual liberty.

Perhaps these are conflicts within the Enlightenment tradition itself. How is it possible to have both liberty and equality? How can we claim inalienable rights on the basis of a secular, scientific creed? How does a faith in human reason lead to revolution? And how can ideas of order or justice avoid the consequences of history and human nature?

The great revolutionary declarations of the Enlightenment embarrass the modern skeptic with their naïve faith in natural laws, their universal prescriptions to cure all ills, and their hypocritical avoidance of slaves, women, and the colonized. The selections by Toussaint L'Ouverture and Abigail Adams, however, remind us that Enlightenment universalism was based not only on cool reason and calculation and the blind arrogance of the powerful. At least some of the great Enlightenment thinkers based their global prescription on the *felt* needs, even the sufferings, of others. For Toussaint, Adams, Olympe de Gouges, and Rammohun Roy, the recognition of human commonality began with a reasoned capacity for empathy that the Enlightenment may have bequeathed to the modern world, even shaping modern sensibility.

21

Capitalism and the Industrial Revolution

Europe and the World, 1750–1900

■ HISTORICAL CONTEXT

Two principal forces have shaped the modern world: capitalism and the industrial revolution. As influential as the transformations discussed in Chapters 19 and 20 (the rise of science and the democratic revolution), these two forces are sometimes considered to be one and the same, because the industrial revolution occurred first in capitalist countries such as England, Belgium, and the United States. In fact, the rise of capitalism preceded the industrial revolution by centuries.

Capitalism denotes a particular economic organization of a society, whereas *industrial revolution* refers to a particular transformation of technology. Specifically, in capitalism market forces (supply and demand) set money prices that determine how goods are distributed. Before 1500, most economic behavior was regulated by family, religion, tradition, and political authority rather than by markets. Increasingly after 1500 in Europe, feudal dues were converted into money rents, periodic fairs became institutionalized, banks were established, modern bookkeeping procedures were developed, and older systems of inherited economic status were loosened. After 1800, new populations of urban workers had to work for money to buy food and shelter; after 1850 in urban areas even clothing was usually purchased in the new "department stores." By 1900, the market had become the operating metaphor of society: One sold oneself; everything had its price. Viewed positively, a capitalist society is one in which buyers and sellers, who together compose the market, make most decisions about the production and distribution of resources. Viewed less favorably, it is the capitalists—those who own the "capital" (resources, stores, factories, and money)—who make the decisions about production and distribution.

The industrial revolution made mass production possible with the use of power-driven machines. Mills driven by waterwheels existed in ancient times, but the construction of identical, replaceable machinery—the machine production of machines—revolutionized industry and enabled the coordination of production on a vast scale, occurring first in England's cotton textile mills at the end of the eighteenth century. The market for such textiles was capitalist, though the demand for many early mass-produced goods, such as muskets and uniforms, was government-driven.

The origins of capitalism are hotly debated among historians. Because the world's first cities, five thousand years ago, created markets, merchants, money, and private ownership of capital, some historians refer to an ancient capitalism. In this text, *capitalism* refers to those societies whose markets, merchants, money, and private ownership became central to the way society operated. As such, ancient Mesopotamia, Rome, and Sung dynasty China, which had extensive markets and paper money a thousand years ago, were not among the first capitalist societies. Smaller societies in which commercial interests and merchant classes took hold to direct political and economic matters were the capitalist forerunners. Venice, Florence, Holland, and England, the mercantile states of the fifteenth to seventeenth centuries, exemplify *commercial capitalism* or mercantile capitalism. Thus, the shift to industrial capitalism was more than a change in scale; it was also a transition from a trade-based economy to a manufacturing-based economy, a difference that meant an enormous increase in productivity, profits, and prosperity.

■ THINKING HISTORICALLY
Distinguishing Historical Processes

When two distinct historical processes occur simultaneously and in mutually reinforcing ways, like the spread of agriculture and languages—or capitalism and industrialization—we might confuse one process of change with the other. This confusion makes it difficult to see exactly what causes what. Here you will be encouraged to distinguish between the latter two historical processes. As you read these selections, keep in mind that capitalism is an economic system that spreads markets, commerce, and the interests of private capital; the industrial revolution was a transformation in technology. How did these two very different processes coincide in the nineteenth century? In what ways were they moving toward different ends, causing different effects, or benefiting different interests?

1

ARNOLD PACEY

Asia and the Industrial Revolution, 1990

Here a modern historian of technology demonstrates how Indian and East Asian manufacturing techniques were assimilated by Europeans, particularly by the English successors of the Mughal Empire, providing a boost to the industrial revolution in Britain. In what ways was Indian technology considered superior prior to the industrial revolution? How did European products gain greater markets than those of India?

THINKING HISTORICALLY

Notice how the author distinguishes between capitalism and the industrial revolution. Was India more industrially advanced than capitalistic? Did the British conquest of India benefit more from capitalism, industry, or something else?

Deindustrialization

During the eighteenth century, India participated in the European industrial revolution through the influence of its textile trade, and through the investments in shipping made by Indian bankers and merchants. Developments in textiles and shipbuilding constituted a significant industrial movement, but it would be wrong to suggest that India was on the verge of its own industrial revolution. There was no steam engine in India, no coal mines, and few machines. . . . [E]xpanding industries were mostly in coastal areas. Much of the interior was in economic decline, with irrigation works damaged and neglected as a result of the breakup of the Mughal Empire and the disruption of war. Though political weakness in the empire had been evident since 1707, and a Persian army heavily defeated Mughal forces at Delhi in 1739, it was the British who most fully took advantage of the collapse of the empire. Between 1757 and 1803, they took control of most of India except the Northwest. The result was that the East India Company now administered major sectors of the economy, and quickly reduced the role of the big Indian bankers by changes in taxes and methods of collecting them.

Meanwhile, India's markets in Europe were being eroded by competition from machine-spun yarns and printed calicoes made in Lancashire, and high customs duties were directed against Indian imports into

Source: Arnold Pacey, *Technology in World Civilization* (Cambridge: MIT Press, 1990), 128–35.

Britain. Restrictions were also placed on the use of Indian-built ships for voyages to England. From 1812, there were extra duties on any imports they delivered, and that must be one factor in the decline in shipbuilding. A few Indian ships continued to make the voyage to Britain, however, and there was one in Liverpool Docks in 1839 when Herman Melville arrived from America. It was the *Irrawaddy* from Bombay and Melville commented: "Forty years ago, these merchantmen were nearly the largest in the world; and they still exceed the generality." They were "wholly built by the native shipwrights of India, who . . . surpassed the European artisans." . . .

Attitudes to India changed markedly after the subcontinent had fallen into British hands. Before this, travellers found much to admire in technologies ranging from agriculture to metallurgy. After 1803, however, the arrogance of conquest was reinforced by the rapid development of British industry. This meant that Indian techniques which a few years earlier seemed remarkable could now be equalled at much lower cost by British factories. India was then made to appear rather primitive, and the idea grew that its proper role was to provide raw materials for western industry, including raw cotton and indigo dye, and to function as a market for British goods. This policy was reflected in 1813 by a relaxation of the East India Company's monopoly of trade so that other British companies could now bring in manufactured goods freely for sale in India. Thus the textile industry, iron production, and shipbuilding were all eroded by cheap imports from Britain, and by handicaps placed on Indian merchants.

By 1830, the situation had become so bad that even some of the British in India began to protest. One exclaimed, "We have destroyed the manufactures of India," pleading that there should be some protection for silk weaving, "the last of the expiring manufactures of India." Another observer was alarmed by a "commercial revolution" which produced "so much present suffering to numerous classes in India."

The question that remains is the speculative one of what might have happened if a strong Mughal government had survived. Fernand Braudel argues that although there was no lack of "capitalism" in India, the economy was not moving in the direction of home-grown industrialization. The historian of technology inevitably notes the lack of development of machines, even though there had been some increase in the use of water-wheels during the eighteenth century both in the iron industry and at gunpowder mills. However, it is impossible not to be struck by the achievements of the shipbuilding industry, which produced skilled carpenters and a model of large-scale organizations. It also trained up draughtsmen and people with mechanical interests. It is striking that one of the Wadia shipbuilders installed gas lighting in his home in 1834 and built a small foundry in which he made parts for steam engines. Given an independent and more prosperous India, it is difficult not to believe that a response to British industrialization might well have taken the form of a spread of skill and innovation from the shipyards into other industries.

As it was, such developments were delayed until the 1850s and later, when the first mechanized cotton mill opened. It is significant that some of the entrepreneurs who backed the development of this industry were from the same Parsi families as had built ships in Bombay and invested in overseas trade in the eighteenth century.

Guns and Rails: Asia, Britain, and America

Britain's "conquest" of India cannot be attributed to superior armaments. Indian armies were also well equipped. More significant was the prior breakdown of Mughal government and the collaboration of many Indians. Some victories were also the result of good discipline and bold strategy, especially when Arthur Wellesley, the future Duke of Wellington, was in command. Wellesley's contribution also illustrates the distinctive western approach to the organizational aspect of technology. Indian armies might have had good armament, but because their guns were made in a great variety of different sizes, precise weapons drill was impossible and the supply of shot to the battlefield was unnecessarily complicated. By contrast, Wellesley's forces standardized on just three sizes of field gun, and the commander himself paid close attention to the design of gun carriages and to the bullocks which hauled them, so that his artillery could move as fast as his infantry, and without delays due to wheel breakages.

Significantly, the one major criticism regularly made of Indian artillery concerned the poor design of gun carriages. Many, particularly before 1760, were little better than four-wheeled trolleys. But the guns themselves were often of excellent design and workmanship. Whilst some were imported and others were made with the assistance of foreign craftworkers, there was many a brass cannon and mortar of Indian design, as well as heavy muskets for camel-mounted troops. Captured field guns were often taken over for use by the British, and after capturing ninety guns in one crucial battle, Wellesley wrote that seventy were "the finest brass ordnance I have ever seen." They were probably made in northern India, perhaps at the great Mughal arsenal at Agra.

Whilst Indians had been making guns from brass since the sixteenth century, Europeans could at first only produce this alloy in relatively small quantities because they had no technique for smelting zinc. By the eighteenth century, however, brass was being produced in large quantities in Europe, and brass cannon were being cast at Woolwich Arsenal near London. Several European countries were importing metallic zinc from China for this purpose. However, from 1743 there was a smelter near Bristol in England producing zinc, using coke[1] as fuel, and zinc smelters were also developed in Germany. At the end of the century, Britain's imports of zinc from the Far East were only about forty tons per year. Nevertheless, a British party which visited China in 1797 took particular note of zinc smelting methods. These were similar to the process used in India, which involved vaporizing the metal and then condensing it. There is a suspicion that the Bristol smelting works of 1743 was based on Indian practice, although the possibility of independent invention cannot be excluded.

A much clearer example of the transfer of technology from India occurred when British armies on the subcontinent encountered rockets, a type of weapon of which they had no previous experience. The basic technology had come from the Ottoman Turks or from Syria before 1500, although the Chinese had invented rockets even earlier. In the 1790s, some Indian armies included very large infantry units equipped with rockets. French mercenaries in Mysore had learned to make them, and the British Ordnance Office was enquiring for somebody with expertise on the subject. In response, William Congreve, whose father was head of the laboratory at Woolwich Arsenal, undertook to design a rocket on Indian lines. After a successful demonstration, about two hundred of his rockets were used by the British in an attack on Boulogne in 1806. Fired from over a kilometre away, they set fire to the town. After this success, rockets were adopted quite widely by European armies, though some commanders, notably the Duke of Wellington, frowned on such imprecise weapons, and they tended to drop out of use later in the century. What happened next, however, was typical of the whole British relationship with India. William Congreve set up a factory to manufacture the weapons in 1817, and part of its output was exported to India to equip rocket troops operating there under British command.

Yet another aspect of Asian technology in which eighteenth-century Europeans were interested was the design of farm implements. Reports on seed drills and ploughs were sent to the British Board of Agriculture from India in 1795. A century earlier the Dutch had found much of interest in ploughs and winnowing machines of a Chinese type which they saw in Java. Then a Swedish party visiting Guangzhou (Canton) took a winnowing machine back home with them. Indeed, several of these machines were imported into different parts of Europe, and similar devices for cleaning threshed grain were soon being made there. The

---

[1] Fuel from soft coal. [Ed.]

inventor of one of them, Jonas Norberg, admitted that he got "the initial idea" from three machines "brought here from China," but had to create a new type because the Chinese machines "do not suit our kinds of grain." Similarly, the Dutch saw that the Chinese plough did not suit their type of soil, but it stimulated them to produce new designs with curved metal mould-boards in contrast to the less efficient flat wooden boards used in Europe hitherto.

In most of these cases, and especially with zinc smelting, rockets, and winnowing machines, we have clear evidence of Europeans studying Asian technology in detail. With rockets and winnowers, though perhaps not with zinc, there was an element of imitation in the European inventions which followed. In other instances, however, the more usual course of technological dialogue between Europe and Asia was that European innovation was challenged by the quality or scale of Asian output, but took a different direction, as we have seen in many aspects of the textile industry. Sometimes, the dialogue was even more limited, and served mainly to give confidence in a technique that was already known. Such was the case with occasional references to China in the writings of engineers designing suspension bridges in Britain. The Chinese had a reputation for bridge construction, and before 1700 Peter the Great had asked for bridge-builders to be sent from China to work in Russia. Later, several books published in Europe described a variety of Chinese bridges, notably a long-span suspension bridge made with iron chains.

Among those who developed the suspension bridge in the West were James Finley in America, beginning in 1801, and Samuel Brown and Thomas Telford in Britain. About 1814, Brown devised a flat, wrought-iron chain link which Telford later used to form the main structural chains in his suspension bridges. But beyond borrowing this specific technique, what Telford needed was evidence that the suspension principle was applicable to the problem he was then tackling. Finley's two longest bridges had spanned seventy-four and ninety-three metres, over the Merrimac and Schuylkill Rivers in the eastern United States. Telford was aiming to span almost twice the larger distance with his 176-metre Menai Bridge. Experiments at a Shropshire ironworks gave confidence in the strength of the chains. But Telford may have looked for reassurance even further afield. One of his notebooks contains the reminder, "Examine Chinese bridges." It is clear from the wording which follows that he had seen a recent booklet advocating a "bridge of chains," partly based on a Chinese example, to cross the Firth of Forth in Scotland.

2

ADAM SMITH

The Wealth of Nations, 1776

An Inquiry into the Nature and Causes of the Wealth of Nations might justly be called the bible of free-market capitalism. Written in 1776 in the context of the British (and European) debate over the proper role of government in the economy, Smith's work takes aim at *mercantilism,* or government supervision of the economy. Mercantilists believed that national economies required government assistance and direction to prosper.

Smith argues that free trade will produce greater wealth than mercantilist trade and that free markets allocate resources more efficiently than the government. His notion of *laissez-faire* (literally "let do") capitalism assumes neither that capitalists are virtuous nor that governments should absent themselves entirely from the economy. However, Smith does believe that the greed of capitalists generally negates itself and produces results that are advantageous to, but unimagined by, the individual. "It is not from the benevolence of the butcher, the brewer, or the baker, that we expect our dinner," Smith writes, "but from their regard of their own interest. We address ourselves not to their humanity, but to their self-love, and never talk to them of our own necessities, but of their advantage."[1] Each person seeks to maximize his or her own gain, thereby creating an efficient market in which the cost of goods is instantly adjusted to exploit changes in supply and demand, while the market provides what is needed at the price people are willing to pay "as if by an invisible hand."

According to Smith, what is the relationship between money and industry, and which is more important? What would Smith say to a farmer or manufacturer who wanted to institute tariffs or quotas to limit the number of cheaper imports entering the country and to minimize competition? What would he say to a government official who wanted to protect an important domestic industry? What would he say to a worker who complained about low wages or boring work? What would Smith think about a "postindustrial" or "service" economy in which few workers actually make products? What would he think of a prosperous country that imported more than it exported?

THINKING HISTORICALLY

The Wealth of Nations was written in defense of free capitalism at a moment when the industrial revolution was just beginning. Some elements

[1] Book I, chapter 2.

Source: Adam Smith, *An Inquiry into the Nature and Causes of the Wealth of Nations* (Indianapolis: Liberty Fund, 1981, a reprint of the Oxford University Press edition of 1976), 1:13–15, 31, 47, 73–74, 449–50, 455–57.

of Smith's writing suggest a preindustrial world, as in the quotation about the butcher, brewer, and baker mentioned earlier. Still, Smith was aware how new industrial methods were transforming age-old labor relations and manufacturing processes. In some respects, Smith recognized that capitalism could create wealth, not just redistribute it, because he appreciated the potential of industrial technology.

As you read this selection, note when Smith is discussing capitalism, the economic system, and the power of the new industrial technology. In his discussion of the division of labor, what relationship does Smith see between the development of a capitalistic market and the rise of industrial technology? To what extent could the benefits that Smith attributes to a free market be attributed to the new system of industrial production?

Book I
Of the Causes of Improvement in the Productive Powers of Labour, and of the Order According to Which Its Produce Is Naturally Distributed among the Different Ranks of the People

Chapter 1: Of the Division of Labour

The greatest improvement in the productive powers of labour, and the greater part of the skill, dexterity, and judgment with which it is anywhere directed, or applied, seem to have been the effects of the division of labour.

The effects of the division of labour, in the general business of society, will be more easily understood by considering in what manner it operates in some particular manufactures. . . .

To take an example, therefore, from a very trifling manufacture; but one in which the division of labour has been very often taken notice of, the trade of the pin-maker; a workman not educated to this business (which the division of labour has rendered a distinct trade), nor acquainted with the use of the machinery employed in it (to the invention of which the same division of labour has probably given occasion), could scarce, perhaps, with his utmost industry, make one pin in a day, and certainly could not make twenty. But in the way in which this business is now carried on, not only the whole work is a peculiar trade, but it is divided into a number of branches, of which the greater part are likewise peculiar trades. One man draws out the wire, another straights it, a third cuts it, a fourth points it, a fifth grinds it at the top for receiving the head; to make the head requires two or three distinct operations; to put it on is a peculiar business, to whiten the pins is another; it is even a trade by itself to put them into the paper; and the important business of making a pin is, in this manner, divided into about eighteen distinct operations, which, in some manufactories, are all performed by distinct hands, though in others the same man will sometimes perform two or three of them. I have seen a small manufactory of this kind where ten men only were employed, and where some of them consequently performed two or three distinct operations. But though they were very poor, and therefore but indifferently accommodated with the necessary machinery, they could, when they exerted themselves, make among them about twelve pounds of pins in a day. There are in a pound upwards of four thousand pins of a middling size. Those ten persons, therefore, could make among them upwards of forty-eight thousand pins in a day. Each person, therefore, making a tenth part of forty-eight thousand pins, might be considered as making four thousand eight hundred pins in a day. But if they had all wrought separately and independently, and without any of them having been educated to this peculiar business, they certainly could not each of them have made twenty, perhaps not one pin in a day; that is, certainly, not the two hundred and fortieth, perhaps not the four thousand eight hundredth part of what they are at present capable of performing, in consequence of a proper division and combination of their different operations.

In every other art and manufacture, the effects of the division of labour are similar to what they are in this very trifling one; though, in many of them, the labour can neither be so much subdivided, nor reduced to so great a simplicity of operation. . . .

Chapter 3: That the Division of Labour Is Limited by the Extent of the Market

As it is the power of exchanging that gives occasion to the division of labour, so the extent of this division must always be limited by the extent of that power, or, in other words, by the extent of the market. When the market is very small, no person can have any encouragement to dedicate himself entirely to one employment, for want of the power to exchange all that surplus part of the produce of his own labour, which is over and above his own consumption, for such parts of the produce of other men's labour as he has occasion for.

There are some sorts of industry, even of the lowest kind, which can be carried on nowhere but in a great town. A porter, for example, can find employment and subsistence in no other place. A village is by much too narrow a sphere for him. . . .

Chapter 5: Of the Real and Nominal Price of Commodities, or Their Price in Labour, and Their Price in Money

Every man is rich or poor according to the degree in which he can afford to enjoy the necessaries, conveniences, and amusements of human life. But after the division of labour has once thoroughly taken place, it is but a very small part of these with which a man's own labour can supply him. The far greater part of them he must derive from the labour of other people, and he must be rich or poor according to the quantity of that labour which he can command, or which he can afford to purchase. The value of any commodity, therefore, to the person who possesses it, and who means not to use or consume it himself, but to exchange it for other commodities, is equal to the quantity of labour which it enables him to purchase or command. Labour, therefore, is the real measure of the exchangeable value of all commodities. . . .

Chapter 7: Of the Natural and Market Price of Commodities

. . . When the quantity of any commodity which is brought to market falls short of the effectual demand, all those who are willing to pay the whole value of the rent, wages, and profit, which must be paid in order to bring it thither, cannot be supplied with the quantity which they want. Rather than want[2] it altogether, some of them will be willing to give more. A competition will immediately begin among them, and the market price will rise more or less above the natural price, according as either the greatness of the deficiency, or the wealth and wanton luxury of the competitors, happen to animate more or less the eagerness of the competition. Among competitors of equal wealth and luxury the same deficiency will generally occasion a more or less eager competition, according as the acquisition of the commodity happens to be of more or less importance to them. Hence the exorbitant price of the necessaries of life during the blockade of a town or in a famine.

When the quantity brought to market exceeds the effectual demand, it cannot be all sold to those who are willing to pay the whole value of the rent, wages, and profit, which must be paid in order to bring it thither. Some part must be sold to those who are willing to pay less, and the low price which they give for it must reduce the price of the whole. The market price will sink more or less below the natural price, according as the greatness of the excess increases more or less the competition of the sellers, or according as it happens to be more or less important to them to get immediately rid of the commodity. The same excess in the importation of perishables will occasion a much greater competition than in that of durable commodities; in the importation of oranges, for example, than in that of old iron.

When the quantity brought to market is just sufficient to supply the effectual demand, and no more, the market price naturally comes to be either exactly, or as nearly as can be judged of, the same with the natural price. The whole quantity upon hand can be disposed of for this price,

---

[2] Be without it. [Ed.]

and cannot be disposed of for more. The competition of the different dealers obliges them all to accept of this price, but does not oblige them to accept of less.

The quantity of every commodity brought to market naturally suits itself to the effectual demand. It is the interest of all those who employ their land, labour, or stock, in bringing any commodity to market, that the quantity never should exceed the effectual demand; and it is the interest of all other people that it never should fall short of that demand.

Book IV
Of Systems of Political Economy

Chapter 1: Of the Principle of the Commercial or Mercantile System

. . . I thought it necessary, though at the hazard of being tedious, to examine at full length this popular notion that wealth consists in money, or in gold and silver. Money in common language, as I have already observed, frequently signifies wealth, and this ambiguity of expression has rendered this popular notion so familiar to us that even they who are convinced of its absurdity are very apt to forget their own principles, and in the course of their reasonings to take it for granted as a certain and undeniable truth. Some of the best English writers upon commerce set out with observing that the wealth of a country consists, not in its gold and silver only, but in its lands, houses, and consumable goods of all different kinds. In the course of their reasonings, however, the lands, houses, and consumable goods seem to slip out of their memory, and the strain of their argument frequently supposes that all wealth consists in gold and silver, and that to multiply those metals is the great object of national industry and commerce. . . .

Chapter 2: Of Restraints upon the Importation from Foreign Countries of Such Goods as Can Be Produced at Home

. . . The produce of industry is what it adds to the subject or materials upon which it is employed. In proportion as the value of this produce is great or small, so will likewise be the profits of the employer. But it is only for the sake of profit that any man employs a capital in the support of industry; and he will always, therefore, endeavour to employ it in the support of that industry of which the produce is likely to be of the greatest value, or to exchange for the greatest quantity either of money or of other goods.

But the annual revenue of every society is always precisely equal to the exchangeable value of the whole annual produce of its industry, or rather is precisely the same thing with that exchangeable value. As every individual, therefore, endeavours as much as he can both to employ his capital in the support of domestic industry, and so to direct that industry that its produce may be of the greatest value; every individual necessarily labours to render the annual revenue of the society as great as he can. He generally, indeed, neither intends to promote the public interest, nor knows how much he is promoting it. By preferring the support of domestic to that of foreign industry, he intends only his own security; and by directing that industry in such a manner as its produce may be of the greatest value, he intends only his own gain, and he is in this, as in many other cases, led by an invisible hand to promote an end which was no part of his intention. Nor is it always the worse for the society that it was no part of it. By pursuing his own interest he frequently promotes that of the society more effectually than when he really intends to promote it. I have never known much good done by those who affected to trade for the public good. It is an affectation, indeed, not very common among merchants, and very few words need be employed in dissuading them from it.

What is the species of domestic industry which his capital can employ, and of which the produce is likely to be of the greatest value, every individual, it is evident, can, in his local situation, judge much better than any statesman or lawgiver can do for him. The statesman who should attempt to direct private people in what manner they ought to employ their capitals would not only load himself with a most unnecessary attention, but assume an authority which could safely be trusted, not only to no single person, but to no council or senate whatever, and which would nowhere be so dangerous as in the hands of a man who had folly and presumption enough to fancy himself fit to exercise it.

To give the monopoly of the home market to the produce of domestic industry, in any particular art or manufacture, is in some measure to direct private people in what manner they ought to employ their capitals, and must, in almost all cases, be either a useless or a hurtful regulation. If the produce of domestic can be brought there as cheap as that of foreign industry, the regulation is evidently useless. If it cannot, it must generally be hurtful. It is the maxim of every prudent master of a family never to attempt to make at home what it will cost him more to make than to buy. The tailor does not attempt to make his own shoes, but buys them of the shoemaker. The shoemaker does not attempt to make his own clothes, but employs a tailor. The farmer attempts to make neither the one nor the other, but employs those different artificers. All of them find it for their interest to employ their whole industry in a way in which they have some advantage over their neighbours, and to purchase with a part of its produce, or what is the same thing, with the price of a part of it, whatever else they have occasion for.

What is prudence in the conduct of every private family can scarce be folly in that of a great kingdom. If a foreign country can supply us with a commodity cheaper than we ourselves can make it, better buy it of them with some part of the produce of our own industry employed in a way in which we have some advantage. The general industry of the country, being always in proportion to the capital which employs it, will not thereby be diminished, no more than that of the abovementioned artificers; but only left to find out the way in which it can be employed with the greatest advantage. It is certainly not employed to the greatest advantage when it is thus directed towards an object which it can buy cheaper than it can make. . . .

3

The Sadler Report of the House of Commons, 1832

Although, for many factory owners, children were among the ideal workers in the factories of the industrial revolution, increasingly their exploitation became a concern of the British Parliament. One important parliamentary investigation, chaired by Michael Sadler, took volumes of testimony from child workers and older people who had worked as children in the mines and factories. The following is a sample of that testimony: an interview with a former child worker named Matthew Crabtree who had worked in a textile factory. The Sadler Commission report led to child-labor reform in the Factory Act of 1833.

What seem to be the causes of Crabtree's distress? How could it have been alleviated? If the owner were asked why he didn't pay more, shorten the workday, provide more time for meals, or provide medical assistance when it was needed, how do you think he would have responded? Do you think Crabtree would have been in favor of reduced hours if it meant reduced wages?

THINKING HISTORICALLY

To what extent are the problems faced by Crabtree the inevitable results of machine production? To what extent are his problems caused by capitalism? How might the owner of this factory have addressed these issues?

Source: From *The Sadler Report: Report from the Committee on the Bill to Regulate the Labour of Children in the Mills and Factories of the United Kingdom* (London: The House of Commons, Parliamentary Papers, 1831–1832), 15:95–97.

Friday, 18 May 1832 — Michael Thomas Sadler, Esquire, in the Chair

Mr. Matthew Crabtree, *called in; and Examined.*

What age are you? — Twenty-two.

What is your occupation? — A blanket manufacturer.

Have you ever been employed in a factory? — Yes.

At what age did you first go to work in one? — Eight.

How long did you continue in that occupation? — Four years.

Will you state the hours of labour at the period when you first went to the factory, in ordinary times? — From 6 in the morning to 8 at night.

Fourteen hours? — Yes.

With what intervals for refreshment and rest? — An hour at noon.

Then you had no resting time allowed in which to take your breakfast, or what is in Yorkshire called your "drinking"? — No.

When trade was brisk what were your hours? — From 5 in the morning to 9 in the evening.

Sixteen hours? — Yes.

With what intervals at dinner[1]? — An hour.

How far did you live from the mill? — About two miles.

Was there any time allowed for you to get your breakfast in the mill? — No.

Did you take it before you left your home? — Generally.

During those long hours of labour could you be punctual; how did you awake? — I seldom did awake spontaneously; I was most generally awoke or lifted out of bed, sometimes asleep, by my parents.

Were you always in time? — No.

What was the consequence if you had been too late? — I was most commonly beaten.

Severely? — Very severely, I thought.

In whose factory was this? — Messrs. Hague & Cook's, of Dewsbury.

Will you state the effect that those long hours had upon the state of your health and feelings? — I was, when working those long hours, commonly very much fatigued at night, when I left my work; so much so that I sometimes should have slept as I walked if I had not stumbled and started awake again; and so sick often that I could not eat, and what I did eat I vomited.

Did this labour destroy your appetite? — It did.

In what situation were you in that mill? — I was a piecener.

Will you state to this Committee whether piecening is a very laborious employment for children, or not? — It is a very laborious employment. Pieceners are continually running to and fro, and on their feet the whole day.

---

[1] The main meal, in the afternoon. Not the evening supper. [Ed.]

The duty of the piecener is to take the cardings from one part of the machinery, and to place them on another? — Yes.

So that the labour is not only continual, but it is unabated to the last? — It is unabated to the last.

Do you not think, from your own experience, that the speed of the machinery is so calculated as to demand the utmost exertions of a child supposing the hours were moderate? — It is as much as they could do at the best; they are always upon the stretch, and it is commonly very difficult to keep up with their work.

State the condition of the children toward the latter part of the day, who have thus to keep up with the machinery. — It is as much as they can do when they are not very much fatigued to keep up with their work, and toward the close of the day, when they come to be more fatigued, they cannot keep up with it very well, and the consequence is that they are beaten to spur them on.

Were you beaten under those circumstances? — Yes.

Frequently? — Very frequently.

And principally at the latter end of the day? — Yes.

And is it your belief that if you had not been so beaten, you should not have got through the work? — I should not if I had not been kept up to it by some means.

Does beating then principally occur at the latter end of the day, when the children are exceedingly fatigued? — It does at the latter end of the day, and in the morning sometimes, when they are very drowsy, and have not got rid of the fatigue of the day before.

What were you beaten with principally? — A strap.

Anything else? — Yes, a stick sometimes; and there is a kind of roller which runs on the top of the machine called a billy, perhaps two or three yards in length, and perhaps an inch and a half, or more in diameter; the circumference would be four or five inches; I cannot speak exactly.

Were you beaten with that instrument? — Yes.

Have you yourself been beaten, and have you seen other children struck severely with that roller? — I have been struck very severely with it myself, so much so as to knock me down, and I have seen other children have their heads broken with it.

You think that it is a general practice to beat the children with the roller? — It is.

You do not think then that you were worse treated than other children in the mill? — No, I was not, perhaps not so bad as some were.

In those mills is chastisement towards the latter part of the day going on perpetually? — Perpetually.

So that you can hardly be in a mill without hearing constant crying? — Never an hour, I believe.

Do you think that if the overlooker were naturally a humane person it would be still found necessary for him to beat the children, in order to keep up their attention and vigilance at the termination of those extraordinary days of labour? — Yes, the machine turns off a regular quantity of cardings, and of course they must keep as regularly to their work the whole of the day; they must keep with the machine, and therefore however humane the slubber may be, as he must keep up with the machine or be found fault with, he spurs the children to keep up also by various means but that which he commonly resorts to is to strap them when they become drowsy.

At the time when you were beaten for not keeping up with your work, were you anxious to have done it if you possibly could? — Yes; the dread of being beaten if we could not keep up with our work was a sufficient impulse to keep us to it if we could.

When you got home at night after this labour, did you feel much fatigued? — Very much so.

Had you any time to be with your parents, and to receive instruction from them? — No.

What did you do? — All that we did when we got home was to get the little bit of supper that was provided for us and go to bed immediately. If the supper had not been ready directly, we should have gone to sleep while it was preparing.

Did you not, as a child, feel it a very grievous hardship to be roused so soon in the morning? — I did.

Were the rest of the children similarly circumstanced? — Yes, all of them; but they were not all of them so far from their work as I was.

And if you had been too late you were under the apprehension of being cruelly beaten? — I generally was beaten when I happened to be too late; and when I got up in the morning the apprehension of that was so great, that I used to run, and cry all the way as I went to the mill.

That was the way by which your punctual attendance was secured? — Yes.

And you do not think it could have been secured by any other means? — No.

Then it is your impression from what you have seen, and from your own experience, that those long hours of labour have the effect of rendering young persons who are subject to them exceedingly unhappy? — Yes.

You have already said it had a considerable effect upon your health? — Yes.

Do you conceive that it diminished your growth? — I did not pay much attention to that; but I have been examined by some persons who said they thought I was rather stunted, and that I should have been taller if I had not worked at the mill.

What were your wages at that time? — Three shillings (per week).

And how much a day had you for overwork when you were worked so exceedingly long? — A halfpenny a day.

Did you frequently forfeit that if you were not always there to a moment? — Yes; I most frequently forfeited what was allowed for those long hours.

You took your food to the mill; was it in your mill, as is the case in cotton mills, much spoiled by being laid aside? — It was very frequently covered by flues from the wool; and in that case they had to be blown off with the mouth, and picked off with the fingers before it could be eaten.

So that not giving you a little leisure for eating your food, but obliging you to take it at the mill, spoiled your food when you did get it? — Yes, very commonly.

And that at the same time that this over-labour injured your appetite? — Yes.

Could you eat when you got home? — Not always.

What is the effect of this piecening upon the hands? — It makes them bleed; the skin is completely rubbed off, and in that case they bleed in perhaps a dozen parts.

The prominent parts of the hand? — Yes, all the prominent parts of the hand are rubbed down till they bleed; every day they are rubbed in that way.

All the time you continue at work? — All the time we are working. The hands never can be hardened in that work, for the grease keeps them soft in the first instance, and long and continual rubbing is always wearing them down, so that if they were hard they would be sure to bleed.

It is attended with much pain? — Very much.

Do they allow you to make use of the back of the hand? — No; the work cannot be so well done with the back of the hand, or I should have made use of that.

4

KARL MARX AND FRIEDRICH ENGELS
The Communist Manifesto, 1848

The Communist Manifesto was written in 1848 in the midst of European upheaval, a time when capitalist industrialization had spread from England to France and Germany. Marx and Engels were Germans who studied and worked in France and England. In the *Manifesto*, they

Source: Karl Marx and Friedrich Engels, *The Communist Manifesto* (1888; Boston: Bedford/ St. Martin's, 1999), 65–72.

imagine a revolution that will transform all of Europe. What do they see as the inevitable causes of this revolution? How, according to their analysis, is the crisis of "modern" society different from previous crises? Were Marx and Engels correct?

THINKING HISTORICALLY

Notice how Marx and Engels describe the notions of capitalism and industrialization without using those words. The term *capitalism* developed later from Marx's classic *Das Kapital* (1859), but the term *bourgeoisie,** as Engels notes in this selection, stands for the capitalist class. For Marx and Engels, the industrial revolution (another later phrase) is the product of a particular stage of capitalist development. Thus, if Marx and Engels were asked whether capitalism or industry was the principal force that created the modern world, what would their answer be?

The Communist Manifesto is widely known as the classic critique of capitalism, but a careful reading reveals a list of achievements of capitalist or "bourgeois civilization." What are these achievements? Did Marx and Engels consider them to be achievements? How could Marx and Engels both praise and criticize capitalism?

Bourgeois and Proletarians[1]

The history of all hitherto existing society is the history of class struggles.

Freeman and slave, patrician and plebeian, lord and serf, guild-master and journeyman, in a word, oppressor and oppressed, stood in constant opposition to one another, carried on an uninterrupted, now hidden, now open fight, a fight that each time ended, either in a revolutionary reconstitution of society at large, or in the common ruin of the contending classes.

In the earlier epochs of history, we find almost everywhere a complicated arrangement of society into various orders, a manifold gradation of social rank. In ancient Rome we have patricians, knights, plebeians, slaves; in the Middle Ages, feudal lords, vassals, guildmasters, journeymen, apprentices, serfs; in almost all of these classes, again, subordinate gradations.

---

* bohr zhwah ZEE

[1] In French *bourgeois* means a town-dweller. *Proletarian* comes from the Latin *proletarius*, which meant a person whose sole wealth was his offspring (*proles*). [Ed.] [Note by Engels] By "bourgeoisie" is meant the class of modern capitalists, owners of the means of social production and employers of wage labor; by "proletariat," the class of modern wage-laborers who, having no means of production of their own, are reduced to selling their labor power in order to live.

The modern bourgeois society that has sprouted from the ruins of feudal society, has not done away with class antagonisms. It has but established new classes, new conditions of oppression, new forms of struggle in place of the old ones.

Our epoch, the epoch of the bourgeoisie, possesses, however, this distinctive feature: It has simplified the class antagonisms. Society as a whole is more and more splitting up into the two great hostile camps, into two great classes directly facing each other—bourgeoisie and proletariat.

From the serfs of the Middle Ages sprang the chartered burghers of the earliest towns. From these burgesses the first elements of the bourgeoisie were developed.

The discovery of America, the rounding of the Cape, opened up fresh ground for the rising bourgeoisie. The East-Indian and Chinese markets, the colonization of America, trade with the colonies, the increase in the means of exchange and in commodities generally, gave to commerce, to navigation, to industry, an impulse never before known, and thereby, to the revolutionary element in the tottering feudal society, a rapid development.

The feudal system of industry, in which industrial production was monopolized by closed guilds, now no longer sufficed for the growing wants of the new markets. The manufacturing system took its place. The guildmasters were pushed aside by the manufacturing middle class; division of labor between the different corporate guilds vanished in the face of division of labor in each single workshop.

Meantime the markets kept ever growing, the demand ever rising. Even manufacture[2] no longer sufficed. Thereupon, steam and machinery revolutionized industrial production. The place of manufacture was taken by the giant, modern industry, the place of the industrial middle class, by industrial millionaires—the leaders of whole industrial armies, the modern bourgeois.

Modern industry has established the world market, for which the discovery of America paved the way. This market has given an immense development to commerce, to navigation, to communication by land. This development has, in its turn, reacted on the extension of industry; and in proportion as industry, commerce, navigation, railways extended, in the same proportion the bourgeoisie developed, increased its capital, and pushed into the background every class handed down from the Middle Ages.

We see, therefore, how the modern bourgeoisie is itself the product of a long course of development, of a series of revolutions in the modes of production and of exchange.

---

[2] By *manufacture* Marx meant the system of production that succeeded the guild system but that still relied mainly on direct human labor for power. He distinguished it from modern industry, which arose when machinery driven by water and steam was introduced. [Ed.]

Each step in the development of the bourgeoisie was accompanied by a corresponding political advance of that class. An oppressed class under the sway of the feudal nobility, it became an armed and self-governing association in the medieval commune; here independent urban republic (as in Italy and Germany), there taxable "third estate" of the monarchy (as in France); afterwards, in the period of manufacture proper, serving either the semifeudal or the absolute monarchy as a counterpoise against the nobility, and, in fact, cornerstone of the great monarchies in general—the bourgeoisie has at last, since the establishment of modern industry and of the world market, conquered for itself, in the modern representative state, exclusive political sway. The executive of the modern state is but a committee for managing the common affairs of the whole bourgeoisie.

The bourgeoisie has played a most revolutionary role in history.

The bourgeoisie, wherever it has got the upper hand, has put an end to all feudal, patriarchal, idyllic relations. It has pitilessly torn asunder the motley feudal ties that bound man to his "natural superiors," and has left no other bond between man and man than naked self-interest, than callous "cash payment." It has drowned the most heavenly ecstasies of religious fervor, of chivalrous enthusiasm, of philistine sentimentalism, in the icy water of egotistical calculation. It has resolved personal worth into exchange value, and in place of the numberless indefensible chartered freedoms, has set up that single, unconscionable freedom—Free Trade. In one word, for exploitation, veiled by religious and political illusions, it has substituted naked, shameless, direct, brutal exploitation.

The bourgeoisie has stripped of its halo every occupation hitherto honored and looked up to with reverent awe. It has converted the physician, the lawyer, the priest, the poet, the man of science, into its paid wage-laborers.

The bourgeoisie has torn away from the family its sentimental veil, and has reduced the family relation to a mere money relation.

The bourgeoisie has disclosed how it came to pass that the brutal display of vigor in the Middle Ages, which reactionaries so much admire, found its fitting complement in the most slothful indolence. It has been the first to show what man's activity can bring about. It has accomplished wonders far surpassing Egyptian pyramids, Roman aqueducts, and Gothic cathedrals; it has conducted expeditions that put in the shade all former migrations of nations and crusades.

The bourgeoisie cannot exist without constantly revolutionizing the instruments of production, and thereby the relations of production, and with them the whole relations of society. Conservation of the old modes of production in unaltered form, was, on the contrary, the first condition of existence for all earlier industrial classes. Constant revolutionizing of production, uninterrupted disturbance of all social conditions, everlasting uncertainty and agitation distinguished the bourgeois epoch from all earlier ones. All fixed, fast-frozen relations, with their train of ancient and venerable prejudices and opinions, are swept away, all new-formed ones become antiquated before they can ossify. All that is solid melts into air, all that is holy is profaned, and man is at last compelled to face with sober senses his real conditions of life and his relations with his kind.

The need of a constantly expanding market for its products chases the bourgeoisie over the whole surface of the globe. It must nestle everywhere, settle everywhere, establish connections everywhere.

The bourgeoisie has through its exploitation of the world market given a cosmopolitan character to production and consumption in every country. To the great chagrin of reactionaries, it has drawn from under the feet of industry the national ground on which it stood. All old-established national industries have been destroyed or are daily being destroyed. They are dislodged by new industries, whose introduction becomes a life and death question for all civilized nations, by industries that no longer work up indigenous raw material, but raw material drawn from the remotest zones; industries whose products are consumed, not only at home, but in every quarter of the globe. In place of the old wants, satisfied by the production of the country, we find new wants, requiring for their satisfaction the products of distant lands and climes. In place of the old local and national seclusion and self-sufficiency, we have intercourse in every direction, universal interdependence of nations. And as in material, so also in intellectual production. The intellectual creations of individual nations become common property. National one-sidedness and narrow-mindedness become more and more impossible, and from the numerous national and local literatures there arises a world literature.

The bourgeoisie, by the rapid improvement of all instruments of production, by the immensely facilitated means of communication, draws all nations, even the most barbarian, into civilization. The cheap prices of its commodities are the heavy artillery with which it batters down all Chinese walls, with which it forces the barbarians' intensely obstinate hatred for foreigners to capitulate. It compels all nations, on pain of extinction, to adopt the bourgeois mode of production; it compels them to introduce what it calls civilization into their midst, i.e., to become bourgeois themselves. In a word, it creates a world after its own image.

The bourgeoisie has subjected the country to the rule of the towns. It has created enormous cities, has greatly increased the urban population as compared with the rural, and has thus rescued a considerable part of the population from the idiocy of rural life. Just as it has made the country dependent on the towns, so it has made barbarian and semi-barbarian countries dependent on the civilized ones, nations of peasants on nations of bourgeois, the East on the West.

More and more the bourgeoisie keeps doing away with the scattered state of the population, of the means of production, and of property. It has agglomerated population, centralized means of production, and has concentrated property in a few hands. The necessary consequence of this was political centralization. Independent, or but loosely connected provinces, with separate interests, laws, governments and systems of taxation, became lumped together into one nation, with one government, one code of laws, one national class interest, one frontier and one customs tariff.

The bourgeoisie, during its rule of scarce one hundred years, has created more massive and more colossal productive forces than have all preceding generations together. Subjection of nature's forces to man, machinery, application of chemistry to industry and agriculture, steam-navigation, railways, electric telegraphs, clearing of whole continents for cultivation, canalization of rivers, whole populations conjured out of the ground—what earlier century had even a presentiment that such productive forces slumbered in the lap of social labor?

We see then that the means of production and of exchange, which served as the foundation for the growth of the bourgeoisie, were generated in feudal society. At a certain stage in the development of these means of production and of exchange, the conditions under which feudal society produced and exchanged, the feudal organization of agriculture and manufacturing industry, in a word, the feudal relations of property became no longer compatible with the already developed productive forces; they became so many fetters. They had to be burst asunder; they were burst asunder.

Into their place stepped free competition, accompanied by a social and political constitution adapted to it, and by the economic and political sway of the bourgeois class.

A similar movement is going on before our own eyes. Modern bourgeois society with its relations of production, of exchange and of property, a society that has conjured up such gigantic means of production and exchange, is like the sorcerer who is no longer able to control the powers of the nether world whom he has called up by his spells. For many a decade past the history of industry and commerce is but the history of the revolt of modern productive forces against modern conditions of production, against the property relations that are the conditions for the existence of the bourgeoisie and of its rule. It is enough to mention the commercial crises that by their periodical return put the existence of the entire bourgeoisie society on trial, each time more threateningly. In these crises a great part not only of the existing products, but also of the previously created productive forces, are periodically destroyed. In these crises there breaks out an epidemic that, in all earlier epochs, would have seemed an absurdity—the epidemic of overproduction. Society suddenly finds itself put back into a state of momentary barbarism; it appears as if a famine, a universal war of devastation had cut off the supply of every means of subsistence; industry and commerce seem to be destroyed. And why? Because there is too much civilization, too much means of subsistence, too much industry, too much commerce. The productive forces at the disposal of society no longer tend to further the development of the conditions of bourgeois property; on the contrary, they have become too powerful for these conditions, by which they are fettered, and no sooner do they overcome these fetters than they bring disorder into the whole of bourgeois society, endanger the existence of bourgeois property. The conditions of bourgeois society are too narrow to comprise the wealth created by them. And how does the bourgeoisie get over these crises? On the one hand by enforced destruction of a mass of productive forces; on the other, by the conquest of new markets, and by the more thorough exploitation of the old ones. That is to say, by paving the way for more extensive and more destructive crises, and by diminishing the means whereby crises are prevented.

The weapons with which the bourgeoisie felled feudalism to the ground are now turned against the bourgeoisie itself.

But not only has the bourgeoisie forged the weapons that bring death to itself; it has also called into existence the men who are to wield those weapons—the modern working class—the proletarians.

In proportion as the bourgeoisie, i.e., capital, is developed, in the same proportion is the proletariat, the modern working class, developed—a class of labourers, who live only so long as they find work, and who find work only so long as their labour increases capital. These labourers, who must sell themselves piece-meal, are a commodity, like every other article of commerce, and are consequently exposed to all the vicissitudes of competition, to all the fluctuations of the market.

Owing to the extensive use of machinery and to division of labour, the work of the proletarians has lost all individual character, and consequently, all charm for the workman. He becomes an appendage of the machine, and it is only the most simple, most monotonous, and most easily acquired knack, that is required of him. Hence, the cost of production of a workman is restricted, almost entirely, to the means of subsistence that he requires for his maintenance, and for the propagation of his race. But the price of a commodity, and therefore also of labour, is equal to its cost of production. In proportion therefore, as the repulsiveness of the work increases, the wage decreases. Nay more, in proportion as the use of machinery and division of labour increases, in the same proportion the burden of toil also increases, whether by prolongation of the working hours, by increase of the work exacted in a given time or by increased speed of the machinery, etc.

Modern industry has converted the little workshop of the patriarchal master into the great factory of the industrial capitalist. Masses of labourers, crowded into the factory, are organised like soldiers.

As privates of the industrial army they are placed under the command of a perfect hierarchy of officers and sergeants. Not only are they slaves of the bourgeois class, and of the bourgeois State; they are daily and hourly enslaved by the machine, by the over-looker, and, above all, by the individual bourgeois manufacturer himself. The more openly this despotism proclaims gain to be its end and aim, the more petty, the more hateful and the more embittering it is.

The less the skill and exertion of strength implied in manual labour, in other words, the more modern industry becomes developed, the more is the labour of men superseded by that of women. Differences of age and sex have no longer any distinctive social validity for the working class. All are instruments of labour, more or less expensive to use, according to their age and sex.

No sooner is the exploitation of the labourer by the manufacturer, so far, at an end, that he receives his wages in cash, than he is set upon by the other portions of the bourgeoisie, the landlord, the shopkeeper, the pawnbroker, etc.

The lower strata of the middle class—the small tradespeople, shopkeepers, retired tradesmen generally, the handicraftsmen and peasants—all these sink gradually into the proletariat, partly because their diminutive capital does not suffice for the scale on which Modern Industry is carried on, and is swamped in the competition with the large capitalists, partly because their specialized skill is rendered worthless by the new methods of production. Thus the proletariat is recruited from all classes of the population.

5

PETER N. STEARNS

The Industrial Revolution outside the West, 1993

Stearns, a modern historian, discusses the export of industrial machinery and techniques outside the West (Europe and North America) in the nineteenth century. Again and again, he finds that initial attempts at industrialization—in Russia, India, Egypt, and South America—led to increased production of export crops and resources but failed to stimulate true industrial revolutions. Consequently, as producers of raw materials, these countries became more deeply dependent on

Source: Peter N. Stearns, *The Industrial Revolution in World History* (Boulder, CO: Westview Press, 1993), 71–79.

Western markets for their products, while at the same time importing from the West more valuable manufactured products like machinery. What common reasons can you find for these failures?

THINKING HISTORICALLY

Did nineteenth-century efforts to ignite industrial revolutions outside the West fail because these societies neglected to develop capitalism, or did they fail because their local needs were subordinated to those of Western capitalists? Explain.

Before the 1870s no industrial revolution occurred outside Western society. The spread of industrialization within western Europe, while by no means automatic, followed from a host of shared economic, cultural, and political features. The quick ascension of the United States was somewhat more surprising—the area was not European and had been far less developed economically during the eighteenth century. Nevertheless, extensive commercial experience in the northern states and the close mercantile and cultural ties with Britain gave the new nation advantages for its rapid imitation of the British lead. Abundant natural resources and extensive investments from Europe kept the process going, joining the United States to the wider dynamic of industrialization in the nineteenth-century West.

Elsewhere, conditions did not permit an industrial revolution, an issue that must be explored in dealing with the international context for this first phase of the world's industrial experience. Yet the West's industrial revolution did have substantial impact. It led to a number of pilot projects whereby initial machinery and factories were established under Western guidance. More important, it led to new Western demands on the world's economies that instigated significant change without industrialization; indeed, these demands in several cases made industrialization more difficult.

Pilot Projects

Russia's contact with the West's industrial revolution before the 1870s offers an important case study that explains why many societies could not follow the lead of nations like France or the United States in imitating Britain. Yet Russia did introduce some new equipment for economic and military-political reasons, and these initiatives did generate change—they were not mere window dressing.

More than most societies not directly part of Western civilization, Russia had special advantages in reacting to the West's industrial lead and special motivation for paying attention to this lead. Russia had been part of Europe's diplomatic network since about 1700. It saw itself as one of Europe's great powers, a participant in international conferences and military alliances. The country also had close cultural ties with western Europe, sharing in artistic styles and scientific developments—though Russian leadership had stepped back from cultural alignment because of the shock of the French Revolution in 1789 and subsequent political disorders in the West. Russian aristocrats and intellectuals routinely visited western Europe. Finally, Russia had prior experience in imitating Western technology and manufacturing: importation of Western metallurgy and shipbuilding had formed a major part of Peter the Great's reform program in the early eighteenth century.

Contacts of this sort explain why Russia began to receive an industrial outreach from the West within a few decades of the advent of the industrial revolution. British textile machinery was imported beginning in 1843. Ernst Knoop, a German immigrant to Britain who had clerked in a Manchester cotton factory, set himself up as export agent to the Russians. He also sponsored British workers who installed the machinery in Russia and told any Russian entrepreneur brash enough to ask not simply for British models but for alterations or adaptations: "That is not your affair; in England they know better than you." Despite the snobbism, a number of Russian entrepreneurs set up small factories to produce cotton, aware that even in Russia's small urban market they could make a substantial profit by underselling traditional manufactured cloth. Other factories were established directly by Britons.

Europeans and Americans were particularly active in responding to calls by the tsar's government for assistance in establishing railway and steamship lines. The first steamship appeared in Russia in 1815, and by 1820 a regular service ran on the Volga River. The first public railroad, joining St. Petersburg to the imperial residence in the suburbs, opened in 1837. In 1851 the first major line connected St. Petersburg and Moscow, along a remarkably straight route desired by Tsar Nicholas I himself. American engineers were brought in, again by the government, to set up a railroad industry so that Russians could build their own locomotives and cars. George Whistler, the father of the painter James McNeill Whistler (and thus husband of Whistler's mother), played an important role in the effort. He and some American workers helped train Russians in the needed crafts, frequently complaining about their slovenly habits but appreciating their willingness to learn.

Russian imports of machinery increased rapidly; they were over thirty times as great in 1860 as they had been in 1825. While in 1851 the nation manufactured only about half as many machines as it imported, by 1860 the equation was reversed, and the number of machine-building factories had quintupled (from nineteen to ninety-nine). The new cotton industry surged forward with most production organized in factories using wage labor.

These were important changes. They revealed that some Russians were alert to the business advantages of Western methods and that some Westerners saw the great profits to be made by setting up shop in a huge but largely agricultural country. The role of the government was vital: The tsars used tax money to offer substantial premiums to Western entrepreneurs, who liked the adventure of dealing with the Russians but liked their superior profit margins even more.

But Russia did not then industrialize. Modern industrial operations did not sufficiently dent established economic practices. The nation remained overwhelmingly agricultural. High percentage increases in manufacturing proceeded from such a low base that they had little general impact. Several structural barriers impeded a genuine industrial revolution. Russia's cities had never boasted a manufacturing tradition; there were few artisans skilled even in preindustrial methods. Only by the 1860s and 1870s had cities grown enough for an artisan core to take shape—in printing, for example—and even then large numbers of foreigners (particularly Germans) had to be imported. Even more serious was the system of serfdom that kept most Russians bound to agricultural estates. While some free laborers could be found, most rural Russians could not legally leave their land, and their obligation to devote extensive work service to their lords' estates reduced their incentive even for agricultural production. Peter the Great had managed to adapt serfdom to a preindustrial metallurgical industry by allowing landlords to sell villages and the labor therein for expansion of ironworks. But this mongrel system was not suitable for change on a grander scale, which is precisely what the industrial revolution entailed.

Furthermore, the West's industrial revolution, while it provided tangible examples for Russia to imitate, also produced pressures to develop more traditional sectors in lieu of structural change. The West's growing cities and rising prosperity claimed rising levels of Russian timber, hemp, tallow, and, increasingly, grain. These were export goods that could be produced without new technology and without altering the existing labor system. Indeed, many landlords boosted the work-service obligations of the serfs in order to generate more grain production for sale to the West. The obvious temptation was to lock in an older economy—to respond to new opportunity by incremental changes within the traditional system and to maintain serfdom and the rural preponderance rather than to risk fundamental internal transformation.

The proof of Russia's lag showed in foreign trade. It rose but rather modestly, posting a threefold increase between 1800 and 1860. Exports of raw materials approximately paid for the imports of some machinery, factory-made goods from abroad, and a substantial volume of luxury products for the aristocracy. And the regions that participated most in the growing trade were not the tiny industrial enclaves (in St. Petersburg, Moscow, and the iron-rich Urals) but the wheat-growing areas of southern Russia where even industrial pilot projects had yet to surface. Russian manufacturing exported nothing at all to the West, though it did find a few customers in Turkey, central Asia, and China.

The proof of Russia's lag showed even more dramatically in Russia's new military disadvantage. Peter the Great's main goal had been to keep Russian military production near enough to Western levels to remain competitive, with the huge Russian population added into the equation. This strategy now failed, for the West's industrial revolution changed the rules of the game. A war in 1854 pitting Russia against Britain and France led to Russia's defeat in its own backyard. The British and French objected to new Russian territorial gains (won at the expense of Turkey's Ottoman Empire) that brought Russia greater access to the Black Sea. The battleground was the Crimea. Yet British and French steamships connected their armies more reliably with supplies and reinforcements from home than did Russia's ground transportation system with its few railroads and mere three thousand miles of first-class roads. And British and French industry could pour out more and higher-quality uniforms, guns, and munitions than traditional Russian manufacturing could hope to match. The Russians lost the Crimean War, surrendering their gains and swallowing their pride in 1856. Patchwork change had clearly proved insufficient to match the military, much less the economic, power the industrial revolution had generated in the West.

After a brief interlude, the Russians digested the implications of their defeat and launched a period of basic structural reforms. The linchpin was the abolition of serfdom in 1861. Peasants were not entirely freed, and rural discontent persisted, but many workers could now leave the land; the basis for a wage labor force was established. Other reforms focused on improving basic education and health, and while change in these areas was slow, it too set the basis for a genuine commitment to industrialization. A real industrial revolution lay in the future, however. By the 1870s Russia's contact with industrialization had deepened its economic gap vis-à-vis the West but had yielded a few interesting experiments with new methods and a growing realization of the need for further change.

Societies elsewhere in the world—those more removed from traditional ties to the West or more severely disadvantaged in the ties that did exist—saw even more tentative industrial pilot projects during the West's industrialization period. The Middle East and India tried some industrial imitation early on but largely failed—though not without generating some important economic change. Latin America also launched some revealingly limited technological change. Only eastern Asia and sub-Saharan Africa were largely untouched by any explicit industrial imitations until the late 1860s or beyond; they were too distant from European culture to venture a response so quickly.

Prior links with the West formed the key variable, as Russia's experience abundantly demonstrated. Societies that had some familiarity with Western merchants and some preindustrial awareness of the West's steady commercial gains mounted some early experiments in industrialization. Whether they benefited as a result compared with areas that did nothing before the late nineteenth century might be debated.

One industrial initiative in India developed around Calcutta, where British colonial rule had centered since the East India Company founded the city in 1690. A Hindu Brahman family, the Tagores, established close ties with many British administrators. Without becoming British, they sponsored a number of efforts to revivify India, including new colleges and research centers. Dwarkanath Tagore controlled tax collection in part of Bengal, and early in the nineteenth century he used part of his profit to found a bank. He also bought up a variety of commercial landholdings and traditional manufacturing operations. In 1834 he joined with British capitalists to establish a diversified company that boasted holdings in mines (including the first Indian coal mine), sugar refineries, and some new textile factories; the equipment was imported from Britain. Tagore's dominant idea was a British-Indian economic and cultural collaboration that would revitalize his country. He enjoyed a high reputation in Europe and for a short time made a success of his economic initiatives. Tagore died on a trip abroad, and his financial empire declined soon after.

This first taste of Indian industrialization was significant, but it brought few immediate results. The big news in India, even as Tagore launched his companies, was the rapid decline of traditional textiles under the bombardment of British factory competition; millions of Indian villagers were thrown out of work. Furthermore, relations between Britain and the Indian elite worsened after the mid-1830s as British officials sought a more active economic role and became more intolerant of Indian culture. One British official, admitting no knowledge of Indian scholarship, wrote that "all the historical information" and science available in Sanskrit was "less valuable than what may be found in the most paltry abridgements used at preparatory schools in England." With these attitudes, the kind of collaboration that might have aided Indian appropriation of British industry became impossible.

The next step in India's contact with the industrial revolution did not occur until the 1850s when the colonial government began to build a significant railroad network. The first passenger line opened in 1853. Some officials feared that Hindus might object to traveling on such smoke-filled monsters, but trains proved very popular and there ensued a period of rapid economic and social change. The principal result, however, was not industrial development but further extension of commercial agriculture (production of cotton and other goods for export) and intensification of British sales to India's interior. Coal mining did expand, but manufacturing continued to shrink. There was no hint of an industrial revolution in India.

Imitation in the Middle East was somewhat more elaborate, in part because most of this region, including parts of North Africa, retained independence from European colonialism. Muslims had long disdained Western culture and Christianity, and Muslim leaders, including the rulers of the great Ottoman Empire, had been very slow to recognize the West's growing dynamism after the fifteenth century. Some Western medicine was imported, but technology was ignored. Only in the eighteenth century did this attitude begin, haltingly, to change. The Ottoman government imported a printing press from Europe and began discussing Western-style technical training, primarily in relationship to the military.

In 1798 a French force briefly seized Egypt, providing a vivid symbol of Europe's growing technical superiority. Later an Ottoman governor, Muhammed Ali, seized Egypt from the imperial government and pursued an ambitious agenda of expansionism and modernization. Muhammed Ali sponsored many changes in Egyptian society in imitation of Western patterns, including a new tax system and new kinds of schooling. He also destroyed the traditional Egyptian elite. The government encouraged agricultural production by sponsoring major irrigation projects and began to import elements of the industrial revolution from the West in the 1830s. English machinery and technicians were brought in to build textile factories, sugar refineries, paper mills, and weapons shops. Muhammed Ali clearly contemplated a sweeping reform program in which industrialization would play a central role in making Egypt a powerhouse in the Middle East and an equal to the European powers. Many of his plans worked well, but the industrialization effort failed. Egyptian factories could not in the main compete with European imports, and the initial experiments either failed or stagnated. More durable changes involved the encouragement to the production of cash crops like sugar and cotton, which the government required in order to earn tax revenues to support its armies and its industrial imports. Growing concentration on cash crops also enriched a new group of Egyptian landlords and merchants. But the shift actually formalized Egypt's dependent position in the world economy, as European businesses and governments increasingly interfered with the internal economy. The Egyptian reaction to the West's industrial revolution, even more than the Russian response, was to generate massive economic redefinition without industrialization, a strategy that locked peasants into landlord control and made a manufacturing transformation at best a remote prospect.

Spurred by the West's example and by Muhammed Ali, the Ottoman government itself set up some factories after 1839, importing equipment from Europe to manufacture textiles, paper, and guns. Coal and iron mining were encouraged. The government established a postal system in 1834, a telegraph system in 1855, and steamships and the beginning of railway construction from 1866 onward. These changes increased the role of European traders and investors in the Ottoman economy and produced no overall industrial revolution. Again, the clearest result of improved transport and communication was a growing emphasis on the export of cash crops and minerals to pay for necessary manufactured imports from Europe. An industrial example had been set, and, as in Egypt, a growing though still tiny minority of Middle Easterners gained some factory experience, but no fundamental transformation occurred. . . .

Developments of preliminary industrial trappings—a few factories, a few railroads—nowhere outside Europe converted whole economies to an industrialization process until late in the nineteenth century, though they provided some relevant experience on which later (mainly after 1870) and more intensive efforts could build. A few workers became factory hands and experienced some of the same upheaval as their Western counterparts in terms of new routines and pressures on work pace. Many sought to limit their factory experience, leaving for other work or for the countryside after a short time; transience was a problem for much the same reasons as in the West: the clash with traditional work and leisure values. Some technical and business expertise also developed. Governments took the lead in most attempts to imitate the West, which was another portent for the future; with some exceptions, local merchant groups had neither the capital nor the motivation to undertake such ambitious and uncertain projects. By the 1850s a number of governments were clearly beginning to realize that some policy response to the industrial revolution was absolutely essential, lest Western influence become still more overwhelming. On balance, however, the principal results of very limited imitation tended to heighten the economic imbalance with western Europe, a disparity that made it easier to focus on nonindustrial exports. This too was a heritage for the future. . . .

6

MARY ANTIN
The Promised Land, 1894/1912

The industrial revolution moved huge capital fortunes and millions of laborers across continents and oceans to places where they could be combined to further new and ever larger capitalist and industrial ventures. Not everyone, however, became a major capitalist or industrial worker. Some like Mary Antin's father played barely supporting roles in the new infrastructure.

Source: Mary Antin, *The Promised Land* (Houghton Mifflin, 1912; Penguin Classics, 1997), 146–49, 153–57.

Mary Antin (1881–1949) grew up in a Jewish family in Polotzk, Russia (now in Bellarus). In 1891 her father sailed to America, three years later calling the rest of the family (Mary, her siblings, and their mother) to join him in Boston. This selection from Antin's memoir contains part of her account of that first year in the United States, initially in Boston and then nearby in Crescent Beach and Chelsea. How did the lives of the Antins change from Polotzk to their first year in the United States? How did they view that change? What connection do you see between immigration and nationalism?

THINKING HISTORICALLY

This selection has numerous references to the material world, capitalism, and the products of the industrial revolution. What are these references? In what ways were their lives in the United States more or less material, capitalist, or industrial than they were in Polotzk?

In our days of affluence in Russia we had been accustomed to upholstered parlors, embroidered linen, silver spoons and candlesticks, goblets of gold, kitchen shelves shining with copper and brass. We had featherbeds heaped halfway to the ceiling; we had clothes presses dusky with velvet and silk and fine woollen. The three small rooms into which my father now ushered us, up one flight of stairs, contained only the necessary beds, with lean mattresses; a few wooden chairs; a table or two; a mysterious iron structure, which later turned out to be a stove; a couple of unornamental kerosene lamps; and a scanty array of cooking-utensils and crockery. And yet we were all impressed with our new home and its furniture. It was not only because we had just passed through our seven lean years, cooking in earthen vessels, eating black bread on holidays and wearing cotton; it was chiefly because these wooden chairs and tin pans were American chairs and pans that they shone glorious in our eyes. And if there was anything lacking for comfort or decoration we expected it to be presently supplied—at least, we children did. Perhaps my mother alone, of us newcomers, appreciated the shabbiness of the little apartment, and realized that for her there was as yet no laying down of the burden of poverty.

Our initiation into American ways began with the first step on the new soil. My father found occasion to instruct or correct us even on the way from the pier to Wall Street, which journey we made crowded together in a rickety cab. He told us not to lean out of the windows, not to point, and explained the word "greenhorn." We did not want to be "greenhorns," and gave the strictest attention to my father's instructions. I do not know when my parents found opportunity to review together the history of Polotzk in the three years past, for we children had no patience with the subject; my mother's narrative was constantly interrupted by irrelevant questions, interjections, and explanations.

The first meal was an object lesson of much variety. My father produced several kinds of food, ready to eat, without any cooking, from little tin cans that had printing all over them. He attempted to introduce us to a queer, slippery kind of fruit, which he called "banana," but had to give it up for the time being. After the meal, he had better luck with a curious piece of furniture on runners, which he called "rocking-chair." There were five of us newcomers, and we found five different ways of getting into the American machine of perpetual motion, and as many ways of getting out of it. One born and bred to the use of a rocking-chair cannot imagine how ludicrous people can make themselves when attempting to use it for the first time. We laughed immoderately over our various experiments with the novelty, which was a wholesome way of letting off steam after the unusual excitement of the day.

In our flat we did not think of such a thing as storing the coal in the bathtub. There was no bathtub. So in the evening of the first day my father conducted us to the public baths. As we moved along in a little procession, I was delighted with the illumination of the streets. So many lamps, and they burned until morning, my father said, and so people did not need to carry lanterns. In America, then, everything was free, as we had heard in Russia. Light was free; the streets were as bright as a synagogue on a holy day. Music was free; we had been serenaded, to our gaping delight, by a brass band of many pieces, soon after our installation on Union Place.

Education was free. That subject my father had written about repeatedly, as comprising his chief hope for us children, the essence of American opportunity, the treasure that no thief could touch, not even misfortune or poverty. It was the one thing that he was able to promise us when he sent for us; surer, safer than bread or shelter. On our second day I was thrilled with the realization of what this freedom of education meant. A little girl from across the alley came and offered to conduct us to school. My father was out, but we five between us had a few words of English by this time. We knew the word school. We understood. This child, who had never seen us till yesterday, who could not pronounce our names, who was not much better dressed than we, was able to offer us the freedom of the schools of Boston! No application made, no questions asked, no examinations, rulings, exclusions; no machinations, no fees. The doors stood open for every one of us. The smallest child could show us the way.

This incident impressed me more than anything I had heard in advance of the freedom of education in America. It was a concrete proof—almost the thing itself. One had to experience it to understand it.

It was a great disappointment to be told by my father that we were not to enter upon our school career at once. It was too near the end of the term, he said, and we were going to move to Crescent Beach in a week or so. We had to wait until the opening of the schools in September. What a loss of precious time—from May till September!

Not that the time was really lost. Even the interval on Union Place was crowded with lessons and experiences. We had to visit the stores and be dressed from head to foot in American clothing; we had to learn the mysteries of the iron stove, the washboard, and the speaking-tube; we had to learn to trade with the fruit peddler through the window, and not to be afraid of the policeman; and, above all, we had to learn English. . . .

I am forgetting the more serious business which had brought us to Crescent Beach. While we children disported ourselves like mermaids and mermen in the surf, our respective fathers dispensed cold lemonade, hot peanuts, and pink popcorn, and piled up our respective fortunes, nickel by nickel, penny by penny. I was very proud of my connection with the public life of the beach. I admired greatly our shining soda fountain, the rows of sparkling glasses, the pyramids of oranges, the sausage chains, the neat white counter, and the bright array of tin spoons. It seemed to me that none of the other refreshment stands on the beach—there were a few—were half so attractive as ours. I thought my father looked very well in a long white apron and shirt sleeves. He dished out ice cream with enthusiasm, so I supposed he was getting rich. It never occurred to me to compare his present occupation with the position for which he had been originally destined; or if I thought about it, I was just as well content, for by this time I had by heart my father's saying, "America is not Polotzk." All occupations were respectable, all men were equal, in America.

If I admired the soda fountain and the sausage chains, I almost worshipped the partner, Mr. Wilner. I was content to stand for an hour at a time watching him make potato chips. In his cook's cap and apron, with a ladle in his hand and a smile on his face, he moved about with the greatest agility, whisking his raw materials out of nowhere, dipping into his bubbling kettle with a flourish, and bringing forth the finished product with a caper. Such potato chips were not to be had anywhere else on Crescent Beach. Thin as tissue paper, crisp as dry snow, and salt as the sea—such thirst-producing, lemonade-selling, nickel-bringing potato chips only Mr. Wilner could make. On holidays, when dozens of family parties came out by every train from town, he could hardly keep up with the demand for his potato chips. And with a waiting crowd around him our partner was at his best. He was as voluble as he was skilful, and as

witty as he was voluble; at least so I guessed from the laughter that frequently drowned his voice. I could not understand his jokes, but if I
could get near enough to watch his lips and his smile and his merry eyes,
I was happy. That any one could talk so fast, and in English, was marvel
enough, but that this prodigy should belong to *our* establishment was a
fact to thrill me. I had never seen anything like Mr. Wilner, except a wedding jester; but then he spoke common Yiddish. So proud was I of the
talent and good taste displayed at our stand that if my father beckoned
to me in the crowd and sent me on an errand, I hoped the people noticed
that I, too, was connected with the establishment.

And all this splendor and glory and distinction came to a sudden
end. There was some trouble about a license—some fee or fine—there
was a storm in the night that damaged the soda fountain and other
fixtures—there was talk and consultation between the houses of Antin
and Wilner—and the promising partnership was dissolved. No more
would the merry partner gather the crowd on the beach; no more would
the twelve young Wilners gambol like mermen and mermaids in the surf.
And the less numerous tribe of Antin must also say farewell to the jolly
seaside life, for men in such humble business as my father's carry their
families, along with their other earthly goods, wherever they go, after
the manner of the gypsies. We had driven a feeble stake into the sand.
The jealous Atlantic, in conspiracy with the Sunday law, had torn it out.
We must seek our luck elsewhere.

In Polotzk we had supposed that "America" was practically synonymous with "Boston." When we landed in Boston, the horizon was
pushed back, and we annexed Crescent Beach. And now, espying other
lands of promise, we took possession of the province of Chelsea, in the
name of our necessity.

In Chelsea, as in Boston, we made our stand in the wrong end of the
town. Arlington Street was inhabited by poor Jews, poor Negroes, and
a sprinkling of poor Irish. The side streets leading from it were occupied
by more poor Jews and Negroes. It was a proper locality for a man without capital to do business. My father rented a tenement with a store in
the basement. He put in a few barrels of flour and of sugar, a few boxes
of crackers, a few gallons of kerosene, an assortment of soap of the
"save the coupon" brands; in the cellar, a few barrels of potatoes, and a
pyramid of kindling-wood; in the showcase, an alluring display of penny
candy. He put out his sign, with a gilt-lettered warning of "Strictly
Cash," and proceeded to give credit indiscriminately. That was the regular way to do business on Arlington Street. My father, in his three years'
apprenticeship, had learned the tricks of many trades. He knew when
and how to "bluff." The legend of "Strictly Cash" was a protection
against notoriously irresponsible customers; while none of the "good"
customers, who had a record for paying regularly on Saturday, hesitated
to enter the store with empty purses.

If my father knew the tricks of the trade, my mother could be counted on to throw all her talent and tact into the business. Of course she had no English yet, but as she could perform the acts of weighing, measuring, and mental computation of fractions mechanically, she was able to give her whole attention to the dark mysteries of the language, as intercourse with her customers gave her opportunity. In this she made such rapid progress that she soon lost all sense of disadvantage, and conducted herself behind the counter very much as if she were back in her old store in Polotzk. It was far more cosey than Polotzk—at least, so it seemed to me; for behind the store was the kitchen, where, in the intervals of slack trade, she did her cooking and washing. Arlington Street customers were used to waiting while the storekeeper salted the soup or rescued a loaf from the oven.

Once more Fortune favored my family with a thin little smile, and my father, in reply to a friendly inquiry, would say, "One makes a living," with a shrug of the shoulders that added "but nothing to boast of." It was characteristic of my attitude toward bread-and-butter matters that this contented me, and I felt free to devote myself to the conquest of my new world. Looking back to those critical first years, I see myself always behaving like a child let loose in a garden to play and dig and chase the butterflies. Occasionally, indeed, I was stung by the wasp of family trouble; but I knew a healing ointment—my faith in America. My father had come to America to make a living. America, which was free and fair and kind, must presently yield him what he sought. I had come to America to see a new world, and I followed my own ends with the utmost assiduity, only, as I ran out to explore, I would look back to see if my house were in order behind me—if my family still kept its head above water.

In after years, when I passed as an American among Americans, if I was suddenly made aware of the past that lay forgotten,—if a letter from Russia, or a paragraph in the newspaper, or a conversation overheard in the street-car, suddenly reminded me of what I might have been,—I thought it miracle enough that I, Mashke, the granddaughter of Raphael the Russian, born to a humble destiny, should be at home in an American metropolis, be free to fashion my own life, and should dream my dreams in English phrases. But in the beginning my admiration was spent on more concrete embodiments of the splendors of America; such as fine houses, gay shops, electric engines and apparatus, public buildings, illuminations, and parades. My early letters to my Russian friends were filled with boastful descriptions of these glories of my new country. No native citizen of Chelsea took such pride and delight in its institutions as I did. It required no fife and drum corps, no Fourth of July procession, to set me tingling with patriotism. Even the common agents and instruments of municipal life, such as the letter carrier and the fire engine, I regarded with a measure of respect. I know what I thought of people who said that Chelsea was a very small, dull, unaspiring town, with no discernible excuse for a separate name or existence.

The apex of my civic pride and personal contentment was reached on the bright September morning when I entered the public school. That day I must always remember, even if I live to be so old that I cannot tell my name. To most people their first day at school is a memorable occasion. In my case the importance of the day was a hundred times magnified, on account of the years I had waited, the road I had come, and the conscious ambitions I entertained.

I am wearily aware that I am speaking in extreme figures, in superlatives. I wish I knew some other way to render the mental life of the immigrant child of reasoning age. I may have been ever so much an exception in acuteness of observation, powers of comparison, and abnormal self-consciousness; none the less were my thoughts and conduct typical of the attitude of the intelligent immigrant child toward American institutions. And what the child thinks and feels is a reflection of the hopes, desires, and purposes of the parents who brought him overseas, no matter how precocious and independent the child may be. Your immigrant inspectors will tell you what poverty the foreigner brings in his baggage, what want in his pockets. Let the overgrown boy of twelve, reverently drawing his letters in the baby class, testify to the noble dreams and high ideals that may be hidden beneath the greasy caftan of the immigrant. Speaking for the Jews, at least, I know I am safe in inviting such an investigation.

7

Italians in Two Worlds: An Immigrant's Letters from Argentina, 1901

One of the distinctive features of the capitalist industrial revolution was the globalization of capital and labor. The capital for the British industrial revolution, beginning toward the end of the eighteenth century, filtered in from the treasures of the Indies — East and West — and owed much to the labor of slaves and legally free workers who were shipped from one end of the world to the other. By the

---

Source: *One Family, Two Worlds: An Italian Family's Correspondence across the Atlantic*, ed. Samuel L. Baily and Franco Ramella, trans. John Lenaghan (New Brunswick: Rutgers University Press, 1988), 34–42.

second half of the nineteenth century, the owners of farms, factories, mines, and railroads called for many more laborers.

Millions of these workers came from Italy alone. From 1860 to 1885, most traveled from northern Italy to South America, mainly Argentina. Between 1890 and 1915, Italian immigration to Argentina continued, but even more came from southern Italy to the United States. By the beginning of the twentieth century, New York City and Buenos Aires each had larger Italian populations than many Italian cities.

This selection contains the first few letters sent back home by one of those Italian immigrants, Oreste Sola, who arrived in Buenos Aires in 1901 from northern Italy. What do these letters tell you about this immigrant's expectations? What sort of work did he do? How did he manage to navigate his new world? What were his challenges? How would you describe his strengths? Based on the few hints of events in Italy, how was his life in Argentina different from what it would have likely been in Italy?

THINKING HISTORICALLY

What signs do you see in these letters of industrialization in Argentina? What signs do you see of a capitalist economic system? How is the life of Oreste shaped by the needs of capitalists? How is it shaped by a capitalist economic system? How is his life shaped by industrialization?

Letter 1

Buenos Ayres, 17 August 1901

Dearest parents,

I have been here since the 5th of this month; I am in the best of health as are my two companions. As soon as we got here, we went to the address of Godfather Zocco, who then introduced us to several people from Valdengo who have been in America for some years and all are doing well more or less. The language here is Castilian, quite similar to Spanish, but you don't hear anyone speaking it. Wherever you go, whether in the hotel or at work, everyone speaks either Piedmontese or Italian, even those from other countries, and the Argentines themselves speak Italian.[1]

---

[1] He does not speak or understand Spanish and therefore does not realize that Spanish and Castilian are the same thing. Although 25 percent of the total population and an even higher percentage of the adult population of Buenos Aires was Italian-born, and therefore the Italian language was indeed spoken in many places, Oreste obviously exaggerates when he claims that everyone speaks it.

This city is very beautiful. There is an enormous amount of luxury. All the streets—they call them *calle* [sic] here—are paved either with hard wood or in cement as smooth as marble, even too smooth since the horses, tram horses as well as carriage horses, which run here, keep slipping constantly. It is not unusual to see twenty or more of them fall in one day. . . .

The piazza Victoria (Plaza de Mayo) is also beautiful, where all around on two sides there are only banks. They are of all nations: English, French, Italian, Spanish, North American, etc., etc. On another side is the government building where the president of the Argentine Republic resides. He is Italian, Rocca by name, the third Italian president in a row who sits on the Argentine throne.[2] There is also the railway station of the south, which is something colossal. With workshops, offices, and the station itself it will cover one million square meters. Now they are at work on a government building for the Congress (Parliament). The architect was an Italian, as is the chief contractor, who is supervising all the work. It is a job which in the end will cost more than 700 million lire. It will occupy an area of a block which is 10,000 square meters and will be surrounded by a square, which, along with the building, will constitute an area of about 100,000 square meters. This work will be better than the first [the railway station], but perhaps I shall not be able to see it finished.

All of this is inside the city, but if you should go outside for a few hours, it's worse than a desert. You only find houses made solely out of mortar, with only a ground floor and a door you have to enter on all fours. Outside you don't see a plant; everything is desert. The plains stretch as far as the eye can see; it takes hours on the train before you come to the mountains. There are a few tracts of land, sort of green, where they may let a few horses loose to graze. Here they let the animals go out no matter what the weather might be. Here you can't find a rock, though you pay its weight in gold for it. All the ground is black like manure, thick and muddy. When it doesn't rain, it gets hard, and if you try to dig, it shoots out as if it were rock.

The food here is pretty good, but it doesn't have much flavor. This is true for all Argentina.

All the guys here are jolly as crazy men. In the evening when we get together before going to bed we split our sides laughing. They would all like to go back to Italy, but they don't ever budge. Perhaps I will do

---

[2] Oreste is in error here. The president to whom he refers, Julio Roca, was Argentine not Italian. The preceding president, José Uriburu, also was not Italian. However, Carlos Pelligrini, president from 1890 to 1892, was the son of a French-Italian father from Savoy.

the same. Here we eat, drink, and laugh and enjoy ourselves; we are in America. . . .

Take one last loving kiss and hug
from your always loving son,
Oreste

Letter 2

Mendoza, 18 September 1901

Dearest parents,

I am still in good spirits and happy that I am in America. I am now at Mendoza instead of Buenos Ayres. I didn't like Buenos Ayres too much because you don't get good wine there; and then every day the temperature changes twenty times, and I was always chilly. Otherwise it was fine.

One day I got the idea, knowing that Secondino's brother-in-law and sister were in Mendoza. Since the boss advanced me the money for the trip,[3] I made up my mind to come here, where you see nothing but hills and mountains in the distance, like at home. You drink very well here; the wine costs half what it does in Buenos Ayres and is pure and delicious. I am living here with Carlo and his wife and a man by the name of Luigi Ferraro from Chiavazza, who has been here for seven years traveling around in America. There are few people here from Biella, but there is no shortage of Italians. I still haven't learned a word of Castilian because, everywhere you go, they speak Italian or Piedmontese.

I am better off here than in Buenos Ayres. I am only sorry to be so far from my friends—they didn't want to come—and from Godfather and the rest.

This city is ugly; it never rains even though it is close to the mountains. I have written a friend to send me the address of my schoolmate Berretta, and I might just go and see him in Peru; it takes four days or more on the train. From Buenos Ayres to Mendoza takes two nights and a day on the railroad without ever changing trains or getting off. The longest stop is a half hour. In the entire journey you don't see a plant. [There are] two or three rivers about 400 meters wide. They are all in the plain, so calm that you can't tell which way the water is going, and yet they flow on in an imperceptible way.

---

[3] The government of the province of Mendoza and many individual employers made a major effort to attract European immigrants during the two decades preceding World War I. It was not unusual for an employer to advance money to pay for the trip from Buenos Aires to Mendoza.

Throughout the journey one meets only horses, cows, and goats, none of which have stables. On the rail line you don't see a house for three hours or more, and everything is like that. . . .

Everyone, Carlo, Cichina, and Luigi, give their regards to you. Tell Secondino to come and see America, to drink and eat and travel.

Time is pressing since I have to work every evening until ten. I work at home after work.

You should write me at:

> El Taller del Ferro Carril G.O.A.
> Mendoza

Goodbye everybody. Kisses to Abele and Narcisa. Tell Abele to study hard and to learn to work. Send him to the technical schools; I imagine he has been promoted. Goodbye, Mom and Dad. Be in good spirits as I am.

> Yours always,
> Orestes

Letter 3

Mendoza, 13 November 1901

Dearest Father, Mother, brother, and sister,

This morning Secondino arrived as you had already indicated he would in your letter of 14 October. He had a very good trip, and he made everyone happy to see him healthy and cheerful—as we are, Carlo, Cichina, and Luigi. He gave me the trousers which you gave him to bring me and the letter written by Dad and Narcisa.

I have been here in Mendoza for about three months, and I am happy that Secondino is here now too. But I don't plan to stay fixed here. I would like to go to Peru with Berretta or to Cuba, where dear Cousin Edvino is staying, since I know that those who are there are doing well now. It wouldn't be bad here except you aren't sure about employment or about anything, especially for the type of work I do. So you can't even be sure of staying in one place. Before leaving I am waiting to get the address of Berretta.

I thought that I could send something, instead I had to make some purchases. Be patient. I think of our family conditions too often to be able to think of anything else. Excuse me if I have been slow in writing. It's because I hoped to get a particular job, and I wanted to let you know. I was waiting for the decision of the company. The job went to another, also Italian, with whom nobody could compete. But let's leave the subject of work because here there are so many professions and so many trades that you can't say what you are doing. Today it's this and tomorrow it's that. I tried to go into the construction business for myself, but it didn't work out. So much effort and expense. Now I am doing something else, and I shall change again soon.

My friends as well as Godfather are still in Buenos Aires. They are fine and want to be remembered to you. I receive news (from Buenos Aires) almost every week.

Pardon me, dear parents, brother, and sister, if I am sometimes slow in writing. It is not that I forget, quite the contrary. Only please don't reproach me the way Narcisa does because, if you knew how painful these reproaches are to us here, especially when they come from the family, you would not believe it. I shall try to write more often.

Narcisa asks me for postcards, Abele for stamps. I cannot satisfy anyone since they don't sell illustrated postcards here even though there would be many beautiful things [to show], like, for example, the ruins of Mendoza of 1860 caused by the earthquake, which often happens here six or seven times a year.[4] If it is a special earthquake, you seem to be in a boat, rocking like at sea. But if it gets a bit strong, you have to lie down so as not to fall. Some attribute it to the various volcanoes, mostly extinct however, which are in the mountains here. Others say it is because of the huge storms of the Pacific meeting the winds that come from the Atlantic. However, no one can verify it.

From what I make out from Dad's letter, he says that he was planning to send me some clothes when I get established here. Excuse me, dear parents, your sacrifices are already excessive. Now it is my job to pay them back at least in part, and I shall do everything possible to that end. But excuse me, I am old enough now to earn my bread. I beg you not to be offended about this. If later I shall be in a position to, I shall send you money and everything. But for now, first of all, I have clothes to wear. I have already purchased here two suits and four pairs of trousers. So don't be upset then. Rather, I repeat, as soon as I am able, I'll see that you get something. Now I cannot; it has gone badly for me before I got started. When I shall again be the way I was in the beginning—but I don't know when because here [in] America [things] can change from one day to the next—you will have some repayment.

I have received your newspapers and bulletins, letters and all, because the telegraph and postal service here is something very precise. I was very pleased to get them. I read also in the bulletin of the professional school that they are asking for the address of members who are living outside the country. If I should send it and then, before publication, I should move, I would be in the same situation I was before. Also they want you to indicate the kind of work you are doing for publication in the bulletin because it will be, I believe, an issue with all the graduates of the professional school, and I can't tell them that. I change from one day to

[4] The earthquake to which he refers occurred on March 20, 1861. It destroyed the entire city of Mendoza and killed much of its population.

the next. At that moment I was a draftsman second grade in the workshop of the Trans Andes railway. It is a direct railway to Chile now under construction. But I am not doing it anymore because the section that the four of us were assigned to work on has been finished.

Now I am working as a smith and various things for the Great Western Railway of Argentina. But since they don't pay me as I want and I have to be first a blacksmith, then work as a planer, then at the lathe, I don't like it. At the first other job that comes along, I'm off. When I find something better, I don't want to work as a laborer for low wages anymore. . . .

> Your most loving son and
> brother,
> Oreste Sola

Letter 4

> Mendoza, 25 November 1901

Dearest ones,

A few days before this letter you will have received another written on the day of Secondino's arrival; a few days later he received some newspapers which indicated that you were on strike.[5] I understand that in this season such a big strike will be very distressing. I, however, right now absolutely cannot, for the moment, help you in any way. If I had been able to get that damned construction job, I assure you I would have "hit the jackpot." From one day to the next another bit of bad luck could come my way; but everything is in doubt, there is then no certainty nor prospect.

Now they are coming here every day on the emigration train, about 600 persons a week. They are then sent out of the city in great numbers; but many remain, and we are beginning to see some unemployment but only in a small way. It's just that working in such conditions you only earn a bare living and with difficulty at that. If I have bad luck, I'm not staying here any longer. I want to go to Cuba with Boffa and the rest since Berretta doesn't answer. Nothing is certain however. The ideas come in crowds, but the execution is just miserable. Still I am not losing heart ever. I have been through a good period at first, then an excellent one, and now I am in a third one that is very tough. But I'll get back on my feet. We are in America.

Be patient then. I too am aware that Mom is working at night, that you are working on Sundays, etc.—things that don't happen here. Here

---

[5] Oreste is referring to the major strike at the Biella textile factory in which [his parents] Luigi and Margherita worked. The strike, which ended in defeat for the workers, was provoked when the owners increased the work load without increasing salaries.

in every profession and everywhere you work nine hours a day and only 'til noon on Saturday. You don't work on Sunday nor after midday meal on Saturday, and you get more respect. When you ask for some improvement in pay, the owners don't say that they will show up with a rifle and fire at the first one who makes trouble, as the famous Giovanni Rivetti used to say.[6] Here, if they don't want to give it to you, they look into it, they review it; but generally they give it to you, and all this without unions or anything. They are capitalists who are more aware; that's all there is to it.

Think always of your loving son who is in America, always in good spirits, even when things are going badly for him.

Oreste Sola

Secondino, like me, is always in good spirits, and we are always together. He sends you his warmest greetings and so does Carlo's family. Secondino would like you to say hello to his wife if it is not too much trouble.

[6] Giovanni Rivetti was one of the owners of the Biella textile factory in which Luigi and Margherita worked. Given the size and importance of the factory, Rivetti's conduct greatly influenced that of the other owners in the entire area.

■ REFLECTIONS

It was because of certain traits in private capitalism that the machine—which was a neutral agent—has often seemed, and in fact has sometimes been, a malicious element in society, careless of human life, indifferent to human interests. The machine has suffered for the sins of capitalism; contrariwise, capitalism has often taken credit for the virtues of the machine.[1]

Our chapter turns the above proposition by writer Lewis Mumford into a series of questions: What has been the impact of capitalism? Is the machine only neutral, or does it have its own effects? How can we distinguish between the economic and the technological chains of cause and effect?

Capitalism and industrialization are difficult concepts to distinguish. Adam Smith illustrated the power of the market and the division of labor by imagining their impact not on a shop or trading firm but on a pin factory, an early industrial enterprise. Karl Marx summarized the achievements of the capitalist age by enumerating "wonders far surpassing Egyptian pyramids," which included chemical industries, steam navigation, railroads, and electric telegraphs. Neither Smith nor

[1] Lewis Mumford, *Technics and Civilization* (New York: Harcourt Brace, 1963), 27.

Marx used the terms *capitalism* or *industrial revolution,* although such variants as *capitalist* and *industrial* were already in circulation. Modern historians fought over their meaning and relevance as explanations of change through most of the last century. To understand the great transformation into modernity, some emphasized the expansion of market capitalism; others emphasized the power of the machine. The rise of state-capitalist and communist industrial societies politicized the debate, but even after the fall of communism, the historical questions remained. Peter Stearns looks for the forces that spread or retarded industrialization. The letters of Oreste Sola support the argument of some historians of Latin America that the continent was modernized more by trade and capital than by industrialization.

After 1900 the industrial revolution spread throughout the world, but its pace was not always revolutionary. Even today some societies are still largely rural, with a majority of workers engaged in subsistence farming or small-scale manufacturing by hand. But over the long course of history people have always tried to replace human labor with machines and increase the production of machine-made goods. In some cases, the transformation has been dramatic. Malaysia, once a languid land of tropical tea and rubber plantations, sprouted enough microchip and electronics factories after 1950 to account for 60 percent of its exports by the year 2000. By the 1990s an already highly industrialized country like Japan could produce luxury cars in factories that needed only a handful of humans to monitor the work of computer-driven robots. Despite occasional announcements of the arrival of a "postindustrial" society, the pressure to mechanize continues unabated in the twenty-first century.

The fate of capitalism in the twentieth century was more varied. The second wave of industrial revolutions—beginning with Germany after 1850 and Japan after 1880—was directed by governments as much as capitalists. Socialist parties won large support in industrial countries in the first half of the twentieth century, creating welfare states in some after World War II. In Russia after 1917, the Communist Party pioneered a model of state-controlled industrialization that attracted imitators from China to Chile and funded anticapitalist movements throughout the world.

The Cold War (1947–1991) between the United States and the Soviet Union, though largely a power struggle between two superpowers, was widely seen as an ideological contest between capitalism and socialism. Thus the demise of the Soviet Union and its Communist Party in 1991 was heralded as the victory of capitalism over socialism. As Russia, China, and other previously communist states embraced market economies, socialism was declared dead.

But could proclaiming the death of socialism be as premature as heralding the end of industrial society? *The Communist Manifesto* of 1848 long predates the Russian Revolution of 1917. Karl Marx died in

1883. Socialists like Rosa Luxembourg criticized Lenin and the Russian communists for misinterpreting Marxism in their impatience to transform Russian society. Socialists, even Marxists, continue to write, advise, and govern today, often urging restraints on the spread of global capital markets and the threat of unregulated capitalism for the global environment. Rarely are they willing to relinquish the advantages of industrial technology; rather, they seek to release the "virtues of the machine."

22

Colonized and Colonizers

Europeans in Africa and Asia, 1850–1930

■ HISTORICAL CONTEXT

The first stage of European colonialism, beginning with Columbus, was a period in which Europeans—led by the Spanish and Portuguese—settled in the Western Hemisphere and created plantations with African labor. From 1492 to 1776, European settlement in Asia was limited to a few coastal port cities where merchants and missionaries operated. The second stage—the years between 1776, when Britain lost most of its American colonies, and 1880, when the European scramble for African territory began—has sometimes been called a period of *free-trade imperialism*. This term refers to the desire by European countries in general and by Britain in particular to expand their zones of free trade. It also refers to a widespread opposition to the expense of colonization, a conviction held especially among the British, who garnered all of the advantages of political empire without the costs of occupation and outright ownership.

The British used to quip that their second global empire was created in the nineteenth century "in a fit of absentmindedness." But colonial policy in Britain and the rest of Europe was more planned and continuous than that comment might suggest. British control of India (including Burma) increased throughout the nineteenth century, as did British control of South Africa, Australia, the Pacific, and parts of the Americas. At the same time, France, having lost most of India to the British, began building an empire that included parts of North Africa, Southeast Asia, and the Pacific.

Thus, a third stage of colonialism, beginning in the mid-nineteenth century, reached a fever pitch with the partition of Africa after 1880. The period between 1888 and 1914 spawned renewed settlement and massive population transfers, with most European migrants settling in the older colonies of the Americas (as well as in South Africa and Australia), where indigenous populations had been reduced. Even where settlement remained light, however, Europeans took political control of large areas of the Earth's surface (see Map 22.1).

■ THINKING HISTORICALLY

Using Literature in History

This chapter also explores how literature can be used in the quest to better understand history. We examine a number of fictional accounts of colonialism, some written by the colonizers, others by the colonized or their descendants, in addition to a critical study of a historical novel and a poem. How do these pieces of literature add to, or detract from, a historical understanding of colonialism? We explore this question because the European colonial experience produced a rich, evocative literature, which, used carefully, can offer a wide range of detail and insight about the period and colonialism.

Historical novels are particularly tricky. The structure of a novel bears certain similarities to history—a description of a place, proper names and biographies, descriptions of human interactions, an accounting of change, and a story. There are also structural differences in a novel—a lot of dialogue, greater attention to physical appearance and character, and a more prominent narrative. These fictional elements are often unattainable for historians. Dialogue, a person's actual words, especially thoughts, are often absent from the historical sources. A good novelist creates these elements based on historical research and familiarity with the time and place. Such details provide a great sense of verisimilitude (resemblance to reality). We feel as if we are there, a feeling that further reinforces our sense of the novel's truth. But in this regard we are captives of the novelist, caught in the web of his or her imagination. In good hands we may see what would otherwise be invisible. In bad hands, we may vividly see what was never there.

A good novel, like a good history, shows us something we did not know, something unexpected, even surprising. But the problem is that we are most easily seduced by what is most familiar to us. Thus, in the hands of the uninformed, we are most likely to believe we have seen the historical truth when we have only projected our own world onto the past. How successfully do the authors of these fictional pieces show you something about the past that is likely true?

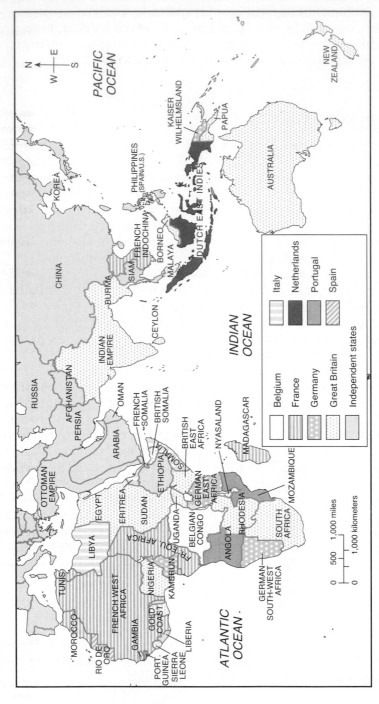

Map 22.1 European Colonialism in Africa and Asia, 1880–1914.

1

GEORGE ORWELL
Burmese Days, 1934

George Orwell, the pen name of Eric Arthur Blair (1903–1950), is best known for such novels as *Animal Farm* (1945) and *Nineteen Eighty-Four* (1949), from which the term *Orwellian* has come to define totalitarianism. *Burmese Days* (1934) was Orwell's first novel, based on his experience in the British police in Burma from 1922 to 1927.

This selection from the novel captures the life of the British colonial class in a remote "upcountry" town in Burma in the 1920s, a hundred years after British conquest and settlement had begun and fifty years after all of Burma had been integrated into the British Indian empire.

The central character is Flory, the only Englishman at all sympathetic to the Burmese. Though he has befriended the Indian physician, Dr. Veraswami, Flory is too weak to propose him as the first "native" member of the club. The other main characters are Westfield, district superintendent of police; Ellis, local company manager and the most racist of the group; Lackersteen, local manager of a timber company who is usually drunk; Maxwell, a forest officer; and Macgregor, deputy commissioner and secretary of the club.

Why does the club loom so large in the lives of these Englishmen? If they complain so much, why are they in Burma? How do you account for the virulent racism of these men? Why does Ellis "correct" the butler's English? What does this story suggest about women in the colonial world?

THINKING HISTORICALLY

Orwell knew Burma quite well. He was born in India in 1903, and his father worked in the Opium Department of the Indian Civil Service. After attending school at Eton in England, Orwell spent five years as a member of the Indian Imperial Police in Burma. Orwell's mother had grown up in Burma, and his grandmother continued to live there in the 1920s. In his various postings, Orwell no doubt spent time in British social clubs like the one that serves as the setting for this chapter. Orwell, therefore, had a broad knowledge of Burma on which to base his story. Is there any way to determine what Orwell invented and what he merely described in this account?

Orwell was politically engaged throughout his life. Would political ideas make him better or worse as a historian or novelist? How so?

Source: George Orwell, *Burmese Days* (1934; reprint, San Diego: Harcourt Brace, 1962), 17–27.

Flory's house was at the top of the maidan,[1] close to the edge of the jungle. From the gate the maidan sloped sharply down, scorched and khaki-coloured, with half a dozen dazzling white bungalows scattered round it. All quaked, shivered in the hot air. There was an English cemetery within a white wall half-way down the hill, and nearby a tiny tin-roofed church. Beyond that was the European Club, and when one looked at the Club—a dumpy one-storey wooden building—one looked at the real centre of the town. In any town in India the European Club is the spiritual citadel, the real seat of the British power, the Nirvana for which native officials and millionaires pine in vain. It was doubly so in this case, for it was the proud boast of Kyauktada Club that, almost alone of Clubs in Burma, it had never admitted an Oriental[2] to membership. Beyond the Club, the Irrawaddy flowed huge and ochreous, glittering like diamonds in the patches that caught the sun; and beyond the river stretched great wastes of paddy fields, ending at the horizon in a range of blackish hills.

The native town, and the courts and the jail, were over to the right, mostly hidden in green groves of peepul trees. The spire of the pagoda rose from the trees like a slender spear tipped with gold. Kyauktada[3] was a fairly typical Upper Burma town, that had not changed greatly between the days of Marco Polo and 1910, and might have slept in the Middle Ages for a century more if it had not proved a convenient spot for a railway terminus. In 1910 the Government[4] made it the headquarters of a district and a seat of Progress—interpretable as a block of law courts, with their army of fat but ravenous pleaders, a hospital, a school, and one of those huge, durable jails which the English have built everywhere between Gibraltar and Hong Kong. The population was about four thousand, including a couple of hundred Indians, a few score Chinese and seven Europeans. There were also two Eurasians named Mr. Francis and Mr. Samuel, the sons of an American Baptist missionary and a Roman Catholic missionary respectively. The town contained no curiosities of any kind, except an Indian fakir[5] who had lived for twenty years in a tree near the bazaar, drawing his food up in a basket every morning.

---

[1] Parade-ground. [Ed.]

[2] The term *Oriental* included all Asians or people of the "East" as opposed to Occidentals or Westerners, as in Rudyard Kipling's *Barrack-room Ballads*: "East is East and West is West, and never the twain [two] shall meet" (1892). But in this case, Orwell means Indians and Burmese as well as the few Chinese. [Ed.]

[3] Fictional name for Katha or Kathar, a town on the Irrawaddy (or Ayeyarwady) River and the railroad, in northern Burma, where Orwell lived from 1926–1927. [Ed.]

[4] The British government eliminated the Burmese monarchy, exiling the king to India, and abolished the traditional role of the Buddhist monks, imposing instead the kind of bureaucracy they used to rule India. [Ed.]

[5] Originally a term for a Muslim Sufi mystic, here used to mean any ascetic, Hindu or Muslim, or even a beggar. [Ed.]

Flory yawned as he came out of the gate. He had been half drunk the night before, and the glare made him feel liverish. "Bloody, bloody hole!" he thought, looking down the hill. And, no one except the dog being near, he began to sing aloud, "Bloody, bloody, bloody, oh, how thou art bloody" to the tune of "Holy, holy, holy, oh how Thou art holy," as he walked down the hot red road, switching at the dried-up grasses with his stick. It was nearly nine o'clock and the sun was fiercer every minute. The heat throbbed down on one's head with a steady, rhythmic thumping, like blows from an enormous bolster. Flory stopped at the Club gate, wondering whether to go in or to go farther down the road and see Dr. Veraswami. Then he remembered that it was "English mail day" and the newspapers would have arrived. He went in, past the big tennis screen, which was overgrown by a creeper with starlike mauve flowers.

In the borders beside the path swathes of English flowers, phlox and larkspur, hollyhock and petunia, not yet slain by the sun, rioted in vast size and richness. The petunias were huge, like trees almost. There was no lawn, but instead a shrubbery of native trees and bushes—gold mohur trees like vast umbrellas of blood-red bloom, frangipanis with creamy, stalkless flowers, purple bougainvillea, scarlet hibiscus, and the pink, Chinese rose, bilious-green crotons, feathery fronds of tamarind. The clash of colours hurt one's eyes in the glare. A nearly naked *mali*,[6] watering-can in hand, was moving in the jungle of flowers like some large nectar-sucking bird.

On the Club steps a sandy-haired Englishman, with a prickly moustache, pale grey eyes too far apart, and abnormally thin calves to his legs, was standing with his hands in the pockets of his shorts. This was Mr. Westfield, the District Superintendent of Police. With a very bored air he was rocking himself backwards and forwards on his heels and pouting his upper lip so that his moustache tickled his nose. He greeted Flory with a slight sideways movement of his head. His way of speaking was clipped and soldierly, missing out every word that well could be missed out. Nearly everything he said was intended for a joke, but the tone of his voice was hollow and melancholy.

"Hullo, Flory me lad. Bloody awful morning, what?"

"We must expect it at this time of year, I suppose," Flory said. He had turned himself a little sideways, so that his birthmarked cheek was away from Westfield.

"Yes, dammit. Couple of months of this coming. Last year we didn't have a spot of rain till June. Look at that bloody sky, not a cloud in it. Like one of those damned great blue enamel saucepans. God! What'd you give to be in Piccadilly now, eh?"

"Have the English papers come?"

---

[6] Gardener. [Ed.]

"Yes. Dear old *Punch, Pink'un,* and *Vie Parisienne.* Makes you home-sick to read 'em, what? Let's come in and have a drink before the ice all goes. Old Lackersteen's been fairly bathing in it. Half pickled already."

They went in, Westfield remarking in his gloomy voice, "Lead on, Macduff." Inside, the Club was a teak-walled place smelling of earthoil, and consisting of only four rooms, one of which contained a forlorn "library" of five hundred mildewed novels, and another an old and mangy billiard-table—this, however, seldom used, for during most of the year hordes of flying beetles came buzzing round the lamps and lit-tered themselves over the cloth. There were also a card-room and a "lounge" which looked towards the river, over a wide veranda; but at this time of day all the verandas were curtained with green bamboo chicks. The lounge was an unhomelike room, with coco-nut matting on the floor, and wicker chairs and tables which were littered with shiny illustrated papers. For ornament there were a number of "Bonzo" pictures,[7] and the dusty skulls of sambhur.[8] A punkah,[9] lazily flapping, shook dust into the tepid air.

There were three men in the room. Under the punkah a florid, fine-looking, slightly bloated man of forty was sprawling across the table with his head in his hands, groaning in pain. This was Mr. Lackersteen, the local manager of a timber firm. He had been badly drunk the night before, and he was suffering for it. Ellis, local manager of yet another company, was standing before the notice board studying some notice with a look of bitter concentration. He was a tiny wiry-haired fellow with a pale, sharp-featured face and restless movements. Maxwell, the acting Divisional Forest Officer, was lying in one of the long chairs read-ing the *Field,* and invisible except for two large-boned legs and thick downy forearms.

"Look at this naughty old man," said Westfield, taking Mr. Lackersteen half affectionately by the shoulders and shaking him. "Example to the young, what? There, but for the grace of God and all that. Gives you an idea what you'll be like at forty."

Mr. Lackersteen gave a groan which sounded like "brandy."

"Poor old chap," said Westfield; "regular martyr to booze, eh? Look at it oozing out of his pores. Reminds me of the old colonel who used to sleep without a mosquito net. They asked his servant why and the ser-vant said: 'At night, master too drunk to notice mosquitoes; in the morn-ing, mosquitoes too drunk to notice master.' Look at him—boozed last night and then asking for more. Got a little niece coming to stay with him, too. Due tonight, isn't she, Lackersteen?"

[7] Bulldog puppy cartoons created by G. E. Studdy in the 1920s for magazines like *Punch.* [Ed.]

[8] Large South Asian deer, like elk. [Ed.]

[9] Large cloth panel fan hanging from the ceiling, usually pulled by a rope to move the air. [Ed.]

"Oh, leave that drunken sot alone," said Ellis without turning round. He had a spiteful cockney voice. Mr. Lackersteen groaned again, "—the niece! Get me some brandy, for Christ's sake."

"Good education for the niece, eh? Seeing uncle under the table seven times a week.—Hey, butler! Bringing brandy for Lackersteen master!"

The butler, a dark, stout Dravidian[10] with liquid, yellow-irised eyes like those of a dog, brought the brandy on a brass tray. Flory and Westfield ordered gin. Mr. Lackersteen swallowed a few spoonfuls of brandy and sat back in his chair, groaning in a more resigned way. He had a beefy, ingenuous face, with a toothbrush moustache. He was really a very simple-minded man, with no ambitions beyond having what he called "a good time." His wife governed him by the only possible method, namely, by never letting him out of her sight for more than an hour or two. Only once, a year after they were married, she had left him for a fortnight, and had returned unexpectedly a day before her time, to find Mr. Lackersteen, drunk, supported on either side by a naked Burmese girl, while a third up-ended a whisky bottle into his mouth. Since then she had watched him, as he used to complain, "like a cat over a bloody mousehole." However, he managed to enjoy quite a number of "good times," though they were usually rather hurried ones.

"My Christ, what a head I've got on me this morning," he said. "Call that butler again, Westfield. I've got to have another brandy before my missus gets here. She says she's going to cut my booze down to four pegs a day when our niece gets here. God rot them both!" he added gloomily.

"Stop playing the fool, all of you, and listen to this," said Ellis sourly. He had a queer wounding way of speaking, hardly ever opening his mouth without insulting somebody. He deliberately exaggerated his cockney accent, because of the sardonic tone it gave to his words. "Have you seen this notice of old Macgregor's? A little nosegay for everyone. Maxwell, wake up and listen!"

Maxwell lowered the *Field*. He was a fresh-coloured blond youth of not more than twenty-five or six—very young for the post he held. With his heavy limbs and thick white eyelashes he reminded one of a carthorse colt. Ellis nipped the notice from the board with a neat, spiteful little movement and began reading it aloud. It had been posted by Mr. Macgregor, who, besides being Deputy Commissioner, was secretary of the Club.

"Just listen to this. 'It has been suggested that as there are as yet no Oriental members of this club, and as it is now usual to admit officials of gazetted rank, whether native or European, to membership of most European Clubs, we should consider the question of following this practice in Kyauktada. The matter will be open for discussion at the next

[10] Dated racial term used to refer to darker-skinned inhabitants of southern India. [Ed.]

general meeting. On the one hand it may be pointed out' — oh, well, no need to wade through the rest of it. He can't even write out a notice without an attack of literary diarrhoea. Anyway, the point's this. He's asking us to break all our rules and take a dear little nigger-boy into this Club. *Dear* Dr. Veraswami, for instance. Dr. Very-slimy, I call him. That *would* be a treat, wouldn't it? Little pot-bellied niggers breathing garlic in your face over the bridge-table. Christ, to think of it! We've got to hang together and put our foot down on this at once. What do you say, Westfield? Flory?"

Westfield shrugged his thin shoulders philosophically. He had sat down at the table and lighted a black, stinking Burma cheroot.

"Got to put up with it, I suppose," he said. "B_____s of natives are getting into all the Clubs nowadays. Even the Pegu Club, I'm told. Way this country's going, you know. We're about the last Club in Burma to hold out against 'em."

"We are; and what's more, we're damn well going to go on holding out. I'll die in the ditch before I'll see a nigger in here." Ellis had produced a stump of pencil. With the curious air of spite that some men can put into their tiniest action, he re-pinned the notice on the board and pencilled a tiny, neat "B. F." against Mr. Macgregor's signature — "There, that's what I think of his idea. I'll tell him so when he comes down. What do *you* say, Flory?"

Flory had not spoken all this time. Though by nature anything but a silent man, he seldom found much to say in Club conversations. He had sat down at the table and was reading G. K. Chesterton's article in the *London News*, at the same time caressing [his dog] Flo's head with his left hand. Ellis, however, was one of those people who constantly nag others to echo their own opinions. He repeated his question, and Flory looked up, and their eyes met. The skin round Ellis's nose suddenly turned so pale that it was almost grey. In him it was a sign of anger. Without any prelude he burst into a stream of abuse that would have been startling, if the others had not been used to hearing something like it every morning.

"My God, I should have thought in a case like this, when it's a question of keeping those black, stinking swine out of the only place where we can enjoy ourselves, you'd have the decency to back me up. Even if that pot-bellied, greasy little sod of a nigger doctor *is* your best pal. *I* don't care if you choose to pal up with the scum of the bazaar. If it pleases you to go to Veraswami's house and drink whisky with all his nigger pals, that's your look-out. Do what you like outside the Club. But, by God, it's a different matter when you talk of bringing niggers in here. I suppose you'd like little Veraswami for a Club member, eh? Chipping into our conversation and pawing everyone with his sweaty hands and breathing his filthy garlic breath in our faces. By God, he'd go out with my boot behind him if ever I saw his black snout inside that door. Greasy, pot-bellied little————!" etc.

This went on for several minutes. It was curiously impressive, because it was so completely sincere. Ellis really did hate Orientals—hated them with a bitter, restless loathing as of something evil or unclean. Living and working, as the assistant of a timber firm must, in perpetual contact with the Burmese, he had never grown used to the sight of a black face. Any hint of friendly feeling towards an Oriental seemed to him a horrible perversity. He was an intelligent man and an able servant of his firm, but he was one of those Englishmen—common, unfortunately—who should never be allowed to set foot in the East.

Flory sat nursing Flo's head in his lap, unable to meet Ellis's eyes. At the best of times his birthmark made it difficult for him to look people straight in the face. And when he made ready to speak, he could feel his voice trembling—for it had a way of trembling when it should have been firm; his features, too, sometimes twitched uncontrollably.

"Steady on," he said at last, sullenly and rather feebly. "Steady on. There's no need to get so excited. *I* never suggested having any native members in here."

"Oh, didn't you? We all know bloody well you'd like to, though. Why else do you go to that oily little babu's house every morning, then? Sitting down at table with him as though he was a white man, and drinking out of glasses his filthy black lips have slobbered over—it makes me spew to think of it."

"Sit down, old chap, sit down," Westfield said. "Forget it. Have a drink on it. Not worth while quarrelling. Too hot."

"My God," said Ellis a little more calmly, taking a pace or two up and down, "my God, I don't understand you chaps. I simply don't. Here's that old fool Macgregor wanting to bring a nigger into this Club for no reason whatever, and you all sit down under it without a word. Good God, what are we supposed to be doing in this country? If we aren't going to rule, why the devil don't we clear out? Here we are, supposed to be governing a set of damn black swine who've been slaves since the beginning of history, and instead of ruling them in the only way they understand, we go and treat them as equals. And all you silly b———s take it for granted. There's Flory, makes his best pal of a black babu who calls himself a doctor because he's done two years at an Indian so-called university. And you, Westfield, proud as Punch of your knock-kneed, bribe-taking cowards of policemen. And there's Maxwell, spends his time running after Eurasian tarts. Yes, you do, Maxwell; I heard about your goings-on in Mandalay with some smelly little bitch called Molly Pereira. I supposed you'd have gone and married her if they hadn't transferred you up here? You all seem to *like* the dirty black brutes. Christ, I don't know what's come over us all. I really don't."

"Come on, have another drink," said Westfield. "Hey, butler! Spot of beer before the ice goes, eh? Beer, butler!"

The butler brought some bottles of Munich beer. Ellis presently sat down at the table with the others, and he nursed one of the cool bottles between his small hands. His forehead was sweating. He was sulky, but not in a rage any longer. At all times he was spiteful and perverse, but his violent fits of rage were soon over, and were never apologised for. Quarrels were a regular part of the routine of Club life. Mr. Lackersteen was feeling better and was studying the illustrations in *La Vie Parisienne*. It was after nine now, and the room, scented with the acrid smoke of Westfield's cheroot, was stifling hot. Everyone's shirt stuck to his back with the first sweat of the day. The invisible *chokra*[11] who pulled the punkah rope outside was falling asleep in the glare.

"Butler!" yelled Ellis, and as the butler appeared, "go and wake that bloody *chokra* up!"

"Yes, master."

"And butler!"

"Yes, master?"

"How much ice have we got left?"

"'Bout twenty pounds, master. Will only last to-day, I think. I find it very difficult to keep ice cool now."

"Don't talk like that, damn you—'I find it very difficult!' Have you swallowed a dictionary? 'Please, master, can't keeping ice cool'—that's how you ought to talk. We shall have to sack this fellow if he gets to talk English too well. I can't stick servants who talk English. D'you hear, butler?"

"Yes, master," said the butler, and retired.

"God! No ice till Monday," Westfield said. "You going back to the jungle, Flory?"

"Yes. I ought to be there now. I only came in because of the English mail."

"Go on tour myself, I think. Knock up a spot of Travelling Allowance. I can't stick my bloody office at this time of year. Sitting there under the damned punkah, signing one chit after another. Paperchewing. God, how I wish the war was on again!"

"I'm going out the day after to-morrow," Ellis said. "Isn't that damned padre coming to hold his service this Sunday? I'll take care not to be in for that, anyway. Bloody knee-drill."

"Next Sunday," said Westfield. "Promised to be in for it myself. So's Macgregor. Bit hard on the poor devil of a padre, I must say. Only gets here once in six weeks. Might as well get up a congregation when he does come."

"Oh, hell! I'd snivel psalms to oblige the padre, but I can't stick the way these damned native Christians come shoving into our church. A

---

[11] Person who pulls the punkah rope that moves a large panel to let in a breeze. [Ed.]

pack of Madrassi servants and Karen[12] school-teachers. And then those two yellow-bellies, Francis and Samuel—they call themselves Christians too. Last time the padre was here they had the nerve to come up and sit on the front pews with the white men. Someone ought to speak to the padre about that. What bloody fools we were ever to let those missionaries loose in this country! Teaching bazaar sweepers they're as good as we are. 'Please, sir, me Christian same like master.' Damned cheek."

[12] An ethnic minority group in Burma. [Ed.]

2

JOSEPH CONRAD
Heart of Darkness, 1899

Although his native tongue was Polish (and French his second language), Joseph Conrad (1857–1924) became one of the leading English novelists of the era of British imperialism. Drawing on his experience as a mariner and ship captain, he secured a post as an officer on river steamboats on the Congo River in 1890. Nine years later he published *Heart of Darkness*, a novel that has introduced generations since to Africa, the Congo, the era of colonialism, and European ideas of "the other."

In this selection from the novel, Conrad's narrator, Marlow, tells of his voyage up the Congo to meet the enigmatic European Kurtz, who has secured prodigious amounts of ivory for his Belgian employer but (we learn at the end of the novel) has lost his mind in the process.

What impression does *Heart of Darkness* give of Africa and Africans? What does it suggest were the motives or intentions of European explorers and traders in Africa? What feeling does this selection convey about European colonization of Africa?

THINKING HISTORICALLY

Like many novels, *Heart of Darkness* is based on the actual experiences of the author. Despite the basis in fact, however, it is very different from historical writing. Imagine Conrad writing a history of the events described in this selection. How would it be different? Would one account be truer, or merely reveal different truths?

Source: Joseph Conrad, *Heart of Darkness*, A Norton Critical Edition (New York: Norton, 1988), 35–39. Originally published by *Blackwood's Magazine* (London, 1899, 1902).

Going up that river was like travelling back to the earliest beginnings of the world, when vegetation rioted on the earth and the big trees were kings. An empty stream, a great silence, an impenetrable forest. The air was warm, thick, heavy, sluggish. There was no joy in the brilliance of sunshine. The long stretches of the waterway ran on, deserted, into the gloom of overshadowed distances. On silvery sandbanks hippos and alligators sunned themselves side by side. The broadening waters flowed through a mob of wooded islands. You lost your way on that river as you would in a desert and butted all day long against shoals trying to find the channel till you thought yourself bewitched and cut off for ever from everything you had known once—somewhere—far away—in another existence perhaps. There were moments when one's past came back to one, as it will sometimes when you have not a moment to spare to yourself; but it came in the shape of an unrestful and noisy dream remembered with wonder amongst the overwhelming realities of this strange world of plants and water and silence. And this stillness of life did not in the least resemble a peace. It was the stillness of an implacable force brooding over an inscrutable intention. It looked at you with a vengeful aspect. I got used to it afterwards. I did not see it any more. I had no time. I had to keep guessing at the channel; I had to discern, mostly by inspiration, the signs of hidden banks; I watched for sunken stones; I was learning to clap my teeth smartly before my heart flew out when I shaved by a fluke some infernal sly old snag that would have ripped the life out of the tin-pot steamboat and drowned all the pilgrims; I had to keep a look-out for the signs of dead wood we could cut up in the night for next day's steaming. When you have to attend to things of that sort, to the mere incidents of the surface, the reality—the reality I tell you—fades. The inner truth is hidden—luckily, luckily. But I felt it all the same; I felt often its mysterious stillness watching me at my monkey tricks. . . .

I managed not to sink that steamboat on my first trip. It's a wonder to me yet. Imagine a blindfolded man set to drive a van over a bad road. I sweated and shivered over that business considerably, I can tell you. After all, for a seaman, to scrape the bottom of the thing that's supposed to float all the time under his care is the unpardonable sin. No one may know of it, but you never forget the thump—eh? A blow on the very heart. You remember it, you dream of it, you wake up at night and think of it—years after—and go hot and cold all over. I don't pretend to say that steamboat floated all the time. More than once she had to wade for a bit, with twenty cannibals splashing around and pushing. We had enlisted some of these chaps on the way for a crew. Fine fellows—cannibals—in their place. They were men one could work with, and I am grateful to them. And, after all, they did not eat each other before my face: they had brought along a provision of hippo-meat which went rotten and made the mystery of the wilderness stink in my nostrils. Phoo! I can sniff it now. I had the Manager on board and three or four pilgrims with their staves—all complete. Sometimes we came upon a station close by the bank clinging to the skirts of the unknown, and the white men rushing out of a tumbledown hovel with great gestures of joy and surprise and welcome seemed very strange, had the appearance of being held there captive by a spell. The word "ivory" would ring in the air for a while—and on we went again into the silence, along empty reaches, round the still bends, between the high walls of our winding way, reverberating in hollow claps the ponderous beat of the stern-wheel. Trees, trees, millions of trees, massive, immense, running up high, and at their foot, hugging the bank against the stream, crept the little begrimed steamboat like a sluggish beetle crawling on the floor of a lofty portico. It made you feel very small, very lost, and yet it was not altogether depressing, that feeling. After all, if you were small, the grimy beetle crawled on—which was just what you wanted it to do. Where the pilgrims imagined it crawled to I don't know. To some place where they expected to get something, I bet! For me it crawled towards Kurtz—exclusively; but when the steam-pipes started leaking we crawled very slow. The reaches opened before us and closed behind, as if the forest had stepped leisurely across the water to bar the way for our return. We penetrated deeper and deeper into the heart of darkness. It was very quiet there. At night sometimes the roll of drums behind the curtain of trees would run up the river and remain sustained faintly, as if hovering in the air high over our heads till the first break of day. Whether it meant war, peace, or prayer we could not tell. The dawns were heralded by the descent of a chill stillness. The woodcutters slept, their fires burned low, the snapping of a twig would make you start. We were wanderers on a prehistoric earth, on an earth that wore the aspect of an unknown planet. We could have fancied ourselves the first of men taking possession of an accursed inheritance, to be subdued at the cost of profound anguish and of excessive toil. But suddenly as we struggled round a bend there would be a glimpse of rush walls, of peaked grass-roofs, a burst of yells, a whirl of black limbs, a mass of hands clapping, of feet stamping, of bodies swaying, of eyes rolling under the droop of heavy and motionless foliage. The steamer toiled along slowly on the edge of a black and incomprehensible frenzy. The prehistoric man was cursing us, praying to us, welcoming us—who could tell? We were cut off from the comprehension of our surroundings; we glided past like phantoms, wondering and secretly appalled, as sane men would be before an enthusiastic outbreak in a madhouse. We could not understand because we were too far and could not remember because we were travelling in the night of first ages, of those ages that are gone, leaving hardly a sign—and no memories.

The earth seemed unearthly. We are accustomed to look upon the shackled form of a conquered monster, but there—there you could look at a thing monstrous and free. It was unearthly and the men were. . . . No they were not inhuman. Well, you know that was the worst of it—this suspicion of their not being inhuman. It would come slowly to one. They howled and leaped and spun and made horrid faces, but what thrilled you was just the thought of their humanity—like yours—the thought of your remote kinship with this wild and passionate uproar. Ugly. Yes, it was ugly enough, but if you were man enough you would admit to yourself that there was in you just the faintest trace of a response to the terrible frankness of that noise, a dim suspicion of there being a meaning in it which you—you so remote from the night of first ages—could comprehend. And why not? The mind of man is capable of anything—because everything is in it, all the past as well as all the future. What was there after all? Joy, fear, sorrow, devotion, valour, rage—who can tell?—but truth—truth stripped of its cloak of time. Let the fool gape and shudder—the man knows and can look on without a wink. But he must at least be as much of a man as these on the shore. He must meet that truth with his own true stuff—with his own inborn strength. Principles? Principles won't do. Acquisitions, clothes, pretty rags—rags that would fly off at the first good shake. No. You want a deliberate belief. An appeal to me in this fiendish row—is there? Very well. I hear, I admit, but I have a voice too, and for good or evil mine is the speech that cannot be silenced. Of course, a fool, what with sheer fright and fine sentiments, is always safe. Who's that grunting? You wonder I didn't go ashore for a howl and a dance? Well, no—I didn't. Fine sentiments, you say? Fine sentiments be hanged! I had no time. I had to mess about with whitelead and strips of woollen blanket helping to put bandages on those leaky steam-pipes—tell you. I had to watch the steering and circumvent those snags and get the tin-pot along by hook or by crook. There was surface-truth enough in these things to save a wiser man. And between whiles I had to look after the savage who was fireman. He was an improved specimen; he could fire up a vertical boiler. He was there below me and, upon my word, to look at him was as edifying as seeing a dog in a parody of breeches and a feather hat walking on his hind legs. A few months of training had done for that really fine chap. He squinted at the steam-gauge and at the water-gauge with an evident effort of intrepidity—and he had filed teeth too, the poor devil, and the wool of his pate shaved into queer patterns, and three ornamental scars on each of his cheeks. He ought to have been clapping his hands and stamping his feet on the bank, instead of which he was hard at work, a thrall to strange witchcraft, full of improving knowledge. He was useful because he had been instructed; and what he knew was this—that should the water in that transparent thing disappear the evil spirit inside the boiler would get angry through the greatness of his thirst and take a terrible vengeance. So he sweated and fired up and watched the glass fearfully (with an impromptu charm, made of rags, tied to his arm and a piece of polished bone as big as a watch stuck flatways through his lower lip) while the wooded banks slipped past us slowly, the shore noise was left behind, the interminable miles of silence—and we crept on, towards Kurtz.

3

CHINUA ACHEBE

An Image of Africa: Racism in Conrad's *Heart of Darkness*, 1975

Chinua Achebe* is modern Africa's most read novelist. His *Things Fall Apart*, about the impact of European missionaries in his native Nigeria at the end of the nineteenth century, is a classic that is as widely read as *Heart of Darkness*. In this selection, which first took form as an address to an American college audience in 1975, Achebe tackles *Heart of Darkness*. What is his argument? Are you persuaded?

THINKING HISTORICALLY

Achebe is a novelist criticizing another novelist for distorting history. Could any of Achebe's criticisms be directed at Orwell? What are the responsibilities of a novelist to historical accuracy? How does a critique of literature like this add to our understanding of the past?

*H*eart *of Darkness* projects the image of Africa as "the other world," the antithesis of Europe and therefore of civilization, a place where man's vaunted intelligence and refinement are finally mocked by triumphant bestiality. The book opens on the River Thames, tranquil, resting, peacefully "at the decline of day after ages of good service done to the

---

* chih NOO ah ah CHEH bay

Source: Chinua Achebe, "An Image of Africa: Racism in Conrad's *Heart of Darkness*," an emended version (1987) of the second Chancellor's Lecture at the University of Massachusetts, Amherst, February 18, 1975; later published in the *Massachusetts Review* 18 (1977): 782–94. Reprinted in *Heart of Darkness*, A Norton Critical Edition (New York: Norton, 1988), 252–54, 257–60.

race that peopled its banks." But the actual story will take place on the River Congo, the very antithesis of the Thames. The River Congo is quite decidedly not a River Emeritus. It has rendered no service and enjoys no old-age pension. We are told that "Going up that river was like travelling back to the earliest beginnings of the world."

Is Conrad saying then that these two rivers are very different, one good, the other bad? Yes, but that is not the real point. It is not the differentness that worries Conrad but the lurking hint of kinship, of common ancestry. For the Thames too "has been one of the dark places of the earth." It conquered its darkness, of course, and is now in daylight and at peace. But if it were to visit its primordial relative, the Congo, it would run the terrible risk of hearing grotesque echoes of its own forgotten darkness, and falling victim to an avenging recrudescence of the mindless frenzy of the first beginnings.

These suggestive echoes comprise Conrad's famed evocation of the African atmosphere in *Heart of Darkness*. In the final consideration his method amounts to no more than a steady, ponderous, fake-ritualistic repetition of two antithetical sentences, one about silence and the other about frenzy. We can inspect samples of this on pages 36 and 37[1] of the present edition: a) *It was the stillness of an implacable force brooding over an inscrutable intention* and b) *The steamer toiled along slowly on the edge of a black and incomprehensible frenzy*. Of course there is a judicious change of adjective from time to time, so that instead of *inscrutable*, for example, you might have *unspeakable*, even plain *mysterious*, etc., etc.

The eagle-eyed English critic F. R. Leavis drew attention long ago to Conrad's "adjectival insistence upon inexpressible and incomprehensible mystery." That insistence must not be dismissed lightly, as many Conrad critics have tended to do, as a mere stylistic flaw; for it raises serious questions of artistic good faith. When a writer while pretending to record scenes, incidents, and their impact is in reality engaged in inducing hypnotic stupor in his readers through a bombardment of emotive words and other forms of trickery much more has to be at stake than stylistic felicity. Generally normal readers are well armed to detect and resist such underhand activity. But Conrad chose his subject well—one which was guaranteed not to put him in conflict with the psychological pre-disposition of his readers or raise the need for him to contend with their resistance. He chose the role of purveyor of comforting myths.

The most interesting and revealing passages in *Heart of Darkness* are, however, about people. I must crave the indulgence of my reader to quote almost a whole page from about the middle of the story when

---

[1] See pp. 858 and 859. [Ed.]

representatives of Europe in a steamer going down the Congo encounter the denizens of Africa.

> We were wanderers on a prehistoric earth, on an earth that wore the aspect of an unknown planet. We could have fancied ourselves the first of men taking possession of an accursed inheritance, to be subdued at the cost of profound anguish and of excessive toil. But suddenly as we struggled round a bend there would be a glimpse of rush walls, of peaked grass-roofs, a burst of yells, a whirl of black limbs, a mass of hands clapping, of feet stamping, of bodies sway-ing, of eyes rolling under the droop of heavy and motionless foliage. The steamer toiled along slowly on the edge of a black and incom-prehensible frenzy. The prehistoric man was cursing us, praying to us, welcoming us—who could tell? We were cut off from the com-prehension of our surroundings; we glided past like phantoms, wondering and secretly appalled, as sane men would be before an enthusiastic outbreak in a madhouse. We could not understand be-cause we were too far and could not remember, because we were travelling in the night of first ages, of those ages that are gone, leav-ing hardly a sign—and no memories.

> The earth seemed unearthly. We are accustomed to look upon the shackled form of a conquered monster, but there—there you could look at a thing monstrous and free. It was unearthly and the men were. . . . No they were not inhuman. Well, you know that was the worst of it—this suspicion of their not being inhuman. It would come slowly to one. They howled and leaped and spun and made horrid faces, but what thrilled you was just the thought of their hu-manity—like yours—the thought of your remote kinship with this wild and passionate uproar. Ugly. Yes, it was ugly enough, but if you were man enough you would admit to yourself that there was in you just the faintest trace of a response to the terrible frankness of that noise, a dim suspicion of there being a meaning in it which you—you so remote from the night of first ages—could comprehend.

Herein lies the meaning of *Heart of Darkness* and the fascination it holds over the Western mind: "What thrilled you was just the thought of their humanity—like yours. . . . Ugly."

Having shown us Africa in the mass, Conrad then zeros in, half a page later, on a specific example, giving us one of his rare descriptions of an African who is not just limbs or rolling eyes:

> And between whiles I had to look after the savage who was fire-man. He was an improved specimen; he could fire up a vertical boiler. He was there below me and, upon my word, to look at him was as edifying as seeing a dog in a parody of breeches and a feather hat walking on his hind legs. A few months of training had done for

that really fine chap. He squinted at the steam-gauge and at the water-gauge with an evident effort of intrepidity—and he had filed his teeth too, the poor devil, and the wool of his pate shaved into queer patterns, and three ornamental scars on each of his cheeks. He ought to have been clapping his hands and stamping his feet on the bank, instead of which he was hard at work, a thrall to strange witchcraft, full of improving knowledge.

As everybody knows, Conrad is a romantic on the side. He might not exactly admire savages clapping their hands and stamping their feet but they have at least the merit of being in their place, unlike this dog in a parody of breeches. For Conrad things being in their place is of the utmost importance.

"Fine fellows—cannibals—in their place," he tells us pointedly. Tragedy begins when things leave their accustomed place, like Europe leaving its safe stronghold between the policeman and the baker to take a peep into the heart of darkness. . . .

The point of my observations should be quite clear by now, namely that Joseph Conrad was a thoroughgoing racist. That this simple truth is glossed over in criticisms of his work is due to the fact that white racism against Africa is such a normal way of thinking that its manifestations go completely unremarked. Students of *Heart of Darkness* will often tell you that Conrad is concerned not so much with Africa as with the deterioration of one European mind caused by solitude and sickness. They will point out to you that Conrad is, if anything, less charitable to the Europeans in the story than he is to the natives, that the point of the story is to ridicule Europe's civilizing mission in Africa. A Conrad student informed me in Scotland that Africa is merely a setting for the disintegration of the mind of Mr. Kurtz.

Which is partly the point. Africa as setting and backdrop which eliminates the African as human factor. Africa as a metaphysical battlefield devoid of all recognizable humanity, into which the wandering European enters at his peril. Can nobody see the preposterous and perverse arrogance in thus reducing Africa to the role of props for the break-up of one petty European mind? But that is not even the point. The real question is the dehumanization of Africa and Africans which this age-long attitude has fostered and continues to foster in the world. And the question is whether a novel which celebrates this dehumanization, which depersonalizes a portion of the human race, can be called a great work of art. My answer is: No, it cannot. I do not doubt Conrad's great talents. Even *Heart of Darkness* has its memorably good passages and moments:

> The reaches opened before us and closed behind, as if the forest had stepped leisurely across the water to bar the way for our return.

Its exploration of the minds of the European characters is often penetrating and full of insight. But all that has been more than fully discussed
in the last fifty years. His obvious racism has, however, not been addressed. And it is high time it was!

Conrad was born in 1857, the very year in which the first Anglican
missionaries were arriving among my own people in Nigeria. It was certainly not his fault that he lived his life at a time when the reputation of
the black man was at a particularly low level. But even after due allowances have been made for all the influences of contemporary prejudice on
his sensibility there remains still in Conrad's attitude a residue of antipathy to black people which his peculiar psychology alone can explain. His
own account of his first encounter with a black man is very revealing:

> A certain enormous buck nigger encountered in Haiti fixed my con-
> ception of blind, furious, unreasoning rage, as manifested in the
> human animal to the end of my days. Of the nigger I used to dream
> for years afterwards.

Certainly Conrad had a problem with niggers. His inordinate love of
that word itself should be of interest to psychoanalysts. Sometimes his
fixation on blackness is equally interesting as when he gives us this brief
description:

> A black figure stood up, strode on long black legs, waving long
> black arms. . .

As though we might expect a black figure striding along on black
legs to wave white arms! But so unrelenting is Conrad's obsession. . . .

Whatever Conrad's problems were, you might say he is now safely
dead. Quite true. Unfortunately his heart of darkness plagues us still.
Which is why an offensive and deplorable book can be described by a
serious scholar as "among the half dozen greatest short novels in the
English language." And why it is today perhaps the most commonly
prescribed novel in twentieth-century literature courses in English
Departments of American universities.

There are two probable grounds on which what I have said so far
may be contested. The first is that it is no concern of fiction to please
people about whom it is written. I will go along with that. But I am not
talking about pleasing people. I am talking about a book which parades
in the most vulgar fashion prejudices and insults from which a section of
mankind has suffered untold agonies and atrocities in the past and continues to do so in many ways and many places today. I am talking about
a story in which the very humanity of black people is called in question.

Secondly, I may be challenged on the grounds of actuality. Conrad,
after all, did sail down the Congo in 1890 when my own father was still
a babe in arms. How could I stand up more than fifty years after his

death and purport to contradict him? My answer is that as a sensible man I will not accept just any traveller's tales solely on the grounds that I have not made the journey myself. I will not trust the evidence even of a man's very eyes when I suspect them to be as jaundiced as Conrad's. And we also happen to know that Conrad was, in the words of his biographer, Bernard C. Meyer, "notoriously inaccurate in the rendering of his own history."

But more important by far is the abundant testimony about Conrad's savages which we could gather if we were so inclined from other sources and which might lead us to think that these people must have had other occupations besides merging into the evil forest or materializing out of it simply to plague Marlow and his dispirited band. For as it happened, soon after Conrad had written his book an event of far greater consequence was taking place in the art world of Europe. This is how Frank Willett, a British art historian, describes it:

> Gaugin had gone to Tahiti, the most extravagant individual act of turning to a non-European culture in the decades immediately before and after 1900, when European artists were avid for new artistic experiences, but it was only about 1904–5 that African art began to make its distinctive impact. One piece is still identifiable; it is a mask that had been given to Maurice Vlaminck in 1905. He records that Derain was "speechless" and "stunned" when he saw it, bought it from Vlaminck and in turn showed it to Picasso and Matisse, who were also greatly affected by it. Ambroise Vollard then borrowed it and had it cast in bronze. . . . The revolution of twentieth century art was under way!

The mask in question was made by other savages living just north of Conrad's River Congo. They have a name too: the Fang people, and are without a doubt among the world's greatest masters of the sculptured form. The event Frank Willett is referring to marked the beginning of cubism and the infusion of new life into European art, which had run completely out of strength.

The point of all this is to suggest that Conrad's picture of the peoples of the Congo seems grossly inadequate even at the height of their subjection to the ravages of King Leopold's International Association for the Civilization of Central Africa.[2]

---

[2] King Leopold II of Belgium established the International Association for the Exploration and Civilization of Central Africa in 1876, with himself as president. The expeditions of the association, particularly those of the explorer Henry Stanley (1880–1884), led to the claim by the association of sovereignty over the Congo basin. The territory of what was then known as the International African Association was reorganized by Leopold as the Congo Free State in 1885. [Ed.]

4

CHINUA ACHEBE
Things Fall Apart, 1958

In this selection from his novel, *Things Fall Apart*, Chinua Achebe imagines the arrival and impact of some of the first Anglican missionaries among the Ibo people of Nigeria — his own ancestors — after 1857. Missionaries were among the earliest European colonialists. The first missionaries went to the Americas with the Spanish conquistadors in the decades after Columbus. But long after the conquistadors were replaced by professional soldiers, administrators, policemen, mining engineers, company agents, and other representatives of a more bureaucratic and industrial age, the missionaries continued to seek out souls to save beyond the frontiers of colonial settlement. What, according to Achebe, were the principal obstacles faced by the missionaries? What elements in Christianity attracted some Africans? What elements repelled others? Judging from this selection, how would you characterize the overall impact of Christianity in Africa?

THINKING HISTORICALLY

Unlike Orwell and Conrad, Achebe is not describing historical events he witnessed, since he is writing about a period before he was born. And yet, he has a firsthand experience of Ibo culture. How does that experience make his fiction different from that of Conrad and Orwell? What does Achebe's fiction add to a historical understanding of missionaries in Africa? How would you compare Achebe with Conrad?

The arrival of the missionaries had caused a considerable stir in the village of Mbanta. There were six of them and one was a white man. Every man and woman came out to see the white man. Stories about these strange men had grown since one of them had been killed in Abame and his iron horse tied to the sacred silk-cotton tree. And so everybody came to see the white man. It was the time of the year when everybody was at home. The harvest was over.

When they had all gathered, the white man began to speak to them. He spoke through an interpreter who was an Ibo man, though his dialect was different and harsh to the ears of Mbanta. Many people laughed at his dialect and the way he used words strangely. Instead of saying

---

Source: Chinua Achebe, *Things Fall Apart* (Oxford: Heinemann, 1958), 101–09.

"myself" he always said "my buttocks." But he was a man of commanding presence and the clansmen listened to him. He said he was one of
them, as they could see from his colour and his language. The other four
black men were also their brothers, although one of them did not speak
Ibo. The white man was also their brother because they were all sons of
God. And he told them about this new God, the Creator of all the world
and all the men and women. He told them that they worshipped false
gods, gods of wood and stone. A deep murmur went through the crowd
when he said this. He told them that the true God lived on high and that
all men when they died went before Him for judgment. Evil men and all
the heathen who in their blindness bowed to wood and stone were
thrown into a fire that burned like palm-oil. But good men who worshipped the true God lived for ever in His happy kingdom. "We have
been sent by this great God to ask you to leave your wicked ways and
false gods and turn to Him so that you may be saved when you die," he
said.

"Your buttocks understand our language," said someone lighthearted-
ly and the crowd laughed.

"What did he say?" the white man asked his interpreter. But before
he could answer, another man asked a question: "Where is the white
man's horse?" he asked. The Ibo evangelists consulted among themselves and decided that the man probably meant bicycle. They told the
white man and he smiled benevolently.

"Tell them," he said, "that I shall bring many iron horses when we
have settled down among them. Some of them will even ride the iron
horse themselves." This was interpreted to them but very few of them
heard. They were talking excitedly among themselves because the white
man had said he was going to live among them. They had not thought
about that.

At this point an old man said he had a question. "Which is this god
of yours," he asked, "the goddess of the earth, the god of the sky, Amadiora of the thunderbolt, or what?"

The interpreter spoke to the white man and he immediately gave his
answer. "All the gods you have named are not gods at all. They are gods
of deceit who tell you to kill your fellows and destroy innocent children.
There is only one true God and He has the earth, the sky, you and me,
and all of us."

"If we leave our gods and follow your god," asked another man,
"who will protect us from the anger of our neglected gods and
ancestors?"

"Your gods are not alive and cannot do you any harm," replied the
white man. "They are pieces of wood and stone."

When this was interpreted to the men of Mbanta they broke into
derisive laughter. These men must be mad, they said to themselves. How

else could they say that Ani and Amadiora were harmless? And Idemili and Ogwugwu too? And some of them began to go away.

Then the missionaries burst into song. It was one of those gay and rollicking tunes of evangelism which had the power of plucking at silent and dusty chords in the heart of an Ibo man. The interpreter explained each verse to the audience, some of whom now stood enthralled. It was a story of brothers who lived in darkness and in fear, ignorant of the love of God. It told of one sheep out on the hills, away from the gates of God and from the tender shepherd's care.

After the singing the interpreter spoke about the Son of God whose name was Jesu Kristi. Okonkwo, who only stayed in the hope that it might come to chasing the men out of the village or whipping them, now said:

"You told us with your own mouth that there was only one god. Now you talk about his son. He must have a wife, then." The crowd agreed.

"I did not say He had a wife," said the interpreter, somewhat lamely.

"Your buttocks said he had a son," said the joker. "So he must have a wife and all of them must have buttocks."

The missionary ignored him and went on to talk about the Holy Trinity. At the end of it Okonkwo was fully convinced that the man was mad. He shrugged his shoulders and went away to tap his afternoon palm-wine.

But there was a young lad who had been captivated. His name was Nwoye, Okonkwo's first son. It was not the mad logic of the Trinity that captivated him. He did not understand it. It was the poetry of the new religion, something felt in the marrow. The hymn about brothers who sat in darkness and in fear seemed to answer a vague and persistent question that haunted his young soul—the question of the twins crying in the bush and the question of Ikemefuna who was killed. He felt a relief within as the hymn poured into his parched soul. The words of the hymn were like the drops of frozen rain melting on the dry plate of the panting earth. Nwoye's callow mind was greatly puzzled.

The missionaries spent their first four or five nights in the market-place, and went into the village in the morning to preach the gospel. They asked who the king of the village was, but the villagers told them that there was no king. "We have men of high title and the chief priests and the elders," they said.

It was not very easy getting the men of high title and the elders together after the excitement of the first day. But the missionaries persevered, and in the end they were received by the rulers of Mbanta. They asked for a plot of land to build their church.

Every clan and village had its "evil forest." In it were buried all those who died of the really evil diseases, like leprosy and smallpox. It was also the dumping ground for the potent fetishes of great medicine-men when they died. An "evil forest" was, therefore, alive with sinister forces and powers of darkness. It was such a forest that the rules of Mbanta gave to the missionaries. They did not really want them in their clan, and so they made them that offer which nobody in his right senses would accept.

"They want a piece of land to build their shrine," said Uchendu to his peers when they consulted among themselves. "We shall give them a piece of land." He paused, and there was a murmur of surprise and disagreement. "Let us give them a portion of the Evil Forest. They boast about victory over death. Let us give them a real battlefield in which to show their victory." They laughed and agreed, and sent for the missionaries, whom they had asked to leave them for a while so that they might "whisper together." They offered them as much of the Evil Forest as they cared to take. And to their greatest amazement the missionaries thanked them and burst into song.

"They do not understand," said some of the elders. "But they will understand when they go to their plot of land tomorrow morning." And they dispersed.

The next morning the crazy men actually began to clear a part of the forest and to build their house. The inhabitants of Mbanta expected them all to be dead within four days. The first day passed and the second and third and fourth, and none of them died. Everyone was puzzled. And then it became known that the white man's fetish had unbelievable power. It was said that he wore glasses on his eyes so that he could see and talk to evil spirits. Not long after, he won his first three converts.

Although Nwoye had been attracted to the new faith from the very first day, he kept it secret. He dared not go too near the missionaries for fear of his father. But whenever they came to preach in the open marketplace or the village playground, Nwoye was there. And he was already beginning to know some of the simple stories they told.

"We have now built a church," said Mr Kiaga, the interpreter, who was now in charge of the infant congregation. The white man had gone back to Umuofia, where he built his headquarters and from where he paid regular visits to Mr Kiaga's congregation at Mbanta.

"We have now built a church," said Mr Kiaga, "and we want you all to come in every seventh day to worship the true God."

On the following Sunday, Nwoye passed and re-passed the little red-earth and thatch building without summoning enough courage to enter. He heard the voice of singing and although it came from a handful of men it was loud and confident. Their church stood on a circular clearing that looked like the open mouth of the Evil Forest. Was it waiting to snap its teeth together? After passing and re-passing by the church, Nwoye returned home.

It was well known among the people of Mbanta that their gods and ancestors were sometimes long-suffering and would deliberately allow a man to go on defying them. But even in such cases they set their limit at seven market weeks or twenty-eight days. Beyond that limit no man was suffered to go. And so excitement mounted in the village as the seventh week approached since the impudent missionaries built their church in the Evil Forest. The villagers were so certain about the doom that awaited these men that one or two converts thought it wise to suspend their allegiance to the new faith.

At last the day came by which all the missionaries should have died. But they were still alive, building a new red-earth and thatch house for their teacher, Mr Kiaga. That week they won a handful more converts. And for the first time they had a woman. Her name was Nneka, the wife of Amadi, who was a prosperous farmer. She was very heavy with child.

Nneka had had four previous pregnancies and childbirths. But each time she had borne twins, and they had been immediately thrown away. Her husband and his family were already becoming highly critical of such a woman and were not unduly perturbed when they found she had fled to join the Christians. It was a good riddance.

One morning Okonkwo's cousin, Amikwu, was passing by the church on his way from the neighbouring village, when he saw Nwoye among the Christians. He was greatly surprised, and when he got home he went straight to Okonkwo's hut and told him what he had seen. The women began to talk excitedly, but Okonkwo sat unmoved.

It was late afternoon before Nwoye returned. He went into the *obi* and saluted his father, but he did not answer. Nwoye turned round to walk into the inner compound when his father, suddenly overcome with fury, sprang to his feet and gripped him by the neck.

"Where have you been?" he stammered.

Nwoye struggled to free himself from the choking grip.

"Answer me," roared Okonkwo, "before I kill you!" He seized a heavy stick that lay on the dwarf wall and hit him two or three savage blows.

"Answer me!" he roared again. Nwoye stood looking at him and did not say a word. The women were screaming outside, afraid to go in.

"Leave that boy at once!" said a voice in the outer compound. It was Okonkwo's uncle Uchendu. "Are you mad?"

Okonkwo did not answer. But he left hold of Nwoye, who walked away and never returned.

He went back to the church and told Mr Kiaga that he had decided to go to Umuofia, where the white missionary had set up a school to teach young Christians to read and write.

Mr Kiaga's joy was very great. "Blessed is he who forsakes his father and his mother for my sake," he intoned. "Those that hear my words are my father and my mother."

Nwoye did not fully understand. But he was happy to leave his father. He would return later to his mother and his brothers and sisters and convert them to the new faith.

As Okonkwo sat in his hut that night, gazing into a log fire, he thought over the matter. A sudden fury rose within him and he felt a strong desire to take up his matchet, go to the church, and wipe out the entire vile and miscreant gang. But on further thought he told himself that Nwoye was not worth fighting for. Why, he cried in his heart, should he, Okonkwo, of all people, be cursed with such a son? He saw clearly in it the finger of his personal god or *chi*. For how else could he explain his great misfortune and exile and now his despicable son's behaviour? Now that he had time to think of it, his son's crime stood out in its stark enormity. To abandon the gods of one's father and go about with a lot of effeminate men clucking like old hens was the very depth of abomination. Suppose when he died all his male children decided to follow Nwoye's steps and abandon their ancestors? Okonkwo felt a cold shudder run through him at the terrible prospect, like the prospect of annihilation. He saw himself and his father crowding round their ancestral shrine waiting in vain for worship and sacrifice and finding nothing but ashes of bygone days, and his children the while praying to the white man's god. If such a thing were ever to happen, he, Okonkwo, would wipe them off the face of the earth.

Okonkwo was popularly called the "Roaring Flame." As he looked into the log fire he recalled the name. He was a flaming fire. How then could he have begotten a son like Nwoye, degenerate and effeminate? Perhaps he was not his son. No! He could not be. His wife had played him false. He would teach her! But Nwoye resembled his grandfather, Unoka, who was Okonkwo's father. He pushed the thought out of his mind. He, Okonkwo, was called a flaming fire. How could he have begotten a woman for a son? At Nwoye's age Okonkwo had already become famous throughout Umuofia for his wrestling and his fearlessness.

He sighed heavily, and as if in sympathy the smouldering log also sighed. And immediately Okonkwo's eyes were opened and he saw the whole matter clearly. Living fire begets cold, impotent ash. He sighed again, deeply.

5

FRANCIS BEBEY

King Albert, 1981

Francis Bebey (1929–2001) was an African writer, artist, and musician from Cameroon. In this novel, he carries the reader to a village called Effidi in the twilight of European imperialism after World War II

Source: Francis Bebey, *King Albert*, trans. Joyce A. Hutchinson (Westport, CT: Lawrence Hill & Co., 1981), 109–18.

but before the late 1950s and early 1960s, when Cameroon and other former colonies became independent states. In this brief selection from the novel, the young Bikounou, whom everyone calls Vespasian because he rides a Vespa Motor Scooter, has returned to Effidi to speak with Chief Ndengué. What is his message? What do his message and his manner of delivery tell you about the chief, the village, and the larger world of which it is a part at this time?

THINKING HISTORICALLY

The dialogue between Bikounou and the chief tells a story about how parts of Africa changed in the period leading up to independence. What are these changes? Where and how did they occur? In a few paragraphs, write a brief history that summarizes these changes. How is your history different from the section in the novel?

The next day, a Sunday, Bikounou went to see Chief Ndengué while the other villagers were at Mass.

"I have come to thank you for the welcome which you permitted the people of Effidi to extend to us, myself and my friend Féfé."

"My son, I permitted nothing. The village spoke for itself. As you could see yourself, nobody bears you any grudge. On the contrary, everybody is very fond of you. But, as a matter of interest, where is your friend Féfé?"

"I wanted to see you alone, Chief Ndengué, to talk to you while the others are not around."

"And what is so important that you need this secrecy?"

"You are the Chief of us all, and you have a right to hear the news first. The others will hear it later if they don't know it already."

"Bikounou, I think I have understood. You are going to get married. That's good, my son, but you know our procedure."

"I'm in a good position to know, Chief Ndengué. But that is not the news I have for you."

"Ah? What do you mean?"

"I mean I want to talk to you about something quite different from my marriage. Besides, as you have just reminded yourself, would you expect me to think of marriage again without consulting all the elders of our community? One should not make the same mistakes more than once in one's life."

"I see, my son. I see that your experience has widened, and you know, I am absolutely delighted. Now I know that you have come back to live among us as we live ourselves, following the laws laid down by our tradition, and not the examples given by people who are not our own people, whether their skin is black or white."

"Chief Ndengué, may all my links with our community be severed if I am not determined to follow the advice of my elders, which is dictated by the experience of generations and generations who lived before our own generation came into the world."

"You speak well, my son."

"But please, let me tell you what brings me here this morning."

"I am listening."

"Now, Chief Ndengué, there is going to be an election."

"What?"

"I am saying there is going to be an election."

"My son, please explain: what does that mean?"

"It means that the whites are going to ask us to choose a person to represent us."

"A person to represent us? But, my son, why do we have to choose someone to represent us? Am I not, myself, the man whom tradition has placed at the head of our community to represent everybody? Am I not the Chief of this community, the person to whom you turn to obtain this or that? The person who says yes, or maybe no, according to whether he sees in his answer some means of benefiting the whole community? Tell me, my son, what is this story you've brought back from the town?"

"Chief Ndengué, I knew you wouldn't understand me straightaway. You are the Chief of our community. You will remain our Chief until the day—when—until the time when—"

"Until my death, my son. Do not be afraid to say so. We are all destined to live for a period and then to die. You know, man is like a flower. He smiles at life as it smiles at the sunlight. Then at the end of his life he closes his eyes just as it droops its head and wilts. There is nothing to be afraid of, Bikounou. I should be lying if I told you that Chief Ndengué would never die. In any case, you would't believe me."

"I am saying, Chief Ndengué, that you will remain at the head of our community until the day when you are no longer with us. So it's not a question of choosing someone to replace you among us."

"Then what is it about?"

"I will explain. You know that our country is governed by the whites?"

"I know, I know. But what have they done now, these whites?"

"Nothing, except that they now realize the need to let us govern our country ourselves."

"What? What country are you talking about, my son?"

"This one, where we live, the country which takes in Effidi, Zaabat, Nkool, Palmtree Village, and even Ngala, as well as other towns."

"My son, what you have just told me is perhaps important, but you can't make me believe that Effidi, Nkool, Zaabat, Palmtree Village, and even Ngala are part of one and the same country and that they will let themselves be governed by one man, one single great Chief! For if you tell me that I shall remain at the head of the community of Effidi, then another chief will be needed to be responsible for governing the whole country, isn't that so?"

"Chief Ndengué, for a long time the whites have occupied our country and governed it in their own way. We, the educated men, have told them that we've had enough and that we wish to govern ourselves, since we are now capable of doing so."

"And the whites agreed?"

"Yes, they have agreed. . . . yes. . . . that is to say that—"

"My son, tell me the exact truth."

"That is to say that they don't believe we are capable of governing ourselves all alone."

"That is exactly what I think, too."

"But, Chief Ndengué, don't take their side! They think we can't govern ourselves alone, but *we* want to prove the opposite. We want to show them that we can live without them and govern ourselves."

"And so?"

"So they have decided to put us to the test."

"By doing what?"

"Precisely, by organizing elections. That's what I wanted—"

"Bikounou, you're mixing everything up—the country, the whites, ourselves, elections. How do you expect me to understand anything in all that?"

"Let me explain it to you, Chief Ndengué. The whites have a way of governing a country which is different from ours. With us, there is a Chief—that's to say, somebody like you—to govern the whole community. But *they* put several people at the head of the country. It is those people who make decisions for the good of the whole country because they have been chosen by the whole country to represent them. It is this new way of governing the country that the whites wish to teach us, and that is why there is going to be an election."

"Now it's becoming clearer," said Chief Ndengué.

He remained plunged in thought for several minutes, during which Bikounou realized that he should say nothing.

"Now, it's becoming clearer," he added. "If I understand correctly, each community like ours will have to choose someone to represent it—"

"In an assembly which will therefore represent the whole country," Bikounou continued.

"Yes, yes, I see."

He thought for a few more moments, then suggested:

"Naturally, if Effidi is asked to choose, I don't see who our brothers will elect to represent them other than myself, do you?"

A logical argument on the part of a village chief incapable of understanding the evolution of a whole of the society of which his community is a part, and only a small part, when all's said and done. Bikounou would not have replied immediately if the Chief had not insisted:

"That is how things will turn out, isn't it?"

"Chief, when you talk about elections, you must not say in advance which man or woman is going to win."

"Which man or woman? What do you mean? Are the women also invited to stand for election? And to represent whom? The men?"

"Chief Ndengué, you must not get carried away. There may well not be a woman presumptuous enough to stand as a candidate in the election. But in the new system that the whites wish to teach us, the women have the right to stand, just like the men."

"What, what are you saying? Is that the kind of thing they wish to introduce here, and for what purpose?"

"Chief Ndengué, times change. Even in this village, which lives in closer proximity to the town than others on account of the road passing through it, people are not sufficiently informed about the evolution of the country."

"Our country is here!" Chief Ndengué shouted. "If you young people and those others educated by the whites wish to sell it, that's different. But, my son, I warn you that there are still enough people at Effidi to oppose such an idea should it ever cross your mind one day. The evolution of the country . . . the evolution of what country? Do you think you know better than old Ndengué what is our country and what it means?"

"Chief Ndengué," said Bikounou, trying to appease him, "you are right. Our country exists inasmuch as you exist as our Chief. All that is built on the tradition of our ancestors."

"Then why have you come back to the village to tell me what other people want, people who have nothing to do with what our ancestors wished this country to be? Why do you all obey these foreigners?"

"Chief Ndengué, you must not give way to sudden anger and refuse to hear the other reasons which bring me here. I can understand your wish to exclude women from any competition concerning the government of the country. The women are in the village to bear children for their husbands and perpetuate the community with boys and girls who will follow traditional ways. I accept it myself, and I shall oppose any person who might seek to give to women the opportunity, the slightest opportunity, of interfering in men's affairs, such as, for example, the government of our society. But, you know, times change. In any case, they have changed a lot since, at the wish of our ancestors, you yourself became our Chief. You have to admit that, these days, you need the support of the whites to make everybody obey you."

"You're lying! You're lying, Bikounou, you're lying! What had the whites to do with your return to the village? Was it not because you felt the ancestral power commanding you to return to your own people that you came back? And this ancestral power, who else but me represents it here?"

"It's true. It's true that what I said was not quite fair. It is not the whites who order all the members of the community to come to you to settle their differences, or to organize tactics about a possible marriage, or to talk about future sowings or the distribution of the harvest to come. But today there is nevertheless something changed about a village chief like yourself. I'm thinking particularly of the allowance paid you by the government."

"Allowance! Look at it! I am compensated because I have the unpleasant task of raising taxes among my people, and you dare call that an allowance? My son, you are too young for me to tell you all I think. But don't force me to believe that you have adopted the mentality of the foreigners who come and make us work for them, in our own country, and afterwards boast that they are doing it for our own good! For, tell me, what happens to all these taxes that I collect each year? Who uses the money that I am responsible for collecting? And after that, you come and defend your bosses and remind me that I am paid by them."

Bikounou wondered what answer he could possibly give to all that. He had come with the firm intention of being submissive, and you, too, must have noticed how diplomatic he was being in order not to shock Chief Ndengué. That is understandable, for it must be realized that, however innocent he might seem, on this Sunday morning when the other inhabitants of Effidi had gone to sing Mass in Latin—too bad for Father Bonsot if he hears about it—the Vespasian had the difficult job of explaining to the old chief that his period of glory and prestige based on tradition was over, and worse still, that new leaders would take his place, chosen with no reference to the law of bygone days. The young man knew what this would mean for this old man accustomed to considering as his personal property what some people would pompously call "power." He therefore decided to introduce into the conversation as much subtlety as was desirable or indeed necessary to lead Chief Ndengué gradually to accept the very principle of an election during which the people of Effidi would be free to choose him or to elect some other candidate.

"If I mentioned an allowance, Chief Ndengué, you must forgive me. You know the village people are not always aware what an unpleasant task the Administration expects you to carry out, and we have all come more or less to believe that you are paid for doing it. I confess that I personally should know something about it, since I work in a government office. In any case, I was joking when I said that, but I'm already at fault for joking with my elder. You must forgive me, Chief Ndengué. I came to see you as an obedient son comes to see his father and not to presume to make you angry."

"Now you're talking sense, my son. So, you inform me there is going to be an election. But tell me, if *I* am not elected, then who will be?"

"I have no idea, Chief Ndengué. What matters now is to know who else at Effidi might intend to stand at this election when you consider all the qualities and the knowledge a person needs to have to represent our community successfully."

"What do you mean?"

"Well, how can I explain it? It must first be understood that the elected representative will have to go to Ngala."

"Each village will have to send someone to Ngala?"

"That is where all the representatives will meet to discuss the measures to be taken concerning the country."

"Then I shall have to go to Ngala?"

"If you are elected by our community, yes."

"That's true. It's true that the community, according to your system, could very well decide that it didn't want me to represent them at Ngala. In any case, I must tell you from the start that, if things really turn out as you have just explained, I am not interested in your story of an election. I have no intention of going to sit at the side of the road every morning and wait for a truck to be kind enough to stop and take me to the town."

Bikounou gave an almost imperceptible sigh of relief. But Chief Ndengué was a crafty old man, who missed no detail of the attitude of those speaking with him. He noticed the suppressed satisfaction of the young man.

"What's the matter? Did I say something unpleasant?"

"No, Chief Ndengué, it's not that. I was in fact wondering whether you realized how difficult it would be for you to make frequent visits to the town if you were elected to represent Effidi."

"I realize it perfectly well. I also realize that in future—if your system works as you have said—it will be someone else who will go to the town to bring back orders to be passed on to the community. Yes, my son, I understand what you were saying just now: times change."

The pathos of these last words was perfectly clear to Bikounou. Nevertheless, he kept his poise, trying to allay the old man's fears:

"Oh, Chief Ndengué, don't take it like that. It's possible that someone else will go to the town to represent our community in the assembly which will meet there, but not to bring back orders, as long as you remain our Chief."

"My son, you are trying to calm me down, but since you began talking to me, I have a feeling that there is to be a change much greater than that suffered by our fathers when the whites arrived."

"There can't be any change more important for our country than when the whites arrived."

"You mean it's a continuation of the same change?"

"Yes and no, Chief Ndengué. Yes, because if the whites had not come, we should perhaps never have felt the need to prove that we are capable of governing ourselves. As a result, there would have been no need to talk of elections. But, on the other hand, we now have to choose from among us people to whom we shall entrust the conduct of our affairs."

"And you believe that, my son? You believe that one day the whites will leave us to manage our own affairs?"

"That is what the younger generation is asking them more and more urgently. They will simply be forced to leave us alone one day."

"Forced? Forced? Who can force them to do anything? These people who manufacture guns and arms who would kill us all if we refused to obey them, who can force them?"

"Chief Ndengué, these people are doubtless very intelligent. They manufacture guns, arms, motor cars, airplanes, the good Lord gives them all they desire. But they overlooked one thing."

"What thing, my son?"

"They overlooked that they shouldn't have taught us to read and write."

"I don't understand what you mean by that."

"You see, by teaching us to read, they gave us the key to their own knowledge, and there we discovered that they spoke of liberty, equality and fraternity."

"So?"

"So they are obliged to give us liberty, equality and fraternity. That's what we're asking for, Chief Ndengué."

"And that is really why there is going to be an election?"

"Actually, this election will not give us liberty, but the assembly which will be established will pave the way for the independence of the whole country."

"My son, I tell you that our country is Effidi!" the Chief growled again.

"You are right, Chief Ndengué, but I tell you that times change. And since times began to change, our country has grown bigger."

"You mean that those savages of Palmtree Village are going to send a representative to the town just like us?"

"They will have the right to do so."

"Like us? With no difference?"

"Like us. But they may be obliged to choose a representative elsewhere than among themselves."

"Why?"

"Well, Chief, because the fact that the elected representative can get to the town fairly often won't be the end of the matter. The representative will also have to be someone educated, someone who understands politics and who—"

"What? What did you say?"

"Politics."

"And poli—, poli—. This thing, what is it?"

"To be exact, it is politics that the representatives will be engaged in when they meet."

"So they won't be speaking?"

"Yes, they will, Chief Ndengué. They will probably speak a great deal. That's what politics is all about. They talk, they talk, they talk. And then they say, good, we will build a road to Nkool, or to Palmtree Village."

Chief Ndengué burst out laughing, and at once, a shaft of sunlight coming through a little hole in the wall and falling on the beaten earth floor in a small luminous circle also began to laugh, with all the particles of fine colored dust dancing in the rainbow that penetrated the half-light. Bikounou wondered what on earth he had said or done that was so amusing.

"My son," said Chief Ndengué at last, "don't be surprised to hear me laugh like this. The fact is that for some time I had been worrying for no reason and it's only now that I've realized my error."

"I don't understand," the Vespasian confessed.

"I will explain," replied the Chief, reverting to his normal serious manner. "This is why I am laughing. Since you began talking to me about your elections, I had become convinced that you were preparing to see someone else take my place at the head of our community, with the help, obviously, of your friends, the white Administrators. And now I see that I was stupid to imagine that. For if the poli—, poli—Oh, what did you say just now the representatives would do in the town?"

"Politics."

"Yes, that's it. If poli—, poli—. If whatever it is consists of talking and saying you're going to build a road, then it will have no effect on Effidi, seeing that we already have our road. Is that not true, my son?"

The serious tone showed that the man wished to be reassured.

"That is to say—I mean, Chief Ndengué—yes, you are right, partly," the Vespasian replied, in a somewhat embarrassed tone. "But I spoke of building a road just as an example. In fact, politics means doing lots and lots of other things."

"Ah?"

"Yes, yes, and that's why I was telling you that we must elect representatives who understand these things. And as I cannot see in Palmtree Village anybody who can claim to understand them, then I think those people will be obliged to choose a representative from outside their own community."

"How shameful for them!"

"I suppose, in fact, that they will not be very proud when they have to come to Effidi to ask if we can provide somebody to represent them in the assembly in the town."

"And if they come, my son, you who understand these things, tell me: what answer do we give these idiots?"

"I don't yet exactly know how these things will work out. But I think we shall be obliged to represent them because, in any case, there will not be a separate representative from each village."

"This business of yours is complicated, my son. I hope that you at least will be able to understand it, so that we don't make a laughing-stock of ourselves in the eyes of our neighbors. You know that they will seize on the slightest opportunity — "

"I'll take care of it, Chief."

The conversation went on into details until the time when the other villagers returned from Mass. It was the Chief's job to announce the news of the coming election, as it had been given him by Bikounou. He did this solemnly, during an evening meeting. The news was received and commented upon in almost as many ways as there were men present at the meeting, for the people of Effidi, outstandingly intelligent, at least in their own opinion, were keen to show that they had understood what they had just been told, and that they would be perfectly capable of playing the new game which was being wished on them by the town. Naturally, many chests swelled with pride at the idea that, once again, the neighboring villagers would remain in the background of the regional scene, since their sons were unable to compete with those of Effidi.

6

RUDYARD KIPLING

The White Man's Burden, 1899

This poem, written by Rudyard Kipling (1865–1936), is often presented as the epitome of colonialist sentiment, though some readers see in it a critical, satirical attitude toward colonialism. Do you find the poem to be for or against colonialism? Can it be both?

THINKING HISTORICALLY

"The White Man's Burden" is a phrase normally associated with European colonialism in Africa. In fact, however, Kipling wrote the poem in response to the annexation of the Philippines by the United States. How does this historical context change the meaning of the poem for you?

Source: Rudyard Kipling, "The White Man's Burden," *McClure's Magazine* 12, no. 4 (February 1899): 290–91.

Neither fiction nor fact, a poem conveys emotions. How does this
poem help us understand something about the feelings of people like
Kipling? How would you describe that feeling?

Take up the White Man's burden—
Send forth the best ye breed—
Go, bind your sons to exile
To serve your captives' need;
To wait, in heavy harness,
On fluttered folk and wild—
Your new-caught sullen peoples,
Half devil and half child.

Take up the White Man's burden—
In patience to abide,
To veil the threat of terror
And check the show of pride;
By open speech and simple,
An hundred times made plain,
To seek another's profit
And work another's gain.

Take up the White Man's burden—
The savage wars of peace—
Fill full the mouth of Famine,
And bid the sickness cease;
And when your goal is nearest
(The end for others sought)
Watch sloth and heathen folly
Bring all your hope to nought.

Take up the White Man's burden—
No iron rule of kings,
But toil of serf and sweeper—
The tale of common things.
The ports ye shall not enter,
The roads ye shall not tread,
Go, make them with your living
And mark them with your dead.

Take up the White Man's burden,
And reap his own reward—
The blame of those ye better

The hate of those ye guard—
The cry of hosts ye humour
(Ah, slowly!) toward the light:—
"Why brought ye us from bondage,
Our loved Egyptian night?"

Take up the White Man's burden—
Ye dare not stoop to less—
Nor call too loud on Freedom
To cloke your weariness.
By all ye will or whisper,
By all ye leave or do,
The silent sullen peoples
Shall weigh your God and you.

Take up the White Man's burden!
Have done with childish days—
The lightly-proffered laurel,
The easy ungrudged praise:
Comes now, to search your manhood
Through all the thankless years,
Cold, edged with dear-bought wisdom,
The judgment of your peers.

▪ REFLECTIONS

Many of the selections within this chapter as well as its title point to
the dual character of colonial society. There are the colonized and the
colonizers, the "natives" and the Europeans, and, as racial categories
hardened in the second half of the nineteenth century, the blacks and
the whites. Colonialism centered on the construction of an accepted inequality. The dominant Europeans invested enormous energy in keeping the double standards, dual pay schedules, and separate rules and
residential areas—the two castes.

One problem with maintaining a neat division between the colonized and the colonizers is that the Europeans were massively outnumbered by the indigenous people. Thus, the colonizers needed a vast
class of middle-status people to staff the army, police, and bureaucracy.
These people might be educated in Paris or London, raised in European
culture, and encouraged to develop a sense of pride in their similarity
to the Europeans ("me Christian, same like master") and their differences from the other "natives." Often, like the Indian Dr. Veraswami,
they were chosen for their ethnic or religious differences from the rest
of the colonized population.

In short, colonialism created a whole class of people who were neither fully colonized nor colonizers. They were in between. To the extent that the colonial enterprise was an extension of European social
class differences, these in-between people could be British as well as
"native." Orwell's Flory is only one of the characters in *Burmese Days*
caught between two worlds. One of the most notorious of this class of
Europeans "gone native" is the Mr. Kurtz that Conrad's crew will meet
upriver. Achebe's point that Africa becomes a setting for the breakup of
a European mind might be generalized to apply to the European perception of the colonial experience. It is certainly one of the dominant
themes of the European colonial novel. Even the great ones often center on the real or imagined rape, ravishing, or corruption of the European by the seething foreign unknown. This attitude also helps us
understand how Kipling could be both anti-imperialist and racist. Imperialism could seem like a thankless act to those who tried to carry
civilization to "sullen peoples, half devil and half child."

All the novels and poetry excerpted in this chapter are well worth
reading in their entirety, and many other excellent colonial novels can
be chosen from this period as well as from the 1930s and 1940s. E. M.
Forster's *A Passage to India* and Paul Scott's *The Raj Quartet* stand out
as fictional introductions to British colonialism in India. (Both have
also received excellent adaptations to film, the latter as the series for
television called *The Jewel in the Crown*.) In addition to Chinua
Achebe, Amos Tutuola and Wole Soyinka have written extensively on
Nigeria. Besides Francis Bebey, Ferdinand Oyono and Mongo Beti
address French colonialism in Cameroon. On South Africa, the work
of Alan Payton, Andre Brink, J. M. Coetzee, Peter Abrams, and James
McClure, among many others, stands out.

The advantage of becoming engrossed in a novel is that we feel part
of the story and have a sense that we are learning something firsthand. Of
course, we are reading a work of fiction, not gaining firsthand experience
or reading an accurate historical account of events. A well-made film poses
an even greater problem. Its visual and aural impact imparts a psychological reality that becomes part of our experience. If it is about a subject of
which we know little, the film quickly becomes our "knowledge" of the
subject, and this knowledge may be incomplete or inaccurate.

On the other hand, a well-written novel or film can whet our
appetite and inspire us to learn more. Choose and read a novel about
colonialism or some other historical subject. Then read a biography
of the author or research his or her background to determine how much
the author knew about the subject. Next, read a historical account of
the subject. How much attention does the historian give to the novelist's
subject? How does the novel add depth to the historical account? How
does the historical account place the novel in perspective? Finally, how
does the author's background place the novel in historical context?

23

Westernization and Nationalism

Japan, India, and the West, 1820–1939

■ HISTORICAL CONTEXT

By the second half of the nineteenth century, the West (meaning Europe and North America) had industrialized, created more representative governments and open societies than the world had known before, and demonstrated the power of its science, technology, and military might by colonizing much of the rest of the world. For those who looked on from outside, the West was a force to be reckoned with.

Some of those observers knew the impact of the West firsthand. The Japanese had experienced Western traders and missionaries since 1543 but had controlled their numbers and influence. The Act of Seclusion in 1636 limited European contact in Japan to a small colony of Dutch traders for the next two hundred years. Not until the appearance of Commodore Perry's steam fleet in 1853 did a new policy toward the West seem necessary.

India had experienced Western colonization and trade since the early 1600s, losing coastal trading cities to various European powers until the English consolidated their hold in the eighteenth century. By 1880 all but a few princely states had come under the rule of the British Indian Empire.

We have then, in these two examples, different degrees of Western influence and penetration. Nevertheless, both of these societies were forced to confront the power of the West. In both cases, the effort to become independent of the West meant considering what might be imitated or borrowed. Broadly speaking, this meant some degree of Westernization.

How did the people of Japan and India answer the challenge of the West? What motivated some to seek to Westernize? What led others to reject Westernization entirely? And what role did nationalism play in the struggle over Westernization?

Nationalism had been a potent force in Europe since the French Revolution, with its national draft army, National Assembly, nationalization of church lands, national flag, national anthem, and celebration of French citizenship. Napoleon's armies inadvertently spread national consciousness among his enemies. Poets and politicians from Vienna to Madrid sought to create and establish the elements of their own national cultures and nation states. European colonization ignited the same spark of national identity in Asia and Africa. Nationalism was itself a Western movement, but nationalism could be built from any indigenous or traditional culture. Extreme Westernizers might be willing to dispense with traditional ways entirely. Extreme anti-Westernizers could invoke nationalism alone. But most thoughtful subjects of Western influence between the mid-nineteenth and mid-twentieth centuries recognized the need to draw on old strengths while borrowing what worked. How did the authors of these selections face the challenge?

■ THINKING HISTORICALLY

Appreciating Contradictions

The process of Westernization, like the experience of conquest and colonization that often preceded it, was fraught with conflict and led to frequent contradictions. Often, the struggle for national independence meant the borrowing of Western practices and ideologies, both Marxist and liberal. Indeed, the idea of national self-determination was a product of the French and American revolutions, as we have seen. Even the words and languages employed in the debate reflected Western origins, as English or French was often the only common language of educated colonized peoples. Therefore, it is not surprising that contradictory behavior and ambivalent relationships were endemic in the post-colonial world, just as they had been under colonialism. These contradictions usually manifested themselves in an individual's cultural identity. How do colonized persons adopt Western ways, embrace traditional culture, and not feel as though their identity has been divided between the two? Such individuals may not fit entirely into either world and so may be torn between who they were and who they have become. The somewhat anguished experiences of these colonized people are difficult to understand. We typically want to accept one view or another, to praise or to blame. But as we have learned, the history of peoples and nations is rarely that clear. In examining some of the fundamental contradictions in the history of Westernization, we might better understand how people were variously affected.

The historical thinking skill one learns in reading documents from people torn between different ideals is the appreciation of contradictions. This operates on a number of levels. We learn that people can hold two contradictory ideas in their minds at the same time; and, in consequence, we learn to do it ourselves. This prevents us from jumping to conclusions or oversimplifying the historical process. In addition, we learn how the struggle over contradictory goals, whether internalized or expressed in group conflict, moves history forward.

1

THEODORE VON LAUE

The World Revolution of Westernization, 1987

Western colonialism, according to von Laue, a modern historian, brought about a "world revolution of Westernization," the victory of Western culture that accompanied Western political domination. What, according to von Laue, are these Western ideas that spread throughout the world during the nineteenth century? Did these ideas spread peacefully or were they forced on non-Western peoples? What groups of people were most attracted to Western ideas? Why did some non-Western people prefer Western culture to their own?

Does von Laue believe that this "world revolution" was a good thing? Does he believe it is over? What, according to von Laue, must still be done?

THINKING HISTORICALLY

Von Laue is particularly interested in the plight of what he calls the "Westernized non-Western intelligentsia." Who are these people? What is their problem? What does von Laue mean when he says that "as a result of their Westernization they became anti-Western nationalists"? How could Westernization make people anti-Western?

Throughout this selection, von Laue discusses paradoxical or ironic behavior. He writes of people learning lessons that were not

Source: Theodore von Laue, *The World Revolution of Westernization* (New York: Oxford University Press, 1987), 27–34.

formally taught and of psychological conflicts or love-hate attitudes. At one point he generalizes this phenomenon of seemingly contradictory behavior by quoting an eighteenth-century maxim that states, "To do just the opposite is also a form of imitation." Is von Laue describing some paradoxical aspect of human nature, or are these conflicts a particular product of colonialism?

While the world revolution of Westernization created a political world order radically above the horizons of all past human experience, it also unhinged, in the revolutionary manner sensed by Lord Lytton,[1] the depths of non-Western societies constituting the bulk of humanity. As he had said, "The application of the most refined principles of European government and some of the most artificial institutions of European society to a . . . vast population in whose history, habits, and traditions they have had no previous existence" was a risky enterprise, perhaps more than he had anticipated.

Examining the history of colonial expansion, one can discern a rough but generally applicable pattern for the revolutionary subversion of non-Western societies. Subversion began at the apex, with the defeat, humiliation, or even overthrow of traditional rulers. The key guarantee of law, order, and security from external interference was thus removed. With it went the continuity of tradition, whether of governance or of all other social institutions down to the subtle customs regulating the individual psyche. Thus ended not only political but also cultural self-determination. Henceforth, the initiatives shaping collective existence came from without, "mysterious formulas of a foreign and more or less uncongenial system" not only of administration but also of every aspect of life.

Once the authority of the ruler (who often was the semi-divine intermediary between Heaven and Earth) was subverted, the Western attack on the other props of society intensified. Missionaries, their security guaranteed by Western arms, discredited the local gods and their guardians, weakening the spiritual foundations of society. At the same time, colonial administrators interfered directly in indigenous affairs by suppressing hallowed practices repulsive to them, including human sacrifice, slavery, and physical cruelty in its many forms. Meanwhile, Western businessmen and their local agents redirected the channels of trade and economic life, making local producers and consumers dependent on a world market beyond their comprehension and control. In a thousand ways the colonial administration and its allies, though not necessarily in agreement with each other, introduced a new set of rewards and punishments, of prestige and authority. The changeover was obvious even in

[1] British viceroy of India from 1876 to 1880.

the externals of dress. Africans became ashamed of their nudity, women covered their breasts; Chinese men cut off their queues and adopted Western clothes. The boldest even tried to become like Westerners "in taste, in opinion, in morals, and intellect."

The pathways of subversion here outlined indicate the general pattern and the directions which it followed over time. Its speed depended on Western policy and the resilience of local society. Things seemingly fell apart quickly in the case of the most vulnerable small-scale societies of Africa and much more slowly in India or China, if at all in Japan. Often the colonial administration itself, under the policy of "indirect rule," slowed the Western impact for fear of causing cultural chaos and making trouble for itself. In all cases, tradition (however subverted) persisted in a thousand forms, merely retreating from the external world into the subliminally conditioned responses of the human psyche, its last refuge. It is still lurking in the promptings of "soul" today.

And did things really fall apart? The world revolution of Westernization prevailed by the arts of both war and peace. Certain aspects of Western power possessed an intrinsic appeal which, even by indigenous judgment, enhanced life. New crops often brought ampler food; European rule often secured peace. Through their command of the seas and of worldwide trade Europeans and Americans opened access to survival and opportunity in foreign lands to countless millions of people in China and India. Or take even the persuasion of raw power: Once convinced of the superiority of European weapons, who would not crave possession of them too? And more generally, being associated with European power also carried weight; it patently held the keys to the future. More directly perhaps, doing business with Westerners promised profit. If they played it right, compradors would get rich.

More subtly, certain categories of the local population eagerly took to foreign ways. Missionaries sheltered outcasts: slaves held for sacrifice, girls to be sold into prostitution or abandoned, or married women feeling abused and oppressed. The struggle for sexual equality is still raging in our midst, yet by comparison even Victorian England offered hope to women in Africa or East Asia. Regarding Japan, Fukuzawa[2] related the story of a highborn dowager lady who "had had some unhappy trials in earlier days." She was told of "the most remarkable of all the Western customs . . . the relations between men and women," where "men and women had equal rights, and monogamy was the strict rule in any class of people. . . ." It was, Fukuzawa reported, "as if her eyes were suddenly opened to something new. . . ." As a messenger of women's rights he certainly had Japanese women, "especially the ladies of the higher society," on his side. In China liberated women rushed to unbind their feet.

---

[2] See selection 2 on page 893. [Ed.]

In addition, the Westerners introduced hospitals and medicines that relieved pain and saved lives, a fact not unappreciated. Besides, whose greed was not aroused by the plethora of Western goods, all fancier than local products: stronger liquor, gaudier textiles, faster transport? Simple minds soon preferred Western goods merely because they were Western. Given the comparative helplessness of local society, was it surprising that everything Western tended to be judged superior?

The Westerners with their sense of mission also introduced their education. It was perhaps not enough, according to anti-Western nationalists suspicious of European desires, to keep the natives down, yet it offered access to Western skills at some sacrifice on the part of teachers willing to forgo the easier life in their own culture. Privileged non-Westerners even attended schools and universities in the West. Thus, as part of the general pattern of Westernization, a new category of cultural half-breeds was created, the Westernized non-Western intelligentsia. It differed somewhat according to cultural origins, but shared a common predicament. Product of one culture, educated in another, it was caught in invidious comparison. As [philosopher] Thomas Hobbes observed "Man, whose Joy consisteth in comparing himselfe with other men, can relish nothing but what is eminent." Riveted to Western preeminence, this intelligentsia struggled for purpose, identity, and recognition in the treacherous no-man's-land in between—and most furiously in lands where skin color added to its disabilities. Talented and industrious, these intellectuals threw themselves heroically into the study of Western society and thought so alien to their own.

Along the way they soon acquired a taste for the dominant ideals of the West, foremost the liberal plea for equality, freedom, and self-determination and the socialists' cry of social justice for all exploited and oppressed peoples and classes. They were delighted by the bitter self-criticism they discovered among Westerners—Western society produced many doubters, especially among its fringes in central and eastern Europe. At the same time, non-Western intellectuals quickly perceived the pride that lurked behind Western humanitarianism. They might be treated as equals in London or Paris, but "east of Aden" on the Indian circuit or anywhere in the colonies, they were "natives"—natives hypersensitive to the hypocrisy behind the Western mission of exporting high ideals without the congenital ingredient of equality. Thus they learned the lessons of power not formally taught by their masters. They needed power—state power—not only to carry the Western vision into practice on their own but also to make equality real.

Inevitably, the non-Western intellectuals turned their lessons to their own use. The ideals of freedom and self-determination justified giving free rein not only to the promptings of their own minds and souls, but also to protests over the humiliation of their countries and cultures. As a result of their Westernization they became anti-Western nationalists, outwardly curtailing, in themselves and their compatriots, the abject imitation of the West. Yet, as an 18th-century German wag had said, "To do just the opposite is also a form of imitation." Anti-Western self-assertion was a form of Westernization copying the cultural self-assertion of the West. Moreover, limiting western influence in fact undercut any chance of matching Western power (and the issue of power was never far from their minds). Thus anti-Western intellectuals were caught in a love-hate attitude toward the West, anti-Western purveyors of further Westernization.

Take Mohandas Gandhi,[3] perhaps the greatest among the Westernized non-Western intellectuals. Born into a prominent tradition-oriented Hindu family and of a lively, ambitious mind, he broke with Hindu taboo and studied English law in London, fashionably dressed and accepted in the best society, though by preference consorting with vegetarians and students of Eastern religion. After his return he confessed that "next to India, [he] would rather live in London than in any other place in the world." From 1892 to 1914, however, he lived in South Africa, using his legal training for defending the local Indian community against white discrimination. There he put together from Indian and Western sources a philosophy as well as a practice of nonviolent resistance, strengthening the self-confidence and civil status of his clients. . . .

One of Gandhi's precursors, Narendranath Datta, better known as Swami Vivekananda, had gone even further. At a lecture in Madras he exhorted his audience: "This is the great ideal before us, and everyone must be ready for it — the conquest of the whole world by India — nothing less than that. . . . Up India and conquer the world with your spirituality." Western globalized nationalism, obviously, was working its way around the world, escalating political ambition and cultural messianism to novel intensity. . . .

. . . [T]he run of Westernized non-Western intellectuals led awkward lives — "in a free state," as [Indian novelist] V. S. Naipaul has put it — forever in search of roots, and certitude; inwardly split, part backward, part Western, camouflaging their imitation of the West by gestures of rejection; forever aspiring to build lofty halfway houses that bridged the disparate cultural universes, often in all-embracing designs, never admitting the fissures and cracks in their lives and opinions; and always covering up their unease with a compensating presumption of moral superiority based on the recognition that the promptings of heart and soul are superior to the dictates of reason. Knowing their own traditions and at least some of the essentials of the West, they sensed that they had a more elevated grasp of human reality; the future belonged to them rather than to the "decadent" West. Out of that existential misery of "heightened consciousness" (as [Russian novelist] Dostoyevsky

---

[3] See selection 6 on page 909. [Ed.]

called it) have come some of the most seminal contributions to the intellectual and political developments of the 20th century, including the anti-Western counterrevolutions.

. . . Let it be said first that the relations between the colonized and the colonizer are exceedingly subtle and complex, subject to keen controversy among all observers, all of them partisans, all of them now judging not by indigenous but by Westernized standards. Western ideals and practices have shaped and intensified the protests of Westernized non-Western intellectuals taking full advantage of the opportunities offered by Western society. Their protests, incidentally, were hardly ever turned against past inhumanities committed by their own kind (because traditionally they were not considered as such).

Next, having already surveyed the not inconsiderable side benefits of Western domination, let us ask: Did the Westerners in their expansion behave toward the non-Westerners worse than they behaved toward themselves? While they never treated their colonial subjects as equals, they never killed as many people in all their colonial campaigns as they did in their own wars at home (the brutality of Europe's cultural evolution has been carefully rinsed out of all current historical accounts). And in their peaceful intercourse with non-Westerners we find the whole range of emotions common in Western society. It was darkness at heart on one extreme and saintliness on the other, and every mix in between, with the balance perhaps tending toward darkness. As one colonial officer in East Africa confided to his diary: "It is but a small percentage of white men whose characters do not in one way or another undergo a subtle process of deterioration when they are compelled to live for any length of time among savage races and under conditions as exist in tropical climates." The colonial district commissioner, isolated among people whose ways sharply contradicted his own upbringing, often suffering from tropical sickness, and scared at heart, found himself perhaps in a worse dilemma than the Westernized non-Western intellectuals. Some of them, no doubt, were unscrupulous opportunists seeking escape from the trammels of civic conformity at home; they turned domineering sadists in the colonies. On the other hand, missionaries often sacrificed their lives, generally among uncomprehending local folk. It was perhaps a credit to the Westerners that the victims of imperialism found considerable sympathy in their own midst. The evils stood out while the good intentions were taken for granted.

Yet—to take a longer view—even compassionate Western observers generally overlook the fact that among all the gifts of the West the two most crucial boons were missing: cultural equality as the basis for political equality and reasonable harmony in the body politic. The world revolution of Westernization perpetuated inequality and ruinous cultural subversion while at the same time improving the material conditions of life. More people survived, forever subject to the agonies of inequality and disorientation resulting from enforced change originating beyond their ken. Collectively and individually, they straddled the border between West and non-West, on the one side enjoying the benefits of Western culture, on the other feeling exploited as victims of imperialism. Indigenous populations always remained backward and dependent, unable to match the resources and skills of a fast-advancing West.

What we should weigh, then, in any assessment of Western colonial expansion before World War I is perhaps not only the actions, good or evil, of the colonial powers, but also the long-run consequences thereafter. The victims of Western colonialism do not include only the casualties of colonial wars but also the far greater multitudes killed or brutalized in the civil commotions in the emerging modern nation-states. Whatever the mitigating circumstances, the anti-Western fury has its justifications indeed.

2

FUKUZAWA YUKICHI

Good-bye Asia, 1885

Fukuzawa* Yukichi (1835–1901) was one of the most important Japanese Westernizers during Japan's late-nineteenth-century rush to catch up with the West. The son of a lower samurai (military) family, his pursuit of Western knowledge took him to a Dutch school in Osaka, where he studied everything from the Dutch language to chemistry, physics, and anatomy, and to Yedo, where he studied English. Due to his privileged background and Western schooling, he was naturally included in the first Japanese mission to the United States in 1860 as well as in the first diplomatic mission to Europe in 1862. After he returned to Japan, he spent many years teaching and writing the books that would make him famous. The best known of these was *Seiyo Jijo* (Things Western), which in 1866 introduced Japanese readers to the daily life and typical institutions of Western society. According to Fukuzawa Yukichi, the main obstacle that prevented Japanese society from catching up with the West was a long heritage of Chinese Confucianism, which stifled educational independence.

In the years after the Meiji Restoration of 1868, in which feudalism was abolished and power was restored to the emperor, Fukuzawa

* foo koo ZAH wah

Source: Fukuzawa Yukichi, "Datsu-a Ron" ("On Saying Good-bye to Asia"), in *Japan: A Documentary History*, ed. David J. Lu (Armonk, NY: M. E. Sharpe, 1997), 2:351–53. From Takeuchi Yoshimi, ed., *Azia Shugi (Asianism) Gendai Nihon Shisō Taikei (Great Compilation of Modern Japanese Thought)* (Tokyo: Chikuma Shobō, 1963), 8:38–40.

Yukichi became the most popular spokesman for the Westernizing policies of the new government. In this essay, "Good-bye Asia," written in 1885, he describes the spread of Western civilization in Japan. Why does he believe that it is both inevitable and desirable? What do you make of his attitude toward Chinese and Korean civilizations?

THINKING HISTORICALLY

Fukuzawa Yukichi is an unapologetic Westernizer. How does his attitude resemble that of a religious convert? Despite his lack of doubt about the advantages of Western ways, however, he does not criticize Japanese culture. He shows how a Westernizer could at the same time be nationalistic. In what ways is his attitude also nationalistic?

Transportation has become so convenient these days that once the wind of Western civilization blows to the East, every blade of grass and every tree in the East follow what the Western wind brings. Ancient Westerners and present-day Westerners are from the same stock and are not much different from one another. The ancient ones moved slowly, but their contemporary counterparts move vivaciously at a fast pace. This is possible because present-day Westerners take advantage of the means of transportation available to them. For those of us who live in the Orient, unless we want to prevent the coming of Western civilization with a firm resolve, it is best that we cast our lot with them. If one observes carefully what is going on in today's world, one knows the futility of trying to prevent the onslaught of Western civilization. Why not float with them in the same ocean of civilization, sail the same waves, and enjoy the fruits and endeavors of civilization?

The movement of a civilization is like the spread of measles. Measles in Tokyo start in Nagasaki and come eastward with the spring thaw. We may hate the spread of this communicable disease, but is there any effective way of preventing it? I can prove that it is not possible. In a communicable disease, people receive only damages. In a civilization, damages may accompany benefits, but benefits always far outweigh them, and their force cannot be stopped. This being the case, there is no point in trying to prevent their spread. A wise man encourages the spread and allows our people to get used to its ways.

The opening to the modern civilization of the West began in the reign of Kaei (1848–58).[1] Our people began to discover its utility and

---

[1] Refers to the Kaei era of the emperor Kōmei (r. 1846–1867). The emperor opposed Western influences but was forced to allow Dutch vaccination in 1849, admit Commodore Perry's U.S. fleet in 1853, permit coaling rights to U.S. ships in 1854, and accept the Treaty of Amity and Commerce in 1859. [Ed.]

gradually and yet actively moved toward its acceptance. However, there was an old-fashioned and bloated government that stood in the way of progress. It was a problem impossible to solve. If the government were allowed to continue, the new civilization could not enter. The modern civilization and Japan's old conventions were mutually exclusive. If we were to discard our old conventions, that government also had to be abolished. We could have prevented the entry of this civilization, but it would have meant loss of our national independence. The struggles taking place in the world civilization were such that they would not allow an Eastern island nation to slumber in isolation. At that point, dedicated men (*shijin*) recognized the principle of "the country is more important than the government," relied on the dignity of the Imperial Household, and toppled the old government to establish a new one.[2] With this, public and the private sectors alike, everyone in our country accepted the modern Western civilization. Not only were we able to cast aside Japan's old conventions, but we also succeeded in creating a new axle toward progress in Asia. Our basic assumptions could be summarized in two words: "Good-bye Asia (*Datsu-a*)."

Japan is located in the eastern extremities of Asia, but the spirit of her people have already moved away from the old conventions of Asia to the Western civilization. Unfortunately for Japan, there are two neighboring countries. One is called China and another Korea. These two peoples, like the Japanese people, have been nurtured by Asiatic political thoughts and mores. It may be that we are different races of people, or it may be due to the differences in our heredity or education; significant differences mark the three peoples. The Chinese and Koreans are more like each other and together they do not show as much similarity to the Japanese. These two peoples do not know how to progress either personally or as a nation. In this day and age with transportation becoming so convenient, they cannot be blind to the manifestations of Western civilization. But they say that what is seen or heard cannot influence the disposition of their minds. Their love affairs with ancient ways and old customs remain as strong as they were centuries ago. In this new and vibrant theater of civilization when we speak of education, they only refer back to Confucianism. As for school education, they can only cite [Chinese philosopher Mencius's] precepts of humanity, righteousness, decorum, and knowledge. While professing their abhorrence to ostentation, in reality they show their ignorance of truth and principles. As for their morality, one only has to observe their unspeakable acts of cruelty

---

[2] The Meiji Restoration (1868). Meiji was a son of Kōmei (who died of smallpox in 1867). Meiji restored the power of the emperor over the Tokugawa Shogunate, a feudal council that had ruled since 1603. Meiji eagerly sought contacts with the West so that Japan would not fall behind. [Ed.]

and shamelessness. Yet they remain arrogant and show no sign of self-examination.

In my view, these two countries cannot survive as independent nations with the onslaught of Western civilization to the East.[3] Their concerned citizens might yet find a way to engage in a massive reform, on the scale of our Meiji Restoration, and they could change their governments and bring about a renewal of spirit among their peoples. If that could happen they would indeed be fortunate. However, it is more likely that would never happen, and within a few short years they will be wiped out from the world with their lands divided among the civilized nations. Why is this so? Simply at a time when the spread of civilization and enlightenment (*bummei kaika*) has a force akin to that of measles, China and Korea violate the natural law of its spread. They forcibly try to avoid it by shutting off air from their rooms. Without air, they suffocate to death. It is said that neighbors must extend helping hands to one another because their relations are inseparable. Today's China and Korea have not done a thing for Japan. From the perspectives of civilized Westerners, they may see what is happening in China and Korea and judge Japan accordingly, because of the three countries' geographical proximity. The governments of China and Korea still retain their autocratic manners and do not abide by the rule of law. Westerners may consider Japan likewise a lawless society. Natives of China and Korea are deep in their hocus pocus of nonscientific behavior. Western scholars may think that Japan still remains a country dedicated to the *yin* and *yang* and five elements.[4] Chinese are meanspirited and shameless, and the chivalry of the Japanese people is lost to the Westerners. Koreans punish their convicts in an atrocious manner, and that is imputed to the Japanese as heartless people. There are many more examples I can cite. It is not different from the case of a righteous man living in a neighborhood of a town known for foolishness, lawlessness, atrocity, and heartlessness. His action is so rare that it is always buried under the ugliness of his neighbors' activities. When these incidents are multiplied, that can affect our normal conduct of diplomatic affairs. How unfortunate it is for Japan.

What must we do today? We do not have time to wait for the enlightenment of our neighbors so that we can work together toward the development of Asia. It is better for us to leave the ranks of Asian nations and cast our lot with civilized nations of the West. As for the way

---

[3] By 1885 China had been "opened" by Western powers in two opium wars (1839–1842, 1856–1860). Korea had been invaded by France (1866) and the United States (1871). Its isolation ended in 1885 by treaty with the United States. [Ed.]

[4] *Yin* and *yang* is a traditional Chinese duality (cold/hot, passive/active, female/male) illustrated by a circle divided by an "s" to show unity within duality. The five elements suggest another traditional, prescientific idea that everything is made of five basic ingredients. [Ed.]

of dealing with China and Korea, no special treatment is necessary just because they happen to be our neighbors. We simply follow the manner of the Westerners in knowing how to treat them. Any person who cherishes a bad friend cannot escape his bad notoriety. We simply erase from our minds our bad friends in Asia.

3

Images from Japan: Views of Westernization, Late Nineteenth Century

This selection consists of two prints by Japanese artists from the Meiji period of Westernization. The first print, Figure 23.1 is called *Monkey Show Dressing Room* (1879), by Honda Kinkachiro. What is this print's message? What is the artist's attitude toward Westernization?

The second piece, Figure 23.2, *The Exotic White Man*, shows a child born to a Western man and a Japanese woman. What is the artist's message? Does the artist favor such unions? What does the artist think of Westerners?

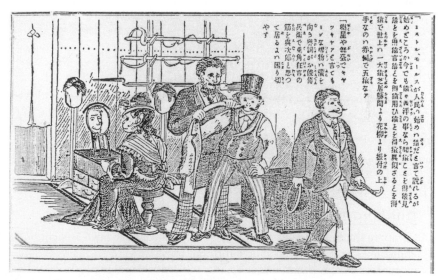

Figure 23.1   Monkey Show Dressing Room.

Source: Honda Kinkachiro, *Monkey Show Dressing Room*, in Julia Meech-Pekarik, *The World of the Meiji Print* (New York: John Weatherhill, 1986).

Figure 23.2   The Exotic White Man.

Source: Japanese color print, late 19th c., Dutch private collection, in C. A. Burland, *The Exotic White Man* (New York: McGraw-Hill, 1969), fig. 38. Werner Forman/Art Resource, NY.

THINKING HISTORICALLY

Compare the attitudes of these artists with that of Fukuzawa Yukichi. Prints, like cartoons, are a shorthand that must capture an easily recognizable trait. What, evidently, were the widely understood Japanese images of the West? Where do you think these stereotypes of the West came from? Do you see any signs in these prints of ambivalence on the part of the artist?

4

KAKUZO OKAKURA

The Ideals of the East, 1904

Kakuzo Okakura (1862–1913) was a Japanese scholar who was responsible for the development and preservation of the arts in Japan. In addition to creating important art schools and journals, he was the director of the Imperial Art School in Tokyo. In 1890 he founded the first Japanese art academy. In later life he worked and lectured in England and the United States, serving as the director of the Chinese and Japanese department at Harvard and, after 1910, as Curator of the Museum of Fine Arts in Boston. He is best known for *The Book of Tea*, which introduced the ritual beauty of the Japanese tea service to a Western audience. He also wrote for a Western audience *The Awakening of Japan* and *The Ideals of the East*, from which this selection is taken.

What are the "ideals of the East" that Okakura celebrates? What are the features of the West that he wants Japan to avoid?

THINKING HISTORICALLY

In Okakura the contradictions abound. He was a cosmopolitan world traveler, living in Europe, the United States, China, and India, as well as Japan. Yet, at the Imperial Art School in Tokyo, he offered no courses in Western Art. He spent his last years in Boston, developing the Asian art collection of an American museum. He wrote all of his major books in English, albeit to extol Asian, especially Japanese, art to the wider world. He was a modern urbanite who sought strength of identity in blood and the past.

How does he use the then popular Western idea of "race" in this selection? How does he negotiate the conflict between Japanese nationalism and a broader Pan-Asian identity? How does he combine love of monarchy with ideas of democracy? How does he reconcile tradition and individualism?

The Range of Ideals

Asia is one. The Himalayas divide, only to accentuate, two mighty civilisations, the Chinese with its communism of Confucius, and the Indian with its individualism of the Vedas. But not even the snowy

---

Source: Kakuzo Okakura, *Ideals of the East: The Spirit of Japanese Art* (Mineola, NY: Dover Publications, Inc., 2005), 1–4, 103–06.

barriers can interrupt for one moment that broad expanse of love for the Ultimate and Universal, which is the common thought-inheritance of every Asiatic race, enabling them to produce all the great religions of the world, and distinguishing them from those maritime peoples of the Mediterranean and the Baltic, who love to dwell on the Particular, and to search out the means, not the end, of life. . . .

For if Asia be one, it is also true that the Asiatic races form a single mighty web. We forget, in an age of classification, that types are after all but shining points of distinctness in an ocean of approximations, false gods deliberately set up to be worshipped, for the sake of mental convenience, but having no more ultimate or mutually exclusive validity than the separate existence of two interchangeable sciences. . . .

Buddhism—that great ocean of idealism, in which merge all the river-systems of Eastern Asiatic thought—is not coloured only with the pure water of the Ganges, for the Tartaric nations[1] that joined it made their genius also tributary, bringing new symbolism, new organisation, new powers of devotion, to add to the treasures of the Faith.

It has been, however, the great privilege of Japan to realise this unity-in-complexity with a special clearness. The Indo-Tartaric blood of this race was in itself a heritage which qualified it to imbibe from the two sources, and so mirror the whole of Asiatic consciousness. The unique blessing of unbroken sovereignty, the proud self-reliance of an unconquered race, and the insular isolation which protected ancestral ideas and instincts at the cost of expansion, made Japan the real repository of the trust of Asiatic thought and culture. Dynastic upheavals, the inroads of Tartar horsemen, the carnage and devastation of infuriated mobs—all these things, sweeping over her again and again, have left to China no landmarks, save her literature and her ruins, to recall the glory of the Tang emperors or the refinement of Sung society. . . .

It is in Japan alone that the historic wealth of Asiatic culture can be consecutively studied through its treasured specimens. The Imperial collection, the Shinto[2] temples, and the opened dolmens, reveal the subtle curves of Hang[3] workmanship. The temples of Nara[4] are rich in representations of Tang culture, and of that Indian art, then in its splendour, which so much influenced the creations of this classic period—natural heirlooms of a nation which has preserved the music, pronunciation, ceremony, and costumes, not to speak of the religious rites and philosophy, of so remarkable an age, intact.

---

[1] He means Central Asian Turks and Mongols. [Ed.]
[2] Traditional Japanese religion. [Ed.]
[3] Han, i.e., classical Chinese. [Ed.]
[4] City in Japan, capital 710–784 (the Nara Period). [Ed.]

The treasure-stores of the daimyos,[5] again, abound in works of art and manuscripts belonging to the Sung and Mongol dynasties, and as in China itself the former were lost during the Mongol conquest, and the latter in the age of the reactionary Ming, this fact animates some Chinese scholars of the present day to seek in Japan the fountain-head of their own ancient knowledge.

Thus Japan is a museum of Asiatic civilisation; and yet more than a museum, because the singular genius of the race leads it to dwell on all phases of the ideals of the past, in that spirit of living Advaitism[6] which welcomes the new without losing the old. The Shinto still adheres to his pre-Buddhistic rites of ancestor-worship; and the Buddhists themselves cling to each various school of religious development which has come in its natural order to enrich the soil.

The Yamato poetry,[7] and Bugaku music,[8] which reflect the Tang ideal under the régime of the Fujiwara aristocracy,[9] are a source of inspiration and delight to the present day, like the sombre Zennism[10] and No-dances,[11] which were the product of Sung illumination. It is this tenacity that keeps Japan true to the Asiatic soul even while it raises her to the rank of a modern power.

The history of Japanese art becomes thus the history of Asiatic ideals—the beach where each successive wave of Eastern thought has left its sand-ripple as it beat against the national consciousness. Yet I linger with dismay on the threshold of an attempt to make an intelligible summary of those art-ideals. For art, like the diamond net of Indra,[12] reflects the whole chain in every link. It exists at no period in any final mould. It is always a growth, defying the dissecting knife of the chronologist. To discourse on a particular phase of its development means to deal with infinite causes and effects throughout its past and present. Art with us, as elsewhere, is the expression of the highest and noblest of our national culture, so that, in order to understand it, we must pass in review the various phases of Confucian philosophy; the different ideals which the Buddhist mind has from time to time revealed; those mighty political cycles which have one after another unfurled the banner of nationality; the reflection in patriotic thought of the lights of poetry and the shadows of heroic characters; and the echoes, alike of the wailing of a multitude, and of the mad-seeming merriment of the laughter of a race. . . .

---

[5] Warlords of feudal Japan. [Ed.]

[6] Indian philosophy of wholeness and immediacy. [Ed.]

[7] Earliest Japanese poetry, seventh–tenth centuries; also period of Tang dynasty in China. [Ed.]

[8] Ceremonial dance music of elite of same period. [Ed.]

[9] Ruling clan in Heian period (794–1185). [Ed.]

[10] Japanese Zen Buddhism. [Ed.]

[11] Highly stylized Japanese dance theater. [Ed.]

[12] Indian god. [Ed.]

The Vista

The simple life of Asia need fear no shaming from that sharp contrast with Europe in which steam and electricity have placed it to-day. The old world of trade, the world of the craftsman and the pedlar, of the village market and the saints'-day fair, where little boats row up and down great rivers laden with the produce of the country, where every palace has some court in which the travelling merchant may display his stuffs and jewels for beautiful screened women to see and buy, is not yet quite dead. And, however its form may change, only at a great loss can Asia permit its spirit to die, since the whole of that industrial and decorative art which is the heirloom of ages has been in its keeping, and she must lose with it not only the beauty of things, but the joy of the worker, his individuality of vision, and the whole age-long humanising of her labour. For to clothe oneself in the web of one's own weaving is to house oneself in one's own house, to create for the spirit its own sphere.

Asia knows, it is true, nothing of the fierce joys of a time-devouring locomotion, but she has still the far deeper travel-culture of the pilgrimage and the wandering monk. For the Indian ascetic, begging his bread of village housewives, or seated at evenfall beneath some tree, chatting and smoking with the peasant of the district, is the real traveller. To him a countryside does not consist of its natural features alone. It is a nexus of habits and associations. Of human elements and traditions, suffused with the tenderness and friendship of one who has shared, if only for a moment, the joys and sorrows of its personal drama. The Japanese peasant-traveller, again, goes from no place of interest on his wanderings without leaving his *hokku* or short sonnet, an art-form within reach of the simplest.

Through such modes of experience is cultivated the Eastern conception of individuality as the ripe and living knowledge, the harmonised thought and feeling of staunch yet gentle manhood. Through such modes of interchange is maintained the Eastern notion of human intercourse, not the printed index, as the true means of culture.

The chain of antitheses might be indefinitely lengthened. But the glory of Asia is something more positive than these. It lies in that vibration of peace that beats in every heart; that harmony that brings together emperor and peasant; that sublime intuition of oneness which commands all sympathy, all courtesy, to be its fruits, making Takakura, Emperor of Japan, remove his sleeping-robes on a winter night, because the frost lay cold on the hearths of his poor; or Taiso, of Tang, forego food, because his people were feeling the pinch of famine. It lies in the dream of renunciation that pictures the Boddhi-Sattva[13] as

---

[13] Buddhist Boddisattva: saint; model of compassion. [Ed.]

refraining from Nirvana till the last atom of dust in the universe shall have passed in before to bliss. It lies in that worship of Freedom which casts around poverty the halo of greatness, imposes his stern simplicity of apparel on the Indian prince, and sets up in China a throne whose imperial occupant—alone amongst the great secular rulers of the world—never wears a sword.

These things are the secret energy of the thought, the science, the poetry, and the art of Asia. Torn from their tradition, India, made barren of that religious life which is the essence of her nationality, would become a worshipper of the mean, the false, and the new; China, hurled upon the problems of a material instead of a moral civilisation, would writhe in the death-agony of that ancient dignity and ethics which long ago made the word of her merchants like the legal bond of the West, the name of her peasants a synonym for prosperity; and Japan, the Fatherland of the race of Ama,[14] would betray the completeness of her undoing in the tarnishing of the purity of the spiritual mirror, the bemeaning of the sword-soul from steel to lead. The task of Asia to-day, then, becomes that of protecting and restoring Asiatic modes. But to do this she must herself first recognise and develop consciousness of those modes. For the shadows of the past are the promise of the future. No tree can be greater than the power that is in the seed. Life lies ever in the return to self. How many of the Evangels have uttered this truth! "Know thyself," was the greatest mystery spoken by the Delphic Oracle. "All in thyself," said the quiet voice of Confucius. And more striking still is the Indian story that carries the same message to its hearers. For once it happened, say the Buddhists, that, the Master having gathered his disciples round him, there shone forth before them suddenly—blasting the sight of all save Vajrapani, the completely-learned—a terrible figure, the figure of Siva, the Great God. Then Vajrapani, his companions being blinded, turned to the Master and said, "Tell me why, searching amongst all the stars and gods, equal in number to the sands of the Ganges, I have nowhere seen this glorious form. Who is he?" And the Buddha said, "He is thyself!" and Vajrapani, it is told, immediately attained the highest.

It was some small degree of this self-recognition that re-made Japan, and enabled her to weather the storm under which so much of the Oriental world went down. And it must be a renewal of the same self-consciousness that shall build up Asia again into her ancient steadfastness and strength. The very times are bewildered by the manifoldness of the possibilities opening out before them. Even Japan cannot, in the tangled skein of the Meiji period,[15] find that single thread which will give

[14] Japanese divers. [Ed.]
[15] 1868–1912. [Ed.]

her the clue to her own future. Her past has been clear and continuous as a mala, a rosary, of crystals. From the early days of the Asuka period,[16] when the national destiny was first bestowed, as the receiver and concentrator, by her Yamato genius, of Indian ideals and Chinese ethics; through the succeeding preliminary phases of Nara and Heian, to the revelation of her vast powers in the unmeasured devotion of her Fujiwara period, in her heroic reaction of Kamakura,[17] culminating in the stern enthusiasm and lofty abstinence of that Ashikaga[18] knighthood who sought with so austere a passion after death — through all these phases the evolution of the nation is clear and unconfused, like that of a single personality. Even through Toyotomi,[19] and Tokugawa,[20] it is clear that after the fashion of the East we are ending a rhythm of activity with the lull of the democratising of the great ideals. The populace and the lower classes, notwithstanding their seeming quiescence and commonplaceness, are making their own the consecration of the Samurai, the sadness of the poet, the divine self-sacrifice of the saint are becoming liberated, in fact, into their national inheritance.

But to-day the great mass of Western thought perplexes us. The mirror of Yamato is clouded, as we say. With the Revolution, Japan, it is true, returns upon her past, seeking there for the new vitality she needs. Like all genuine restorations, it is a reaction with a difference. For that self-dedication of art to nature which the Ashikaga inaugurated has become now a consecration to the race, to man himself. We know instinctively that in our history lies the secret of our future, and we grope with a blind intensity to find the clue. But if the thought be true, if there be indeed any spring of renewal hidden in our past, we must admit that it needs at this moment some mighty reinforcement, for the scorching drought of modern vulgarity is parching the throat of life and art.

We await the flashing sword of the lightning which shall cleave the darkness. For the terrible hush must be broken, and the raindrops of a new vigour must refresh the earth before new flowers can spring up to cover it with their bloom. But it must be from Asia herself, along the ancient roadways of the race, that the great voice shall be heard.

Victory from within, or a mighty death without.

---

[16] 552–645. [Ed.]

[17] 1185–1333. [Ed.]

[18] 1336–1573, Feudal period. [Ed.]

[19] Toyotomi Hideyoshi (1537–1598). A feudal lord who ended feudalism. [Ed.]

[20] Tokugawa Ieyasu (1543–1616). Founder and first shogun of the Tokugawa Shogunate (1603–1868). [Ed.]

5

RAMMOHUN ROY
Letter on Indian Education, 1823

India's Westernization was less voluntary than Japan's. While Japan
successfully limited European colonialism to a few seaports in the
seventeenth century and was not forced to deal with the West again
until after Commodore Perry's steam-age arrival in 1853, India
became increasingly colonized by England throughout the eighteenth
and nineteenth centuries. Because of India's long history as a British
colony, aspects of Westernization there were deeper and more complex, the most obvious being use of the English language.

A colonial and foreign tongue, English had the advantage of uniting a country with dozens of regional languages (some of which were
also imposed by foreign conquerors), while at the same time providing access to universities and a body of knowledge and literature as
advanced as any in the world. English instruction—rather than
ancient Sanskrit or Hindi or another Indian regional language—was
championed by Britons who thought it would make Indians loyal and
by Indians who thought it would unite them as a nation. The Indian
use of English had its detractors, too: Britons who thought it dangerous or unseemly, and Britons and Indians who thought it patronizing
and demeaning.

The debate over teaching English or Indian languages was part of
a larger debate about the relative value of Western and Indian
culture. Increasingly, toward the end of the nineteenth century as
science took center stage in English culture, Indians found themselves
torn between the claim of science and the appeal of traditional
Indian religious knowledge.

Rammohun Roy (1772–1833) was an Indian social and religious
reformer, as well as one of the earliest proponents of English
education. Roy was an accomplished linguist who knew Latin, Greek,
Hebrew, Arabic, Persian, and ancient Indian Sanskrit as well as his
native Bengali. Yet when the British proposed to build a new Sanskrit
school in Calcutta, Roy fired off the following letter to the British
prime minister. Why did Roy object to a school that taught Sanskrit,
the sacred language of ancient Hindu culture? What were his reasons
for preferring English education for Indians?

Source: Rammohun Roy, Letter on Indian Education, in H. Sharp, ed., *Selections from
Educational Records, Part I, 1781–1839* (Calcutta: Superintendent Government Printing,
1920; reprint, Delhi: National Archives of India, 1965), 98–101.

THINKING HISTORICALLY

To effectively communicate his ideas on Indian education, Roy had to strike a delicate balance in expressing deference to the British government while asserting enough authority to be taken seriously. How did he accomplish this dual task? How did he suggest that he knew more about the issue than his superiors in the English government, without seeming arrogant or ungrateful? How does his letter show that he was an Indian who benefited from an English education but did not pose a threat to British rule? What does his letter reveal about the inherent tensions in colonial India, within individuals and the society as a whole?

To His Excellency the Right Hon'ble William Pitt, Lord Amherst
My Lord,

Humbly reluctant as the natives of India are to obtrude upon the notice of Government the sentiments they entertain on any public measure there are circumstances when silence would be carrying this respectful feeling to culpable excess. The present Rulers of India, coming from a distance of many thousand miles to govern a people whose language, literature, manners, customs, and ideas are almost entirely new and strange to them, cannot easily become so intimately acquainted with their real circumstances, as the natives of the country are themselves. We should therefore be guilty of a gross dereliction of duty to ourselves, and afford our Rulers just ground of complaint at our apathy, did we omit on occasions of importance like the present to supply them with such accurate information as might enable them to devise and adopt measures calculated to be beneficial to the country, and thus second by our local knowledge and experience their declared benevolent intentions for its improvement.

The establishment of a new Sanskrit School in Calcutta evinces the laudable desire of Government to improve the Natives of India by Education, a blessing for which they must ever be grateful; and every well wisher of the human race must be desirous that the efforts made to promote it should be guided by the most enlightened principles, so that the stream of intelligence may flow into the most useful channels.

When this Seminary of learning was proposed, we understood that the Government in England had ordered a considerable sum of money to be annually devoted to the instruction of its Indian Subjects. We were filled with sanguine hopes that this sum would be laid out in employing European Gentlemen of talents and education to instruct the natives of India in Mathematics, Natural Philosophy, Chemistry, Anatomy and other useful Sciences, which the Nations of Europe have carried to a degree of perfection that has raised them above the inhabitants of other parts of the world.

While we looked forward with pleasing hope to the dawn of knowledge thus promised to the rising generation, our hearts were filled with mingled feelings of delight and gratitude; we already offered up thanks to Providence for inspiring the most generous and enlightened of the Nations of the West with the glorious ambitions of planting in Asia the Arts and Sciences of modern Europe.

We now find that the Government are establishing a Sanskrit school under Hindu Pundits to impart such knowledge as is already current in India. This Seminary (similar in character to those which existed in Europe before the time of Lord Bacon[1]) can only be expected to load the minds of youth with grammatical niceties and metaphysical distinctions of little or no practicable use to the possessors or to society. The pupils will there acquire what was known two thousand years ago, with the addition of vain and empty subtilties [sic] since produced by speculative men, such as is already commonly taught in all parts of India.

The Sanskrit language, so difficult that almost a life time is necessary for its perfect acquisition, is well known to have been for ages a lamentable check on the diffusion of knowledge; and the learning concealed under this almost impervious veil is far from sufficient to reward the labour of acquiring it. But if it were thought necessary to perpetuate this language for the sake of the portion of the valuable information it contains, this might be much more easily accomplished by other means than the establishment of a new Sanskrit College; for there have been always and are now numerous professors of Sanskrit in the different parts of the country, engaged in teaching this language as well as the other branches of literature which are to be the object of the new Seminary. Therefore their more diligent cultivation, if desirable, would be effectually promoted by holding out premiums and granting certain allowances to those most eminent Professors, who have already undertaken on their own account to teach them, and would by such rewards be stimulated to still greater exertions.

From these considerations, as the sum set apart for the instruction of the Natives of India was intended by the Government in England, for the improvement of its Indian subjects, I beg leave to state, with due deference to your Lordship's exalted situation, that if the plan now adopted be followed, it will completely defeat the object proposed; since no improvement can be expected from inducing young men to consume a dozen of years of the most valuable period of their lives in acquiring the niceties of the Byakurun or Sanskrit Grammar. For

---

[1] Francis Bacon (1561–1626), English philosopher often credited with developing the scientific method. [Ed.]

instance, in learning to discuss such points as the following: *Khad* signifying to eat, *khaduti,* he or she or it eats. Query, whether does the word *khaduti,* taken as a whole, convey the meaning *he, she,* or *it eats,* or are separate parts of this meaning conveyed by distinct portions of the word? As if in the English language it were asked, how much meaning is there in the *eat,* how much in the *s*? and is the whole meaning of the word conveyed by those two portions of it distinctly, or by them taken jointly?

Neither can much improvement arise from such speculations as the following, which are the themes suggested by the Vedanta: In what manner is the soul absorbed into the deity? What relation does it bear to the divine essence? Nor will youths be fitted to be better members of society by the Vedantic doctrines, which teach them to believe that all visible things have no real existence; that as father, brother, etc., have no actual entirety, they consequently deserve no real affection, and therefore the sooner we escape from them and leave the world the better. Again, no essential benefit can be derived by the student of the Meemangsa from knowing what it is that makes the killer of a goat sinless on pronouncing certain passages of the Vedas, and what is the real nature and operative influence of passages of the Veda, etc.

Again the student of the Nyaya Shastra cannot be said to have improved his mind after he has learned from it into how many ideal classes the objects in the Universe are divided, and what speculative relation the soul bears to the body, the body to the soul, the eye to the ear, etc.

In order to enable your Lordship to appreciate the utility of encouraging such imaginary learning as above characterised, I beg your Lordship will be pleased to compare the state of science and literature in Europe before the time of Lord Bacon, with the progress of knowledge made since he wrote.

If it had been intended to keep the British nation in ignorance of real knowledge the Baconian philosophy would not have been allowed to displace the system of the schoolmen, which was the best calculated to perpetuate ignorance. In the same manner the [Sanskrit] system of education would be the best calculated to keep this country in darkness, if such had been the policy of the British Legislature. But as the improvement of the native population is the object of the Government, it will consequently promote a more liberal and enlightened system of instruction, embracing mathematics, natural philosophy, chemistry and anatomy, with other useful sciences which may be accomplished with the sum proposed by employing a few gentlemen of talents and learning educated in Europe, and providing a college furnished with the necessary books, instruments, and other apparatus.

In representing this subject to your Lordship I conceive myself discharging a solemn duty which I owe to my countrymen and also to that enlightened Sovereign and Legislature which have extended their benevolent cares to this distant land actuated by a desire to improve its inhabitants and I therefore humbly trust you will excuse the liberty I have taken in thus expressing my sentiments to your Lordship.

I have, etc.,

Rammohun Roy
Calcutta;
The 11th December 1823

6

MOHANDAS K. GANDHI
Hind Swaraj, 1921

Mohandas K. Gandhi (1869–1948), the father of Indian independence, combined the education of an English lawyer with the temperament of an Indian ascetic to lead a national resistance movement against the British. In the century that followed British-supported reforms to the Indian education system (in the early nineteenth century), British rule had become far more pervasive and increasingly hostile toward Indian culture. Unlike Indian educational reformers, who had embraced Western culture as a means to uplift Indians, Gandhi became extremely critical of Western culture as he witnessed the havoc British rule wreaked on his country.

Gandhi began to develop his ideas of *Hind Swaraj,** or Indian Home Rule, in 1909 while he sailed from England to South Africa, where he served as a lawyer for fellow Indians. An early version of this essay, published then, was reissued in its present form in 1921, two years after he returned to his birthplace, India, and again in 1938, in the last years of struggle against British rule.

After Gandhi's introduction, the essay takes the form of questions and answers. The questions are posed by a presumed "reader" of Gandhi's pamphlet. As "editor," Gandhi explains what he means. How does Gandhi compare life in Europe and India? What does he think of the possibility of Hindus and Muslims living together? What

---

* hihnd swah RAHJ

Source: M. K. Gandhi, *Hind Swaraj* (Ahmedabad, India: Navajivan, 1938), 31–33, 44–45, 58–59, 69–71.

does he mean by passive resistance or soul-force (Satyagraha)? Why does he think it is preferable to violence, or body-force? Gandhi was assassinated by a Hindu extremist in 1948 before he had a chance to shape the new nation. What kind of India would Gandhi have tried to create had he lived? Compare Gandhi's response to the West with that of Rammohan Roy in the previous selection. In what respects is his attitude like his contemporary, Kakuzo Okakura?

THINKING HISTORICALLY

Some historians have argued that Gandhi's contradictory roles—Hindu philosopher espousing secular nationalism and anti-modernist revolutionary—were ultimately unbridgeable. Notice how Gandhi makes a lawyer's case for traditional Indian values. How does he combine both religious and secular goals for India? How does he combine Hindu religious ideas with respect for Muslims? Were Gandhi's contradictions a fatal flaw, or could they have been his strength?

Civilization

READER   Now you will have to explain what you mean by civilization.

EDITOR   Let us first consider what state of things is described by the word "civilization." Its true test lies in the fact that people living in it make bodily welfare the object of life. We will take some examples. The people of Europe today live in better-built houses than they did a hundred years ago. This is considered an emblem of civilization, and this is also a matter to promote bodily happiness. Formerly, they wore skins, and used spears as their weapons. Now, they wear long trousers, and, for embellishing their bodies, they wear a variety of clothing, and, instead of spears, they carry with them revolvers containing five or more chambers. If people of a certain country, who have hitherto not been in the habit of wearing much clothing, boots, etc., adopt European clothing, they are supposed to have become civilized out of savagery. Formerly, in Europe, people ploughed their lands mainly by manual labour. Now, one man can plough a vast tract by means of steam engines and can thus amass great wealth. This is called a sign of civilization. Formerly, only a few men wrote valuable books. Now, anybody writes and prints anything he likes and poisons people's minds. Formerly, men travelled in waggons. Now, they fly through the air in trains at the rate of four hundred and more miles per day. This is considered the height of civilization. It has been stated that, as men progress, they shall be able to travel in airship and reach any part of the world in a few hours. Men will not need the use of their hands and feet. They will press a button, and they will have their clothing at their side. They will press another button, and they will have their newspaper. A third, and motor-car will be in waiting for them. They will have a variety of delicately dished up food. Everything will be done by machinery. Formerly, when people wanted to fight with one another, they measured between them their bodily strength; now it is possible to take away thousands of lives by one man working behind a gun from a hill. This is civilization. Formerly, men worked in the open air only as much as they liked. Now thousands of workmen meet together and for the sake of maintenance work in factories or mines. Their condition is worse than that of beasts. They are obliged to work, at the risk of their lives, at most dangerous occupations, for the sake of millionaires. Formerly, men were made slaves under physical compulsion. Now they are enslaved by temptation of money and of the luxuries that money can buy. There are now diseases of which people never dreamt before, and an army of doctors is engaged in finding out their cures, and so hospitals have increased. This is a test of civilization. Formerly, special messengers were required and much expense was incurred in order to send letters; today, anyone can abuse his fellow by means of a letter for one penny. True, at the same cost, one can send one's thanks also. Formerly, people had two or three meals consisting of home-made bread and vegetables; now, they require something to eat every two hours so that they have hardly leisure for anything else. What more need I say? . . . Even a child can understand that in all I have described above there can be no inducement to morality.

The Hindus and the Mahomedans

READER   Has the introduction to Mahomedanism [Islam] not unmade the nation?

EDITOR   India cannot cease to be one nation because people belonging to different religions live in it. The introduction of foreigners does not necessarily destroy the nation; they merge in it. A country is one nation only when such a condition obtains in it. That country must have a faculty for assimilation. India has ever been such a country. In reality there are as many religions as there are individuals; but those who are conscious of the spirit of nationality do not interfere with one another's religion. If they do, they are not fit to be considered a nation. If the Hindus believe that India should be peopled only by Hindus, they are living in dreamland. The Hindus, the Mahomedans, the Parsis and the Christians who have made India their country are fellow-countrymen, and they will have to live in unity, if only for their own interest. In no part of the world are one nationality and one religion synonymous terms; nor has it ever been so in India.

READER   But what about the inborn enmity between Hindus and
    Mahomedans?
EDITOR   That phrase has been invented by our mutual enemy. When the
    Hindus and Mahomedans fought against one another, they certainly
    spoke in that strain. They have long since ceased to fight. How, then,
    can there be any inborn enmity? Pray remember this too, that we did
    not cease to fight only after British occupation. The Hindus flour-
    ished under Moslem sovereigns and Moslems under the Hindu. Each
    party recognized that mutual fighting was suicidal, and that neither
    party would abandon its religion by force of arms. Both parties,
    therefore, decided to live in peace. With the English advent quarrels
    recommenced. . . .

How Can India Become Free?

READER   If Indian civilization is, as you say, the best of all, how do you
    account for India's slavery?
EDITOR   This civilization is unquestionably the best, but it is to be ob-
    served that all civilizations have been on their trial. That civilization
    which is permanent outlives it. Because the sons of India were found
    wanting, its civilization has been placed in jeopardy. But its strength
    is to be seen in its ability to survive the shock. Moreover, the whole
    of India is not touched. Those alone who have been affected by
    Western civilization have become enslaved. We measure the universe
    by our own miserable foot-rule. When we are slaves, we think that
    the whole universe is enslaved. Because we are in an abject condition,
    we think that the whole of India is in that condition. As a matter of
    fact, it is not so, yet it is as well to impute our slavery to the whole of
    India. But if we bear in mind the above fact, we can see that if we
    become free, India is free. And in this thought you have a definition
    of Swaraj. It is Swaraj when we learn to rule ourselves. It is, there-
    fore, in the palm of our hands. Do not consider this Swaraj to be like
    a dream. There is no idea of sitting still. The Swaraj that I wish to
    picture is such that, after we have once realized it, we shall endeav-
    our to the end of our life-time to persuade others to do likewise. But
    such Swaraj has to be experienced, by each one for himself. One
    drowning man will never save another. Slaves ourselves, it would be
    a mere pretension to think of freeing others. Now you will have seen
    that it is not necessary for us to have as our goal the expulsion of the
    English. If the English become Indianized, we can accommodate
    them. If they wish to remain in India along with their civilization,
    there is no room for them. It lies with us to bring about such a state
    of things. . . .

Passive Resistance

READER   Is there any historical evidence as to the success of what you have called soul-force or truth-force? No instance seems to have happened of any nation having risen through soul-force. I still think that the evil-doers will not cease doing evil without physical punishment.

EDITOR   The [Hindu] poet Tulsidas [1532–1623] has said: "Of religion, pity, or love, is the root, as egotism of the body. Therefore, we should not abandon pity so long as we are alive." This appears to me to be a scientific truth. We have evidence of its working at every step. The universe would disappear without the existence of that force. . . .

 The fact that there are so many men still alive in the world shows that it is based not on the force of arms but on the force of truth or love. Therefore, the greatest and most unimpeachable evidence of the success of this force is to be found in the fact that, in spite of the wars of the world, it still lives on.

 Thousands, indeed tens of thousands, depend for their existence on a very active working of this force. Little quarrels of millions of families in their daily lives disappear before the exercise of this force. Hundreds of nations live in peace. History does not and cannot take note of this fact. History is really a record of every interruption of the even working of the force of love or of the soul. Two brothers quarrel; one of them repents and re-awakens the love that was lying dormant in him; the two again begin to live in peace; nobody takes note of this. But if the two brothers, through the intervention of solicitors or some other reason take up arms or go to law — which is another form of the exhibition of brute force, — their doings would be immediately noticed in the press, they would be the talk of their neighbours and would probably go down to history. And what is true of families and communities is true of nations. There is no reason to believe that there is one law for families and another for nations. History, then, is a record of an interruption of the course of nature. Soul-force, being natural, is not noted in history.

READER   According to what you say, it is plain that instances of this kind of passive resistance are not to be found in history. It is necessary to understand this passive resistance more fully. It will be better, therefore, if you enlarge upon it.

EDITOR   Passive resistance is a method of securing rights by personal suffering; it is the reverse of resistance by arms. When I refuse to do a thing that is repugnant to my conscience, I use soul-force. For instance, the Government of the day has passed a law which is applicable to me. I do not like it. If by using violence I force the Government to repeal the law, I am employing what may be termed body-force. If I do not obey the law and accept the penalty for its breach, I use soul-force. It involves sacrifice of self.

7

JAWAHARLAL NEHRU

Gandhi, 1936

Mohandas K. Gandhi and Jawaharlal Nehru* were the two most important leaders of India's national independence movement. In 1936 Nehru published his autobiography, excerpted here, in which he had much to say about the importance of Gandhi in his life. Though they worked together and Nehru was Gandhi's choice as the first Indian prime minister, they expressed in their personalities and ideas two very different Indias. How would you describe these two Indias? Was it Gandhi's or Nehru's vision of the future that was realized? Who do you think was a better guide for India? Why?

THINKING HISTORICALLY

Think of Gandhi and Nehru as the two sides of the Indian struggle for independence. Did India benefit from having both of these sides represented? What would have happened if there had been only Gandhi's view or only Nehru's?

How was the debate in India about the influence of the West different from the debate in Japan?

I imagine that Gandhiji[1] is not so vague about the objective as he sometimes appears to be. He is passionately desirous of going in a certain direction, but this is wholly at variance with modern ideas and conditions, and he has so far been unable to fit the two, or to chalk out all the

---

* jah wah HAHR lahl   NAY roo
[1] Term of endearment for Gandhi. [Ed.]

Source: Jawaharlal Nehru, *An Autobiography* (New Delhi: Allied Publishers, 1942–1962), 510–11.

intermediate steps leading to his goal. Hence the appearance of vague-ness and avoidance of clarity. But his general inclination has been clear enough for a quarter of a century, ever since he started formulating his philosophy in South Africa. I do not know if those early writings still represent his views. I doubt if they do so in their entirety, but they do help us to understand the background of his thought.

"India's salvation consists," he wrote in 1909, "in unlearning what she has learned during the last fifty years. The railways, telegraphs, hos-pitals, lawyers, doctors, and suchlike have all to go; and the so-called upper classes have to learn consciously, religiously, and deliberately the simple peasant life, knowing it to be a life giving true happiness." And again: "Every time I get into a railway car or use a motor bus I know that I am doing violence to my sense of what is right"; "to attempt to reform the world by means of highly artificial and speedy locomotion is to attempt the impossible."

All this seems to me utterly wrong and harmful doctrine, and impos-sible of achievement. Behind it lies Gandhiji's love and praise of poverty and suffering and the ascetic life. For him progress and civilization con-sist not in the multiplication of wants, of higher standards of living, "but in the deliberate and voluntary restriction of wants, which promotes real happiness and contentment, and increases the capacity for service." If these premises are once accepted, it becomes easy to follow the rest of Gandhiji's thought and to have a better understanding of his activities. But most of us do not accept those premises, and yet we complain later on when we find that his activities are not to our liking.

Personally I dislike the praise of poverty and suffering. I do not think they are at all desirable, and they ought to be abolished. Nor do I appre-ciate the ascetic life as a social ideal, though it may suit individuals. I understand and appreciate simplicity, equality, self-control; but not the mortification of the flesh. Just as an athlete requires to train his body, I believe that the mind and habits have also to be trained and brought under control. It would be absurd to expect that a person who is given to too much self-indulgence can endure much suffering or show unusual self-control or behave like a hero when the crisis comes. To be in good moral condition requires at least as much training as to be in good physical condition. But that certainly does not mean asceticism or self-mortification.

Nor do I appreciate in the least the idealization of the "simple peas-ant life." I have almost a horror of it, and instead of submitting to it myself I want to drag out even the peasantry from it, not to urbaniza-tion, but to the spread of urban cultural facilities to rural areas. Far from his life's giving me true happiness, it would be almost as bad as impris-onment for me. What is there in "The Man with the Hoe" to idealize over? Crushed and exploited for innumerable generations, he is only little removed from the animals who keep him company.

Who made him dead to rapture and despair,
A thing that grieves not and that never hopes,
Stolid and stunned, a brother to the ox?[2]

This desire to get away from the mind of man to primitive conditions where mind does not count, seems to me quite incomprehensible. The very thing that is the glory and triumph of man is decried and discouraged, and a physical environment which will oppress the mind and prevent its growth is considered desirable. Present-day civilization is full of evils, but it is also full of good; and it has the capacity in it to rid itself of those evils. To destroy it root and branch is to remove that capacity from it and revert to a dull, sunless, and miserable existence. But even if that were desirable it is an impossible undertaking. We cannot stop the river of change or cut ourselves adrift from it, and psychologically we who have eaten of the apple of Eden cannot forget that taste and go back to primitiveness.

[2] From poem by Edwin Markam, "The Man with the Hoe" (1899), which was a response to the painting of the same title by Jean Millet. [Ed.]

■ REFLECTIONS

We have looked at the conflict between Westernization and nationalism through windows on Japan and India. For the Japanese, the borrowing of Western institutions and ideas provided an escape from colonization. By the time India gained political independence in 1947, it had become partially Westernized by three hundred years of colonialism. Yet in both countries there were those who resisted Western ways, those who embraced them, and others still who developed ambivalent feelings toward the West.

This last response—often accepting the contradictions: treasuring the traditional while trying the new—may have been the most difficult, but ultimately the most useful. It must have been far easier to cast off everything Asian, as Fukuzawa Yukichi urged, or make fun of any contact with the West as monkeying around or frightful miscegenation, as the Japanese cartoons suggested. Japan may have made the most successful non-Western transition to industrial modernity because it steered a path between Fukuzawa Yukichi's prescription for wholesale cultural capitulation and the cartoonists' blanket rejection of anything new and foreign.

India, with older indigenous traditions than Japan but also a longer period confronting the influence of Western culture, approached independence in 1947 with a political elite trained in English law, liberal and Marxist political parties, a literate English-speaking middle class, and a long-suppressed hunger for economic freedom and material well-being. Gandhi feared violence, anticolonial in 1909 and anti-Muslim in 1947, more than the repressions of the old society. While he sought a new social cohesion in traditional religious spiritualism, Nehru hoped to forge a new solidarity along the Western industrial socialist model.

Some may find the nationalist vision of Okakura more unsettling. Certainly his celebration of Asian art was long overdue. Though Japanese art, especially, was well known to a Western elite of artists and collectors (Gaughin for one made it his own), most Westerners ignorantly dismissed it. It is interesting that even today many college courses in art history ignore Asian art, relegating it at best to a separate course. In introducing Asian art to the West, Okakura began a Herculean task, still not fully accomplished. But Okakura's nationalism had a sharp edge that cut aggressively in the next generation. In his eagerness to embrace a deep Asian past as his own, he adopted for Japan centuries of oppressive Asian dynasties including the Mongols, in the process turning cultural heritage into racial inheritance. The idea of race, initially a Western pseudo-science to rationalize dominion, would be turned against the West with consequences as devastating as those experienced in Europe and the United States in the 1930s and 1940s. That is not to blame Okakura for later Japanese nationalism. He merely participated in a kind of nationalism that turned lethal.

Nationalism could always turn inward or outward. Even when it turned outward, it did not have to denigrate "the other." The idea that the nation consisted of those who lived on the same soil and the idea that each nation had its own individual attributes were beliefs of what historians have come to call "liberal nationalism," the nationalist movement that prevailed especially in the first half of the nineteenth century. The antagonistic idea that national identity was in the blood, and that, therefore, not only are some nations better than others, but their superiority is in their genes, were beliefs of the "ethnic nationalism" that developed along with racism at the end of the century. A belief that nations were based on blood would help spawn two world wars.

24

World War I and
Its Consequences

Europe and the World, 1914–1929

■ HISTORICAL CONTEXT

The Europe that so many non-European intellectuals sought to imitate
or reject between 1880 and 1920 came very close to self-destructing between 1914 and 1918, and bringing many of the world's peoples from
Asia, Africa, and the Americas down with it. The orgy of bloodletting,
then known as the "Great War," put seventy million men in uniform, of
whom ten million were killed and twenty million were wounded. Most
of the soldiers were Western European, though Russia contributed
more soldiers than France or Germany, while Japan enlisted as many as
the Austro-Hungarian Empire that began the war. Enlisted men also
came from the United States, Canada, Australia, New Zealand, South
Africa, and the colonies: India, French West Africa, and German East
Africa, among others. The majority of soldiers were killed in Europe,
especially along the German Western Front—four hundred miles of
trenches that spanned from Switzerland to the English Channel, across
northeastern France. But battles were also fought along the borders of
German, French, and English colonies in Africa, and there were high
Australian casualties on the coast of Gallipoli in Ottoman Turkey.

The selections in this chapter focus on the lives and deaths of the
soldiers, as well as the efforts of some of their political leaders to
redefine the world around them. We examine the experiences of
soldiers and how the war changed the lives of those who survived its
devastating toll. We compare the accounts of those who fought on both
sides of the great divide. Germany and the Austro-Hungarian Empire,
joined by the Ottoman Empire, formed an alliance called the Central
Powers (see Map 24.1). In opposition, England, France, and Russia,

918

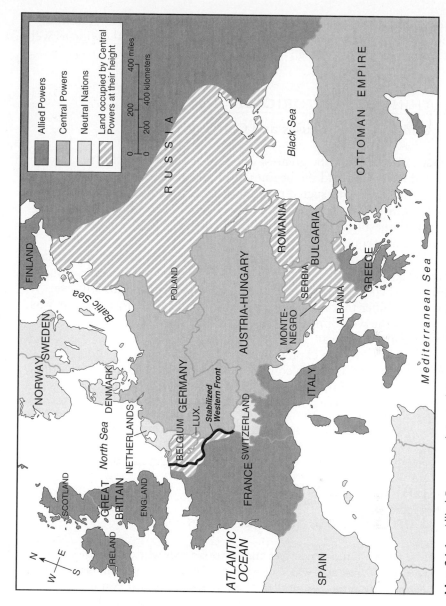

Map 24.1 Allied Powers and Central Powers in World War I.

the Allied Powers, were later joined by Italy, Greece, Japan, and the United States. We compare views across the generational divide as well as from the trenches and government offices.

■ THINKING HISTORICALLY

Understanding Causes and Consequences

From 1914 to 1920, the greatest divide was the war itself. It marked the end of one era and the beginning of another. Few events have left the participants with such a profound sense of fundamental change. And so our study of the war is an appropriate place to ask two of the universal questions of major historical change: What caused it? What were the consequences?

The *causes* are those events or forces that came before; the *consequences* are the results, what the war itself prompted to occur. Thus, causes and consequences are part of the same continuum. Still, we must remember that not everything that happened before the war was a cause of the war. Similarly, not everything that happened afterward was a result of the war.

In this chapter we explore specific ideas about cause and consequence. Our goal is not to compile a definitive list of either but, rather, to explore some of the ways that historians and thoughtful readers can make sense of the past.

1

DAVID FROMKIN

Europe's Last Summer, 2004

The author, a modern lawyer and historian, has written extensively on the Middle East as it was shaped by the First World War. In his book *Europe's Last Summer*, subtitled "Who Started the Great War in 1914?," he argues that Germany most wanted the war. In this selection from that work, he discusses three of the background causes of the war: imperialism, social-class conflicts, and nationalism. According to Fromkin, how did the clash of empires become more severe in the last decade or so of the nineteenth century? How did domestic social conflicts increase the chances of war? How did nationalism undermine the European peace?

Source: David Fromkin, *Europe's Last Summer* (New York: Vintage Books, 2005), 17–27.

THINKING HISTORICALLY

While the development of imperialism, social-class conflicts, and nationalism are often counted as background causes of World War I, there is little agreement among historians as to which of the three is the most important. What factors would you weigh or what questions would you ask to make such a determination? Secondly, historians might argue that there were other background causes. Even in this brief selection, Fromkin touches on other changes in Europe that might be considered background causes. What are these? How important are they?

Empires Clash

At the start of the twentieth century Europe was at the peak of human accomplishment. In industry, technology, and science it had advanced beyond all previous societies. In wealth, knowledge, and power it exceeded any civilization that ever had existed.

Europe is almost the smallest of the continents: 3 or 4 million square miles in extent, depending on how you define its eastern frontiers. By contrast, the largest continent, Asia, has 17 million square miles. Indeed, some geographers viewed Europe as a mere peninsula of Asia.

Yet, by the beginning of the 1900s, the Great Powers of Europe—a mere handful of countries—had come to rule most of the earth. Between them, Austria-Hungary, France, Germany, Great Britain, Italy, and Russia dominated Europe, Africa, Asia, the Pacific, and even substantial parts of the Western Hemisphere. Of what little remained, much belonged to less powerful European states: Belgium, Holland, Portugal, and Spain. When all of its empires were added together, Europe spanned the globe.

But the European empires were of greatly unequal size and strength, an imbalance that led to instability; and as they were rivals, their leaders were continuously matching them against one another in their minds, trying to guess who would defeat whom in case of war and with whom, therefore, it would be best to ally. Military prowess was seen as a supreme value in an age that mistakenly believed Charles Darwin's survival of the fittest to refer to the most murderous rather than (as we now understand it) to the best adapted.

The British Empire was the wealthiest, most powerful, and largest of the Great Powers. It controlled over a quarter of the land surface and a quarter of the population of the globe, and its navy dominated the world ocean that occupies more than 70 percent of the planet. Germany, a newly created confederation led by militarist Prussia, commanded the most powerful land army. Russia, the world's largest country, a backward giant that sprawled across two continents, remained an enigma;

enfeebled by a war it lost to Japan in 1904–05, and by the revolution of 1905, it turned itself around by industrializing and arming with financial backing from France. France, despite exploiting a large empire, no longer was a match for Germany and therefore backed Russia as a counterweight to Teutonic power. The Dual Monarchy of Austria-Hungary ruled a variety of nationalities who were restless and often in conflict. Italy, a new state, as a latecomer aspiring to take its place among the powers, hungered to be treated as an equal.

It was commonly believed at the time that the road to wealth and greatness for European powers was through the acquisition of more colonies. The problem was that the Great Powers already controlled so much of the world that there was little left for others to take. Repeatedly, in going forward, the European powers ran up against one another. Time and again, war threatened, and only skilled diplomacy and self-restraint enabled them to pull back from the brink. The decades before 1914 were punctuated by crises, almost any one of which might have led to war.

It was no accident that some of the more conspicuous of these crises resulted from moves by Germany. It was because Germany's emperor—the Kaiser, or Caesar—in changing his Chancellor in 1890 also changed his government's policy. Otto von Bismarck, the iron-willed leader who had created Germany in 1870–71, was skeptical of imperialism.[1] Far from believing that overseas colonies bring additional wealth and power, he apparently viewed them as a drain on both. In order to distract France from thoughts of recovering territories in Europe that Germany had seized—in Alsace-Lorraine—Bismarck encouraged and supported France in seeking new acquisitions in North Africa and Asia. As such a policy would bring France into frequent collisions with imperial England and Russia, thus dividing Germany's potential rivals, it suited all of Bismarck's purposes.

Post-Bismarck Germany coveted the overseas territories that the Iron Chancellor had regarded as mere fool's gold. It positioned itself to take part in the coming partition of China. But the rulers in Berlin had come to the game too late. Germany no longer could win an empire on a scale proportioned to its position as the greatest military power in Europe. There was not world enough. No more continents were there for the taking: no more Africas, no more Americas. Nonetheless—heedlessly—Wilhelmine Germany displayed an interest in overseas land.

As France moved deeper into Morocco at the beginning of the twentieth century to round out its North African empire, Germany, instead of offering encouragement and support, as Bismarck would have done, stepped in to oppose. These German moves misfired and sparked two of the more high-profile international crises of those years:

---

[1] For reasons not entirely clear, Bismarck briefly departed from this policy in the early 1880s, when Germany acquired a small number of colonies.

the Morocco crises of 1905–06 and of 1911. To the German government these maneuvers may have been mere probes, but they caused genuine alarm in Europe.

In retrospect, it is clear the problem was that Germany's post-1890 hunger for empire could no longer be satisfied except by taking overseas territories away from the other European countries. This was not something likely to be accomplished by peaceful means. Could Germany therefore content itself with remaining the leading military and industrial power on the Continent but with African and Asian empires smaller than those of England or France? Germans themselves disagreed, of course, about what the answer to that question ought to be, and the climate of opinion was changing. Germany in 1914 was the only country on the Continent with more industrial than farm workers, and the growing strength of its socialist and working-class masses suggested that the nation might be compelled to focus its attention on solving problems at home rather than on adventures abroad. Alternatively, it suggested that Germany's leaders would have to pursue an aggressive foreign policy in order to distract attention from problems at home that remained unsolved.

Classes Struggle

Nor was Germany alone in being divided against itself. Europe before the war was in the grip of social and economic upheavals that were reshaping its structure and its politics. The Industrial Revolution that had begun in eighteenth-century France and England continued, at an accelerated pace, to effect radical changes in those two countries, as well as in Germany, and was making similar changes in others. Agrarian Europe, in part still feudal, and smokestack Europe, bringing modernity, lived literally at the same time but figuratively centuries apart. Some still were living as though in the fourteenth century, with their pack animals and their slow, almost unchanging village rhythms, while others inhabited the crowded, sprawling cities of the twentieth century, driven by the newly invented internal combustion machine and informed by the telegraph.

At the same time, the growth of an urban factory-working population in the Industrial Revolution brought conflict between that population and factory owners over wages and working conditions. It also pitted both workers and manufacturers, on the one hand, who could expand their exports only in a free-trade world, against farmers, who needed protection, and the cash-poor landed gentry on the other. Class became a line of division and loyalty—the chief line according to many. Domestic strife threatened all the countries of Western Europe.

In Britain, the Labour party was formed to speak for a working class no longer content to be represented by the Liberal party, which sympathized with wage-earners but spoke as the voice of the professional classes and even some of the well-born. On the Continent, labor also turned to socialism, with growing success at the polls: in the German elections of 1912, the Social Democrats emerged as the largest single party in the Reichstag. It should have been some consolation to German and British conservatives that workers in their countries usually expressed their socialism peacefully by voting rather than (as Syndicalists did in France, Spain, and Italy) by strikes, riots, and terrorist attacks. But governments, in these times of frequent war crises, worried that their peoples might not support them if war broke out. The issue had another side to it: foreign adventures could distract from class and social conflict and bring the people instead to rally around the flag. Which would it be? Would class and social clashes divide, or would international conflicts unite?

Nations Quarrel

To socialist internationalism, the rival was nationalism, a passion that increasingly was taking priority over all else in the minds and hearts of Europeans as the nineteenth century departed and the twentieth arrived. Even Britain contracted the fever. Ireland—or at any rate its Roman Catholic majority—agitated violently for autonomy or independence, and clashed with the Protestants of Ulster who prepared to take up arms to defend the union with Great Britain.

Edwardian England already was a surprisingly violent country, torn by such issues as industrial wages and working conditions and also by the cause of woman suffrage. It was rocked, too, by a constitutional crisis that was also a class crisis. The crisis focused on two interrelated issues: the budget, and the power of the hereditary House of Lords to veto legislation enacted by the popularly elected House of Commons. Between them these conflicts eroded the sense of national solidarity.

Now that the country also was polarized on the question of home rule for Ireland, large sections of the army and of the Unionist-Conservative party seemed prepared to defy law and government in order to hold on to the union with Ireland. The precedent set by the United States in 1861 was troubling. Would there be a British civil war?

On the continent of Europe the flames of nationalism threatened to burn down even structures that had endured for centuries. Hapsburg-ruled Austria, a holdover from the Middle Ages that until recently had been headed by the so-called Holy Roman Empire, remained, as it had been in the nineteenth century, the principal enemy of European nationalism. The two great new nations of Germany and Italy had been carved out of domains that the Hapsburgs once had dominated. At universities, coffeehouses, and in the dimly lit hiding places of secret societies and terrorists, in the Balkans and Central Europe in the early years of the twentieth century, plans were being hatched by ethnic groups that aspired to achieve something similar. The nationalists were in contact with one another and with nihilists, anarchists, socialists, and others who lived and conspired in the obscurity of the political underground. It was there that Serbs, Croats, Czechs, and others plotted to disrupt and destroy the Austrian Empire.

The Hapsburgs were a dynasty that over the course of a thousand years had come to rule a motley collection of territories and peoples — a multinational empire that held no prospect of ever becoming a homogeneous national state. Centered in German-speaking Vienna, Austria-Hungary encompassed a variety of languages, ethnic groups, and climates. Its 50 million people comprised perhaps eleven or so nations or parts thereof. Many of its lands originally had been dowries that had come with marriage to territorial heiresses: whatever else you might say about them, the Hapsburg family wedded well. At its height in the sixteenth century, when it included Spain and much of the New World, the Hapsburg family holdings comprised the largest empire in the world. Hapsburg roots went back to Christmas Day 800, when Charlemagne the Frank was crowned emperor of the Roman Empire in the West by the pope. As Holy Roman Emperor, a post to which a Hapsburg was almost always elected from the fifteenth century until it was abolished in the early nineteenth century, the Hapsburgs dominated Central Europe, including its many German- and Italian-speaking political entities. In the aftermath of the 1848 revolutions, they lost their Italian possessions to the newly unified Italy, and they were excluded from Prussian-organized, newly unified Germany in 1870–71. Once the leader of Europe's Germans and Italians, the Hapsburg emperor was left as the odd man out.

Left alone with a German core — of Austria's 28 million inhabitants, only 10 million were German — and a restive empire of Central European and Balkan peoples, mostly Slavs, the Hapsburg ruler Franz Joseph found himself presiding over a political entity that arguably was not viable. The solution that he found in 1867 was a compact between Austria and a Hungary that was ruled by its Magyar minority, in which Franz Joseph served both as emperor of Austria and king of Hungary. The Dual Monarchy, as it was called, was a state in which Austria and Hungary each had its own parliament and its own Prime Minister, but there was only one foreign minister, one war minister, one finance minister — and, of course, only one monarch of both the Austrian empire and the Hungarian kingdom. The peoples who ruled were the minority Germans of Austria and the Magyar minority in Hungary. What they attempted to rule, in the words of one Hapsburg statesman, was "eight nations, seventeen countries, twenty parliamentary groups, twenty-seven parties" — and a spectrum of peoples and religions.

Europe was rapidly becoming a continent of nation-states. As it entered the twentieth century, a chief weakness of Austria-Hungary was that it was on what looked to be the wrong side of history. But what was threatening to bring it down was a force that was not entirely progressive either; nationalism had its atavistic aspects.

Whether considered to be a political philosophy or its contrary, a type of mass delirium, nationalism was ambivalent. It was the democratic belief that each nation had the right to become independent and to rule itself. But it also was the illiberal insistence that nonmembers of the nation should assimilate, be denied civic rights, be expelled, or even be killed. Nationalism was hating some as an expression of loving others. To add to the murkiness, there was no agreement on what constitutes a nationality. The 1911 edition of the *Encyclopaedia Britannica* calls it a "vague term" and remarked that "a 'nationality'. . . represents a common feeling and an organized claim rather than distinct attributes which can be comprised in a strict definition." So there was no general agreement on which groups were nations and which were not. It was one more issue for Europe to fight about. Some thought—some still think—that it was the main thing that Europe had to fight about.

In the absence of scientific measurement of public opinion through polls, historians are unable to tell us with any certainty what the people of Europe thought or felt in the pre-1914 age. This leaves a gap in our knowledge. It is not so great a gap as it would be today, for a century ago the public played little role in the formation of foreign policy. But public opinion was of some significance, in that decision-makers presumably did take it into account—to the extent that they knew what it was.

Evidence suggests that the most widespread feeling in Europe at the time was xenophobia: a great deal of hostility toward one another. The ethnic groups of the Balkans provided a conspicuous example of mutual hatred, but countries far more advanced exhibited such tendencies too.

England is a case in point. It had been in conflict or at war with France on and off since the eleventh century—in other words, for about a thousand years. Anti-French feeling remained high well into the twentieth century. Even during the First World War, in which the two countries were allies, British and French officers schemed and maneuvered against one another to take control of the postwar Arab Middle East.

Britain came into collision with Russia much later than it did with France, but once they did clash it was all across the board. The two countries opposed each other on one point after another, economically, politically, militarily, and ideologically, until Britons grew to object to Russians not merely for what they did but for who they were. The story is recounted at length in a classic: *The Genesis of Russophobia in Great Britain* by John Howes Gleason.

Germany came into existence as a state only in 1871, and seemed to be a possible ally—the idea was discussed at the highest levels more than once—

but the British became suspicious of Germany and then antagonistic. This was for a variety of reasons, thoroughly discussed in Paul Kennedy's definitive account, *The Rise of the Anglo-German Antagonism.*

So the British, though they believed themselves to be open-minded, detested the peoples of the next three ranking Great Powers: the French, the Russians, and the Germans.

The questions that European statesmen attempted to resolve at the dawn of the twentieth century therefore were being faced against a background of peoples who harbored hostile, sometimes warlike, sentiments.

The rise of independent mass-circulation newspapers in the nineteenth century in such European countries as England and France brought to bear upon decision-making yet another powerful influence impossible to calculate precisely. Appealing to popular fears and prejudices in order to win circulation, the press seems to have exacerbated hatred and divisions among Europeans. Of the anti-German British press and the anti-British German press, the German emperor wrote to the King of England in 1901: "The Press is awful on both sides."

2

ERICH MARIA REMARQUE
All Quiet on the Western Front, 1929

All Quiet on the Western Front, one of the most famous war novels ever written, follows the daily routines of the German army on the "Western Front," the long line of trenches that stretched across northern France from Switzerland to the English Channel for most of the war between 1914 and 1918. Born in Germany, Erich Maria Remarque (1898–1970) served on the Western Front during the war until he was wounded. In this selection from the beginning of the novel, the narrator recalls how his teacher, Kantorek, induced him and his friends to enlist. Now one of them, Franz Kemmerich, has been seriously wounded and the group of friends visit him. What does this selection suggest about the types of people recruited to serve in the army? How do they experience the war, and how does it change them? Do you imagine these German soldiers behaved very differently from French or English soldiers?

Source: Erich Maria Remarque, *All Quiet on the Western Front*, trans. A. W. Wheen (New York: Fawcett Books, 1929), 1–18.

THINKING HISTORICALLY

Remarque's novel is not intended as an explanation of the causes of war, but this excerpt sheds light on what caused men to support the war and enlist. How might you use material from this novel, assuming that it is based on fact, to propose at least one cause of World War I?

In this brief selection, the author also suggests something about the consequences of the war. What are the war's likely outcomes projected here?

Kantorek had been our schoolmaster, a stern little man in a grey tail-coat, with a face like a shrew mouse. He was about the same size as Corporal Himmelstoss, the "terror of Klosterberg." It is very queer that the unhappiness of the world is so often brought on by small men. They are so much more energetic and uncompromising than the big fellows. I have always taken good care to keep out of sections with small company commanders. They are mostly confounded little martinets.

During drill-time Kantorek gave us long lectures until the whole of our class went, under his shepherding, to the District Commandant and volunteered. I can see him now, as he used to glare at us through his spectacles and say in a moving voice: "Won't you join up, Comrades?"

These teachers always carry their feelings ready in their waistcoat pockets, and trot them out by the hour. But we didn't think of that then.

There was, indeed, one of us who hesitated and did not want to fall into line. That was Joseph Behm, a plump, homely fellow. But he did allow himself to be persuaded, otherwise he would have been ostracized. And perhaps more of us thought as he did, but no one could very well stand out, because at that time even one's parents were ready with the word "coward"; no one had the vaguest idea what we were in for. The wisest were just the poor and simple people. They knew the war to be a misfortune, whereas those who were better off, and should have been able to see more clearly what the consequences would be, were beside themselves with joy.

Katczinsky said that was a result of their upbringing. It made them stupid. And what Kat said, he had thought about.

Strange to say, Behm was one of the first to fall. He got hit in the eye during an attack, and we left him lying for dead. We couldn't bring him with us, because we had to come back helter-skelter. In the afternoon suddenly we heard him call, and saw him crawling about in No Man's Land. He had only been knocked unconscious. Because he could not see, and was mad with pain, he failed to keep under cover, and so was shot down before anyone could go and fetch him in.

Naturally we couldn't blame Kantorek for this. Where would the world be if one brought every man to book? There were thousands of

Kantoreks, all of whom were convinced that they were acting for the best—in a way that cost them nothing.

And that is why they let us down so badly.

For us lads of eighteen they ought to have been mediators and guides to the world of maturity, the world of work, of duty, of culture, of progress—to the future. We often made fun of them and played jokes on them, but in our hearts we trusted them. The idea of authority, which they represented, was associated in our minds with a greater insight and a more humane wisdom. But the first death we saw shattered this belief. We had to recognize that our generation was more to be trusted than theirs. They surpassed us only in phrases and in cleverness. The first bombardment showed us our mistake, and under it the world as they had taught it to us broke in pieces.

While they continued to write and talk, we saw the wounded and dying. While they taught that duty to one's country is the greatest thing, we already knew that death-throes are stronger. But for all that we were no mutineers, no deserters, no cowards—they were very free with all these expressions. We loved our country as much as they; we went courageously into every action; but also we distinguished the false from true, we had suddenly learned to see. And we saw that there was nothing of their world left. We were all at once terribly alone; and alone we must see it through.

Before going over to see Kemmerich we pack up his things: He will need them on the way back.

In the dressing station there is great activity: It reeks as ever of carbolic, pus, and sweat. We are accustomed to a good deal in the billets, but this makes us feel faint. We ask for Kemmerich. He lies in a large room and receives us with feeble expressions of joy and helpless agitation. While he was unconscious someone had stolen his watch.

Müller shakes his head: "I always told you that nobody should carry as good a watch as that."

Müller is rather crude and tactless, otherwise he would hold his tongue, for anybody can see that Kemmerich will never come out of this place again. Whether he finds his watch or not will make no difference, at the most one will only be able to send it to his people.

"How goes it, Franz?" asks Kropp.

Kemmerich's head sinks.

"Not so bad . . . but I have such a damned pain in my foot."

We look at his bed covering. His leg lies under a wire basket. The bed covering arches over it. I kick Müller on the shin, for he is just about to tell Kemmerich what the orderlies told us outside: that Kemmerich has lost his foot. The leg is amputated. He looks ghastly, yellow and wan. In his face there are already the strained lines that we know so well, we have seen them now hundreds of times. They are not so much lines as marks. Under the skin the life no longer pulses, it has already pressed out the boundaries of the body. Death is working through from within. It already has command in the eyes. Here lies our comrade, Kemmerich, who a little while ago was roasting horse flesh with us and squatting in the shellholes. He it is still and yet it is not he any longer. His features have become uncertain and faint, like a photographic plate from which two pictures have been taken. Even his voice sounds like ashes.

I think of the time when we went away. His mother, a good plump matron, brought him to the station. She wept continually, her face was bloated and swollen. Kemmerich felt embarrassed, for she was the least composed of all; she simply dissolved into fat and water. Then she caught sight of me and took hold of my arm again and again, and implored me to look after Franz out there. Indeed he did have a face like a child, and such frail bones that after four weeks' pack-carrying he already had flat feet. But how can a man look after anyone in the field!

"Now you will soon be going home," says Kropp. "You would have had to wait at least three or four months for your leave."

Kemmerich nods. I cannot bear to look at his hands, they are like wax. Under the nails is the dirt of the trenches, it shows through blue-black like poison. It strikes me that these nails will continue to grow like lean fantastic cellar-plants long after Kemmerich breathes no more. I see the picture before me. They twist themselves into corkscrews and grow and grow, and with them the hair on the decaying skull, just like grass in a good soil, just like grass, how can it be possible——

Müller leans over. "We have brought your things, Franz."

Kemmerich signs with his hands. "Put them under the bed."

Müller does so. Kemmerich starts on again about the watch. How can one calm him without making him suspicious?

Müller reappears with a pair of airman's boots. They are fine English boots of soft, yellow leather which reach to the knees and lace up all the way—they are things to be coveted.

Müller is delighted at the sight of them. He matches their soles against his own clumsy boots and says: "Will you be taking them with you then, Franz?"

We all three have the same thought; even if he should get better, he would be able to use only one—they are no use to him. But as things are now it is a pity that they should stay here; the orderlies will of course grab them as soon as he is dead.

"Won't you leave them with us?" Müller repeats.

Kemmerich doesn't want to. They are his most prized possessions.

"Well, we could exchange," suggests Müller again. "Out here one can make some use of them." Still Kemmerich is not to be moved.

I tread on Müller's foot; reluctantly he puts the fine boots back again under the bed.

We talk a little more and then take our leave.

"Cheerio, Franz."

I promise him to come back in the morning. Müller talks of doing so, too. He is thinking of the lace-up boots and means to be on the spot.

Kemmerich groans. He is feverish. We get hold of an orderly outside and ask him to give Kemmerich a dose of morphia.

He refuses. "If we were to give morphia to everyone we would have to have tubs full———"

"You only attend to officers properly," says Kropp viciously.

I hastily intervene and give him a cigarette. He takes it.

"Are you usually allowed to give it, then?" I ask him.

He is annoyed. "If you don't think so, then why do you ask?"

I press a few more cigarettes into his hand. "Do us the favour———"

"Well, all right," he says.

Kropp goes in with him. He doesn't trust him and wants to see. We wait outside.

Müller returns to the subject of the boots. "They would fit me perfectly. In these boots I get blister after blister. Do you think he will last till tomorrow after drill? If he passes out in the night, we know where the boots———"

Kropp returns. "Do you think———?" he asks.

"Done for," said Müller emphatically.

We go back to the huts. I think of the letter that I must write tomorrow to Kemmerich's mother. I am freezing. I could do with a tot of rum. Müller pulls up some grass and chews it. Suddenly little Kropp throws his cigarette away, stamps on it savagely, and looking around him with a broken and distracted face, stammers "Damned shit, the damned shit!"

We walk on for a long time. Kropp has calmed himself; we understand, he saw red; out there every man gets like that sometime.

"What has Kantorek written to you?" Müller asks him.

He laughs. "We are the Iron Youth."

We all three smile bitterly, Kropp rails: He is glad that he can speak.

Yes, that's the way they think, these hundred thousand Kantoreks! Iron Youth! Youth! We are none of us more than twenty years old. But young? Youth? That is long ago. We are old folk.

World War I Propaganda Posters, 1915–1918

Posters were the communication medium of the First World War. In an age when governments had still not taught most people how to read but increasingly needed their consent or compliance, images often spoke louder than words, but those images had to be *persuasive*.

The American poster from 1917 and the German poster from 1915–1916 (Figures 24.1 and 24.3) implore men to enlist in the army; the Italian poster from 1917 (Figure 24.2) encourages people

Figure 24.1   Recruiting Poster for U.S. Army, 1917.
Source: Library of Congress.

Figure 24.2 Italian Poster for National War Loan, 1917.
Source: Snark/Art Resource, NY.

to buy war bonds. What do you think accounts for the similar graphic style used in these three posters? How effective do you think they were, and why?

Another strategy for promoting loyalty, patriotism, and support for a war that was lasting far longer than anyone had anticipated was to demonize or ridicule the enemy. What feelings does the

Figure 24.3   Recruiting Poster for German Army, 1915–1916.
Source: Library of Congress.

U.S. anti-German poster from 1917–1918 (Figure 24.4) attempt to provoke in viewers, and how does the scene shown achieve this?

Women contributed to the war in various ways. Figure 24.5 asks German women to contribute their gold. Figure 24.6 urges women in London to come to work in the munitions industry. What images of women do these posters portray? Finally, Figure 24.7 asks Americans to support Armenian refugees from the Ottoman Empire in newly proclaimed independent Armenia and Syria. What response is the image of woman and child supposed to evoke?

THINKING HISTORICALLY

When war broke out overseas in 1914, President Woodrow Wilson declared it a European matter that had nothing to do with the United

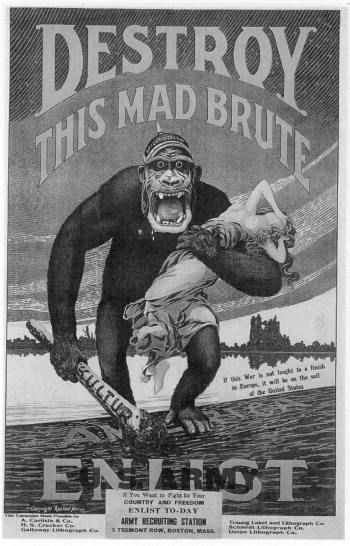

Figure 24.4 Propaganda Poster, United States, 1917–1918.

States, and most Americans agreed. Indeed, the United States did not join the war and throw its crucial weight behind the Allied Powers until April 1917. What role do you think propaganda such as Figure 24.4 played in swaying public opinion? This and the other posters illustrate both sides' efforts to promote and sustain the cause of war. What do they tell you about the causes of the war? What do they tell you about the consequences?

Figure 24.5 German Appeal to Women: Gold for the War.
Source: Library of Congress.

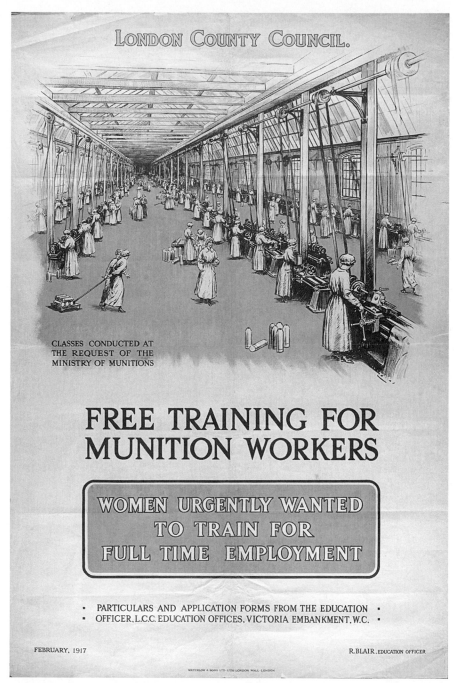

Figure 24.6   English Appeal to Women: Munitions Work.

Source: World War Poster Collection (MSS36), University of Minnesota Libraries, Archives and Special Collections, Minneapolis, MN.

Figure 24.7 "Your Bit Saves a Life."
Source: World War Poster Collection (MSS36), University of Minnesota Libraries, Archives and Special Collections, Minneapolis, MN.

4

WILFRED OWEN

Dulce et Decorum Est, 1917

Wilfred Owen (1893–1918) enlisted in the British Army in 1915, was wounded in 1917, and was hospitalized, released, and sent back to the front, where he died on November 4, 1918, one week before the end of the war. In this poem, he describes a poison gas attack. Like the machine gun and the airplane, gas was a common element of the new mechanized mass warfare. Owen describes how physically debilitating the effects of gas were. Why was gas such an effective and deadly weapon? How, according to Owen, had the nature of war changed?

THINKING HISTORICALLY

The concluding phrase, which means "Sweet and proper it is to die for one's country," was a Latin declaration of patriotic duty that English students repeated as a lesson, not only in Latin classes but, more important, in their political education as subjects of the British Empire. How does Owen portray this lesson as a cause of the war? What does he imagine to be the consequences of fighting a war with such patriotic slogans in mind? How does Owen's attitude toward patriotism compare with that of Remarque?

Dulce et Decorum Est

Bent double, like old beggars under sacks,
Knock-kneed, coughing like hags, we cursed through sludge,
Till on the haunting flares we turned our backs
And towards our distant rest began the trudge.
Men marched asleep. Many had lost their boots
But limped on, blood-shod. All went lame; all blind;
Drunk with fatigue; deaf even to the hoots
Of tired, outstripped Five-Nines[1] that dropped behind.

Gas! GAS! Quick, boys!—An ecstasy of fumbling,
Fitting the clumsy helmets just in time;
But someone still was yelling out and stumbling,
And flound'ring like a man in fire or lime. . . .

---

[1] German artillery shells. [Ed.]

Source: Wilfred Owen, *Poems*, ed. Siegfried Sassoon (London: Chatto and Windus, 1920).

Dim, through the misty panes and thick green light,
As under a green sea, I saw him drowning.

In all my dreams, before my helpless sight,
He plunges at me, guttering, choking, drowning.

If in some smothering dreams you too could pace
Behind the wagon that we flung him in,
And watch the white eyes writhing in his face,
His hanging face, like a devil's sick of sin;
If you could hear, at every jolt, the blood
Come gargling from the froth-corrupted lungs,
Obscene as cancer, bitter as the cud
Of vile, incurable sores on innocent tongues,
My friend, you would not tell with such high zest,
To children ardent for some desperate glory.
The old Lie: Dulce et decorum est
Pro patria mori.

5

Memories of Senegalese Soldiers, 1914–1918/1981–1999

Not only did the roots of the First World War lie in competing imperial claims, but some of the fighting took place along imperial divides of colonies as well. Africans in French and English colonies were mobilized to fight Africans in neighboring German colonies, and vice versa. In addition, many Africans were mobilized to fight in Europe, especially after European troops suffered heavy losses along the Western Front. Over 140,000 West Africans were recruited into the French Army between 1914 and 1918 to serve in Europe. Some 45,000 never returned. Senegal mobilized more than other colonies: 29,000, probably more than one-third of the men of military age.

Source: Joe Lunn, *Memoirs of the Maelstrom: A Senegalese Oral History of the First World War* (Portsmouth, NH: Heinemann, 1999), 40, 42, 78–79, 97–98, 102–3, 110, 137, 165–66, 172–73, 174, 108–9, 190, 230, 232–33. Headings added, individual names and footnotes deleted.

The historian Joe Lunn interviewed eighty-five of these Senegalese veterans for his book *Memoirs of the Maelstrom: A Senegalese Oral History of the First World War,* from which these selections are drawn. What do these various Senegalese voices tell you about the African experience in the First World War? How was their experience of the war different from that of European soldiers? How were Senegalese soldiers recruited, and why did they enlist? What were their expectations?

THINKING HISTORICALLY

These memories provide greater insight into the consequences than the causes of World War I. How did the war change the lives of those African troops who survived? How did it change the way the Senegalese and French thought of themselves and each other?

[Recruitment]

Many of the young men fled from the village [when the *chef de canton* came to take soldiers]. [But] they used to arrest their fathers [if] they [did not] come back. [And] often their mothers used to say to their sons [when they returned from the countryside for food]: "You know that your name has been written [down by the *che de canton*] and [yet] you ran away. And now your father has been arrested and he will be taken [to] prison. So go and enter the army." And often they used to go and enter the army [so that] their fathers [would be] released.

In each family they only took one young man, never two. And my father decided that I should go and enter the army instead of my elder brother. Because, he told me: "If I die, your elder brother could care for the family, but you are too young for that." That's why he sent me into the army. I was not happy to go, [but] because I was very close to my father . . . I felt obliged to.

I was in Bamako [on leave] when Blaise Diagne and Galandou Diouf[1] came to recruit soldiers. [And my friend and I] attended the meeting he called for recruitment. [And] Blaise Diagne's propaganda [at] this meeting [was very effective]. Because, before he came, he had made the son of the

---

[1] Blaise Diagne (1872–1934), from Senegal, became in 1914 the first black African elected to the French national parliament where he fought for and won the right of urban Senegalese to be citizens and soldiers. He was appointed by French prime minister George Clemenceau to head the recruitment drive in French West Africa during the war. Galandou Diouf (1875–1941), the first black African elected (in 1909) to the Senegalese assembly, was Diagne's assistant. They argued that military service was a vehicle to full and equal citizenship for Africans. [Ed.]

chef de quartier in Bamako a lieutenant. [So] almost all the town was there, because the chief had called everybody, and there were a lot, a lot, a lot of people! The fact that Blaise Diagne had made his son a lieutenant was a very important thing for him personally, because . . . for the Bambara becoming an officer in the army was a very great honor. [And Diagne came] with many, many people—August Brunet [the lieutenant governor of Haut-Sénégal et Niger] and [other] French administrators. [And] he was [accompanied by] some Bambara soldiers too. But they were not simple soldiers; all of them had *"grades."*[2] [And after speeches by Galandou Diouf, the *chef de quartier*, and his son, Diagne spoke.] [And although] I have forgotten almost all his speech, I remember that he told them that he was sent by the President of the Republic of France who needed [more] soldiers to go on fighting. And after [he finished], he introduced the son of the *chef de quartier* to [all] the other parents that were at the meeting. [And he told them:] "I want some other soldiers to enter the army, so perhaps they too can become lieutenants." So as soon as he said that, everybody gave him the name of his son. And the secretary was writing down their names. [And] that's why he succeeded with his recruitment mission [among the Bambara]—[because] everybody was expecting his son to become an officer one day.

[Becoming Soldiers]

We all joined the same army—the French army. . . . So we did not think about our [previous] way of living, our behavior, our [former] kingdoms. We were bound to follow the French regulations and their way of thinking about all these things. [And although] little arguments sometimes [occurred] between soldiers from the same country, [the status of a man's family] wasn't stressed. . . . There wasn't any [social] differentiation [with regard to slaves] because we were following another system—another [way of] life—which was the French one.

[Departures]

We [sailed from Dakar] on a boat called *l'Afrique* on May 9, 1916. There was a French officer with us—[a lieutenant called Oeuvre]—[who] was a very very bad man. We spent [the first] three days [being allowed to go on deck] in the boat . . . and we had a good journey. [But] when we arrived at a place called "the Gulf" [Golfe de Gascogne] . . . this French officer said that all the soldiers had to go downstairs—deep inside the ship. And he put [a guard] at the door [to prevent] any of us

[2] Ranks. [Ed.]

from going out. . . . And we [were confined for] the [next] six days in the bottom [of the boat near] the keel. [And] we suffered a lot in the bottom of the ship because there was no air. From time to time they opened the [portholes] to let some air [in, but] after that they closed them [again]. And even during meals, we were eating in the bottom of the ship. And it was very hot [there] and it was very tight.

[In France]

When we went [to the camps in France,] Diagne joined us [there] to see about our conditions. Whenever you had problems, he came and solved them. Sometimes the food was bad or insufficient, for example. [So] when Diagne came, if we said the food was not good, he called the officers together and asked [them] why. He said, "I brought soldiers to fight for you and to help you. And I don't see why you treat them like this!" So he would tear off the ranks [of insignia] of the officers and put them on the table.

We felt very proud after the attack because the French had tried many times to retake the fort, but finally, we [were the ones] that took it. . . . And when we were leaving the fort, our officers told us not to wash our uniforms even though they were very dirty and covered with mud. But we were told: "Don't wash your uniforms. Cross the country as you are so that everyone who meets you will know that you made the attack on Fort Douaumont." And we took the train [and traveled] for three days between Douaumont and St. Raphäel. And in every town we crossed, the French were clapping their hands and shouting: "Vive les tirailleurs sénégalais!" . . . And afterwards, whenever we were walking in the country—everywhere we used to go—if we told people that we made the attack on Fort Douaumont, the French were looking at us with much admiration.

One day I was in the [mess hall] in the camp [where] we used to eat. And often after eating, we used to drink coffee in cups. But before drinking it, we used to make "cheers" with the other soldiers. So on this day, I took my cup and I wanted to make "cheers" with a French soldier who was sitting next to me. So I made the "cheers," [but] the soldier said to me, "don't touch my cup, you are too dirty!" And [this made] me very angry. [So] I punched him and we began to fight. And when they went to get the captain, the captain told me that I was right, and he told the French soldier that he would be punished. But afterwards, I became very friendly with this same soldier.

I had a very good [French] friend—his name was Perout—[and we] were in the same unit. . . . I was his only African friend, [but] we spent a lot of time together. [And] I often went to his house [when on leave]. He invited me [there] for lunch, or dinner, and sometimes I spent the night. . . . And when his [family] came to visit him, they kissed me before they kissed him—his father, his mother, and his sisters.

"*Marraine de guerre*" . . . was the term used by the soldiers to say "my girlfriend"; instead of saying "my girlfriend," they said "my *marraine de guerre.*" [And] the African soldiers in France had their *marraines de guerre* too. They were not prostitutes. They were girls of good families who saw us and knew that we were [far from] our countries. [And they realized] we needed some affection and some money . . . to buy cigarettes with, to go to the movies, and so on.

[And we met them] on the street or in cafés. A French girl saw you and felt very pleased by [your appearance]. And she said to you that she wanted to take you to her house to present you to her parents. And you got [an adopted] French family in that way. [But] it wasn't necessary to have love affairs [with them]. From time to time some *marraines de guerre* fell in love with the soldiers they invited home. But generally, they were only friendly relations.

Some of the French who had never seen a "black" man used to pay to come and see us. [And the European soldiers] were making money selling tickets. [They] used to take us to a hidden place and told us: "Stay here. We are going to bring some Frenchmen who have never seen 'black' people before." [But] we didn't know they were making money in that way.

[And after they] got the money, they used to bring the *Tubabs*[3] to look at us. And [they] said: "This one is a Senegalese, this one is a Somalian, [and so forth]." And the *Tubabs* were touching us, and peeking, creeping very close to us because we [looked so different].

[Return]

One day [we were on] the ship that brought us back to Senegal from Bordeaux. . . . There were [many] Senegalese soldiers [aboard, and sometimes] they got into arguments with some of the "white" men who treated them like "dirty niggers." . . . And one of these soldiers—a citizen from Goree—was [called] a "*sale nègre*" by a "white" man. . . . I think maybe the [French]man was not well educated, or perhaps he was drunk. [And the soldier hit] him hard . . . and [they] started fighting. [And] we all [joined in] and started to give our friend some help. And we beat [the Frenchman] badly until he asked to be forgiven. He was crying and said that he would never do it again.

[3] Europeans. [Ed.]

So what happened [afterwards]? Nothing! We were within our rights, because discrimination between people [was no longer tolerated] at that time, [and] we were French citizens like anybody else. [If] the "white" man wanted to start acting like that, we [could retaliate] and nothing happened. [But] if the same thing had happened before the war, [we] would not have done the same thing. Because we had less power then, and [we] were treated badly like this [by the French] all the time.

[The parents of those who had been killed] knew the number of soldiers who went to the war together, and they [also] knew the number of soldiers who came back. So no one [had to tell] them that their sons were dead; they guessed it [on their own]. [But afterward], we told them how they died. Those [of us who] knew their sons had died explained to their families [what had happened to them]. . . . [I had to do this once.] . . . A son [from my grandfather's family] was lost in Champagne. . . . And [they] knew that we went [to the war] together. But when I came back, they didn't see him. And after a while, they began to ask me where he was. And I told them: "He is dead; you have to make the sacrifices."

[After the War]

We went to France, we fought for France, and the French took us by force to fight for them. [But] we learned nothing [there]—[not] even the French language. They only taught us some rudimentary [commands], [in order] to use us in the war. But they didn't care about teaching us the structure and the sound of their language. So [although we] went to the war, [we] came back here without any real knowledge of the French language.

I received many lasting things from the war. I demonstrated my dignity and courage, and [I] won the respect of the people and the [colonial] government. And whenever the people of the village had something to contest [with the French]—and they didn't dare do it [themselves] because they were afraid of them—I used to do it for them. And many times when people had problems with the government, I used to go with my decorations and arrange the situation for [them]. Because whenever the *Tubabs* saw your decorations, they knew that they [were dealing with] a very important person. . . . And I gained this ability—of obtaining justice over a *Tubab*—from the war.

The war changed many, many things. At first, when we joined the army, when you had an argument or a problem with a "white" man, what happened? You were wrong; you were [always] wrong. But later, those things changed. [Then] they looked into the matter and determined who was wrong or right. [But] before that time, the "black" man didn't mean anything. So that [change] was something [very important]. [And] the respect we gained [from] the war [continued] increasing; it never [diminished]. [And this] respect [continued] increasing day to day—up until [it culminated in] the Independence Day.

6

V. I. LENIN

War and Revolution, 1917

One of the great casualties of the First World War was the Russian Empire, including the czar, his family, many of the members of their class, and its centuries-old autocratic system. The burden of war was simply too much for Russian society to bear. The disillusionment in the army and civilian society, along with the overwhelming costs of war, fueled uprisings among civilians and the army, and Czar Nicholas II was forced to abdicate in February of 1917. The government that emerged, under Alexander Kerensky, proved unable to satisfy the growing demands of peasants, veterans, and urban workers for "land, peace, and bread," a slogan that V. I. Lenin (1870–1924) and the communists exploited, successfully seizing power from the moderate parliamentarians in October of that year.

As a Marxist, Lenin believed that he could establish a socialist society in Russia, but he argued that Russian conditions (such as economic underdevelopment; the devastation of war; the opposition of Europe, the United States, and Russian nobles to the revolution) made a democratic transition impossible. According to Lenin, a self-appointed government acting in the interests of the working class was the only way to a socialist Soviet Union. Lenin called this government "the dictatorship of the proletariat." Lenin delivered his "War and Revolution" address in May of 1917, during the fateful summer that followed the liberal February revolution and preceded the Bolshevik revolution in October. How did Lenin view the First World War and Russia's continued participation in it? What did he hope to accomplish in the summer of 1917? How did he hope to accomplish it? The most important news for Russia's allies, England and France, in the summer of 1917 was the United States' entry into the war on their behalf. What was Lenin's reaction to this development?

Source: V. I. Lenin, *Collected Works*, 4th English ed. (Moscow: Progress Publishers, 1964), 24:398–421.

THINKING HISTORICALLY

According to Lenin, what were the causes of the First World War? What did he believe to be the main cause of the Russian revolution that occurred in February? What were the consequences of that revolution? What did he think would be the causes of a new revolution in Russia?

What we have at present is primarily two leagues, two groups of capitalist powers. We have before us all the world's greatest capitalist powers—Britain, France, America, and Germany—who for decades have doggedly pursued a policy of incessant economic rivalry aimed at achieving world supremacy, subjugating the small nations, and making threefold and tenfold profits on banking capital, which has caught the whole world in the net of its influence. That is what Britain's and Germany's policies really amount to. . . .

These policies show us just one thing—continuous economic rivalry between the world's two greatest giants, capitalist economies. On the one hand we have Britain, a country which owns the greater part of the globe, a country which ranks first in wealth, which has created this wealth not so much by the labour of its workers as by the exploitation of innumerable colonies, by the vast power of its banks which have developed at the head of all the others into an insignificantly small group of some four or five super-banks handling billions of rubles, and handling them in such a way that it can be said without exaggeration that there is not a patch of land in the world today on which this capital has not laid its heavy hand, not a patch of land which British capital has not enmeshed by a thousand threads. . . .

On the other hand, opposed to this, mainly Anglo-French group, we have another group of capitalists, an even more rapacious, even more predatory one, a group who came to the capitalist banqueting table when all the seats were occupied, but who introduced into the struggle new methods for developing capitalist production, improved techniques, and superior organization, which turned the old capitalism, the capitalism of the free-competition age, into the capitalism of giant trusts, syndicates, and cartels. This group introduced the beginnings of state-controlled capitalist production, combining the colossal power of capitalism with the colossal power of the state into a single mechanism and bringing tens of millions of people within the single organization of state capitalism. Here is economic history, here is diplomatic history, covering several decades, from which no one can get away. It is the one and only guide-post to a proper solution of the problem of war; it leads you to the conclusion that the present war, too, is the outcome of the policies of the classes who have come to grips in it, of the two supreme giants, who, long before the war, had caught the whole world, all countries, in the net of financial exploitation and economically divided the globe up among themselves. They were bound to clash, because a redivision of this supremacy, from the point of view of capitalism, had become inevitable. . . .

The present war is a continuation of the policy of conquest, of the shooting down of whole nationalities, of unbelievable atrocities committed by the Germans and the British in Africa, and by the British and the Russians in Persia—which of them committed most it is difficult to say. It was for this reason that the German capitalists looked upon them as their enemies. Ah, they said, you are strong because you are rich? But we are stronger, therefore we have the same "sacred" right to plunder. That is what the real history of British and German finance capital in the course of several decades preceding the war amounts to. That is what the history of Russo-German, Russo-British, and German-British relations amounts to. There you have the clue to an understanding of what the war is about. That is why the story that is current about the cause of the war is sheer duplicity and humbug. Forgetting the history of finance capital, the history of how this war had been brewing over the issue of redivision, they present the matter like this: Two nations were living at peace, then one attacked the other, and the other fought back. All science, all banks are forgotten, and the peoples are told to take up arms, and so are the peasants, who know nothing about politics. . . .

What revolution did we make? We overthrew Nicholas. The revolution was not so very difficult compared with one that would have overthrown the whole class of landowners and capitalists. Who did the revolution put in power? The landowners and capitalists—the very same classes who have long been in power in Europe. . . . The [February] Russian revolution has not altered the war, but it has created organizations which exist in no other country and were seldom found in revolutions in the West. . . . We have all over Russia a network of Soviets of Workers', Soldiers', and Peasants' Deputies. Here is a revolution which has not said its last word yet. . . .

In the two months following the revolution the industrialists have robbed the whole of Russia. Capitalists have made staggering profits; every financial report tells you that. And when the workers, two months after the revolution, had the "audacity" to say they wanted to live like human beings, the whole capitalist press throughout the country set up a howl.

On the question of America entering the war I shall say this. People argue that America is a democracy, America has the White House.

I say: Slavery was abolished there half a century ago. The anti-slave war ended in 1865. Since then multimillionaires have mushroomed. They have the whole of America in their financial grip. They are making ready to subdue Mexico and will inevitably come to war with Japan over a carve-up of the Pacific. This war has been brewing for several decades. All literature speaks about it. America's real aim in entering the war is to prepare for this future war with Japan. The American people do enjoy considerable freedom and it is difficult to conceive them standing for compulsory military service, for the setting up of an army pursuing any aims of conquest—a struggle with Japan, for instance. The Americans have the example of Europe to show them what this leads to. The American capitalists have stepped into this war in order to have an excuse, behind a smoke-screen of lofty ideals championing the rights of small nations, for building up a strong standing army. . . .

Tens of millions of people are facing disaster and death; safeguarding the interests of the capitalists is the last thing that should bother us. The only way out is for all power to be transferred to the Soviets, which represent the majority of the population. Possibly mistakes may be made in the process. No one claims that such a difficult task can be disposed of offhand. We do not say anything of the sort. We are told that we want the power to be in the hands of the Soviets, but they don't want it. We say that life's experience will suggest this solution to them, and the whole nation will see that there is no other way out. We do not want a "seizure" of power, because the entire experience of past revolutions teaches us that the only stable power is the one that has the backing of the majority of the population. "Seizure" of power, therefore, would be adventurism, and our Party will not have it. . . .

Nothing but a workers' revolution in several countries can defeat this war. The war is not a game, it is an appalling thing taking a toll of millions of lives, and it is not to be ended easily.

. . . The war has been brought about by the ruling classes and only a revolution of the working class can end it. Whether you will get a speedy peace or not depends on how the revolution will develop.

Whatever sentimental things may be said, however much we may be told: Let us end the war immediately—this cannot be done without the development of the revolution. When power passes to the Soviets the capitalists will come out against us. Japan, France, Britain—the governments of all countries will be against us. The capitalists will be against, but the workers will be for us. That will be the end of the war which the capitalists started. There you have the answer to the question of how to end the war.

ROSA LUXEMBURG

The Problem of Dictatorship, 1918

Events moved very quickly in Russia in 1917. In May, Lenin insisted that the February revolution was incomplete. Remaking Russian society could not be achieved by a seizure of the state alone, but would also require mobilizing the support of a majority of the country's workers. The new Soviets, or workers' organizations, were to provide the foundation for this grassroots revolution. Futher, Lenin believed that workers throughout Europe needed to be liberated through revolution before peace and stability could be attained. The realities of the October revolution, however, obscured many of these original ideas. By the fall, Lenin and his Bolshevik party seized power without majority support while civil war still raged in Russia. The success of the Bolshevik revolution in October required a new revolutionary ideology.

Rosa Luxemburg (1870–1919) was born in Russian Poland, but at the age of nineteen fled to Switzerland, where she earned a doctorate in law and political science. At twenty-five she migrated to Germany where, as a journalist and theorist, she became an impassioned and influential voice in the German democratic socialist movement. She criticized its bureaucratic leadership and excoriated its submission to war hysteria. Her opposition to the war led to frequent imprisonment. While Luxemburg was imprisoned, Lenin seized power, and she composed her thoughts on the Russian Revolution in 1918.

As a cofounder of the German Spartacus League (which later became the German Communist Party), Luxemburg believed that the Bolshevik Revolution could mean the liberation of working people throughout Russia, then Germany and the rest of Europe. But since 1904 she disagreed with Lenin's ideas of centralized control and party discipline. What objections does she make to Lenin's revolution? What do you think of her arguments?

Ironically, the apparent success of Lenin's strategy in Russia led many in the German Spartacus League to agitate for a similar seizure of power in Germany at the end of the war. Rosa Luxemburg tried to dissuade them, believing it to be suicidal. Outvoted, she joined their uprising in Berlin in January 1919 and was subsequently arrested and murdered by the police.

Source: Rosa Luxemburg, *The Russian Revolution and Leninism or Marxism?* (Ann Arbor: The University of Michigan Press, 1961), 68–72. Introduction by Bertram D. Wolfe.

THINKING HISTORICALLY

Causes and consequences are often different sides of the same event. We might say that the First World War was a cause of the Russian Revolution or, conversely, that the Russian Revolution was a consequence of the First World War. Lenin argued that one of the consequences of the First World War was the particular sort of revolution he advocated, on the grounds that a democratic revolution was impossible under the circumstances. What do you think of that argument? Rosa Luxemburg disagreed that such draconian measures were necessary, and she argued that Lenin's revolutionary strategy would have its own consequences. Why did she think a dictatorial revolution could only lead to a dictatorial society?

Freedom only for the supporters of the government, only for the members of one party—however numerous they may be—is no freedom at all. Freedom is always and exclusively freedom for the one who thinks differently. Not because of any fanatical concept of "justice" but because all that is instructive, wholesome and purifying in political freedom depends on this essential characteristic, and its effectiveness vanishes when "freedom" becomes a special privilege.

The Bolsheviks themselves will not want, with hand on heart, to deny that, step by step, they have to feel out the ground, try out, experiment, test now one way now another, and that a good many of their measures do not represent priceless pearls of wisdom. Thus it must and will be with all of us when we get to the same point—even if the same difficult circumstances may not prevail everywhere.

The tacit assumption underlying the Lenin-Trotsky theory of dictatorship is this: that the socialist transformation is something for which a ready-made formula lies completed in the pocket of the revolutionary party, which needs only to be carried out energetically in practice. This is, unfortunately—or perhaps fortunately—not the case. Far from being a sum of ready-made prescriptions which have only to be applied, the practical realization of socialism as an economic, social and juridical system is something which lies completely hidden in the mists of the future. What we possess in our program is nothing but a few main signposts which indicate the general direction in which to look for the necessary measures, and the indications are mainly negative in character at that. Thus we know more or less what we must eliminate at the outset in order to free the road for a socialist economy. But when it comes to the nature of the thousand concrete, practical measures, large and small, necessary to introduce socialist principles into economy, law and all social relationships, there is no key in any socialist party program or textbook. That is not a shortcoming but rather the very thing that makes scientific socialism superior to the utopian varieties.

The socialist system of society should only be, and can only be, an historical product, born out of the school of its own experiences, born in the course of its realization, as a result of the developments of living history, which—just like organic nature of which, in the last analysis, it forms a part—has the fine habit of always producing along with any real social need the means to its satisfaction, along with the task simultaneously the solution. However, if such is the case, then it is clear that socialism by its very nature cannot be decreed or introduced by *ukase*. It has as its prerequisite a number of measures of force—against property, etc. The negative, the tearing down, can be decreed; the building up, the positive, cannot. New Territory. A thousand problems. Only experience is capable of correcting and opening new ways. Only unobstructed, effervescing life falls into a thousand new forms and improvisations, brings to light creative new force, itself corrects all mistaken attempts. The public life of countries with limited freedom is so poverty-stricken, so miserable, so rigid, so unfruitful, precisely because, through the exclusion of democracy, it cuts off the living sources of all spiritual riches and progress. (Proof: the year 1905 and the months from February to October 1917.)[1] There it was political in character; the same thing applies to economic and social life also. The whole mass of the people must take part in it. Otherwise, socialism will be decreed from behind a few official desks by a dozen intellectuals.

Public control is indispensably necessary. Otherwise the exchange of experiences remains only with the closed circle of the officials of the new regime. Corruption becomes inevitable. (Lenin's words, Bulletin No. 29) Socialism in life demands a complete spiritual transformation in the masses degraded by centuries of bourgeois rule. Social instincts in place of egotistical ones, mass initiative in place of inertia, idealism which conquers all suffering, etc., etc. No one knows this better, describes it more penetratingly; repeats it more stubbornly than Lenin. But he is completely mistaken in the means he employs. Decree, dictatorial force of the factory overseer, draconian penalties, rule by terror—all these things are but palliatives. The only way to a rebirth is the school of public life itself, the most unlimited, the broadest democracy and public opinion. It is rule by terror which demoralizes.

---

[1] In both 1905 and February/March of 1917, uprisings could not become revolutions because democracy was so thin. Only authoritarian regimes could carry out a revolution, as Lenin did in October/November 1917. [Ed.]

Syrian Congress Memorandum, 1919

As it became clear that the Allies would defeat the Central Powers, they began considering the nature of the peace and how they would construct the postwar world. On the issue of how to treat a defeated Germany after the war, the insistence of the French on stiff financial retribution fanned the embers for the next generation. Almost as important in the eyes of the victors was how to treat the defeated Ottoman Empire. In January, 1918, President Woodrow Wilson gave a speech to the U.S. Congress in which he listed "Fourteen Points" intended to ensure a just and lasting peace. An overall theme was the need for "national self-determination."

Point XII began: "The Turkish portions of the present Ottoman Empire should be assured a secure sovereignty, but the other nationalities which are now under Turkish rule should be assured an undoubted security of life and an absolutely unmolested opportunity of autonomous development." The Arabs of the Middle East constituted at least one of these "other nationalities," and many of them expected their independence after the war. Instead the Paris Peace Conference instituted a system of "mandates" by which the victorious European powers maintained control over enemy colonies, including the Ottoman Arab territories, until the Europeans determined the colonies were prepared for independence.

This selection details the Syrians' objections to this arrangement, sent as a memorandum to the King-Crane Commission, the body responsible for overseeing the transfer of Ottoman territory. What were their objections? What evidence did they give to support their position? What did they want?

THINKING HISTORICALLY

Do you think this conflict could have been an expected consequence of the First World War? Do you think Wilson's Fourteen Points made the Syrian demands more likely? Do you think the European powers expected this response? What were the consequences of the failure of the Allies to settle these grievances?

We the undersigned members of the General Syrian Congress, meeting in Damascus on Wednesday, July 2nd 1919, . . . provided with credentials

Source: "The King-Crane Commission Report," in *Papers Relating to the Foreign Relations of the United States: Paris Peace Conference, 1919* (Washington, DC: GPO, 1947), 12:780–81.

and authorizations by the inhabitants of our various districts, Muslims, Christians, and Jews, have agreed upon the following statement of the desires of the people of the country who have elected us to present them to the American Section of the International Commission; the fifth article was passed by a very large majority; all the other articles were accepted unanimously.

1. We ask absolutely complete political independence for Syria within these boundaries. The Taurus System on the North; Rafah and a line running from Al Jauf to the south of the Syrian and the Hejazian line to Akaba on the south; the Euphrates and Khabur Rivers and a line extending east of Abu Kamal to the east of Al Jauf on the east; and the Mediterranean on the west.

2. We ask that the Government of this Syrian country should be a democratic civil constitutional Monarchy on broad decentralization principles, safeguarding the rights of minorities, and that the King be the Emir Feisal, who carried on a glorious struggle in the cause of our liberation and merited our full confidence and entire reliance.

3. Considering the fact that the Arabs inhabiting the Syrian area are not naturally less than other more advanced races and that they are by no means less developed than the Bulgarians, Serbians, Greeks, and Romanians at the beginning of their independence, we protest against Article 22 of the Covenant of the League of Nations, placing us among the nations in their middle stage of development which stand in need of a mandatory power.

4. In the event of the rejection by the Peace Conference of this just protest for certain considerations that we may not understand, we, relying on the declarations of President Wilson that his object in waging war was to put an end to the ambition of conquest and colonization, can only regard the mandate mentioned in the Covenant of the League of Nations as equivalent to the rendering of economical and technical assistance that does not prejudice our complete independence. And desiring that our country should not fall a prey to colonization and believing that the American Nation is furthest from any thought of colonization and has no political ambition in our country, we will seek the technical and economical assistance from the United States of America, provided that such assistance does not exceed 20 years.

5. In the event of America not finding herself in a position to accept our desire for assistance, we will seek this assistance from Great Britain, also provided that such assistance does not infringe the complete independence and unity of our country and that the duration of such assistance does not exceed that mentioned in the previous article.

6. We do not acknowledge any right claimed by the French Government in any part whatever of our Syrian country and refuse that she should assist us or have a hand in our country under any circumstances and in any place.

7. We oppose the pretensions of the Zionists to create a Jewish commonwealth in the southern part of Syria, known as Palestine, and oppose Zionist migration to any part of our country; for we do not acknowledge their title but consider them a grave peril to our people from the national, economical, and political points of view. Our Jewish compatriots shall enjoy our common rights and assume the common responsibilities.

8. We ask that there should be no separation of the southern part of Syria, known as Palestine, nor of the littoral western zone, which includes Lebanon, from the Syrian country. We desire that the unity of the country should be guaranteed against partition under whatever circumstances.

9. We ask complete independence for emancipated Mesopotamia and that there should be no economic barriers between the two countries.

10. The fundamental principles laid down by President Wilson in condemnation of secret treaties impel us to protest most emphatically against any treaty that stipulates the partition of our Syrian country and against any private engagement aiming at the establishment of Zionism in the southern part of Syria; therefore we ask the complete annulment of these conventions and agreements.

The noble principles enunciated by President Wilson strengthen our confidence that our desires emanating from the depths of our hearts, shall be the decisive factor in determining our future; and that President Wilson and the free American people will be our supporters for the realization of our hopes, thereby proving their sincerity and noble sympathy with the aspiration of the weaker nations in general and our Arab people in particular.

We also have the fullest confidence that the Peace Conference will realize that we would not have risen against the Turks, with whom we had participated in all civil, political, and representative privileges, but for their violation of our national rights, and so will grant us our desires in full in order that our political rights may not be less after the war than they were before, since we have shed so much blood in the cause of our liberty and independence.

We request to be allowed to send a delegation to represent us at the Peace Conference to defend our rights and secure the realization of our aspirations.

■ REFLECTIONS

By studying causes and consequences of world events, we learn how things change; more important, we learn how to avoid repeating past mistakes. History is full of lessons that breed humility as well as confidence. In *The Origins of the First World War*,[1] historian James Joll points out how unprepared people were for the war as late as

---

[1] James Joll, *The Origins of the First World War* (London: Longman, 1992), 200.

the summer of 1914. Even after the Austrian ultimatum to Serbia was issued on July 23 (almost a month after the assassination of the Archduke Franz Ferdinand on June 28), diplomats across Europe left for their summer holidays. By August, all of Europe was at war, though the expectation was that it would be over in a month.

We could make a good case for diplomatic blundering as an important cause of the First World War. It is safe to say that few statesmen had any inkling of the consequences of their actions in 1914. And yet, if we concentrate on the daily decisions of diplomats that summer, we may pay attention only to the tossing of lit matches by people sitting on powder kegs rather than on the origins of the powder kegs themselves.

President Wilson blamed secret diplomacy, the international system of alliances, and imperialism as the chief causes of the war. On the importance of imperialism, Wilson's conclusion was the same as that of Lenin, though he certainly did not share Lenin's conviction that capitalism was the root cause of imperialism, and in 1919 neither alliances nor imperialism was regarded as un-American or likely to end anytime soon. Still, Wilson's radical moral aversion to reviving Old World empires might have prevented a new stage of imperialism, as it developed in the mandate system. One of the consequences of a Wilsonian peace might have been the creation of independent states in the Middle East and Africa a generation earlier.

The principle of the "self-determination of nations" that Wilson espoused, however, was a double-edged sword. The fact that the war had been "caused" by a Bosnian Serb nationalist assassin in 1914 might have been a warning that national self-determination could become an infinite regress in which smaller and smaller units sought to separate themselves from "foreign" domination.

The rise of nationalist movements and the rise of international organizations were only two consequences of the First World War. Historians have attributed many other aspects of the twentieth century to the war. Stephen O'Shea offers a striking list of cultural changes:

> It is generally accepted that the Great War and its fifty-two months of senseless slaughter encouraged, or amplified, among other things: the loss of a belief in progress, a mistrust of technology, the loss of religious faith, the loss of a belief in Western cultural superiority, the rejection of class distinctions, the rejection of traditional sexual roles, the birth of the Modern [in art], the rejection of the past, the elevation of irony to a standard mode of apprehending the world, the unbuttoning of moral codes, and the conscious embrace of the irrational.[2]

Evidence of any of these consequences is only barely visible in the accounts of a chapter that ends in 1920, but many of the developments described in the next few chapters were consequences of World War I as well.

---

[2] Stephen O'Shea, *Back to the Front: An Accidental Historian Walks the Trenches of World War I* (New York: Avon Books, 1996), 9.

25

World War II and Mass Killing

Germany, the Soviet Union, Japan, and the United States, 1926–1945

■ HISTORICAL CONTEXT

In some ways World War II resembled World War I. At the European core, England and France again fought Germany and Austria. As in World War I, the United States eventually came to the aid of England and France, playing a decisive role. In both conflicts Russia also fought against Germany, only until the Soviet revolution in 1917, but fiercely and at great cost as the Soviet Union from 1941 to 1945. By contrast, Japan, an enemy of Germany in World War I, became an important German ally in World War II, and the pro-German Ottoman Empire of World War I was an independent, neutral Turkey in World War II.

While the main combatants were aligned on the same sides, and both wars ended in the defeat of Germany and its allies, the causes and consequences of the two wars were significantly different. The causes of World War II are clearer than those of World War I. German aggression was a factor in both wars, but in the buildup to World War I, there was much blame to go around. World War II, on the other hand, followed the aggressive conquests of Japan and Germany. Both countries had been militarized by extreme nationalist regimes. Similar "fascist" movements took power in Italy and Eastern Europe, partly in response to the economic hardship of the Great Depression of the 1930s. These movements, like the German Nazi Party, were led by demagogues—Hitler in Germany, Mussolini in Italy—who called for dictatorial power, the expulsion or conquest of foreigners, colonial expansion, and aggressive, violent solutions to social and economic problems. Similarly, the military party that took power in Japan sought an empire in China and Southeast Asia to ensure its economic prosperity.

957

The aggressions of Germany and Japan unleashed forces of violence that also distinguished World War II from World War I. New technologies of warfare (machine guns, biplanes, and gas in World War I) that had been directed almost entirely at soldiers in trenches were transformed by World War II into missiles and warheads that rained down on civilian populations. Even the victorious Allies directed previously unheard of violence against civilian populations in the fire-bombing of cities like Dresden and Tokyo and the use of nuclear bombs on Hiroshima and Nagasaki.

Despite the pounding barbarity of the Western Front, the era of World War I still contained features of earlier gentlemanly conflict. Like chivalric jousters, aristocratic World War I pilots displayed colorful scarves and saluted their falling rivals. But the extreme nationalist and racist movements of the interwar years instilled a hatred of the enemy that eviscerated any possibility of compassion or fellow feeling. Totalitarian governments indoctrinated mass citizen armies with a hatred that sometimes made the new technologies of violence redundant. Millions of newly designated enemies—neighbors as well as foreigners—were murdered by hand.

This chapter begins with selections on Nazi Germany: excerpts from Hitler's *Mein Kampf*, a Nazi speech on the extermination of Jews, and a description of the workings of one death camp, Treblinka. Then a recent historical essay places the holocaust of German Jews in a larger perspective. An even larger global view of the war and genocide brings us to Dr. Robert Wilson's letters about Japanese atrocities in China. We conclude this chapter on the war that killed so many millions by reflecting on its ending in mass death by a new weapon of far greater magnitude. We ask how, amidst the greatest technological progress the world had ever seen, the lives of ordinary people became so cheap.

■ THINKING HISTORICALLY

Thinking about the Unthinkable

To be able to think about the unthinkable is to be able to understand without excusing. Occasionally when we learn of something horrendous, we simply say, "I don't believe it." Our disbelief harbors two feelings: first, our sense of outrage and anger, a rejection of what was done; second, our unwillingness to believe that such a thing could happen or did happen. Our choice of words expresses the difficulty we have making sense of the senseless.

We must try, however, to understand such catastrophes so that we can help to prevent similar horrors in our own time. Understanding reprehensible acts requires a level of empathy that is often difficult to arouse. As you read these selections, you will be encouraged to understand and explain events that are easier to not think about. To understand what is offensive is not to excuse it, but to be better prepared to avoid it in the future.

1

ADOLF HITLER
Mein Kampf, 1926

Hitler (1889–1945) wrote *Mein Kampf* (My Struggle) in prison where he was jailed after an unsuccessful attempt to take over the German government in Munich in 1923. As he wrote in the Epilogue, included at the end of this selection, the German National Socialist Labor (Nazi) Party, banned after the attempted coup in 1923, was revived by 1926 to become a force in German politics.

We read from this rambling 700-page book today because of what happened in the years after its publication in 1926. In the context of the global depression after 1929, the Nazi party grew to be the largest party in the German Parliament by 1932 with 37 percent of the popular vote. In January 1933 Hitler was appointed chancellor by President Paul von Hindenburg. He proceeded to concentrate all power in his hands as *Fuhrer* (Dictator), militarize the German economy, and mobilize for war. In 1938, while the rest of Europe stood by, he annexed his native Austria and German-speaking regions of Czechoslovakia. In March 1939, he added the rest of Czechoslovakia. On September 1, 1939, the German invasion of Poland triggered World War II in Europe.

During the same period the Nazi regime imposed increasingly discriminatory restrictions on German Jews. As early as 1933, Jews were banned from government service, law practice, some medical careers and some schools, and Dachau, the first concentration camp in Germany, was built. In 1935 the Nuremburg laws outlawed any civic life for Jews and any sexual contact between Jews and non-Jews. In the next couple of years Jews were banned from all other occupations, Jewish children were banned from public schools, and German properties were seized. With the outbreak of war, Jews in Germany and in German-occupied countries were rounded up and put in concentration

Source: Adolf Hitler, *Mein Kampf*, translated by Ralph Manheim (Boston: Houghton Mifflin, 1999), 11–13, 15, 20–21, 34, 51–52, 56–58, 65, 78, 126, 134–36.

camps where they were forced to work in factories for private corporations or government producers of war materials. In 1941 the Nazis began building extermination camps, first in Poland, to annihilate Jews, Poles, and other enemies of the Nazis. These included communists, socialists, political dissenters, homosexuals, Romani (Gypsies), Slavs, and other ethnic and religious minorities. By 1945, upwards of 11 million Jews and other "undesirables" had been killed.

It would be a mistake to try to see all of this in embryo in a young artist in Vienna twenty years before, or even in the vitriolic ruminations of a prison inmate ten years later, but what do these selections suggest to you about Hitler's motivations and the roots of Nazism?

THINKING HISTORICALLY

To understand the unthinkable it is necessary to resist the temptation to demonize. To call someone a "Devil" or "Evil Incarnate" obviates the need to understand and learn. The English word *understand* is equivalent to the German word *verstehen*, which social scientists have used to connote empathetic knowledge: relating to another human, putting oneself in their shoes. This is a technique to gain knowledge; it has nothing to do with excusing or forgiving. Try this with probably the hardest subject in history: How did that aspiring art student become Hitler? What went wrong? How did his background, environment, and experience produce a future monster?

In the House of My Parents

Today it seems to me providential that Fate should have chosen Braunau on the Inn as my birthplace. For this little town lies on the boundary between two German states which we of the younger generation at least have made it our life work to reunite by every means at our disposal.

German-Austria must return to the great German mother country, and not because of any economic considerations. No, and again no: even if such a union were unimportant from an economic point of view; yes, even if it were harmful, it must nevertheless take place. One blood demands one Reich. Never will the German nation possess the moral right to engage in colonial politics until, at least, it embraces its own sons within a single state. Only when the Reich borders include the very last German, but can no longer guarantee his daily bread, will the moral right to acquire foreign soil arise from the distress of our own people. Their sword will become our plow, and from the tears of war the daily bread of future generations will grow. . . .

I, too, while still comparatively young, had an opportunity to take part in the struggle of nationalities in old Austria. Collections were taken for the *Südmark*[1] and the school association; we emphasized our convictions by wearing corn-flowers[2] and red, black, and gold colors; 'Heil' was our greeting, and instead of the imperial anthem we sang '*Deutschland über Alles*,' despite warnings and punishments. In this way the child received political training in a period when as a rule the subject of a so-called national state knew little more of his nationality than its language. It goes without saying that even then I was not among the lukewarm. In a short time I had become a fanatical 'German Nationalist,' though the term was not identical with our present party concept.

This development in me made rapid progress; by the time I was fifteen I understood the difference between dynastic '*patriotism*' and folkish '*nationalism*'; and even then I was interested only in the latter. . . .

Did we not know, even as little boys, that this Austrian state had and could have no love for us Germans?

Our historical knowledge of the works of the House of Habsburg was reinforced by our daily experience. In the north and south the poison of foreign nations gnawed at the body of our nationality, and even Vienna was visibly becoming more and more of an un-German city. The Royal House Czechized wherever possible, and it was the hand of the goddess of eternal justice and inexorable retribution which caused Archduke Francis Ferdinand, the most mortal enemy of Austrian-Germanism, to fall by the bullets which he himself had helped to mold. For had he not been the patron of Austria's Slavization from above! . . .

Years of Study and Suffering in Vienna

When after the death of my mother I went to Vienna for the third time, to remain for many years, the time which had meanwhile elapsed had restored my calm and determination. My old defiance had come back to me and my goal was now clear and definite before my eyes. I wanted to become an architect, and obstacles do not exist to be surrendered to, but only to be broken. I was determined to overcome these obstacles, keeping before my eyes the image of my father, who had started out as the child of a village shoemaker, and risen by his own efforts to be a government official. I had a better foundation to build on, and hence my possibilities in the struggle were easier, and what then seemed to be the harshness of Fate, I praise today as wisdom and Providence. While the

---

[1] Another term for Austria. Apparently devised in imitation of the old imperial Marks by the *Verein für Deutschtum im Ausland*, founded in 1881 to defend the endangered nationality of Germans in the border territories.

[2] The corn-flower was the emblem of Germans loyal to the imperial House of Hohenzollern and of the Austrian Pan-Germans.

Goddess of Suffering took me in her arms, often threatening to crush me, my will to resistance grew, and in the end this will was victorious.

I owe it to that period that I grew hard and am still capable of being hard. And even more, I exalt it for tearing me away from the hollowness of comfortable life; for drawing the mother's darling out of his soft downy bed and giving him 'Dame Care' for a new mother; for hurling me, despite all resistance, into a world of misery and poverty, thus making me acquainted with those for whom I was later to fight.

In this period my eyes were opened to two menaces of which I had previously scarcely known the names, and whose terrible importance for the existence of the German people I certainly did not understand: Marxism and Jewry. . . .

In the years 1909 and 1910, my own situation had changed somewhat in so far as I no longer had to earn my daily bread as a common laborer. By this time I was working independently as a small draftsman and painter of watercolors. Hard as this was with regard to earnings—it was barely enough to live on—it was good for my chosen profession. Now I was no longer dead tired in the evening when I came home from work, unable to look at a book without soon dozing off. My present work ran parallel to my future profession. Moreover, I was master of my own time and could apportion it better than had previously been possible.

I painted to make a living and studied for pleasure. . . .

Today it is difficult, if not impossible, for me to say when the word 'Jew' first gave me ground for special thoughts. At home I do not remember having heard the word during my father's lifetime. I believe that the old gentleman would have regarded any special emphasis on this term as cultural backwardness. In the course of his life he had arrived at more or less cosmopolitan views which, despite his pronounced national sentiments, not only remained intact, but also affected me to some extent.

Likewise at school I found no occasion which could have led me to change this inherited picture.

At the *Realschule*, to be sure, I did meet one Jewish boy who was treated by all of us with caution, but only because various experiences had led us to doubt his discretion and we did not particularly trust him; but neither I nor the others had any thoughts on the matter.

Not until my fourteenth or fifteenth year did I begin to come across the word 'Jew,' with any frequency, partly in connection with political discussions. This filled me with a mild distaste, and I could not rid myself of an unpleasant feeling that always came over me whenever religious quarrels occurred in my presence.

At that time I did not think anything else of the question.

There were few Jews in Linz. In the course of the centuries their outward appearance had become Europeanized and had taken on a human look; in fact, I even took them for Germans. The absurdity of this idea did not dawn on me because I saw no distinguishing feature but the strange religion. The fact that they had, as I believed, been persecuted on this account sometimes almost turned my distaste at unfavorable remarks about them into horror.

Thus far I did not so much as suspect the existence of an organized opposition to the Jews.

Then I came to Vienna.

Preoccupied by the abundance of my impressions in the architectural field, oppressed by the hardship of my own lot, I gained at first no insight into the inner stratification of the people in this gigantic city. Notwithstanding that Vienna in those days counted nearly two hundred thousand Jews among its two million inhabitants, I did not see them. In the first few weeks my eyes and my senses were not equal to the flood of values and ideas. Not until calm gradually returned and the agitated picture began to clear did I look around me more carefully in my new world, and then among other things I encountered the Jewish question. . . .

Once, as I was strolling through the Inner City, I suddenly encountered an apparition in a black caftan and black hair locks. Is this a Jew? was my first thought.

For, to be sure, they had not looked like that in Linz. I observed the man furtively and cautiously, but the longer I stared at this foreign face, scrutinizing feature for feature, the more my first question assumed a new form:

Is this a German?

As always in such cases, I now began to try to relieve my doubts by books. For a few hellers I bought the first anti-Semitic pamphlets of my life. Unfortunately, they all proceeded from the supposition that in principle the reader knew or even understood the Jewish question to a certain degree. Besides, the tone for the most part was such that doubts again arose in me, due in part to the dull and amazingly unscientific arguments favoring the thesis.

I relapsed for weeks at a time, once even for months.

The whole thing seemed to me so monstrous, the accusations so boundless, that, tormented by the fear of doing injustice, I again became anxious and uncertain.

Yet I could no longer very well doubt that the objects of my study were not Germans of a special religion, but a people in themselves; for since I had begun to concern myself with this question and to take cognizance of the Jews, Vienna appeared to me in a different light than before. Wherever I went, I began to see Jews, and the more I saw, the more sharply they became distinguished in my eyes from the rest of humanity. Particularly the Inner City and the districts north of the Danube Canal swarmed with a people which even outwardly had lost all resemblance to Germans. . . .

What had to be reckoned heavily against the Jews in my eyes was when I became acquainted with their activity in the press, art, literature, and the theater. All the unctuous reassurances helped little or nothing. It sufficed to look at a billboard, to study the names of the men behind the horrible trash they advertised, to make you hard for a long time to come. This was pestilence, spiritual pestilence, worse than the Black Death of olden times, and the people were being infected with it! . . .

If, with the help of his Marxist creed, the Jew is victorious over the other peoples of the world, his crown will be the funeral wreath of humanity and this planet will, as it did thousands of years ago, move through the ether devoid of men.

Eternal Nature inexorably avenges the infringement of her commands.

Hence today I believe that I am acting in accordance with the will of the Almighty Creator: *by defending myself against the Jew, I am fighting for the work of the Lord.* . . .

Political Reflections Arising out of My Sojourn in Vienna

The Western democracy of today is the forerunner of Marxism which without it would not be thinkable. It provides this world plague with the culture in which its germs can spread. In its most extreme form, parliamentarianism created a 'monstrosity of excrement and fire,' in which, however, sad to say, the 'fire' seems to me at the moment to be burned out. . . .

Munich

In the spring of 1912 I came at last to Munich. . . .

. . . A *German* city! What a difference from Vienna! I grew sick to my stomach when I even thought back on this Babylon of races. In addition, the dialect, much closer to me, which particularly in my contacts with Lower Bavarians, reminded me of my former childhood. . . .

Assuredly at a certain time the whole of humanity will be compelled, in consequence of the impossibility of making the fertility of the soil keep pace with the continuous increase in population, to halt the increase of the human race and either let Nature again decide or, by self-help if possible, create the necessary balance, though, to be sure, in a more correct way than is done today. But then this will strike all peoples, while today only those races are stricken with such suffering which no longer possess the force and strength to secure for themselves the necessary territories in this world. For as matters stand there are at the present time on this earth immense areas of unused soil, only waiting for the men to till them. But it is equally true that Nature as such has not reserved this soil for the future possession of any particular nation or race; on the contrary, this soil exists for the people which possesses the force to take it and the industry to cultivate it.

Nature knows no political boundaries. First, she puts living creatures on this globe and watches the free play of forces. She then confers the master's right on her favorite child, the strongest in courage and industry.

When a people limits itself to internal colonization because other races are clinging fast to greater and greater surfaces of this earth, it will be forced to have recourse to self-limitation at a time when the other peoples are still continuing to increase. . . .

For us Germans the slogan of 'inner colonization' is catastrophic, if for no other reason because it automatically reinforces us in the opinion that we have found a means which, in accordance with the pacifistic tendency, allows us 'to earn' our right to exist by labor in a life of sweet slumbers. Once this doctrine were taken seriously in our country, it would mean the end of every exertion to preserve for ourselves the place which is our due. Once the average German became convinced that he could secure his life and future in this way, all attempts at an active, and hence alone fertile, defense of German vital necessities would be doomed to failure. In the face of such an attitude on the part of the nation any really beneficial foreign policy could be regarded as buried, and with it the future of the German people as a whole.

Taking these consequences into account, it is no accident that it is always primarily the Jew who tries and succeeds in planting such mortally dangerous modes of thought in our people. He knows his customers too well not to realize that they gratefully let themselves be swindled by any gold-brick salesman who can make them think he has found a way to play a little trick on Nature, to make the hard, inexorable struggle for existence superfluous, and instead, sometimes by work, but sometimes by plain doing nothing, depending on how things 'come out,' to become the lord of the planet.

It cannot be emphasized sharply enough *that any German internal colonization must serve to eliminate social abuse particularly to withdraw the soil from widespread speculation, but can never suffice to secure the future of the nation without the acquisition of new soil.*

If we do not do this, we shall in a short time have arrived, not only at the end of our soil, but also at the end of our strength. . . .

Conclusion

On November 9, 1923, in the fourth year of its existence, the National Socialist German Workers' Party was dissolved and prohibited in the whole Reich territory. Today in November, 1926, it stands again free before us, stronger and inwardly firmer than ever before.

All the persecutions of the movement and its individual leaders, all vilifications and slanders, were powerless to harm it. The correctness of its ideas, the purity if its will, its supporters' spirit of self-sacrifice, have caused it to issue from all repressions stronger than ever.

If, in the world of our present parliamentary corruption, it becomes more and more aware of the profoundest essence of its struggle, feels itself to be the purest embodiment of the value of race and personality and conducts itself accordingly, it will with almost mathematical certainty some day emerge victorious from its struggle. Just as Germany must inevitably win her rightful position on this earth if she is led and organized according to the same principles.

A state which in this age of racial poisoning dedicates itself to the care of its best racial elements must some day become lord of the earth.

May the adherents of our movement never forget this if ever the magnitude of the sacrifices should beguile them to an anxious comparison with the possible results.

2

HEINRICH HIMMLER

Speech to the SS, 1943

Heinrich Himmler (1900–1945) was one of the most powerful leaders of Nazi Germany. He was the head of the SS, or *Schutzstaffel,* an elite army that was responsible for, among other things, running the many concentration camps. Hitler gave Himmler the task of implementing the "final solution of the Jewish question": attempted genocide of the Jewish population of Germany and the other countries the Nazis occupied. The horror that resulted is today often referred to by the word *holocaust* (literally, holy burnt offering).

The following reading is an excerpt from a speech Himmler gave to SS leaders on October 4, 1943. What was Himmler's concern in this speech? What kind of general support for the extermination of the Jews does this excerpt suggest existed?

THINKING HISTORICALLY

Psychiatrists say that people use various strategies to cope when they must do something distasteful. We might summarize these strategies as

Source: Heinrich Himmler, "Secret Speech at Posen," in *A Holocaust Reader*, ed. Lucy S. Dawidowicz (New York: Behrman House, 1976), 132–33.

denial, distancing, compartmentalizing, ennobling, rationalizing, and scapegoating. *Denial* is pretending that something has not happened. *Distancing* removes the idea, memory, or reality from the mind, placing it at a distance. *Compartmentalizing* separates one action, memory, or idea from others, allowing one to "put away" certain feelings. *Ennobling* makes the distasteful act a matter of pride rather than guilt, nobility rather than disgrace. *Rationalizing* creates "good" reasons for doing something, while *scapegoating* puts blame on someone else.

What evidence do you see of these strategies in Himmler's speech? Judging from the speech, which of these strategies do you think his listeners used to justify their actions?

I also want to make reference before you here, in complete frankness, to a really grave matter. Among ourselves, this once, it shall be uttered quite frankly; but in public we will never speak of it. Just as we did not hesitate on June 30, 1934, to do our duty as ordered, to stand up against the wall comrades who had transgressed,[1] and shoot them, so we have never talked about this and never will. It was the tact which I am glad to say is a matter of course to us that made us never discuss it among ourselves, never talk about it. Each of us shuddered, and yet each one knew that he would do it again if it were ordered and if it were necessary.

I am referring to the evacuation of the Jews, the annihilation of the Jewish people. This is one of those things that are easily said. "The Jewish people is going to be annihilated," says every party member. "Sure, it's in our program, elimination of the Jews, annihilation—we'll take care of it." And then they all come trudging, 80 million worthy Germans, and each one has his one decent Jew. Sure, the others are swine, but this one is an A-1 Jew. Of all those who talk this way, not one has seen it happen, not one has been through it. Most of you must know what it means to see a hundred corpses lie side by side, or five hundred, or a thousand. To have stuck this out—excepting cases of human weakness—to have kept our integrity, that is what has made us hard. In our history, this is an unwritten and never-to-be-written page of glory, for we know how difficult we would have made it for ourselves if today—amid the bombing raids, the hardships, and the deprivations of war—we still had the Jews in every city as secret saboteurs, agitators, and demagogues. If the Jews were still ensconced in the body of the German nation, we probably would have reached the 1916–17 stage by now.[2]

---

[1] A reference to the "Night of the Long Knives," when Hitler ordered the SS to murder the leaders of the SA, a Nazi group he wished to suppress. [Ed.]

[2] Here Himmler is apparently referring to the stalemate on Germany's Western Front in World War I. [Ed.]

The wealth they had we have taken from them. I have issued a strict order, carried out by SS-Obergruppenfuhrer Pohl, that this wealth in its entirety is to be turned over to the Reich as a matter of course. We have taken none of it for ourselves. Individuals who transgress will be punished in accordance with an order I issued at the beginning, threatening that whoever takes so much as a mark of it for himself is a dead man. A number of SS men — not very many — have transgressed, and they will die, without mercy. We had the moral right, we had the duty toward our people, to kill this people which wanted to kill us. But we do not have the right to enrich ourselves with so much as a fur, a watch, a mark, or a cigarette, or anything else. Having exterminated a germ, we do not want, in the end, to be infected by the germ, and die of it. I will not stand by and let even a small rotten spot develop or take hold. Wherever it may form, we together will cauterize it. All in all, however, we can say that we have carried out this heaviest of our tasks in a spirit of love for our people. And our inward being, our soul, our character has not suffered injury from it.

3

JEAN-FRANÇOIS STEINER

Treblinka, 1967

Treblinka, in Poland, was one of several Nazi extermination camps (see Map 25.1). In these "death factories," the Nazis murdered millions of Jews as well as Roma and Sinti, communists, socialists, Poles, Soviet prisoners of war, and other people. Extermination of Jews became official Nazi policy in 1942. Extermination camps were built to supplement earlier concentration camps used to contain political prisoners, Jews, and other forced laborers (many of whom also died there). In this selection, Steiner describes some of the elaborate study and preparation that went into the design of an extermination camp, focusing on the work of Kurt Franz, whom the prisoners called Lalka. What were the problems the Nazis faced in building an extermination camp? How did they solve them? What does this level of efficiency and scientific planning tell you about the Nazi regime or the people involved?

THINKING HISTORICALLY

Try to imagine what went through the mind of Lalka as he designed the extermination process at Treblinka. How did concerns for

Source: Jean-François Steiner, *Treblinka* (New York: Simon & Schuster, 1967), 153–54, 155–58, 159–60.

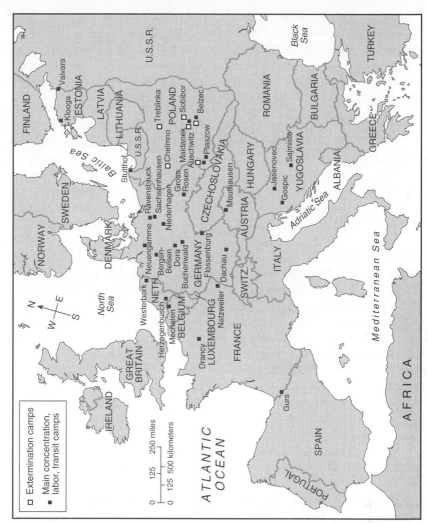

Map 25.1 Major Nazi Concentration Camps in World War II.

969

efficiency and humanity enter into his deliberations? Do you think he found his work distasteful? If so, which of the strategies mentioned in the previous selection did he adopt?

What would it have been like to be a sign-painter, guard, or hair-cutter at Treblinka? What do you imagine went through the minds of the victims?

Each poorly organized debarkation [of deportees from trains arriving at Treblinka] gave rise to unpleasant scenes—uncertainties and confusion for the deportees, who did not know where they were going and were sometimes seized with panic.

So, the first problem was to restore a minimum of hope. Lalka had many faults, but he did not lack a certain creative imagination. After a few days of reflection he hit upon the idea of transforming the platform where the convoys [trains] arrived into a false station. He had the ground filled in to the level of the doors of the cars in order to give the appearance of a train platform and to make it easier to get off the trains. . . . On [a] wall Lalka had . . . doors and windows painted in gay and pleasing colors. The windows were decorated with cheerful curtains and framed by green blinds which were just as false as the rest. Each door was given a special name, stencilled at eye level: "Stationmaster," "Toilet," "Infirmary" (a red cross was painted on this door). Lalka carried his concern for detail so far as to have his men paint two doors leading to the waiting rooms, first and second class. The ticket window, which was barred with a horizontal sign reading, "Closed," was a little masterpiece with its ledge and false perspective and its grill, painted line for line. Next to the ticket window a large timetable announced the departure times of trains for Warsaw, Bialystok, Wolkowysk, etc. . . . Two doors were cut into the [wall]. The first led to the "hospital," bearing a wooden arrow on which "Wolkowysk" was painted. The second led to the place where the Jews were undressed; that arrow said "Bialystok." Lalka also had some flower beds designed, which gave the whole area a neat and cheery look. . . .

Lalka also decided that better organization could save much time in the operations of undressing and recovery of the [deportees'] baggage. To do this you had only to rationalize the different operations, that is, to organize the undressing like an assembly line. But the rhythm of this assembly line was at the mercy of the sick, the old, and the wounded, who, since they were unable to keep the pace, threatened to bog down the operation and make it proceed even more slowly than before. . . . Individuals of both sexes over the age of ten, and children under ten, at a maximum rate of two children per adult, were judged fit to follow the complete circuit,[1] as long as they did not show serious wounds or marked disability. Victims who did not correspond to the norms were to be conducted to the "hospital" by members of the blue commando and turned over to the Ukrainians [guards] for special treatment. A bench was built all around the ditch of the "hospital" so that the victims would fall of their own weight after receiving the bullet in the back of the head. This bench was to be used only when Kurland[2] was swamped with work. On the platform, the door which these victims took was surmounted by the Wolkowysk arrow. In the Sibylline language of Treblinka, "Wolkowysk" meant the bullet in the back of the neck or the injection. "Bialystok" meant the gas chamber.

Beside the "Bialystok" door stood a tall Jew whose role was to shout endlessly, "Large bundles here, large bundles here!" He had been nicknamed "Groysse Pack." As soon as the victims had gone through, Groysse Pack and his men from the red commando carried the bundles at a run to the sorting square, where the sorting commandos immediately took possession of them. As soon as they had gone through the door came the order, "Women to the left, men to the right." This moment generally gave rise to painful scenes.

While the women were being led to the left-hand barracks to undress and go to the hairdresser,[3] the men, who were lined up double file, slowly entered the production line. This production line included five stations. At each of these a group of "reds" shouted at the top of their lungs the name of the piece of clothing that it was in charge of receiving. At the first station the victim handed over his coat and hat. At the second, his jacket. (In exchange, he received a piece of string.) At the third he sat down, took off his shoes, and tied them together with the string he had just received. Until then the shoes were not tied together in pairs, and since the yield was at least fifteen thousand pairs of shoes per day, they were all lost, since they could not be matched up again. At the fourth station the victim left his trousers, and at the fifth his shirt and underwear.

After they had been stripped, the victims were conducted, as they came off the assembly line, to the right-hand barracks and penned in until the women had finished: ladies first. However, a small number, chosen from among the most able-bodied, were singled out at the door to carry the clothing to the sorting square. They did this while running naked between two rows of Ukrainian guards. Without stopping once

---

[1] The "complete" circuit was getting off the train, walking along the platform through the door to the men's or women's barracks, undressing, and being led to the gas chamber "showers." [Ed.]

[2] Kurland was a Jew assigned to the "hospital," where he gave injections of poison to those who were too ill or crippled to make the complete circuit. [Ed.]

[3] Haircutter. [Ed.]

they threw their bundles onto the pile, turned around, and went back for another.

Meanwhile the women had been conducted to the barracks on the left. This barracks was divided into two parts: a dressing room and a beauty salon. "Put your clothes in a pile so you will be able to find them after the shower," they were ordered in the first room. The "beauty salon" was a room furnished with six benches, each of which could seat twenty women at a time. Behind each bench twenty prisoners of the red commando, wearing white tunics and armed with scissors, waited at attention until all the women were seated. Between haircutting sessions they sat down on the benches and, under the direction of a *kapo* [prisoner guard] who was transformed into a conductor, they had to sing old Yiddish melodies.

Lalka, who had insisted on taking personal responsibility for every detail, had perfected the technique of what he called the "Treblinka cut." With five well-placed slashes the whole head of hair was transferred to a sack placed beside each hairdresser for this purpose. It was simple and efficient. How many dramas did this "beauty salon" see? From the very beautiful young woman who wept when her hair was cut off, because she would be ugly, to the mother who grabbed a pair of scissors from one of the "hairdressers" and literally severed a Ukrainian's arm; from the sister who recognized one of the "hairdressers" as her brother to the young girl, Ruth Dorfman, who, suddenly understanding and fighting back her tears, asked whether it was difficult to die and admitted in a small brave voice that she was a little afraid and wished it were all over.

When they had been shorn the women left the "beauty salon" double file. Outside the door, they had to squat in a particular way also specified by Lalka, in order to be intimately searched. Up to this point, doubt had been carefully maintained. Of course, a discriminating eye might have observed that . . . the smell was the smell of rotting bodies. A thousand details proved that Treblinka was not a transient camp, and some realized this, but the majority had believed in the impossible for too long to begin to doubt at the last moment. The door of the barracks, which opened directly onto the "road to heaven," represented the turning point. Up to here the prisoners had been given a minimum of hope, from here on this policy was abandoned.

This was one of Lalka's great innovations. After what point was it no longer necessary to delude the victims? This detail had been the subject of rather heated controversy among the Technicians. At the Nuremberg trials, Rudolf Höss, Commandant of Auschwitz, criticized Treblinka where, according to him, the victims knew that they were going to be killed. Höss was an advocate of the towel distributed at the door to the gas chamber. He claimed that this system not only avoided disorder, but was more humane, and he was proud of it. But Höss did not invent this "towel technique"; it was in all the manuals, and it was utilized at Treblinka until Lalka's great reform.

Lalka's studies had led to what might be called the "principle of the cutoff." His reasoning was simple: Since sooner or later the victims must realize that they were going to be killed, to postpone this moment was only false humanity. The principle "the later the better" did not apply here. Lalka had been led to make an intensive study of this problem upon observing one day completely by chance, that winded victims died much more rapidly than the rest. The discovery had led him to make a clean sweep of accepted principles. Let us follow his industrialist's logic, keeping well in mind that his great preoccupation was the saving of time. A winded victim dies faster. Hence, a saving of time. The best way to wind a man is to make him run—another saving of time. Thus Lalka arrived at the conclusion that you must make the victims run. A new question had then arisen: At what point must you make the victims run and thus create panic (a further aid to breathlessness)? The question had answered itself: As soon as you have nothing more to make them do. Franz located the exact point, the point of no return: the door of the barracks.

The rest was merely a matter of working out the details. Along the "road to heaven" and in front of the gas chambers he stationed a cordon of guards armed with whips, whose function was to make the victims run, to make them rush into the gas chambers of their own accord in search of refuge. One can see that this system is more daring than the classic system, but one can also see the danger it represents. Suddenly abandoned to their despair, realizing that they no longer had anything to lose, the victims might attack the guards. Lalka was aware of this risk, but he maintained that everything depended on the pace. "It's close work," he said, "but if you maintain a very rapid pace and do not allow a single moment of hesitation, the method is absolutely without danger." There were still further elaborations later on, but from the first day, Lalka had only to pride himself on his innovation: It took no more than three quarters of an hour, by the clock, to put the victims through their last voyage, from the moment the doors of the cattle cars were unbolted to the moment the great trap doors of the gas chamber were opened to take out the bodies. . . .

But let us return to the men. The timing was worked out so that by the time the last woman had emerged from the left-hand barracks, all the clothes had been transported to the sorting square. The men were immediately taken out of the right-hand barracks and driven after the women into the "road to heaven," which they reached by way of a special side path. By the time they arrived at the gas chambers the toughest, who had begun to run before the others to carry the bundles, were just as winded as the weakest. Everyone died in perfect unison for the greater satisfaction of that great Technician Kurt Franz, the Stakhanovite [model worker] of extermination.

TIMOTHY SNYDER

Holocaust: The Ignored Reality, 2009

The mass killing of Jews was a policy of the Nazis fueled by long-standing anti-Semitism, aggravated by German economic collapse and propaganda that linked Jews to both communist laborer agitation and the bankers at the upper levels of finance capitalism. This anti-Semitism was not limited to Germany, however. It was especially pervasive throughout Eastern Europe, where most Jews lived. Thus, it would be a mistake, according to the author of this selection, to think of the Holocaust solely in terms of Germany and German Jews. What are the broader dimensions of the Holocaust that the author describes? Further, if the Holocaust refers only to the killing of Jews, how might a focus on this genocide alone minimize the scale of civilian casualties in World War II?

THINKING HISTORICALLY

The process of understanding without excusing is a struggle between the intellect and the emotions. No historical study can be entirely divorced from the emotions, but subjects like mass slaughter make it harder than many other subjects to be objective. Other factors might inhibit the historian's ability to get to the truth. One difficulty, for instance, lies with sources. What limitations does Snyder see in the sources that have been available to understand the Holocaust? How representative are survivors? What can we learn from the perpetrators? How do statistics help and hinder our understanding? What is gained, and lost, by distinguishing between such events as holocaust, genocide, war crimes, massacres, civilian casualties, and "collateral damage"?

Though Europe thrives, its writers and politicians are preoccupied with death. The mass killings of European civilians during the 1930s and 1940s [see Map 25.2] are the reference of today's confused discussions of memory, and the touchstone of whatever common ethics Europeans may share. The bureaucracies of Nazi Germany and the Soviet Union turned individual lives into mass death, particular humans into quotas of those to be killed. The Soviets hid their mass shootings in dark woods and falsified the records of regions in which they had

Source: Timothy Snyder, "Holocaust: The Ignored Reality," *New York Review of Books* 56, no. 12 (July 16, 2009), http://www.nybooks.com/articles/22875.

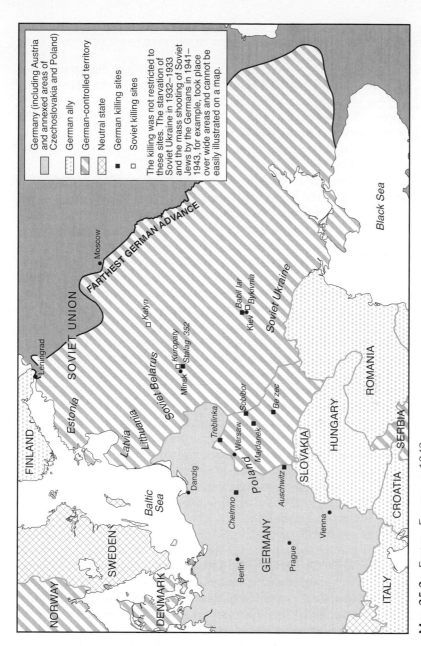

Map 25.2 Eastern Europe, c. 1942.

Source: Courtesy of the New York Review of Books.

starved people to death; the Germans had slave laborers dig up the bodies of their Jewish victims and burn them on giant grates. Historians must, as best we can, cast light into these shadows and account for these people. This we have not done. Auschwitz, generally taken to be an adequate or even a final symbol of the evil of mass killing, is in fact only the beginning of knowledge, a hint of the true reckoning with the past still to come.

The very reasons that we know something about Auschwitz warp our understanding of the Holocaust: we know about Auschwitz because there were survivors, and there were survivors because Auschwitz was a labor camp as well as a death factory. These survivors were largely West European Jews, because Auschwitz is where West European Jews were usually sent. After World War II, West European Jewish survivors were free to write and publish as they liked, whereas East European Jewish survivors, if caught behind the iron curtain, could not. In the West, memoirs of the Holocaust could (although very slowly) enter into historical writing and public consciousness.

This form of survivors' history, of which the works of Primo Levi[1] are the most famous example, only inadequately captures the reality of the mass killing. *The Diary of Anne Frank* concerns assimilated European Jewish communities, the Dutch and German, whose tragedy, though horrible, was a very small part of the Holocaust. By 1943 and 1944, when most of the killing of West European Jews took place, the Holocaust was in considerable measure complete. Two thirds of the Jews who would be killed during the war were already dead by the end of 1942. The main victims, the Polish and Soviet Jews, had been killed by bullets fired over death pits or by carbon monoxide from internal combustion engines pumped into gas chambers at Treblinka, Be zec,[2] and Sobibor in occupied Poland.

Auschwitz as symbol of the Holocaust excludes those who were at the center of the historical event. The largest group of Holocaust victims—religiously Orthodox and Yiddish-speaking Jews of Poland, or, in the slightly contemptuous German term, *Ostjuden*[3]—were culturally alien from West Europeans, including West European Jews. To some degree, they continue to be marginalized from the memory of the Holocaust. The death facility Auschwitz-Birkenau was constructed on territories that are today in Poland, although at the time they were part of the German Reich. Auschwitz is thus associated with today's Poland by anyone who visits, yet relatively few Polish Jews and almost no Soviet Jews died there. The two largest groups of victims are nearly missing from the memorial symbol.

[1] Primo Levi (1919–1987), Italian chemist, poet, essayist, novelist. Author of the memoir *Survival in Auschwitz*. [Ed.]

[2] Also rendered as Belzec. [Ed.]

[3] Eastern Jews (from Eastern Europe). [Ed.]

An adequate vision of the Holocaust would place Operation Reinhardt, the murder of the Polish Jews in 1942, at the center of its history. Polish Jews were the largest Jewish community in the world, Warsaw the most important Jewish city. This community was exterminated at Treblinka, Be zec, and Sobibor. Some 1.5 million Jews were killed at those three facilities, about 780,863 at Treblinka alone. Only a few dozen people survived these three death facilities. Be zec, though the third most important killing site of the Holocaust, after Auschwitz and Treblinka, is hardly known. Some 434,508 Jews perished at that death factory, and only two or three survived. About a million more Polish Jews were killed in other ways, some at Chelmno, Majdanek, or Auschwitz, many more shot in actions in the eastern half of the country.

All in all, as many if not more Jews were killed by bullets as by gas, but they were killed by bullets in easterly locations that are blurred in painful remembrance. The second most important part of the Holocaust is the mass murder by bullets in eastern Poland and the Soviet Union. It began with SS Einsatzgruppen shootings of Jewish men in June 1941, expanded to the murder of Jewish women and children in July, and extended to the extermination of entire Jewish communities that August and September. By the end of 1941, the Germans (along with local auxiliaries and Romanian troops) had killed a million Jews in the Soviet Union and the Baltics. That is the equivalent of the total number of Jews killed at Auschwitz during the entire war. By the end of 1942, the Germans (again, with a great deal of local assistance) had shot another 700,000 Jews, and the Soviet Jewish populations under their control had ceased to exist.

There were articulate Soviet Jewish witnesses and chroniclers, such as Vassily Grossman. But he and others were forbidden from presenting the Holocaust as a distinctly Jewish event. Grossman discovered Treblinka as a journalist with the Red Army in September 1944. Perhaps because he knew what the Germans had done to Jews in his native Ukraine, he was able to guess what had happened there, and wrote a short book about it. He called Treblinka "hell," and placed it at the center of the war and of the century. Yet for Stalin, the mass murder of Jews had to be seen as the suffering of "citizens." Grossman helped to compile a *Black Book* of German crimes against Soviet Jews, which Soviet authorities later suppressed. If any group suffered especially under the Germans, Stalin maintained wrongly, it was the Russians. In this way Stalinism has prevented us from seeing Hitler's mass killings in proper perspective.

In shorthand, then, the Holocaust was, in order: Operation Reinhardt, Shoah[4] by bullets, Auschwitz; or Poland, the Soviet Union, the rest. Of the 5.7 million or so Jews killed, roughly 3 million were pre-war Polish citizens, and another 1 million or so pre-war Soviet citizens:

[4] Mass murder. [Ed.]

taken together, 70 percent of the total. (After the Polish and Soviet Jews, the next-largest groups of Jews killed were Romanian, Hungarian, and Czechoslovak. If these people are considered, the East European character of the Holocaust becomes even clearer.)

Yet even this corrected image of the Holocaust conveys an unacceptably incomplete sense of the scope of German mass killing policies in Europe. The Final Solution, as the Nazis called it, was originally only one of the exterminatory projects to be implemented after a victorious war against the Soviet Union. Had things gone the way that Hitler, Himmler, and Göring expected, German forces would have implemented a Hunger Plan in the Soviet Union in the winter of 1941–1942. As Ukrainian and south Russian agricultural products were diverted to Germany, some 30 million people in Belarus, northern Russia, and Soviet cities were to be starved to death. The Hunger Plan was only a prelude to Generalplan Ost, the colonization plan for the western Soviet Union, which foresaw the elimination of some 50 million people.

The Germans did manage to carry out policies that bore some resemblance to these plans. They expelled half a million non-Jewish Poles from lands annexed to the Reich. An impatient Himmler ordered a first stage of Generalplan Ost implemented in eastern Poland: ten thousand Polish children were killed and a hundred thousand adults expelled. The Wehrmacht[5] purposefully starved about one million people in the siege of Leningrad, and about a hundred thousand more in planned famines in Ukrainian cities. Some three million captured Soviet soldiers died of starvation or disease in German prisoner-of-war camps. These people were purposefully killed: as with the siege of Leningrad, the knowledge and intention to starve people to death was present. Had the Holocaust not taken place, this would be recalled as the worst war crime in modern history.

In the guise of anti-partisan actions, the Germans killed perhaps three quarters of a million people, about 350,000 in Belarus alone, and lower but comparable numbers in Poland and Yugoslavia. The Germans killed more than a hundred thousand Poles when suppressing the Warsaw Uprising of 1944. Had the Holocaust not happened, these "reprisals" too would be regarded as some of the greatest war crimes in history. In fact they, like the starvation of Soviet prisoners of war, are scarcely recalled at all beyond the countries directly concerned. German occupation policies killed non-Jewish civilians in other ways as well, for example by hard labor in prison camps. Again: these were chiefly people from Poland or the Soviet Union.

The Germans killed somewhat more than ten million civilians in the major mass killing actions, about half of them Jews, about half of them non-Jews. The Jews and the non-Jews mostly came from the same part of Europe. The project to kill all Jews was substantially realized;

[5] German Army. [Ed.]

the project to destroy Slavic populations was only very partially implemented.

Auschwitz is only an introduction to the Holocaust, the Holocaust only a suggestion of Hitler's final aims. Grossman's novels *Forever Flowing* and *Life and Fate* daringly recount both Nazi and Soviet terror, and remind us that even a full characterization of German policies of mass killing is incomplete as a history of atrocity in mid-century Europe. It omits the state that Hitler was chiefly concerned to destroy, the other state that killed Europeans en masse in the middle of the century: the Soviet Union. In the entire Stalinist period, between 1928 and 1953, Soviet policies killed, in a conservative estimate, well over five million Europeans. Thus when one considers the total number of European civilians killed by totalitarian powers in the middle of the twentieth century, one should have in mind three groups of roughly equal size: Jews killed by Germans, non-Jews killed by Germans, and Soviet citizens killed by the Soviet state. As a general rule, the German regime killed civilians who were not German citizens, whereas the Soviet regime chiefly killed civilians who were Soviet citizens. Soviet repressions are identified with the Gulag, much as Nazi repressions are identified with Auschwitz. The Gulag,[6] for all of the horrors of slave labor, was not a system of mass killing. If we accept that mass killing of civilians is at the center of political, ethical, and legal concerns, the same historical point applies to the Gulag as to Auschwitz. We know about the Gulag because it was a system of labor camps, but not a set of killing facilities. The Gulag held about 30 million people and shortened some three million lives. But a vast majority of those people who were sent to the camps returned alive. Precisely because we have a literature of the Gulag, most famously Aleksandr Solzhenitsyn's *Gulag Archipelago*, we can try to imagine its horrors—much as we can try to imagine the horrors of Auschwitz.

Yet as Auschwitz draws attention away from the still greater horrors of Treblinka, the Gulag distracts us from the Soviet policies that killed people directly and purposefully, by starvation and bullets. Of the Stalinist killing policies, two were the most significant: the collectivization famines of 1930–1933 and the Great Terror of 1937–1938. It remains unclear whether the Kazakh famine of 1930–1932 was intentional, although it is clear that over a million Kazakhs died of starvation. It is established beyond reasonable doubt that Stalin intentionally starved to death Soviet Ukrainians in the winter of 1932–1933. Soviet documents reveal a series of orders of October–December 1932 with evident malice and intention to kill. By the end, more than three million inhabitants of Soviet Ukraine had died.

---

[6] A system of Soviet labor camps, many in remote locations, where political prisoners were sent and sometimes disappeared. [Ed.]

What we read of the Great Terror[7] also distracts us from its true nature. The great novel and the great memoir are Arthur Koestler's *Darkness at Noon* and Alexander Weissberg's *The Accused*. Both focus our attention on a small group of Stalin's victims, urban Communist leaders, educated people, sometimes known in the West. This image dominates our understanding of the Great Terror, but it is incorrect. Taken together, purges of Communist Party elites, the security police, and military officers claimed not more than 47,737 lives.

The largest action of the Great Terror, Operation 00447, was aimed chiefly at "kulaks," which is to say peasants who had already been oppressed during collectivization.[8] It claimed 386,798 lives. A few national minorities, representing together less than 2 percent of the Soviet population, yielded more than a third of the fatalities of the Great Terror. In an operation aimed at ethnic Poles who were Soviet citizens, for example, 111,091 people were shot. Of the 681,692 executions carried out for alleged political crimes in 1937 and 1938, the kulak operation and the national operations accounted for 633,955, more than 90 percent of the total. These people were shot in secret, buried in pits, and forgotten.

The emphasis on Auschwitz and the Gulag understates the numbers of Europeans killed, and shifts the geographical focus of the killing to the German Reich and the Russian East. Like Auschwitz, which draws our attention to the Western European victims of the Nazi empire, the Gulag, with its notorious Siberian camps, also distracts us from the geographical center of Soviet killing policies. If we concentrate on Auschwitz and the Gulag, we fail to notice that over a period of twelve years, between 1933 and 1944, some 12 million victims of Nazi and Soviet mass killing policies perished in a particular region of Europe, one defined more or less by today's Belarus, Ukraine, Poland, Lithuania, and Latvia. More generally, when we contemplate Auschwitz and the Gulag, we tend to think of the states that built them as systems, as modern tyrannies, or totalitarian states. Yet such considerations of thought and politics in Berlin and Moscow tend to overlook the fact that mass killing happened, predominantly, in the parts of Europe between Germany and Russia, not in Germany and Russia themselves.

The geographic, moral, and political center of the Europe of mass killing is the Europe of the East, above all Belarus, Ukraine, Poland, and the Baltic States, lands that were subject to sustained policies of atrocity by both regimes. The peoples of Ukraine and Belarus, Jews above all but not only, suffered the most, since these lands were both part of the Soviet Union during the terrible 1930s and subject to the worst of the German

---

[7] Period in 1930s of Stalin's purges of political rivals and anyone who voiced criticism. Here refers to 1937–1938. [Ed.]

[8] Soviet policy from 1928 to 1940 to end private property in farmland and create large farming communes. Forced collectivization of peasant kulaks led to mass starvation. [Ed.]

repressions in the 1940s. If Europe was, as Mark Mazower[9] put it, a dark continent, Ukraine and Belarus were the heart of darkness.

Historical reckonings that can be seen as objective, such as the counting of victims of mass killing actions, might help to restore a certain lost historical balance. German suffering under Hitler and during the war, though dreadful in scale, does not figure at the center of the history of mass killing. Even if the ethnic Germans killed during flight from the Red Army, expulsion from Poland and Czechoslovakia in 1945–1947, and the firebombings in Germany are included, the total number of German civilians killed by state power remains comparatively small. . . .

The main victims of direct killing policies among German citizens were the 70,000 "euthanasia" patients and the 165,000 German Jews. The main German victims of Stalin remain the women raped by the Red Army and the prisoners of war held in the Soviet Union. Some 363,000 German prisoners died of starvation and disease in Soviet captivity, as did perhaps 200,000 Hungarians. At a time when German resistance to Hitler receives attention in the mass media, it is worth recalling that some participants in the July 1944 plot to kill Hitler were right at the center of mass killing policies: Arthur Nebe, for example, who commanded Einsatzgruppe B in the killing fields of Belarus during the first wave of the Holocaust in 1941; or Eduard Wagner, the quartermaster general of the Wehrmacht, who wrote a cheery letter to his wife about the need to deny food to the starving millions of Leningrad.

It is hard to forget Anna Akhmatova: "It loves blood, the Russian earth." Yet Russian martyrdom and heroism, now loudly proclaimed in Putin's Russia, must be placed against the larger historical background. Soviet Russians, like other Soviet citizens, were indeed victims of Stalinist policy: but they were much less likely to be killed than Soviet Ukrainians or Soviet Poles, or members of other national minorities. During World War II several terror actions were extended to eastern Poland and the Baltic states, territories absorbed by the Soviet Union. In the most famous case, 22,000 Polish citizens were shot in 1940 at Katyn and four other sites; tens of thousands more Poles and Balts died during or shortly after deportations to Kazakhstan and Siberia. During the war, many Soviet Russians were killed by the Germans, but far fewer proportionately than Belarusians and Ukrainians, not to mention Jews. Soviet civilian deaths are estimated at about 15 million. About one in twenty-five civilians in Russia was killed by the Germans during the war, as opposed to about one in ten in Ukraine (or Poland) or about one in five in Belarus.

Belarus and Ukraine were occupied for much of the war, with both German and Soviet armies passing through their entire territory twice, in attack and retreat. German armies never occupied more than a small portion of Russia proper, and that for shorter periods. Even taking into

[9]Historian, author of *The Dark Continent: Europe's Twentieth Century* (2000). [Ed.]

account the siege of Leningrad and the destruction of Stalingrad, the toll taken on Russian civilians was much less than that on Belarusians, Ukrainians, and Jews. Exaggerated Russian claims about numbers of deaths treat Belarus and Ukraine as Russia, and Jews, Belarusians, and Ukrainians as Russians: this amounts to an imperialism of martyrdom, implicitly claiming territory by explicitly claiming victims. This will likely be the line propounded by the new historical committee appointed by President Dmitri Medvedev to prevent "falsifications" of the Russian past. Under legislation currently debated in Russia, statements such as those contained in this paragraph would be a criminal offense.

Ukrainian politicians counter Russia's monopolization of common suffering, and respond to Western European stereotypes of Ukrainians as Holocaust collaborators, by putting forward a narrative of suffering of their own: that millions of Ukrainians were deliberately starved by Stalin. President Viktor Yushchenko does his country a grave disservice by claiming ten million deaths, thus exaggerating the number of Ukrainians killed by a factor of three; but it is true that the famine in Ukraine of 1932–1933 was a result of purposeful political decisions, and killed about three million people. With the exception of the Holocaust, the collectivization famines were the greatest political disaster of the European twentieth century. Collectivization nevertheless remained the central element of the Soviet model of development, and was copied later by the Chinese Communist regime, with the predictable consequence: tens of millions dead by starvation in Mao's Great Leap Forward.[10]

The preoccupation with Ukraine as a source of food was shared by Hitler and Stalin. Both wished to control and exploit the Ukrainian breadbasket, and both caused political famines: Stalin in the country as a whole, Hitler in the cities and the prisoner-of-war camps. Some of the Ukrainian prisoners who endured starvation in those camps in 1941 had survived the famine in 1933. German policies of starvation, incidentally, are partially responsible for the notion that Ukrainians were willing collaborators in the Holocaust. The most notorious Ukrainian collaborators were the guards at the death facilities at Treblinka, Be zec, and Sobibor. What is rarely recalled is that the Germans recruited the first cadres of such men, captured Soviet soldiers, from their own prisoner-of-war camps. They rescued some people from mass starvation, one great crime in the east, in order to make them collaborators in another, the Holocaust.

Poland's history is the source of endless confusion. Poland was attacked and occupied not by one but by both totalitarian states between 1939 and 1941, as Nazi Germany and the Soviet Union, then allies, exploited its territories and exterminated much of its intelligentsia at

---

[10] Chinese communist collectivization (1958–1961) under Mao Zedong, which failed. [Ed.]

that time. Poland's capital was the site of not one but two of the major uprisings against German power during World War II: the ghetto[11] uprising of Warsaw Jews in 1943,[12] after which the ghetto was leveled; and the Warsaw Uprising of the Polish Home Army in 1944, after which the rest of the city was destroyed. These two central examples of resistance and mass killing were confused in the German mass media in August 1994, 1999, and 2004, on all the recent five-year anniversaries of the Warsaw Uprising of 1944, and will be again in August 2009.

If any European country seems out of place in today's Europe, stranded in another historical moment, it is Belarus under the dictatorship of Aleksandr Lukashenko. Yet while Lukashenko prefers to ignore the Soviet killing fields in his country, wishing to build a highway over the death pits at Kuropaty, in some respects Lukashenko remembers European history better than his critics. By starving Soviet prisoners of war, shooting and gassing Jews, and shooting civilians in anti-partisan actions, German forces made Belarus the deadliest place in the world between 1941 and 1944. Half of the population of Soviet Belarus was either killed or forcibly displaced during World War II: nothing of the kind can be said of any other European country.

Belarusian memories of this experience, cultivated by the current dictatorial regime, help to explain suspicions of initiatives coming from the West. Yet West Europeans would generally be surprised to learn that Belarus was both the epicenter of European mass killing and the base of operations of anti-Nazi partisans who actually contributed to the victory of the Allies. It is striking that such a country can be entirely displaced from European remembrance. The absence of Belarus from discussions of the past is the clearest sign of the difference between memory and history.

Just as disturbing is the absence of economics. Although the history of mass killing has much to do with economic calculation, memory shuns anything that might seem to make murder appear rational. Both Nazi Germany and the Soviet Union followed a path to economic self-sufficiency, Germany wishing to balance industry with an agrarian utopia in the East, the USSR wishing to overcome its agrarian backwardness with rapid industrialization and urbanization. Both regimes were aiming for economic autarky in a large empire, in which both sought to control Eastern Europe. Both of them saw the Polish state as a historical aberration;[13] both saw Ukraine and its rich soil as indispensable. They defined different groups as the enemies of their designs, although the German plan to kill every Jew is unmatched by any Soviet policy in the totality of its aims. What is crucial is that the ideology that legitimated mass death

[11] Ghettos were urban areas in which Jews were forced to live, apart from the rest of the society. [Ed.]

[12] Revolt of Polish Jews in April 1943 in opposition to removal to Treblinka. Crushed by German troops in May. [Ed.]

[13] Polish territory had often been part of one or more larger states. [Ed.]

was also a vision of economic development. In a world of scarcity, particularly of food supplies, both regimes integrated mass murder with economic planning.

They did so in ways that seem appalling and obscene to us today, but which were sufficiently plausible to motivate large numbers of believers at the time. Food is no longer scarce, at least in the West; but other resources are, or will be soon. In the twenty-first century, we will face shortages of potable water, clean air, and affordable energy. Climate change may bring a renewed threat of hunger.

If there is a general political lesson of the history of mass killing, it is the need to be wary of what might be called privileged development: attempts by states to realize a form of economic expansion that designates victims, that motivates prosperity by mortality. The possibility cannot be excluded that the murder of one group can benefit another, or at least can be seen to do so. That is a version of politics that Europe has in fact witnessed and may witness again. The only sufficient answer is an ethical commitment to the individual, such that the individual counts in life rather than in death, and schemes of this sort become unthinkable.

The Europe of today is remarkable precisely in its unity of prosperity with social justice and human rights. Probably more than any other part of the world, it is immune, at least for the time being, to such heartlessly instrumental pursuits of economic growth. Yet memory has made some odd departures from history, at a time when history is needed more than ever. The recent European past may resemble the near future of the rest of the world. This is one more reason for getting the reckonings right.

5

DR. ROBERT WILSON

Letters from Nanking, 1937–1938

In 1946 the American-led International Military Tribunal for the Far East brought charges against the defeated Iwane Matsui, former Commander of the Japanese Shanghai Expeditionary Forces, for what was already being called "the Rape of Nanking." Matsui was charged with leading an army that systematically killed 200,000 defenseless Chinese civilians, committed 20,000 cases of rape, and stole or burned much of the property in the city.

Source: *Documents on the Rape of Nanking*, ed. Timothy Brook (Ann Arbor: University of Michigan Press, 1999), 210–11, 214–17, 250–54.

Dr. Robert Wilson was one of three American medical doctors, and the only surgeon, who remained at the University Hospital in Nanking when the Chinese defenders retreated and Japanese troops occupied the city in December, 1937. He wrote these letters to his family, even after he realized he wouldn't be able to mail them, as a kind of diary of events between December 1937 and March 1938.

What does Wilson's diary tell you about the Japanese occupation of Nanking? What does it tell you about Japanese forces? What are "war crimes" in the midst of war?

THINKING HISTORICALLY

It would be difficult to get into the shoes, much less the minds, of these Japanese troops from the viewpoint of a single American observer. Nevertheless, how might Robert Wilson account for their behavior? How do you make sense of it?

Tuesday, December 14

. . . On Monday morning the 13th, exactly four months after the trouble started in Shanghai, the Japanese entered the city by several gates at once. Some came in Hoping Men [Gate] in the north and some in Hansi and Kwanghua Mens in the west and south-east respectively. By night they had complete control of the city and numerous Japanese flags flew from various places including their former embassy.

The entire remaining population of Nanking, some 150 or 200 thousand individuals, were crowded into the zone I have described earlier as the refugee zone. The International Committee[1] are doing a tremendous job with them and there is no doubt but that they have saved thousands of lives by their efforts. At the last moment thousands of Chinese soldiers threw away their uniforms and equipment and donned looted civilian clothes and crowded into the zone. Handling them is a grave problem in itself. Doubly grave has it become since the Japanese have not been fooled and are rounding them up by the hundreds and shooting them, putting their bodies in the conveniently handy dugouts built for air-raid protection.

Any civilian who shows no signs of fear and goes quietly about his business in the daytime seems relatively safe. Nobody is safe at night. Last night Mr. Chi, architect for the university and left behind to look after the buildings as best he could, was only saved from shooting by the intervention of Charlie Riggs, who stoutly maintained that Chi was his

---

[1] The European (including German) and North American governors of the International Zone (non-Asian). [Ed.]

coolie.[2] They then came over to our place with another Chinese University staff man, Mr. Ku, and all three stayed the night on some cots we put up in the living room. Steele of the *Chicago Daily News* also slept there and we totalled eleven people sleeping on the main floor and up, and I completely lost track of the innumerable Chinese that slept in the basement. The servants are rightly scared to death. To finish this paragraph more or less as it began, any civilian that shows signs of fear or tries to run away is promptly bayonetted. I sewed up one severed trachea this afternoon and we have had several dozen cases of bayonetting.

This morning we were treated to a thorough though unofficial inspection by thirty or so Japanese troops with fixed bayonets. They poked into everything. [Dr. James] McCallum, [Dr. C. S.] Trimmer and I showed them around and they would jabber away in Japanese while we would jabber away in both Chinese and English and neither had any idea what the other was saying. They lined up some of the nurses and took away their pens, flashlights and wrist watches. They did a pretty good job of looting the nurses' dormitory, taking all kinds of petty things. So far there has been no physical violence done to any of our staff.

Wednesday, December 15

. . . The slaughter of civilians is appalling. I could go on for pages telling of cases of rape and brutality almost beyond belief. Two bayonetted cases are the only survivors of seven street cleaners who were sitting in their headquarters when Japanese soldiers came in without warning or reason and killed five of their number and wounded the two that found their way to the hospital. I wonder when it will stop and we will be able to catch up with ourselves again.

Saturday, December 18

Today marks the sixth day of the modern Dante's Inferno, written in huge letters with blood and rape. Murder by the wholesale and rape by the thousands of cases. There seems to be no stop to the ferocity, lust and atavism of the brutes. At first I tried to be pleasant to them to avoid arousing their ire but the smile has gradually worn off and my stare is fully as cool and fishy as theirs.

Tonight as I came back from supper to stay here for the night I found three soldiers had ransacked the place. Miss [Iva] Hynds had accompanied them to the back gate. Two of them arrived and the other had disappeared. He must be hiding somewhere around the place. I motioned

---

[2] Word used for usually Chinese workers. [Ed.]

to the others outside stating in no uncertain terms that this was a Bei-koku Byoyen [American hospital]. How do you like that? The two that were there allowed themselves to be led out. They had taken Miss Hynds' watch and several other watches and fountain pens as well.

Let me recount some instances occurring in the last two days. Last night the house of one of the Chinese staff members of the university was broken into and two of the women, his relatives, were raped. Two girls about 16 were raped to death in one of the refugee camps. In the University Middle School where there are 8,000 people the Japs came in ten times last night, over the wall, stole food, clothing, and raped until they were satisfied. They bayonetted one little boy, killing him, and I spent an hour and a half this morning patching up another little boy of eight who had five bayonet wounds including one that penetrated his stomach, a portion of omentum was outside the abdomen. I think he will live.

I just took time out because the third soldier had been found. He was on the fourth floor of the nurses' dormitory where there were fifteen nurses. They were scared within an inch of their lives. I don't know how much he had done before I arrived but he didn't do anything afterwards. He had a watch or two and was starting off with one of the girls' cameras. I motioned for him to give it back to her and to my surprise he obeyed. I then accompanied him to the front door and bade him a fond farewell. Unfortunately he didn't get the swift kick that I mentally aimed at him. One of the earlier ones was toying around with a rather formidable looking pistol which I'm thankful he didn't use.

One man I treated today had three bullet holes. He is the sole survivor of a group of eighty, including an eleven year old boy, who were led out of two buildings within the so-called safety zone and taken into the hills west of Tibet Road and there slaughtered. He came to after they had left and found the other seventy-nine dead about him. His three bullet wounds are not serious. To do the Japanese justice there were in the eighty a few ex-soldiers.

One girl I have is a half-wit with some sort of birth injury, I believe. She didn't have any more sense than to claw at a Japanese soldier who was taking away her only bedding. Her reward was a bayonet thrust that cut half the muscles of one side of her neck.

Another girl of seventeen has a terrific gash in her neck and is the only survivor of her family, the rest of them were finished off. She was employed by the International Export Company.

As I left the hospital for supper after finishing my rounds on the 150 cases now under my care, the full moon was rising over Purple Mountain and was indescribably beautiful, and yet it looked down on a Nanking that was more desolate than it has been since the Taiping Rebellion [1853–64]. Nine-tenths of the city are totally deserted by Chinese and contain only roving bands of plundering Japanese. The remaining tenth contains almost two hundred thousand terrified citizens.

Last night [Plumer] Mills, [Lewis] Smythe and [George] Fitch went over in Fitch's car to escort Mills to Ginling [College]. Minnie [Vautrin] holds the fort there with several thousand women. When they got to the front gate they were held up by a patrol of Japanese soldiers under command of a pugnacious, impudent lieutenant. He lined the men on one side and Miss Vautrin, Mrs. Chen [Shui-fang] and Mrs. [deWitt] Twinem on the other side. He snatched the hats off the men and ordered everyone off the place including the women. Fitch told him he didn't have a place for them to stay but he insisted. They just got into the car when he ordered them back again and again harangued them for some minutes, finally sending the men back where they came from. Later we learned that while this was going on some Japanese soldiers had climbed over the wall and helped themselves to sixteen women.

The population faces famine in the near future and there is no provision for winter's fuel. It is not a pleasant winter that we look forward to. It is too bad that the newspaper reporters left on the day they did instead of two days or so later when they could have been more detailed in their reports of the Reign of Terror.

Another interruption to usher two Japanese soldiers off the premises.

As I probably won't get much sleep tonight I had better turn in dressed to get what I can.

Thursday, February 10

[. . .] The proportion of medical [to] surgical cases at the hospital is steadily increasing so that now Trim has about 50 patients to my 100. Today for the first time I went to our regular surgical clinic at 2 p.m., starting my operative schedule at 3:30. I shall try to continue that as the clinic certainly needs a guiding hand and there have been a lot of complaints about the way people are being treated there. This afternoon a woman came in with her face badly burned. She had returned to her home, on the orders of the Japanese, four days ago. Several Japanese soldiers promptly visited the house and demanded girls. She had only one 11 year old and one 12 year old and as these did not satisfy the soldiers they set fire to her house burning up the 11 year old girl in the building.

We are getting a large number of women from 16 to 30, most of them nice looking girls who are ridden with venereal disease from frequent raping. All of them have gonorrhea, most have syphilis and a large proportion have chancroid as well. That aspect of the clinic is certainly a heartbreaking one. It doesn't take long for any remote respect for the Japanese soldiers to evaporate permanently.

When our two cases of beri-beri showed up the other day we got immediate action and a boat is starting from Shanghai tomorrow with 100 tons of green beans. We hope to cut down any further incidence.

Yesterday I tried my first heterogeneous skin graft using pinch grafts from a father to his daughter. The graft looked fine today but it is much too early to tell. This afternoon I admitted a horribly burned little girl who has all the skin off her lower abdomen and anterior thighs. It happened six days ago and the mother had put on a concoction of mice boiled in oil and ground up. I had to give the child a general anaesthesia to clean it up. Her father had been shot offhand by the Japs about a month ago and the mother had not been able to give the child the attention she wanted to.

We get up to the tune of Jap airplanes and hear them all day long. Every now and then we think some Chinese planes come to the outskirts but we have no direct confirmation except occasional radio reports from Hankow. [. . .]

Sunday, February 13

[. . .] Last night we finally had the members of the Japanese Embassy to dinner. Three of the four came, the fourth having celebrated the previous day too vigorously. The previous day was the Anniversary of the founding of the Empire. Mssrs. Fukui, Fukuda and Kasuya were the guests. We put our excellent radio upstairs and played some classical records for them. We settled the problem of what to talk about by finding that two of them played bridge so that a bridge game was quickly organized. Fitch and Fukuda playing Riggs and Fukui. Unfortunately they stayed until ten-fifteen so that we didn't get any of the news broadcasts. Ordinarily we listen to Manila at 8:50, Hongkong at 9:30 and Shanghai at 10:10. Occasionally London at 6:00 and now and then Melbourne or some other place that happens to be giving the news.

Another cheerful tale came to my attention yesterday. Two weeks ago six Japanese soldiers entered the town of Liulangchiao some miles southwest of our town. They proceeded with their usual system of rape and looting. Some of the men in the town organized some resistance and killed three of the soldiers, the other three getting away. The three soon returned with several hundred who quickly threw a cordon around the town. A town of 500 inhabitants, it had only about 300 at the time. These 300 were all tied together in groups of six to eight and thrown in the icy river. They then leveled the town so that there wasn't a wall standing. The story was told me by a man who had gone from Nanking to Tanyangchen, a village just beyond Liulangchiao. He talked with the few terrified inhabitants of the surrounding territory and saw the ruins. Coming back he passed two soldiers on sentry duty at Yuhwatai just outside of South Gate. He was with his wife and child. They had passed the sentries about fifty yards when one of them casually shot in their direction, the bullet going through his flank but fortunately not entering the peritoneum. He is anxious to get out and return to Tanyangchen.

Only tonight four Jap soldiers came in and robbed several people in the University Library at the point of pistols of several hundred dollars. I guess the millennium is not here yet.

March 7

[. . .] The fall of Nanking on December 13 was immeasurably hastened by the incompetence and defection of T'ang Sheng-chih who was supposed to coordinate the defence. I shall not go into details on that here but will some day when the opportunity affords. If anyone had mentioned to us on December 12 that the entry of the Japanese would be the signal for a reign of terror almost beyond description we would have laughed at their fears. We had urged our Chinese staff to stay in the firm belief that, once the much vaunted Japanese Imperial army had taken control, lives would be safe and, while there might be some interference in the conduction of affairs, it would be only petty annoyances and that we need not be overconcerned.

When the mass murder, rapine, looting and arson began shortly after the entry of the Japanese troops we at first could not believe our eyes but were effectively convinced in a very short time. We had experienced no trouble whatever at the hands of Chinese soldiers even during the night of December 12 when tens of thousands of them streamed northward through the city to their slaughter at Hsia Kwan. It is true that they had burned some of the buildings just outside of the city walls in preparation for a defence of the walls that was never made, but outside of that and the burning of the Ministry of Communications, which burned on December 12th and therefore was presumably burned by Chinese, no destruction was carried out.

The Red Swastika Society[3] has for the last month been feverishly burying bodies from all parts of the city outside the zone and from the surrounding countryside. A conservative estimate of the number of people slaughtered in cold blood is somewhere about 100,000, including of course thousand of soldiers that had thrown down their arms. A few pitiful survivors of many of the mass murders managed to get to the hospital to tell their tale. I will record only one incident to illustrate.

At the University where the haphazard registration was going on of the twenty thousand people occupying the new library and compound and the main University buildings and compound, speeches were made urging all those that had been connected with the military to acknowledge it. They were promised that if they did so they would be made into labor gangs and their lives would be spared. If they did not acknowledge it and for any reason the Japanese suspected they had been connected

---

[3] Nazi German imitation of Red Cross Society. [Ed.]

with the military they would be summarily shot. About two hundred came forward and gave themselves up. I treated several survivors of that group. They were separated into several gangs and joined with hundreds of others picked up elsewhere. One bunch was taken into the hills beyond Ginling College, a few machine guns sprayed on them, several gallons of gasoline doused over their heads and they were set afire. Two survivors later died in the hospital burned almost beyond recognition, one not even having been hit by the machine guns, and the other having his jaw torn open.

6

President Truman's Announcement of the Dropping of an Atom Bomb on Hiroshima, 1945

In World War II the aerial bombing of civilian populations became increasingly common. A war that began for the British in a Nazi blitzkrieg of bombs and missiles on London, and that began for the United States in a Japanese air attack on the naval base at Pearl Harbor, came to a conclusion with an increased intensity of allied aerial attacks on the populated cities of Germany and Japan. In February of 1945, 1,300 U.S. and British bombers dropped 3,900 tons of explosives on the medieval German city of Dresden, unleashing a firestorm that claimed tens of thousands of lives. Tokyo was bombed throughout the war, but in March of 1945, a single bombing run of 179 new long-range B-29s took well over a hundred thousand lives. By the end of the war 50 percent of Tokyo, the most densely populated city in the world, had been leveled, an area that had once housed one and a half million people. By the summer of 1945, a new kind of weapon was about to harness the atom for even greater destruction.

The U.S. effort to make an atomic bomb had been a secret wartime project, begun initially by President Franklin D. Roosevelt out of fear that Germany was already developing one. Work continued in 1945, despite the death of Roosevelt in April and the surrender of Germany in May, as the United States and its allies turned their attention to defeating the Japanese in the Pacific. President Truman was also interested in the propaganda value of the bomb to ward off possible Soviet

Source: "Statement by the President Announcing the Use of the A-Bomb at Hiroshima," Truman Library, http://www.trumanlibrary.org/calendar/viewpapers.php?pid=100.

intentions in China and Japan. On August 6, 1945, the United States dropped the world's first atomic bomb on the city of Hiroshima, Japan. Three days later, a second atomic bomb was dropped on the Japanese city of Nagasaki. On August 15, Japan surrendered.

This selection is President Truman's address after the bombing of Hiroshima. What reasons does he give for the use of such a weapon? How does he relate the atomic bomb to the use of other weapons of war? How does he relate it to the issue of peace?

THINKING HISTORICALLY

President Truman was aware there would be controversy about the use of an atomic bomb. He had received a petition from atomic scientists urging him to first demonstrate the power of the weapon to the Japanese by exploding it in an uninhabited area. He heard his secretary of war Stimson compare the army's imprecise bombing and high civilian casualties to Nazi atrocities. On the very day he gave the order to drop the bomb, July 25, 1945, he wrote in his diary: "I have told the Sec. of War, Mr. Stimson, to use it so that military objectives and soldiers and sailors are the target and not women and children. . . . The target will be a purely military one."[1] However, the order contained no such language.

What signs do you see in this announcement of an effort to counter some of these concerns? How might Truman have shielded himself from recognizing some of the consequences of his decision?

Sixteen hours ago an American airplane dropped one bomb on Hiroshima, an important Japanese Army base. That bomb had more power than 20,000 tons of T.N.T. It had more than two thousand times the blast power of the British "Grand Slam" which is the largest bomb ever yet used in the history of warfare.

The Japanese began the war from the air at Pearl Harbor. They have been repaid many fold. And the end is not yet. With this bomb we have now added a new and revolutionary increase in destruction to supplement the growing power of our armed forces. In their present form these bombs are now in production and even more powerful forms are in development.

It is an atomic bomb. It is a harnessing of the basic power of the universe. The force from which the sun draws its power has been loosed against those who brought war to the Far East.

Before 1939, it was the accepted belief of scientists that it was theoretically possible to release atomic energy. But no one knew any practical

---

[1] Truman quoted in Robert H. Ferrell, *Off the Record: The Private Papers of Harry S. Truman* (New York: Harper and Row, 1980), 55–56.

method of doing it. By 1942, however, we knew that the Germans were working feverishly to find a way to add atomic energy to the other engines of war with which they hoped to enslave the world. But they failed. We may be grateful to Providence that the Germans got the V-1's and the V-2's late and in limited quantities and even more grateful that they did not get the atomic bomb at all.

The battle of the laboratories held fateful risks for us as well as the battles of the air, land and sea, and we have now won the battle of the laboratories as we have won the other battles.

Beginning in 1940, before Pearl Harbor, scientific knowledge useful in war was pooled between the United States and Great Britain, and many priceless helps to our victories have come from that arrangement. Under that general policy the research on the atomic bomb was begun. With American and British scientists working together we entered the race of discovery against the Germans.

The United States had available the large number of scientists of distinction in the many needed areas of knowledge. It had the tremendous industrial and financial resources necessary for the project and they could be devoted to it without undue impairment of other vital war work. In the United States the laboratory work and the production plants, on which a substantial start had already been made, would be out of reach of enemy bombing, while at that time Britain was exposed to constant air attack and was still threatened with the possibility of invasion. For these reasons Prime Minister Churchill and President Roosevelt agreed that it was wise to carry on the project here. We now have two great plants and many lesser works devoted to the production of atomic power. Employment during peak construction numbered 125,000 and over 65,000 individuals are even now engaged in operating the plants. Many have worked there for two and a half years. Few know what they have been producing. They see great quantities of material going in and they see nothing coming out of these plants, for the physical size of the explosive charge is exceedingly small. We have spent two billion dollars on the greatest scientific gamble in history — we won.

But the greatest marvel is not the size of the enterprise, its secrecy, nor its cost, but the achievement of scientific brains in putting together infinitely complex pieces of knowledge held by many men in different fields of science into a workable plan. And hardly less marvelous has been the capacity of industry to design, and of labor to operate, the machines and methods to do things never done before so that the brain child of many minds came forth in physical shape and performed as it was supposed to do. Both science and industry worked under the direction of the United States Army, which achieved a unique success in managing so diverse a problem in the advancement of knowledge in an amazingly short time. It is doubtful if such another combination could be got together in the world. What has been done is the greatest achievement of organized science in history. It was done under high pressure and without failure.

We are now prepared to obliterate more rapidly and completely every productive enterprise the Japanese have above ground in any city. We shall destroy their docks, their factories, and their communications. Let there be no mistake; we shall completely destroy Japan's power to make war.

It was to spare the Japanese people from utter destruction that the ultimatum of July 26 was issued at Potsdam.[2] Their leaders promptly rejected that ultimatum.[3] If they do not now accept our terms they may expect a rain of ruin from the air, the like of which has never been seen on this earth. Behind this air attack will follow sea and land forces in such numbers and power as they have not yet seen and with the fighting skill of which they are already well aware.

The Secretary of War, who has kept in personal touch with all phases of this project, will immediately make public a statement giving further details.

His statement will give facts concerning the sites of Oak Ridge near Knoxville, Tennessee, and at Richland near Pasco, Washington, and an installation near Santa Fe, New Mexico. Although the workers at the sites have been making materials to be used in producing the greatest destructive force in history they have not themselves been in danger beyond that of many other occupations, for the utmost care has been taken of their safety.

The fact that we can release atomic energy ushers in a new era in man's understanding of nature's forces. Atomic energy may in the future supplement the power that now comes from coal, oil, and falling water, but at present it cannot be produced on a basis to compete with them commercially. Before that comes there must be a long period of intensive research.

It has never been the habit of the scientists of this country or the policy of the Government to withhold from the world scientific knowledge. Normally, therefore, everything about the work with atomic energy would be made public.

But under present circumstances it is not intended to divulge the technical processes of production or all the military applications, pending further examination of possible methods of protecting us and the rest of the world from the danger of sudden destruction. I shall recommend that the Congress of the United States consider promptly the establishment of an appropriate commission to control the production and use of atomic power within the United States. I shall give further consideration and make further recommendations to the Congress as to how atomic power can become a powerful and forceful influence towards the maintenance of world peace.

[2] Potsdam proclamation called for immediate unconditional surrender or "complete and utter destruction." [Ed.]
[3] Japan wanted the condition that it could keep the emperor (which the Allies later allowed). [Ed.]

AKIHIRO TAKAHASHI

Memory of Hiroshima, 1945/1986

The author of this selection, Akihiro Takahashi, was fourteen years old on August 6, 1945, when the United States bombed Hiroshima. He was standing in line with other students in the courtyard of the Hiroshima Municipal Junior High School. His and other survivors' recollections of that day and its aftermath were recorded, transcribed, and translated some forty years later by a Japanese peace project called "The Voice of Hibakusha."[1] How do you weigh the experience of Akihiro Takahashi against the reasons given by President Truman for dropping the bomb?

THINKING HISTORICALLY

One of the difficulties in thinking about the unthinkable is remembering the details we want to forget. Trauma victims often repress memories that are too painful to bear. In some cases time revives memories as well as heals. Akihiro Takahashi's recollections display both a prodigious and courageous memory. How might this process of remembering and telling be helpful to him? How might it be helpful to others?

. . . [W]e saw a B-29 approaching and about fly over us. All of us were looking up the sky, pointing out the aircraft. Then the teachers came out from the school building and the class leaders gave the command to fall in. Our faces were all shifted from the direction of the sky to that of the platform. That was the moment when the blast came. And then the tremendous noise came and we were left in the dark. I couldn't see anything at the moment of explosion just like in this picture. We had been blown by the blast. Of course, I couldn't realize this until the darkness disappeared. I was actually blown about 10 m. My friends were all marked down on the ground by the blast just like this. Everything collapsed for as far as I could see. I felt the city of Hiroshima had disappeared all of a sudden. Then I looked at myself and found my clothes had turned into rags due to the heat. I was probably burned at the back of the head, on my back, on both arms and both legs. My skin was peeling and hanging like this. Automatically I began to walk heading west

---

[1] Japanese term for the victims of Hiroshima and Nagasaki: literally, the "explosion-affected people."

Source: "The Voice of Hibakusha," Testimony of Akihiro Takahashi in Atomic Archive, http://www.atomicarchive.com/Docs/Hibakusha/Akihiro.shtml.

because that was the direction of my home. After a while, I noticed somebody calling my name. I looked around and found a friend of mine who lived in my town and was studying at the same school. His name was Yamamoto. He was badly burnt just like myself. We walked toward the river. And on the way we saw many victims. I saw a man whose skin was completely peeled off the upper half of his body and a woman whose eye balls were sticking out. Her whole body was bleeding. A mother and her baby were lying with a skin completely peeled off. We desperately made away crawling. And finally we reached the river bank. At the same moment, a fire broke out. We made a narrow escape from the fire. If we had been slower by even one second, we would have been killed by the fire. Fire was blowing into the sky, becoming 4 or even 5 m high. There was a small wooden bridge left, which had not been destroyed by the blast. I went over to the other side of the river using that bridge. But Yamamoto was not with me any more. He was lost somewhere. I re-member I crossed the river by myself and on the other side, I purged myself into the water three times. The heat was tremendous. And I felt like my body was burning all over. For my burning body the cold water of the river was as precious as a treasure. Then I left the river, and I walked along the railroad tracks in the direction of my home. On the way, I ran into another friend of mine, Tokujiro Hatta. I wondered why the soles of his feet were badly burnt. It was unthinkable to get burned there. But it was an undeniable fact that the soles were peeling and red muscle was exposed. Even though I myself was terribly burnt, I could not go home ignoring him. I made him crawl using his arms and knees. Next, I made him stand on his heels and I supported him. We walked heading toward my home repeating the two methods. When we were resting because we were so exhausted, I found my grandfather's brother and his wife, in other words, great uncle and great aunt, coming toward us. That was quite a coincidence. As you know, we have a proverb about meeting Buddha in Hell. My encounter with my relatives at that time was just like that. They seemed to be the Buddha to me wandering in the living hell.

Afterwards I was under medical treatment for one year and half and I miraculously recovered. Out of sixty junior high school classmates, only ten of us are alive today. Yamamoto and Hatta soon died from the acute radiation disease. The radiation corroded their bodies and killed them. I myself am still alive on this earth suffering after-effects of the bomb. I have to see regularly an ear doctor, an eye doctor, a dermatolo-gist and a surgeon. I feel uneasy about my health every day. Further, on both of my hands, I have keloids.[2] My injury was most serious on my right hand and I used to have terrible keloids right here. I had them removed by surgery in 1954, which enabled me to move my wrist a little

[2] Scars. [Ed.]

bit like this. For my four fingers are fixed just like this, and my elbow is fixed at one hundred twenty degrees and doesn't move. The muscle and bones are attached [to] each other. Also the fourth finger of my right hand doesn't have a normal nail. It has a black nail. A piece of glass which was blown by the blast stuck here and destroyed the cells of the base of the finger. That is why a black nail continues to grow and from now on, too, it will continue to be black and never become normal. Anyway I'm alive today together with nine of my classmates for this forty years. I've been living believing that we can never waste the deaths of the victims. I've been living on, dragging my body full of sickness, and from time to time I question myself; I wonder if it is worth living in such hardship and pain and I become desperate. But it's time I manage to pull myself together and I tell myself once my life was saved, I should fulfill my mission as a survivor; in other words, it has been and it is my belief that those who survived must continue to talk about our experiences. To hand down the awful memories to future generations representing the silent voices of those who had to die in misery. Throughout my life, I would like to fulfill this mission by talking about my experience both here in Japan and overseas.

■ REFLECTIONS

Short of war, the world community has adopted three strategies to counter genocide and the mass killing of civilians. The first is the trial of war criminals. At the conclusion of World War II, the victorious Allies conducted war-crime trials of leading Nazi and Japanese officials. Twelve high Nazi officials and seven Japanese leaders, including Iwane Matsui for the "Rape of Nanking," were sentenced to death. Many others served prison sentences. Critics argued that some of the alleged crimes ("wars of aggression" and "crimes against peace") were vague and that the victorious Allies might be guilty of these as well. Other charges—specifically "war crimes" and "crimes against humanity"— were devised as a response to the trials, an ex post facto (after the fact) violation of standard procedure where prosecution must be based on criminal statutes.

The problem was that the technology and practice of warfare had largely outrun international agreements. The first Geneva Conventions, dating from 1864, were mainly concerned with the treatment of the wounded and prisoners. Therefore, the second strategy was developing and refining international laws regarding human rights and the protection of civilians. In 1948, the "Universal Declaration of Human Rights" passed by the United Nations, itself a shaper and guardian of international law, offered a recognized standard and continuing process for defining and preventing genocide, mass murder, and "crimes against humanity." A fourth Geneva Convention in 1949 added the destruction of civilian populations in time of war to the list of war crimes for which a country would be held responsible. In addition, the precedent of the "International Military Tribunal" that tried Nazi and Japanese officials led to the creation of international laws and courts for the prosecution of war crimes and mass murder. The legacy continues. In 2002, the United Nations' International Court of Criminal Justice in the Hague, Netherlands, brought President Milošević of Yugoslavia to trial for the "ethnic cleansing" of Muslims in Kosovo and Bosnia, and (at this writing) the court continues with the prosecution of others. An International Tribunal for Genocide in Rwanda is similarly trying Hutu Rwandans charged with the mass murder of Tutsi fellow citizens in 1994.

A third strategy has emerged in recent years, largely where human rights abuses or civilian casualties have occurred within a national population. Often without the benefit of international courts or agencies, governments seeking to put past grievances aside, rather than prosecute offenders, have created "truth and reconciliation" commissions. In 1995, after decades of racist violence, the new South African government under Nelson Mandela established such a commission. Former white officials were guaranteed immunity from prosecution in return for complete and remorseful testimony of their crimes. Similarly, in El Salvador after a decade of violence in the 1980s, a new government established a Truth Commission in 1992 with United Nations assistance.

Finding the truth is the beginning of any strategy toward renewal. To promote understanding, archives must be opened, press and Internet censorship must be challenged, and laws such as the Freedom of Information Act must be used aggressively. But in addition, we must develop sensitivity to the plight of victims, knowledge of the victimizers' motives, and understanding about the ways that the horrendous can happen.

26

The Cold War and the Third World

Vietnam, Cuba, Argentina, and Afghanistan, 1945–1989

■ HISTORICAL CONTEXT

The United States and the Union of Soviet Socialist Republics (USSR or Soviet Union) were allies during World War II. Meetings between the heads of state could be strained, but the Allies cooperated in the war and reached many agreements on the peace that followed, including the division of Europe and the creation of the United Nations and other international organizations. The Cold War developed within these agreements about postwar Europe and in the debates of the new international organizations, but it also festered from prewar ideological differences and antagonisms. U.S. troops were sent to fight "communist" Latin American regimes throughout the first half of the century; the Soviets never forgot Western efforts to reverse the Russian Revolution of 1917, and they never imagined that capitalism would outlast socialism.

World War II ended with the devastation of Germany and Japan and the exhaustion of England and France. One of the casualties turned out to be the colonial system that had fed and served the imperial powers. Some German colonies in Africa and Japanese colonies in Asia were turned over to the Allies after the war, but the postwar decades eventually brought an end to English and French colonies as well: British India as early as 1947, French Vietnam (Indochina) in 1954, and most of Africa by the early 1960s.

Although the Soviet Union had suffered enormous losses, it emerged with the United States as one of the two great "superpowers" of the postwar world. Both countries hoped to build a new world in which they would play a dominant role. Both professed opposition to imperialism, by which the Soviets meant the capitalist commercial and military expansion that they believed caused two world wars and by which the Americans meant the expansion of Soviet military power in Eastern Europe and communist governments in China and beyond. Both the United States and the Soviet Union championed the emergence of new independent nations from the ashes of colonialism, but neither wanted these new states to ally with the other power. In response, leaders of some of these new states declared themselves "noncommitted" to communism or capitalism—they were members of a "Third World" caught between the first two. Many Third World leaders were nationalists who sought help where they could find it, and some found the road to independence blockaded at either end. The Cold War had much to do with the effort by the United States and the Soviet Union to woo these new nations to capitalism or communism and into American or Soviet spheres of influence.

■ THINKING HISTORICALLY

Detecting Ideological Language

> The great enemy of clear language is insincerity. When there is a gap between one's real and one's declared aims, one turns as it were instinctively to long words and exhausted idioms, like a cuttlefish spurting out ink. In our age there is no such thing as "keeping out of politics." All issues are political issues, and politics itself is a mass of lies, evasions, folly, hatred, and schizophrenia.
>
> —George Orwell, "Politics and the English Language"

In his 1946 essay, George Orwell flagged the Big Lies of Hitler, Stalin, and fascist dictatorships, but he also ruminated on the ways that political language served the interest of the ruling political belief system (for "ideology") rather than the truth. The result of language that deluded the speaker as well as the audience was poor, often self-defeating policy.

Since Orwell confronted the political distortions of language in the period of the developing Cold War, a term he coined, we will use our study of the Cold War as an opportunity to examine the use of ideological language. It was an era of new mass media like television; government efforts to control public opinion through pollsters, advertisers, and public relations; and a competitive struggle between superpowers to win the "hearts and minds" of the world. Thus, many of the efforts of political writers were devoted to propaganda. But propagandists were not the only ones to choose their words for political purposes. Political practitioners did so as well, and often without realizing that the words they chose trapped them in dogma, fantasy, or fog.

1

HEONIK KWON

Origins of the Cold War, 2010

Heonik Kwon is a modern specialist on Korean and Cold War history. He is one of a growing number of Cold War scholars who are examining the many "hot wars" that were caused by the "cold" conflict between the United States and the Soviet Union. In this selection he mentions the Korean War, but he is mainly concerned with examining the causes of the Cold War. How, according to Kwon, does the establishment of a beginning date and cause of the Cold War become a moral issue? What alternate starting dates for the Cold War does Kwon discuss? Which of these do you find most convincing? How do the ideas of George Kennan and J. Edgar Hoover help us understand the causes of the Cold War?

THINKING HISTORICALLY

One goal of propaganda is to convert rational analysis into powerful emotions, frequently fear. How do the writings included here of Kennan, Hoover, and Eisenhower do this? The line between propaganda and self-delusion can be very thin. Do you think these important people believed what they said? How did the Cold War psychology become so pervasive?

The story of the cold war, like that of any other war in human history, begins somewhere and ends somewhere. There is no consensus about the question of beginning. The origin of the cold war is an unsettled issue that continues to engender instructive debate among historians. Reflecting on the diverse ways to think about the origin of the cold war means rethinking the political history of the twentieth century and therefore considering the changing conditions of the contemporary

Source: Heonik Kwon, *The Other Cold War* (New York: Columbia University Press, 2010), 1–3, 70–73.

world in new historical perspectives. However, this openness to historical reasoning and imagining does not extend to the other end of the story. There is a strong consensus in contemporary literature that the end of the cold war is a fait accompli, a universal historical reality. The question of the end has no room for diversity and generates no such positive interpretive controversies like those about the origin. The story of the cold war we tell ourselves today, therefore, has an open-ended beginning and a closed ending.

The term *cold war* refers to the prevailing condition of the world in the second half of the twentieth century, divided into two separate paths of political modernity and economic development. In a narrower sense, it means the contest of power and will between the two dominant states, the United States and the Soviet Union, that (according to George Orwell, who coined the term in 1945) set out to rule the world between them under an undeclared state of war, being unable to conquer one another. In a wide definition, however, the global cold war also entails the unequal relations of power among the political communities that pursued or were driven to pursue a specific path of progress within the binary structure of the global order. The "contest-of-power" dimension of the cold war has been an explicit and central element in cold war historiography; in contrast, the "relation-of-domination" aspect has been a relatively marginal, implicit element. The debates about the origins of the cold war contribute to disclosing how complex the great bifurcation in the project of modernity has been for both nations and communities. The origin of the cold war is not merely a question of time but also, in significant measure, a moral question: Which side of the bi-polarized human community was more responsible for bringing about the global order and engendering political and military crises? The moral question is intertwined with the chronological one, and their connected-ness is more apparent in places where the bipolar conflict was waged in a violent form.

Imagining the political future of Korea, for example, is inseparable from locating the origin of the Korean War. For people who date the origin of the war to 1950, the culpability for the devastating civil war rests unquestionably with the northern Communist regime, which launched, with endorsement and support from Mao Zedong and Joseph Stalin, an all-out surprise offensive against the southern territory in June of that year. For those who trace the war's origin to earlier years, the blame is apportioned equally to the belligerent, strongly anti-Communist southern regime, which instigated a series of border skirmishes and crushed domestic radical nationalist forces in a ruthless manner from 1947 to 1950. The latter measure provoked the outbreak of armed partisan activities in parts of the southern territory, which were effectively in a state of war from 1948 on. For those who associate the origin of the Korean

War with the end of the Pacific War in 1945, however, the main responsibility for the civil war lies instead with the United States and the Soviet Union, which partitioned and separately occupied the postcolonial nation after the surrender of Japan. (And we should add to these divergent views the official position taken by North Korea, which continues to paint its part in the war as an act of self-defense against the unprovoked aggression from South Korea, orchestrated by the United States, despite a wealth of evidence that points to the contrary.) These diverse perspectives on the origin of one of the first violent manifestations of the bipolar global order are not merely matters of scholarly debate. They are also deeply ingrained in the society that endured what was at once a civil war and an international war, provoking heated public debate and developing conflicting political voices and forces. In this context, the origin of the cold war is largely the origin of the war-induced wounds felt in the society, thereby making the very concept of a "cold" war somewhat contradictory, so that claiming a particular version of the origin is simultaneously an act of asserting a particular vision of the nation's history and future.

In the wider terrain, too, the cold war's temporal identity continues to be revised as to the question of its origin. Conventional knowledge associates the origin of the cold war with the end of World War II and the breakdown of the wartime alliance between the Western powers and the Soviet state. However, several scholars have challenged this conventional view. For example, Melvyn Leffler retraces the origin to the period following the Russian Revolution of 1917, whereas William Appleman Williams famously argues that the seeds of the cold war were sown much earlier, during the nineteenth-century contest for global supremacy between the established European imperial powers and the newly rising American power. Each of these revisions of the cold war's origin is simultaneously an attempt to reinterpret the meaning of the global conflict in modern history. Leffler's scheme foregrounds the importance of ideology (the antagonistic view to communism as a radically alien way of life incompatible with the market-based liberal world) in the construction of the cold war global order, whereas Williams shows how the perception of the alien ideological other mirrored for the United States at the turn of the twentieth century the nation's own ideological self-image defined in terms of so-called Manifest Destiny—the idea that America, as a sole benevolent and progressive power, confronts the backward and confused world infested with imperialist excess and colonial miseries. . . .

Two important documents of the early cold war show how the ideological "other" was imagined both from within and from without. George Kennan, an American diplomat considered the "father of containment policy," wrote in his famous "Long Telegram" sent from the U.S. Embassy in Moscow to the U.S. State Department in February 1946:

> At bottom of [the] Kremlin's neurotic view of world affairs is the traditional and instinctive Russian sense of insecurity. Originally, this was the insecurity of a peaceful agricultural people trying to live on a vast exposed plain in the neighborhood of fierce nomadic peoples. To this was added, as Russia came into contact with the economically advanced West, fear of more competent, more powerful, more highly organized societies in that area. . . . For this reason they have always feared foreign penetration, feared direct contact between [the] Western world and their own, feared what would happen if Russians learned the truth about the world without or if foreigners learned the truth about the world within. And they have learned to seek security only [in] a patient but deadly struggle for total destruction of rival power, never in compacts and compromises with it.

In September of the same year, J. Edgar Hoover, director of the U.S. Federal Bureau of Investigation, spoke at the San Francisco Conference of the American Legion:

> During the past five years, American Communists have made their deepest inroads upon our national life. In our vaunted tolerance for all peoples the Communist has found our "Achilles' heel." . . . The Communist Party in this country is not working for the general welfare of all our people—it is working against our people. It is not interested in providing for the common defense. It has for its purpose the shackling of America and its conversion to the Godless, Communist way of life. . . . We, of this generation, have faced two great menaces in America—Fascism and Communism. Both are materialistic; both are totalitarian; both are anti-religious; both are degrading and inhuman. In fact, they differ little except in name. Communism has bred Fascism and Fascism spawns Communism. Both are the antithesis of the American belief in liberty and freedom. If the peoples of other countries want Communism, let them have it, but it has no place in America.

Kennan highlighted the "traditional and instinctive Russian sense of insecurity": just as their "neurotic" leaders ruthlessly destroyed all domestic oppositions to their rule, he argued, so would they act in a similar fashion toward their defined enemies abroad. Kennan's "Long Telegram" was mainly about the threats to the West's security in the international sphere, and it was Hoover who epitomized the flip side of the "two-pronged policy of containment"—the commitment to containing communism both at home and abroad. In his book A *Study of Communism*, Hoover explored what he called the biggest mystery of his time: "How anyone who enjoys the rights and privileges of

American citizenship [can] bring himself to join a [Communist] movement which is such an outspoken foe of our entire way of life."

As the views of these influential state officials were circulated and were becoming a consensus in policy circles and public opinion, by the end of 1946 "the basic Cold War psychology" was taking hold of the U.S. administration. The Soviet maneuvers in northern Iran and incursions to the Turkish border in 1946 strengthened the belief in the United States that the Russians were hell bent on expansion and that only a united, preponderant counterforce could stop it. At the same time, Stalin encouraged the idea of encirclement by hostile Western forces to justify his brutal terror campaigns against his own population. The rise of the so-called cold war security culture was to a large measure, according to Mary Kaldor, a reciprocal action between opposing powers and had an "inertial logic" of mutually reinforcing external threats and internal fears. She argues that the construction of the cold war was thus a "joint venture" between the contending political blocs.

Hoover stated that "if the peoples of other countries want Communism, let them have it, but it has no place in America." It is argued in recent studies that American foreign politics in the mid–twentieth century was based on a broad bipartisan compromise between the Republican-dominated militancy against domestic labor and civil rights unrests and the largely Democrat-led initiatives to aggressively counter Communist threats in foreign soils. These studies show that although the U.S. administration perceived the threats of communism to be coming both from within the society and from overseas, the formulation of security threats was initially complicated by bipartisan politics in which contending groups lay emphasis on either the domestic dimension or the foreign dimension of containment. These two dimensions of perceived Communist threats gradually merged into a rhetorical whole; the polemics against the enemy within (such as Hoover's) and the polemics against the external enemies (such as Kennan's) became increasingly indistinguishable. In the beginning of the 1960s, therefore, Hoover advocated radical measures against overseas Communist threats to Asia and Europe, whereas Kennan lamented the lack of spiritual vigilance and moral solidarity against communism within the Western world. Hence, we should add to Kaldor's idea of "joint venture" another dimension — how the vision of the ideological enemy inside and the vision of the enemy outside colluded with each other, thereby augmenting the intensity of anti-Communist politics.

Dwight D. Eisenhower aptly summed up the emerging Manichean worldview in his inaugural speech in 1953: "The forces of good and evil are massed and armed and opposed as rarely before in history. Freedom is pitted against slavery; lightness against the dark." This anti-Communist worldview drew on an epidemiological model of society as a vulnerable organism. Hoover saw communism as "a condition akin to disease that spreads like an epidemic and like an epidemic a quarantine is necessary to keep it from infecting the nation." In 1950, an important report from the U.S. National Security Council known as *NSC-68* described the Soviet Union as aiming to "contaminate" the Western world by means of its preferred technique of infiltrating "labor unions, civic enterprises, schools, churches, and all media for influencing opinion." The document argued that, in parallel with the urgency to stop domestic contagion, there was a need internationally "to quarantine a growing number of [states] infected [by the disease of communism]."

2

The Vietnamese Declaration of Independence, 1945

Although this document may predate the Cold War, it demonstrates the importance of the anticolonial struggle to create new states at the end of World War II. Vietnam had been part of French Indochina from 1887 until World War II, when it was occupied by Japan. This Declaration of Independence represented an effort by Vietnamese nationalists to prevent the French from retaking the country from the defeated Japanese.

The author of the declaration, Ho Chi Minh (1890–1969), is a prime example of the kind of new national leader torn between the appeals of Washington and Moscow. A founder of the French Communist Party in 1921 as well as the Vietnamese Communist Party in 1930, he was also the leader of the Viet Minh, the Vietnamese nationalist movement, even enjoying the secret help of the United States during World War II in the battle against Japan.

What, according to Ho Chi Minh, were the effects of French colonialism in Vietnam? What reasons does he give for Vietnamese independence?

THINKING HISTORICALLY

Since this document was intended as a declaration of Vietnamese nationalism, delivered in Vietnamese to the Vietnamese people, one is struck by the use of ideological language from both the U.S. Declaration of Independence and the French Declaration of the Rights of Man and Citizen. What other signs do you see that Ho Chi Minh may have been interested in attracting the favor of a U.S. or French audience? What purpose would such a strategy serve?

Source: *Ho Chi Minh, Selected Works* (Hanoi, 1960–1962), 3:17–21.

"All men are created equal. They are endowed by their Creator with certain inalienable rights, among these are Life, Liberty, and the pursuit of Happiness."

This immortal statement was made in the *Declaration of Independence* of the United States of America in *1776*. In a broader sense, this means: All the peoples on the Earth are equal from birth, all the peoples have a right to live, to be happy and to be free.

The Declaration of the *French Revolution* made in *1791* on *the Rights of Man and the Citizen* also states: "All men are born free and with equal rights, and must always remain free and have equal rights."

Those are undeniable truths.

Nevertheless, for more than eighty years, the French imperialists, abusing the standard of *Liberty, Equality, and Fraternity*,[1] have violated our Motherland and oppressed our fellow-citizens. They have acted contrary to the ideals of humanity and justice. In the field of politics, they have deprived our people of every democratic liberty.

They have enforced inhuman laws; they have set up three distinct political regimes in the North, the Center and the South of Vietnam in order to wreck our national unity and prevent our people from being united.

They have built more prisons than schools. They have mercilessly slain our patriots—they have drowned our uprisings in rivers of blood. They have fettered public opinion; they have practised obscurantism against our people. To weaken our race they have forced us to use opium and alcohol.

In the fields of economics, they have fleeced us to the backbone, impoverished our people, and devastated our land.

They have robbed us of our rice fields, our mines, our forests, and our raw materials. They have monopolised the issuing of bank-notes and the export trade. They have invented numerous unjustifiable taxes and reduced our people, especially our peasantry, to a state of extreme poverty.

They have hampered the prospering of our national bourgeoisie; they have mercilessly exploited our workers.

In the autumn of 1940, when the Japanese Fascists violated Indochina's territory to establish new bases in their fight against the Allies, the French imperialists went down on their bended knees and handed over our country to them.

Thus, from that date, our people were subjected to the double yoke of the French and the Japanese. Their sufferings and miseries increased. The result was that from the end of last year to the beginning of this year, from Quang Tri province to the North of Vietnam, more than two

---

[1] This was the rallying cry of the French Revolution of 1789. (*Fraternity* means brotherhood.) [Ed.]

million of our fellow-citizens died from starvation. On March 9, the French troops were disarmed by the Japanese. The French colonialists either fled or surrendered, showing that not only were they incapable of "protecting" us, but that, in the span of five years, they had twice sold our country to the Japanese.

On several occasions before March 9, the Vietminh League urged the French to ally themselves with it against the Japanese. Instead of agreeing to this proposal, the French colonialists so intensified their terrorist activities against the Vietminh members that before fleeing they massacred a great number of our political prisoners detained at Yen Bai and Cao Bang.

Notwithstanding all this, our fellow-citizens have always manifested toward the French a tolerant and humane attitude. Even after the Japanese putsch of March 1945, the Vietminh League helped many Frenchmen to cross the frontier, rescued some of them from Japanese jails, and protected French lives and property.

From the autumn of 1940, our country had in fact ceased to be a French colony and had become a Japanese possession.

After the Japanese had surrendered to the Allies, our whole people rose to regain our national sovereignty and to found the Democratic Republic of Vietnam.

The truth is that we have wrested our independence from the Japanese and not from the French.

The French have fled, the Japanese have capitulated, Emperor Bao Dai has abdicated. Our people have broken the chains which for nearly a century have fettered them and have won independence for the Fatherland. Our people at the same time have overthrown the monarchic regime that has reigned supreme for dozens of centuries. In its place has been established the present Democratic Republic.

For these reasons, we, members of the Provisional Government, representing the whole Vietnamese people, declare that from now on we break off all relations of a colonial character with France; we repeal all the international obligation that France has so far subscribed to on behalf of Vietnam and we abolish all the special rights the French have unlawfully acquired in our Fatherland.

The whole Vietnamese people, animated by a common purpose, are determined to fight to the bitter end against any attempt by the French colonialists to reconquer their country.

We are convinced that the Allied nations which at Tehran and San Francisco have acknowledged the principles of self-determination and equality of nations, will not refuse to acknowledge the independence of Vietnam.

A people who have courageously opposed French domination for more than eighty years, a people who have fought side by side with the Allies against the Fascists during these last years, such a people must be free and independent.

For these reasons, we, members of the Provisional Government of the Democratic Republic of Vietnam, solemnly declare to the world that Vietnam has the right to be a free and independent country and in fact it already has been so. The entire Vietnamese people are determined to mobilise all their physical and mental strength, to sacrifice their lives and property in order to safeguard their independence and liberty.

3

EDWARD LANSDALE

Report on CIA Operations in Vietnam, 1954–1955

France did not cede independence to Vietnam in 1945; nor did the United States support the Viet Minh against the French. The newly declared Democratic Republic of Vietnam controlled only the north while French forces controlled the south. Ho Chi Minh and the Viet Minh forces continued their struggle against the French, finally defeating them at the battle of Dien Bien Phu in 1954. An international peace conference at Geneva called for a temporary division of northern and southern Vietnam to be followed in two years by a national election for a unified government. However, in the wake of the Chinese communist victory in China in 1949 and the American fear of its further spread in the Korean War (1950–1953), the United States increasingly saw Ho Chi Minh and the Viet Minh as part of the expansion of communism rather than a national independence movement. In 1954 President Eisenhower voiced belief in a "falling domino" theory in which the loss of Vietnam would lead to communist victories throughout Southeast Asia and beyond. Fearing that Ho Chi Minh would win 80 percent of the vote in a general Vietnamese election, Eisenhower created a separate South Vietnamese government and army in violation of the Geneva Accords, and he sent U.S. advisors and resources to make this division along the 17th parallel permanent. But one of the problems was that many pro-French Catholics lived in the north where the Viet Minh were strongest, and many Viet Minh lived and operated in the south. Thus, the creation of a southern Republic of Vietnam required large-scale population transfers as well as efforts to bolster the resources and legitimacy of an untried southern government and army.

Source: Edward Lansdale, "Report on CIA Operations in Vietnam, 1954–55," in *The Pentagon Papers*, abr. ed., ed. George C. Herring (New York: McGraw-Hill, 1993), 23–36.

In this selection, Edward Lansdale informs his CIA superiors of some of the activities of one of the teams of advisors sent by the United States to accomplish these tasks. Lansdale was a legendary early CIA operative, known for his work in defeating a similar communist and nationalist movement in the Philippines. What did Lansdale's team attempt to do in the north? What was the purpose of the first rumor campaign? How would you judge the tactics and success of the Saigon Military Mission (SMM) team in the north? What did the CIA do in the south? How successful were its efforts?

THINKING HISTORICALLY

What do you make of Lansdale's quotation marks around "cold war"? What does Lansdale's use of the word *team* suggest to you? What does Lansdale mean by "the Geneva Agreements . . . imposed restrictive rules on all official Americans"? Notice how Lansdale uses terms such as *Vietminh* and *Vietnamese*, the "government," and "security forces." How might others use these terms? What do you think of Lansdale's praise of American reporters for giving "the U.S. an objective account of events in Vietnam"? How does Lansdale describe the differences between the Viet Minh and the "Vietnamese national army"? What conclusions does he draw from the differences between those two armies? What different conclusions could one draw?

Foreword

. . . It was often a frustrating and perplexing year, up close. The Geneva Agreements signed on 21 July 1954 imposed restrictive rules upon all official Americans, including the Saigon Military Mission. An active and intelligent enemy made full use of legal rights to screen his activities in establishing his stay-behind organizations south of the 17th Parallel and in obtaining quick security north of that Parallel. The nation's economy and communications system were crippled by eight years of open war. The government, including its Army and other security forces, was in a painful transition from colonial to self rule, making it a year of hot-tempered incidents. Internal problems arose quickly to points where armed conflict was sought as the only solution. The enemy was frequently forgotten in the heavy atmosphere of suspicion, hatred and jealousy.

The Saigon Military Mission received some blows from allies and the enemy in this atmosphere, as we worked to help stabilize the government and to beat the Geneva time-table of Communist takeover in the north. However, we did beat the time-table. The government did become stabilized. The Free Vietnamese are now becoming unified and learning how to cope with the Communist enemy. We are thankful that we had a chance to help in this work in a critical area of the world, to be positive and constructive in a year of doubt. . . .

Highlights of the Year

a. Early Days

. . . Working in close cooperation with George Hellyer, USIS[1] Chief, a new psychological warfare campaign was devised for the Vietnamese Army and for the government in Hanoi. Shortly after, a refresher course in combat psywar was constructed and Vietnamese Army personnel were rushed through it. A similar course was initiated for the Ministry of Information. Rumor campaigns were added to the tactics and tried out in Hanoi. It was almost too late.

The first rumor campaign was to be a carefully planted story of a Chinese Communist regiment in Tonkin taking reprisals against a Vietminh village whose girls the Chinese had raped, recalling Chinese Nationalist troop behavior in 1945 and confirming Vietnamese fears of Chinese occupation under Vietminh rule; the story was to be planted by soldiers of the Vietnamese Armed Psywar Company in Hanoi dressed in civilian clothes. The troops received their instructions silently, dressed in civilian clothes, went on the mission, and failed to return. They had deserted to the Vietminh. . . .

Ngo Dinh Diem[2] arrived on 7 July, and within hours was in despair as the French forces withdrew from the Catholic provinces of Phat Diem and Nam Dinh in Tonkin.[3] . . . The Tonkinese had hopes of American friendship and listened to the advice given them. Governor [name illegible] died, reportedly by poison. Tonkin's government changed as despair grew. On 21 July, the Geneva Agreement was signed. Tonkin was given to the Communists. Anti-Communists turned to SMM[4] for help in establishing a resistance movement and several tentative initial arrangements were made. . . .

---

[1] United States Information Service, the overseas offices of the United States Information Agency (USIA), which was created by President Eisenhower in 1953 to project a positive image of the United States in the world. [Ed.]

[2] Ngo Dinh Diem (1901–1963), a Catholic, became a favorite of the United States while in exile. He returned to Vietnam in 1954 and became first president of South Vietnam as the French withdrew; he was deposed and killed in a coup in 1963. [Ed.]

[3] Area of northern Vietnam. French Indochina consisted of Cambodia, Laos, and three areas now making up Vietnam: Tonkin in the north, Annam in the center, and Cochinchina in what is now southernmost Vietnam. [Ed.]

[4] Saigon Military Mission, the group run by Lansdale. [Ed.]

b. August 1954

An agreement had been reached that the personnel ceiling of U.S. military personnel with MAAG[5] would be frozen at the number present in Vietnam on the date of the cease-fire, under the terms of the Geneva Agreement. In South Vietnam this deadline was to be 11 August. It meant that SMM might have only two members present, unless action were taken. General O'Daniel agreed to the addition of ten SMM men under MAAG cover, plus any others in the Defense pipeline who arrived before the deadline. A call for help went out. Ten officers in Korea, Japan, and Okinawa were selected and rushed to Vietnam.

SMM had one small MAAG house. Negotiations were started for other housing, but the new members of the team arrived before housing was ready and were crammed three and four to a hotel room for the first days. Meetings were held to assess the new members' abilities. None had had political-psychological warfare experience. Most were experienced in paramilitary and clandestine intelligence operations. Plans were made quickly, for time was running out in the north; already the Vietminh had started taking over secret control of Hanoi and other areas of Tonkin still held by French forces.

Major Conein was given responsibility for developing a paramilitary organization in the north, to be in position when the Vietminh took over. . . . [His] . . . team was moved north immediately as part of the MAAG staff working on the refugee problem. The team had headquarters in Hanoi, with a branch in Haiphong. Among cover duties, this team supervised the refugee flow for the Hanoi airlift,[6] organized by the French. One day, as a CAT C-46[7] finished loading, they saw a small child standing on the ground below the loading door. They shouted for the pilot to wait, picked the child up and shoved him onto the aircraft, which they promptly taxied out for its takeoff in the constant air shuffle. A Vietnamese man and woman ran up to the team, asking what they had done with their small boy, whom they'd brought to say goodbye to relatives. The chagrined team explained, finally talked the parents into going south to Free Vietnam, put them in the next aircraft to catch up with their son in Saigon. . . .

c. September 1954

. . . Towards the end of the month, it was learned that the largest printing establishment in the north intended to remain in Hanoi and

---

[5] Military Assistance Advisory Group: military advisors sent to Vietnam by President Truman beginning in 1950 to train a Vietnamese national army for South Vietnam. [Ed.]

[6] To fly Catholics from the northern city of Hanoi to South Vietnam. [Ed.]

[7] A plane; Civil Air Transport was established in Shanghai in 1946 as a Chinese airline and was owned and used by the CIA after 1950. The C-46 was a military transport and cargo plane made by the Curtiss-Wright Company. [Ed.]

do business with the Vietminh. An attempt was made by SMM to destroy the modern presses, but Vietminh security agents already had moved into the plant and frustrated the attempt. This operation was under a Vietnamese patriot whom we shall call Trieu; his case officer was Capt. Arundel. Earlier in the month they had engineered a black psywar strike in Hanoi: leaflets signed by the Vietminh instructing Tonkinese on how to behave for the Vietminh takeover of the Hanoi region in early October, including items about property, money reform, and a three-day holiday of workers upon takeover. The day following the distribution of these leaflets, refugee registration tripled. Two days later Vietminh currency was worth half the value prior to the leaflets. The Vietminh took to the radio to denounce the leaflets; the leaflets were so authentic in appearance that even most of the rank and file Vietminh were sure that the radio denunciations were a French trick. . . .

d. October 1954

Hanoi was evacuated on 9 October. The northern SMM team left with the last French troops, disturbed by what they had seen of the grim efficiency of the Vietminh in their takeover, the contrast between the silent march of the victorious Vietminh troops in their tennis shoes and the clanking armor of the well-equipped French whose Western tactics and equipment had failed against the Communist military-political-economic campaign.

The northern team had spent the last days of Hanoi in contaminating the oil supply of the bus company for a gradual wreckage of the engines in the buses, in taking the first actions for delayed sabotage of the railroad (which required teamwork with a CIA special technical team in Japan who performed their part brilliantly), and in writing detailed notes of potential targets for future paramilitary operations. (U.S. adherence to the Geneva Agreement prevented SMM from carrying out the active sabotage it desired to do against the power plant, water facilities, harbor, and bridge.) The team had a bad moment when contaminating the oil. They had to work quickly at night, in an enclosed storage room. Fumes from the contaminant came close to knocking them out. Dizzy and weak-kneed, they masked their faces with handkerchiefs and completed the job.

Meanwhile, Polish and Russian ships had arrived in the south to transport southern Vietminh to Tonkin under the Geneva Agreement. This offered the opportunity for another black psywar strike. A leaflet was developed by Binh with the help of Capt. Arundel, attributed to the Vietminh Resistance Committee. Among other items, it reassured the Vietminh they would be kept safe below decks from imperialist air and submarine attacks, and requested that warm clothing be brought; the warm clothing item would be coupled with a verbal rumor campaign that Vietminh were being sent into China as railroad laborers. . . .

f. December 1954

. . . Till and Peg Durdin of the N.Y. Times, Hank Lieberman of the N.Y. Times, Homer Bigart of the N.Y. Herald-Tribune, John Mecklin of Life-Time and John Roderick of Associated Press, have been warm friends of SMM and worked hard to penetrate the fabric of French propaganda and give the U.S. an objective account of events in Vietnam. The group met with us at times to analyze objectives and motives of propaganda known to them, meeting at their own request as U.S. citizens. These mature and responsible news correspondents performed a valuable service for their country. . . .

g. January 1955

The Vietminh long ago had adopted the Chinese Communist thought that the people are the water and the army is the fish. Vietminh relations with the mass of the population during the fighting had been exemplary, with a few exceptions; in contrast, the Vietnamese National Army had been like too many Asian armies, adept at cowing a population into feeding them, providing them with girls. SMM had been working on this problem from the beginning. Since the National Army was the only unit of government with a strong organization through the country and with good communications, it was the key to stabilizing the situation quickly on a nation-wide basis. If Army and people could be brought together into a team, the first strong weapon against Communism could be forged. . . .

4

TIME MAGAZINE

Nikita Khrushchev: "We Will Bury You," November 26, 1956

The first years of the Cold War pitted former World War II allies Soviet Premier Joseph Stalin and Presidents Roosevelt, Truman, and Eisenhower against each other. Stalin died in 1953, to be followed by two inconsequential leaders[1] and then longtime Communist Party leader Nikita Khrushchev, premier from 1955 to 1964. Khrushchev initiated the Soviet space and missile program, but he attempted to reduce the size of the army and strengthen the consumer sector of the

---

[1] Georgy Malenkov and Nikolai Bulganin.

Source: "We Will Bury You!" *Time*, November 26, 1956.

economy. In February 1956, Khrushchev startled party members with a speech denouncing Stalin as a brutal dictator. The speech expressed long suppressed grievances, especially in the dependent Soviet satellite states of Poland, East Germany, Romania, and Hungary.

Hungarians opposed to continued Soviet rule saw an opportunity in the new climate and took to the streets in protest in October 1956. On November 1 their leader Imre Nagy declared an independent Hungarian government and asked for UN recognition. On November 4 Soviet troops invaded Hungary, crushing the revolution by November 10. This selection is a *Time* magazine report of a routine event the following week.

On November 17 Khrushchev attended a reception at the Polish Embassy hosted by visiting Polish communist leader Wladyslaw Gomulka, who also invited representatives of Western countries. At the reception, Khrushchev compared Soviet troops in Hungary and Eastern Europe with Western troops in two areas. What are these areas? What do you think of these comparisons? What was Khrushchev's attitude toward the United States and Western capitalist countries? What was his attitude toward colonialism?

THINKING HISTORICALLY

No four words better raised the fear of a Soviet threat for Americans during the Cold War than Khrushchev's "We will bury you." Numerous American political leaders, commentators, and citizens referred to that quote in the following years to underscore Soviet aggressive intentions. With those four words, the reformist premier who de-Stalinized Kremlin policy and later traveled through the United States arguing for nuclear disarmament and peaceful coexistence could be pictured as a dangerous belligerent.

What do you think Khrushchev meant by those four words? Why do you think *Time* magazine chose them to headline the article? How else might you summarize the evening at the Polish Embassy? What would be your headline?

At the final reception for Poland's visiting Gomulka, stubby Nikita Khrushchev planted himself firmly with the Kremlin's whole hierarchy at his back, and faced the diplomats of the West, and the satellites, with an intemperate speech that betrayed as much as it threatened.

"We are Bolsheviks!" he declared pugnaciously. "We stick firmly to the Lenin precept—don't be stubborn if you see you are wrong, but don't give in if you are right." "When are you right?" interjected First Deputy Premier Mikoyan—and the crowd laughed. Nikita plunged on, turning to the Western diplomats. "About the capitalist states, it doesn't depend on you whether or not we exist. If you don't like us, don't accept our invitations, and don't invite us to come to see you. Whether you like it or not, history is on our side. We will bury you!"

Just the day before, ambassadors of twelve NATO nations had walked out on a Khrushchev tirade that lumped Britain, France and Israel as bandits. Now Khrushchev was off again.

The Kremlin men cheered. Gomulka laughed. Red-faced and gesticulating, Nikita rolled on: "The situation is favorable to us. If God existed, we would thank him for this. On Hungary—we had Hungary thrust upon us. We are very sorry that such a situation exists there, but the most important thing is that the counterrevolution must be shattered. They accuse us of interfering in Hungary's internal affairs. They find the most fearful words to accuse us. But when the British, French and Israelis cut the throats of the Egyptians,[2] that is only a police action aimed at restoring order! The Western powers are trying to denigrate Nasser,[3] although Nasser is not a Communist. Politically, he is closer to those who are waging war on him, and he has even put Communists in jail."

"He had to," offered Soviet President Kliment Voroshilov.[4] Khrushchev turned on him and said: "Don't try to help me."

"Nasser is the hero of his nation, and our sympathies are on his side. We sent sharp letters to Britain, France and Israel—well, Israel, that was just for form, because, as you know, Israel carries no weight in the world, and if it plays any role, it was just to start a fight. If Israel hadn't felt the support of Britain, France and others, the Arabs would have been able to box her ears and she would have remained at peace. I think the British and French will be wise enough to withdraw their forces, and then Egypt will emerge stronger than ever."

Turning again to the Westerners, Khrushchev declared: "You say we want war, but you have now got yourselves into a position I would call idiotic" ("Let's say delicate," offered Mikoyan) "but we don't want to profit by it. If you withdraw your troops from Germany, France and Britain—I'm speaking of American troops—we will not stay one day in Poland, Hungary and Rumania." His voice was scornful as he added: "But we, Mister Capitalists, we are beginning to understand your methods."

By this time, the diplomats—who, in turn, have come to understand Mister Khrushchev's methods—had already left the room.

---

[2] On November 5, 1956, combined British and French forces invaded Egypt in retaliation for Egyptian nationalization of the Suez Canal, while Israel occupied the Egyptian Sinai Peninsula. [Ed.]

[3] Gamal Abdel Nasser (1918–1970), nationalist leader and president of Egypt, 1956–1970. Nasser was a socialist, a leader of neutral "nonaligned nations," and sought help from the United States, Soviet Union, and China. [Ed.]

[4] Chairman of the Presidium of the Supreme Soviet, the head of state but a largely symbolic office compared to the premier or the head of the Communist Party, both of which positions Khrushchev held. [Ed.]

5

NEW YORK TIMES

"Khrushchev Tirade Again Irks Envoys," November 19, 1956

The day after the Polish reception in Moscow described in document 4, the *New York Times* published the following story. Why did the Western diplomats walk out? Notice how the *Times* account emphasizes the conflict in the Middle East more than that in Eastern Europe. Notice how the Soviets wanted to talk about the Middle East while the Westerners wanted to talk about Hungary. What accounts for these different agendas?

THINKING HISTORICALLY

Notice the different words Khrushchev and the Westerners use to describe the military action in Egypt by the British, French, and Israelis. Why do these verbal differences cause so much trouble? How would you characterize the attitude of the reporter from the *New York Times*? In what ways is this report similar to that of *Time* magazine? How is it different? What is missing from the *New York Times* account? How might you explain this omission?

Special to the New York Times

MOSCOW, Nov. 18—Envoys from nations of the North Atlantic pact and Israel walked out of a reception here for the second time in twenty-four hours, because of a speech by Nikita S. Khrushchev, Soviet Communist leader.

The reason for the walkout was remarks by the party secretary that, among other things, charged the British, French and Israelis with having "cut the throats of the Egyptians" while pretending that their attack on Egypt was a police action aimed at restoring order.

As a sign of respect for the Poles, at whose embassy the reception was being held, the Western and Israeli envoys did not leave the building, but merely moved into another room, where Mr. Khrushchev's voice was inaudible. The Soviet leader was scornful about the origin of the attack on Egypt. In his mention of the contention by the British and French that they had gone into Egypt to restore order, he said:

Source: "Khrushchev Tirade Again Irks Envoys," *New York Times*, November 19, 1956.

"What kind of order is this? It is the order of colonizers, the order of enslavement, domination of the strong over the weak."

Mr. Khrushchev apologized to Wladyslaw Gomulka, Polish Communist leader, for "making such a speech on the territory of a foreign state." The reception marked the conclusion of a new Polish-Soviet Government and party accord.

The Western powers are trying to "defame" President Gamal Abdel Nasser of Egypt, Mr. Khrushchev said, adding:

"Actually Nasser is not a Communist and politically he is closer to those waging war on him."

Nasser Is Chided

"He has even put Communists in jail," he continued, in what is nowadays unusual Soviet criticism of the Egyptian leader.

"He had to," said Marshal Kliment Y. Voroshilov, in an apparent allusion to the Soviet contention that Egypt had been dominated by the anti-Communist Western powers until recently.

"Don't try to help me," Mr. Khrushchev admonished the elderly chief of the Soviet state, and continued:

"But Nasser is fighting for national independence, he is the hero of his nation and our sympathies are on his side."

Mr. Khrushchev reserved his most scathing sallies for Israel, which "carries no weight in the world and if it plays any role it is to start a fight."

The Soviet Union protested to Israel "just for form," he said, at the time it called on Britain and France to halt the war in Egypt.

Without British-French backing, Mr. Khrushchev continued, Israel would have had her "ears boxed" by the Arabs and peace would have been preserved.

Mr. Khrushchev promised that the Soviet Union would seek a Middle East settlement because it realized the situation in Egypt was serious and "the fire must be put out."

Withdrawal Urged

He predicted Britain and France would be "wise enough" to withdraw their troops from the Suez Canal zone and Egypt would emerge stronger than ever. He ignored Moscow's threat to send "volunteers" to help the Egyptians.

Mr. Khrushchev's estimate of the outlook was considerably more conciliatory and optimistic than anything heard here in recent days.

"We must seek a rapprochement," the party leader said. "We must seek a settlement so coexistence can be peaceful and advantageous."

Admitting the seriousness of the crisis he said the Soviet leaders were "realists" and would not seek to exploit it for their own purposes. He said the new Soviet disarmament proposals attested to Moscow's desire for peace.

The Soviet press reported this morning that Egypt had not requested Chinese Communist "volunteers" because of her "belief" that the United Nations resolutions on the withdrawal of troops would be carried out.

Mistakes Conceded

MOSCOW, Nov. 18 (AP) — Mr. Khrushchev told the Western envoys at the Polish Embassy tonight:

"It you don't like us, don't accept our invitations and don't invite us to come to see you."

The Soviet Communist party chief said many mistakes had been made in building socialism in the Soviet Union because of the lack of examples and the lack of personnel.

He continued:

"If we could have the revolution over again, we would carry it out more sensibly and with smaller losses. But history does not repeat itself. The situation is favorable for us. If God existed, we would thank Him for this."

6

WELLES HANGEN

"Pravda Modifies Khrushchev Slur," November 20, 1956

The day after its article about a second walkout at the Polish Embassy because of a speech by Soviet leader Nikita S. Khrushchev (document 5), the *New York Times* published a follow-up article on the Polish reception. The ostensible rationale for another article was to examine and critique the coverage of the event in the official Soviet communist newspaper, *Pravda*. The *Times* often showed how *Pravda* misinformed its readers, especially by omission of important news. But how, according to the *Times*, did *Pravda* change the tone of

Source: Welles Hangen, "*Pravda* Modifies Khrushchev Slur," *New York Times*, November 20, 1956.

Khrushchev's remarks? Why might *Pravda* want to do that? What was
the "Khrushchev slur" that *Pravda* modified? What other reason might
the *Times* have for the follow-up piece?

THINKING HISTORICALLY

The *Times* publishes daily, *Time* magazine weekly. Reporters often discussed their stories before they were published. Notice the paragraph
below that begins: "For example." What does it suggest to you about
the evolving story described in documents 4, 5, and 6? What, if anything, did that paragraph add to the charge of distortion by *Pravda*?
What value did that paragraph have for the *Times*? If this article is an
accurate rendition of Khrushchev's remarks, what did he likely mean?
What Soviet ideological belief did Khrushchev's words affirm? What
American ideological belief did *Time* magazine affirm?

Special to the New York Times

MOSCOW, Nov. 19—The biting remarks of Nikita S. Khrushchev that
caused Western diplomats to leave a Polish reception last night were
presented to the Soviet public today as a judicious call for coexistence.

The remarks of the First Secretary of the Soviet Communist Party
were published in expurgated form by Pravda, Communist party
newspaper.

Correspondents who heard Mr. Khrushchev make scathing comments about the West last night had difficulty recognizing the Pravda
version.

For example, in commenting on coexistence last night Mr. Khrushchev
said communism did not have to resort to war to defeat capitalism.
"Whether you like it or not, history is on our side," he said. "We will
bury you."

Missing from the Pravda account was any biting sallies on the part
of Mr. Khrushchev. Attacks on Western "imperialism" made by the
party leader last night were omitted. So were criticisms by Anastas I.
Mikoyan, a First Deputy Premier; Marshal Kliment Y. Voroshilov, Soviet
chief of state, and other Soviet leaders.

On the political level the party chief's charge that British, French and
Israelis were out to "cut the throats of the Egyptians" was turned into a
simple accusation of "aggression" in the Pravda account.

The "sharp letters" that Mr. Khrushchev said Moscow had sent to
Britain, France and Israel became just "fairly candid" in Pravda's version.

Mr. Khrushchev's ridicule of Israel as a Western puppet whose only
role was to start a fight was omitted entirely. His hope that the Arabs
could have "boxed her ears" was absent.

Similarly, the party chief's remark that Gamal Abdel Nasser, President of Egypt, had imprisoned Communists and was closer to the West politically than to the Soviet Union was expunged.

The West, Pravda said, finds itself in a "very, very embarrassing situation"—this instead of the "idiotic predicament" Mr. Khrushchev described last night.

The comments published in Pravda contained nothing unusually offensive—at least by Mr. Khrushchev's standards—and might be used by Soviet propagandists in denouncing the envoys' departure. The new version also spares President Nasser's feelings and Arab sympathies for the Soviet Union at a time when Moscow wishes to pose as the Arabs' best friend.

Even when Mr. Khrushchev spoke about relations among the Communists, all of whom are presumably accustomed to blunt talk, Pravda's editors found it necessary to recast his comments. For example, Mr. Khrushchev's apparently inadvertent reference to the "Yugoslavian" brand of communism was deleted to conform with sharp criticism of Marshal Tito, Yugoslav President, appearing on another page of Pravda.

7

Soviet Telegram on Cuba,
September 7, 1962

On January 1, 1959, Cuban revolutionaries under Fidel Castro overthrew the government of U.S.-backed dictator Fulgencio Batista. The Castro government increasingly faced opposition from the United States and relied on the support of the Soviet Union. U.S. efforts to depose Castro included a failed CIA-sponsored invasion by Cuban exiles at the Cuban Bay of Pigs, April 17–19, 1961, three months after John F. Kennedy came into office. Expecting further U.S. attempts at toppling the regime, the Castro government received from the Soviet Union midrange nuclear missiles. President Kennedy learned of their existence on October 14, 1962. He demanded they be withdrawn and ordered a naval blockade of

---

Source: Telegram of Soviet Ambassador to Cuba A. I. Alekseev to the USSR Ministry of Foreign Affairs (MFA), 7 September 1962 at Woodrow Wilson International Center for Scholars, Cold War International History Project, Virtual Archive: http://www.wilsoncenter. org/index.cfm?topic_id=1409&fuseaction=va2.document&identifier=5034DA8F-96B6-175C-97D258B27DC3A0E6&sort=Collection&item=Cuban%20Missile%20Crisis. [Source: Archive of Foreign Policy of the Russian Federation (AVP RF), Moscow, copy courtesy of National Security Archive (NSA), Washington, DC; translation by Mark H. Doctoroff.]

Cuban ports. The confrontation, known as the Cuban Missile Crisis, October 18–29, came dangerously close to erupting into a nuclear war. The crisis ended with Khrushchev withdrawing the missiles and the United States pledging not to invade Cuba and to withdraw American missiles from Turkey.

This document reveals Cuban and Soviet attitudes shortly after the Cuban receipt of the missiles but a month before the crisis. The document is a telegram, dated September 7, 1962, from the Soviet ambassador in Cuba to the Soviet Foreign Ministry in Moscow. In it he informs Moscow about recent events on the island. What seems to be happening? What conclusions does the Soviet ambassador draw? What does the ambassador want the Soviet government to do? How well informed does the ambassador seem to be about events in Cuba, the United States, and Latin America? Do you think President Kennedy would have been less alarmed if he had read this telegram?

THINKING HISTORICALLY

How are the words that the Soviet ambassador uses to describe the situation in Cuba different from the way Americans would understand it? How significant were the Soviet missiles for the ambassador? Why are the charges of aggressive activity by the United States against Cuba more believable in this document than they would be in a magazine article or a public speech?

Recently, the ruling circles of the USA have noticeably activated a policy of provocation against Cuba;[1] military preparations and its political isolation. Nearly every day, the air space and territorial waters of Cuba are violated by American airplanes, submarines and ships trying to establish permanent control over the territory of Cuba and diverting passenger and transport ships bound for Cuba. The landing of counter-revolutionary bands of spies and arms has been increased.

The constant acts of provocation are carried out from the territory of the USA base at Guantanamo, most often in the form of shooting at Cuban patrols. Especially noteworthy among all these provocations are far reaching acts like the August 24 shelling of the hotel in which mainly live Soviet specialists, and also the lies published by the Kennedy Administration about the alleged August 30 attack, in international

---

[1] In November 1961, President Kennedy initiated Operation Mongoose, a secret plan to stimulate a rebellion in Cuba, bring Cuban exiles into the U.S. army for training, undermine the regime, and assassinate Castro. General Edward Lansdale was put in charge of operations. The program was stepped up in the spring of 1962. The CIA also continued to support internal resistance to Castro and engaged the assistance of organized crime figures who had interests in Cuba to assassinate Castro. [Ed.]

waters, on an American airplane from two small Cuban ships. In the USA government's announcement, it is noted that in the event of a repeat of "an incident of this type," the armed forces of the United States "will take all necessary retaliatory measures." It is entirely evident that this carries a great danger for Cuba, since it gives the most reactionary anti-Cuban authorities in the USA an opening at any moment to organize a provocation and unleash aggressive actions against Cuba.

In regard to the above two last actions undertaken by the USA, the government of Cuba came forward with corresponding official declarations signed by Fidel Castro. Both of these declarations were circulated as official documents to the UN. The goal of these declarations is to attract the attention of the appropriate international organizations and all of world public opinion to the provocative and far-reaching acts of the USA, to unmask the aggressive schemes of the United States in relation to Cuba, and to ward them off. In these declarations the government of Cuba precisely makes the point that the anti-Cuban actions and schemes of the USA present a threat not only to Cuba, but to the whole world.

The series of provocations is now accompanied by a whipped up, broad anti-Cuba campaign in the USA press, striving with all its might to convince the population of the United States of the alleged presence in Cuba of large contingents of Soviet troops and of the fact that Cuba has turned into a military base of "world Communism" which presents a grave threat to the USA and all Latin American countries. Under this pretext, the press, certain American senators and other public figures demand of the Kennedy administration the revival of the Monroe Doctrine,[2] establishment of a sea and air blockade of Cuba, the bringing into force of the Treaty of Rio de Janeiro,[3] and the military occupation of Cuba.

Following the signing in Moscow of the Soviet-Cuban communiqué in which the agreement of the Soviet government to provide assistance in strengthening its armed forces is noted, Kennedy in a public statement on September 4 pointed to the defensive nature of Cuba's military preparations and noted that Soviet military specialists are in Cuba to teach the Cubans how to use defensive equipment presented by the Soviet Union. Several USA press agencies, commenting on that part of Kennedy's statement, underline the evidence of the fact that the president of the USA obviously preferred an attempt to calm down those circles in the USA which are supporting quick, decisive actions against Cuba. Along with this, in Kennedy's statement there are contained insinuations of purported aggressive Cuban schemes regarding influence on the American continent and a threat to use "all necessary means" to "defend" the continent.

[2] The Monroe Doctrine (1823) warned European nations that any efforts by them to interfere in affairs of the Americas would be viewed as aggression requiring U.S. intervention. [Ed.]

[3] The Inter-American Treaty of Reciprocal Assistance (1947) held that any attack on one nation of the Americas would be viewed as an attack on them all. [Ed.]

According to certain information, the USA State Department through its ambassadors notified the governments of Latin American countries that they can expect changes in the situation in the Caribbean basin "if Castro's government does not come to its senses." More probably, in the near future the USA, using the pretext of an allegedly growing threat to the Western hemisphere, will embark on a long process of increasing the pressure on governments of the Latin-American countries and will probably convene a meeting of foreign ministers of the member-countries of the OAS[4] to work out supplementary sanctions against Cuba. One can also assume that the most wildly aggressive powers in the USA (the Pentagon, the Cuban external counter-revolution,[5] and others) will continue to exert pressure on Kennedy in order to realize the most decisive actions against Cuba.

The campaign of anti-Cuban hysteria has been conveyed via American propaganda to Latin American countries too. There the publication of articles and transmissions of radio programs of anti-Cuban and anti-Soviet content is constantly encouraged, while the external Cuban counter-revolution and local reaction put constant pressure on the governments of those countries, conduct loud demonstrations and terrorize individuals and organizations which speak out in defense of the Cuban revolution, and by means of bribery and blackmail get a range of people who have visited Cuba to make anti-Cuban statements, and so forth.

Simultaneously, the USA continues actively to conduct purely military preparations,[6] aimed at repressing possible centers of the national-liberation movement in Latin America, and, given the appropriate circumstances, the Cuban revolution itself. This is shown by such facts as the organization by the United States of schools for instruction in methods of street-fighting and anti-partisan struggle in many Latin American countries (in Panama, Peru, Colombia, Equador, Bolivia, and others); continuing intensive instruction of Cuban counter-revolutionaries in camps located on the territory of the USA, in Puerto Rico and in several Central American countries; many inspection trips to these bases, schools, and camps by responsible American military officials and the heads of the Cuban counter-revolution, including Miro Cardona;[7]

[4] Organization of American States. A State Department memo dated May 17, 1962, lists Operation Mongoose "Task 1" as "obtain some special and significant action within the OAS organization against the Castro-Communist regime." For this and following U.S. security memos, see http://www.globalsecurity.org/intell/library/reports. [Ed.]

[5] "External counter-revolution" refers to Cuban exiles in the United States and elsewhere, including veterans of the Bay of Pigs, who were still organized to topple Castro. [Ed.]

[6] Whether President Kennedy was willing to mount another military operation is uncertain, but active preparations were made to train exiles, prepare a blockade, and consider all options, including military. [Ed.]

[7] Jose Miro Cardona (1902–1974): briefly prime minister of Cuba in 1959; went into exile and led anti-Castro Cubans in the United States. Was to be president if Bay of Pigs invasion succeeded. [Ed.]

unflagging efforts of the USA aimed at strengthening the unity of the external Cuban counter-revolution and unity in the action of counter-revolutionary organizations active in Cuba itself, etc.

At the same time, the USA is actively continuing to conduct its efforts towards the political isolation of Cuba, particularly in Latin America. The USA is concentrating on putting pressure on the governments of Mexico and Brazil,[8] which continue to express their support for the principle of non-interference and self-determination of peoples. This pressure is applied through economic means, and also by exploiting the domestic reaction. The realization of Kennedy's visit to Mexico, following which he was to have quickly visited Brazil too (this visit was put off to the last months of the year), served the goals of determining the likelihood of attracting these two countries to the anti-Cuban plans of the USA.

Until now none of the attempts of the USA to attract Brazil and Mexico to its anti-Cuban adventures has had any success.

Under pressure from the USA, in a majority of Latin American countries the local authorities are applying the harshest measures aimed at forbidding or tightly limiting visits of any groups or individuals to Cuba, and also their contacts with Cuban delegations in third countries. People who visit Cuba or make contact with Cuban delegations in third countries are subject to arrest, repression, investigations upon return to their homeland. The USA does not lack means for organizing broad and loud provocations against Cuban delegations taking part in international quorums, as took place recently in Finland[9] and Jamaica.

Referring to the decision taken at the meeting at Punta-del-Este about the exclusion of Cuba from the OAS, the USA is undertaking all measures to deny Cuba participation in any organizations connected with the inter-American system. In particular, they recently undertook an attempt to secure the exclusion of Cuba from the Pan American Health Organization (PAHO). The unlawful denial of Cuba's application to join the so-called Latin American Free Trade Association is another example.[10] In response to the American policy towards Cuba of provocation, military threats, and political isolation, the Cuban government is intensifying its efforts on strengthening its own armed forces, struggling with the internal counter-revolution, unmasking before world public opinion the aggressive designs of the USA, and broadening its anti-American propaganda in

[8] Mexico and Brazil were thought particularly important propaganda targets by the United States. [Ed.]

[9] U.S. State Department memo, June 27, 1962: "it is important to work with the forthcoming youth festival in Helsinki (where there will be 2,000 Latin American students) to take the festival away from the Communists and ensure a good amount of anti-Communist propaganda emanating from this support." [Ed.]

[10] Memo from Lansdale on Operation Mongoose, July 5, 1962: "State reports that diplomatic efforts are being made to block Cuba's application for accreditation to the European Economic Community. Similarly, efforts are being made to exclude Cuba from the proposed Latin American Free Trade area." [Ed.]

Latin America. At the end of August, taking into account the activization of provocative actions by the USA and the possible increase in the unleashing of counter-revolutionary bands and manifestations of domestic counter-revolution, preventive arrests were carried out in the country and strengthened control was established over many registered [known] counter-revolutionary elements and the places where they gather.

The Cuban leaders are paying serious attention to the question of strengthening the devotion to the revolution of the cadres of its diplomatic missions, particularly in Latin American countries; they are taking every opportunity, as was the case with their presentation at the Latin American Free Trade Association, to widen the sphere of their activity in Latin America; they are strengthening their connections with the Latin American peoples by inviting to Cuba society delegations and individual Latin American officials; in timely fashion and aggressively, they speak at international organizations, unmasking the aggressive schemes and actions of the USA; they are striving to take part in any international forums at which there is a possibility to expose the aggressive character of American imperialism; they are strengthening Cuba's ties with African and Asian countries, etc.

The Cuban leadership believes, however, that the main guarantee of the development of the Cuban Revolution under conditions of possible direct American aggression is the readiness of the Soviet government to provide military assistance to Cuba and simultaneously to warn the USA of that fact. From this position, the joint Soviet-Cuban communiqué about [Ernesto "Che"] Guevara's visit to Moscow was greeted by the Cuban leaders and the vast majority of the Cuban people with great enthusiasm and gratitude. The Cuban leadership and Fidel Castro himself suggest that these warnings will help to prevail against those forces in the USA that are warning of the outbreak now of a world conflict, and are staving off a direct American attack on Cuba in the near future.

In our opinion, in the near future the ruling circles of the USA will continue to expand the attacks on Cuba by all the above-mentioned means: provocations, the propaganda campaign, military preparations, and actions of the domestic counter-revolution, political isolation, and so forth. Their success in drawing the Latin American countries into their aggressive actions will most depend on the positions of the governments of Mexico and Brazil.

We also suggest that the question of direct American actions against Cuba will be decided by the correlation of forces in American ruling circles which have differing approaches to questions of war and peace in the present period, and the struggle between them on these issues.

The mood of the overwhelming majority of the Cuban people is defiant, and regardless of the reality of the threat of intervention, no panic or fear before the threat which is hanging over Cuba is observed in the masses of the people. The American provocations make possible an ever-tighter unity of the Cuban workers and raise the political consciousness of the masses.

Regarding the provocations, the influence of the Soviet Union in Cuba has grown as never before, and our cooperation with the Cuban leaders has been strengthened even more.

In the interest of future productive work with our Cuban friends it would be desirable to receive from you for dispatch to the Cuban leaders information which we have about the plans of the USA government toward Cuba.

8

U.S. Government Meeting Transcript and Telegram on Military Coup in Argentina, 1976

On March 24, 1976, a right-wing military coup d'état led by General Jorge Videla overthrew the government of President Isabel Perón of Argentina. Even before the coup, right-wing generals in the Argentine military had secretly joined forces with other extreme anti-leftists in Uruguay, Bolivia, Brazil, Peru, and Chile in "Operation Condor." Named after the national bird of Chile, Operation Condor was run by the Chilean dictator Augusto Pinochet, who in 1973 had led a military coup against the government of Salvatore Allende, the first legally elected socialist president in South America. Condor enabled Pinochet to seek out, abduct, torture, and kill those Chilean socialists and their allies who were able to escape Chile in the aftermath of his coup and bloody repression. Generals and right-wing politicians in other "Southern Cone" countries of South America, especially in Argentina and Uruguay, participated in the alliance in order to get rid of leftists in their own countries. These countries, internally divided by huge economic disparities, had given birth to various socialist, communist, and guerilla movements, including the Tupamaros of Uruguay and the ERP (People's Revolutionary Army) in Argentina. The communist ERP launched a guerilla campaign in 1969 against a previous military dictatorship, continuing their attacks on the military and carrying out bank robberies and kidnappings of the wealthy, including foreign business executives well into the 1970s.

In the "Dirty War" of state terrorism that followed, the police and military targeted not only communists but students, pacifists,

---

Source: Documents posted at The National Security Archive, The George Washington University. http://www.gwu.edu/~nsarchiv/NSAEBB/NSAEBB185/index.htm

academics, critics, and everyone on the left who they believed supported the web of terrorism. In October 1975 the coup-leader General Jorge Videla promised that "in order to guarantee the security of the state all the necessary people will die," defining "subversives" as "anyone who opposed the Argentine way of life."[1] Estimates of the dead and "disappeared" from 1975 to 1978 vary between 22,000 and 30,000.

Based on these two documents from March 1976, what seems to be the attitude of the United States toward the coup and the military government? What appeared to be the concerns and interests of the United States? Would you call the United States involved or detached? Does it appear that the United States was globalizing the Cold War or that the Argentine right wing was using the United States to accomplish its own objectives?

THINKING HISTORICALLY

The Dirty War of "disappearing" Argentines had already begun before the coup. To some degree, the coup occurred because Isabel Perón was not sufficiently compliant with military requests to ratchet up the violent response to the ERP. At the State Department Staff Meeting, what concerns does the prospect of greater violent repression raise? How thoroughly do Secretary of State Henry Kissinger and the twenty men at the meeting discuss this? How do they decide to deal with that prospect?

In the telegram from U.S. Ambassador to Argentina Robert C. Hill, the subject line reads: "Videla's Moderate Line Prevails." What does Ambassador Hill mean by that, and how do the contents of the telegram support that judgment? What, according to Hill, are the two sides that Videla was moderating? What signs do you see of Hill's support for the military coup? What words, phrases, or passages in the telegram strike you as euphemisms that downplay the military violence? What examples of ideological language can you find in this and the previous document?

Secret Staff Meeting Transcript, Secretary of State Henry Kissinger, Chairman, March 26, 1976

SECRETARY KISSINGER Bill?

MR. ROGERS The chief negotiator in Panama has resigned. It looks as though for personal reasons he's going to be succeeded, in all probability, by Guerra, who's a former Foreign Minister.

---

[1] John Simpson and Jana Bennett, *The Disappeared and the Mothers of the Plaza* (New York: St. Martin's, 1985), 75–76.

SECRETARY KISSINGER   I don't think Tack[2] is such a great loss, is he?

MR. ROGERS   No, sir. It wouldn't seem that way — even in Panama.

In Argentina, although the junta[3] has had some pretty good success, we're trying to make whatever estimates we can about what's going to happen. We've asked both the Mission and Washington to do their own visualizations — to compare them. But I think the preliminary estimate has got to be that it's going to go downhill. This junta is testing the basic proposition that Argentina is not governable, so they're going to succeed where everybody else has failed. I think that's a distinctly odds-on choice.

I think we're going to look for a considerable effort to involve the United States — particularly in the financial field. I think we're going to see a good deal —

SECRETARY KISSINGER   Yes, but that's in our interest.

MR. ROGERS   If there's a chance of it succeeding and if they're not asking us to put too much up on the table. What we're going to try to do, when and if they come up with such a plan, is what we were prepared to do about six months ago. We had worked out as intermediaries a sensible program for international assistance, using the private banks and monetary institutions.

Whether we can pull that off again, I don't know; but I think we're going to hear from them very early on in terms of financial programs.

I think also we've got to expect a fair amount of repression, probably a good deal of blood, in Argentina before too long. I think they're going to have to come down very hard not only on the terrorists but on the dissidents of trade unions and their parties.

SECRETARY KISSINGER   But —

MR. ROGERS   The point I'm making is that although they have good press today, the basic line of all the interference was they had to do it because she[4] couldn't run the country. So I think the point is that we ought not at this moment to rush out and embrace this new regime — that three–six months later will be considerably less popular with the press.

SECRETARY KISSINGER   But we shouldn't do the opposite either.

MR. ROGERS   Oh, no; obviously not.

MR. McCLOSKEY   What do we say about recognition?

---

[2] Panamanian foreign minister Juan Antonio Tack; in 1974 he negotiated an agreement with Secretary of State Henry Kissinger on eight principles to serve as a guide for a new treaty on the Panama Canal to eliminate increasing conflict between Panamanian nationalists and the United States. [Ed.]

[3] Government of military officers who seized power in a coup. [Ed.]

[4] President Isabel Perón of Argentina. [Ed.]

MR. ROGERS Well, we're going to recognize this morning a formal note in response to their request for recognition—as have virtually all the other countries of Latin America. But beyond that, Hill will keep his mouth shut.

SECRETARY KISSINGER Yes, but what does that mean concretely? Whatever chance they have, they will need a little encouragement from us. What is he telling them?

MR. ROGERS What? Oh, nothing. He has not been talking with them yet. He has not been invited to talk with them. He's ready to go in and talk with them when and if they request a meeting. But the Generals who are now presently occupying the Ministerial positions are there very temporarily—probably for the week—until the junta can make its final decisions as to whom they're going to appoint. They will make decisions on who they will appoint within a week. We think we know who's the Foreign Minister—which is the key appointment.

SECRETARY KISSINGER Who?

MR. ROGERS Probably a fellow named Vanek, who we have worked with in the past. And if he is appointed, then I think we're in a position to work with him.

SECRETARY KISSINGER But can I see some instructions on what you're going to tell Hill if somebody should come in—

MR. ROGERS Yes.

SECRETARY KISSINGER —because I do want to encourage them. I don't want to give the sense that they're harassed by the United States.

MR. ROGERS No. What I was basically concerned about in the first instance was the public posture.

SECRETARY KISSINGER I agree with that. . . .

Telegram from U.S Ambassador to Argentina, Robert C. Hill, to Secretary of State Henry Kissinger, March 30, 1976

1. *Summary*: It is too early to make any firm predictions concerning final success of the experiment in govt undertaken by the Armed Forces on Mar 24. Even so, with Videla now named Pres and his new cabinet now named, it is perhaps a convenient moment to report several short-term conclusions: a) Videla is at least for the time being in a strong enough position to keep the hardliners in check and impose a moderate approach; b) *The terrorists are likely to keep a relatively low profile for the next few weeks*, especially in view of the fact that the Armed Forces have launched a massive drive against them; c) The new govt has not yet presented its full economic program, but the approach evidenced so far is encouragingly pragmatic and deliberate, and d) Once the govt begins

to impose an austerity program, labor reaction may stiffen, but so far it has been almost nonexistent; indeed, absenteeism reportedly ceased to be a problem almost the day after the coup. The USG[5] of course should not become overly identified with the Junta, but so long as the new govt can hew to a moderate line the USG should encourage it by examining sympathetically any requests for assistance. *End Summary.*

2. The *coup d'etat* which culminated during the early hours of Mar 24 can now definitely be judged as moderate in character. In their first statements the three members of the Junta indicated they had taken power only to save the country and that their takeover was not directed at any group or sector. They did not attack the memory of Gen Peron, nor did they say anything derogatory about Peronism or any other party. They have arrested some high officials such as Raul Lastiri, Julio Gonzalez and Gov Carlos Menem who are believed to be guilty of malfeasance or abuse of power and they have rounded up a good number of suspected terrorists. But it is now clear that there have been no massive arrests. No one has been put against a wall and no one has been pulled in simply because they happened to be a Peronist or because they served in the last govt. Most congressmen, governors and other deposed officials have simply been told to go home. Mrs. Peron herself is in custody but clearly the Junta does not intend to make a martyr of her. If there is an investigation of her questionable activities, it will probably be a fair one, and if she is convicted, her sentence is likely to be nothing more than exile. Indeed, many in the military would like to put her on a plane to Madrid even without an investigation.

3. Several extreme left-wing parties, mostly Trotskyite and Maoist in orientation, have been banned, but the charters of other parties, including the orthodox Communist Party (PCA), remain in force. Political activity is suspended temporarily and the various parties have had to remove signs and slogans from their headquarters. Their organizations are intact, however, and several of the Embassy's sources within the parties have expressed hope that limited political activity may resume within six months or so.

4. Prior to the coup, there had been fears that hardline commanders in the field might exceed their orders and arbitrarily shoot or arrest any labor leader, Peronist or leftist they did not like. As indicated above, however, this did not happen. Videla and his moderate colleagues kept the hawks[6] in line. Further, the smoothness with which the coup was carried out and the way in which it was accepted by the people did much to enhance Videla's image. Probably at least for the next several months, therefore, his position relative to that of the hardliners will be overpowering. It is most unlikely that any of them would try to move against him. If they did, they would lose. Thus, for now, Videla's moderate policies seem safe.

---

[5] United States Government. [Ed.]
[6] Those favoring more violent repression of labor and leftists. [Ed.]

5. If fending off the hawks was Videla's first concern, coming to grips with the terrorists was his second. Indeed, in order of importance the second outranks the first, but the new govt needed a firm political base in order effectively to confront the terrorists and thus its first thought had to be for institutional unity. With that now assured, at least for the time being, the Armed Forces have launched a nationwide effort against the terrorists. Many suspected terrorists have been rounded up. Widespread searches are being conducted and shifting roadblocks have resulted in the capture of several guerrillas in Cordoba and elsewhere.

6. For their part, the guerrillas are likely to continue some hit-and-run operations such as *today's assassination* of a *Police Commissioner*, but they will probably keep a fairly low profile for the next few weeks. Tactically, they will probably want to get the lay of the land and wait for the military to drop its guard. Strategically, they probably hope popular opinion will begin to swing against the military govt within a few weeks. That would be the time to move. They may have some recalculating to do, however, for so far the military have not behaved in the repressive way the terrorists seem to have expected. If Videla can hold to his moderate course, the guerrillas may be surprised to find several weeks from now that the govt continues to enjoy popular support.

7. Equally as pressing as the terrorist problem is that of the economy. The govt has not yet had a chance to present its plan, but the economic team is now in place and looks impressive. The contacts the Embassy has had so far with Econ Min Martinez de Hoz and some of his assistants indicate they have a firm grasp of the problems and hopefully will have a practical approach to their solution. Detailed analysis of economic program will follow ASAP.

8. As encouraging as the new govt's own performance so far has been public reaction to it. Most Argentines were glad to be rid of Mrs. Peron's pathetically incompetent govt. But they did not rush into the streets to cheer the Armed Forces or jeer the Peronists. They approve of what the Armed Forces have done, but they have some healthy reservations. They have seen military govts start off well before, only to fail further down the road. They hope this one will be different and at this point are willing to give it their support. But no one seems to expect miracles, and that is one of the most mature phenomenon about this coup.

9. Even Labor so far is quiescent. Absenteeism, for example, disappeared as a major problem on Mar 25. Many labor leaders have made their peace with the military and are willing to cooperate. For its part, the Junta has handled Labor intelligently and with prudence. Some of the more corrupt labor leaders have been arrested, but most leaders have been left alone. The CGT[7] is intervened but most unions within it are functioning more or less normally. The crunch, however, has not yet

---

[7] General Confederation of Labor; includes most unions and workers. [Ed.]

come and will not until the govt introduces its econ program and begins to impose austerity measures.

10. *US Position.* This was probably the best executed and most civilized coup in Argentine history. It was unique in other ways too. The US has not been accused of being behind it, except by *Nuestra Palabra,*[8] the organ of the PCA. The Embassy hopes to keep it that way. Clearly, we should not become overly identified with the Junta. That would not be good for them or for us. Nonetheless, Argentina's best interests, and ours, lie in the success of the moderate govt now led by Gen Videla. He has a chance of pulling Argentina together again, stopping terrorism and getting the economy going. His govt, moreover, has promised to solve quickly our various investment problems (Exxon, Chase Manhattan, Standard Electric, etc.) and to bring about a better climate in general for foreign investment. Should Videla's govt fail, that might on the one hand open the door to the hardliners, who would return Argentina to the polarization of the past and who, being more nationalistically inclined than the moderates, would not take as favorable an attitude toward the US and US investments. On the other side, Videla's failure could also bring about conditions under which the extreme left might have an opportunity to make a bid for power, which would clearly run contrary to all our interests.

11. Thus, while we should move discreetly and keep our distance, we should also, so long as the Videla govt sticks to a moderate course, look sympathetically on any requests for assistance it may direct to us.

[8] Argentine Communist Party periodical. [Ed.]

9

Telephone Transcript: Soviet Premier and Afghan Prime Minister, 1979

The Soviet war in Afghanistan (1979–1989), which eventually contributed to the dissolution of the Soviet Union itself, began, like the American war in Vietnam, with seemingly small steps on behalf of a client who lacked widespread support. This document reveals one of the first of those steps. The Soviet client was Nur Mohammed Taraki, a leader of the communist movement in Afghanistan who came to the Afghan presidency as a result of a military coup in April 1978.

Source: Transcript of telephone conversation between Soviet premier Alexei Kosygin and Afghan prime minister Nur Mohammed Taraki, March 18, 1979. Cold War International History Project Bulletin, Issues 8–9, Winter 1996/1997, 145–46. Available at http://wilsoncenter.org/topics/pubs/ACF193.pdf.

His ambitious program of radical social reform alienated tribal and religious leaders. After only a year of an Afghan communist experiment, he was seeking aid from Moscow—an effort captured in this document. It is a transcript of a telephone conversation between the Soviet premier Alexei Kosygin and the Afghan prime minister Nur Mohammed Taraki on March 18, 1979, about six months before the Soviets sent troops into Afghanistan. Alexei Kosygin succeeded Khrushchev as Soviet premier, serving from 1964 to 1980.

It was common in the Cold War period to speak of clients of the big powers, like Taraki, as "puppets," but historians have since recognized that such collaborators had considerable power. What are the different powers that Kosygin and Taraki exert in this conversation? How are their differences expressed and resolved?

THINKING HISTORICALLY

Notice that Kosygin uses different words than Taraki to describe the Afghan people. What are these differences, and how do you explain them? How did Soviet ideology hinder Soviet policy?

KOSYGIN   Ask Comrade Taraki, perhaps he will outline the situation in Afghanistan.

TARAKI   The situation is bad and getting worse.

KOSYGIN   Do you have support among the workers, city dwellers, the petty bourgoisie, and the white collar workers in Herat? Is there still anyone on your side?

TARAKI   There is no active support on the part of the population. It is almost wholly under the influence of Shiite slogans—follow not the heathens, but follow us. The propaganda is underpinned by this.

KOSYGIN   Are there many workers there?

TARAKI   Very few—between 1,000 and 2,000 people in all.

KOSYGIN   What are the prospects?

TARAKI   We are convinced that the enemy will form new units and will develop an offensive.

KOSYGIN   Do you not have the forces to rout them?

TARAKI   I wish it were the case.

KOSYGIN   What, then, are your proposals on this issue?

TARAKI   We ask that you extend practical and technical assistance, involving people and arms.

KOSYGIN   It is a very complex matter.

TARAKI   Iran and Pakistan are working against us, accordingly to the same plan. Hence, if you now launch a decisive attack on Herat, it will be possible to save the revolution.

KOSYGIN   The whole world will immediately get to know this. The rebels have portable radio transmitters and will report it directly.

TARAKI   I ask that you extend assistance.

KOSYGIN   We must hold consultations on this issue. Do you not have connections with Iran's progressives? Can't you tell them that it is currently the United States that is your and their chief enemy? The Iranians are very hostile toward the United States and evidently this can be put to use as propaganda. What foreign policy activities or statements would you like to see coming from us? Do you have any ideas on this question, propaganda-wise?

TARAKI   Propaganda help must be combined with practical assistance. I suggest that you place Afghan markings on your tanks and aircraft and no one will be any the wiser. Your troops could advance from the direction of Kushka and from the direction of Kabul. In our view, no one will be any the wiser. They will think these are Government troops.

KOSYGIN   I do not want to disappoint you, but it will not be possible to conceal this. Two hours later the whole world will know about this. Everyone will begin to shout that the Soviet Union's intervention in Afghanistan has begun. If we quickly airlift tanks, the necessary ammunition and make mortars available to you, will you find specialists who can use these weapons?

TARAKI   I am unable to answer this question. The Soviet advisers can answer that.

KOSYGIN   Hundreds of Afghan officers were trained in the Soviet Union. Where are they all now?

TARAKI   Most of them are Moslem reactionaries. We are unable to rely on them, we have no confidence in them.

KOSYGIN   Can't you recruit a further 50,000 soldiers if we quickly airlift arms to you? How many people can you recruit?

TARAKI   The core can only be formed by older secondary school pupils, students, and a few workers. The working class in Afghanistan is very small, but it is a long affair to train them. But we will take any measures, if necessary.

KOSYGIN   We have decided to quickly deliver military equipment and property to you and to repair helicopters and aircraft. All this is for free. We have also decided to deliver to you 100,000 tons of grain and to raise gas prices from $21 per cubic meter to $37.

TARAKI   That is very good, but let us talk of Herat. Why can't the Soviet Union send Uzbeks, Tajiks, and Turkmens in civilian clothing? No one will recognize them. We want you to send them. They could drive tanks, because we have all these nationalities in Afghanistan. Let them don Afghan costume and wear Afghan badges and no one will recognize them. It is very easy work, in our view. If Iran's and Pakistan's experience is anything to go by, it is clear that it is easy to do this work, they have already shown how it can be done.

KOSYGIN   You are, of course, oversimplifying the issue. It is a complex political and international issue, but, irrespective of this, we will hold consultations again and will get back to you.

TARAKI   Send us infantry fighting vehicles by air.

KOSYGIN   Do you have anyone to drive them?

TARAKI   We will find drivers for between 30 and 35 vehicles.

KOSYGIN   Are they reliable? Won't they flee to the enemy, together with their vehicles? After all, our drivers do not speak the language.

TARAKI   Send vehicles together with drivers who speak our language—Tajiks and Uzbeks.

KOSYGIN   I expected this kind of reply from you. We are comrades and are waging a common struggle and that is why we should not stand on ceremony with each other. Everything must be subordinate to this.

■ REFLECTIONS

The Cold War used to be ancient history. It ended at such breathtaking speed and with such pronounced results that few imagined tomorrow would have anything to do with yesterday. The Soviet Union collapsed in 1991, like the Berlin Wall in 1989, into an irretrievable heap of rubble. Commissars became capitalists, the USSR awoke as Russia, Leningrad turned back into St. Petersburg, and the red flag with hammer and sickle was exchanged for a French-like tricouleur of red, white, and blue stripes. Shoppers replaced placeholders as waiting lines disappeared; shelves of pricey foreign delicacies appeared fully stocked.

Whole countries cracked off along the periphery of what had been a great empire. Baltic city-states breathed their own air and minted their own money. Newly independent Central Asian countries built mosques and elected new dictators. These non-Soviet "stans" sent Russians back to Russia, from which they emigrated by the millions to Toledo and Tel Aviv. Some of those who stayed turned nationalized industries into personal possessions. Others lost their jobs, their savings, their homes, and half their life expectancies. New classes emerged—the "Russian mafia" from the KGB, the plutocrats from the bureaucrats—except they were often the same people in better clothes.

So too the view from America. Reagan's "Evil Empire" of 1983 became a partner in peace. In 1990 Mikhail Gorbachev received the Nobel Prize for ending the Cold War. *Time* magazine—the same magazine that brought America the Cold War—named Gorbachev "Man of the Year." Ex-president Nixon—the same Nixon who had made a career of anticommunism, coming into national prominence in a "kitchen debate" with Khrushchev in 1959—said Gorbachev should have been "Man of the Decade." Times had changed.

But the New World Order of nuclear disarmament, shrunken military budgets, and global cooperation that Gorbachev and Reagan envisioned never quite arrived. A CIA director became president of the United States, shortly followed by his son, and a KGB secret policeman from the old USSR became president of the new Russia. George W. Bush, the son, said he looked into the eyes of Vladimir Putin, the KGB man, and saw his soul. Putin saw a partner. That was in June 2001. In the following years, the United States became more militarized and chose to show it could fight two major wars (in Iraq and Afghanistan) at the same time, while Putin, as president and prime minister, closed down the budding democracy of Russia faster than one could say Ivan the Terrible.

From the vantage point of 2012, the Cold War has certainly not returned. But its history has become more current. Russia and the United States are more often at variance in choosing friends and at odds over global issues than they were in the halcyon 1990s. The United States has lessons to learn from the old Soviet Union's misadventures in Afghanistan. And if Russia is a shadow of its Soviet self, China has become a giant. The give and take of superpowers may not be far ahead. One hopes the lessons will not lag too far behind.

27

New Democracy Movements

The World, 1977 to the Present

■ HISTORICAL CONTEXT

One of the most striking developments in world history has been the recent rise in the number of democracies and the increasing consensus that democracy is desirable and achievable. Before 1945, democracy was limited to a few Western countries, many of which ruled colonial empires like despots. The end of World War II brought an end to those colonial empires. But the newly created independent states of Asia and Africa did not always opt for democracy. India, which became independent in 1947, did create what is still called today "the world's largest democracy," but elsewhere many newly independent regimes established single-party dictatorships to replace colonial rule.

In some ways the Cold War made things worse. The United States and the Soviet Union demanded loyalty above all from their client states. For the Soviet Union that meant the domination of puppet Communist Parties in Eastern Europe. For the United States, the desired loyalty was to vigorous anticommunism at home and abroad. Dictators delivered better than democrats, who were often too sympathetic to popular forces, communists and socialists included. Consequently the Cold War superpowers extinguished budding national democracies and democratic movements. At least for the duration of the conflict, nondemocratic regimes in Eastern Europe, Latin America, and even much of Africa were rewarded with financial and military assistance that enabled them to continue old feuds, social conflicts, or civil wars, as long as they remained loyal to their patron.

As the Cold War came to an end in the late 1980s, the exhausted and indebted former enemies cared less about who governed in Poland, South Africa, or Argentina, thus allowing new democratic movements to rise and rule. After the Soviet Union was replaced by the Russian

Federation in 1991, independent states mushroomed throughout the Baltic region and Eastern Europe. Similarly, in Latin America, military dictatorships were replaced by democratic governments, some of which even called themselves "socialist." Before 1991, it was inconceivable that Russian or American governments would ever have allowed such a change.

In a perverse way, the Cold War had undermined the popular legitimacy of democratic movements. Since both the United States and the Soviet Union claimed to be democratic, while subverting democratic movements abroad, nationalist leaders, especially in Africa, derided democracy as an imperialist ideology. But since 1991, it has become easier to see democracy and human rights as universal goals.

Our chapter spans the Cold War and post–Cold War periods. This allows us to see how democratic movements developed in the context of the Cold War and have thrived since its end. During the last decade of the Cold War, demands for democracy were voiced *against* the clients of the Soviet Union and the United States, as we see in the protests of the "Mothers of the Plaza de Mayo" in Argentina, and *by* the leaders of those superpowers, as we see in Mikhail Gorbachev's policy of *Perestroika*. After the Cold War, countries like East Germany or South Africa were freed by their patrons to pursue their own destinies, as indicated here in the address by Nelson Mandela that is included in the chapter.

In recent years, democracy movements have continued to develop in Eastern Europe and Latin America, but the newest breakthroughs have been in the Middle East. These began in Tunisia in December 2010, when a young street vendor set himself on fire after his goods had been taken and he had been denied a hearing by government authorities. Massive street protests followed, bringing down the ruler of the country, forcing him, his family, and aides into exile. The example of Tunisia sparked popular protests in Egypt against President Mubarak in January 2011, resulting in his resignation by February. As similar movements for popular government broke out in Bahrain, Yemen, and Libya, these and other Arab countries were swept up in what was called an "Arab Spring." This is perhaps most remarkable because the Middle East had been for so long dominated by oil-rich autocratic sheiks, super-privileged royal families, and, as a consequence of the Cold War and the creation of Israel, United States–supplied military regimes: Iran and Iraq at various times and Egypt throughout.

Whether the Arab Spring turns into a truly democratic summer is complicated by continued high unemployment, remaining members of the old ruling class, sectarian conflicts, and global politics, but the hunger for popular representation and responsive government, once tasted, is unlikely to disappear. A powerful model, the Arab Spring has raised democratic aspirations from China to Chile.

■ THINKING HISTORICALLY

Using Connections and Context to Interpret the Past

When historians ask about causes, as they frequently do, they look to connections with past events and the general context in which the event takes place. These are two different ways of understanding the causes of anything. To take an example from our discussion of the Arab Spring, we might ask to what extent the events in Egypt in early 2011 were connected to (that is, a continuation of or influenced by) the events in Tunisia, and to what extent the Egyptian revolution was a product of the Egyptian context (its unique problems, politics, etc.). Obviously both played a role; that is why historians frequently study connections and context together, but it is always valuable to understand which, if either, was more important.

In this chapter we will search the primary source documents for signs of connections to earlier events and for the impact of the local and immediate context of the events under discussion. An explanation of an historical event that ignores either outside influences or the internal context is almost always incomplete. We may or may not be able to conclude which was more important, but we will learn to look in both directions.

1

HEBE DE BONAFINI AND MATILDE SÁNCHEZ

The Madwomen at the Plaza de Mayo, 1977/2002

The history of Latin America is pockmarked by the rule of caudillos, generals, and military juntas. During the Cold War, with the blessings of the United States, anticommunist military dictatorships ruled throughout Central and South America. Since the end of the Cold War, democracies have created a new Latin America. We might date

Source: Hebe de Bonafini and Matilde Sánchez, "The Madwomen at the Plaza de Mayo," trans. Patricia Owen Steiner in *The Argentina Reader: History, Culture, Politics*, eds. Gabriela Nouzeilles and Graciela Montaldo (Durham: Duke University Press, 2002), 430–37.

the origins of these new democracies to the protests against the military juntas of the Cold War. Under some of the most brutal of these terrorist states, dedicated to repress any opposition, some people found the strength to say "no."

In the previous chapter, we looked at the impact of the military coup and Dirty War in Argentina (document 8). Between 1975 and 1978, 22,000–30,000 people were killed by the military. In addition to hundreds of communist revolutionaries who had already declared war on the military, tens of thousands of ordinary citizens were rounded up, interrogated, tortured, and ultimately "disappeared" with a bullet in the back of the head or the drop of a broken body into the Atlantic Ocean from an army helicopter. Infants were taken from their condemned parents and given to their torturers to be raised as their own. Students left one day for school, and never returned. And so it was the mothers of teenagers and the grand-mothers of infants suddenly disappeared who began asking for an accounting. As the women began to gather in the Plaza de Mayo of Buenos Aires, the police mocked them as the "Madwomen" of the Plaza, insinuating that they had been driven mad by misbehaved children who ran away from home. But the constant presence of these women, each Thursday afternoon in the Plaza, allowed the world to see the Mothers for who they were and listen to their stories.

Hebe de Bonafini was one of these "Madwomen," having lost two sons to the repression. Here, with the help of journalist Matilde Sánchez, Hebe de Bonafini tells what happened after she was denied informa-tion about her eldest son Jorge Omar in March 1977. What enabled her and the other Mothers to challenge the junta? Of course, the women were not asking for democracy *per se*; they were demanding the return of their children and at the very least they wanted informa-tion. But how did these demands grow to challenge an antidemo-cratic regime?

THINKING HISTORICALLY

We read nothing here to suggest that Hebe de Bonafini read past democratic theorists or borrowed ideas of democracy from historical sources. In fact, she says nothing about democracy. The eruption of the force of the Mothers sprang from the specific context of Argen-tina: foremost the military dictatorship and the state terrorism against leftists. But as we indicated in the previous chapter, the Argentine coup had connections to military planners throughout the hemisphere. Further, on a personal level, women made connections with each other. How did the forging of these connections among the women contribute to the strength of the protest? And how did connections to outside observers provide a stage and an audience much larger than could be gathered in the Plaza de Mayo?

I was beginning to notice that the faces were repeating themselves in the courts and police stations of La Plata. But I didn't say hello to the other women. And it was obvious that what had happened to me had happened to them because after a time I had exhausted all the possibilities in La Plata and absolutely had to go to Buenos Aires, where I began to run into those same faces in the courts, in the Ministry of the Interior, which was located at the time in the Casa Rosada itself. But we gave each other only shy, sideways glances. For my part, at first there was only a disguised effort to fish for a little information. Since we were all standing in the same lines, there was no need to ask questions. Each of us had to repeat her own story of the crime dozens of times to the changing faces at the little windows.

It was in April, I believe, when I first started to talk with some of the women. Our conversations were limited to the habeas corpus petitions[1] and the best way of writing them and of identifying the judges that weren't granting them. But I didn't give any of the women my name or my telephone number. We were anonymous, distrustful people, united by the paperwork and the lives we were trying to recover. Faces of mothers without children, wives without husbands or brothers. Women looking for other people, we were a precarious company in the aloneness of bureaucracy. . . .

On the train from La Plata to Buenos Aires, one of those faces that I used to see in those days in the offices of the capital was already approaching its dreadful destiny. That afternoon my steps and my itinerary matched those of that gray-haired woman with the dark circles under her eyes whom I had spotted days before on the train when I went to the First Army Corps. We both made the change to the subway at Constitución and rode together to the Plaza de Mayo, to the offices of Interior Minister Albano Harguindeguy. I greeted her. We didn't meet again for two weeks.

"We could go back on a bus if that seems like a good idea to you," the woman finally said one afternoon when we saw each other again. "It's a little more expensive, but it's a much more comfortable ride."

I agreed. We sat down in the back of the bus. We were silent. Then I began to ask myself why I had accepted her invitation if I intended to remain mute. In reality, I was wondering if she had a child missing. Perhaps her child might be sharing the cell and some meals with my son while we were sharing the bus seat, mute, not knowing how to get to know each other under such circumstances. She was the one who spoke. She didn't give her name. She was looking for her twenty-four-year-old daughter. They had taken her away five months ago. She was pregnant.

---

[1] The women were encouraged to file petitions of "habeas corpus," which would release a prisoner from unlawful detention, but the petitions were routinely denied without explanation. [Ed.]

I was overwhelmed by astonishment: her case seemed unbelievable. How could that woman go on living if her daughter was a prisoner and about to give birth? I refused to believe that things were really so harsh, so crude. I didn't know the woman's name, but I began to feel a tremendous sense of solidarity with her pain. I was beginning to think that my case was not as serious, although it was my own case that was hurting me. Yet as the bus sped along—probably late because it was leaving lines of passengers standing at every stop—I felt a bond of sisterhood with that woman. I felt understood. She went on talking about her daughter, about the paperwork she had done. But although she sounded sad, she seemed a little released from her own suffering, as if she had gotten past the moments of confusion that I was now living through myself. "We are many more than you believe," she finally said, "and we are beginning to work."

"To work?" I asked. I had no idea what that could mean in this case The woman responded that a group of mothers were doing their paperwork together and were arranging for interviews with influential people who could help them. I asked her if my presence would do any good. . . .

The woman smiled; that initial distance between us had evaporated. She said that next Thursday afternoon a group of mothers would be getting together at the Plaza de Mayo. They were going to sign a petition or meet with a priest. It wouldn't be a bad idea to come—"the more mothers, the better." I said that I'd think it over (something in me was still asking if we weren't creating too much of a scandal over nothing, over some confusion that would surely be cleared up sooner or later). The woman stood up and shook hands with me and began to walk down the aisle of the bus.

"Don't forget. Thursday at two, on the dot." . . .

I walked around; it wasn't two o'clock yet. I hadn't seen the woman from the train with the dark circles under her eyes. I was feeling nervous; I wanted to be sure she would be in the Plaza before I arrived. Suddenly I asked myself why I was afraid: what was wrong, when you came right down to it, with my joining those women? The billboards on Bolívar Street proclaimed the official slogan, "The country is advancing," in sky-blue letters on a white background, like the national flag. I followed that street back to the Plaza.

Some women were already there, near the obelisk, on the right, standing together beside a bench. There were no more than ten: the woman from the train hadn't arrived yet, but another woman walked toward me. She had brown hair and strong, attractive features. She was short, with strong arms and workers' hands, and her body made you think of a great fortress. The weather was cool for April, but she was wearing a loose cotton T-shirt. I tried to explain who I was and how I happened to be there: "A lady from La Plata told me on the bus." It was all very vague, but the woman began to smile. "Ah! Yes." she said at last. "She mentioned you. She said you'd be here. Come on over."

They all appeared extremely rushed. They were talking quickly, softly, their voices bumping into one another. They were passing around a piece of paper. "By chance we managed to get hold of a typewriter," the woman whispered to me. "We wrote a letter to President Videla pleading for our children. Now we're signing it, before we deliver it to the secretary. Sign it if you want.". . .

The women continued passing around the paper and explaining what it was about to the latest women to arrive. Behind us, the city kept on at its rhythm; it didn't seem to realize that we were there. Men were hurrying because the banks were closing; some retired men, completely indifferent, were lying in the sun. We women might well be alumnae of some school, meeting to arrange another reunion. Most of us were about my age or somewhere in their fifties; Azucena moved quickly, like a young woman, but she was a little older. She and I became friends. I agreed with the petition, and I signed. I did it with a large, clear signature so that the president would read my name and it would be engraved on his eyes. Also, so that he would know that my son's name gave me no shame.

We left saying that we would see each other again the following Thursday in the Plaza. At that time, none of us thought that our waiting without children would be longer than a couple of months or that the initial search would someday be transformed into this painful story. . . .

Toward the end of September 1977, we are already more than fifty women, and our feelings grow closer with our growing numbers. Every time there are more of us. Every time we feel stronger and less afraid. Every time we feel safer together. But every time there are more children missing. At the benches on the side of the Plaza we feel defiant, almost invincible for a few minutes. The truth is, they don't know what to do with us. If there is anything left in their hearts, it is the line from all those macho tangos about "my poor old lady." That keeps us safe for the moment. They think that we are crazed by grief, that we'll last until we get tired of standing there with all our varicose veins or until one of us has a heart attack. . . .

They dispatch the police. "This is a demonstration, and the country is under a state of siege. Move on, ladies, move on." We begin to walk together in pairs, arm in arm. Then they make us walk separately.

The Plaza is big, the pairs break up, nobody can make us out from the other women who are just out for a walk. We know that the most important thing is to keep closing the circle, but imperceptibly, a little closer to the obelisk each time, so that they don't have time to realize it. There are more of them all the time; but every Thursday there are more of us, and the police bring reinforcements. They stand in front of the obelisk and keep us from getting close to it. We walk around talking in pairs, watching the necks of the pair of mothers in front of us. . . .

September 1977: . . . Azucena said it would be a good idea for all of us to join the annual pilgrimage to Luján "because people talk a lot on the way and we can stand out." We agreed: besides, there were also many Catholic mothers with us who wanted to go to pray the rosary. The problem is that not all of them wanted to go on foot: some would meet in Haedo, others in Moreno or Castelar. "We all have to agree clearly on where we'll meet."

"I know," said Eva, a mother who usually preferred to keep quiet. "We have to wear something that can be spotted from far away so we can find each other. A kerchief on our heads, for example."

"Or a mantilla. But we don't all have mantillas. Better a kerchief."

"Yes," says another woman. "Or better still a baby diaper; it looks like a kerchief, but it'll make us feel better, closer to our children.". . .

The husbands come along that day, but they always keep a little to the side. As soon as they enter the crowd, they see many other white-headed women like their wives. The diapers leap out at the sun in the sea of people walking along: we begin to come together, first two, then three. Further on, we come across another small group. The diapers multiply and stun the rest of the pilgrims who have already ceased to see them as a coincidence. When we get to the plaza across from the basilica in Luján, we're a good-sized group. Fifteen or twenty of us come together, and, standing in a circle, we pray the rosary for the children who no longer are. For the children who have disappeared.

Naturally the word *disappeared* bursts out. What does it mean? someone asks. The term is explicit: only someone who didn't want to understand could fail to understand. The word is multiplied many times by our mouths. It is repeated with the Ave Marias of the rosary. It embraces all the impunity of the situation. One woman, then another, comes over to talk with us. Their children are also "disappeared," they want to see us again, to pray with us, even with diapers on their heads. People look on, listening to the rosary in the plaza. In the basilica, in front of the altar, some of the devoted women are taking communion or praying for world peace. We are, in some way, the horrible worm that has wriggled out of a shining Argentina "that is advancing." Advancing toward what? Toward those graves without crosses. Toward the bottom of the river. . . .

A few days before the World Cup, a final blow struck "our family." On 25 May, in the afternoon, military forces abducted a group of women in a pastry shop in Lomas de Zamora. One of them was María Elena Bugnone, who was looking for her husband, her brother-in-law Raúl, her sister, and her sister's husband. Not one of that group of women ever returned. Later information from released prisoners indicated that María Elena was held for two years in the prison at Ezeiza. . . .

We know that the World Cup will fill the country with tourists and media professionals from all over the world. I said, "The question is how do we take advantage of those TV cameras for our own cause, to ask for our children and produce a juicy scandal for the government."

"But we don't know how to talk very well, Hebe. We know how to keep house, and we have learned how to do the paperwork, but what are we going to answer if they ask us something in English?"

"It's easy, Clarita," said a mother who had just joined but had plenty of energy. "You look at the journalist, and you say, 'We want our children. We want them to tell us where they are.'"

Our slogans and our rallying cries were being born: later on, they would shatter our silent circling of the obelisk at the center of the Plaza. But for the month of May they wouldn't let us circle: the police were there waiting punctually at three o'clock and charged whenever they saw more than three women together. But we fought them as long as we could. They threw us out one side, and we slipped back in the other. They dragged us out of one flower bed, and, after going around the block, we turned up next to the other. This game of cat and mouse that so exasperated them had for us the almost symbolic objective of occupying the obelisk, the center of the Plaza. From there people would see us better.

And the World Cup began: Argentine flags, confetti thrown from every office window. This meant the indifference of others, of all those Argentines who didn't want to know anything about death but preferred to celebrate to the end the mad fiesta power had offered them, stuffing themselves full with the four TV channels until they were sick or thoroughly brainwashed.

Meanwhile, we women worked to spread the news about our group. We sent hundreds of letters to foreign politicians, and we sought interviews with different world TV networks. Those men listened to us wide-eyed, some became indignant, and all considered us news. We had made it.

2

MIKHAIL GORBACHEV

Perestroika and Glasnost, 2000

Mikhail Gorbachev (b. 1931) was the head (General Secretary) of the Communist Party of the Soviet Union (1985–1991) and president of the Soviet Union (1988–1991). He led the party and the state through the wrenching changes of its liberalization, democratization, and demise. Beginning in 1985, Gorbachev envisioned the democratic reform

Source: Gorbachev, *On My Country and the World* (New York: Columbia University Press, 2000), 55–61.

of the party and state. His formula was *perestroika* (restructuring) and *glasnost* (opening). In this selection from his memoir, he describes that effort.

In what ways was the democratization of the Soviet Union, as described here, different from that of Argentina (see chapter 26, document 8 and the previous document)?

THINKING HISTORICALLY

In what ways does Gorbachev connect his democratization with the ideas and efforts of others? In what ways does he attribute it to the particular context of the Soviet Union and the world in the late 1980s?

There has been a continuing debate over when reform actually began in our country. Politicians and journalists have been trying to locate the exact point at which all our dramatic changes began. Some assert that reforms in Russia did not really begin until 1992.

The basis for reform was laid by Khrushchev.[1] His break with the repressive policies of Stalinism was a heroic feat of civic action. Khrushchev also tried, though without much success, to make changes in the economy. Significant attempts were made within the framework of the so-called Kosygin reforms. Then came a long period of stagnation and a new attempt by Yuri Andropov[2] to improve the situation in our society. An obvious sign that the times were ripe for change was the activity of the dissidents. They were suppressed and expelled from the country, but their moral stand and their proposals for change (for example, the ideas of Andrei Sakharov[3]) played a considerable role in creating the spiritual preconditions for perestroika.

Of course external factors were also important. Thus the Prague Spring of 1968 sowed the seeds of profound thought and reflection in our society. The invasion of Czechoslovakia, dictated by fear of the "democratic infection," was not only a crude violation of the sovereignty and rights of the Czechoslovak people. It had the effect, for years, of putting the brakes on moves toward change, although change was long overdue both in our country and throughout the so-called socialist camp. I should also acknowledge the role of such phenomena as Willy Brandt's[4]

[1] Nikita Khrushchev, First Secretary of the Communist Party of the Soviet Union from 1953 to 1964; responsible for early de-Stalinization reforms. See chapter 26, selections 4, 5, and 6. [Ed.]

[2] General Secretary of the Communist Party of the Soviet Union from November 1982 until February 1984. [Ed.]

[3] Soviet nuclear scientist who became a human rights activist. [Ed.]

[4] Mayor of West Berlin 1957–1966, Chancellor of West Germany 1969–1974, and leader of the socialist Social Democratic Party of Germany (SPD) 1964–1987. His Eastern policy was an effort to improve relations with communist East Germany, Poland, and the Soviet Union. [Ed.]

"Eastern policy" and the search for new avenues toward social progress by those who were called Euro-Communists. All this contributed to deeper reflection in our country, reflection on the values of democracy, freedom, and peace and the ways to achieve them.

Thus we see that attempts at change were made, quite a few of them in fact. But none of them produced results. This is not surprising: After all, none of these attempts touched the essence of the system—property relations, the power structure, and the monopoly of the party on political and intellectual life. The suppression of dissidence continued in spite of everything.

Clearly what was needed was not particular measures in a certain area, even if they were substantial, but rather an entirely different policy, a new political path. Since early 1985, especially after the April plenum of the CPSU Central Committee,[5] this kind of policy began to be formulated. A new course was taken.

Today, in retrospect, one can only be amazed at how quickly and actively our people, the citizens of our country, supported that new course. Apathy and indifference toward public life were overcome. This convinced us that change was vitally necessary. Society awakened.

Perestroika was born out of the realization that problems of internal development in our country were ripe, even overripe, for a solution. New approaches and types of action were needed to escape the downward spiral of crisis, to normalize life, and to make a breakthrough to qualitatively new frontiers. It can be said that to a certain extent perestroika was a result of a rethinking of the Soviet experience since October.[6]

The vital need for change was dictated also by the following consideration. It was obvious that the whole world was entering a new stage of development—some call it the postindustrial age, some the information age. But the Soviet Union had not yet passed through the industrial stage. It was lagging further and further behind those processes that were making a renewal in the life of the world community possible. Not only was a leap forward in technology needed but fundamental change in the entire social and political process.

Of course it cannot be said that at the time we began perestroika we had everything thought out. In the early stages we all said, including myself, that perestroika was a continuation of the October revolution. Today I believe that that assertion contained a grain of truth but also an element of delusion.

The truth was that we were trying to carry out fundamental ideas that had been advanced by the October revolution but had not been realized: overcoming people's alienation from government and property, giving

---

[5] The Central Committee of the Communist Party of the Soviet Union was the governing body between party congress meetings. [Ed.]

[6] October 1917, the Bolshevik Revolution. [Ed.]

power to the people (and taking it away from the bureaucratic upper echelons), implanting democracy, and establishing true social justice.

The delusion was that at the time I, like most of us, assumed this could be accomplished by improving and refining the existing system. But as experience accumulated, it became clear that the crisis that had paralyzed the country in the late 1970s and early 1980s was systemic and not the result of isolated aberrations. The logic of how matters developed pointed to the need to penetrate the system to its very foundations and change it, not merely refine or perfect it. We were already talking about a gradual shift to a social market economy, to a democratic political system based on rule of law and the full guarantee of human rights.

This transition turned out to be extremely difficult and complicated, more complicated than it had seemed to us at first. Above all, this was because the totalitarian system possessed tremendous inertia. There was resistance from the party and government structures that constituted the solid internal framework of that system. The nomenklatura encouraged resistance. And this is understandable: Since it held the entire country in its hands, it would have to give up its unlimited power and privileges. Thus the entire perestroika era was filled with struggles—concealed at first and then more open, more fully exposed to public view—between the forces for change and those who opposed it, those who, especially after the first two years, simply began to sabotage change.

The complexity of the struggle stemmed from the fact that in 1985 the entire society—politically, ideologically, and spiritually—was still in the thrall of old customs and traditions. Great effort was required to overcome these traditions, as mentioned above. There was another factor. Destroying the old system would have been senseless if we did not simultaneously lay the foundations for a new life. And this was genuinely unexplored territory. The six-year perestroika era was a time filled with searching and discovery, gains and losses, breakthroughs in thought and action, as well as mistakes and oversights. The attempted coup in August 1991 interrupted perestroika. After that there were many developments, but they were along different lines, following different intentions. Still, in the relatively short span of six years we succeeded in doing a great deal. The reforms in China, incidentally, have been going on since 1974, and their most difficult problems still remain unsolved.

What specifically did we accomplish as a result of the stormy years of perestroika? The foundations of the totalitarian system were eliminated. Profound democratic changes were begun. Free general elections were held for the first time, allowing real choice. Freedom of the press and a multiparty system were guaranteed. Representative bodies of government were established, and the first steps toward a separation of powers were taken. Human rights (previously in our country these were only "so-called," reference to them invariably made only in scornful quotation marks) now became an unassailable principle. And freedom of conscience was also established.

Movement began toward a multistructured, or mixed, economy providing equality of rights among all forms of property. Economic freedom was made into law. The spirit of enterprise began to gain strength, and processes of privatization and the formation of joint stock companies got under way. Within the framework of our new land law, the peasantry was reborn and private farmers made their appearance. Millions of hectares of land were turned over to both rural and urban inhabitants. The first privately owned banks also came on the scene. The different nationalities and peoples were given the freedom to choose their own course of development. Searching for a democratic way to reform our multinational state, to transform it from a unitary state in practice into a national federation, we reached the threshold at which a new union treaty was to be signed, based on the recognition of the sovereignty of each republic along with the preservation of a common economic, social, and legal space that was necessary for all, including a common defense establishment.

The changes within our country inevitably led to a shift in foreign policy. The new course of perestroika predetermined renunciation of stereotypes and the confrontational methods of the past. It allowed for a rethinking of the main parameters of state security and the ways to ensure it. . . .

In other words, the foundations were laid for normal, democratic, and peaceful development of our country and its transformation into a normal member of the world community.

These are the decisive results of perestroika. Today, however, looking back through the prism of the past few years and taking into account the general trends of world development today, it seems insufficient to register these as the only results. Today it is evidently of special interest to state not only *what* was done but also *how* and *why* perestroika was able to achieve its results, and what its mistakes and miscalculations were.

Above all, *perestroika would have been simply impossible if there had not been a profound and critical reexamination not only of the problems confronting our country but a rethinking of all realities—both national and international.*

Previous conceptions of the world and its developmental trends and, correspondingly, of our country's place and role in the world were based, as we have said, on dogmas deeply rooted in our ideology, which essentially did not permit us to pursue a realistic policy. These conceptions had to be shattered and fundamentally new views worked out regarding our country's development and the surrounding world.

This task turned out to be far from simple. We had to renounce beliefs that for decades had been considered irrefutable truths, to reexamine the very methods and principles of leadership and action, indeed to rethink our surroundings entirely on a scientific basis (and not according to schemes inherited from ideological biases).

The product of this effort was the new thinking, which became the basis for all policy—both foreign and domestic—during perestroika. The point of departure for the new thinking was an attempt to evaluate everything not from the viewpoint of narrow class interests or even national interests but from the broader perspective: that of giving priority to the interests of all humanity with consideration for the increasingly apparent wholeness of the world, the interdependence of all countries and peoples, the humanist values formed over centuries.

The practical work of perestroika was to *renounce stereotypical ideological thinking and the dogmas of the past. This required a fresh view of the world and of ourselves with no preconceptions, taking into account the challenges of the present and the already evident trends of the future in the third millennium.*

During perestroika, and often now as well, the initiators of perestroika have been criticized for the absence of a "clear plan" for change. The habit developed over decades of having an all-inclusive regimentation of life. But the events of the perestroika years and of the subsequent period have plainly demonstrated the following: *At times of profound, fundamental change in the foundations of social development it is not only senseless but impossible to expect some sort of previously worked out "model" or a clear-cut outline of the transformations that will take place. This does not mean, however, the absence of a definite goal for the reforms, a distinct conception of their content and the main direction of their development.*

All this was present in perestroika: a profound democratization of public life and a guarantee of freedom of social and political choice. These goals were proclaimed and frequently reaffirmed. This did not exclude but presupposed the necessity to change one's specific reference points at each stage as matters proceeded and to engage in a constant search for optimal solutions.

An extremely important conclusion follows from the experience of perestroika: Even in a society formed under totalitarian conditions, democratic change is possible by *peaceful evolutionary means.* The problem of revolution and evolution, of the role and place of reforms in social development, is one of the eternal problems of history. In its inner content perestroika of course was a revolution. But in its form it was an evolutionary process, a process of reform.

Historically the USSR had grown ripe for a profound restructuring much earlier than the mid-1980s. But if we had not decided to begin this restructuring at the time we did, even though we were quite late in doing so, an explosion would have taken place in the USSR, one of tremendous destructive force. It would certainly have been called a revolution, but it would have been the catastrophic result of irresponsible leadership.

In the course of implementing change we did not succeed in avoiding bloodshed altogether. But that was a consequence solely of resistance by the opponents of perestroika in the upper echelons of the nomenklatura. On the whole the change from one system to another took place peacefully and by evolutionary means. Our having chosen a policy course that was supported from below by the masses made this peaceful transition possible. And our policy of glasnost played a decisive role in mobilizing the masses and winning their support.

Radical reforms in the context of the Soviet Union could only have been initiated from above by the leadership of the party and the country. This was predetermined by the very "nature" of the system—supercentralized management of all public life. This can also be explained by the inert condition of the masses, who had become used to carrying out orders and decisions handed down from above.

From the very beginning of the changes our country's leadership assigned primary importance to open communication with the people, including direct disclosure in order to explain the new course. Without the citizens' understanding and support, without their participation, it would not have been possible to move from dead center. That is why we initiated the policies of perestroika and glasnost simultaneously.

Like perestroika itself, glasnost made its way with considerable difficulty. The nomenklatura on all levels, which regarded the strictest secrecy and protection of authorities from criticism from below as the holy of holies of the regime, opposed glasnost in every way they could, both openly and secretly, trampling its first shoots in the local press. Even among the most sincere supporters of perestroika, the tradition over many years of making everything a secret made itself felt. But it was precisely glasnost that awakened people from their social slumber, helped them overcome indifference and passivity and become aware of the stake they had in change and of its important implications for their lives. Glasnost helped us to explain and promote awareness of the new realities and the essence of our new political course. In short, without glasnost there would have been no perestroika.

The question of the relation between ends and means is one of the key aspects of politics and of political activity. If the means do not correspond to the ends, or, still worse, if the means contradict the ends, this will lead to setbacks and failure. The Soviet Union's experience is convincing evidence of this. When we began perestroika as a process of democratic change, we had to ensure that the means used to carry out these changes were also democratic.

In essence, glasnost became the means for drawing people into political activity, for including them in the creation of a new life, and this, above all, corresponded to the essence of perestroika. Glasnost not only created conditions for implementing the intended reforms but also made it possible to overcome attempts to sabotage the policy of change.

We are indebted to glasnost for a profound psychological transformation in the public consciousness toward democracy, freedom, and the humanist values of civilization. Incidentally, this was one of the guarantees that the fundamental gains of this period would be irreversible.

Perestroika confirmed once again that the normal, democratic development of society rules out universal secrecy as a method of administration. Democratic development presupposes glasnost—that is, openness, freedom of information for all citizens and freedom of expression by them of their political, religious, and other views and convictions, freedom of criticism in the fullest sense of the word.

Why, then, did perestroika not succeed in achieving all its goals? The answer primarily involves the question of "harmonization" between political and economic change.

The dominant democratic aspect of perestroika meant that the accent was inevitably placed on political reform. The dialectic of our development during those years was such that serious changes in the economic sphere proved to be impossible without emancipating society politically, without ensuring freedom—that is, breaking the political structures of totalitarianism. And this was accomplished. But economic change lagged behind political change, and we did not succeed in developing economic change to the full extent.

3

NELSON MANDELA
Nobel Peace Prize Address, 1993

Democracy for South Africa meant racial democracy: political equality for all South Africans regardless of the color of their skin. It meant the end of apartheid, a system of legal racial segregation in jobs, housing, and access to the political process. It meant the end of the political domination of the 80 percent of South Africans who were black by the 10 percent who were white. In practice, it meant the defeat of the white-supremacist National Party that had ruled South Africa since 1948 and the victory of the mainly black African National Congress party, led by Nelson Mandela despite his imprisonment from 1962 to 1990.

A change of this magnitude was made even more momentous by the fact that it occurred relatively peacefully when National Party

---

Source: Acceptance Speech of the President of the African National Congress, Nelson Mandela, at the Nobel Peace Prize Award Ceremony: Oslo, Norway. December 10, 1993. At http://www.nobelprize.org/nobel_prizes/peace/laureates/1993/mandela-lecture.html

leader and South African president F. W. de Klerk released Mandela from prison in 1990 and scheduled elections that would include the previously outlawed African National Congress for 1994. As a consequence, the Noble Peace Prize committee awarded the 1993 prize jointly to Mandela and de Klerk.

The Nobel Peace Prize is not, of course, a democracy prize. Still, the realization of a political democracy in black-majority South Africa is what the Nobel committee celebrated. Mandela humbly accepted the prize, knowing the challenges that lay ahead in creating a democratic state in South Africa. What did he see as the elements of the democracy he hoped to create? What were his goals? What, if any, elements of democracy did he not include? How was his vision of democracy different from that of Gorbachev?

THINKING HISTORICALLY

The end of institutional racism in South Africa came about after domestic protests, starting in the black township of Soweto in 1976, attracted international attention. Western campaigns to boycott South African goods and investments gained support during the following decade. By the end of the Cold War, the support of anti-communist white South Africa by the United States became unnecessary as well as untenable. Thus, the Nobel Peace Prize acknowledged both a national and an international achievement. How does Mandela recognize the national context of the South African democratic revolution? How does he connect the arrival of democracy in South Africa with the global development of democracy and human rights?

Your Majesty the King,
Your Royal Highness,
Honourable Prime Minister,
Madame Gro Brundtland,
Ministers,
Members of Parliament and Ambassadors,
Esteemed Members of the Norwegian Nobel Committee,
Fellow Laureate, Mr. F. W. de Klerk,
Distinguished guests,
Friends, ladies and gentlemen:

I am indeed truly humbled to be standing here today to receive this year's Nobel Peace Prize.

I extend my heartfelt thanks to the Norwegian Nobel Committee for elevating us to the status of a Nobel Peace Prize winner.

I would also like to take this opportunity to congratulate my compatriot and fellow laureate, State President F. W. de Klerk, on his receipt of this high honour.

Together, we join two distinguished South Africans, the late Chief Albert Luthuli and His Grace Archbishop Desmond Tutu, to whose seminal contributions to the peaceful struggle against the evil system of apartheid you paid well-deserved tribute by awarding them the Nobel Peace Prize.

It will not be presumptuous of us if we also add, among our predecessors, the name of another outstanding Nobel Peace Prize winner, the late African-American statesman and internationalist, the Rev. Martin Luther King Jr.

He, too, grappled with and died in the effort to make a contribution to the just solution of the same great issues of the day which we have had to face as South Africans.

We speak here of the challenge of the dichotomies of war and peace, violence and non-violence, racism and human dignity, oppression and repression and liberty and human rights, poverty and freedom from want.

We stand here today as nothing more than a representative of the millions of our people who dared to rise up against a social system whose very essence is war, violence, racism, oppression, repression and the impoverishment of an entire people.

I am also here today as a representative of the millions of people across the globe, the anti-apartheid movement, the governments and organisations that joined with us, not to fight against South Africa as a country or any of its peoples, but to oppose an inhuman system and sue for a speedy end to the apartheid crime against humanity.

These countless human beings, both inside and outside our country, had the nobility of spirit to stand in the path of tyranny and injustice, without seeking selfish gain. They recognised that an injury to one is an injury to all and therefore acted together in defence of justice and a common human decency.

Because of their courage and persistence for many years, we can, today, even set the dates when all humanity will join together to celebrate one of the outstanding human victories of our century.

When that moment comes, we shall, together, rejoice in a common victory over racism, apartheid and white minority rule.

That triumph will finally bring to a close a history of five hundred years of African colonisation that began with the establishment of the Portuguese empire.

Thus, it will mark a great step forward in history and also serve as a common pledge of the peoples of the world to fight racism wherever it occurs and whatever guise it assumes.

At the southern tip of the continent of Africa, a rich reward is in the making, an invaluable gift is in the preparation, for those who suffered in the name of all humanity when they sacrificed everything—for liberty, peace, human dignity and human fulfilment.

This reward will not be measured in money. Nor can it be reckoned in the collective price of the rare metals and precious stones that rest in the bowels of the African soil we tread in the footsteps of our ancestors. It will and must be measured by the happiness and welfare of the children, at once the most vulnerable citizens in any society and the greatest of our treasures.

The children must, at last, play in the open veld, no longer tortured by the pangs of hunger or ravaged by disease or threatened with the scourge of ignorance, molestation and abuse, and no longer required to engage in deeds whose gravity exceeds the demands of their tender years.

In front of this distinguished audience, we commit the new South Africa to the relentless pursuit of the purposes defined in the World Declaration on the Survival, Protection and Development of Children.

The reward of which we have spoken will and must also be measured by the happiness and welfare of the mothers and fathers of these children, who must walk the earth without fear of being robbed, killed for political or material profit, or spat upon because they are beggars.

They too must be relieved of the heavy burden of despair which they carry in their hearts, born of hunger, homelessness and unemployment.

The value of that gift to all who have suffered will and must be measured by the happiness and welfare of all the people of our country, who will have torn down the inhuman walls that divide them.

These great masses will have turned their backs on the grave insult to human dignity which described some as masters and others as servants, and transformed each into a predator whose survival depended on the destruction of the other.

The value of our shared reward will and must be measured by the joyful peace which will triumph, because the common humanity that bonds both black and white into one human race, will have said to each one of us that we shall all live like the children of paradise.

Thus shall we live, because we will have created a society which recognises that all people are born equal, with each entitled in equal measure to life, liberty, prosperity, human rights and good governance.

Such a society should never allow again that there should be prisoners of conscience nor that any person's human rights should be violated.

Neither should it ever happen that once more the avenues to peaceful change are blocked by usurpers who seek to take power away from the people, in pursuit of their own, ignoble purposes.

In relation to these matters, we appeal to those who govern Burma that they release our fellow Nobel Peace Prize laureate, Aung San Suu Kyi, and engage her and those she represents in serious dialogue, for the benefit of all the people of Burma.

We pray that those who have the power to do so will, without further delay, permit that she uses her talents and energies for the greater good of the people of her country and humanity as a whole.

Far from the rough and tumble of the politics of our own country, I would like to take this opportunity to join the Norwegian Nobel Committee and pay tribute to my joint laureate, Mr. F. W. de Klerk.

He had the courage to admit that a terrible wrong had been done to our country and people through the imposition of the system of apartheid.

He had the foresight to understand and accept that all the people of South Africa must, through negotiations and as equal participants in the process, together determine what they want to make of their future.

But there are still some within our country who wrongly believe they can make a contribution to the cause of justice and peace by clinging to the shibboleths that have been proved to spell nothing but disaster.

It remains our hope that these, too, will be blessed with sufficient reason to realise that history will not be denied and that the new society cannot be created by reproducing the repugnant past, however refined or enticingly repackaged.

We live with the hope that as she battles to remake herself, South Africa will be like a microcosm of the new world that is striving to be born.

This must be a world of democracy and respect for human rights, a world freed from the horrors of poverty, hunger, deprivation and ignorance, relieved of the threat and the scourge of civil wars and external aggression and unburdened of the great tragedy of millions forced to become refugees.

The processes in which South Africa and Southern Africa as a whole are engaged, beckon and urge us all that we take this tide at the flood and make of this region a living example of what all people of conscience would like the world to be.

We do not believe that this Nobel Peace Prize is intended as a commendation for matters that have happened and passed.

We hear the voices which say that it is an appeal from all those, throughout the universe, who sought an end to the system of apartheid.

We understand their call, that we devote what remains of our lives to the use of our country's unique and painful experience to demonstrate, in practice, that the normal condition for human existence is democracy, justice, peace, non-racism, non-sexism, prosperity for everybody, a healthy environment and equality and solidarity among the peoples.

Moved by that appeal and inspired by the eminence you have thrust upon us, we undertake that we too will do what we can to contribute to the renewal of our world so that none should, in future, be described as the wretched of the earth.

Let it never be said by future generations that indifference, cynicism or selfishness made us fail to live up to the ideals of humanism which the Nobel Peace Prize encapsulates.

Let the strivings of us all prove Martin Luther King Jr. to have been correct, when he said that humanity can no longer be tragically bound to the starless midnight of racism and war.

Let the efforts of us all, prove that he was not a mere dreamer when he spoke of the beauty of genuine brotherhood and peace being more precious than diamonds or silver or gold.

Let a new age dawn!

Thank you.

4

GENE SHARP

From Dictatorship to Democracy, 1993

Gene Sharp (b. 1928) is the founder of The Albert Einstein Institution and author of numerous books on nonviolent political struggle. His theoretical and "how to" writings have been instrumental in new democracy movements in Southeast Asia and Eastern Europe. These have included the peaceful "Orange Revolution" in Ukraine in 2004–2005 and similar successful nonviolent democratic movements in Serbia, Georgia, Belarus, and the Baltic countries.

During the "Arab Spring" of 2011, the *New York Times* and *London Daily Telegraph* (among others) published articles that claimed this "unknown professor" was behind the democratic revolutions shaking the Arab world. Many Egyptians disputed this, along with Sharp himself who insisted that the Egyptian revolution showed that Egyptians could do it themselves, without the intervention of Western actors.

Nevertheless, Sharp's study of nonviolent revolutions has led him to an analysis of the exercise of state power that would be useful to many democratic revolutionaries. He challenges the more popular view that nonviolence is rarely successful and that violence is always the most powerful weapon. He argues instead that nonviolence is always *tactically* (as well as morally) preferable against superior power. What do you think of his argument? What does he teach you about fighting dictators? How might this argument be more persuasive in our contemporary age than it would have been in the past?

THINKING HISTORICALLY

How does Sharp undermine the arguments of those who seek to export democracy? How does he support them? How does he show the importance of every particular context? How does he show the value of connections to history?

Centers of Democratic Power

One characteristic of a democratic society is that there exist independent of the state a multitude of nongovernmental groups and institutions.

Source: Gene Sharp, *From Dictatorship to Democracy: A Conceptual Framework for Liberation*, 4th U.S. edition (Boston: The Albert Einstein Institution, 2010), pp. 21–23, 31–34, 62–64, 69.

These include, for example, families, religious organizations, cultural associations, sports clubs, economic institutions, trade unions, student associations, political parties, villages, neighborhood associations, gardening clubs, human rights organizations, musical groups, literary societies, and others. These bodies are important in serving their own objectives and also in helping to meet social needs.

Additionally, these bodies have great political significance. They provide group and institutional bases by which people can exert influence over the direction of their society and resist other groups or the government when they are seen to impinge unjustly on their interests, activities, or purposes. Isolated individuals, not members of such groups, usually are unable to make a significant impact on the rest of the society, much less a government, and certainly not a dictatorship.

Consequently, if the autonomy and freedom of such bodies can be taken away by the dictators, the population will be relatively helpless. Also, if these institutions can themselves be dictatorially controlled by the central regime or replaced by new controlled ones, they can be used to dominate both the individual members and also those areas of the society. However, if the autonomy and freedom of these independent civil institutions (outside of government control) can be maintained or regained they are highly important for the application of political defiance. The common feature of the cited examples in which dictatorships have been disintegrated or weakened has been the courageous *mass* application of political defiance by the population and its institutions. . . .

During the Hungarian Revolution of 1956–1957 a multitude of direct democracy councils emerged, even joining together to establish for some weeks a whole federated system of institutions and governance. In Poland during the late 1980s workers maintained illegal Solidarity unions and, in some cases, took over control of the official, Communist-dominated, trade unions. Such institutional developments can have very important political consequences. . . .

Methods of Nonviolent Struggle

In contrast to military means, the methods of nonviolent struggle can be focused directly on the issues at stake. For example, since the issue of dictatorship is primarily political, then political forms of nonviolent struggle would be crucial. These would include denial of legitimacy to the dictators and noncooperation with their regime.

Noncooperation would also be applied against specific policies. At times stalling and procrastination may be quietly and even secretly practiced, while at other times open disobedience and defiant public demonstrations and strikes may be visible to all. On the other hand, if the dictatorship is vulnerable to economic pressures or if many of the popular grievances against it are economic, then economic action, such as boycotts or strikes, may be appropriate resistance methods. The dictators' efforts to exploit the economic system might be met with limited general strikes, slowdowns, and refusal of assistance by (or disappearance of) indispensable experts. Selective use of various types of strikes may be conducted at key points in manufacturing, in transport, in the supply of raw materials, and in the distribution of products.

Some methods of nonviolent struggle require people to perform acts unrelated to their normal lives, such as distributing leaflets, operating an underground press, going on hunger strike, or sitting down in the streets. These methods may be difficult for some people to undertake except in very extreme situations. Other methods of nonviolent struggle instead require people to continue approximately their normal lives, though in somewhat different ways. For example, people may report for work, instead of striking, but then deliberately work more slowly or inefficiently than usual. "Mistakes" may be consciously made more frequently. One may become "sick" and "unable" to work at certain times. Or, one may simply refuse to work. One might go to religious services when the act expresses not only religious but also political convictions.

One may act to protect children from the attackers' propaganda by education at home or in illegal classes. One might refuse to join certain "recommended" or required organizations that one would not have joined freely in earlier times. The similarity of such types of action to people's usual activities and the limited degree of departure from their normal lives may make participation in the national liberation struggle much easier for many people.

Since nonviolent struggle and violence operate in fundamentally different ways, even limited resistance violence during a political defiance campaign will be counterproductive, for it will shift the struggle to one in which the dictators have an overwhelming advantage (military warfare). Nonviolent discipline is a key to success and must be maintained despite provocations and brutalities by the dictators and their agents. . . .

Openness, Secrecy, and High Standards

Secrecy, deception, and underground conspiracy pose very difficult problems for a movement using nonviolent action. It is often impossible to keep the political police and intelligence agents from learning about intentions and plans. From the perspective of the movement, secrecy is not only rooted in fear but contributes to fear, which dampens the spirit of resistance and reduces the number of people who can participate in a given action. It also can contribute to suspicions and accusations, often unjustified, within the movement, concerning who is an informer or agent for the opponents.

Secrecy may also affect the ability of a movement to remain nonviolent. In contrast, openness regarding intentions and plans will not only have the opposite effects, but will contribute to an image that the resistance movement is in fact extremely powerful. The problem is of course more complex than this suggests, and there are significant aspects of resistance activities that may require secrecy. A well informed assessment will be required by those knowledgeable about both the dynamics of nonviolent struggle and also the dictatorship's means of surveillance in the specific situation.

The editing, printing, and distribution of underground publications, the use of illegal radio broadcasts from within the country, and the gathering of intelligence about the operations of the dictatorship are among the special limited types of activities where a high degree of secrecy will be required. . . .

Planning Political Defiance

During the planning and implementation of political defiance and non-cooperation, it is highly important to pay close attention to all of the dictators' main supporters and aides, including their inner clique, political party, police, and bureaucrats, but especially their army.

The degree of loyalty of the military forces, both soldiers and officers, to the dictatorship needs to be carefully assessed and a determination should be made as to whether the military is open to influence by the democratic forces. Might many of the ordinary soldiers be unhappy and frightened conscripts? Might many of the soldiers and officers be alienated from the regime for personal, family, or political reasons? What other factors might make soldiers and officers vulnerable to democratic subversion?

Early in the liberation struggle a special strategy should be developed to communicate with the dictators' troops and functionaries. By words, symbols, and actions, the democratic forces can inform the troops that the liberation struggle will be vigorous, determined, and persistent. Troops should learn that the struggle will be of a special character, designed to undermine the dictatorship but not to threaten their lives. Such efforts would aim ultimately to undermine the morale of the dictators' troops and finally to subvert their loyalty and obedience in favor of the democratic movement. Similar strategies could be aimed at the police and civil servants.

The attempt to garner sympathy from and, eventually, induce disobedience among the dictators' forces ought not to be interpreted, however, to mean encouragement of the military forces to make a quick end to the current dictatorship through military action. Such a scenario is not likely to install a working democracy, for (as we have discussed) a coup d'état does little to redress the imbalance of power relations between the populace and the rulers. Therefore, it will be necessary to plan how sympathetic military officers can be brought to understand that neither a military coup nor a civil war against the dictatorship is required or desirable. Sympathetic officers can play vital roles in the democratic struggle, such as spreading disaffection and noncooperation in the military forces, encouraging deliberate inefficiencies and the quiet ignoring of orders, and supporting the refusal to carry out repression.

Military personnel may also offer various modes of positive nonviolent assistance to the democracy movement, including safe passage, information, food, medical supplies, and the like. The army is one of the most important sources of the power of dictators because it can use its disciplined military units and weaponry directly to attack and to punish the disobedient population.

Defiance strategists should remember that it will be exceptionally difficult, or impossible, to disintegrate the dictatorship if the police, bureaucrats, and military forces remain fully supportive of the dictatorship and obedient in carrying out its commands. Strategies aimed at subverting the loyalty of the dictators' forces should therefore be given a high priority by democratic strategists.

The democratic forces should remember that disaffection and disobedience among the military forces and police can be highly dangerous for the members of those groups. Soldiers and police could expect severe penalties for any act of disobedience and execution for acts of mutiny. The democratic forces should not ask the soldiers and officers that they immediately mutiny. Instead, where communication is possible, it should be made clear that there are a multitude of relatively safe forms of "disguised disobedience" that they can take initially. For example, police and troops can carry out instructions for repression inefficiently, fail to locate wanted persons, warn resisters of impending repression, arrests, or deportations, and fail to report important information to their superior officers. Disaffected officers in turn can neglect to relay commands for repression down the chain of command. Soldiers may shoot over the heads of demonstrators. Similarly, for their part, civil servants can lose files and instructions, work inefficiently, and become "ill". . . .

Escalating Freedom

Combined with political defiance during the phase of selective resistance, the growth of autonomous social, economic, cultural, and political institutions progressively expands the "democratic space" of the society and shrinks the control of the dictatorship. As the civil institutions of the society become stronger vis-à-vis the dictatorship, then, whatever the dictators may wish, the population is incrementally building an independent society outside of their control. If and when the dictatorship intervenes to halt this "escalating freedom," nonviolent struggle can be applied in defense of this newly won space and the dictatorship will be faced with yet another "front" in the struggle.

In time, this combination of resistance and institution building can lead to *de facto* freedom, making the collapse of the dictatorship and the formal installation of a democratic system undeniable because the power relationships within the society have been fundamentally altered.

5

WAEL GHONIM
Revolution 2.0, 2012

Wael Ghonim (b. 1980) was an Egyptian computer engineer working for Google in the Middle East when in June 2010 a friend posted pictures on his Facebook Wall of the bloody body of a young man, Khaled Said, who had been beaten to death by Egyptian police. Unable to stop crying at an image that crystallized for him the police state that had developed under Hosni Mubarak, Ghonim decided to devote all of his computer and marketing ability to bring justice for Khaled Said. He created a Facebook page called *Kullena Khaled Said* ("We are all Khaled Said") and within two minutes 300 had joined the page. Within an hour it had grown to 3,000. In the following weeks, Ghonim used the page to engage supporters and then promote peaceful demonstrations, the first of which was a Silent Stand along the banks of the Nile in both Alexandria and Cairo. By the end of June there were 100,000 members, many of whom were young people who had never done anything political.

In *Revolution 2.0*, Ghonim captures the next eight months of what became, in no small part thanks to his efforts and those who joined him, the Arab Spring of democratic revolution. This selection is drawn from the end of the book. It describes the last days of massive peaceful protest in Tahrir Square Cairo, as Ghonim, recognized as the administrator of the Facebook page and imprisoned for eleven days, is called by the minister of the interior to negotiate on behalf of the people in Tahrir. *Kullena Khaled Said* then had 1,650,000 members.

Source: Wael Ghonim, *Revolution 2.0* (Boston: Houghton Mifflin Harcourt, 2012), 282–94.

Ghonim is promised a meeting with Mubarak but after a long wait he drives home. He picks up the story there.

From the title of his book to the epilogue, Ghonim displays the power of technology: television as well as social media on the Internet (though he also mentions the power of Friday prayers and sermons). How important were these new technologies, perhaps especially new media, to the protests in Egypt? In what ways was this Revolution 2.0? Is Revolution 2.0 easier than Revolution 1.0?

THINKING HISTORICALLY

Ghonim writes about the importance of connections to foreigners and events outside of Egypt. He also writes with a great deal of national pride and knowledge of conditions in Egypt. In explaining the fall of Mubarak, how do you balance the impact of these connections with the immediate Egyptian context? What foreign connections were important? To what extent was this Egyptian revolution a continuation of events in Tunisia? To what extent was it a distinctly Egyptian event?

Everyone in Tahrir Square was cheering, and news channels started asking people there to comment on the to-be-confirmed news that Mubarak was stepping down. Al Arabiya[1] asked me for a phone interview to congratulate the Egyptian people. I said we had finally succeeded in realizing the objective of the president's resignation and it was now time to go home and think of rebuilding Egypt. . . .

After speaking to Al Arabiya, I decided to watch the resignation speech from Tahrir Square. I had spoken to many people there who were very happy with the news and eagerly awaiting the speech.

Mubarak began his speech much later than expected, and a wave of suspense washed over us as we waited. But he spoke in his traditional manner. He reminded us of his role in war and in peace, and of his achievements and history. And although he spent a moment offering condolences for the lives of the martyrs, it wasn't half as emotional as the moment when he expressed his pain at Tahrir Square's depiction of him. He even referred to the martyrs as "your martyrs," unwittingly reinforcing his clear disconnection from the square. Mubarak invited everyone to give precedence to Egypt's interests over everything else. He said he had lived on Egyptian soil and would die on Egyptian soil. Then, during the final thirty seconds of the speech, Mubarak said he delegated his authority to Vice President Omar Soliman. It was not actually a resignation from power.

---

[1] Saudi-owned Arabic television channel. [Ed.]

In Tahrir Square, thousands of disappointed yet determined people started chanting, "Leave means go, in case you did not know!" A group of people in the square gathered around me. "What will we do? This is unbelievable. Don't these people understand?" they exclaimed. I had nothing to say to them except that we were the stronger ones and would not give up until our goal was reached. We desired a real resignation and not a murky delegation of power. Disappointed, I left Tahrir with a friend who drove me home.

Two surprising pieces of news surfaced when I met my friends to discuss our next steps. The first was that the Middle East News Agency reported that I had issued a statement inviting all Egyptians at Tahrir to return to their homes following the president's speech. The second was that hundreds of angry protesters had begun marching from Tahrir Square toward the presidential palace to force the president to step down. It was an extremely dangerous development. Everyone was talking about how this could lead to a bloodbath. The presidential guard would attack anyone who approached the palace. I was devastated by this news and extremely apprehensive about the consequences. . . .

I received a call from the TV host Amr al-Laithy, who asked that I call in during his show and declare my opinion of events and of the president's decision. I accepted.

On the air, I clarified that I had not made any statements and that, like everyone else, I was not happy with Mubarak's speech. The president was not resigning but delegating authority to his vice president while remaining president. Amr al-Laithy asked . . . me to say something to the people marching toward the palace. I said that it was not for me to address the protesters and asked him and others to stop trying to influence them, because the protesters were not watching television. My final comment was that I would formulate my position after completing an opinion poll on the Facebook page, asking members how they evaluated the events on the ground, as I had done before.

A huge burden of responsibility lay on my shoulders. It was true that my statements might not influence the masses and that rallying through the Facebook page might not be as effective as it had been, since heroes on the ground were now the ones who controlled the course of events. Yet I still sensed — for the first time — that my computer keyboard had become a machine gun, firing bullets with every keystroke. I felt a new sense of responsibility for everything I wrote, and I became very tense.

I designed a questionnaire to canvass people's reactions to the president's speech and find out what they thought the next steps should be, including the idea of marching toward the palace. My plan was to base my own decision on the majority's opinion. We would then all shoulder the responsibility for our actions, even if the result was gunfire from the presidential guard that claimed the lives of hundreds of young Egyptians.

Moments after posting the questionnaire, the polling service that I had been using for months stopped working. The main server that hosted the service suddenly froze because of a burst of user traffic. Thousands, or maybe tens of thousands, of website visitors wanted to participate and share their opinions, which created more traffic than their server could handle. I tried several times to revive the server, without success. I announced the failure of the polling service on the page as some members accused me of cowardice, lies, and deception. At that point I was physically worn out beyond imagination. I decided to go home, not knowing what I would post next. . . .

I entered my family home with my emotions transparent on my face. My mother asked our relatives, who lived in the same building, to come to my room and try to talk to me, but I asked everyone to leave me alone. Then I vented through the Facebook page.

> Dear God, you know our intentions best and that we are seeking our rights and our freedom . . . Dear God, inspire us to do what is right and increase the strength of each and every one of us.
>
> 👍 15,095 Likes   💬 19,690 Comments   1,405,565 Views

I tried to think as I lay down in bed, but before I knew it I was fast asleep, after a day full of unexpected events. For the first time since my release from detainment, I slept for more than seven hours. When I woke up, I was no longer confused. I was determined — and angry. I was angry that we had been used to broadcast an image of "dialogue" to undermine the revolution. I was angry that my name had been used in a press statement to dissuade the protesters from continuing their sit-in. Once again I expressed my complete support for the revolution and its demands on the Facebook page.

> I'm with all of you, I'm with our rights and our freedom. I'm with taking all the corrupt people to justice. I'm with ending over 30 years of violation of the basic rights of Egyptians and their dignity.
>
> 👍 6,632 Likes   💬 2,540 Comments   1,538,294 Views

Mostafa al-Nagar called and said that we must make a media appearance to tell the story of our deception the night before. He suggested appearing with the famous TV host Hafiz al-Mirazi on Al Arabiya.

Later Mostafa arrived at my house with a formal statement he and other political activists had prepared for the army, containing a number of demands. The statement was based on the army's announcement the day before. It began by saluting the SCAF's[2] involvement and went on to outline our demands: confirmation of the complete resignation of the president and his irrevocable removal from power; dissolution of the National Democratic Party and the free formation of political parties; removal of the restrictions placed on candidate nominations for presidential elections; immediate suspension of the emergency law; new rounds of parliamentary elections in all the constituencies in which the court had ruled the previous ballot results illegitimate; monitoring of all elections by local and international civil society, as well as facilitation of the voting process by allowing all resident citizens to use their national ID card and allowing expatriate Egyptians to vote from abroad; the release of all arrested protesters from detainment; the bringing to justice of all the murderers responsible for crimes against Egyptian youth; the bringing to justice of corrupt politicians and the confiscation of all assets stolen from the Egyptian people; and re-creation of the security apparatus on a base of transparency that would prevent monstrous acts of torturing and terrorizing the citizens.

On our way to Al Arabiya, we learned that the numbers at the presidential palace were still limited but increasing as the time for Friday prayers approached. Meanwhile, Tahrir was flooded with hundreds of thousands of protesters and a march had taken off toward the state television building, which was guarded by army forces to prevent it from being raided. By the time my Al Arabiya interview began, I was angrier than I had ever been. I told Hafiz al-Mirazi, the interviewer, that Egypt was experiencing an immense crisis of trust. I said that the country was like a girl who had been raped continually for thirty years, and as soon as she had obtained a knife to fight back, her rapist was begging her to "dialogue" and give up revenge. I read our statement of demands aloud. Mostafa al-Nagar declared that complying with these demands was necessary because martyrs' blood had been shed.

I told the interviewer how Mostafa had held a dying protester in his arms after the man had been shot in the chest. "Mostafa, are we on the right side?" he had asked. "Will I die a martyr?" Speaking through tears as he held him, Mostafa had replied, "Yes, of course." Then the wounded man let out his last breath.

Then my voice rose. "Our tears are not tears of weakness but a sign of strength. Our tears are stronger than the bullets to our chests from Omar Soliman and his men. I am stronger than Omar Soliman and stronger than Hosni Mubarak." Although I ended my statement in the first person, to me it felt as if the protesters had just uttered those words. There was no way we were going to give up our dream, especially not because of fear.

[2] Supreme Council of Egyptian Armed Forces.

Outside on the street after the interview, people crowded around us once again. I wanted to depart quickly to follow the updates and access the Facebook page. The scene at Tahrir Square was magnificent that Friday. It was clear evidence that the majority of Jan 25 protesters had not been satisfied by Mubarak's mere delegation of powers to his vice president. I soon discovered that national television had broadcast the army's approval of the protesters' demands. They even mentioned specific demands, including the ones in our statement. We became hopeful once again.

Message to the regime: The people on the streets raise the level of their demands with every passing hour. The current demand that needs to be fulfilled as fast as possible is for the president to step down and leave Egypt.

👍 5,514 Likes   💬 5,030 Comments   1,013,841 Views

At about 5 p.m., television stations announced that an important statement would be broadcast "shortly." After the experience of the previous night, anything was possible. So we decided not to celebrate just yet.

This time Vice President Omar Soliman appeared on national television, looking very serious. "In the name of God, most gracious, most merciful," Soliman read, "my fellow citizens, in the difficult circumstances our country is experiencing, President Muhammad Hosni Mubarak has decided to give up the office of the president of the republic and instructed the Supreme Council of the Armed Forces to manage the affairs of the country. May God guide our steps."

I could not believe it. The dream had been realized. What was impossible for years had been achieved in eighteen days. I went around hugging everyone in the vicinity: my mother, sister, brother, aunt, and friends. We all started singing the national anthem, raising our voices high. I called my wife and said, "You won't believe it! Mubarak is gone!"

"Are you serious?"

"Yes!" I exclaimed. "He's gone! He's gone! He's gone!" I kept repeating it hysterically.

One minute later I updated the Facebook page:

Congratulations, Egypt! This is the historical moment we have been longing to witness!

👍 15,190 Likes   💬 10,832 Comments   968,496 Views

. . . The rejoicing and celebrations in the streets were incredible. Car horns, fireworks, screams, chants, and applause were heard everywhere. It was a defining moment of Egypt's modern history. The will of the people vanquished the will of the rulers.

I went out on the street surrounded by neighbors and friends. Together we stopped the passing cars and chanted with all our might, "Mubarak is gone! The Egyptian people are free!" Celebrations continued throughout the night. We began at Mostafa Mahmoud Square in Mohandeseen and moved all the way to Tahrir Square, which was now filled with people as never before. There I got on the main stage and recited the opening chapter of the Qur'an, "Al-Fatihah," in tribute to the martyrs, and I called on a young Christian to lead a prayer for the martyrs as well. Everyone started chanting, "Muslims and Christians, we are all Egyptians!". . .

I returned home after midnight with my head held high. I updated the *"Kullena Khaled Said"* page before I went to bed:

Proud to be Egyptian!

👍 9,413 Likes   💬 2,539 Comments   655,359 Views

Epilogue

. . . Something changed when Egyptians stood up to the Mubarak regime. That change is not limited to our country or to our revolution—it is happening in many countries in the Middle East and on the streets of many cities around the world. Now that so many people can easily connect with one another, the world is less hospitable to authoritarian regimes. Humanity will always be cursed with power-hungry people, and the rule of law and justice will not automatically flourish in all places at all times. But thanks to modern technology, participatory democracy is becoming a reality. Governments are finding it harder and harder to keep their people isolated from one another, to censor information, and to hide corruption and issue propaganda that goes unchallenged. Slowly but surely, the weapons of mass oppression are becoming extinct.

The Egyptian revolution showed us that the great mass of people who are normally risk-averse, aren't normally activists, can become extraordinarily brave and active when they unite together as one. It was like an offline Wikipedia, with everyone anonymously and selflessly contributing efforts toward a common goal. . . .

Revolutions of the past have usually had charismatic leaders who were politically savvy and sometimes even military geniuses. Such revolutions followed what we can call the Revolution 1.0 model. But the revolution in Egypt was different: it was truly a spontaneous movement led by nothing other than the wisdom of the crowd. One day revolution seemed utterly impossible, and there were just a few people dreaming of change. And then, after the brave people of Tunisia ignited a fire that had been smoldering in the hearts of Egyptians and many other Arab people, the impossible quickly became possible. People who would only post comments in cyberspace became willing to stand in public; then those protesters, among many others, made the great leap to become marchers and chanters, and grew into a critical mass that toppled a brutal and tyrannical regime.

6

China's "Charter 08," 2008

In 1979 the Chinese Communist Party began to introduce markets and open the Chinese economy to national and foreign capitalists. But the Party maintained a tight grip on all political offices and public media, sometimes brutally silencing criticism. Various efforts at political liberalization, like the China Democracy Movement in 1989, were met by fierce military suppression and efforts to substitute material well-being for political participation and freedom of expression. The exponential growth of the Chinese economy since then was largely successful in pacifying the population. But critics did not disappear.

This 2008 Chinese democratic manifesto was originally signed by 350 Chinese human rights activists, lawyers, artists, writers, intellectuals, and even some former communist officials. Today over 10,000 have signed. It was immediately banned in China and many of the signers were harassed or jailed. One of the authors, Liu Xiaobo, was awarded the Nobel Peace Prize in 2010 while in a Chinese prison, where he remains as of this writing.

What does the fact that these ideas and demands were so threatening tell you about the struggle for democracy in China today? How would the realization of these demands create a democratic China?

THINKING HISTORICALLY

The name given to this democratizing effort, "Charter 08," recognized a similar set of demands signed by prominent citizens of

---

Source: "Charter 08," translated by "Human Rights in China." http://www.hrichina.org/crf/article/3203

Czechoslovakia in 1977 called "Charter 77." Many of the signers of Charter 77 were active in the Velvet Revolution of 1989 in which the Czechoslovakian Communist Party relinquished power. Making a connection to that earlier event was evidently important to the drafters of Charter 08 in China. In addition, the authors make a point of connecting their charter with earlier Chinese reform movements. Beyond that, many of the statements and demands of Charter 08 reflect an emerging global consensus about human rights and democracy. As such, they form a connection to other charters, constitutions, and revolutionary pronouncements going back to the Enlightenment. On the other hand, some of the demands reflect the specific context of contemporary China. Which passages in the document are connected to earlier, foreign, or universal issues? Which stem from a particular Chinese context?

Preamble

This year marks 100 years since China's [first] Constitution, the 60th anniversary of the promulgation of the *Universal Declaration of Human Rights*,[1] the 30th anniversary of the birth of the Democracy Wall,[2] and the 10th year since the Chinese government signed the *International Covenant on Civil and Political Rights*.[3] Having experienced a prolonged period of human rights disasters and challenging and tortuous struggles, the awakening Chinese citizens are becoming increasingly aware that freedom, equality, and human rights are universal values shared by all humankind, and that democracy, republicanism, and constitutional government make up the basic institutional framework of modern politics. A "modernization" bereft of these universal values and this basic political framework is a disastrous process that deprives people of their rights, rots away their humanity, and destroys their dignity. . . .

The tremendous historic changes of the mid-19th century exposed the decay of the traditional Chinese autocratic system and set the stage for the greatest transformation China had seen in several thousand years. The Self-Strengthening Movement [1861–1895] sought improvements in China's technical capability by acquiring manufacturing techniques, scientific knowledge, and military technologies from the West;

---

[1] List of individual rights adopted by the UN General Assembly, December 1948. [Ed.]

[2] Brick wall in Beijing where political statements were posted in the Chinese democracy movement of 1978. [Ed.]

[3] Treaty adopted by UN General Assembly, December 1966, in force in 1976, signed by China in 1998. [Ed.]

China's defeat in the first Sino-Japanese War [1894–1895] once again exposed the obsolescence of its system; the Hundred Days' Reform [1898] touched upon the area of institutional innovation, but ended in failure due to cruel suppression by the die-hard faction [at the Qing court]. The Xinhai Revolution [1911], on the surface, buried the imperial system that had lasted for more than 2,000 years and established Asia's first republic. But, because of the particular historical circumstances of internal and external troubles, the republican system of government was short lived, and autocracy made a comeback.

The failure of technical imitation and institutional renewal prompted deep reflection among our countrymen on the root cause of China's cultural sickness, and the ensuing May Fourth [1919] and New Culture Movements[4] [1915–1921] under the banner of "science and democracy." But the course of China's political democratization was forcibly cut short due to frequent civil wars and foreign invasion. The process of a constitutional government began again after China's victory in the War of Resistance against Japan [1937–1945], but the outcome of the civil war between the Nationalists and the Communists plunged China into the abyss of modern-day totalitarianism. The "New China" established in 1949 is a "people's republic" in name, but in reality it is a "party domain." The ruling party monopolizes all the political, economic, and social resources. It has created a string of human rights disasters, such as the Anti-Rightist Campaign, the Great Leap Forward, the Cultural Revolution, June Fourth,[5] and the suppression of unofficial religious activities and the rights defense movement, causing tens of millions of deaths, and exacting a disastrous price from both the people and the country.

The "Reform and Opening Up" of the late 20th century extricated China from the pervasive poverty and absolute totalitarianism of the Mao Zedong era, and substantially increased private wealth and the standard of living of the common people. Individual economic freedom and social privileges were partially restored, a civil society began to grow, and calls for human rights and political freedom among the people increased by the day. . . . In 2004, the National People's Congress amended the Constitution to add that "[the State] respects and guarantees human rights." And this year, the government has promised to formulate and implement a "National Human Rights Action Plan." But so

---

[4] Chinese turn from Confucianism to embrace Western democratic values as universal. [Ed.]

[5] First three were campaigns of Mao Zedong against capitalism, the middle class, and political and personal enemies. The Great Leap Forward was also a campaign by Mao to radically collectivize the economy. It failed, causing much hardship instead. June 4th is the Chinese term for the democracy movement in 1989 called in the West the Tiananmen Square protest and massacre. [Ed.]

far, this political progress has largely remained on paper: there are laws, but there is no rule of law; there is a constitution, but no constitutional government; this is still the political reality that is obvious to all. The ruling elite continues to insist on its authoritarian grip on power, rejecting political reform. This has caused official corruption, difficulty in establishing rule of law, the absence of human rights, moral bankruptcy, social polarization, abnormal economic development, destruction of both the natural and cultural environment, no institutionalized protection of citizens' rights to freedom, property, and the pursuit of happiness, the constant accumulation of all kinds of social conflicts, and the continuous surge of resentment. . . .

Our Fundamental Concepts

At this historical juncture that will decide the future destiny of China, it is necessary to reflect on the modernization process of the past hundred and some years and reaffirm the following concepts:

Freedom: Freedom is at the core of universal values. The rights of speech, publication, belief, assembly, association, movement, to strike, and to march and demonstrate are all the concrete expressions of freedom. Where freedom does not flourish, there is no modern civilization to speak of.

Human Rights: Human rights are not bestowed by a state; they are inherent rights enjoyed by every person. Guaranteeing human rights is both the most important objective of a government and the foundation of the legitimacy of its public authority; it is also the intrinsic requirement of the policy of "putting people first." . . . People are the mainstay of a nation; a nation serves its people; government exists for the people.

Equality: The integrity, dignity, and freedom of every individual, regardless of social status, occupation, gender, economic circumstances, ethnicity, skin color, religion, or political belief, are equal. The principles of equality before the law for each and every person and equality in social, economic, cultural, and political rights of all citizens must be implemented.

Republicanism: Republicanism is "joint governing by all, peaceful coexistence," that is, the separation of powers for checks and balances and the balance of interests; that is, a community comprising many diverse interests, different social groups, and a plurality of cultures and faiths, seeking to peacefully handle public affairs on the basis of equal participation, fair competition, and joint discussion.

Democracy: The most fundamental meaning is that sovereignty resides in the people and the government elected by the people. Democracy has the following basic characteristics: (1) The legitimacy of political power comes from the people; the source of political power is the people. (2) Political control is exercised through choices made by the people. (3) Citizens enjoy the genuine right to vote; officials in key positions at all levels of government must be the product of elections at regular intervals. (4) Respect the decisions of the majority while protecting the basic human rights of the minority. In a word, democracy is the modern public instrument for creating a government "of the people, by the people, and for the people."

Constitutionalism: Constitutionalism is the principle of guaranteeing basic freedoms and rights of citizens as defined by the constitution through legal provisions and the rule of law, restricting and defining the boundaries of government power and conduct, and providing appropriate institutional capability to carry this out. In China, the era of imperial power is long gone, never to return; in the world at large, the authoritarian system is on the wane; citizens ought to become the true masters of their states. The fundamental way out for China lies only in dispelling the subservient notion of reliance on "enlightened rulers" and "upright officials," promoting public consciousness of rights as fundamental and participation as a duty, and putting into practice freedom, engaging in democracy, and respecting the law.

Our Basic Positions

Thus, in the spirit of responsible and constructive citizens, we put forth the following specific positions regarding various aspects of state administration, citizens' rights and interests, and social development:

1. **Constitutional Amendment:** Based on the aforementioned values and concepts, amend the Constitution, deleting clauses in the current Constitution that are not in conformity with the principle that sovereignty resides in the people, so that the Constitution can truly become a document that guarantees human rights and allows for the exercise of public power, and become the enforceable supreme law that no individual, group, or party can violate, establishing the foundation of the legal authority for democratizing China.

2. **Separation of Powers and Checks and Balances:** Construct a modern government that separates powers and maintains checks and balances among them, that guarantees the separation of legislative, judicial, and

executive powers. Establish the principle of statutory administration and responsible government to prevent excessive expansion of executive power; government should be responsible to taxpayers; . . . the central power must be clearly defined and mandated by the Constitution, and the localities must exercise full autonomy.

3. **Legislative Democracy:** Legislative bodies at all levels should be created through direct elections; maintain the principle of fairness and justice in making law; and implement legislative democracy.

4. **Judicial Independence:** The judiciary should transcend partisanship, be free from any interference, exercise judicial independence, and guarantee judicial fairness; it should establish a constitutional court and a system to investigate violations of the Constitution, and uphold the authority of the Constitution. . . .

5. **Public Use of Public Instruments:** Bring the armed forces under state control. Military personnel should render loyalty to the Constitution and to the country. Political party organizations should withdraw from the armed forces; raise the professional standards of the armed forces. All public employees including the police should maintain political neutrality. Abolish discrimination in hiring of public employees based on party affiliation; there should be equality in hiring regardless of party affiliation.

6. **Human Rights Guarantees:** Guarantee human rights in earnest; protect human dignity. Set up a Commission on Human Rights, responsible to the highest organ of popular will, to prevent government abuse of public authority and violations of human rights, and, especially, to guarantee the personal freedom of citizens. No one shall suffer illegal arrest, detention, subpoena, interrogation, or punishment. Abolish the Reeducation-Through-Labor system.

7. **Election of Public Officials:** Fully implement the system of democratic elections to realize equal voting rights based on "one person, one vote." Systematically and gradually implement direct elections of administrative heads at all levels. Regular elections based on free competition and citizen participation in elections for legal public office are inalienable basic human rights.

8. **Urban-Rural Equality:** Abolish the current urban-rural two-tier household registration system to realize the constitutional right of equality before the law for all citizens and guarantee the citizens' right to move freely.

9. **Freedom of Association:** Guarantee citizens' right to freedom of association. Change the current system of registration upon approval for community groups to a system of record-keeping. Lift the ban on political parties. Regulate party activities according to the Constitution and law; abolish the privilege of one-party monopoly on power; establish the principles of freedom of activities of political parties and fair competition for political parties; normalize and legally regulate party politics.

10. **Freedom of Assembly:** Freedoms to peacefully assemble, march, demonstrate, and express [opinions] are citizens' fundamental freedoms stipulated by the Constitution; they should not be subject to illegal interference and unconstitutional restrictions by the ruling party and the government.

11. **Freedom of Expression:** Realize the freedom of speech, freedom to publish, and academic freedom; guarantee the citizens' right to know and right to supervise [public institutions]. Enact a "News Law" and a "Publishing Law," lift the ban on reporting, repeal the "crime of inciting subversion of state power" clause in the current *Criminal Law*, and put an end to punishing speech as a crime.

12. **Freedom of Religion:** Guarantee freedom of religion and freedom of belief, and implement separation of religion and state so that activities involving religion and faith are not subjected to government interference. Examine and repeal administrative statutes, administrative rules, and local statutes that restrict or deprive citizens of religious freedom; ban management of religious activities by administrative legislation. Abolish the system that requires that religious groups (and including places of worship) obtain prior approval of their legal status in order to register, and replace it with a system of record-keeping that requires no scrutiny.

13. **Civic Education:** Abolish political education and political examinations that are heavy on ideology and serve the one-party rule. Popularize civic education based on universal values and civil rights, establish civic consciousness, and advocate civic virtues that serve society.

14. **Property Protection:** Establish and protect private property rights, and implement a system based on a free and open market economy; guarantee entrepreneurial freedom, and eliminate administrative monopolies; set up a Committee for the Management of State-Owned Property, responsible to the highest organ of popular will; launch reform of property rights in a legal and orderly fashion, and clarify the ownership of property rights and those responsible; launch a new land movement,

advance land privatization, and guarantee in earnest the land property rights of citizens, particularly the farmers.

15. **Fiscal Reform:** Democratize public finances and guarantee taxpayers' rights. Set up the structure and operational mechanism of a public finance system with clearly defined authority and responsibilities, and establish a rational and effective system of decentralized financial authority among various levels of government; carry out a major reform of the tax system, so as to reduce tax rates, simplify the tax system, and equalize the tax burden. Administrative departments may not increase taxes or create new taxes at will without sanction by society obtained through a public elective process and resolution by organs of popular will. Pass property rights reform to diversify and introduce competition mechanisms into the market; lower the threshold for entry into the financial field and create conditions for the development of privately-owned financial enterprises, and fully energize the financial system.

16. **Social Security:** Establish a social security system that covers all citizens and provides them with basic security in education, medical care, care for the elderly, and employment.

17. **Environmental Protection:** Protect the ecological environment, promote sustainable development, and take responsibility for future generations and all humanity; clarify and impose the appropriate responsibilities that state and government officials at all levels must take to this end; promote participation and oversight by civil society groups in environmental protection.

18. **Federal Republic:** Take part in maintaining regional peace and development with an attitude of equality and fairness, and create an image of a responsible great power. Protect the free systems of Hong Kong and Macau. On the premise of freedom and democracy, seek a reconciliation plan for the mainland and Taiwan through equal negotiations and cooperative interaction. Wisely explore possible paths and institutional blueprints for the common prosperity of all ethnic groups, and establish the Federal Republic of China under the framework of a democratic and constitutional government.

19. **Transitional Justice:** Restore the reputation of and give state compensation to individuals, as well as their families, who suffered political persecution during past political movements; release all political prisoners and prisoners of conscience; release all people convicted for their beliefs; establish a Commission for Truth Investigation to find the truth of historical events, determine responsibility, and uphold justice; seek social reconciliation on this foundation.

7

Occupy Wall Street, 2011

In the wake of a global financial crisis in 2008 and the following "Great Recession" that in some countries duplicated the effects of the Great Depression of the 1930s, a number of movements sprang up in opposition to what were seen as the progenitors of the crisis: Wall Street, corporations, crony capitalism, government support of big money, and economic inequality. One of the most visible of these protests, because of its location, was Occupy Wall Street. But similar groups sprang up in cities in the United States and throughout the world. Here we see a declaration from the New York group as well as images from protests on both Wall Street and in Adelaide, New Zealand.

Critics of the protests frequently said that it was not clear what the protesters wanted. What does the New York document tell you about the demands of the protesters? Do they seem to be all over the map, or is there a unifying theme? In what ways would the realization of these goals increase democracy? How are these economic demands different from the more political demands of previous movements documented in this chapter?

Finally, look at the two photos. Do they suggest diverse protests across the globe or a considerable degree of consensus? Are these images from opposite sides of the world distinct or interchangeable?

THINKING HISTORICALLY

The demands in the New York declaration spring from the specific context of the financial crisis in the United States. Yet the authors reach out to connect with movements throughout the world. How does a national context become a global context? What phrases or stylistic features connect this document to other declarations or manifestos of the past?

Declaration of the Occupation of New York City

This document was accepted by the NYC General Assembly on September 29, 2011.

As we gather together in solidarity to express a feeling of mass injustice, we must not lose sight of what brought us together. We write so that all people who feel wronged by the corporate forces of the world can know that we are your allies.

Source: http://www.nycga.net/resources/declaration/ or http://occupywallst.org/forum/first-official-release-from-occupy-wall-street/

As one people, united, we acknowledge the reality: that the future of the human race requires the cooperation of its members; that our system must protect our rights, and upon corruption of that system, it is up to the individuals to protect their own rights, and those of their neighbors; that a democratic government derives its just power from the people, but corporations do not seek consent to extract wealth from the people and the Earth; and that no true democracy is attainable when the process is determined by economic power. We come to you at a time when corporations, which place profit over people, self-interest over justice, and oppression over equality, run our governments. We have peaceably assembled here, as is our right, to let these facts be known.

- They have taken our houses through an illegal foreclosure process, despite not having the original mortgage.
- They have taken bailouts from taxpayers with impunity, and continue to give Executives exorbitant bonuses.
- They have perpetuated inequality and discrimination in the workplace based on age, the color of one's skin, sex, gender identity and sexual orientation.
- They have poisoned the food supply through negligence, and undermined the farming system through monopolization.
- They have profited off of the torture, confinement, and cruel treatment of countless animals, and actively hide these practices.
- They have continuously sought to strip employees of the right to negotiate for better pay and safer working conditions.
- They have held students hostage with tens of thousands of dollars of debt on education, which is itself a human right.
- They have consistently outsourced labor and used that outsourcing as leverage to cut workers' healthcare and pay.
- They have influenced the courts to achieve the same rights as people, with none of the culpability or responsibility.
- They have spent millions of dollars on legal teams that look for ways to get them out of contracts in regards to health insurance.
- They have sold our privacy as a commodity.
- They have used the military and police force to prevent freedom of the press.
- They have deliberately declined to recall faulty products endangering lives in pursuit of profit.
- They determine economic policy, despite the catastrophic failures their policies have produced and continue to produce.
- They have donated large sums of money to politicians, who are responsible for regulating them.
- They continue to block alternate forms of energy to keep us dependent on oil.

- They continue to block generic forms of medicine that could save people's lives or provide relief in order to protect investments that have already turned a substantial profit.
- They have purposely covered up oil spills, accidents, faulty book-keeping, and inactive ingredients in pursuit of profit.
- They purposefully keep people misinformed and fearful through their control of the media.
- They have accepted private contracts to murder prisoners even when presented with serious doubts about their guilt.
- They have perpetuated colonialism at home and abroad.
- They have participated in the torture and murder of innocent civilians overseas.
- They continue to create weapons of mass destruction in order to receive government contracts.

To the people of the world,

We, the New York City General Assembly occupying Wall Street in Liberty Square, urge you to assert your power.

Exercise your right to peaceably assemble; occupy public space; create a process to address the problems we face, and generate solutions accessible to everyone.

Figure 27.1   Occupy Wall Street, 2011.
Source: Tomas Abad/Alamy.

Figure 27.2   Occupy Aukland, New Zealand, 2011.
Source: EPA/Kim Ludbrook/Landov.

To all communities that take action and form groups in the spirit of direct democracy, we offer support, documentation, and all of the resources at our disposal.

Join us and make your voices heard!

8

WILLIAM MOSS WILSON

Just Don't Call Her Che, 2012

This piece from the *New York Times* is interesting in a number of ways. As a media phenomenon: Camila Vallejo, a striking unknown becomes a global media sensation. It is also interesting in that it turns our study of new democracy movements full circle since many of the

Source: William Moss Wilson, "Just Don't Call Her Che" (*New York Times*, January 29, 2012), SR 5.

democratic movements since 1977 were related to the fall of communism in the Soviet Union and its satellites, and this woman declares
herself a communist. Further, Chile is already perceived as something
of a democratic success story: The age of dictator Augusto Pinochet
has been discredited, and democratic elections have brought new
leaders from the socialist party that elected Salvador Allende in 1970.
And yet, as Wilson writes, Chile is still the thirteenth most unequal
country in the world and that inequality manifests itself glaringly in
the meager state support for public education.

So this article raises some important questions in Chile that might
be asked in the United States and other countries that have already
experienced democratic revolutions. How important is education to
democracy? How important is equal access to education? What is
the impact of high fees, heavy loans, private institutions for the
wealthy, separate educational tracks for rich and poor? Is education
a human right? Is equal access to education a necessary ingredient of
democracy in the modern knowledge economy?

THINKING HISTORICALLY

Asking about connections and context (or what is borrowed from elsewhere and what is invented in the local context) in a political movement
is difficult enough when we have a primary source to draw on. Here we
have only the journalist's account. Nevertheless, what in Wilson's description of this movement suggests possible connections to Gene Sharp
or Wael Ghonim? What strikes you as more likely local or Chilean?

Late last month the British newspaper *The Guardian* asked readers to
vote for its person of the year. The candidates included household names
like German Chancellor Angela Merkel, the Egyptian techno-revolutionary
Wael Ghonim and the Burmese pro-democracy leader Daw Aung San Suu
Kyi. All placed far behind a striking, nose-ringed student from Chile
named Camila Vallejo.

Though far from a familiar face in the United States, the 23-year-old
Ms. Vallejo has gained rock-star status among the global activist class.
Since June she has led regular street marches of up to 200,000 people
through Santiago's broad avenues — the largest demonstrations since the
waning days of the Pinochet regime in the late 1980s. Under her leadership, the mobilization, known as the Chilean Winter, has gained nation-
wide support; one of its slogans, "We are the 90 percent," referred to its
approval rating in late September.

Ms. Vallejo's charismatic leadership has led commentators to make
the obligatory comparisons to other Latin American leftist icons like
Subcomandante Marcos and Che Guevara. Yet "Commander Camila,"
as her followers call her, has become a personality in her own regard.

She skewers senators in primetime TV debates and stays on message with daytime talk-show hosts hungry for lurid details about her personal life, while her eloquence gives her a preternatural ability to connect with an audience far beyond her left-wing base.

In perhaps the most poignant set piece in the year of the protester, Ms. Vallejo addressed a dense ring of photographers and reporters in August while kneeling within a peace sign made of spent teargas shells, where she calmly mused about how many educational improvements could have been bought with the $100,000 worth of munitions at her feet.

Ms. Vallejo, like many of her fellow student leaders, is an avowed communist. But while she has publicly commended other regional leftists like Presidents Evo Morales of Bolivia and Rafael Correa of Ecuador, she and her generation have little in common with the older left of Fidel Castro or Hugo Chávez. They are less ideological purists than change-seeking pragmatists, even if that means working within the existing political order.

Still, there's no question that the movement is upending Chilean society. True, it is centered on a policy question, namely reforming an educational system that disproportionally favors the children of wealthy families. But the earth-shaking Paris protests in 1968 also began with calls for university reform — before spiraling into street battles between radicalized students and truncheon-wielding gendarmes, opposing symbols in the culture war between old and new France.

The same process is under way in Chile. As the protests increasingly devolve into rock and tear-gas exchanges between students and the police, it's becoming clear that more than education policy is at stake: a nonviolent social revolution in which disaffected, politically savvy youth are trying to overthrow the mores of an older generation, one they feel is still tainted by the legacy of Pinochet. It is not just about policy reform, but also about changing the underlying timbers of Chilean society.

It's no surprise that the movement should be led by someone as charismatic as Ms. Vallejo. Paris 1968 had its celebrity protesters, handsome faces that brought hundreds of thousands into the streets, photogenic young men like Jacques Sauvageot and Daniel Cohn-Bendit. Chile has Ms. Vallejo.

Chile is perhaps Latin America's greatest success story. After decades of authoritarian rule, it has spent the last 20 years building a thriving economy with a renewed democratic culture and a booming, educated middle class. But it is also confronting a dangerous imbalance: While the liberalization of higher education has led to improvements in access, tuition has consistently outpaced inflation and now represents 40 percent of the average household's income.

At the same time, protesters say that wealthy students from private and expensive, co-pay charter schools have unfair access to elite universities, while the rest struggle to meet entrance standards at under-financed public institutions.

Criticism of the university system has been growing for years, but it was only in April that, energized by protests against a dam in Patagonia, students finally took to the streets. The protests grew over the winter; by the first press conference held by the national confederation of student unions, known as the Confech, Ms. Vallejo had emerged as its leader.

Echoing 1960s street activism, the Chilean Winter dabbled in the absurd, but with a high-tech, social-media twist. Thousands gathered in front of the presidential palace in June dressed as zombies, then broke into a choreographed dance to Michael Jackson's "Thriller." In July, students again gathered in front of the palace for a huge "kiss-in."

Though the ideas came, said Giorgio Jackson, former student president of Chile's Catholic University, from "everywhere, absolutely every local space," the movement's success hinged on the leadership's ability to channel such creativity while maintaining a unified front to government and the media. The organization used a Web site to gather ideas and disseminate content for placards and posters. And it has used Ms. Vallejo's 300,000-plus Twitter followers to quickly initiate huge "cacerolazos," a form of dictatorship-era protest where people walk the streets banging on pots and pans.

While they vow to continue until all their lofty demands are met, the students have already scored some political victories. The government's proposed 2012 budget has a $350 million increase for higher education, with promises to finance scholarships for qualifying students from families up to the 60th percentile in household income. Meanwhile, the year began with the naming of Chile's third education minister in six months.

It was only a matter of time, perhaps, before the movement's focus on education began to broaden. As more support for the movement came from outside the universities, its interests changed accordingly. "This year we have already started talking about political reforms and tax reforms, and we think the students and youth in general play an important role in profound reforms in the country," said Noam Titelman, the new student president at Catholic University.

Tax reform is, not coincidentally, now at the top of the government's agenda. And rightly so: though it has the largest economy in Latin America, Chile is the 13th most unequal country in the world.

"Something very powerful that has come out of the heart of this movement is that people are really questioning the economic policies of the country," Ms. Vallejo said. "People are not tolerating the way a small number of economic groups benefit from the system. Having a market economy is really different from having a market society. What we are asking for, via education reform, is that the state take on a different role."

The movement has also begun to spread regionally. Ms. Vallejo lent her star power to Brazilian student protests in August, while in November students demonstrated in France, Germany and several other countries in support of Confech's Latin American March for Education.

"The student movement here is permanently connected to other student movements, principally in Latin America, but also in the world," Ms. Vallejo said. "We believe this reveals something fundamental: that there is a global demand for the recovery and defense of the right to education."

But the students clearly have a lot to learn about real-world politics. Ms. Vallejo and other student leaders spent weeks lobbying in Parliament, only to be left out of the final budget negotiations.

Frustration with Ms. Vallejo's strategy propelled a rival leftist, Gabriel Boric, to challenge her in the latest round of student-government elections. On Dec. 7, national TV news crews lingered past 5 a.m. outside the University of Chile to cover a stunning defeat for the world's most famous student leader.

Yet even in her early-morning concession speech, Ms. Vallejo claimed victory, recognizing that the movement was greater than any one figure. Indeed, her rise has barely broken stride. She just left for a speaking tour in Europe, while her first book, a collection of her speeches and essays for the last year, is rising through the best-seller ranks. And she is being heavily courted by the Communist Party to run at the top of its list for the Chilean Congress in the 2013 elections.

For all its recent stumbles, the movement's prospects of getting a woman under 26 elected to Congress would help fulfill one of its underlying aims, to kindle young people's interest in traditional politics. This may be Ms. Vallejo's greatest contribution: to restore faith in a discredited system by showing a new generation that politics can be responsive to the people's demands.

■ REFLECTIONS

This chapter has argued that democracy is new and spreading, especially in recent years and decades. But any argument has to bear the burden of a counterargument. How might we counter the argument of this chapter?

First we might point out that a claim for recent years or decades is always subject to the near-sightedness of the present. Recent events and movements that seem important now may well disappear from the longer view a hundred or five hundred years from now. A century from now, will the six years of Gorbachev's reform become a blip, possibly like the Russian Revolution of 1905 or even that of 1917, in a long history of continued Czarism from Saint Vladimir I's rule during the tenth century through Putin VI's rule in the twenty-second century? Will the Arab Spring seem like the seasonal change the term implies rather than the beginning of a new age? Has Egypt seen its last pharaoh or was Mubarak only the most recent?

This line of questioning rests, I think too much, on a belief that the past is far more continuous than it is. Many other fifty-year periods of the past experienced as many protests as our own age. Many other historical periods produced protests of the have-nots against the haves. But the ideas and vocabulary of democracy are certainly new at least to recent centuries. No peasant uprising of the ancient or medieval world called for elected representatives, universal suffrage, equality before the law, the people as source of the law, freedom of expression, belief, and religion, universal education, social justice, and human rights. These are all principles and practices that have evolved and developed over the last couple of centuries. They all have earlier roots, but taken together they form a set of hopes, expectations, and experiences that are distinctly modern. Times *do* change.

A second line of criticism might run like this. Even if democracy is a modern idea and experience, how can we certify a flowering in a couple of protests, many of which have been thwarted or defeated? Gorbachev's democratization, after all, occurred twenty-five years ago and even Russians do not remember it fondly. Some of the democratic gains that were won by Gorbachev by 1991 receded in the following years under Boris Yeltsin, first President of the Russian Federation (1991–1999), and Vladimir Putin (president and prime minister since 1999). To take one indicator of glasnost—press freedom—since 1993 over 200 Russian journalists have been murdered, making Russia the third most dangerous country in the world for a free press. Gorbachev today calls for a new wave of democratic protests in Russia: something like the Arab Spring. And what about the Arab Spring? Only a year after 2011 the optimism of the Arab Spring has soured for many Egyptians who thrilled to the prospect of a liberal civic society for all Egyptians— Christian and Muslim—as the Muslim Brotherhood Party's struggle against the unyielding military squeezes out secular democrats. In more secular Tunisia, the achievement of democratic revolution, one Tunisian recently quipped, is that now "everyone is above the law."[1] In Libya, the revolution that deposed Gaddafi reverted to tribal war, the uprising in Syria led to sectarian conflict and civil war, and those of Bahrain and Yemen were crushed (with some U.S. support).

To this argument, I would respond that the Arab revolution is definitely a work in progress. It occurs in a part of the world where democracy was least expected. The same might be said of the former Soviet Union. Gorbachev started a process that unleashed democratic and national independence movements throughout the former Soviet dominions. Some of these continue to be controlled by single parties or strong men, but not all. Czechoslovakia managed a peaceful Velvet Revolution and then a peaceful divorce between the Czech Republic

---

[1] Quoted by Michael J. Totten, Dispatches, April 18, 2012, at http://www .worldaffairsjournal.org/blogs/michael-j-totten.

and Slovakia. Poland and Hungary have become viable democracies. The Baltic states—Estonia, Lithuania, and Latvia—are independent republics. Many of the former Soviet states like Ukraine, Belarus, and "the stans" are independent. And, perhaps most remarkably of all, the former East Germany became independent, then part of a unified German state, one of the most democratic in Europe. One can carp about backsliding in Russia and the rise of supernationalists in Hungary, but there is no way to dismiss the numbers of people or countries who now govern themselves. Their example and the example of even temporarily successful democratic revolutions from the Philippines to Paraguay have buttressed the expectation that self-government in a free society is the right of all.

Democracy is not a light turned on, or off. It is a process that advances, or recedes. Still the advances are more contagious and longer lasting, at least in the mind. Few want to return to the conditions of dictatorship. But the process is rarely smooth. There are those in any society who lose privilege or power in a democratic revolution. And they are, by definition, the privileged and powerful.

The Mothers of the Disappeared still gather around the Plaza de Mayo; they still seek a full accounting for the acts of state terrorism under the military junta of the 1970s. Students in Chile are fighting battles fought by their parents and grandparents. Latin Americans celebrate democratic and independence movements that go back hundreds of years, but that have still not been fully realized. Indeed, in the Americas and the rest of the world the goalposts have moved since the days when democratic states accepted enslaved Africans, invisible Indians, and colonial subjects. Recent claims for human rights, freedom from sexual or gender discrimination, international jurisdiction over war crimes and genocide are all extensions of our democratic expectations. Failure or retrenchment can be seen as the setting of the next battle rather than a sign that democracy failed or, worse, that it doesn't work.

Democratic demands in the twenty-first century reach further than ever before. Likewise, the conditions for achieving democracy have also expanded. A democracy that was limited to white men of the propertied class could function with an educational system that ignored everyone else. A mass democracy requires a mass citizenry educated to think and participate intelligently. It requires what Franklin D. Roosevelt called "freedom from want" to allow all citizens the time and resources to participate. And it requires the level playing field, unencumbered by special interests with private agendas. The early years of modern liberal democracy heard the call for the separation of church and state. Today we hear the call for the separation of corporations and the state. The effort to create the public space where citizens can create their common world continues.

28

Globalization

The World, 1990 to the Present

■ HISTORICAL CONTEXT

Globalization is a term used by historians, economists, politicians, religious leaders, social reformers, business people, and average citizens to describe large-scale changes and trends in the world today. It is often defined as a complex phenomenon whereby individuals, nations, and regions of the world become increasingly integrated and interdependent, while national and traditional identities are diminished. Although it is a widely used term, *globalization* is also a controversial and widely debated topic. Is globalization really a new phenomenon, or is it a continuation of earlier trends? Is it driven by technological forces or economic forces, or both? Does it enrich or impoverish? Is it democratizing or antidemocratic? Is it generally a positive or negative thing?

Some limit the definition of globalization to the global integration driven by the development of the international market economy in the last twenty to forty years. Worldwide integration dates back much further, however, and has important technological, cultural, and political causes as well. In fact, all of human history can be understood as the story of increased interaction on a limited planet. Ancient empires brought diverse peoples from vast regions of the world together under single administrations. These empires, connected by land or maritime routes, interacted with each other through trade and exploration, exchanging goods as well as ideas. The unification of the Eastern and Western hemispheres after 1492 was a major step in the globalization of crops, peoples, cultures, and diseases. The industrial revolution joined countries and continents in ever vaster and faster transportation and communication networks. The great colonial empires that developed during the eighteenth and nineteenth centuries integrated the populations of far-flung areas of the world. The commercial aspects of these developments cannot be divorced from religious zeal, technological innovations, and political motives, which were often driving factors.

The current era of economic globalization is largely a product of the industrial capitalist world, roughly dating back to the middle of the nineteenth century. We might call the period between 1850 and 1914 the first great age of globalization in the modern sense. It was the age of ocean liners, mass migrations, undersea telegraph cables, transcontinental railroads, refrigeration, and preserved canned foods, when huge European empires dramatically reduced the number of sovereign states in the world. The period ended with World War I, which not only dug trenches between nations and wiped out a generation of future migrants and visitors, but also planted seeds of animosity that festered for decades, strangling the growth of international trade, interaction, and immigration.

Since the conclusion of World War II in 1945, and increasingly since the end of the Cold War in 1989, political and technological developments have enabled economic globalization on a wider scale and at a faster pace than occurred during the previous age of steamships and telegraphs. The collapse of the Soviet Union and international communism unleashed the forces of market capitalism as never before. Jet travel, satellite technology, mobile phones, and the World Wide Web have revived global integration and enabled the global marketplace. The United States, the World Bank, and the International Monetary Fund led in the creation of regional and international free-trade agreements, the reduction of tariffs, and the removal of national trade barriers, touting these changes as agents of material progress and democratic transformation. Yet these changes have also elicited wide-ranging resistance in peaceful protests, especially against the West's economic dominance, and violent ones against the West's political and cultural domination, such as the terrorist attacks on September 11, 2001.

Multinational companies are now able to generate great wealth by moving capital, labor, raw materials, and finished products through international markets at increasing speeds and with lasting impact. This economic globalization has profound cultural ramifications; increasingly the peoples of the world are watching the same films and television programs, speaking the same languages, wearing the same clothes, enjoying the same amusements, and listening to the same music. Whether free-market capitalism lifts all boats, or only yachts, is a hotly debated issue today.

■ THINKING HISTORICALLY

Understanding Process

What are the most important ways in which the world is changing? What are the most significant and powerful forces of change? What is the engine that is driving our world? These are the big questions raised at the end of historical investigation. They also arise at the beginning, as the assumptions that shape our specific investigations. *Globalization* is one of the words most frequently used to describe the big changes that are occurring in our world. All of the readings in this chapter assume or describe some kind of global integration as a dominant driver of the world in which we live. This chapter asks you to think about large-scale historical processes. It asks you to examine globalization as one of the most important of these processes. It asks you to reflect on what globalization means, and what causes it. How does each of these authors use the term? Do the authors see this process as primarily commercial and market-driven, or do they view it as a matter of culture or politics? Does globalization come from one place or many, from a center outwards, or from one kind of society to another? Is globalization linear or unidirectional, or does it have differing, even opposite effects? What do these writers, thinkers, and activists believe about the most important changes transforming our world? And what do you think?

1

SHERIF HETATA

Dollarization, 1998

Sherif Hetata is an Egyptian intellectual, novelist, and activist who was originally trained as a medical doctor. He and his wife, the prominent feminist writer Nawal El-Saadawi, have worked together to promote reform in Egypt and the larger Arab world. In this presentation given at a conference on globalization, Hetata outlines the global economy's homogenizing effects on culture. Through what historic lens does Hetata view globalization? What links does he make between globalization and imperialism? What do you think of his argument?

Source: Sherif Hetata, "Dollarization, Fragmentation, and God," in *The Cultures of Globalization*, ed. Fredric Jameson and Masao Miyoshi (Durham, NC: Duke University Press, 1998), 273–74, 276–80.

THINKING HISTORICALLY

What, according to Hetata, is the main process that is changing the world? Does he think the engine of world change is primarily technological, commercial, or cultural?

As a young medical student, born and brought up in a colony, like many other people in my country, Egypt, I quickly learned to make the link between politics, economics, culture, and religion. Educated in an English school, I discovered that my English teachers looked down on us. We learned Rudyard Kipling by heart, praised the glories of the British Empire, followed the adventures of Kim in India, imbibed the culture of British supremacy, and sang carols on Christmas night.

At the medical school in university, when students demonstrated against occupation by British troops it was the Moslem Brothers who beat them up, using iron chains and long curved knives, and it was the governments supported by the king that shot at them or locked them up.

When I graduated in 1946, the hospital wards taught me how poverty and health are linked. I needed only another step to know that poverty had something to do with colonial rule, with the king who supported it, with class and race, with what was called imperialism at the time, with cotton prices falling on the market, with the seizure of land by foreign banks. These things were common talk in family gatherings, expressed in a simple, colorful language without frills. They were the facts of everyday life. We did not need to read books to make the links: They were there for us to see and grasp. And every time we made a link, someone told us it was time to stop, someone in authority whom we did not like: a ruler or a father, a policeman or a teacher, a landowner, a *maulana* (religious leader or teacher), a Jesuit, or a God.

And if we went on making these links, they locked us up.

For me, therefore, coming from this background, cultural studies and globalization open up a vast horizon, one of global links in a world where things are changing quickly. It is a chance to learn and probe how the economics, the politics, the culture, the philosophical thought of our days connect or disconnect, harmonize or contradict.

Of course, I will not even try to deal with all of that. I just want to raise a few points to discuss under the title of my talk, "Dollarization, Fragmentation, and God." Because I come from Egypt, my vantage point will be that of someone looking at the globe from the part we now call South, rather than "third world" or something else.

A New Economic Order: Gazing North at the Global Few

Never before in the history of the world has there been such a concentration and centralization of capital in so few nations and in the hands of so few people. The countries that form the Group of Seven,[1] with their 800 million inhabitants, control more technological, economic, informatics, and military power than the rest of the approximately 4.3 billion who live in Asia, Africa, Eastern Europe, and Latin America.

Five hundred multinational corporations account for 80 percent of world trade and 75 percent of investment. Half of all the multinational corporations are based in the United States, Germany, Japan, and Switzerland. The OECD (Organisation for Economic Cooperation and Development) group of countries contributes 80 percent of world production. . . .

A Global Culture for a Global Market

To expand the world market, to globalize it, to maintain the New Economic Order, the multinational corporations use economic power and control politics and the armed forces. But this is not so easy. People will always resist being exploited, resist injustice, struggle for their freedom, their needs, security, a better life, peace.

However, it becomes easier if they can be convinced to do what the masters of the global economy want them to do. This is where the issue of culture comes in. Culture can serve in different ways to help the global economy reach out all over the world and expand its markets to the most distant regions. Culture can also serve to reduce or destroy or prevent or divide or outflank the resistance of people who do not like what is happening to them, or have their doubts about it, or want to think. Culture can be like cocaine, which is going global these days: from Kali in Colombia to Texas, to Madrid, to the Italian mafiosi in southern Italy, to Moscow, Burma, and Thailand, a worldwide network uses the methods and the cover of big business, with a total trade of $5 billion a year, midway between oil and the arms trade.

At the disposal of global culture today are powerful means that function across the whole world: the media, which, like the economy, have made it one world, a bipolar North/South world. If genetic engineering gives scientists the possibility of programming embryos before children are born, children, youth, and adults are now being programmed after

---

[1] Canada, France, Germany, Italy, Japan, the United Kingdom, and the United States meet as the G7. [Ed.]

they are born in the culture they imbibe mainly through the media, but also in the family, in school, at the university, and elsewhere. Is this an exaggeration? an excessively gloomy picture of the world?

To expand the global market, increase the number of consumers, make sure that they buy what is sold, develop needs that conform to what is produced, and develop the fever of consumerism, culture must play a role in developing certain values, patterns of behavior, visions of what is happiness and success in the world, attitudes toward sex and love. Culture must model a global consumer.

In some ways, I was a "conservative radical." I went to jail, but I always dressed in a classical, subdued way. When my son started wearing blue jeans and New Balance shoes, I shivered with horror. He's going to become like some of those crazy kids abroad, the disco generation, I thought! Until the age of twenty-five he adamantly refused to smoke. Now he smokes two packs of Marlboros a day (the ones that the macho cowboy smokes). That does not prevent him from being a talented film director. But in the third-world, films, TV, and other media have increased the percentage of smokers. I saw half-starved kids in a marketplace in Mali buying single imported Benson & Hedges cigarettes and smoking.

But worse was still to come. Something happened that to me seemed impossible at one time, more difficult than adhering to a leftwing movement. At the age of seventy-one, I have taken to wearing blue jeans and Nike shoes. I listen to rock and reggae and sometimes rap. I like to go to discos and I sometimes have other cravings, which so far I have successfully fought! And I know these things have crept into our lives through the media, through TV, films, radio, advertisements, newspapers, and even novels, music, and poetry. It's a culture and it's reaching out, becoming global.

In my village, I have a friend. He is a peasant and we are very close. He lives in a big mud hut, and the animals (buffalo, sheep, cows, and donkeys) live in the house with him. Altogether, in the household, with the wife and children of his brother, his uncle, the mother, and his own family, there are thirty people. He wears a long *galabeya* (robe), works in the fields for long hours, and eats food cooked in the mud oven.

But when he married, he rode around the village in a hired Peugeot car with his bride. She wore a white wedding dress, her face was made up like a film star, her hair curled at the hairdresser's of the provincial town, her finger and toe nails manicured and polished, and her body bathed with special soap and perfumes. At the marriage ceremony, they had a wedding cake, which she cut with her husband's hand over hers. Very different from the customary rural marriage ceremony of his father. And all this change in the notion of beauty, of femininity, of celebration, of happiness, of prestige, of progress happened to my peasant friend and his bride in one generation.

The culprit, or the benevolent agent, depending on how you see it, was television.

In the past years, television has been the subject of numerous studies. In France, such studies have shown that before the age of twelve a child will have been exposed to an average 100,000 TV advertisements. Through these TV advertisements, the young boy or girl will have assimilated a whole set of values and behavioral patterns, of which he or she is not aware, of course. They become a part of his or her psychological (emotional and mental) makeup. Linked to these values are the norms and ways in which we see good and evil, beauty and ugliness, justice and injustice, truth and falseness, and which are being propagated at the same time. In other words, the fundamental values that form our aesthetic and moral vision of things are being inculcated, even hammered home, at this early stage, and they remain almost unchanged throughout life.

The commercial media no longer worry about the truthfulness or falsity of what they portray. Their role is to sell: beauty products, for example, to propagate the "beauty myth" and a "beauty culture" for both females and males alike and ensure that it reaches the farthest corners of the earth, including my village in the Delta of the Nile. Many of these beauty products are harmful to the health, can cause allergic disorders or skin infections or even worse. They cost money, work on the sex drives, and transform women and men, but especially women, into sex objects. They hide the real person, the natural beauty, the process of time, the stages of life, and instill false values about who we are, can be, or should become.

Advertisements do not depend on verifiable information or even rational thinking. They depend for their effect on images, colors, smart technical production, associations, and hidden drives. For them, attracting the opposite sex or social success or professional achievement and promotion or happiness do not depend on truthfulness or hard work or character, but rather on seduction, having a powerful car, buying things or people. . . .

Thus the media produce and reproduce the culture of consumption, of violence and sex to ensure that the global economic powers, the multinational corporations can promote a global market for themselves and protect it. And when everything is being bought or sold everyday and at all times in this vast supermarket, including culture, art, science, and thought, prostitution can become a way of life, for everything is priced. The search for the immediate need, the fleeting pleasure, the quick enjoyment, the commodity to buy, excess, pornography, drugs keeps this global economy rolling, for to stop is suicide.

PHILIPPE LEGRAIN

Cultural Globalization Is Not Americanization, 2003

Philippe Legrain, an economist, journalist, and former advisor to the World Trade Organization, takes aim at what he calls the myths of globalization in the following article. What, according to him, are these myths? What are the consequences of globalization according to Legrain? What evidence does he cite to support his argument? How does his view differ from that of Hetata?

THINKING HISTORICALLY

Does Legrain believe the driving force of globalization is economic or cultural? How important does he think globalization is? How, according to the author, is globalization changing the world?

Fears that globalization is imposing a deadening cultural uniformity are as ubiquitous as Coca-Cola, McDonald's, and Mickey Mouse. Europeans and Latin Americans, left-wingers and right, rich and poor — all of them dread that local cultures and national identities are dissolving into a crass All-American consumerism. That cultural imperialism is said to impose American values as well as products, promote the commercial at the expense of the authentic, and substitute shallow gratification for deeper satisfaction.

. . . If critics of globalization were less obsessed with "Cocacolonization," they might notice a rich feast of cultural mixing that belies fears about Americanized uniformity. Algerians in Paris practice Thai boxing; Asian rappers in London snack on Turkish pizza; Salman Rushdie delights readers everywhere with his Anglo-Indian tales. Although — as with any change — there can be downsides to cultural globalization, this cross-fertilization is overwhelmingly a force for good.

The beauty of globalization is that it can free people from the tyranny of geography. Just because someone was born in France does not mean they can only aspire to speak French, eat French food, read French books, visit museums in France, and so on. A Frenchman — or an American, for that matter — can take holidays in Spain or Florida, eat sushi or spaghetti for dinner, drink Coke or Chilean wine, watch a Hollywood blockbuster or an Almodóvar, listen to bhangra or rap, practice yoga or

---

Source: Philippe Legrain, "Cultural Globalization Is Not Americanization," *Chronicle of Higher Education* 49, no. 35 (May 9, 2003): B7.

kickboxing, read *Elle* or *The Economist*, and have friends from around the world. That we are increasingly free to choose our cultural experiences enriches our lives immeasurably. We could not always enjoy the best the world has to offer.

Globalization not only increases individual freedom, but also revitalizes cultures and cultural artifacts through foreign influences, technologies, and markets. Thriving cultures are not set in stone. They are forever changing from within and without. Each generation challenges the previous one; science and technology alter the way we see ourselves and the world; fashions come and go; experience and events influence our beliefs; outsiders affect us for good and ill.

Many of the best things come from cultures mixing: V. S. Naipaul's Anglo-Indo-Caribbean writing, Paul Gauguin painting in Polynesia, or the African rhythms in rock 'n' roll. Behold the great British curry. Admire the many-colored faces of France's World Cup–winning soccer team, the ferment of ideas that came from Eastern Europe's Jewish diaspora, and the cosmopolitan cities of London and New York. Western numbers are actually Arabic; zero comes most recently from India; Icelandic, French, and Sanskrit stem from a common root.

John Stuart Mill was right: "The economical benefits of commerce are surpassed in importance by those of its effects which are intellectual and moral. It is hardly possible to overrate the value, for the improvement of human beings, of things which bring them into contact with persons dissimilar to themselves, and with modes of thought and action unlike those with which they are familiar. . . . It is indispensable to be perpetually comparing [one's] own notions and customs with the experience and example of persons in different circumstances. . . . There is no nation which does not need to borrow from others."

It is a myth that globalization involves the imposition of Americanized uniformity, rather than an explosion of cultural exchange. For a start, many archetypal "American" products are not as all-American as they seem. Levi Strauss, a German immigrant, invented jeans by combining denim cloth (or "serge de Nîmes," because it was traditionally woven in the French town) with Genes, a style of trousers worn by Genoese sailors. So Levi's jeans are in fact an American twist on a European hybrid. Even quintessentially American exports are often tailored to local tastes. MTV in Asia promotes Thai pop stars and plays rock music sung in Mandarin. CNN en Español offers a Latin American take on world news. McDonald's sells beer in France, lamb in India, and chili in Mexico.

In some ways, America is an outlier, not a global leader. Most of the world has adopted the metric system born from the French Revolution; America persists with antiquated measurements inherited from its British-colonial past. Most developed countries have become intensely secular, but many Americans burn with fundamentalist fervor—like

Muslims in the Middle East. Where else in the developed world could there be a serious debate about teaching kids Bible-inspired "creationism" instead of Darwinist evolution?

America's tastes in sports are often idiosyncratic, too. Baseball and American football have not traveled well, although basketball has fared rather better. Many of the world's most popular sports, notably soccer, came by way of Britain. Asian martial arts—judo, karate, kickboxing—and pastimes like yoga have also swept the world.

People are not only guzzling hamburgers and Coke. Despite Coke's ambition of displacing water as the world's drink of choice, it accounts for less than 2 of the 64 fluid ounces that the typical person drinks a day. Britain's favorite takeaway is a curry, not a burger: Indian restaurants there outnumber McDonald's six to one. For all the concerns about American fast food trashing France's culinary traditions, France imported a mere $620 million in food from the United States in 2000, while exporting to America three times that. Nor is plonk[1] from America's Gallo displacing Europe's finest: Italy and France together account for three-fifths of global wine exports, the United States for only a twentieth. Worldwide, pizzas are more popular than burgers, Chinese restaurants seem to sprout up everywhere, and sushi is spreading fast. By far the biggest purveyor of alcoholic drinks is Britain's Diageo, which sells the world's best-selling whiskey (Johnnie Walker), gin (Gordon's), vodka (Smirnoff), and liqueur (Baileys).

In fashion, the ne plus ultra is Italian or French. Trendy Americans wear Gucci, Armani, Versace, Chanel, and Hermès. On the high street and in the mall, Sweden's Hennes & Mauritz (H&M) and Spain's Zara vie with America's Gap to dress the global masses. Nike shoes are given a run for their money by Germany's Adidas, Britain's Reebok, and Italy's Fila.

In pop music, American crooners do not have the stage to themselves. The three artists who were featured most widely in national Top Ten album charts in 2000 were America's Britney Spears, closely followed by Mexico's Carlos Santana and the British Beatles. Even tiny Iceland has produced a global star: Björk. Popular opera's biggest singers are Italy's Luciano Pavarotti, Spain's José Carreras, and the Spanish-Mexican Placido Domingo. Latin American salsa, Brazilian lambada, and African music have all carved out global niches for themselves. In most countries, local artists still top the charts. According to the IFPI, the record-industry bible, local acts accounted for 68 percent of music sales in 2000, up from 58 percent in 1991.

One of the most famous living writers is a Colombian, Gabriel García Márquez, author of *One Hundred Years of Solitude*. Paulo Coelho,

---

[1] British slang for cheap, low-quality alcohol. [Ed.]

another writer who has notched up tens of millions of global sales with *The Alchemist* and other books, is Brazilian. More than 200 million Harlequin romance novels, a Canadian export, were sold in 1990; they account for two-fifths of mass-market paperback sales in the United States. The biggest publisher in the English-speaking world is Germany's Bertelsmann, which gobbled up America's largest, Random House, in 1998.

Local fare glues more eyeballs to TV screens than American programs. Although nearly three-quarters of television drama exported worldwide comes from the United States, most countries' favorite shows are homegrown.

Nor are Americans the only players in the global media industry. Of the seven market leaders that have their fingers in nearly every pie, four are American (AOL Time Warner, Disney, Viacom, and News Corporation), one is German (Bertelsmann), one is French (Vivendi), and one Japanese (Sony). What they distribute comes from all quarters: Bertelsmann publishes books by American writers; News Corporation broadcasts Asian news; Sony sells Brazilian music.

The evidence is overwhelming. Fears about an Americanized uniformity are over-blown: American cultural products are not uniquely dominant; local ones are alive and well.

3

MIRIAM CHING YOON LOUIE

Sweatshop Warriors: Immigrant Women Workers Take On the Global Factory, 2001

Sherif Hetata and Philippe Legrain highlight the impact of globalization on consumers, but it is also important to examine how it affects workers. Free-trade policies have removed barriers to international trade, with global consequences. An example of such change can be witnessed along the border between Mexico and the United States, especially in the export factories, or *maquiladoras,** that are run by international corporations on both the U.S. and Mexican sides of the border. In the following excerpt, Miriam Ching Yoon Louie, a writer

---

* mah kee lah DOH rahs

Source: Miriam Ching Yoon Louie, *Sweatshop Warriors: Immigrant Women Workers Take On the Global Factory* (Cambridge, MA: South End Press, 2001), 65–71, 87–89.

and activist, interviews Mexican women who work in these factories and explores both the challenges they face and the strength they show in overcoming these challenges. What is the impact of liberalized trade laws on women who work in the *maquiladoras*? What is neoliberalism, and how is it tied to globalization? Why are women particularly vulnerable to these policies?

THINKING HISTORICALLY

According to Louie, how far back do neoliberalism and economic globalization date? How does Louie's assessment of economic globalization differ from the views expressed by Legrain? How might they both be right?

Many of today's *nuevas revolucionarias*[1] started working on the global assembly line as young women in northern Mexico for foreign transnational corporations. Some women worked on the U.S. side as "commuters" before they moved across the border with their families. Their stories reveal the length, complexity, and interpenetration of the U.S. and Mexican economies, labor markets, histories, cultures, and race relations. The women talk about the devastating impact of globalization, including massive layoffs and the spread of sweatshops on both sides of the border. *Las mujeres*[2] recount what drove them to join and lead movements for economic, racial, and gender justice, as well as the challenges they faced within their families and communities to assert their basic human rights. . . .

Growing Up Female and Poor

Mexican women and girls were traditionally expected to do all the cooking, cleaning, and serving for their husbands, brothers, and sons. For girls from poor families, shouldering these domestic responsibilities proved doubly difficult because they also performed farm, sweatshop, or domestic service work simultaneously. . . .

Petra Mata, a former seamstress for Levi's whose mother died shortly after childbirth, recalls the heavy housework she did as the only daughter:

> Aiyeee, let me tell you! It was very hard. In those times in Mexico, I was raised with the ideal that you have to learn to do everything— cook, make tortillas, wash your clothes, and clean the house—just the way they wanted you to. My grandparents were very strict. I always

[1] New revolutionaries. [Ed.]
[2] moo HAIR ace   The women. [Ed.]

had to ask their permission and then let them tell me what to do. I was not a free woman. Life was hard for me. I didn't have much of a childhood; I started working when I was 12 or 13 years old.

Neoliberalism and Creeping Maquiladorization

These women came of age during a period of major change in the relationship between the Mexican and U.S. economies. Like Puerto Rico, Hong Kong, South Korea, Taiwan, Malaysia, Singapore, and the Philippines, northern Mexico served as one of the first stations of the global assembly line tapping young women's labor. In 1965 the Mexican government initiated the Border Industrialization Program (BIP) that set up export plants, called *maquiladoras* or *maquilas*, which were either the direct subsidiaries or subcontractors of transnational corporations. Mexican government incentives to U.S. and other foreign investors included low wages and high productivity; infrastructure; proximity to U.S. markets, facilities, and lifestyles; tariff loopholes; and pliant, pro-government unions. . . .

Describing her quarter-century-long sewing career in Mexico, Celeste Jiménez ticks off the names of famous U.S. manufacturers who hopped over the border to take advantage of cheap wages:

> I sewed for twenty-four years when I lived in Chihuahua in big name factories like Billy the Kid, Levi Strauss, and Lee *maquiladoras*. Everyone was down there. Here a company might sell under the brand name of Lee; there in Mexico it would be called Blanca García.

Transnational exploitation of women's labor was part of a broader set of policies that critical opposition movements in the Third World have dubbed "neoliberalism," i.e., the new version of the British Liberal Party's program of laissez faire capitalism espoused by the rising European and U.S. colonial powers during the late eighteenth and nineteenth centuries. The Western powers, Japan, and international financial institutions like the World Bank and International Monetary Fund have aggressively promoted neoliberal policies since the 1970s. Mexico served as an early testing ground for such standard neoliberal policies as erection of free trade zones; commercialization of agriculture; currency devaluation; deregulation; privatization; outsourcing; cuts in wages and social programs; suppression of workers', women's, and indigenous people's rights; free trade; militarization; and promotion of neoconservative ideology.

Neoliberalism intersects with gender and national oppression. Third World women constitute the majority of migrants seeking jobs as maids, vendors, *maquila* operatives, and service industry workers. Women also pay the highest price for cuts in education, health and housing programs, and food and energy subsidies and increases in their unpaid labor. . . .

The deepening of the economic crisis in Mexico, especially under the International Monetary Fund's pressure to devaluate the peso in 1976, 1982, and 1994, forced many women to work in both the formal and informal economy to survive and meet their childbearing and household responsibilities. María Antonia Flores was forced to work two jobs after her husband abandoned the family, leaving her with three children to support. She had no choice but to leave her children home alone, *solitos,* to look after themselves. Refugio Arrieta straddled the formal and informal economy because her job in an auto parts assembly *maquiladora* failed to bring in sufficient income. To compensate for the shortfall, she worked longer hours at her *maquila* job and "moonlighted" elsewhere:

> We made chassis for cars and for the headlights. I worked lots! I worked 12 hours more or less because they paid us so little that if you worked more, you got more money. I did this because the schools in Mexico don't provide everything. You have to buy the books, notebooks, *todos, todos* [everything]. And I had five kids. It's very expensive. I also worked out of my house and sold ceramics. I did many things to get more money for my kids.

In the three decades following its humble beginnings in the mid-1960s, the *maquila* sector swelled to more than 2,000 plants employing an estimated 776,000 people, over 10 percent of Mexico's labor force. In 1985, *maquiladoras* overtook tourism as the largest source of foreign exchange. In 1996, this sector trailed only petroleum-related industries in economic importance and accounted for over U.S. $29 billion in export earnings annually. The *maquila* system has also penetrated the interior of the country, as in the case of Guadalajara's electronics assembly industry and Tehuacán's jeans production zones. Although the proportion of male *maquila* workers has increased since 1983, especially in auto-transport equipment assembly, almost 70 percent of the workers continue to be women.

As part of a delegation of labor and human rights activists, this author met some of Mexico's newest proletarians[3] — young indigenous women migrant workers from the Sierra Negra to Tehuacán, a town famous for its refreshing mineral water springs in the state of Puebla, just southeast of Mexico City. Standing packed like cattle in the back of the trucks each morning the women headed for jobs sewing for name

[3] Workers, especially exploited ones (a Marxist term derived from Latin for lower classes). [Ed.]

brand manufacturers like Guess?, VF Corporation (producing Lee brand clothing), Gap, Sun Apparel (producing brands such as Polo, Arizona, and Express), Cherokee, Ditto Apparel of California, Levi's, and others. The workers told U.S. delegation members that their wages averaged U.S. $30 to $50 a week for 12-hour work days, six days a week. Some workers reported having to do *veladas* [all-nighters] once or twice a week. Employees often stayed longer without pay if they did not finish high production goals.

Girls as young as 12 and 13 worked in the factories. Workers were searched when they left for lunch and again at the end of the day to check that they weren't stealing materials. Women were routinely given urine tests when hired and those found to be pregnant were promptly fired, in violation of Mexican labor law. Although the workers had organized an independent union several years earlier, Tehuacán's Human Rights Commission members told us that it had collapsed after one of its leaders was assassinated.

Carmen Valadez and Reyna Montero, long-time activists in the women's and social justice movements, helped found Casa de La Mujer Factor X in 1977, a workers' center in Tijuana that organizes around women's workplace, reproductive, and health rights, and against domestic violence. Valadez and Montero say that the low wages and dangerous working conditions characteristic of the *maquiladoras* on the Mexico-U.S. border are being "extended to all areas of the country and to Central America and the Caribbean. NAFTA represents nothing but the *'maquiladorization'* of the region."

Elizabeth "Beti" Robles Ortega, who began working in the *maquilas* at the age of fourteen and was blacklisted after participating in independent union organizing drives on Mexico's northern border, now works as an organizer for the Servicio, Desarrollo y Paz, AC 520 (SEDEPAC) [Service, Development and Peace organization]. Robles described the erosion of workers' rights and women's health under NAFTA:

> NAFTA has led to an increase in the workforce, as foreign industry has grown. They are reforming labor laws and our constitution to favor even more foreign investment, which is unfair against our labor rights. For example, they are now trying to take away from us free organization which was guaranteed by Mexican law. Because foreign capital is investing in Mexico and is dominating, we must have guarantees. The government is just there with its hands held out; it's always had them out but now even more shamelessly. . . . Ecological problems are increasing. A majority of women are coming down with cancer—skin and breast cancer, leukemia, and lung and heart problems. There are daily deaths of worker women. You can see and feel the contamination of the water and the air. As soon

as you arrive and start breathing the air in Acuña and Piedras Ne-
gras [border cities between the states of Coahuila and Texas], you
sense the heavy air, making you feel like vomiting.

Joining the Movement

Much of the education and leadership training the women received took
place "on the job." The women talked about how much their participation in the movement had changed them. They learned how to analyze
working conditions and social problems, who was responsible for these
conditions, and what workers could do to get justice. They learned to
speak truth to power, whether this was to government representatives,
corporate management, the media, unions, or co-ethnic gatekeepers.
They built relations with different kinds of sectors and groups and organized a wide variety of educational activities and actions. Their activism
expanded their world view beyond that of their immediate families to
seeing themselves as part of peoples' movements fighting for justice. . . .

Through her participation in the movement, [María del Carmen
Domínguez] developed her skills, leadership, and awareness:

> When I stayed at work in the factory, I was only thinking of myself
> and how am I going to support my family—nothing more, nothing
> less. And I served my husband and my son, my girl. But when I
> started working with La Mujer Obrera I thought, "I need more re-
> spect for myself. We need more respect for ourselves." (laughs) . . .
> . . . I learned about the law and I learned how to organize
> classes with people, whether they were men or women like me.

4

BENJAMIN BARBER

Jihad vs. McWorld, 1995

Not everyone views the world as coming together, for better or worse,
under the umbrella of globalization. Benjamin Barber, a political
scientist, uses the terms *Jihad* and *McWorld* to refer to what he sees as
the two poles of the modern global system. *McWorld* is the force of
Hollywood, fast-food outlets, jeans, and Americanization. *Jihad* (the

Source: Benjamin Barber, *Jihad vs. McWorld: How Globalism and Tribalism Are Reshaping
the World* (New York: Ballantine, 1995), 3–9, 17–20.

Arab word for "struggle") is used to symbolize all the nationalist, fundamentalist, ethnocentric, and tribal rejections of McWorld. Barber's argument is that these forces have largely shaped modern culture and that despite their opposition to each other, they both prevent the development of civic society and democracy. According to Barber, in what ways do both Jihad and McWorld stymie this development? What do you think of his argument? Can the world really be divided into these two groups? What sort of future does Barber predict?

THINKING HISTORICALLY

Barber argues that Jihad originated in opposition to McWorld and that the two play off each other in a way that gives them both substance and support. Which is a greater force toward globalization? Does Barber see Jihad and McWorld as primarily cultural or economic forces? How is Barber's idea of the process of global change different from that of the previous authors?

History is not over.[1] Nor are we arrived in the wondrous land of techné[2] promised by the futurologists. The collapse of state communism has not delivered people to a safe democratic haven, and the past, fratricide and civil discord perduring, still clouds the horizon just behind us. Those who look back see all of the horrors of the ancient slaughterbench reenacted in disintegral nations like Bosnia, Sri Lanka, Ossetia, and Rwanda and they declare that nothing has changed. Those who look forward prophesize commercial and technological interdependence — a virtual paradise made possible by spreading markets and global technology — and they proclaim that everything is or soon will be different. The rival observers seem to consult different almanacs drawn from the libraries of contrarian planets.

Yet anyone who reads the daily papers carefully, taking in the front page accounts of civil carnage as well as the business page stories on the mechanics of the information superhighway and the economics of communication mergers, anyone who turns deliberately to take in the whole 360-degree horizon, knows that our world and our lives are caught between what [Irish poet] William Butler Yeats called the two eternities of race and soul: that of race reflecting the tribal past, that of soul anticipating the cosmopolitan future. Our secular eternities are

---

[1] This is a response to the argument of Francis Fukuyama in "The End of History" (1989) that with the downfall of communism, there were no more fundamental conflicts to challenge the universalization of liberal democracy. [Ed.]

[2] Technology. [Ed.]

corrupted, however, race reduced to an insignia of resentment, and soul sized down to fit the demanding body by which it now measures its needs. Neither race nor soul offers us a future that is other than bleak, neither promises a polity that is remotely democratic.

The first scenario rooted in race holds out the grim prospect of a retribalization of large swaths of humankind by war and bloodshed: a threatened balkanization of nation-states in which culture is pitted against culture, people against people, tribe against tribe, a Jihad in the name of a hundred narrowly conceived faiths against every kind of interdependence, every kind of artificial social cooperation and mutuality: against technology, against pop culture, and against integrated markets; against modernity itself as well as the future in which modernity issues. The second paints that future in shimmering pastels, a busy portrait of onrushing economic, technological, and ecological forces that demand integration and uniformity and that mesmerize peoples everywhere with fast music, fast computers, and fast food—MTV, Macintosh, and McDonald's—pressing nations into one homogenous global theme park, one McWorld tied together by communications, information, entertainment, and commerce. Caught between Babel and Disneyland, the planet is falling precipitously apart and coming reluctantly together at the very same moment.

Some stunned observers notice only Babel, complaining about the thousand newly sundered "peoples" who prefer to address their neighbors with sniper rifles and mortars; others—zealots in Disneyland—seize on futurological platitudes and the promise of virtuality, exclaiming "It's a small world after all!" Both are right, but how can that be?

We are compelled to choose between what passes as "the twilight of sovereignty" and an entropic end of all history, or a return to the past's most fractious and demoralizing discord; to "the menace of global anarchy," to [John] Milton's capital of hell, Pandaemonium; to a world totally "out of control."

The apparent truth, which speaks to the paradox at the core of this book, is that the tendencies of both Jihad *and* McWorld are at work, both visible sometimes in the same country at the very same instant. Iranian zealots keep one ear tuned to the mullahs urging holy war and the other cocked to [Australian media mogul] Rupert Murdoch's Star television beaming in *Dynasty, Donahue,* and *The Simpsons* from hovering satellites. Chinese entrepreneurs vie for the attention of party cadres in Beijing and simultaneously pursue KFC franchises in cities like Nanjing, Hangzhou, and Xian where twenty-eight outlets serve over 100,000 customers a day. The Russian Orthodox church, even as it struggles to renew the ancient faith, has entered a joint venture with California businessmen to bottle and sell natural waters under the rubric Saint Springs Water Company. Serbian assassins wear Adidas sneakers and listen to Madonna on Walkman headphones as they take aim through their gunscopes at scurrying Sarajevo civilians looking to fill family watercans. Orthodox Hasids and brooding neo-Nazis have both turned to rock music to get their traditional messages out to the new generation, while fundamentalists plot virtual conspiracies on the Internet.

Now neither Jihad nor McWorld is in itself novel. History ending in the triumph of science and reason or some monstrous perversion thereof (Mary Shelley's Doctor Frankenstein) has been the leitmotiv of every philosopher and poet who has regretted the Age of Reason since the Enlightenment. [W. B.] Yeats lamented "the center will not hold, mere anarchy is loosed upon the world," and observers of Jihad today have little but historical detail to add. The Christian parable of the Fall and of the possibilities of redemption that it makes possible captures the eighteenth-century ambivalence — and our own — about past and future. I want, however, to do more than dress up the central paradox of human history in modern clothes. It is not Jihad and McWorld but the relationship between them that most interests me. For, squeezed between their opposing forces, the world has been sent spinning out of control. Can it be that what Jihad and McWorld have in common is anarchy: the absence of common will and that conscious and collective human control under the guidance of law we call democracy?

Progress moves in steps that sometimes lurch backwards; in history's twisting maze, Jihad not only revolts against but abets McWorld, while McWorld not only imperils but re-creates and reinforces Jihad. They produce their contraries and need one another. My object here then is not simply to offer sequential portraits of McWorld and Jihad, but while examining McWorld, to keep Jihad in my field of vision, and while dissecting Jihad, never to forget the context of McWorld. Call it a dialectic[3] of McWorld: a study in the cunning of reason that does honor to the radical differences that distinguish Jihad and McWorld yet that acknowledges their powerful and paradoxical interdependence.

There is a crucial difference, however, between my modest attempt at dialectic and that of the masters of the nineteenth century. Still seduced by the Enlightenment's faith in progress, both [G. W. F.] Hegel and [Karl] Marx believed reason's cunning was on the side of progress. But it is harder to believe that the clash of Jihad and McWorld will issue in some overriding good. The outcome seems more likely to pervert than to nurture human liberty. The two may, in opposing each other, work to the same ends, work in apparent tension yet in covert harmony, but democracy is not their beneficiary. In East Berlin, tribal communism has yielded to capitalism. In Marx-Engelsplatz, the stolid, overbearing

---

[3] Interaction; *dialectic* is a term borrowed from the German philosopher G. W. F. Hegel and the philosopher and revolutionary Karl Marx that described historical change as the product of competing systems — of ideas for Hegel, and of social-economic systems for Marx. [Ed.]

statues of Marx and [Friedrich] Engels face east, as if seeking distant solace from Moscow: but now, circling them along the streets that surround the park that is their prison are chain eateries like T.G.I. Friday's, international hotels like the Radisson, and a circle of neon billboards mocking them with brand names like Panasonic, Coke, and GoldStar. New gods, yes, but more liberty?

What then does it mean in concrete terms to view Jihad and McWorld dialectically when the tendencies of the two sets of forces initially appear so intractably antithetical? After all, Jihad and McWorld operate with equal strength in opposite directions, the one driven by parochial hatreds, the other by universalizing markets, the one recreating ancient subnational and ethnic borders from within, the other making national borders porous from without. Yet Jihad and McWorld have this in common: They both make war on the sovereign nation-state and thus undermine the nation-state's democratic institutions. Each eschews civil society and belittles democratic citizenship, neither seeks alternative democratic institutions. Their common thread is indifference to civil liberty. Jihad forges communities of blood rooted in exclusion and hatred, communities that slight democracy in favor of tyrannical paternalism or consensual tribalism. McWorld forges global markets rooted in consumption and profit, leaving to an untrustworthy, if not altogether fictitious, invisible hand issues of public interest and common good that once might have been nurtured by democratic citizenries and their watchful governments. Such governments, intimidated by market ideology, are actually pulling back at the very moment they ought to be aggressively intervening. What was once understood as protecting the public interest is now excoriated as heavy-handed regulatory browbeating. Justice yields to markets, even though, as [New York banker] Felix Rohatyn has bluntly confessed, "there is a brutal Darwinian logic to these markets. They are nervous and greedy. They look for stability and transparency, but what they reward is not always our preferred form of democracy." If the traditional conservators of freedom were democratic constitutions and Bills of Rights, "the new temples to liberty," [literary critic and philosopher] George Steiner suggests, "will be McDonald's and Kentucky Fried Chicken."

In being reduced to a choice between the market's universal church and a retribalizing politics of particularist identities, peoples around the globe are threatened with an atavistic return to medieval politics where local tribes and ambitious emperors together ruled the world entire, women and men united by the universal abstraction of Christianity even as they lived out isolated lives in warring fiefdoms defined by involuntary (ascriptive) forms of identity. This was a world in which princes and kings had little real power until they conceived the ideology of nationalism. Nationalism established government on a scale greater than the tribe yet less cosmopolitan than the universal church and in

time gave birth to those intermediate, gradually more democratic institutions that would come to constitute the nation-state. Today, at the far
end of this history, we seem intent on re-creating a world in which our
only choices are the secular universalism of the cosmopolitan market
and the everyday particularism of the fractious tribe.

In the tumult of the confrontation between global commerce and
parochial ethnicity, the virtues of the democratic nation are lost and the
instrumentalities by which it permitted peoples to transform themselves
into nations and seize sovereign power in the name of liberty and the
commonweal are put at risk. Neither Jihad nor McWorld aspires to re-
secure the civic virtues undermined by its denationalizing practices; neither global markets nor blood communities service public goods or
pursue equality and justice. Impartial judiciaries and deliberate assemblies play no role in the roving killer bands that speak on behalf of newly
liberated "peoples," and such democratic institutions have at best only
marginal influence on the roving multinational corporations that speak
on behalf of newly liberated markets. Jihad pursues a bloody politics of
identity, McWorld a bloodless economics of profit. Belonging by default
to McWorld, everyone is a consumer; seeking a repository for identity,
everyone belongs to some tribe. But no one is a citizen. Without citizens,
how can there be democracy? . . .

Jihad is, I recognize, a strong term. In its mildest form, it betokens
religious struggle on behalf of faith, a kind of Islamic zeal. In its strongest political manifestation, it means bloody holy war on behalf of partisan identity that is metaphysically defined and fanatically defended.
Thus, while for many Muslims it may signify only ardor in the name of
a religion that can properly be regarded as universalizing (if not quite
ecumenical), I borrow its meaning from those militants who make the
slaughter of the "other" a higher duty. I use the term in its militant construction to suggest dogmatic and violent particularism of a kind known
to Christians no less than Muslims, to Germans and Hindis as well as to
Arabs. The phenomena to which I apply the phrase have innocent
enough beginnings: identity politics and multicultural diversity can represent strategies of a free society trying to give expression to its diversity.
What ends as Jihad may begin as a simple search for a local identity,
some set of common personal attributes to hold out against the numbing
and neutering uniformities of industrial modernization and the colonizing culture of McWorld. . . .

McWorld is a product of popular culture driven by expansionist
commerce. Its template is American, its form style. Its goods are as much
images as matériel, an aesthetic as well as a product line. It is about
culture as commodity, apparel as ideology. Its symbols are Harley-
Davidson motorcycles and Cadillac motorcars hoisted from the roadways, where they once represented a mode of transportation, to the

marquees of global market cafés like Harley-Davidson's and the Hard Rock where they become icons of lifestyle. You don't drive them, you feel their vibes and rock to the images they conjure up from old movies and new celebrities, whose personal appearances are the key to the wildly popular international café chain Planet Hollywood. Music, video, theater, books, and theme parks—the new churches of a commercial civilization in which malls are the public squares and suburbs the neighborless neighborhoods—are all constructed as image exports creating a common world taste around common logos, advertising slogans, stars, songs, brand names, jingles, and trademarks. Hard power yields to soft, while ideology is transmuted into a kind of videology that works through sound bites and film clips. Videology is fuzzier and less dogmatic than traditional political ideology: it may as a consequence be far more successful in instilling the novel values required for global markets to succeed.

McWorld's videology remains Jihad's most formidable rival, and in the long run it may attenuate the force of Jihad's recidivist tribalisms. Yet the information revolution's instrumentalities are also Jihad's favored weapons. Hutu or Bosnian Serb identity[4] was less a matter of real historical memory than of media propaganda by a leadership set on liquidating rival clans. In both Rwanda and Bosnia, radio broadcasts whipped listeners into a killing frenzy. As New York Times rock critic Jon Pareles has noticed, "regionalism in pop music has become as trendy as microbrewery beer and narrowcasting cable channels, and for the same reasons."[5] The global culture is what gives the local culture its medium, its audience, and its aspirations. Fascist pop and Hasid rock are not oxymorons; rather they manifest the dialectics of McWorld in particularly dramatic ways. Belgrade's radio includes stations that broadcast Western pop music as a rebuke to hard-liner Milosevic's supernationalist government and stations that broadcast native folk tunes laced with antiforeign and anti-Semitic sentiments. Even the Internet has its neo-Nazi bulletin boards and Turk-trashing Armenian "flamers" (who assail every use of the word turkey, fair and fowl alike, so to speak), so that the abstractions of cyberspace too are infected with a peculiar and rabid cultural territoriality all their own.

The dynamics of the Jihad-McWorld linkage are deeply dialectical. Japan has, for example, become more culturally insistent on its own traditions in recent years even as its people seek an ever greater purchase on McWorld. In 1992, the number-one restaurant in Japan measured by

---

[4] This is a reference to the attempted genocide of Tutsis by Hutus in Rwanda (1994) and of Muslim Bosnians by Serbian Bosnians in what was Yugoslavia (1992–1995). In both cases the "other" was so indistinguishable that the perpetrators demanded identity cards. [Ed.]

[5] Jon Pareles, "Striving to Become Rock's Next Seattle," The New York Times, July 17, 1994, Section 2, p. 1.

volume of customers was McDonald's, followed in the number-two spot by the Colonel's Kentucky Fried Chicken. In France, where cultural purists complain bitterly of a looming Sixième République ("la République Américaine"),[6] the government attacks "franglais" even as it funds EuroDisney park just outside of Paris. In the same spirit, the cinema industry makes war on American film imports while it bestows upon Sylvester Stallone one of France's highest honors, the Chevalier des arts et lettres. Ambivalence also stalks India. Just outside of Bombay, cheek by jowl with villages still immersed in poverty and notorious for the informal execution of unwanted female babies or, even, wives, can be found a new town known as SCEEPZ—the Santa Cruz Electronic Export Processing Zone—where Hindi-, Tamil-, and Mahratti-speaking computer programmers write software for Swissair, AT&T, and other labor-cost-conscious multinationals. India is thus at once a major exemplar of ancient ethnic and religious tensions and "an emerging power in the international software industry."[7] To go to work at SCEEPZ, says an employee, is "like crossing an international border." Not into another country, but into the virtual nowhere-land of McWorld.

More dramatic even than in India, is the strange interplay of Jihad and McWorld in the remnants of Yugoslavia. In an affecting *New Republic* report, Slavenka Drakulic recently told the brief tragic love story of Admira and Bosko, two young star-crossed lovers from Sarajevo: "They were born in the late 1960's," she writes. "They watched Spielberg movies; they listened to Iggy Pop; they read John le Carré; they went to a disco every Saturday night and fantasized about traveling to Paris or London."[8] Longing for safety, it seems they finally negotiated with all sides for safe passage, and readied their departure from Sarajevo. Before they could cross the magical border that separates their impoverished land from the seeming sanctuary of McWorld, Jihad caught up to them. Their bodies lay along the riverbank, riddled with bullets from anonymous snipers for whom safe passage signaled an invitation to target practice. The murdered young lovers, as befits émigrés to McWorld, were clothed in jeans and sneakers. So too, one imagines, were their murderers.

Further east, tourists seeking a piece of old Russia that does not take them too far from MTV can find traditional Matryoshka nesting dolls (that fit one inside the other) featuring the nontraditional visages of (from largest to smallest) Bruce Springsteen, Madonna, Boy George, Dave Stewart, and Annie Lennox.

---

[6] "Sixth Republic"; the present French government is the Fifth Republic. [Ed.]

[7] National Public Radio, *All Things Considered,* December 2, 1993, from the broadcast transcription.

[8] Slavenka Drakulic, "Love Story: A True Tale from Sarajevo," *The New Republic,* October 26, 1993, pp. 14–16.

In Russia, in India, in Bosnia, in Japan, and in France too, modern history then leans both ways: toward the meretricious inevitability of McWorld, but also into Jihad's stiff winds, heaving to and fro and giving heart both to the Panglossians and the Pandoras,[9] sometimes for the very same reasons. The Panglossians bank on EuroDisney and Microsoft, while the Pandoras await nihilism and a world in Pandaemonium. Yet McWorld and Jihad do not really force a choice between such polarized scenarios. Together, they are likely to produce some stifling amalgam of the two suspended in chaos. Antithetical in every detail, Jihad and McWorld nonetheless conspire to undermine our hard-won (if only half-won) civil liberties and the possibility of a global democratic future. In the short run the forces of Jihad, noisier and more obviously nihilistic than those of McWorld, are likely to dominate the near future, etching small stories of local tragedy and regional genocide on the face of our times and creating a climate of instability marked by multimicrowars inimical to global integration. But in the long run, the forces of McWorld are the forces underlying the slow certain thrust of Western civilization and as such may be unstoppable. Jihad's microwars will hold the headlines well into the next century, making predictions of the end of history look terminally dumb. But McWorld's homogenization is likely to establish a macropeace that favors the triumph of commerce and its markets and to give to those who control information, communication, and entertainment ultimate (if inadvertent) control over human destiny. Unless we can offer an alternative to the struggle between Jihad and McWorld; the epoch on whose threshold we stand—postcommunist, postindustrial, postnational, yet sectarian, fearful, and bigoted—is likely also to be terminally postdemocratic.

[9] Extreme optimists and pessimists, respectively. [Ed.]

5

THE WORLD BANK

World Development Report: Gender and Development, 2012

The World Bank and its sister organization, The International Monetary Fund, were created by the United States and European Allies in 1944 as World War II was coming to an end. Its purpose was to

Source: The World Bank, *2012 World Development Report: Gender and Development*, chapter 6: "Globalization's impact on gender equality: What's happened and what's needed," 255–72.

promote international trade. In recent decades it has concentrated on problems of the developing countries, looking to finance projects to reduce poverty, child mortality, illiteracy, and gender inequality. In this regard, the bank issues reports like the one selected here from 2012.

What according to the authors is the relationship between globalization and gender inequality? In what ways does globalization improve the lives of women?

THINKING HISTORICALLY

For the purposes of this report, what does the World Bank mean by "globalization"? How does their definition correspond to, and differ from, others in this chapter?

The world is becoming more and more integrated. What started with greater trade openness is translating into growing global economic integration and interdependence, as transnational movements of people and capital accelerate and information becomes ever more accessible. Technological developments are rapidly changing the way people learn, work, and communicate. And the world population is concentrating in medium and large cities.

The new forces associated with globalization—understood as the combination of economic integration, technological diffusion, and greater access to information—have operated through markets, formal institutions, and informal institutions to lift some of the constraints to greater gender equality.

First, trade openness and the diffusion of new information and communication technologies (ICTs) have translated into more jobs and stronger connections to markets for many women, increasing their access to economic opportunities. In some countries and sectors, women's wages have also increased relative to those of men.

Second, gender inequality has more costs in an integrated world. It can diminish countries' ability to compete internationally—particularly for countries with export potential in goods and services with high female employment. And given growing global awareness of women's rights, continued gender inequality can also hurt a country's international standing. These factors strengthen the incentives for policy action toward gender equality around the world.

Third, greater access to information has allowed many in developing countries to learn about life and mores in other parts of the world, including those pertaining to the role of women, possibly affecting attitudes and behaviors. A shift toward more egalitarian gender roles and norms has also been facilitated and, in some cases, reinforced by women's economic empowerment.

But in the absence of public policy, globalization alone cannot and will not reduce gender inequality. Despite significant increases in agency and in access to economic opportunities for many women in many countries, the rising tide has not lifted everybody. Those often left behind are women for whom the existing constraints are most binding. That is why public action aimed at closing existing gender gaps in endowments, agency, and access to economic opportunities is necessary for countries to fully capitalize on the potential of globalization as a force for development and greater gender equality. . . .

Female Workers Wanted

The early years of trade liberalization were mainly characterized by the move of textile and information technology manufacturing from developed to developing countries. New employment in manufacturing often consisted of labor-intensive assembly line jobs, and the initial gains in manufacturing employment were greatest in countries with abundant unskilled labor and a comparative advantage in producing basic manufactures.

This shift in geographic location of production promoted female labor force participation and the feminization of employment in manufacturing in developing countries—particularly in Asia and Central America. . . .

In the past 15 years, the spread of ICTs has expanded trade in services and has, to a lesser extent, promoted the growth of ICT sectors in developing countries. As a result employment shifted from manufacturing, where jobs could be automated, to services. In the process, demand for nimble fingers on the assembly line gave way to demand for computer literacy as the tasks became more sophisticated and direct interaction with clients and customers more common.

As technology advanced, low-skilled women in light manufacturing were often displaced by men. . . .

New ICT-enabled jobs in services—particularly information processing in banking, insurance, printing, and publishing—were mainly taken up by women, but not the same women who lost their manufacturing jobs, because the new jobs required a different set of skills, including keyboarding, English, and sometimes French. Female employment in data entry and processing was initially highest in Barbados, Jamaica, and the Philippines. Later, ICT-related jobs were concentrated in software, call centers, and geographical information systems, and clustered in Malaysia and India, particularly in Delhi and Mumbai, where call centers employ more than 1 million people, most of them women.

In both manufacturing and service exports, growth in female employment was faster than ever before and faster than in other sectors. And although exports in many countries initially accounted for a small fraction of total female employment, their importance grew over time as a result of rapid employment growth. . . .

But the feminization of employment through exports appears to be less common in agricultural economies. Growth in traditional agricultural exports has benefited men more than women because women are less likely to work on commercial crops and are crowded out of traditionally female-intensive crops when these corps become commercial. . . .

Higher female employment in exports has often (but not always) been accompanied by wage gains. Transnational and exporting companies may be able to pay higher wages than locally owned firms and firms producing for the domestic market. They also may be better able to insulate their workers from economic cycles—and their workers may be better protected by labor legislation and are more likely to be unionized and thus eligible for benefits. That is why female wages are frequently higher and the gender wage gap is lower in exports than in other sectors, even after controlling for worker characteristics. . . .

More Connected and Better Informed—ICTs Have Increased Women's Access to Markets

ICTs can improve access to markets and increase participation in market work by reducing transaction costs associated with time and mobility constraints. They facilitate the gathering and transmission of price and other information and increase the flexibility in where and when economic activities can occur. Because women often face more restrictions than men in their mobility and available time, they stand to benefit more from these developments. . . .

Cell phone access and use can alleviate time and mobility constraints for women by increasing the ability to coordinate their family and work lives, reducing the cost of money transfers, and cutting down the physical labor or travel required to discover information (including avoiding fruitless trips to get supplies or meet customers). In Senegal, female fishmongers report that access to cell phones facilitates communication with their clients and suppliers, reducing travel time and costs, and with their families while they are away from home. Similarly, 41 percent of women interviewed in Bolivia, the Arab Republic of Egypt, India, and Kenya declared that owning a mobile phone had increased their income and their access to economic opportunities. . . .

In many cases, women, particularly rural women, were willing to reduce expenditures on other items to have access to a mobile phone, suggesting that the perceived benefits outweighed the costs, which averaged 3.5 percent of household income among those surveyed. . . .

The picture is quite different for the Internet. Low private access in the developing world, especially in rural areas, has severely limited its impact on access to economic opportunities—beyond the impact of ICTs on outsourcing and service export employment discussed earlier. Governments and development agencies have set up village "telecenters" for public use, generally as a fee for service, to increase access to basic ICT services among underserved populations. These centers generally offer computers linked to the Internet and are available for word processing and graphics work, faxes, e-mail, photocopying, and phone lines. They may also feature training on the equipment, and some incorporate radio broadcasts or video resources. . . .

Adapt or Miss the Boat

Trade openness, technological diffusion, and access to information have fundamentally changed the way countries interact and compete with each other in the global economy. Because gender (and other) inequality has more costs in a globalized world, these changes could translate into stronger incentives for both firms and governments to move toward gender equality. Specifically in countries with a comparative advantage in female goods, gender differences in access to market work and persistent employment segregation by gender could severely undermine the country's capacity to compete internationally and ultimately hamper economic growth.

Added to this economic reality is growing international pressure for countries to grant and enforce formal rights for women. International action in this area has translated into agreements sponsored by international organizations, primarily the International Labour Organization (ILO) and the United Nations (UN), followed by strong international pressure on countries to formally adhere to these agreements either directly or indirectly as part of broader trade and other economic agreements. . . .

Pressure from media and consumers in developed countries can also lead multinational firms to offer better working conditions to their workers in developing countries. For instance, both wages and nonwage working conditions (such as hours worked, accidents, contractual characteristics, work environment, and other benefits) among formal workers (most of them women) in the export textile and apparel industries in Cambodia, El Salvador, and Indonesia were found to be at or above the average in the rest of the economy. Similarly, antisweatshop campaigns in Indonesia led to large wage increases in foreign-owned and export firms, with some costs to the firms in the form of reduced investment, falling profits, and increased probability of closure for smaller plants, but no significant impact on employment. . . .

Globalization Could Also Promote More Egalitarian Gender Roles and Norms

The changes unleashed by globalization—especially the greater access to economic opportunities and information among women—could also influence existing gender roles and norms, ultimately promoting more egalitarian views. . . .

Women turned income earners may be able to leverage their new position to change gender roles in their households by influencing the allocation of time and resources among household members, shifting relative power within the households, and more broadly exercising stronger agency. In fact, women appear to gain more control over their income by working in export-oriented activities, although the impact on well-being and agency is more positive for women working in manufacturing and away from their male relatives than for those working in agriculture. Women in factories feel their status has improved. They are more likely to marry and have their first baby later than other women of similar socioeconomic status and to have better quality housing and access to modern infrastructure. They also report greater self-esteem and decision-making capacity, with benefits extending to other family members. In contrast, women in agriculture have not experienced significant changes in decision-making capacity or agency as a result of commercialization and higher export orientation, even when typical "women's crops" are promoted.

Beyond the economic sphere, increased access to information, primarily through higher exposure to television and the Internet, has also exposed many in developing countries to the roles women play in other parts of the world, which may affect gender roles and outcomes. For instance, in Brazil, a country where soap opera watching is ubiquitous and cuts across social classes, the presence of the Globo signal (a television channel that offers many popular Brazilian soap operas) has led to lower fertility, measured as the number of live births for women ages 15–49. . . .

Access to economic opportunities has also brought change in the public sphere. In Bangladesh, the employment of hundreds of thousands of women in the ready-made garment industry feminized the urban public space, creating more gender-equitable norms for women's public mobility and access to public institutions. In the process, Bangladeshi women had to redefine and negotiate the terms of *purdah*, typically reinterpreting it as a state of mind in contrast to its customary expression as physical absence from the public space, modest clothing, and quiet demeanor. . . .

Is The Glass Half Full or Half Empty?
The Need for Public Action

What, then, are we to conclude from the discussion in this chapter? The evidence suggests that employment in the export sector represents an attractive option for a large number of women in the developing world. These jobs enable women to contribute to household income, increase their economic empowerment within the household, and allow for greater social participation. . . .

But persistent gender differences in endowments, time availability, access to productive inputs and agency, and pervasive employment segregation by gender, mean that not all women have fully benefited from the economic opportunities brought about by globalization. And even among women who did benefit, remaining gaps, primarily in wages and working conditions, still need to be closed.

As long as these differences persist, globalization alone cannot—and will not—make gender inequality go away. Public action to close gender gaps is therefore critical for countries to fully capitalize on the potential of globalization as a force for development and greater gender equality. Such action is also urgent in light of the rising costs of gender inequality in a globalized world.

6

Cartoons on Globalization, 2000s

The following are editorial cartoons. Each addresses economic components of globalization, and each in some way addresses the relationship between those in the most developed part of the world and those in the developing world.

Figure 28.1, "As an Illegal Immigrant," raises questions about increased labor and capital mobility, allowing the import of migrant workers and the export of capital for foreign factories. What is the point of the cartoon? How would you describe its attitude toward globalization?

Figure 28.2, "Help Is on the Way, Dude," focuses on an irony of some well-intentioned efforts to protect the environment and exploited foreign laborers. What is the irony? How might you solve the problem posed by the cartoon?

Figure 28.3, "Cheap Chinese Textiles," explores the problem of low-cost manufacturing countries flooding global markets with cheap

Figure 28.1 "As an Illegal Immigrant."

Source: Gary Markstein.

Figure 28.2 "Help Is on the Way, Dude."

Source: By permission of Chip Bok and Creators Syndicate, Inc.

Figure 28.3 "Cheap Chinese Textiles."

Source: Patrick Chappatte/Globe Cartoon.

Figure 28.4 "Keep the Europeans Out."

Source: Bruce MacKinnon/artizans.com.

Figure 28.5 "I Don't Mean to Hurry You."

Source: J. McGillen/Cartoonstock.com.

products. What is the meaning of the comment by the representative
of the European Union (EU)? What is the meaning of the cartoon?

Figure 28.4, "Keep the Europeans Out," examines a concern of
North American farmers, here expressed on a placard of a Canadian
farmer. What is that concern, and what is the farmer's solution? What
is the point of the cartoon? What does this cartoon say about the use
of tariffs, quotas, or other protectionist barriers to limit global competition? Compare this cartoon to the previous one on this issue.

Figure 28.5, "I Don't Mean to Hurry You," asks about the wishes
of people in the developing world. What is the point of the cartoon?
Compare the cartoon with the analysis of Barber.

THINKING HISTORICALLY

All of these cartoonists explore a process of economic globalization.
What are the economic forces that bring about the globalization
depicted in these cartoons? To what extent does the humor in these
cartoons depend on a realization that globalization is inevitable?
To what extent is that attitude shared by the authors of the other
selections in this chapter?

■ REFLECTIONS

Globalization is not one process, but many. It is as technological as the
Internet, smart phones, and the latest flu vaccine. It is as cultural as
international film festivals, sushi, and disappearing languages. It is as
political as the United Nations, time zones, and occupying armies.
Perhaps most important, it is economic. People migrate for jobs,
factories move for cheaper labor, and neither consumers nor corporations care about country of origin. Since the end of communism, the
entire world has become a single market.

Is this a good thing? It depends on whom you ask. Sherif Hetata
sees overcommercialization undermining national traditions. Philippe
Legrain applauds the new menu of possibilities. Life is clearly hard for
the women working in the sweatshops of international corporations, as
Miriam Ching Yoon Louie points out; but is economic globalization
responsible for their suffering, or does it provide women like them with
new opportunities? Benjamin Barber explains why some choose jihad
in response to the effects of world trade. More than any of the other
authors, he is skeptical of the inevitability of globalization, but his
prognosis is not pretty. The World Bank offers a way forward, but
acknowledges that only with public action will global inequalities
change.

It is the duty of citizens, not historians, to decide what outcomes are good or bad, better or worse. But historians can help us decide by showing us where we are—by deepening the temporal dimension of our awareness.

Understanding the process of change is the most useful "habit of mind" we gain from studying the past. Although the facts are many and the details overwhelming, the historical process appears to us only through the study of the specifics. And we must continually check and revise our interpretations to conform to new information. But like a storyteller without a plot, we are lost without some overall understanding of how our world is changing.

More important, understanding change does not mean that we have to submit to it. Of the processes of globalization discussed in this chapter—trade and technological transfers, cultural homogenization and competition, commercialization and market expansion—some may seem inevitable, some strong, some even reversible. Intelligent action requires an appreciation of the possible as well as the identification of the improbable.

History is not an exact science. Fortunately, human beings are creators, as well as subjects, of change. Even winds that cannot be silenced can be deflected, harnessed, or made to chime. Which way is the world moving? What are we becoming? What can we do? What kind of world can we create? These are questions that can only be answered by studying the past, both distant and recent, and trying to understand the overarching changes that are shaping our lives. Worlds of history converge upon us, but only one world will emerge from our wishes, our wisdom, and our will.

Acknowledgments

Chapter 1

1   Natalie Angier. "Furs for Evening, But Cloth Was the Stone Age Standby" from the *New York Times*, December 14, 1999. Copyright © 1999 by The New York Times Company. All rights reserved. Used by permission and protected by the Copyright Laws of the United States. The printing, copying, redistribution, or retransmission of this Content without express written permission is prohibited.
3   Marjorie Shostak. From *Nisa: The Life and Words of a !Kung Woman*. Reprinted by permission of the publisher from *Nisa: The Life and Words of a !Kung Woman* by Marjorie Shostak, pp. 51, 56–59, 61–62, 89–90, Cambridge, Mass.: Harvard University Press. Copyright © 1981 by Marjorie Shostak.
4   Margaret Ehrenberg. Excerpts from "The First Farmers" from *Women in Prehistory*, University of Oklahoma. Reproduced with permission of the publisher in the format republished in a book via Copyright Clearance Center.
5   Catherine Clay, Chandrika Paul, and Christine Senecal. "Women in the First Urban Communities" from *Envisioning Women in World History: Prehistory to 1500*, 1/e. Copyright © 2009. Reprinted by permission of McGraw-Hill, Inc.

Chapter 2

1   Kevin Reilly. "Cities and Civilization" from *West and the World: A History of Civilization*, Volume 2. Copyright © 1988 by Kevin Reilly. Reprinted by permission of Pearson Education, Inc., Upper Saddle River, NJ.
2   Anonymous. Excerpt from *The Epic of Gilgamesh*, trans. N. K. Sanders. Copyright © 1972 by N. K. Sanders. Used by permission of Penguin Group (UK).
3   Martha T. Roth. Excerpt from *Law Collections from Mesopotamia and Asia Minor*, Second Edition. Copyright © 1997. Reprinted with the permission of the Society of Biblical Literature.
4   From *Tale of Sinuhe and Other Ancient Egyptian Poems, 1940–1640* B.C.E., trans. with an introduction by R. B. Parkinson (1997): "The Tale of the Eloquent Peasant" (pp. 54–88). By permission of Oxford University Press.
6   Martha T. Roth. Excerpt from *Law Collections from Mesopotamia and Asia Minor*, Second Edition. Copyright © 1997. Reprinted with the permission of the Society of Biblical Literature.
7   "First City in the New World?" from Smithsonian.com, August 2002.

Chapter 3

1   William H. McNeill. "Greek and Indian Civilization" from *A World History*, Second Edition. Copyright © 1971 by Oxford University Press. Reprinted by permission of the author.

2   Ainslee T. Embree. Excerpt from "The Rig Veda: Sacrifice as Creation" from *Sources of Indian Tradition*, Second Edition. Copyright © 1988 by Columbia University Press. Reprinted with permission of the publisher.

3   From *The Thirteen Principal Upanishads*, ed. and trans. by R. E. Hume (1954): "Brihad Aranyka, IV: 4: 5–6" (pp. 140–41). By permission of Oxford University Press, USA.

4   Anonymous. Excerpt from "The Upanishads: Brahman and Atman" from "Chandogya Upanishad" in *The Upanishads*, trans. Juan Mascaro. Copyright © 1965 by Juan Mascaro. Used by permission of Penguin Group (UK).

5   Barbara Stoler Miller. From *Bhagavad Gita*, trans. Barbara Stoler Miller. Translation copyright © 1986 by Barbara Stoler Miller. Used by permission of Bantam Books, a division of Random House, Inc.

6   Aristotle. "The Athenian Constitution: Territorial Sovereignty,"trans. by John Warrington, from *Aristotle, Politics, and the Athenian Constitution* (J. M. Dent & Sons, 1959) is reproduced by permission of Everyman's Library, an imprint of Alfred A. Knopf.

Chapter 4

1   From *The Government of the Qin and Han Empires, 221 B.C.E.–220 C.E.*, trans. Michael Loewe. Copyright © 2006 by Hackett Publishing Company, Inc. Reprinted by permission of Hackett Publishing Company, Inc. All rights reserved.

2   Sima Qian. From *Records of the Historian,* trans. Burton Watson. Copyright © Columbia University Press. Reprinted by permission of the publisher.

4   Hai Fei. From *Sources of Chinese Tradition*, Volume 1, ed. William Theodore de Bary. Copyright © 1963 by Columbia University Press. Reprinted with the permission of the publisher.

5   From *Sources of Chinese Tradition*, Second Edition, ed. Wm. Theodore de Bary and Irene Bloom. Copyright © Columbia University Press. Reprinted with permission of the publisher.

6   From *The Oxford History of the Classical World: The Roman World*, ed. John Boardman, Jasper Griffin & Oswyn Murray (1988). Extract of 734 words from "Rome: The Arts of Government" (pp. 154, 155, 156, 170–74, 175–77). By permission of Oxford University Press.

8   Pliny the Younger. Reprinted by permission of the publishers and the Trustees of the Loeb Classical Library from *Pliny the Younger: Volume II*, Loeb Classical Library Volume 59, translated by Betty Radice, pp. 285–93, Cambridge, Mass.: Harvard University Press, Copyright © 1969 by the President and Fellows of Harvard College. Loeb Classical Library® is a registered trademark of the President and Fellows of Harvard College.

Chapter 5

1   Sarah Shaver Hughes and Brady Hughes. "Women in Ancient Civilizations" from *Women's History in Global Perspective*, Volume II, edited by Bonnie G. Smith. Copyright © 2005.

2   Ban Zhao. "Lessons for Women" excerpt from *Pan Chao: Foremost Woman Scholar of China, First Century A.D.: Background, Ancestry, Life and Writings of*

the Most Celebrated Chinese Woman of Letters, trans. Nancy Lee Swann. Copyright © East Asian Library and the Gest Collection, Princeton University.

5 Ovid. "The Art of Love," trans. A. S. Kline. Reprinted with permission.

Chapter 6

1 Anonymous. "Svetasvatara Upanished" from *The Upanishads: Breath of the Eternal,* trans. Swami Prabhavananda and Frederick Manchester. Copyright © 1948, 1957 by The Vedanta Society of Southern California.

3 From *The Buddhist Tradition in India, China, and Japan,* ed. William Theodore de Bary, copyright © 1969 by William Theodore de Bary and renewed 1997. Used by permission of Random House, Inc.

4 From *The Dharma Flower Sutra,* Volume 2, Chapter 1. Introduction with the commentary of Tripitaka Master Hua translated into English by The Buddhist Text Translation Society, 1977, pp. 324–27, 337.

5 Scripture taken from the Holy Bible, New International Version®. Copyright © 1973, 1978, 1984 by Biblica, Inc. Used by permission of Zondervan. All rights reserved.

6 Scripture taken from the Holy Bible, New International Version®. Copyright © 1973, 1978, 1984 by Biblica, Inc. Used by permission of Zondervan. All rights reserved.

7 Scripture taken from the Holy Bible, New International Version®. Copyright © 1973, 1978, 1984 by Biblica, Inc. Used by permission of Zondervan. All rights reserved.

8 Scripture taken from the Holy Bible, New International Version®. Copyright © 1973, 1978, 1984 by Biblica, Inc. Used by permission of Zondervan. All rights reserved.

Chapter 7

1 Shlomo Sand. From *The Invention of the Jewish People,* trans. Yael Lotan. Copyright © Verso 2007, translation copyright © Yael Lotan. Reprinted by permission of Verso.

4 From *The Buddhist Tradition in India, China, and Japan,* ed. William Theodore de Bary, copyright © 1969 by William Theodore de Bary and renewed 1997. Used by permission of Random House, Inc.

5a Michael Sells. From The Koran, Chapters 1, 91, 109, and 112, excerpt from *Approaching the Qur'an: The Early Revelations.* Copyright © 1999. Published by White Cloud Press. Reprinted by permission of White Cloud Press in the format textbook via Copyright Clearance Center.

5b Chapters 2, 4 from The Koran from *The New On-Line Translation of the Qur'an,* copyright © Noor Foundation International Inc. www.islamusa.org.

6 Richard C. Foltz. "The Islamization of the Silk Road" from *Religions of the Silk Road: Overland Trade and Cultural Exchange from Antiquity to the Fifteenth Century,* Palgrave Macmillan, 2010.

7 From *Islam, Volume 1: Politics and War,* ed. and trans. Bernard Lewis (1987): "Peace Terms with Jerusalem" (pp. 235–36, 600 words). By permission of Oxford University Press, USA. Copyright © 1974 by Bernard Lewis.

8   From *Sunjata: A West African Epic of the Mande Peoples,* trans. David C. Conrad and narrated by Djanka Tassey Conde. Copyright © 2004 Hackett Publishing Company, Inc. Reprinted by permission of Hackett Publishing Company, Inc. All rights reserved.

Chapter 8

1   Patrick Manning. From *Migration in World History,* copyright © 2005 Patrick Manning, published by Routledge. Reproduced by permission of Taylor & Francis Books UK.
2   Lynda Norene Shaffer. "Southernization" from *Journal of World History* 5 (Spring 1994): 1–21. Copyright © 1994. Reprinted with the permission of University of Hawai'i Press.
4   Ibn Battuta. Excerpt from *The Travels of Ibn Battutah,* abridged and annotated by Tim Mackintosh-Smith, copyright © 1958, 1962, 1971, 1994, 2000 the Hakluyt Society, originally published by the Hakluyt Society in four volumes, 1958–1994. Reprinted by permission of David Higham Associates.

Chapter 9

1a   Kevin Reilly, "Love in Medieval Europe, India, and Japan" from *The West and the World,* Third Edition. Copyright © 1997 by Kevin Reilly. Reprinted with the permission of Markus Wiener Publishers.
1b   Sei Shonagon. From *Pillow Book of Sei Shonagon,* ed. and trans. by Ivan Morris (1967): 225 words. Copyright © Ivan Morris 1967. By permission of Oxford University Press and Columbia University Press.
2   From Ulrich von Lichtenstein's "Service of Ladies" by Jim Dean. Copyright © 1969 by the University of North Carolina. Used by permission of the publisher, www.uncpress.unc.edu.
3   Andreas Capellanus. Excerpt from *The Art of Courtly Love,* trans. John J. Parry. Copyright © Columbia University Press. Reprinted with permission of the publisher.
4   Excerpt from *The Secret History,* trans. Richard Atwater.
5   Kalidasa. From *Theater of Memory,* ed. and trans. Barbara Stoler Miller. Copyright © Columbia University Press. Reprinted with permission of the publisher.
6   Murasaki Shikibu. From *The Tale of Genji,* trans. Royall Tyler, translation copyright © 2001 by Royall Tyler. Used by permission of Viking Penguin, a division of Penguin Group (USA) Inc.
7   Zhou Daguan. Excerpt from *A Record of Cambodia: The Land and Its People,* trans. Peter Harris. Copyright © 2007 by Peter Harris. Reprinted with permission of Silkworm Books.

Chapter 10

1   Fulcher of Chartres. "Pope Urban at Clermont" from *The First Crusade: The Chronicle of Fulcher of Chartres and Other Source Materials,* ed. Edward Peters. Copyright © 1998. Reprinted by permission of the University of Pennsylvania Press.
2   Solomon bar Simson. "Chronicle of Solomon bar Simson" from *The Jews and the Crusaders: The Hebrew Chronicles of the First and Second Crusades,* ed. and trans.

Shlomo Eidelberg. Copyright © 1977. Reprinted with the permission of Shlomo Eidelberg.

3   Ibn al-Athir. From *Arab Historians of the Crusades*, ed. and trans. Francesco Gabrieli. Copyright © 1969 by Routledge & Kegan Paul Ltd. Published by the University of California Press. Reprinted by permission of the publisher.

4   From *The Alexiad of the Princess Anna Comnena*, trans. Elizabeth A. S. Dawes. Reproduced by permission of Taylor & Francis Books UK.

5   Fulcher of Chartres. "The Siege of Antioch" from *The First Crusade: The Chronicle of Fulcher of Chartres and Other Source Materials*, ed. Edward Peters. Copyright © 1998. Reprinted by permission of the University of Pennsylvania Press.

8   Ibn al-Athir. From *Arab Historians of the Crusades*, ed. and trans. Francesco Gabrieli. Copyright © 1969 by Routledge & Kegan Paul Ltd. Published by the University of California Press. Reprinted by permission of the publisher.

9   "Letter from a Jewish Pilgrim in Egypt" from "Contemporary Letters on the Capture of Jerusalem by the Crusaders" in *Journal of Jewish Studies* 3, No. 4, 1952, trans. S. D. Goitein. Copyright © 1952 by S. D. Goitein. Reprinted with the permission of the Journal of Jewish Studies.

Chapter 11

1   Gregory Guzman. Excerpt from "Were the Barbarians a Negative or Positive Factor in Ancient and Medieval History?" from *The Historian* 50, August 1988. Reprinted by permission of Gregory Guzman.

2   Ibn Fadlan. "Ibn Fadlan's Account of Scandinavian Merchants on the Volga in 1922" from *Journal of English and Germanic Philology* 22:1, 1923, pp. 56–63. Copyright © 1923 by the Board of Trustees of the University of Illinois. Used with permission of the authors and the University of Illinois Press.

3   Barry Cunliffe. "The Western Vikings" from *Facing the Ocean and Its Peoples*. Copyright © 2001 by Barry Cunliffe. Reprinted with the permission of Oxford University Press, Ltd.

4   "Eirik's Saga" from *The Vinland Sagas: The Norse Discovery of America*, trans. Magnus Magnusson and Hermann Palsson. Copyright © 1965 by Magnus Magnusson and Hermann Palsson. Reprinted by permission of Penguin UK.

6   K. Reilly. "The Secret History of the Mongols" adapted from R. P. Lister, *Genghis Khan*. Reprinted with the permission of Barnes and Noble Books.

8   John of Plano Carpini. "History of the Mongols" from *Mission to Asia: Narratives and Letters of the Franciscan Missionaries in Mongolia and China in the Thirteenth and Fourteenth Centuries*, translated by a nun of Stanbrook Abbey, edited by Christopher Dawson Sheed and Ward, an imprint of Bloomsbury Publishing Plc.

Chapter 12

2   Gabriel de' Mussis. "Origins of the Black Death" from *The Black Death*, by Rosemary Horrox (trans. and ed.), 1996, Manchester University Press, Manchester, UK.

3   Giovanni Boccacio. "The Plague in Florence" from the *Decameron*, trans. G. H. McWilliam. Copyright © 1972 by G. H. McWilliam. Reprinted by permission of Penguin UK.

2   Ma Huan. From *The Overall Survey of the Ocean Shores*, ed. and trans. Feng Ch'eng Chun, originally published by Hakluyt Society, 1970. Reprinted by permission of David Higham.

4   Christopher Columbus. "Letter to King Ferdinand and Queen Isabella" from *The Four Voyages of Columbus*, ed. Cecil Jane, Dover, 1988.

5   Kirkpatrick Sale. Excerpt from *The Conquest of Paradise*. Copyright © 1990 by Kirkpatrick Sale. Used by permission of The Joy Harris Literary Agency.

Chapter 16

1   Bernal Díaz. Excerpt from *The Conquest of New Spain*, trans. J. M. Cohen, Penguin UK, 1963. Reprinted by permission of Penguin UK.

2   From *The Broken Spears: The Aztec Account of the Conquest of Mexico*, ed. Miguel Leon-Portilla, trans. Lysander Kemp, Beacon Press, 1990.

3   Bartolomé de Las Casas. From *The Devastation of the Indies: A Brief Account*, trans. Herma Briffault. Copyright © 1974. Reproduced with permission of Continuum Publishing Company in the format Textbook via Copyright Clearance Center.

5   Nzinga Mbemba. "Appeal to the King of Portugal" from *The African Past*, ed. Basil Davidson. Copyright © 1964 by Basil Davidson. Reprinted by permission of Curtis Brown, Ltd.

7   J. B. Romaigne. From *Journal of a Slave Ship Voyage*, Dover Publications. Reprinted by permission of the publisher.

Chapter 17

1   Jonathan D. Spence. From *Emperor of China*, copyright © 1974, copyright renewed 2002 by Jonathan D. Spence. Used by permission of Alfred A. Knopf, a division of Random House.

2   From *Japan: A Documentary History*, ed. David J. Lu (Armonk, NY: M. E. Sharpe, 1997), pp. 219–20. English translation copyright © 1997 by David J. Lu. Reprinted with permission from M. E. Sharpe, Inc.

3   Abdul Qadir Bada'uni. From *Muntakhab-ut-Tawarikh*, Volume 2, by G. S. A. Ranking and W. H. Lowe. Copyright © Columbia University Press. Reprinted with permission of the publisher.

5   Benjamin J. Kaplan. *Divided by Faith: Religious Conflict and the Practice of Toleration in Early Modern Europe*, pp. 28–32, 100–03, Cambridge, Mass.: The Belknap Press of Harvard University Press. Copyright © 2007 by Benjamin J. Kaplan. Reprinted by permission of Harvard University Press.

Chapter 18

1   Miu Family of Guangdong Province. "Family Instructions for the Miu Lineage," trans. Clara Yu, from *Chinese Civilization: A Sourcebook*, Second Edition, ed. Patricia Ebrey, Free Press, 1993.

2   Pu Songling. "The Lady Knight-Errant" from Liao-chai chih-i, translated by Lorraine S. Y. Lieu, Y. W. Ma and Joseph S. M. Lau, from *Traditional Chinese Stories: Themes and Variations*, ed. Y. W. Ma and Joseph S. M. Lau, copyright ©

1986 by Cheng & Tsui Company, Inc. Originally published by Columbia University Press in 1978. Used by permission of Cheng & Tsui Company, Inc.

4   Anna Bijns. "Unyoked Is Best! Happy the Woman without a Man," trans. by Kristiaan P. G. Aercke, from *Women and Writers of the Renaissance and Reformation*, ed. Katharina M. Wilson, The University of Georgia Press, 1987.

6   Countess de Rochefort. "Diary of the Countess de Rochefort" from *Not in God's Image,* eds. Julia O'Faolain and Lauro Martines, HarperCollins Publishers. Used by permission of the author.

7   "Court Case on Marriage in High Court of Aix" from *Not in God's Image,* eds. Julia O'Faolain and Lauro Martines, HarperCollins Publishers. Used by permission of the author.

8   Mary Jo Maynes and Ann Waltner. "Childhood, Youth, and the Female Life Cycle: Women's Life-Cycle Transitions in a World-Historical Perspective: Comparing Marriage in China and Europe" from *Journal of Women's History* 12:4. Copyright © 2001 Journal of Women's History. Reprinted with permission of The Johns Hopkins University Press.

Chapter 19

1   Jack Goldstone. Excerpt from *Why Europe? The Rise of the West in World History 1500–1850.* Copyright © 2009 by Jack Goldstone. Reprinted with the permission of The McGraw-Hill Companies, Inc.

4   Bonnie S. Anderson and Judith P. Zinsser. From *A History of Their Own: Women in Europe from Prehistory to the Present,* Volume I. Copyright © 1988 by Bonnie S. Anderson and Judith Zinsser. Reprinted by permission of HarperCollins Publishers.

6   Lynda Norene Shaffer. "China, Technology, and Change" from *World History Bulletin* 4, no. 1 (Fall/Winter 1986–1987) pages 1–6.

7   Sugita Gempaku. From *Japan: A Documentary History*, ed. David J. Lu (Armonk, NY: M. E. Sharpe, 1997), pp. 219–20. English translation copyright © 1997 by David J. Lu. Reprinted with permission from M. E. Sharpe, Inc.

Chapter 20

7   Toussaint L'Ouverture. "Letter to the Directory, November 5, 1797" from *The Black Jacobins*, ed. C.L.R. James, Vintage Books, 1989. Reproduced with permission of Curtis Brown Group Ltd., London on behalf of the Estate of C.L.R. James. Copyright © The Estate of C.L.R. James.

9   Chakrabarty, Dipesh. From *Provincializing Europe*. © 2000 Princeton University Press. Reprinted by permission of Princeton University Press.

Chapter 21

1   Arnold Pacey. *Technology in World Civilization: A Thousand-Year History,* pp.128–35, copyright © Massachusetts Institute of Technology, by permission of The MIT Press.

5   Peter N. Stearns. Excerpt from *The Industrial Revolution in World History.* Copyright © 1993 Stearns, Peter N. Reprinted by permission of Westview Press, a member of the Perseus Books Group.

7 Samuel L. Bailey and Franco Ramella. *One Family, Two Worlds: An Italian Family's Correspondence Across the Atlantic.* Copyright © 1988 by Rutgers, the State University. Reprinted by permission of Rutgers University Press.

Chapter 22

1 George Orwell. From *Burmese Days*, copyright © 1934 by George Orwell and renewed 1962 by Sonia Pitt-Rivers, reprinted by permission of Houghton Mifflin Harcourt Publishing Company. All rights reserved.

3 "An Image of Africa: Racism in Conrad's *Heart of Darkness*" from *Hopes and Impediments* by Chinua Achebe. Copyright © 1988 by Chinua Achebe, used by permission of The Wylie Agency LLC.

4 Chinua Achebe. From *Things Fall Apart*, 1958. Reprinted by permission.

Chapter 23

1 Theodore von Laue, Excerpt from *The World Revolution of Westernization: The Twentieth Century in Global Perspective*, Oxford University Press, 1987.

2 Fukuzawa Yukichi. From *Japan: A Documentary History*, ed. David J. Lu (Armonk, NY: M. E. Sharpe, 1997), pp. 351–53. English translation copyright © 1997 by David J. Lu. Reprinted with permission from M. E. Sharpe, Inc.

6 Mohandas K. Gandhi. Excerpt from *Hind Swaraj*, Navajivan, 1938. Reprinted by permission of The Navajivan Trust.

Chapter 24

1 David Fromkin. From *Europe's Last Summer: Who Started the Great War in 1914?* Copyright © 2004 by David Fromkin. Used by permission of Alfred A. Knopf, a division of Random House, Inc.

2 Erich Maria Remarque. Excerpt from *All Quiet on the Western Front*, trans. A. W. Wheen. Copyright © 1928 by Ullstein, A. G., renewed © 1956 by Erich Maria Remarque. Copyright © 1929, 1930 by Little, Brown and Company, renewed © 1957, 1958, by Erich Maria Remarque. Reprinted with the permission of the Estate of Paulette Goddard Remarque, c/o Pryor, Cashman, Sherman & Flynn, New York, NY. All rights reserved.

5 Joe Lunn. Reprinted with permission from *Memoirs of the Maelstrom: A Senegalese Oral History of the First World War* by Joe Lunn. Copyright © 1999 by Joe Lunn. Published by Heinemann, Portsmouth, NH. All rights reserved.

Chapter 25

1 Adolf Hitler. Excerpts from *Mein Kampf*, trans. Ralph Manheim. Published by Hutchinson. Copyright © 1943, renewed 1971 by Houghton Mifflin Harcourt Publishing Company. Reprinted by permission of Houghton Mifflin Harcourt Publishing Company and The Random House Group Limited. All rights reserved.

2 Heinrich Himmler. From *A Holocaust Reader*, trans. Lucy Dawidowicz. Copyright © Behrman House, Inc., reprinted with permission www.behrmanhouse.com.

3   Jean-François Steiner. Reprinted with the permission of Simon & Schuster, Inc. from *Treblinka* by Jean-François Steiner. English translation copyright © 1967 Simon & Schuster, Inc. Original French language edition copyright © 1966 Librairie Artheme Fayard.

4   Timothy Snyder. "Holocaust: The Ignored Reality." From *The New York Review of Books.* Copyright © 2009 Timothy Snyder.

5   Dr. Robert Wilson. From *Documents on the Rape of Nanking*, ed. Timothy Brook, the University of Michigan Press. Reprinted by permission.

7   Akihiro Takahashi. "The Voice of Hibakusha" from *Testimony of Akihiro Takahashi in the video Hiroshima Witness,* produced by Hiroshima Peace Cultural Center and NHK. Reprinted with permission of Hiroshima Peace Culture Foundation and Akihiro Takahashi.

Chapter 26

1   Heonik Kwon. From *Origins of the Cold War.* Copyright © Columbia University Press. Reprinted with permission of the publisher.

2   Edward Lansdale. Excerpts from "Report on CIA Operations, 1954–1955" in *The Pentagon Papers,* Abridged Edition, ed. George C. Herring. Copyright © 1993 by McGraw-Hill, Inc. Reprinted by permission of the McGraw Hill Companies.

3   Ho Chi Minh. From *Ho Chi Minh, Selected Works.* Copyright © The Gioi Publishers. Reprinted by permission of The Gioi Publishers.

4   "Nikita Khrushchev: We Will Bury You." Copyright © Time Inc. Reprinted by permission. Time is a registered trademark of Time Inc. All rights reserved.

5   "Khrushchev Tirade Again Irks Envoys," the *New York Times,* November 19, 1956. All rights reserved. Used by permission and protected by the Copyright Laws of the United States. The printing, copying, redistribution, or retransmission of this Content without express written permission is prohibited.

6   Welles Hangen. "*Pravda* Modifies Khrushchev Slur," the *New York Times,* November 20, 1956. All rights reserved. Used by permission and protected by the Copyright Laws of the United States. The printing, copying, redistribution, or retransmission of this Content without express written permission is prohibited.

8a   Secret Staff Meeting Transcript, Secretary of State Henry Kissinger, Chairman, March 26, 1976. These materials are reproduced from www.nsarchive.org with the permission of the National Security Archive.

8b   Telegram from U.S Ambassador to Argentina, Robert C. Hill, to Secretary of State Henry Kissinger, March 30, 1976. These materials are reproduced from www.nsarchive.org with the permission of the National Security Archive.

9   "Transcript of telephone conversation between Soviet Premier Alexei Kosygin and Afghan Prime Minister Nur Mohammad Taraki" (March 18, 1979) from *Cold War International History Project Bulletin* 8–9 (Winter 1996/1997): 145–46. Available at www.CWIHP.org.

Chapter 27

1   Hebe de Bonafini and Matilde Sánchez. "The Madwomen at the Plaza de Mayo," excerpted from *The Argentina Reader: History, Culture, Politics* (Durham: Duke University Press, 2002). Reprinted by permission of the authors.

2   Mikhail Gorbachev. From *On My Country and the World*. Copyright © Columbia University Press. Reprinted with permission of the publisher.

3   Nobel Peace Prize Address by Nelson Mandela. © The Nobel Foundation 1993. Used by permission.

4   Gene Sharp. Excerpt from "Dictatorship to Democracy," The Albert Einstein Institution.

5   Wael Ghonim. Excerpt from *Revolution 2.0: The Power of the People is Greater than the People in Power*. Copyright © 2012 by Wael Gohnim. Reprinted by permission of Houghton Mifflin Harcourt Publishing Company. All rights reserved.

6   "Charter 08," http://www.hrichina.org/crf/article/3203.

7   General Assembly of Occupy Wall Street. "Declaration of the Occupation of New York City."

8   William Moss Wilson. "Just Don't Call Her Che," the *New York Times*, January 29, 2012. All rights reserved. Used by permission and protected by the Copyright Laws of the United States. The printing, copying, redistribution, or retransmission of this Content without express written permission is prohibited.

Chapter 28

1   Sherif Hetata. "Dollarization, Fragmentation, and God" from *The Cultures of Globalization,* eds. Frederic Jameson and Masasao Miyoshi. Copyright © 1998 Duke University Press. All rights reserved. Reprinted by permission of the publisher. www.dukepress.edu.

2   Philippe Legrain. "Cultural Globalization Is Not Americanization" from *The Chronicle of Higher Education,* May 9, 2003. Reprinted with the permission of the author.

3   Miriam Ching Yoon Louie. Excerpt from *Sweatshop Warriors: Immigrant Women Workers Take On the Global Factory*. Copyright © 2001 by Miriam Chin Yoon Louie. Reprinted by permission of South End Press.

4   Benjamin Barber. From *Jihad vs. McWorld: How the Planet Is Both Falling Apart and Coming Together and What This Means for Democracy*. Copyright © 1995 by Benjamin Barber. Used by permission of Times Books, a division of Random House, Inc.

About the Author

Kevin Reilly is a professor of humanities at Raritan Valley College and has taught at Rutgers, Columbia, and Princeton Universities. Cofounder and first president of the World History Association, Reilly has written numerous articles on the teaching of history and has edited works including *The Introductory History Course* for the American Historical Association. A specialist in immigration history, Reilly incorporated his research in creating the "Modern Global Migrations" globe at Ellis Island. His work on the history of racism led to the editing of *Racism: A Global Reader.* He was a Fulbright scholar in Brazil and Jordan and an NEH fellow in Greece, Oxford (UK), and India. Awards include the Community College Humanities Association's Distinguished Educator of the Year and the World History Association's Pioneer Award. He has also served the AHA in various capacities, including the governing council. He is currently writing a global history of racism.

About the Cover Images

Egyptian Wall Painting, c. 1450 B.C.E. (left), and *Trade in the Gulf of Cambay*, India, c. 1410 C.E. (right). These scenes, from the tomb of the Egyptian scribe Ounsu and from an illustration in *The Travels of Marco Polo,* show the importance of trade goods and trade networks in the spread of culture.

***Spring Scything* in China, 1974 (left), and Candido Portinari, *Coffee,* 1935 (right).** The agricultural revolution five thousand years ago was one of the most important events in human history. While agricultural processes have changed over time, so too have they endured, as these images of workers in a rice field in China and coffee-pickers in Brazil attest.

Popular Value Packages from Bedford/St. Martin's

For more information on packages and discounts, visit **bedfordstmartins.com/highschool/reilly/catalog** or contact your Bedford/St. Martin's representative.

Strayer, *Ways of the World*, Second Edition
bedfordstmartins.com/highschool/strayer/catalog

Also available in e-book format.

The Bedford Series in History and Culture
bedfordstmartins.com/history/series

Guides • bedfordstmartins.com/history/guides

Trade Books • bedfordstmartins.com/tradeup
Hill & Wang • Farrar, Straus and Giroux • Palgrave • and other fine imprints from Macmillan